A GUITARISTS' GUIDE TO COMMON CHORD PROGRESSIONS

ISBN 978-1-291-10657-2

Contents

Contents

Appendices

HOW TO USE THIS BOOK

(Italicised words are defined in the Glossary at the back of the book. Other technical terms are explained in more detail in the main text).

While more experienced guitarists can use this book as a reference to dip into as required, it is designed for beginners to work through in a systematic way in order to develop a comprehensive chord repertoire, and fluency in making the chord changes which appear most frequently in popular and classical music.

It should be noted the the exercises are laid out in *key signature* order, rather than in order of difficulty. I therefore recommend that students do not attempt to master each exercise before moving on to the next. Rather, practise one or more exercises in a different key each day - returning to the first key at the end of the cycle. In this way, new chords are learnt at a comfortable pace, while familiar chords are constantly reinforced.

As the chord changes become more fluent, you should incorporate right-hand technique into the exercises, by experimenting with different strumming rhythms and picking patterns.

WHAT YOU WILL LEARN

The chord progressions which occur most frequently in the European tradition, from the Baroque to contemporary pop and rock, are the I-IV-V, ii-V-I, and vi-ii-V-I (if you are not familiar with these naming conventions, don't worry, they are explained within the book). This book teaches these in all major and minor keys, in *triad* and seventh-chord form, with alternative voicings chosen for their practical utility.

In addition to practical exercises, the basics of classical harmony are explained, with illustrations of the harmonisation of the remaining *degrees* of the scale.

Fluency in lead and melody playing is developed with exercises relating arpeggios, pentatonics, scales and modes to the chord progressions.

Additional sections deal briefly with suspensions and sixth chords, augmented and diminished chords, substitution of chords within the common progressions, and alternative scales, such as the melodic minor and blues scales. In-depth study of these topics is beyond the scope of this book.

WHAT IS NOT COVERED

The exercises do not include harmonisations beyond the seventh degree of the scale (the ninth, eleventh and thirteenth chords), or any more exotic chords. However the grounding given in basic harmony theory should provide a sound basis on which to explore more advanced chording concepts.

Although some examples are written out in musical notation, it is not essential to understand this to use the book and no instruction is given. Basic guidance is given on reading chord charts and tablature, and this should be sufficient for non-readers to follow the exercises with ease.

The book assumes familiarity with the system of key signatures, and the *intervals* of the major and natural minor scales, and these are not explained in the text. (The practical exercises can still be followed without understanding these concepts).

AN IMPORTANT NOTE ON TRANSPOSITION

For each chord progression, one example is given in each key. You should always bear in mind that any fingering which includes no open strings can be easily *transposed* to any other key, simply by moving the whole pattern up or down the fretboard. I have tried to avoid repeating these patterns in different keys where an alternative voicing is available. Thus by transposing the exercises between keys, the number of alternative voicings available to you in each key will be greatly increased.

HOW TO READ THE CHORD DIAGRAMS

The chord diagrams in this book are in the form of a grid showing the six strings of the guitar as if held upright, facing you with the lowest (E) string on the left. Most of the diagrams show the first (lowest) six frets, as follows:

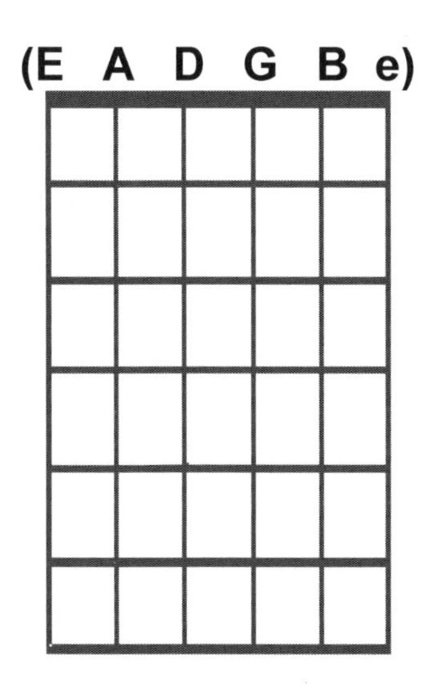

For chords above the sixth fret, the diagram will appear as follows, with the position indicated by a fret number to the left of the diagram:

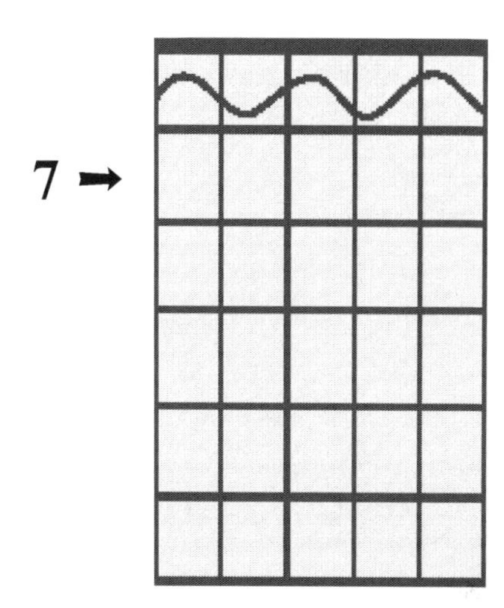

Finger positions are given by dots on the diagram. Numbers within the dots give suggested fingerings where 1 = index finger, 2 = middle finger, 3 = ring finger and 4 = little finger. In some cases, possible alternative fingerings are given by two numbers separated by a slash. Often other choices of fingering are possible and you should feel free to experiment and find the one which suits you best.

e.g.  

A white dot always indicates the *root* note of the chord; other notes are marked with a black dot. A dot with no finger number is used to indicate where an open string should be played. An "X" marked on the nut indicates that the string should not be sounded.

Markings in brackets are optional. For example in the following "Em7" chord, including the 3rd fret, 2nd string results in doubling the *seventh* (D - the open 4th string) at the octave; leaving the 2nd string open doubles the *fifth* (B - 2nd fret, 5th string). Either way, the chord has the same name:

In this example a chord of C major can be played i) with the third finger at fret 3, string 5 (C) and omitting string 6 (E) to create a *root-position* chord; ii) with the open string 6 sounded to create a first-*inversion* C chord;or iii) with the third finger at fret 3, string 6 (G) and the fourth finger at fret 3, string 5 to create a second-inversion C chord:

BARRE CHORDS

"Barre" chords are played by holding down several (usually all six) strings with the first finger laid flat across the fretboard. The first finger position for these chords is indicated on the diagrams by a brace connecting the top and bottom notes of the range, as in this example of an F Major chord:

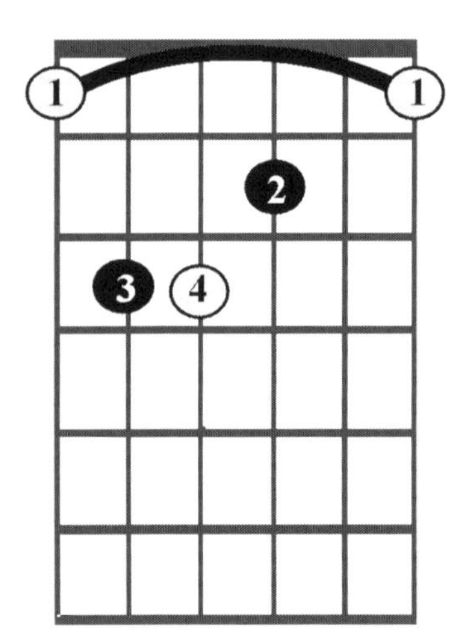

ATTENTION BEGINNERS: Barre chords are notoriously tricky to master at first - so don't be disheartened if your first attempts sound dreadful. Move on and work your way through a set of exercises as described above, and you will notice a progressive improvement each time you repeat the cycle.

HOW TO READ TABLATURE

Arpeggio and scale exercises are given in standard music notation and tablature (tab for short). In tablature the 6 strings of the guitar are represented in diagrammatic form with string 6 (low E) at the bottom i.e. upside-down. Numbers on the "strings" represent fret numbers (counting from 0 = open string) and are played reading from left to right as normal. Suggested fingerings are given beneath the tab (once again, experiment with your own alternatives). Thus the following arpeggio of C major is played: 2nd finger, fret 3, string 5; 1st finger, fret 2, string 4; 4th finger, fret 5, string 4:

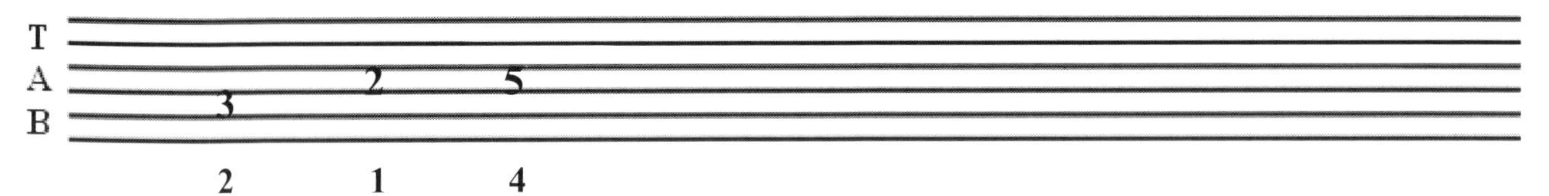

HOW TO READ FINGERING CHARTS

Many of the arpeggio and scale exercises in this book are written as generic fingering charts which can be transposed to any position on the fretboard . To write them out in all keys would be a waste of effort, since the fingering patterns are identical. Each of these charts is a schematic representation of a section of the fretboard, similar to the chord diagrams, but laid out horizontally. Like the chord diagrams, fingerings are given in numbered circles, with a white circle representing the root of the relevant chord, and black circles representing the remaining chord tones. Like the tablature diagrams, these fingering charts show string 6 (low E) at the bottom of the diagram. The example below shows a major triad arpeggio spanning 2 octaves, with the root on string 6:

ORGANISING YOUR PRACTICE SCHEDULE

Only you can determine the time you have available for practice, and the pace at which you like to work. However I strongly recommend that the arpeggio and scale exercises are practised alongside the corresponding chord examples in the same key, working in a new key each day. This will help you to become familiar with the relationship between chord structures and the melodic elements of music.

PART ONE

I - IV - V

MAJOR KEYS
TRIADS

WHY I - IV - V?

Chords are numbered according to the *degree* of the scale which forms the *root* of the chord. By convention, upper-case Roman numerals (e.g. I, V) are used for *major* chords, and lower-case Roman numerals (e.g. ii, vi) for *minor* chords. Thus, in the key of C, the first note of the scale (C) is the root of chord I; the fourth note of the scale (F) is root of chord IV, and the fifth (G) is the root of chord V, giving the chord progression C - F - G.

More often than not, the root will be the lowest (bass) note of the chord. However, sometimes another of the chord tones will appear in the bass, in which case the chord is said to be an *inversion*. Chords may be inverted for musical reasons (e.g. to make a melody note the top note of the chord), but sometimes inversions are used merely for a more convenient fingering.

HARMONISING THE SCALE

Chords are constructed from a scale by stacking *intervals* of a *third*, or, to put it more simply, by using alternate notes of the scale. Thus the I chord consists of the first, third and fifth notes of the scale; the IV chord contains the fourth, sixth and eighth notes of the scale, and the V chord contains the fifth, seventh and ninth notes (the ninth note is the same note as the second, one *octave* higher).

In the key of C, this gives us the chord progression:

I (C) = C + E + G
IV (F) = F + A + C
V (G) = G + B + D

THE IMPORTANCE OF THE I - IV - V PROGRESSION

I - IV - V is the most common chord progression in western music, from the baroque to contemporary pop/rock. One reason is that this set of chords contains all the notes of the major scale, so a basic accompaniment to any *diatonic* melody can be constructed using just these three chords.

Furthermore, the movement from the V back to the I chord forms the classical "perfect *cadence*" and is the most widely used chord change for ending a piece (or section) of music. The movement from IV to I (the "plagal cadence"), is also common.

The I - IV - V progression is also the basis of the blues, from which is derived an enormous range of popular music, from jazz to country, latin, heavy rock and more. A typical 12-bar blues sequence might be:

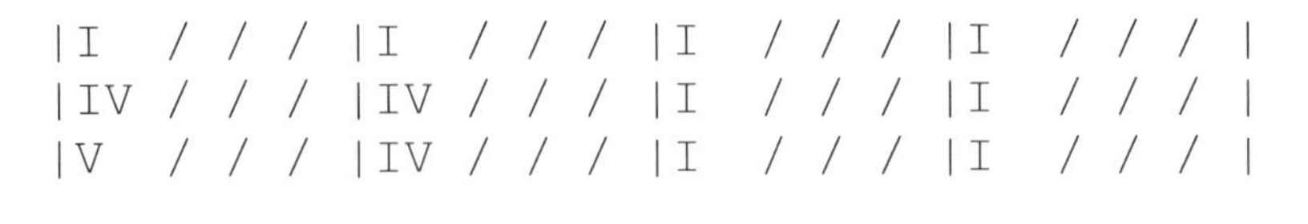

A variation:

```
|I  / / / |IV / / / |I  / / / |I  / / / |
|IV / / / |IV / / / |I  / / / |I  / / / |
|V  / / / |IV / / / |I  / / / |I  / V / |
```


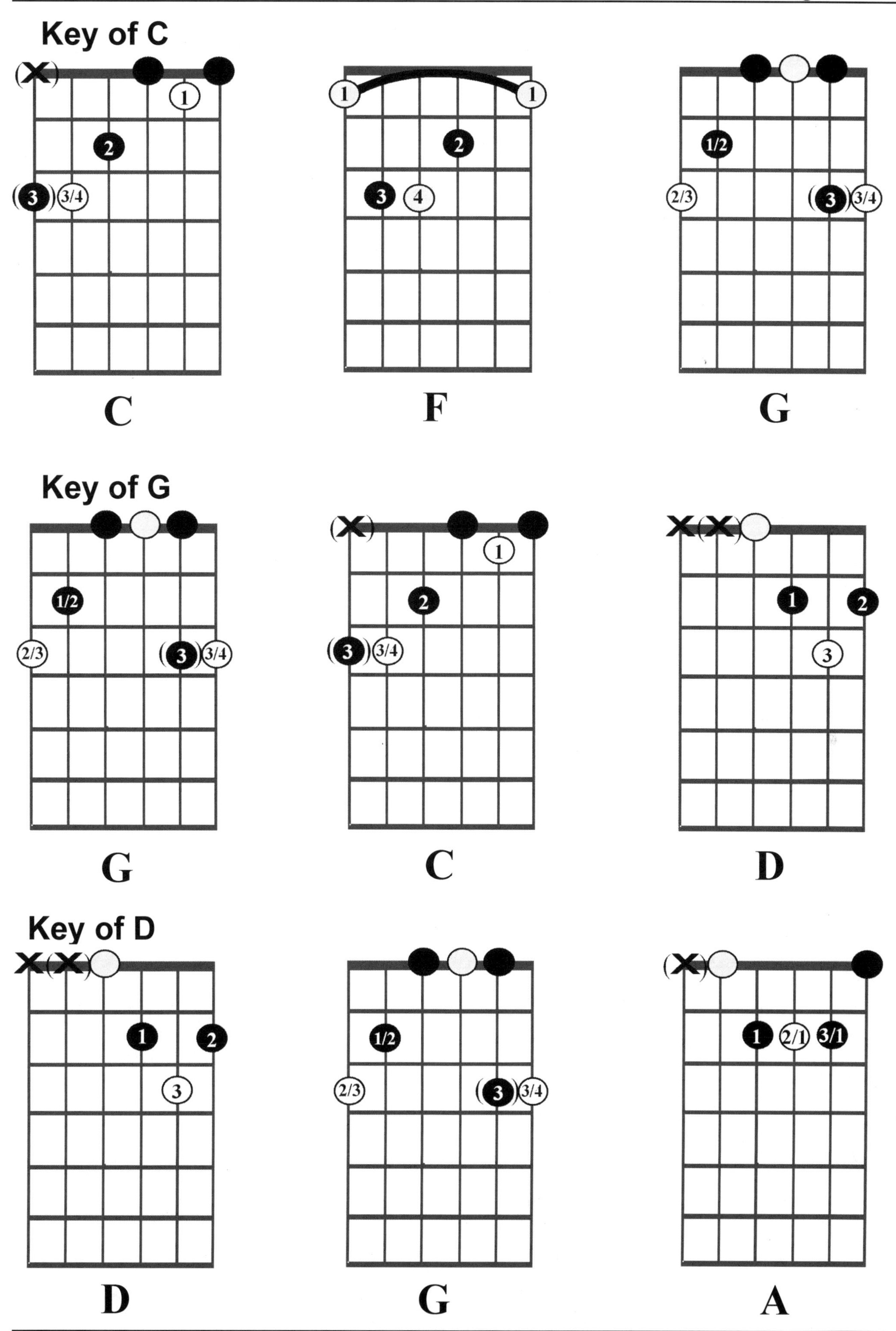
Key of C
C
F
G
Key of G
G
C
D
Key of D
D
G
A

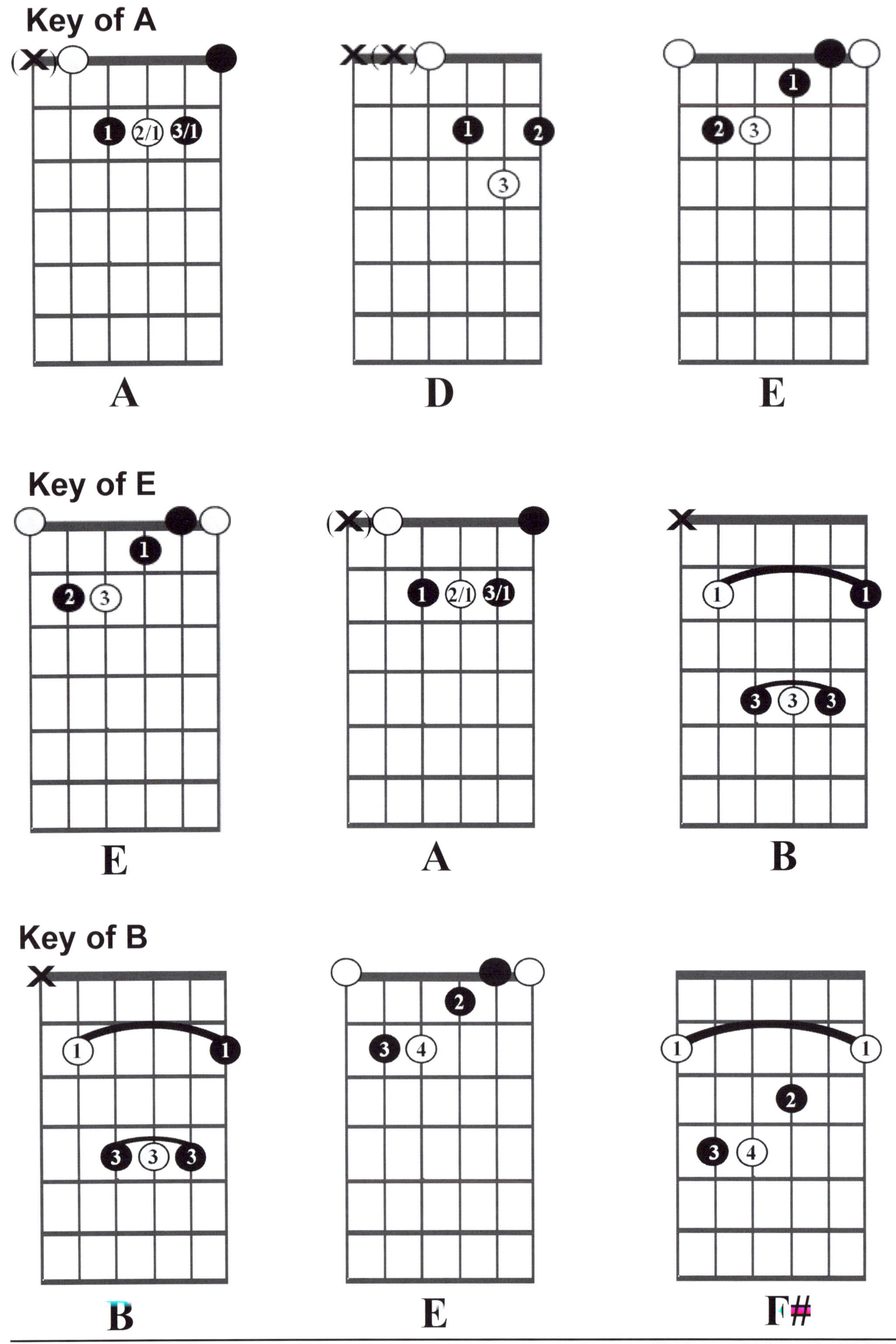
Key of A
A
D
E
Key of E
E
A
B
Key of B
B
E
F#

Key of F#

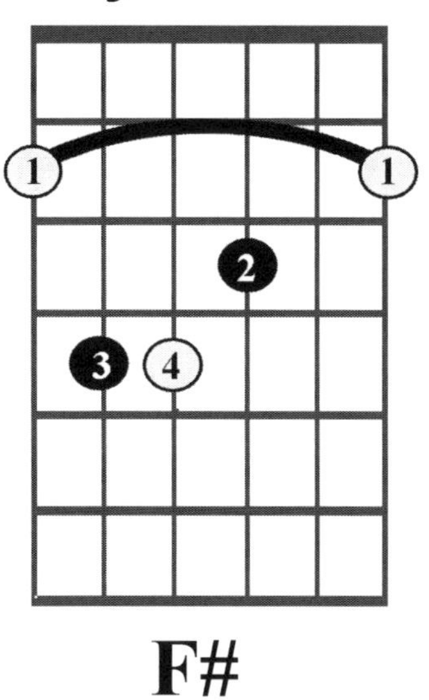

F#

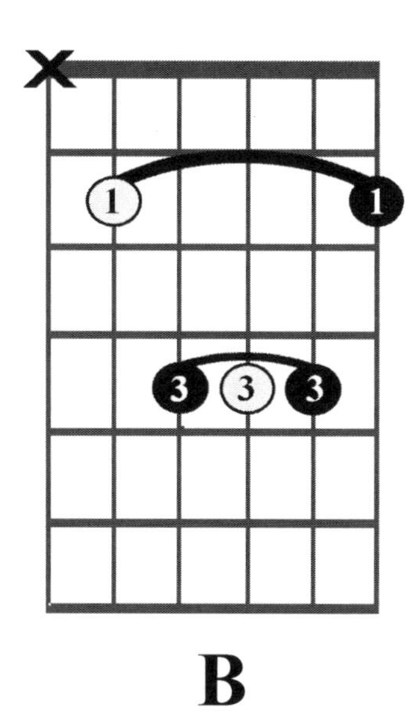

B

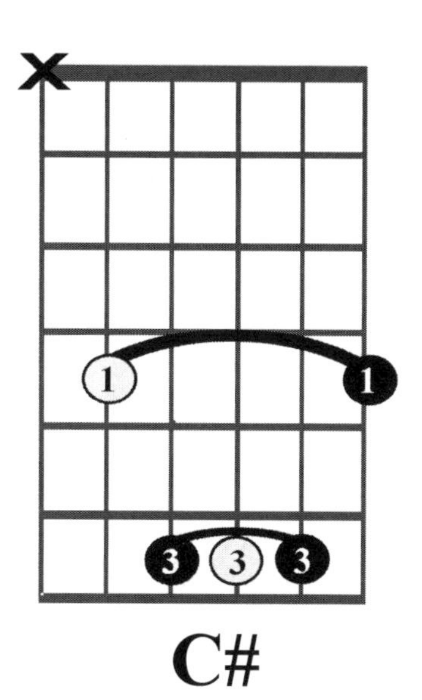

C#

Key of C#

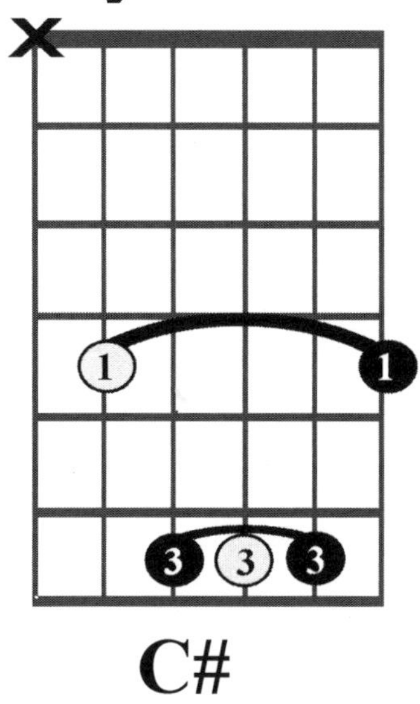

C#

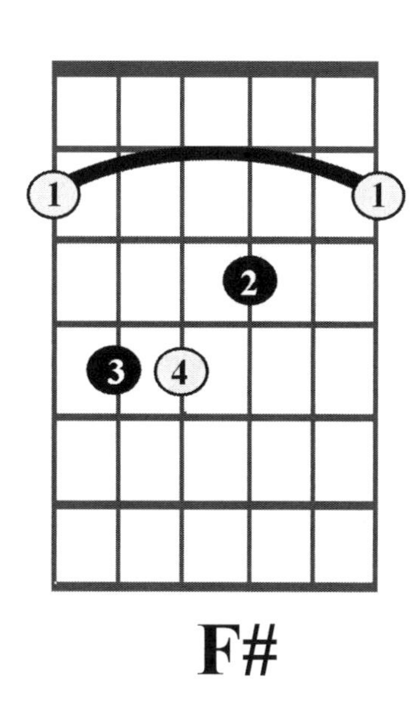

F#

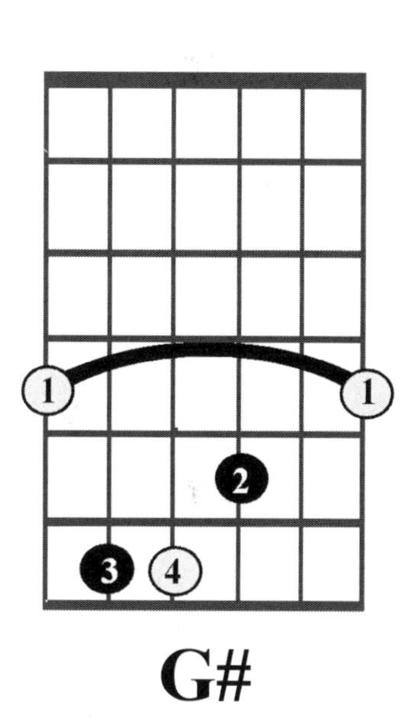

G#

Key of A♭

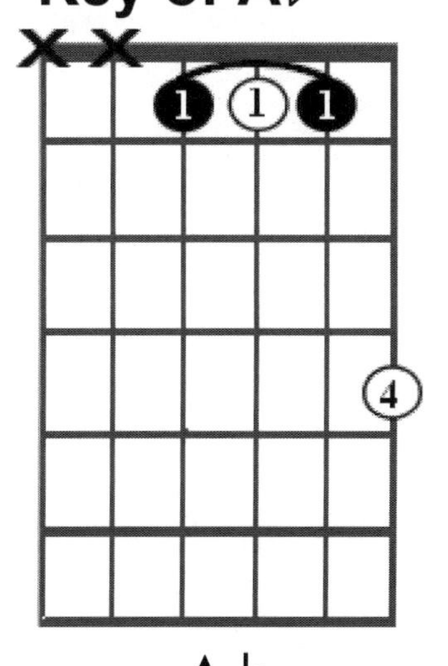

A♭

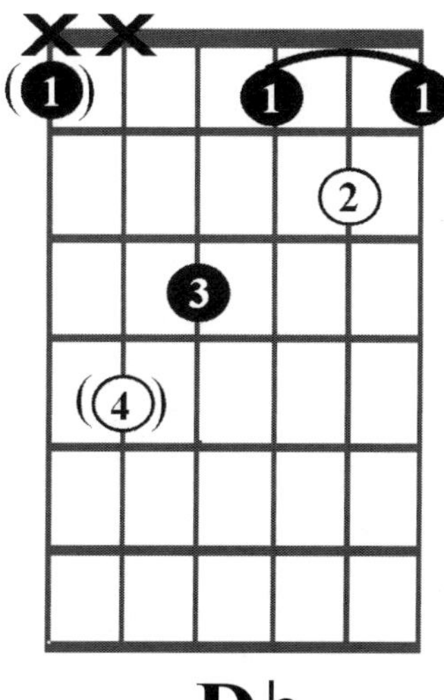

D♭

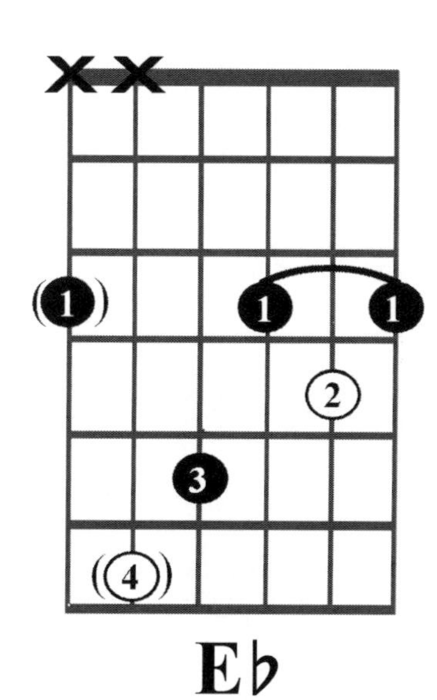

E♭

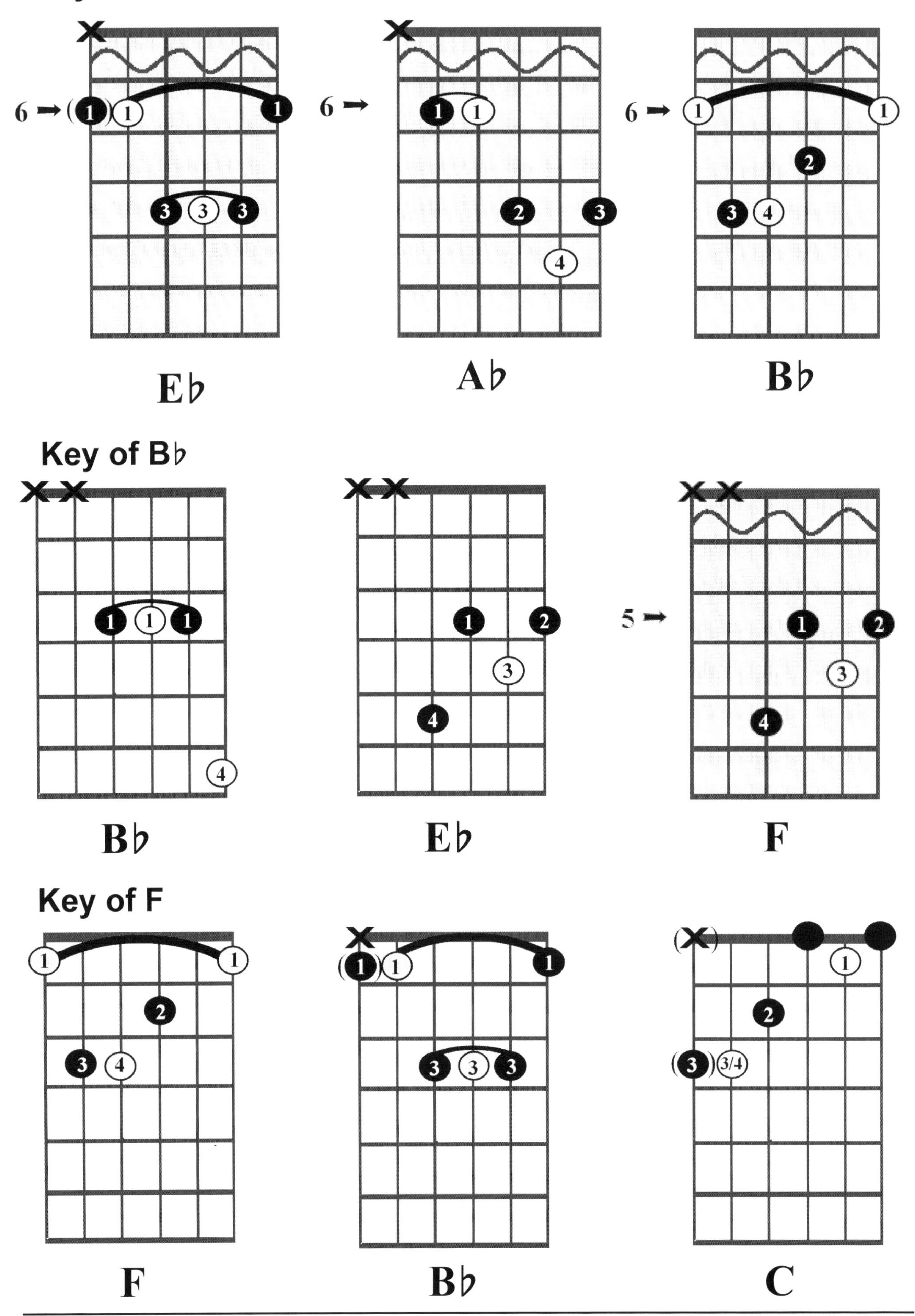
Key of E♭
6
6
6
E♭
A♭
B♭
Key of B♭
5
B♭
E♭
F
Key of F
F
B♭
C

PART TWO

ii - V - I

MAJOR KEYS
TRIADS

FURTHER HARMONISATION

In the previous exercise, we saw how we can build a chord on each *degree* of the scale by adding alternate scale notes to the *root*. In the case of the 1st, 4th and 5th degrees of the scale, the first *interval* (e.g. C to E, F to A, G to B) is a *major third* (two tones), making each of the I, IV, and V chords a major chord. If we apply the same principle to the second degree of the scale (taking the 2nd, 4th and 6th notes of the scale), the first interval is one *semitone* smaller - i.e. a *minor* third (one and a half tones), creating a minor chord, which we denote by using lower-case roman numerals: ii.

This exercise, therefore, will introduce you to all of the minor *triads*. The I and V chords will be familiar from the previous exercise.

USE OF THE ii - V - I PROGRESSION

We have seen that the "perfect *cadence*" (V - I) is the most frequently used way end a piece, or a passage, of music. Preceding the cadence with the ii chord usually works well - perhaps because the movement of the chord root from 2 to 5 (an interval of a fourth) is the same as that from 5 back to 1. We can see an example of its use in this slightly more elaborate version of a 12-bar blues:

```
|I  / / / |IV / / / |I  / / / |I  / / / |
|IV / / / |IV / / / |I  / / / |I  / / / |
|V  / / / |IV / / / |ii / V / |I  / V / |
```

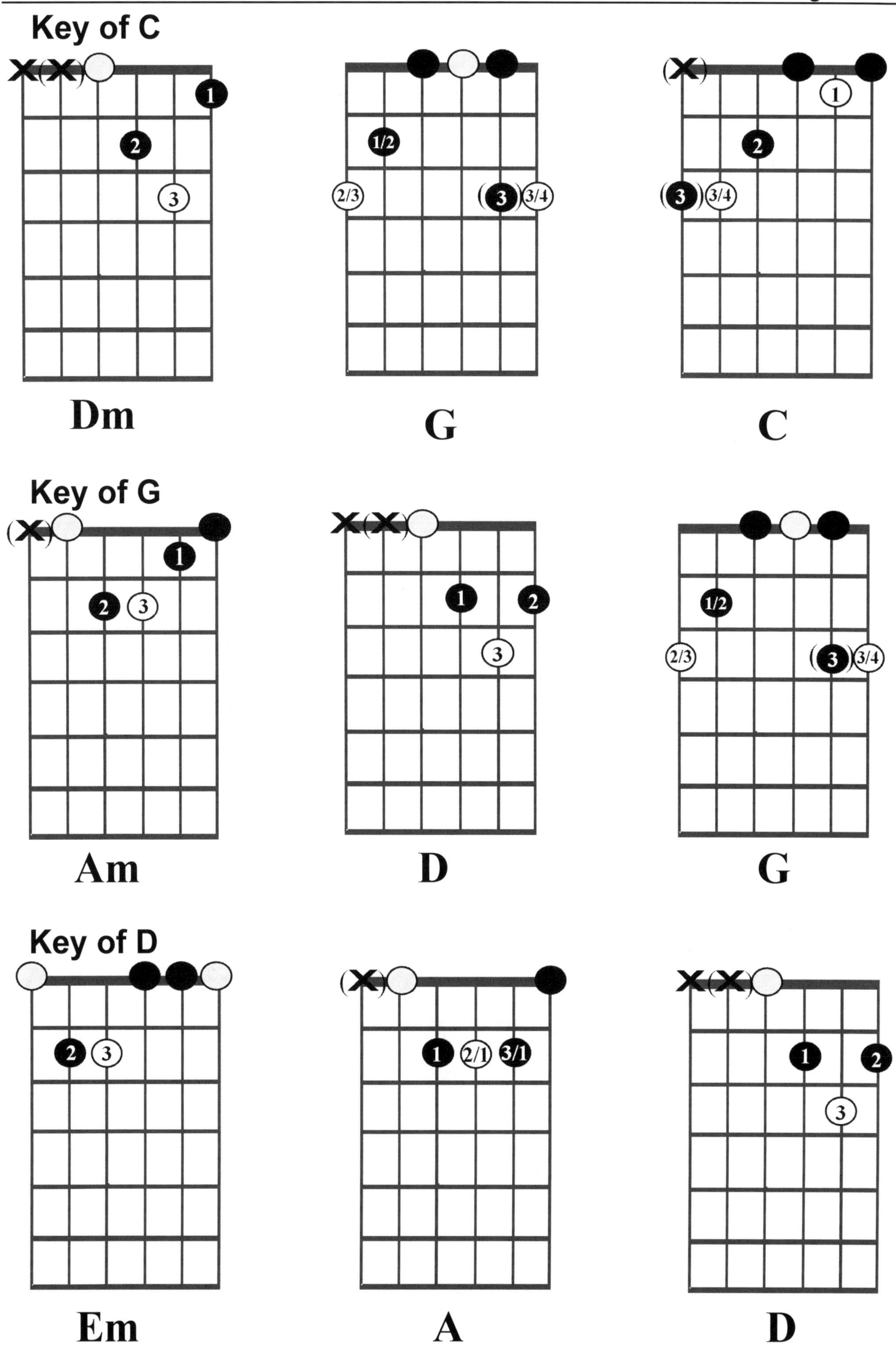
Key of C
Dm
G
C
Key of G
Am
D
G
Key of D
Em
A
D

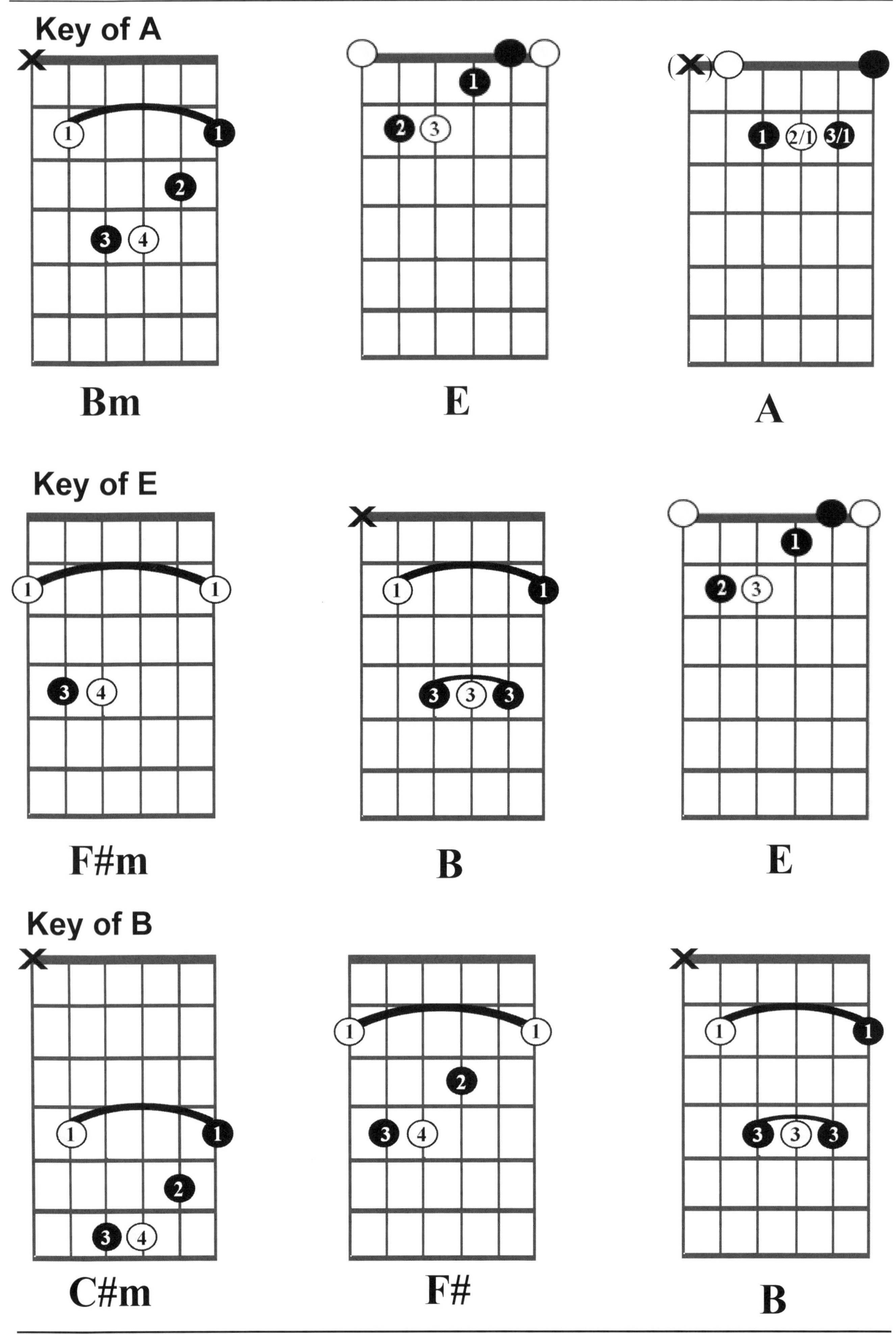
Key of A
Bm
E
A
Key of E
F#m
B
E
Key of B
C#m
F#
B

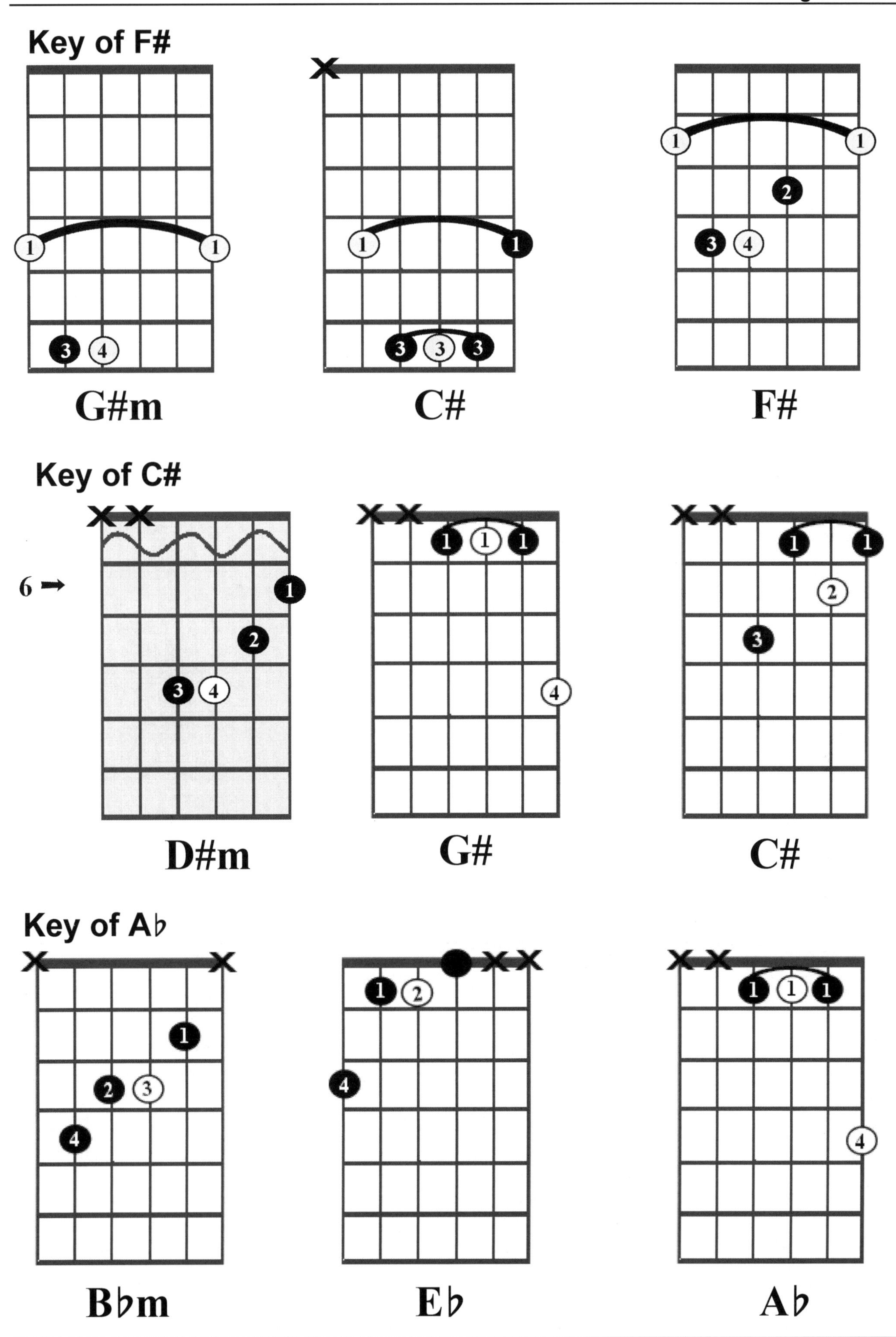
Key of F#
G#m
C#
F#
Key of C#
6
D#m
G#
C#
Key of A♭
B♭m
E♭
A♭

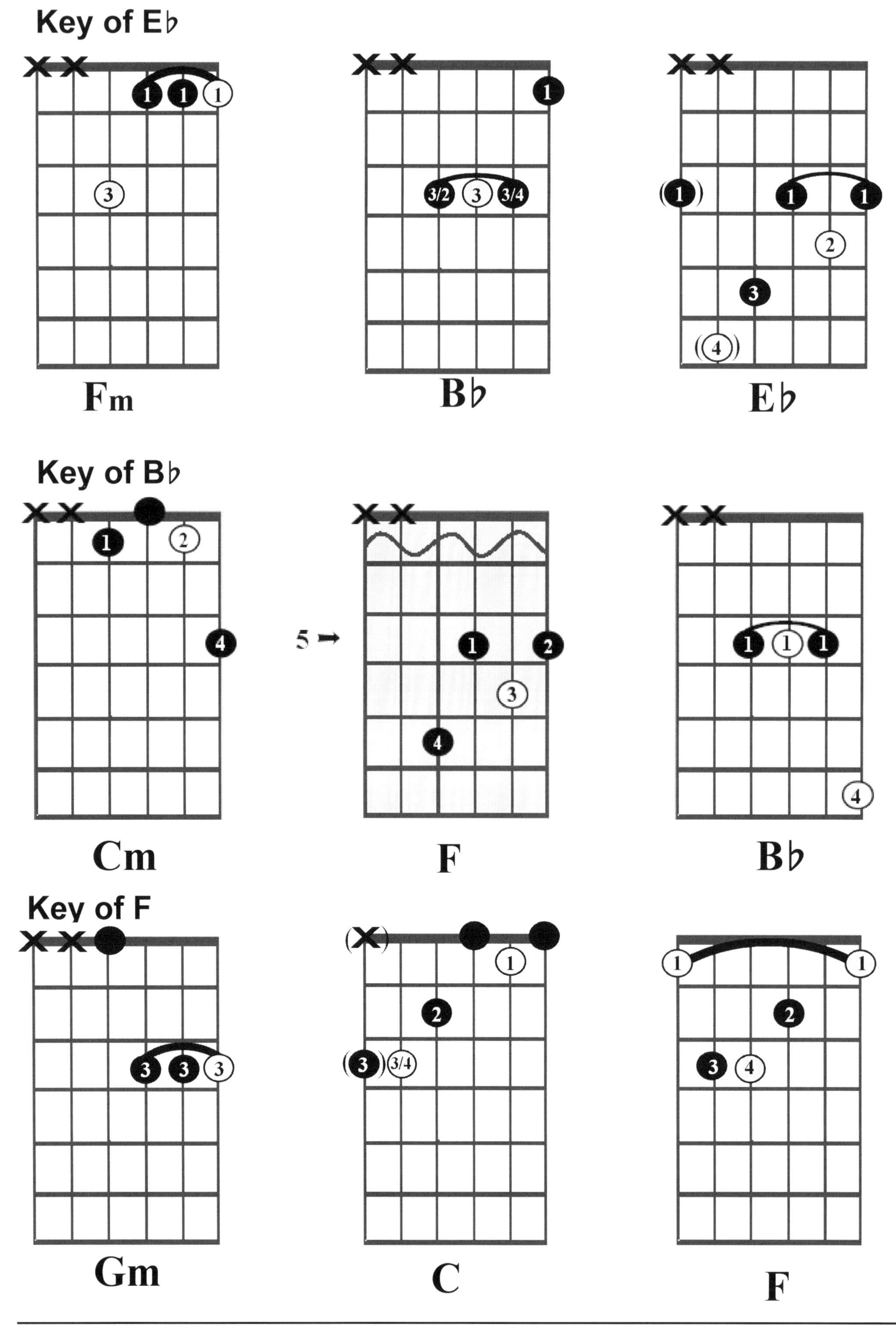
Key of E♭
Fm
B♭
E♭
Key of B♭
5
Cm
F
B♭
Key of F
Gm
C
F

PART THREE

vi - ii - V - I

MAJOR KEYS
TRIADS

HARMONISING THE SIXTH

There are no new chords introduced in this exercise (though there are some new variant voicings). Following the system of harmonising the scale for the sixth note (using notes 6, 8 (=1) & 10 (=3)) of the *major* scale) produces another *minor* chord. Thus the vi - ii - V - I progression is an extension of the

ii - V - I progression, using the chords you have already learned.

You will see that the *root* notes of the chords continue to move in steps of a *fourth*. You may also have noticed that the fourth and fifth intervals are inversions of each other, so that if you reverse the sequence

(I - V - ii - vi), the root note moves by a fifth at each chord change. Chord movements by a fourth or a fifth are by far the most common in most genres of European music.

A BRIEF DIGRESSION ON KEY CHANGES

More often than not, a piece of any significant length will change key at some point. Though any key change is possible, you will find once again that the two encountered most frequently move by an interval of a fifth or a fourth. The reason for this is that these are closely related keys, in that only one note changes in the *key signature* (so six out of seven notes are common to the two keys). When the *tonic* (key note) moves by a fifth, one note is sharpened in the key signature; when the tonic moves by a fourth, one note is flattened. For example, the key of C contains no sharps or flats; the key of G (a fifth above C) contains one sharp (F#); the key of F (a fourth above C) contains one flat (B♭). See the Glossary (under "Key Signature") for a complete description of the cycles of fifths and fourths.

Chord movements of a fifth or fourth can therefore be useful in creating a *modulation* between keys - e.g. using a chord common to both keys to form a smooth transition between the keys.

USE OF THE vi - ii - V - I PROGRESSION

The vi - ii - V - I progression, like the ii - V - I, is often used as an extended *cadence* in classical music. This progression is also extremely popular in jazz (particularly of the bebop era and later). Plentiful examples can be found elsewhere.

Here is a 12-bar sequence modified to use the vi - ii - V - I progression:

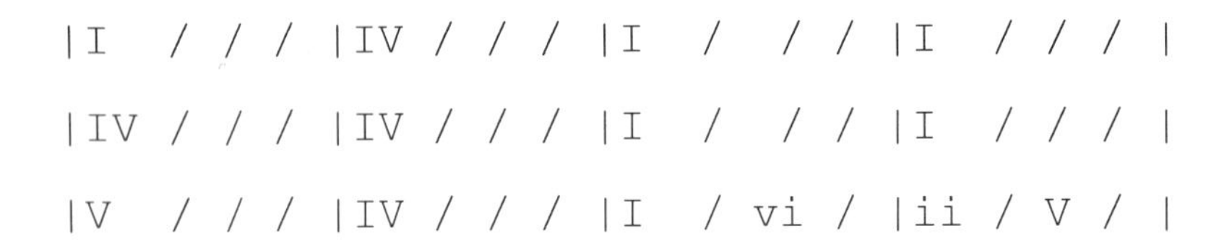

```
|I  / / / |IV / / / |I  /  / / |I  / / / |
|IV / / / |IV / / / |I  /  / / |I  / / / |
|V  / / / |IV / / / |I  / vi / |ii / V / |
```

(With the I chord falling on the first beat of the next verse).

Key of C

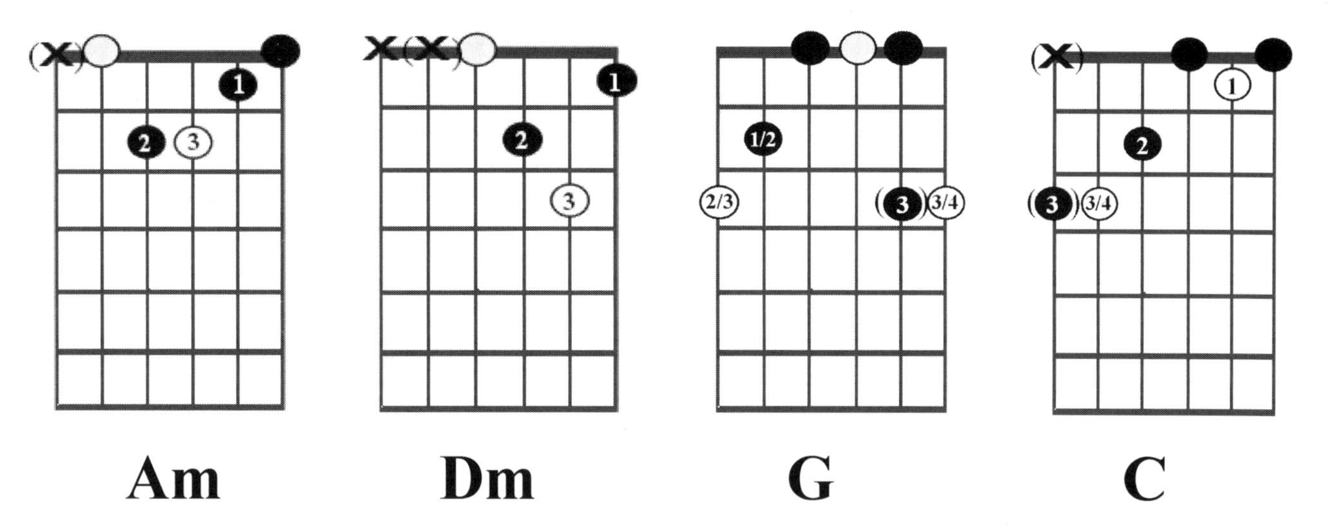

Key of G

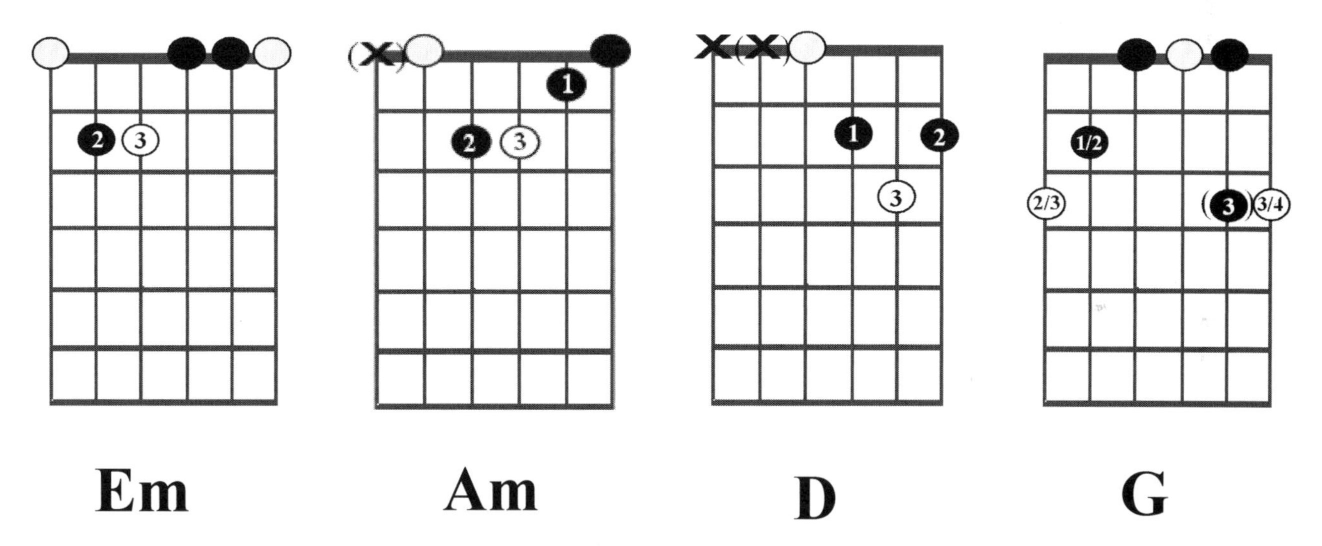

Key of D

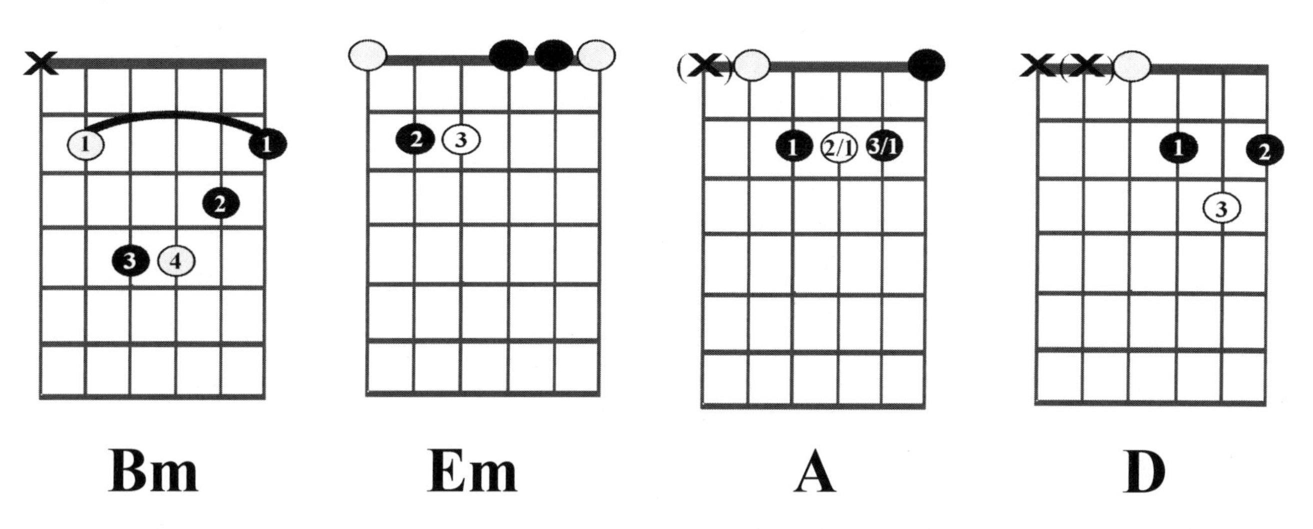

Key of A

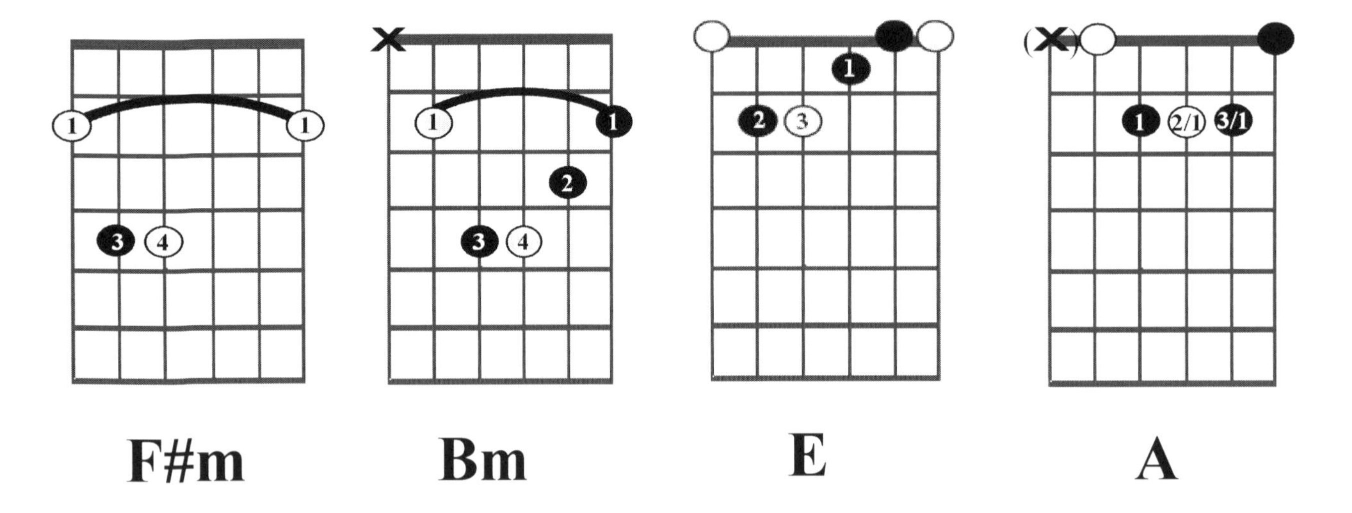

Key of E

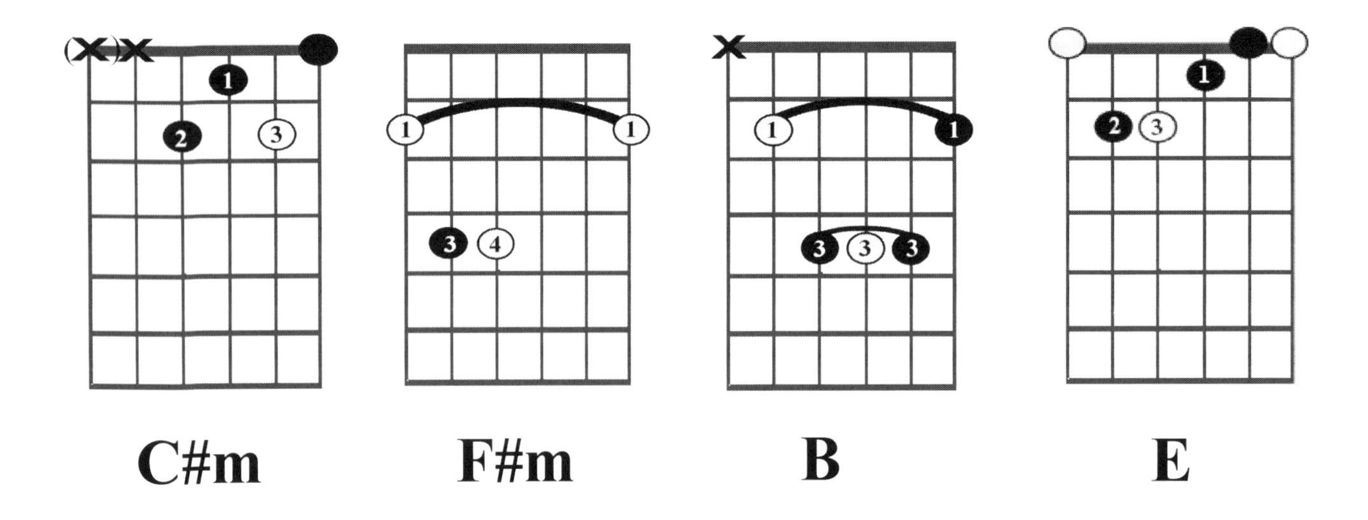

Key of B

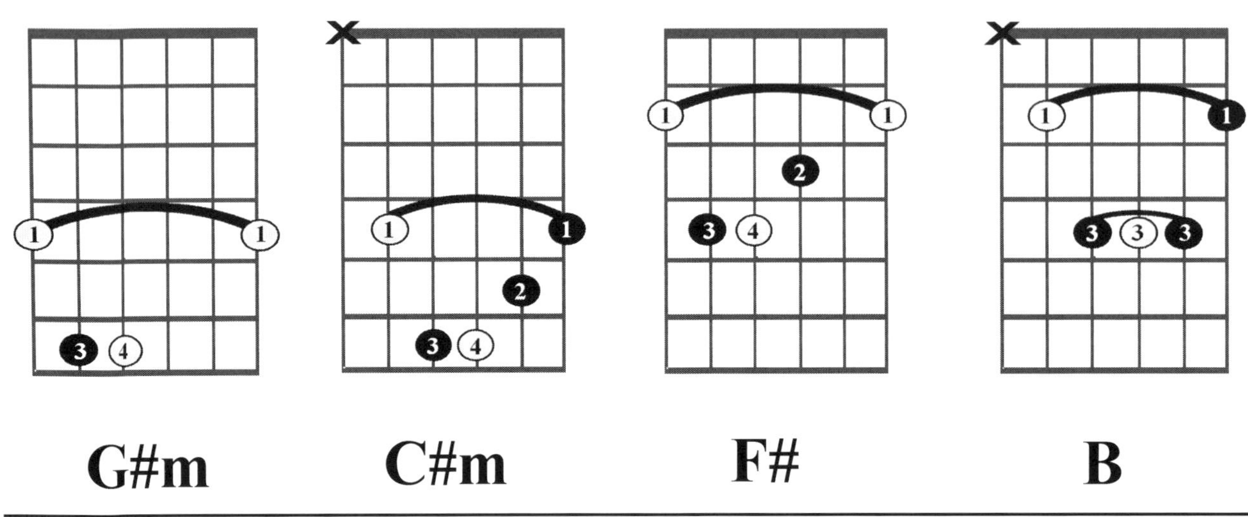

Key of F#

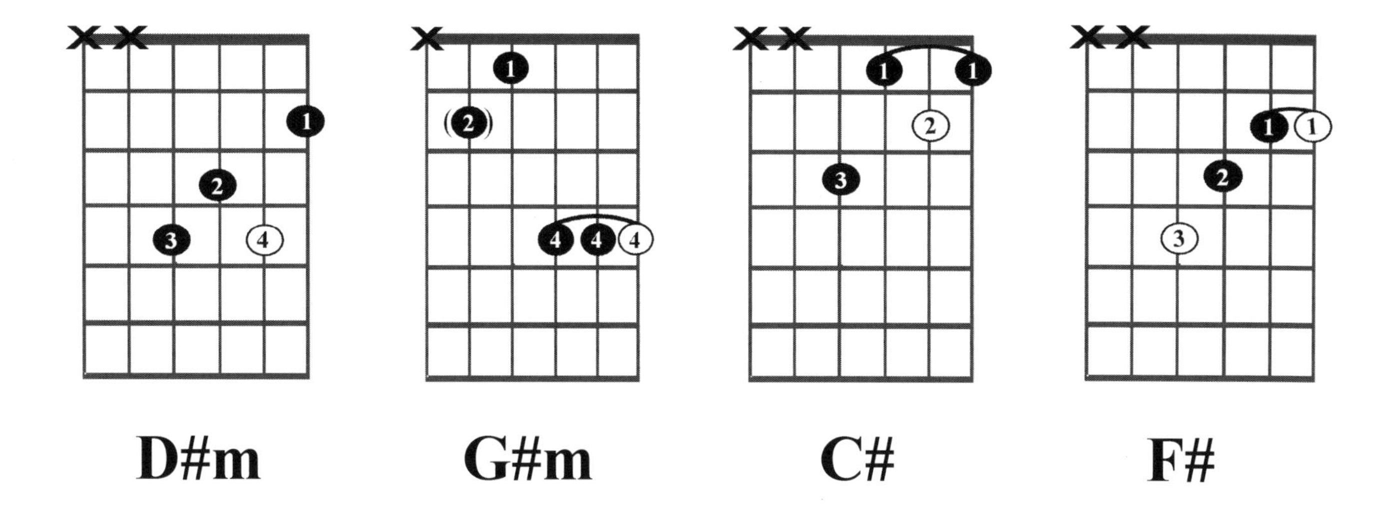

Key of C#

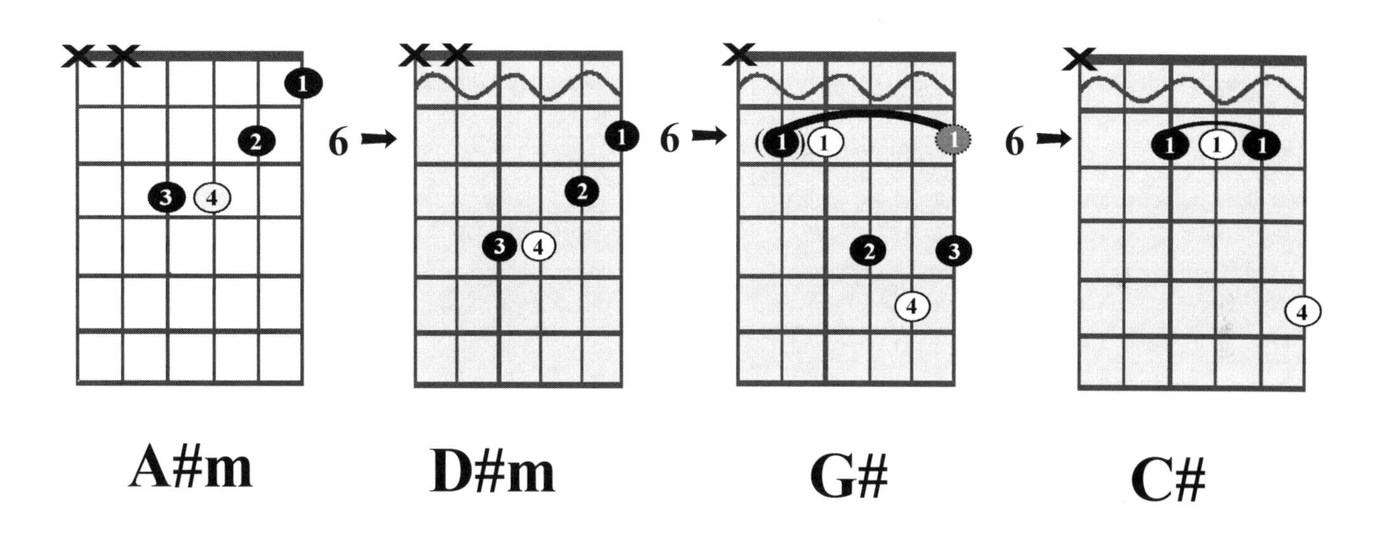

Key of A♭

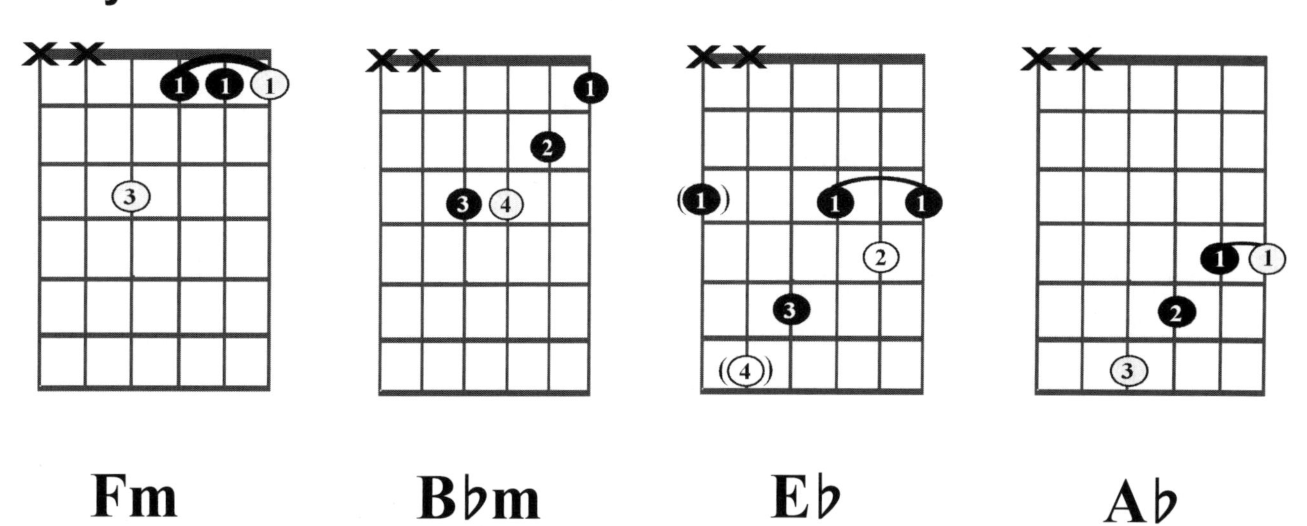

Key of E♭

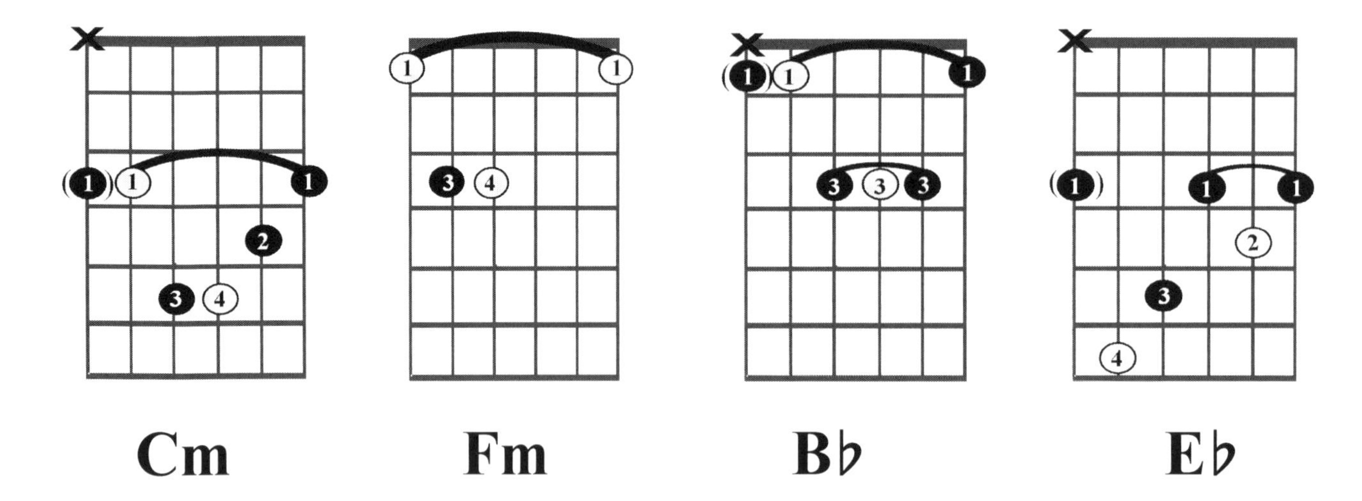

Key of B♭

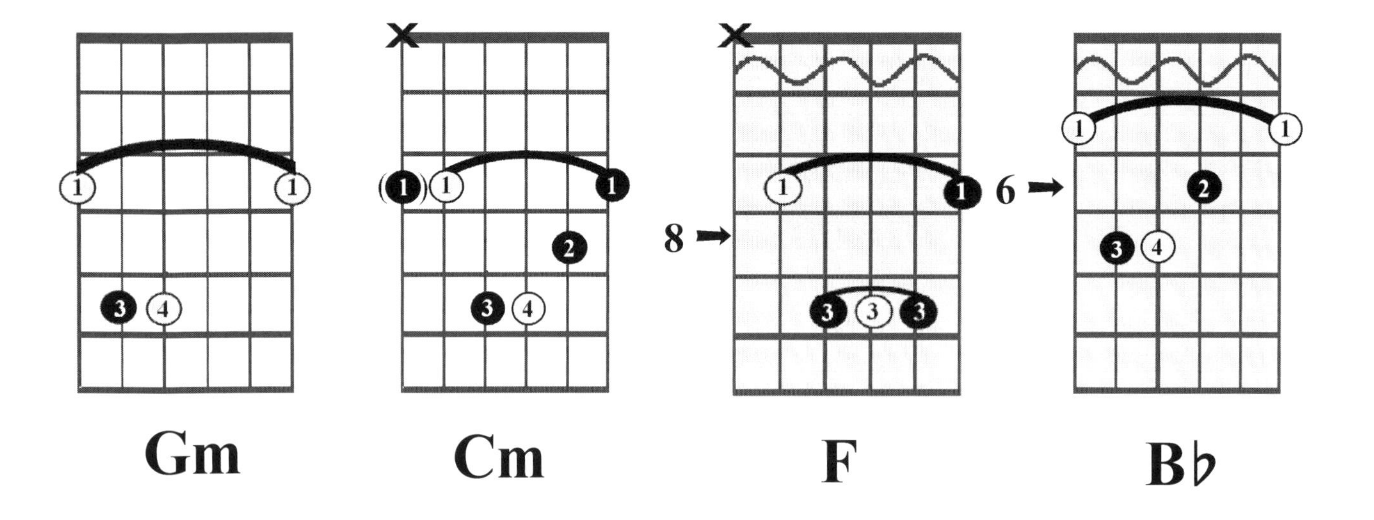

Key of F

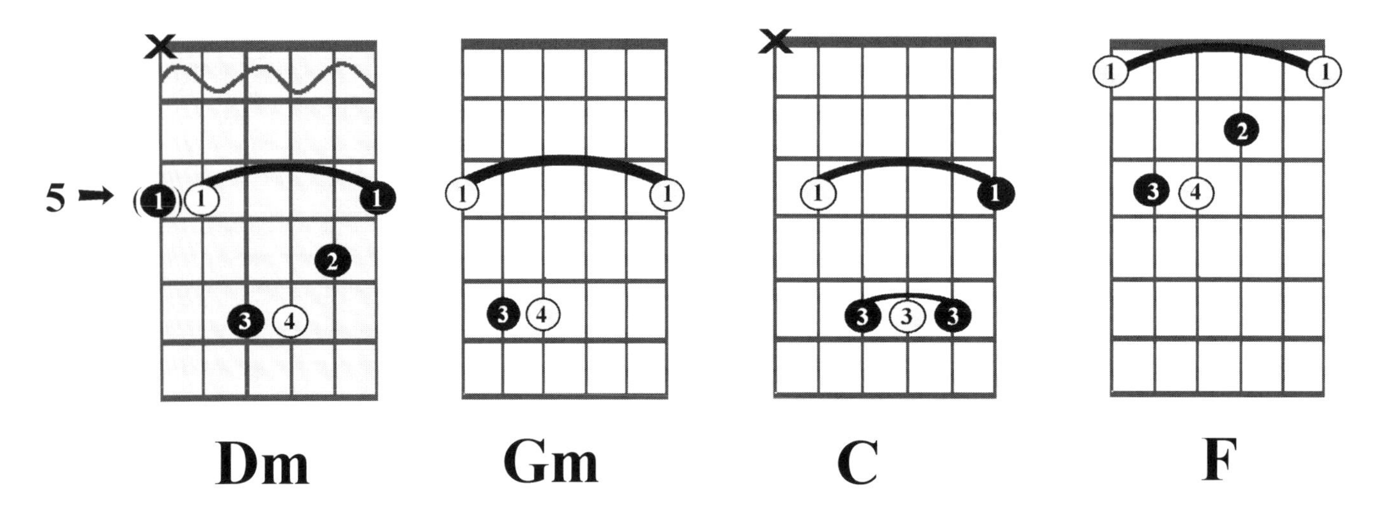

PART FOUR

i - iv - V

MINOR KEYS
TRIADS

RELATIVE MAJOR AND MINOR KEYS

For each of the *major* keys, there is a corresponding (or "relative") *minor* key, which is made up of the same notes, and therefore has the same *key signature*. For example, the key of C major contains the notes C, D, E, F, G, A, & B (no sharps or flats); the relative minor key of A minor consists of the notes A, B, C, D, E, F, & G. In general, the sixth note of any major key is the *tonic* note of the relative minor key, and the third note of any minor key is the tonic note of the relative major key.

The minor scale formed in this way is called the natural minor scale.

THE V CHORD IN MINOR KEYS

Following the same system of harmonisation as we used for the major keys, i.e. stacking intervals of a third, you will find that a minor chord is formed on the fifth degree of the scale. Nevertheless it is extremely common for a V (major) chord to be used instead, and the following exercises use this convention.

The reason for this is that much of the character of the V-I (or V-i) chord progression derives from the *semitone* movement between the *third* of the V chord and the root of the I chord. This semitone movement is lost if the v chord is minor. This chord progression (the "perfect *cadence*" - remember?) is so important in European music that this substitution of a major for a minor chord has long been deemed not only acceptable but, more often than not, desirable, even though one of the chord tones now falls outside the key signature.

The sharpened note in the V chord corresponds to the seventh degree of the natural minor scale. Sharpening this note within the scale creates the "harmonic" minor scale. See part forty-one for further discussion of this and other variations of the minor scale.

Of course, there is nothing "wrong" with the minor v chord in minor keys and it can be freely used.

Key of Am

Am

Dm

E

Key of Em

Em

Am

B

Key of Bm

Bm

Em

F#

Key of F#m

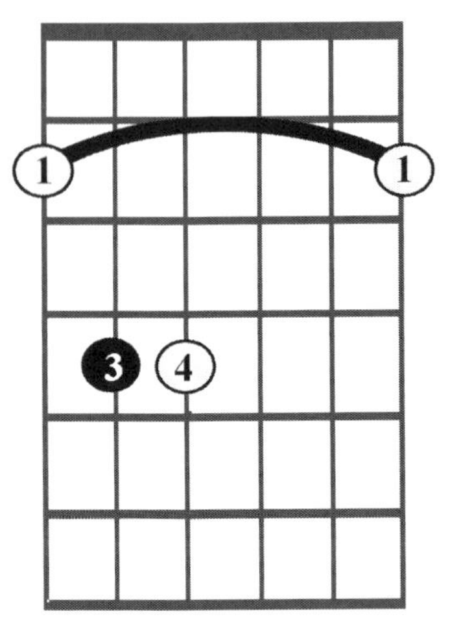

F#m

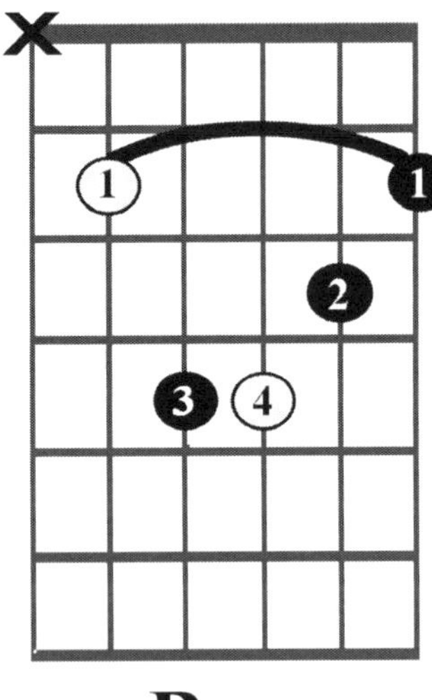

Bm

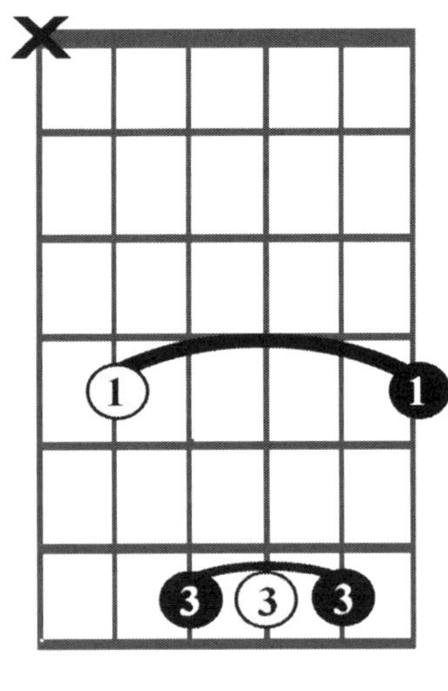

C#

Key of C#m

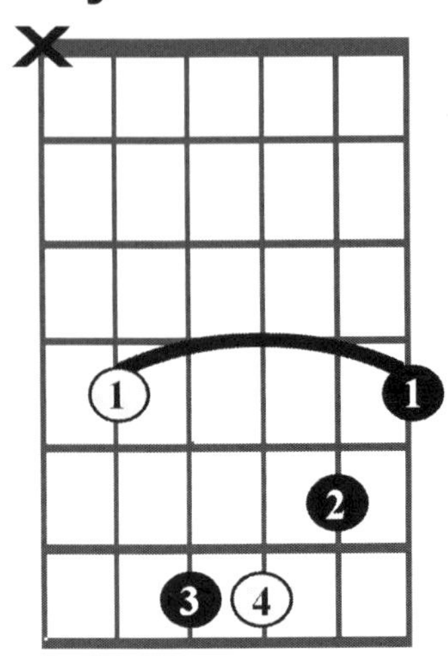

C#m

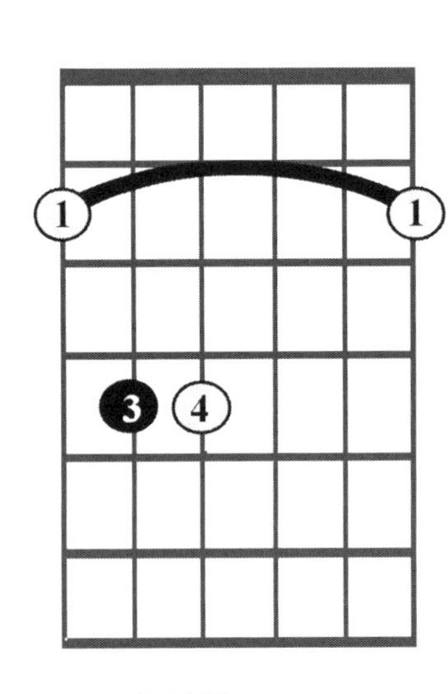

F#m

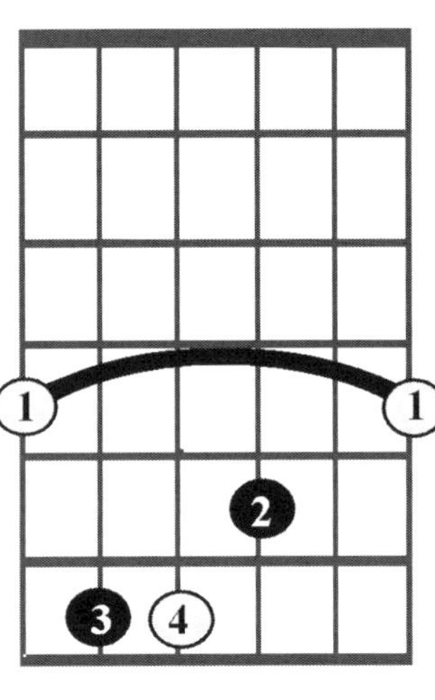

G#

Key of A♭m

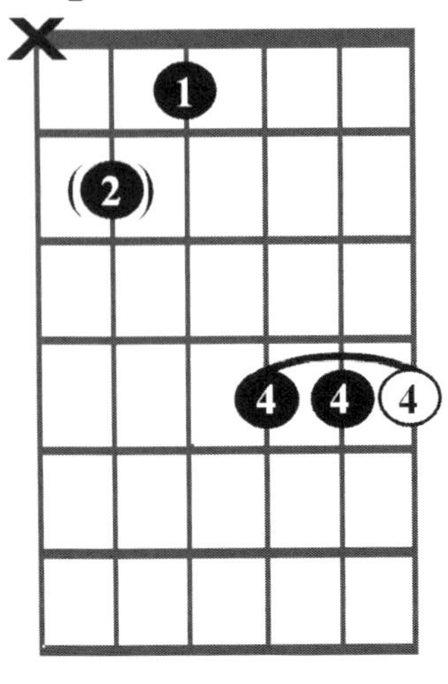

A♭m

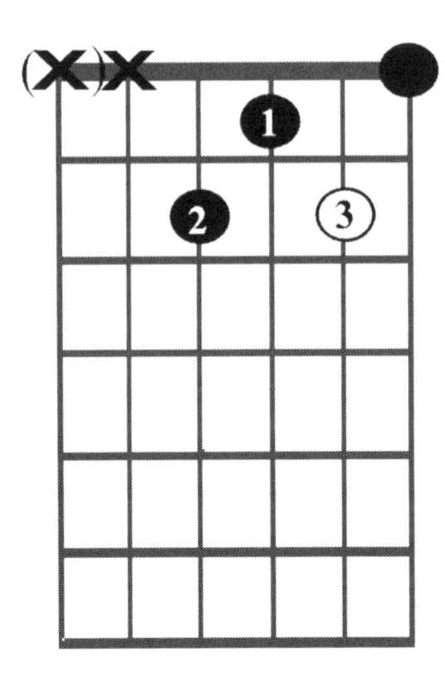

D♭m

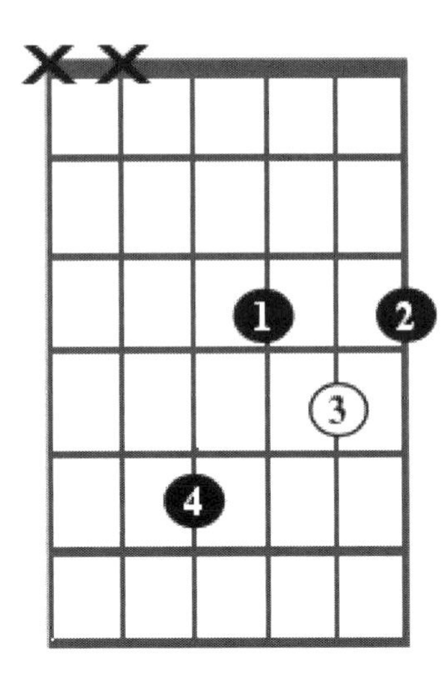

E♭

Key of E♭m

E♭m

A♭m

B♭

Key of B♭m

B♭m

E♭m

F

Key of Fm

Fm

B♭m

C

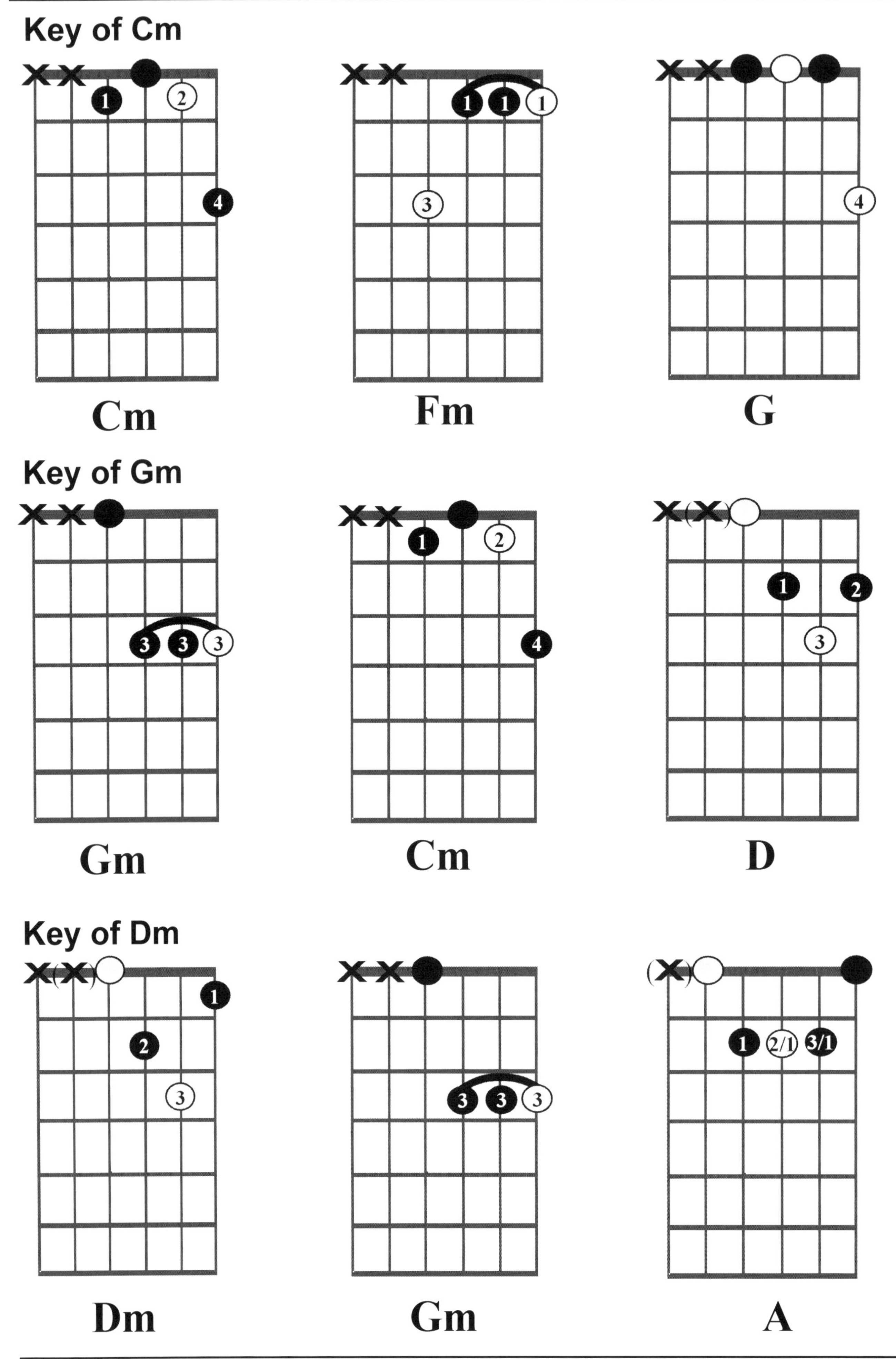
Key of Cm
Cm
Fm
G
Key of Gm
Gm
Cm
D
Key of Dm
Dm
Gm
A

PART FIVE

ii - V - i

MINOR KEYS
TRIADS

A NEW TYPE OF CHORD

So far, all our chords have been constructed from two *intervals* - a (*major* or *minor*) *third*, and a (*perfect*) *fifth*. The fifth is, in classical harmony, termed a "perfect" interval, as it does not vary between the major and minor scales and chords. Only the third varies between the normal major and minor triads. However when the second *degree* of the minor scale (corresponding to the seventh degree of the major scale) is harmonised, the chord which is formed has a minor third and a flattened fifth. This chord is called the "minor flat five" chord, sometimes referred to as a minor *diminished* fifth chord and is written (e.g.) Cm♭5 or Cm-5.

Key of Am

Bm♭5

E

Am

Key of Em

F#m♭5

B

Em

Key of Bm

C#m♭5

F#

Bm

Key of F#m

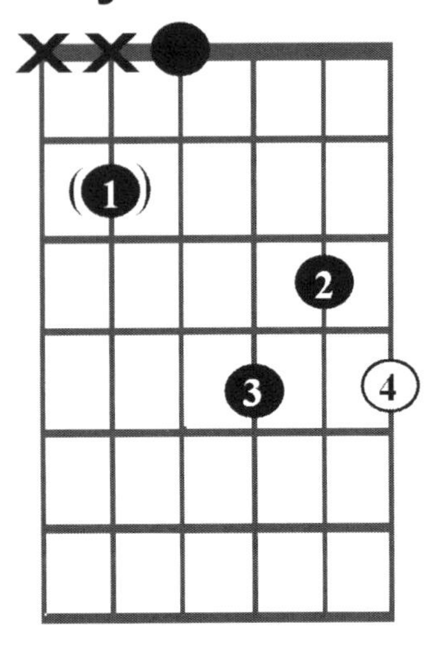

G#m♭5

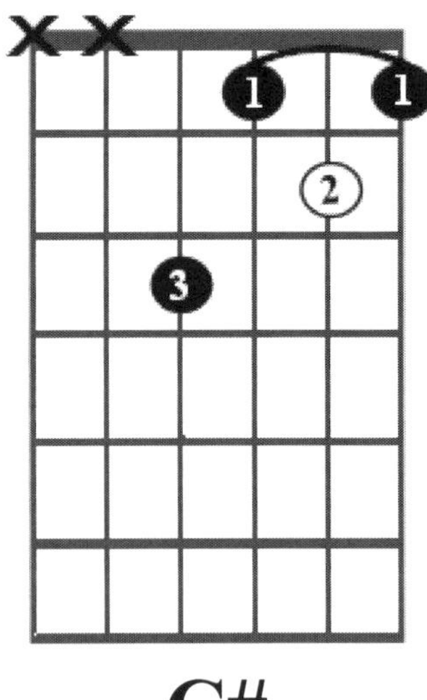

C#

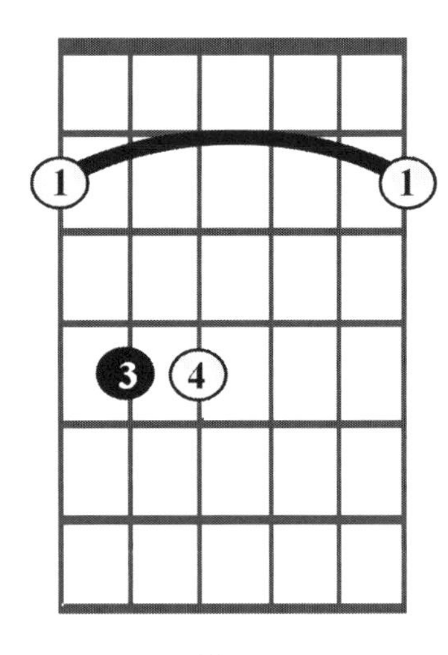

F#m

Key of C#m

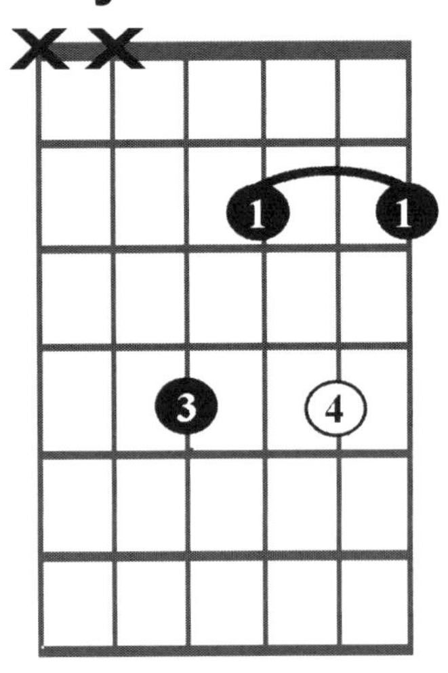

D#m♭5

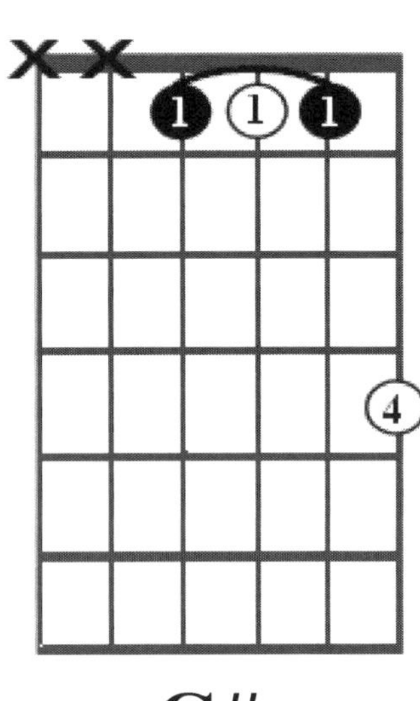

G#

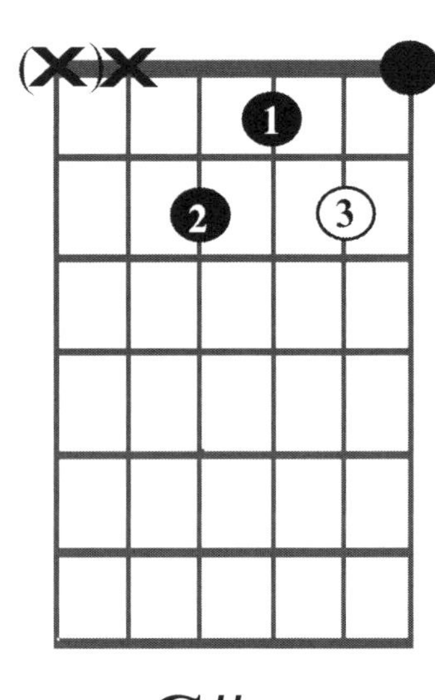

C#m

Key of A♭m

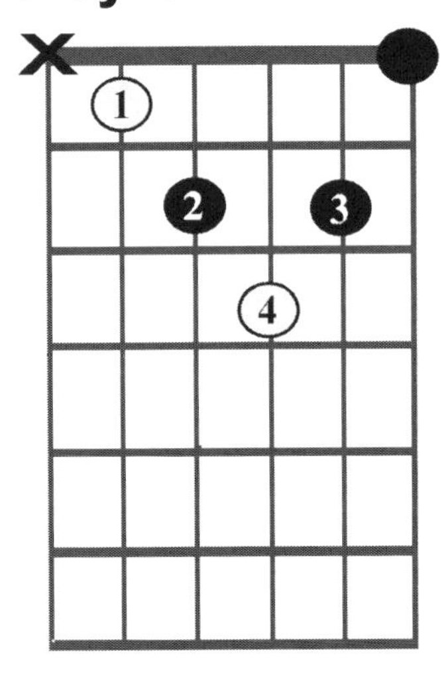

B♭m♭5

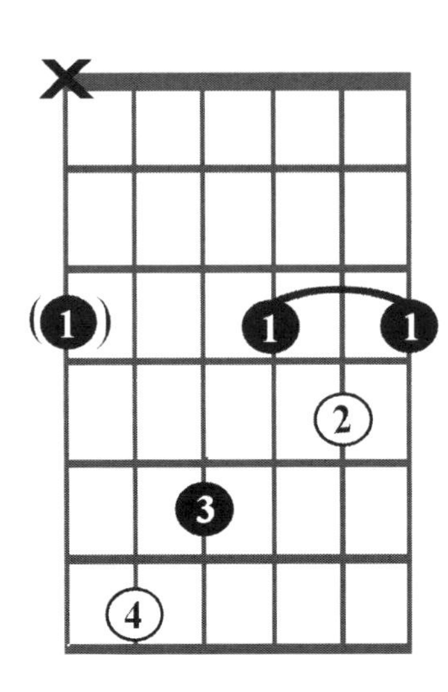

E♭

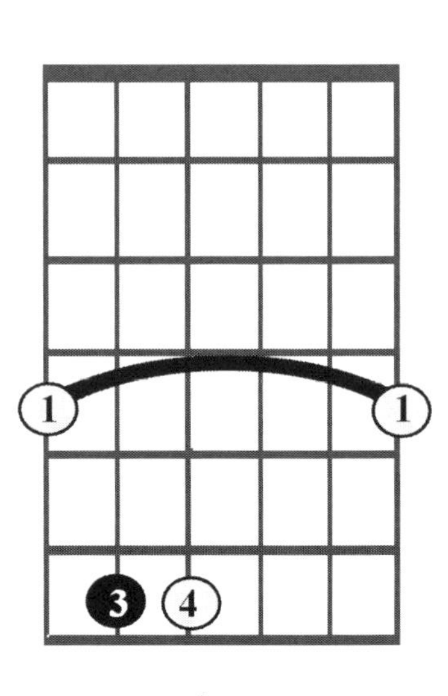

A♭m

Key of E♭m

Fm♭5

B♭

E♭m

Key of B♭m

7 ➡

Cm♭5

8 ➡

F

6 ➡

B♭m

Key of Fm

Gm♭5

C

Fm

Key of Cm

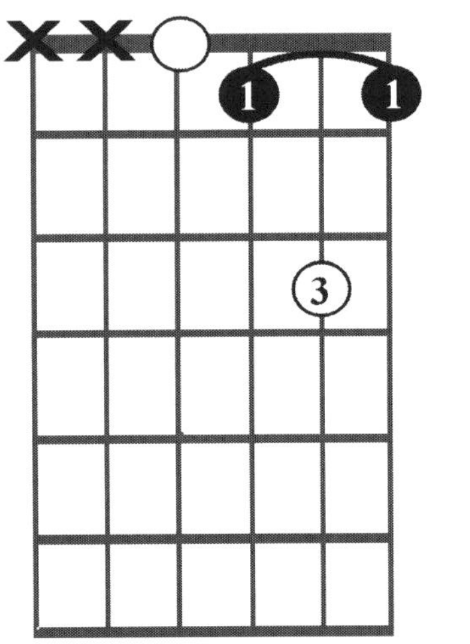

Dm♭5 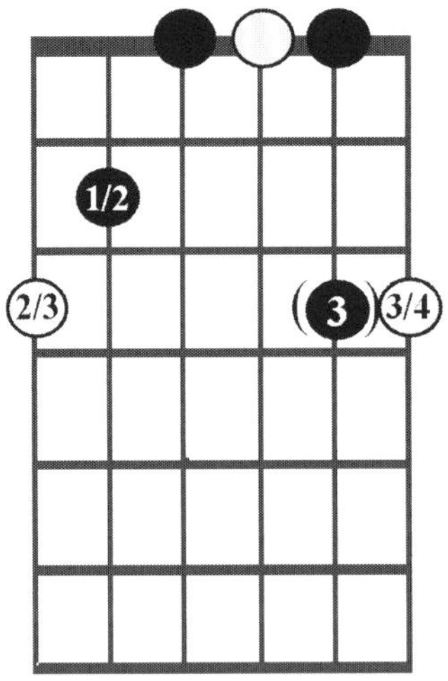 G 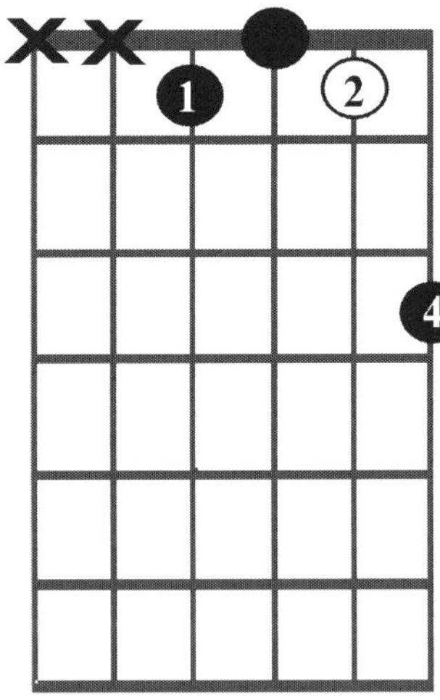 Cm

Key of Gm

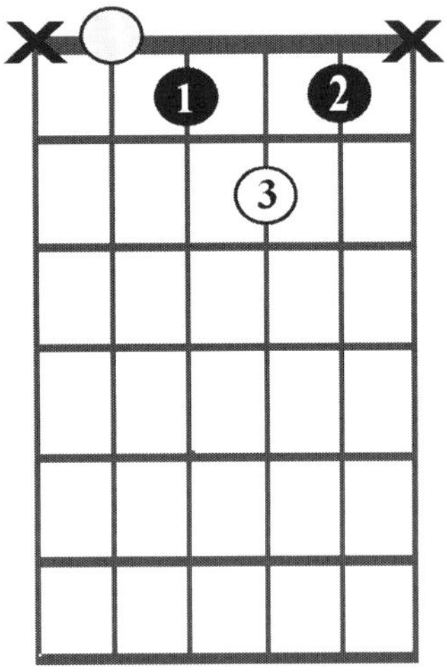

Am♭5 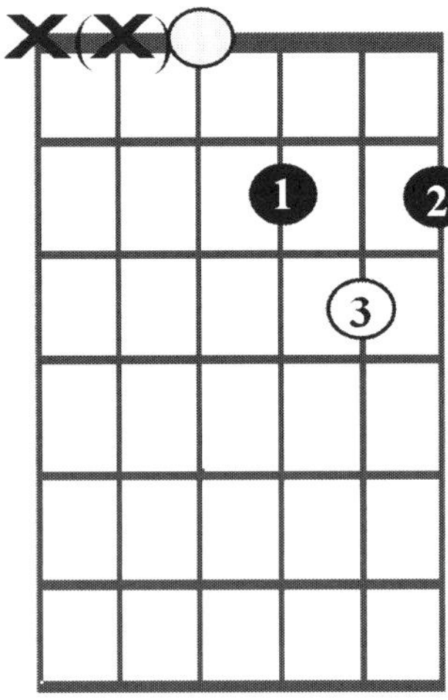 D 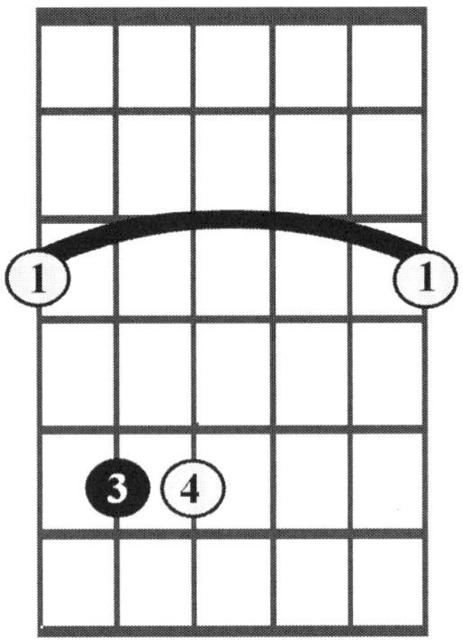 Gm

Key of Dm

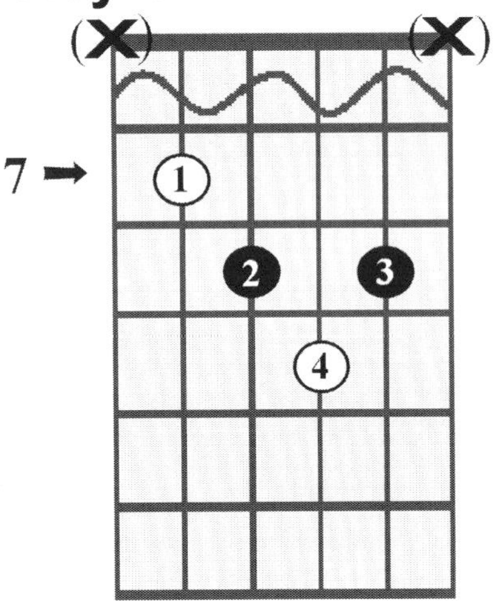

7 ➡

Em♭5 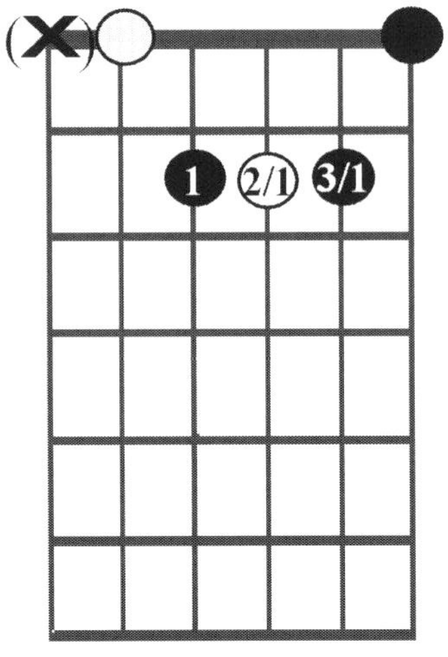 A 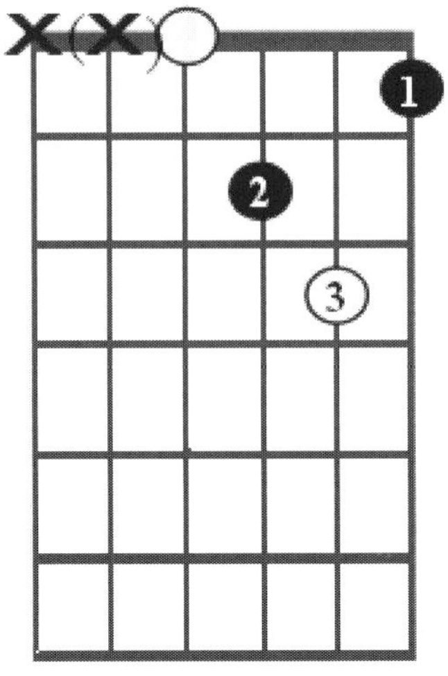 Dm

PART SIX

VI - ii - V - i

MINOR KEYS
TRIADS

THE VI CHORD

If you compare a *minor* scale with its relative *major* scale, you will see that the 6th *degree* of the minor scale corresponds the the 4th degree of the major scale. Thus, when the scale is harmonised, a major chord is formed on this note.

As with the major vi-ii-V-I exercises, no new chords are introduced in this section, though some new voicings and/or fingerings will appear. The alternative voicings, are, of course, interchangeable with the voicings you already know, and you should also explore further possibilities for yourself.

Key of Am

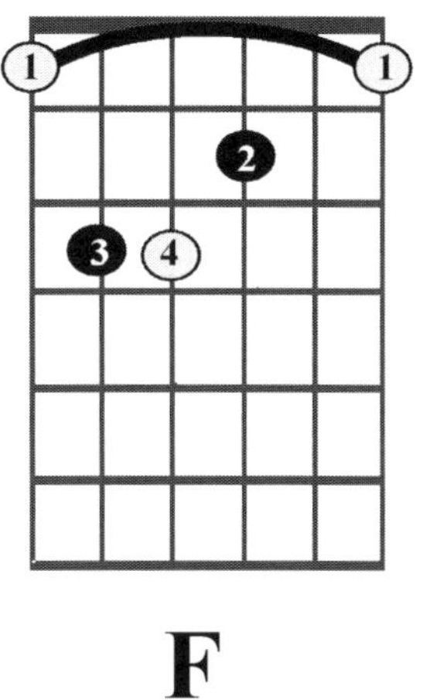

F

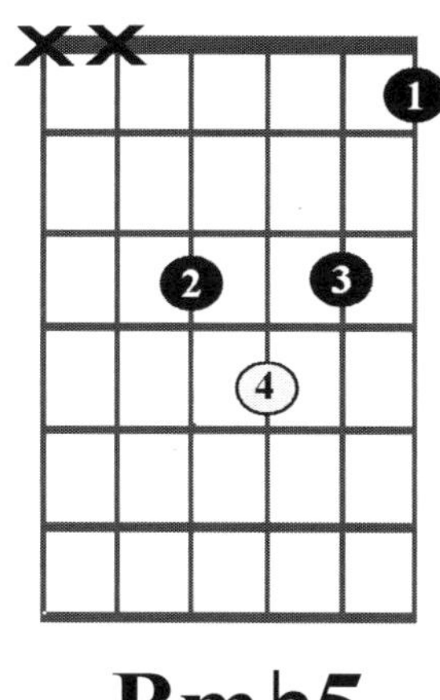

Bm♭5

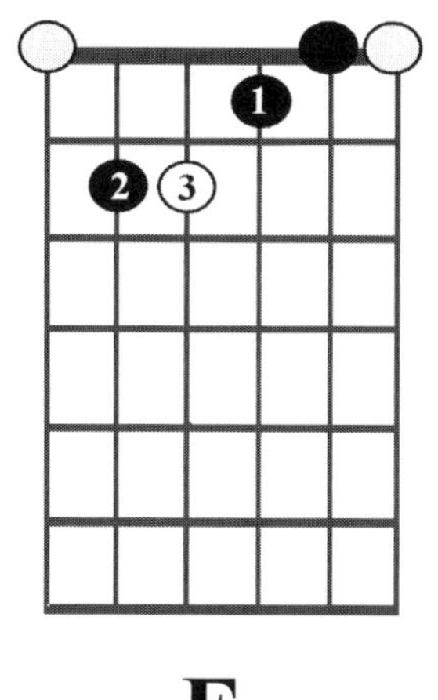

E

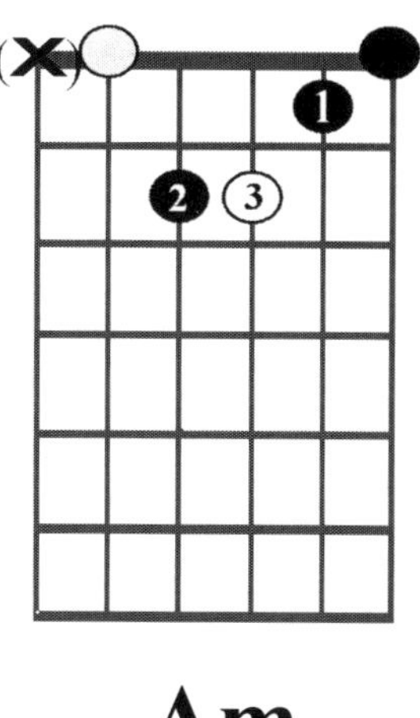

Am

Key of Em

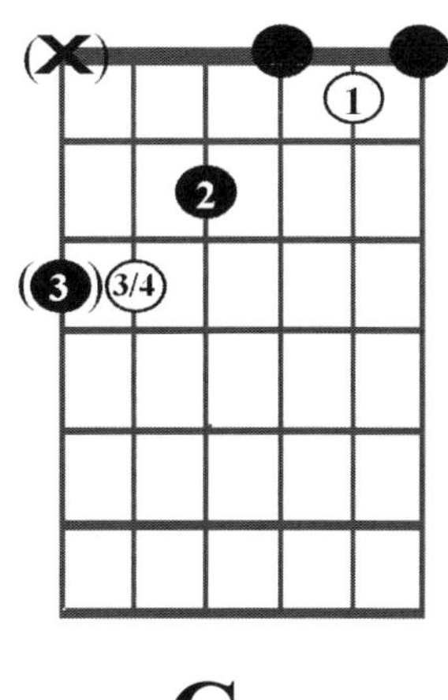

C

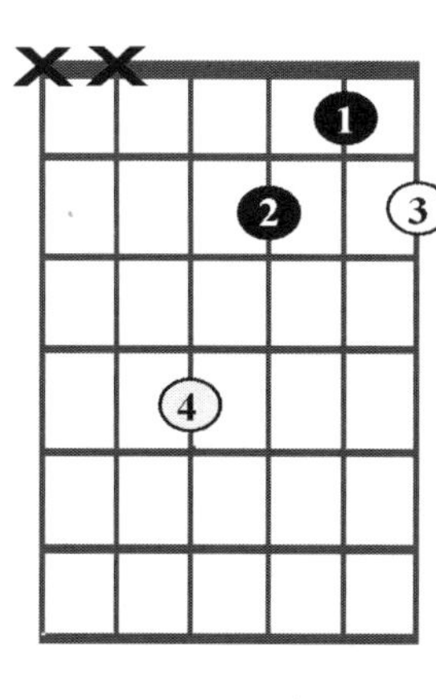

F#m♭5

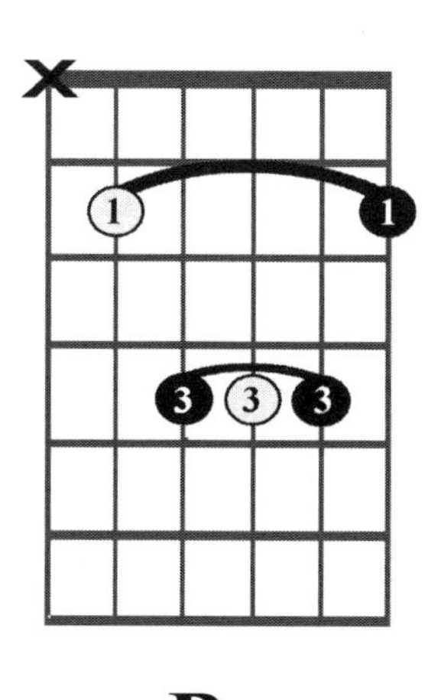

B

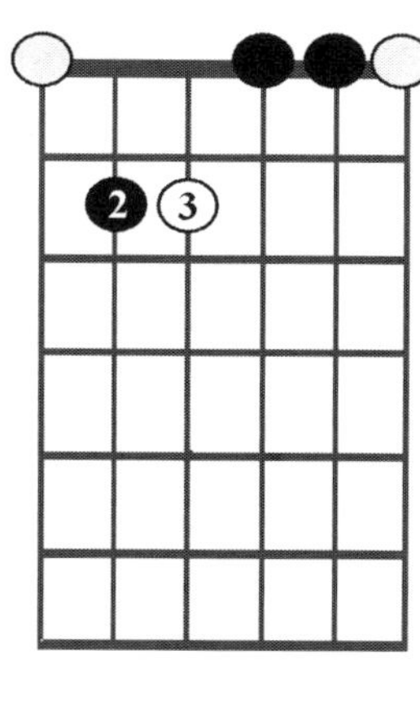

Em

Key of Bm

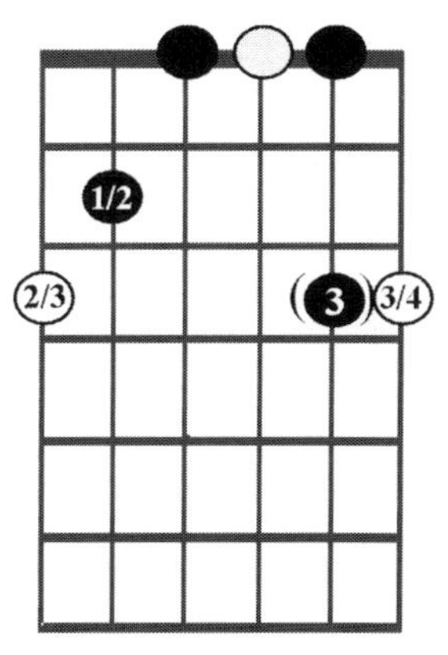

G

C#m♭5

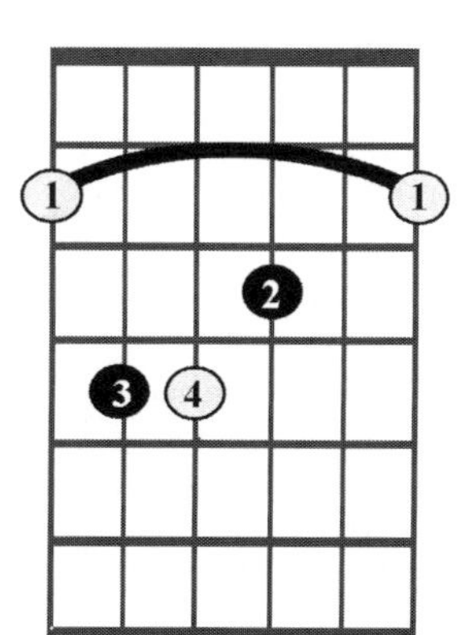

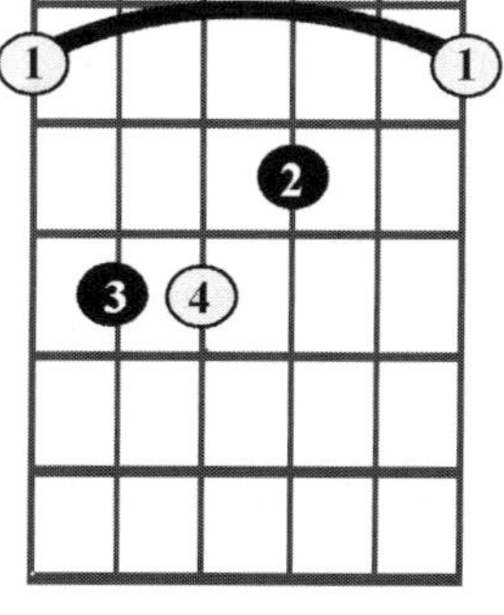

F#

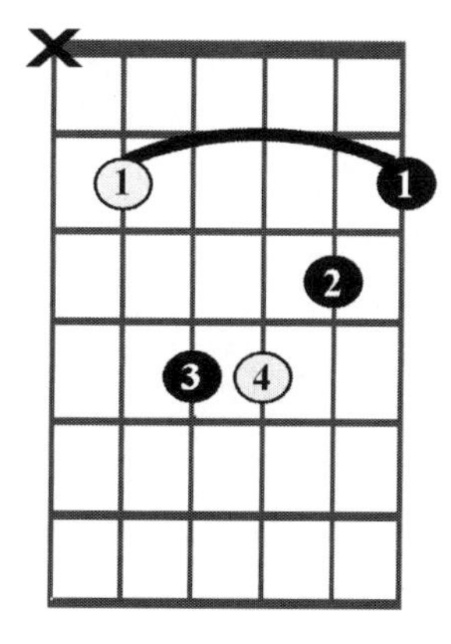

Bm

Key of F#m

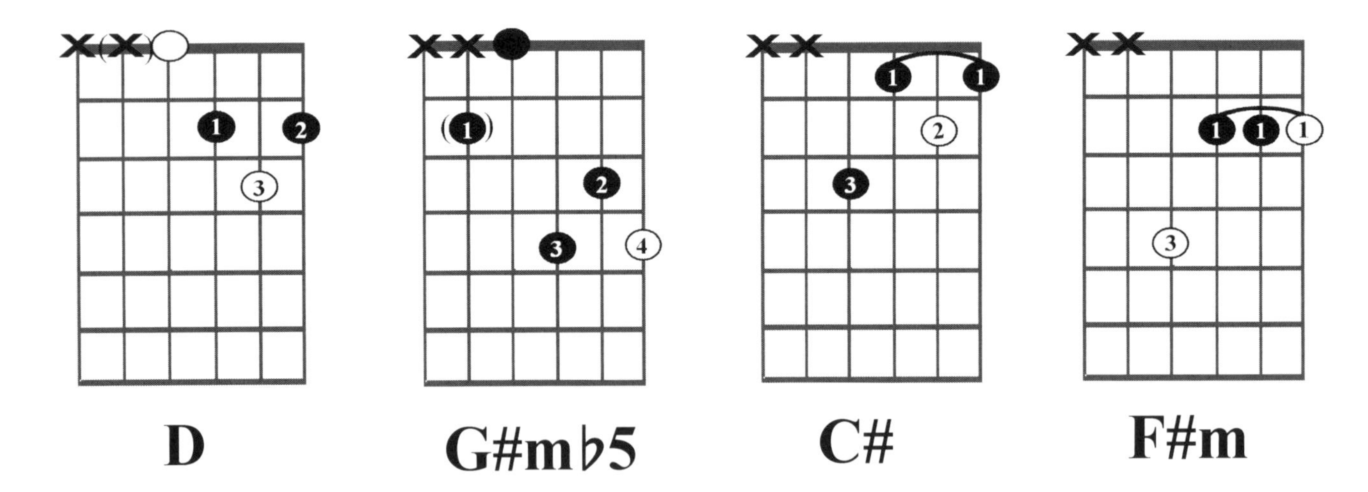

Key of C#m

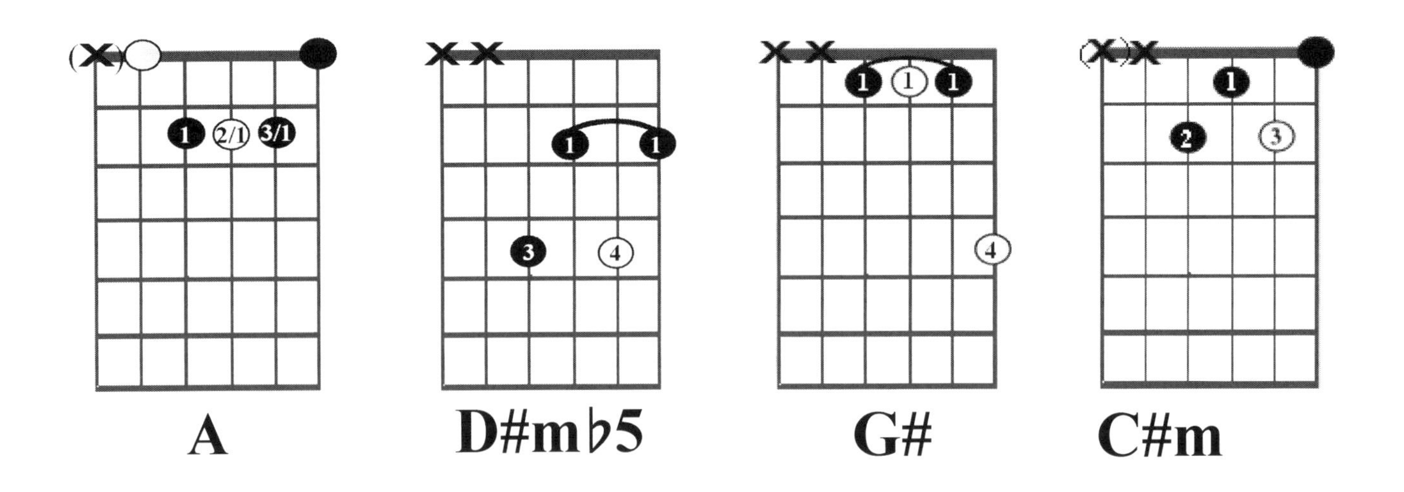

Key of A♭m

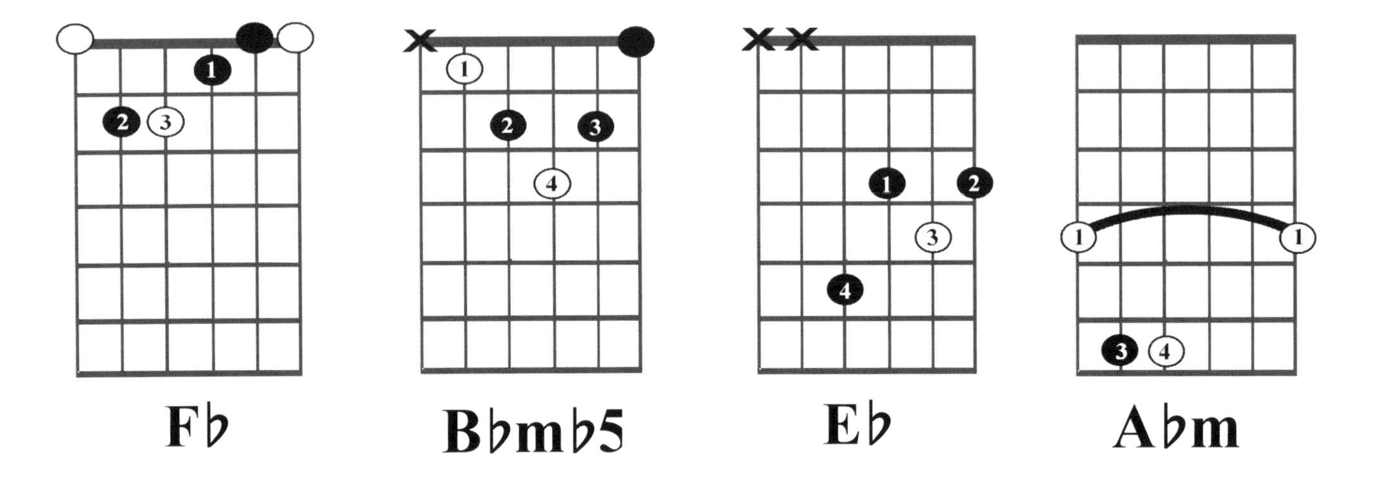

Key of E♭m

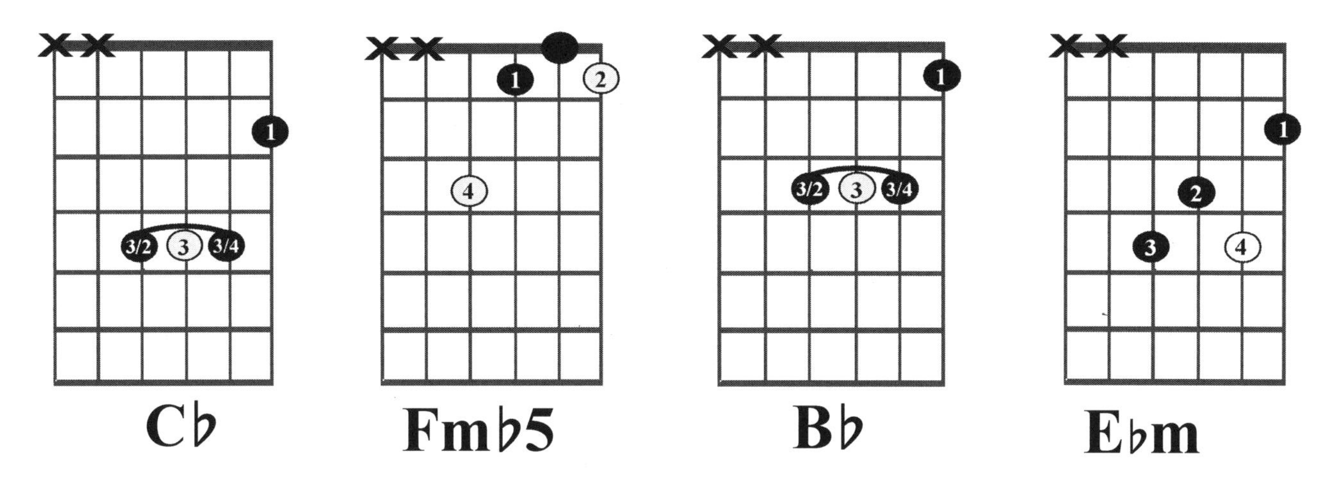

Key of B♭m

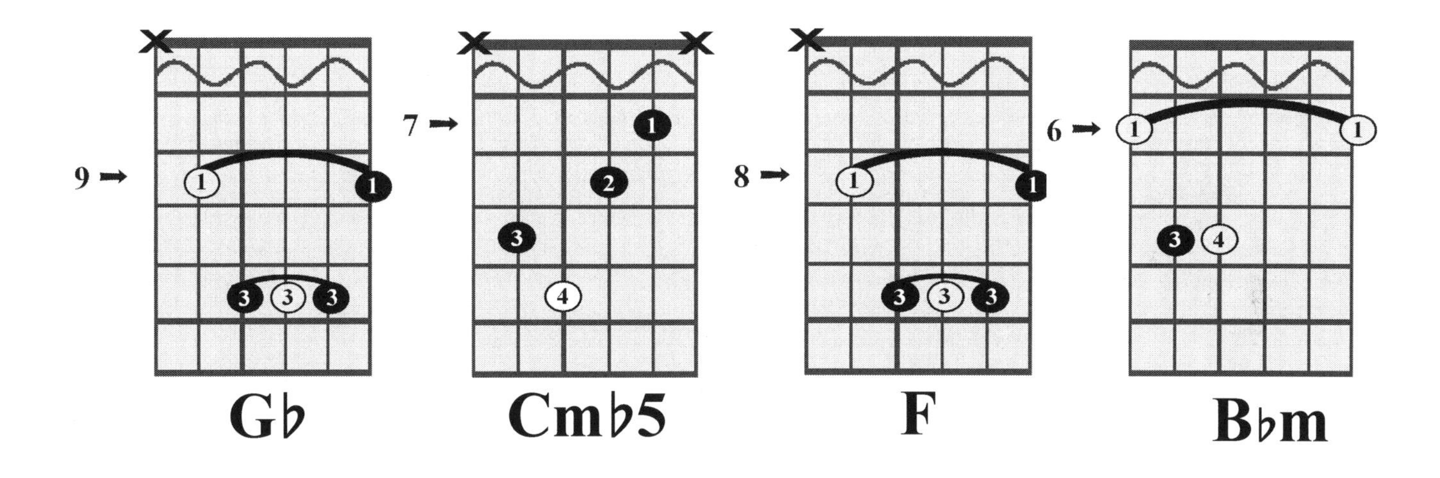

Key of Fm

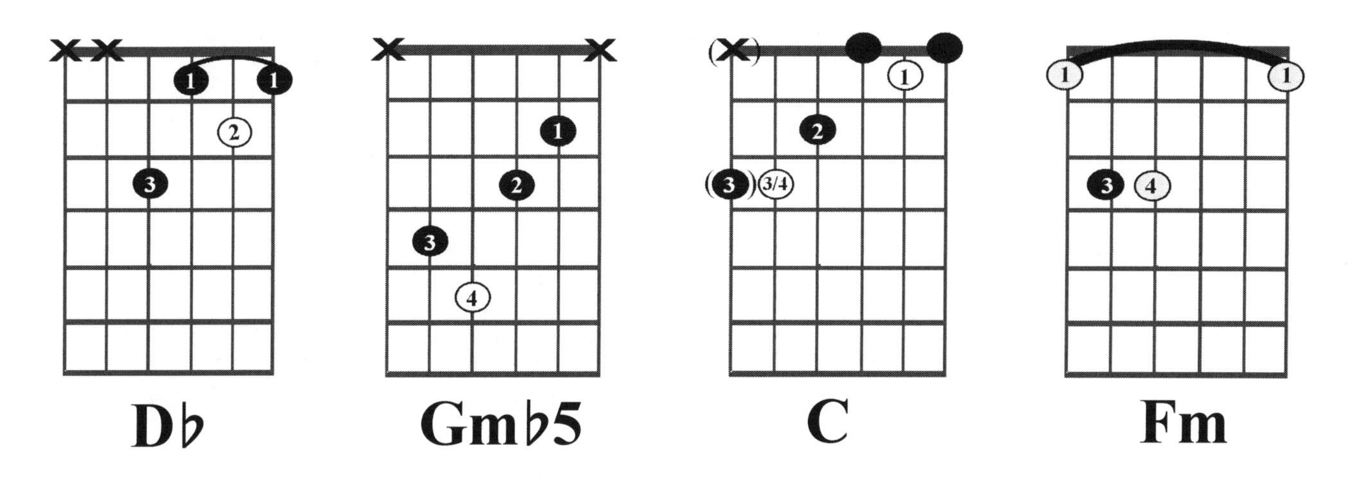

Key of Cm

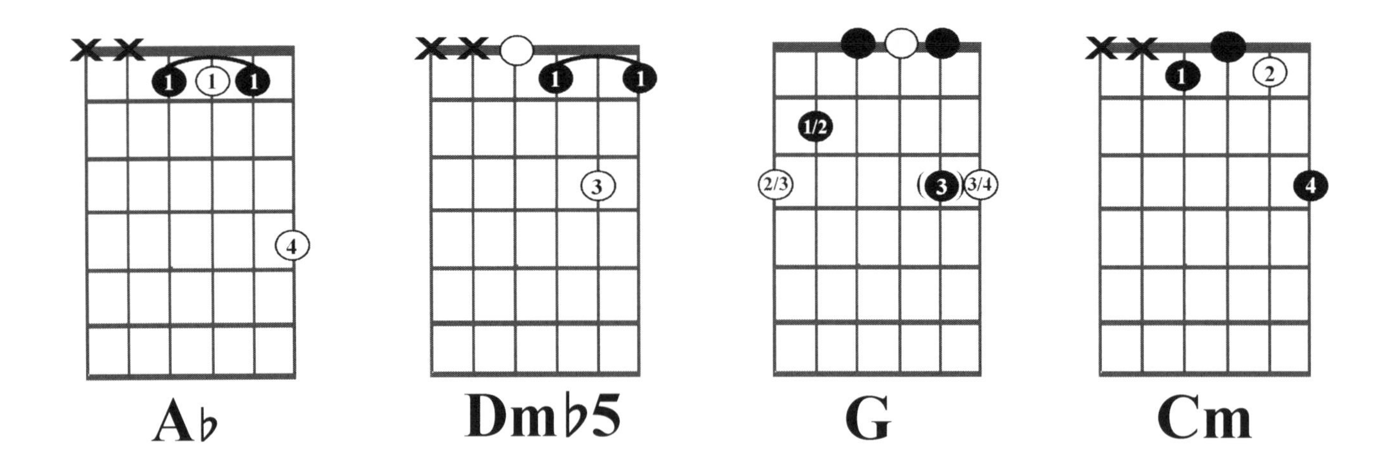

Key of Gm

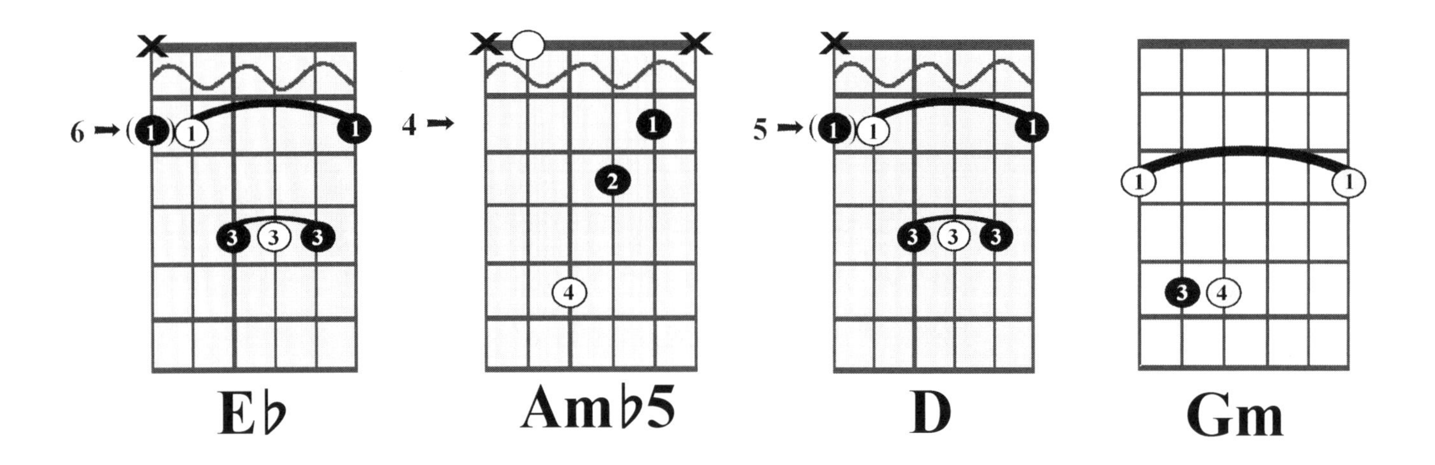

Key of Dm

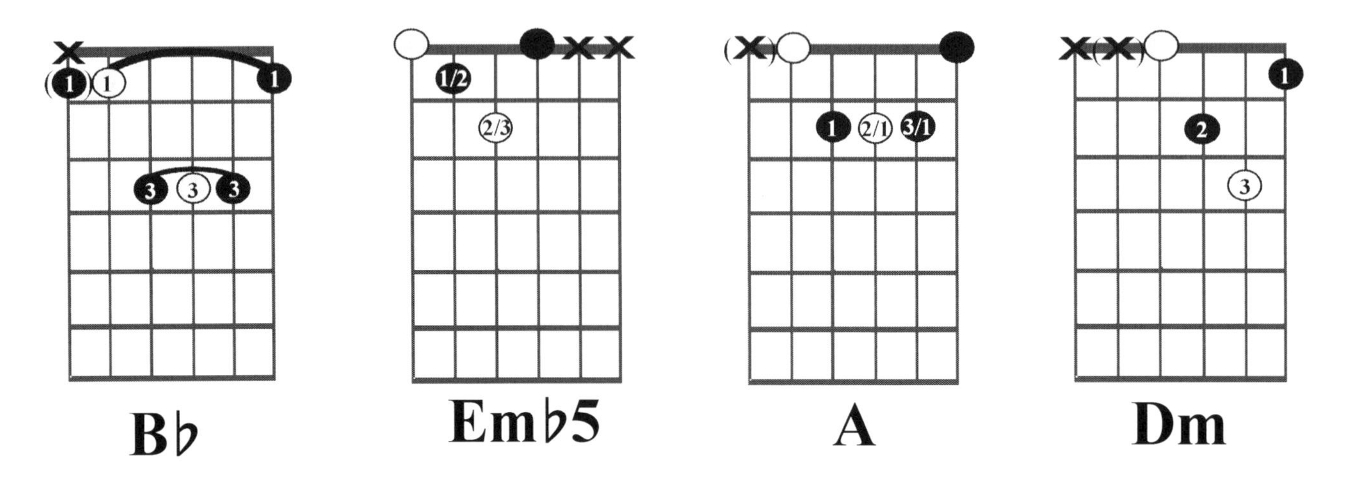

PART SEVEN

I - IV - V

MAJOR KEYS
SEVENTH CHORDS

FURTHER HARMONISATION

All the chords we have encountered so far have been *triads* - that is to say that there only three unique notes in each chord: the *root*, *third* and *fifth*. Since the chords are played across four, five or six strings of the guitar, one or more notes of the chord are doubled in each example.

In the next sections, the harmonisation of the scale is extended to add a fourth note, the *seventh* (so called since the *interval* corresponds to that between the *tonic* (first) and seventh notes of the scale). Seventh chords come in four varieties:

i) *Major* Seventh: **M7** (the interval from the root to the seventh is the same as that from the tonic to the seventh of a major scale; the chord also contains a major third and a *perfect* fifth). Major seventh chords are formed on the first and fourth *degrees* of the major scale, corresponding to the third and sixth degrees of the minor scale.

ii) *Minor* Seventh: **m7** - (the interval from the root to the seventh is the same as that from the tonic to the seventh of a minor scale; the chord also contains a minor third and a perfect fifth). Minor seventh chords are formed on the second, third and sixth degrees of the major scale, corresponding to the fourth, fifth and first degrees of the minor scale. However it is common practice to substitute a dominant seventh (see below) for the minor v chord.

iii) Dominant Seventh: **7** - often just referred to as a "Seventh"; any time you encounter a 7 chord unqualified by "major" or "minor", you can assume a dominant seventh is intended. This chord has a major third, perfect fifth and minor seventh and is formed on the fifth degree of the major scale (the seventh degree of the minor scale). The name "dominant" comes from the classical system of naming the degrees of the scale where 1 = tonic; 2 = supertonic; 3 = mediant; 4 = subdominant; 5 = dominant; 6 = submediant; 7 = leading note. Hence the V chord is the "dominant" chord, and the V7 chord the "dominant seventh".

iv) Minor Seven Flat Five: **m7♭5** - Also called a Minor Seventh *Diminished* Fifth, or "half-diminished" chord. This chord contains a minor third, a flattened (or "diminished") fifth, and a minor seventh, and is formed on the seventh degree of the major scale (the second degree of the minor scale).

Triads and seventh chords can be freely mixed and matched within a chord progression. A popular compositional technique is to end a chord sequence predominantly in triads with a V7-I progression. In major keys, the cadential movement is enhanced, since the semitone movement from the third of the V7 chord to the root of the I chord is mirrored by a downward semitone movement from the seventh of the V7 chord to the third of the I chord.

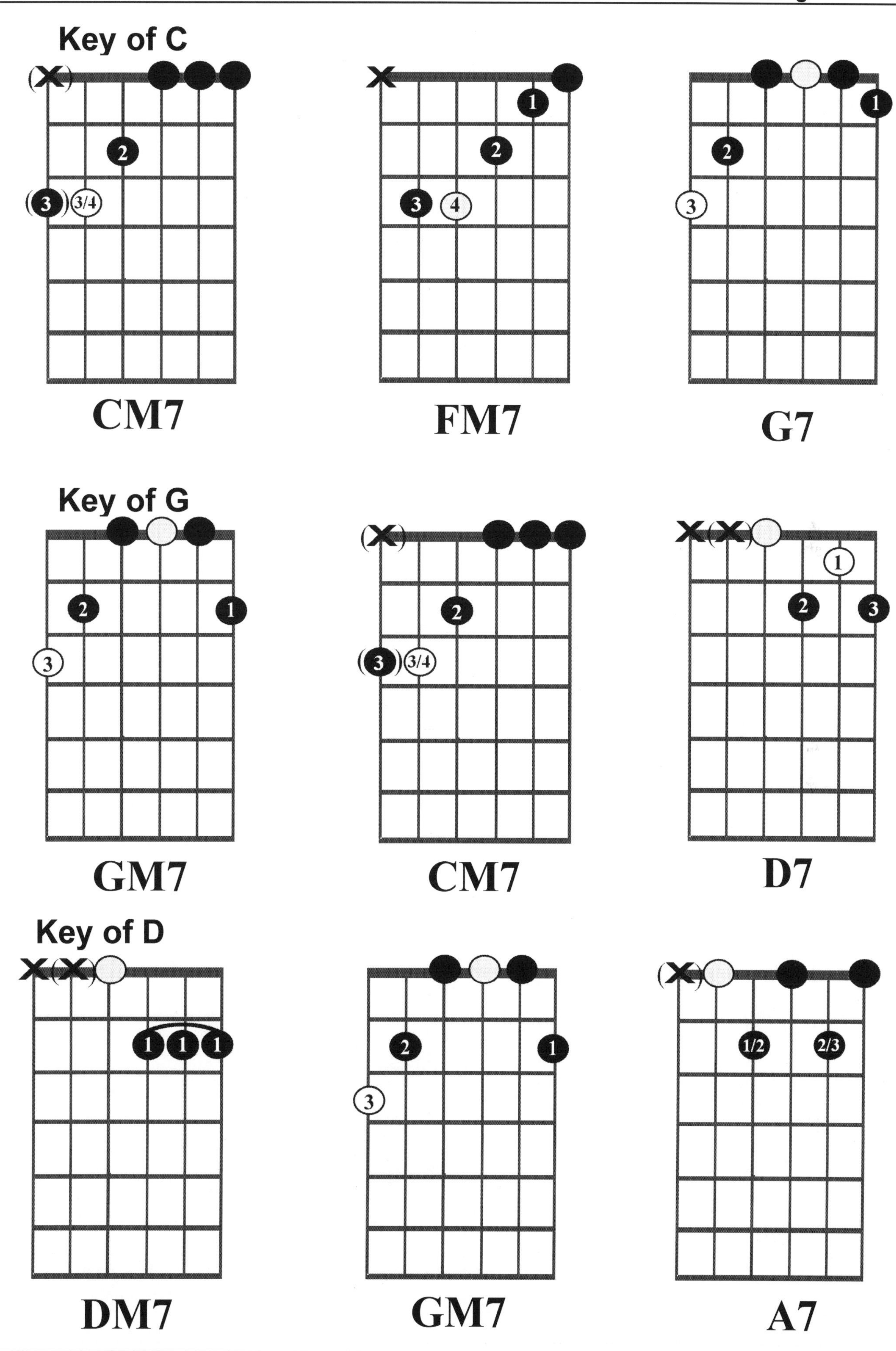
Key of C
CM7
FM7
G7
Key of G
GM7
CM7
D7
Key of D
DM7
GM7
A7

Key of A

AM7

DM7

E7

Key of E

EM7

AM7

B7

Key of B

BM7

EM7

F#7

Key of F#

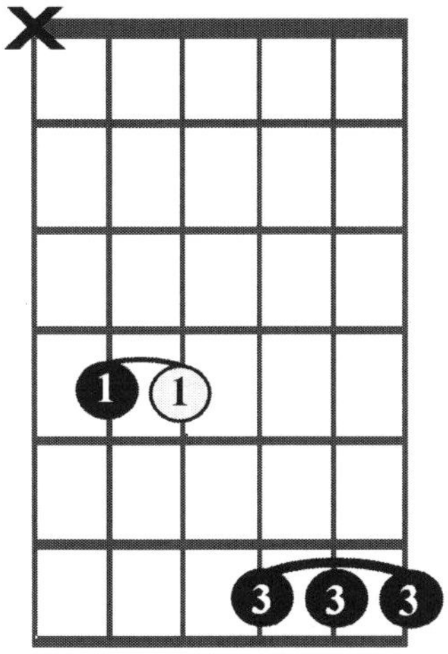

F#M7

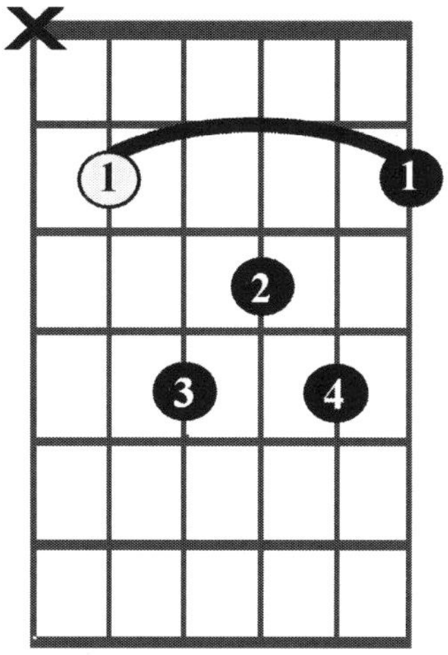

BM7

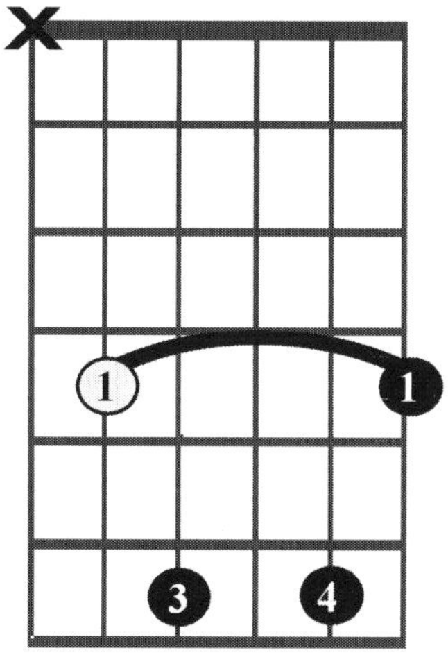

C#7

Key of C#

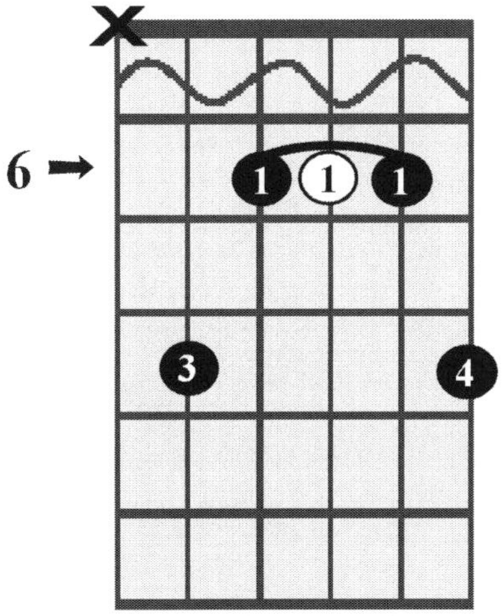

6 ➡

C#M7

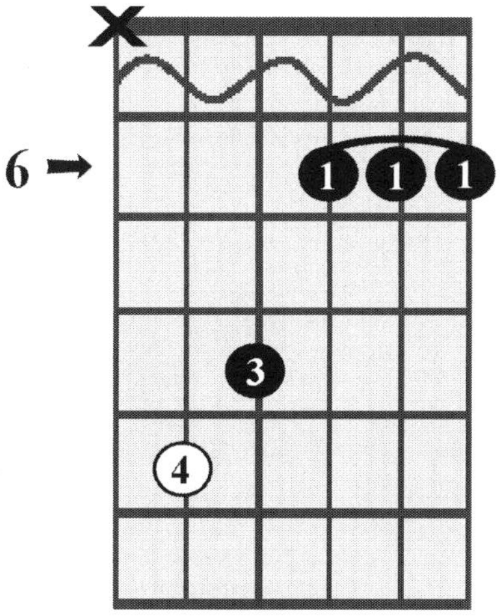

6 ➡

F#M7

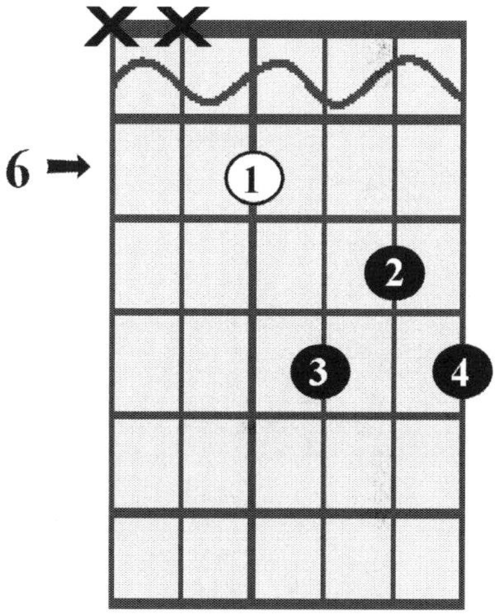

6 ➡

G#7

Key of A♭

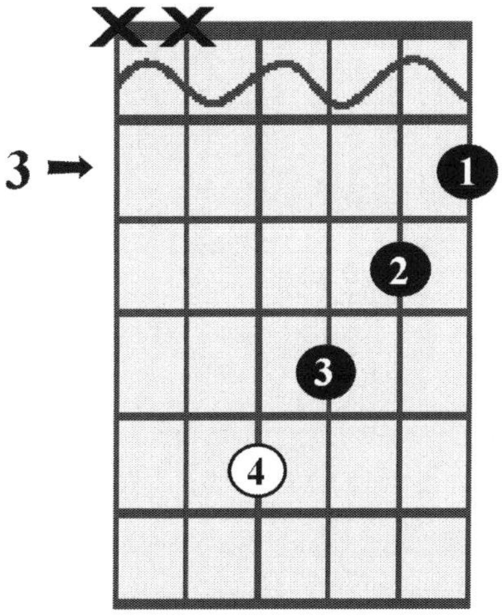

3 ➡

A♭M7

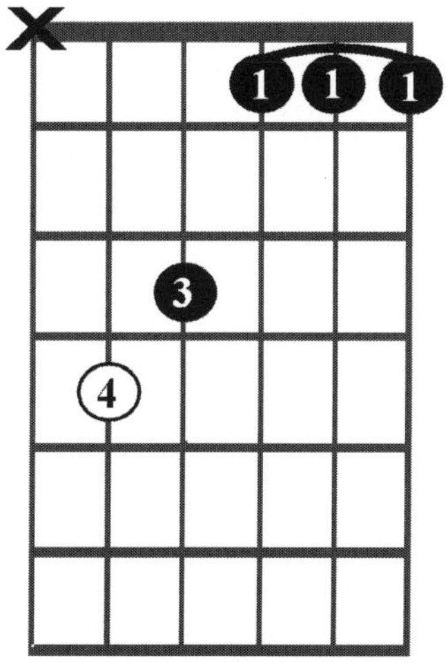

D♭M7

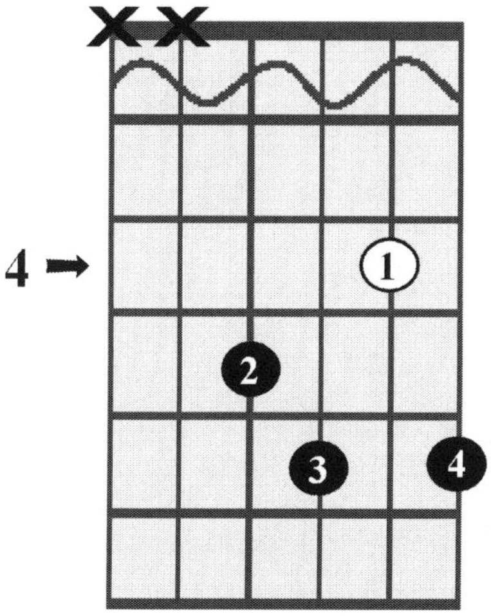

4 ➡

E♭7

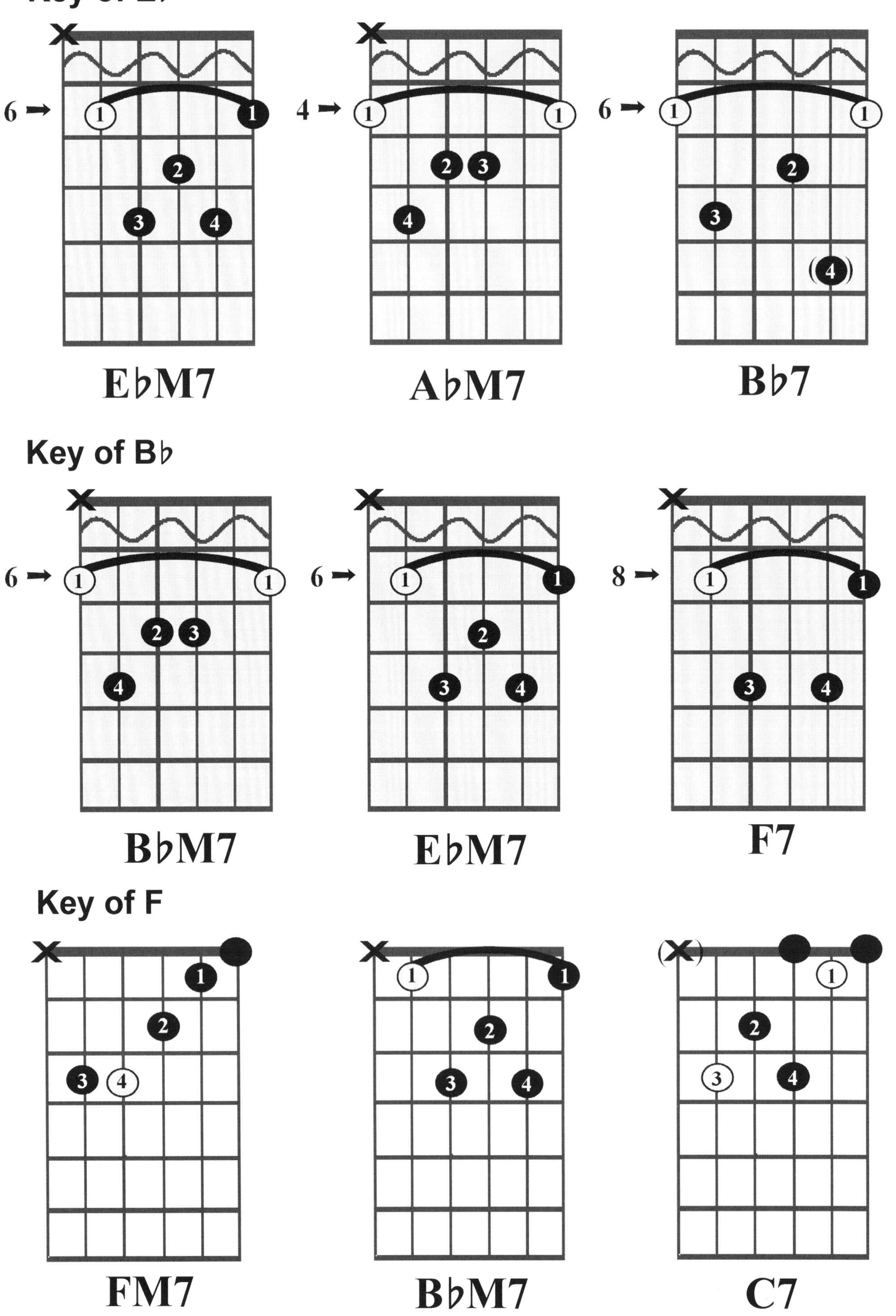
Key of E♭
6 →
E♭M7
4 →
A♭M7
6 →
B♭7
Key of B♭
6 →
B♭M7
6 →
E♭M7
8 →
F7
Key of F
FM7
B♭M7
C7

PART EIGHT

ii - V - I

MAJOR KEYS
SEVENTH CHORDS

A BRIEF PAUSE FOR THOUGHT

If you have been working systematically through this book, you will undoubtedly have found by now that some of the chord fingerings are considerably trickier than others. It is therefore worth emphasising that many of the chord voicings are interchangeable, particularly the transposable voicings (and most particularly the barre chords).

Throughout this book, I have endeavoured to include as many alternative chord voicings as I can - although a completely comprehensive list of all possible variants and combinations would be impractical. At the same time, I have tried to combine the chord voicings within each progression in a way that makes sense, both from a musical point of view, and with a view to ease of movement between the chords. In reality, some of the fingerings given will rarely be used in everyday playing, unless there is an overriding musical reason to do so (perhaps in order to create a melody line from the top notes, or a bass line from the bass notes).

It follows that if an example in any one key is proving overly troublesome, an easier alternative can often be found by transposing either the complete progression or individual chords from one of the other examples. Of course, I recommend practising all of the examples, whether or not you intend to use them in performance, in order to develop your technique to the maximum.

You will also no doubt have noticed that some of the examples sound very different in character in alternative keys - this may result from the *inversion* of the chord; the register (i.e. how far up or down the fretboard the chords are played); how many strings are used; which note is the highest etc. Except for the open-position chords, which are not transposable, the chosen key does not restrict you to using these voicings (it's just that this book is limited to one example per key). Once again, bear in mind that any transposable chord shape is available to use in **any** key, and in any appropriate chord progression.

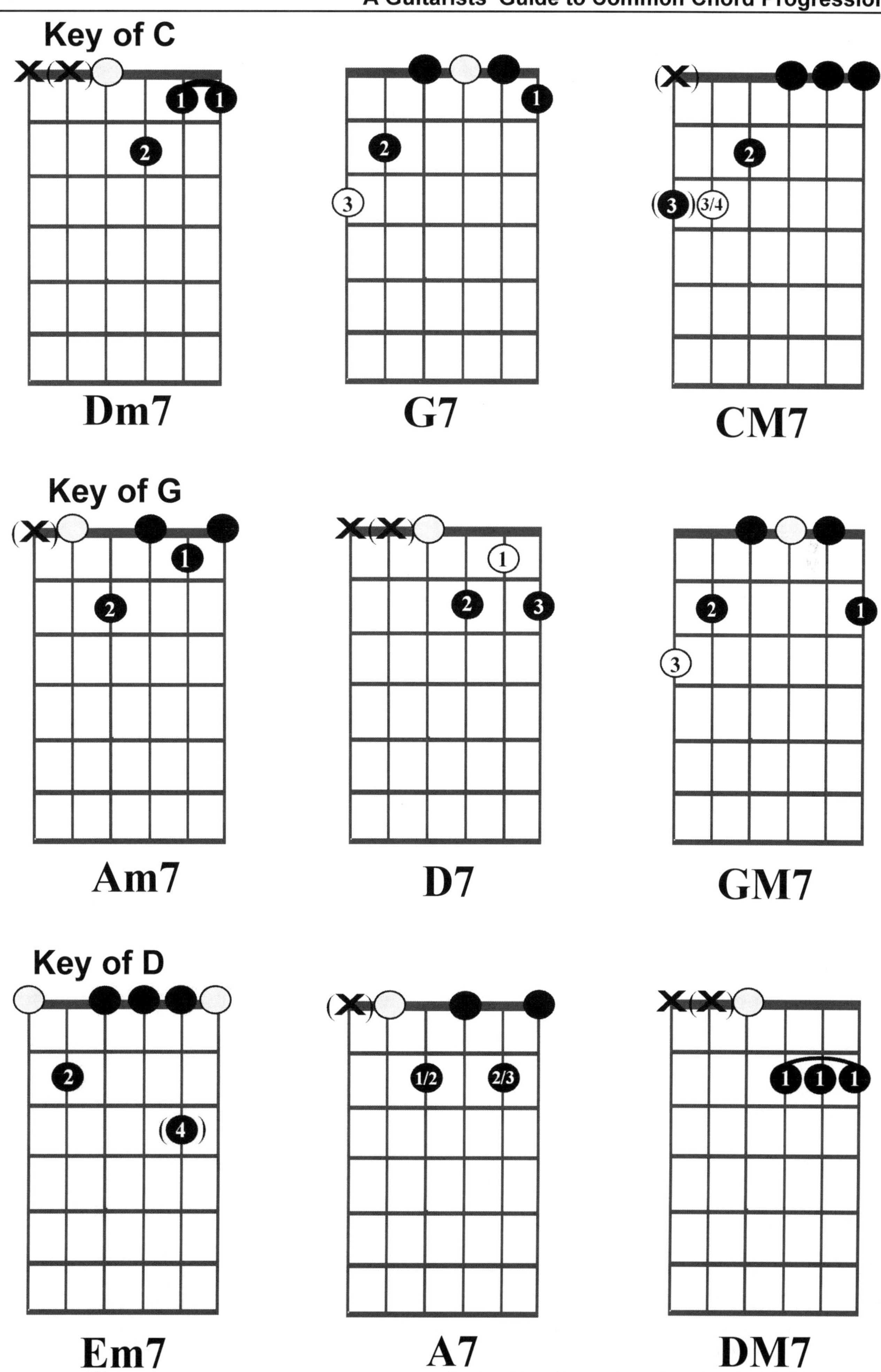
Key of C
Dm7
G7
CM7
Key of G
Am7
D7
GM7
Key of D
Em7
A7
DM7

Key of A

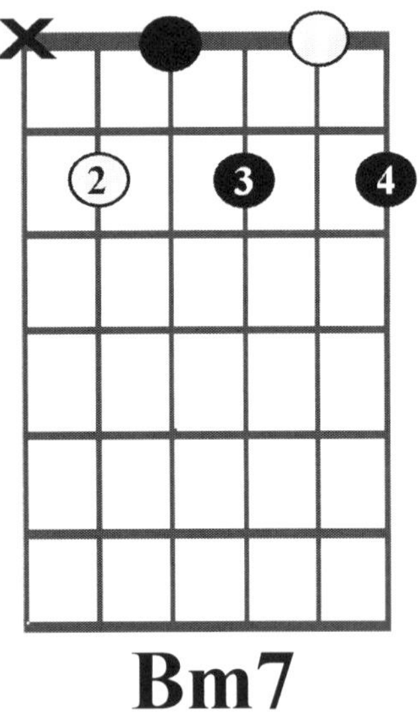

Bm7

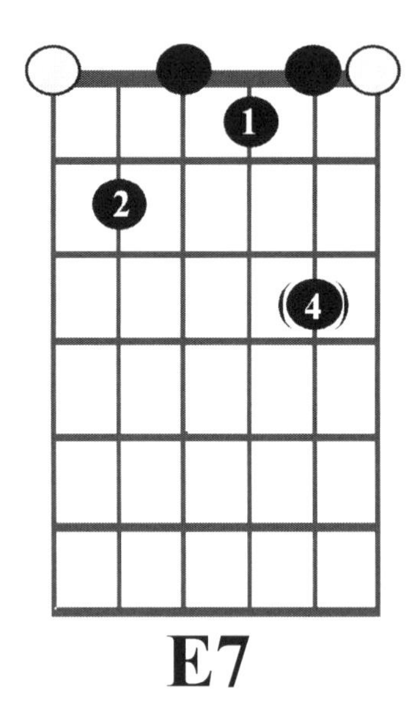

E7

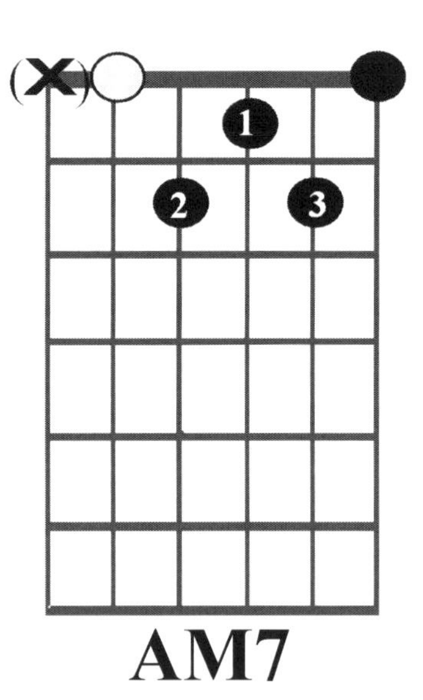

AM7

Key of E

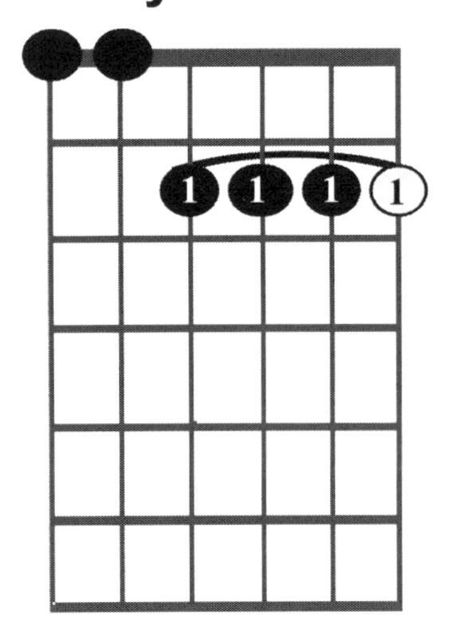

F#m7

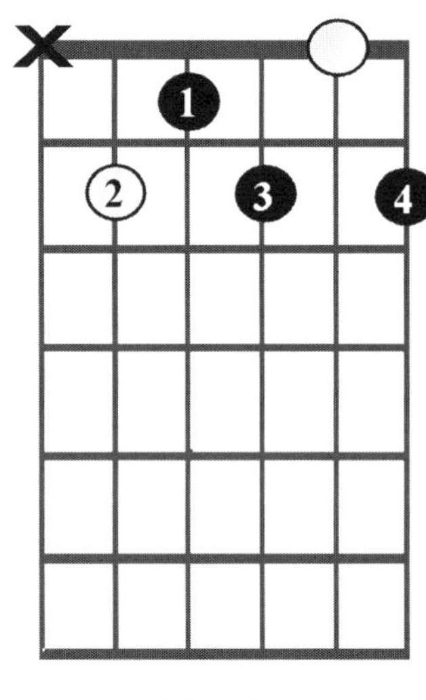

B7

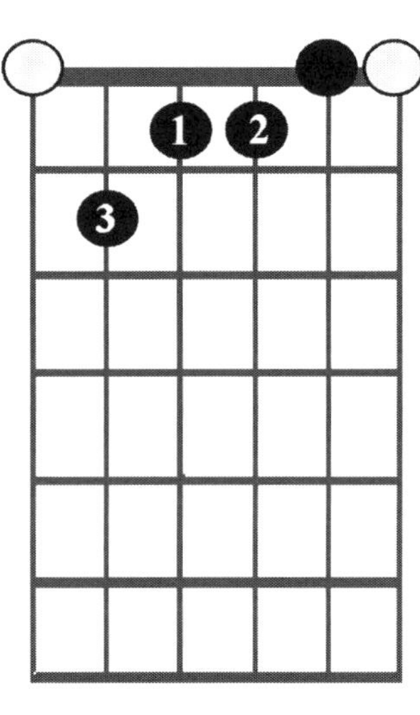

EM7

Key of B

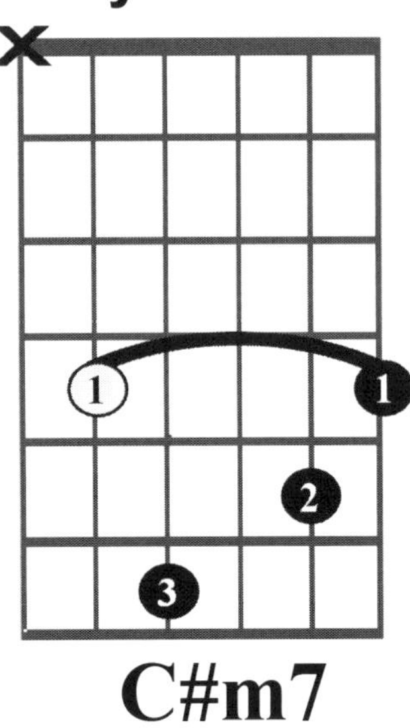

C#m7

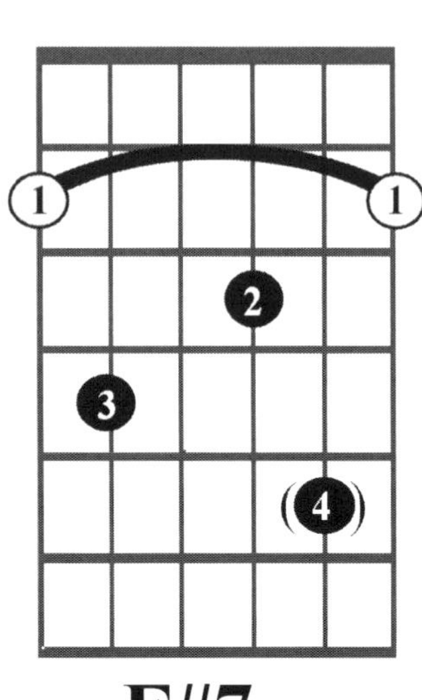

F#7

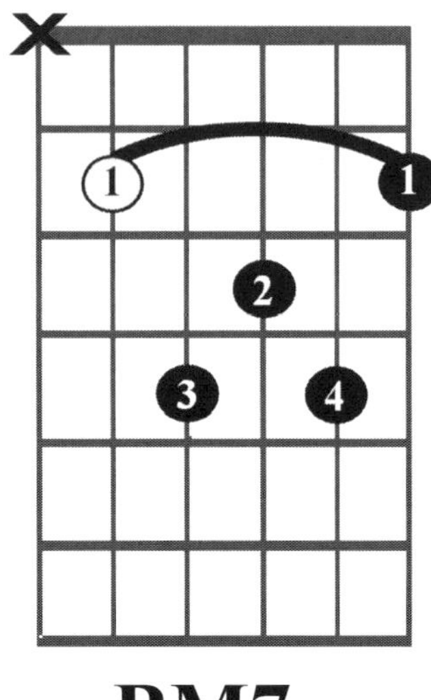

BM7

Key of F#

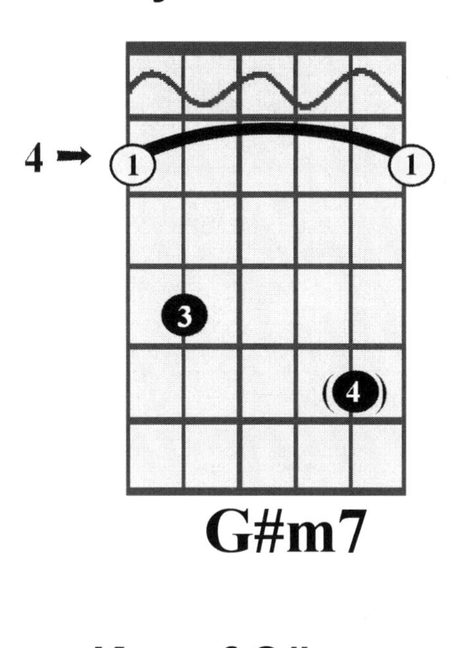

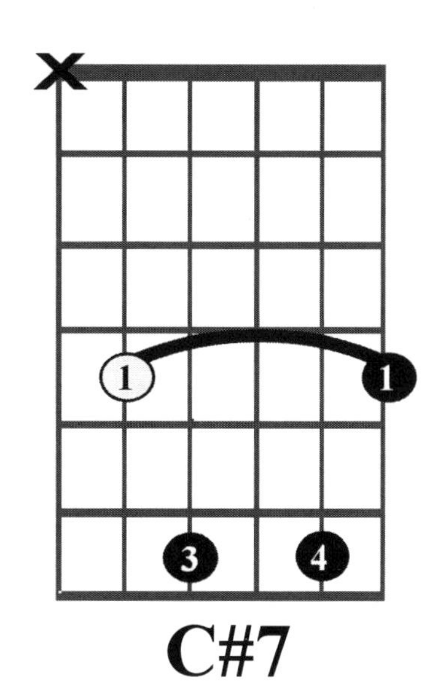

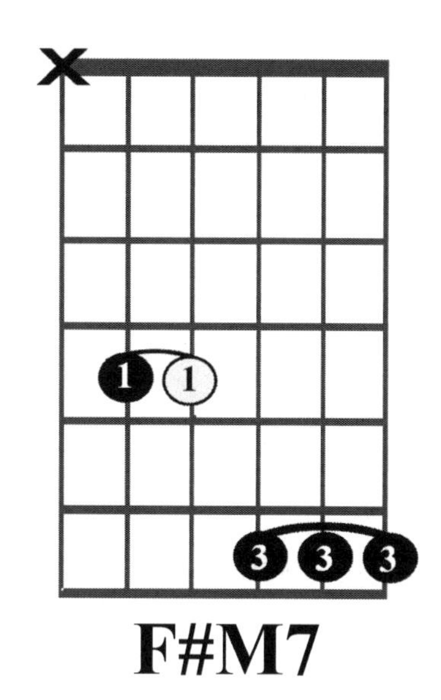

Key of C#

D#m7

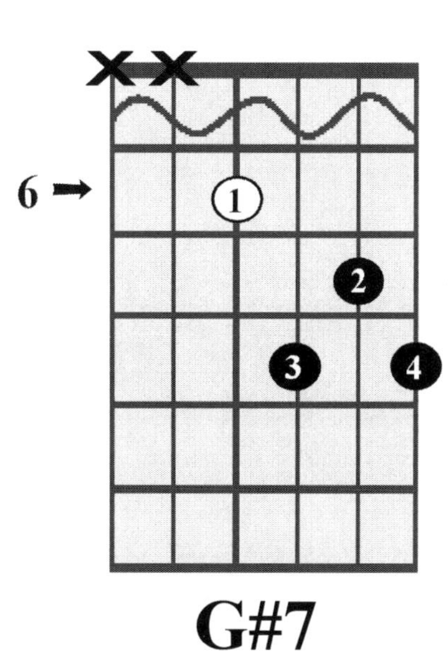

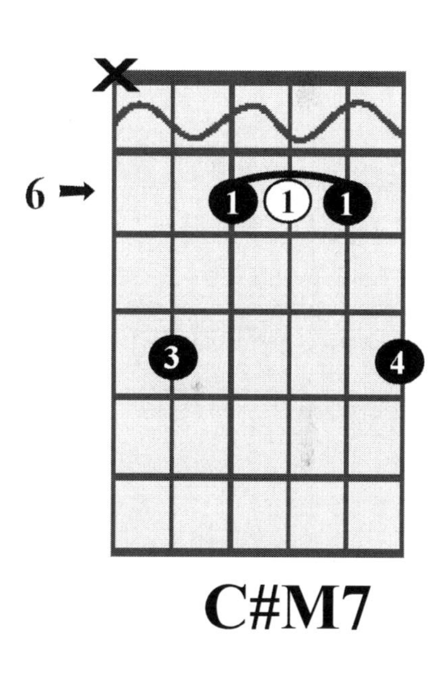

Key of A♭

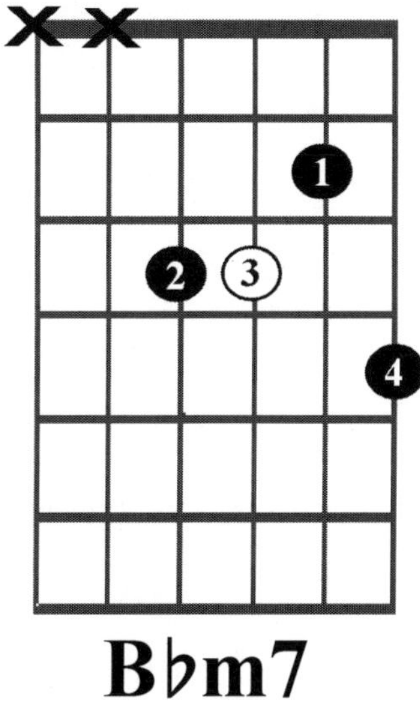

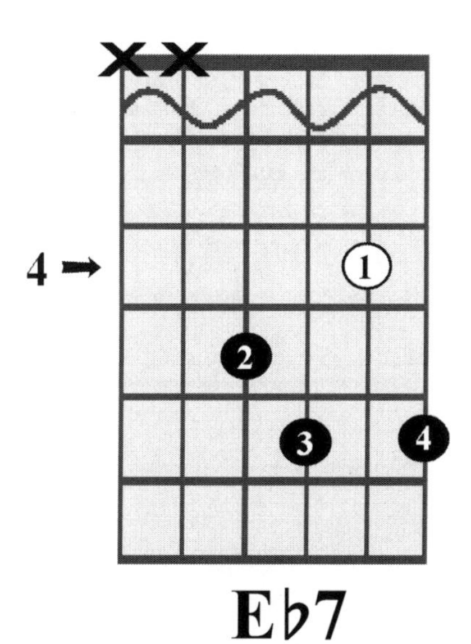

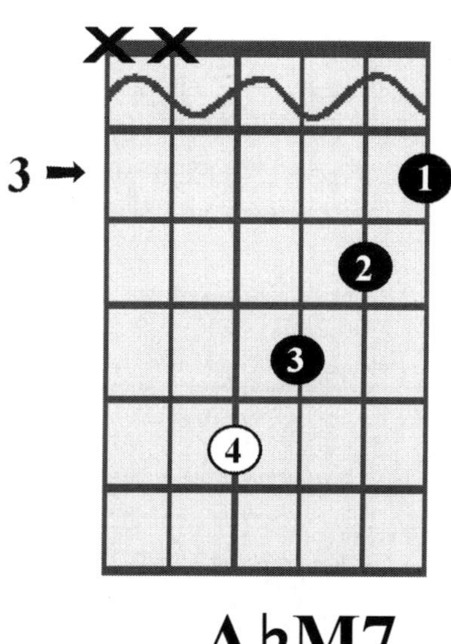

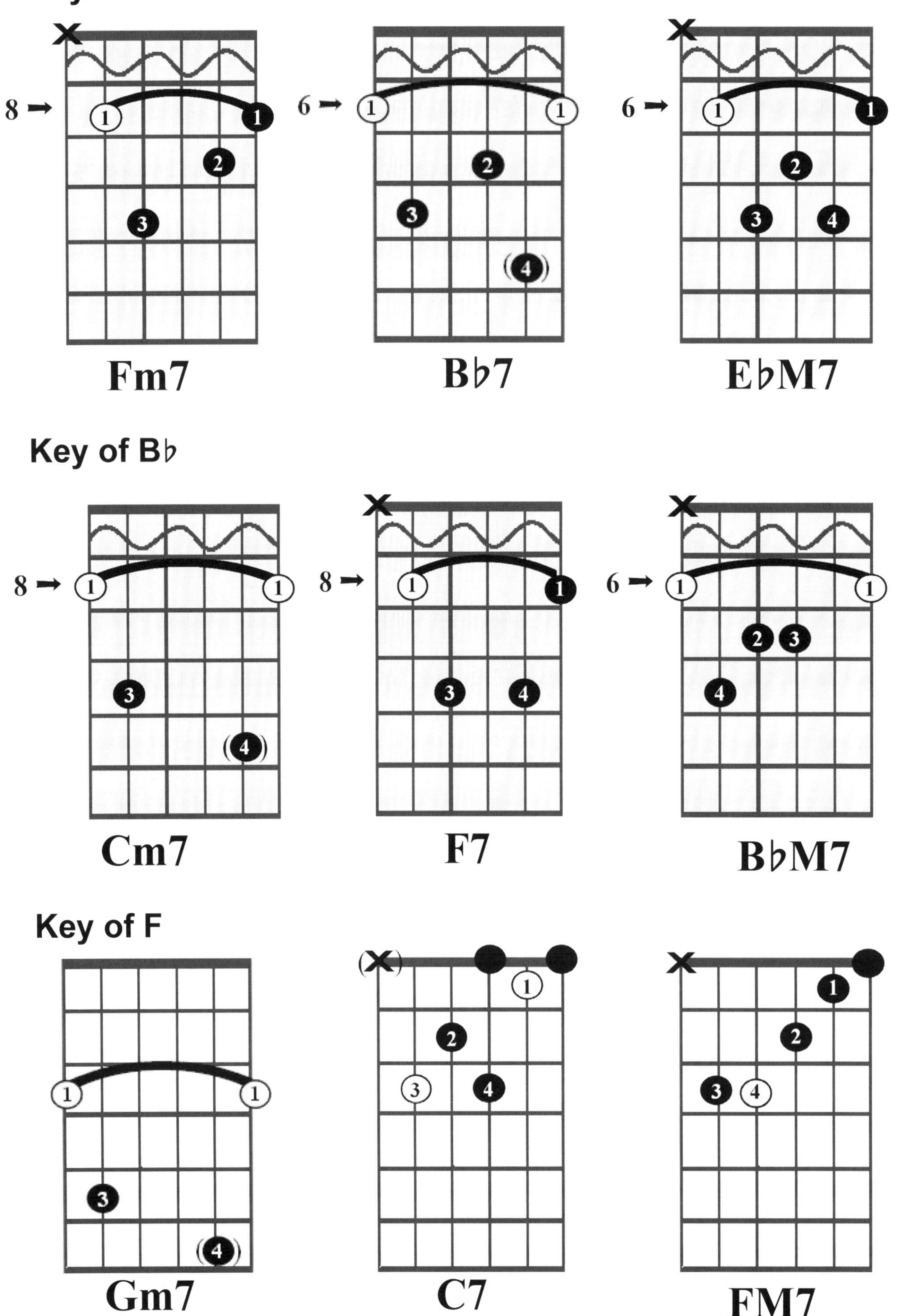
Key of E♭
8
6
6
Fm7
B♭7
E♭M7
Key of B♭
8
8
6
Cm7
F7
B♭M7
Key of F
Gm7
C7
FM7

PART NINE

vi - ii - V - I

MAJOR KEYS
SEVENTH CHORDS

Key of C

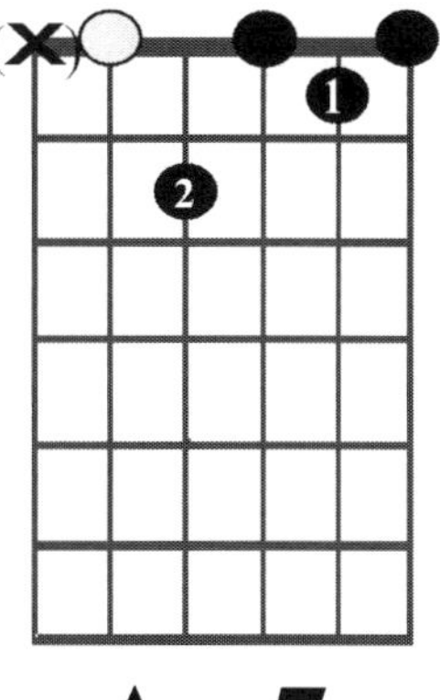

Am7

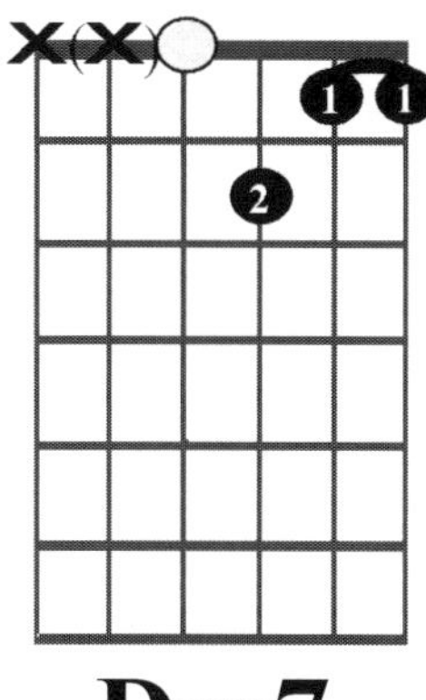

Dm7

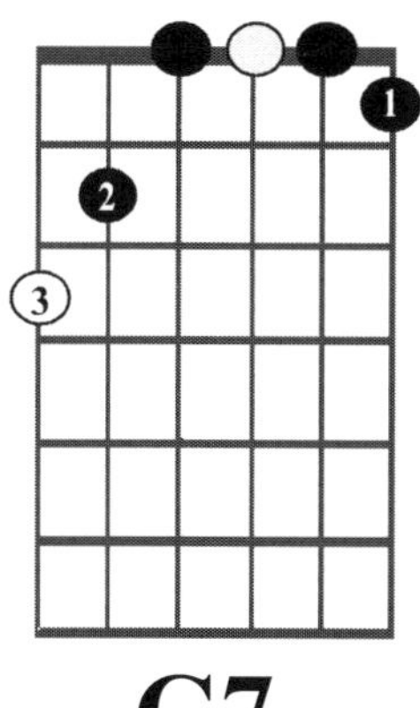

G7

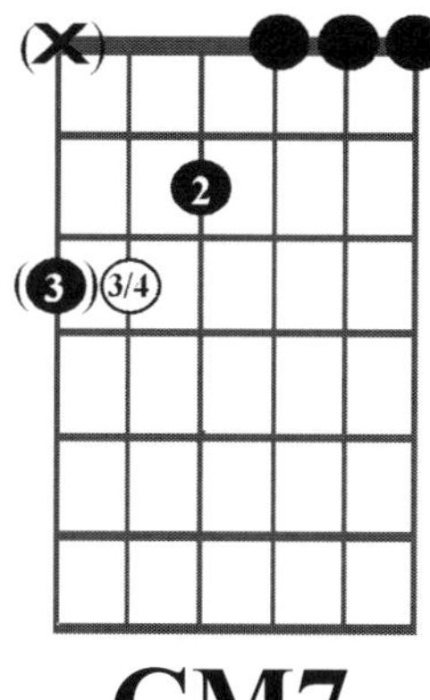

CM7

Key of G

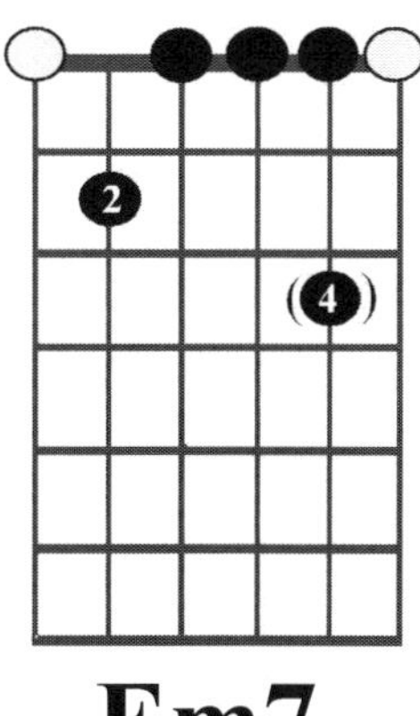

Em7

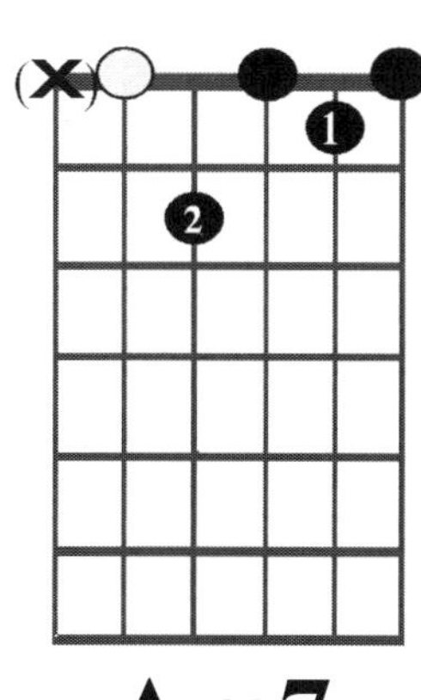

Am7

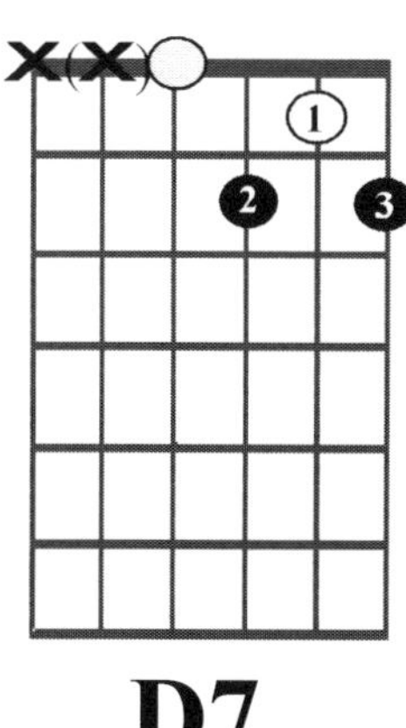

D7

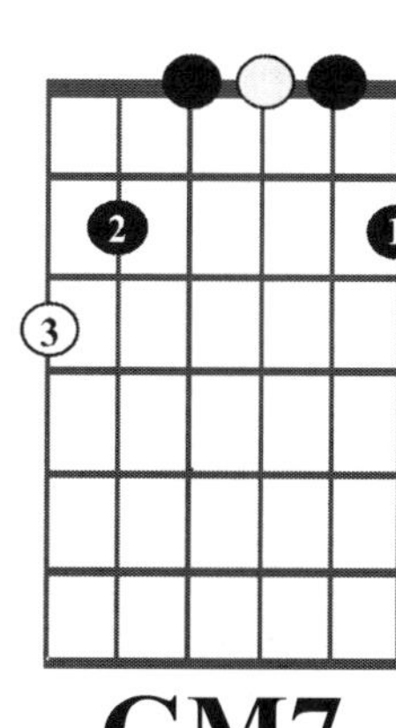

GM7

Key of D

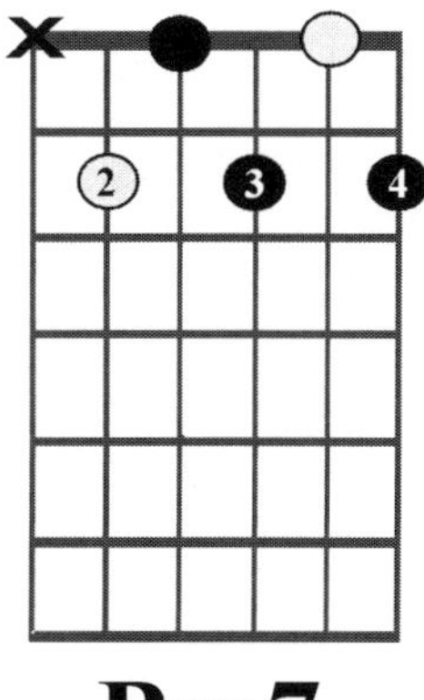

Bm7

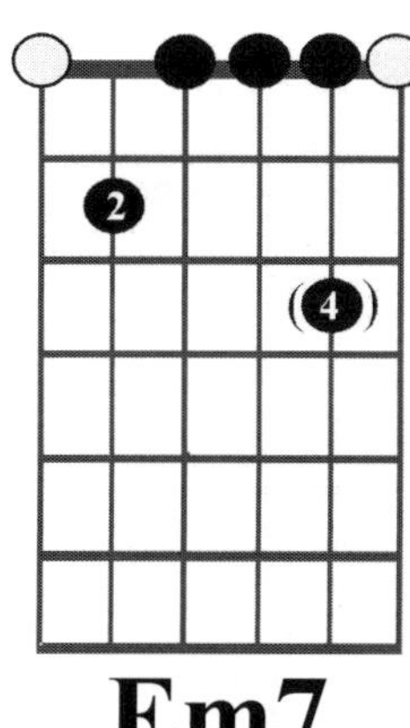

Em7

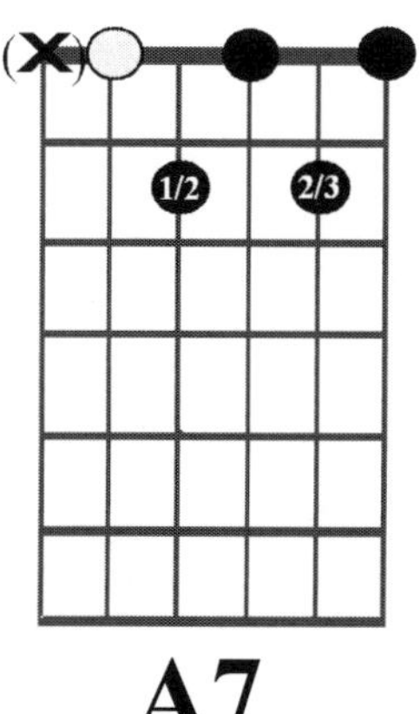

A7

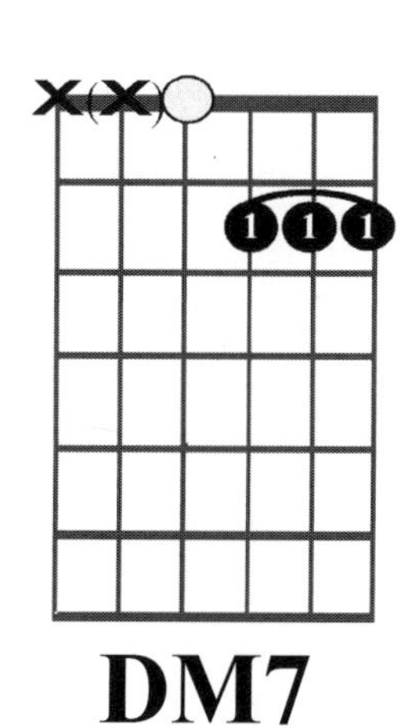

DM7

Key of A

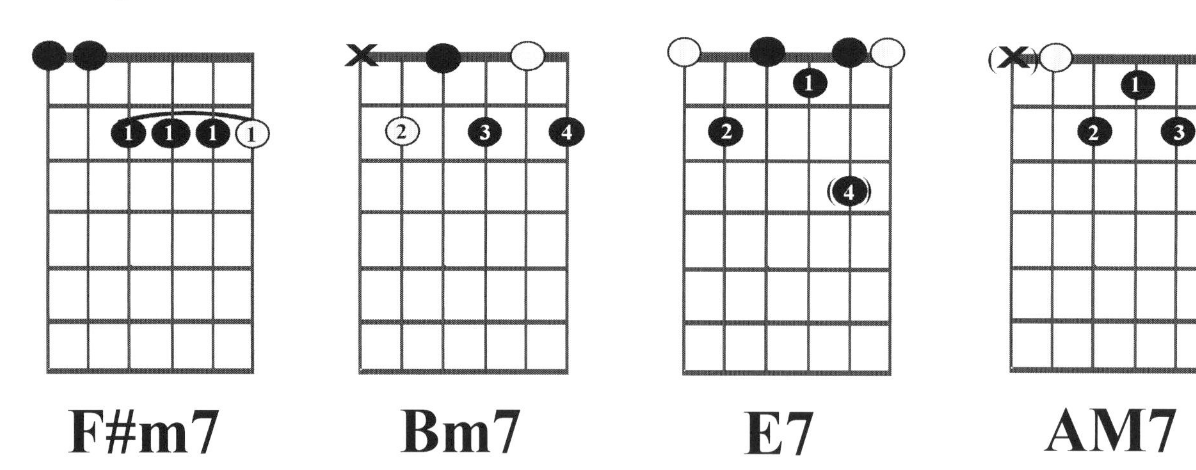

Key of E

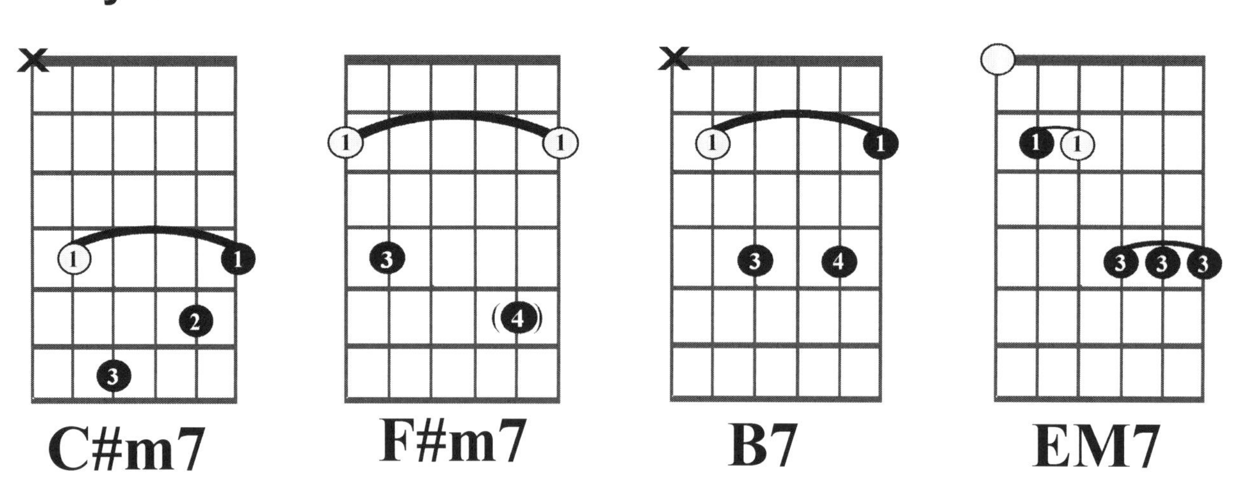

Key of B

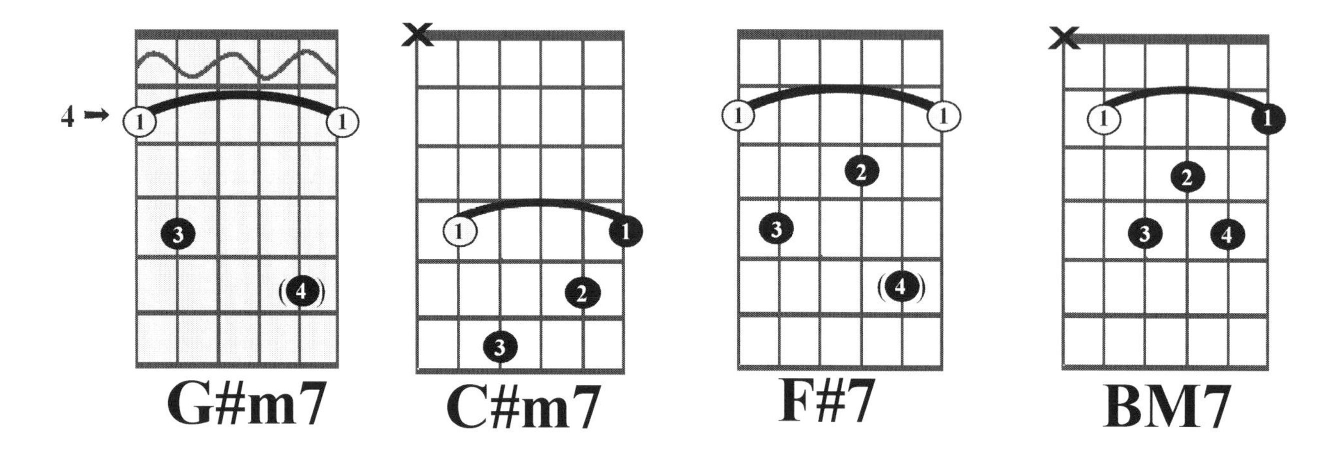

Key of F#

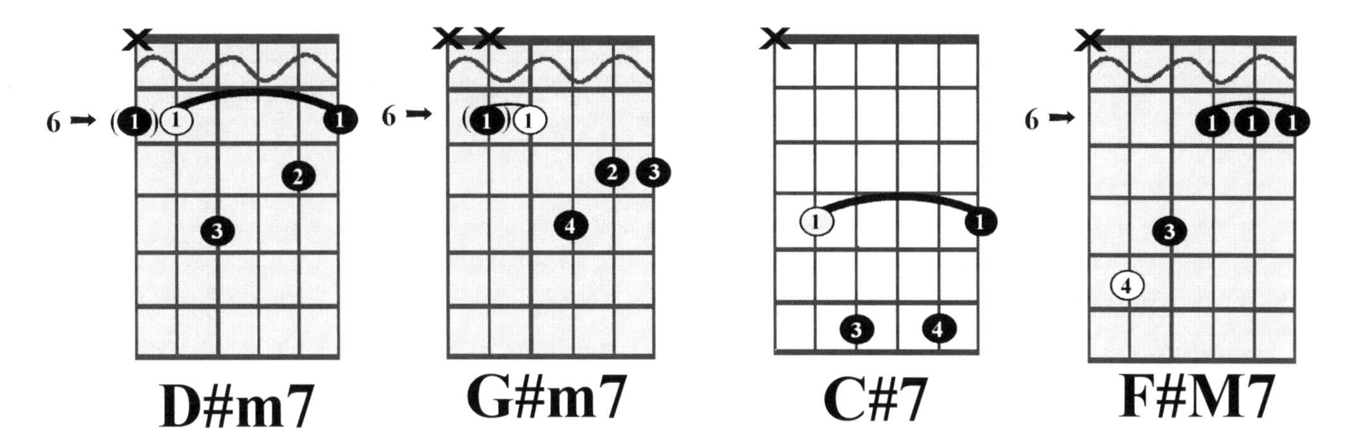

Key of C#

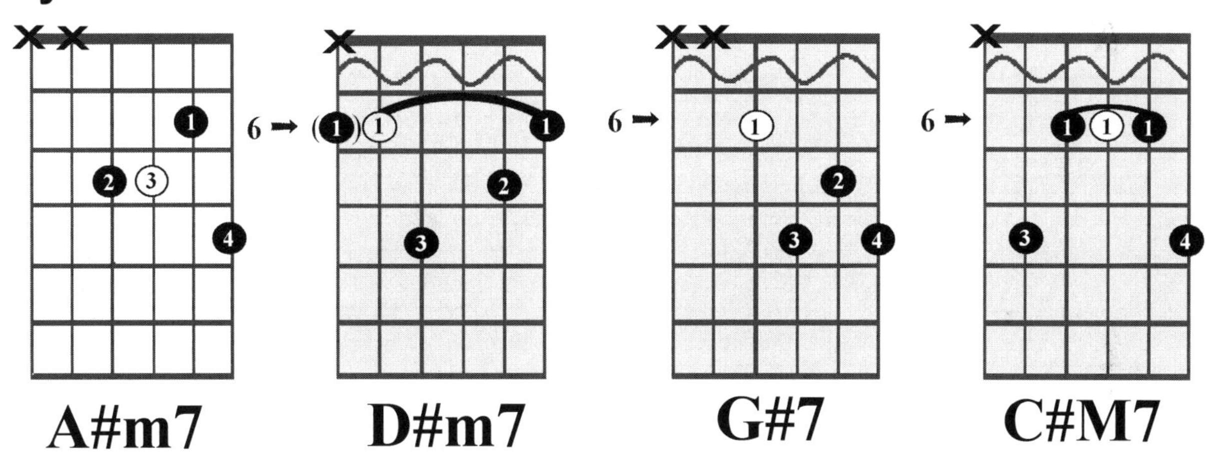

Key of A♭

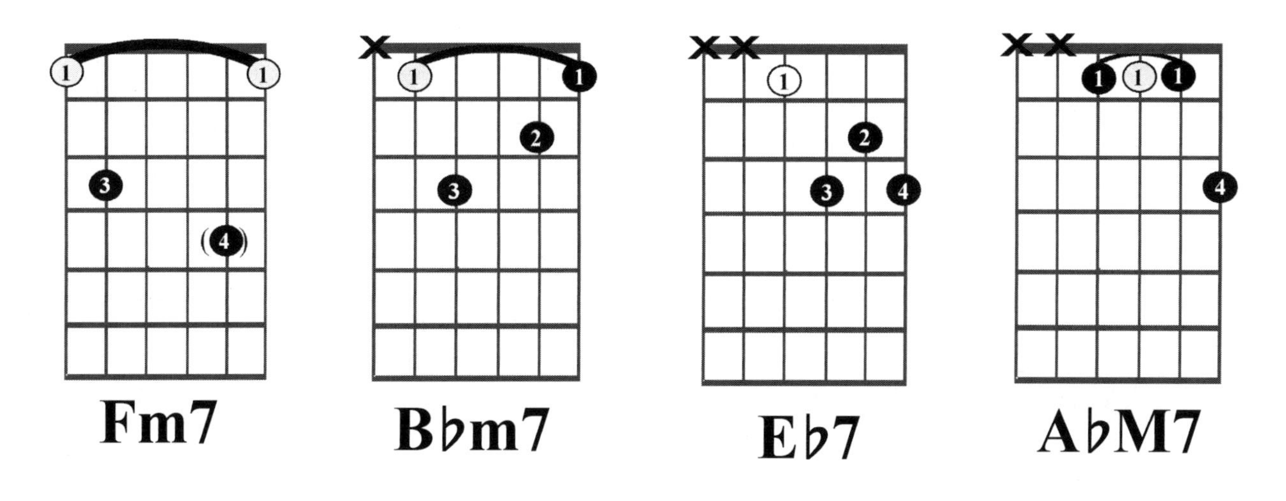

Key of E♭

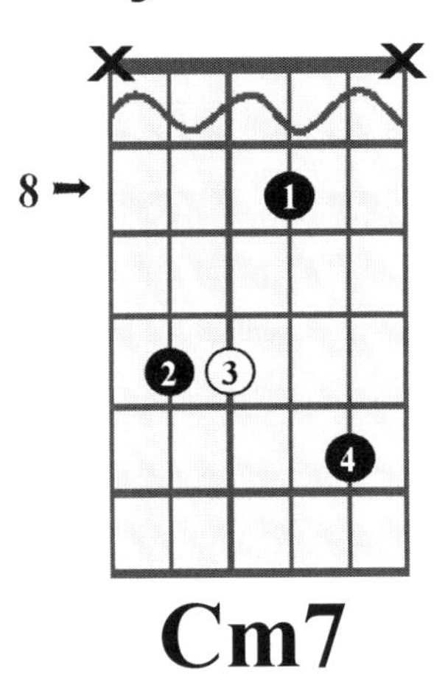

Cm7

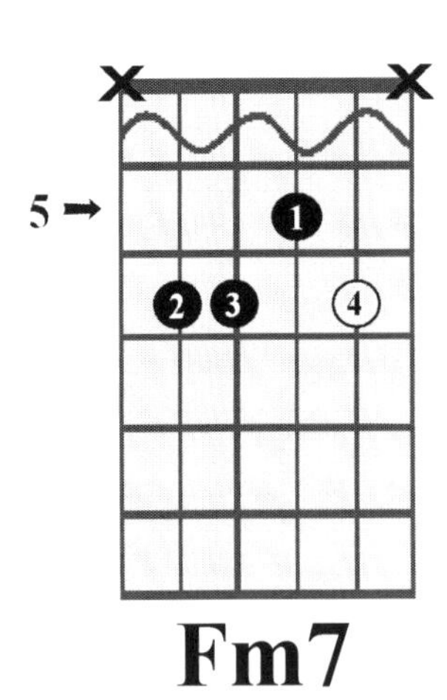

Fm7

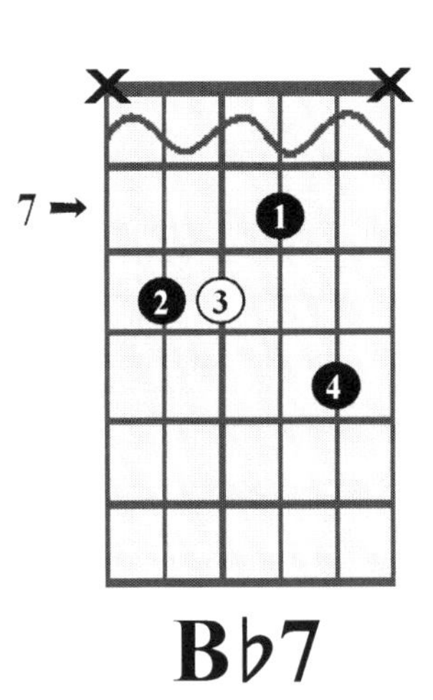

B♭7

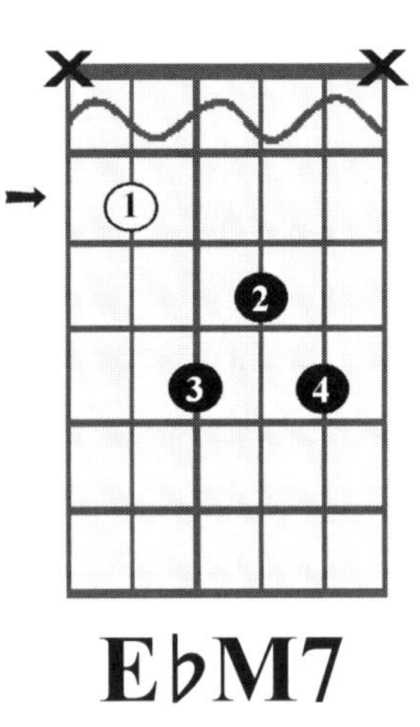

E♭M7

Key of B♭

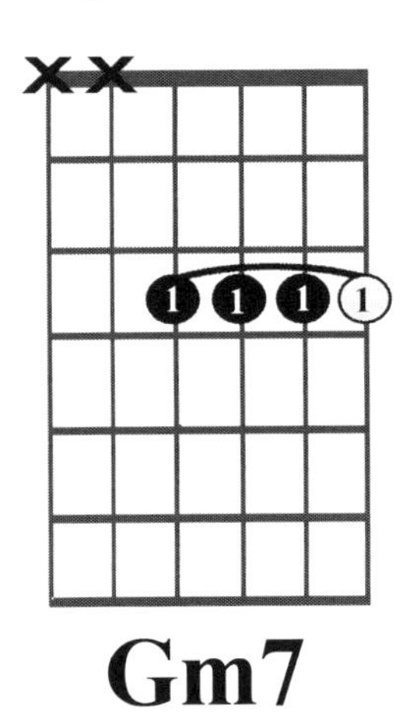

Gm7

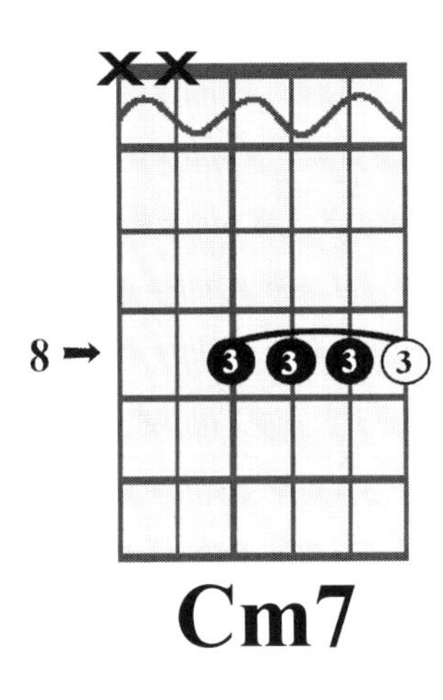

Cm7

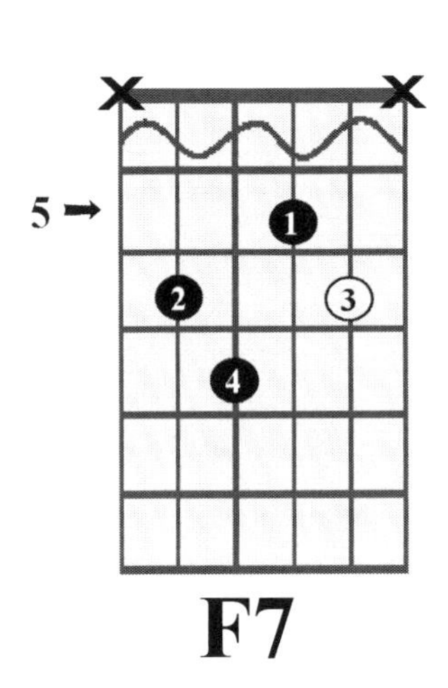

F7

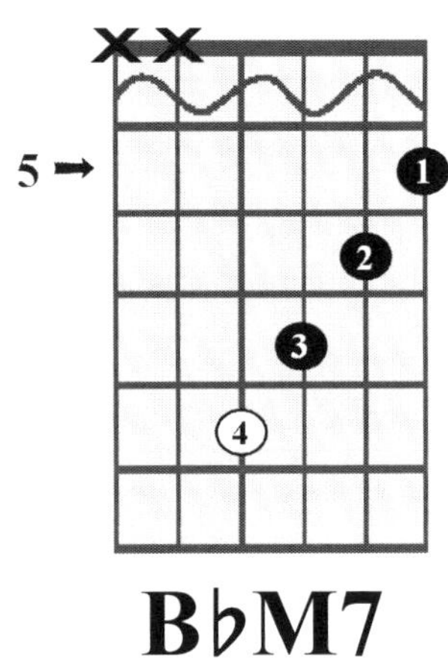

B♭M7

Key of F

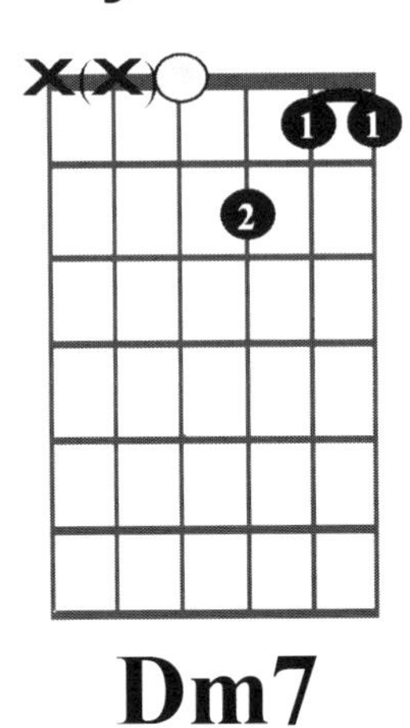

Dm7

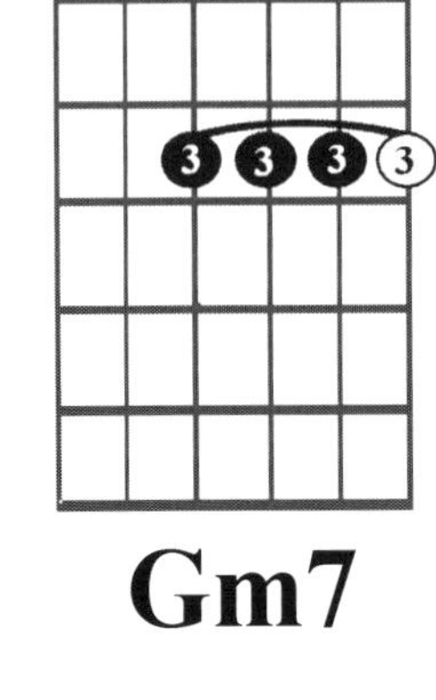

Gm7

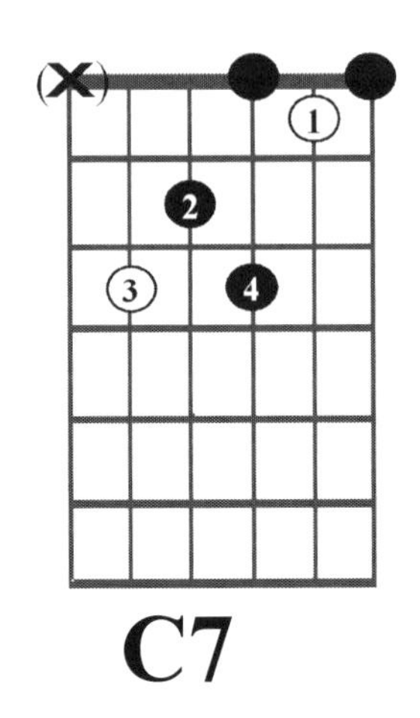

C7

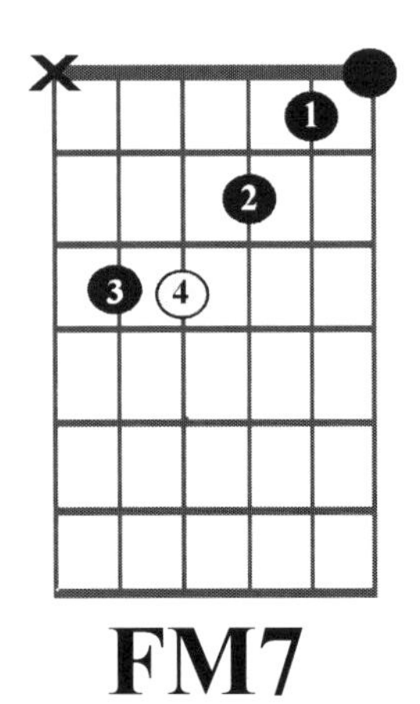

FM7

PART TEN

i - iv - V

MINOR KEYS
SEVENTH CHORDS

THE V7 CHORD IN MINOR KEYS

The following exercises observe the same convention that was introduced in the *minor* key *triad* exercises, in that the V7 chord is played with a major *third*, even though the strict harmonisation of the natural minor scale would produce a minor 7th chord.

The vm7 chord is therefore an acceptable substitute for the V7 - its use is a matter for personal taste and the "feel" of a particular piece of music.

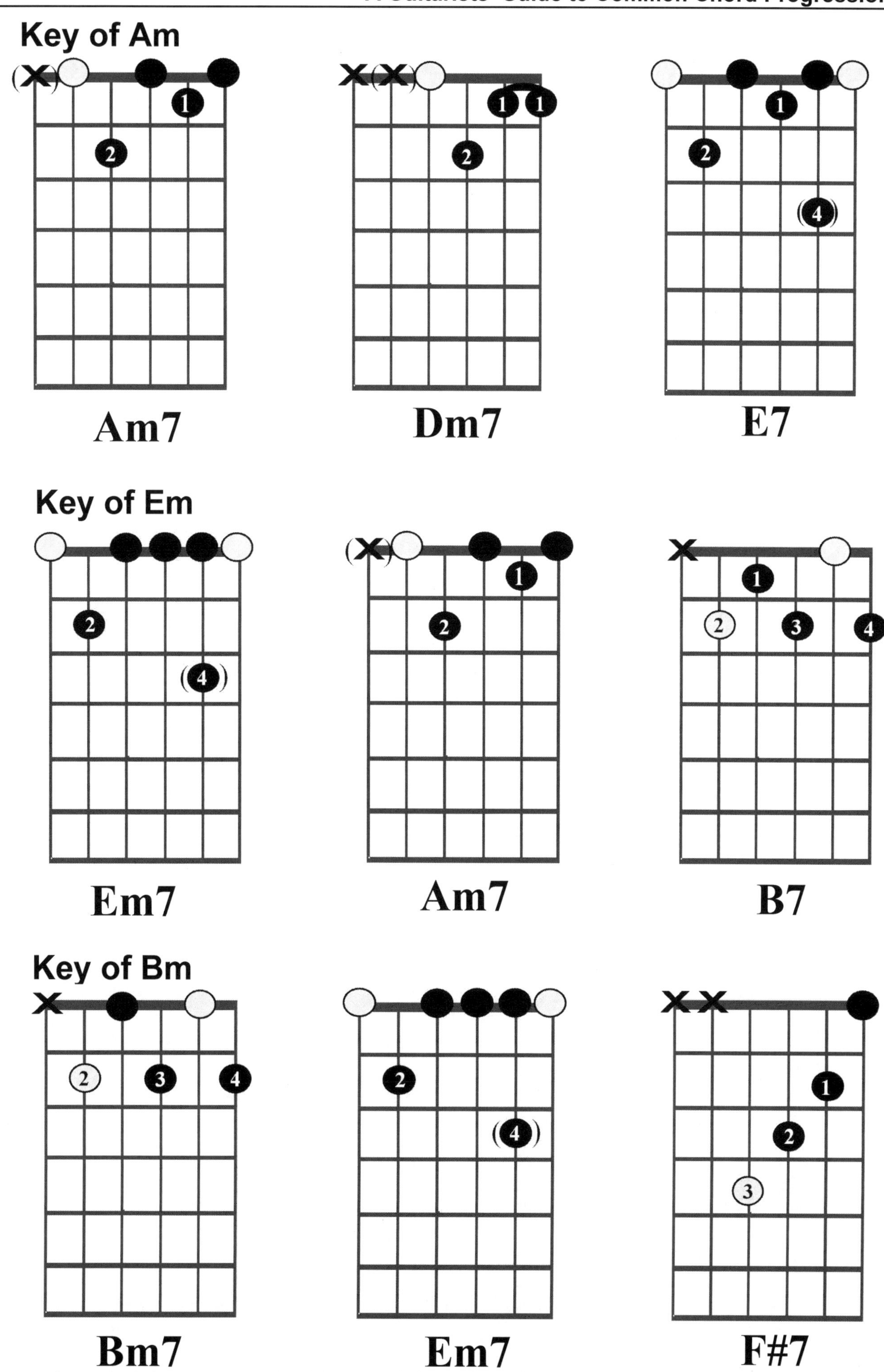
Key of Am
1
2
1
1
2
1
2
(4)
Am7
Dm7
E7
Key of Em
2
(4)
1
2
1
2
3
4
Em7
Am7
B7
Key of Bm
2
3
4
2
(4)
1
2
3
Bm7
Em7
F#7

Key of F#m

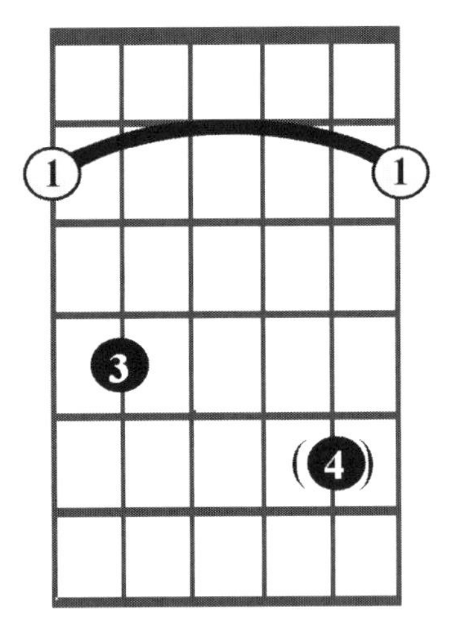

F#m7

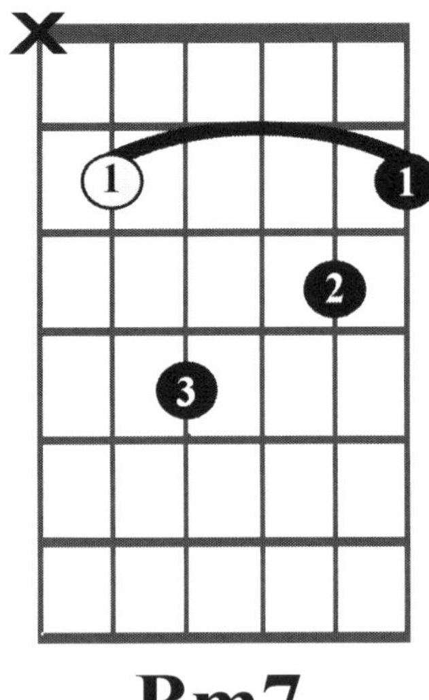

Bm7

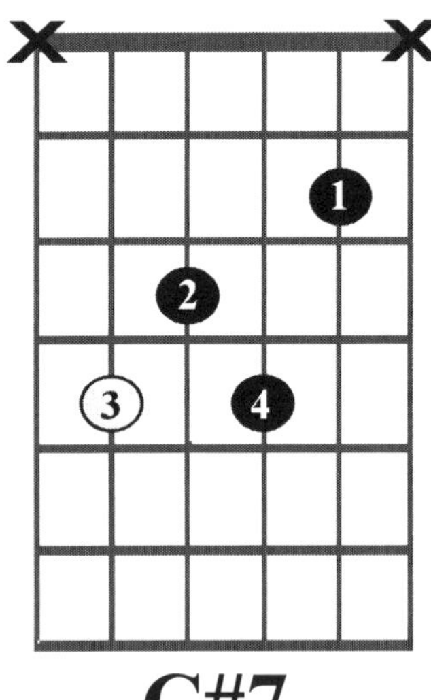

C#7

Key of C#m

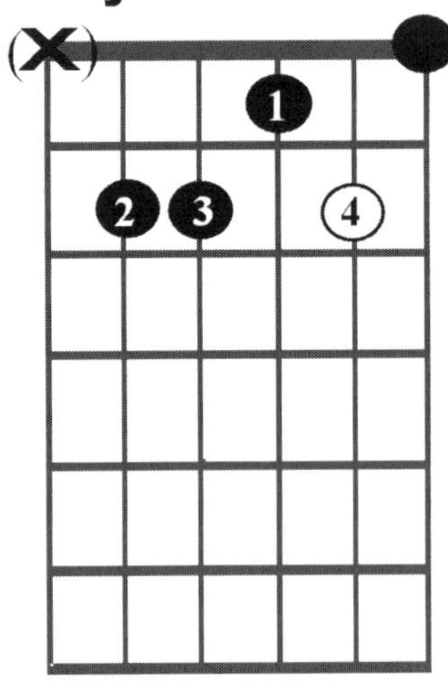

C#m7

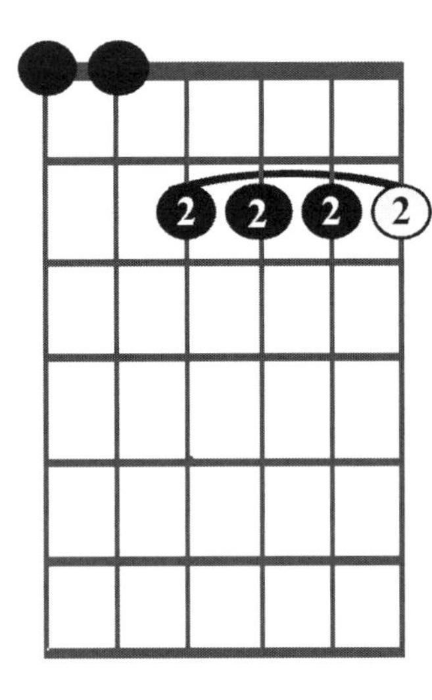

F#m7

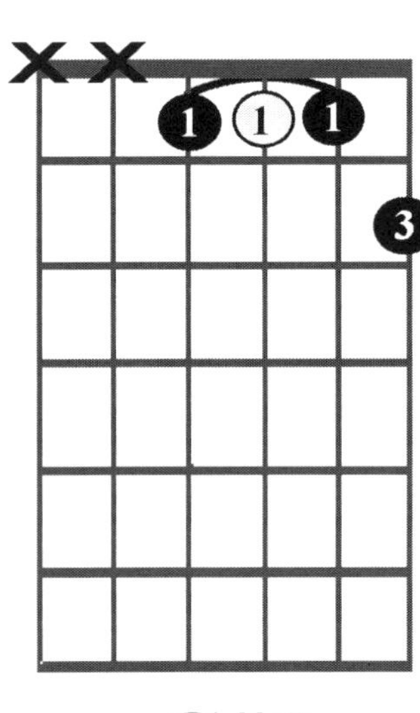

G#7

Key of A♭m

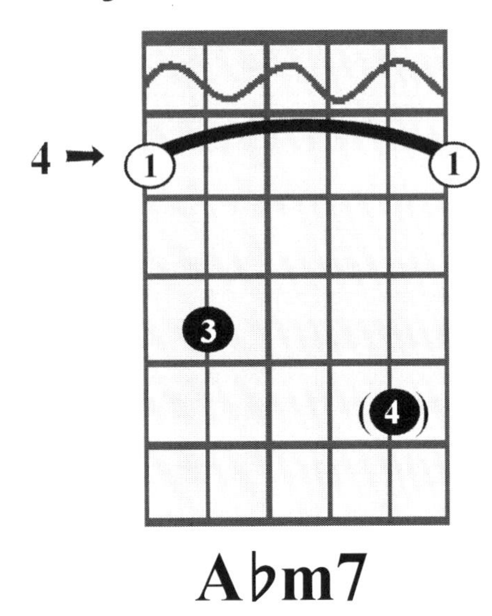

A♭m7

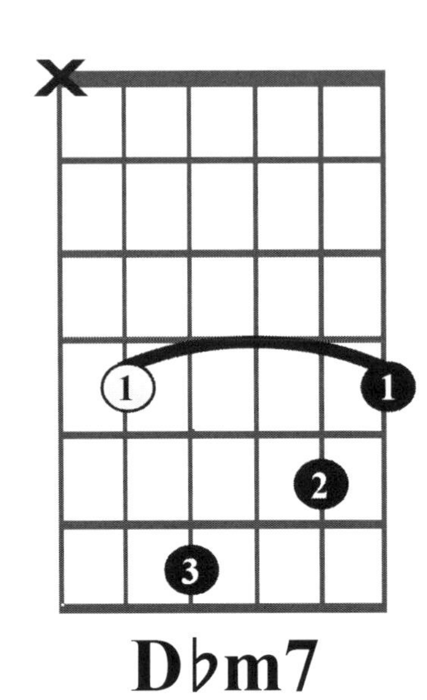

D♭m7

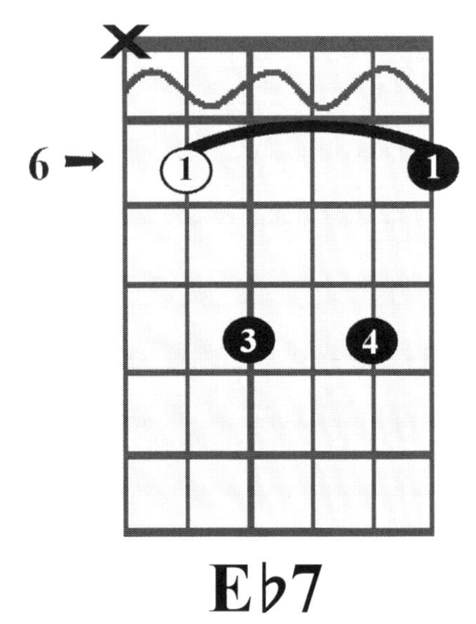

E♭7

Key of E♭m

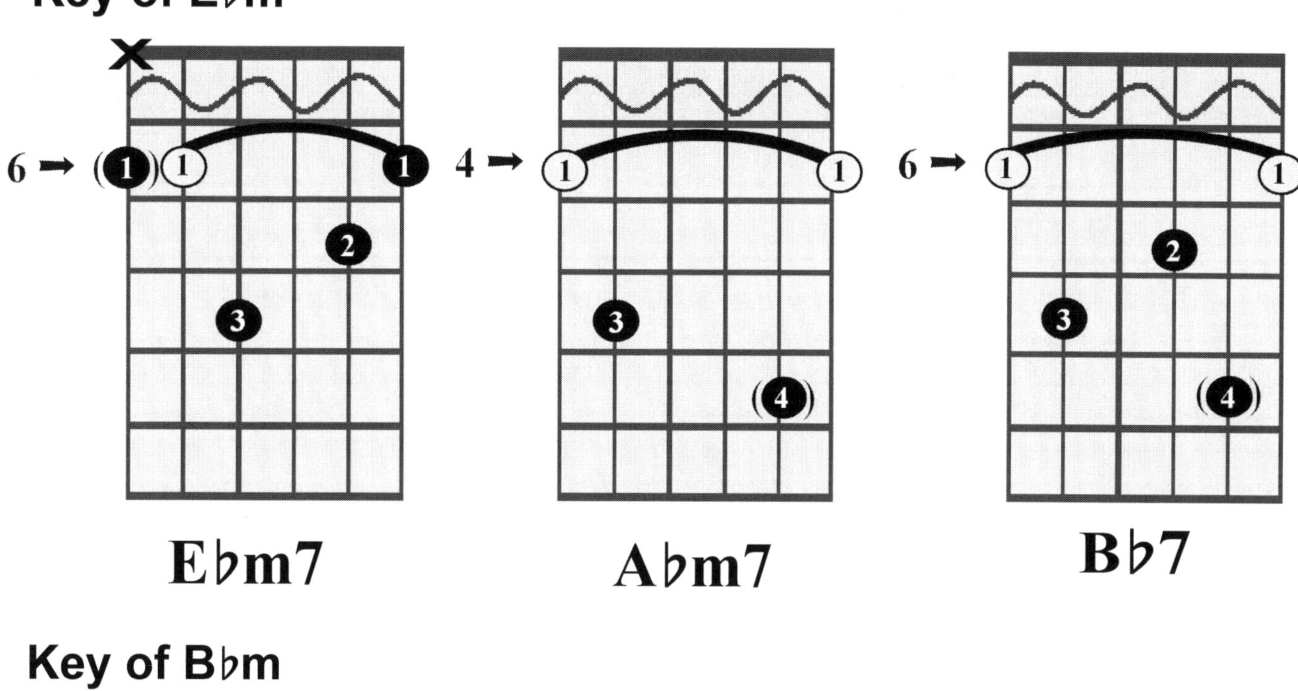

E♭m7 A♭m7 B♭7

Key of B♭m

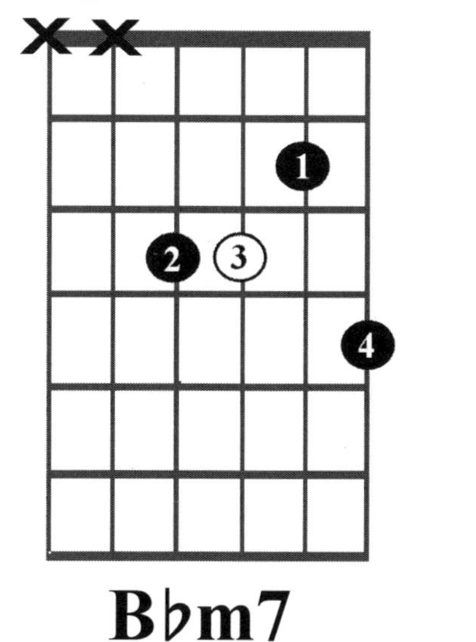

B♭m7

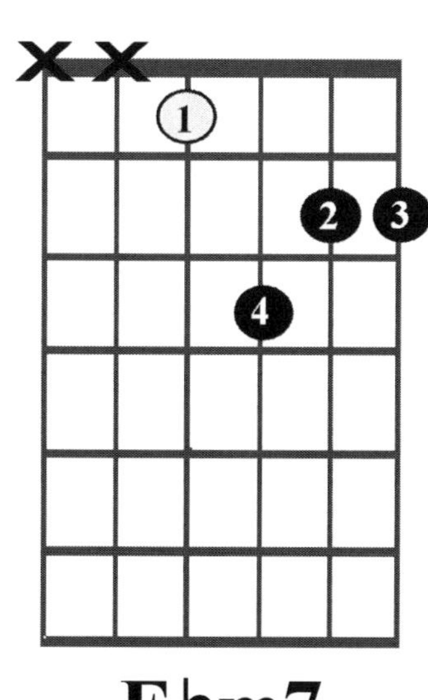

E♭m7

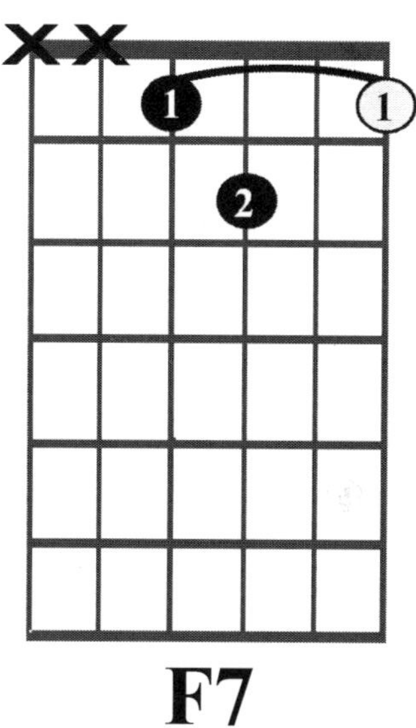

F7

Key of Fm

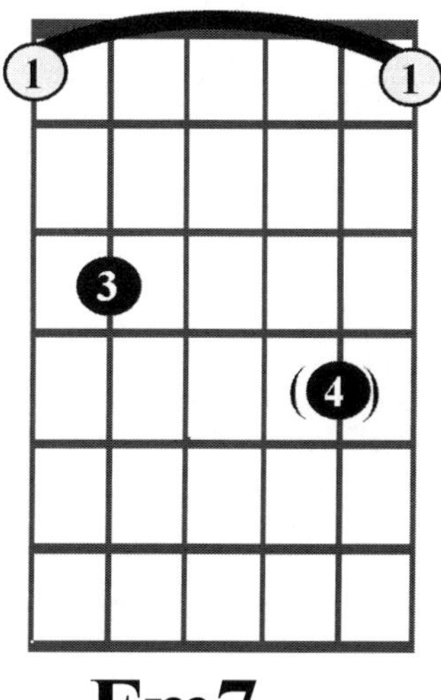

Fm7

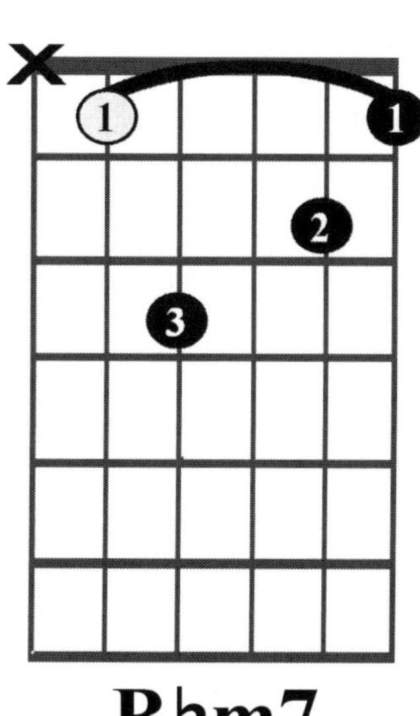

B♭m7

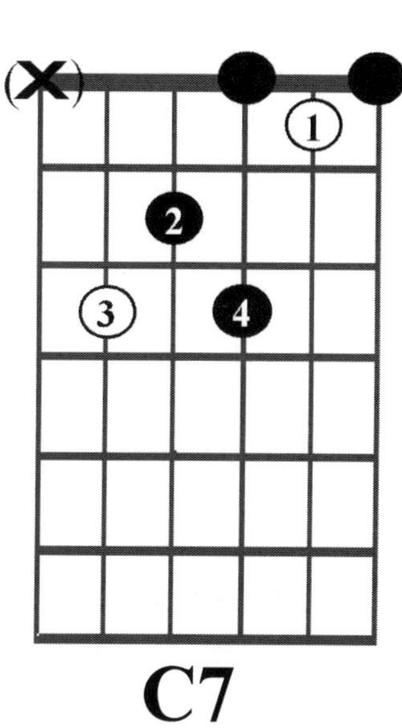

C7

Key of Cm

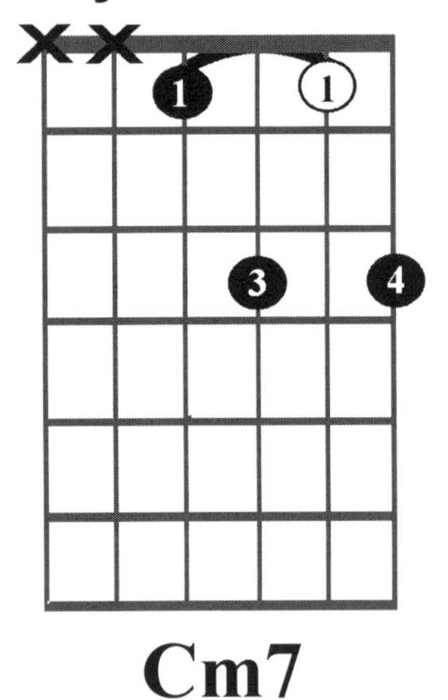

Cm7

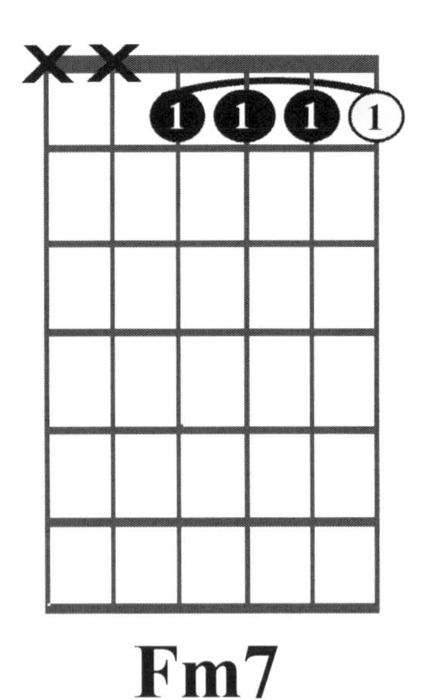

Fm7

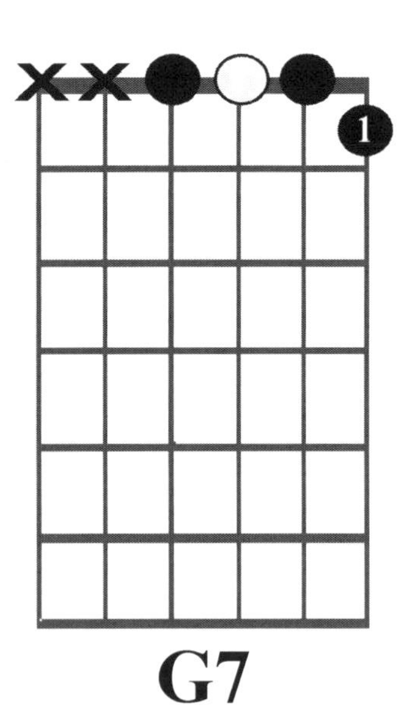

G7

Key of Gm

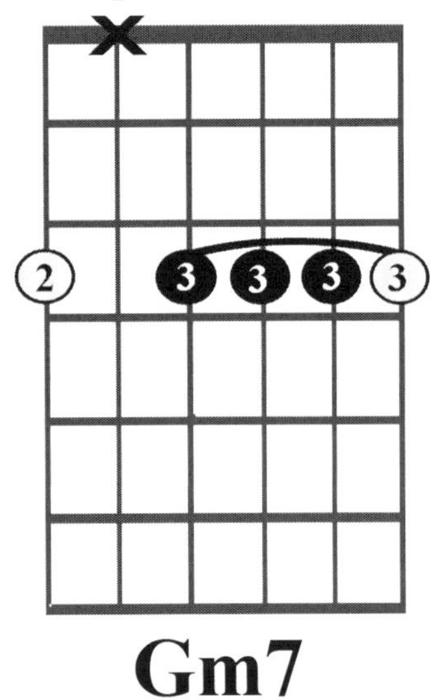

Gm7

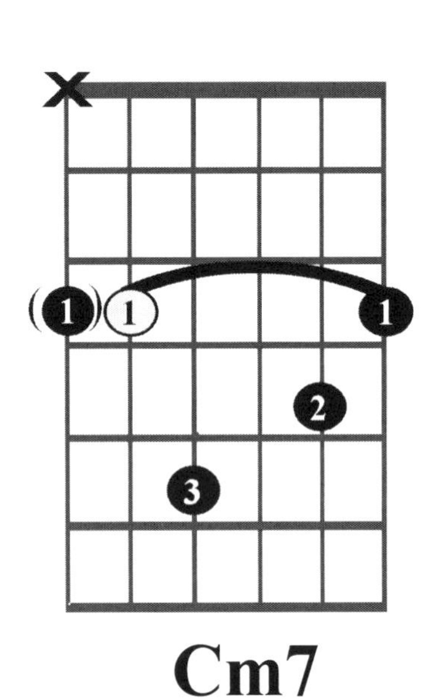

Cm7

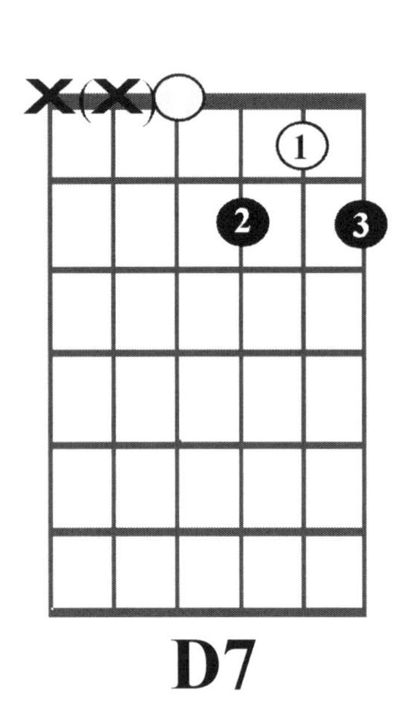

D7

Key of Dm

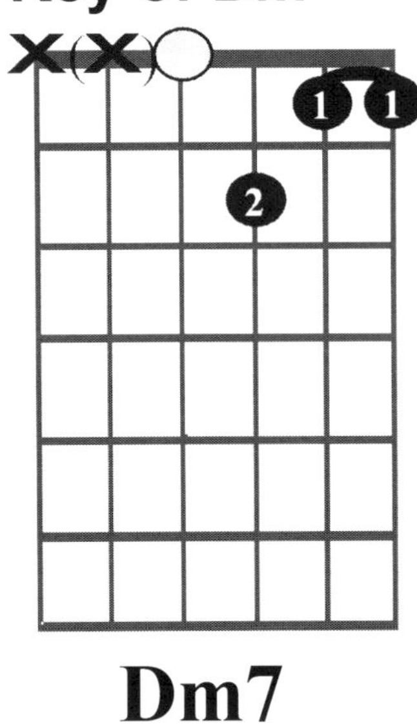

Dm7

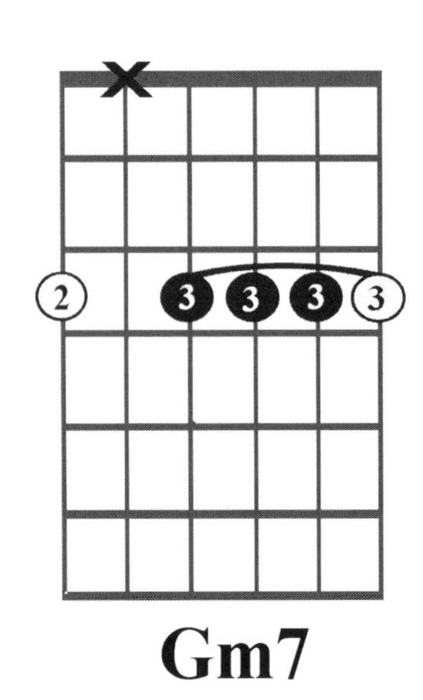

Gm7

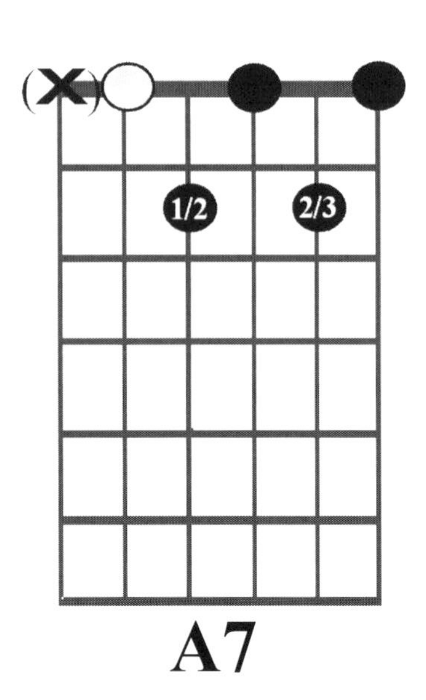

A7

PART ELEVEN

ii - V - i

MINOR KEYS
SEVENTH CHORDS

THE MINOR 7/FLAT 5 CHORD

These exercises introduce the final chord type derived from the harmonised scale. This is the seventh chord formed on the second *degree* of the *minor* scale (equivalent to the seventh degree of the *major* scale), and contains a minor *third*, a flattened *fifth*, and a minor *seventh*. This is the minor 7/flat5 chord (m7♭5 or m7-5), also referred to as a "minor 7/*diminished* 5th" or "half-diminished" chord.

(Remember that further harmonisation of the scale is possible to derive the 9th, 11th and 13th chords, but is beyond the scope of this book, and don't forget to experiment with alternative voicings and fingerings of your own).

Key of Am

Bm7♭5

E7

Am7

Key of Em

F#m7♭5

B7

Em7

Key of Bm

C#m7♭5

F#7

Bm7

Key of F#m

G#m7♭5

C#7

F#m7

Key of C#m

D#m7♭5

G#7

C#m7

Key of A♭m

6 ➡

B♭m7♭5

6 ➡

E♭7

4 ➡

A♭m7

Key of E♭m

Fm7♭5

B♭7

E♭m7

Key of B♭m

Cm7♭5

F7

B♭m7

Key of Fm

Gm7♭5

C7

Fm7

Key of Cm

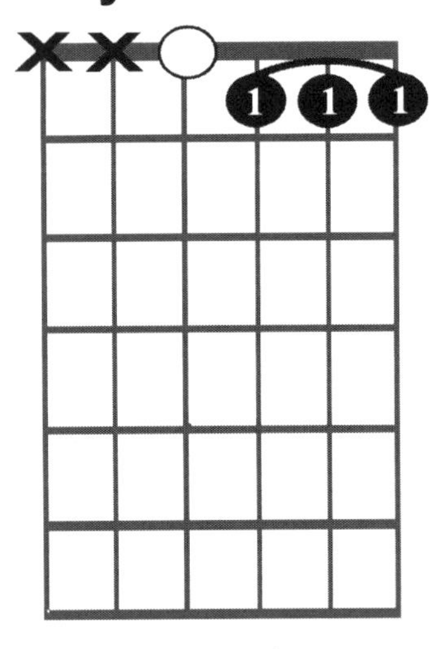

Dm7♭5

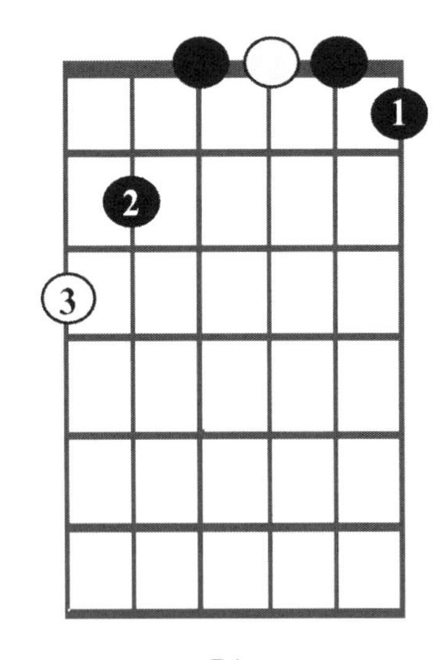

G7

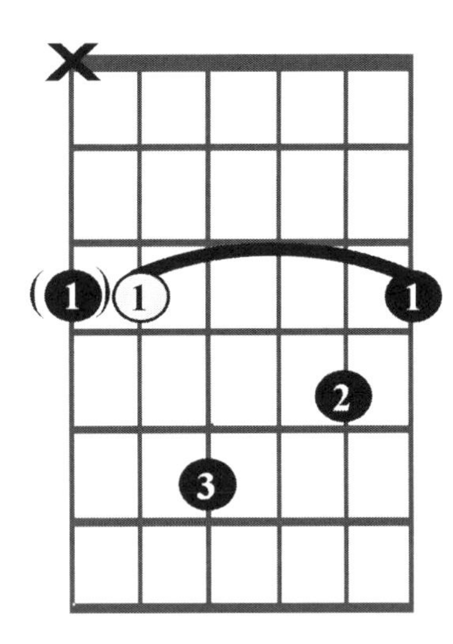

Cm7

Key of Gm

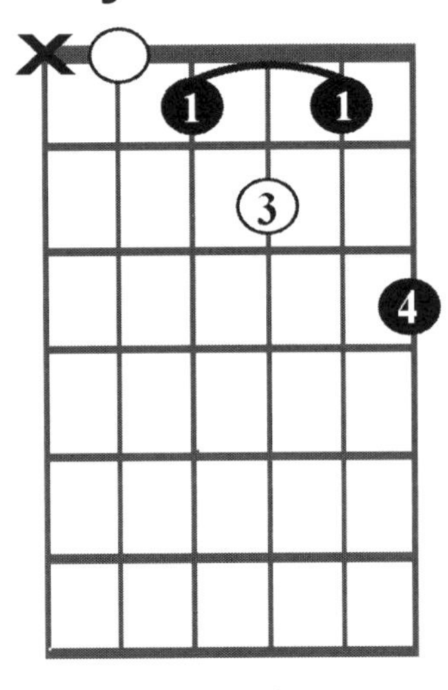

Am7♭5

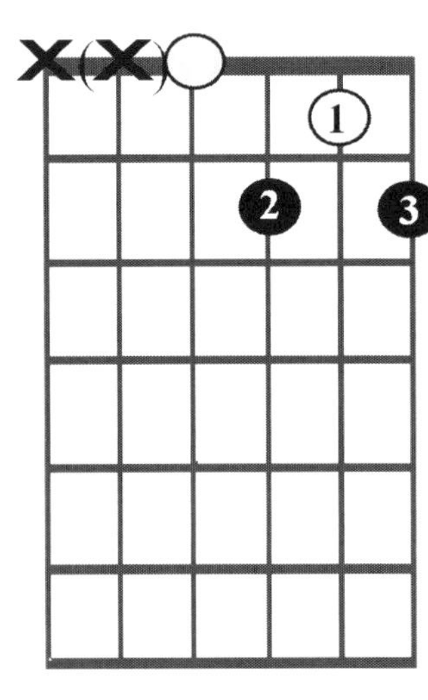

D7

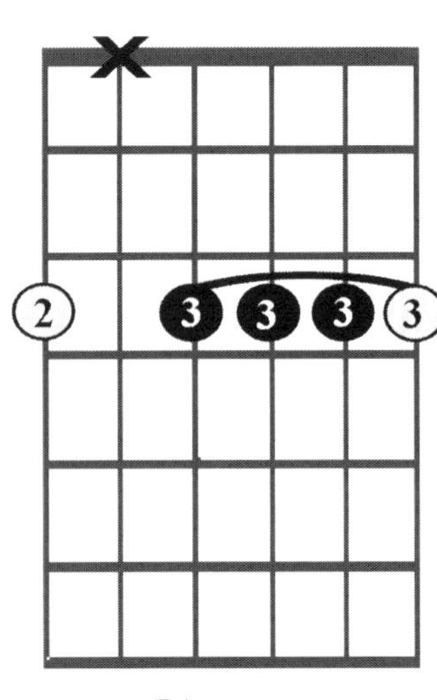

Gm7

Key of Dm

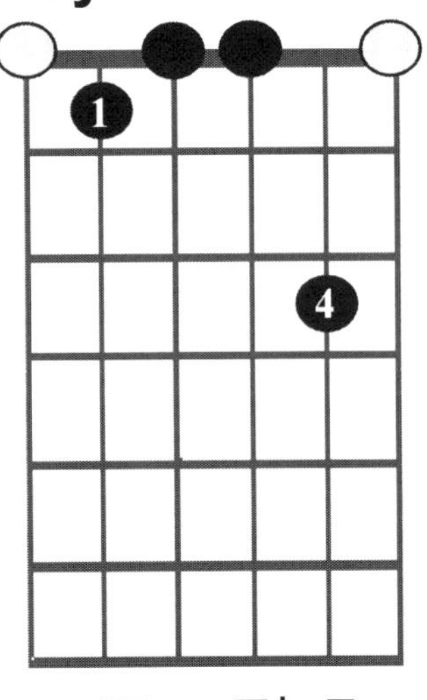

Em7♭5

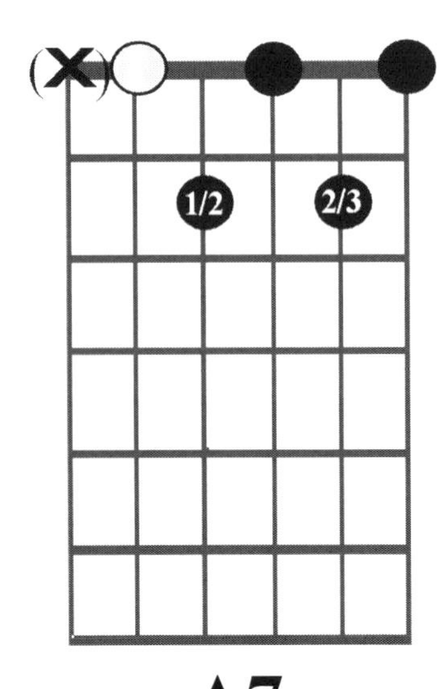

A7

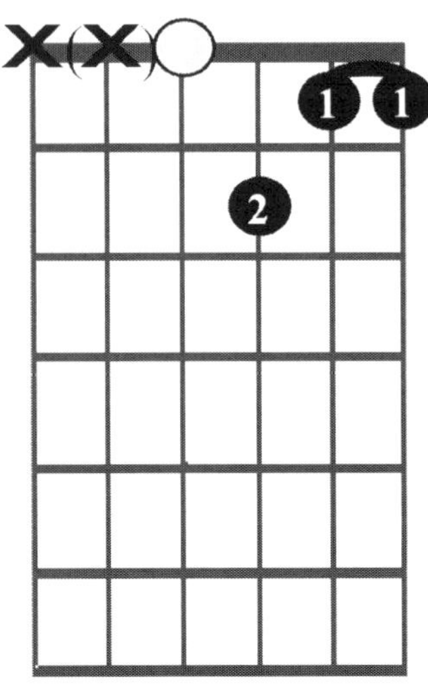

Dm7

PART TWELVE

VI - ii - V - i

MINOR KEYS SEVENTH CHORDS

THE VIM7 CHORD

Since the 6th *degree* of the *minor* scale corresponds the the 4th degree of the major scale, when the scale is harmonised, a *major* seventh chord is formed on this note.

Key of Am

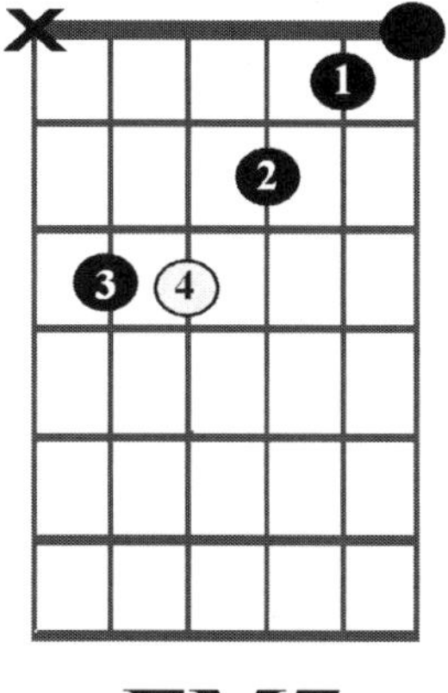

FM7

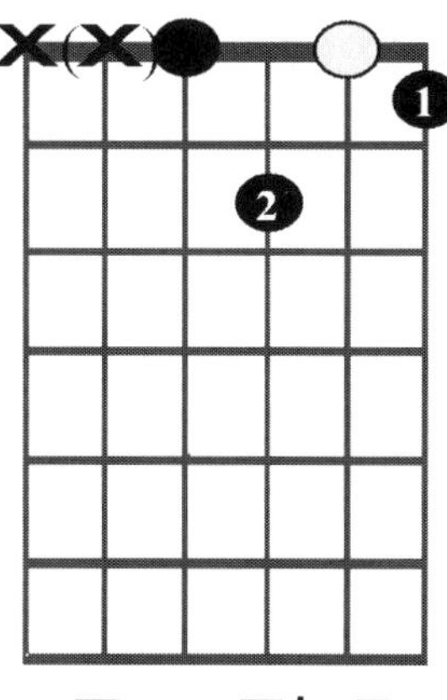

Bm7♭5

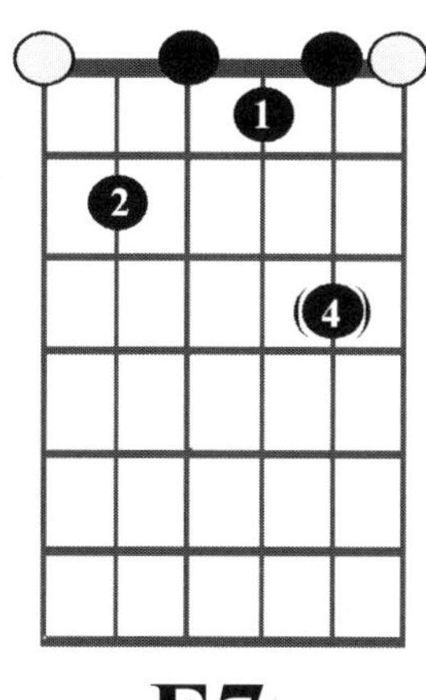

E7

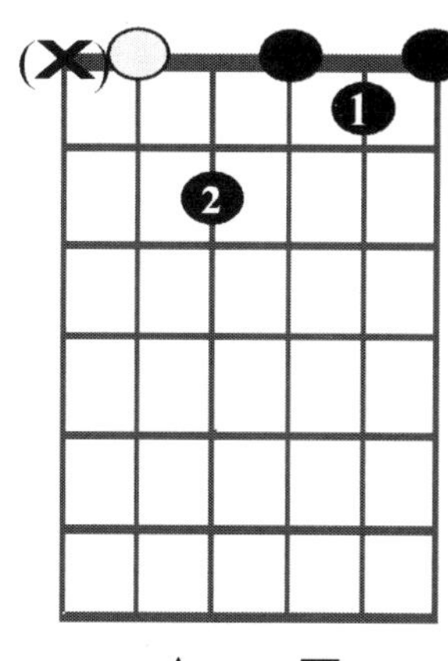

Am7

Key of Em

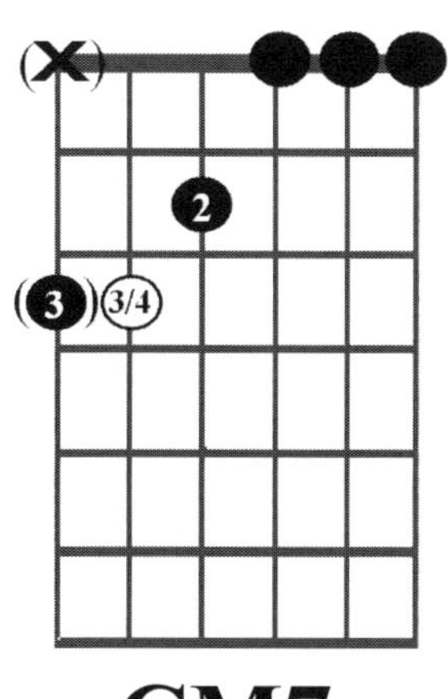

CM7

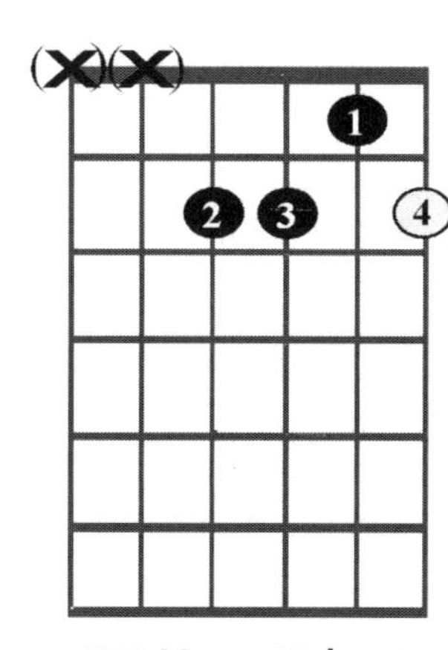

F#m7♭5

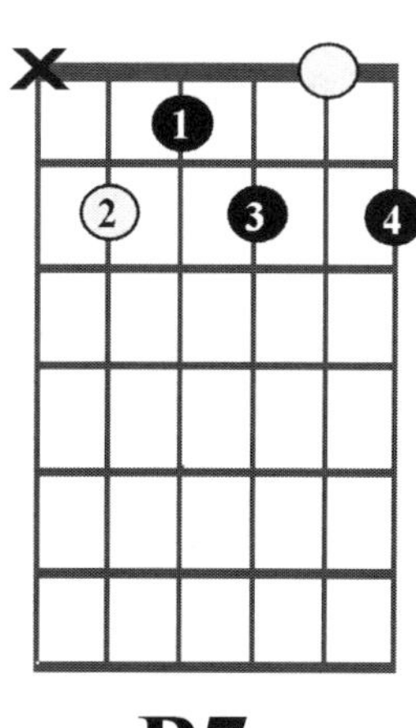

B7

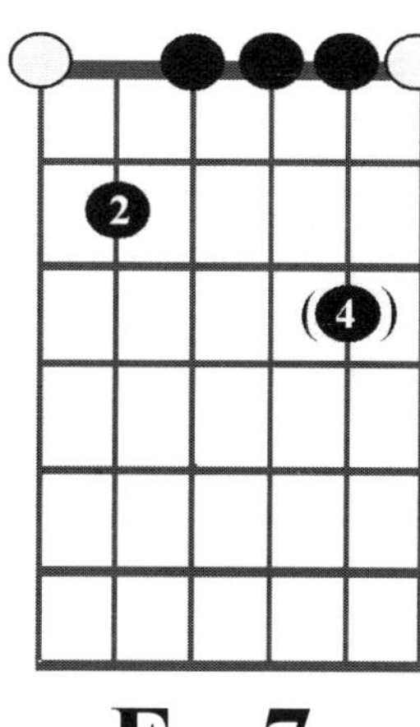

Em7

Key of Bm

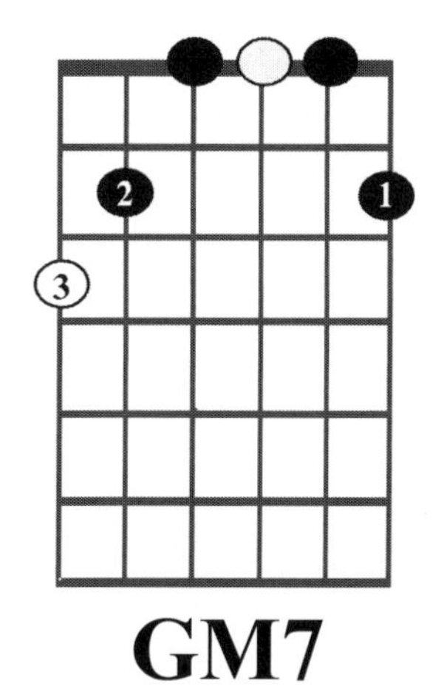

GM7

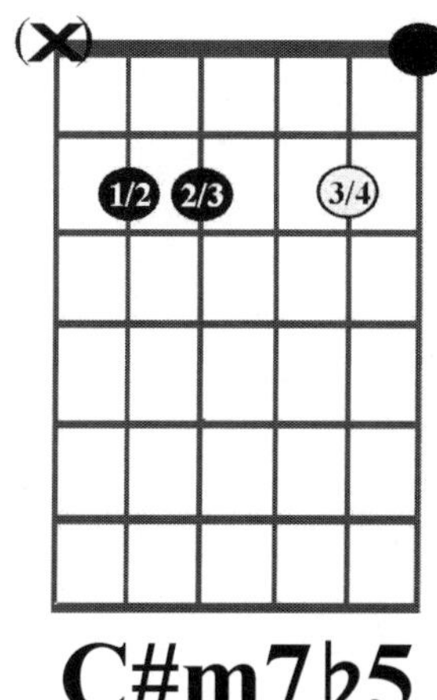

C#m7♭5

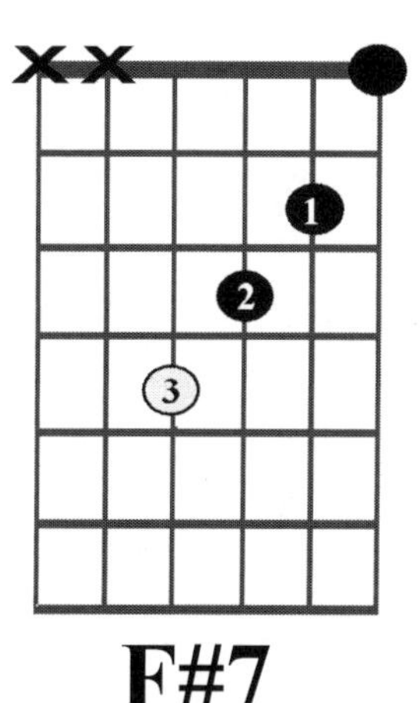

F#7

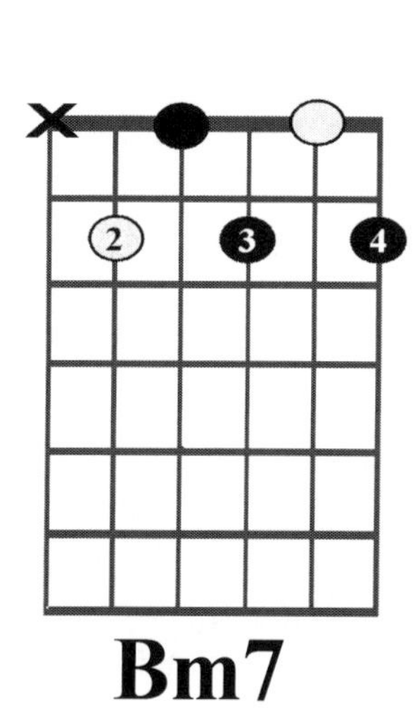

Bm7

Key of F#m

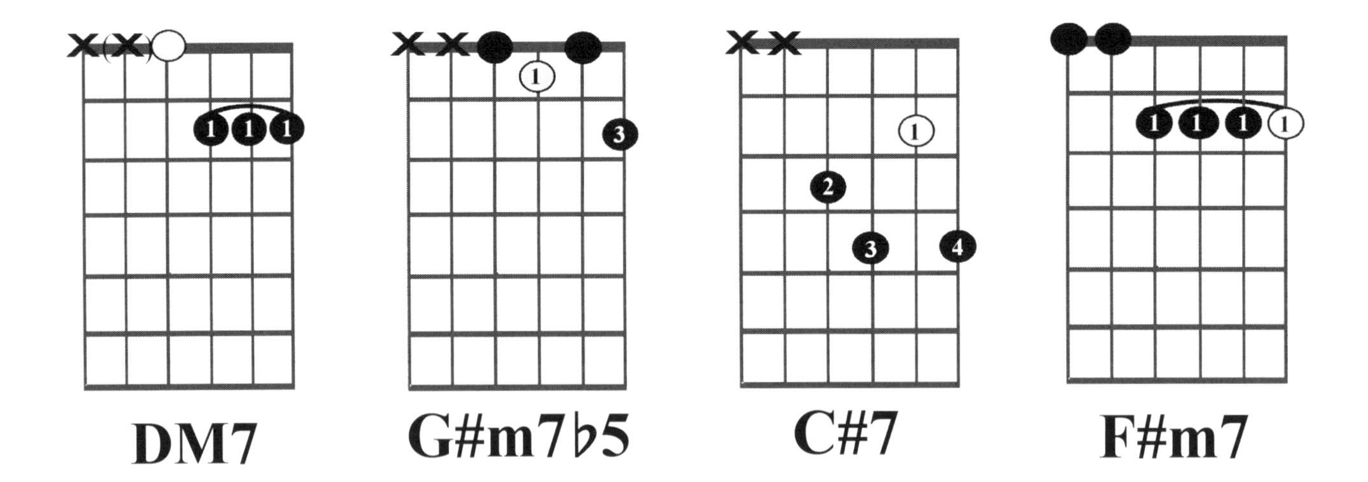

Key of C#m

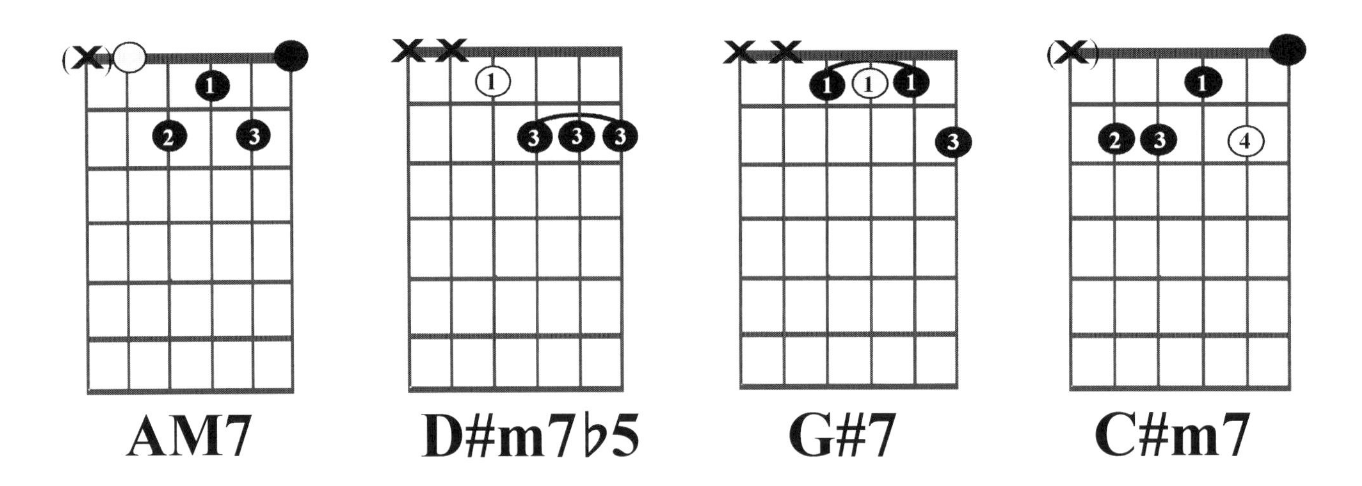

Key of A♭m

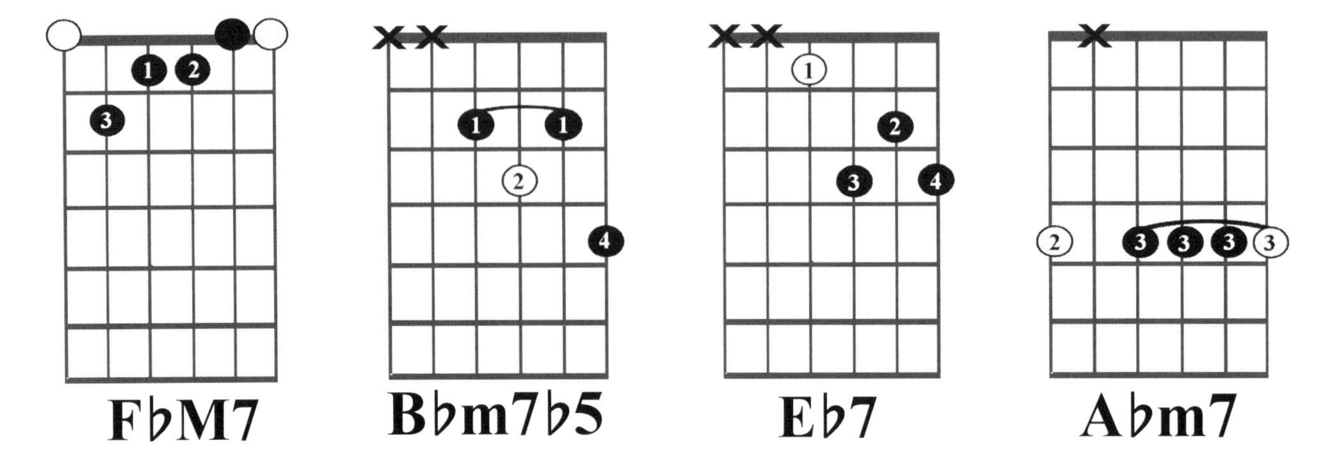

Key of E♭m

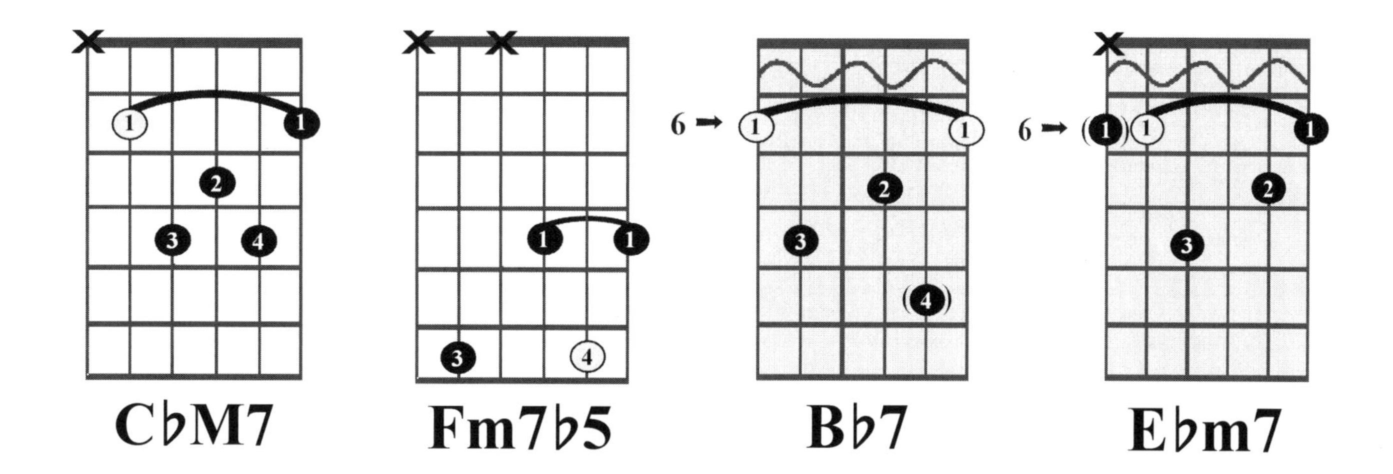

Key of B♭m

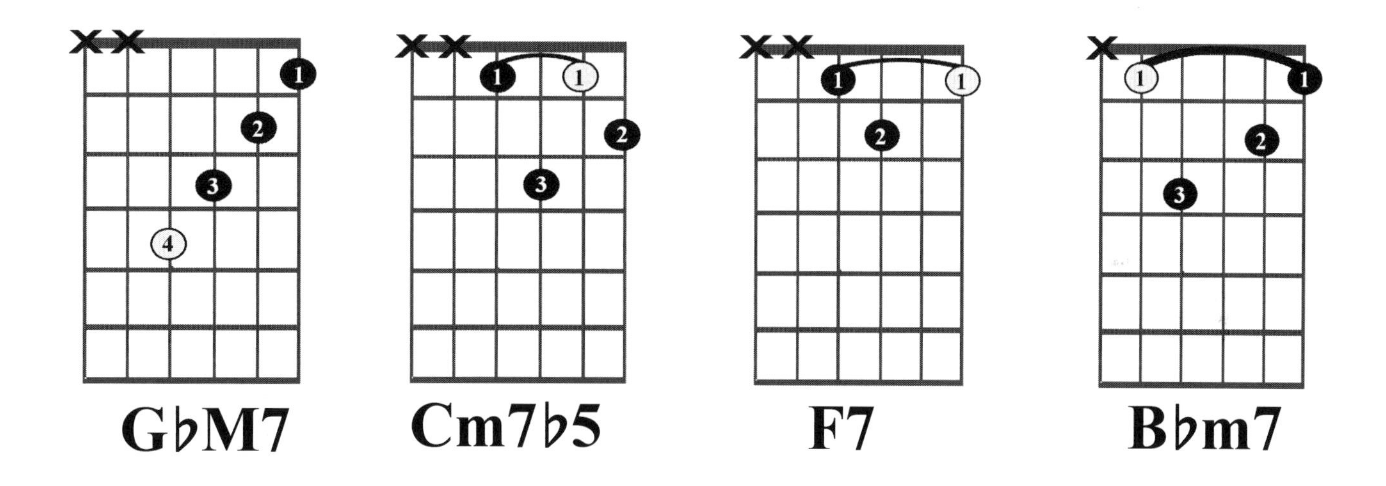

Key of Fm

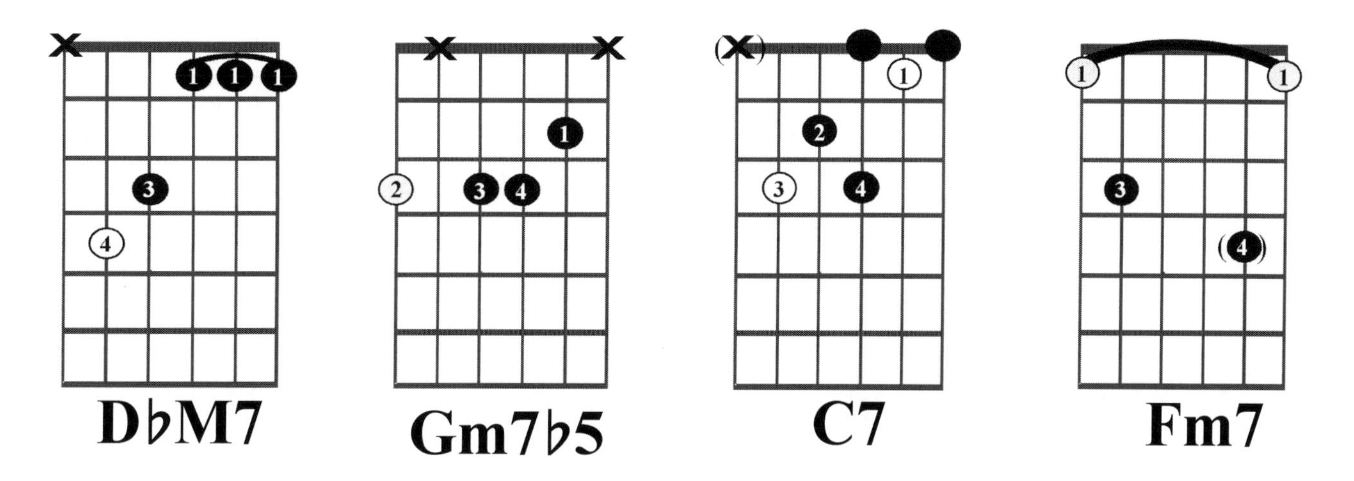

Key of Cm

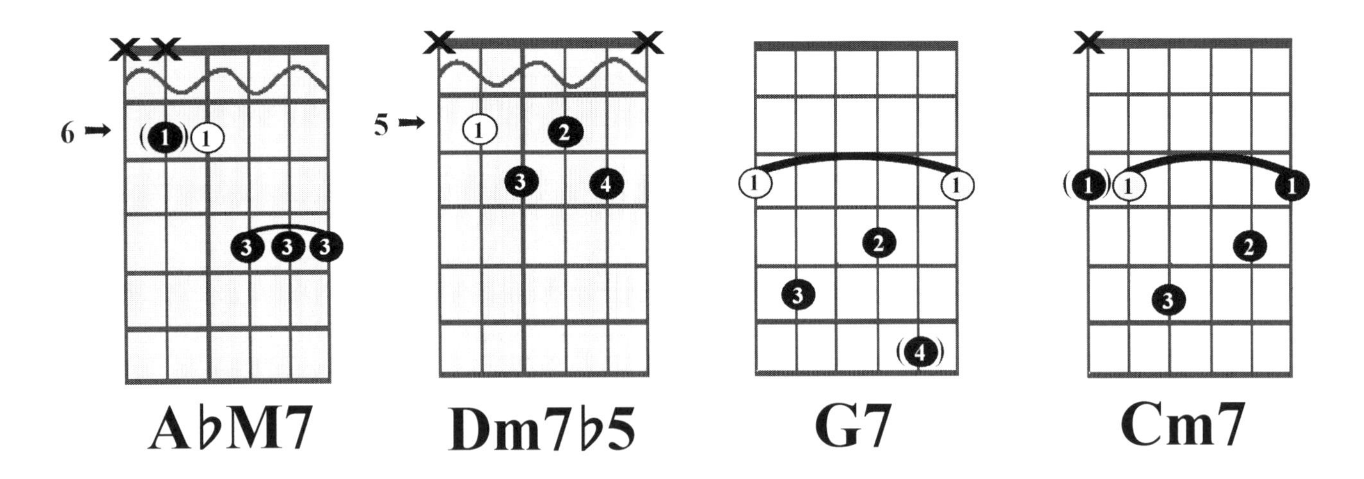

Key of Gm

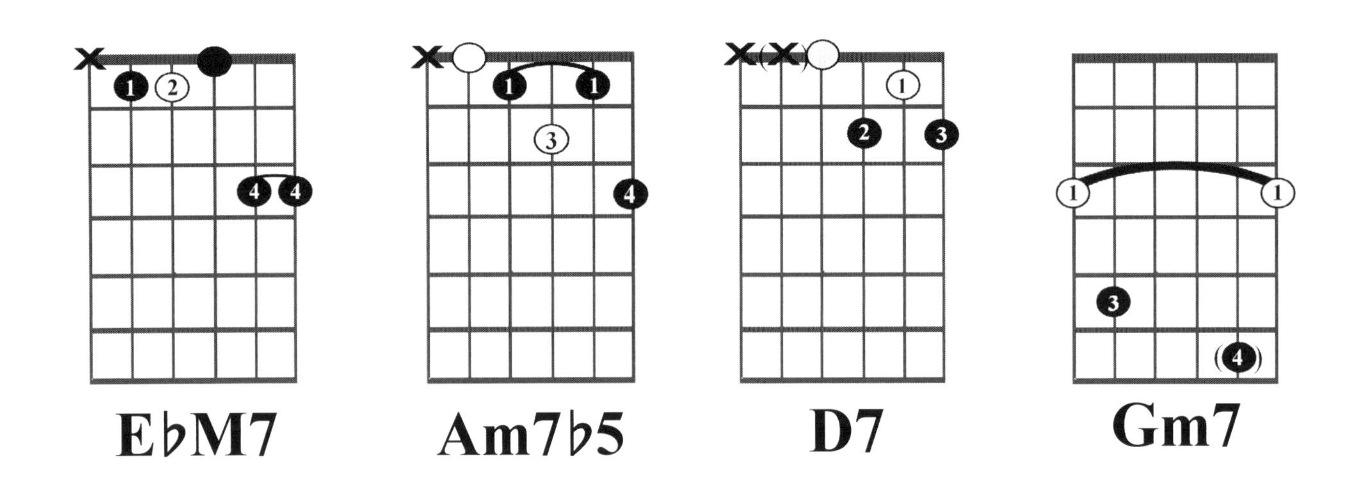

Key of Dm

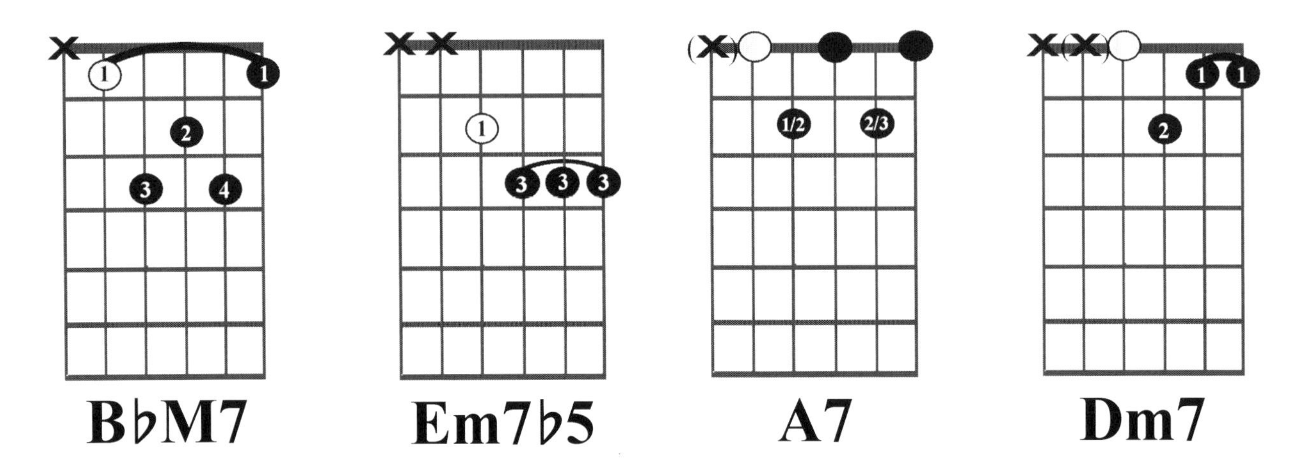

PART THIRTEEN

I - IV - V

MAJOR KEYS
TRIADS
ARPEGGIOS

INTRODUCING ARPEGGIOS

An arpeggio is simply the individual notes of a given chord, played as a melodic pattern. Arpeggios are the basic building blocks from which melodies and improvised lead lines are constructed since, logically, any melody constructed using only chord tones is guaranteed to fit with the underlying harmony. More sophisticated melodies can then be constructed by adding notes from the scale, or indeed *chromatic* notes, between the chord tones.

THE ARPEGGIO EXERCISES

The arpeggio exercises in this book follow the same system as the preceding chord exercises. For each chord sequence, examples are given of one-octave arpeggios in the "open" position (covering the lowest four frets and using open strings where necessary) for all keys. In addition, these exercises are followed by generic fingering charts for arpeggio patterns which can be *transposed* to any key. These are given in nine positions, starting with the first, second and fourth/third fingers on each of the lowest three strings. These exercises should also be practiced in all keys.

FINGERINGS

For this first set of exercises, fingerings shown are strictly "in-position", i.e. finger 1 always plays fret 1, finger 2, fret 2, finger 3, fret 3, and finger 4, fret 4. You will quickly find that this creates some awkward jumps when moving between arpeggios on the same finger. Subsequent chapters will explore alternative fingerings to circumvent these problems - you may like to pre-empt these by finding your own solutions.

Because of the way the guitar is tuned, you will see that, in many positions the *fifth* and *octave* fall on adjacent strings, at the same fret, and can be played with the same finger. In these cases the finger tip should be placed flat across the strings, like a partial barre.

PRACTISING ARPEGGIOS

The arpeggios should be played from the lowest note to the highest, backwards (high to low), and back-and-forth. Practice the arpeggios individually, then in sequence following the chord patterns. You might also like to extend the arpeggios by finding additional chord tones below and above the *root* notes in each position.

Tip: when practising arpeggios back-and-forth, in sequence, move to the root of the next arpeggio instead of returning to the root of the current arpeggio - then the fingering should flow smoothly and the patterns fit neatly into a triple (3/4 or 6/8) *time signature*.

Each two-*octave* pattern can, of course be broken down into one-octave, or smaller, units and recombined in numerous ways to create further alternatives.

Key of C

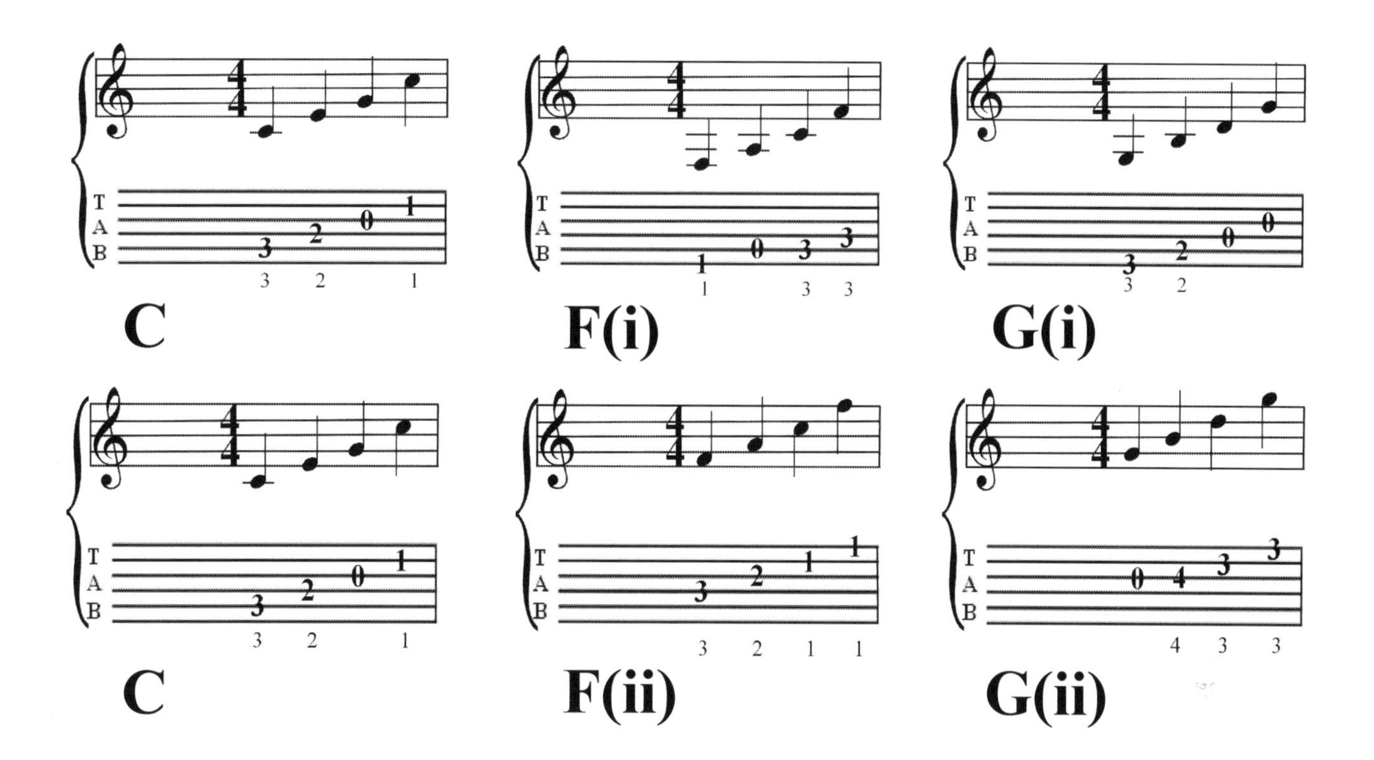

Key of G

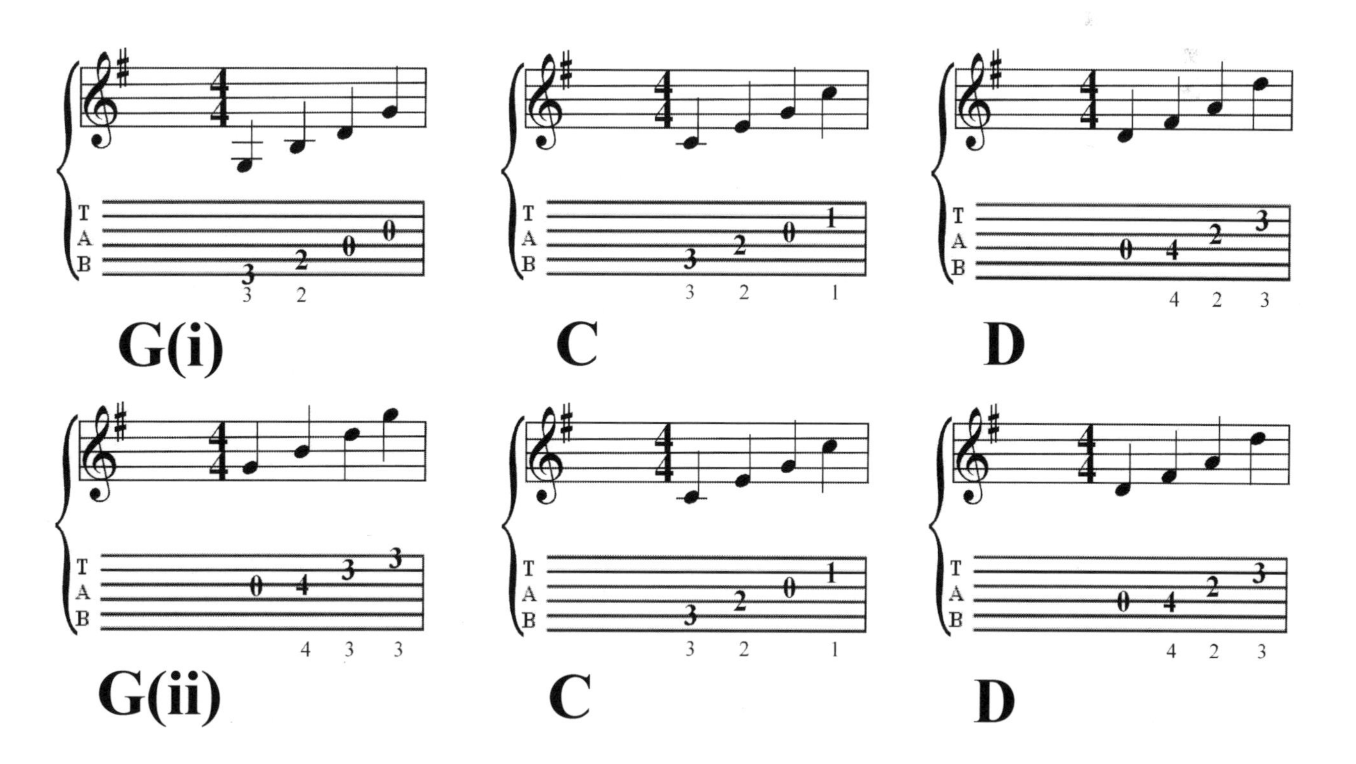

Key of D

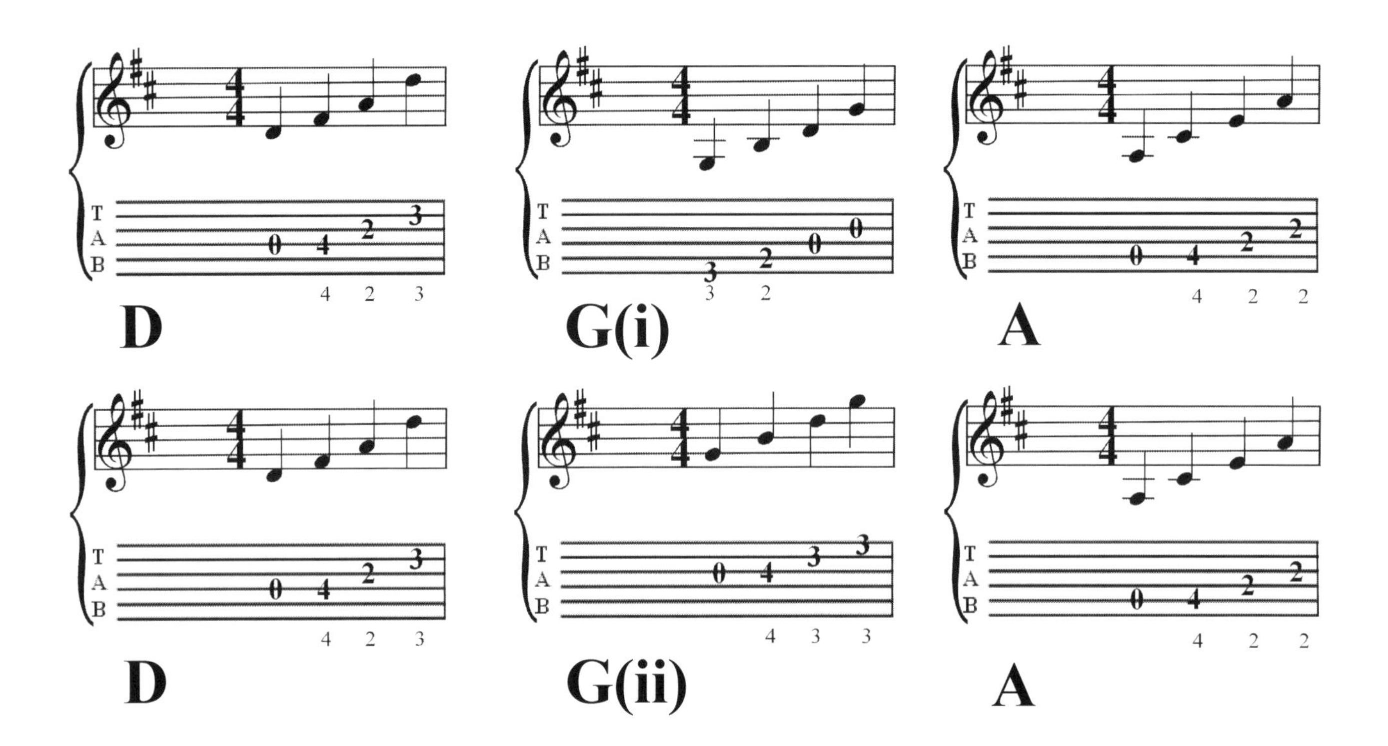

Key of A

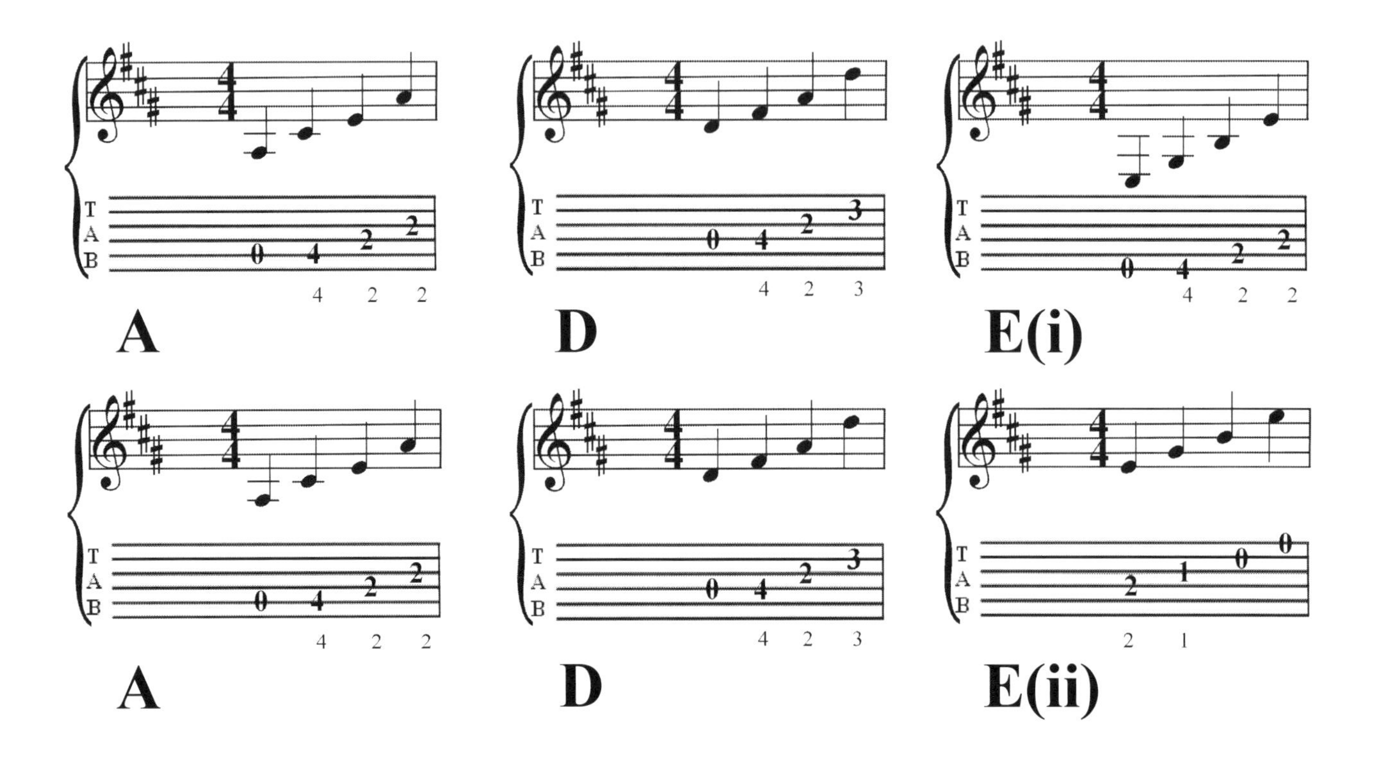

Key of E

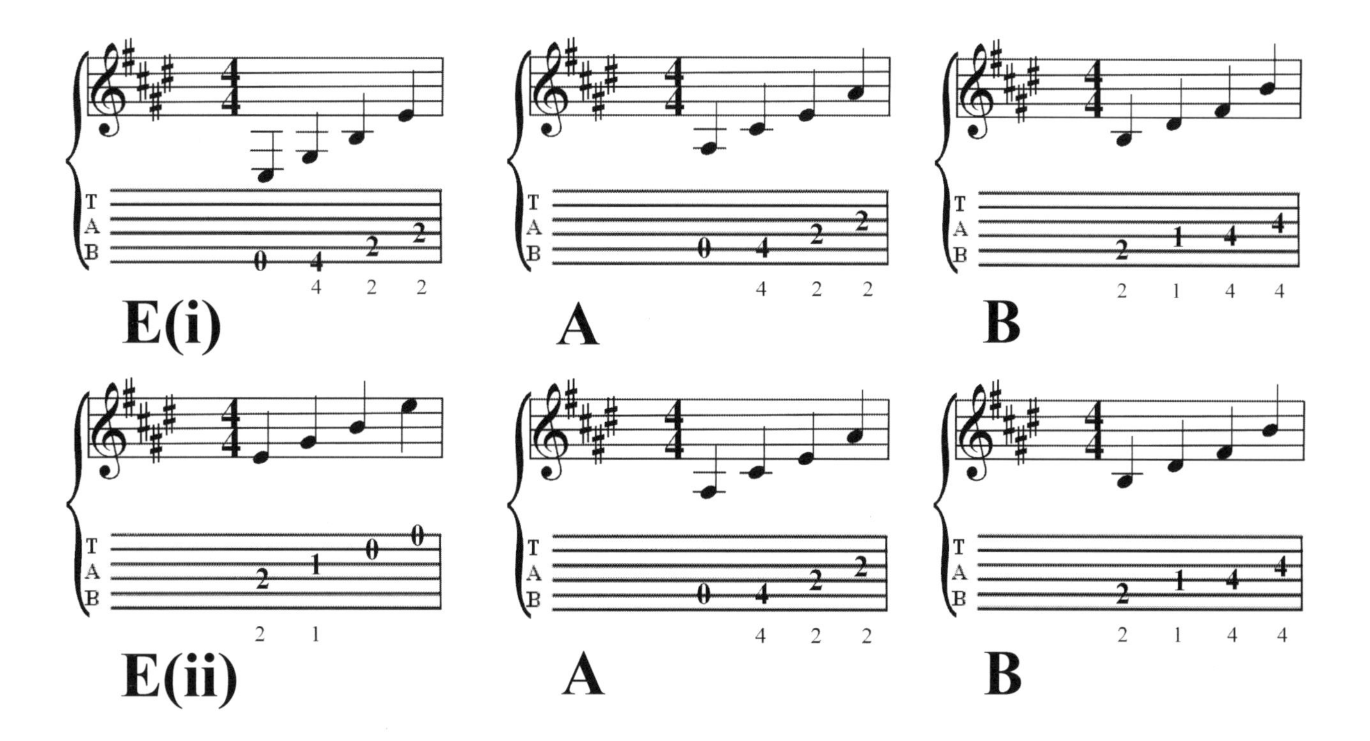

Key of B

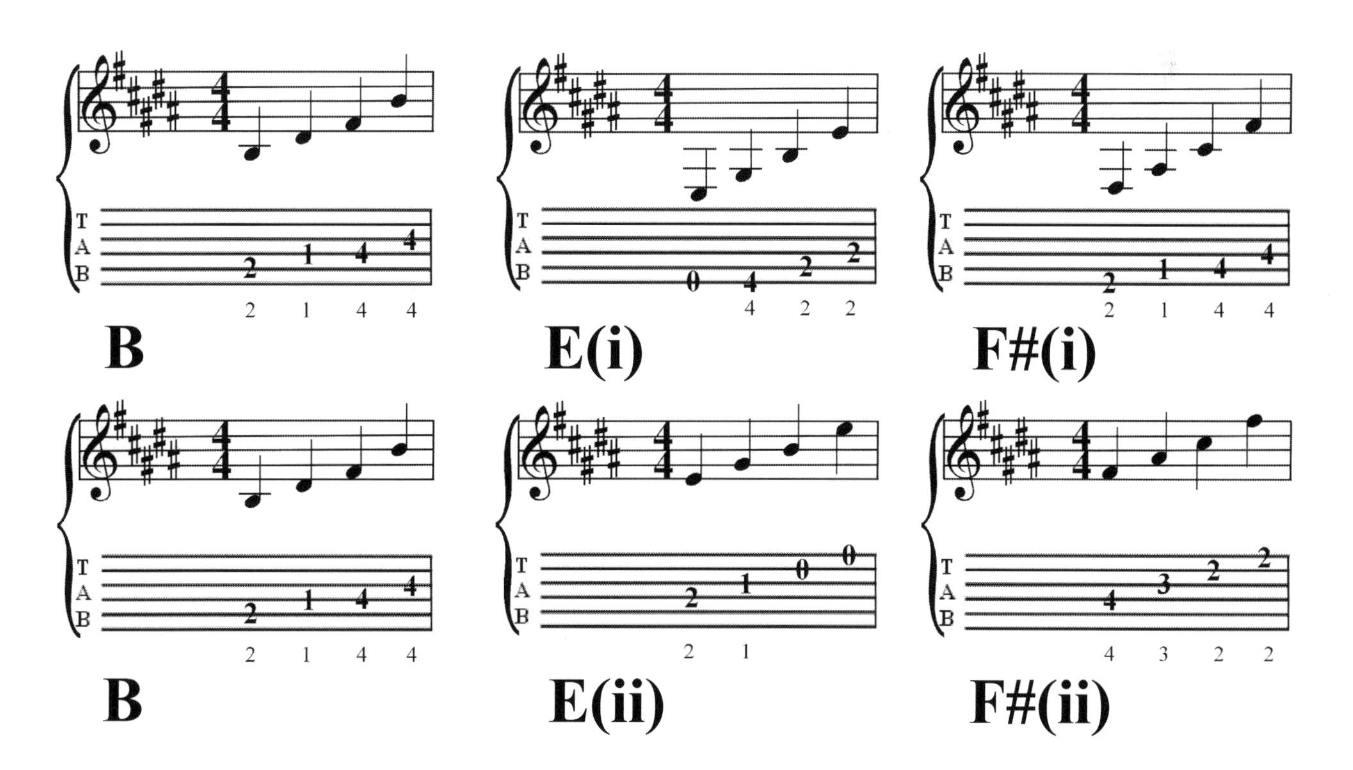

Key of F#

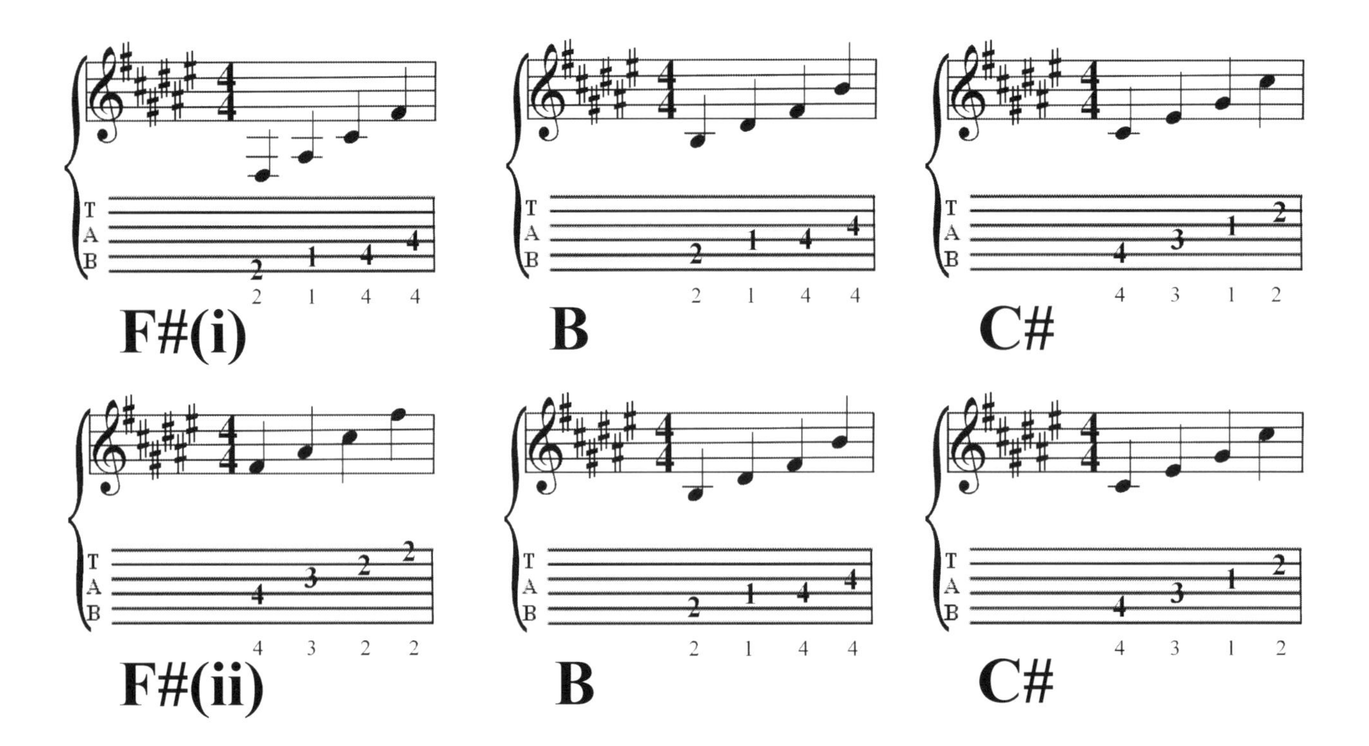

Key of C#

Key of A♭

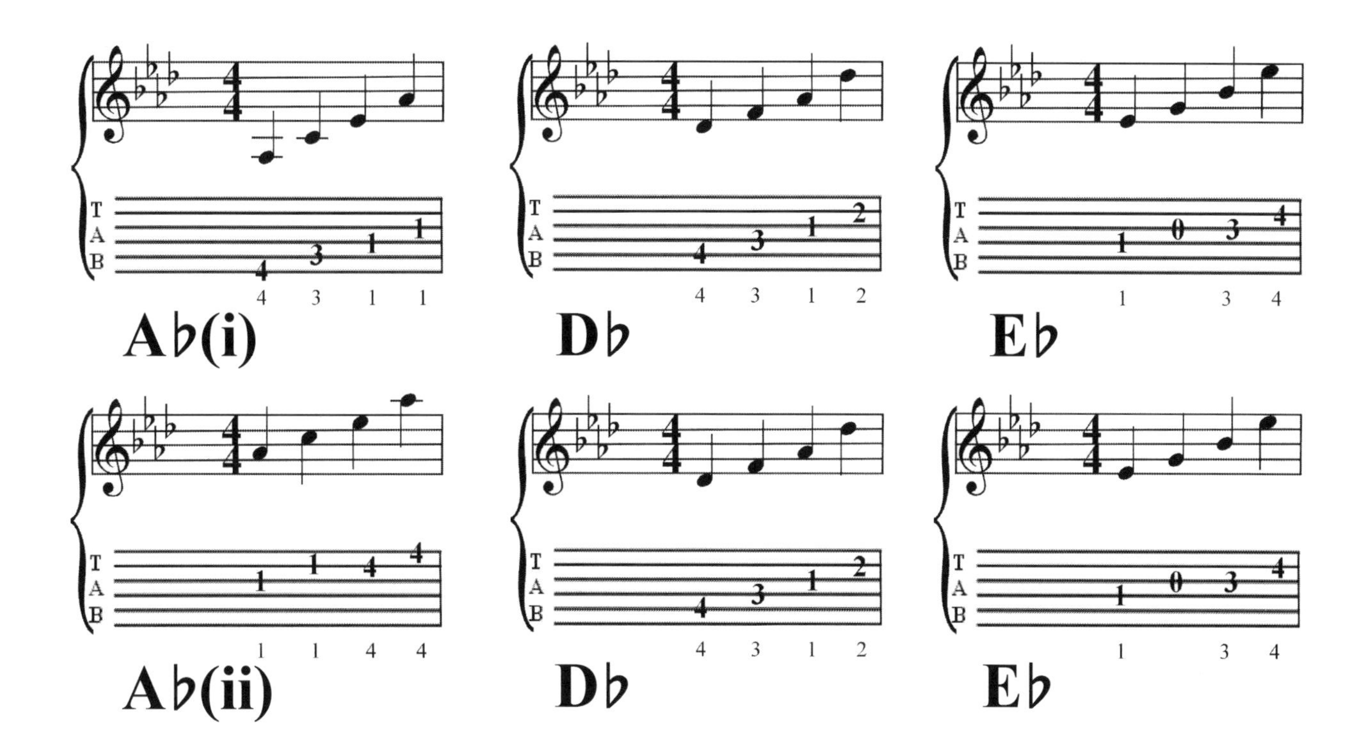

Key of E♭

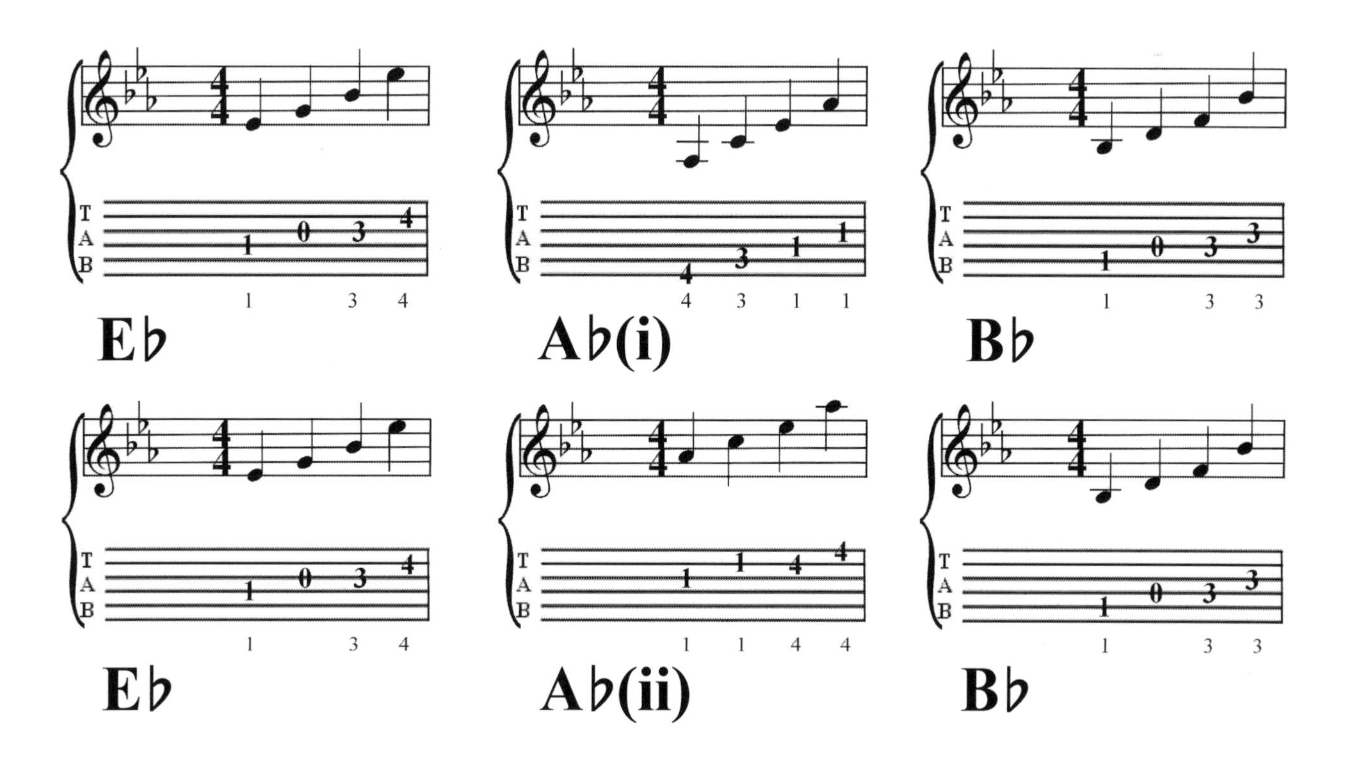

Key of B♭

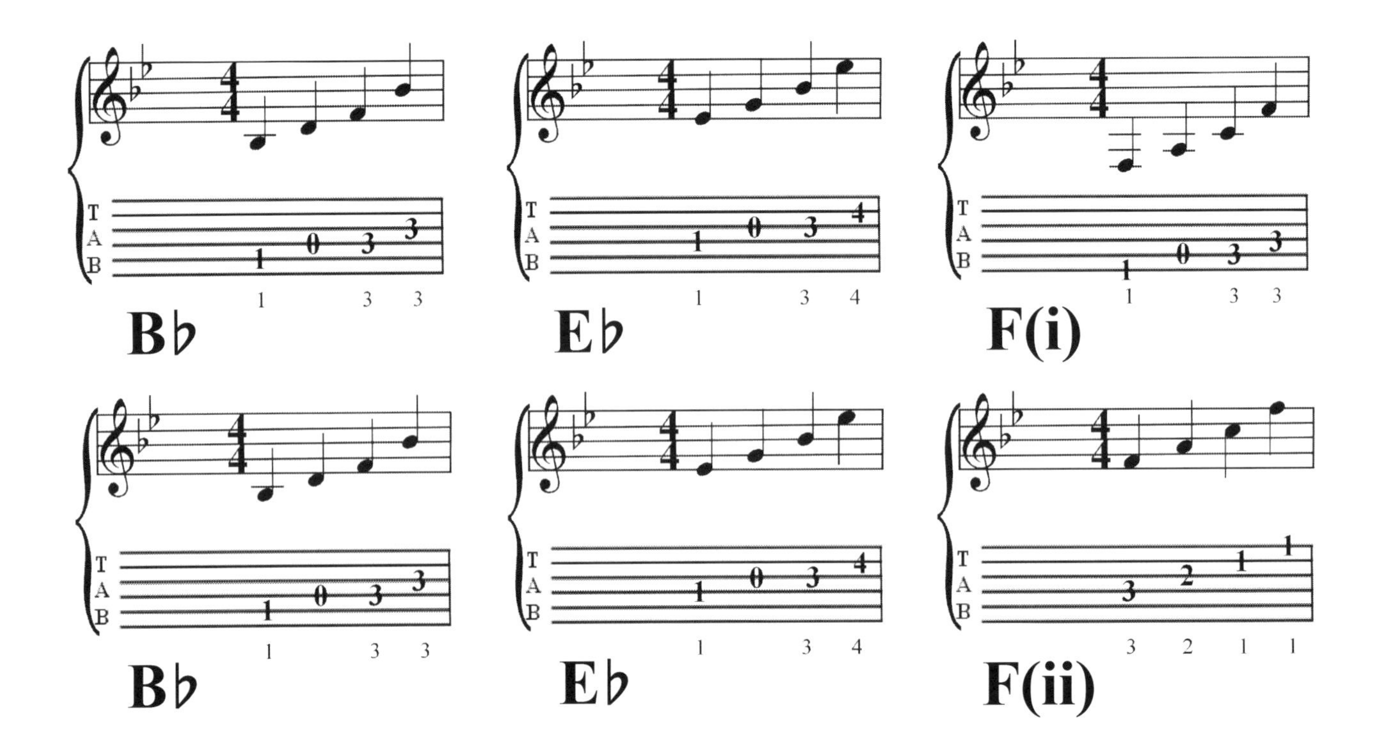

Key of F

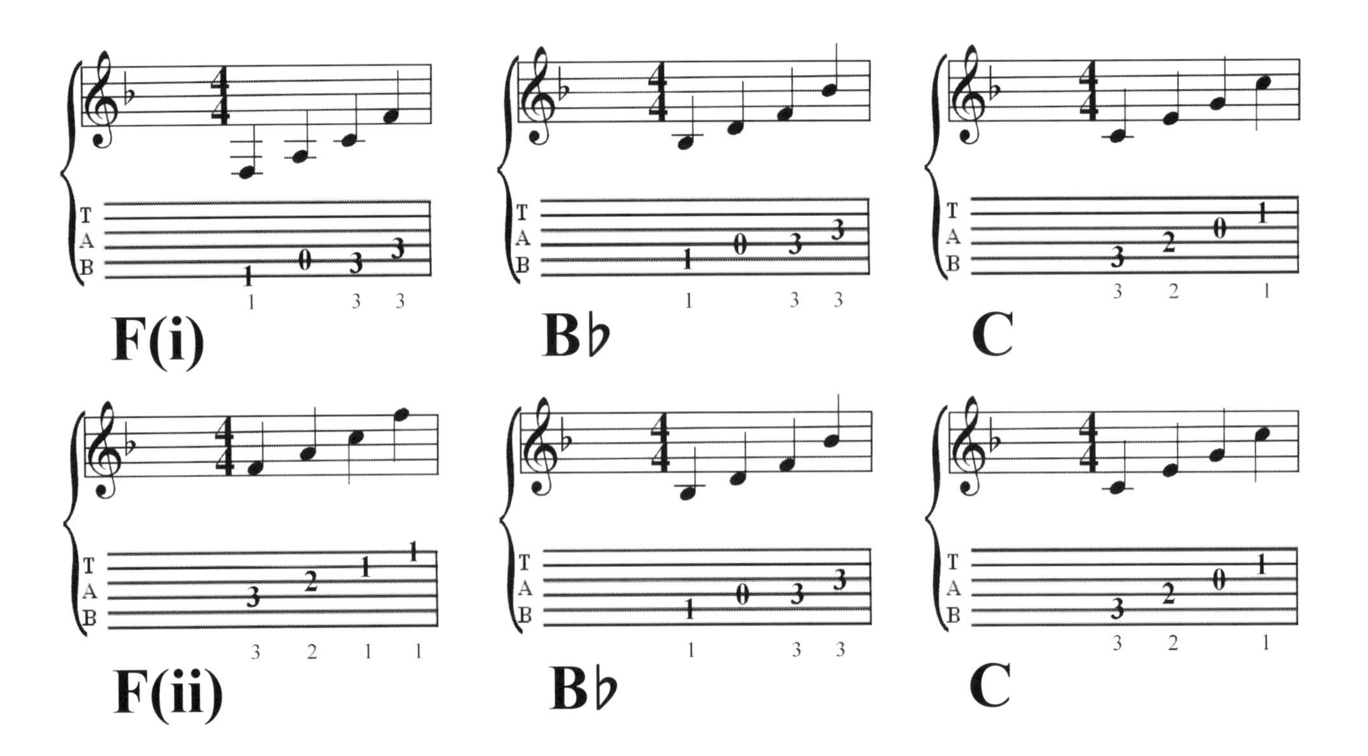

All Keys (i)

I

IV

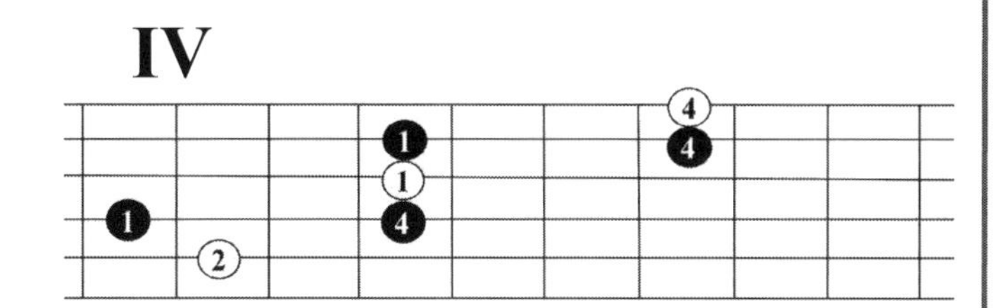

V

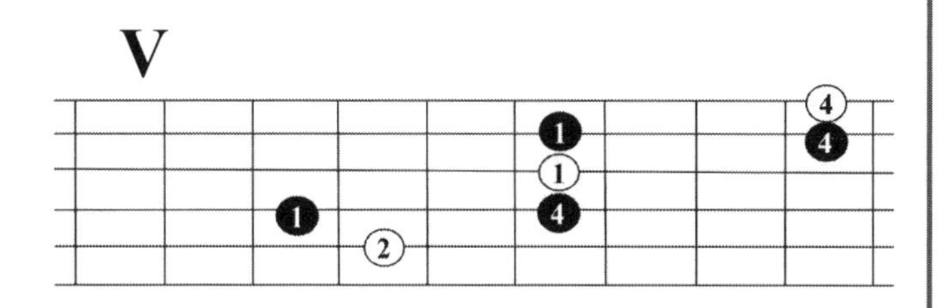

All Keys (ii)

I

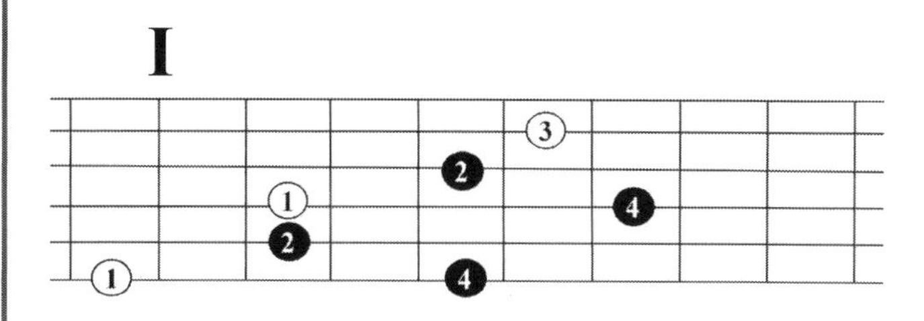

IV

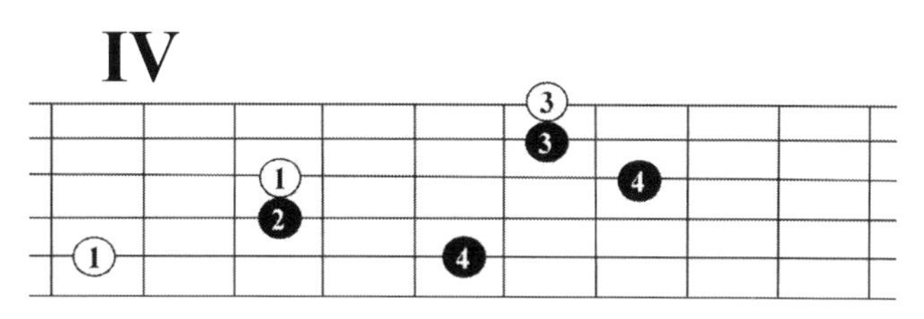

V

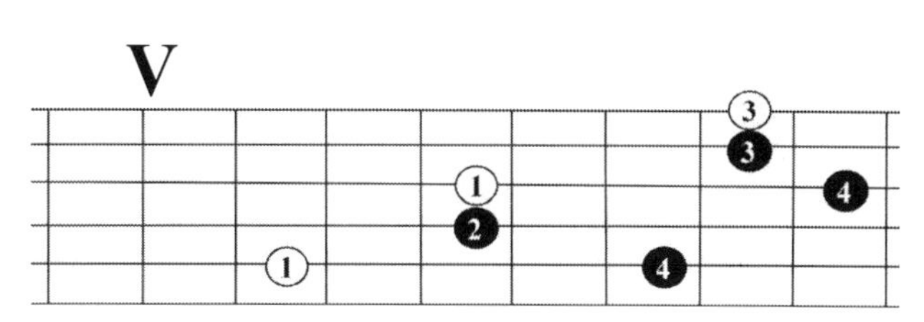

All Keys (iii)

I

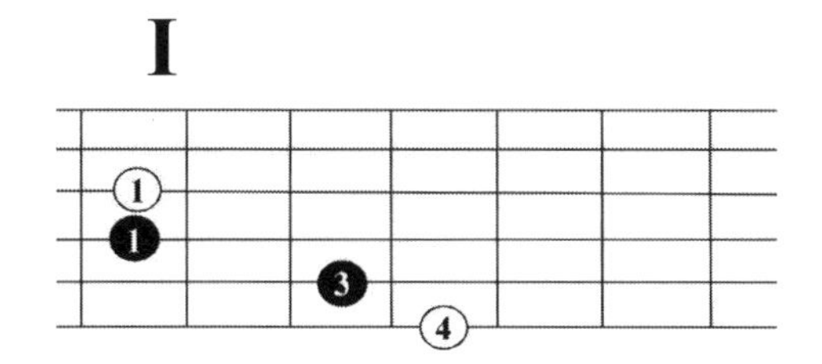

IV

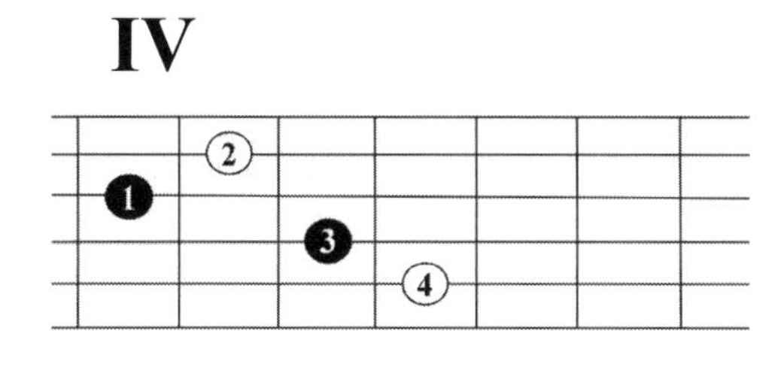

V

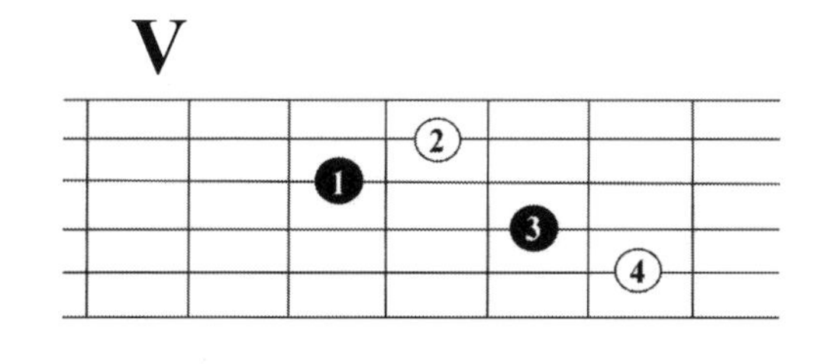

All Keys (iv)

I

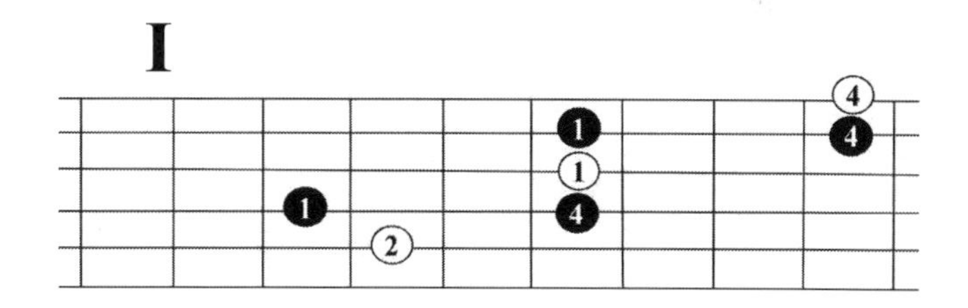

IV

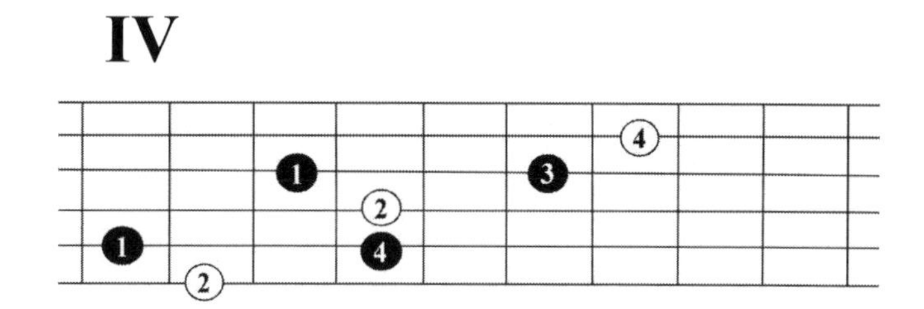

V

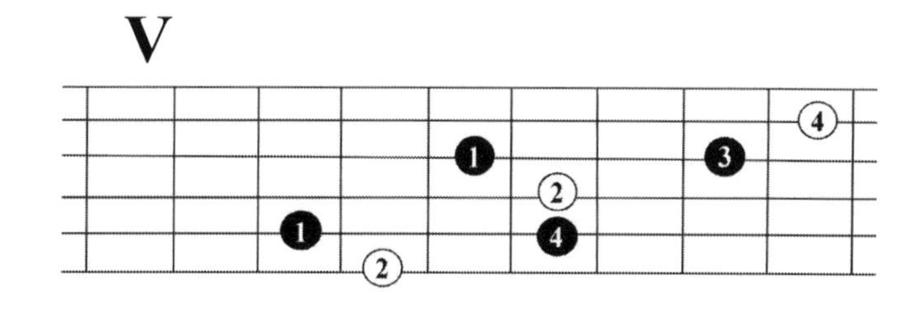

All Keys (v)

I

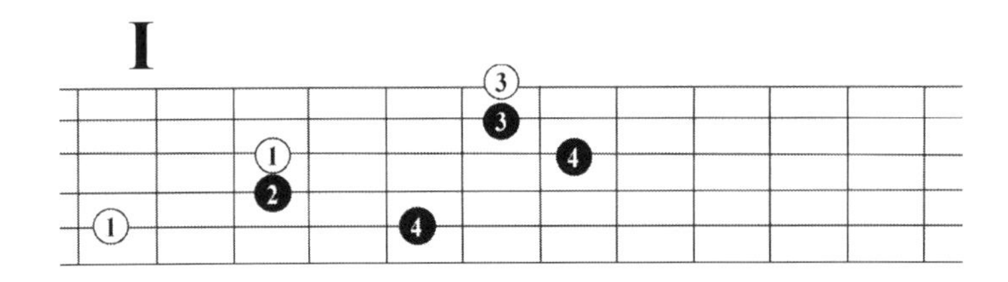

IV

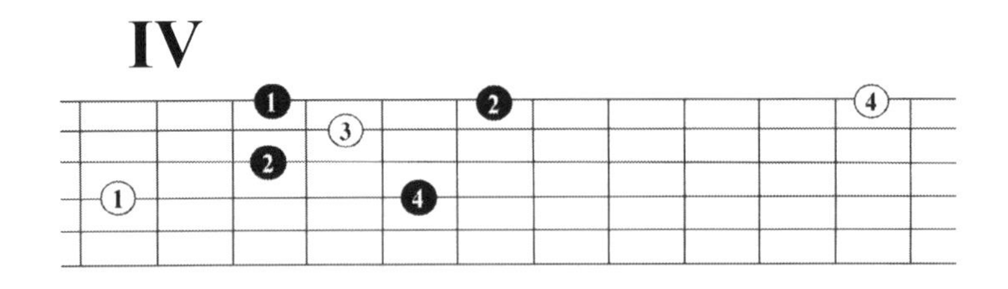

V

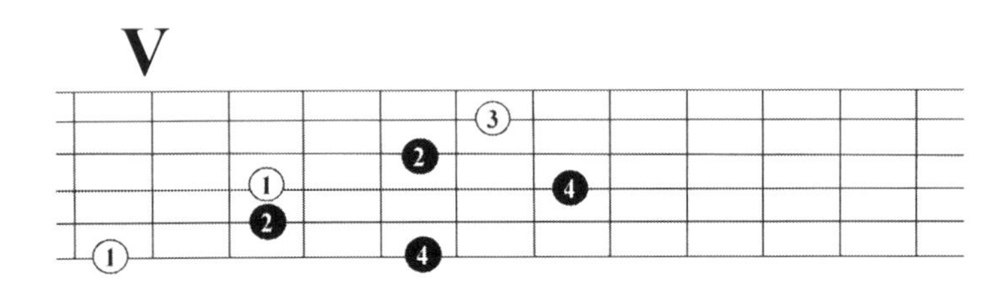

All Keys (vi)

I

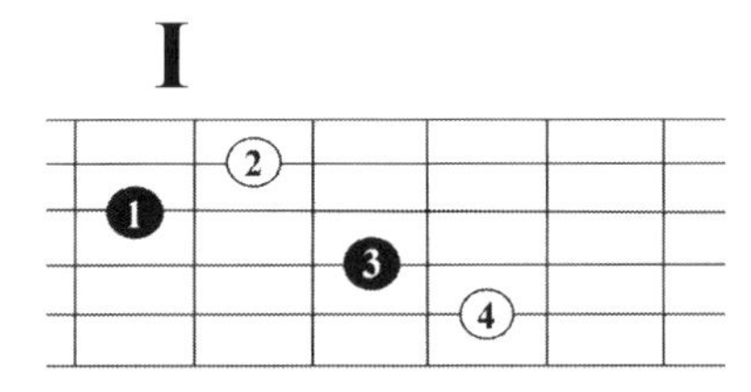

IV

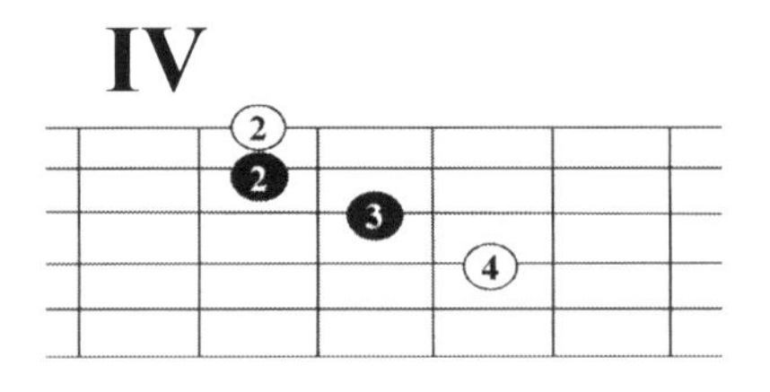

V

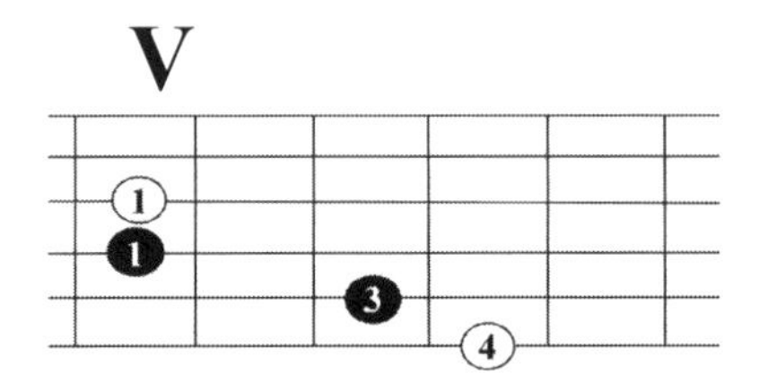

All Keys (vii)

I

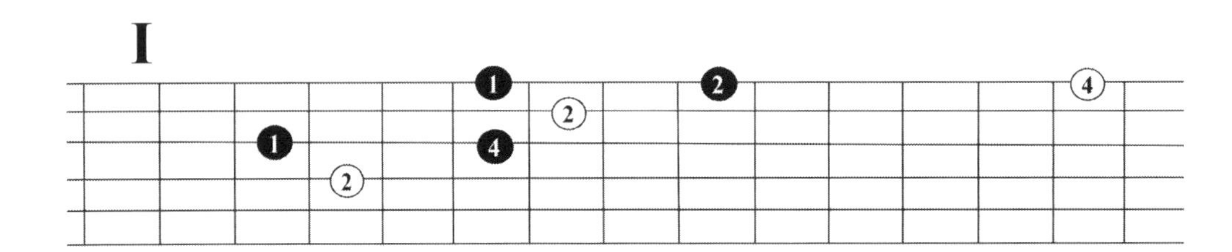

IV

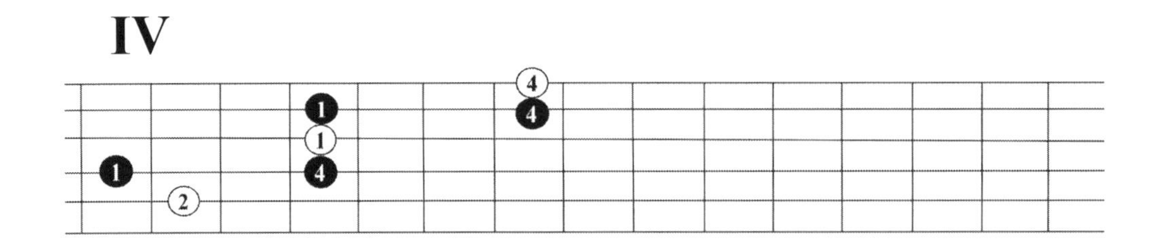

V

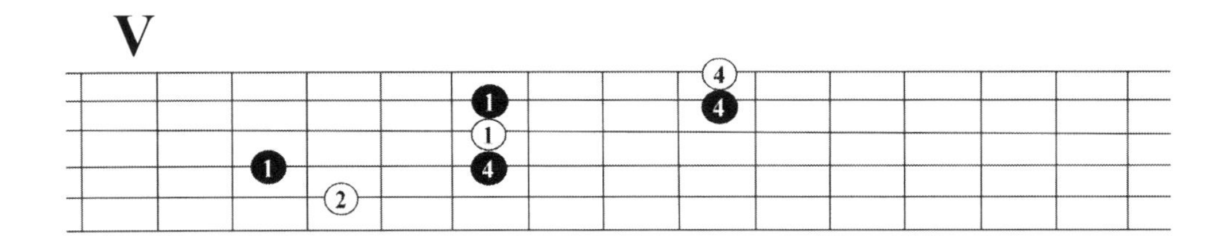

All Keys (viii)

I

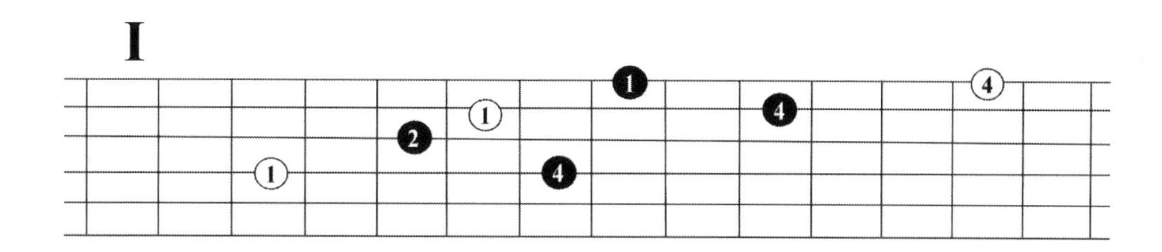

IV

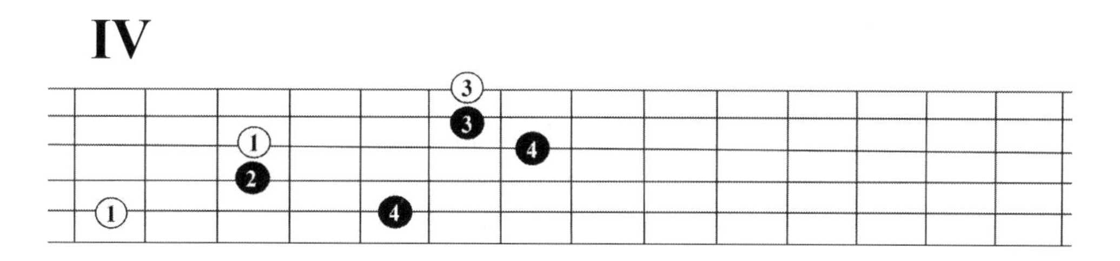

V

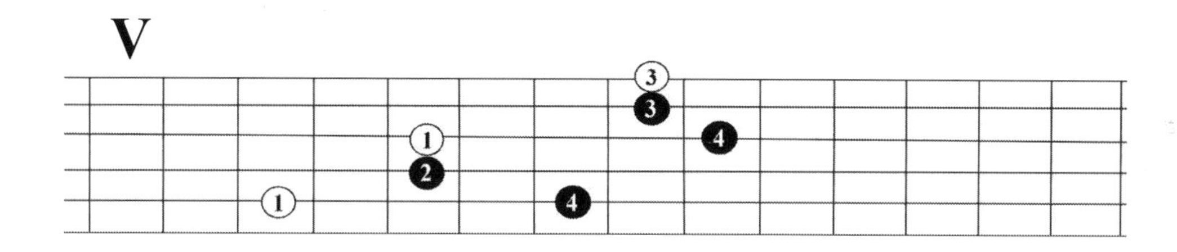

All Keys (ix)

I

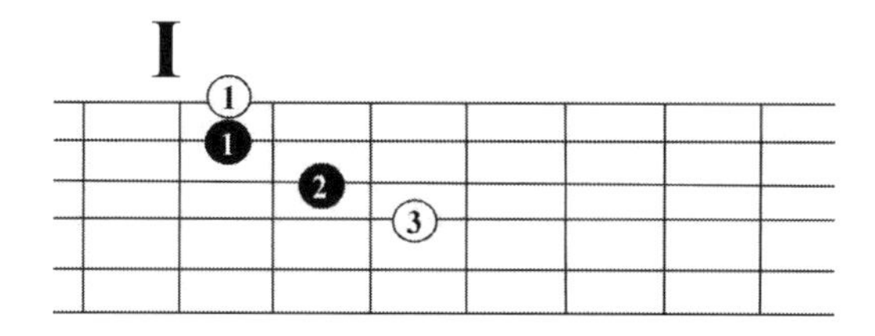

IV

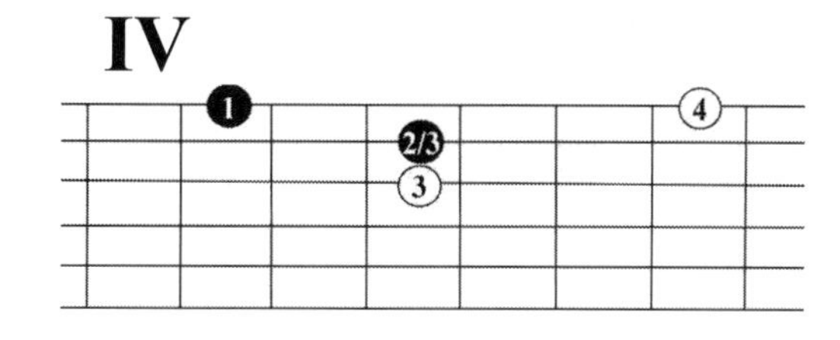

V

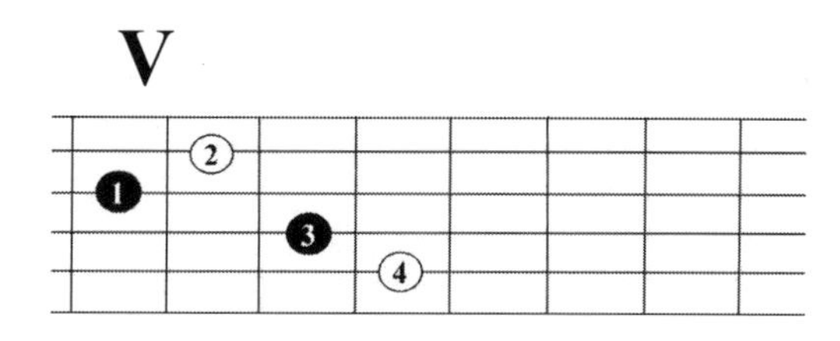

PART FOURTEEN

ii - V - I

MAJOR KEYS
TRIADS
ARPEGGIOS

A NOTE ON FINGERINGS

The next set of exercises introduces some alternative fingerings for some of the arpeggios. You should try to become comfortable with a variety of alternatives for each arpeggio pattern. Where these are given, they will appear in brackets next to the "normal" fingering, e.g. 3(4), on the tablature, or separated by a slash, e.g. 3/4, on the fingering charts. One important use of variant fingerings is to avoid playing consecutive notes with the same finger when moving from one arpeggio to the next. Experiment using different fingerings for the ascending and descending patterns. Try new fingerings of your own.

You can also mix up the arpeggio **shapes** from different exercises (e.g. playing one shape ascending, another descending). There isn't space here to print all the alternative combinations, so once again, don't be afraid to experiment.

Fingerings for the A (*minor* and *Major*) arpeggios in the open position now include the arpeggio in the upper *octave*, which requires a stretch to the 5th fret with the 4th finger. This breaks the "in position" rule we've been following, but it is a very minor transgression which allows us to complete the two-octave arpeggio. By omitting the top A, the arpeggio can, of course, be played in position.

Key of C

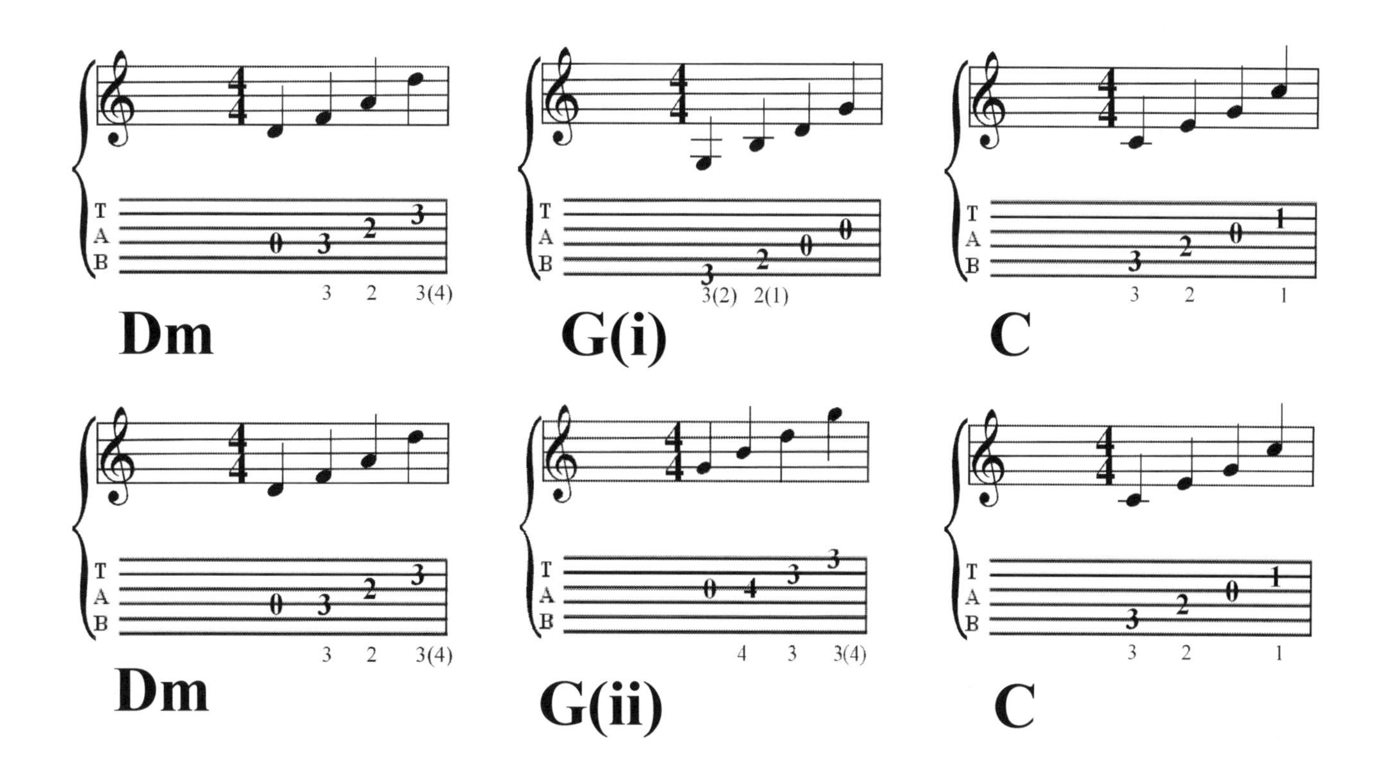

Key of G

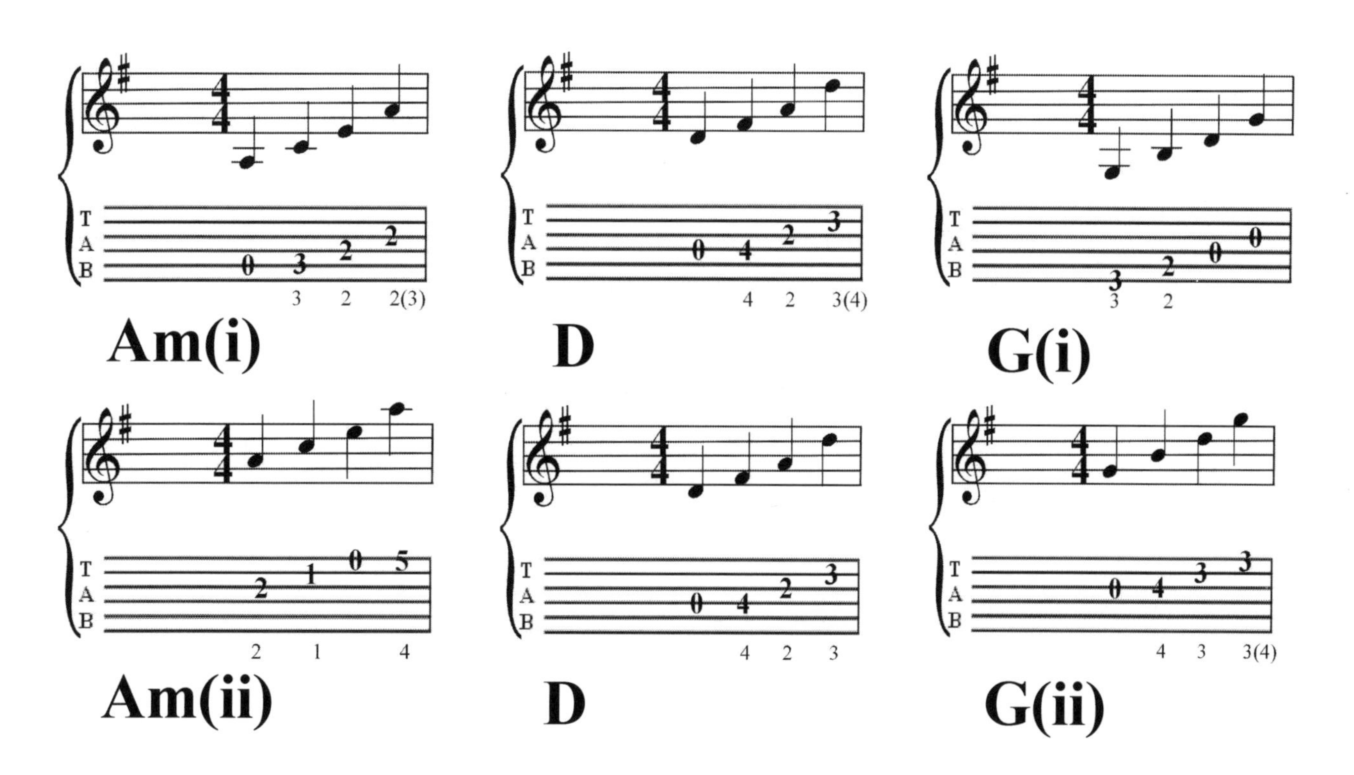

Key of D

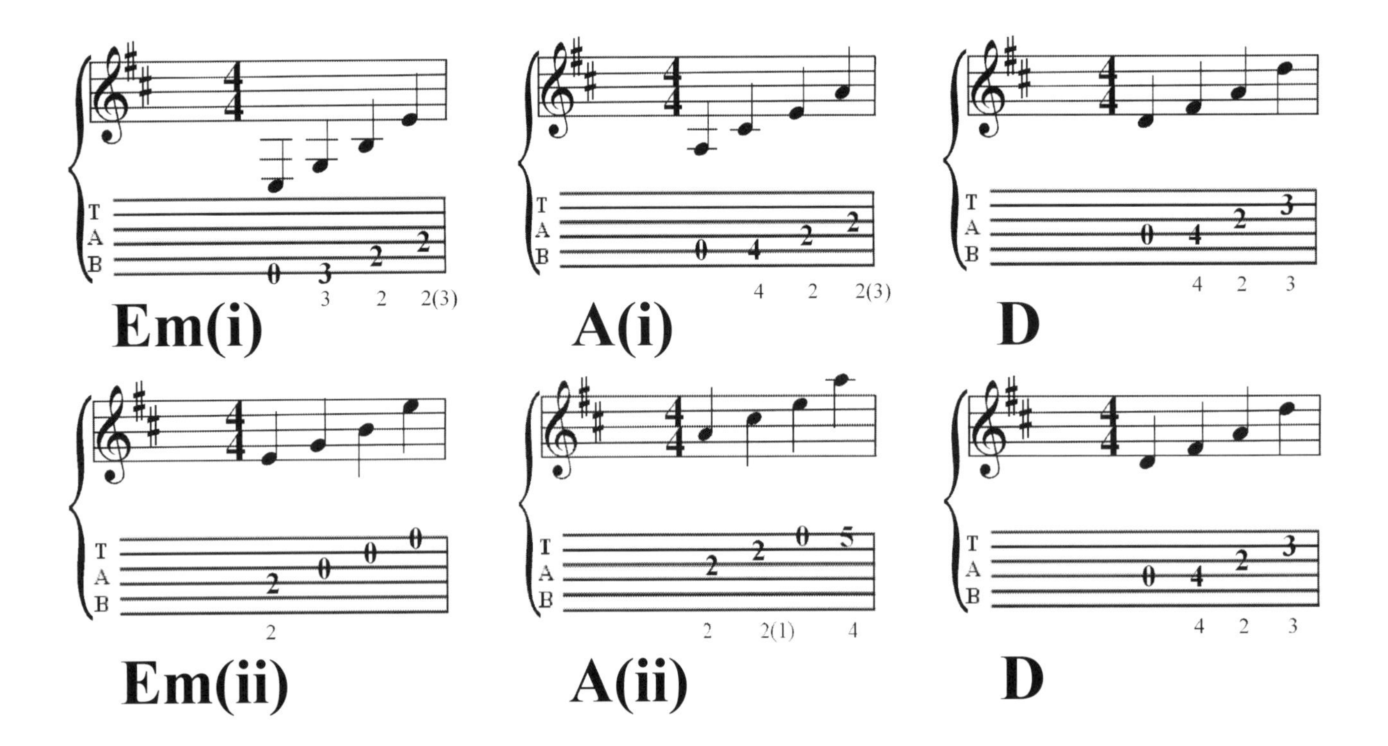

Key of A

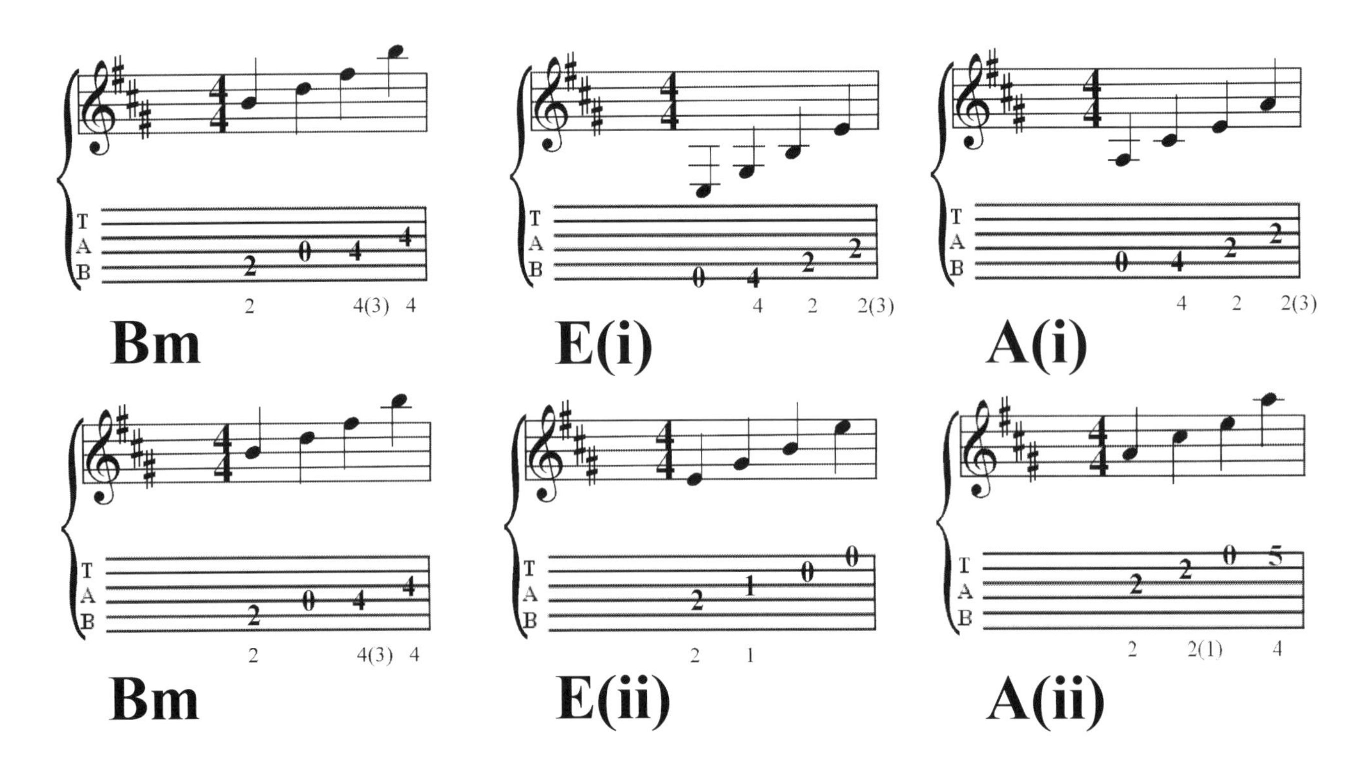

Key of E

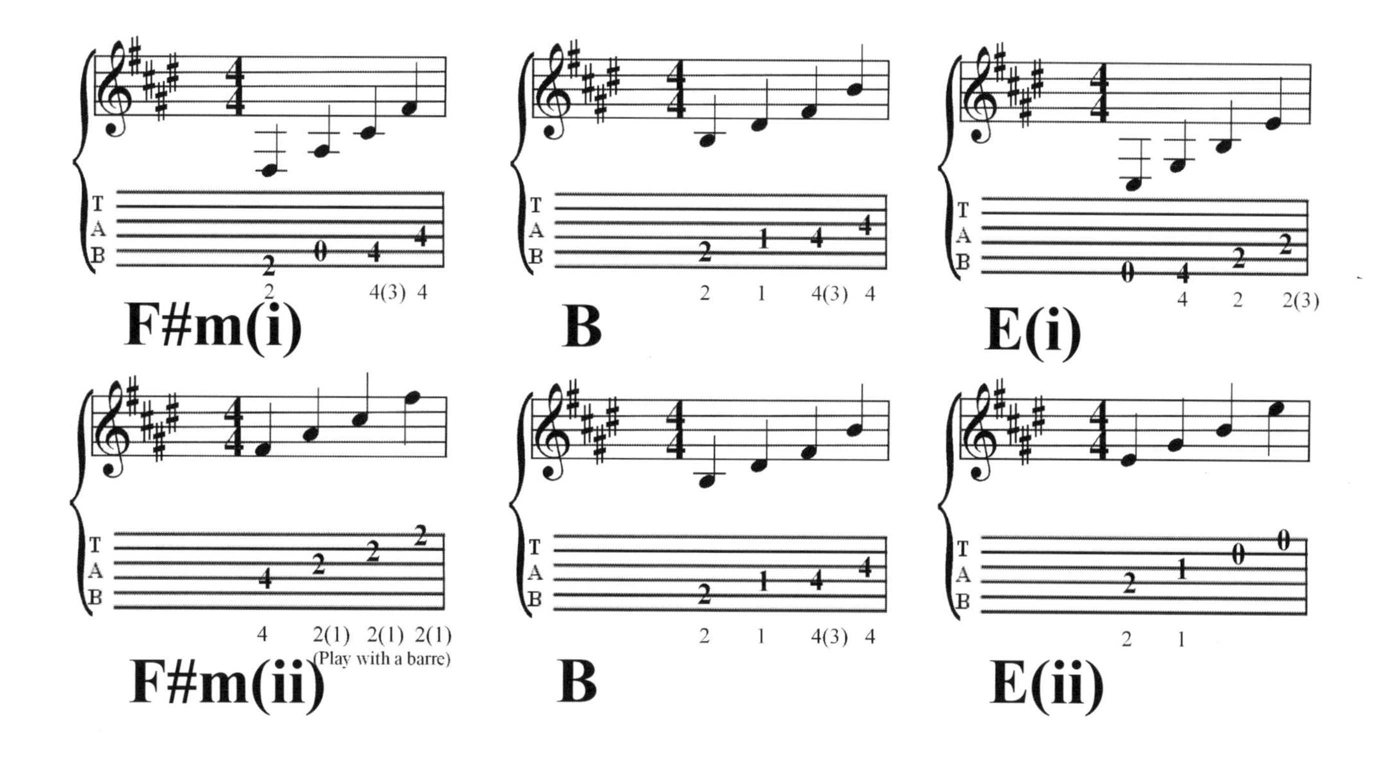

Key of B

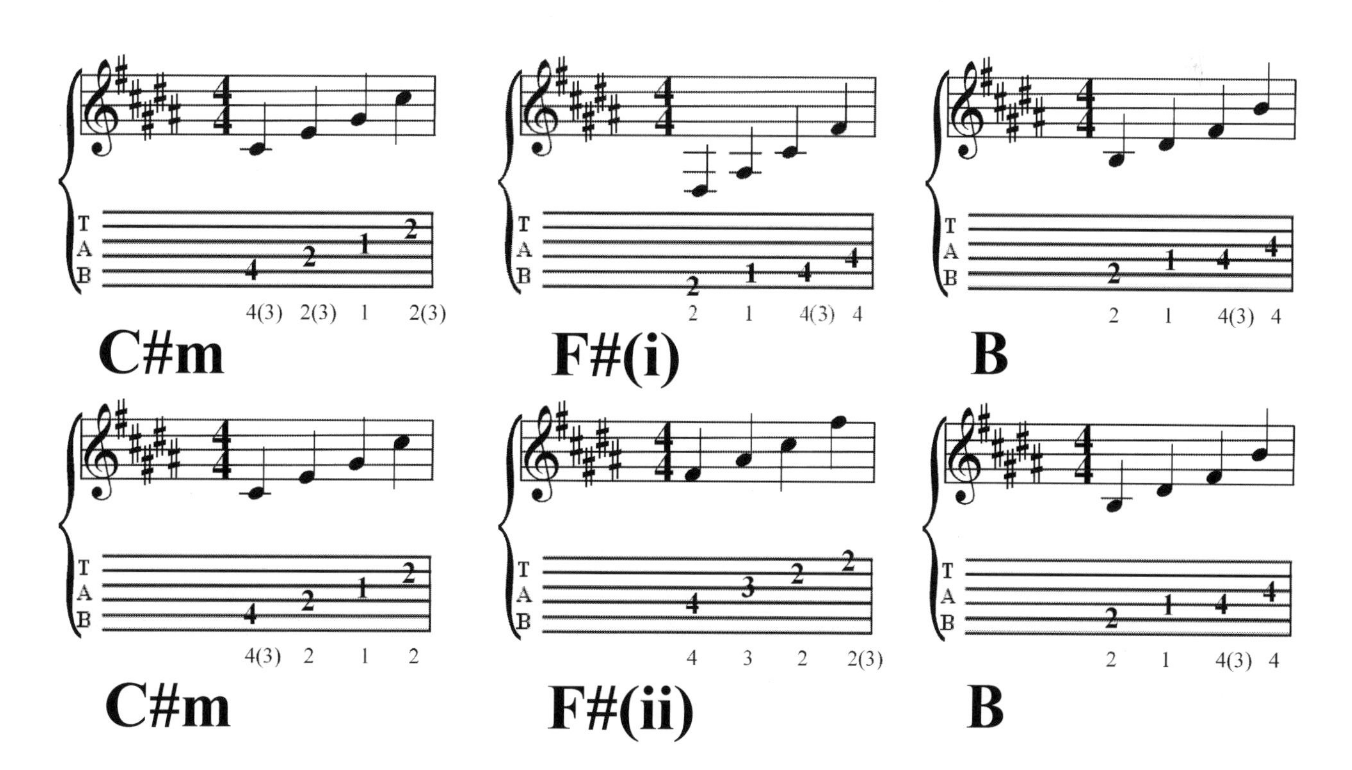

Key of F#

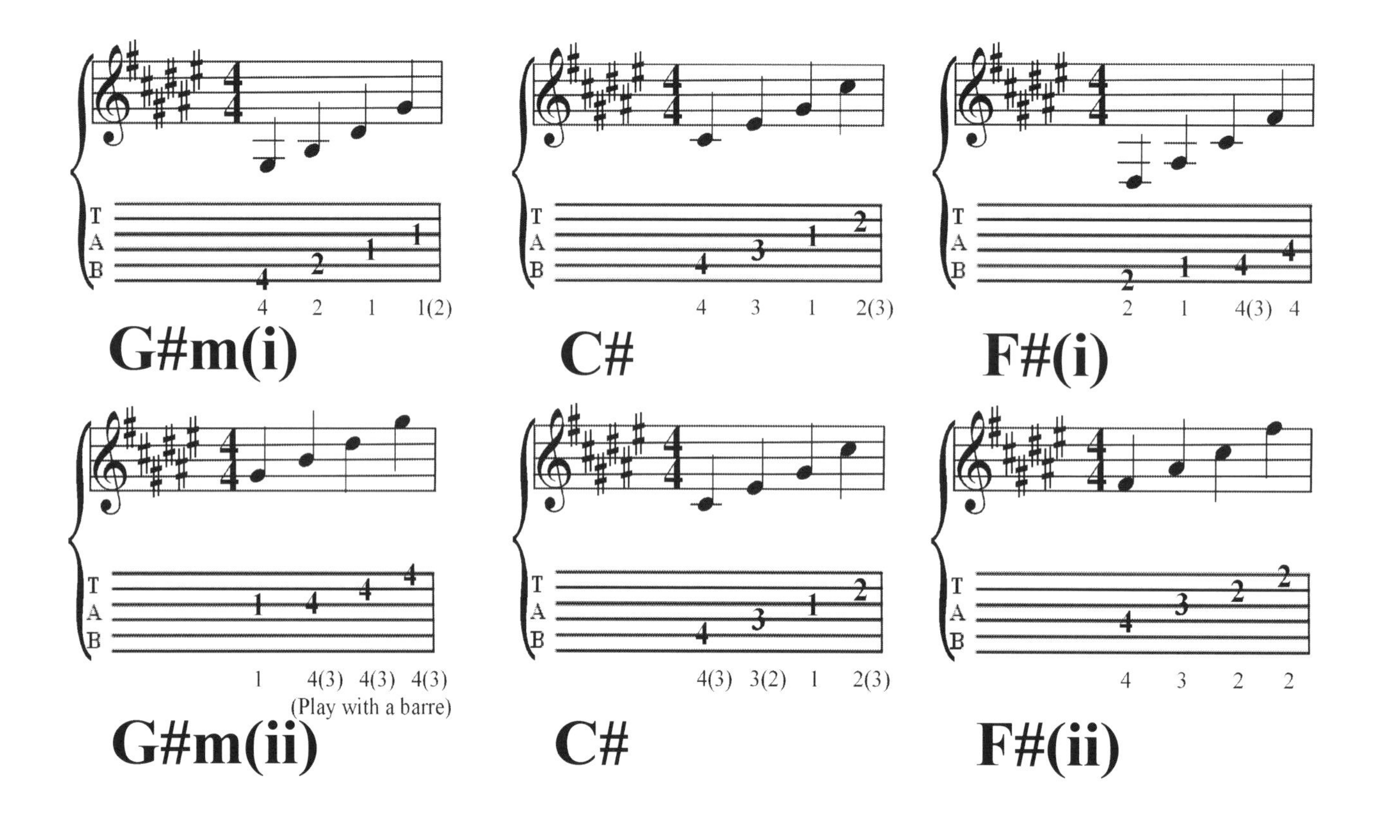

Key of C#

Key of A♭

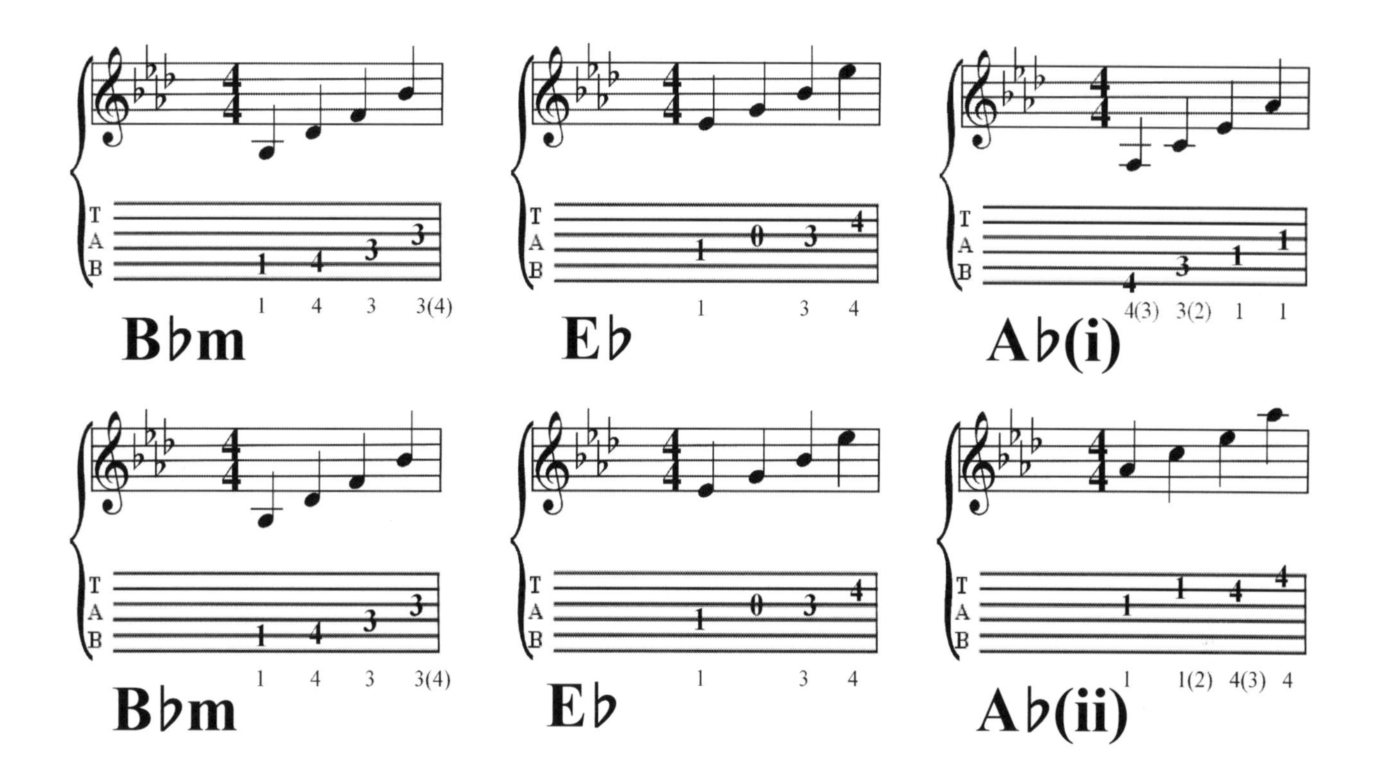

Key of E♭

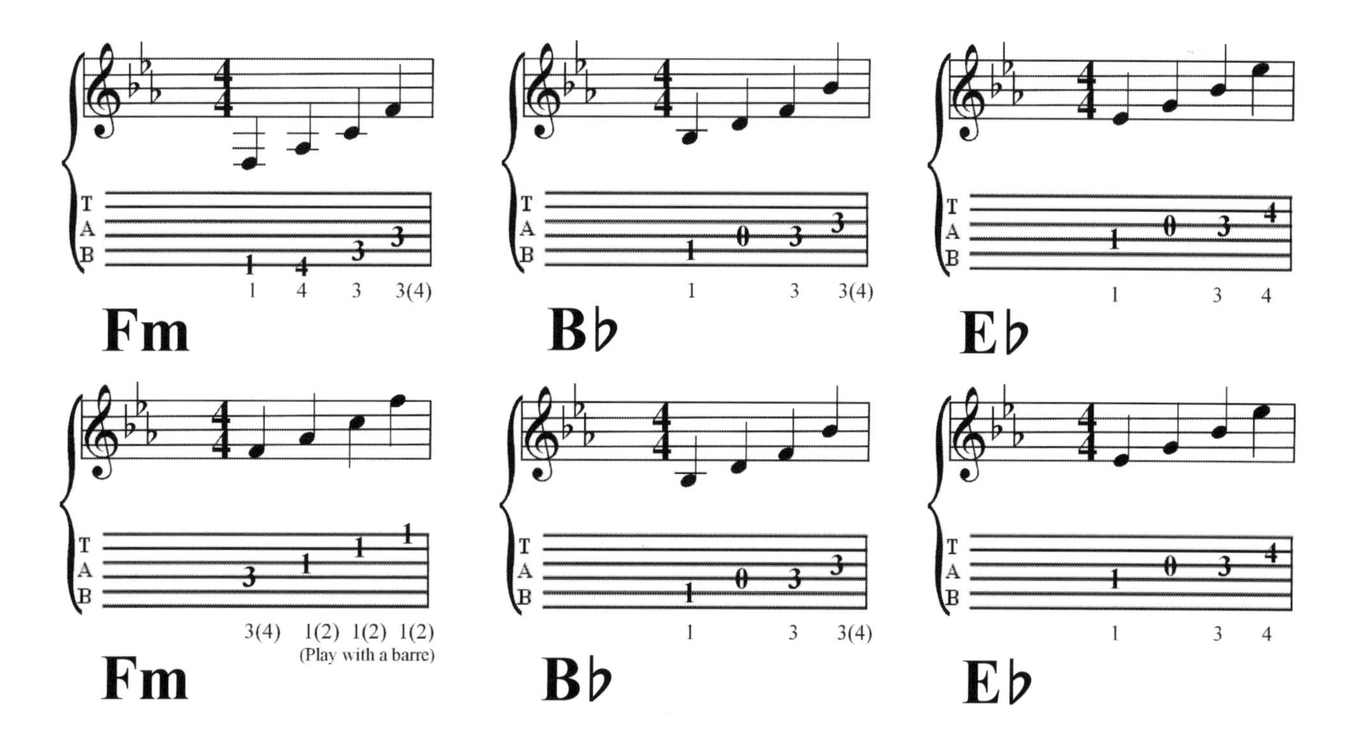

Key of B♭

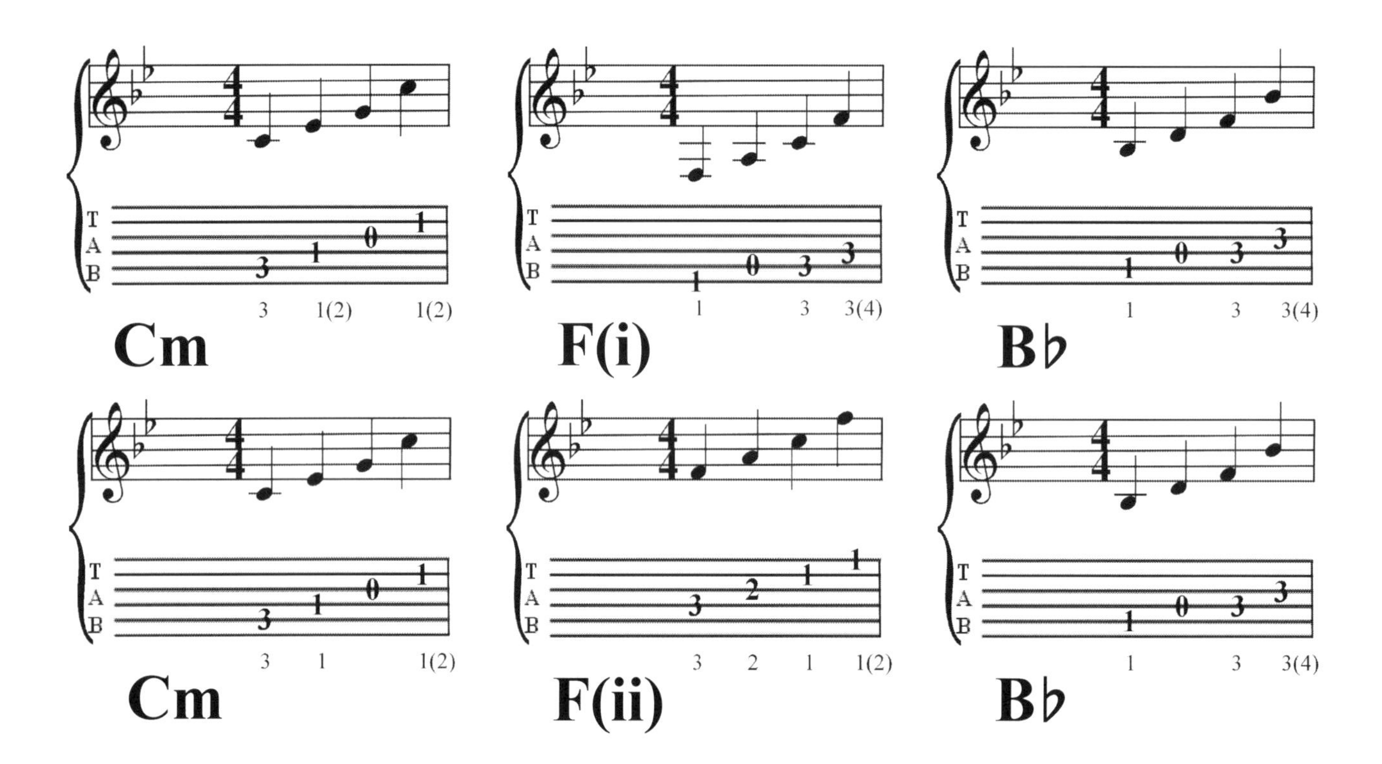

Key of F

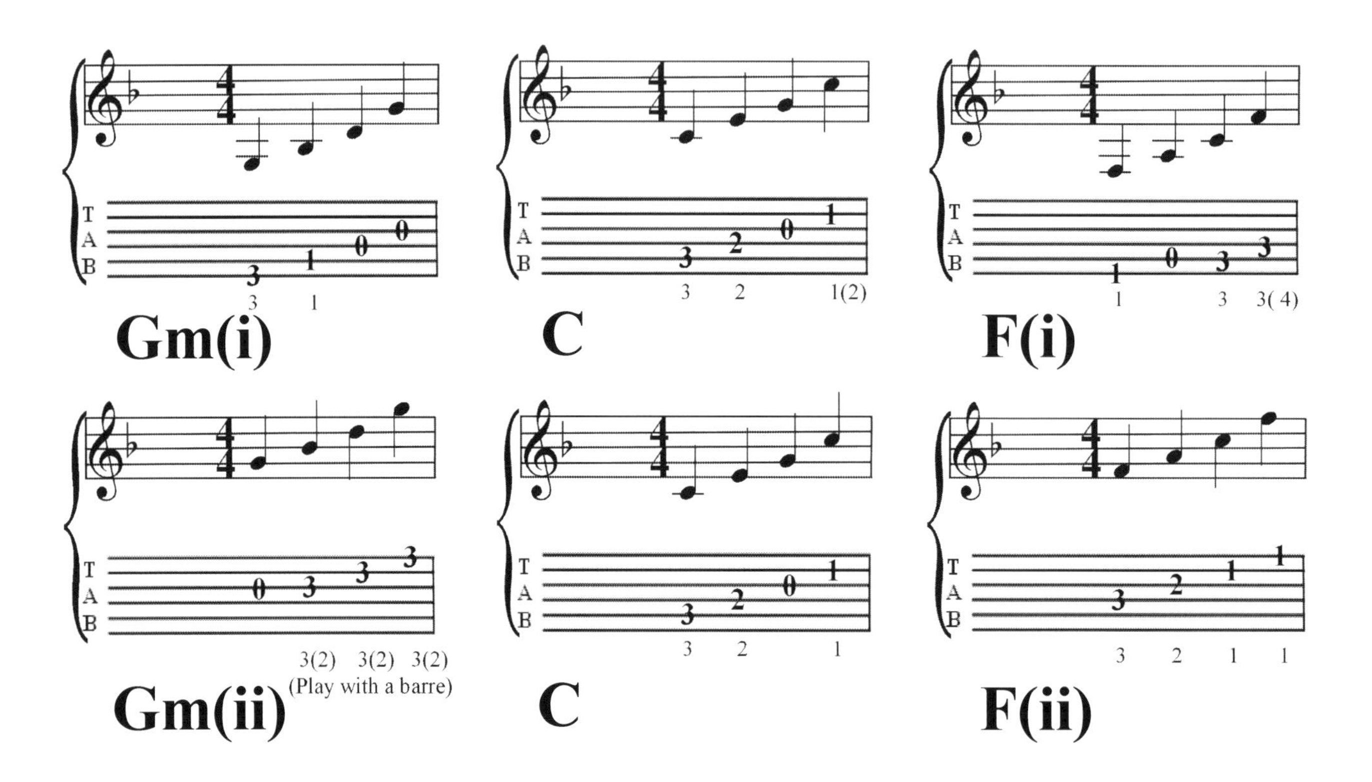

All Keys (i)

ii

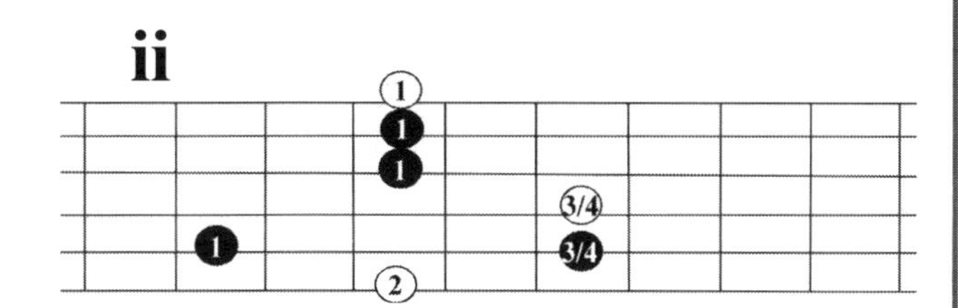

V

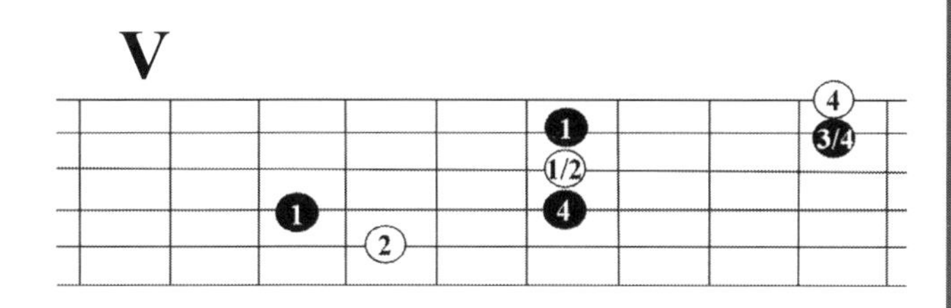

I

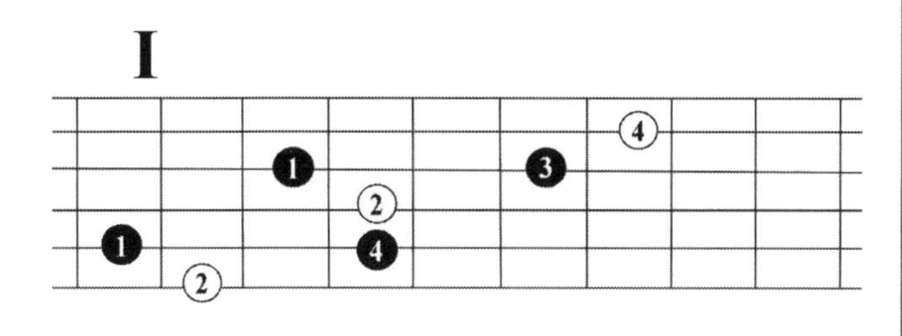

All Keys (ii)

ii

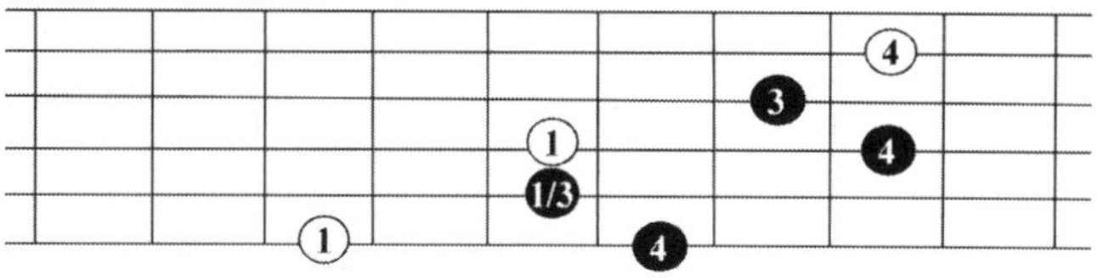

V

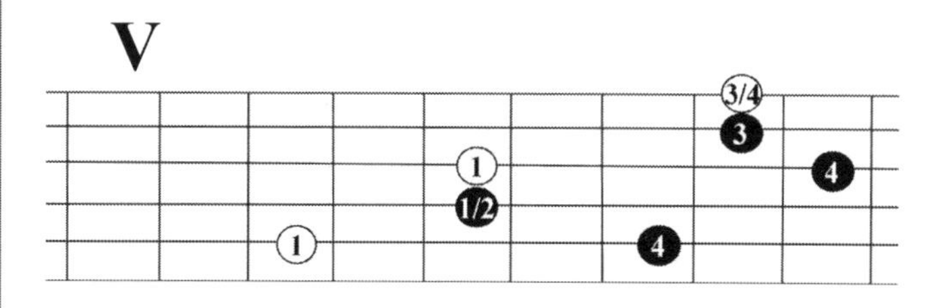

I

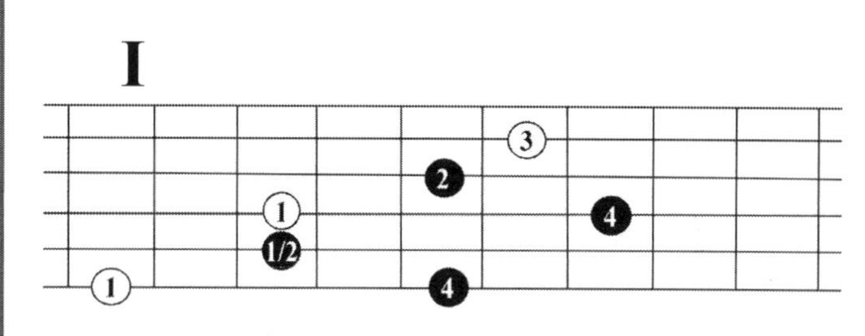

All Keys (iii)

ii

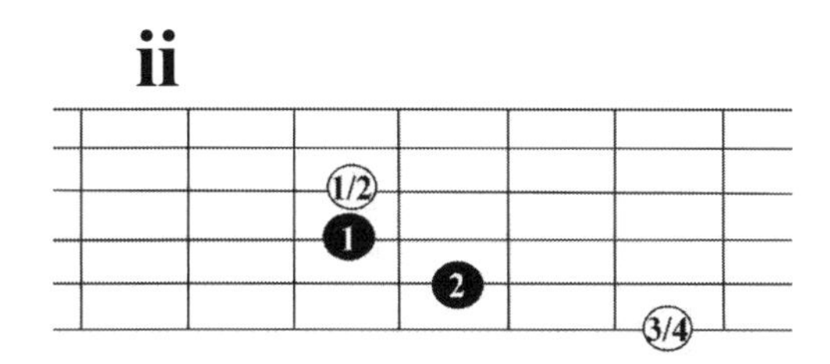

V

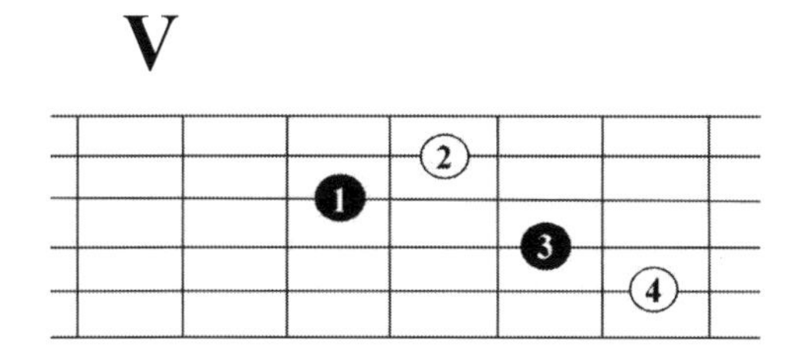

I

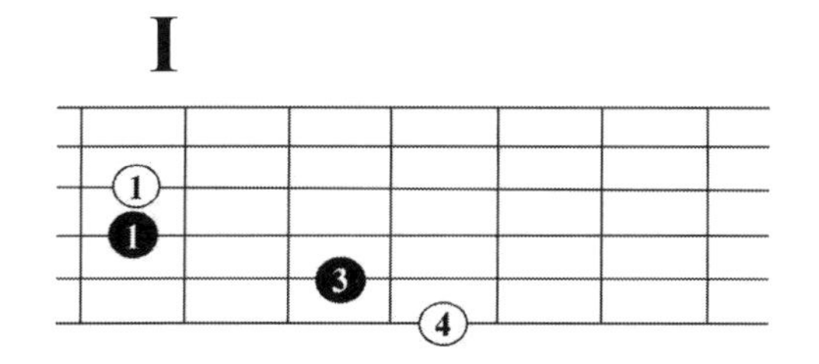

All Keys (iv)

ii

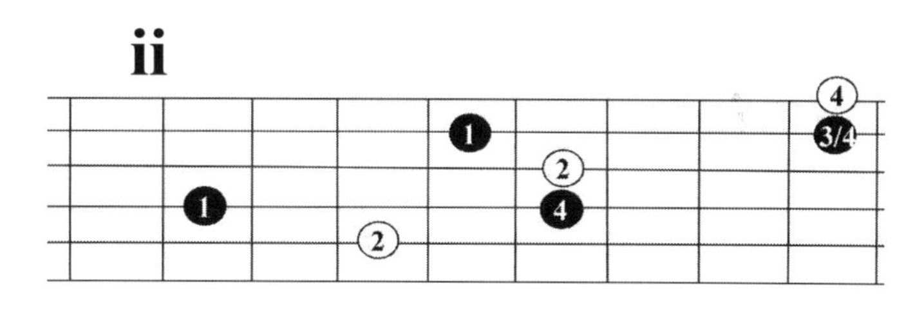

V

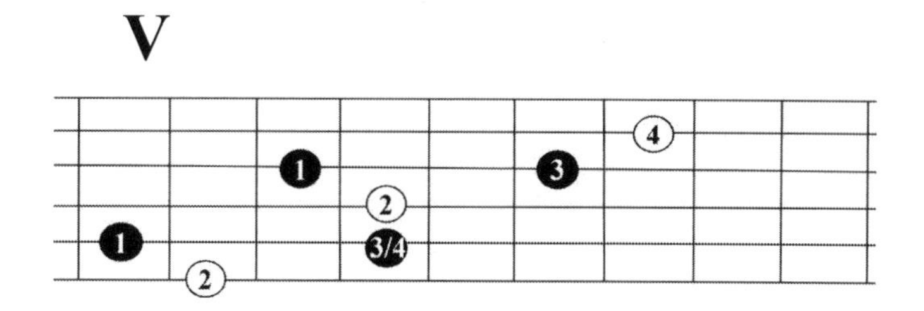

I

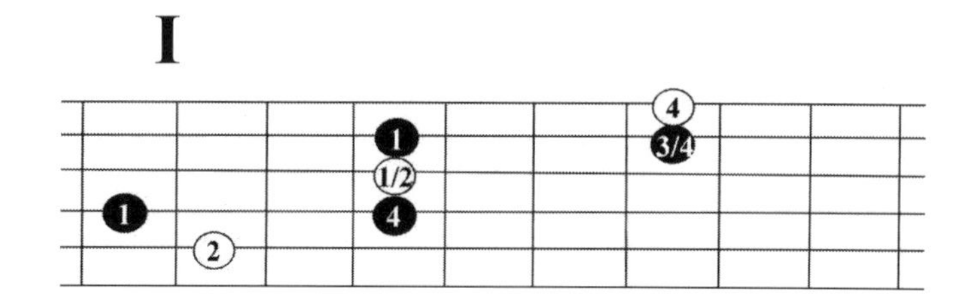

All Keys (v)

ii

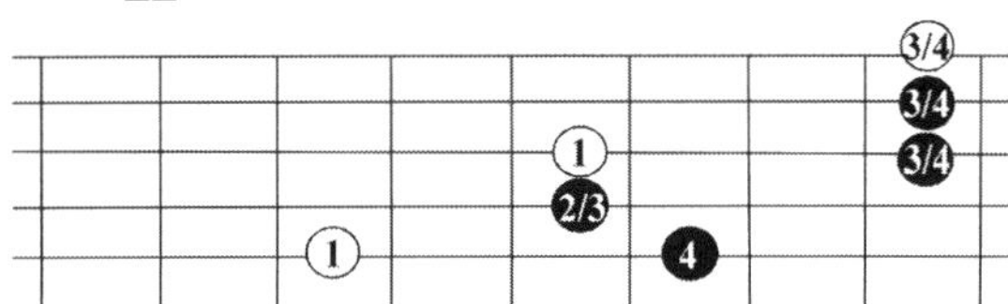

V

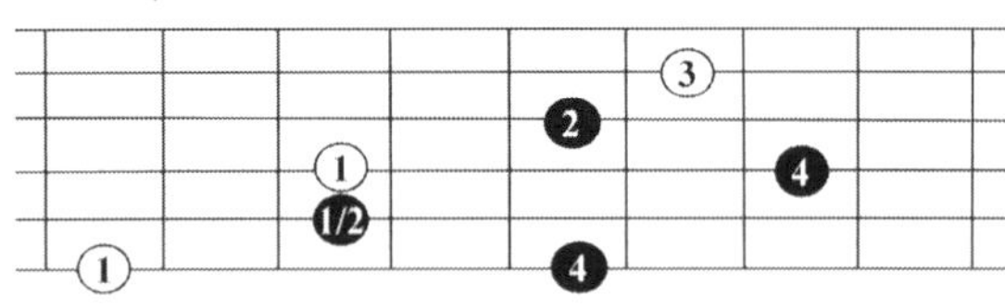

I

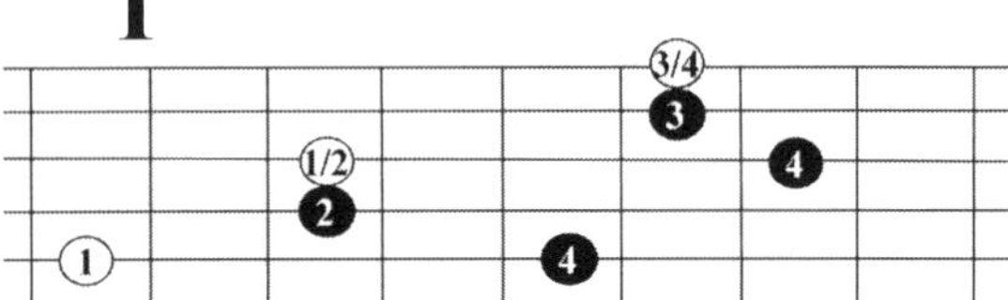

All Keys (vi)

ii

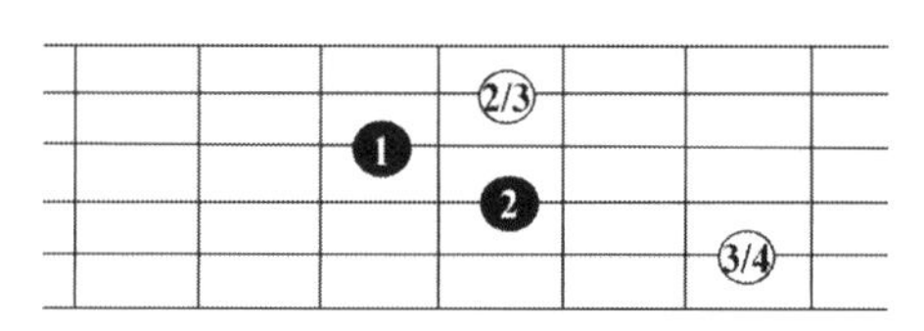

V

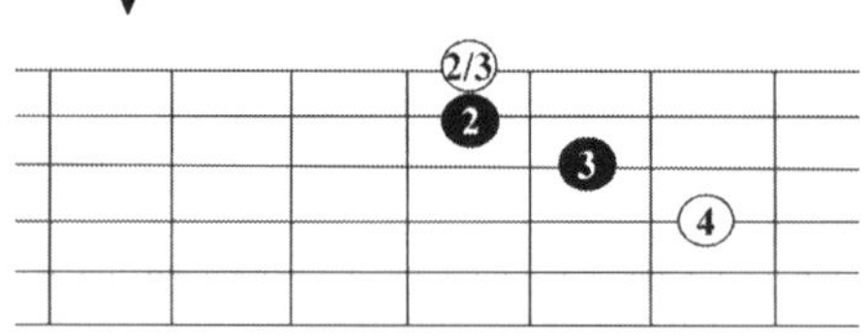

I

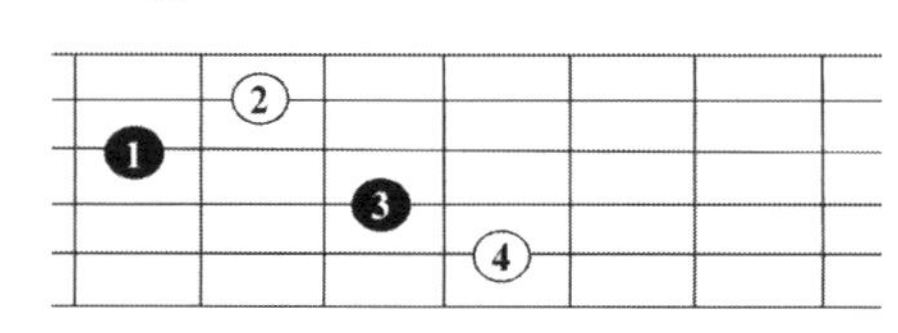

All Keys (vii)

ii

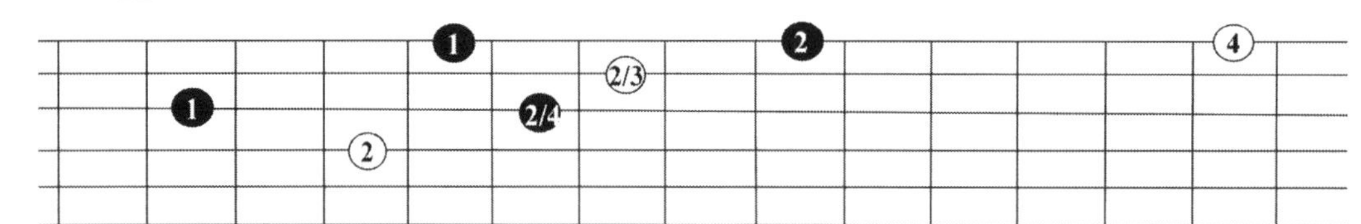

V

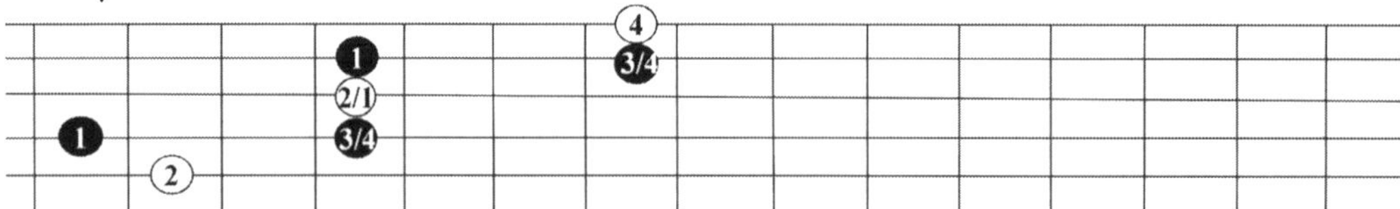

I

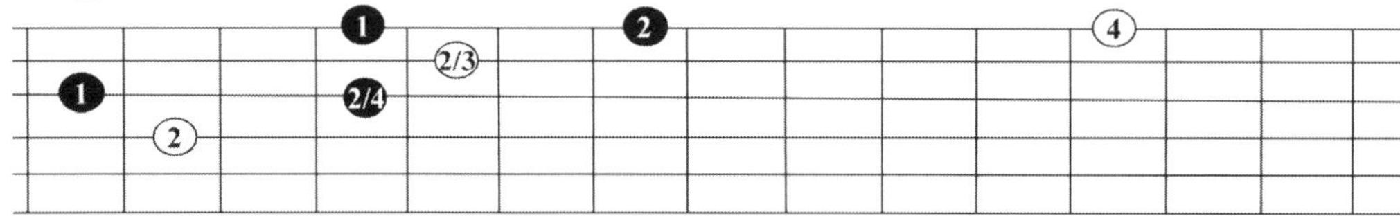

All Keys (viii)

ii

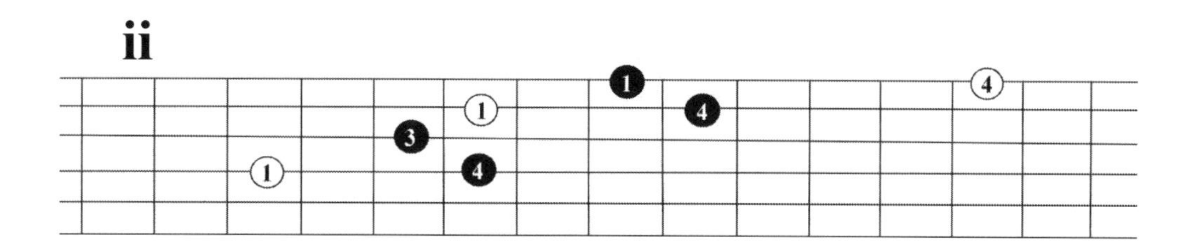

V

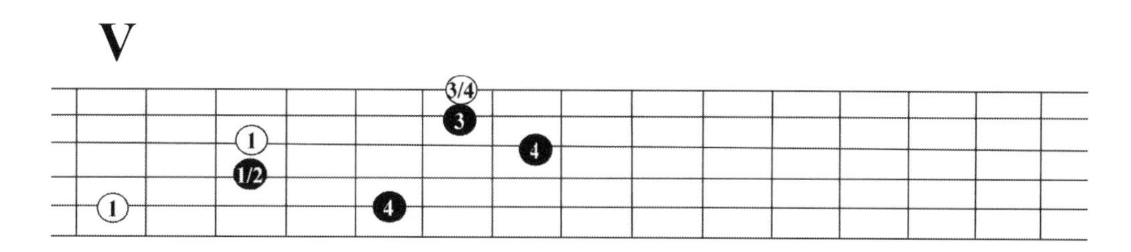

I

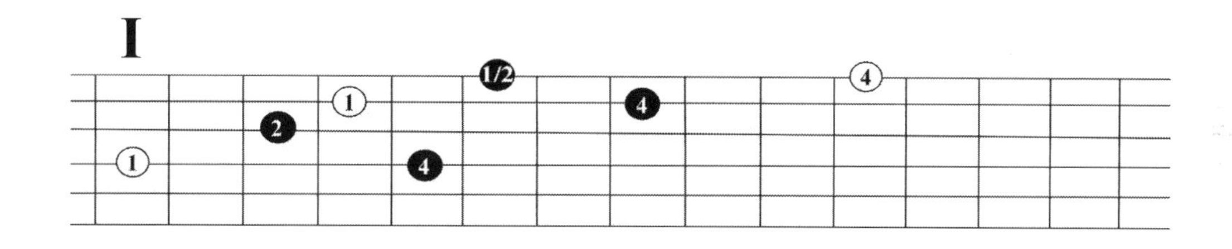

All Keys (ix)

ii

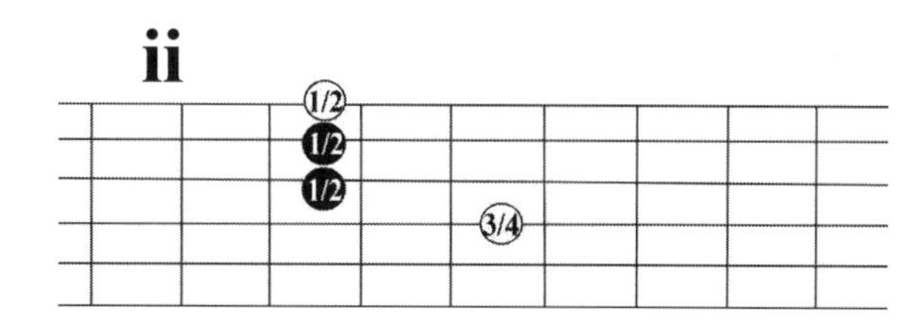

V

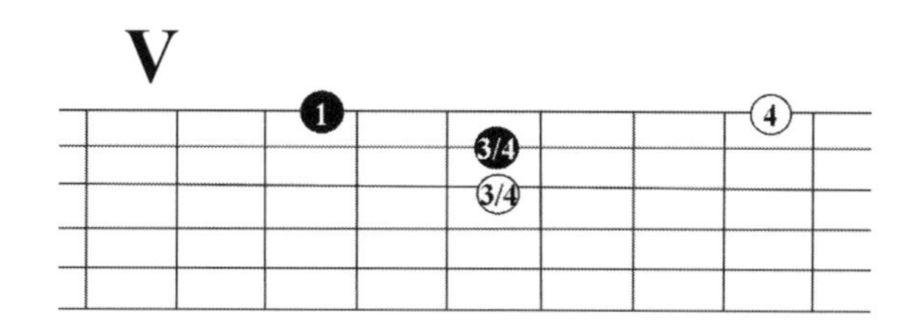

I

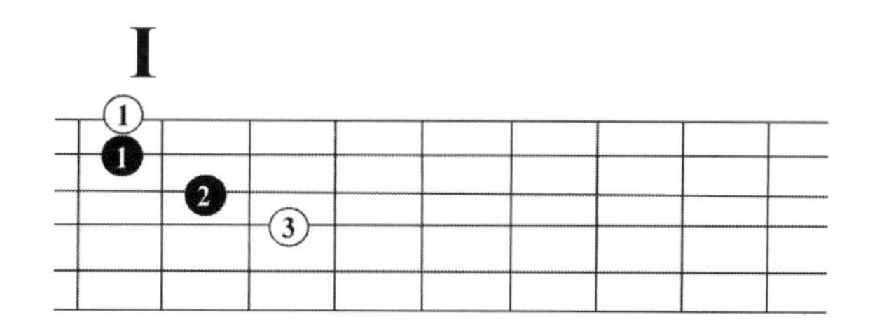

PART FIFTEEN

vi - ii - V - I

MAJOR KEYS
TRIADS
ARPEGGIOS

Key of C

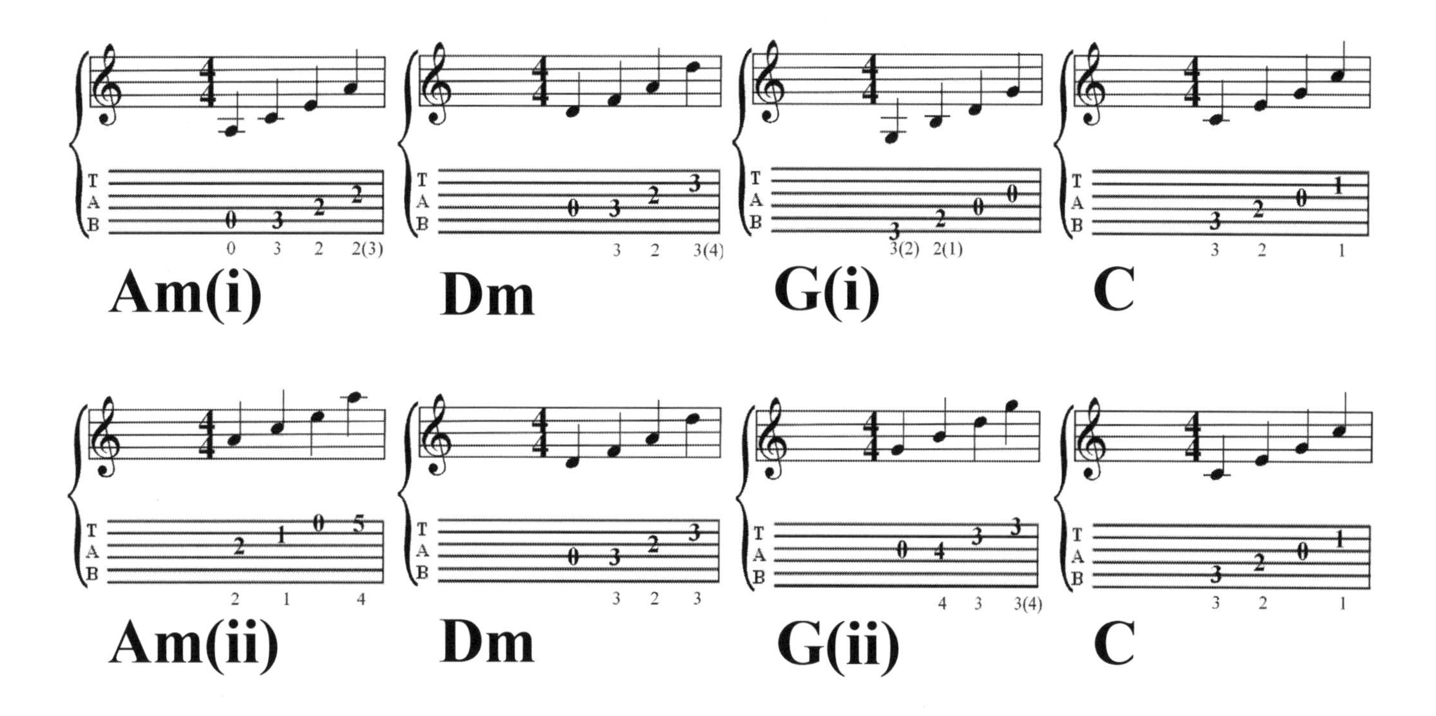

Key of G

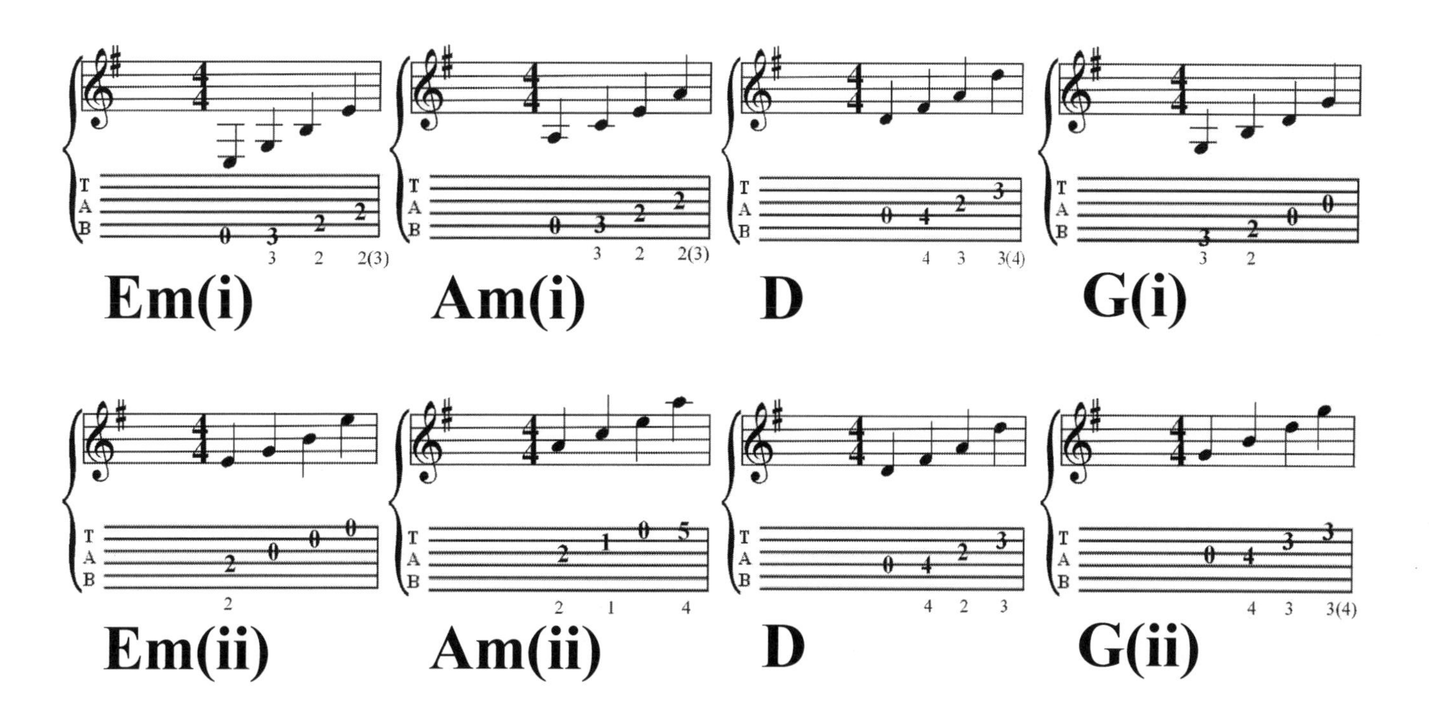

Key of D

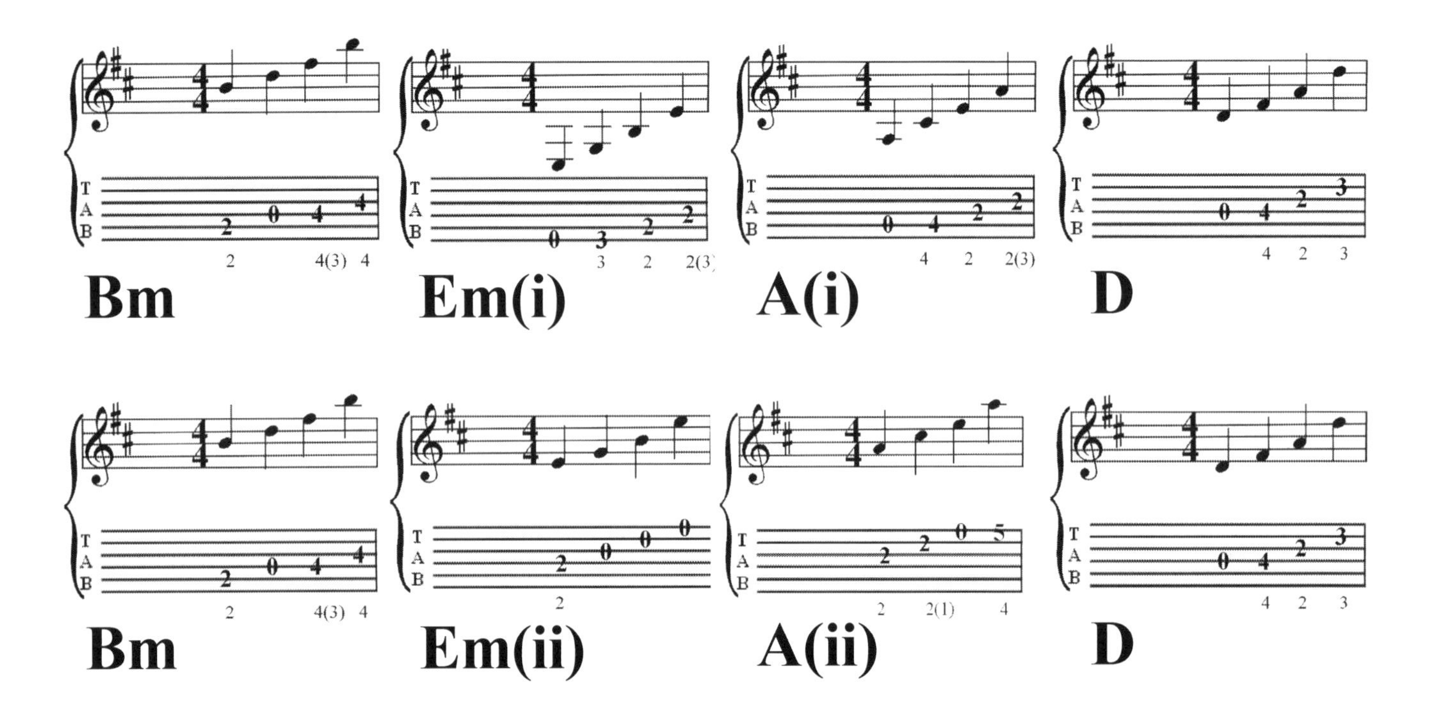

Key of A

Key of E

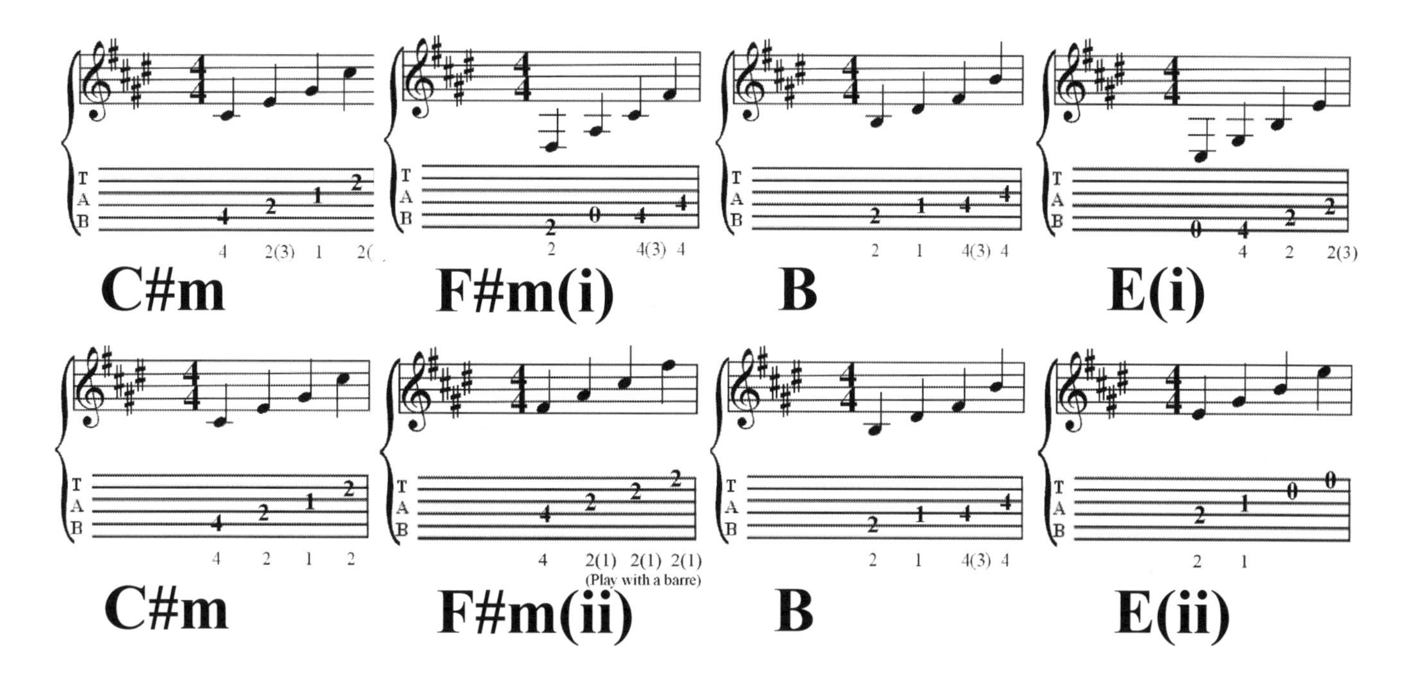

Key of B

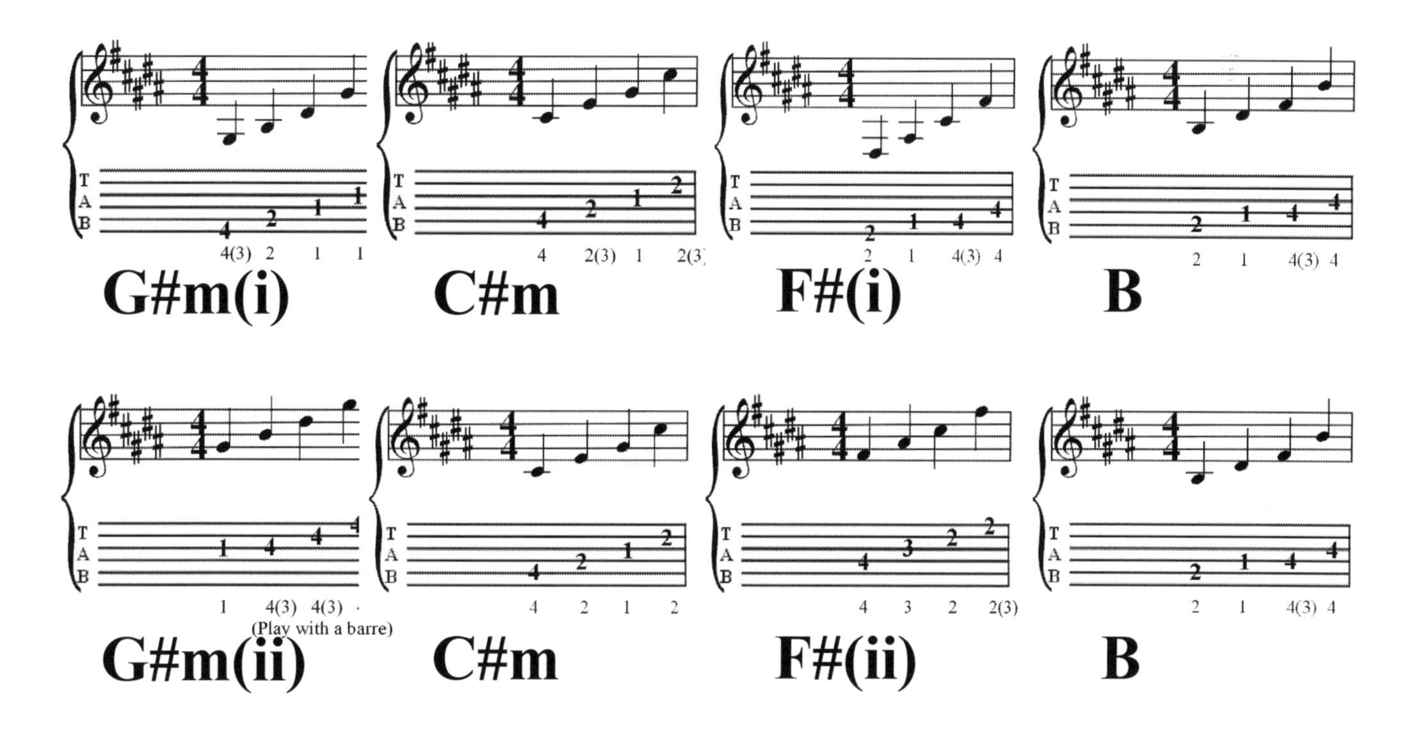

Key of F#

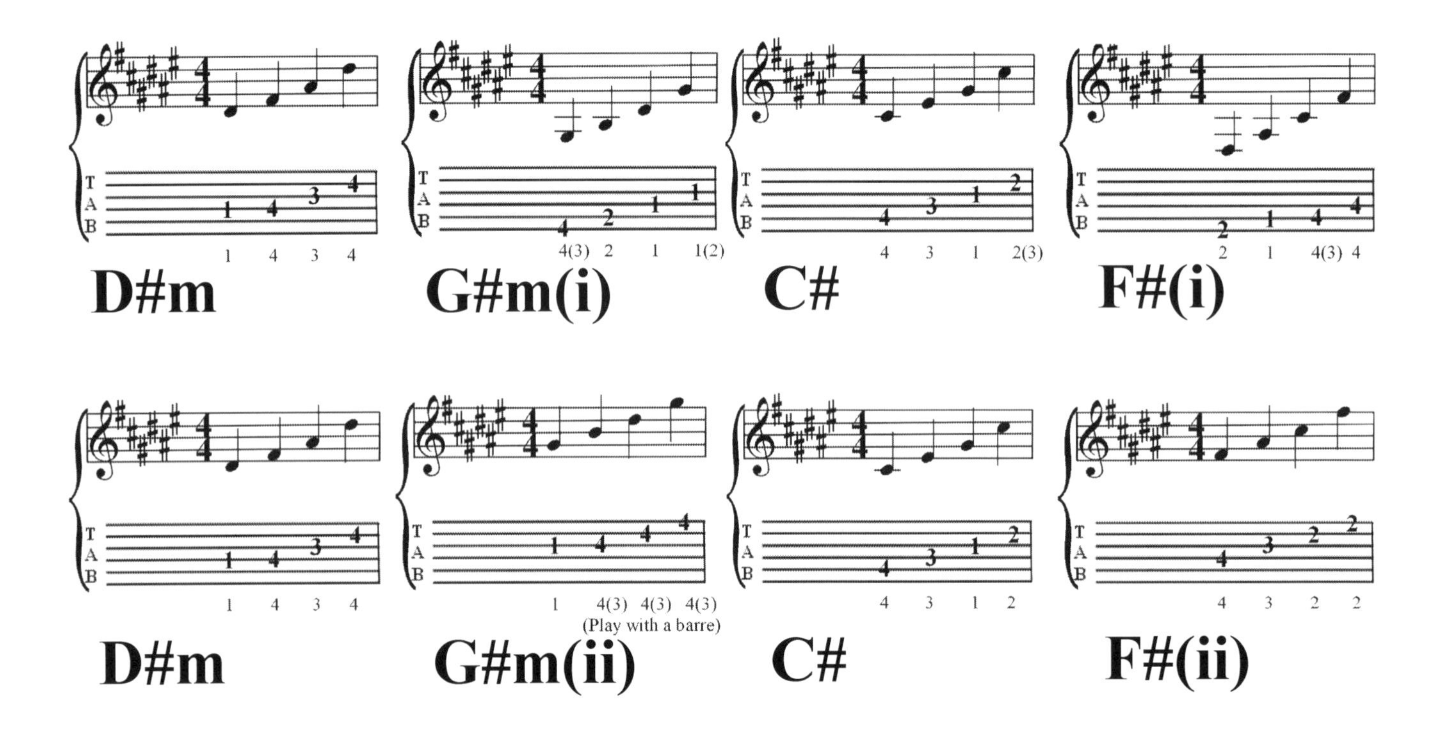

Key of C#

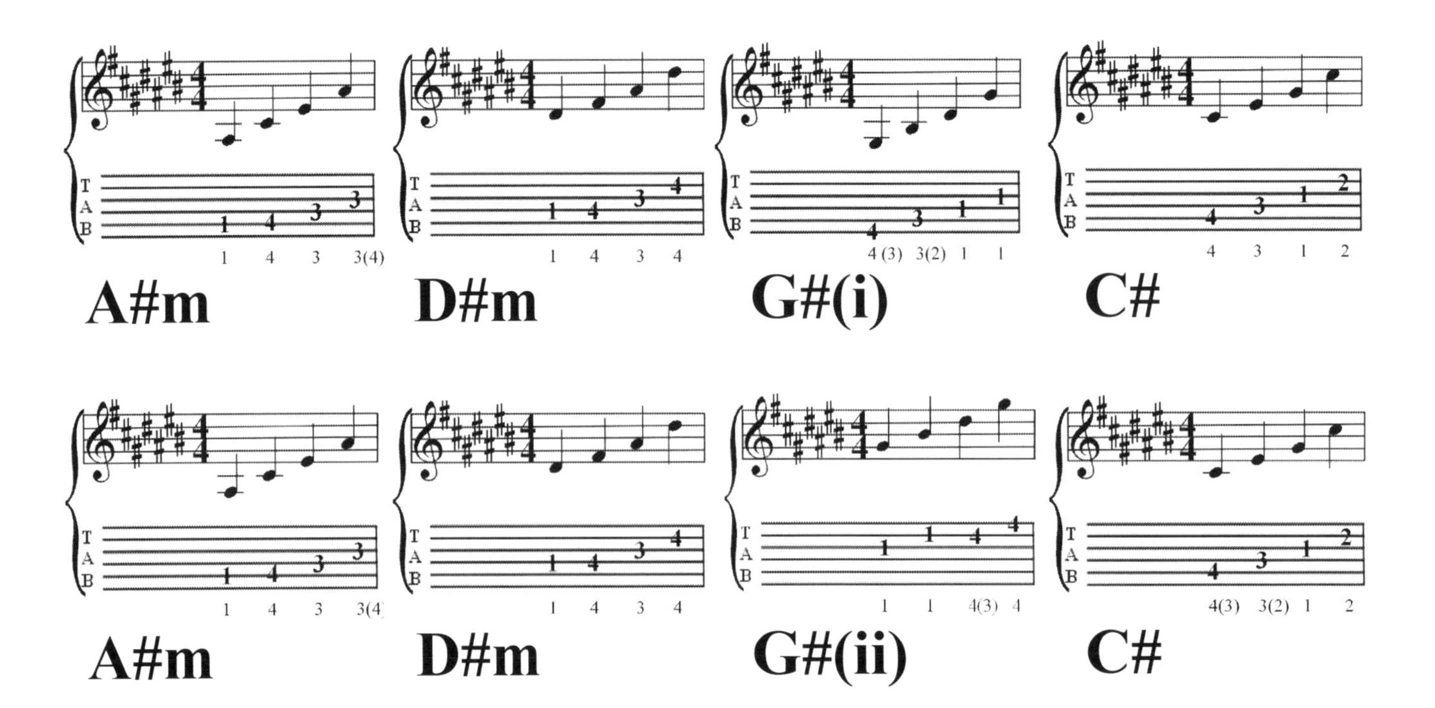

Key of A♭

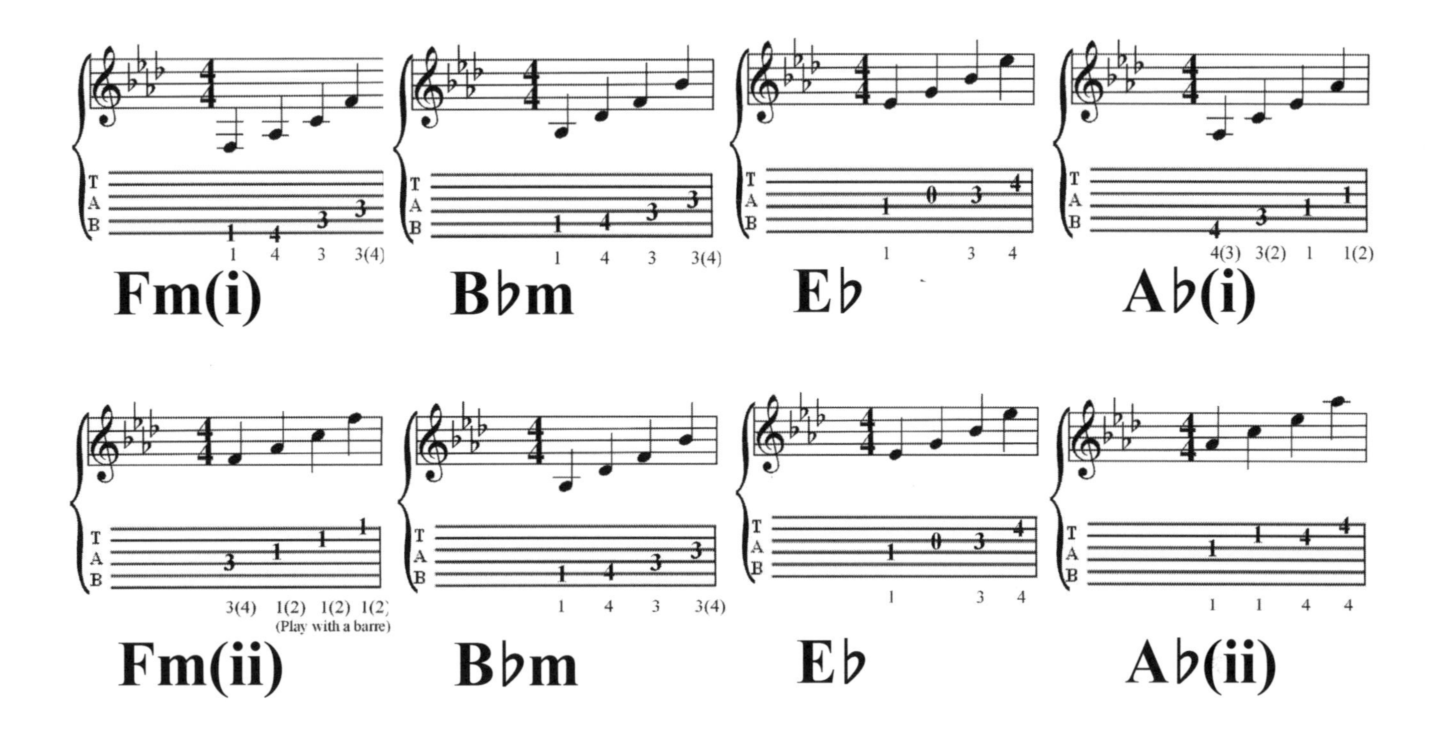

Key of E♭

Key of B♭

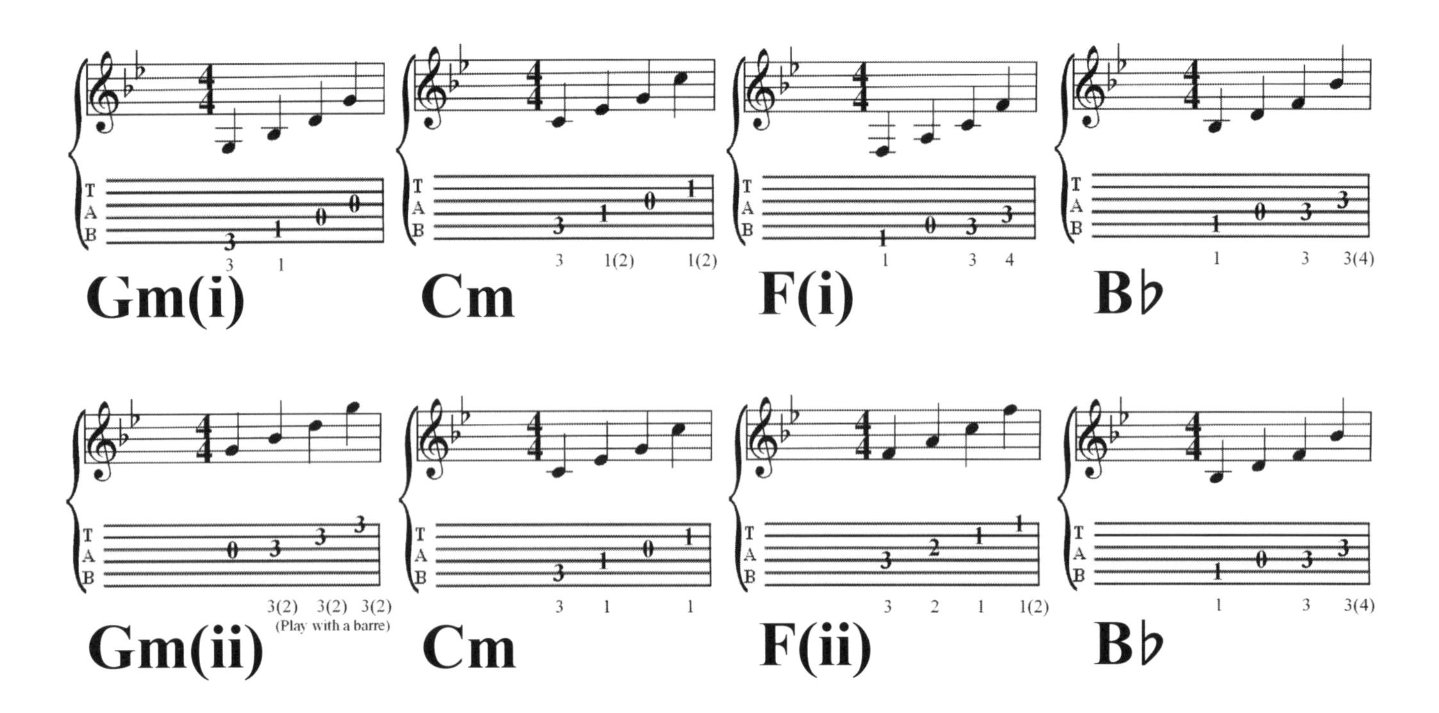

Key of F

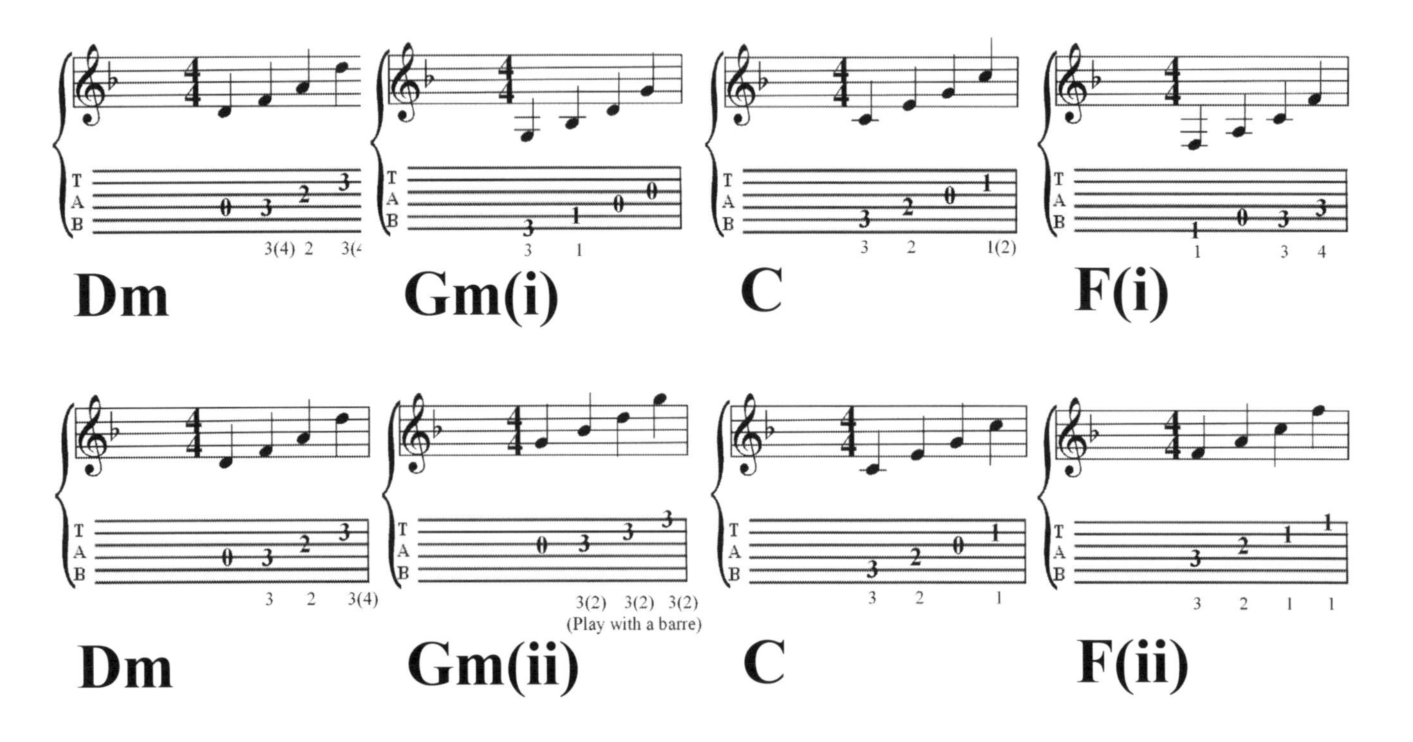

All Keys (i)

vi

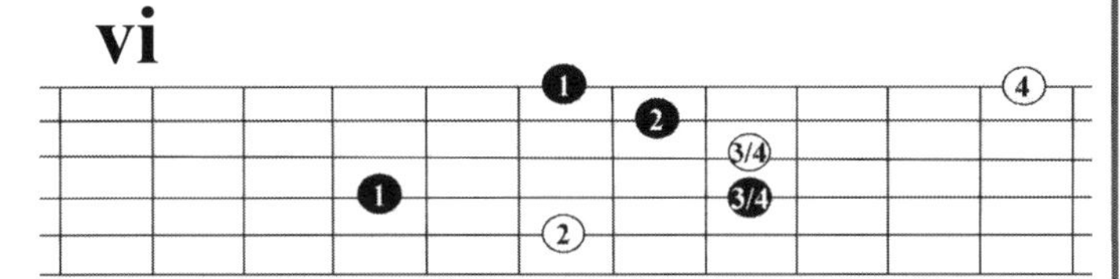

ii

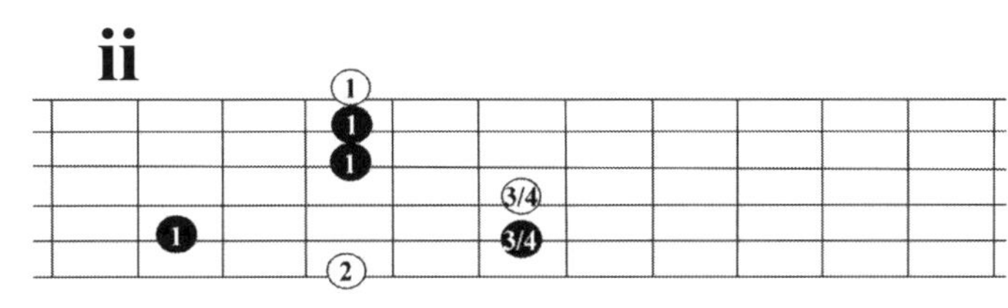

V

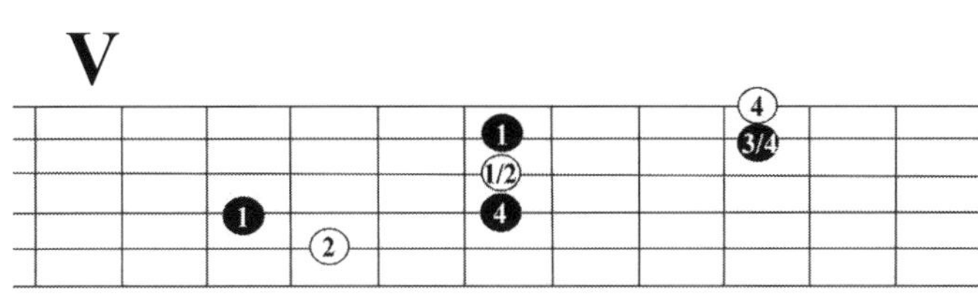

I

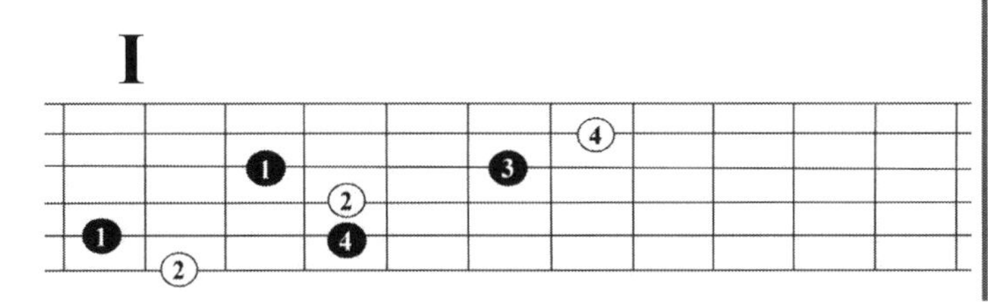

All Keys (ii)

vi

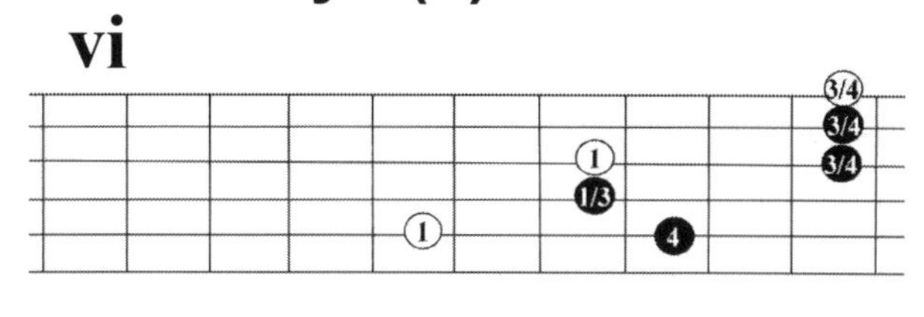

ii

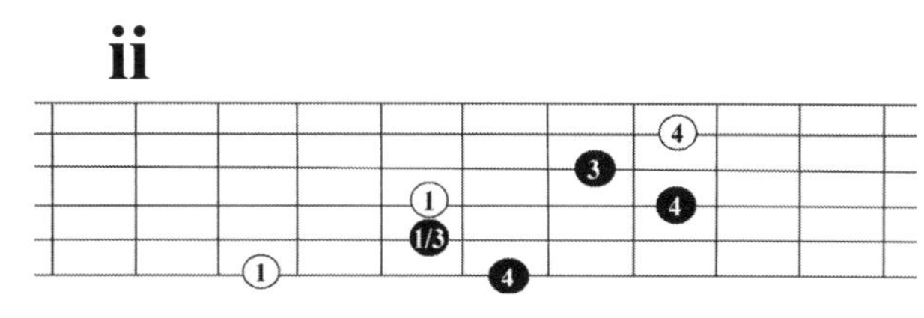

V

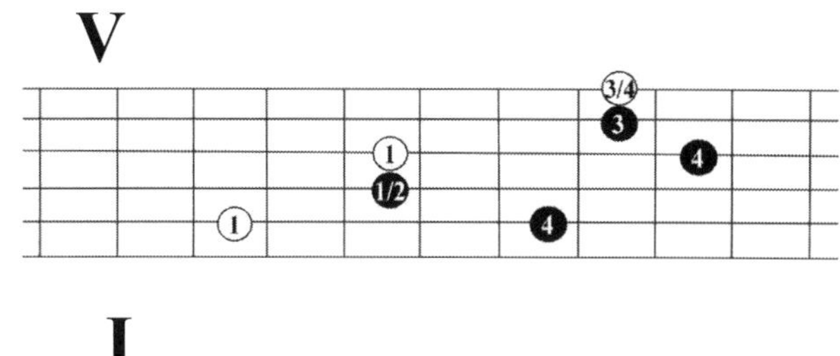

I

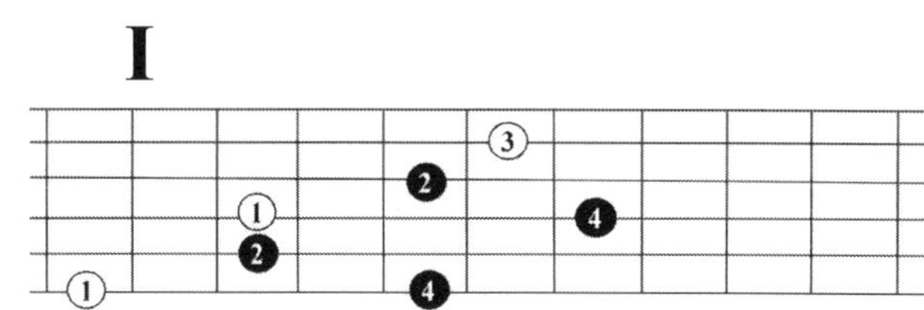

All Keys (iii)

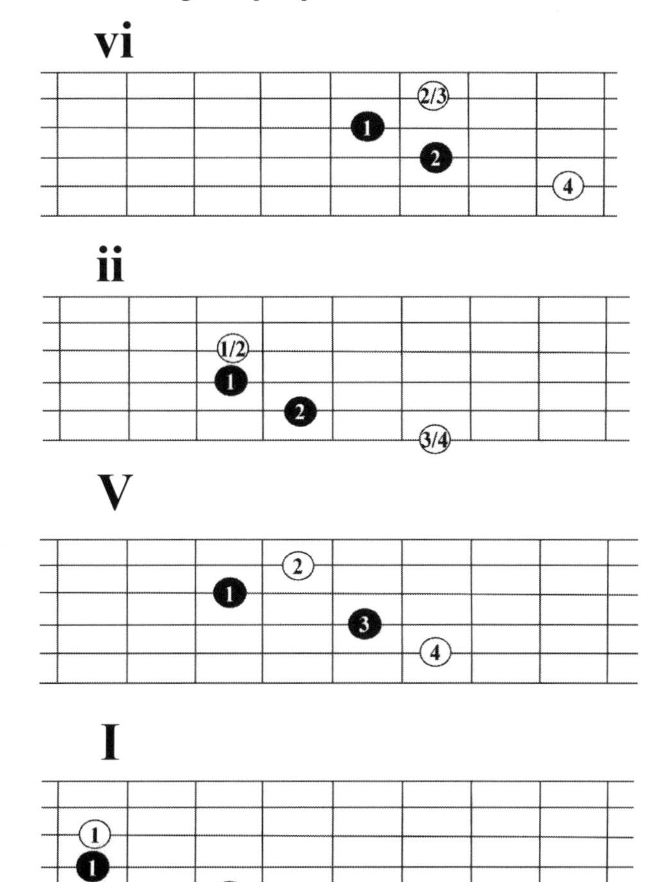

All Keys (iv)

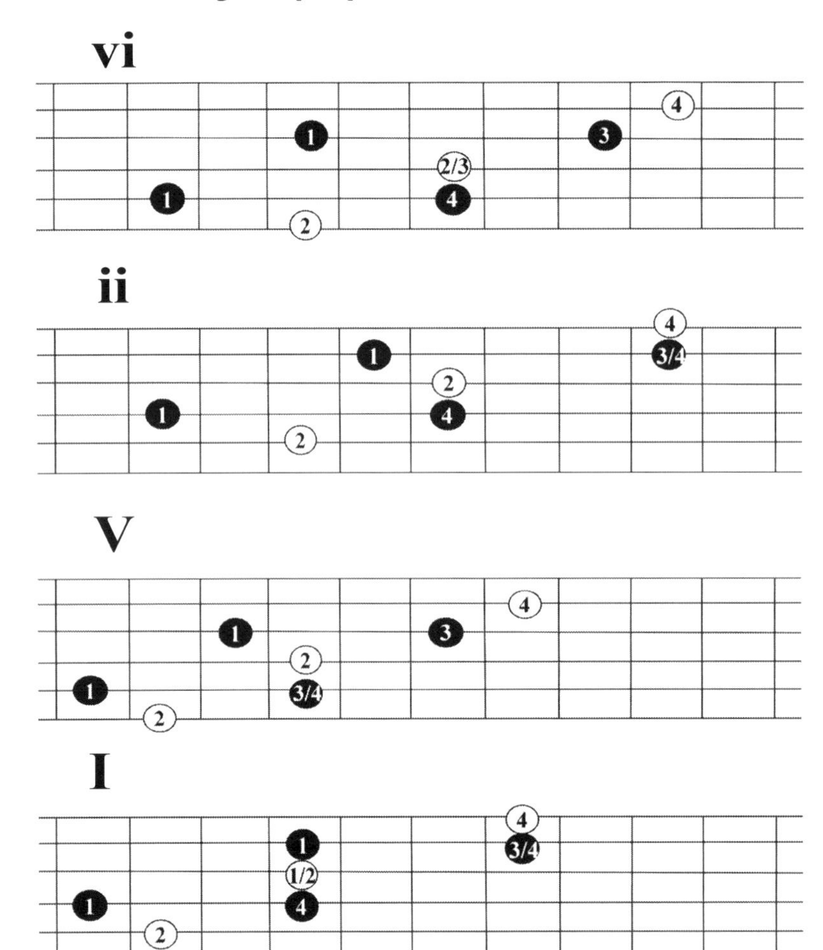

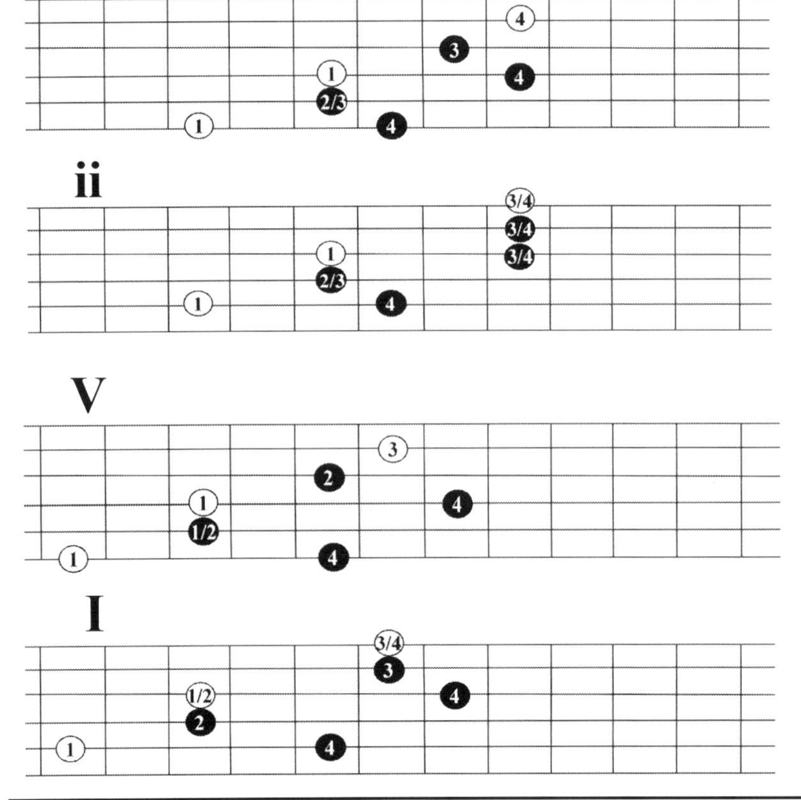

All Keys (vi)

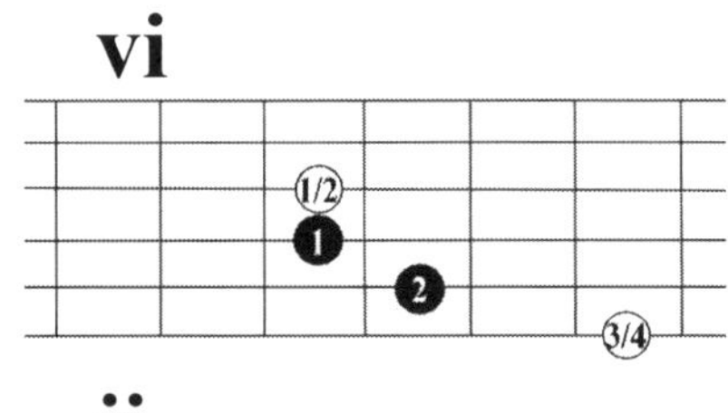

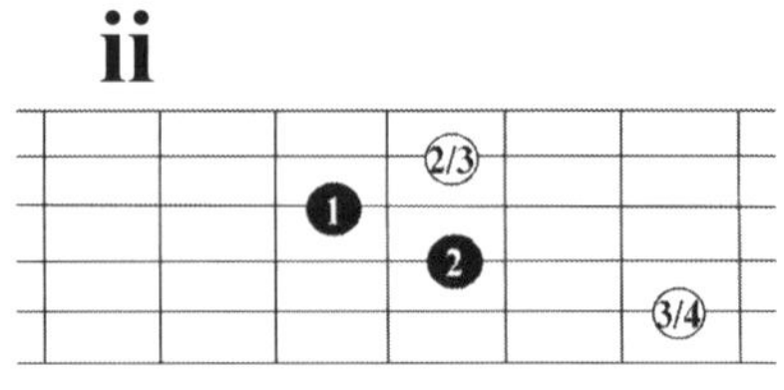

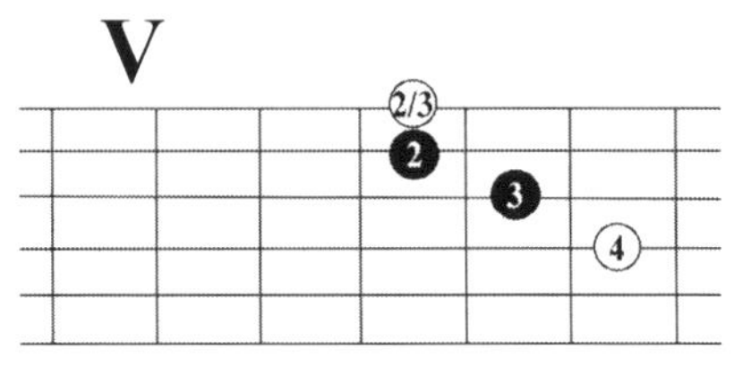

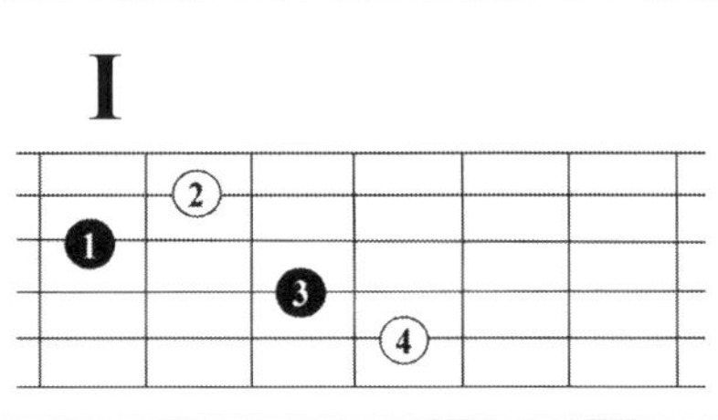

All Keys (vii)

vi

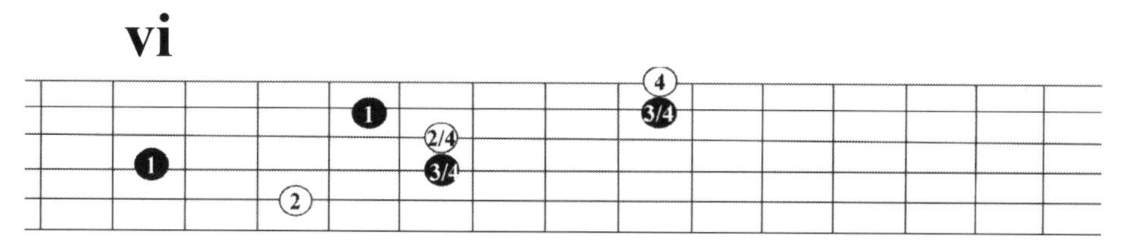

ii

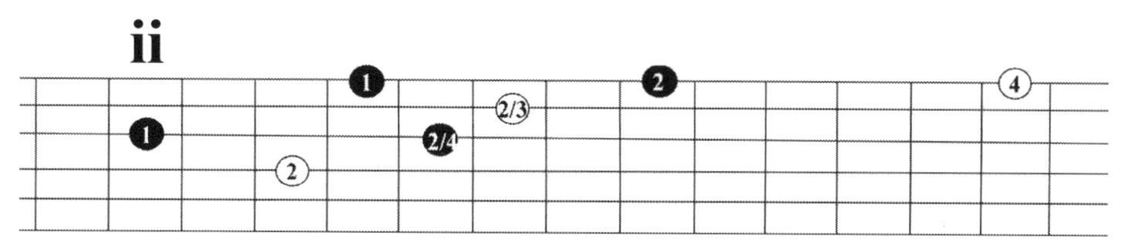

V

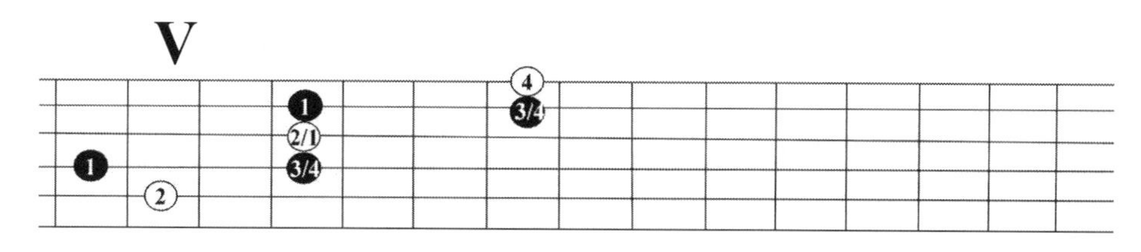

I

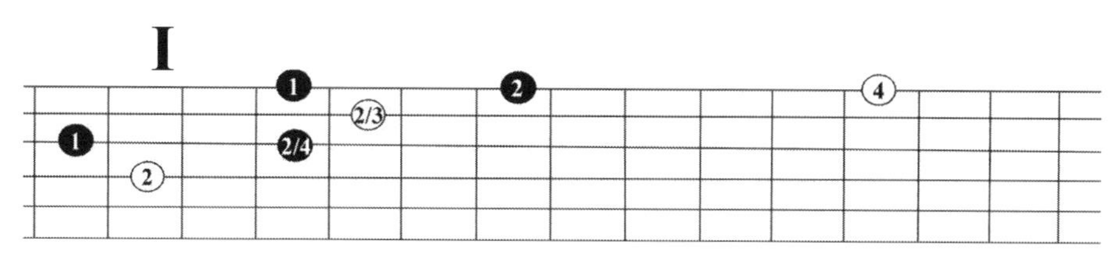

All Keys (viii)

vi

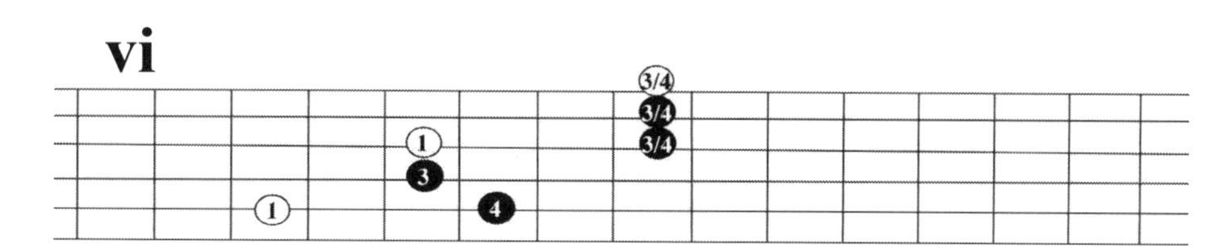

ii

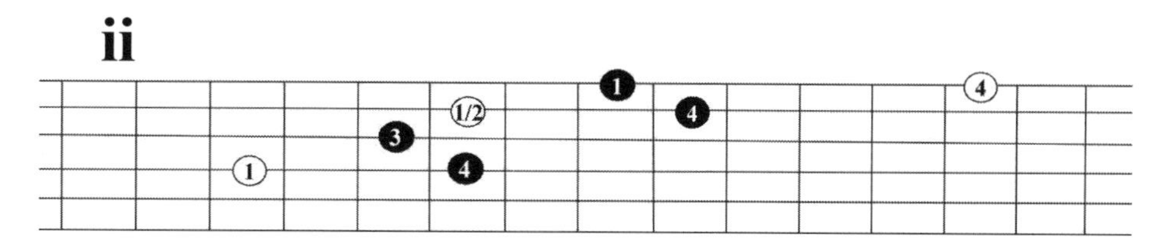

V

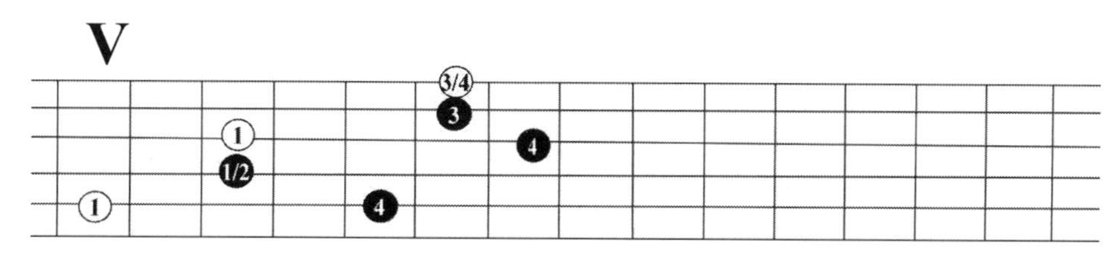

I

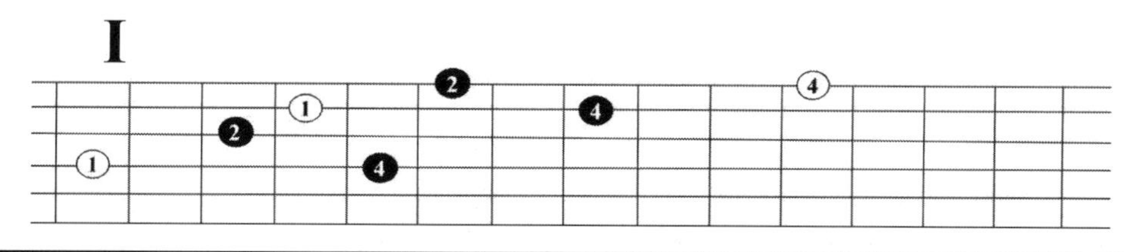

All Keys (ix)

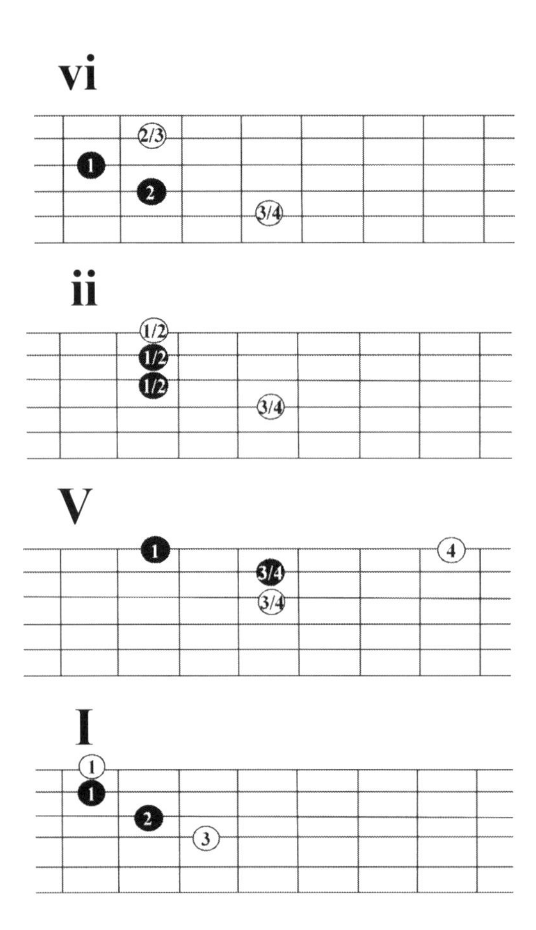

PART SIXTEEN

i - iv - V

MINOR KEYS
TRIADS
ARPEGGIOS

Key of Am

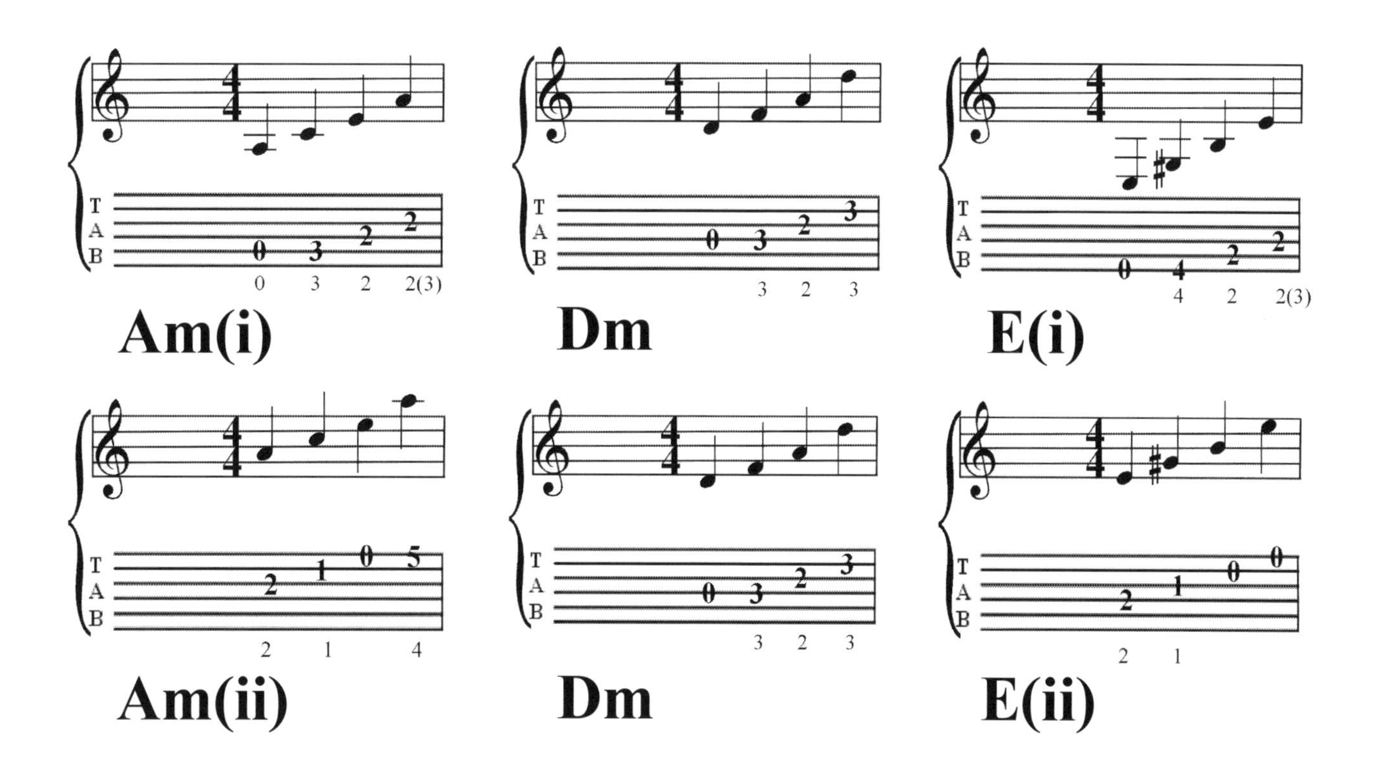

Key of Em

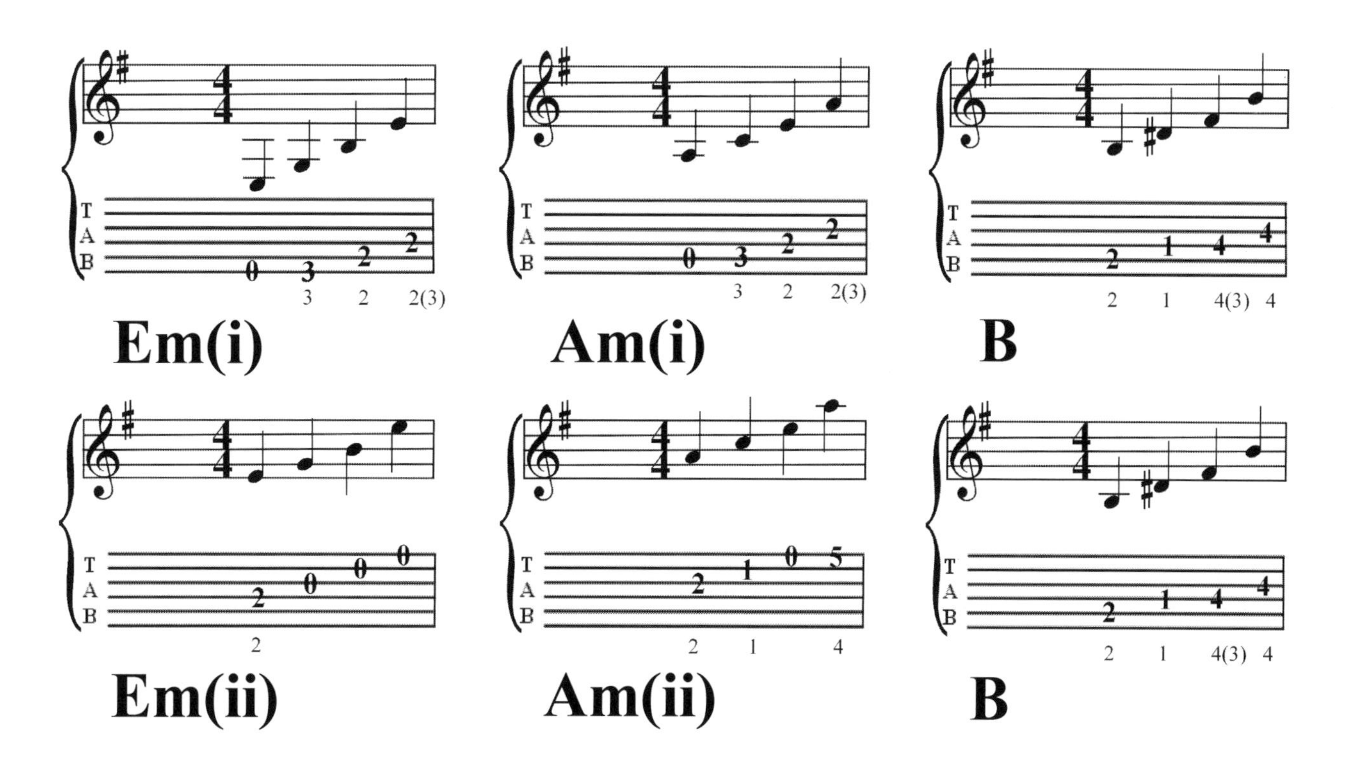

Key of Bm

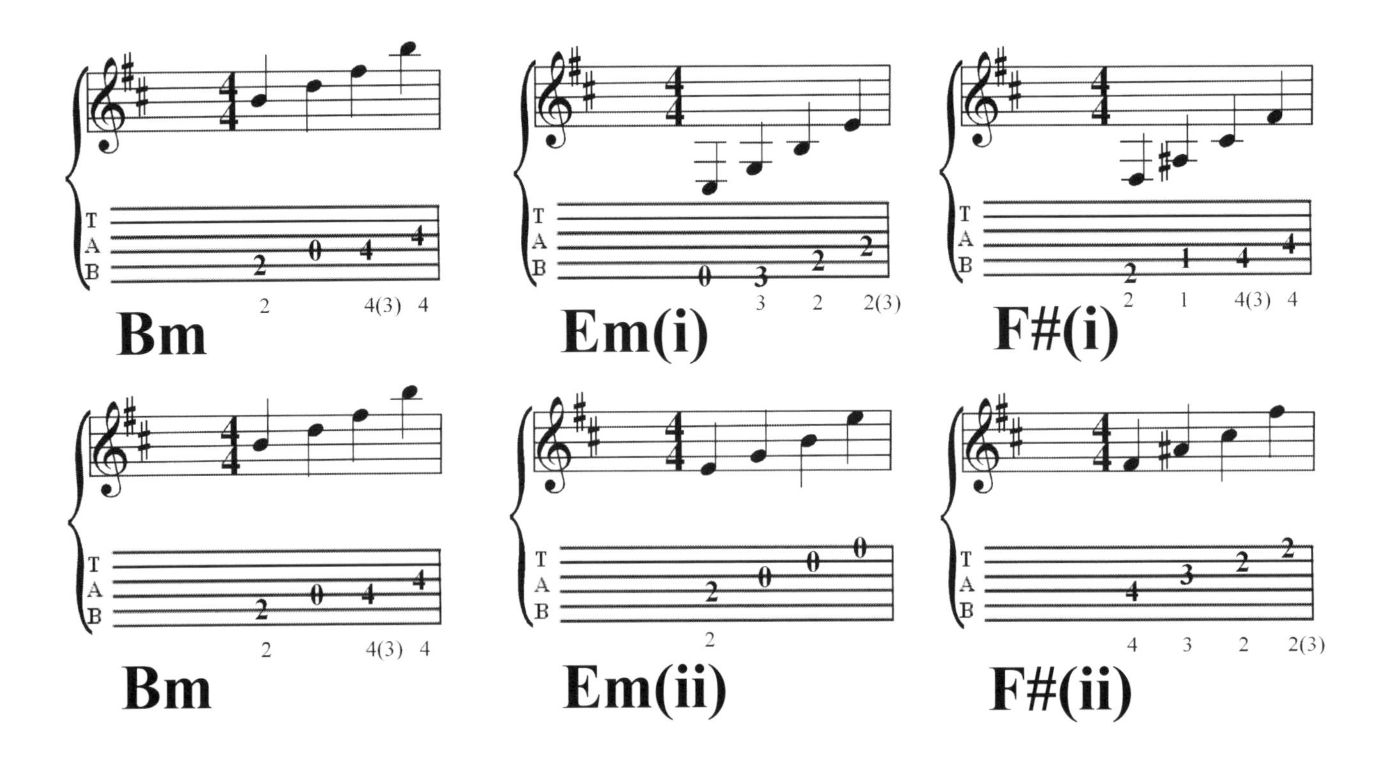

Key of F#m

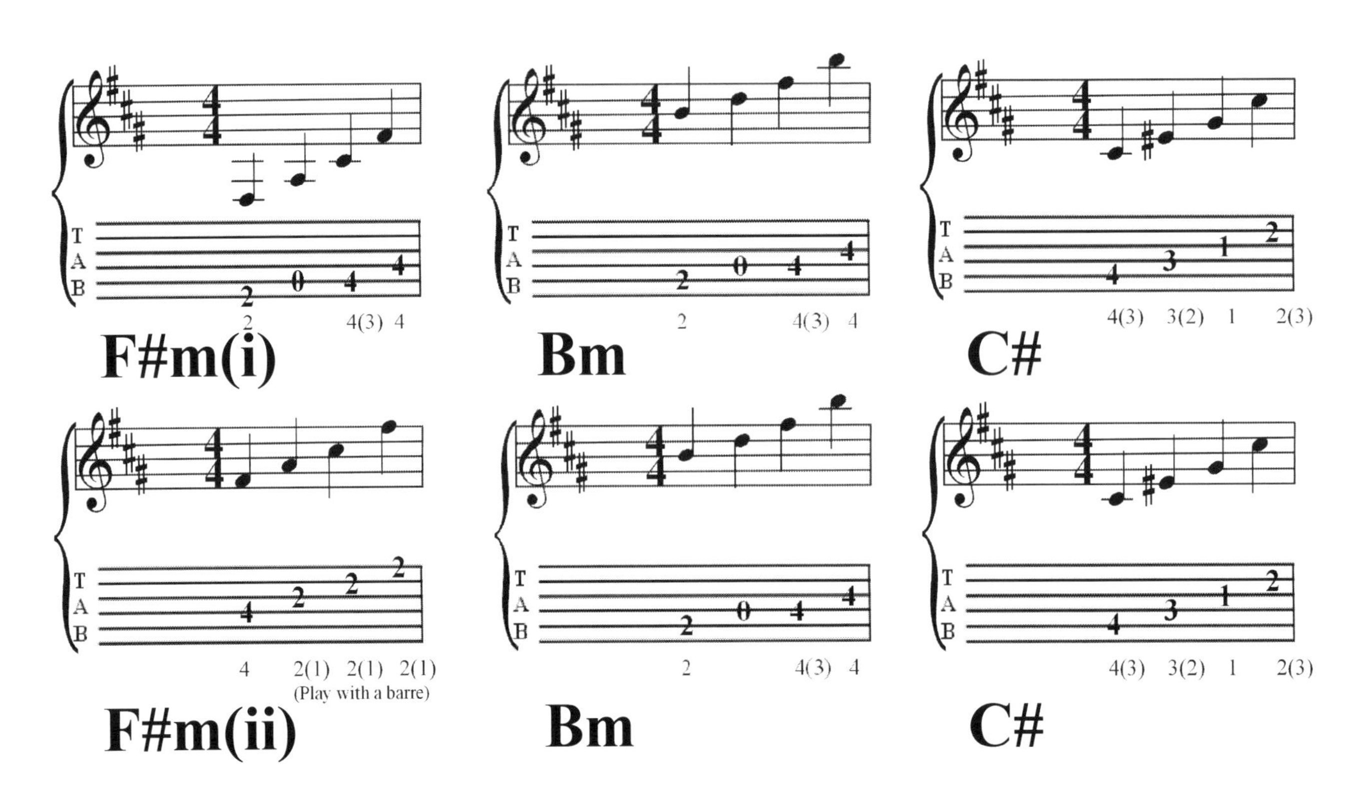

Key of C#m

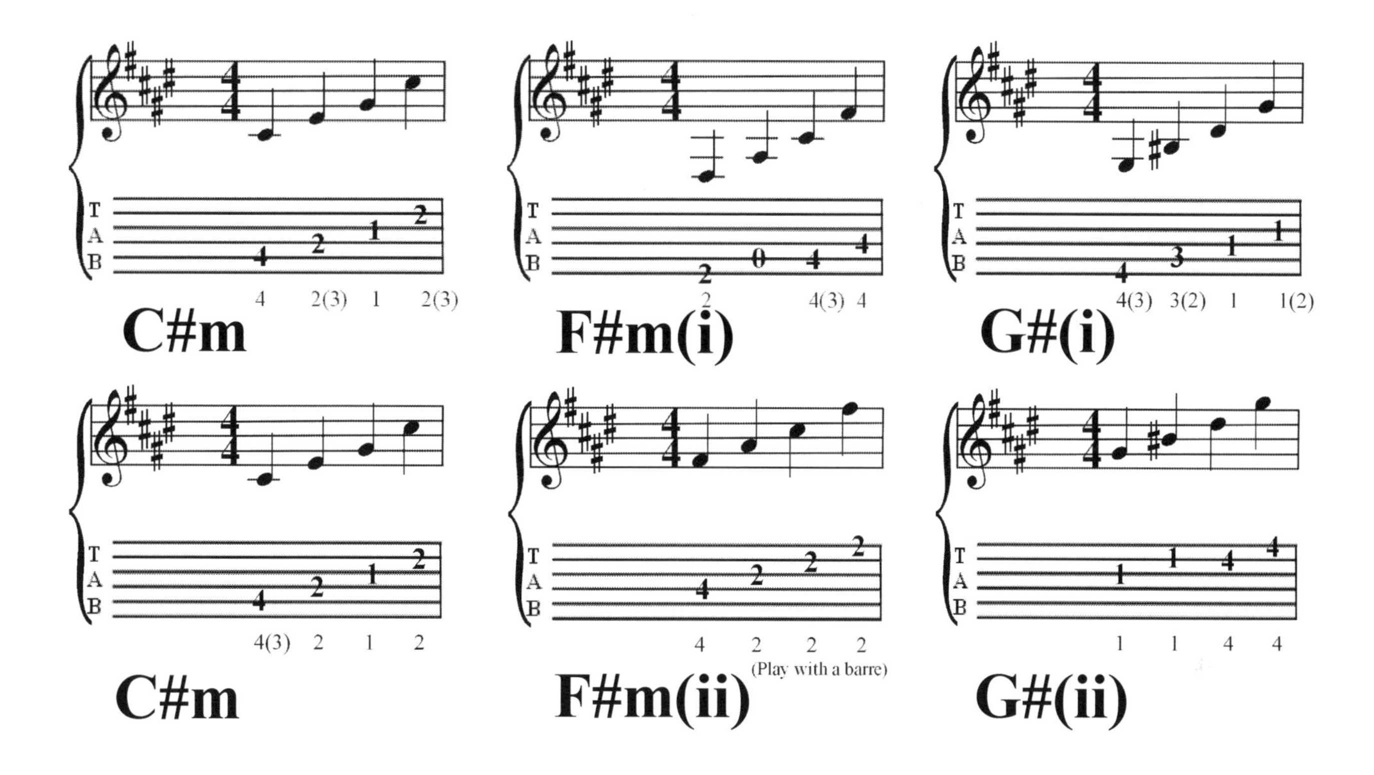

Key of A♭m

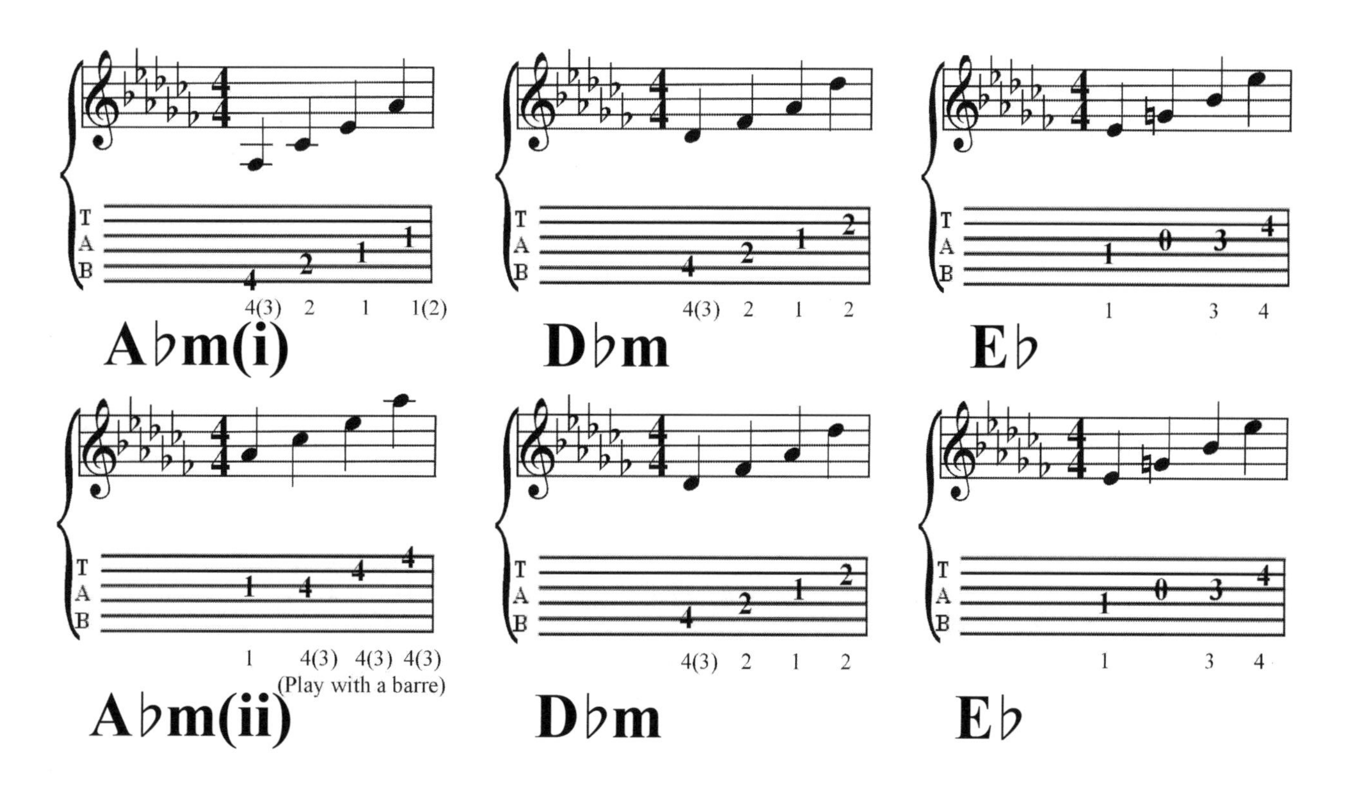

Key of E♭m

Key of B♭m

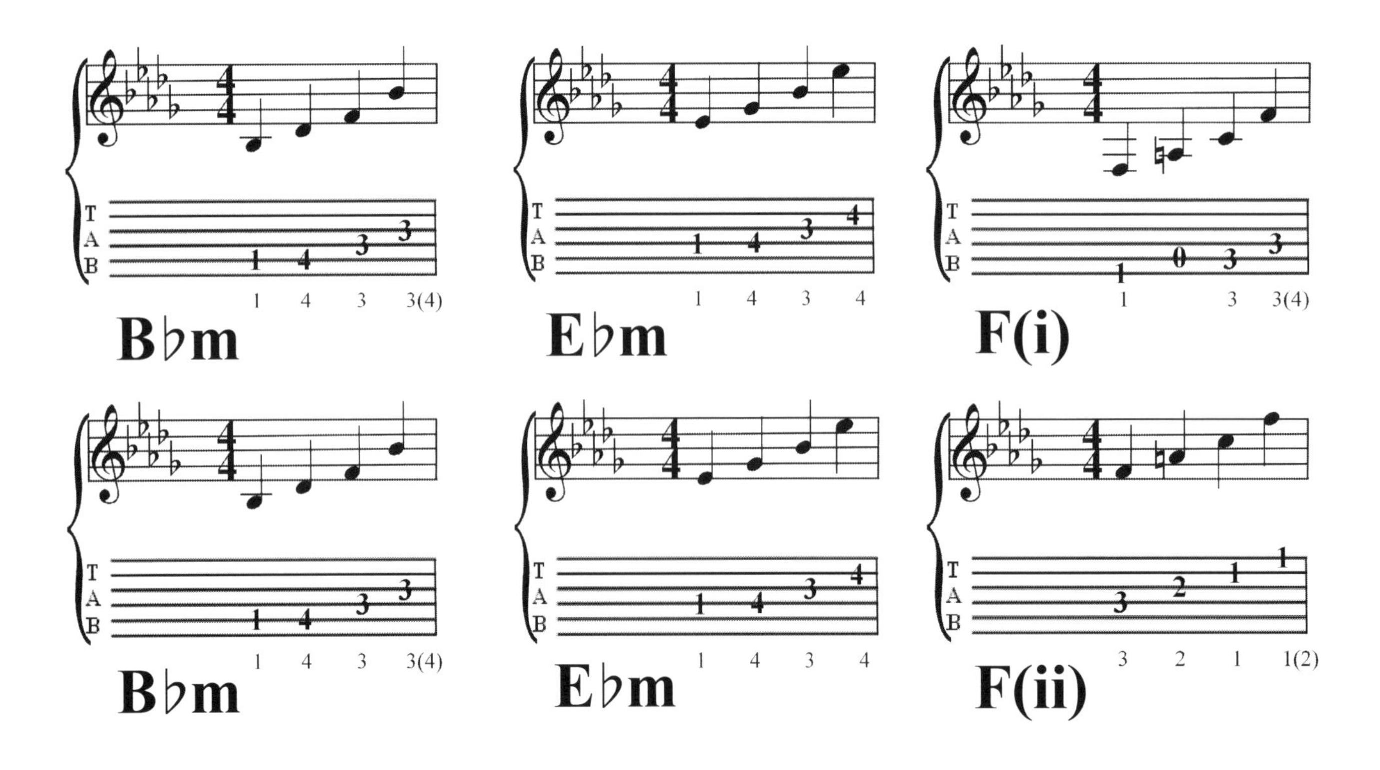

Key of Fm

Key of Cm

Key of Gm

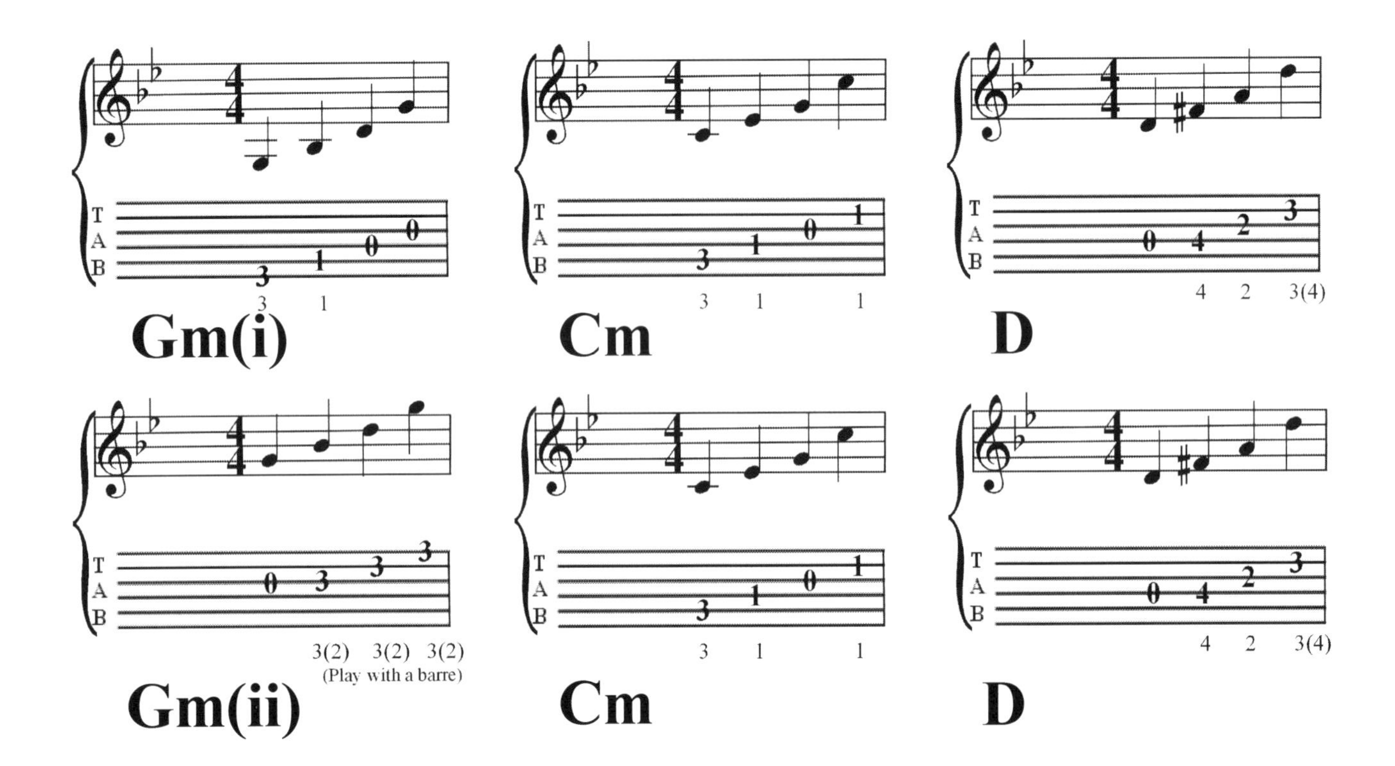

Key of Dm

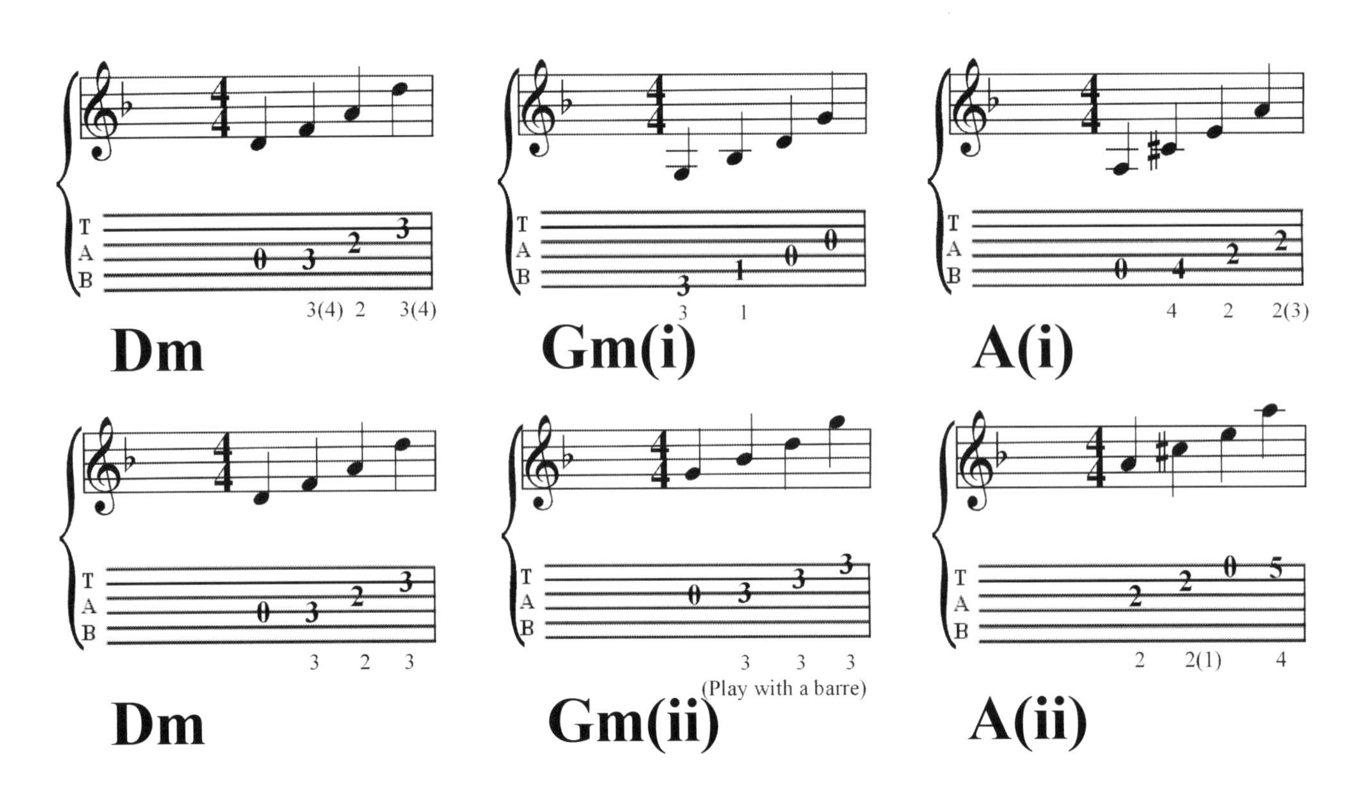

All Keys (i)

i

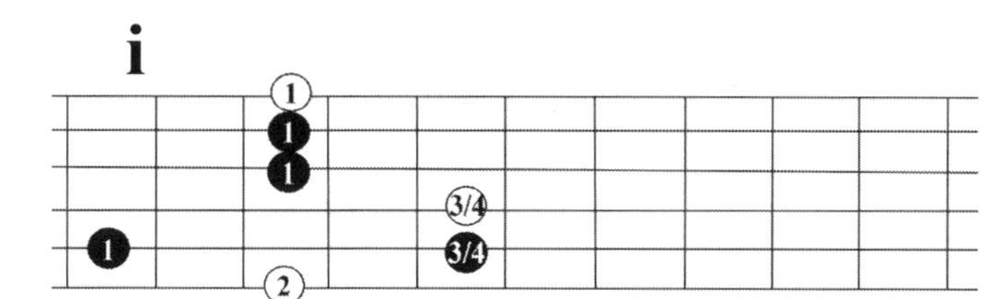

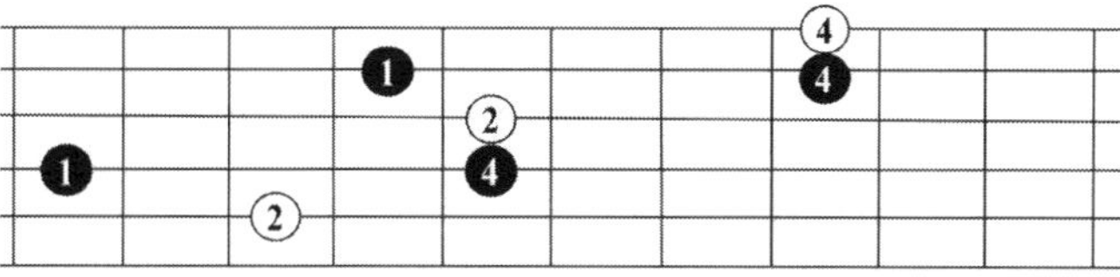

V

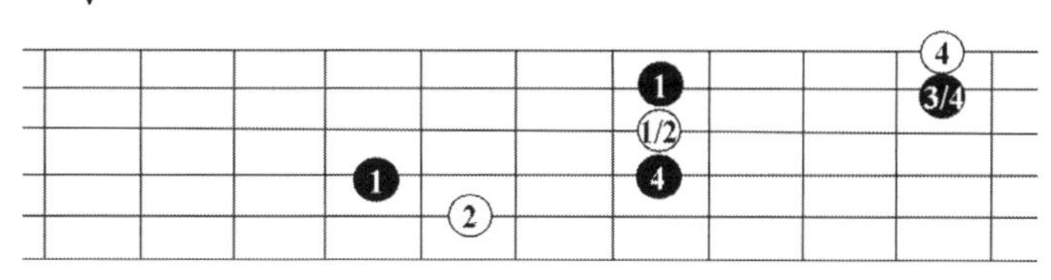

All Keys (ii)

i

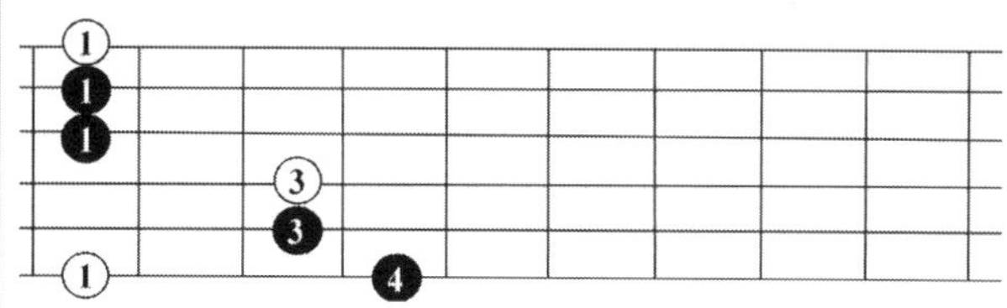

iv

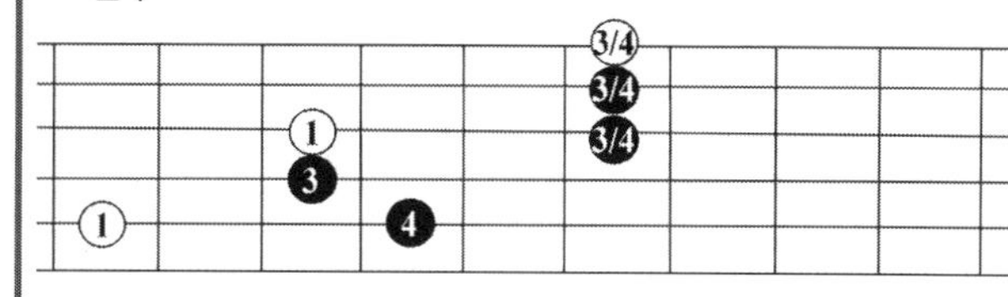

V

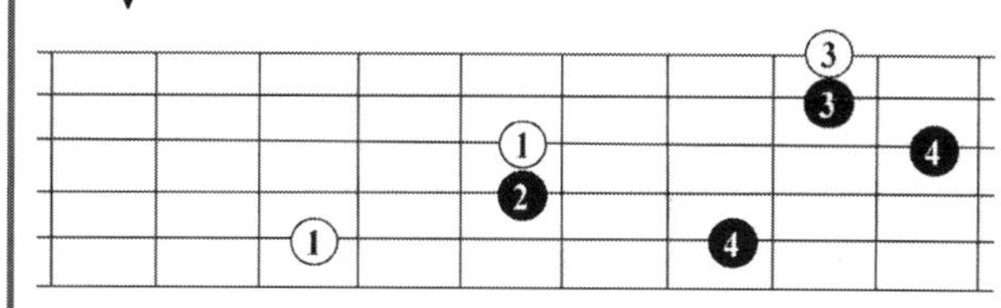

All Keys (iii)

i

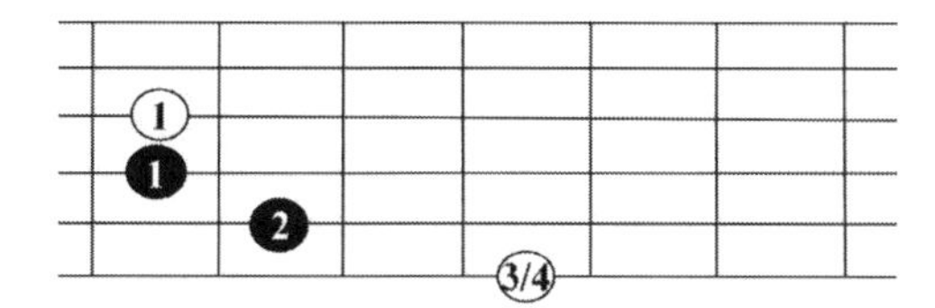

iv

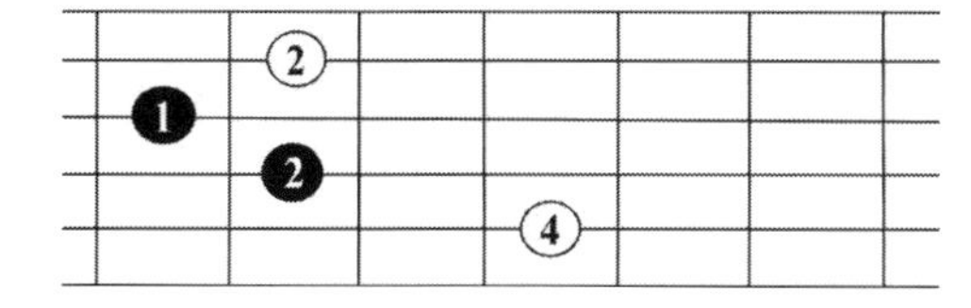

V

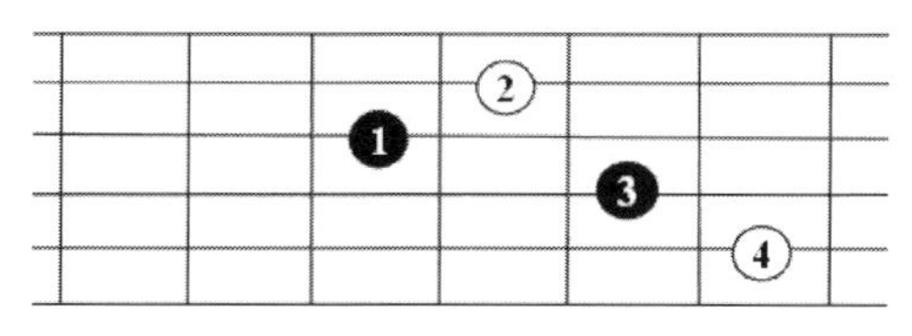

All Keys (iv)

i

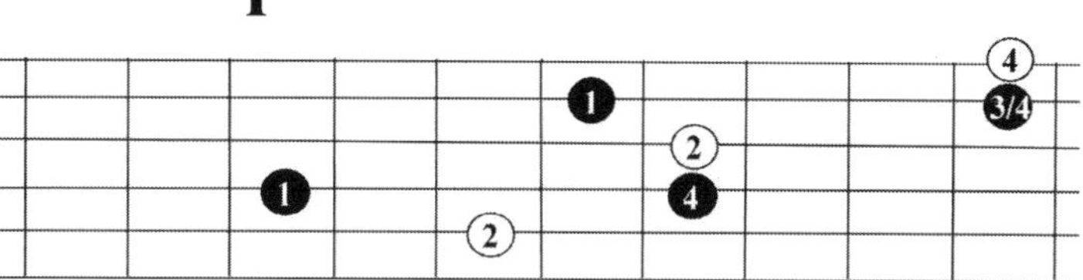

iv

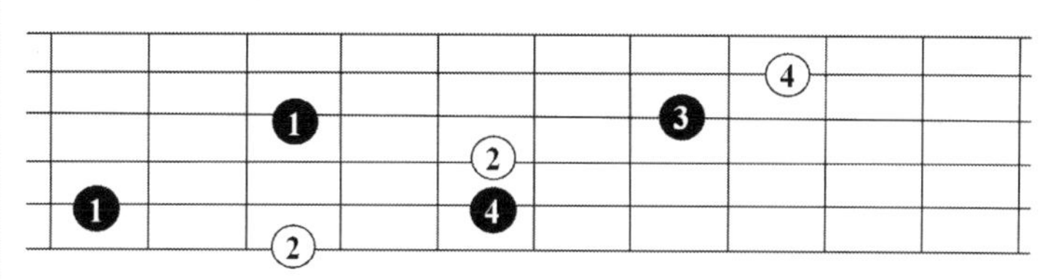

V

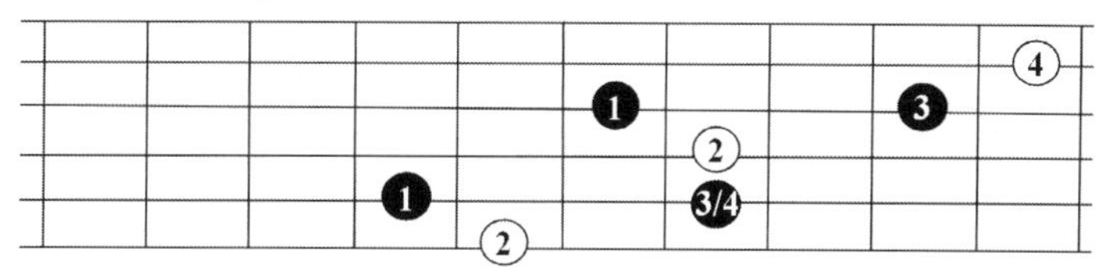

All Keys (v)

i

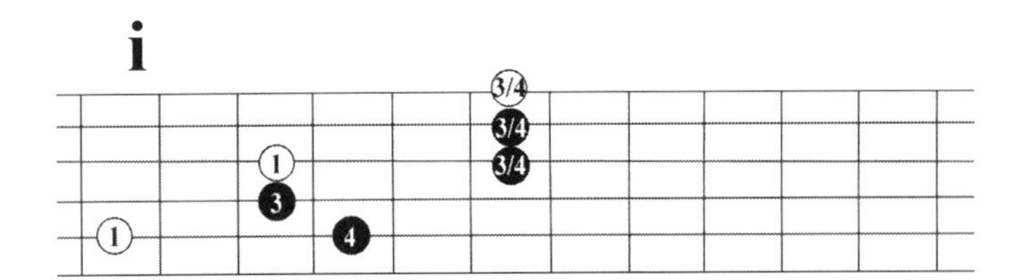

iv

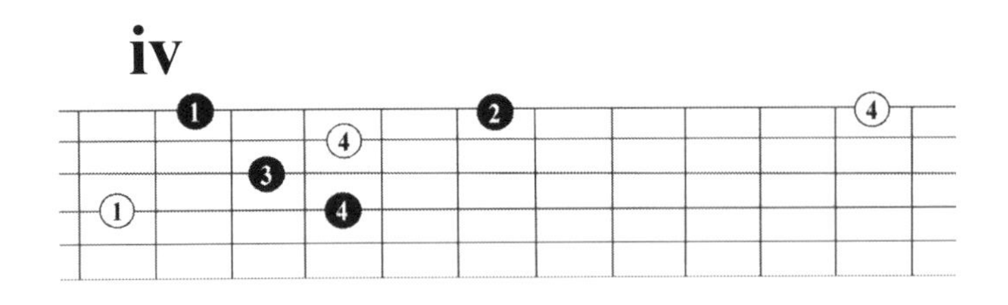

V

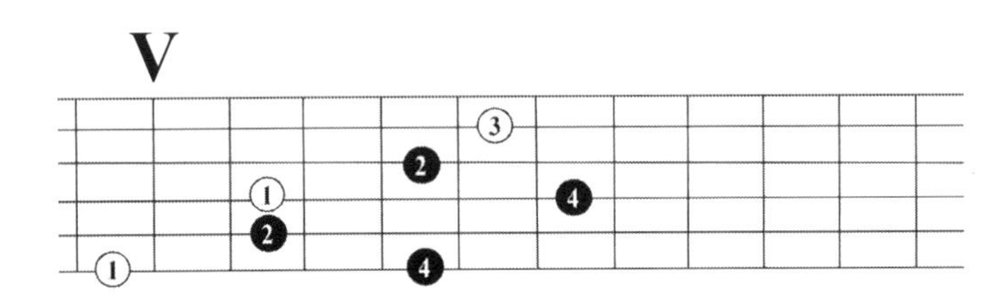

All Keys (vi)

i

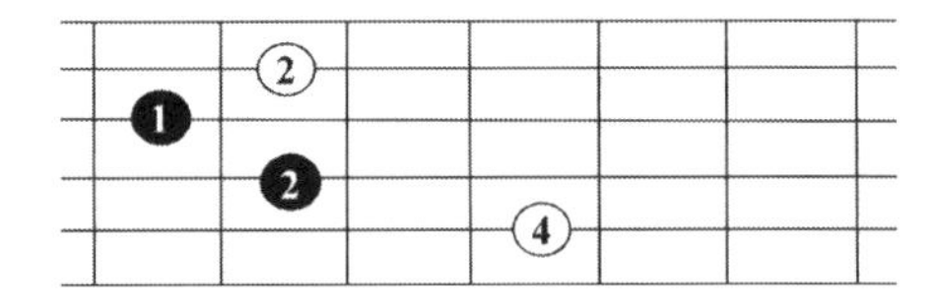

iv

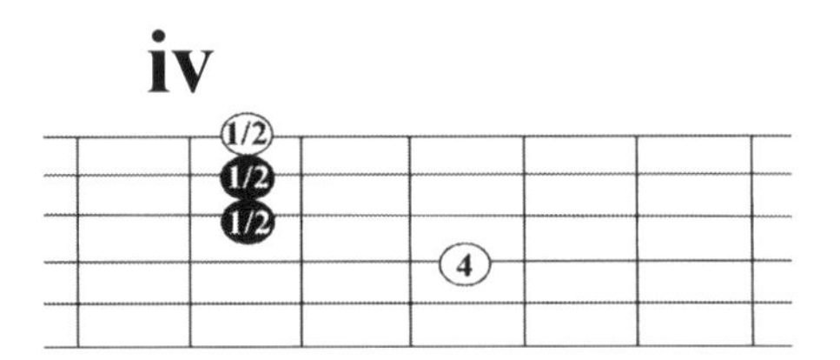

V

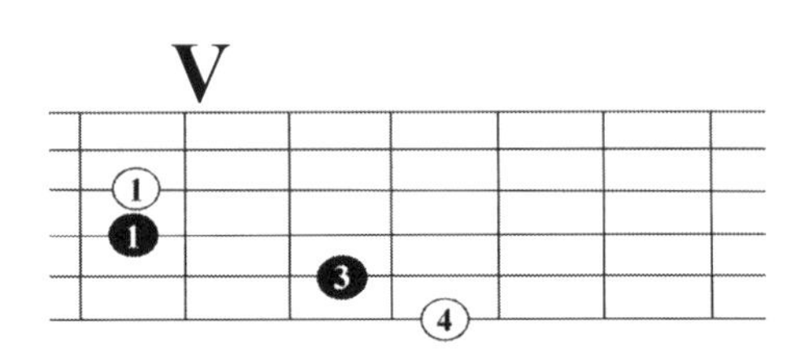

All Keys (vii)

i

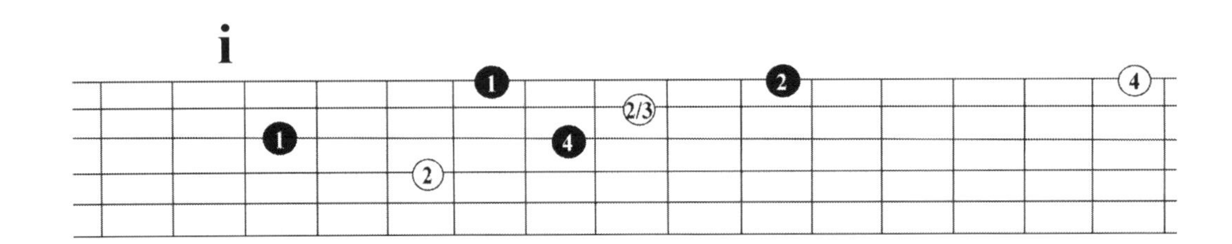

iv

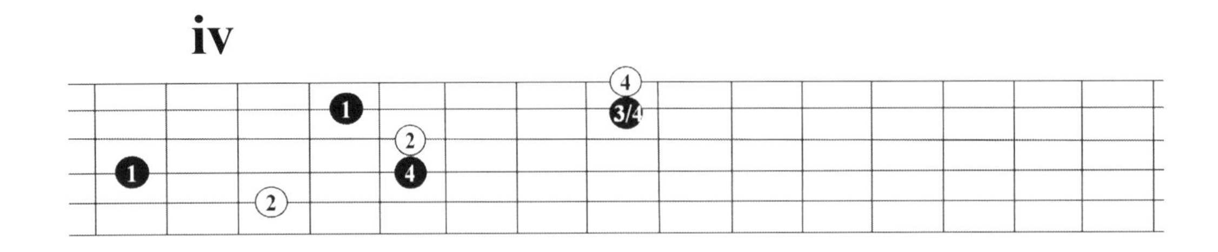

V

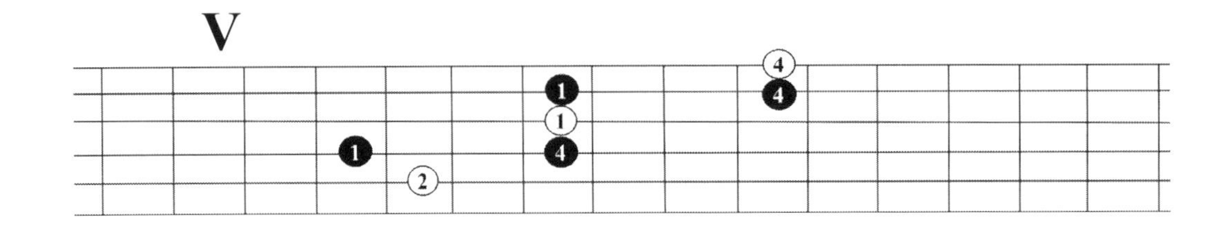

All Keys (viii)

i

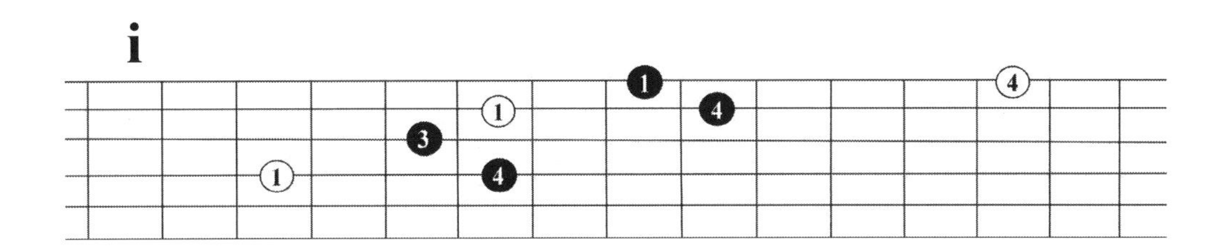

iv

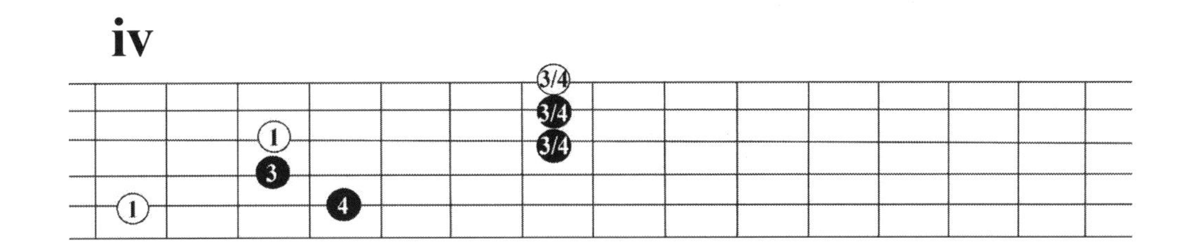

V

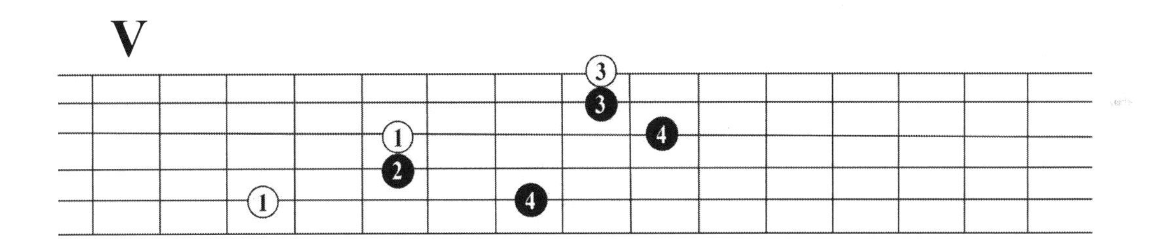

All Keys (ix)

i

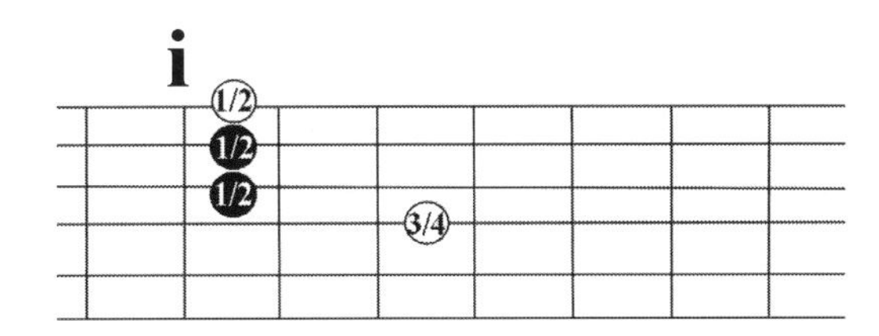

iv

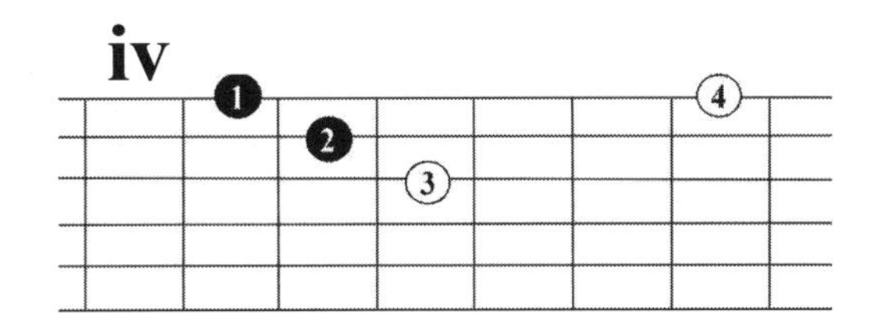

V

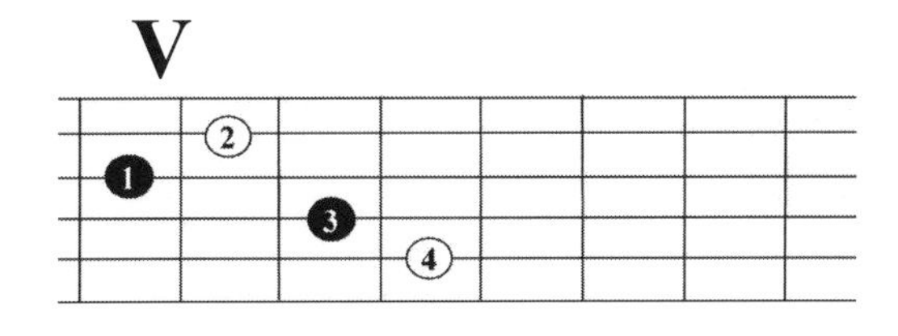

PART SEVENTEEN

ii - V - i

MINOR KEYS
TRIADS
ARPEGGIOS

Key of Am

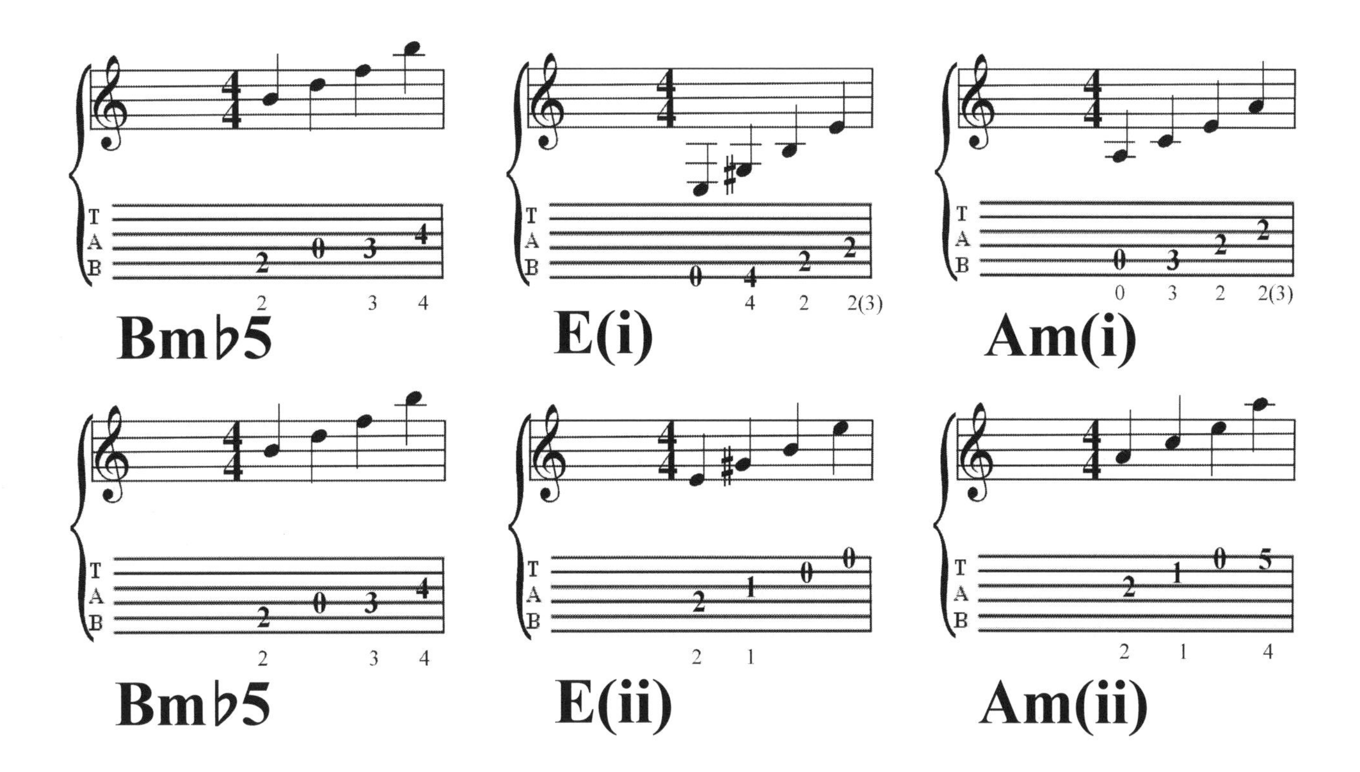

Key of Em

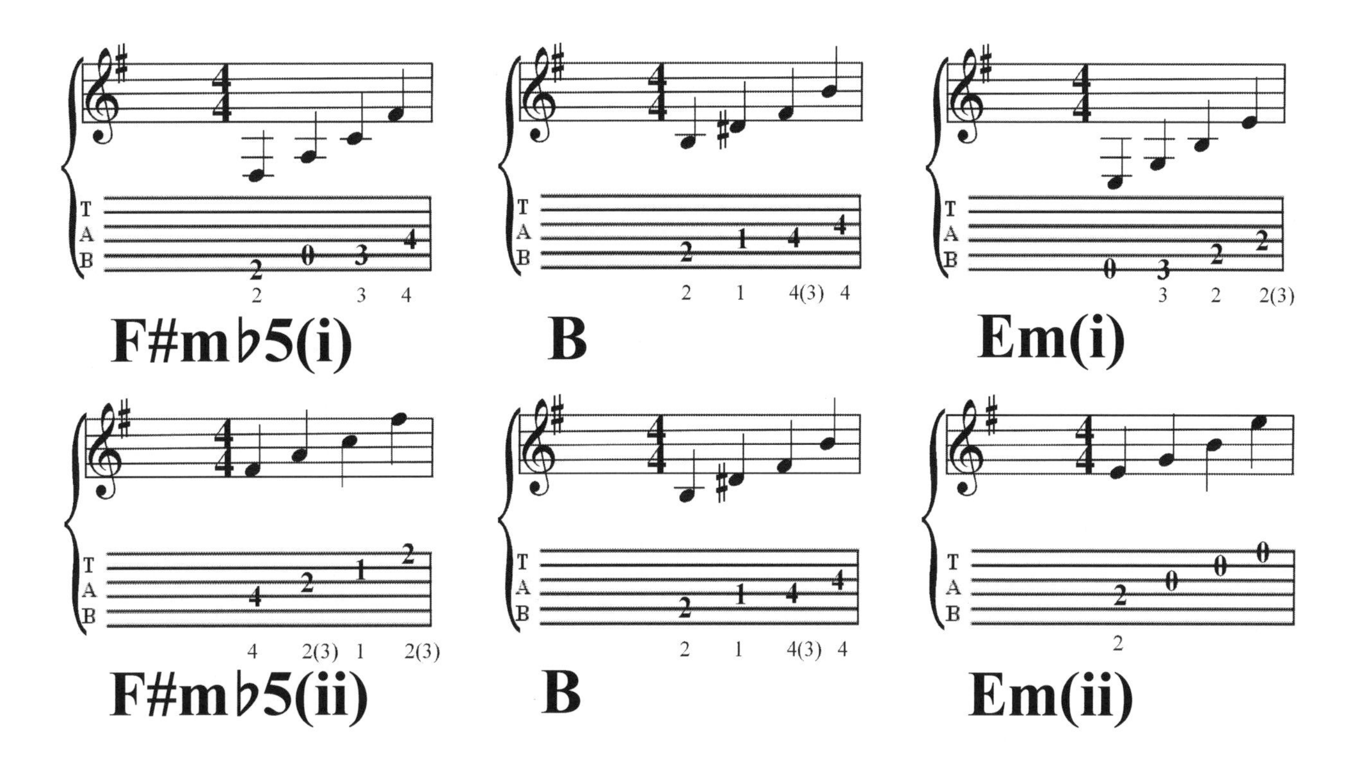

Key of Bm

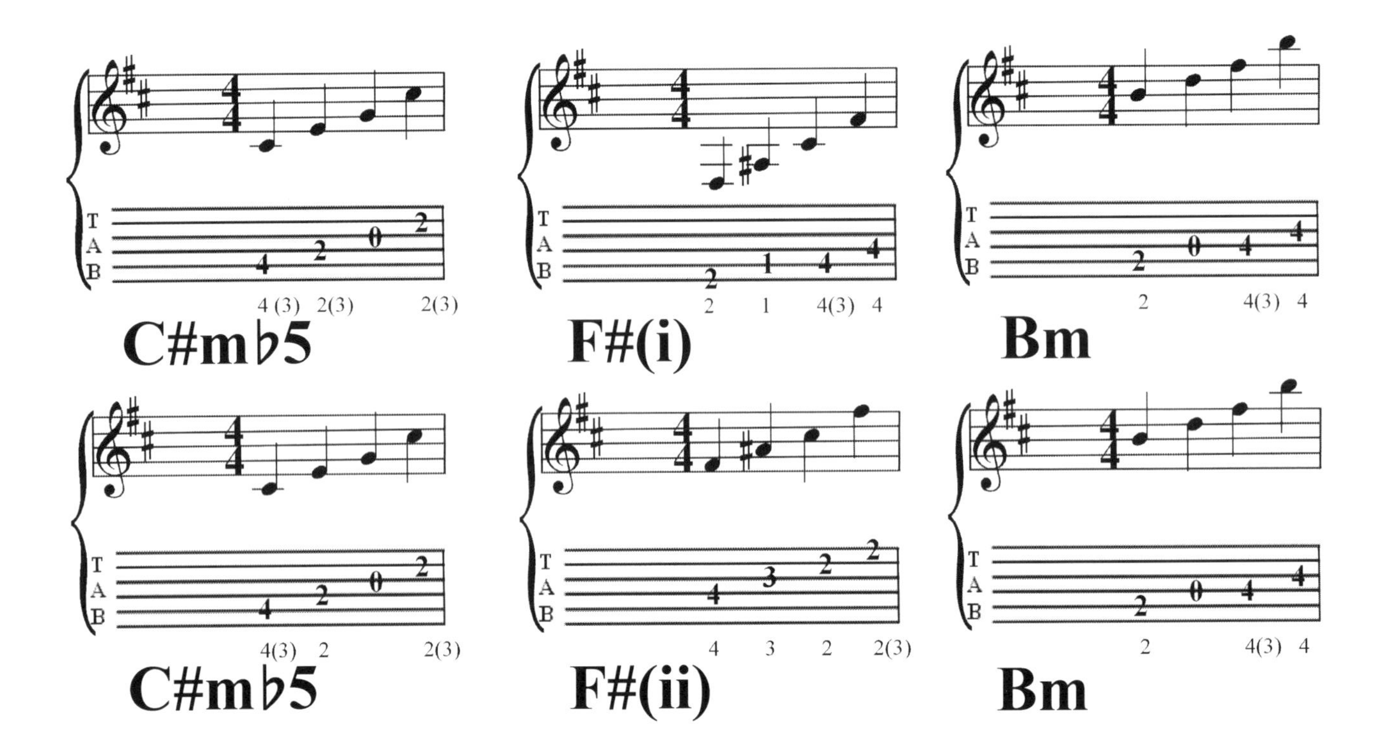

Key of F#m

Key of C#m

Key of A♭m

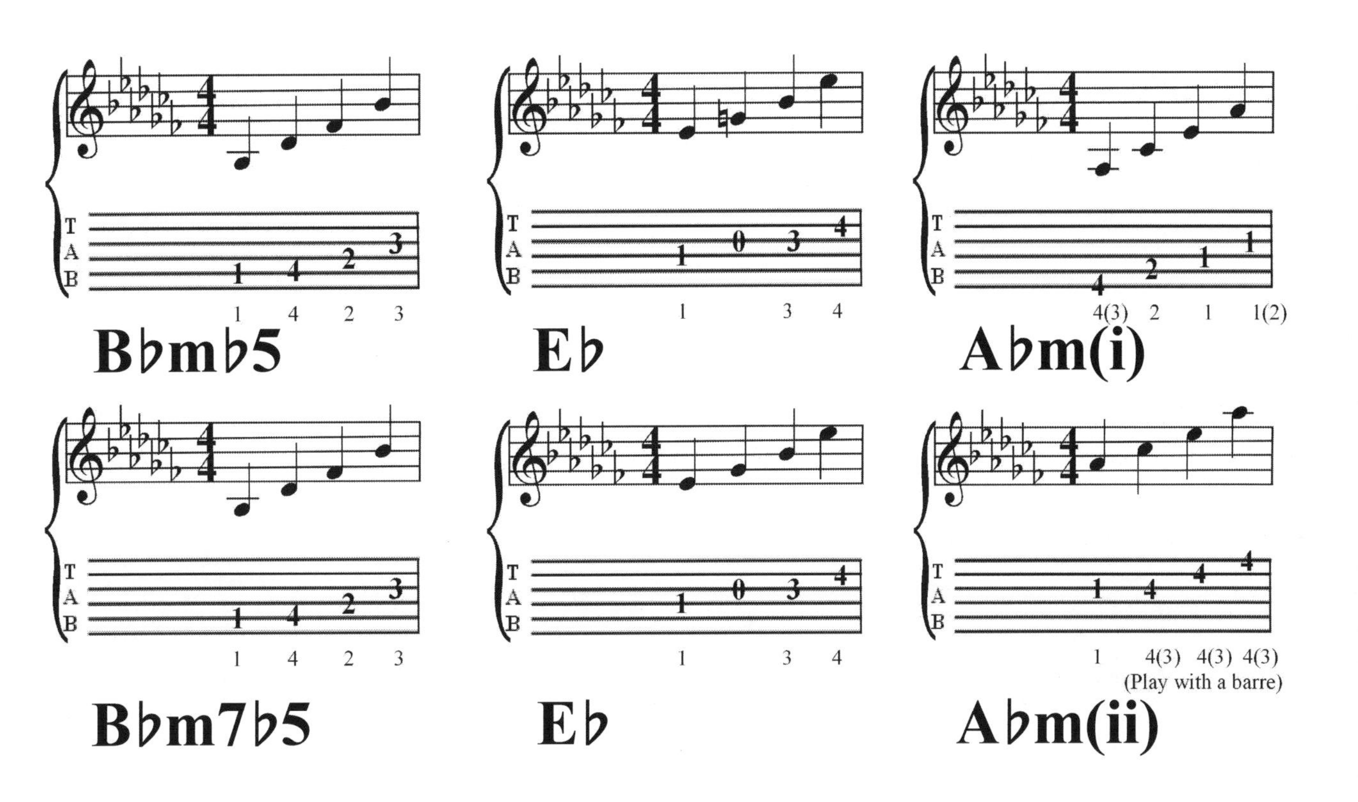

Key of E♭m

Key of B♭m

Key of Fm

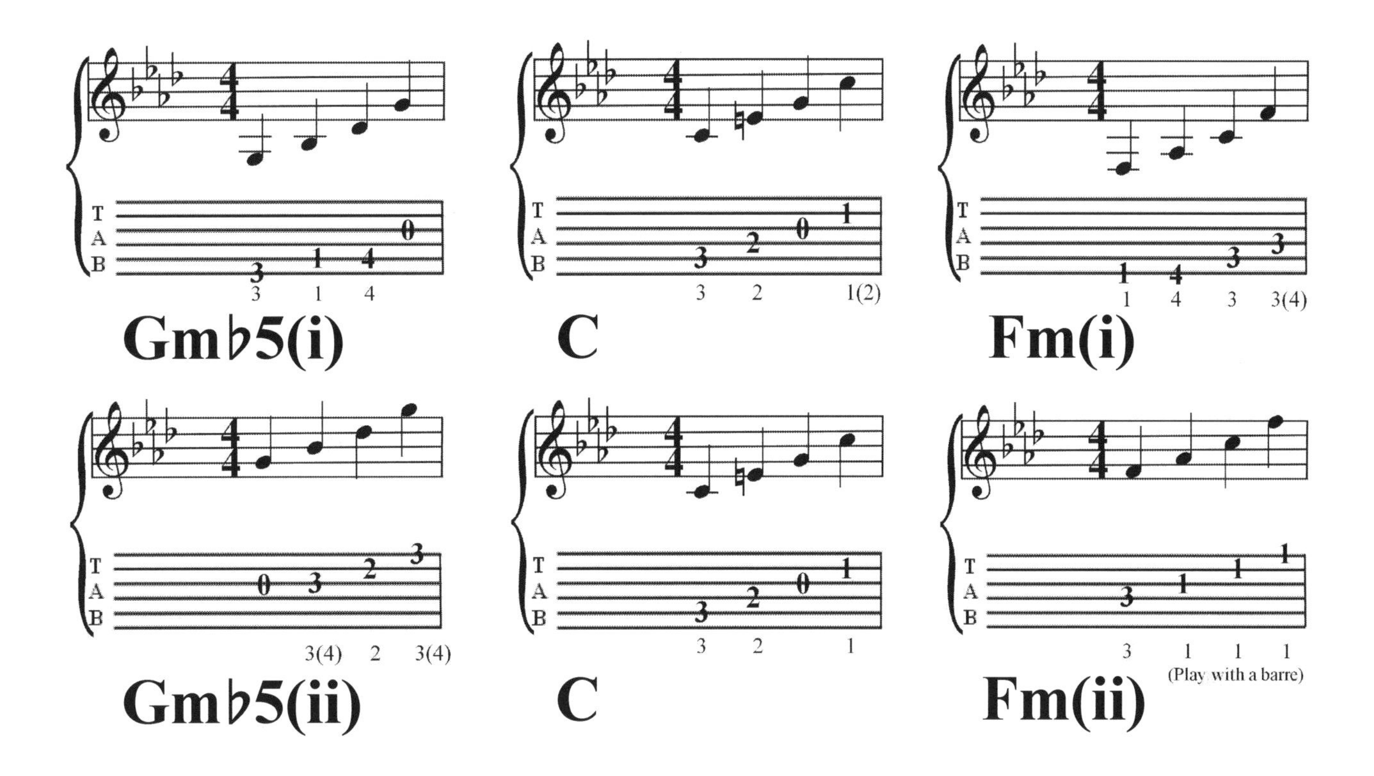

Key of Cm

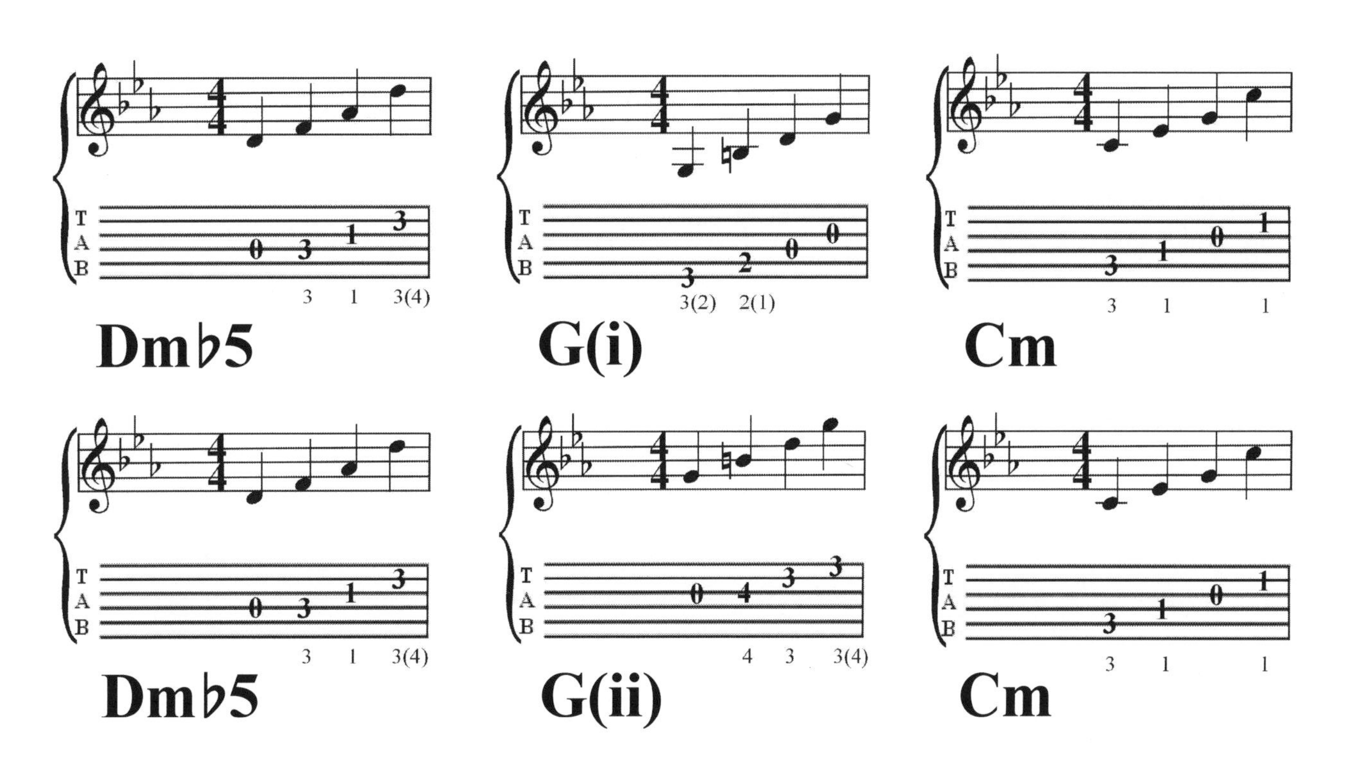

Key of Gm

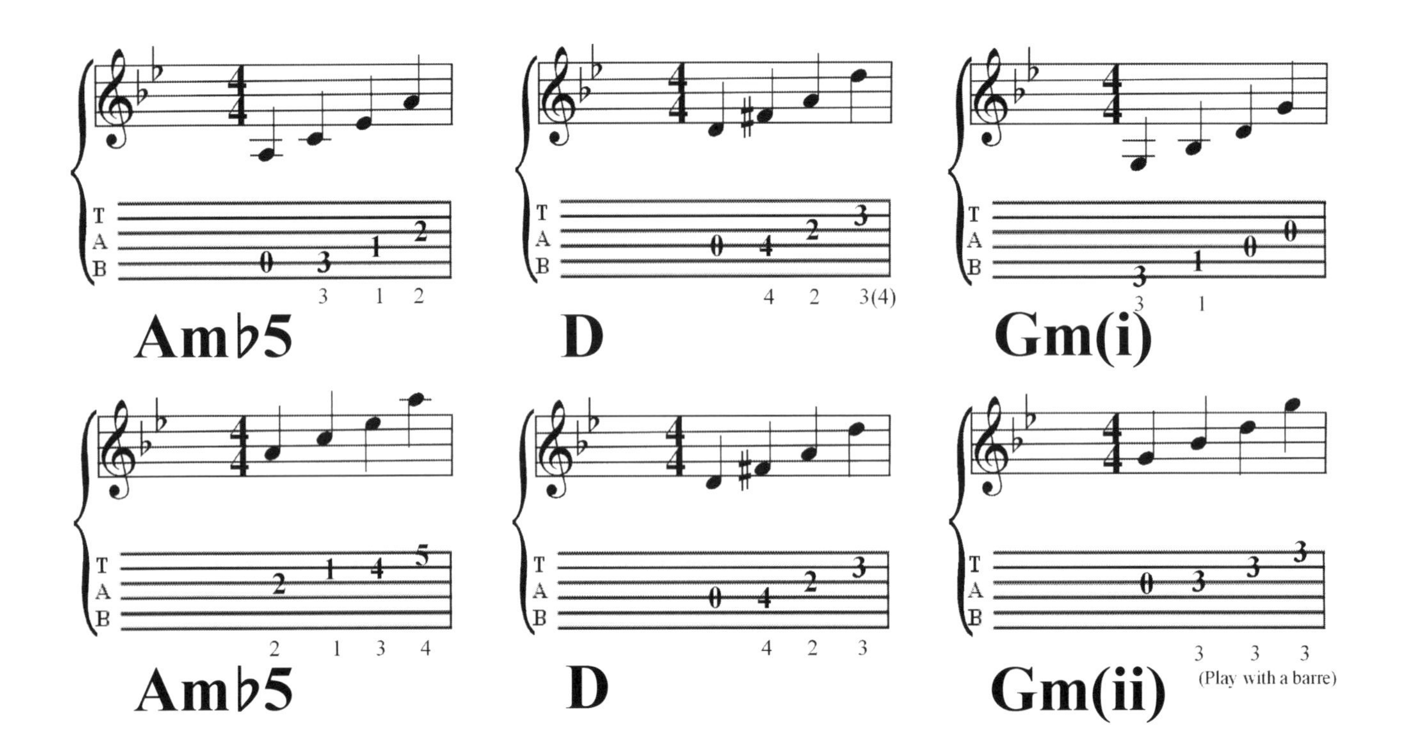

Key of Dm

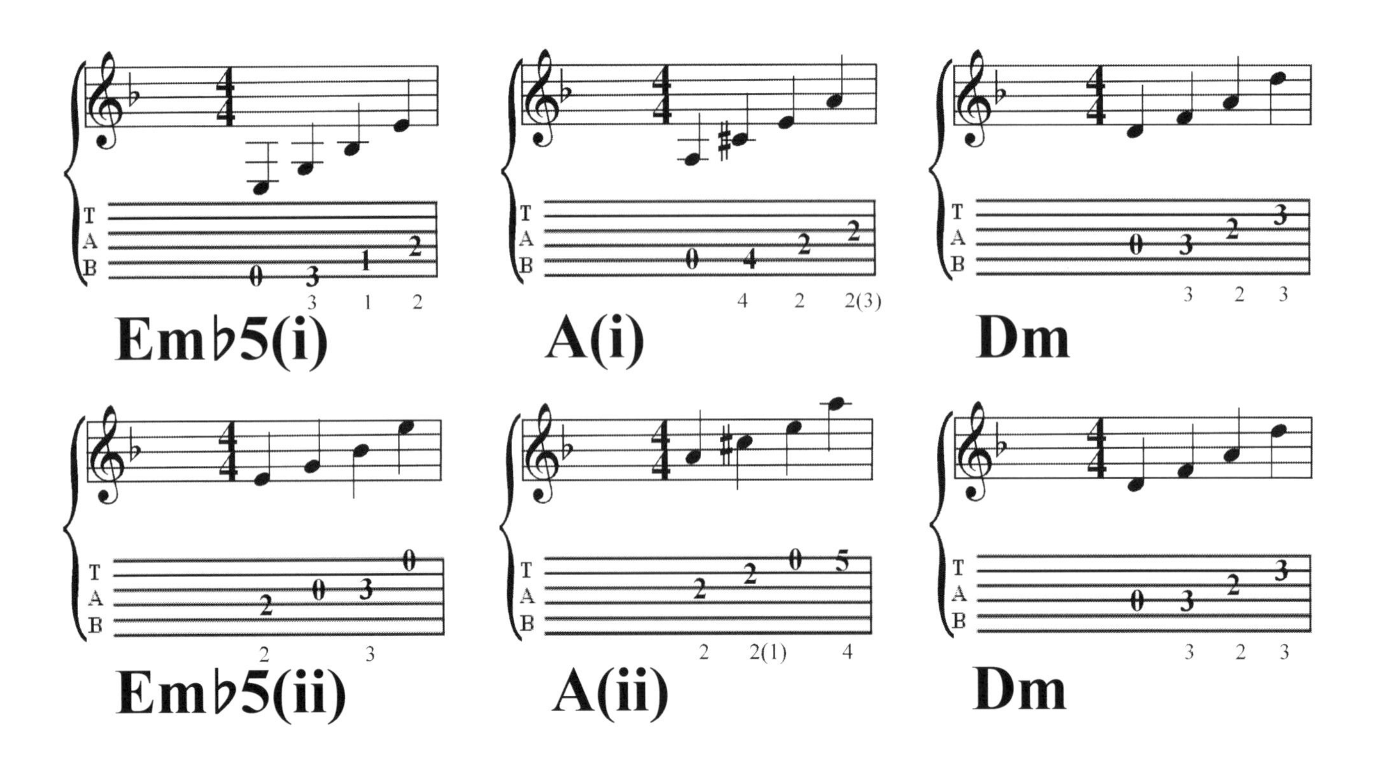

All Keys (i)

ii

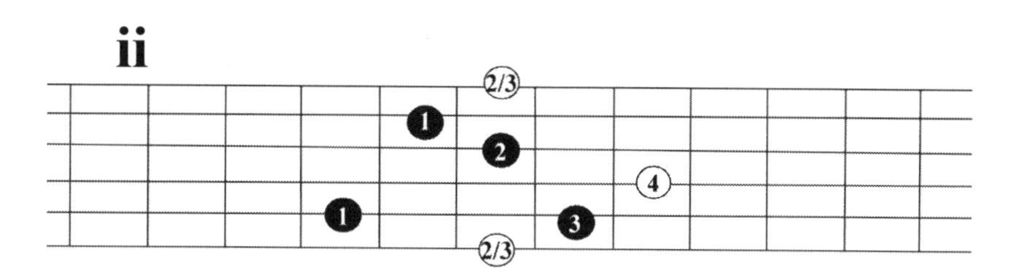

V

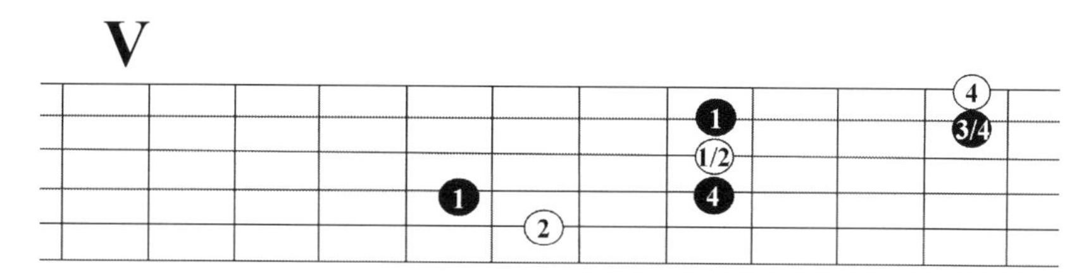

i

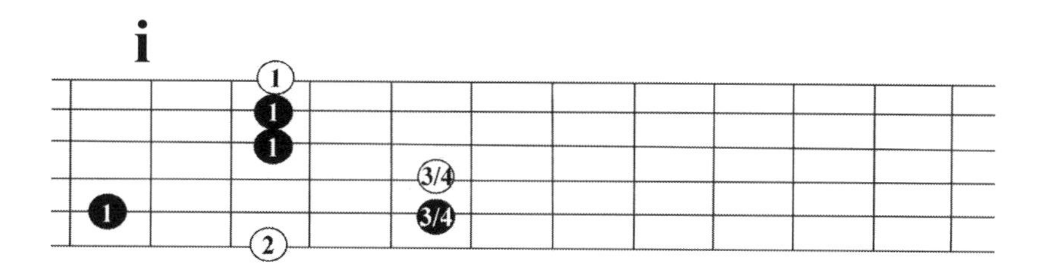

All Keys (ii)

ii

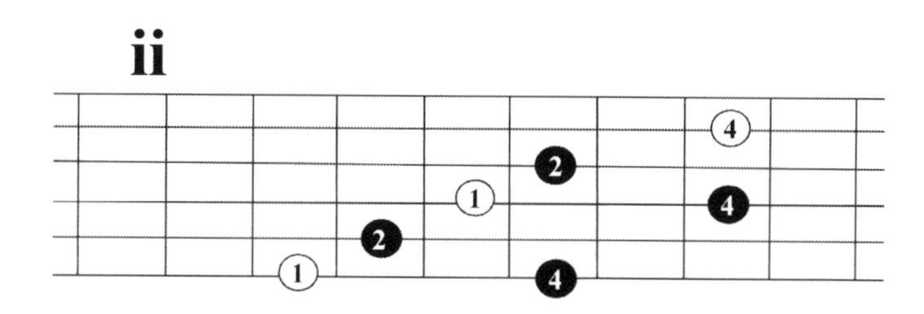

V

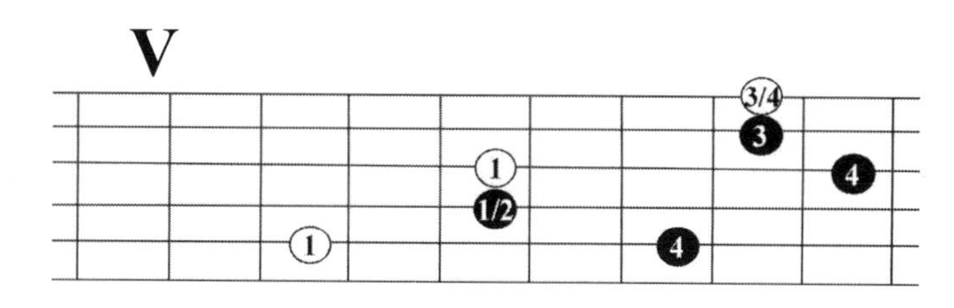

i

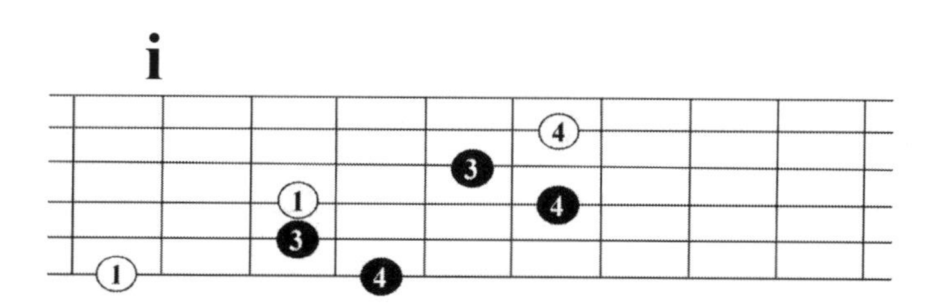

All Keys (iii)

ii

V

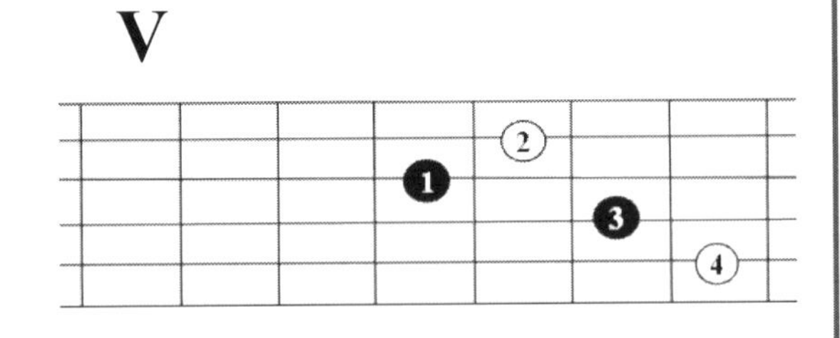

i

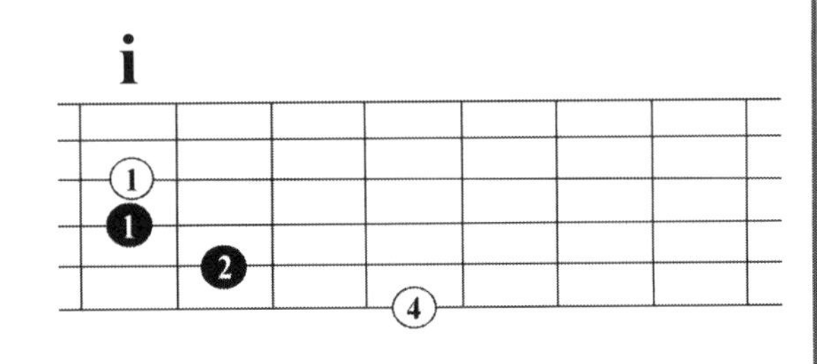

All Keys (iv)

ii

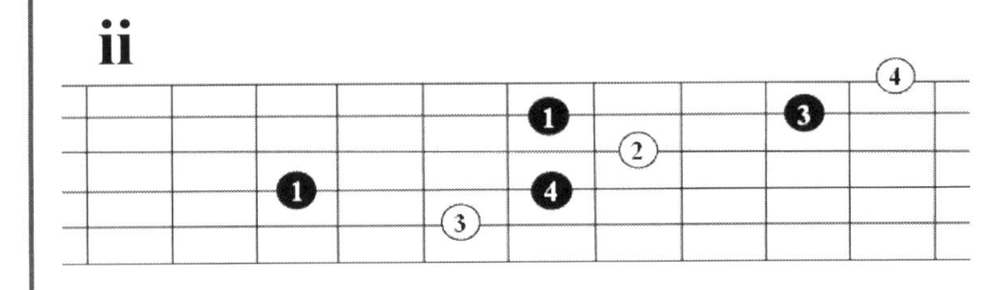

V

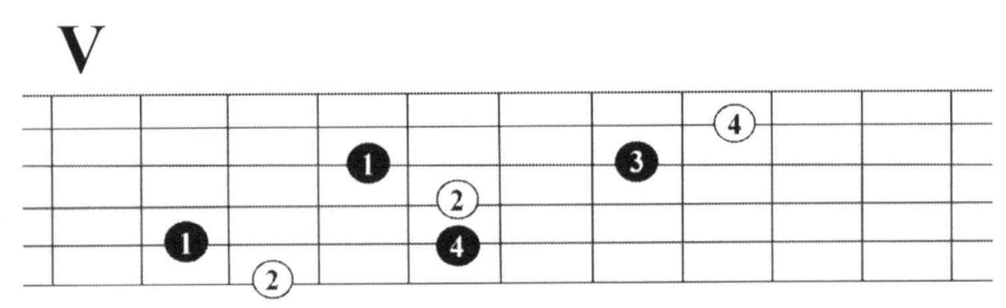

i

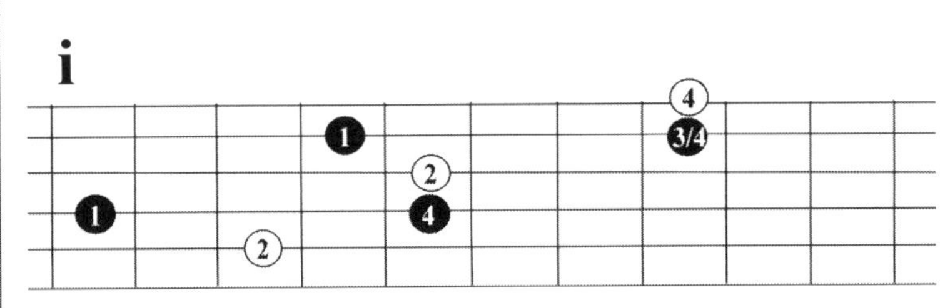

All Keys (v)

ii

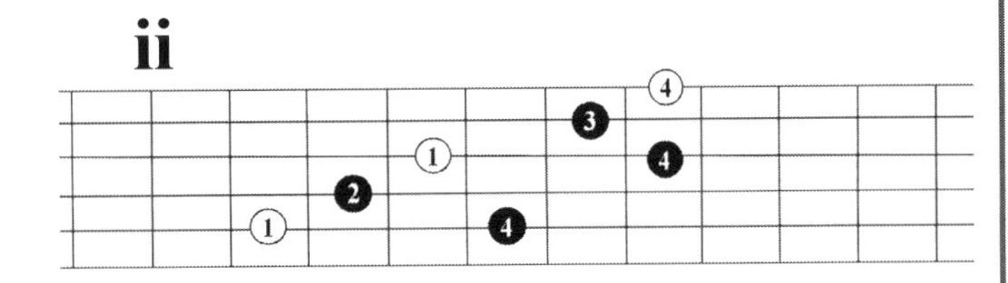

V

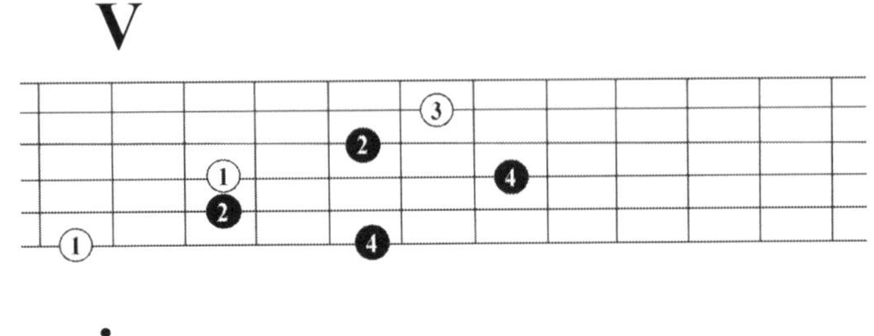

i

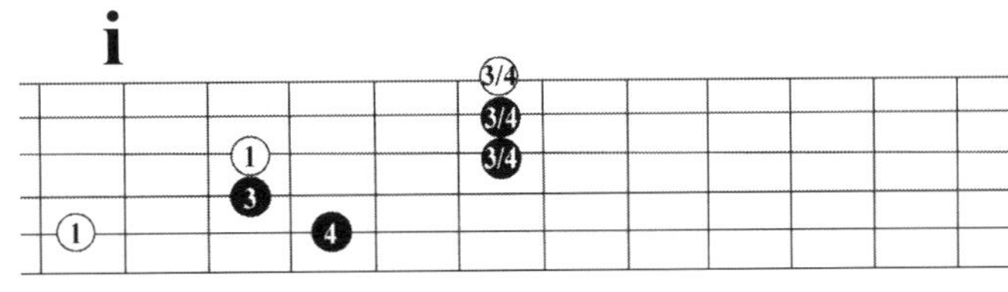

All Keys (vi)

ii

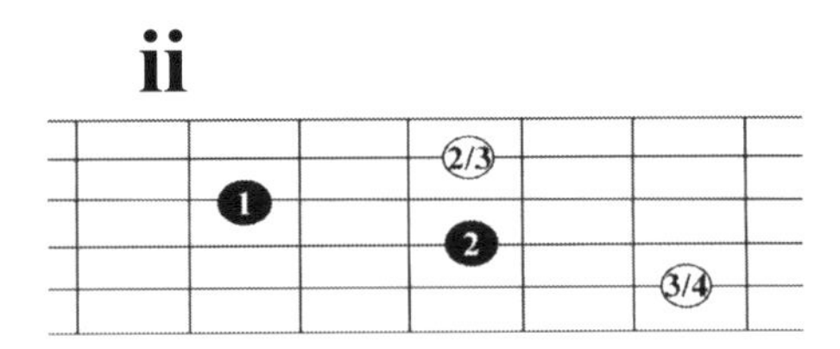

V

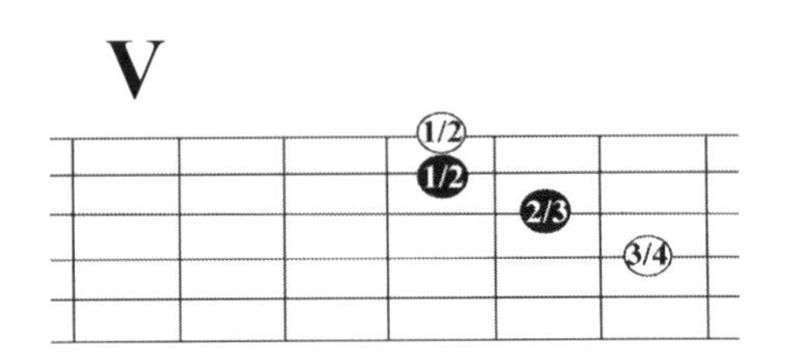

i

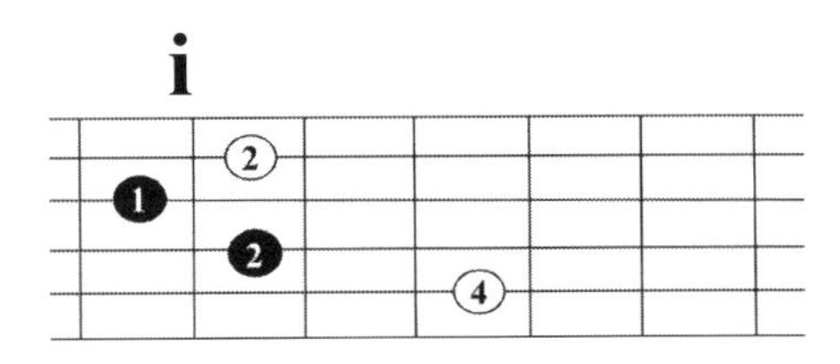

All Keys (vii)

ii

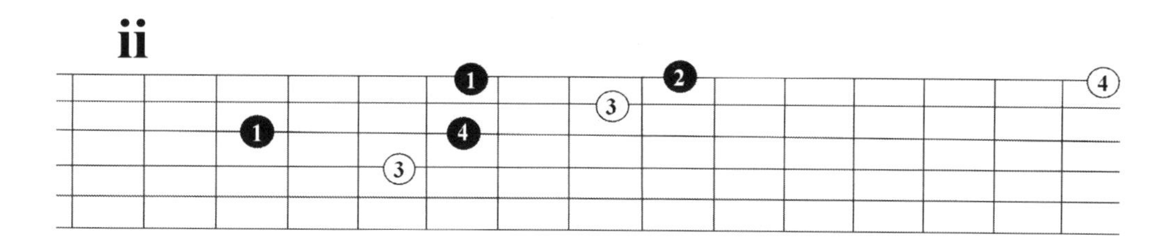

V

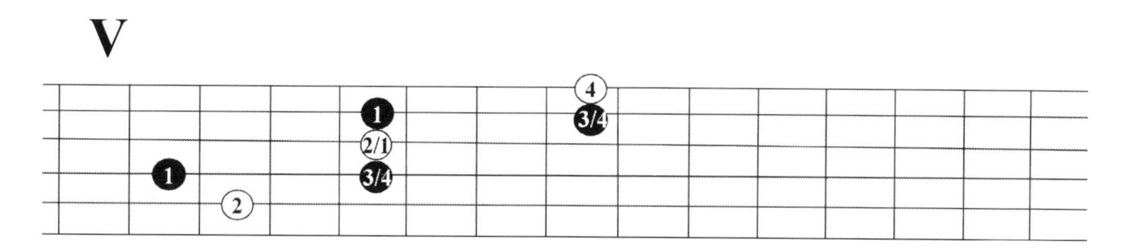

i

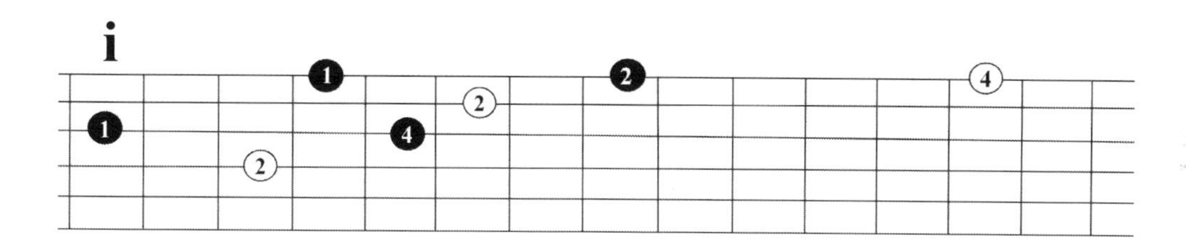

All Keys (viii)

ii

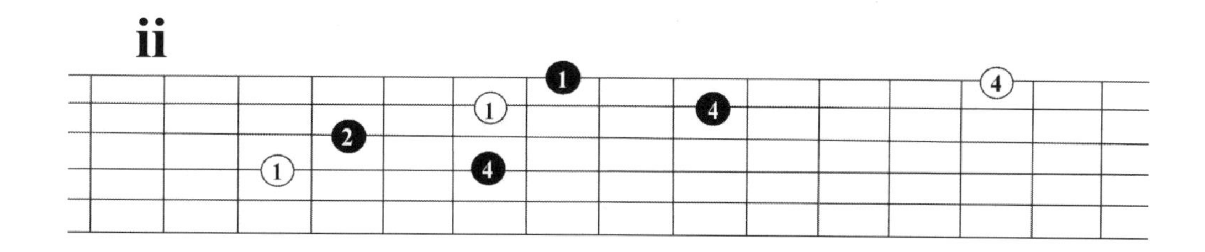

V

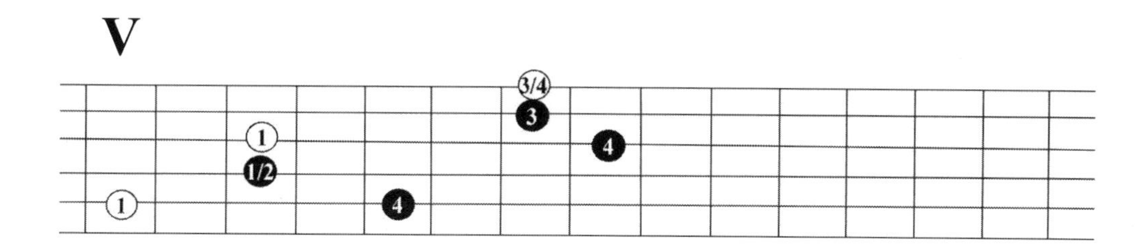

i

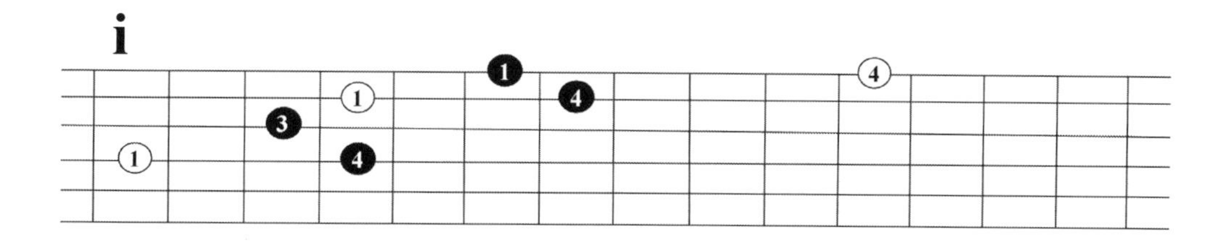

All Keys (ix)

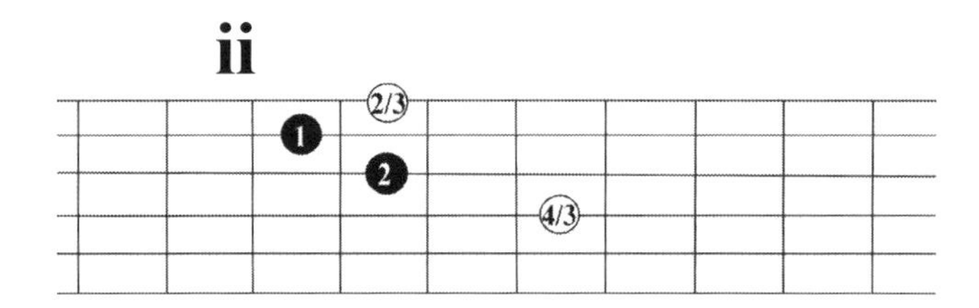

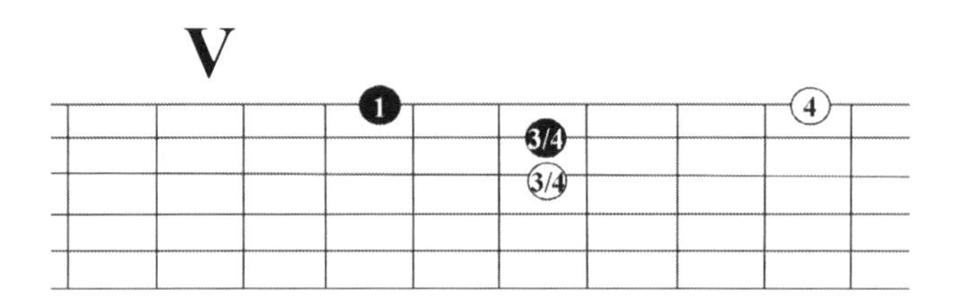

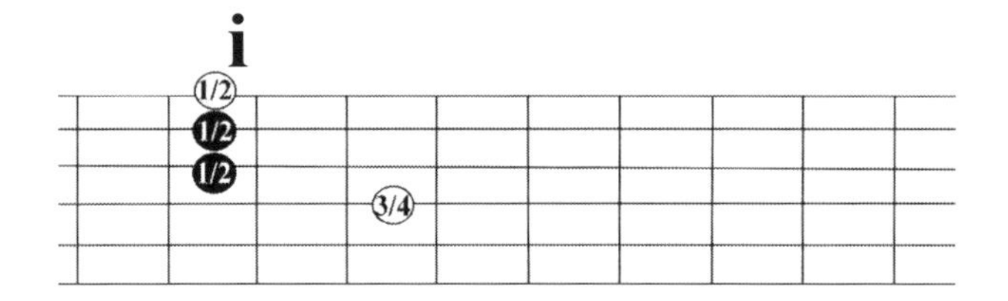

PART EIGHTEEN

VI - ii - V - i

MINOR KEYS
TRIADS
ARPEGGIOS

Key of Am

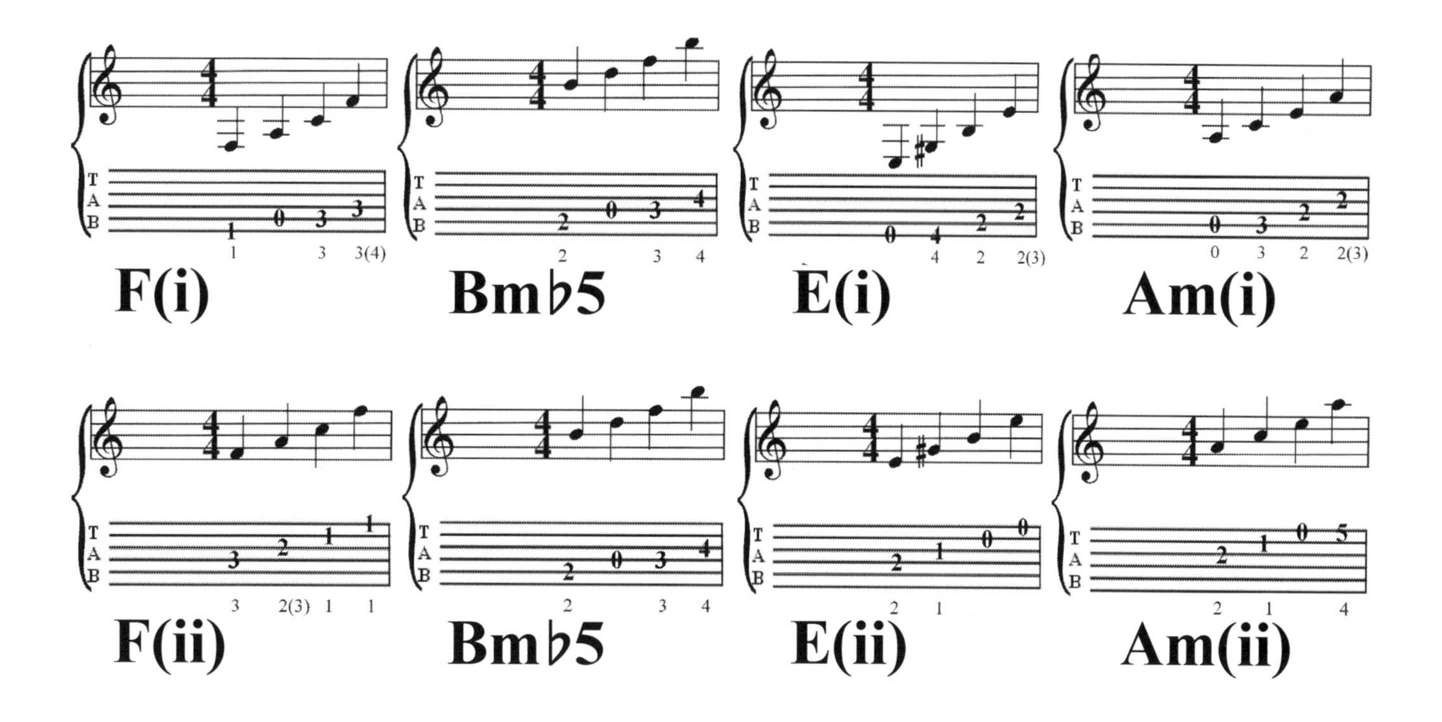

Key of Em

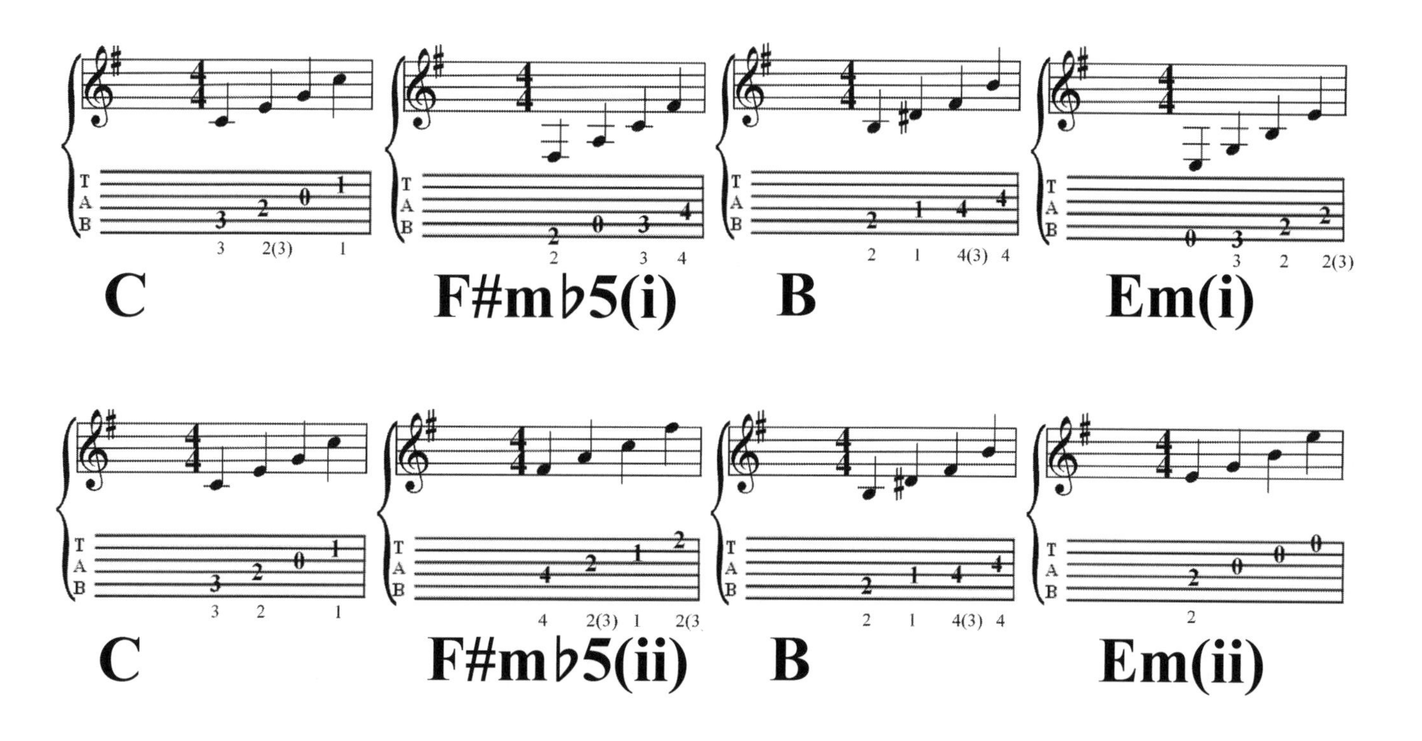

Key of Bm

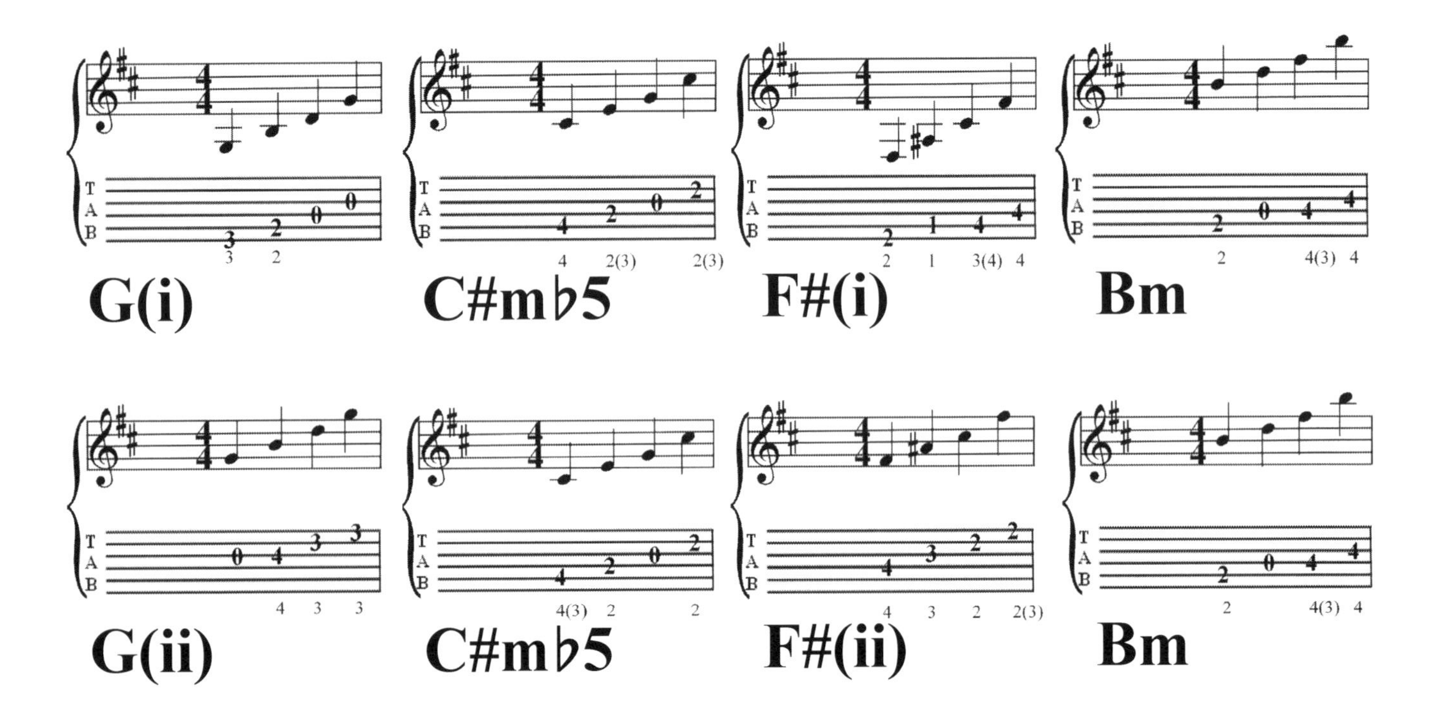

Key of F#m

Key of C#m

Key of A♭m

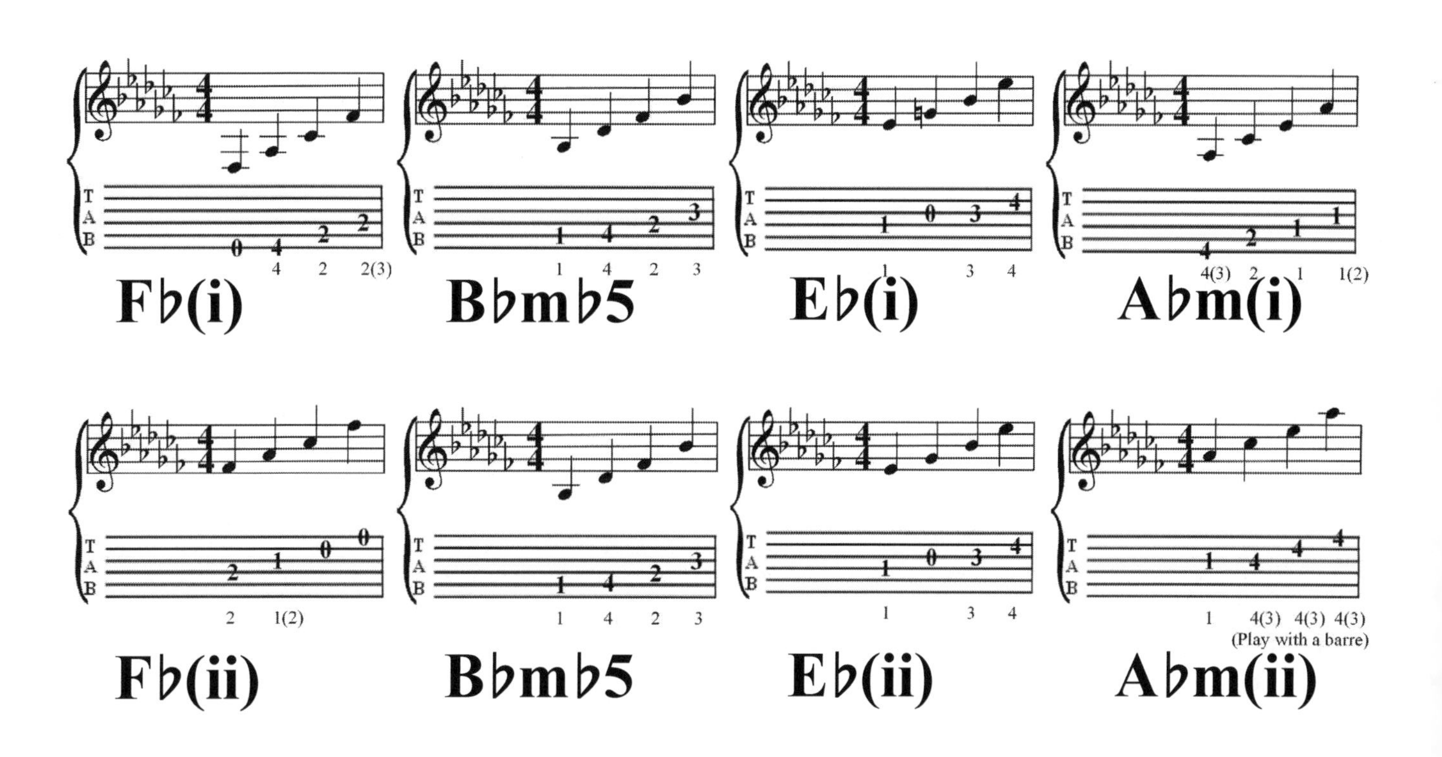

Key of E♭m

Key of B♭m

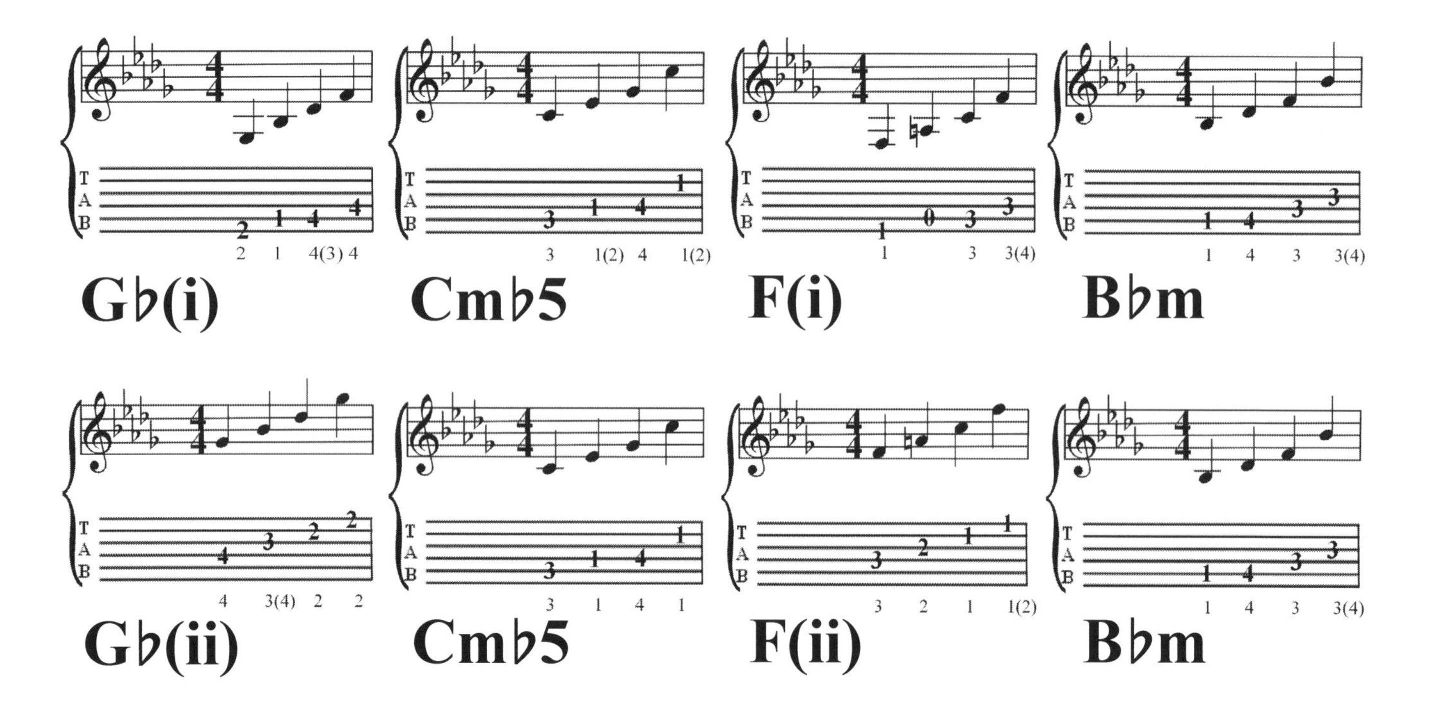

Key of Fm

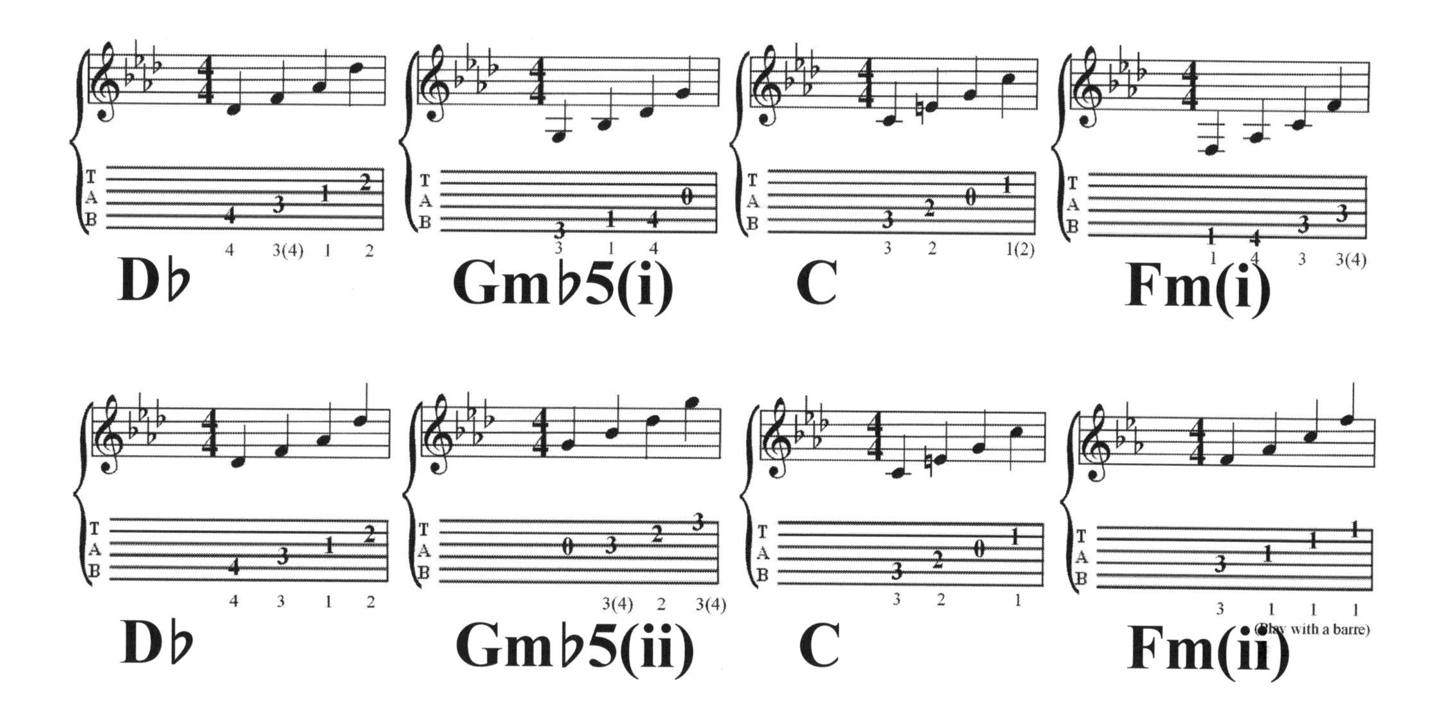

Key of Cm

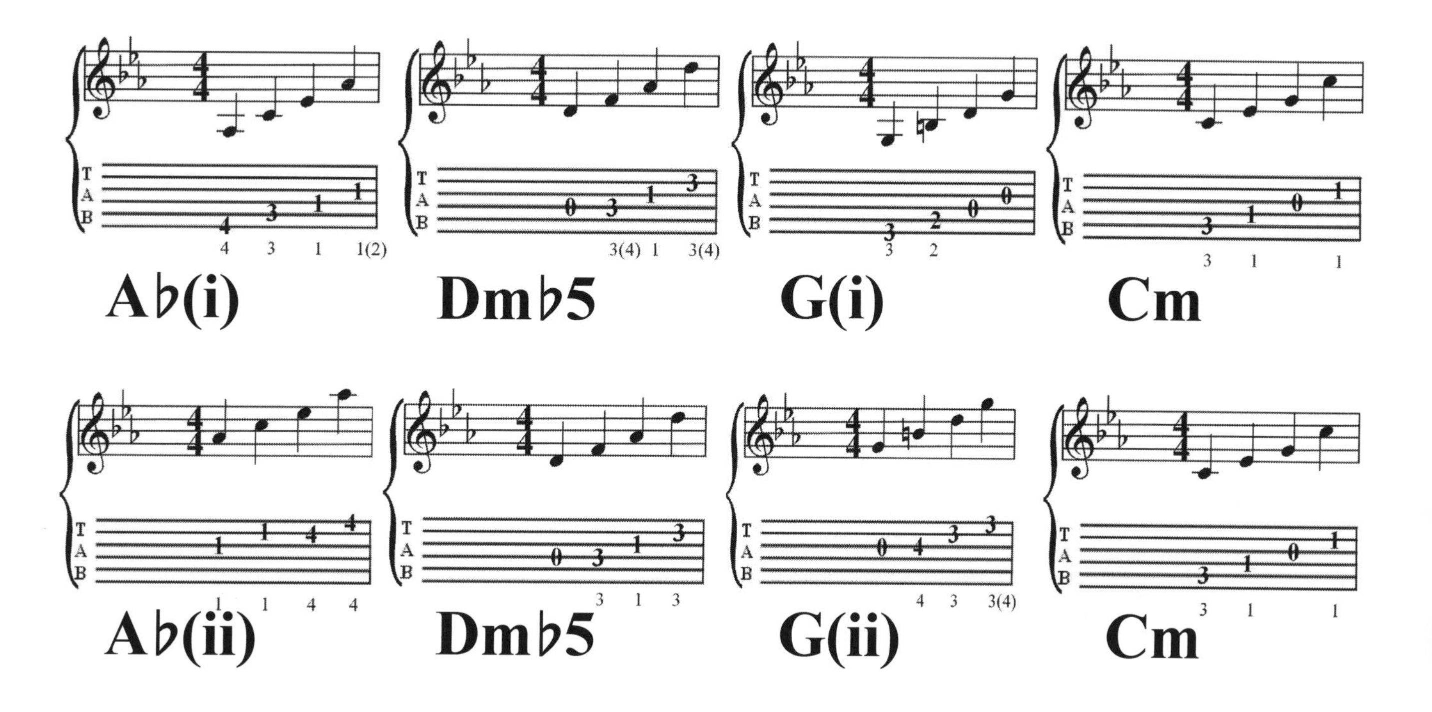

Key of Gm

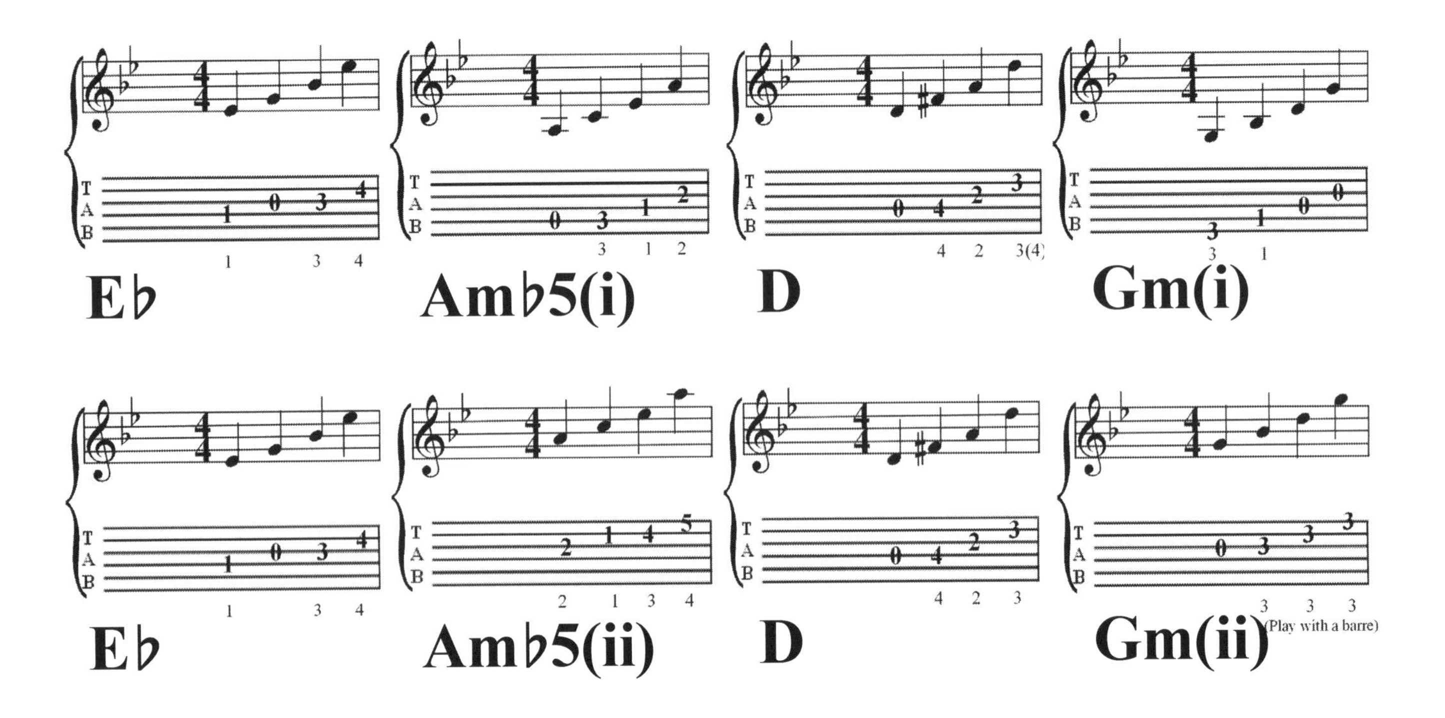

Key of Dm

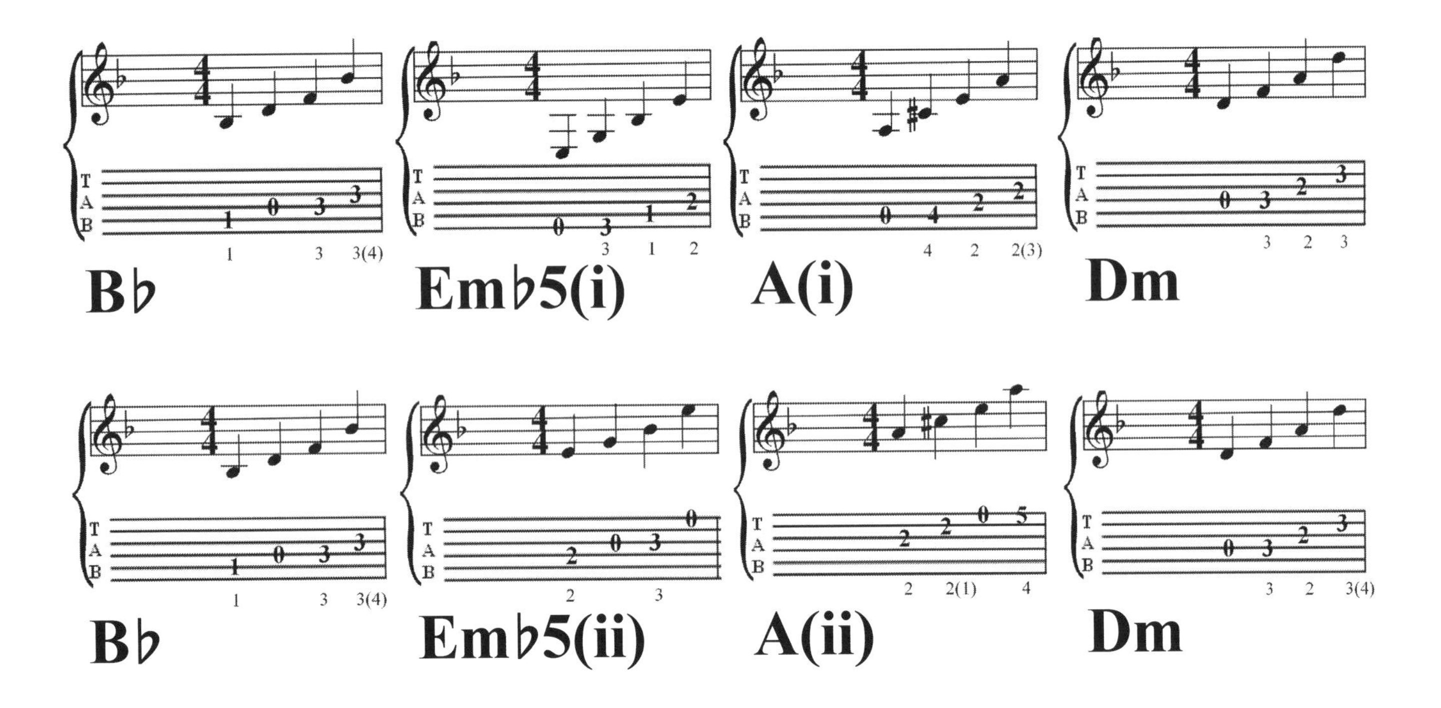

All Keys (i)

VI

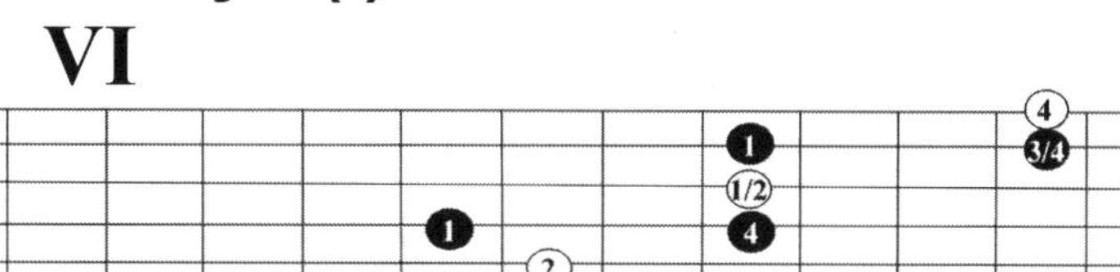

ii

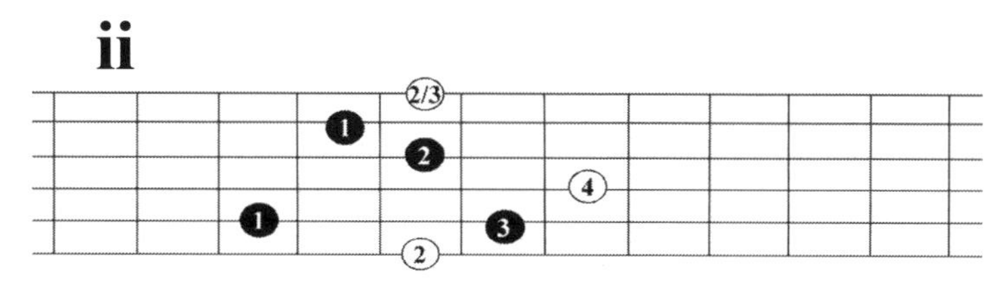

V

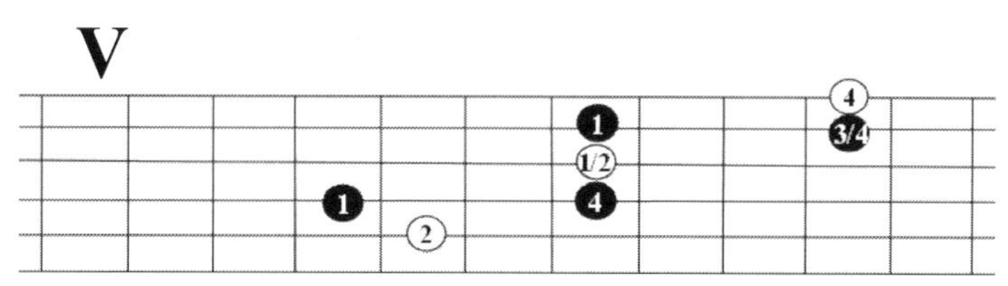

i

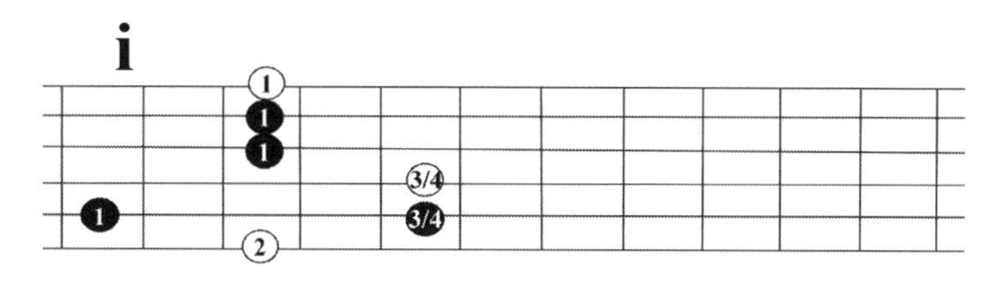

All Keys (ii)

VI

ii

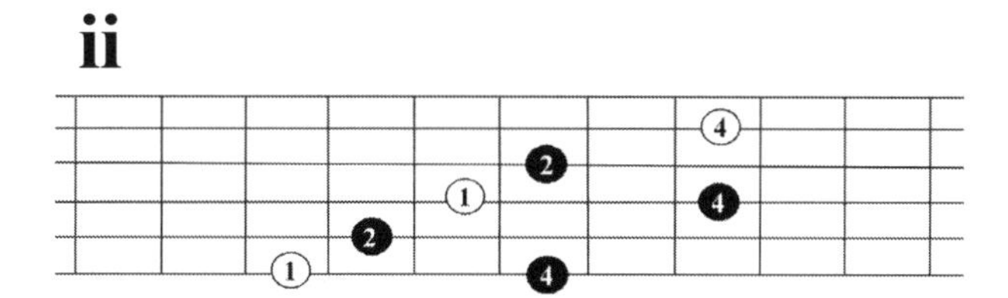

V

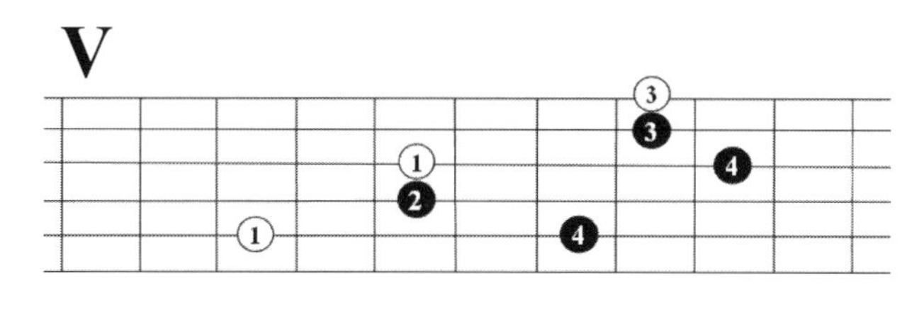

i

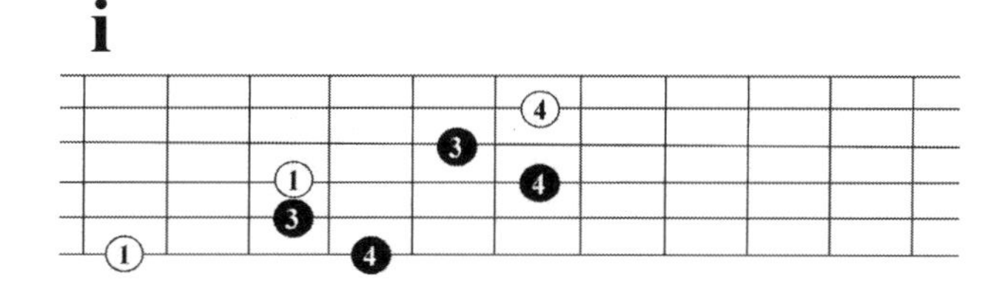

All Keys (iii)

VI

ii

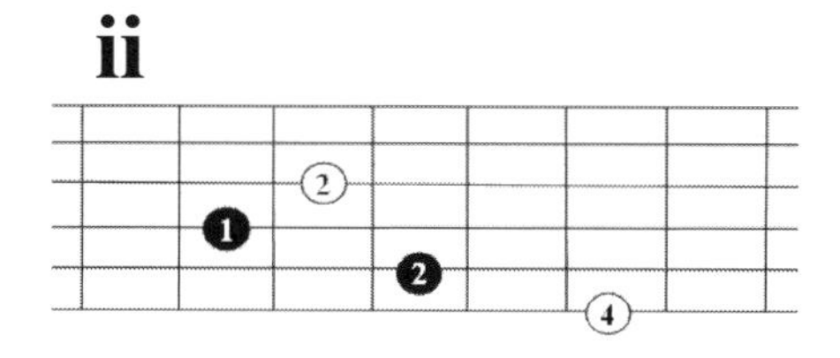

V

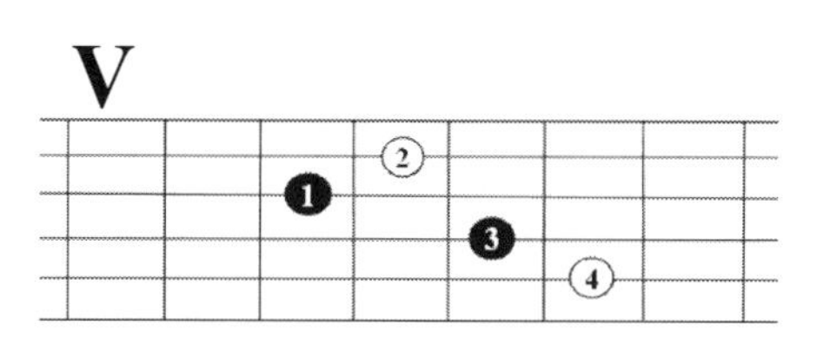

i

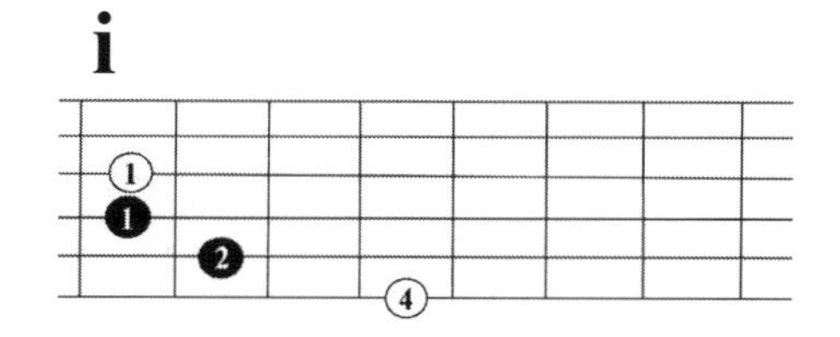

All Keys (iv)

VI

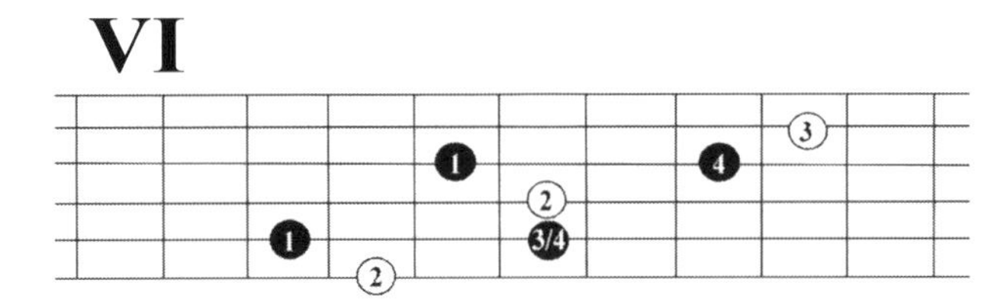

ii

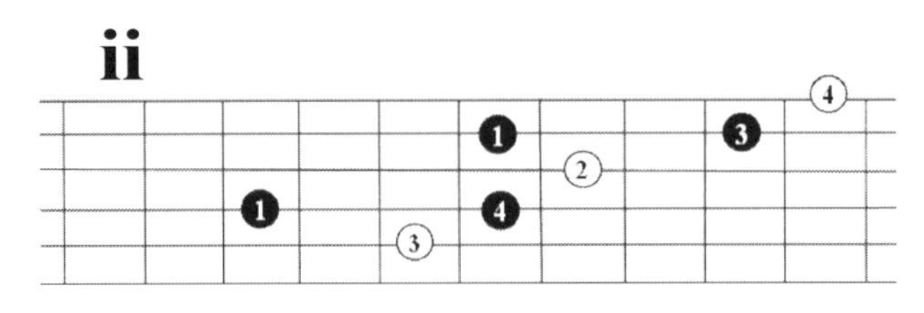

V

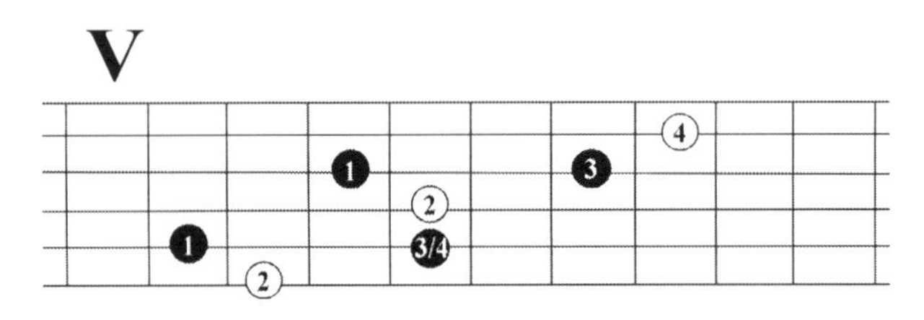

i

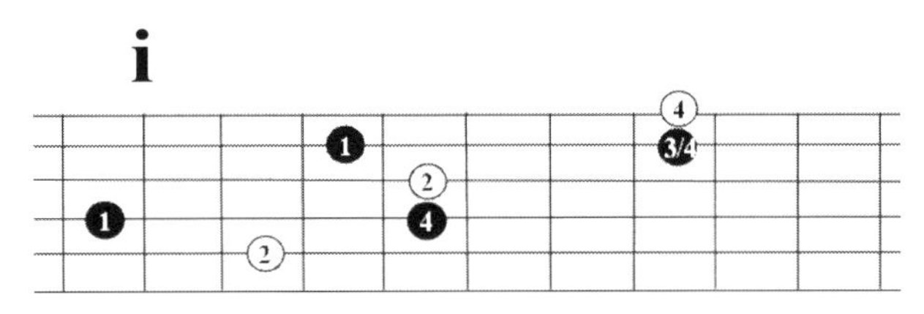

All Keys (v)

VI

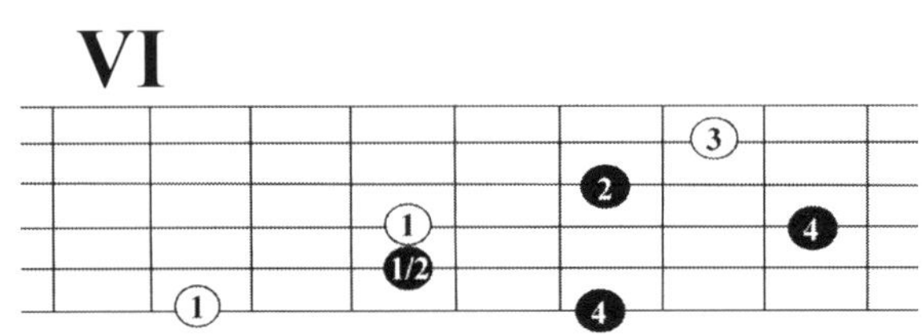

ii

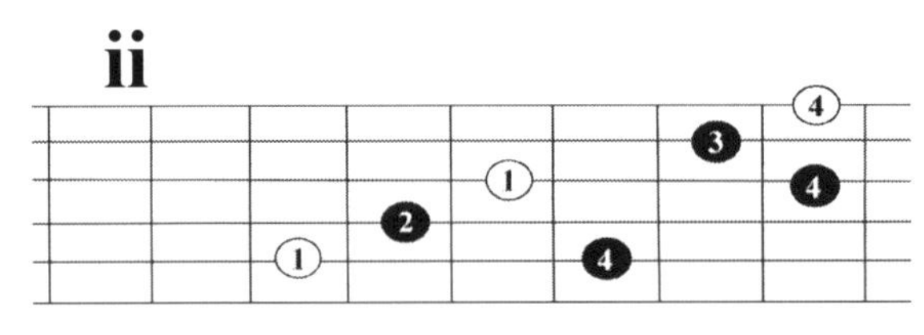

V

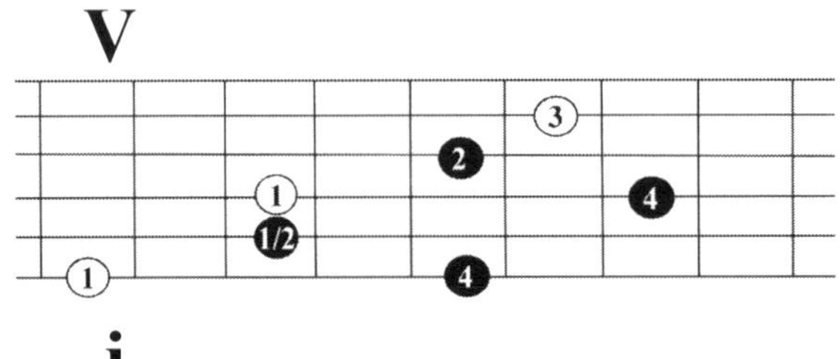

i

All Keys (vi)

VI

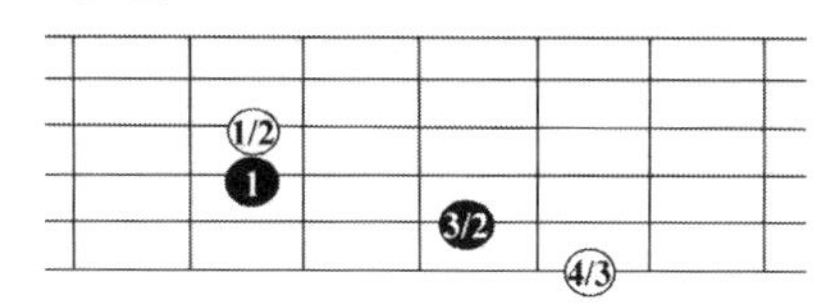

ii

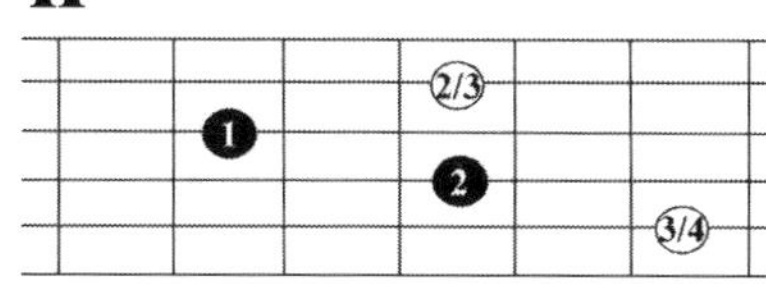

V

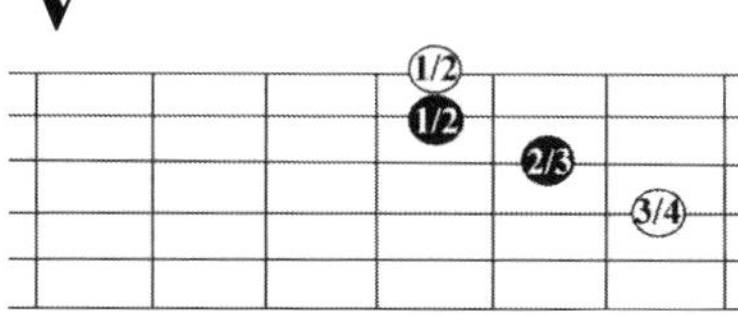

i

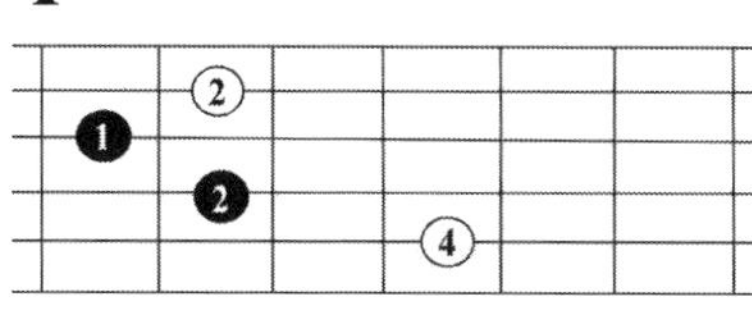

All Keys (vii)

VI

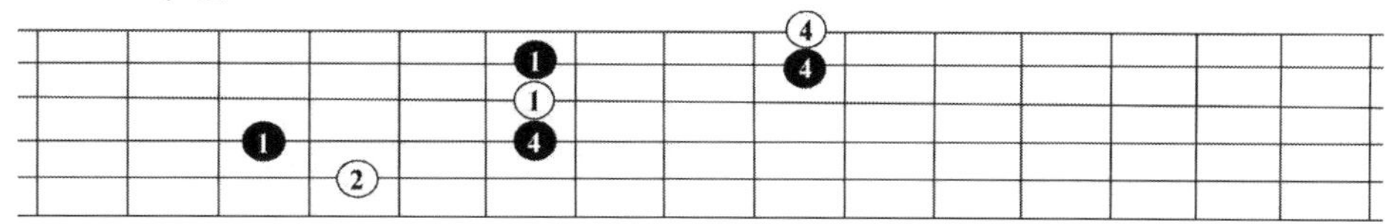

ii

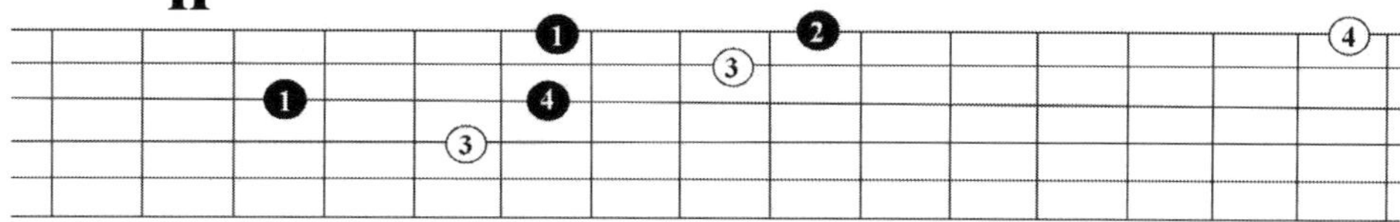

V

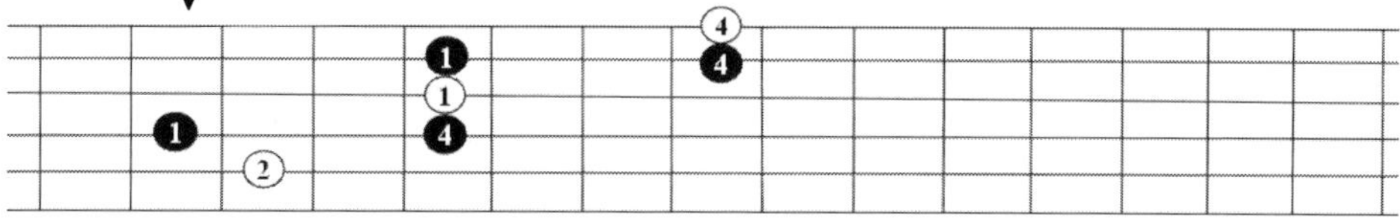

i

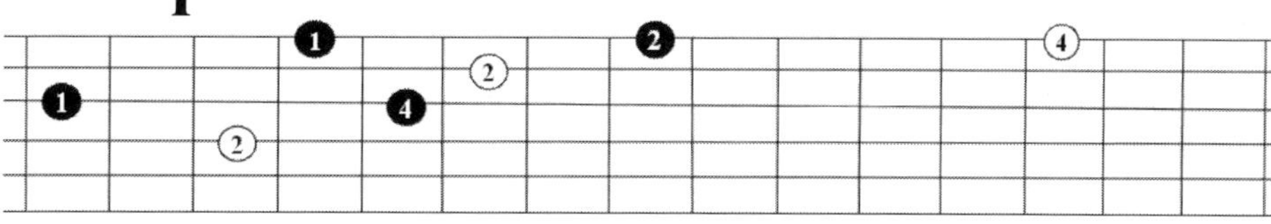

All Keys (viii)

VI

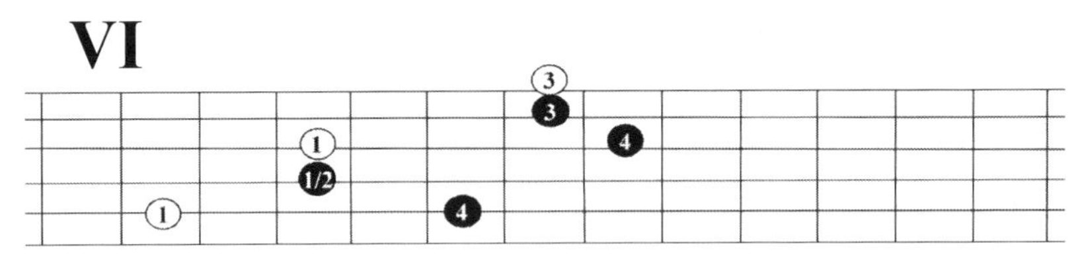

ii

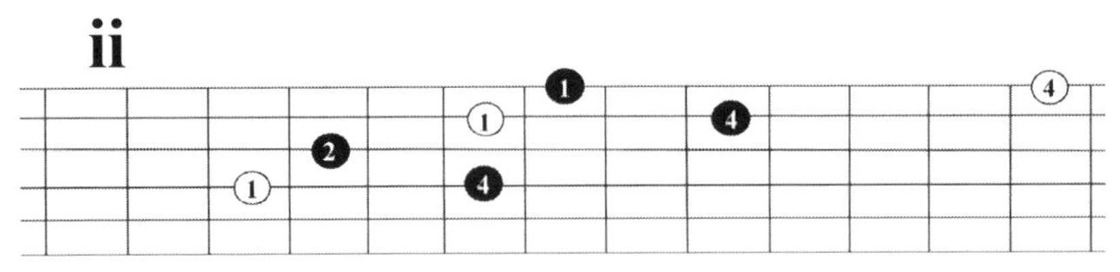

V

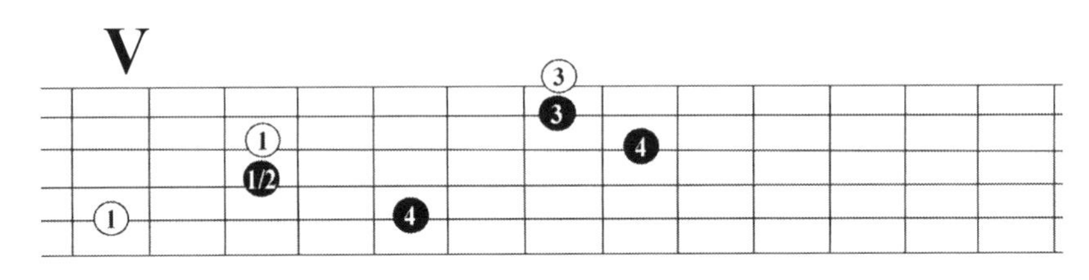

i

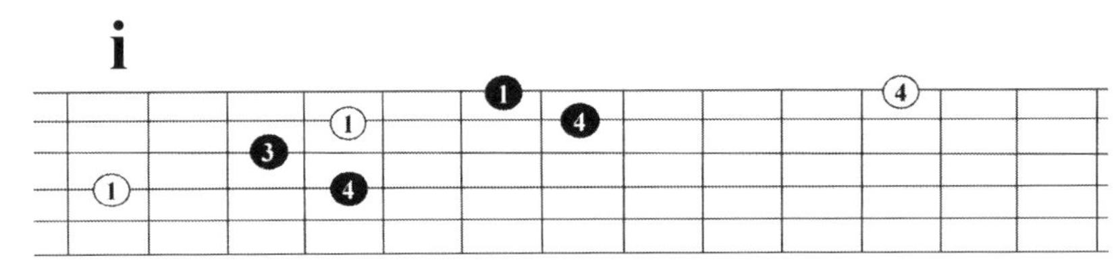

All Keys (ix)

VI

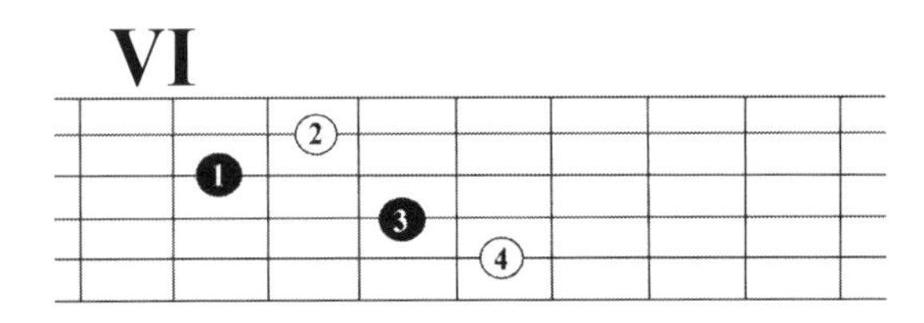

ii

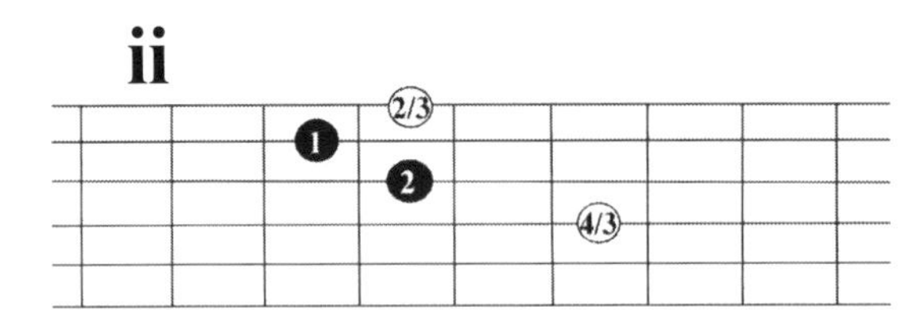

V

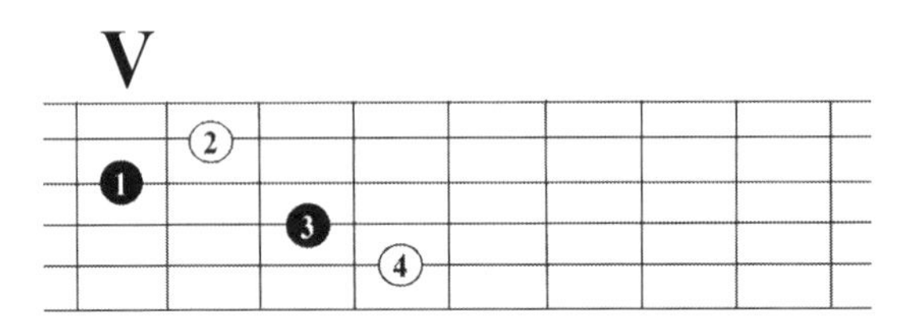

i

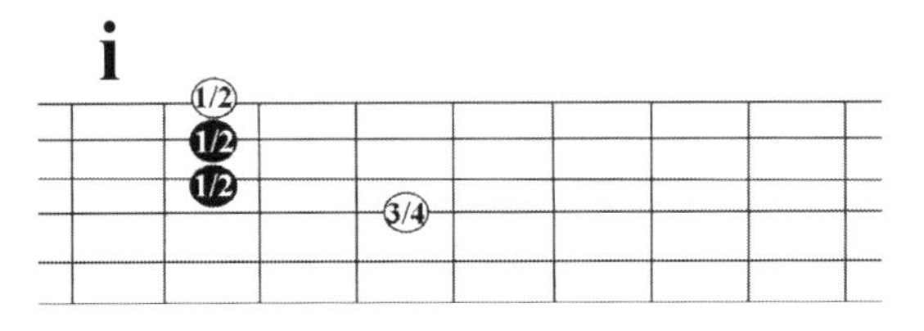

PART NINETEEN

I - IV - V

MAJOR KEYS
SEVENTH CHORDS
ARPEGGIOS

SEVENTH CHORD ARPEGGIOS

The following exercises introduce the arpeggio forms of the *seventh* chords: *major* seventh (M7), *minor* seventh (m7), dominant seventh (7) and minor seven/flat 5 (m7♭5). The sequence of exercises follows the same pattern as the previous *triad* arpeggio exercises. As previously - try out alternative fingerings of your own.

When playing each arpeggio back-and-forth, moving on to the next arpeggio without returning to the *root* of the current arpeggio (as suggested for the triad arpeggios) will keep the whole cycle in a steady 4/4 time signature. The substitute fingerings indicated have been chosen to facilitate this pattern.

FURTHER ARPEGGIOS

Although a detailed account of harmonisation beyond the seventh is outside the scope of this book, I suggest that you experiment with your own fingerings for arpeggios of the ninth, eleventh and thirteenth chords, using the system of harmonisation described earlier in the book (a quick reminder - use alternate notes of the relevant major or minor scale...). See part fourty-four "Chord Substitution" for an overview of these chords and their structure.

Key of C

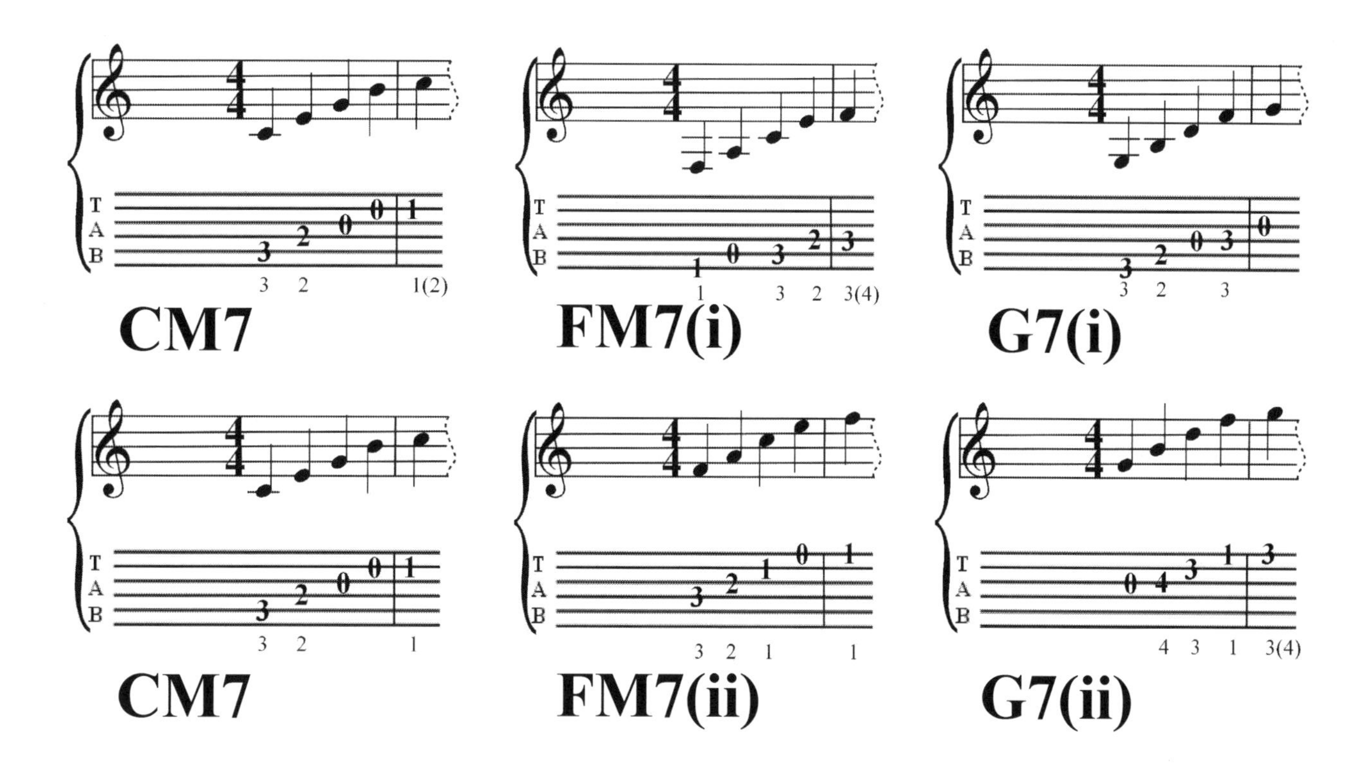

Key of G

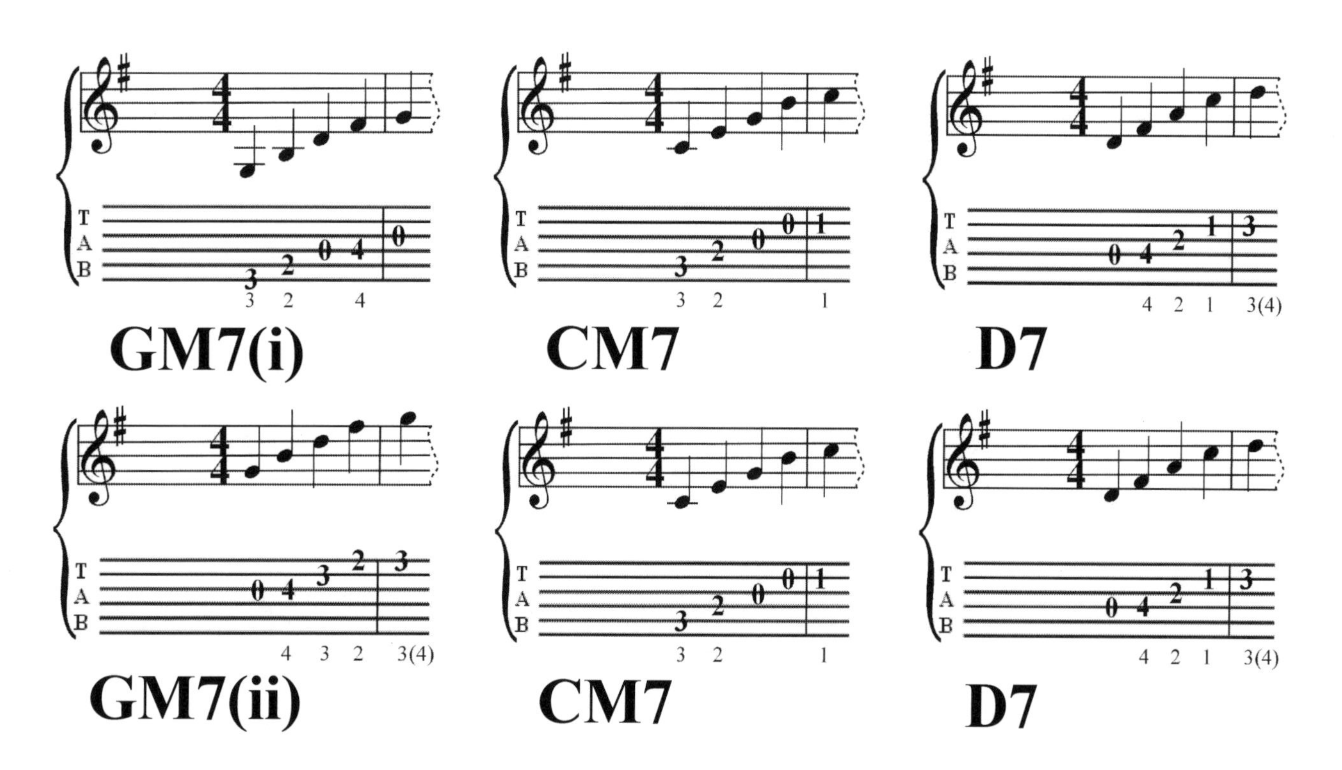

Key of D

Key of A

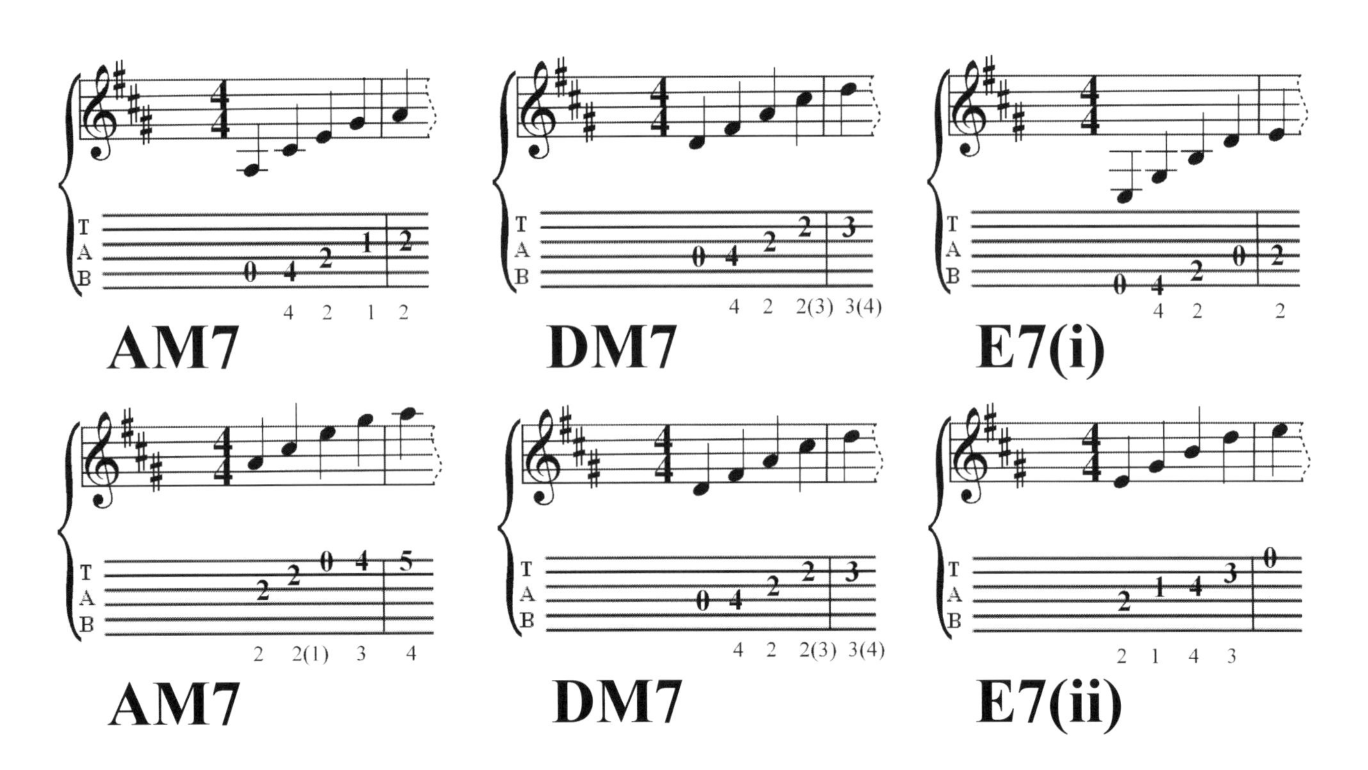

Key of E

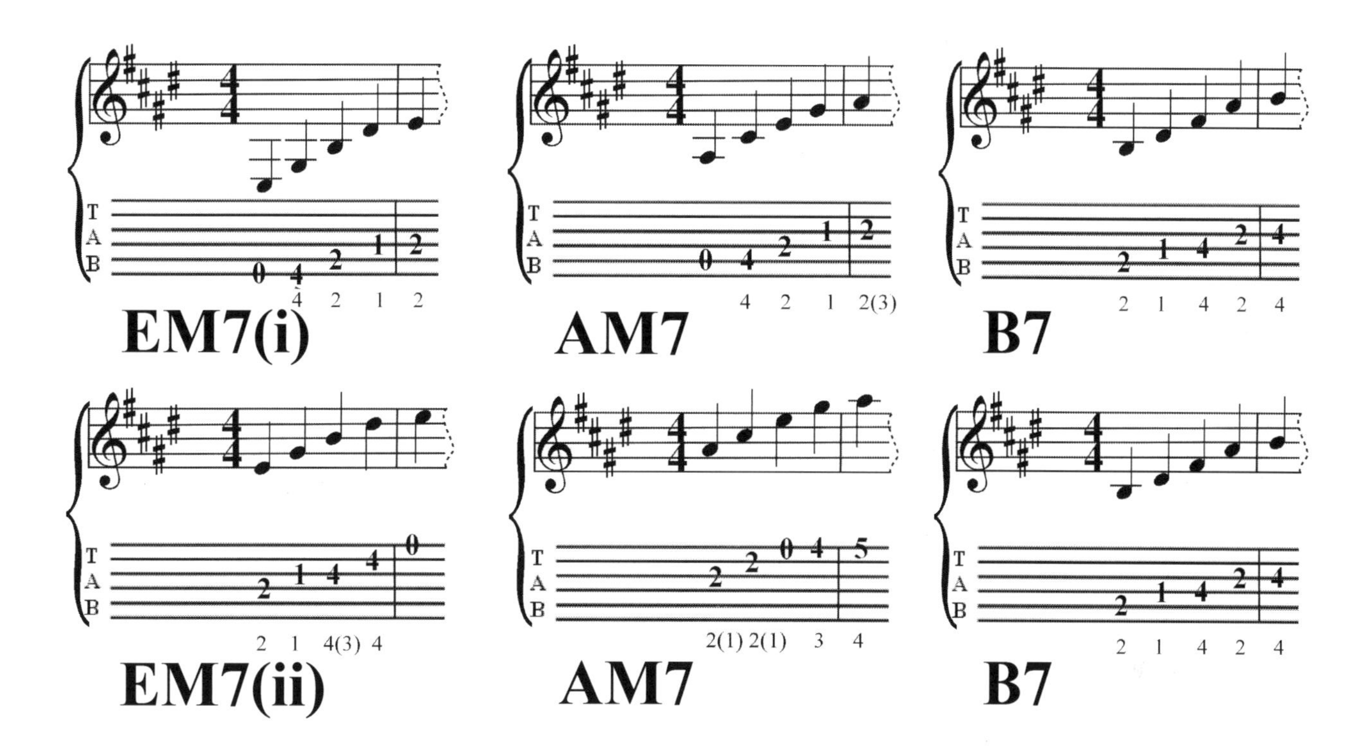

Key of B

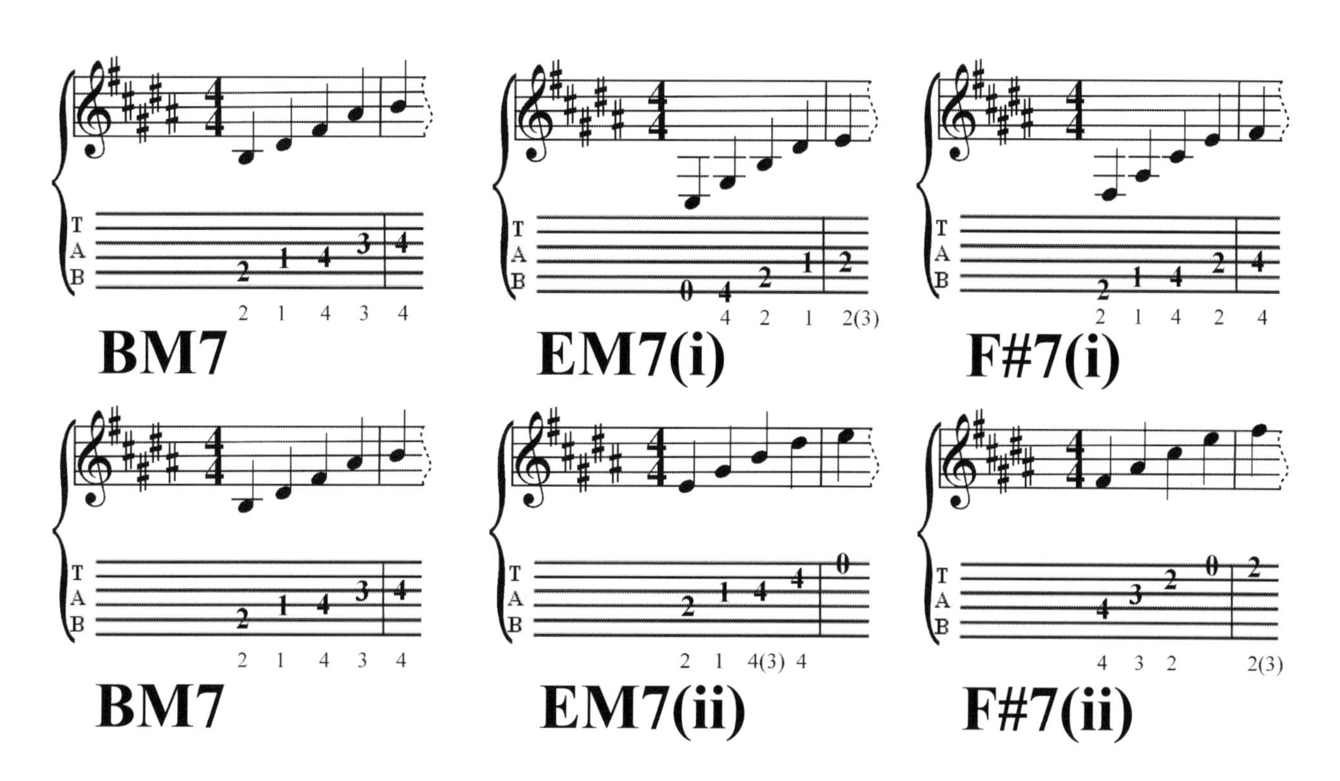

Key of F#

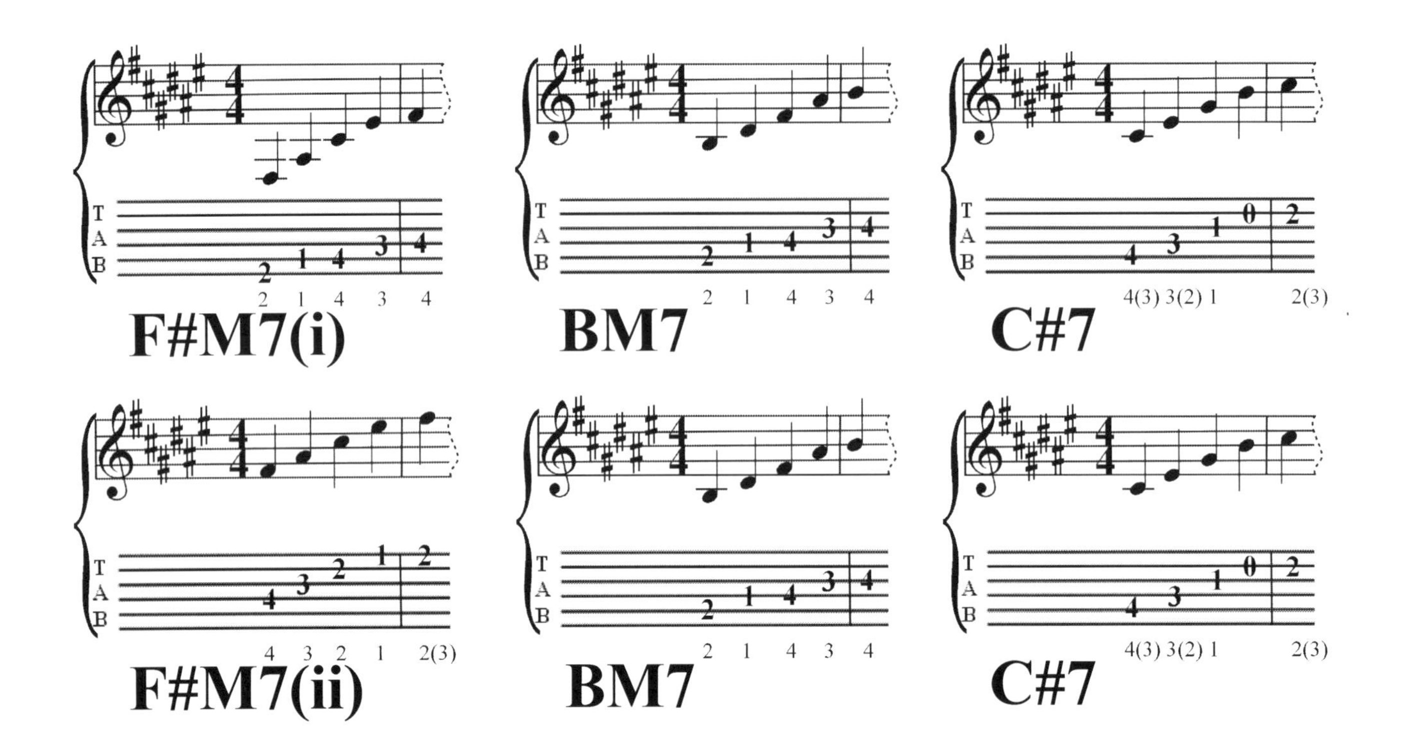

Key of C#

Key of A♭

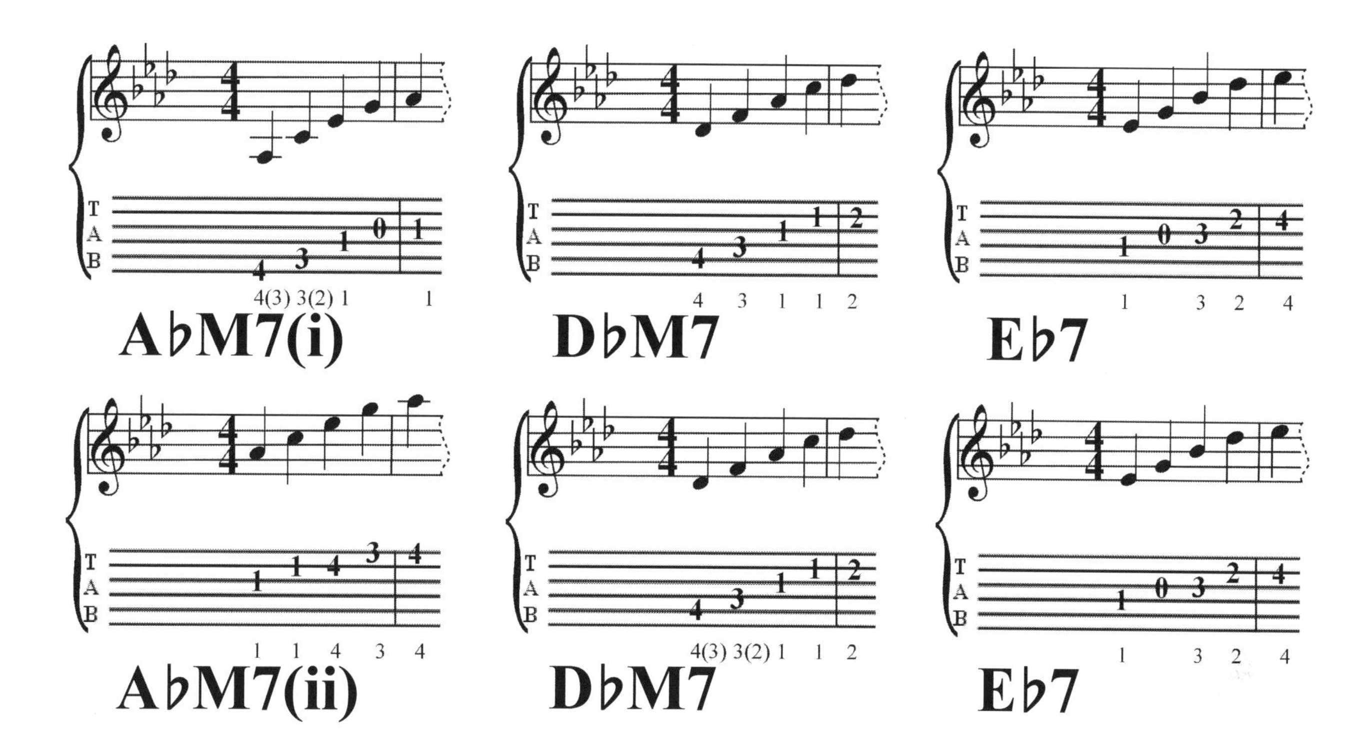

Key of E♭

Key of B♭

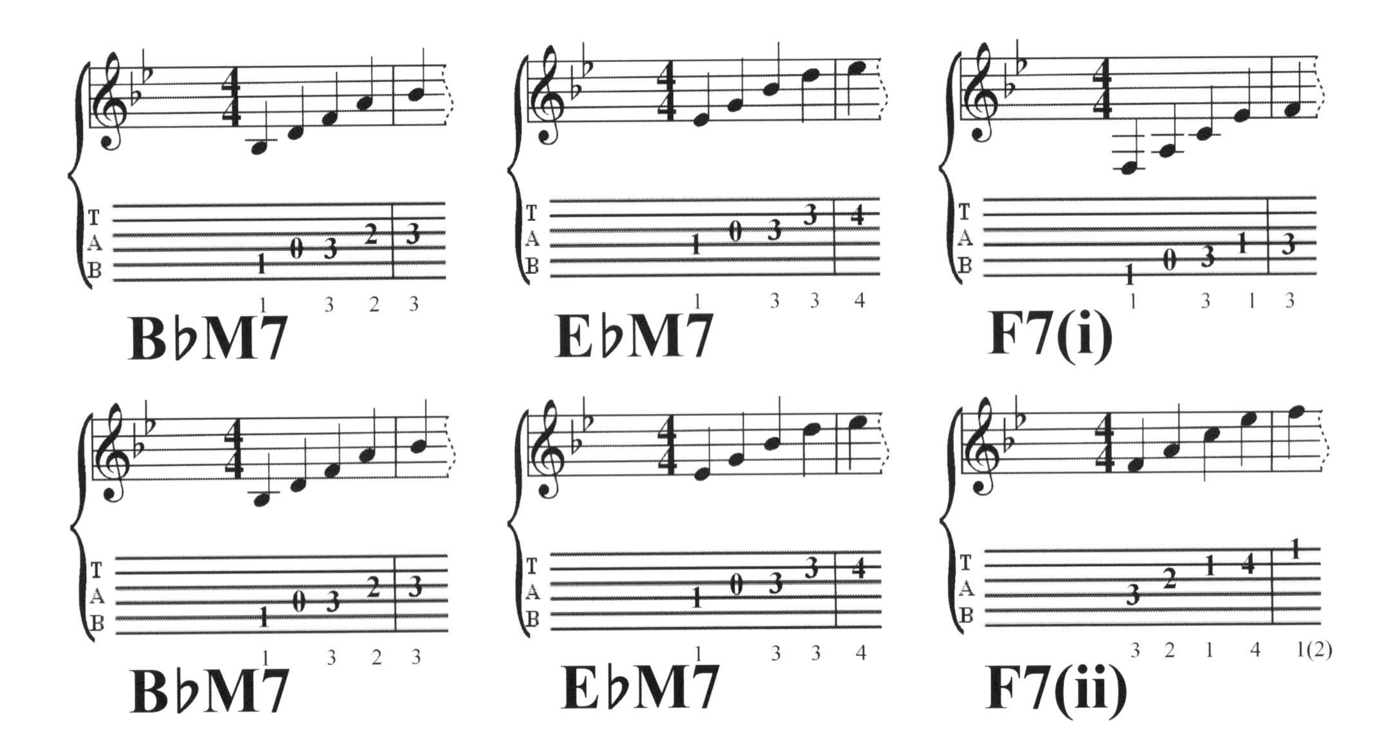

Key of F

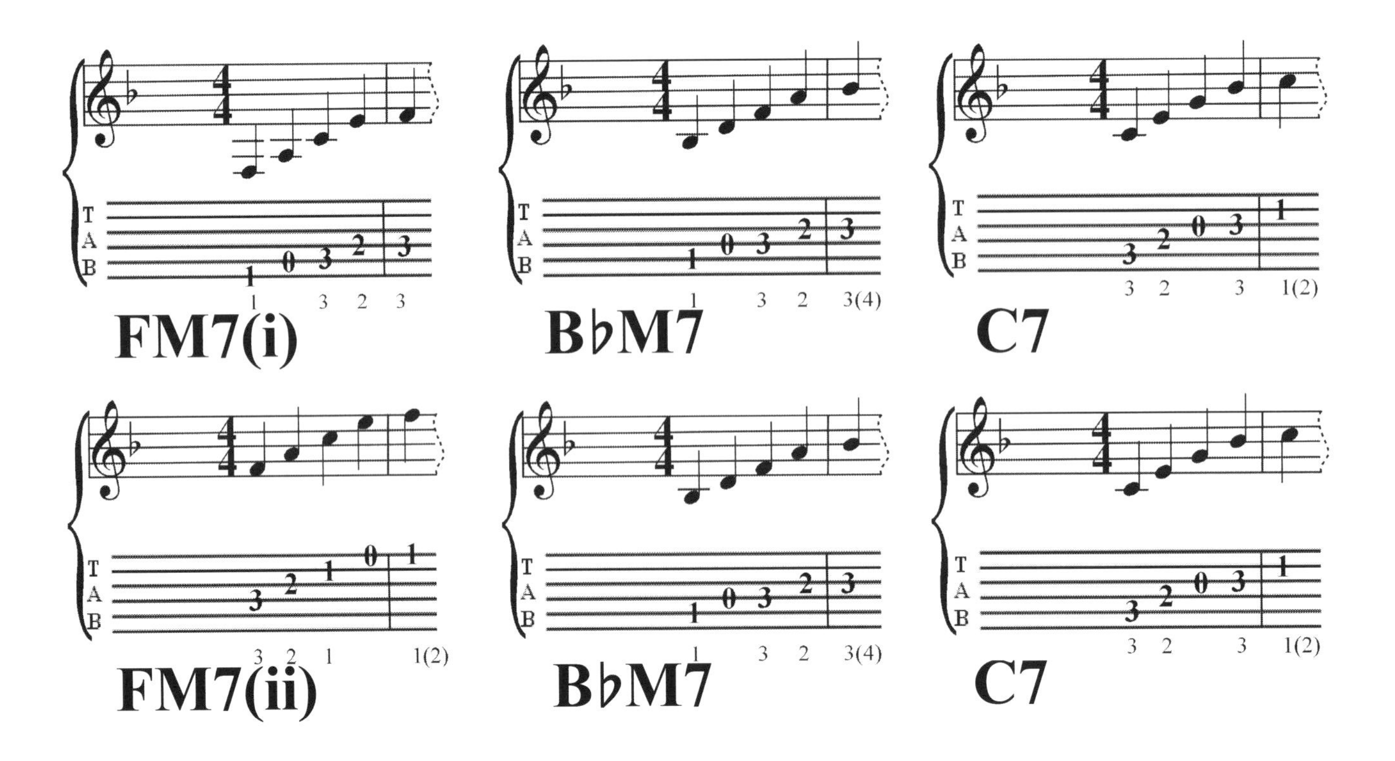

All Keys (i)

I

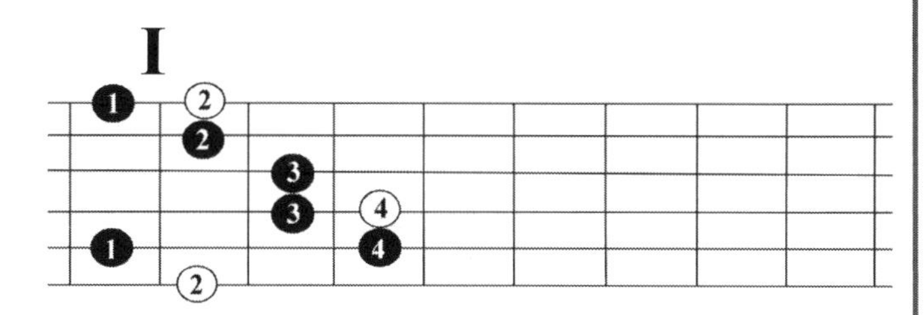

IV

V

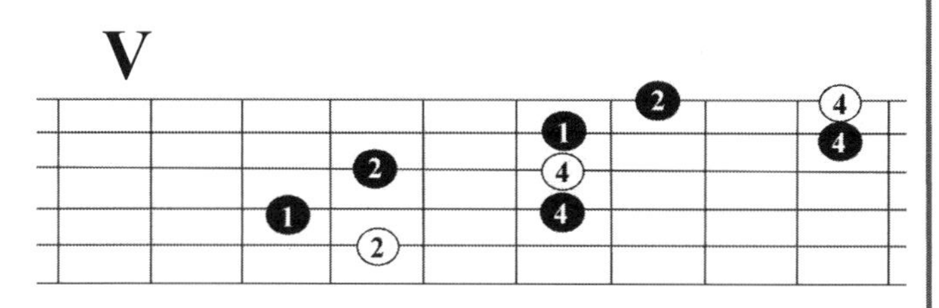

All Keys (ii)

I

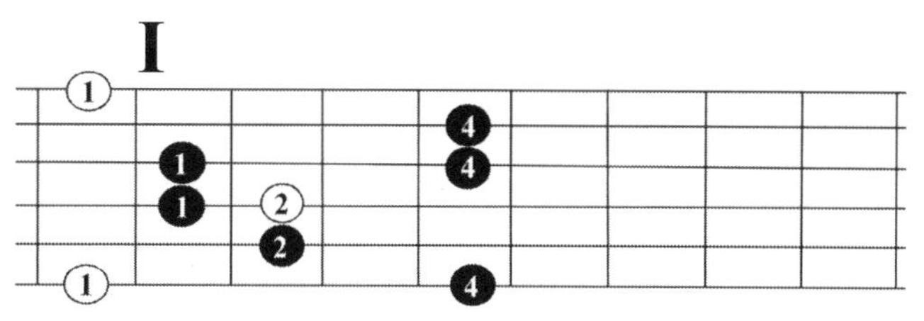

IV

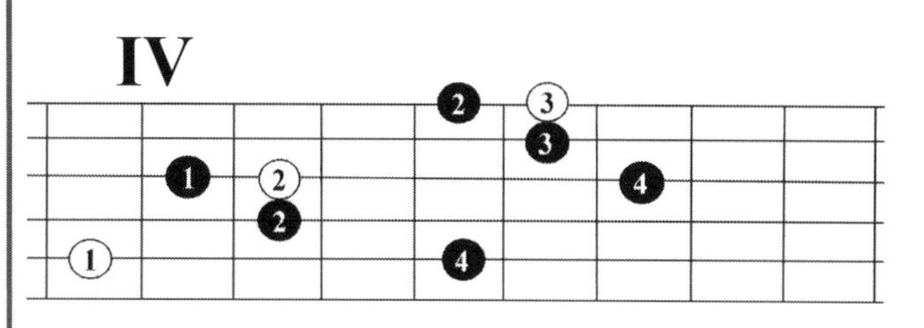

V

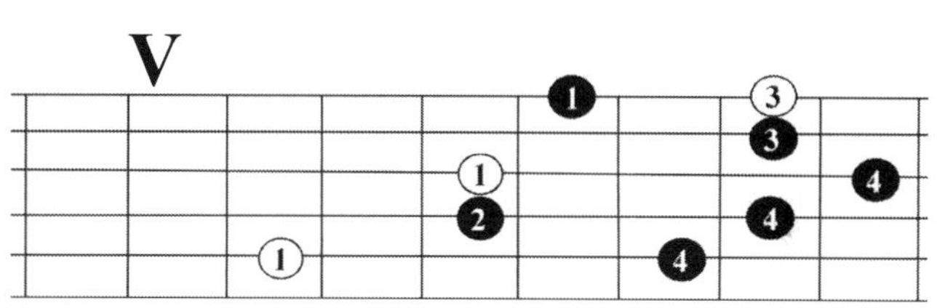

All Keys (iii)

I

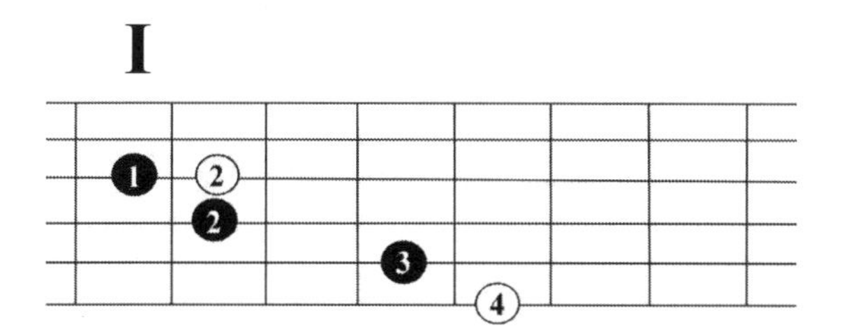

IV

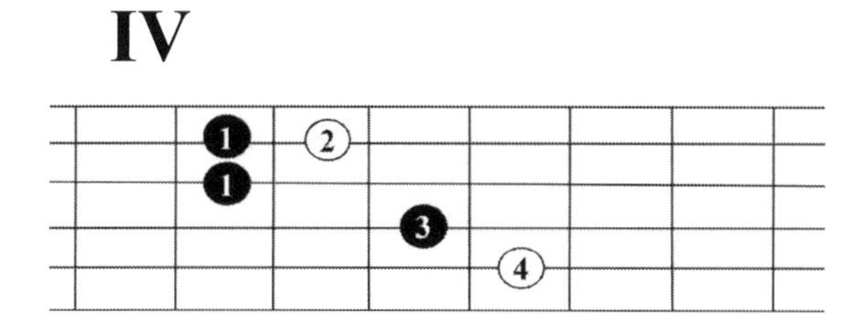

V

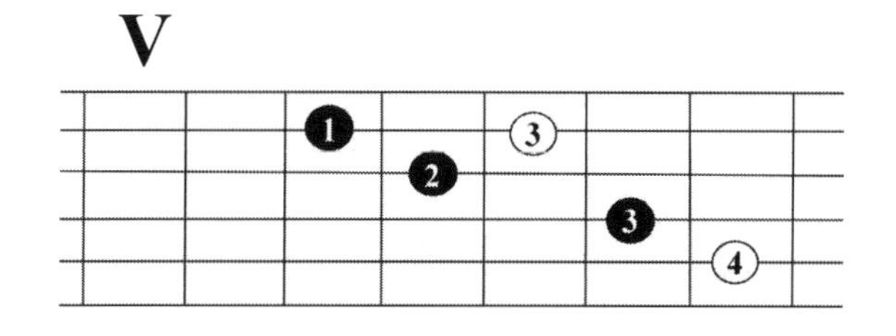

All Keys (iv)

I

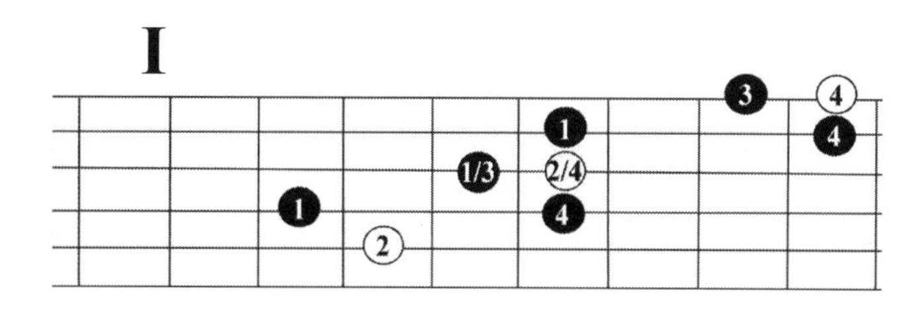

IV

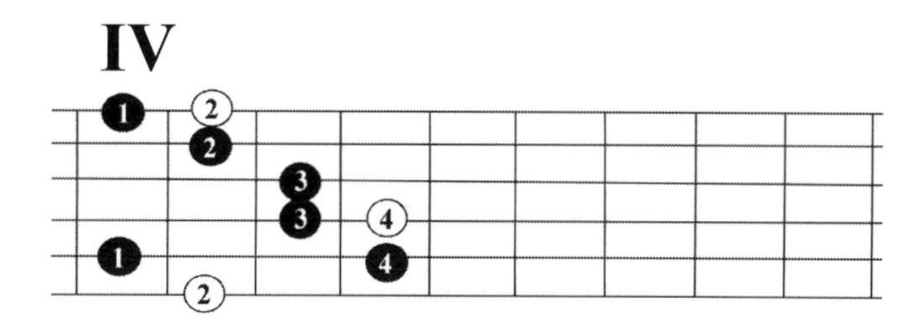

V

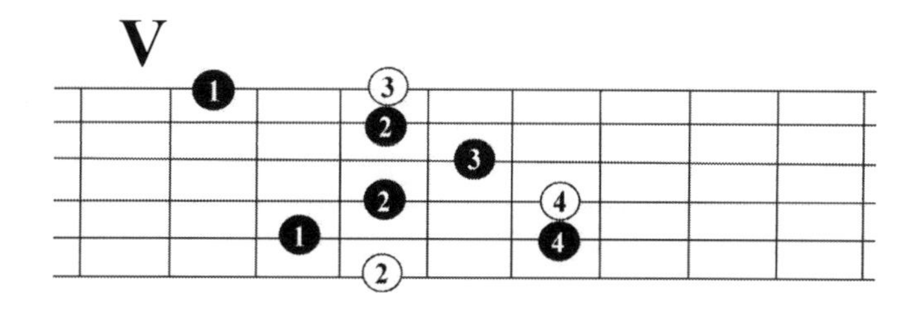

All Keys (v)

I

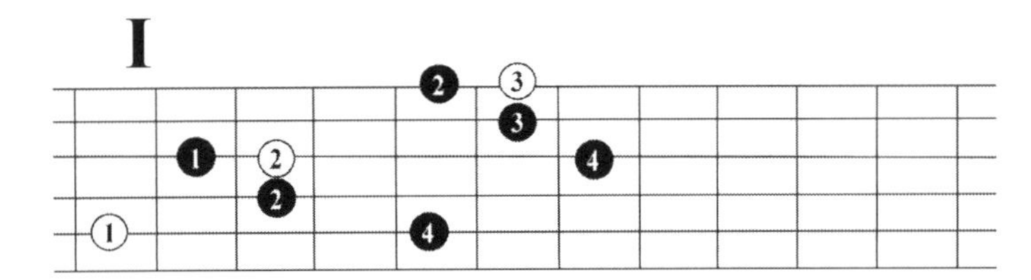

IV

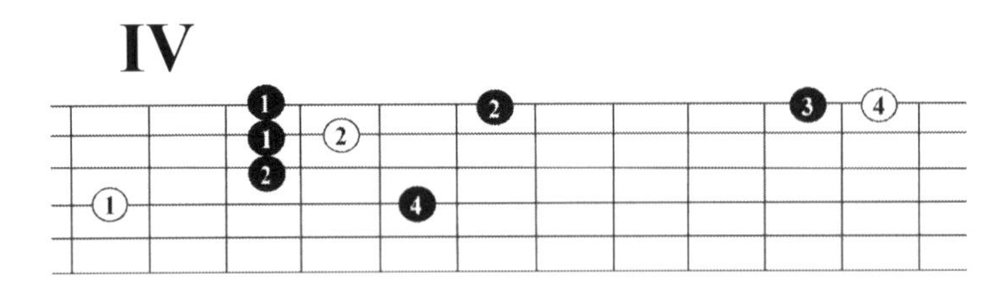

V

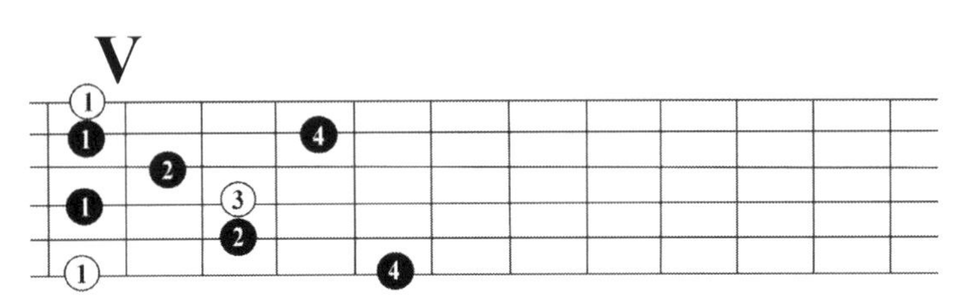

All Keys (vi)

I

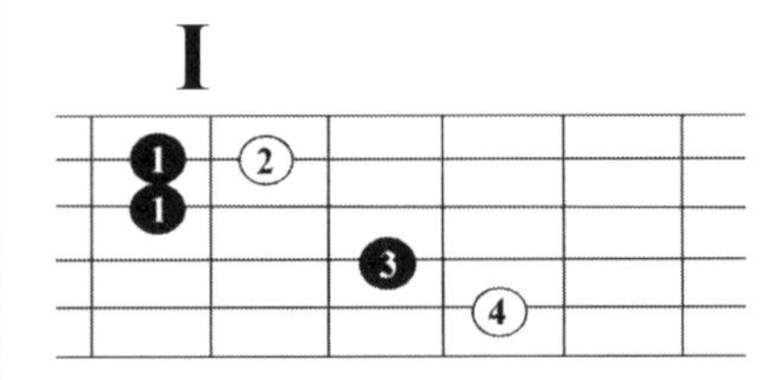

IV

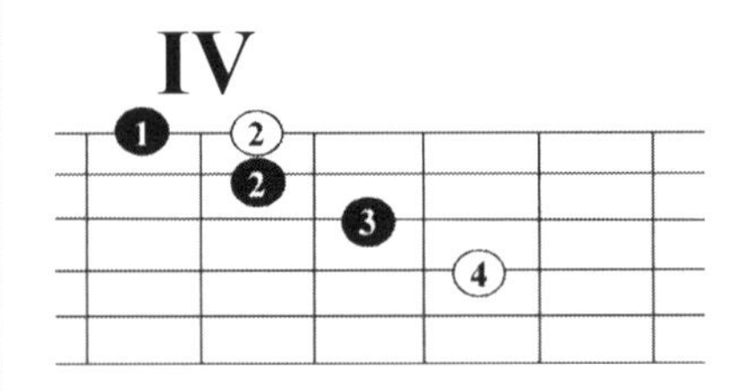

V

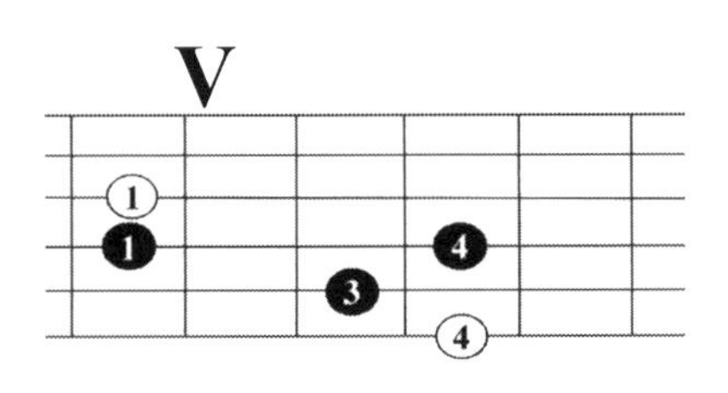

All Keys (vii)

I

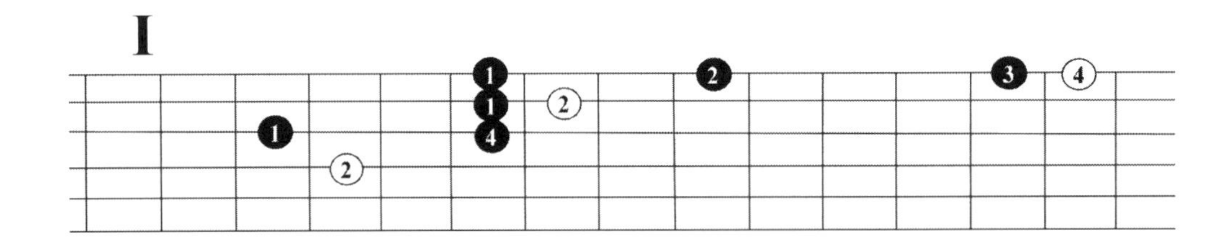

IV

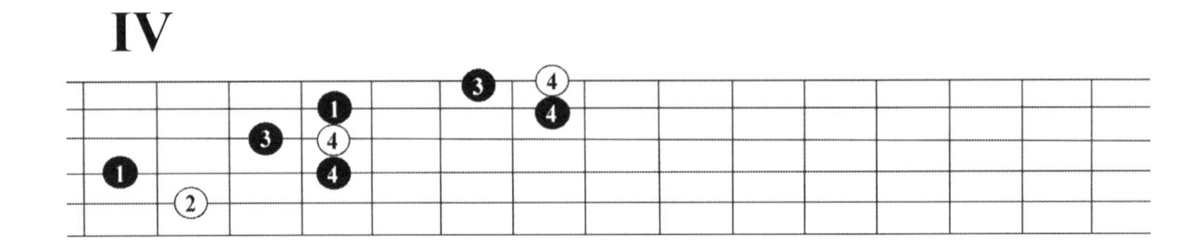

V

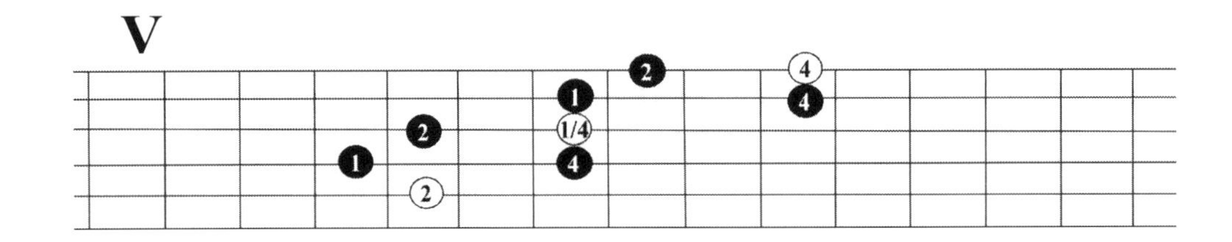

All Keys (viii)

I

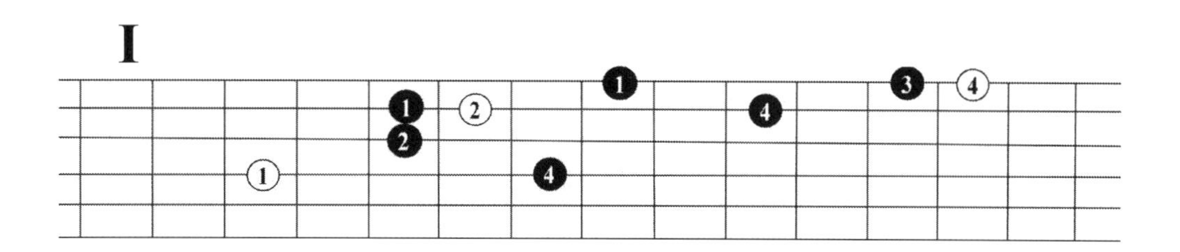

IV

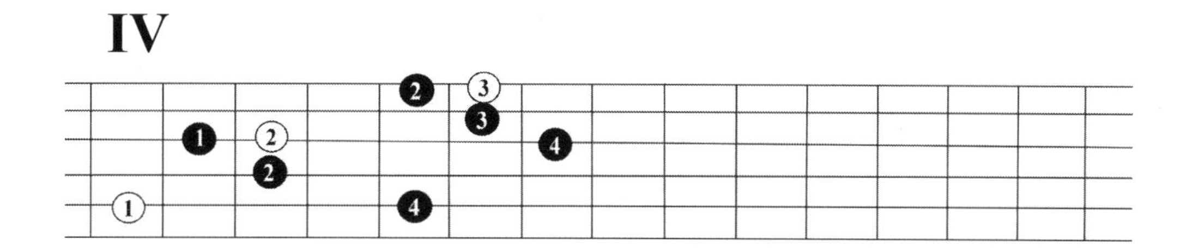

V

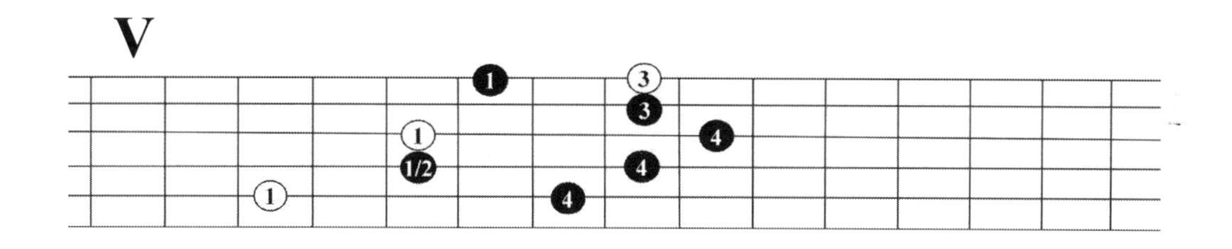

All Keys (ix)

I

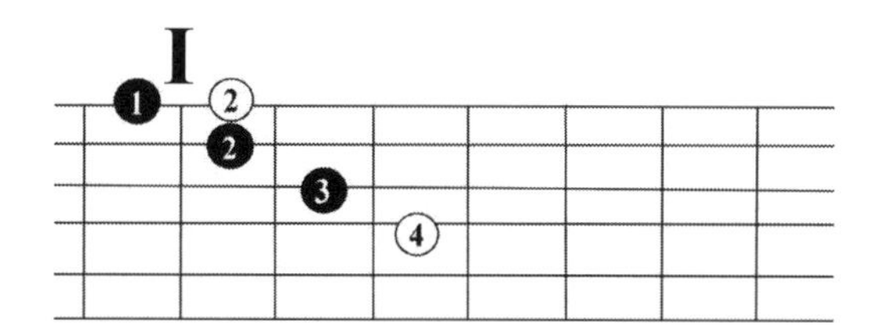

IV

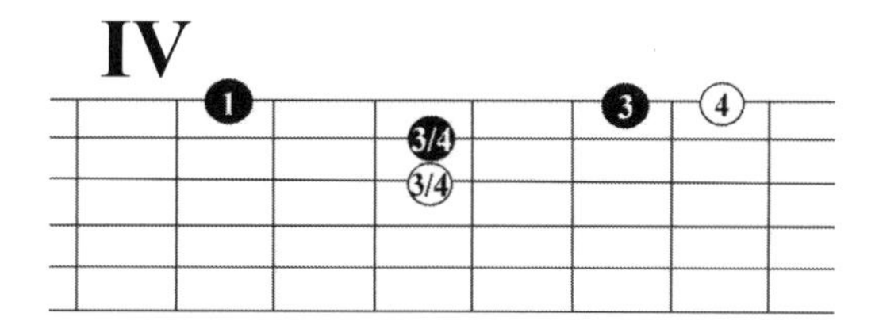

V

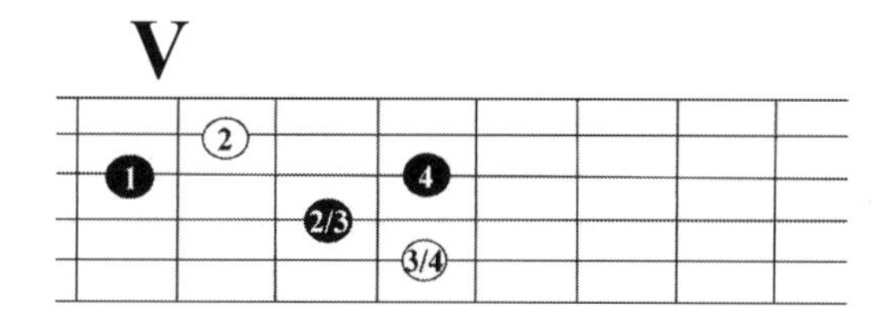

PART TWENTY

ii - V - I

MAJOR KEYS
SEVENTH CHORDS
ARPEGGIOS

Key of C

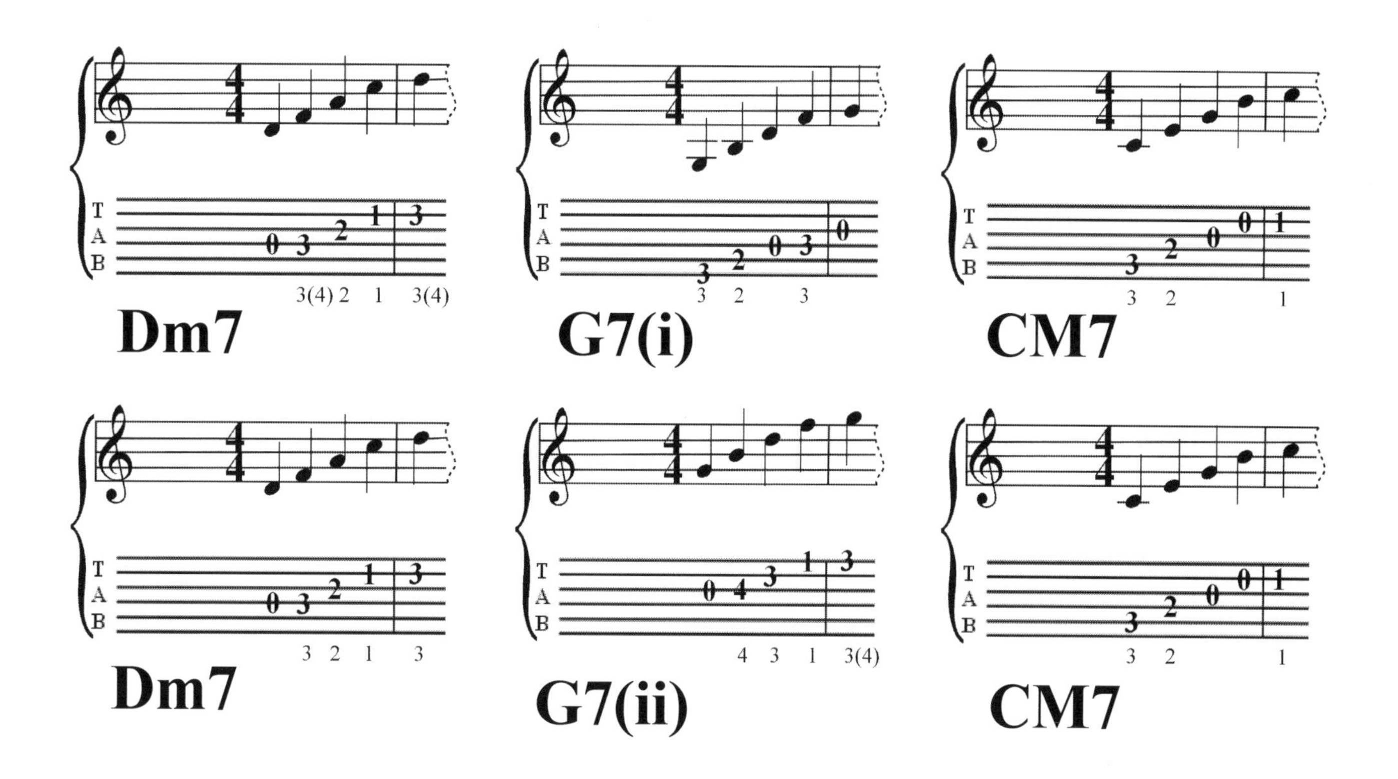

Key of G

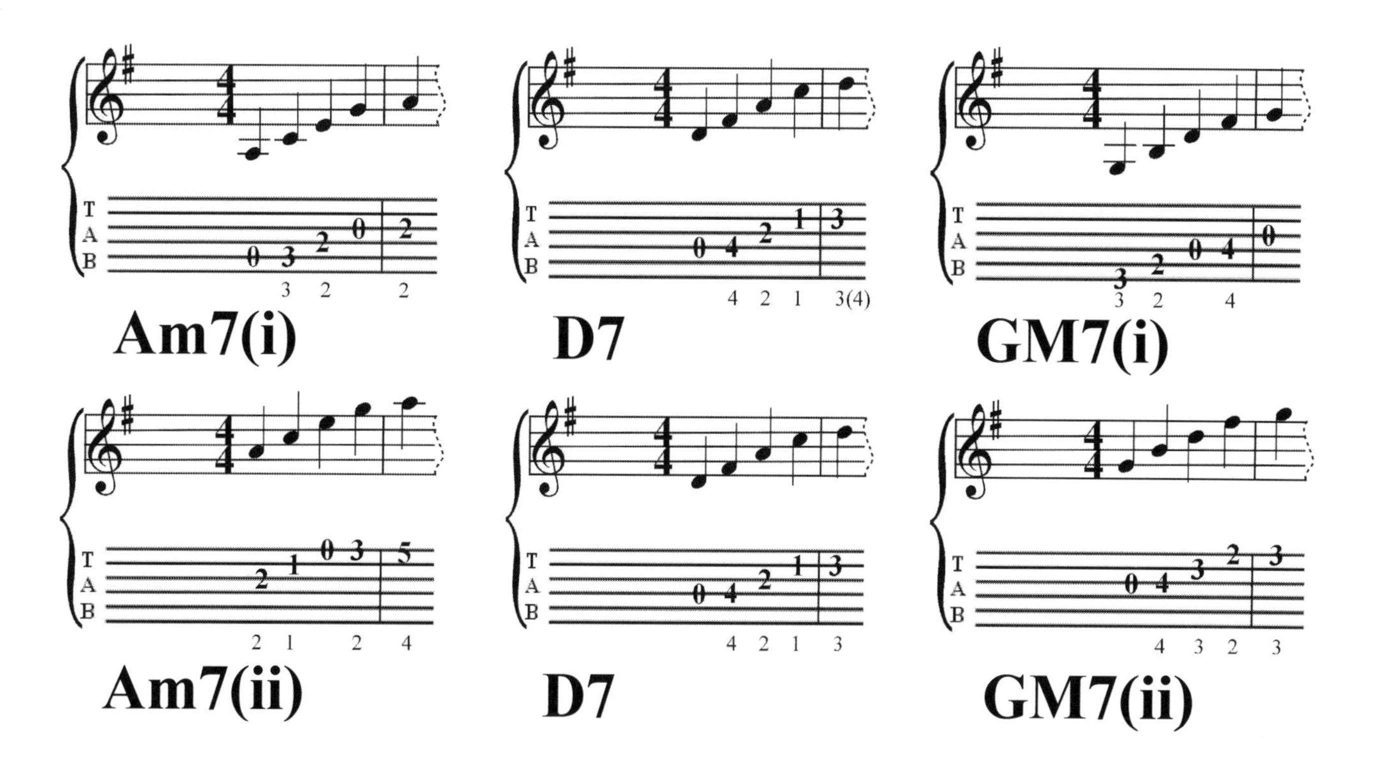

Key of D

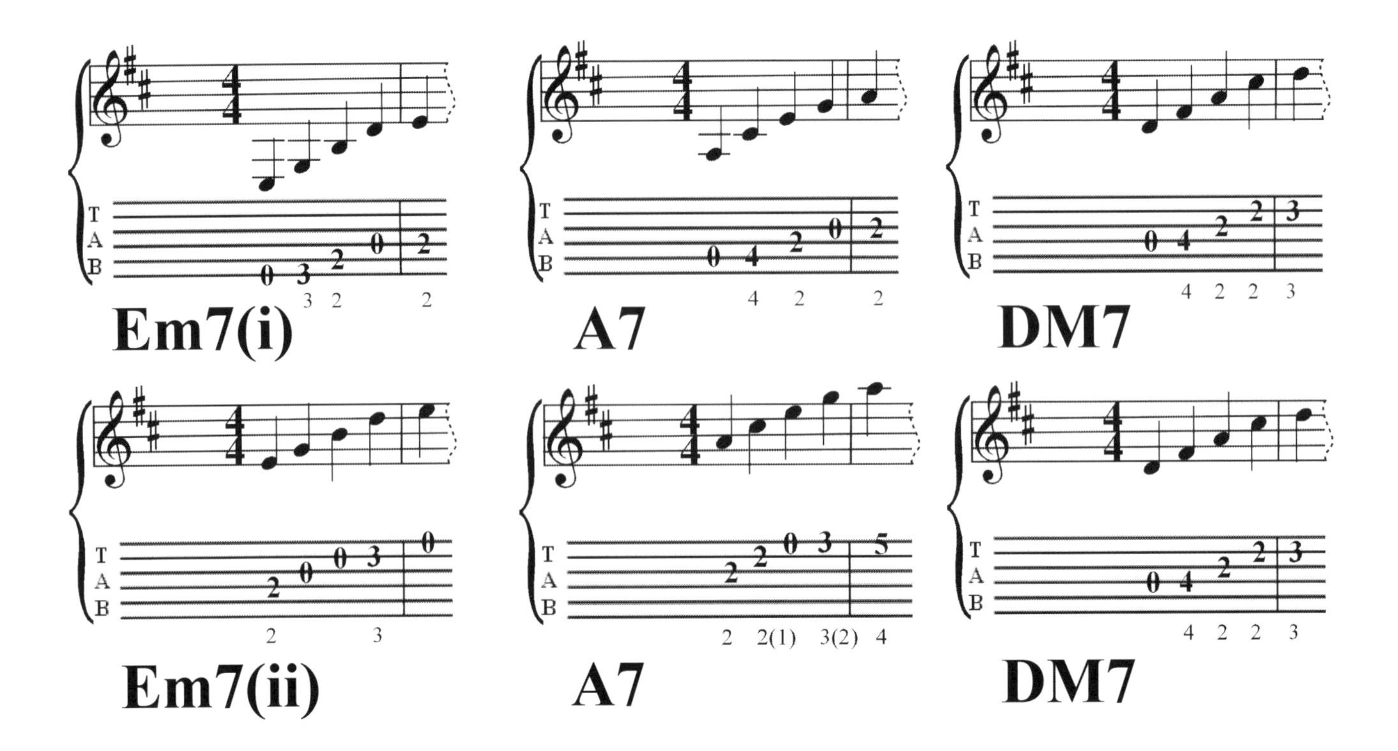

Key of A

Key of E

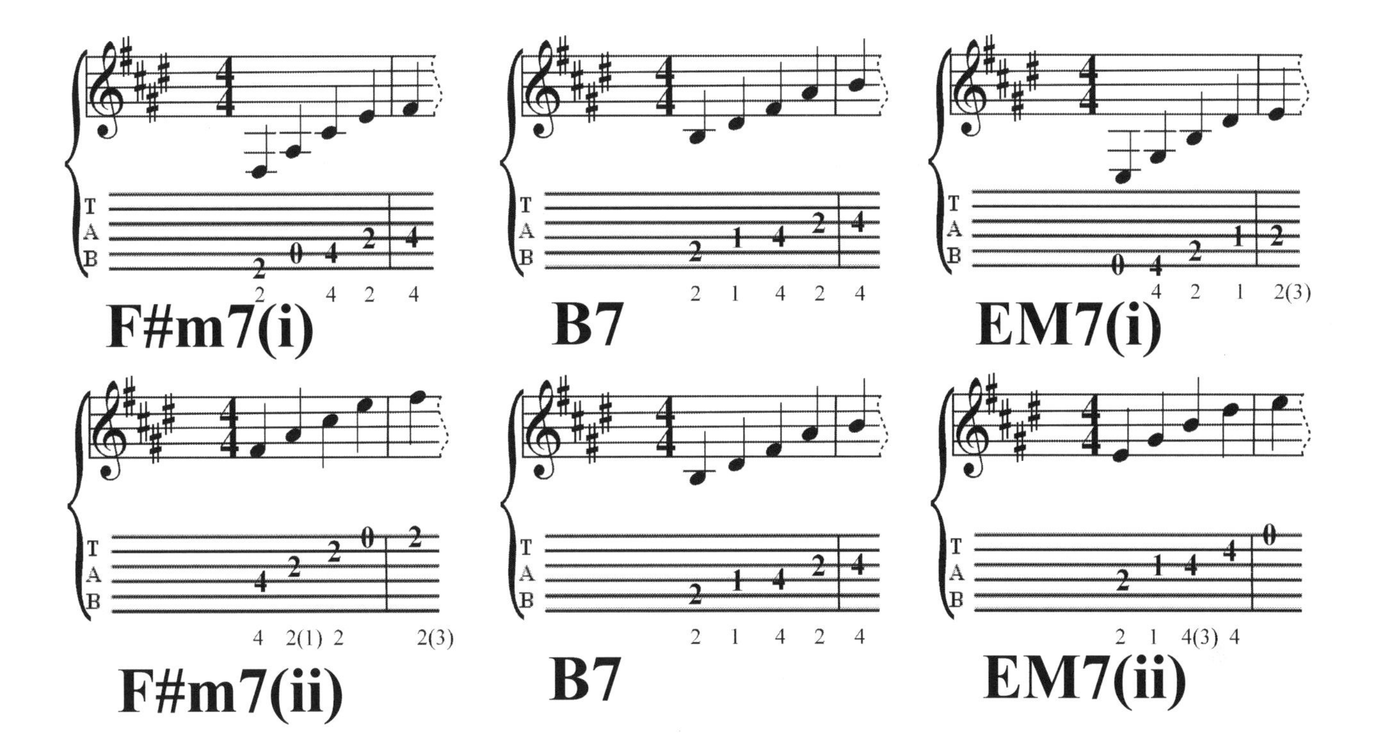

Key of B

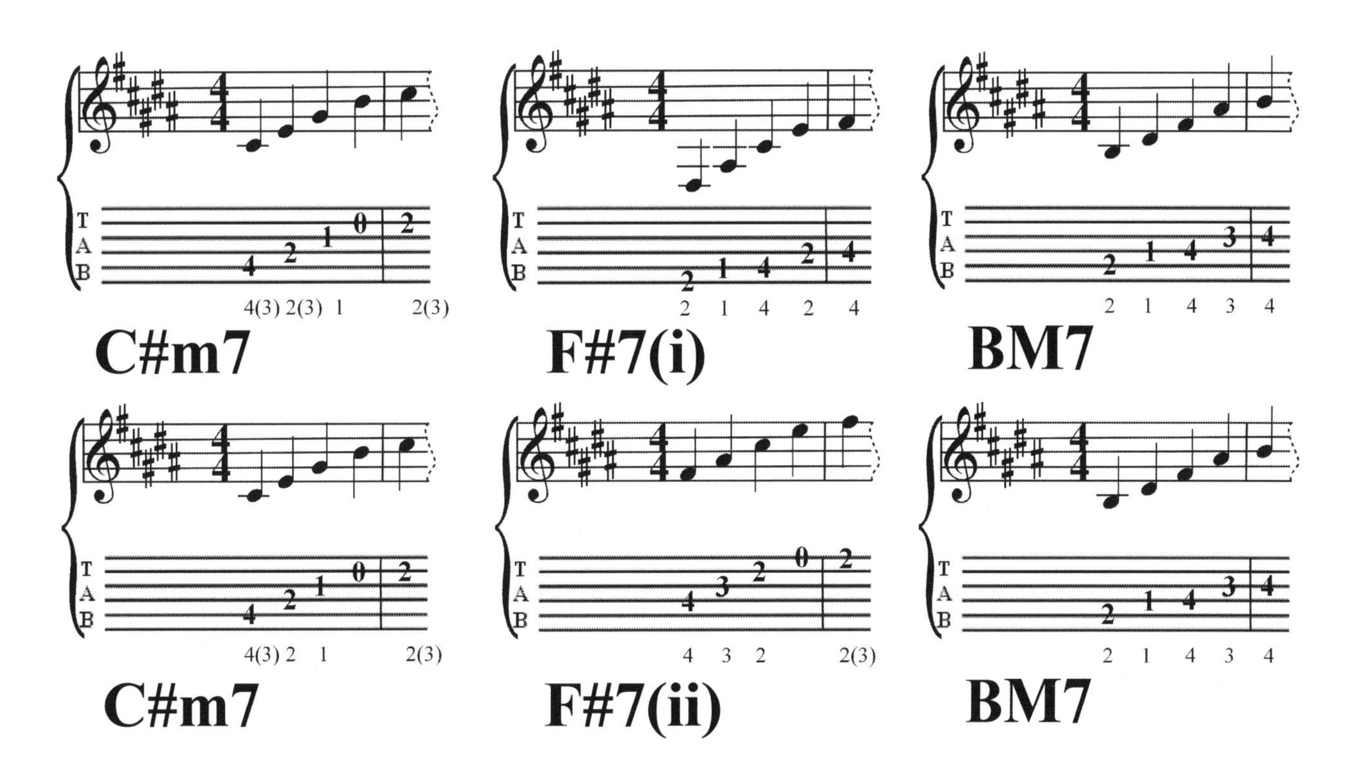

Key of F#

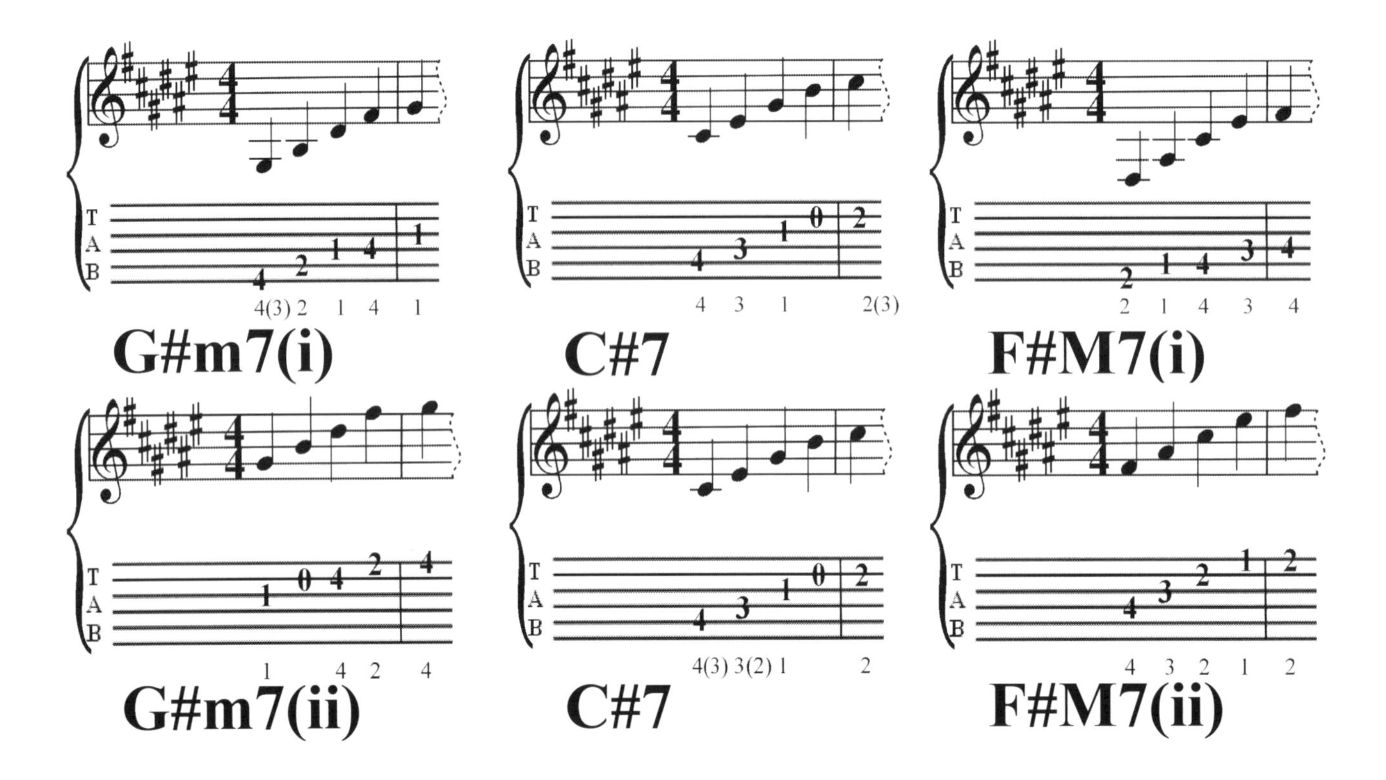

Key of C#

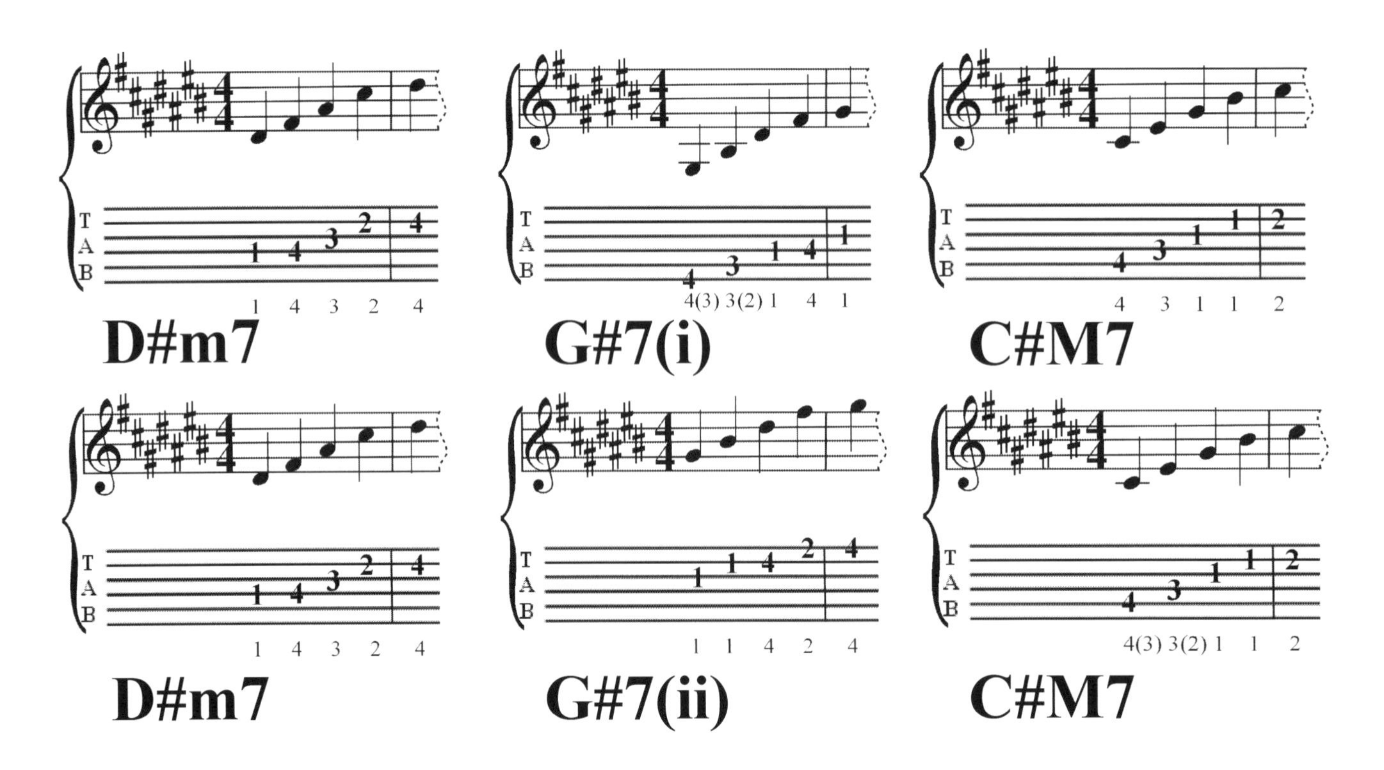

Key of A♭

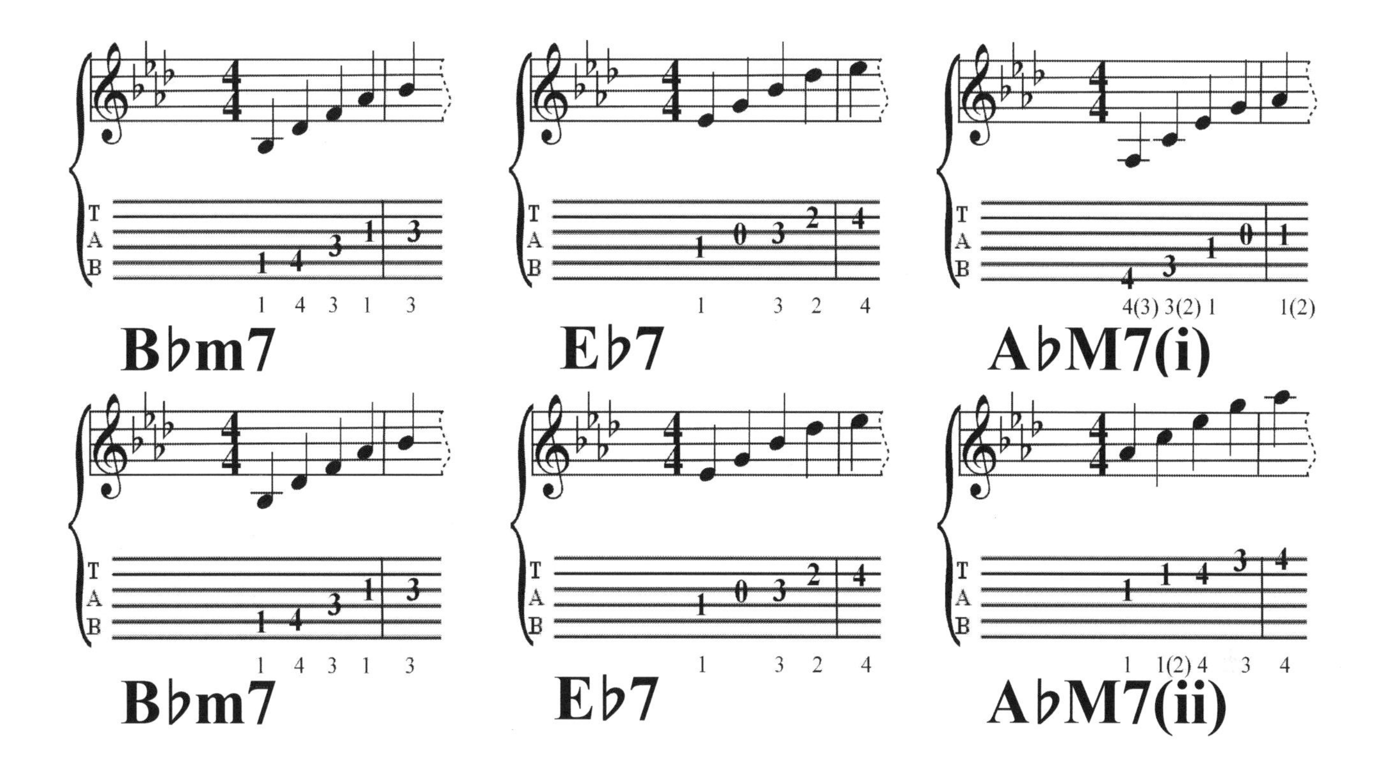

Key of E♭

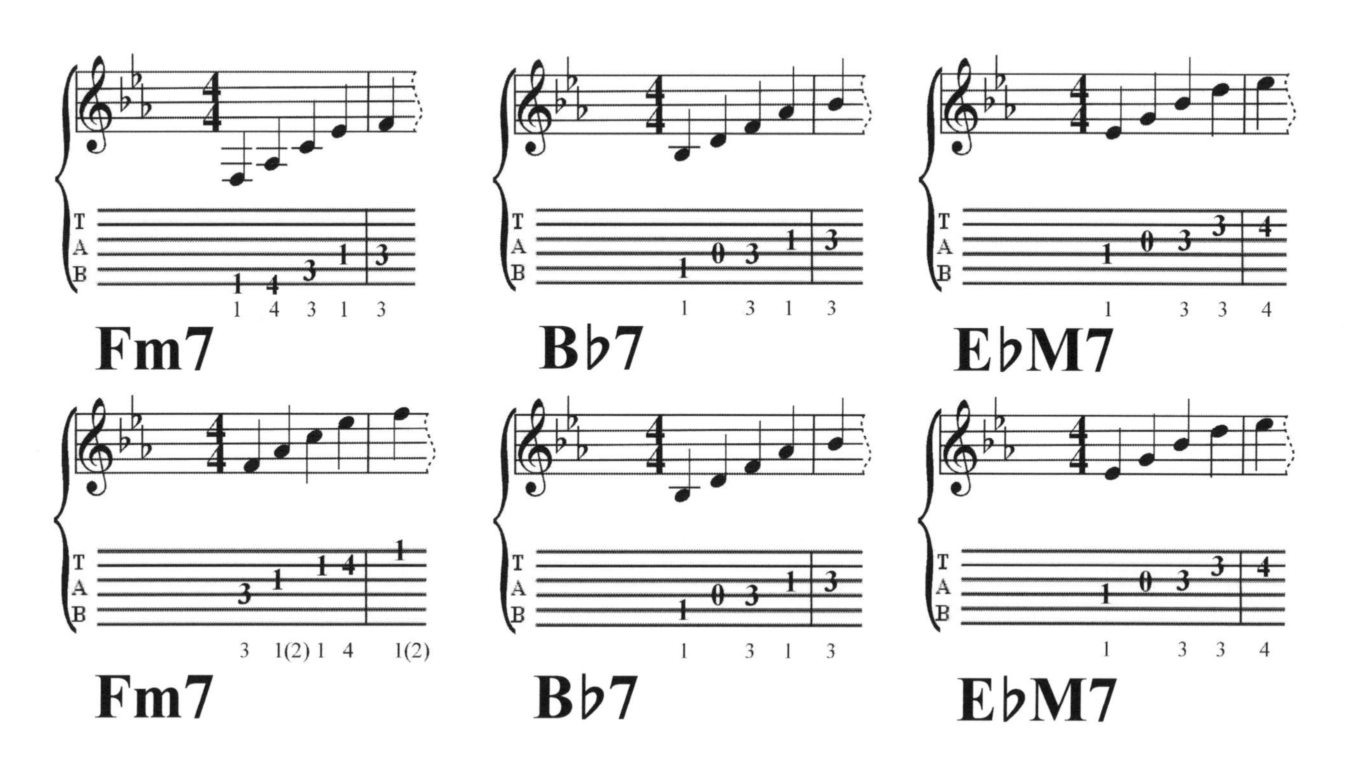

Key of B♭

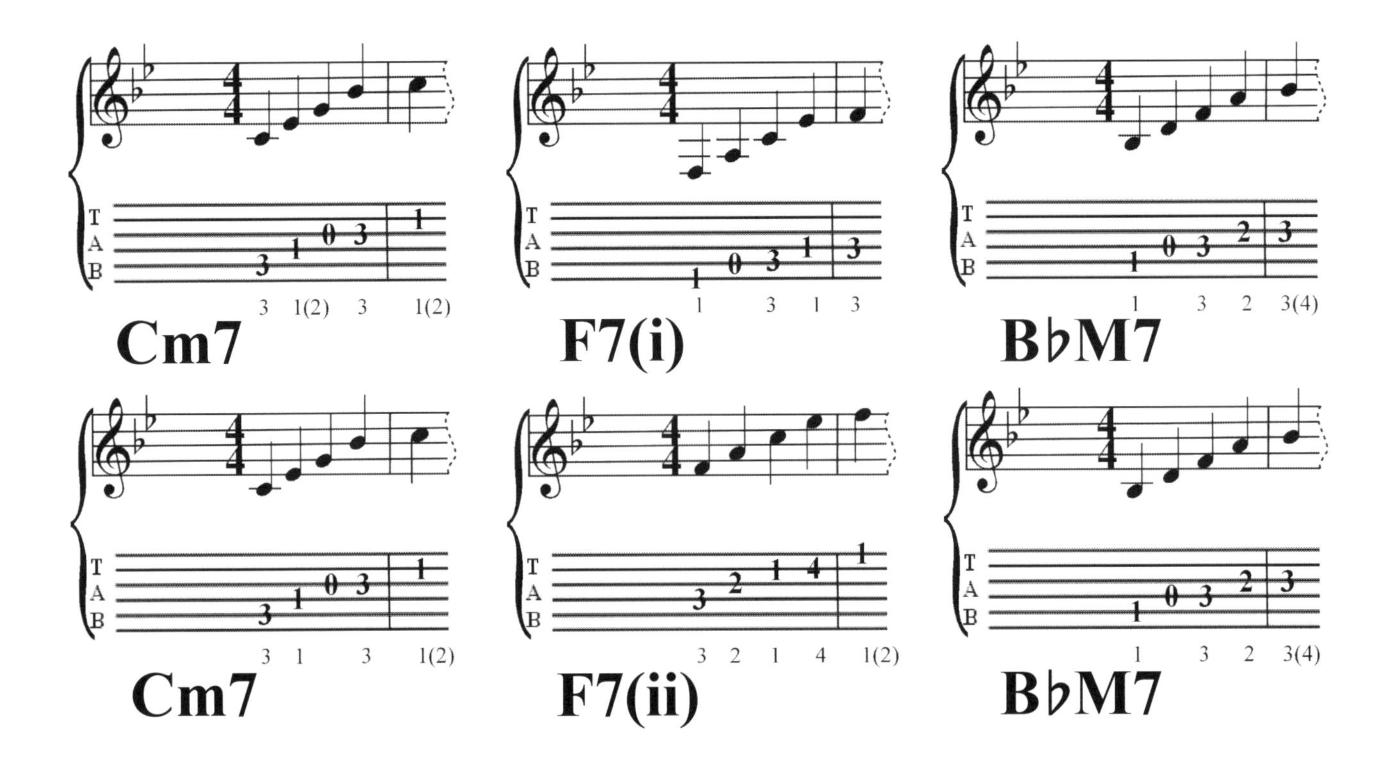

Key of F

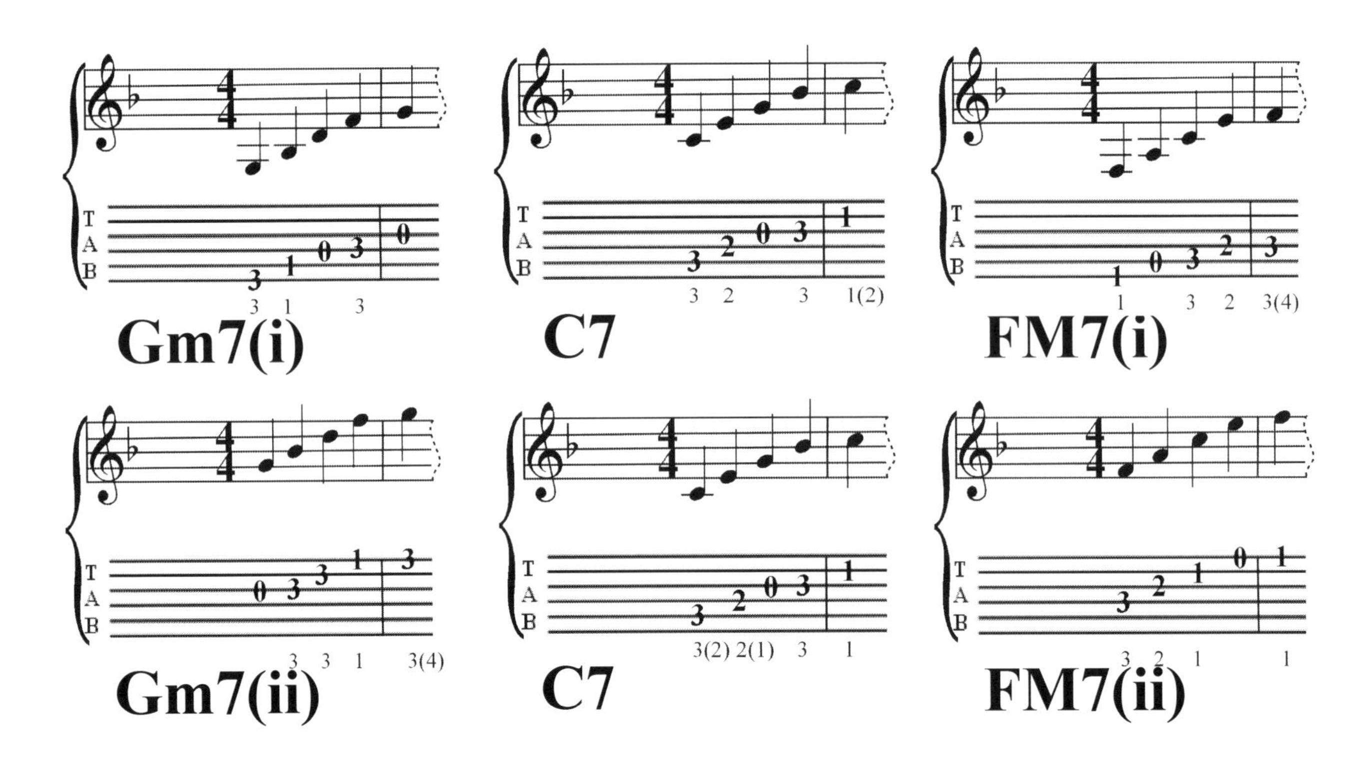

All Keys (i)

ii

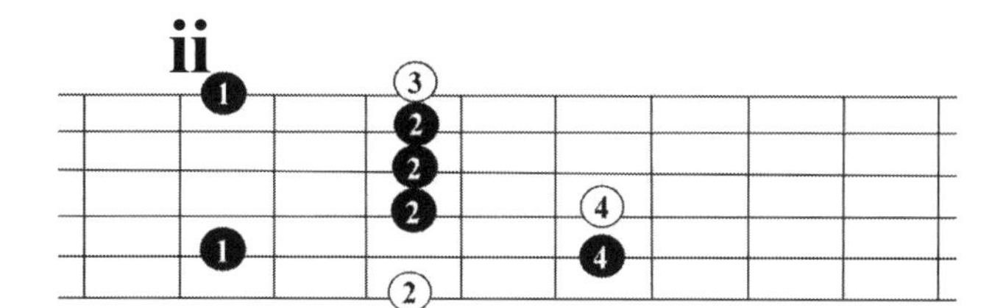

V

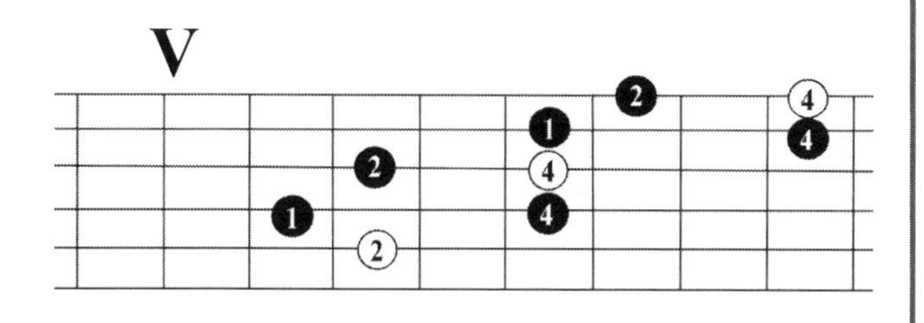

I

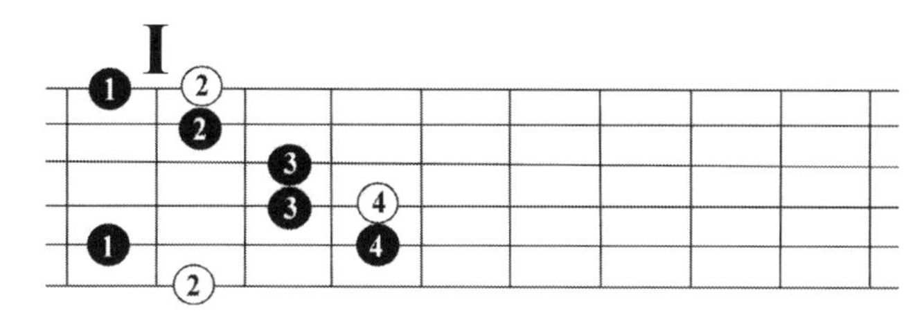

All Keys (ii)

ii

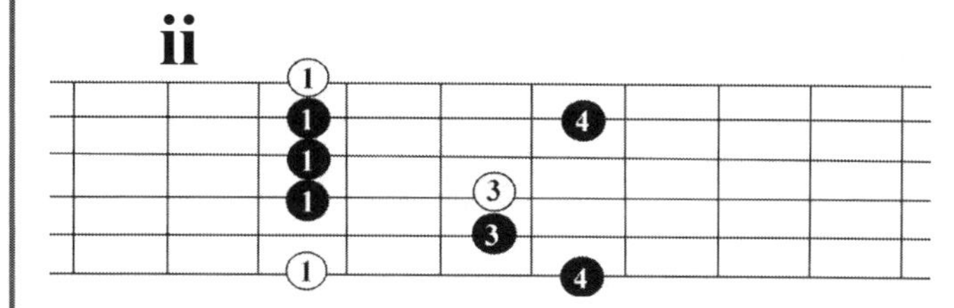

V

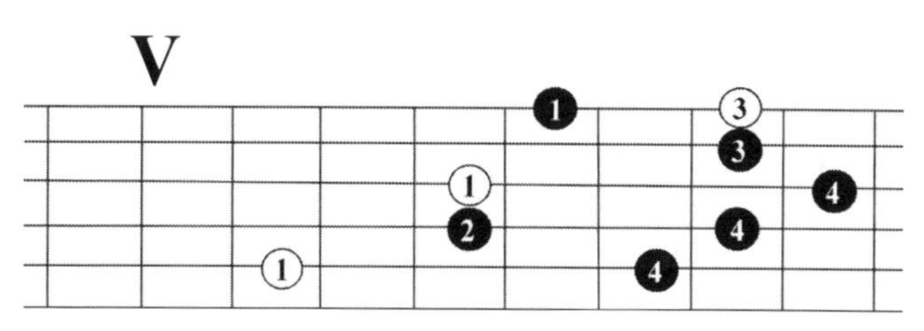

I

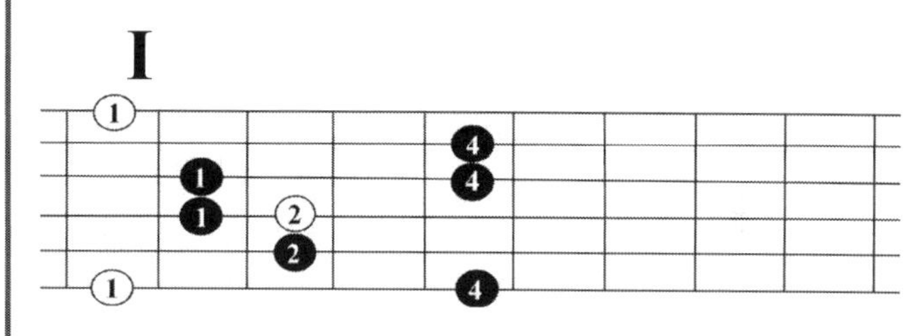

All Keys (iii)

ii

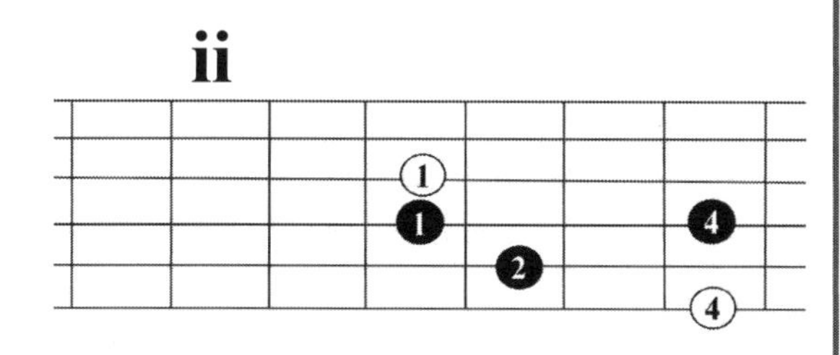

V

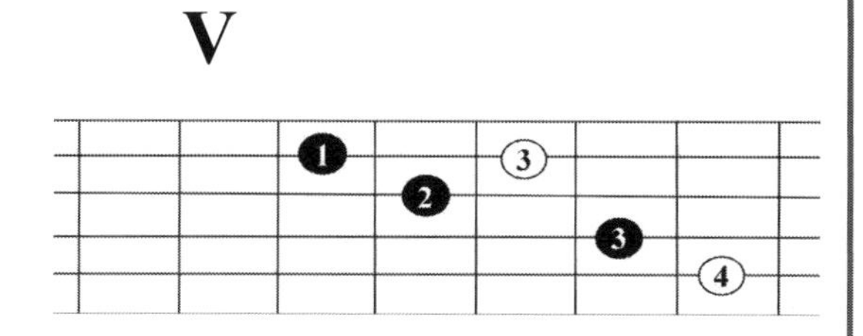

I

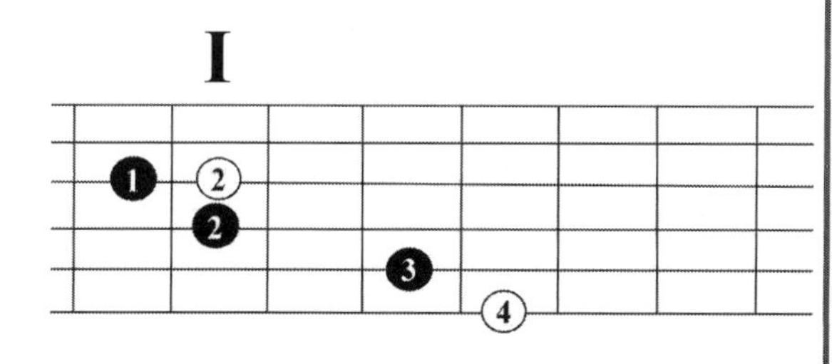

All Keys (iv)

ii

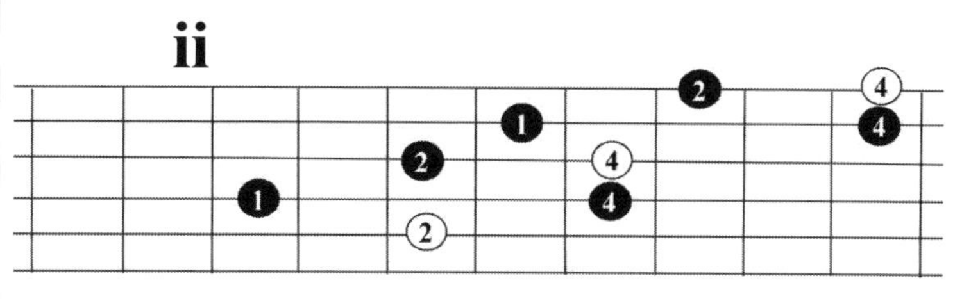

V

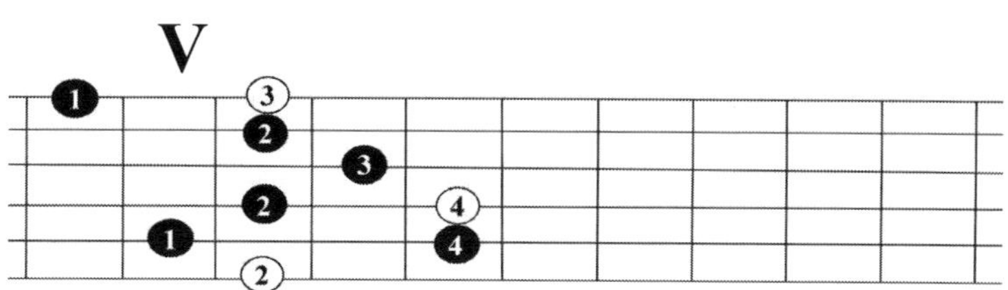

I

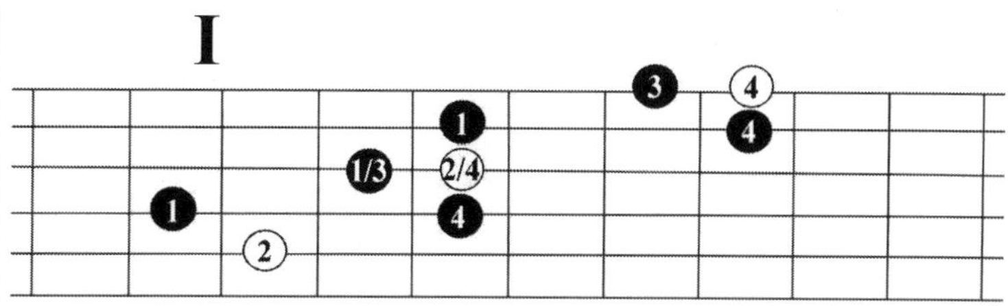

All Keys (v)

ii

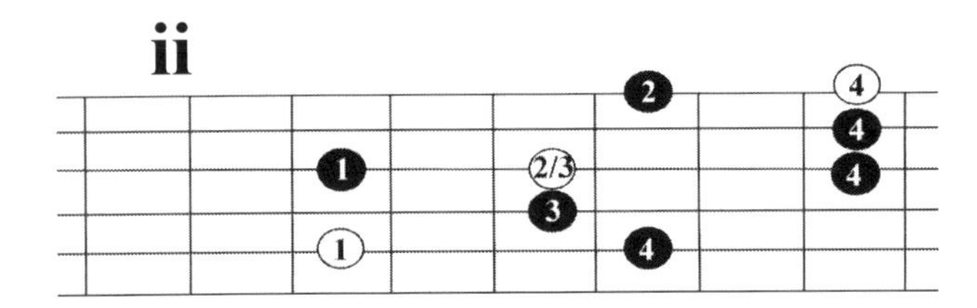

V

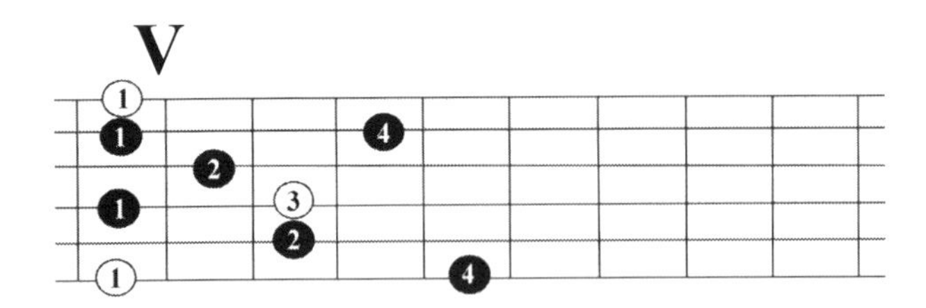

I

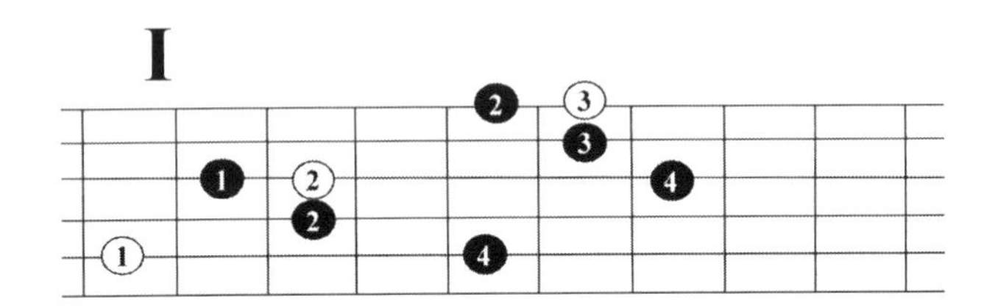

All Keys (vi)

ii

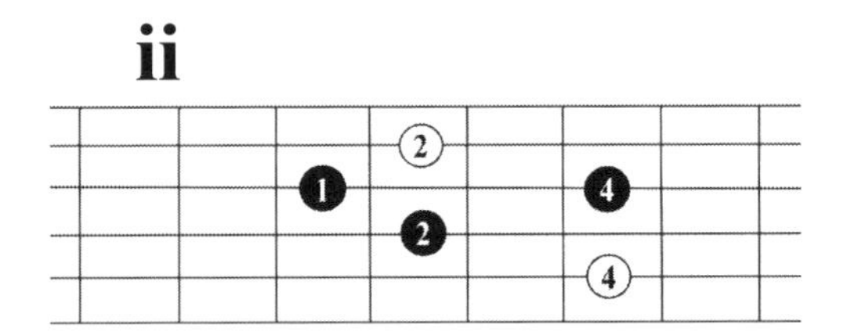

V

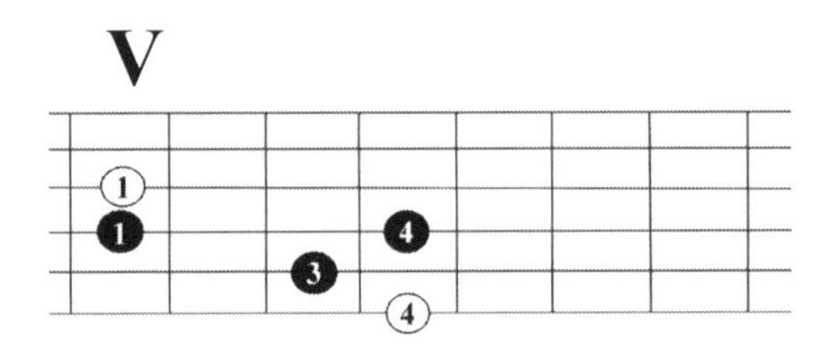

I

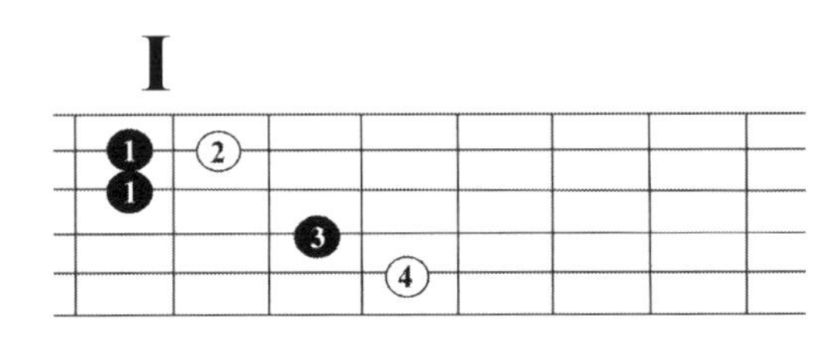

All Keys (vii)

ii

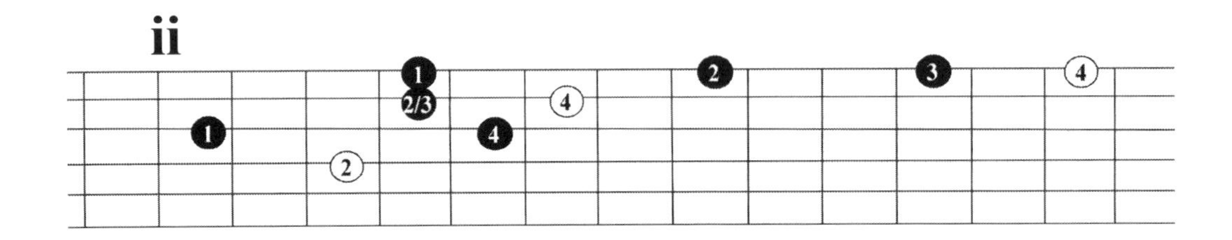

V

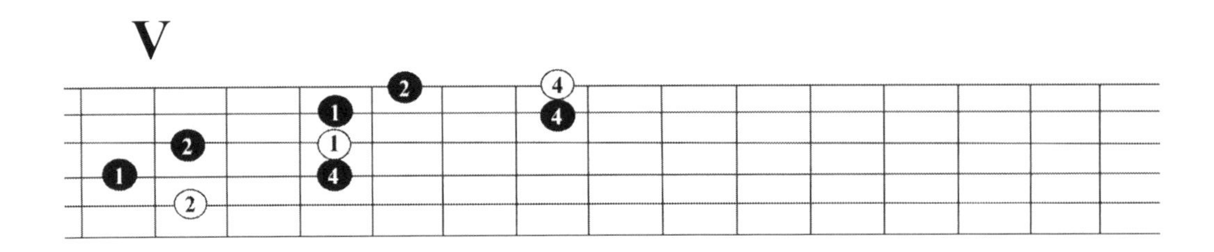

I

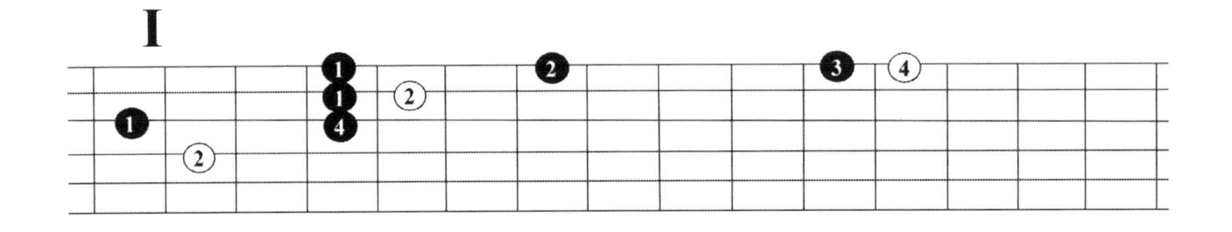

All Keys (viii)

ii

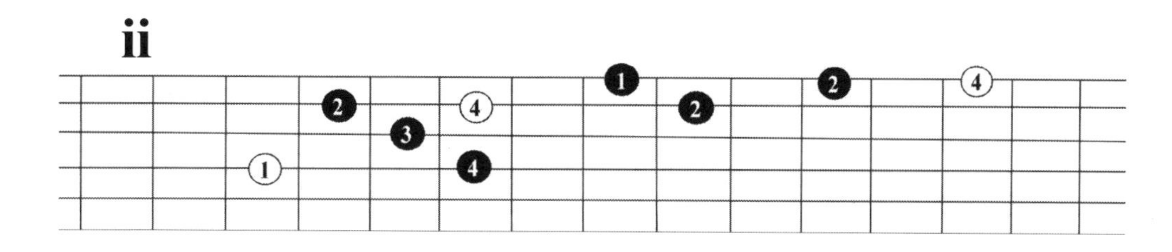

V

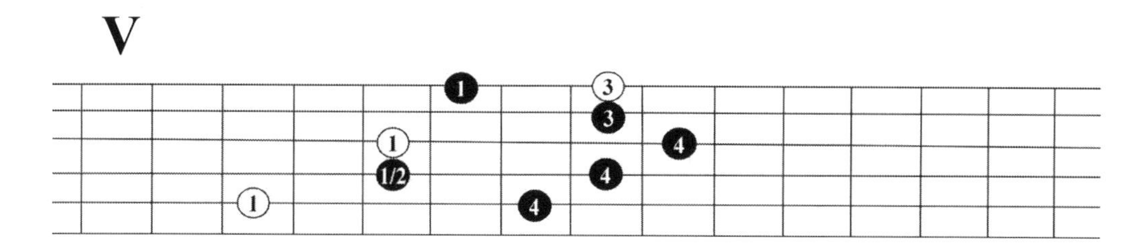

I

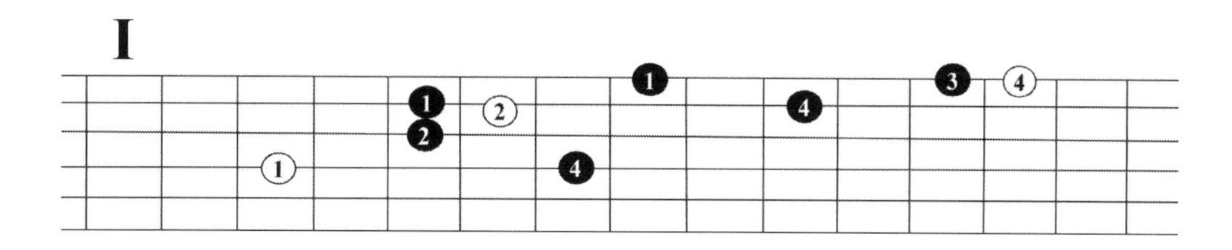

All Keys (ix)

ii

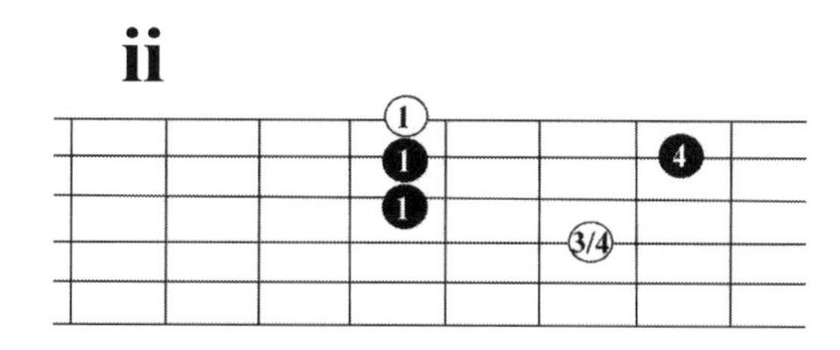

V

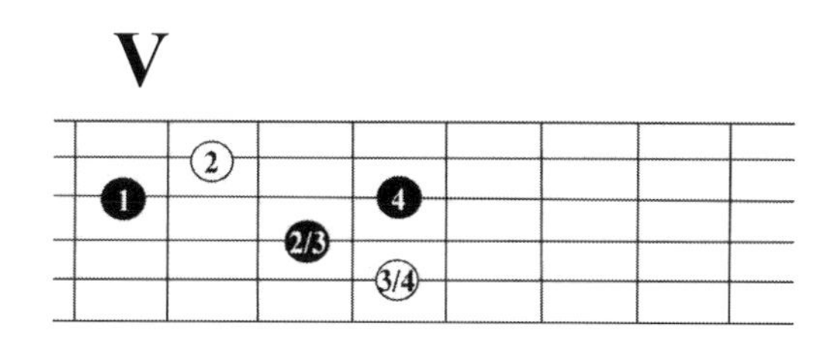

I

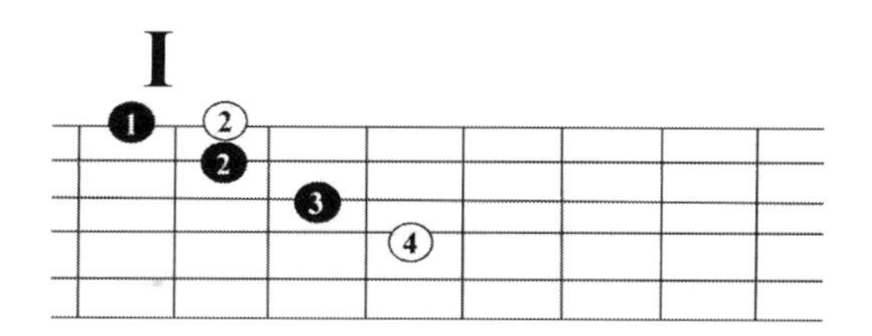

PART TWENTY-ONE

vi - ii - V - I

MAJOR KEYS
SEVENTH CHORDS
ARPEGGIOS

Key of C

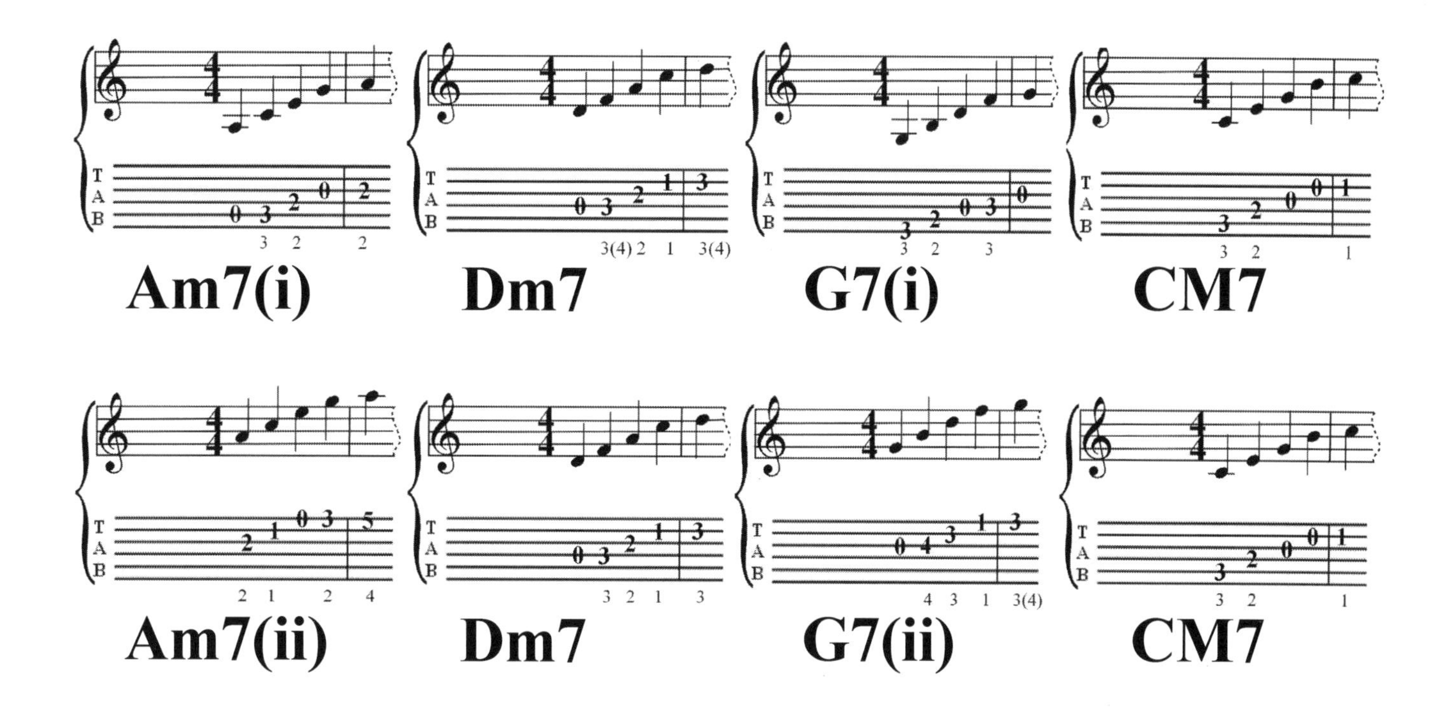

Key of G

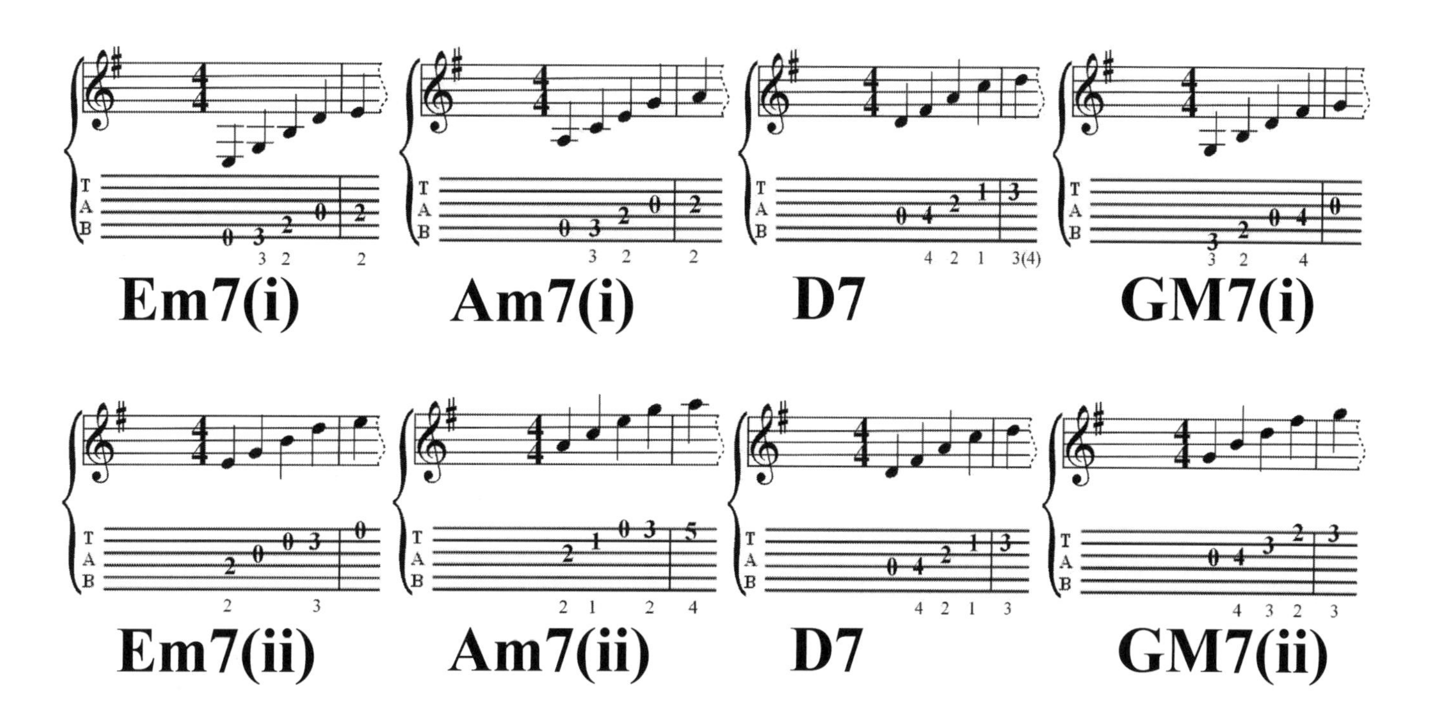

Key of D

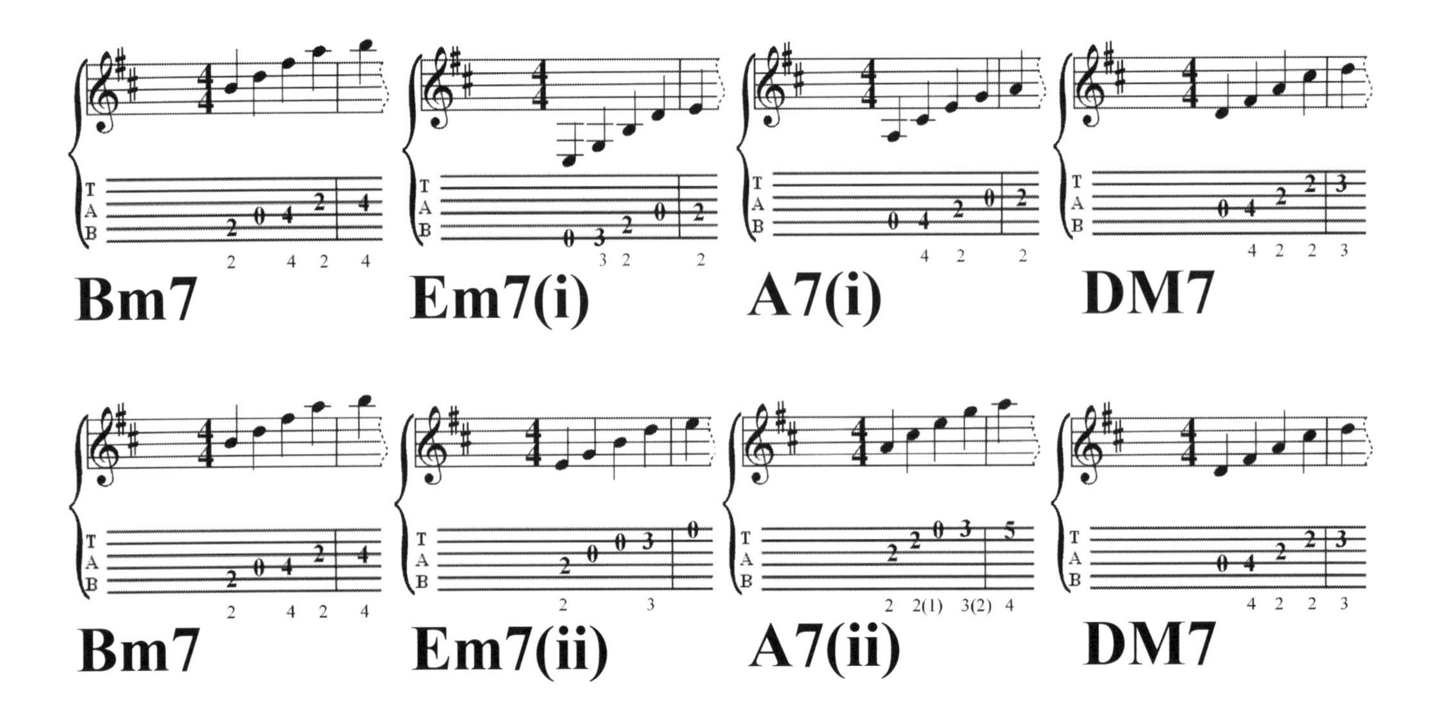

Key of A

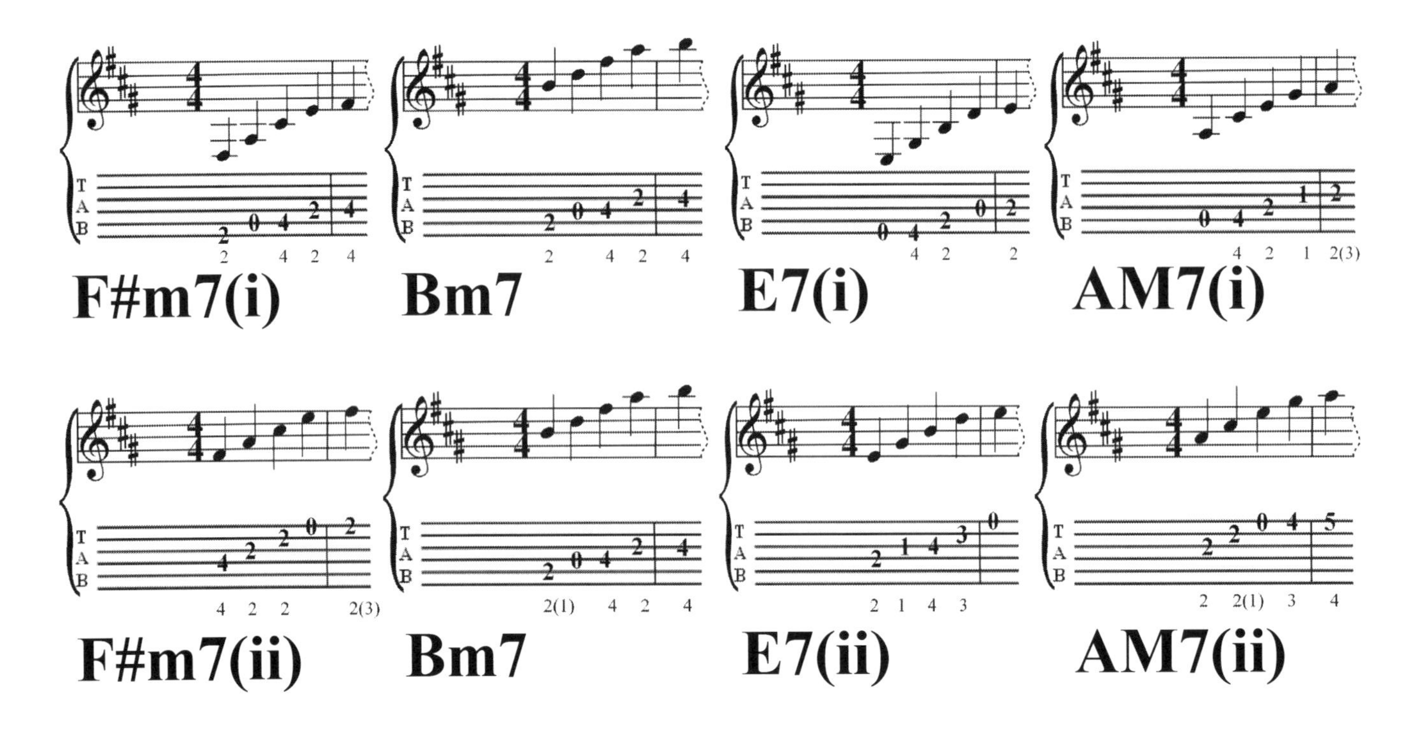

Key of E

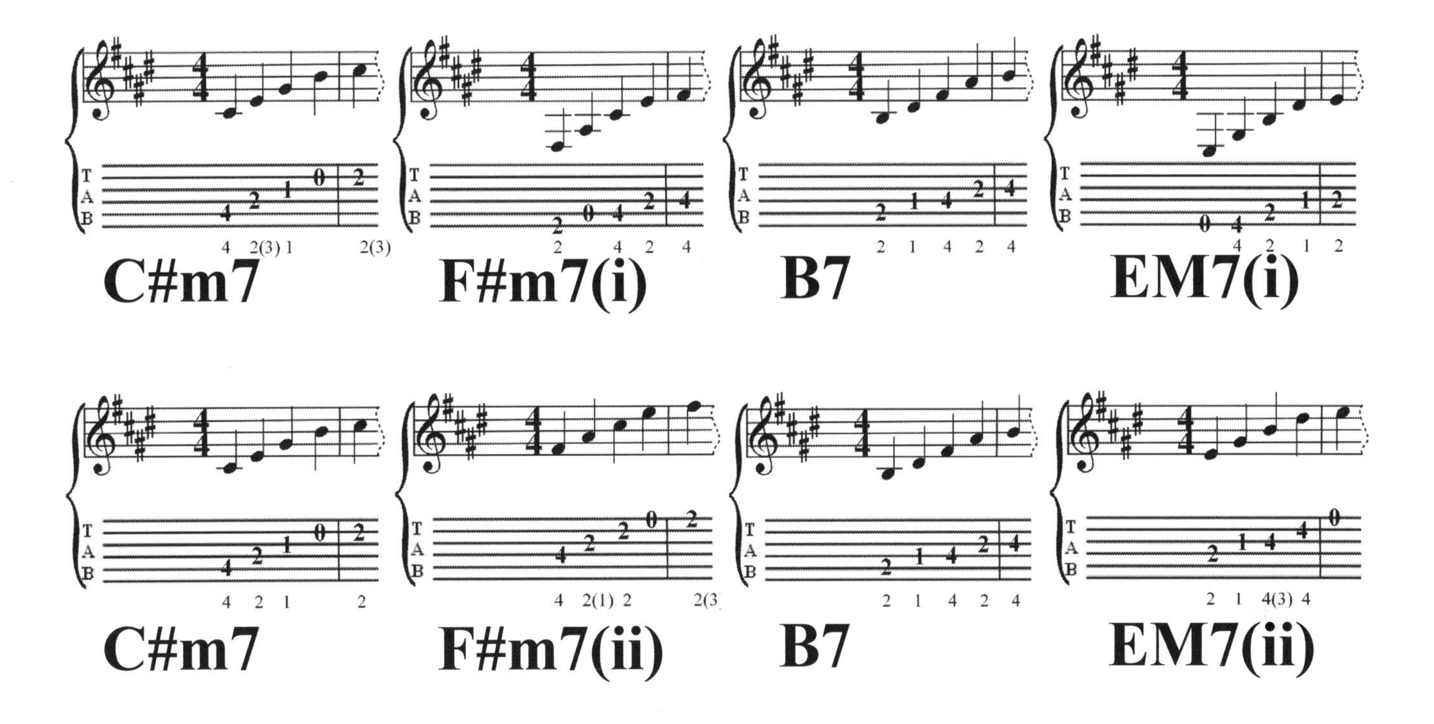

Key of B

Key of F#

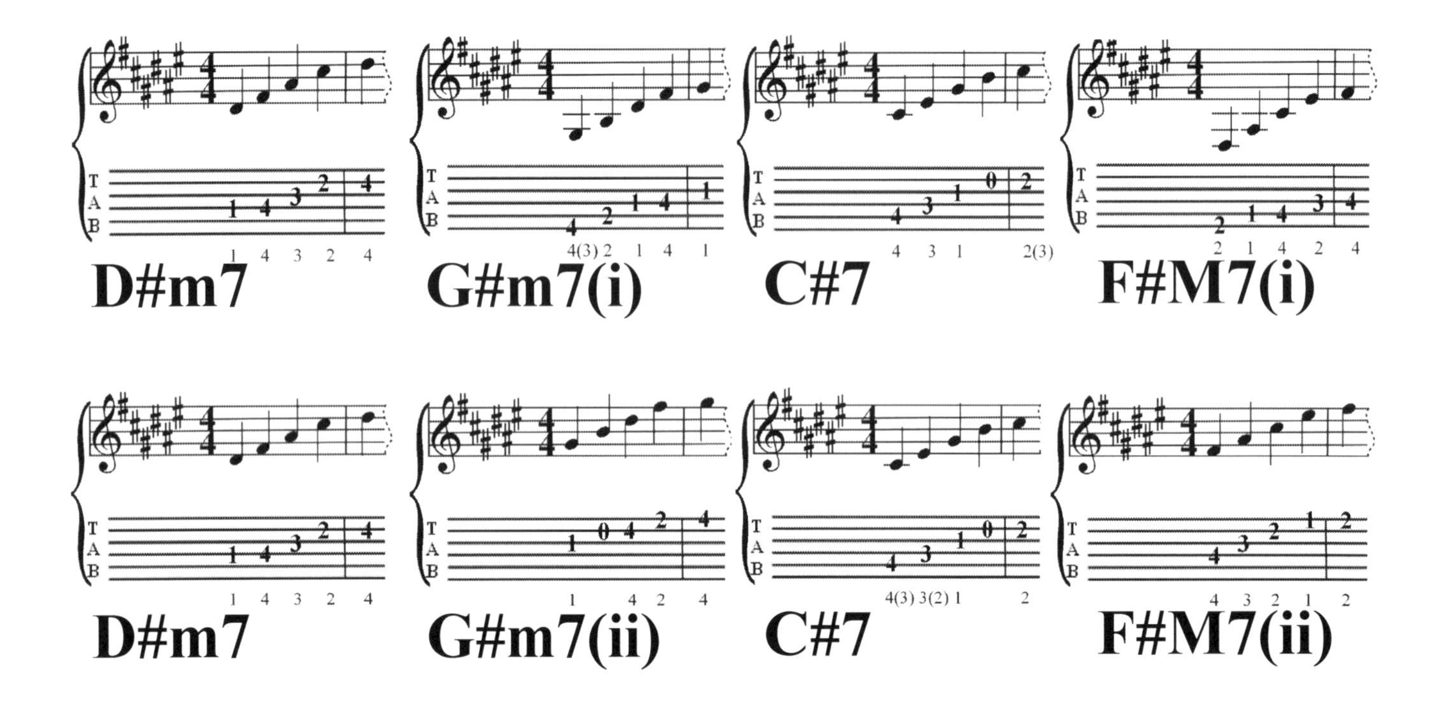

Key of C#

Key of A♭

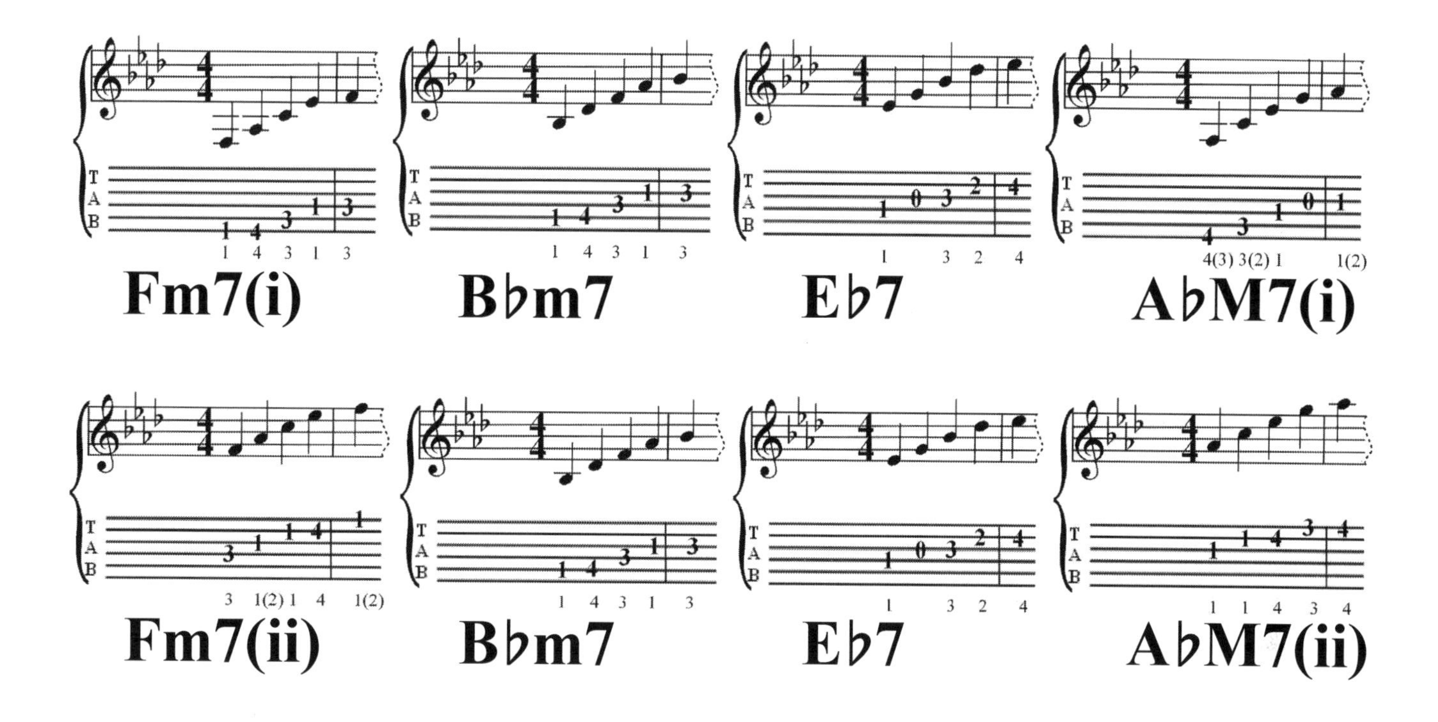

Key of E♭

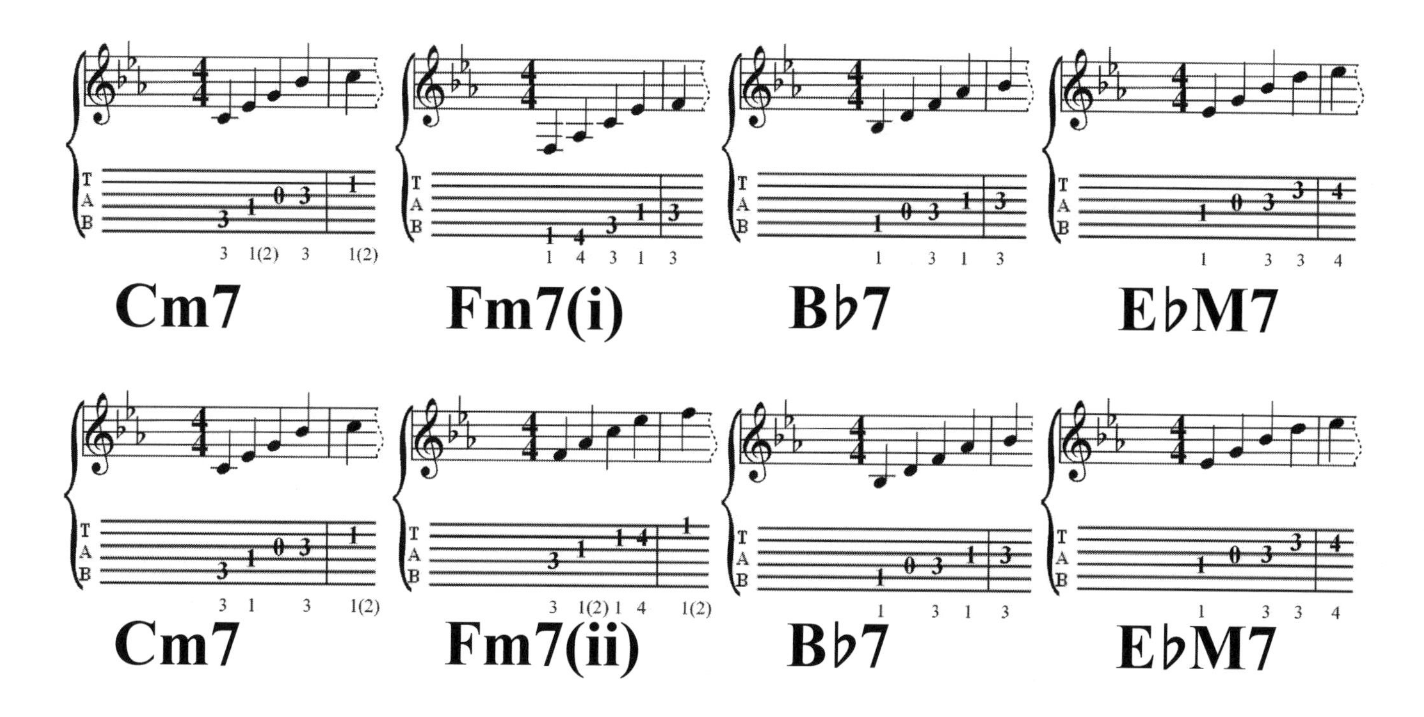

Key of B♭

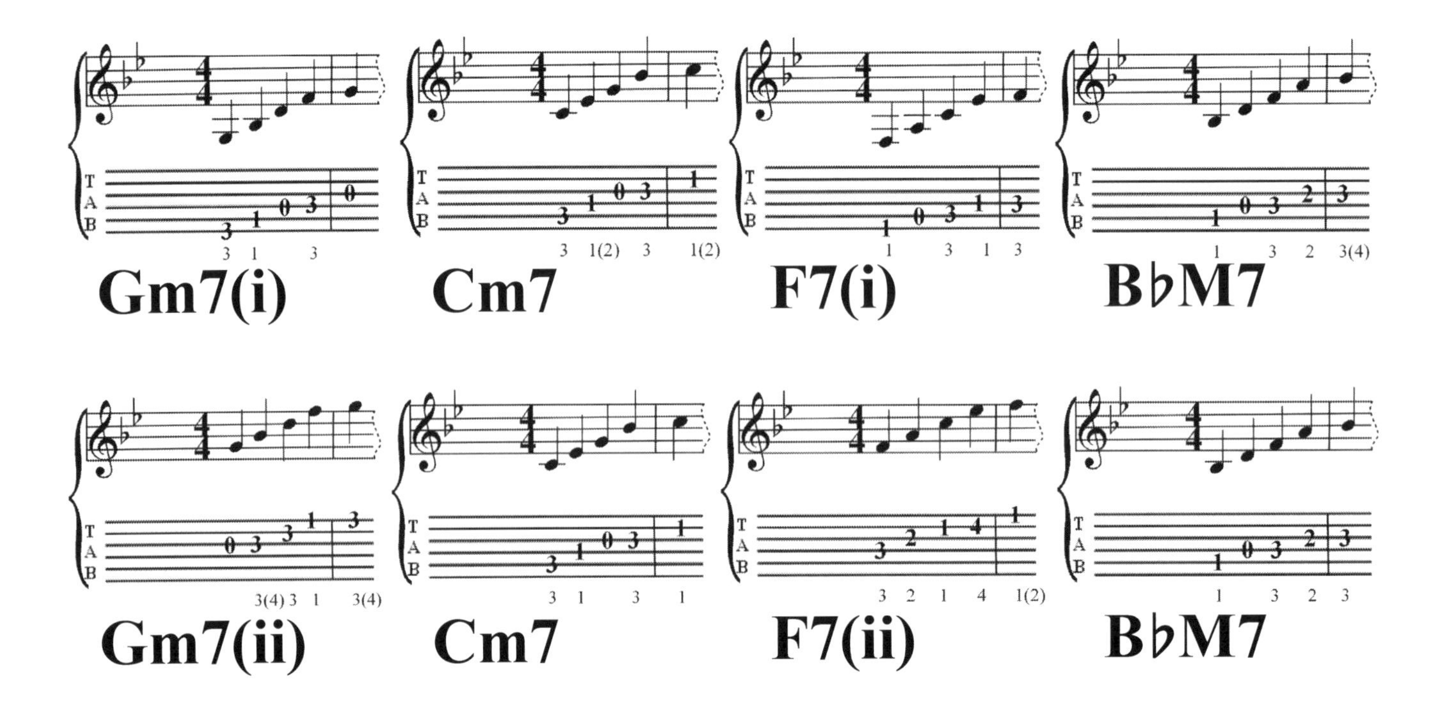

Key of F

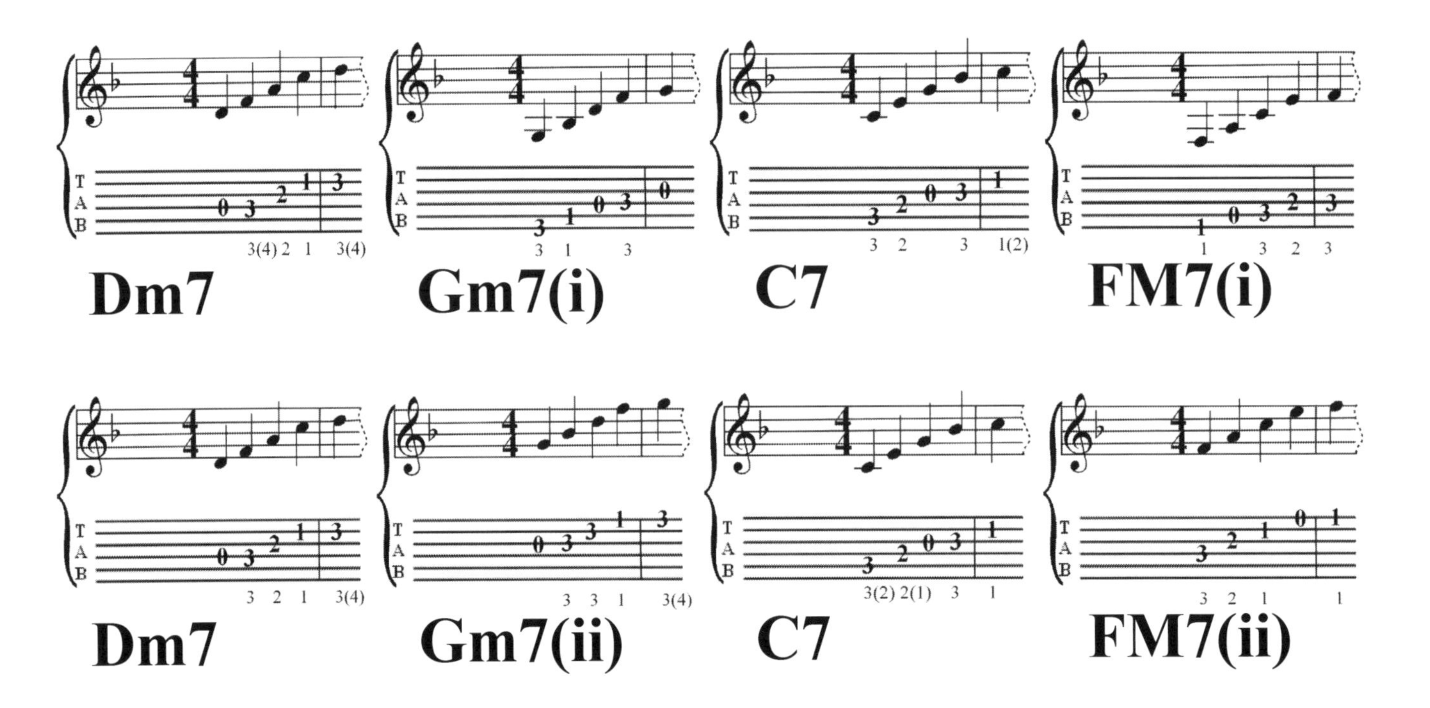

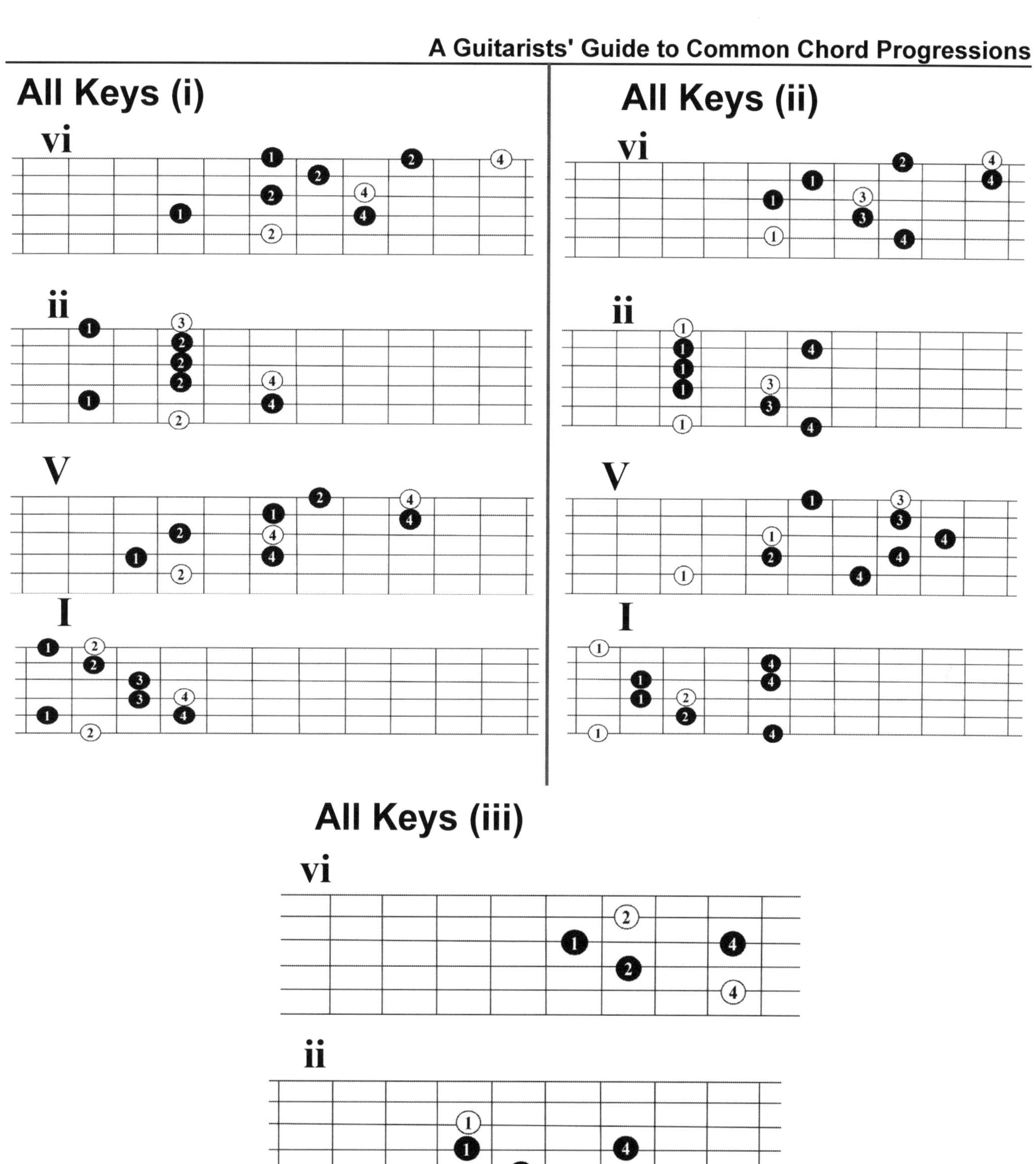

V

I

All Keys (iv)

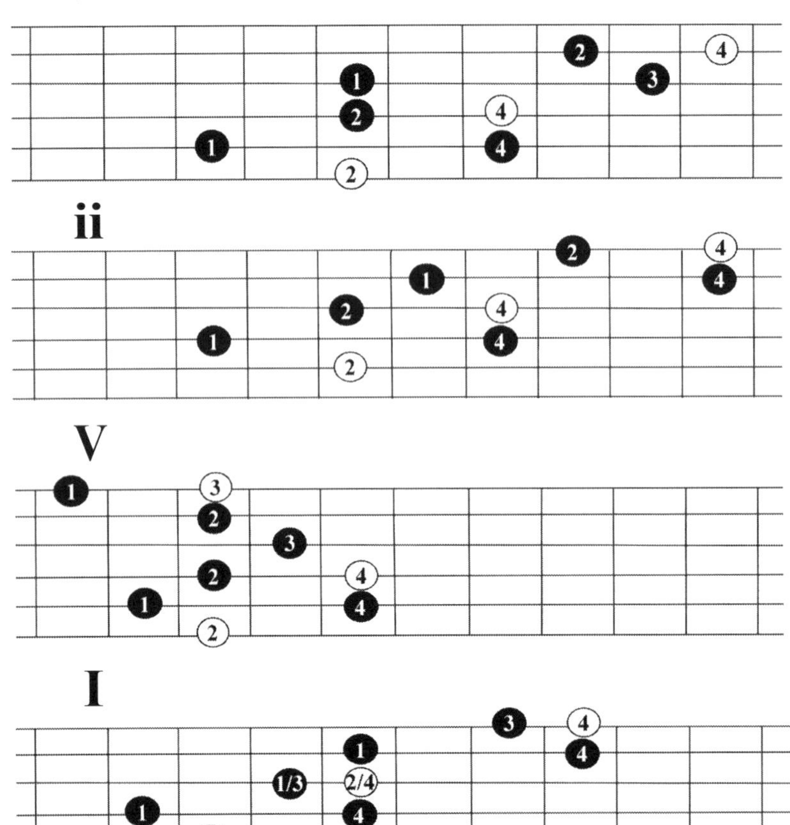

All Keys (v)

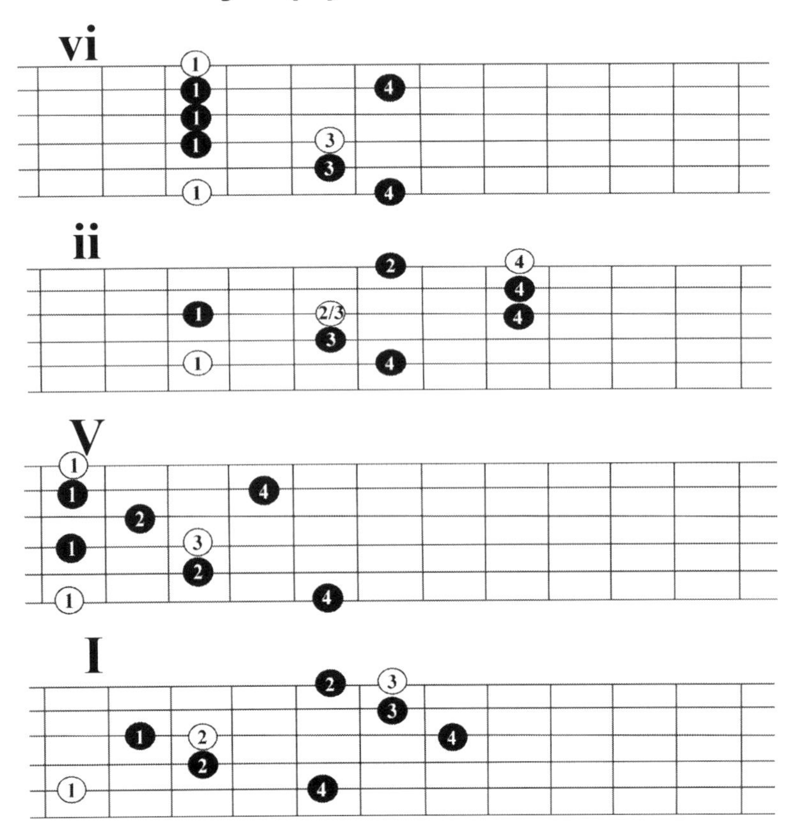

All Keys (vi)

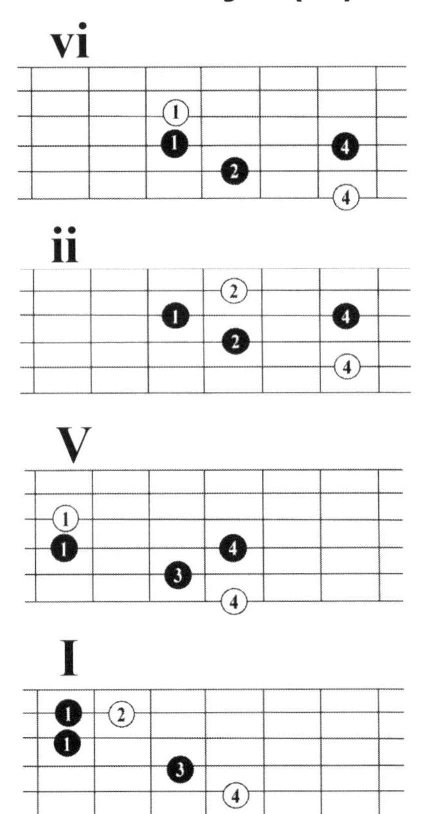

All Keys (vii)

vi

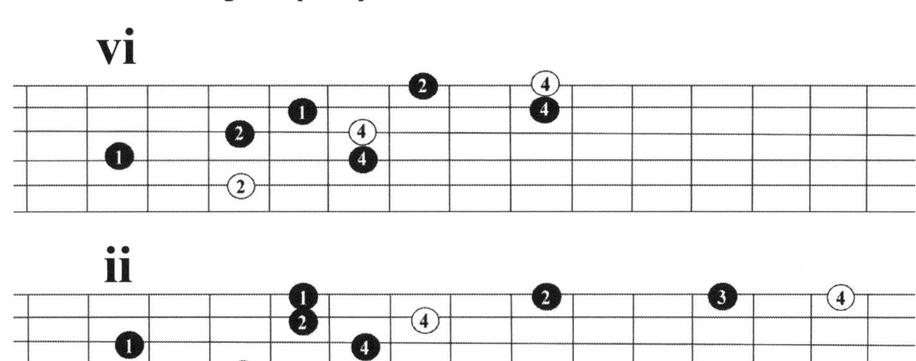

ii

V

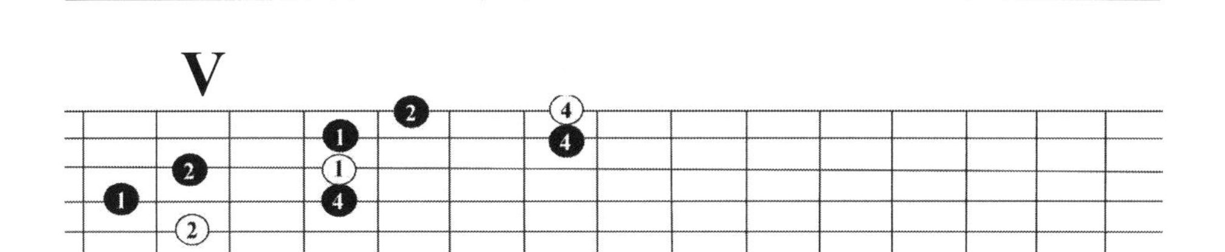

I

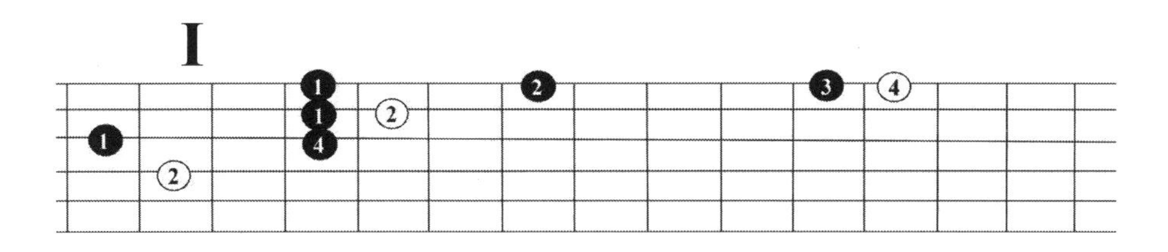

All Keys (viii)

vi

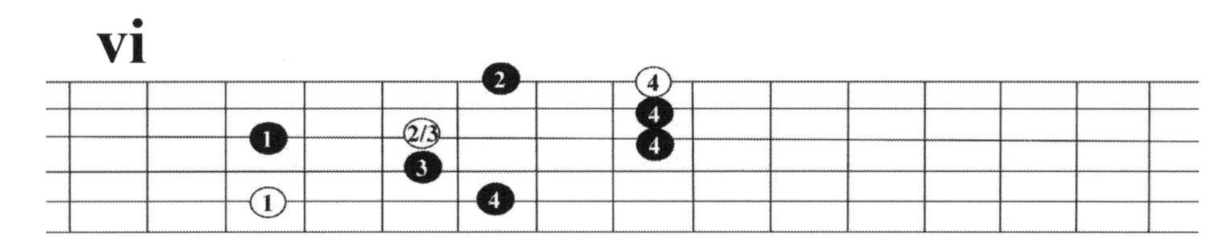

ii

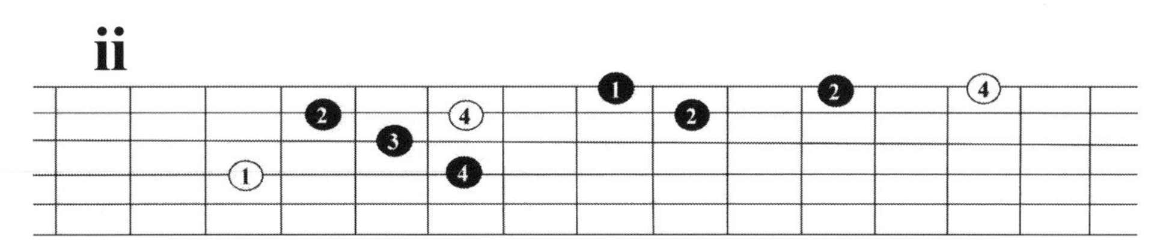

V

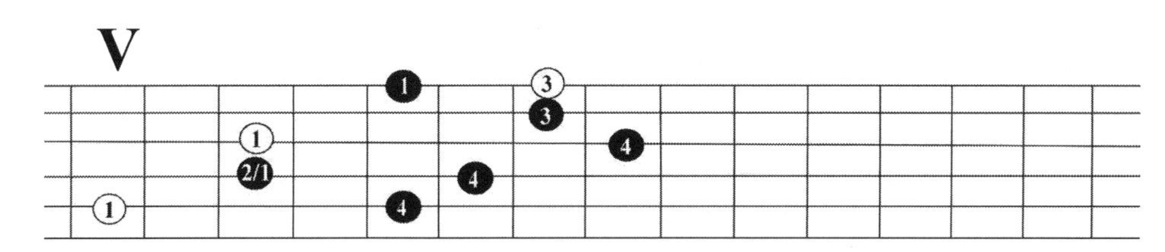

I

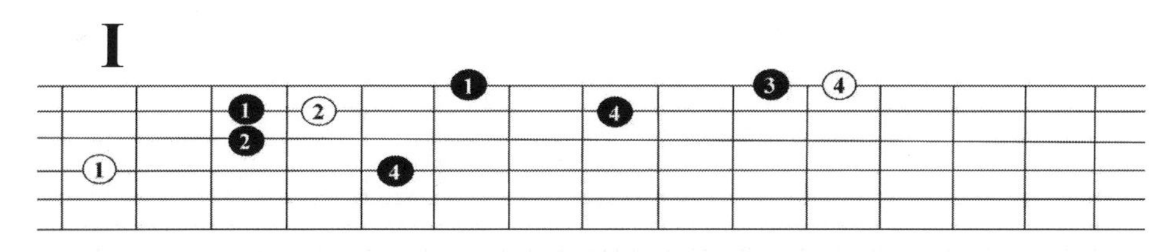

All Keys (ix)

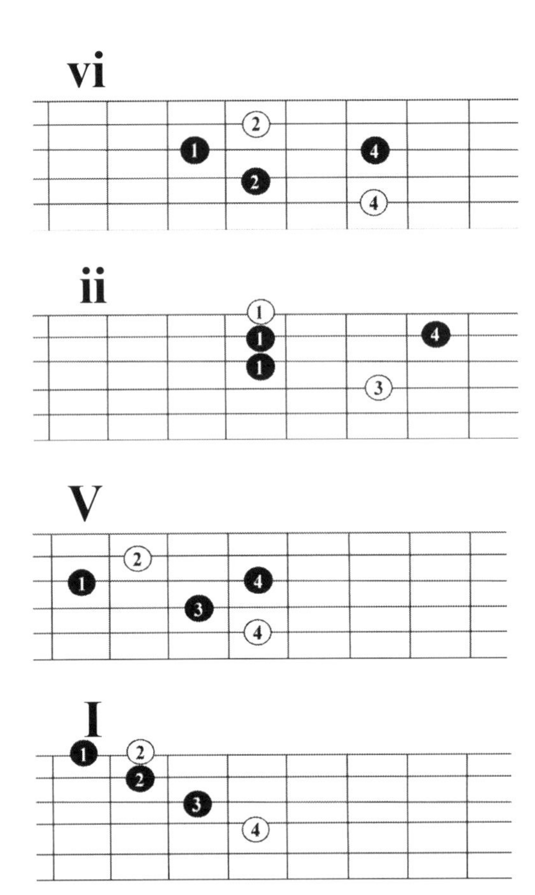

PART TWENTY-TWO

i - iv - V

MINOR KEYS
SEVENTH CHORDS
ARPEGGIOS

Key of Am

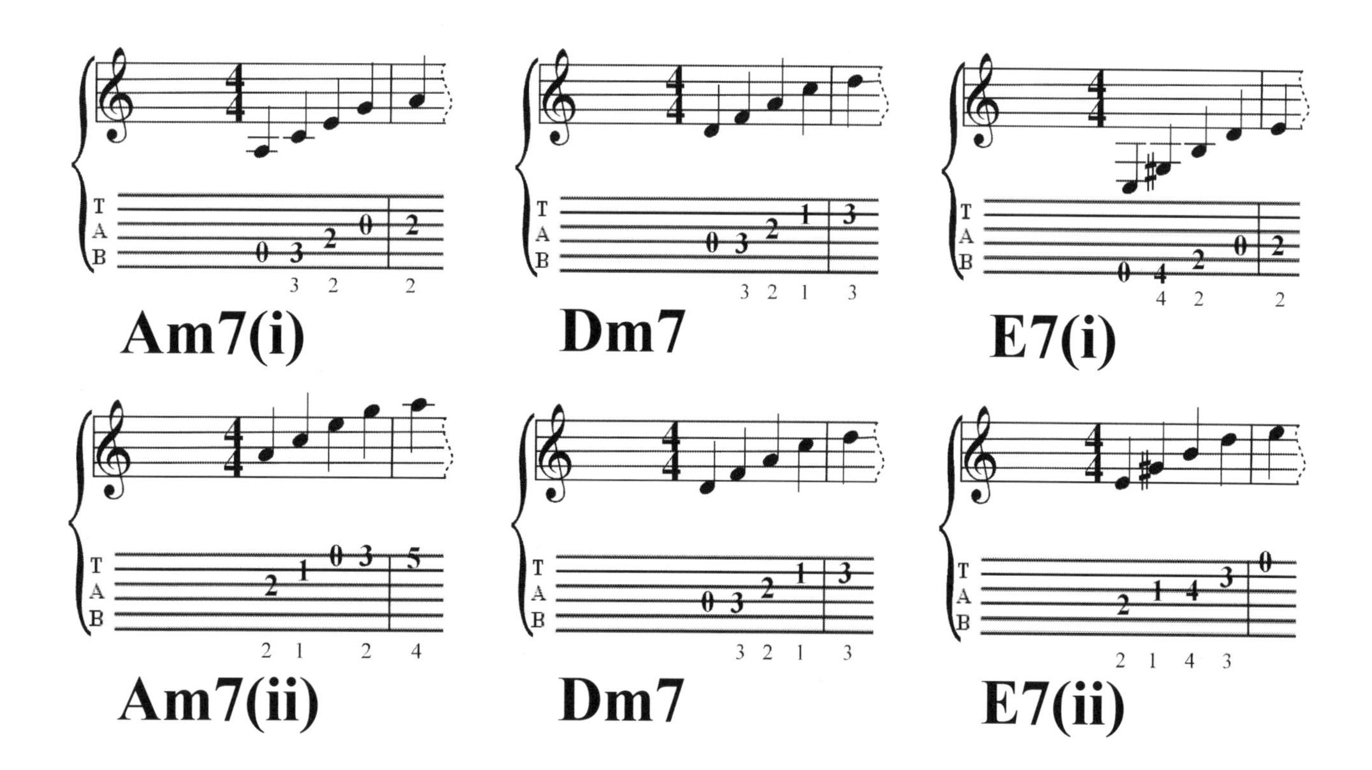

Key of Em

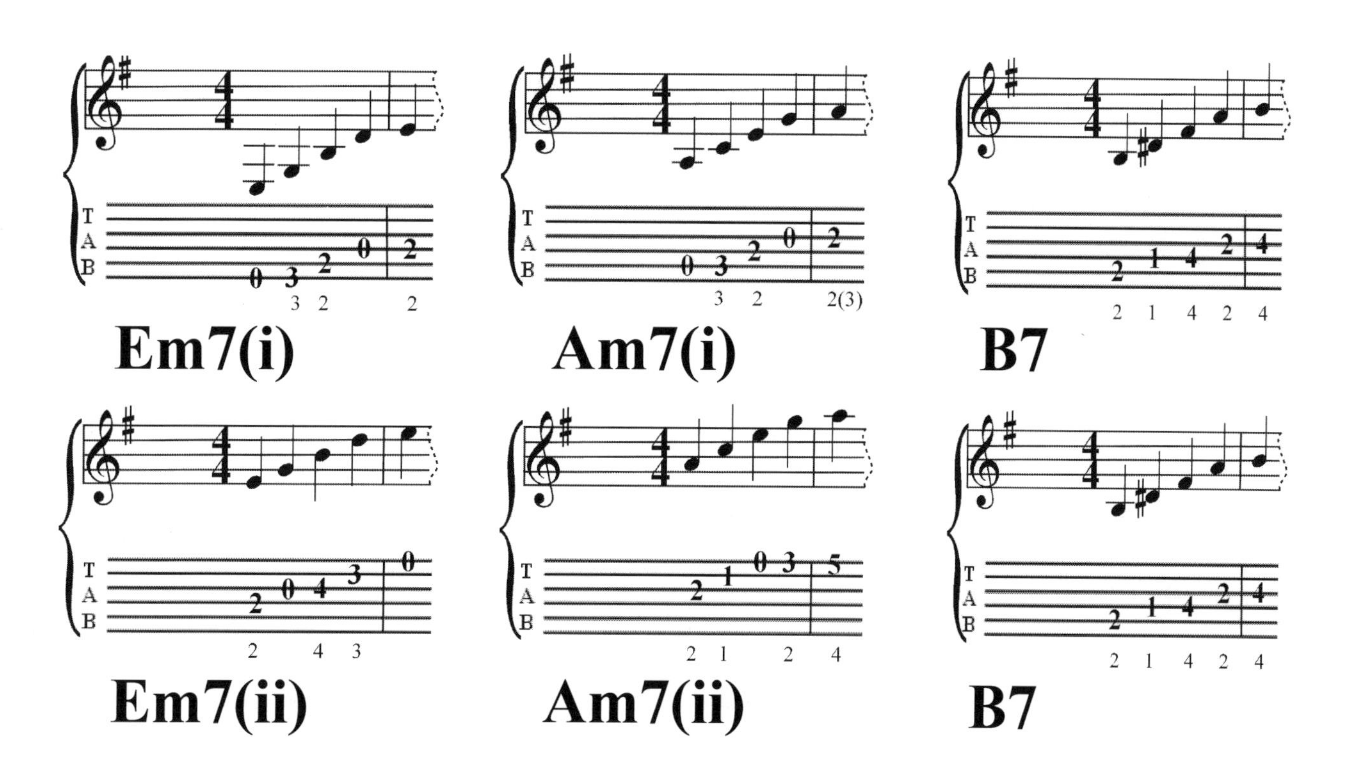

Key of Bm

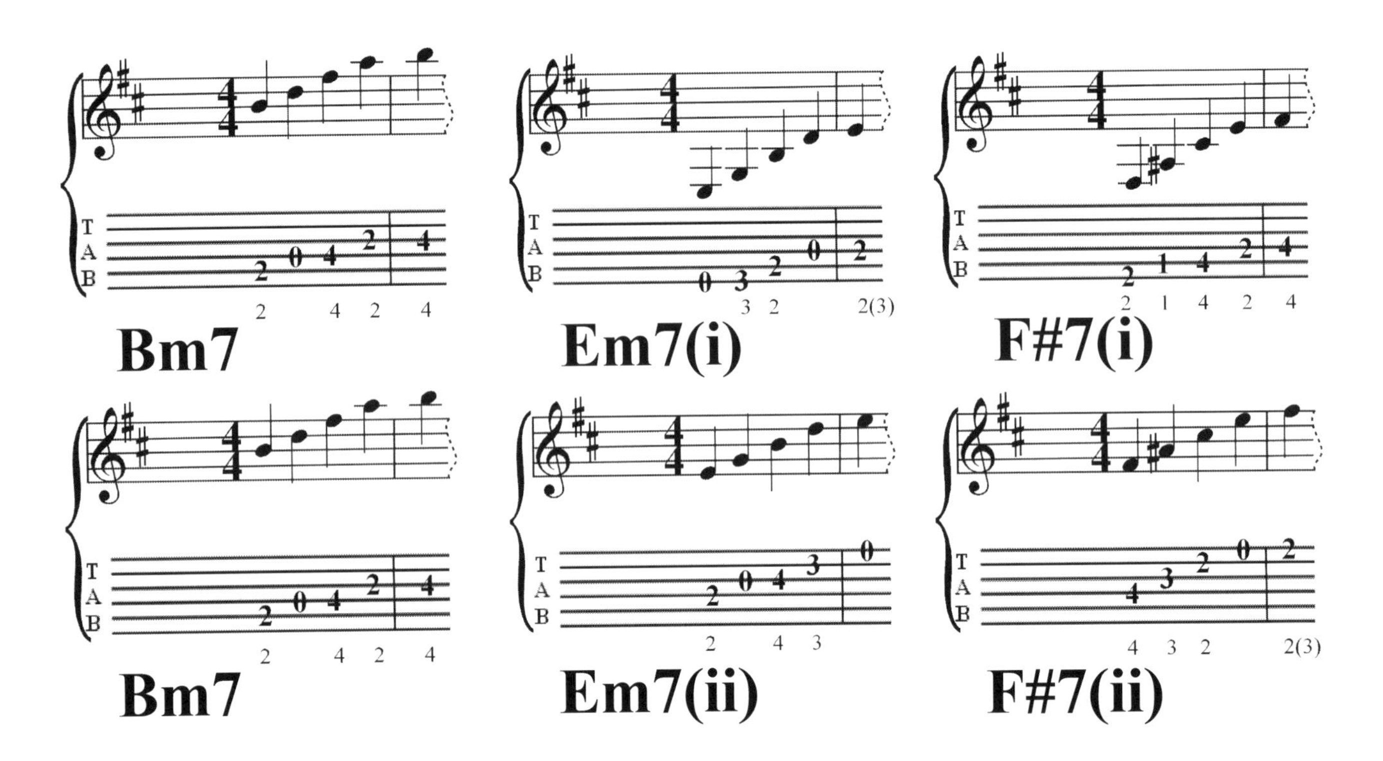

Key of F#m

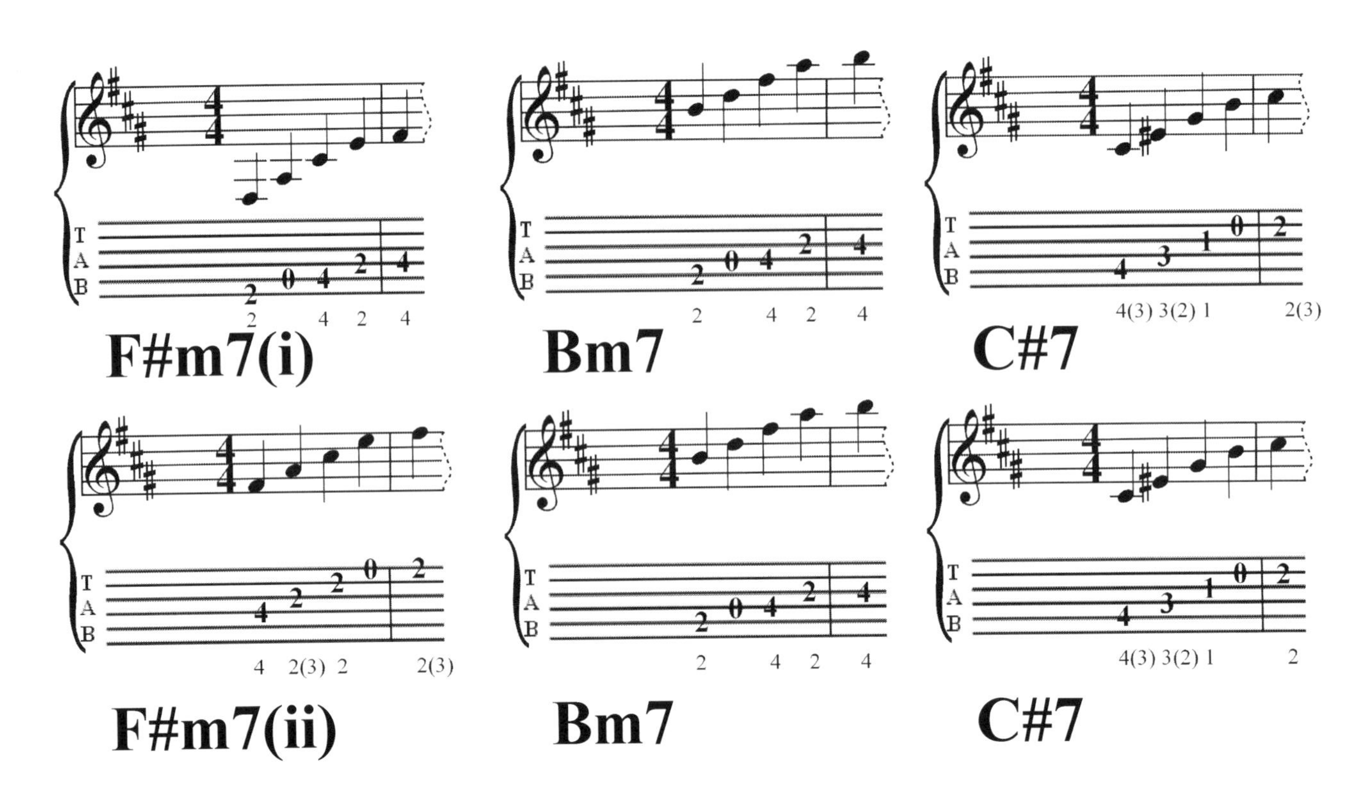

Key of C#m

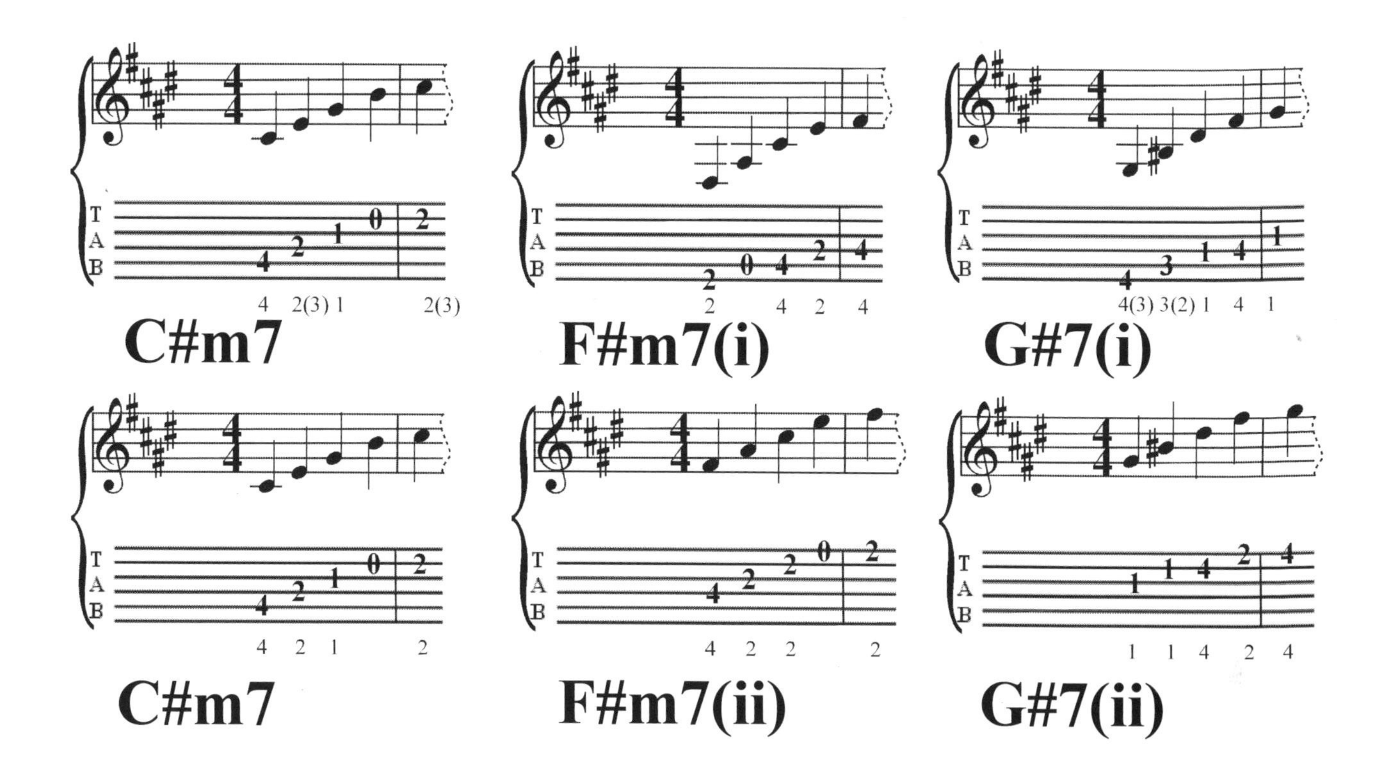

Key of A♭m

Key of E♭m

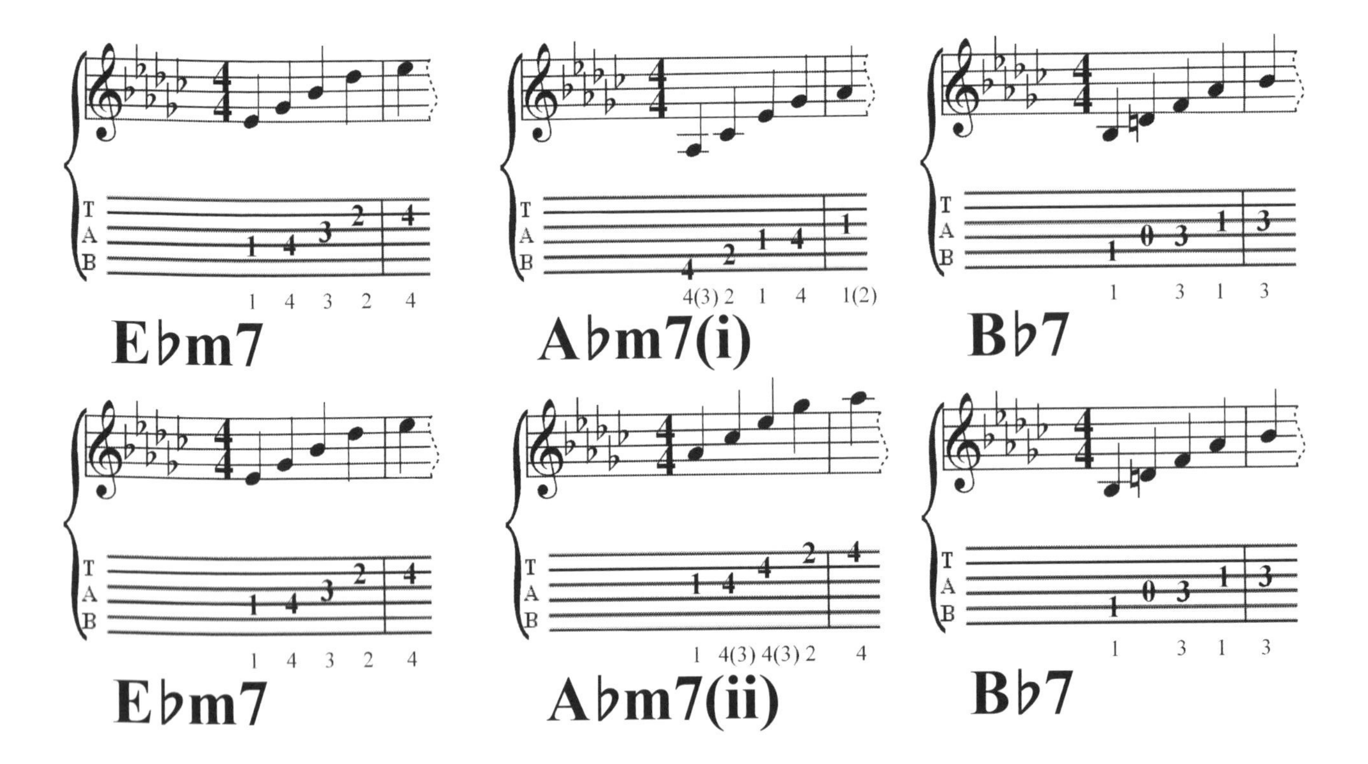

Key of B♭m

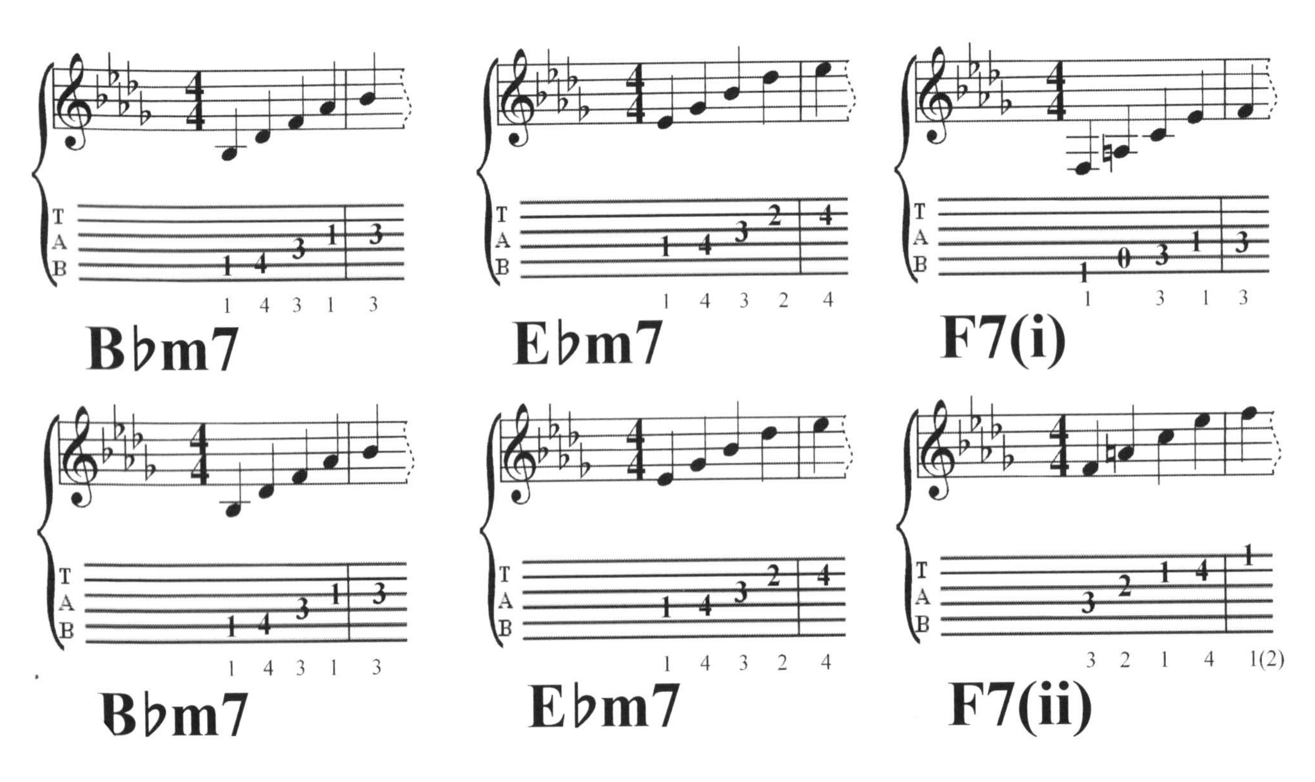

Key of Fm

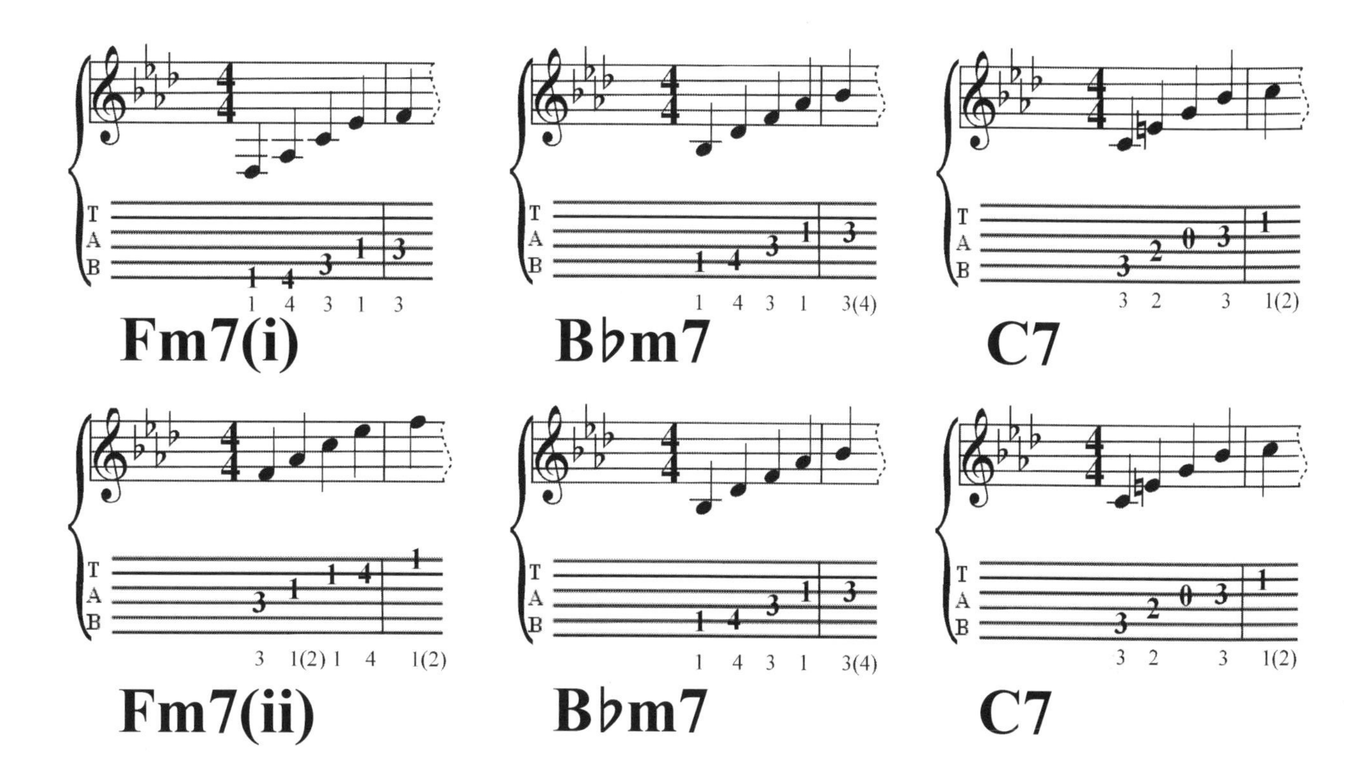

Key of Cm

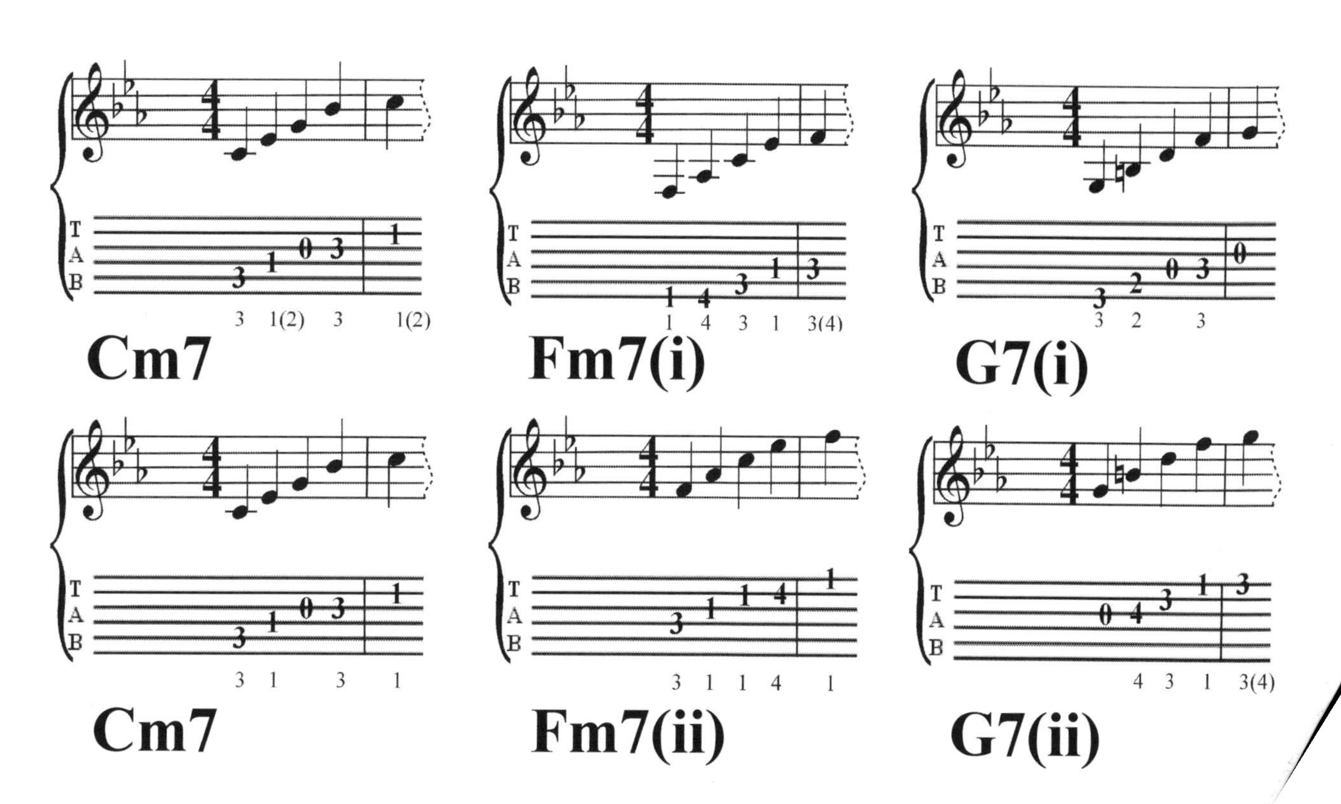

Key of Gm

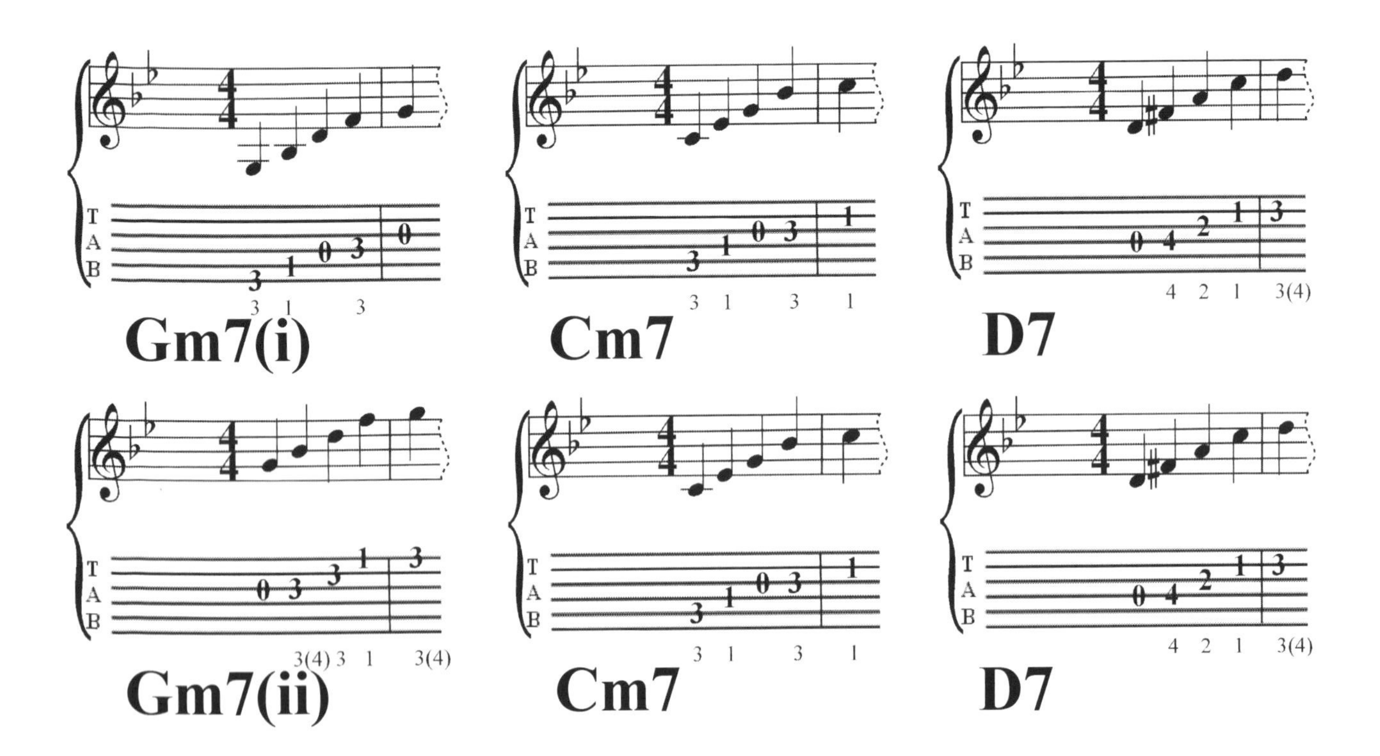

Key of Dm

All Keys (i)

i

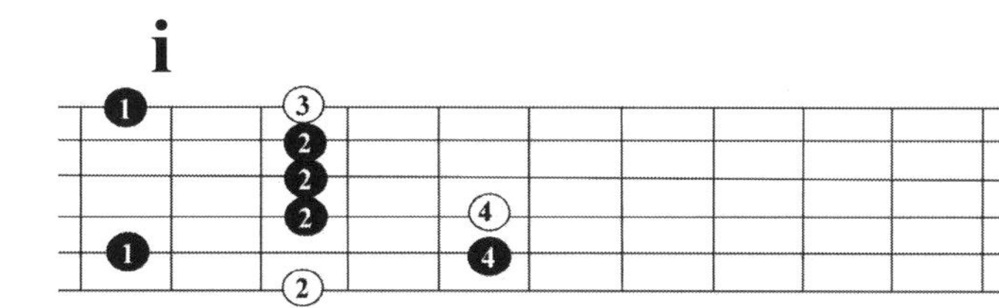

iv

V

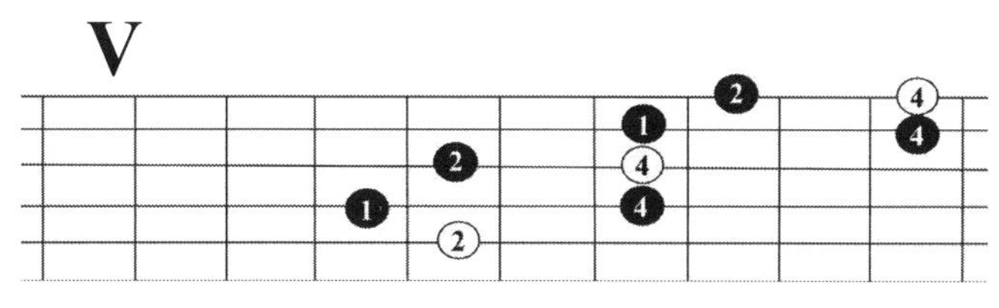

All Keys (ii)

i

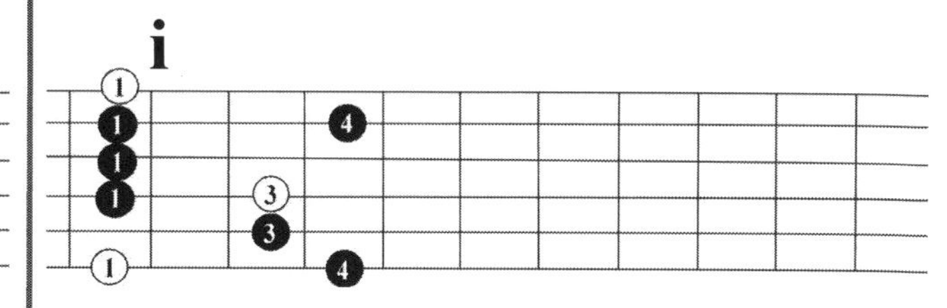

iv

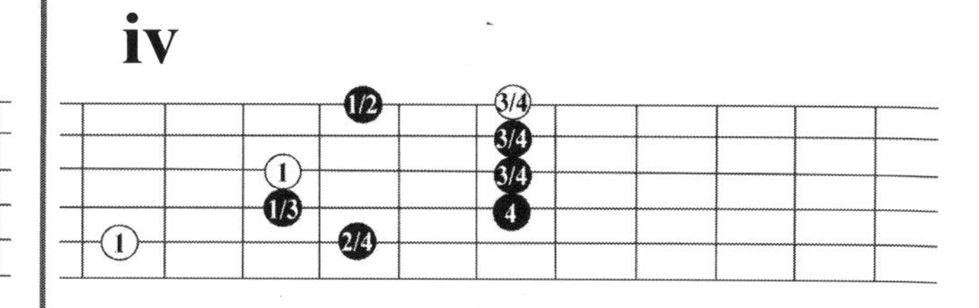

V

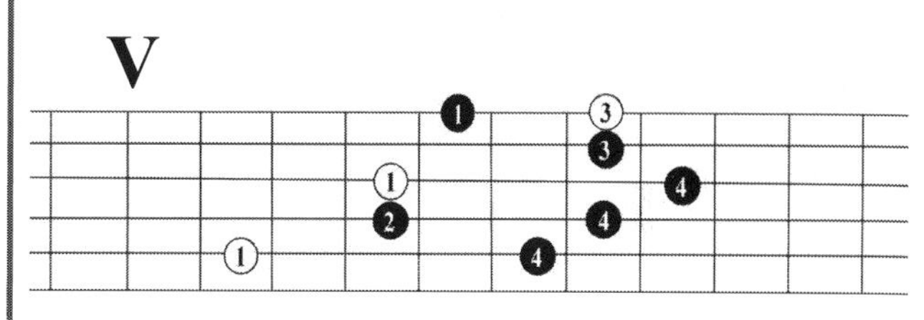

All Keys (iii)

i

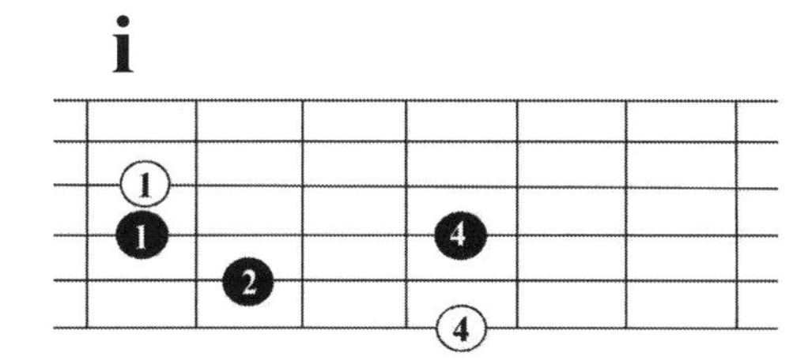

iv

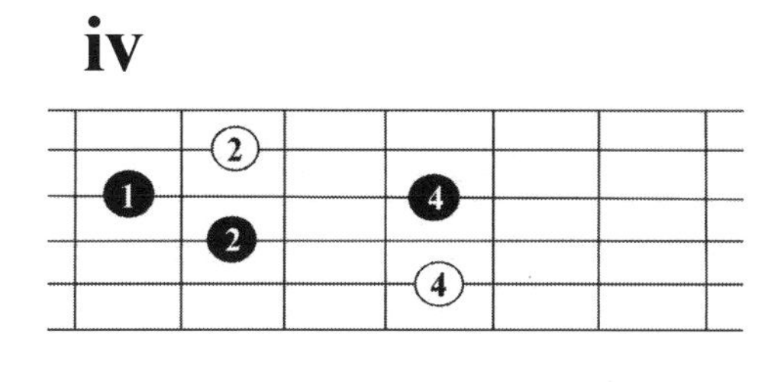

V

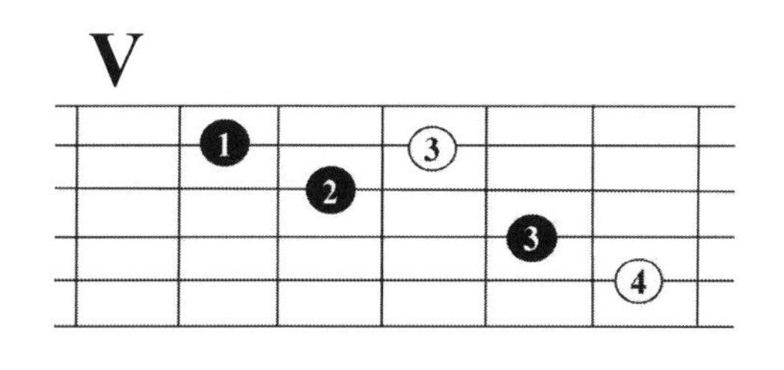

All Keys (iv)

i

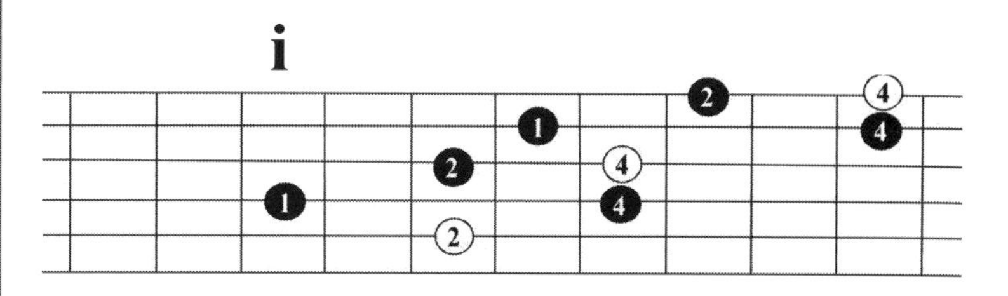

iv

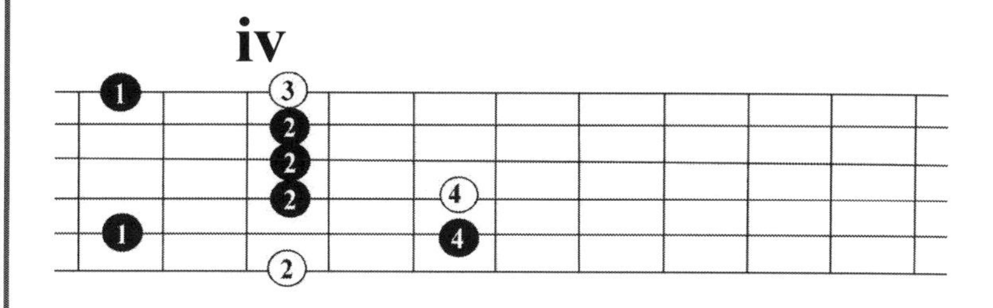

V

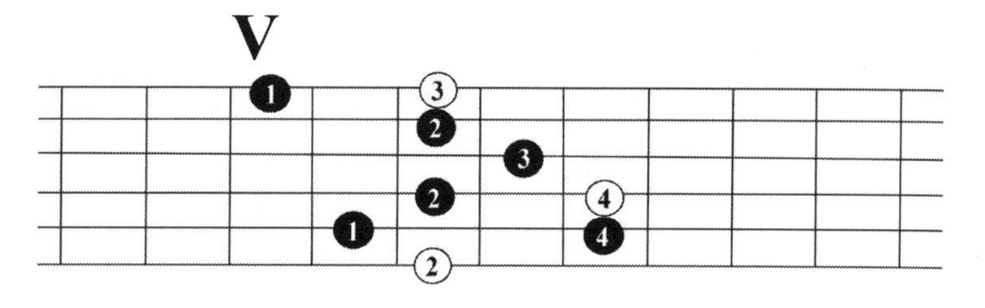

All Keys (v)

i

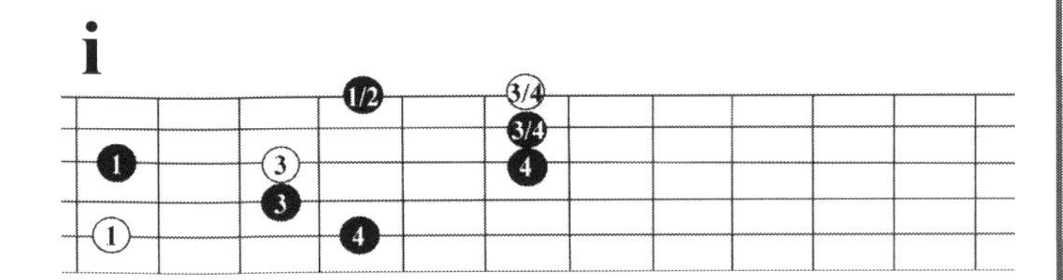

iv

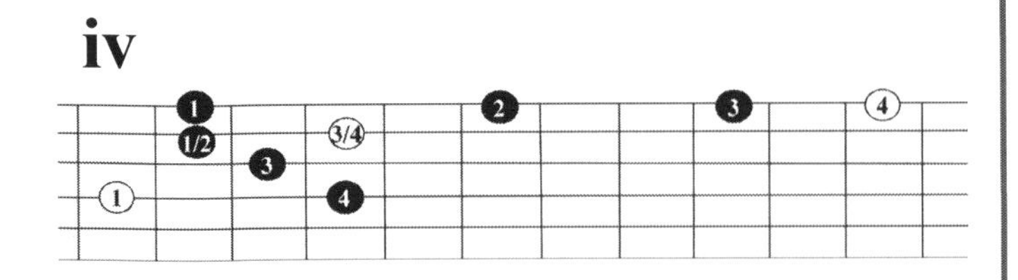

V

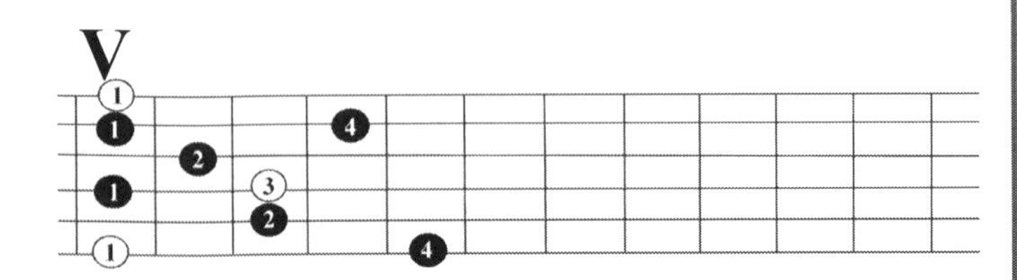

All Keys (vi)

i

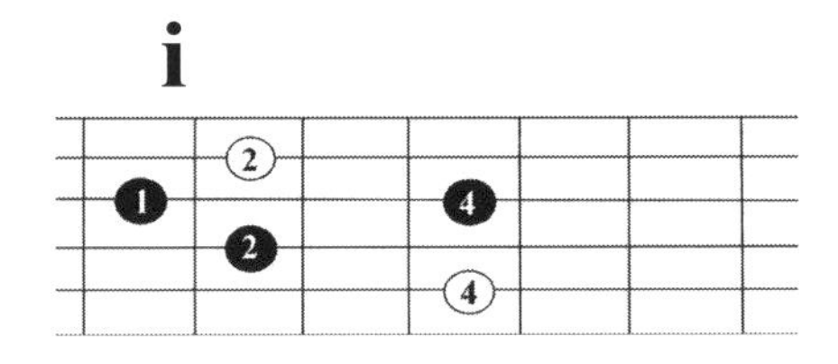

iv

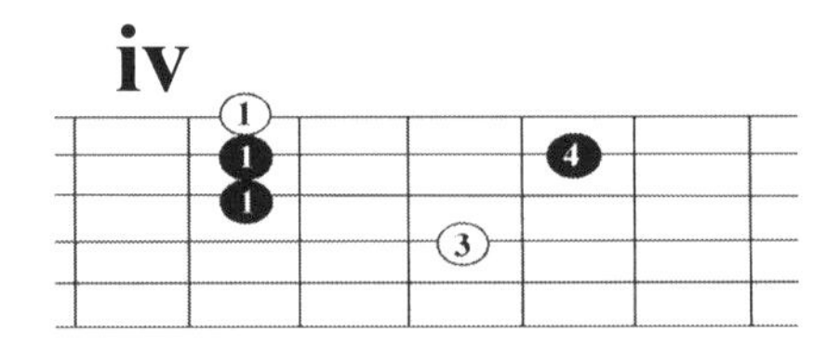

V

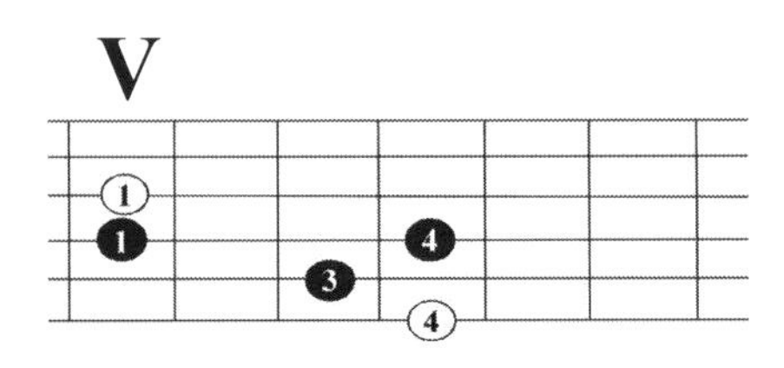

All Keys (vii)

i

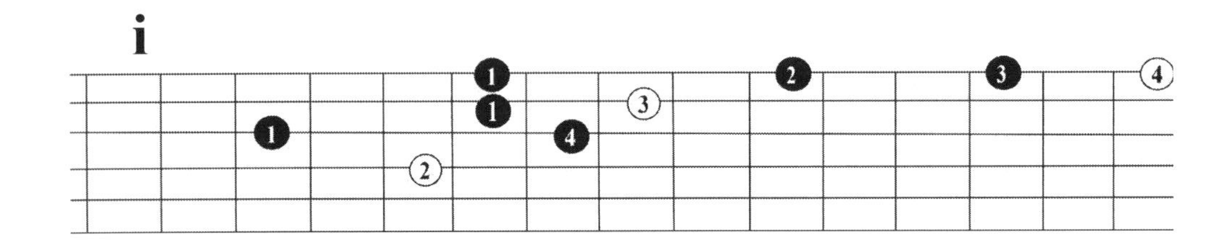

iv

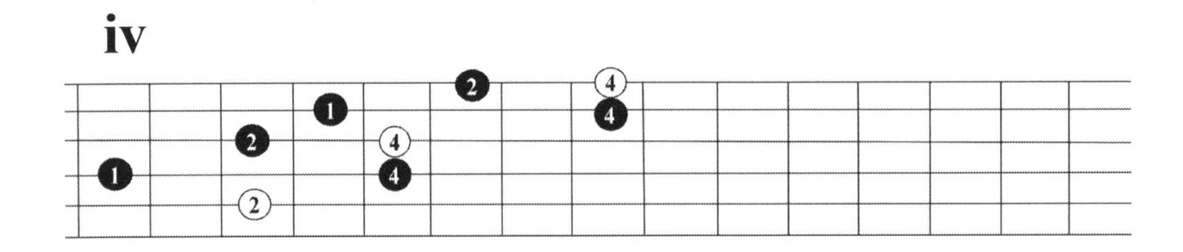

V

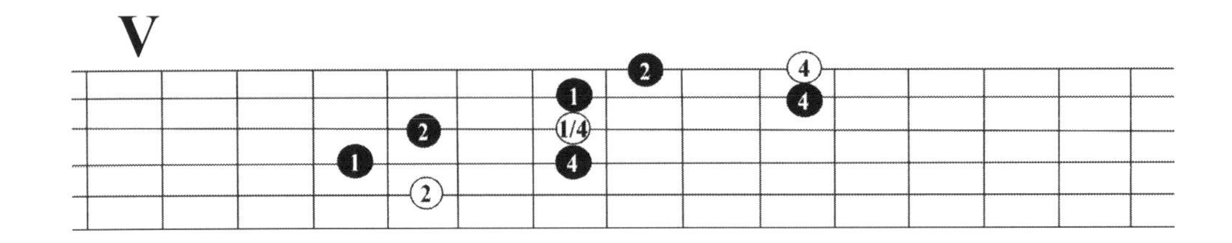

All Keys (viii)

i

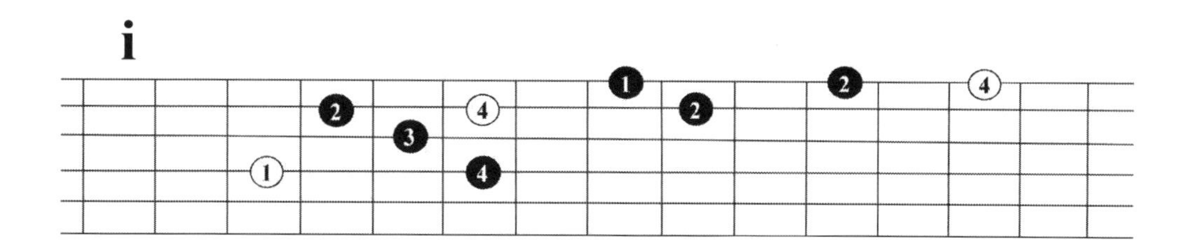

iv

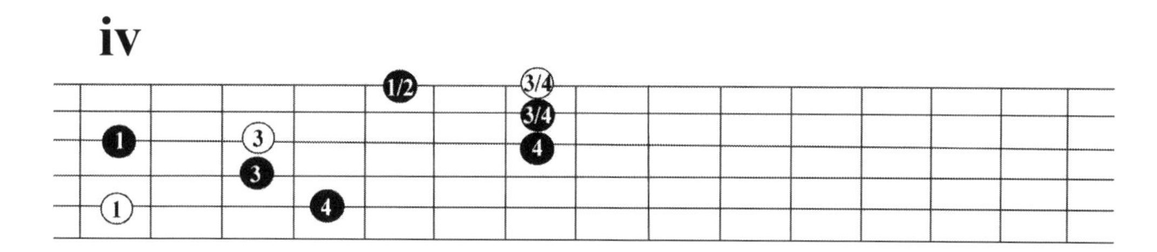

V

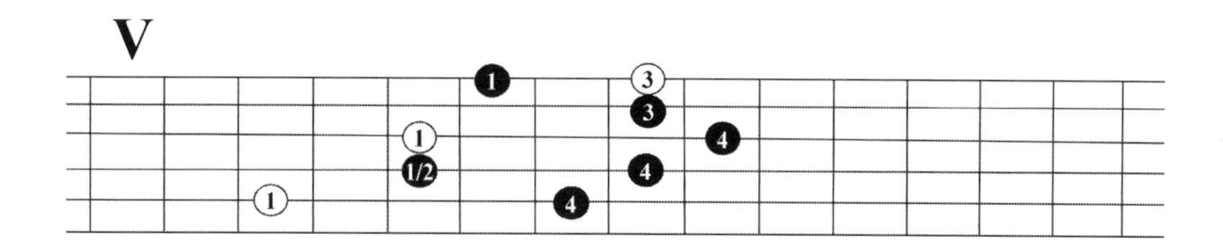

All Keys (ix)

i

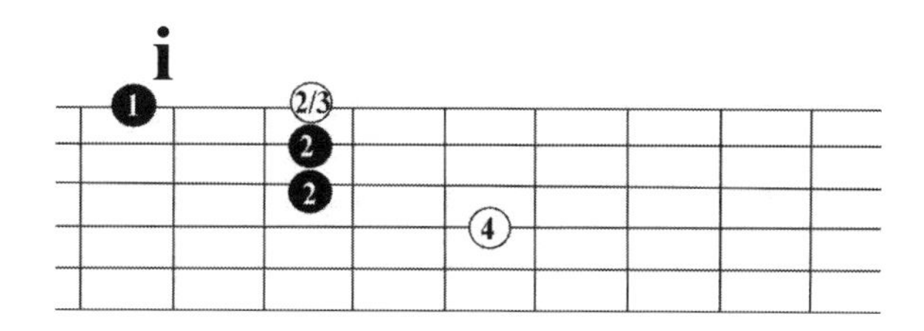

iv

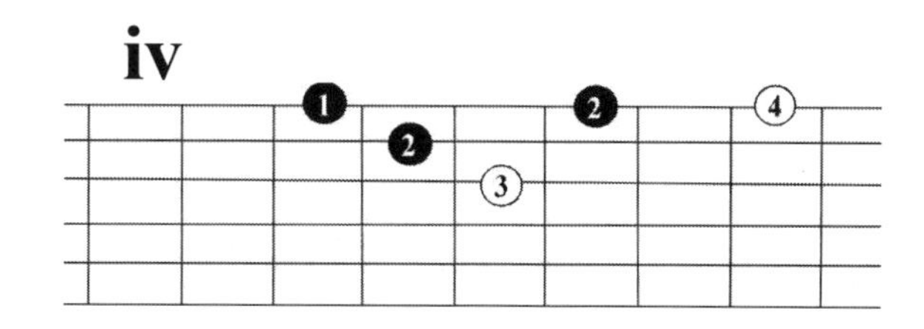

V

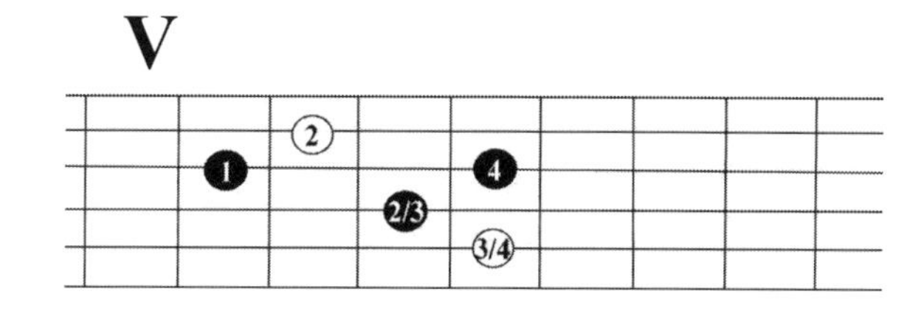

PART TWENTY-THREE

ii - V - i

MINOR KEYS
SEVENTH CHORDS
ARPEGGIOS

Key of Am

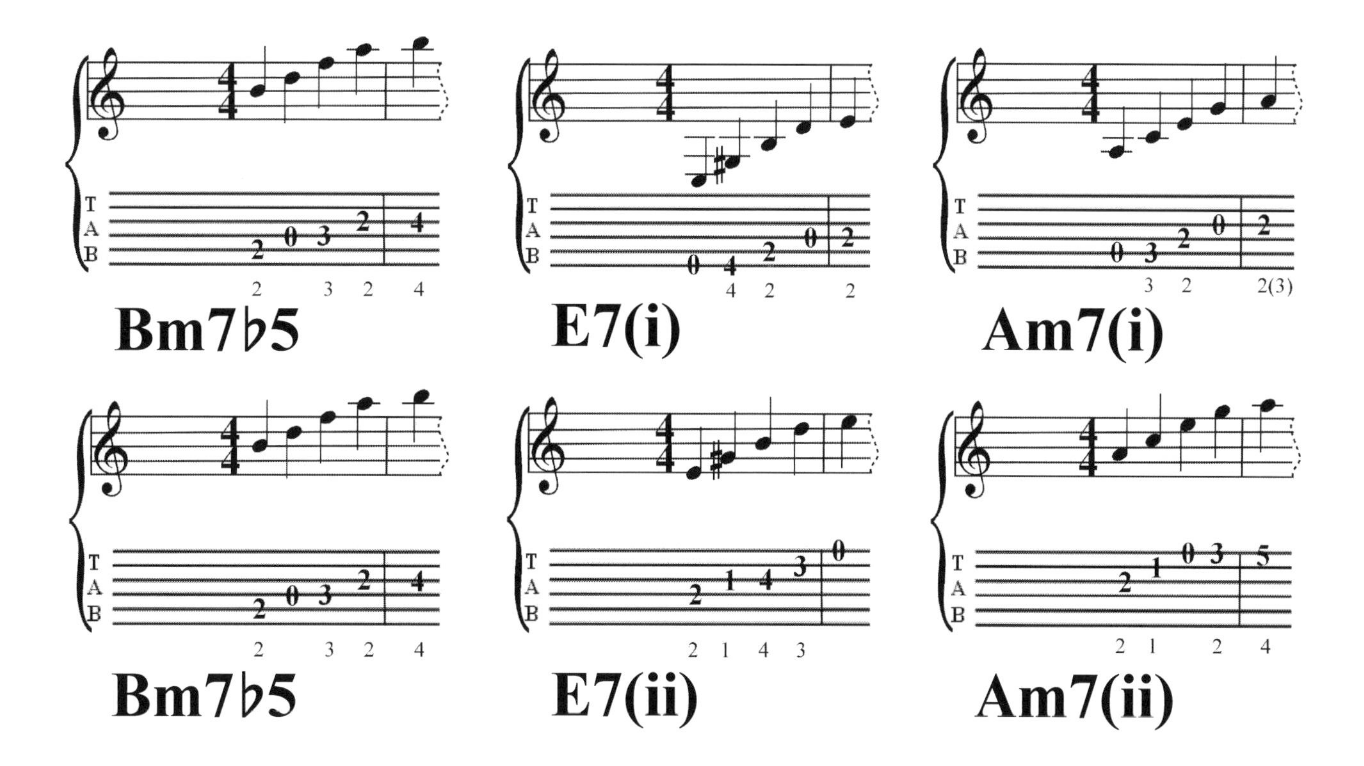

Key of Em

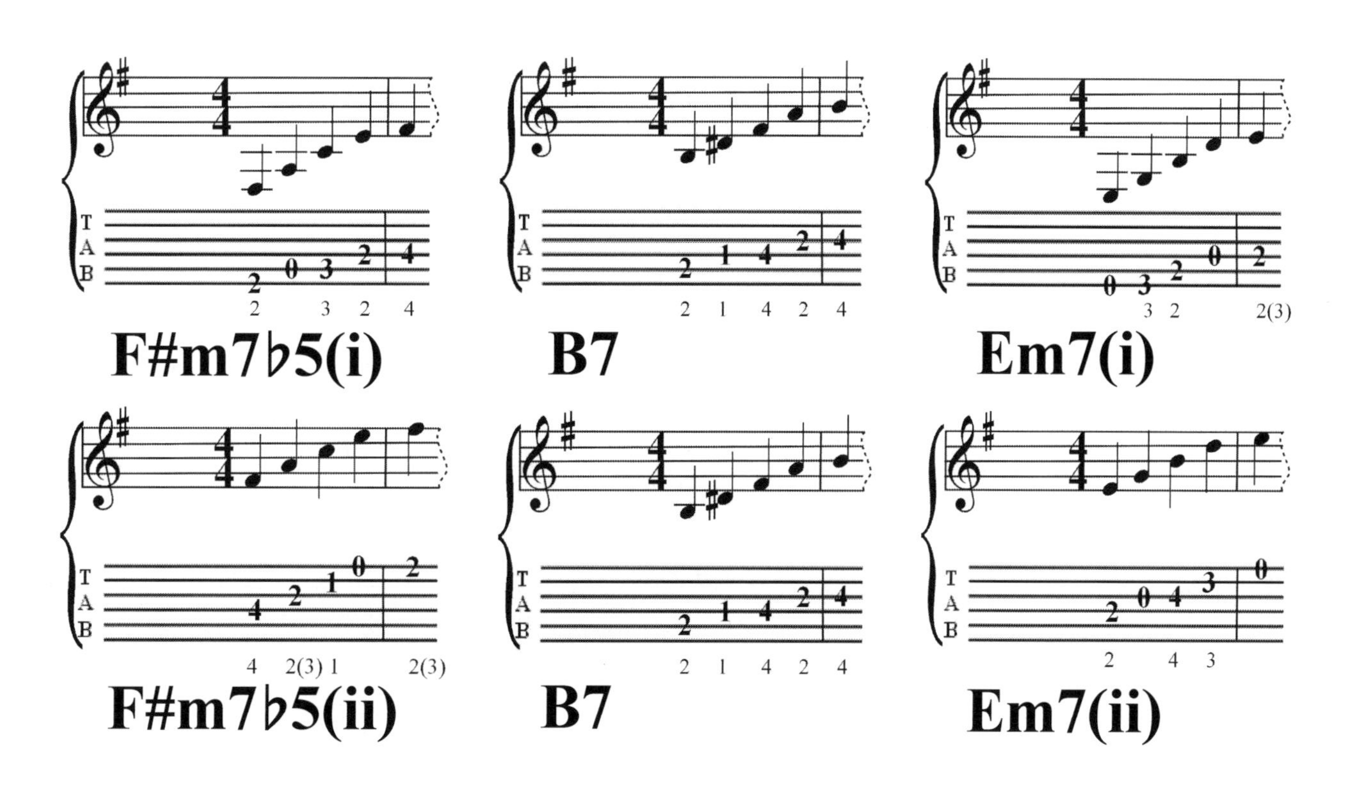

Key of Bm

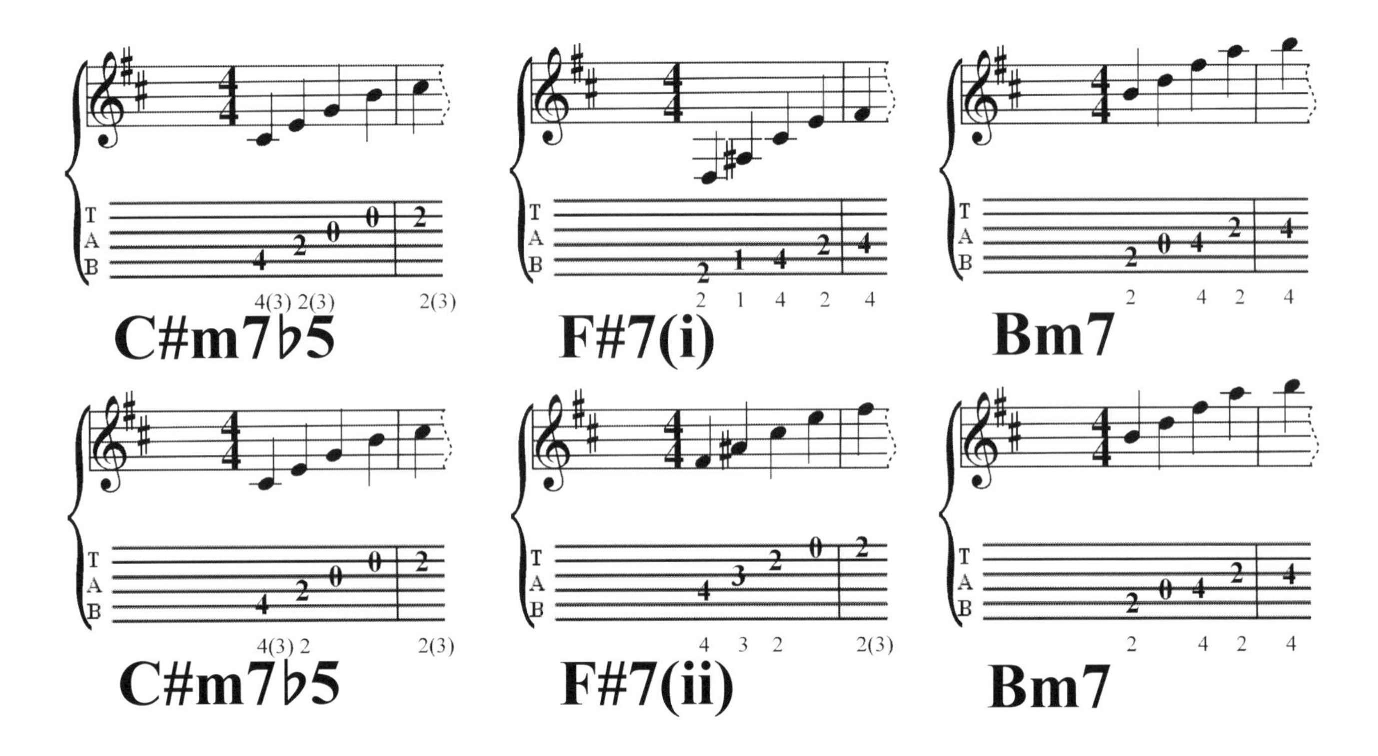

Key of F#m

Key of C#m

Key of A♭m

Key of E♭m

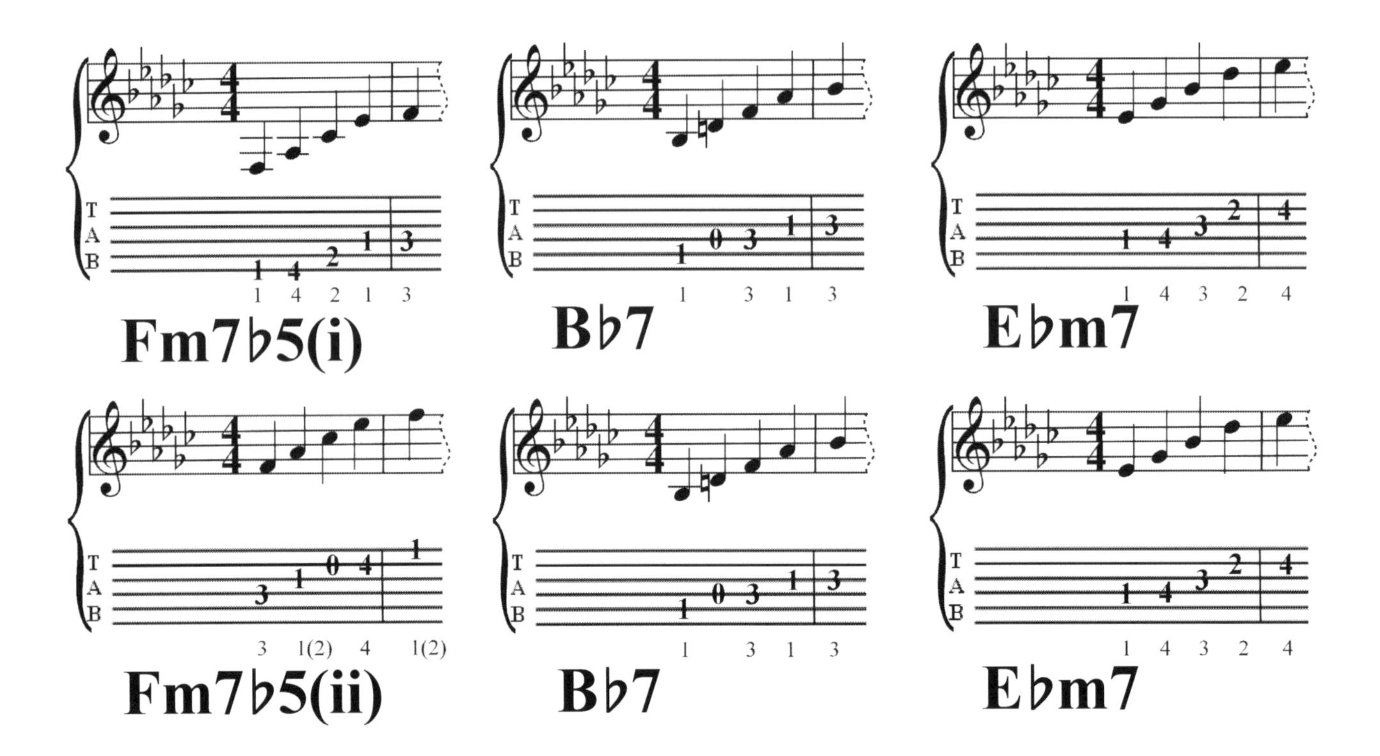

Key of B♭m

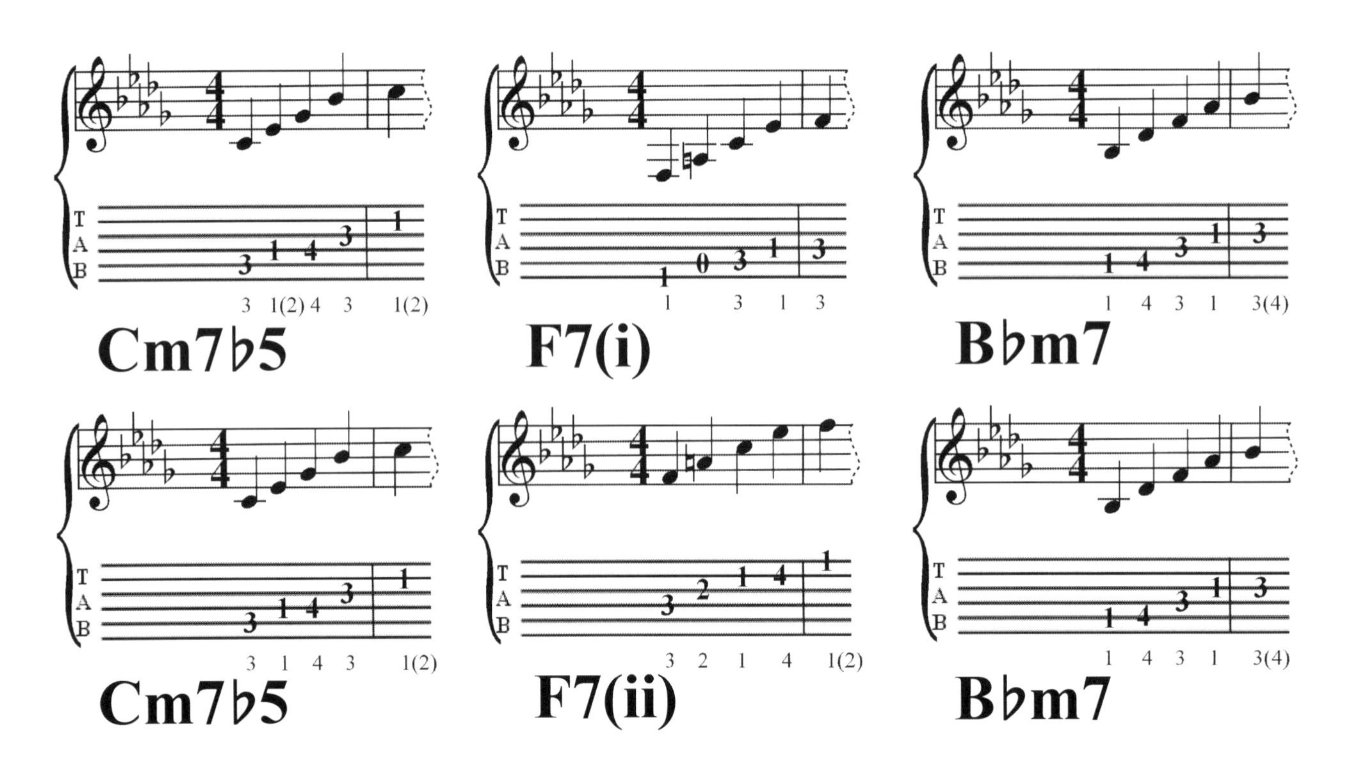

Key of Fm

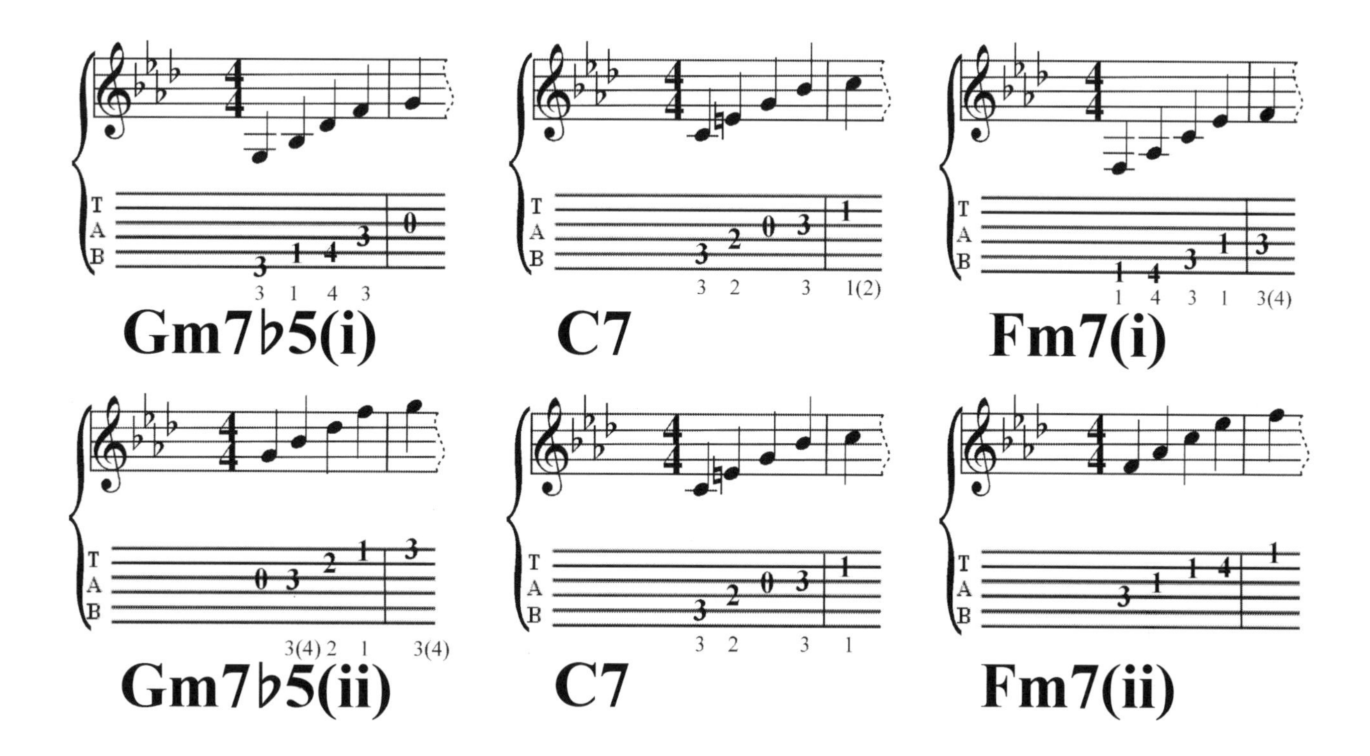

Key of Cm

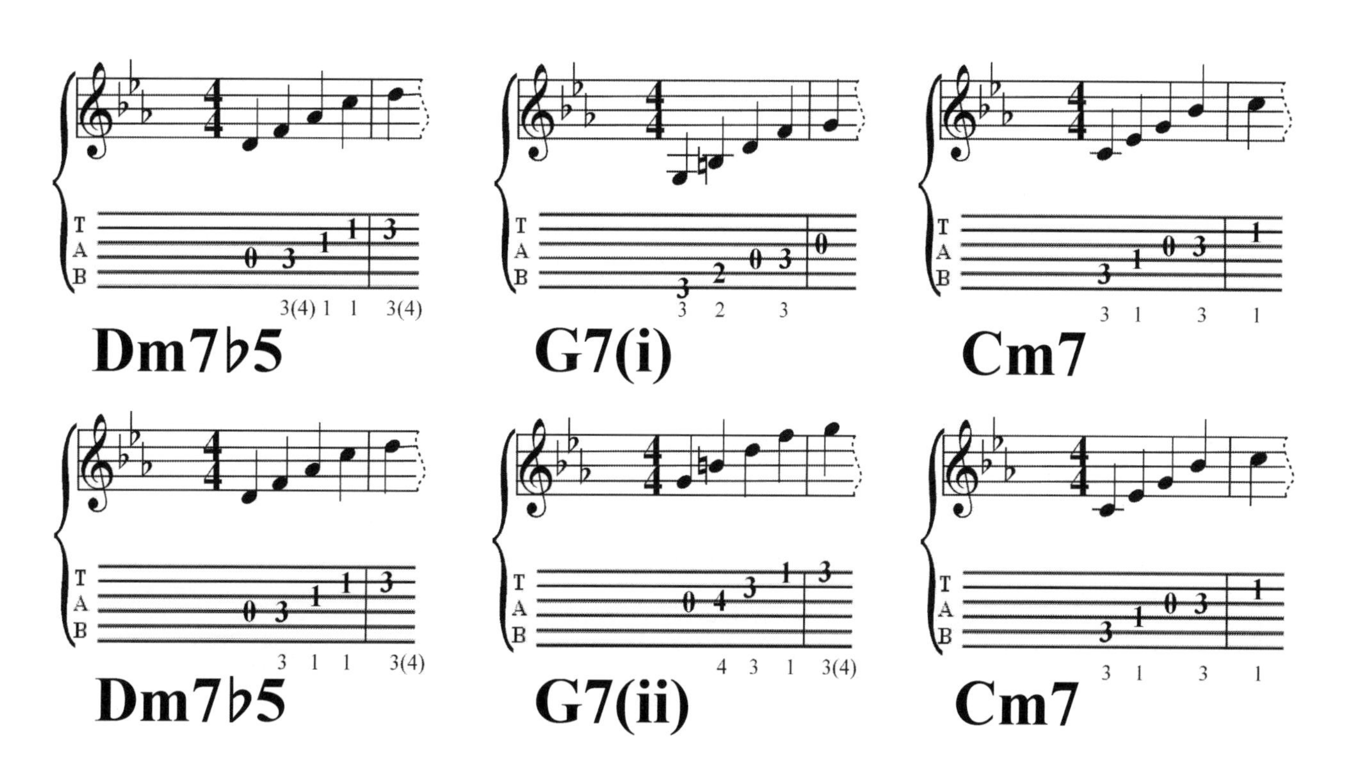

Key of Gm

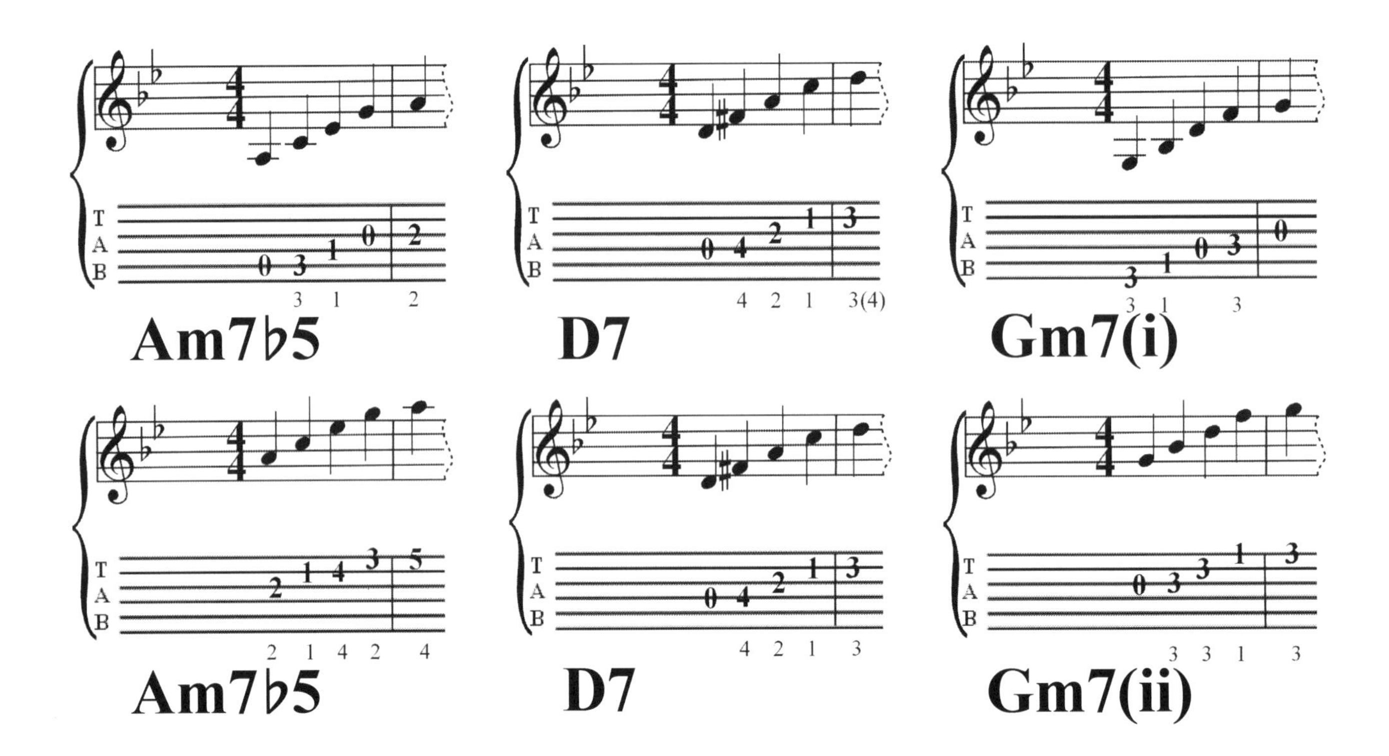

Key of Dm

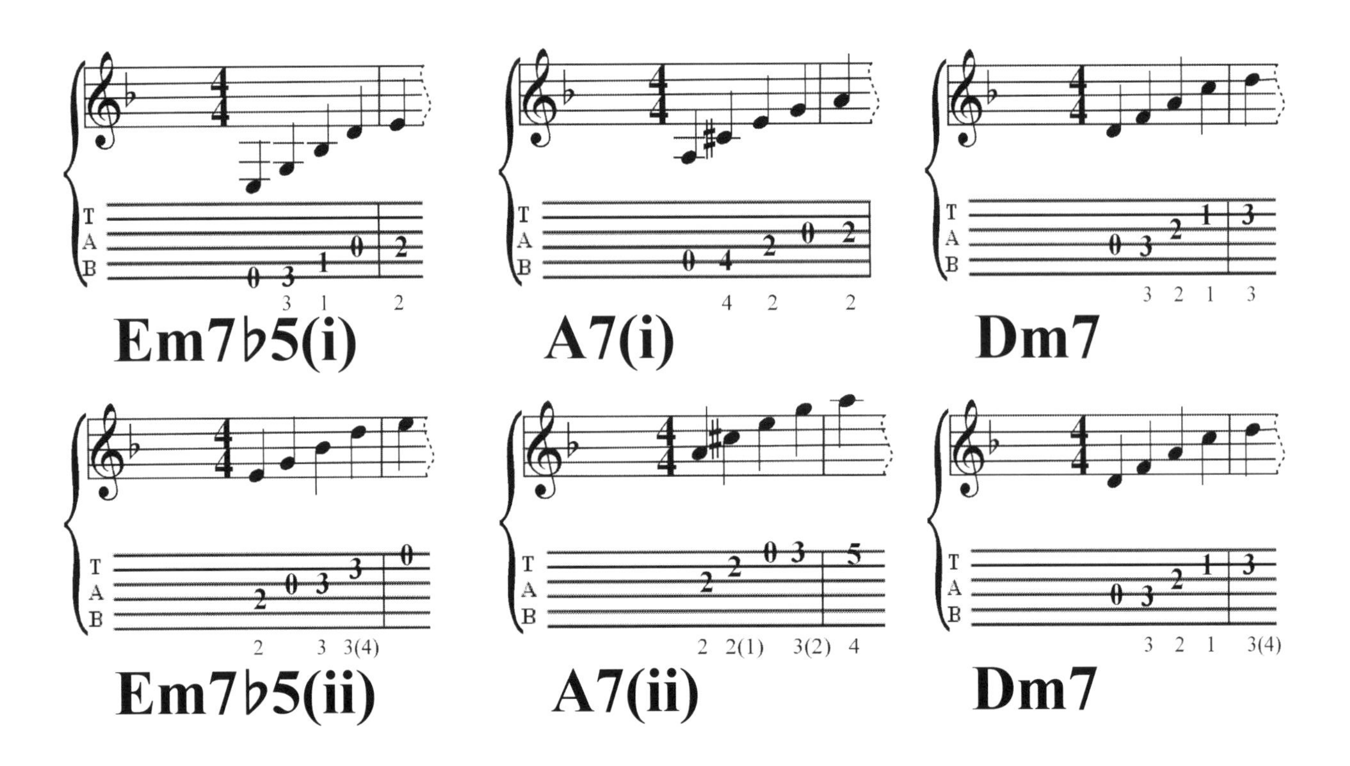

All Keys (i)

ii

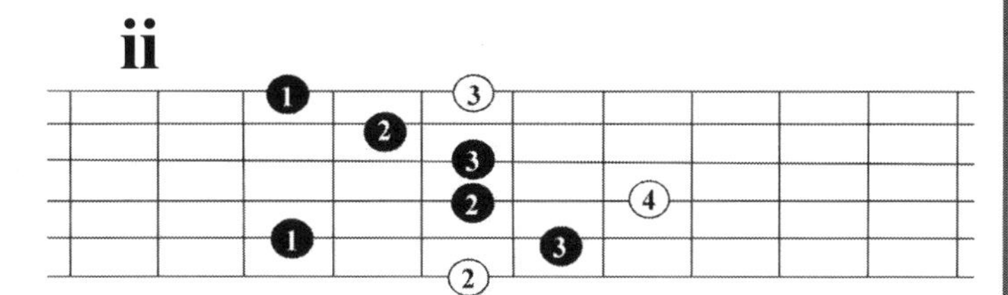

V

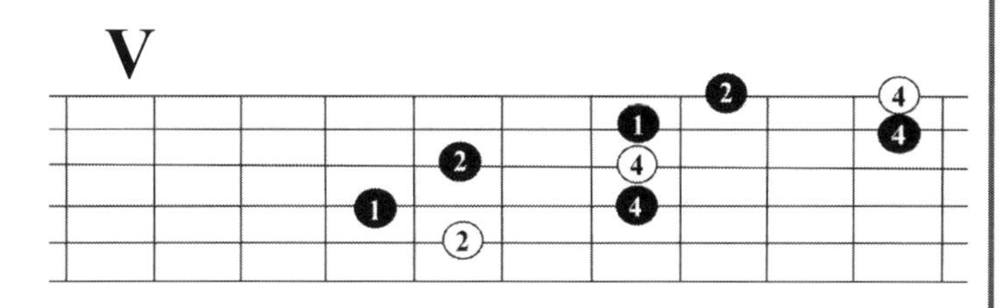

i

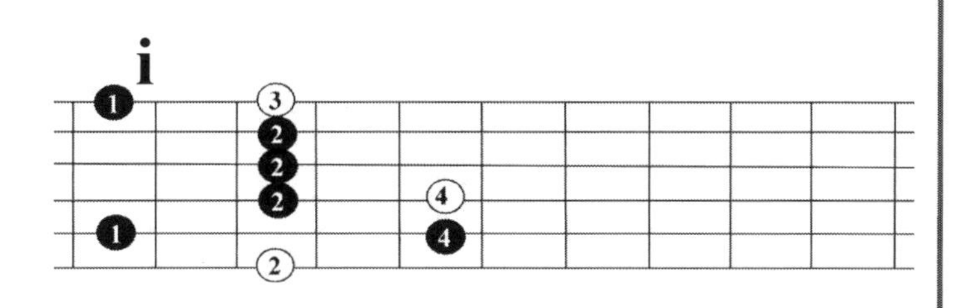

All Keys (ii)

ii

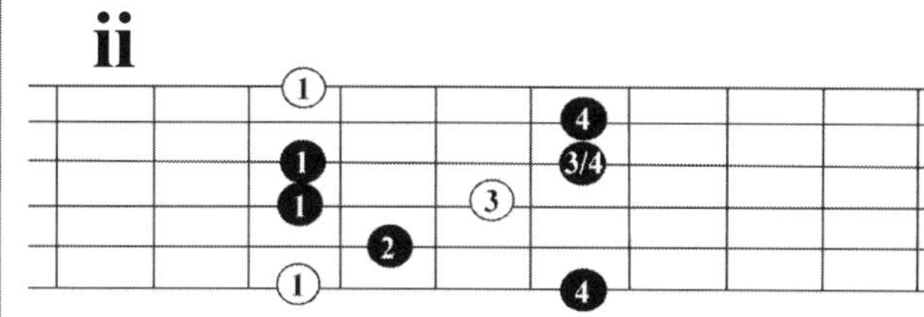

V

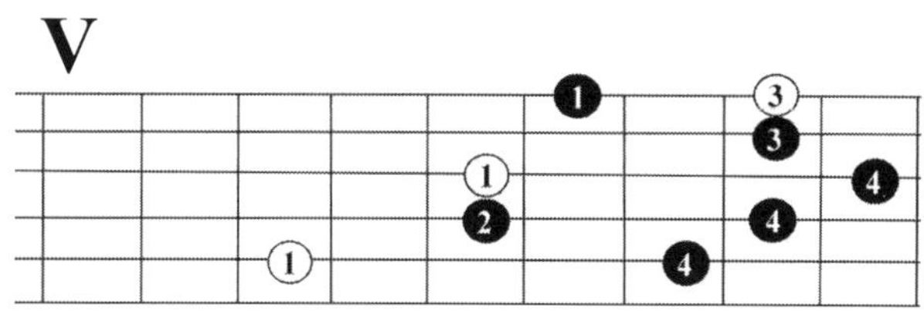

i

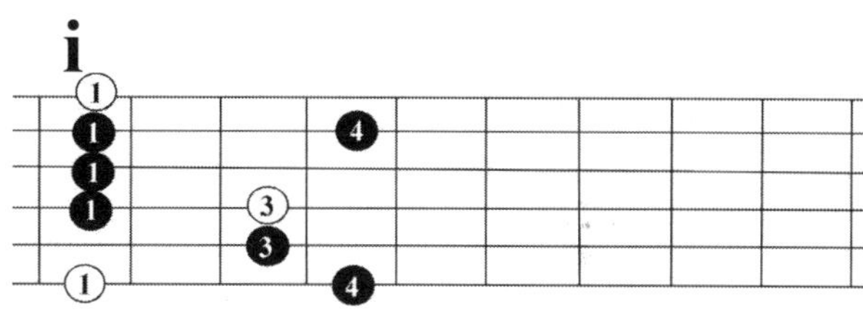

All Keys (iii)

ii

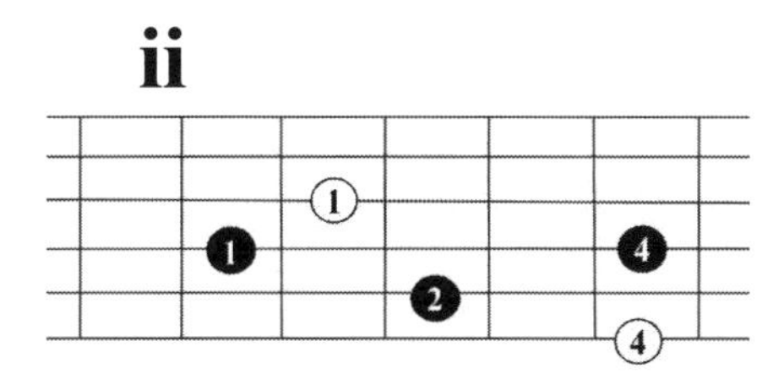

V

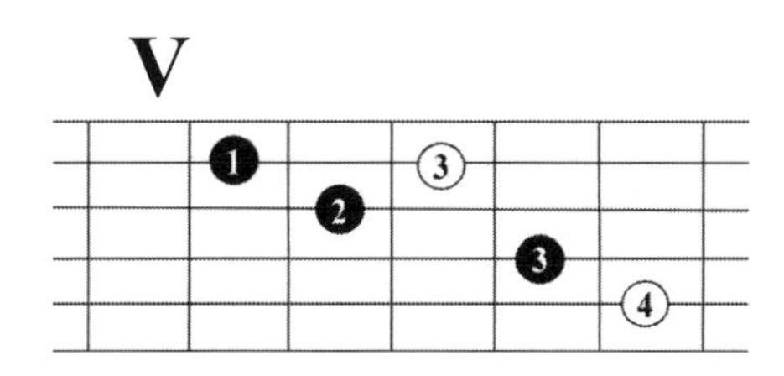

i

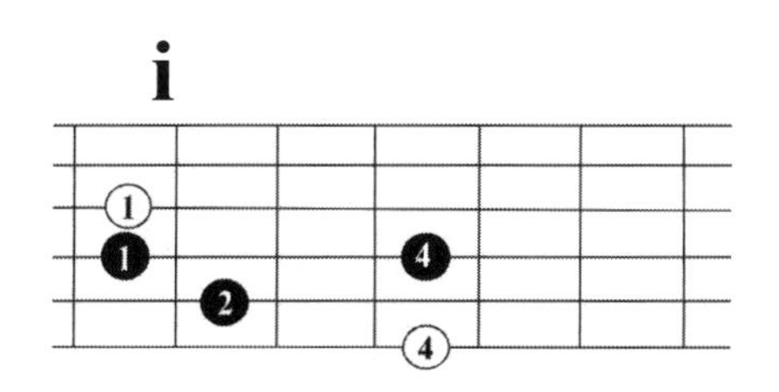

All Keys (iv)

ii

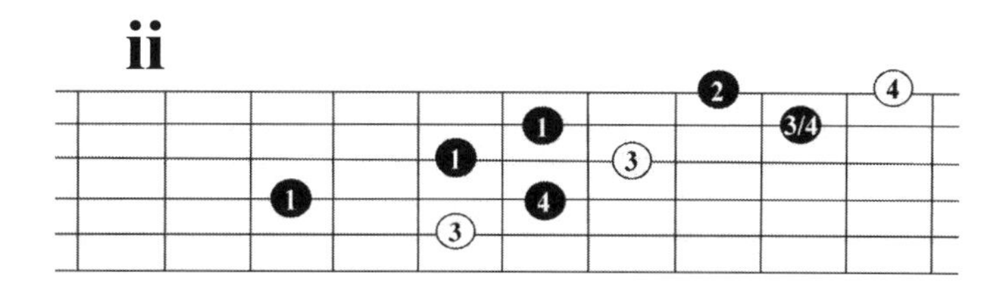

V

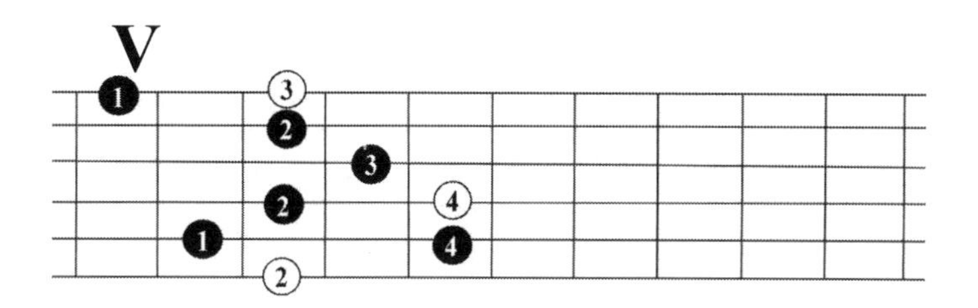

i

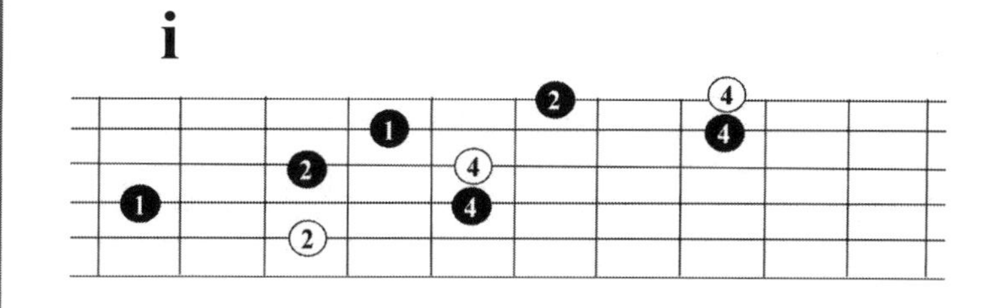

All Keys (v)

ii

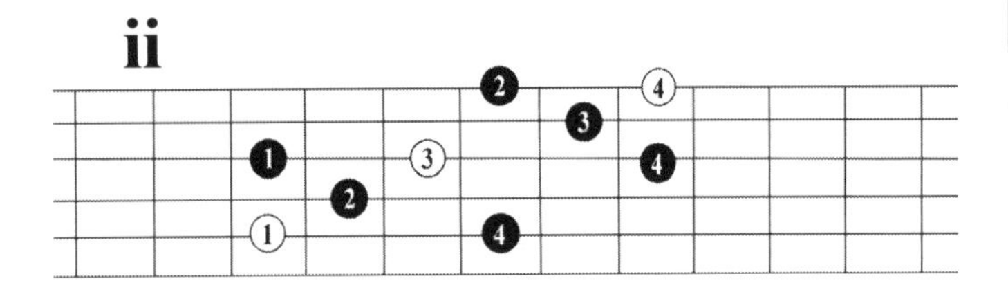

V

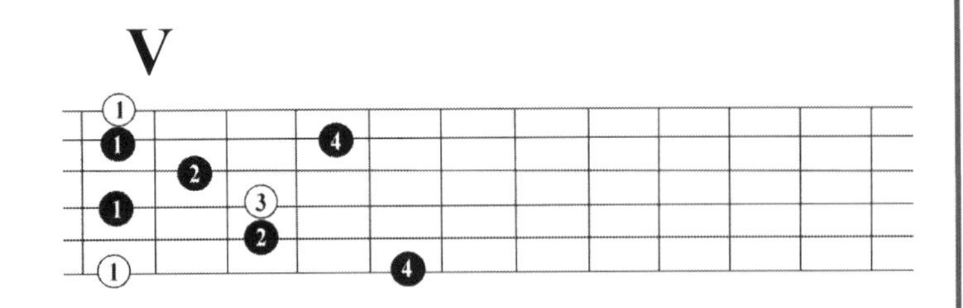

i

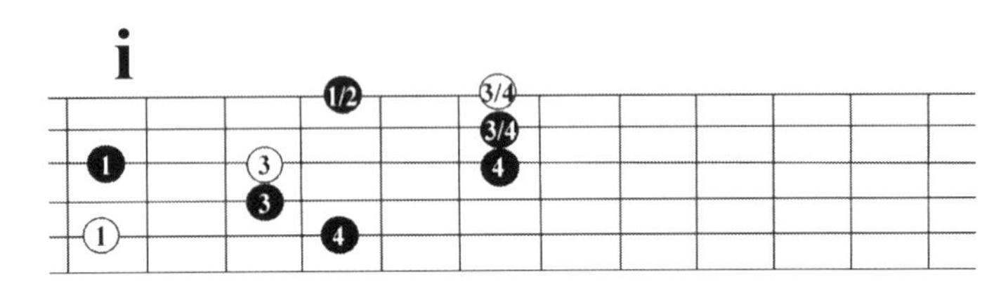

All Keys (vi)

ii

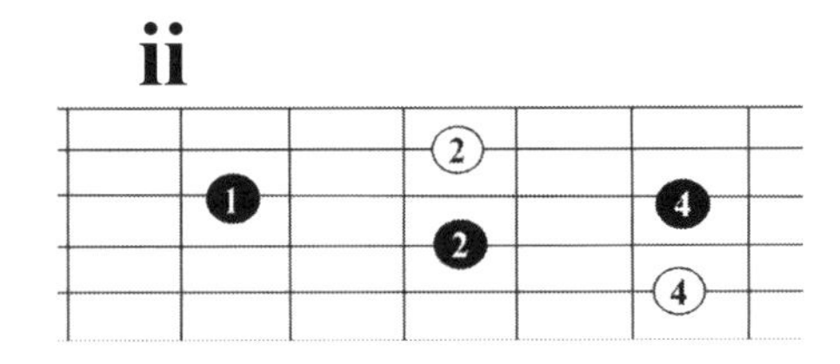

V

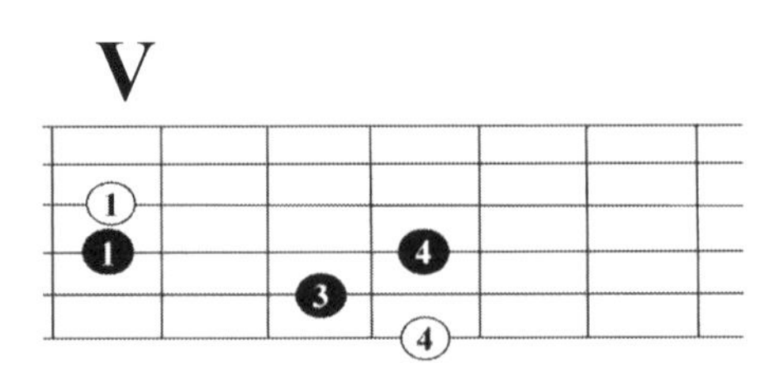

i

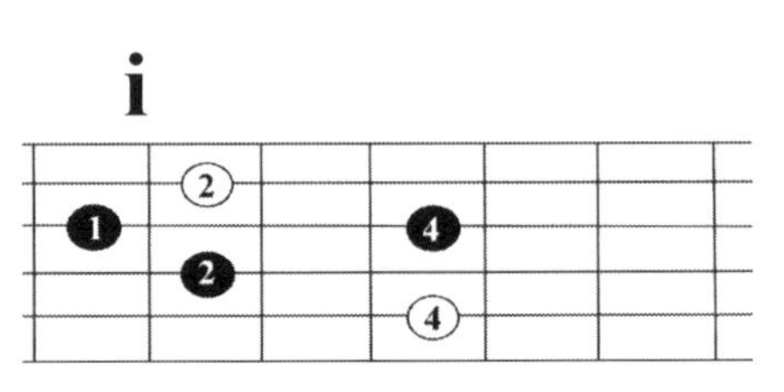

All Keys (vii)

ii

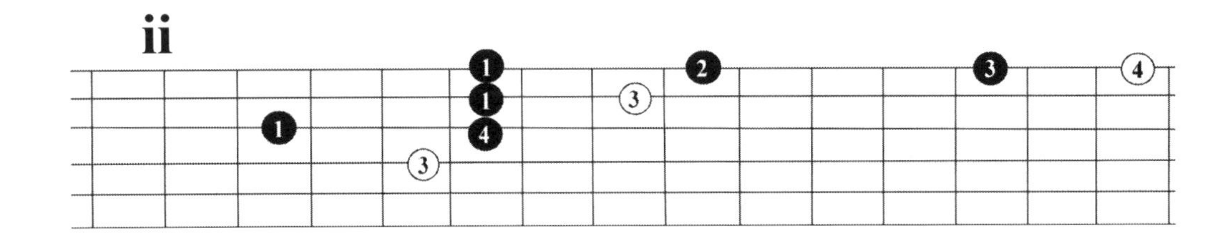

V

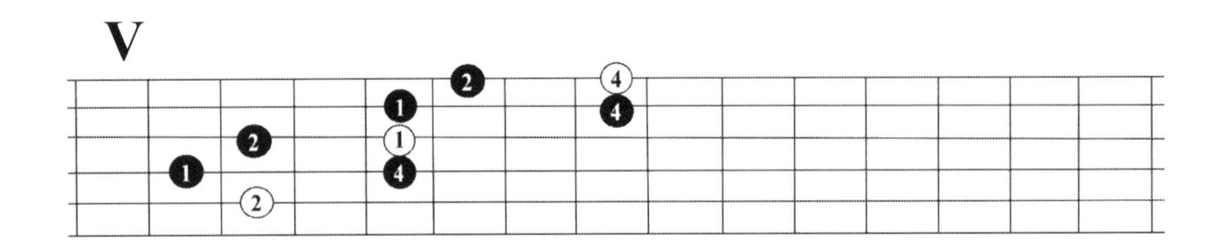

i

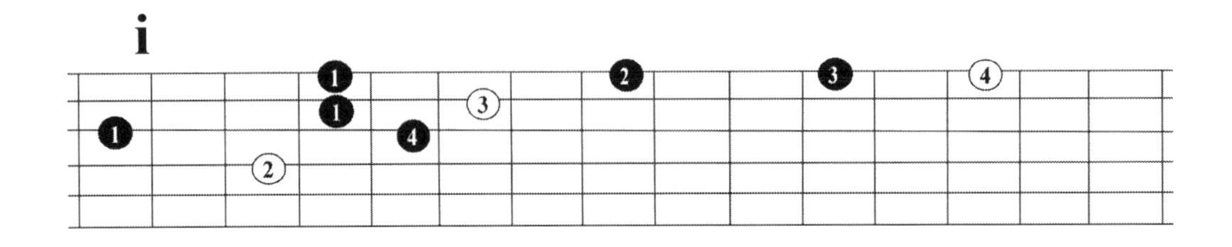

All Keys (viii)

ii

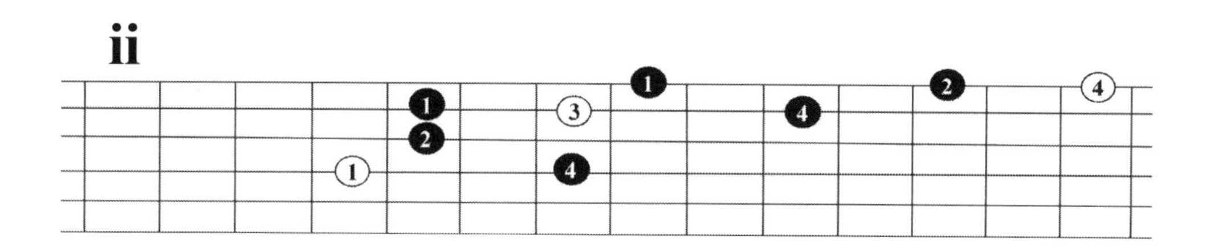

V

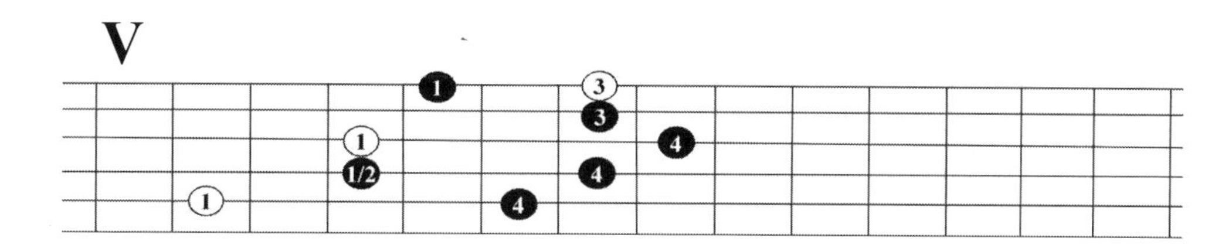

i

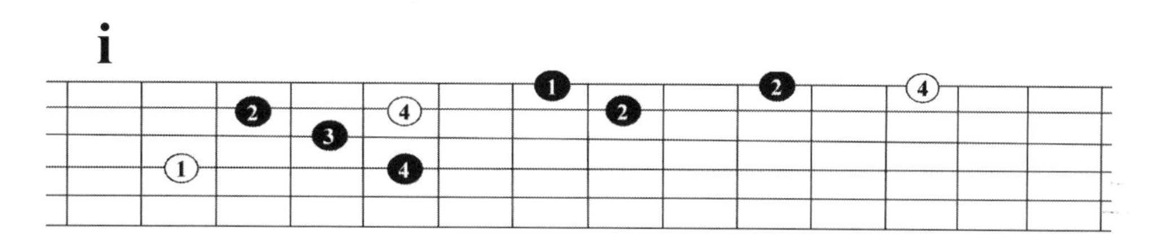

All Keys (ix)

ii

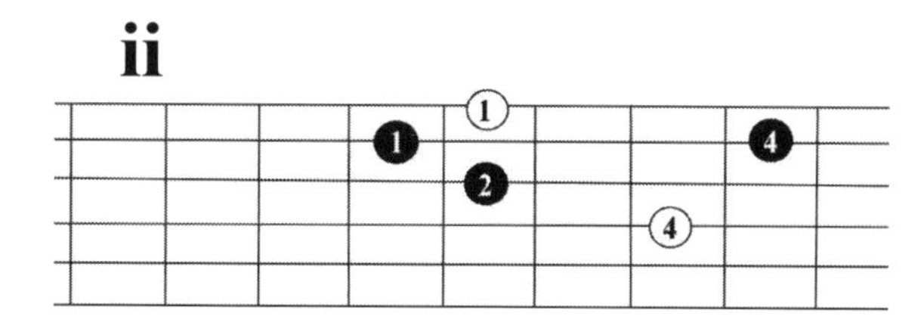

V

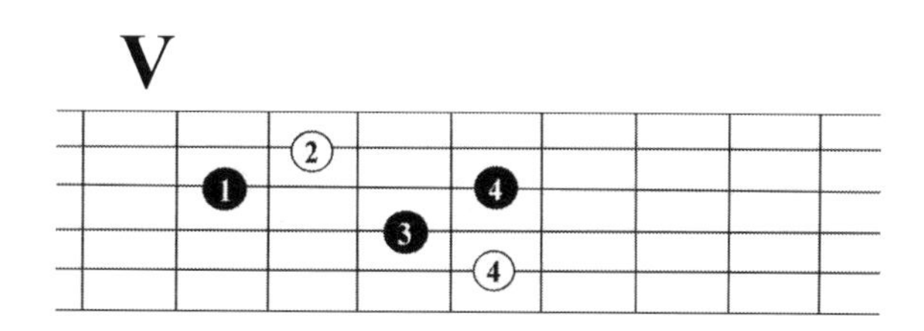

i

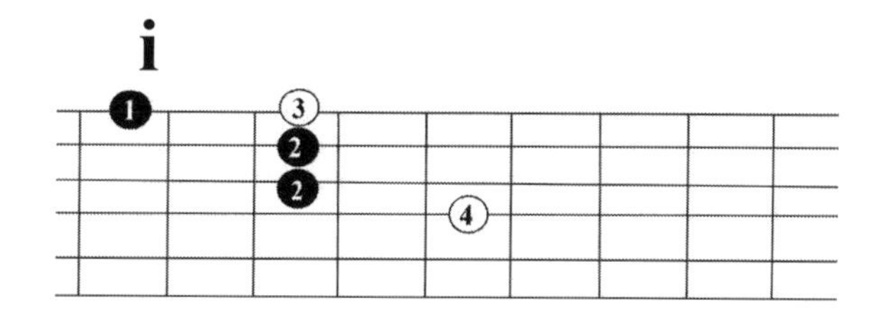

PART TWENTY-FOUR

VI - ii - V - i

MINOR KEYS
SEVENTH CHORDS
ARPEGGIOS

Key of Am

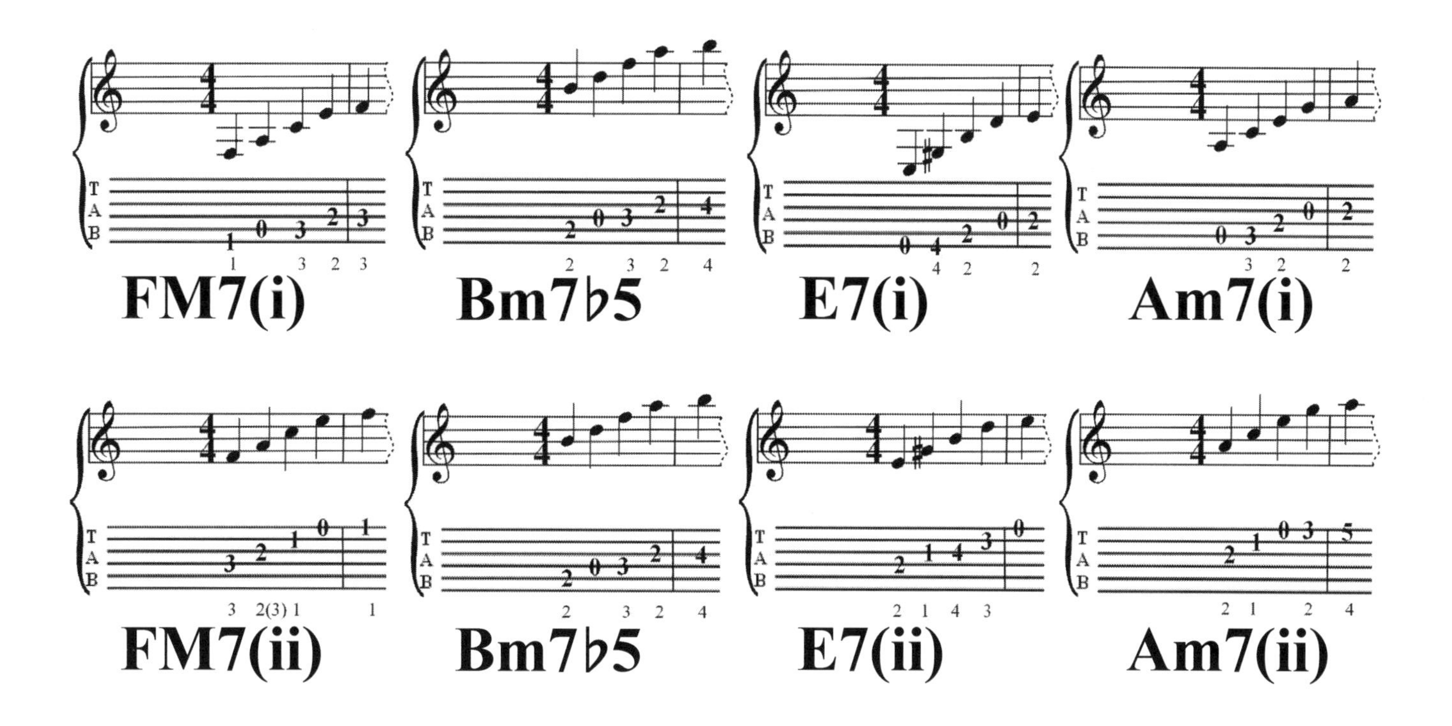

Key of Em

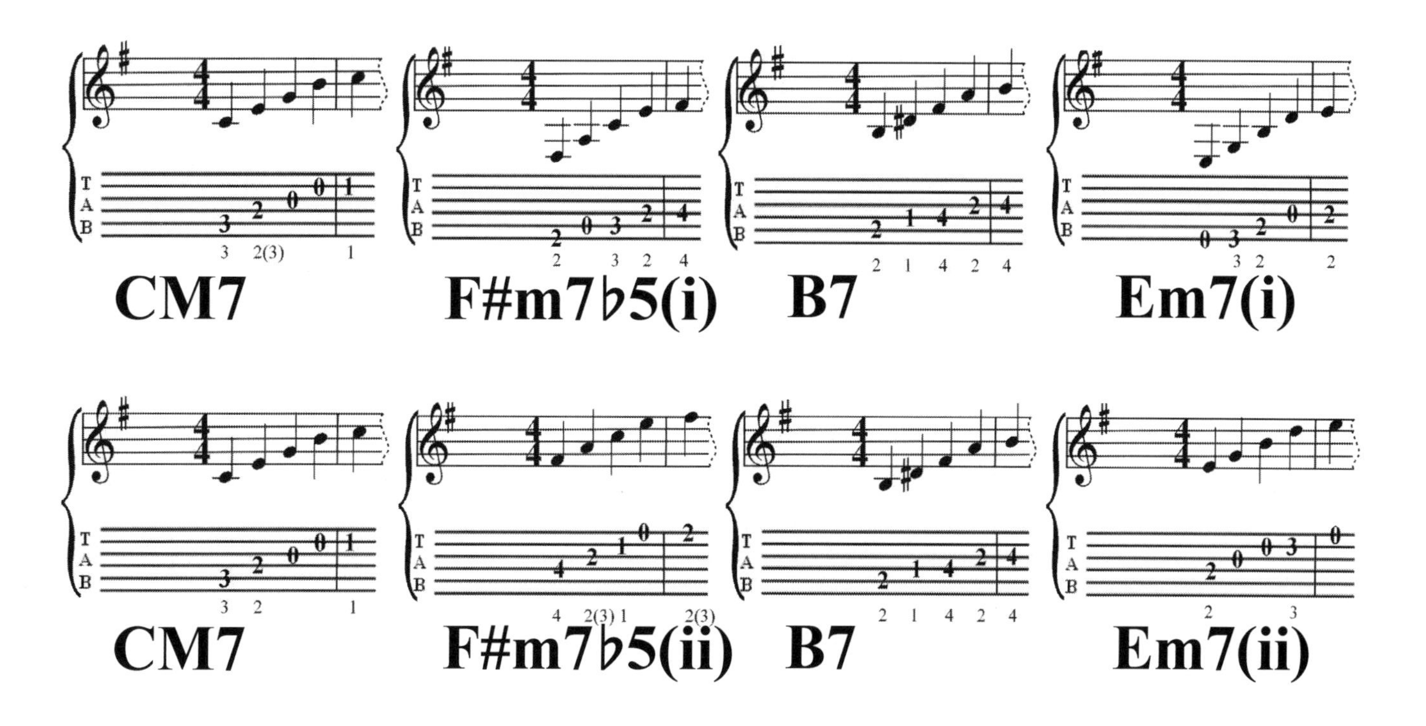

Key of Bm

Key of F#m

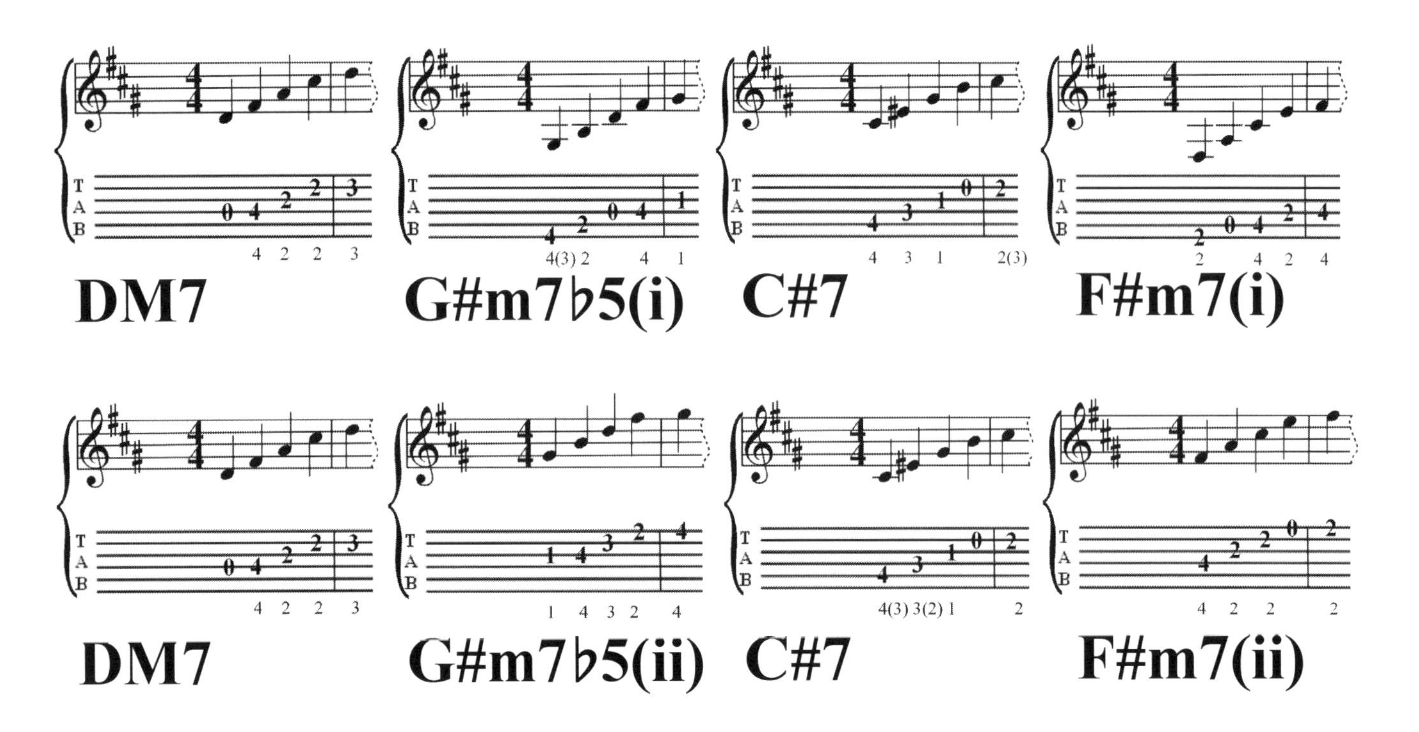

Key of C#m

Key of A♭m

Key of E♭m

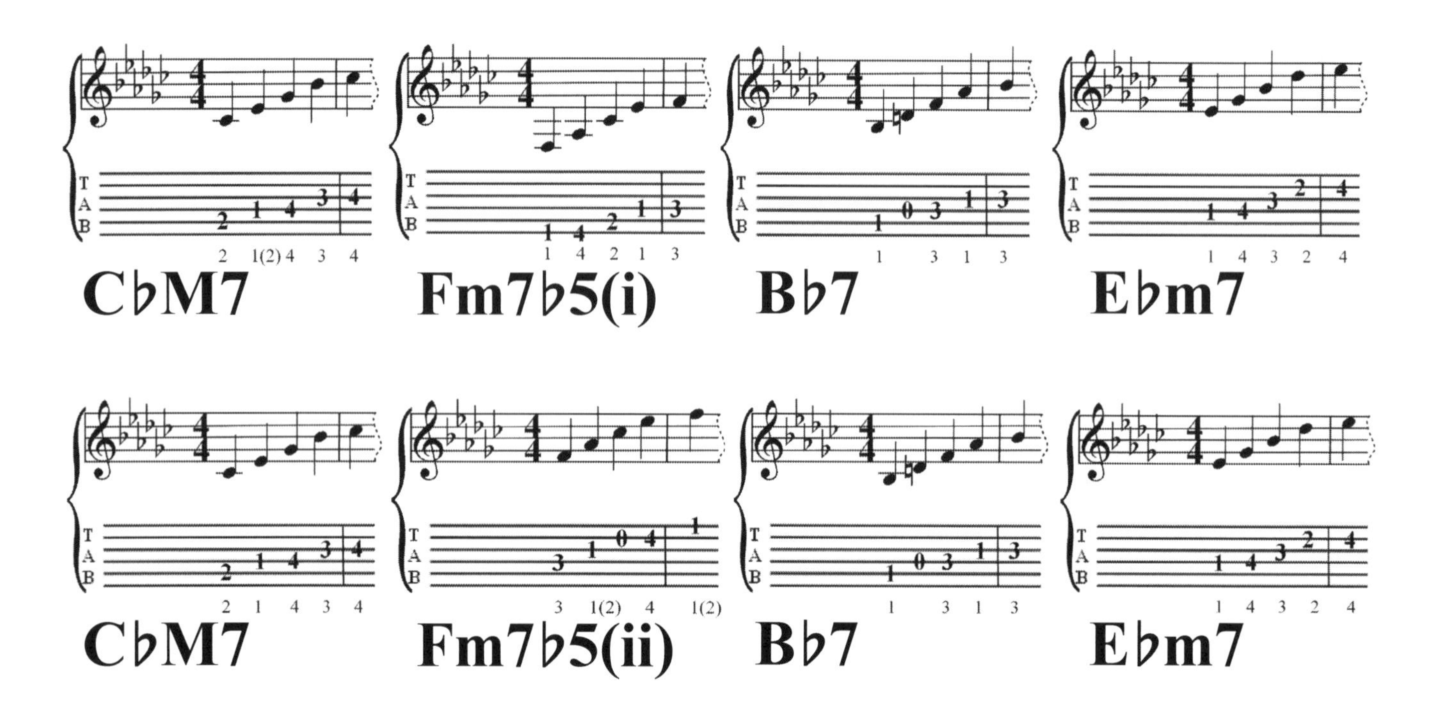

Key of B♭m

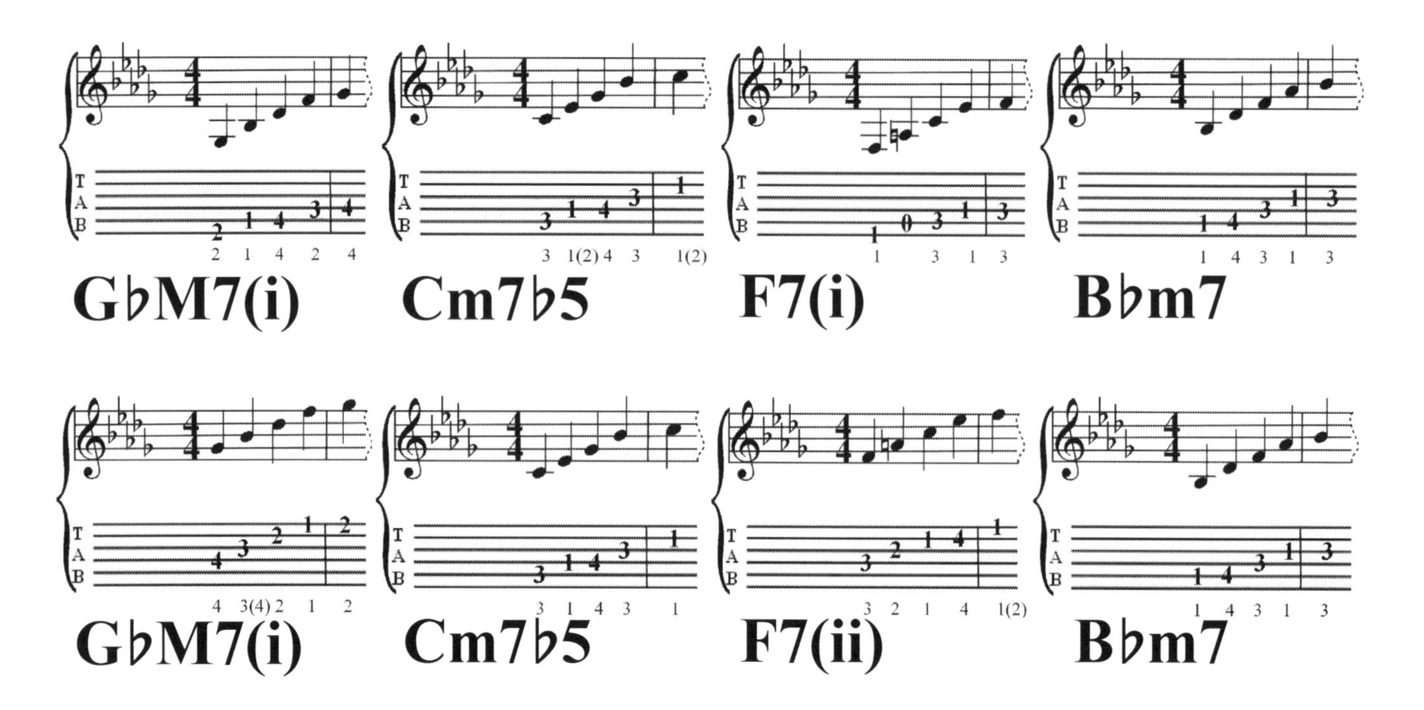

Key of Fm

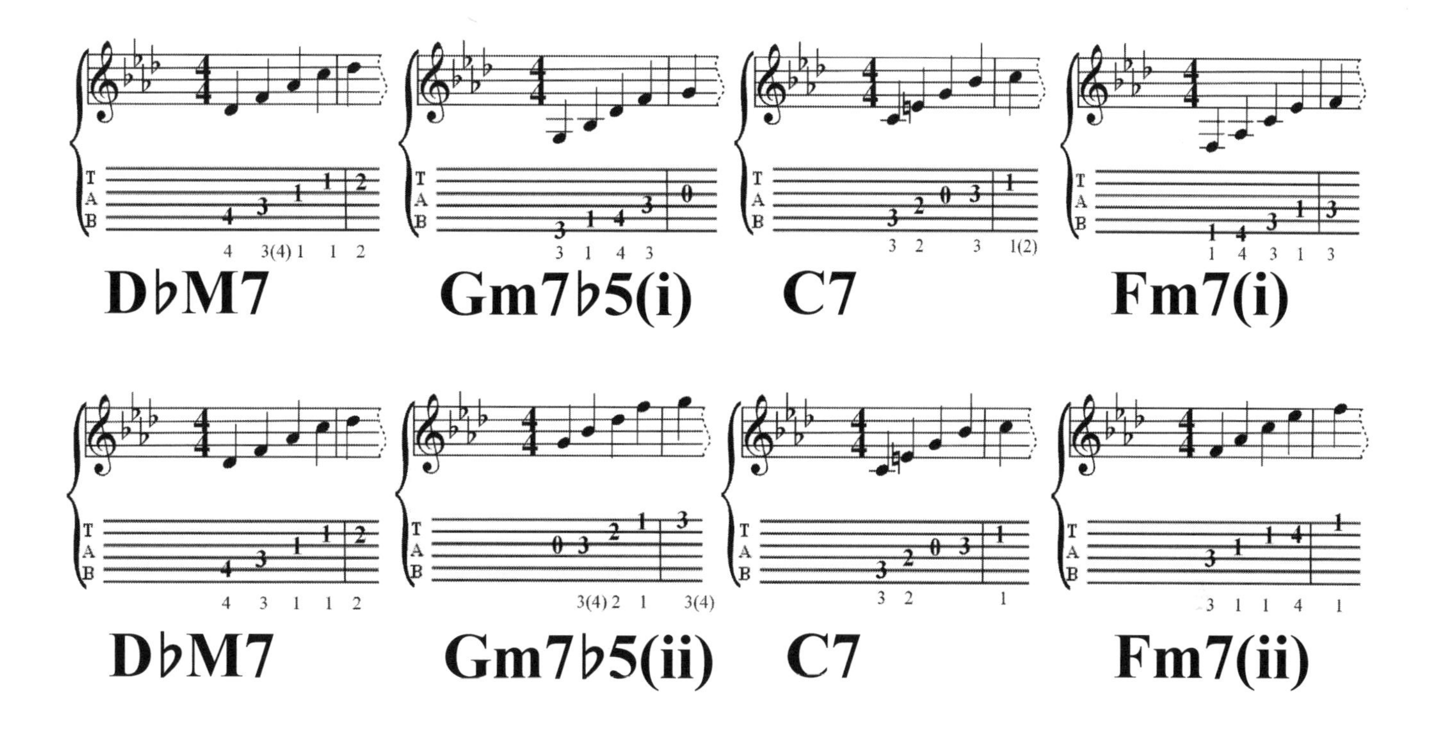

Key of Cm

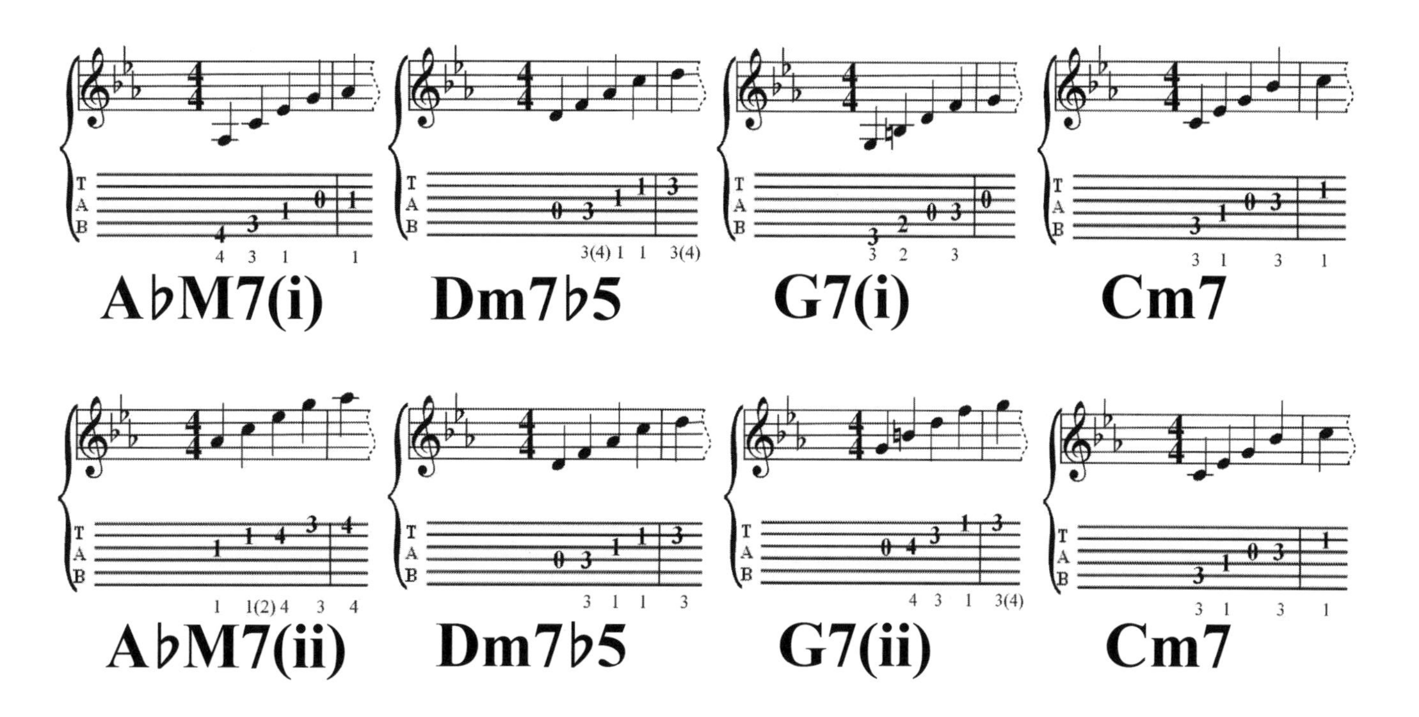

Key of Gm

Key of Dm

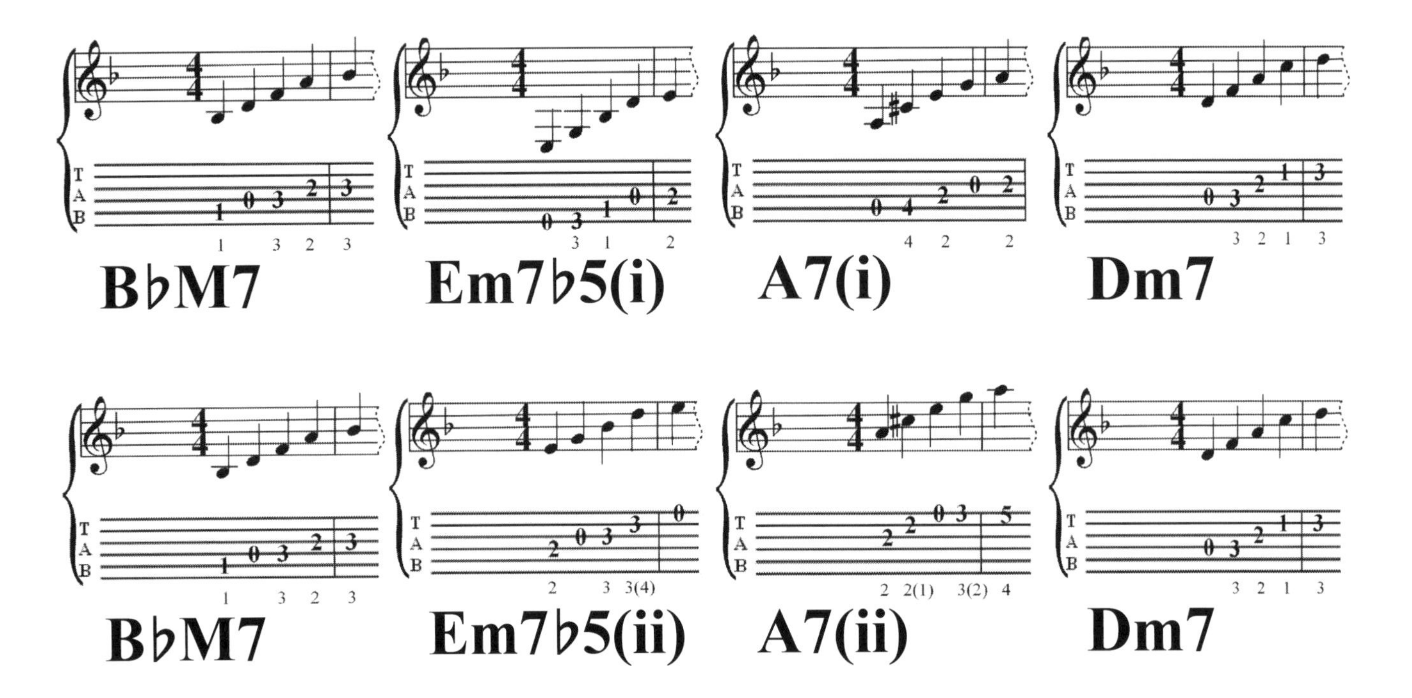

All Keys (i)

VI

ii

V

i

All Keys (ii)

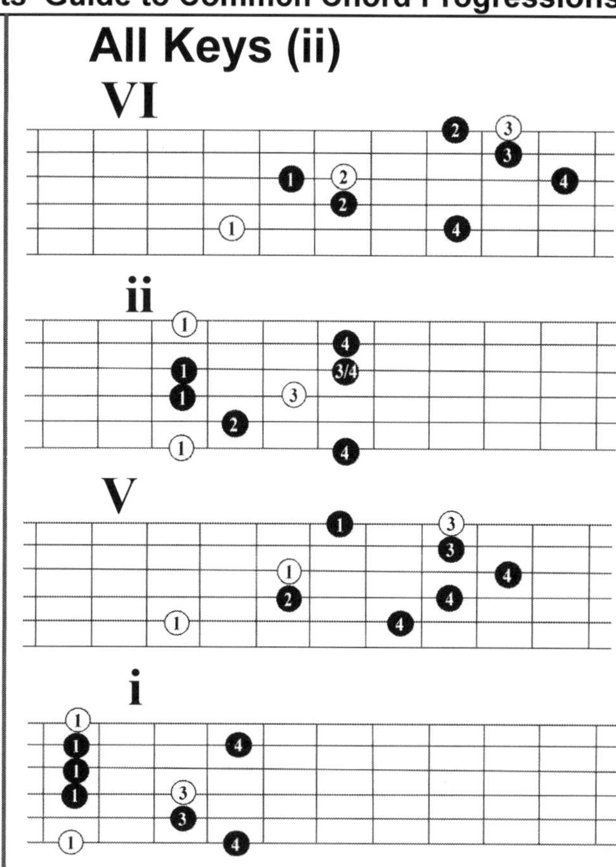

All Keys (iii)

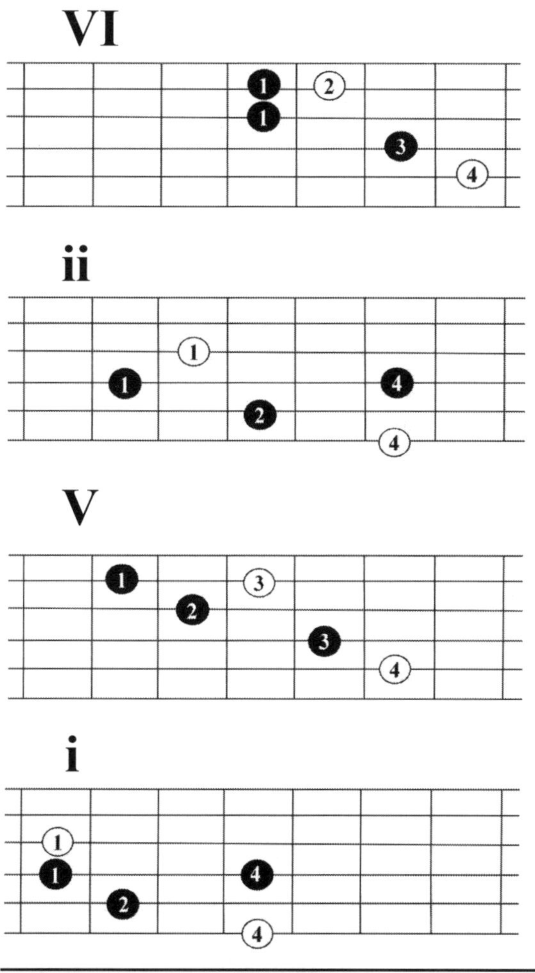

All Keys (iv)

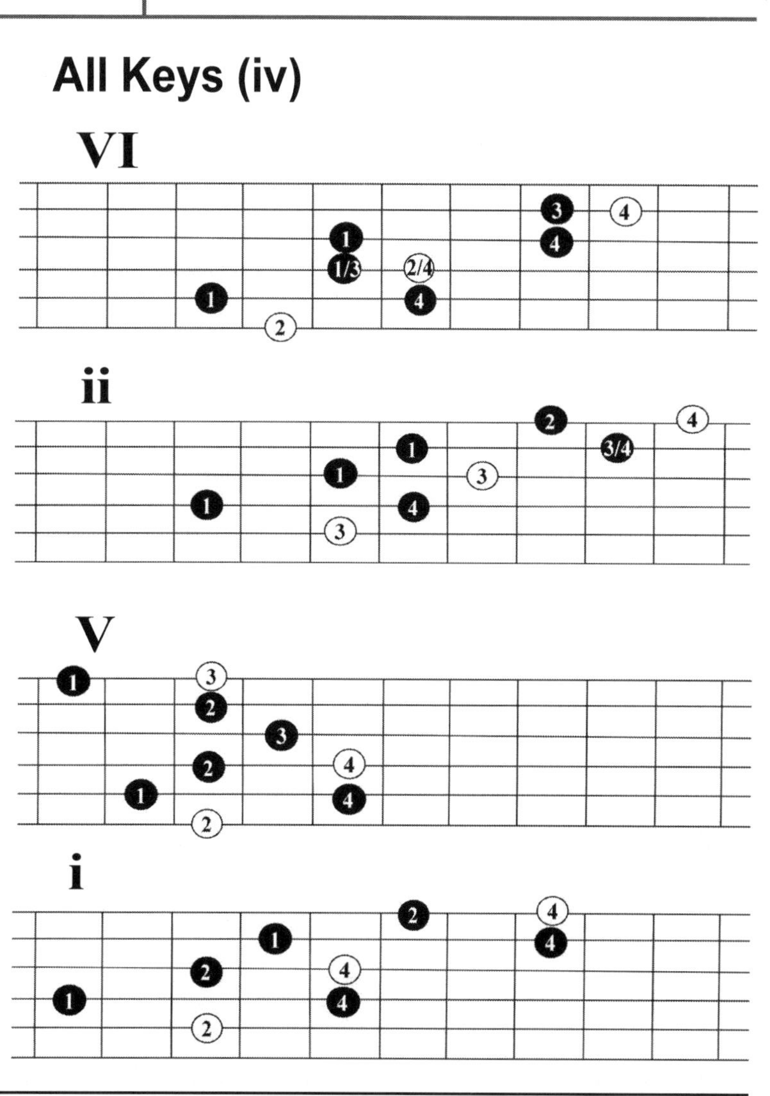

All Keys (v)

VI

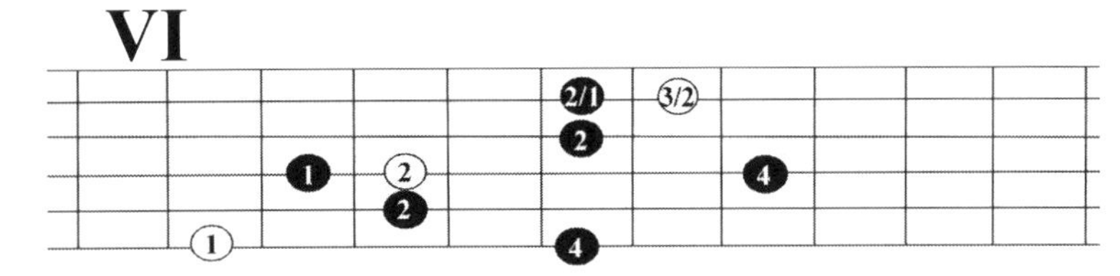

ii

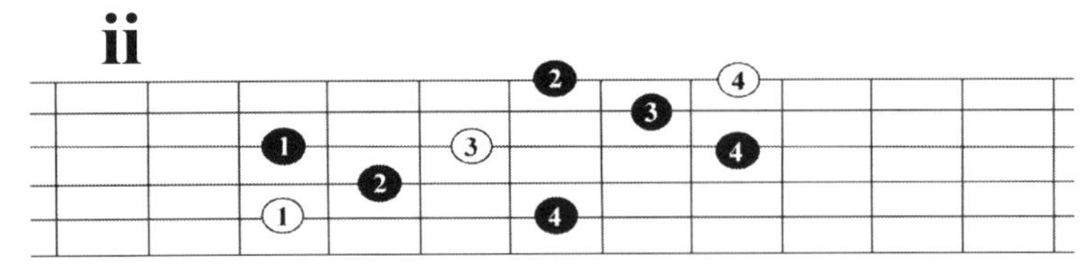

V

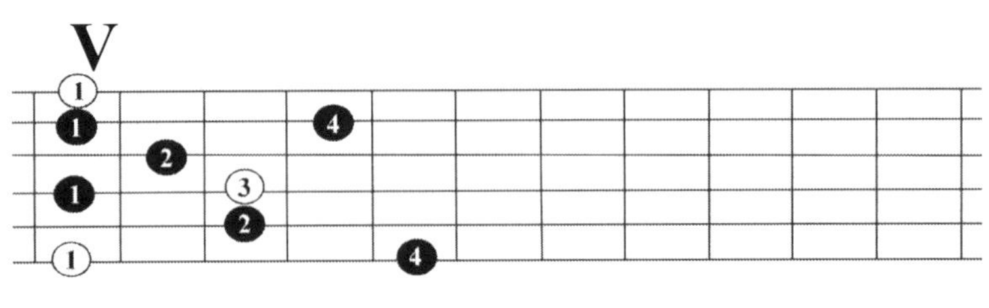

i

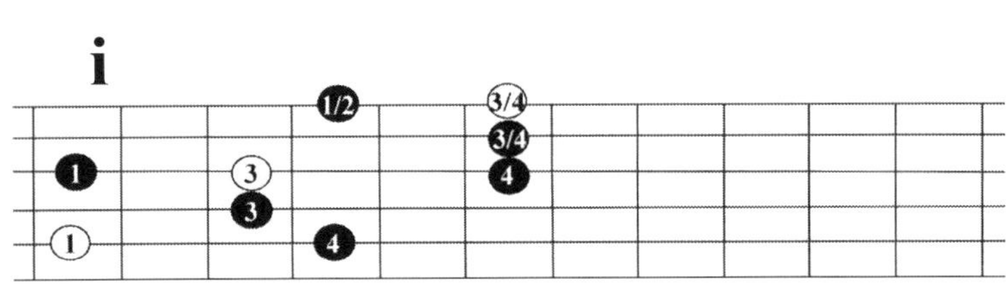

All Keys (vi)

VI

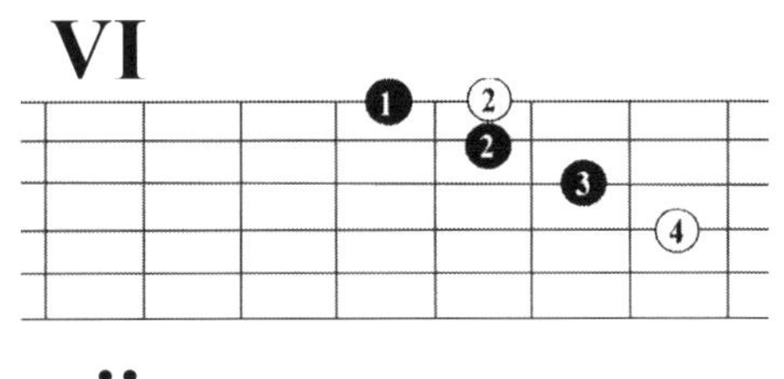

ii

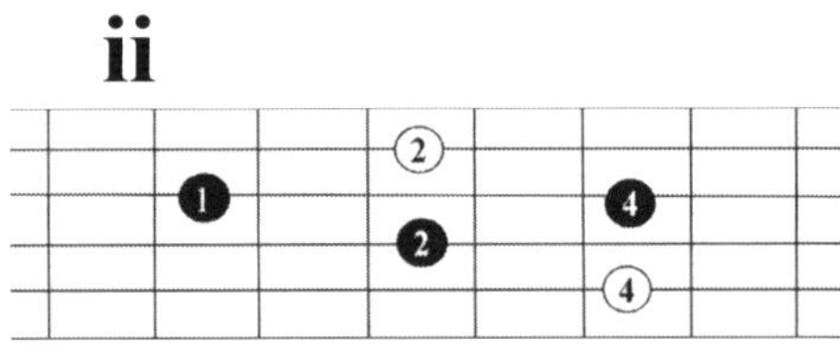

V

i

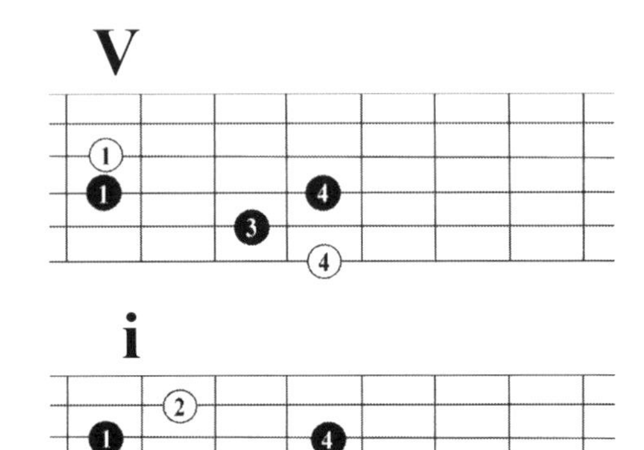

All Keys (vii)

VI

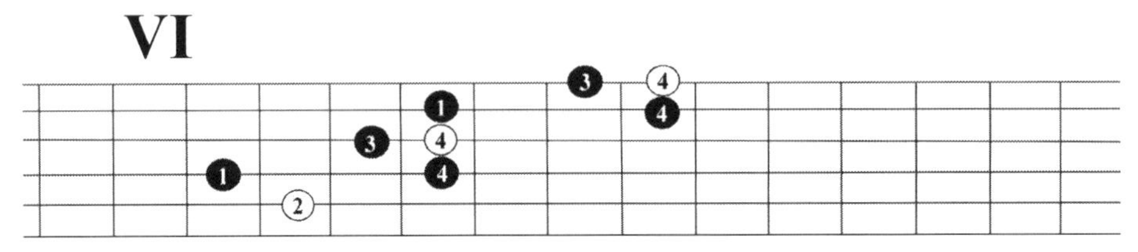

ii

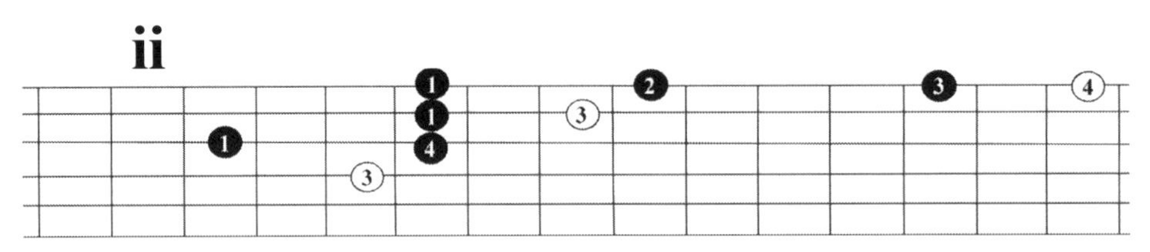

V

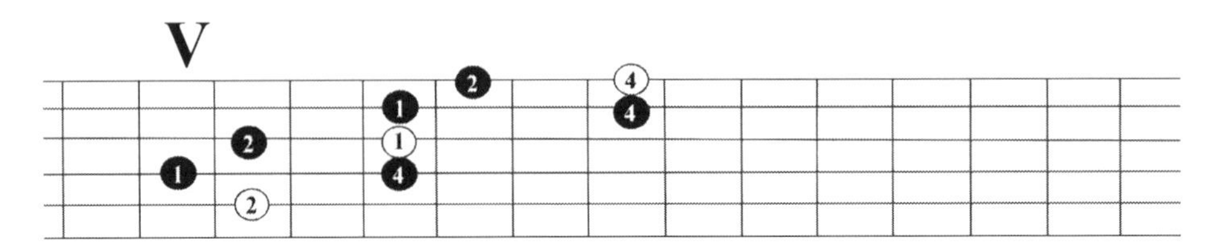

i

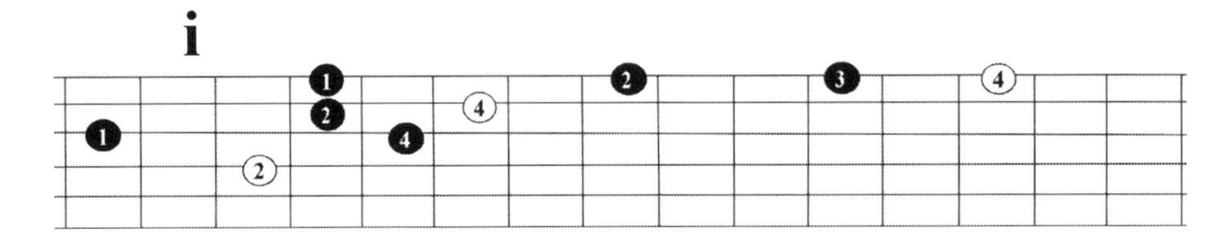

All Keys (viii)

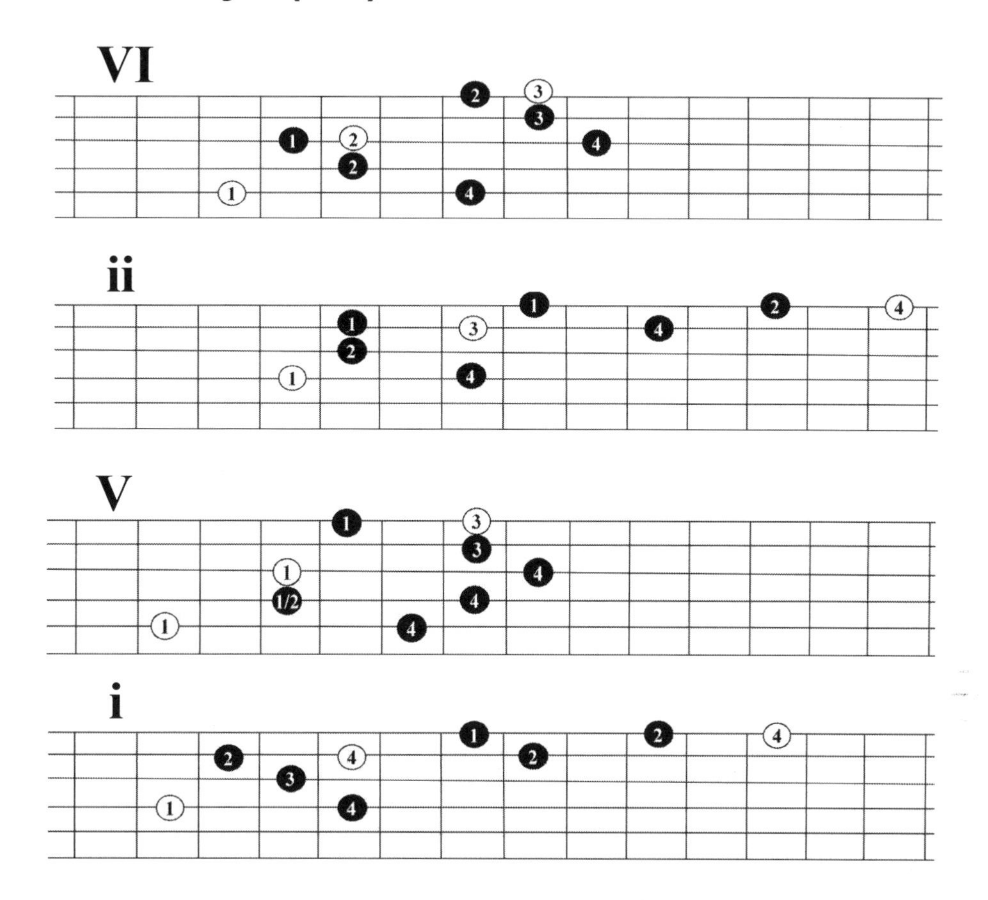

All Keys (ix)

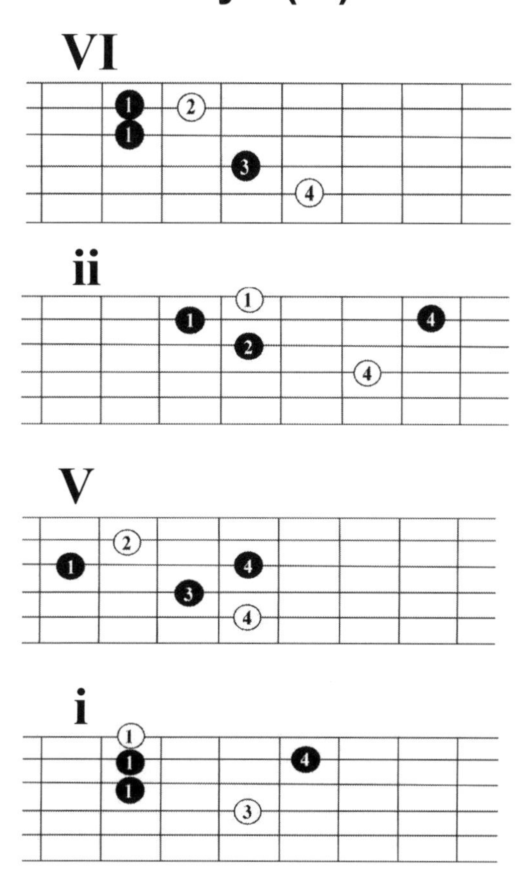

PART TWENTY-FIVE

I - IV - V

MAJOR KEYS PENTATONICS

WHAT ARE PENTATONIC SCALES?

A pentatonic scale is simply a scale which contains five *intervals* within the *octave*, as compared to the seven intervals of the classical (or "*diatonic*") *major* and *minor* scales. Pentatonic scales form the basis of much traditional and folk music throughout the world, but are also used a great deal in jazz, pop and rock music - in building melodies, and particularly in improvisation. For the guitarist, one big advantage of pentatonic patterns is that, in many positions, they can be played with two notes per string. This makes it relatively easy to develop very fast "motors" in your fingers for playing these patterns.

HOW ARE PENTATONIC SCALES CONSTRUCTED?

In principle, any five intervals between a note and its octave can form a pentatonic scale, and I recommend you to spend some time experimenting with the possibilities. However, the most common pentatonics, as used in this book, can be derived by eliminating the *semitone* intervals from the seven-interval scales and modes of the diatonic system. (If you are not familiar with the concept of modes, they are dealt with in detail in a later section of this book - by all means skip ahead for an overview).

THE I (Major or M7) CHORD

The semitone intervals of the major scale occur between the *third* and *fourth*, and the *seventh* and octave. Since the *root* and third define the essential character of the chord, these are retained, so that the major pentatonic scale loses the fourth and seventh. For example, in the key of C, the notes and intervals of the major scale are:

C *(tone)* **D** *(tone)* **E** *(semitone)* **F** *(tone)* **G** *(tone)* **A** *(tone)* **B** *(semitone)* **C**

So the C major pentatonic scale will contain:

C *(tone)* **D** *(tone)* **E** *(minor third)* **G** *(tone)* **A** *(minor third)* **C**

THE IV (Major or M7) CHORD

The major pentatonic pattern above will work perfectly well for the IV chord. However the mode built on the fourth *degree* of the scale distinctively contains a sharpened fourth - this can be substituted for the fifth to create an alternative pentatonic as follows (example given for a chord of F in the key of C):

F *(tone)* **G** *(tone)* **A** *(tone)* **B** *(minor third)* **D** *(minor third)* **F**

THE V (Major or 7) CHORD

Once again, the basic major pentatonic will work with the V chord. An alternative pentatonic exploits the fact that the V chord and its corresponding mode, uniquely, contain a major third and a flattened (minor) seventh - this can replace the sixth giving (for example - chord of G in the key of C):

G *(tone)* **A** *(tone)* **B** *(minor third)* **D** *(minor third)* **F** *(tone)* **G**

Using these variants of the major pentatonic scale for the IV and V chords helps to emphasise the tonality (i.e. key) of the piece as a whole. Using the basic major pentatonic for all the chords introduces an element of tonal ambiguity which you may wish to exploit - perhaps especially in passages which *modulate* between keys. Similar considerations will apply to the minor pentatonic scales introduced in the following chapters.

Throughout this book, the exercises will use the variant pentatonic forms, so that all patterns are practised thoroughly.

PRACTICE TIP

In order to keep the exercises in a regular, simple time signature, I recommend that the back-and-forth patterns are played in complete scales, repeating the octave and returning to the root so that the ascending and descending patterns each contain 6 notes (in contrast to the recommendations for the arpeggio exercises) - making the time signature 6/4 throughout. Substitute fingerings have been chosen with this pattern in mind.

Key of C

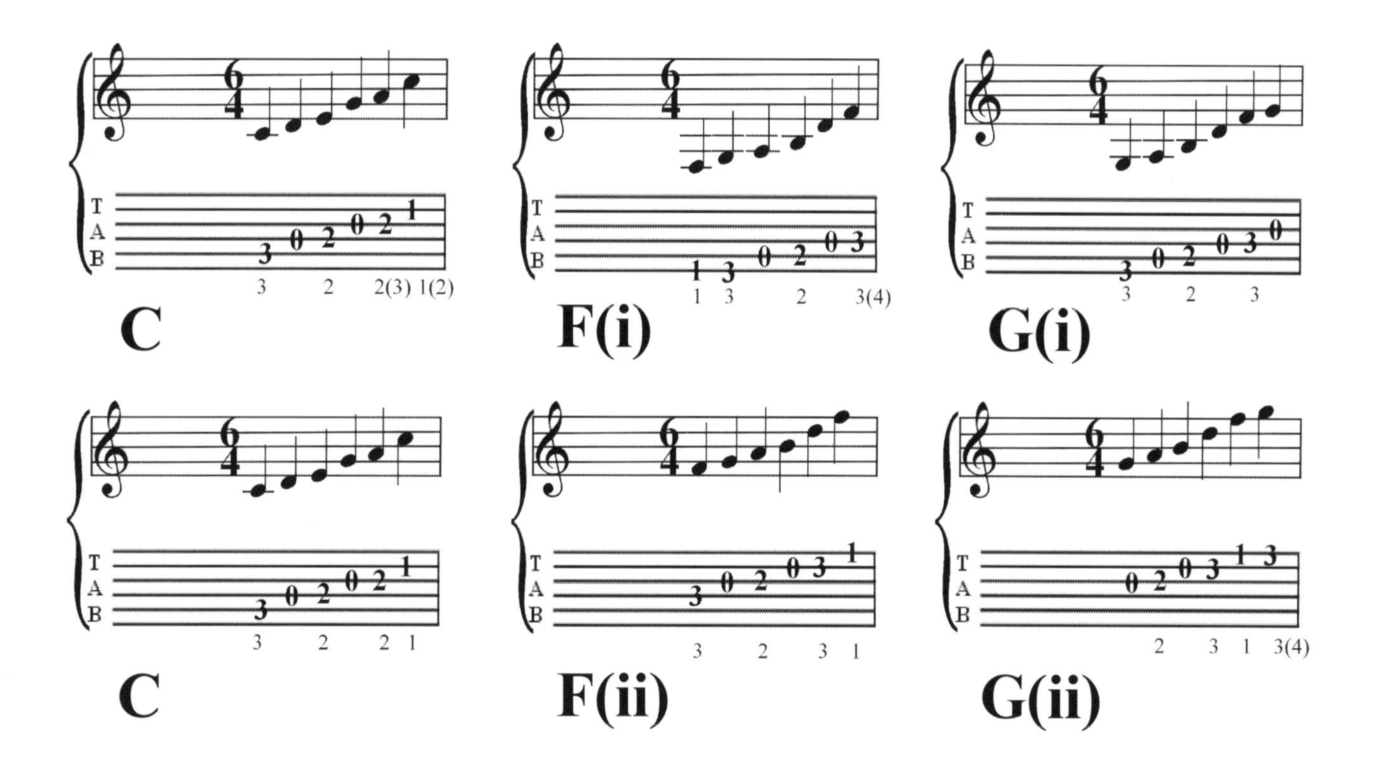

Key of G

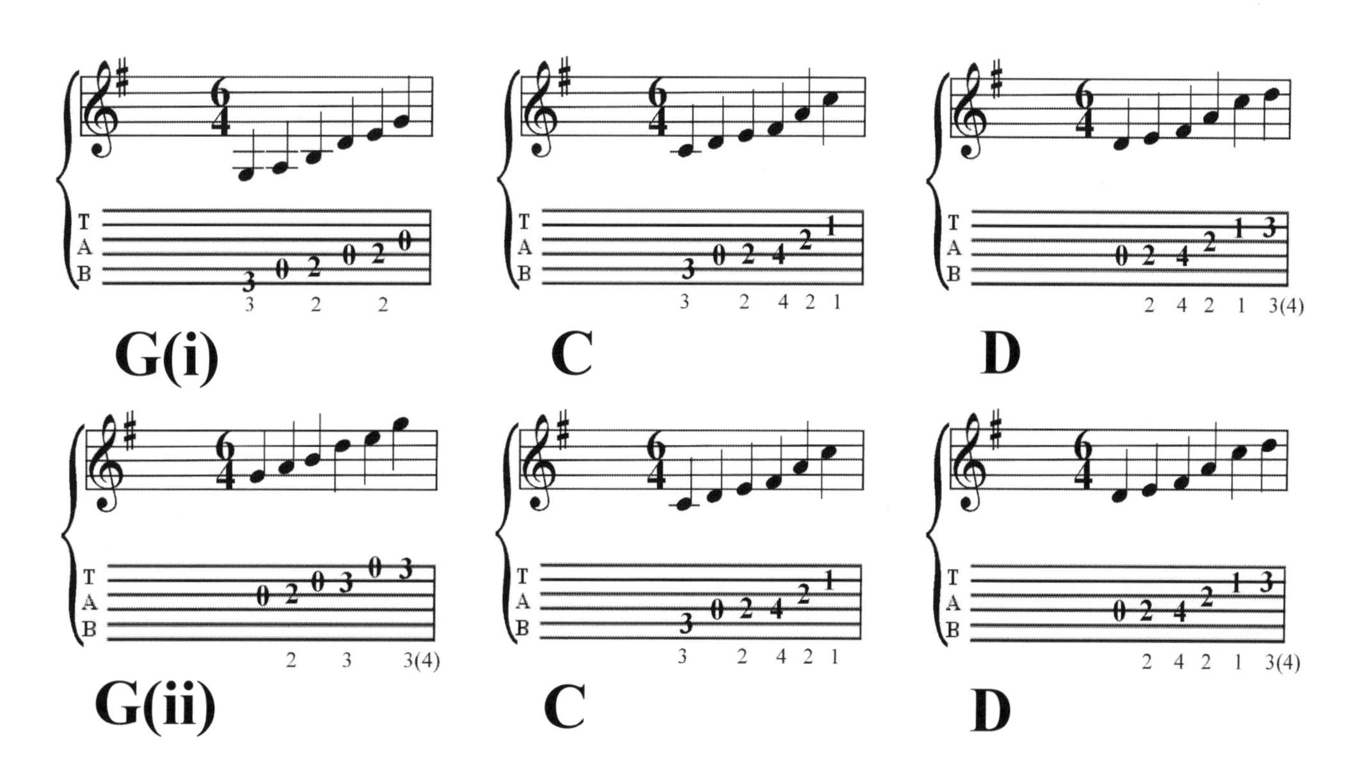

Key of D

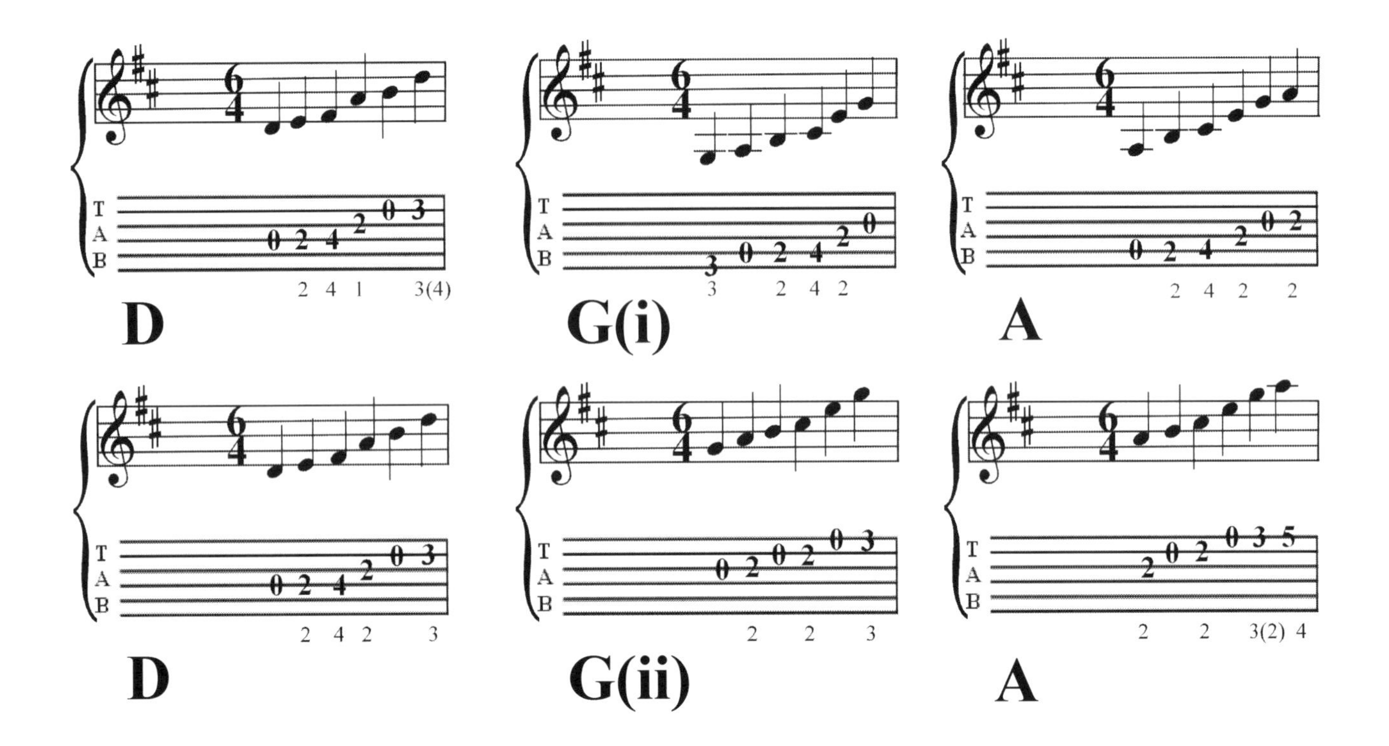

Key of A

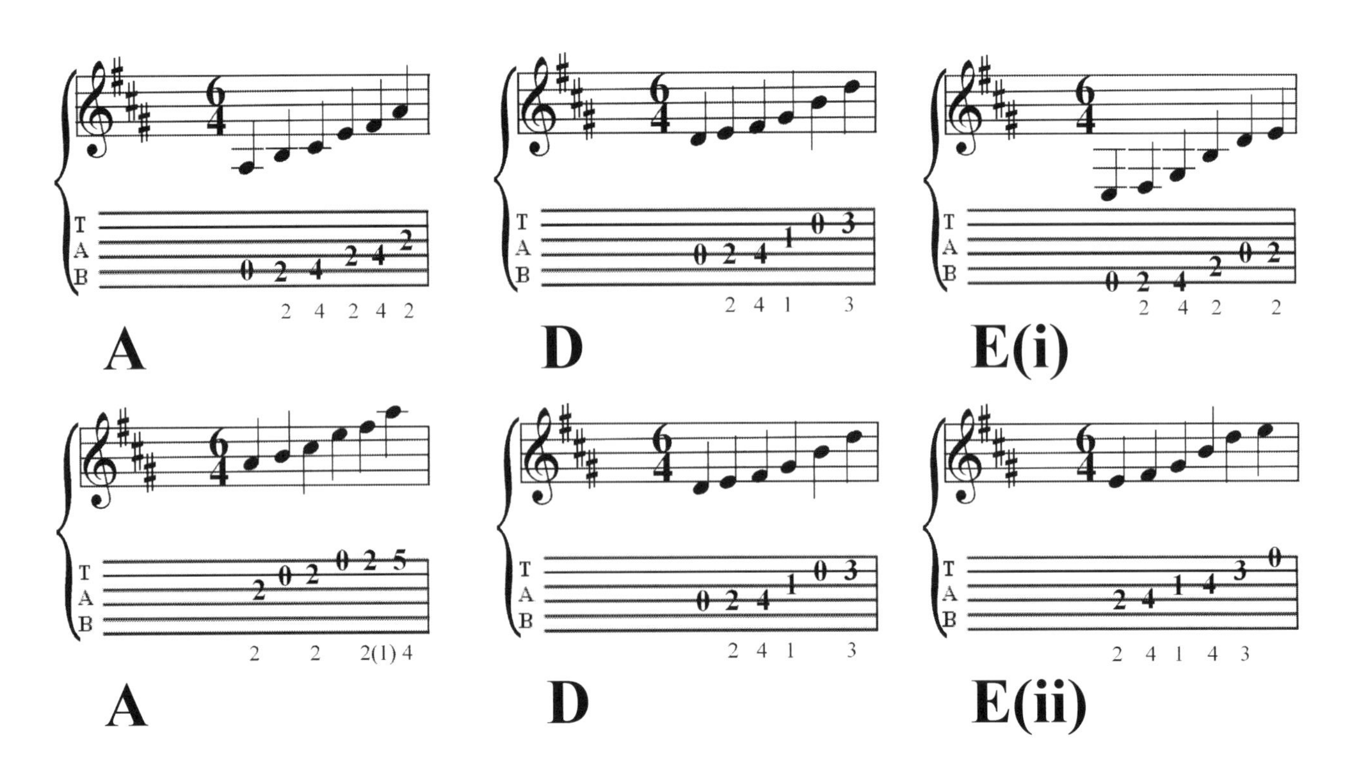

Key of E

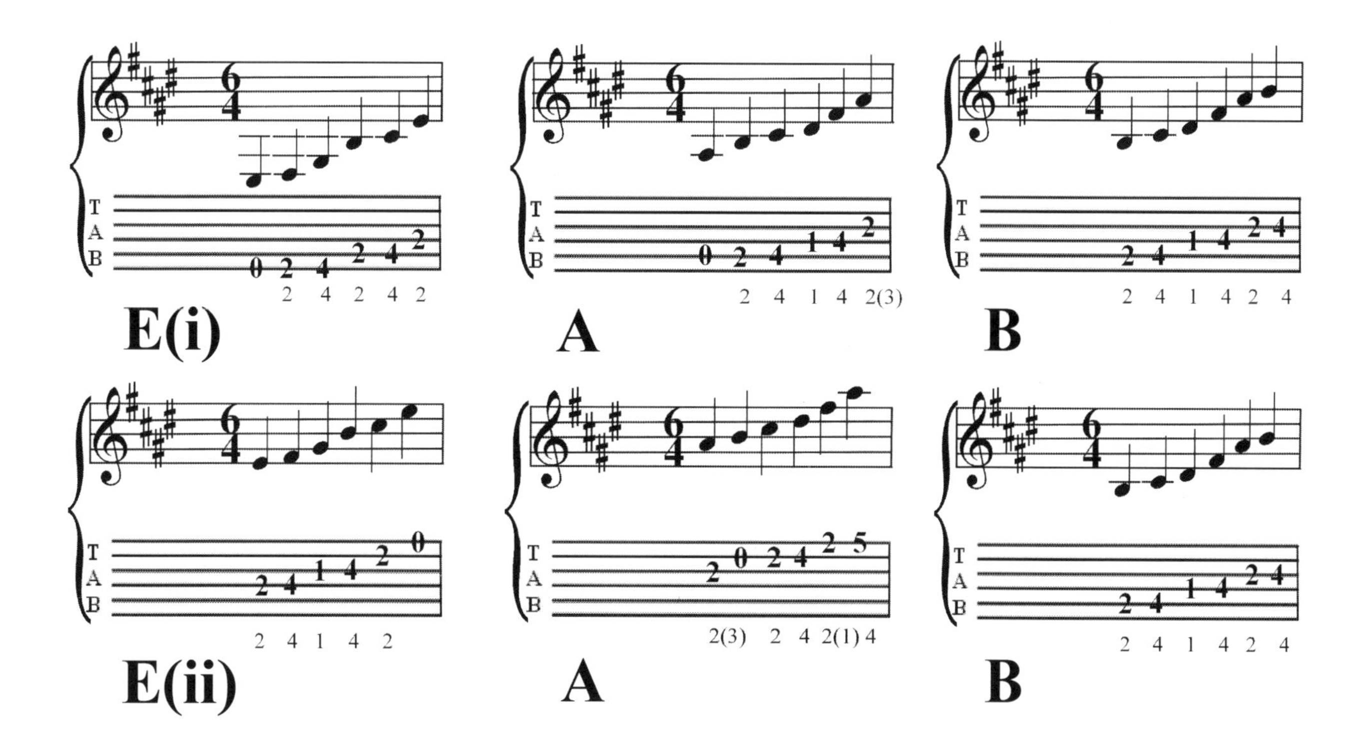

Key of B

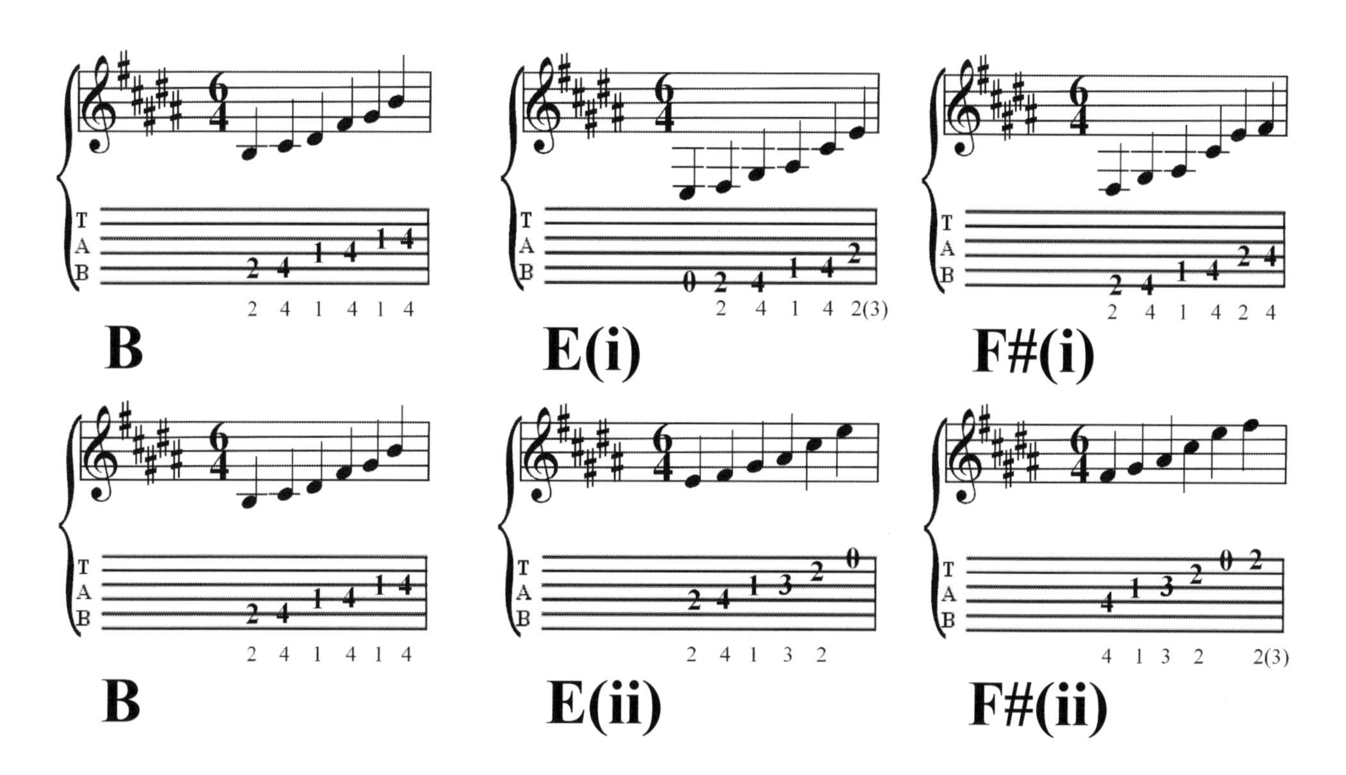

Key of F#

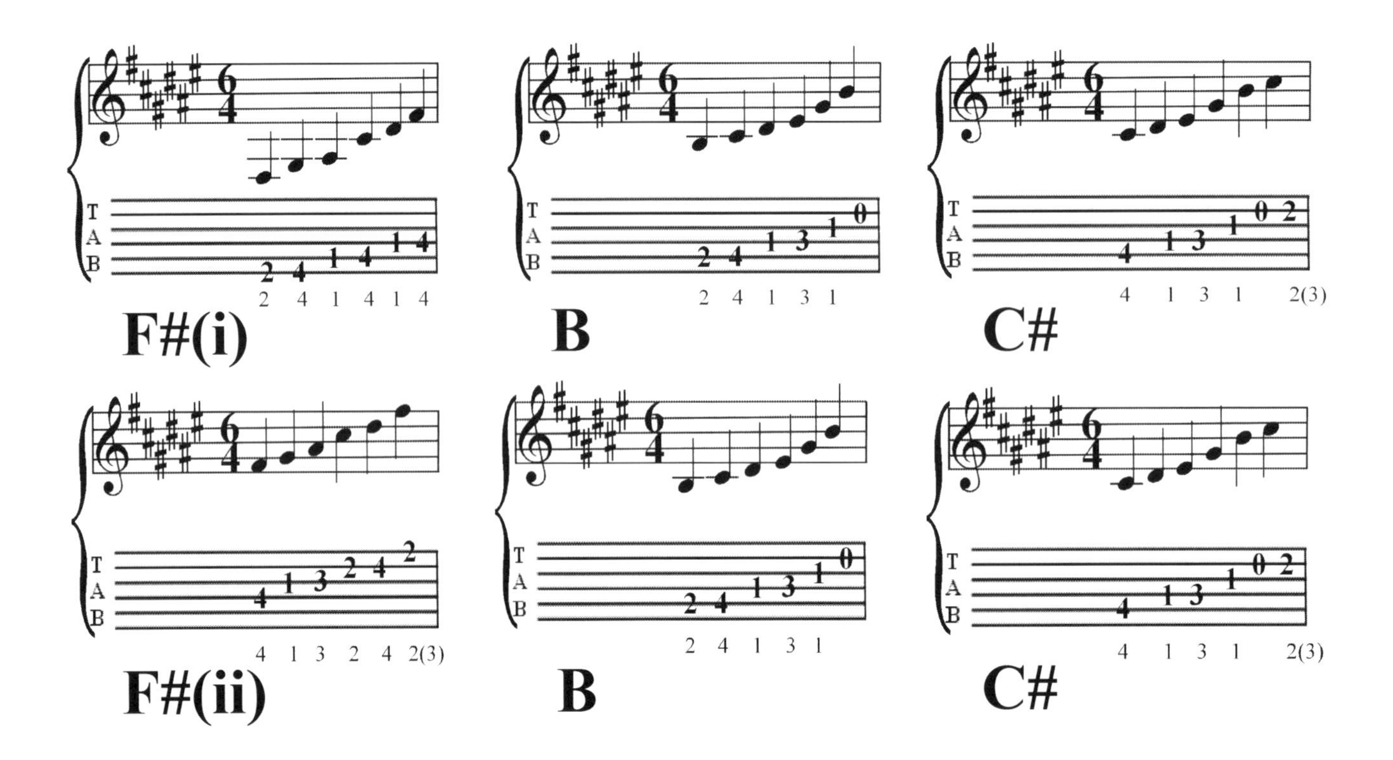

Key of C#

Key of A♭

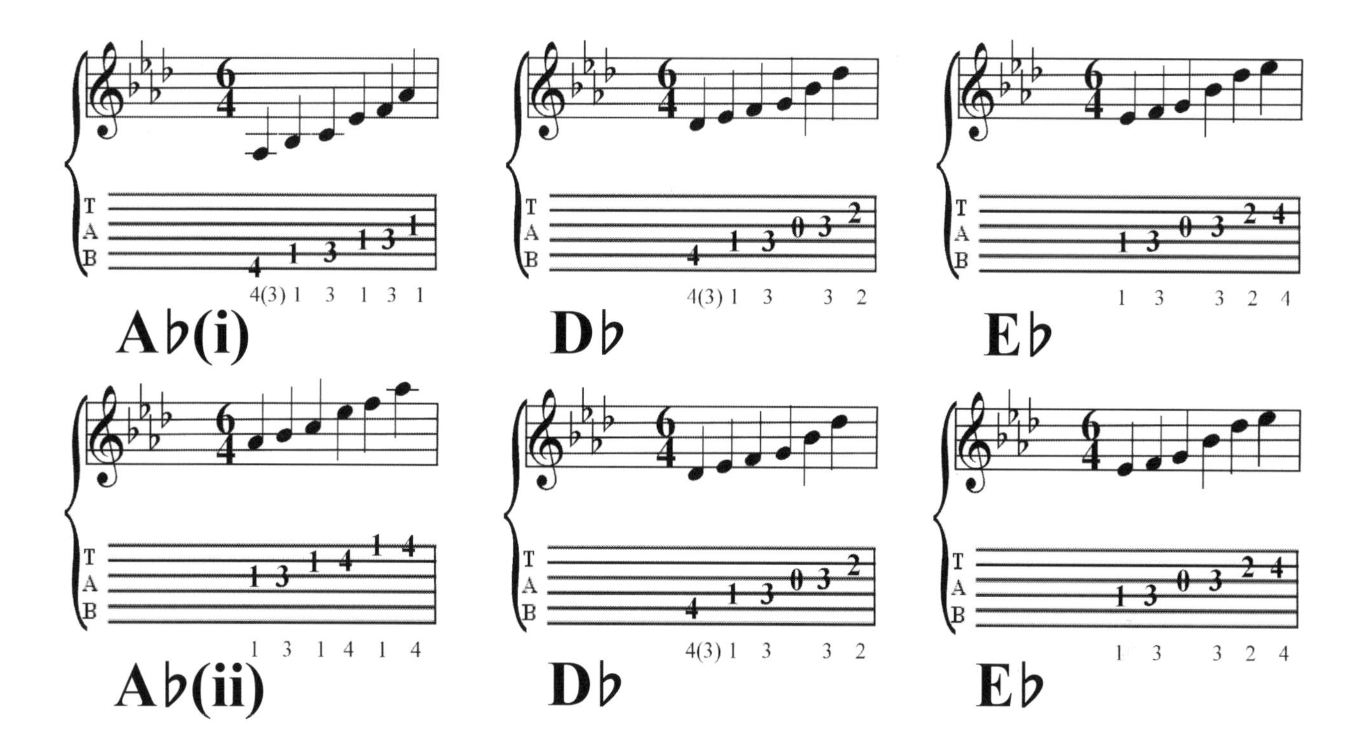

Key of E♭

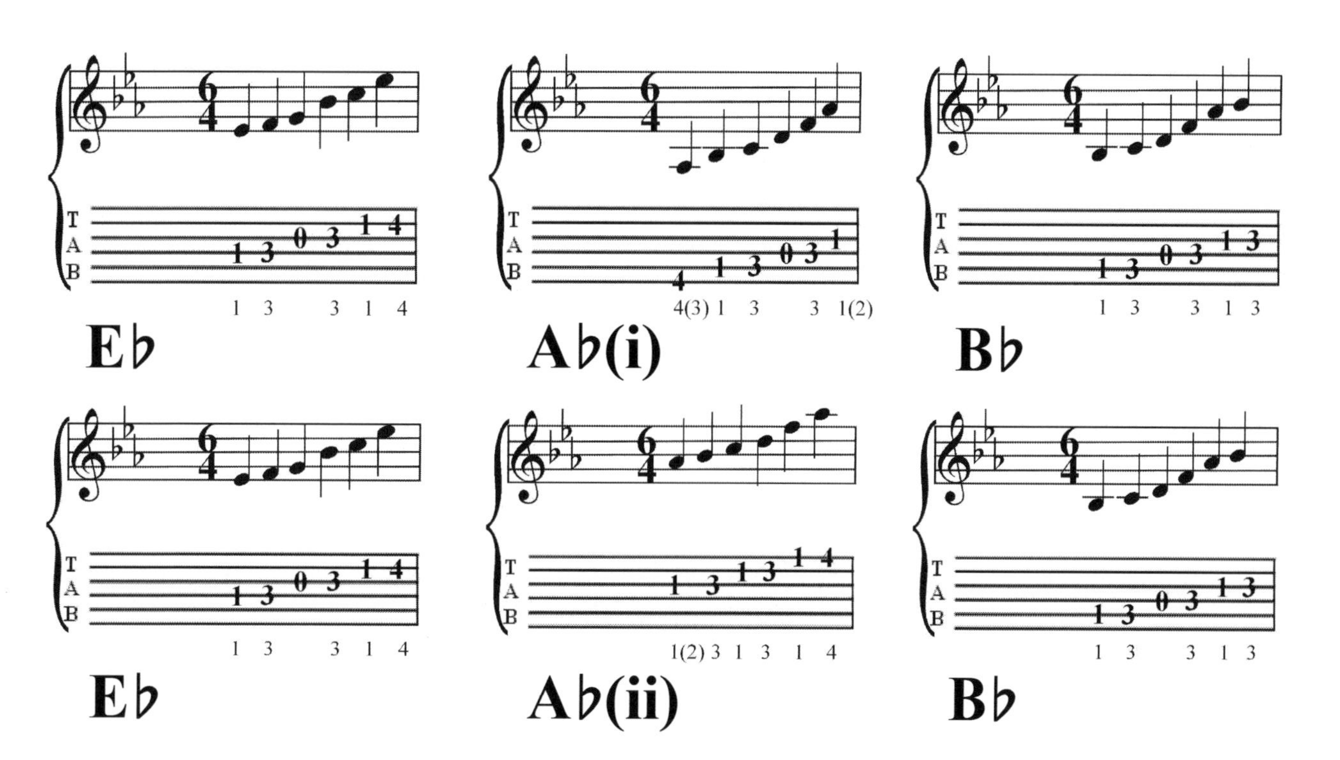

Key of B♭

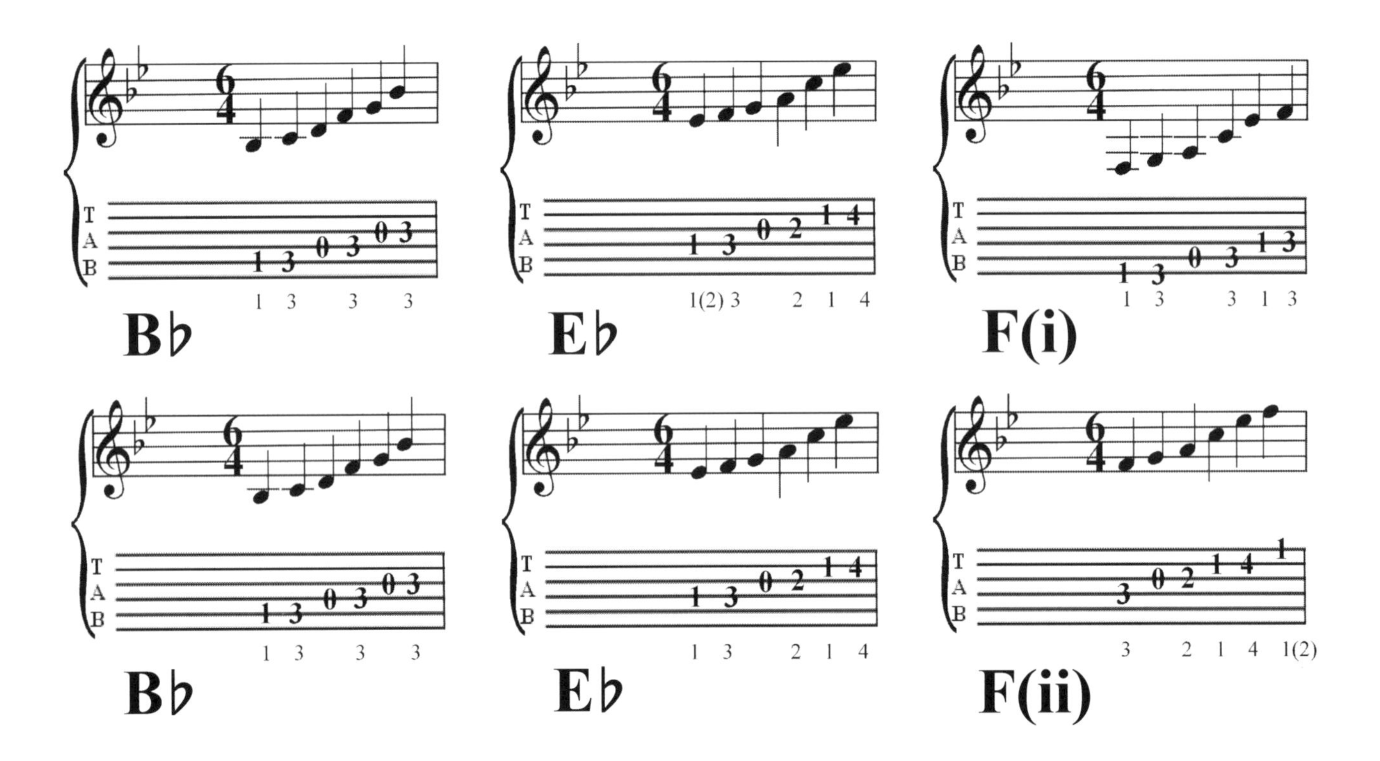

Key of F

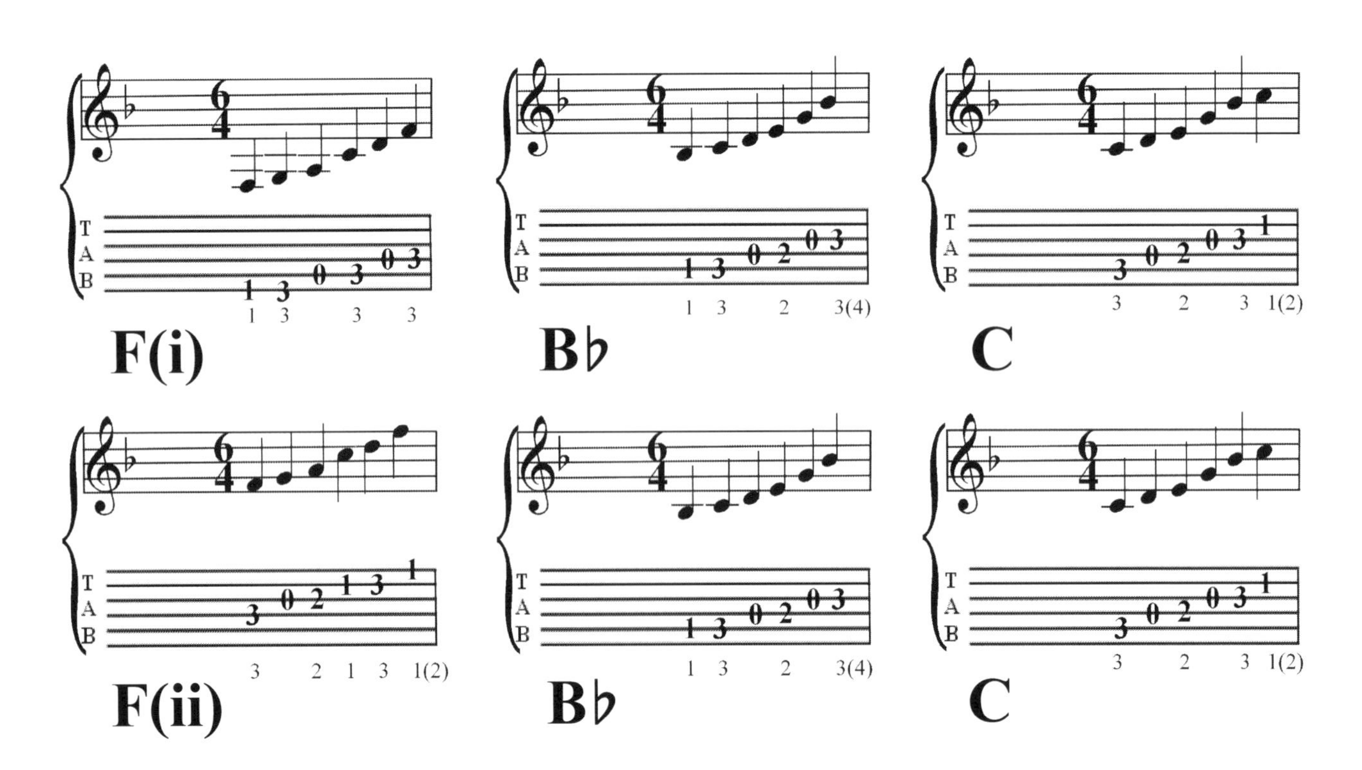

All Keys (i)

I

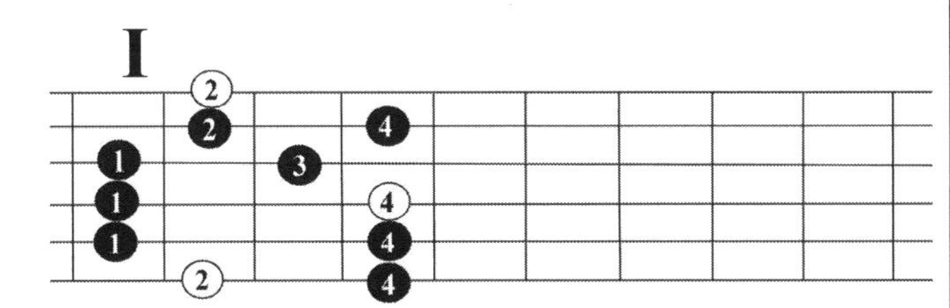

IV

V

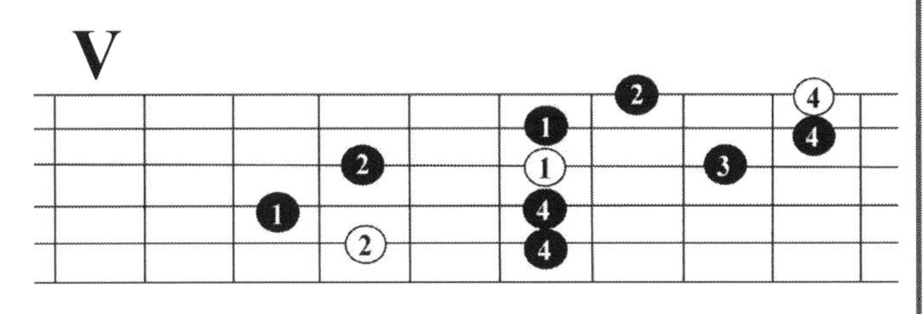

All Keys (ii)

I

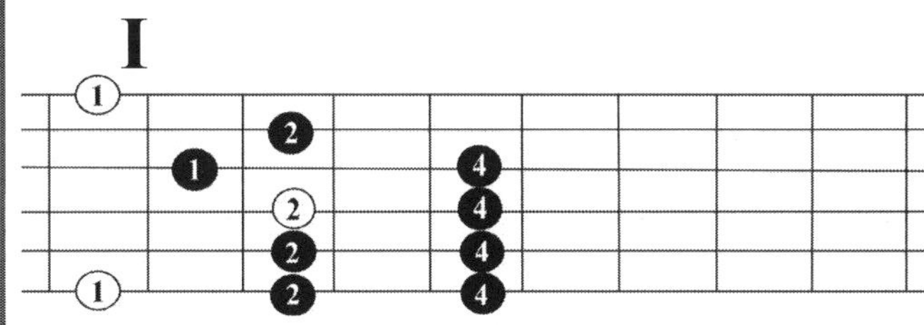

IV

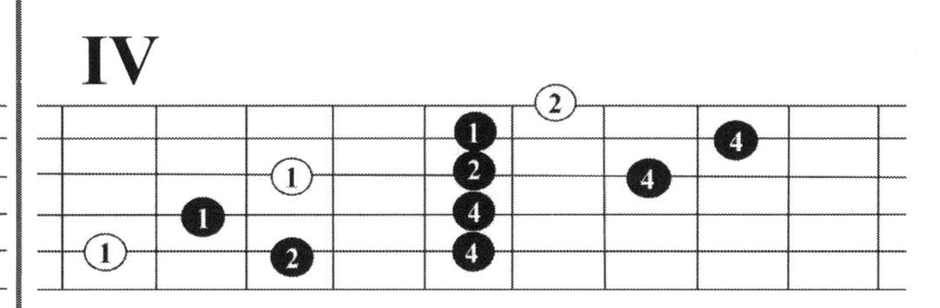

V

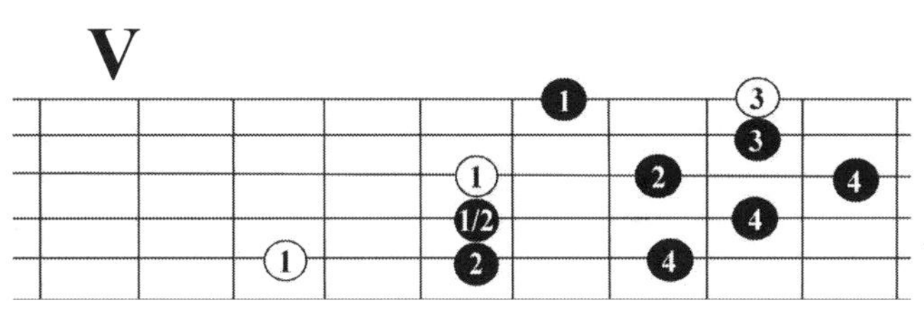

All Keys (iii)

I

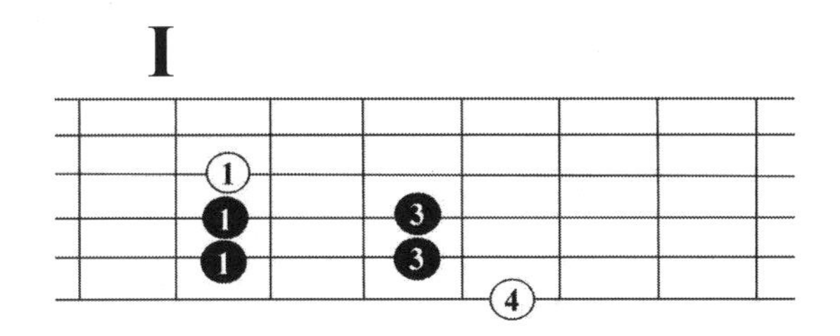

IV

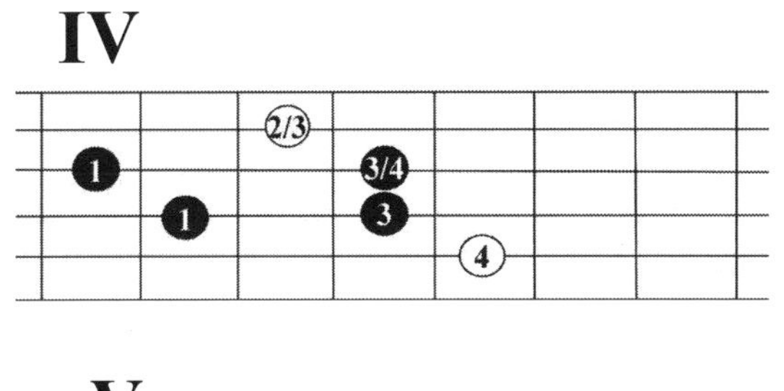

V

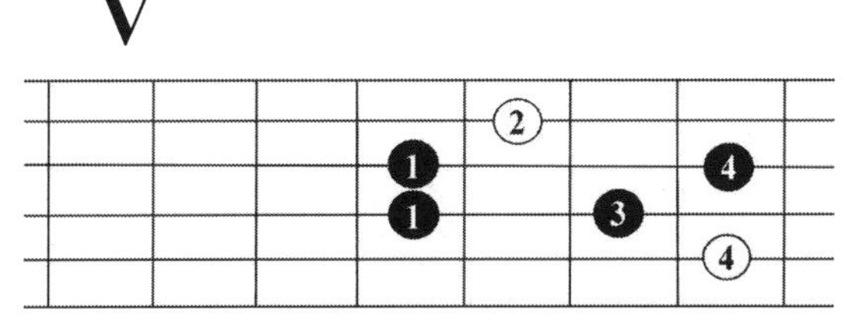

All Keys (iv)

I

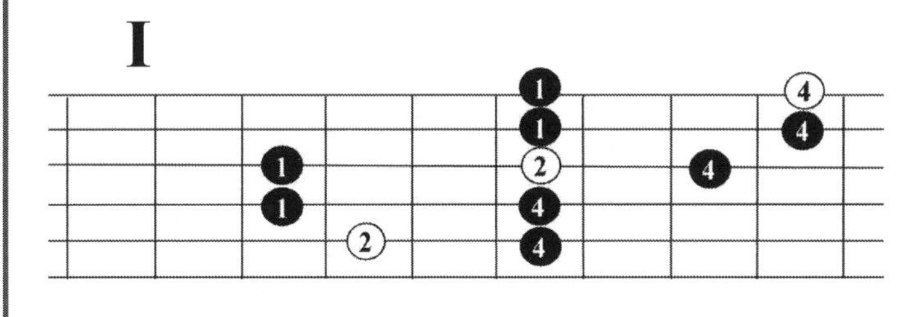

IV

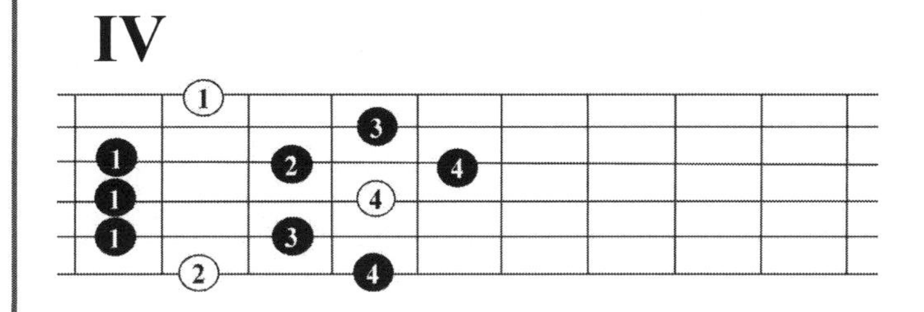

V

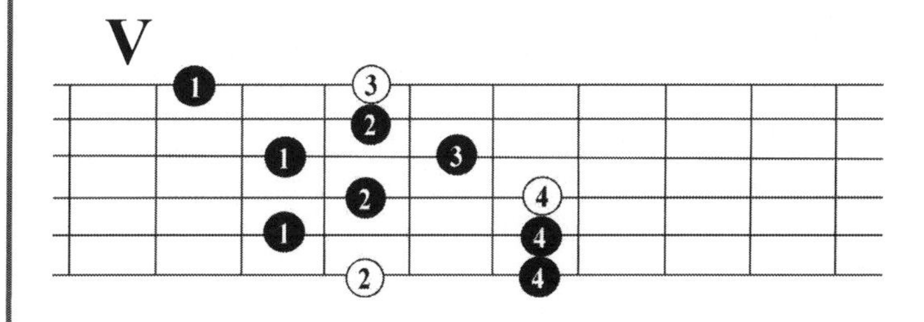

All Keys (v)

I

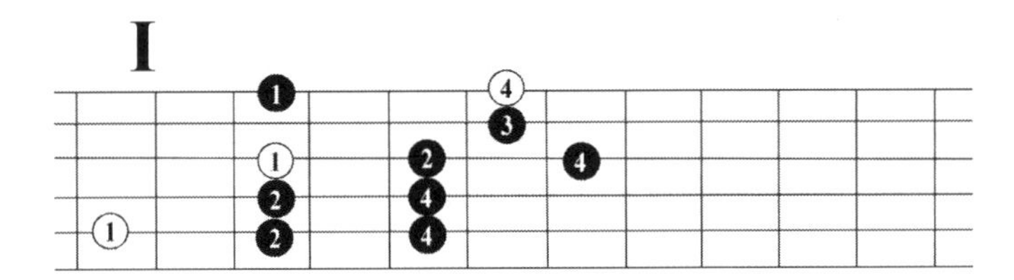

IV

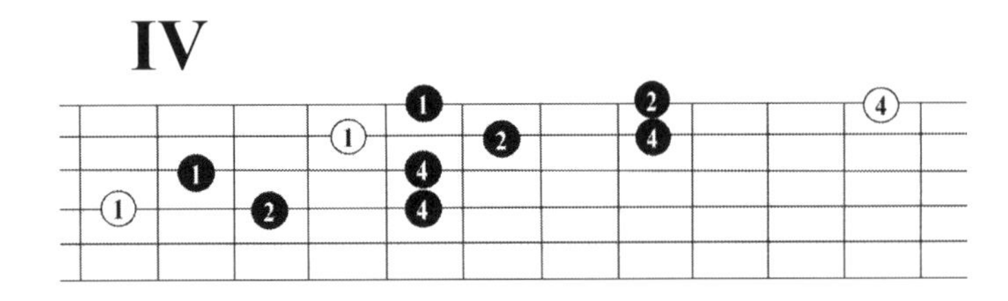

V

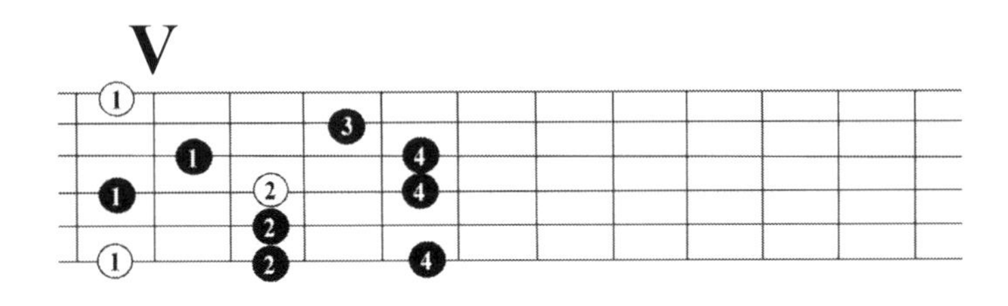

All Keys (vi)

I

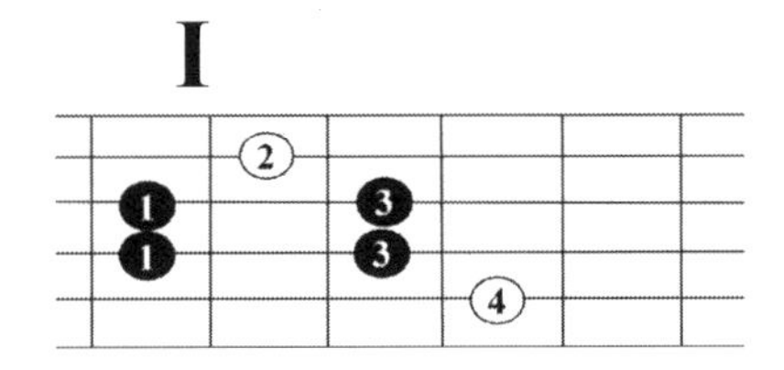

IV

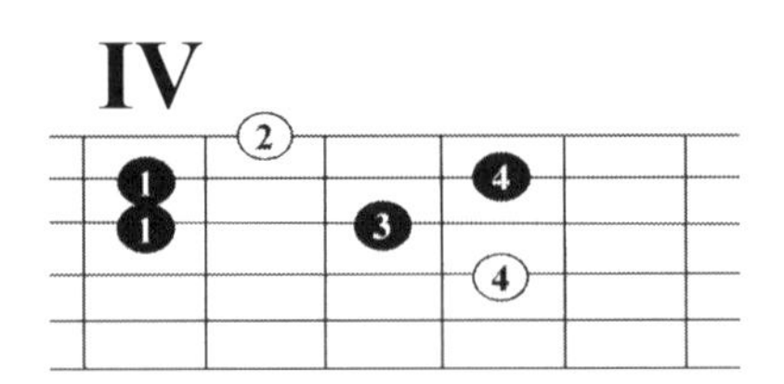

V

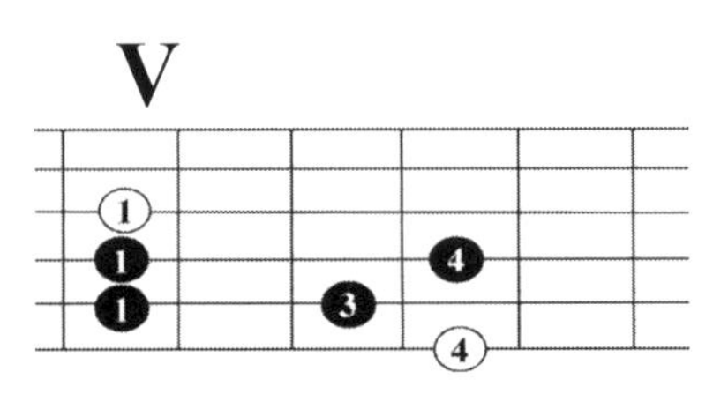

All Keys (vii)

I

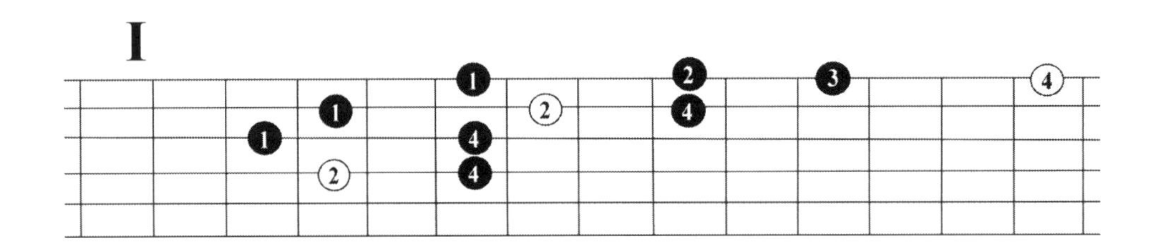

IV

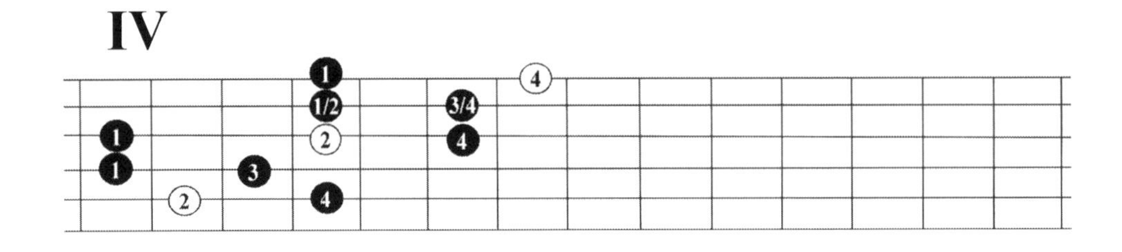

V

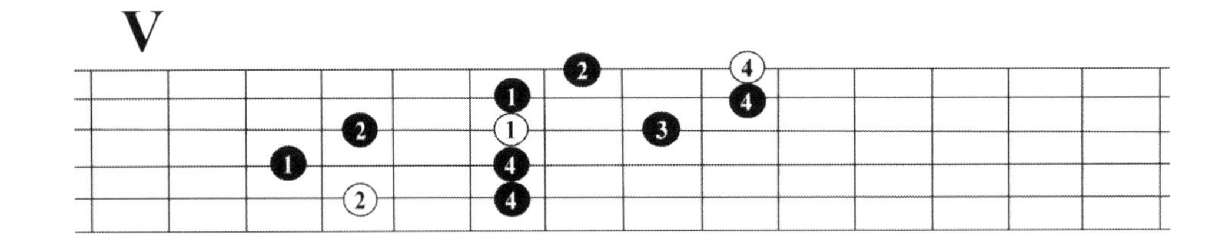

All Keys (viii)

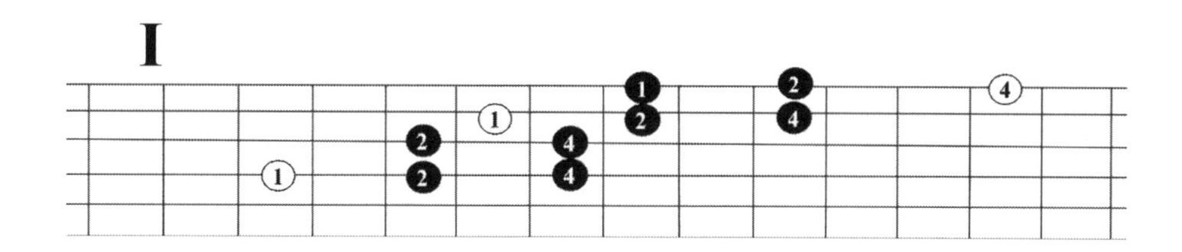

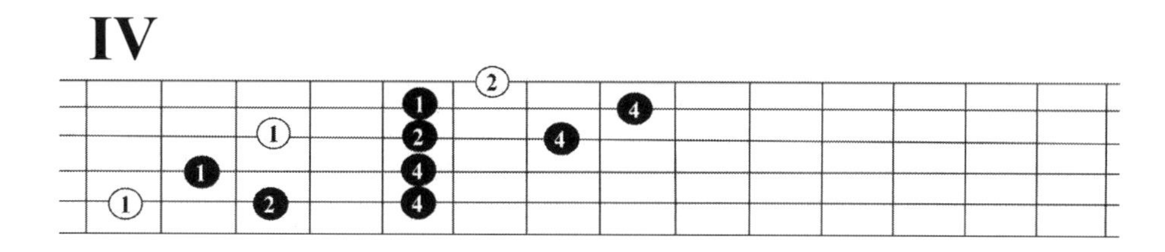

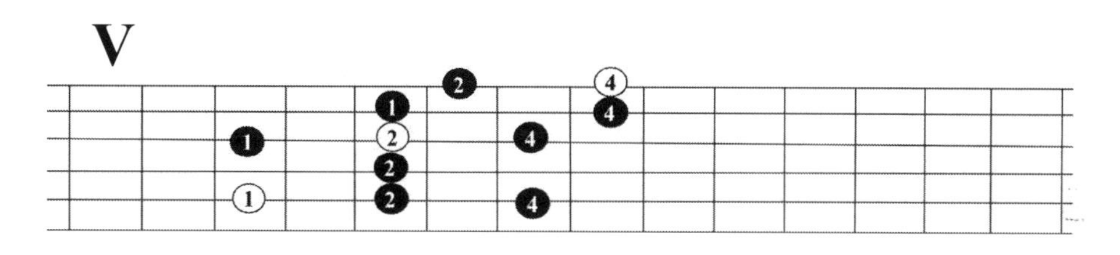

All Keys (ix)

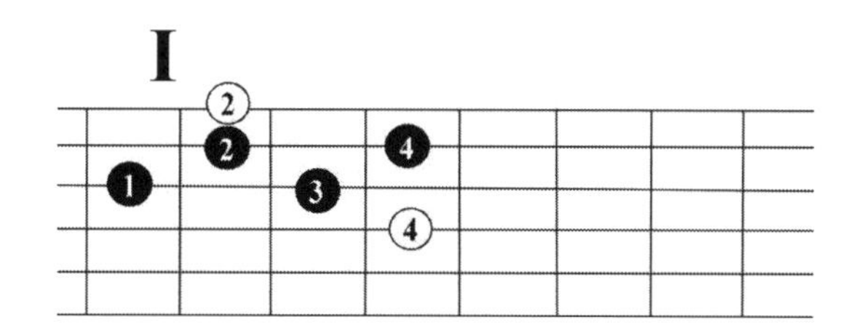

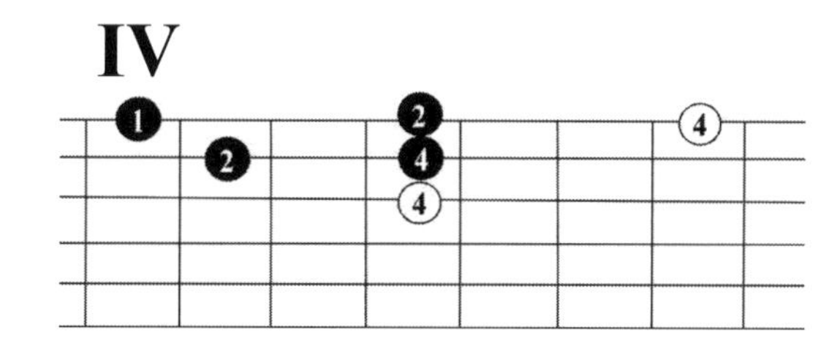

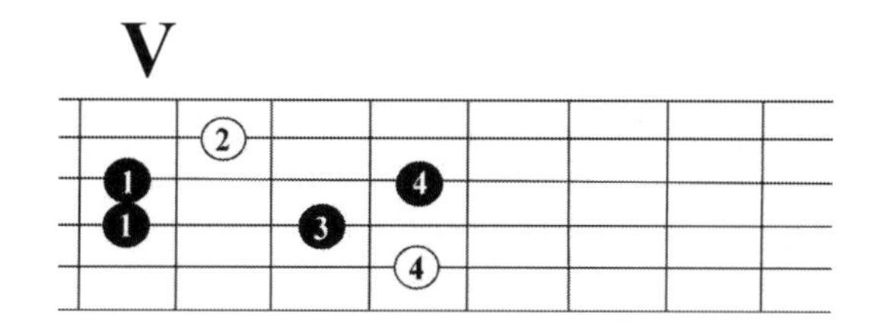

PART TWENTY-SIX

ii - V - i

MAJOR KEYS PENTATONICS

THE ii (minor or m7) CHORD

A full account of *minor* pentatonic scales is given in the sections on pentatonics in the minor keys.

For the moment, I would just like to note that the ii chord in a *major* key corresponds to the iv chord in the relative minor key, and the pentatonic pattern used for these exercises contains a *root*, minor *third*, *fourth*, *fifth*, major *sixth*, and *octave*. e.g., for a chord of D in the key of C:

D *(minor third)* **F** *(tone)* **G** *(tone)* **A** *(tone)* **B** *(minor third)* **D**

Key of C

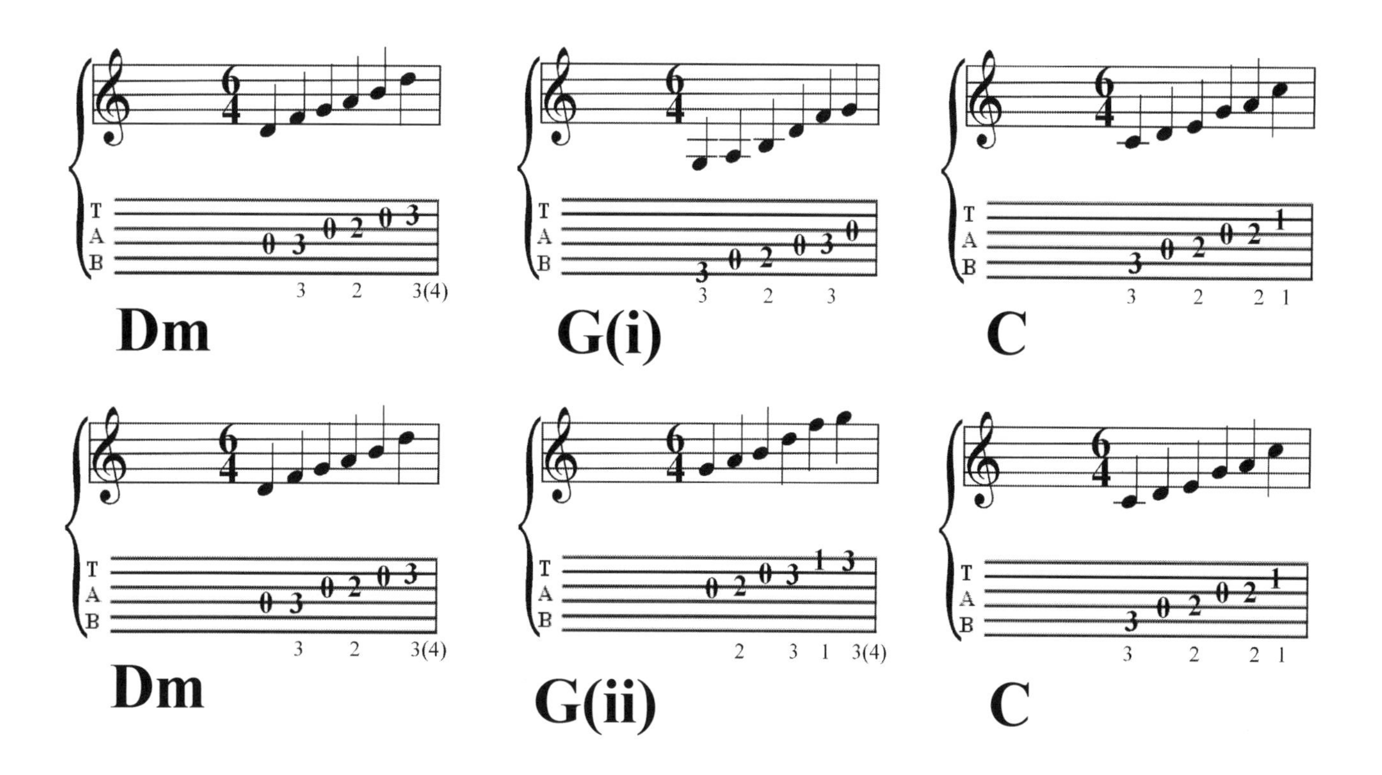

Key of G

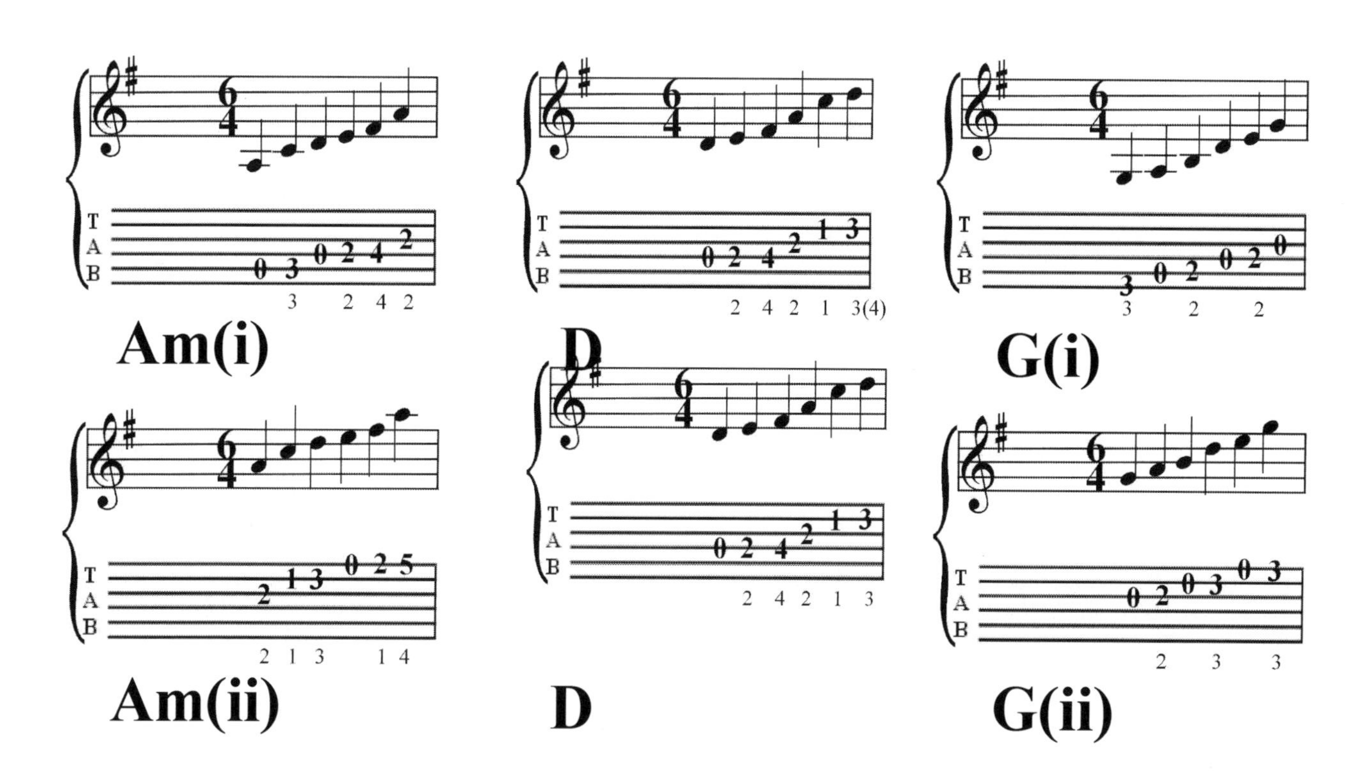

Key of D

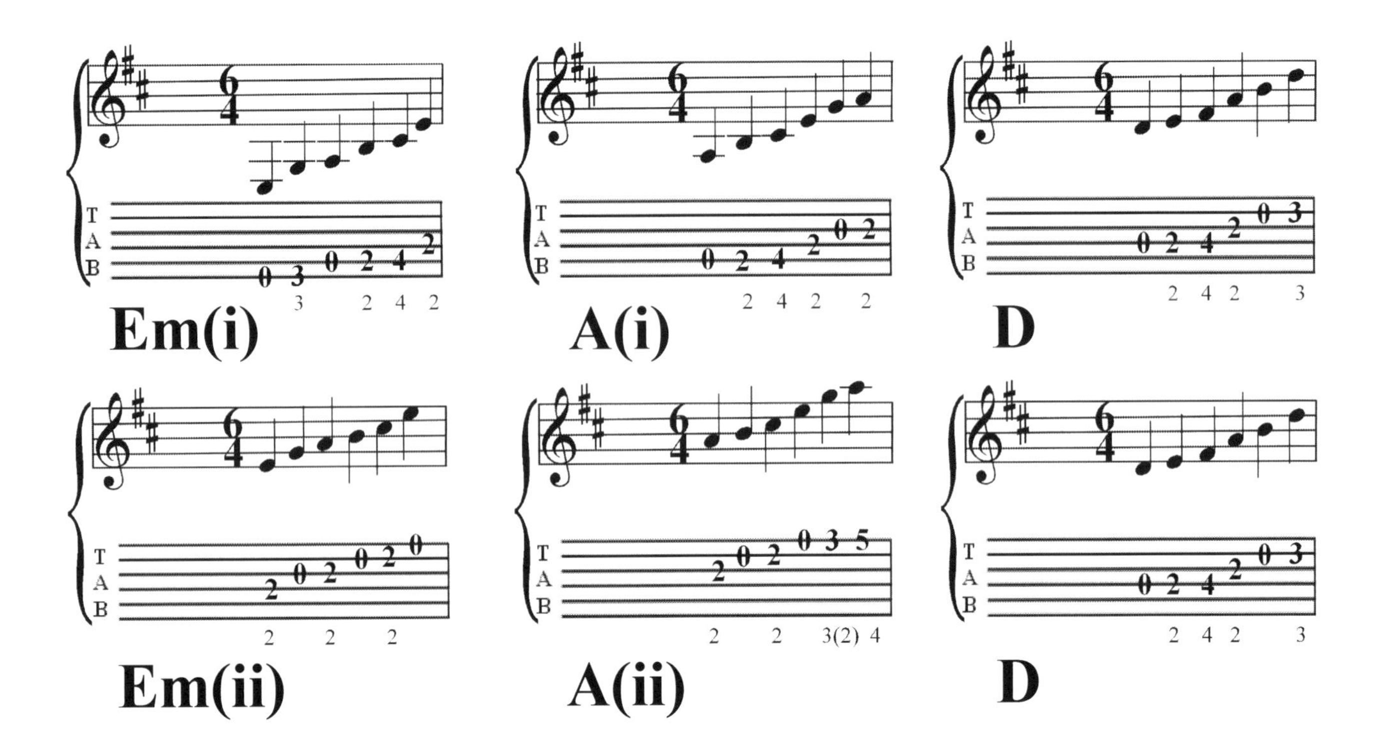

Key of A

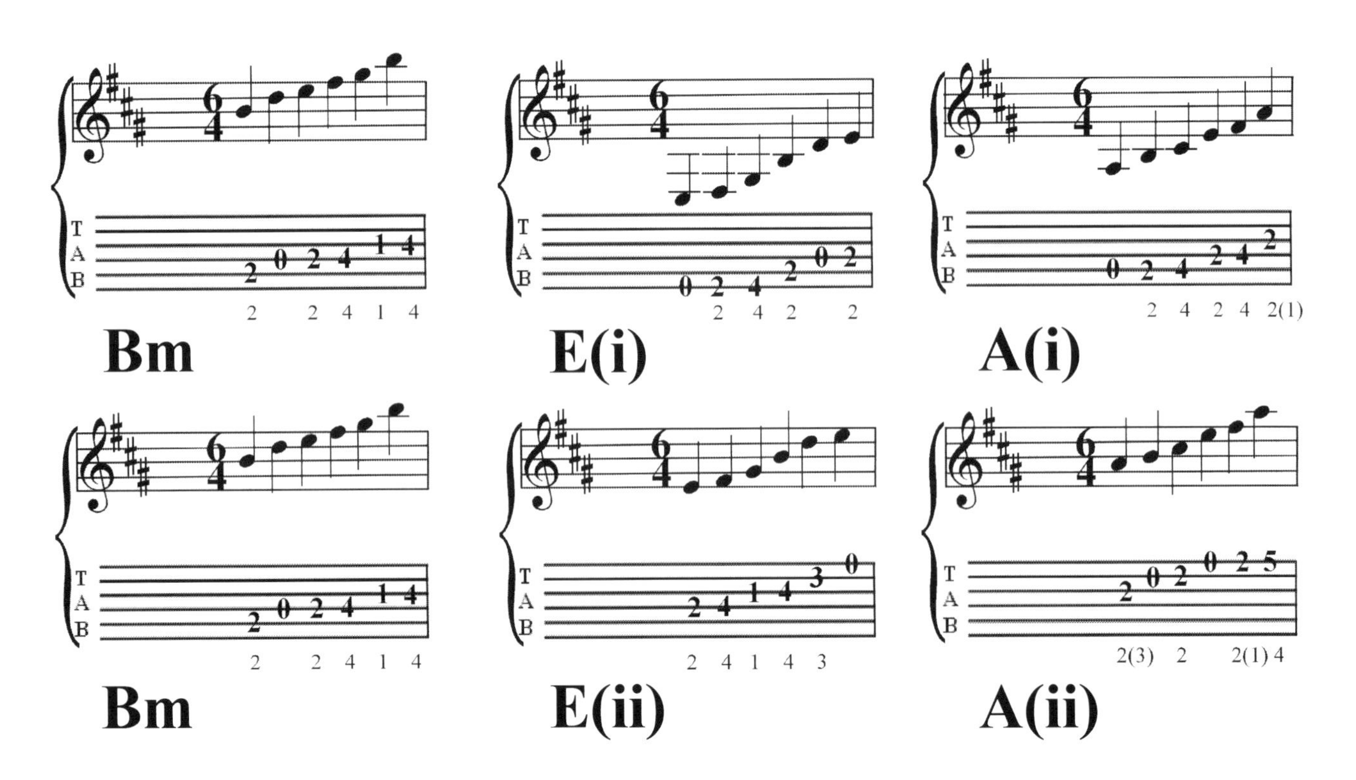

Key of E

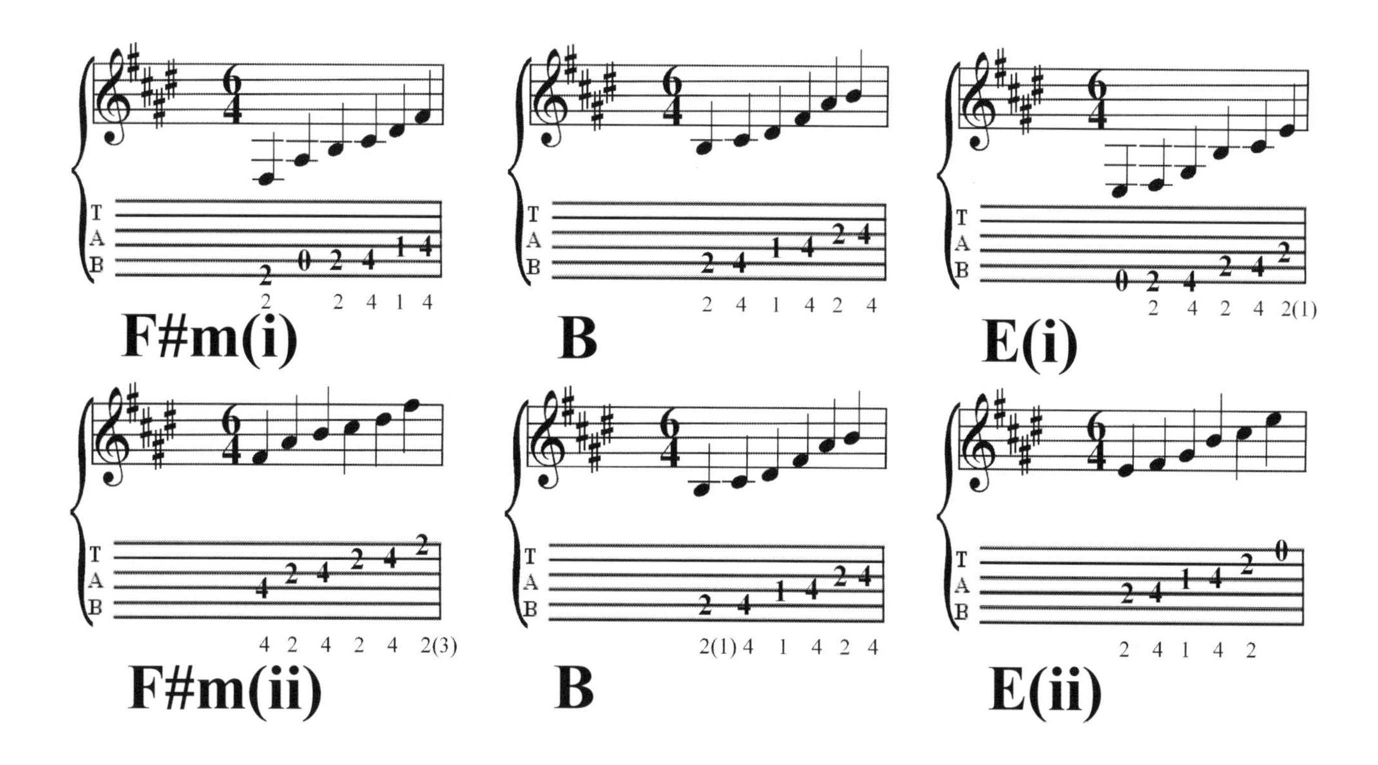

Key of B

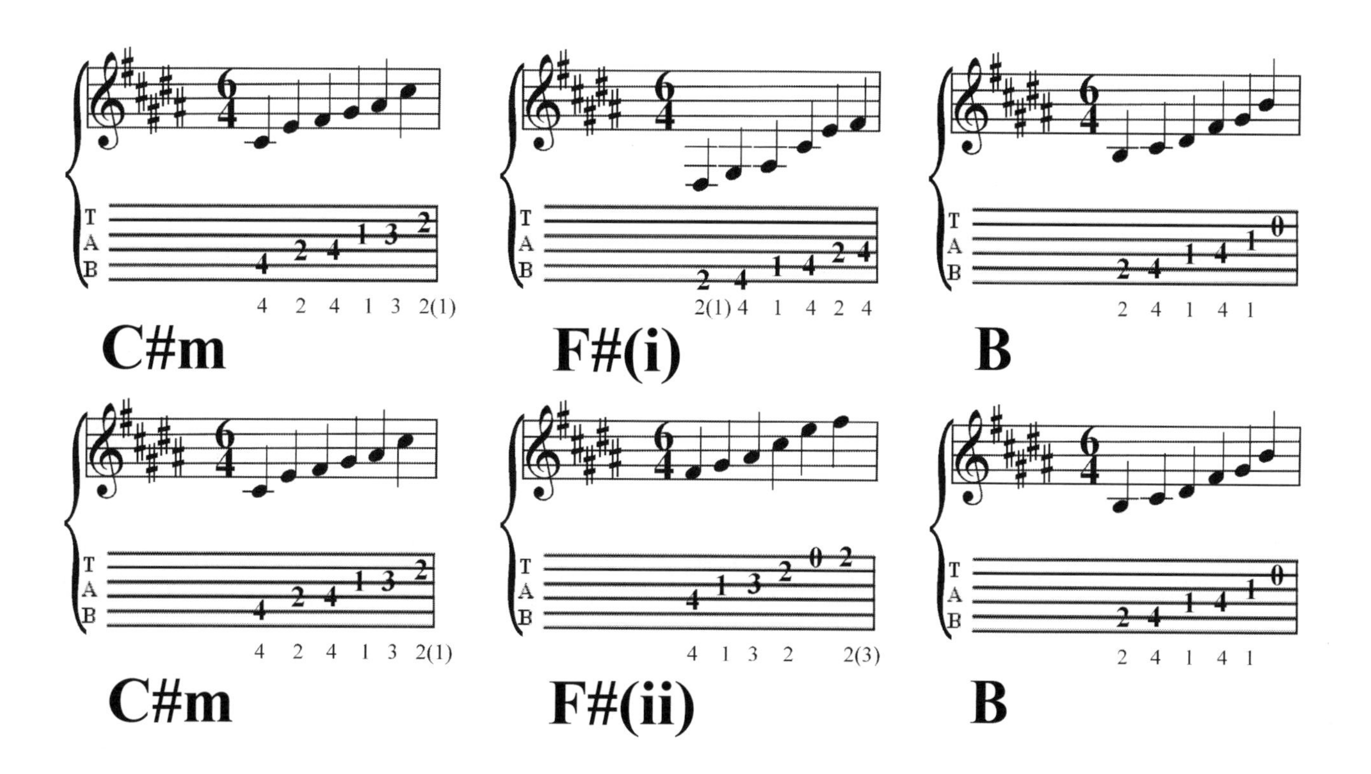

Key of F#

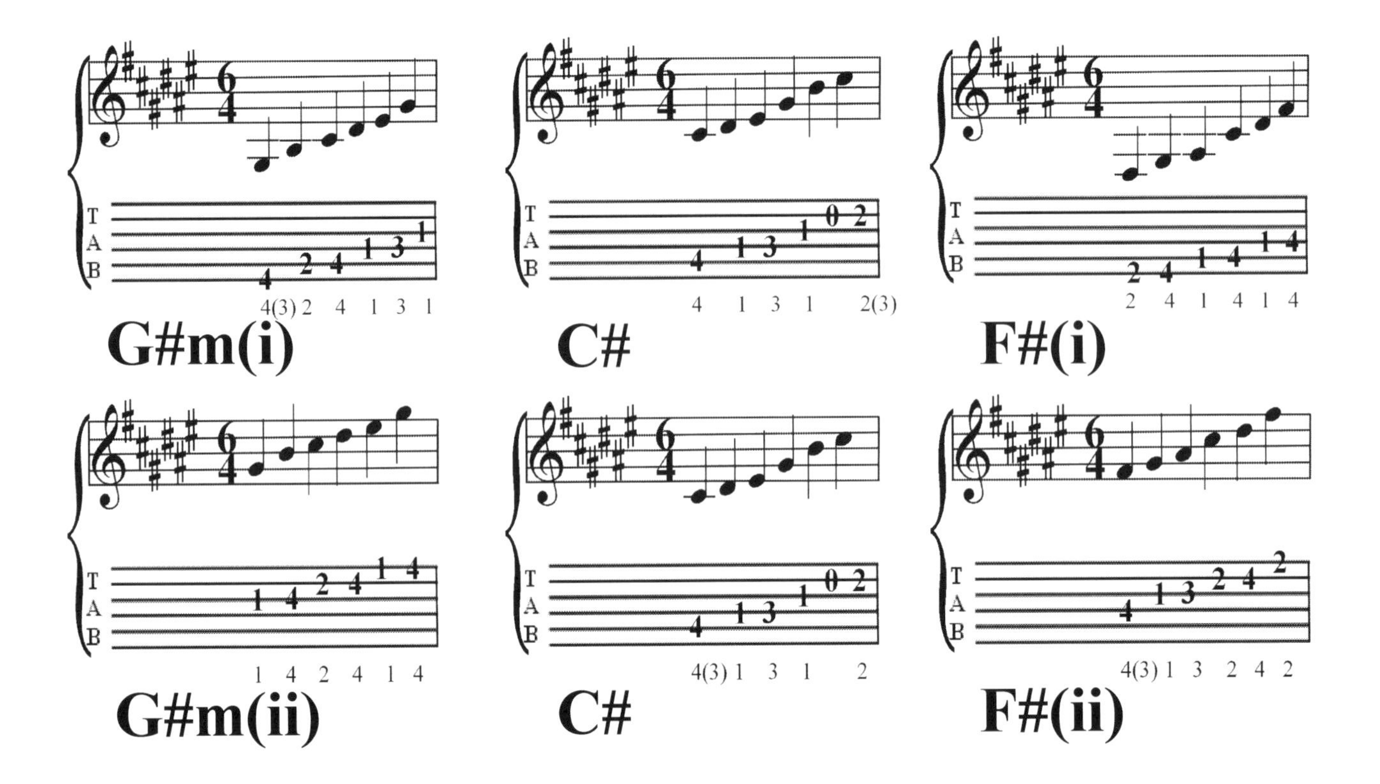

Key of C#

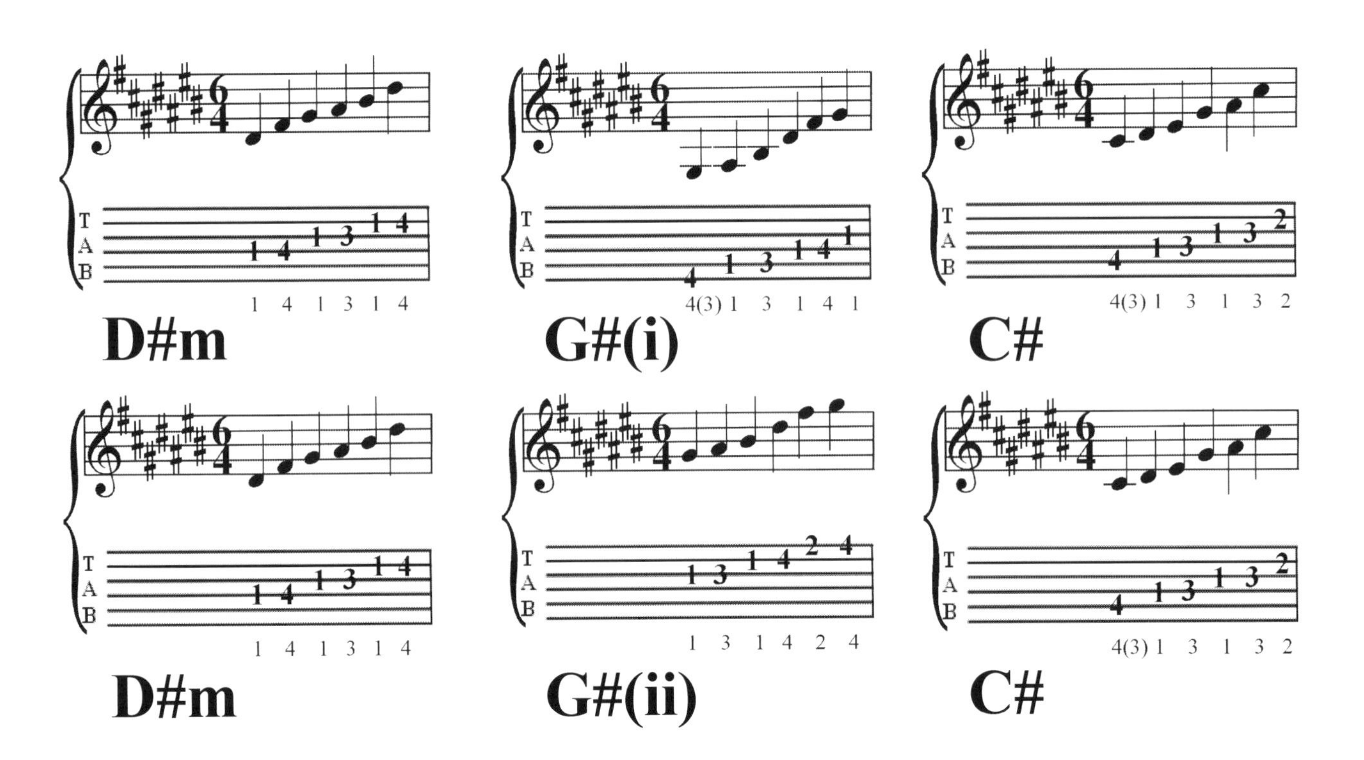

Key of A♭

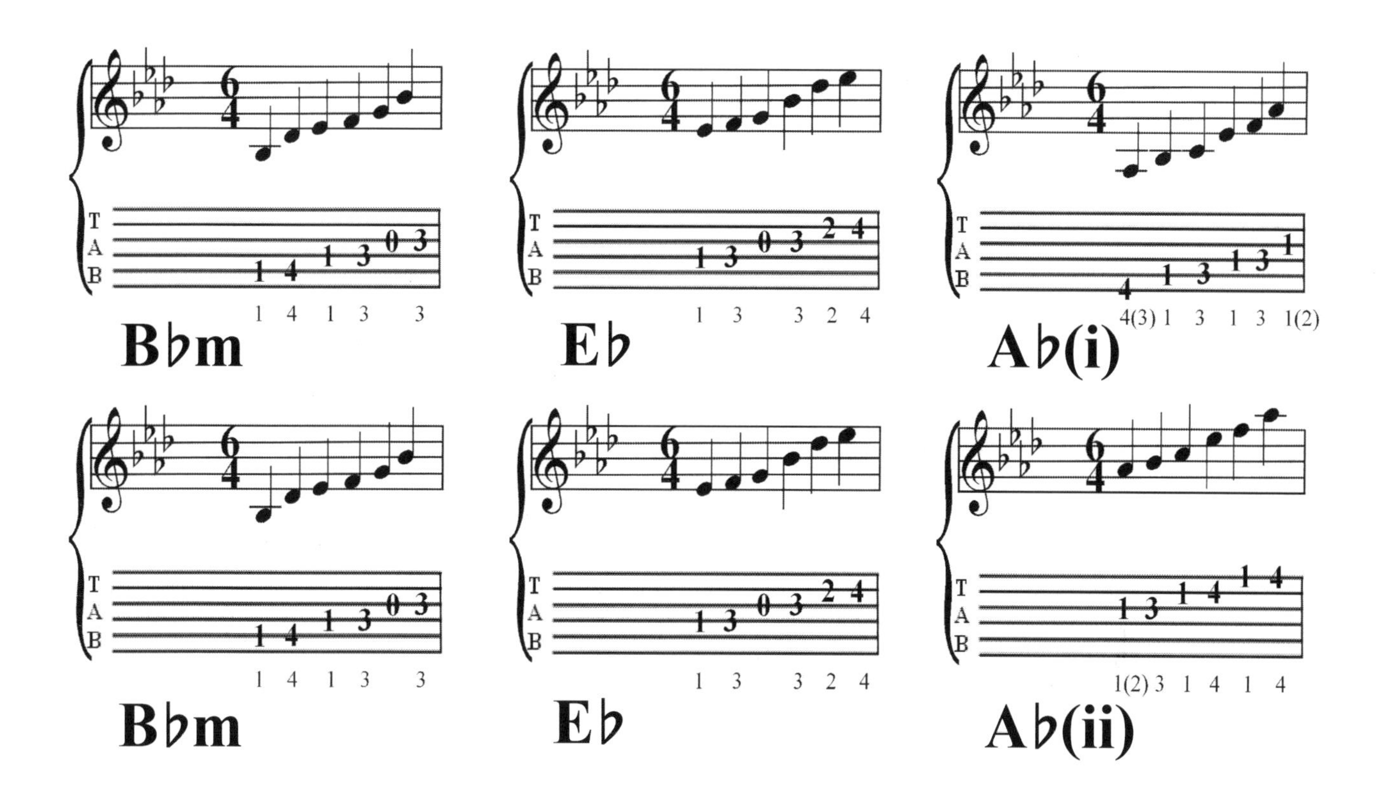

Key of E♭

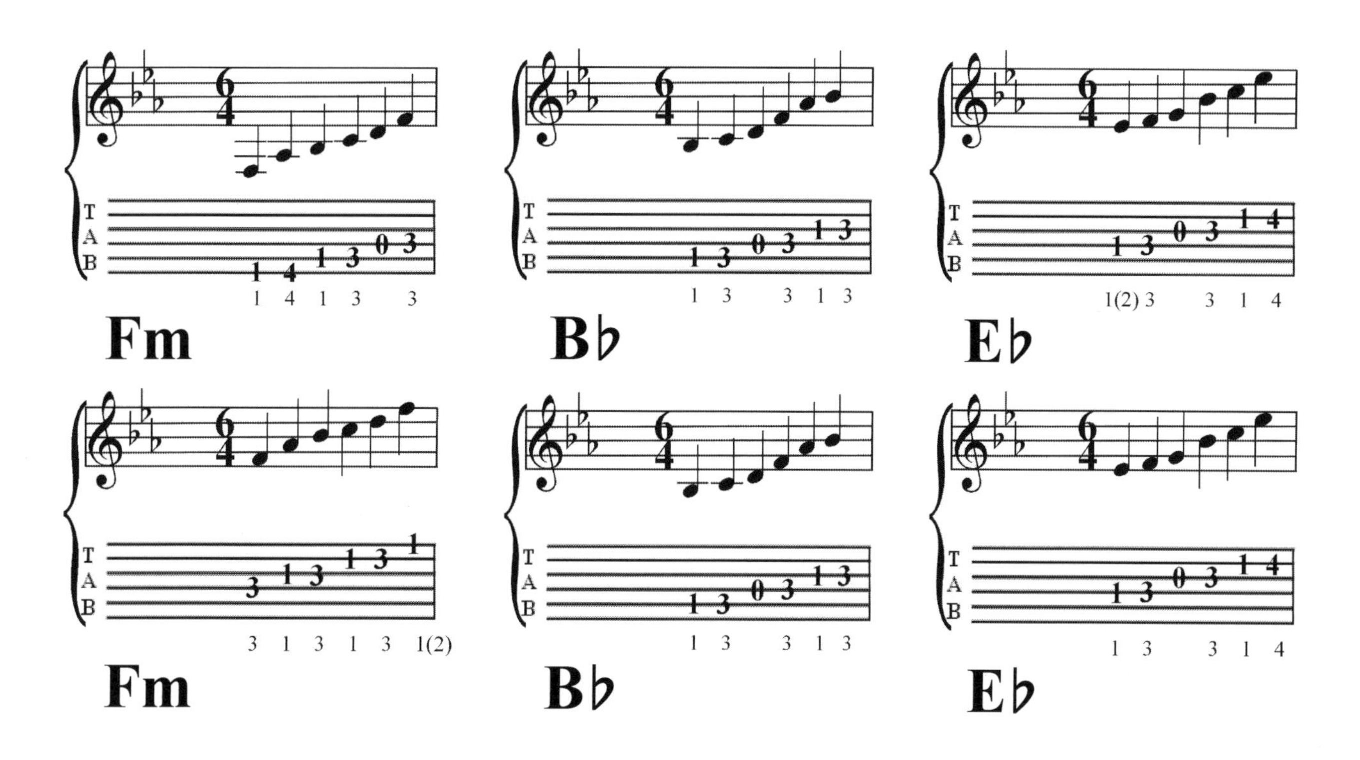

Key of B♭

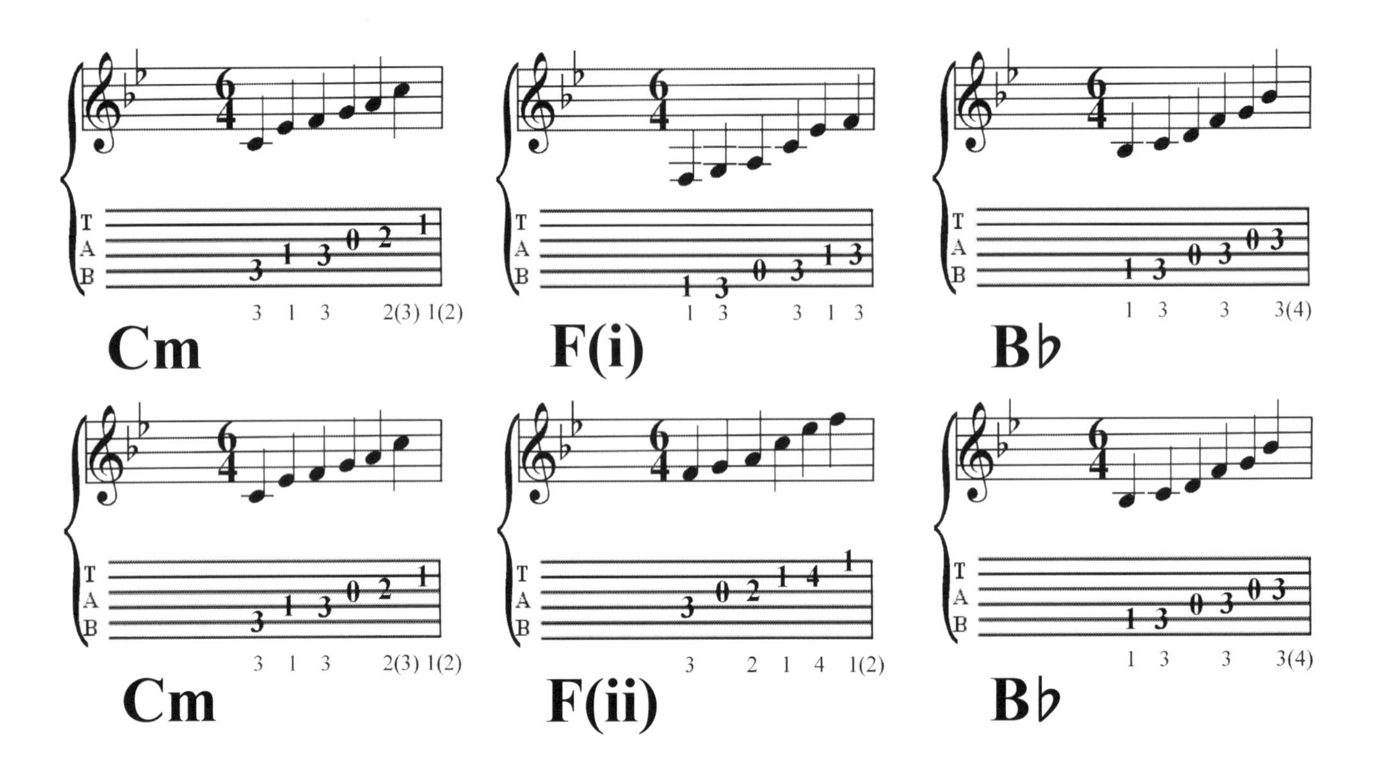

Key of F

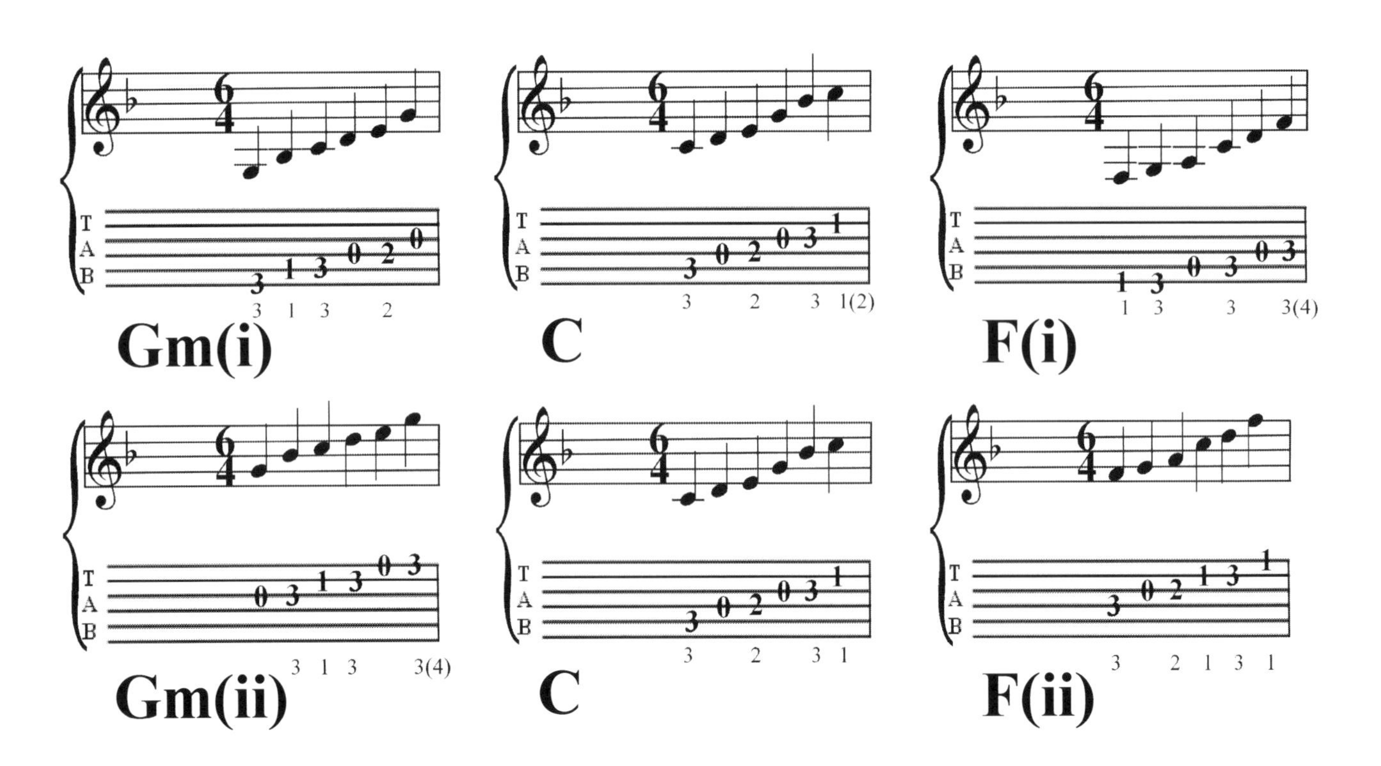

All Keys (i)

ii

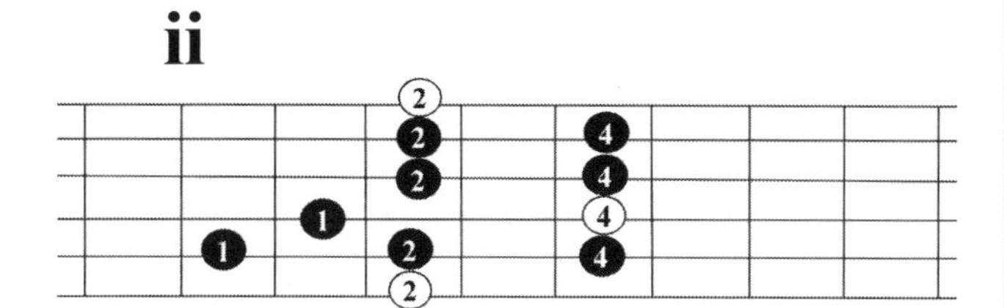

V

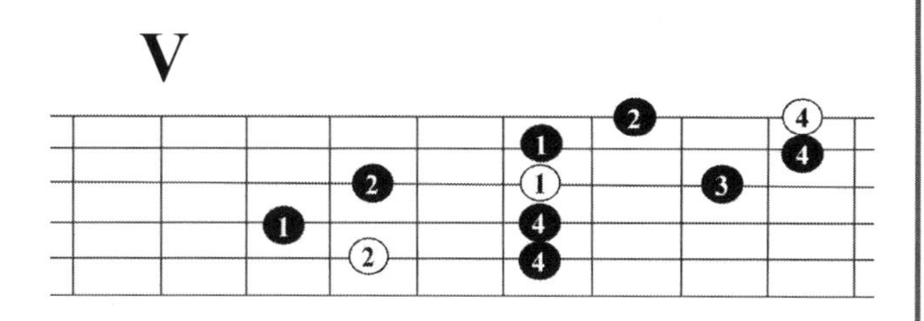

I

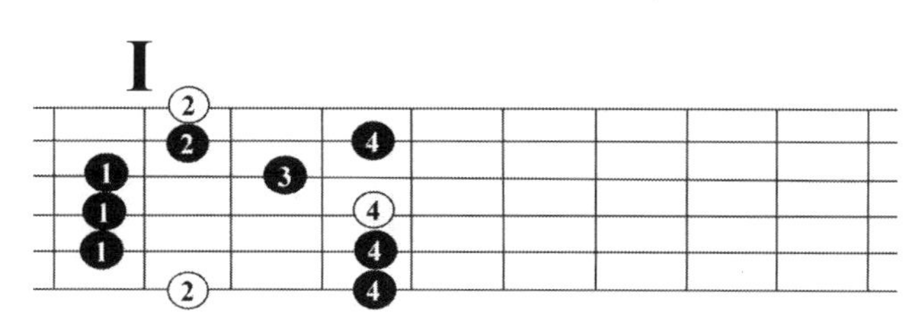

All Keys (ii)

ii

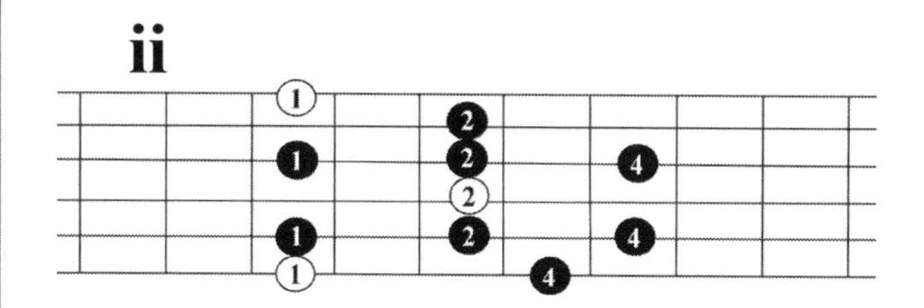

V

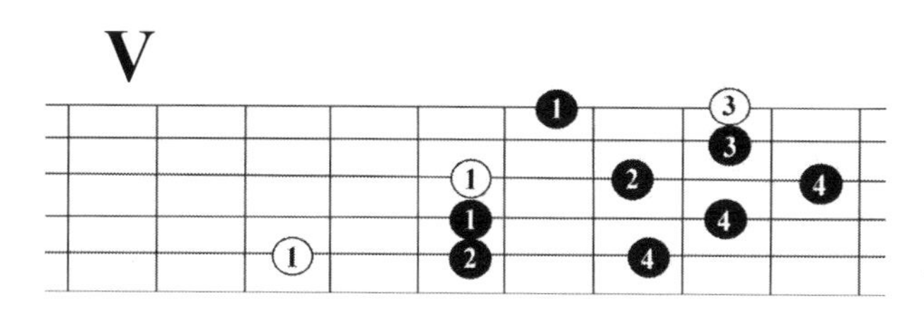

I

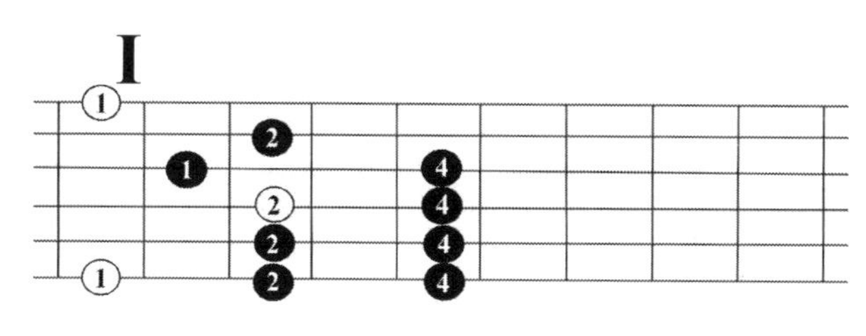

All Keys (iii)

ii

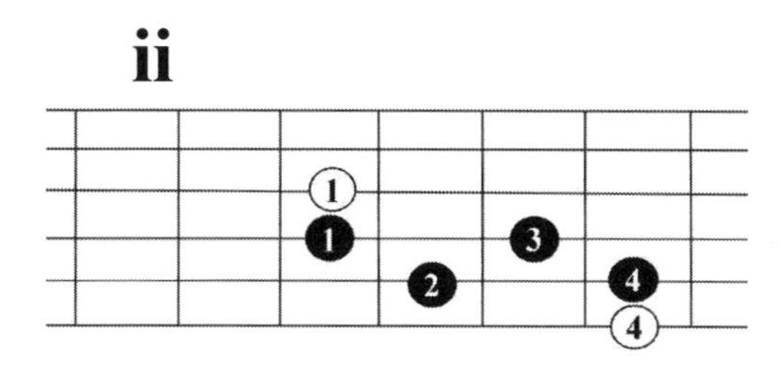

V

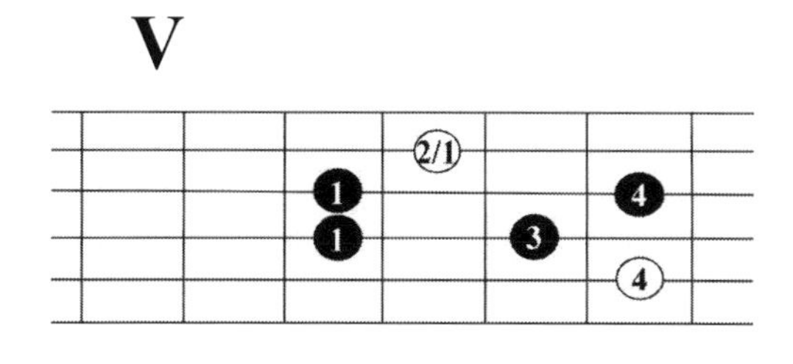

I

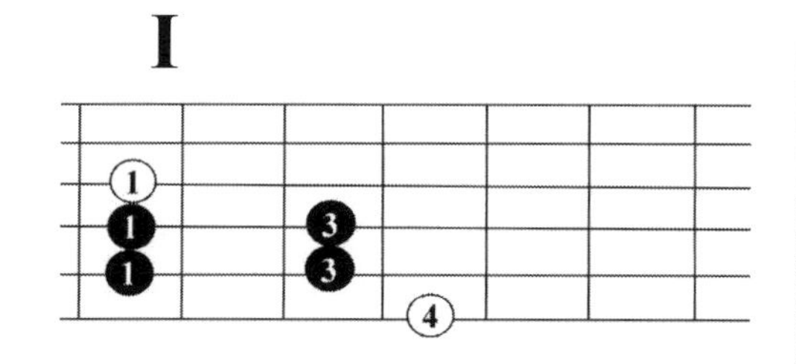

All Keys (iv)

ii

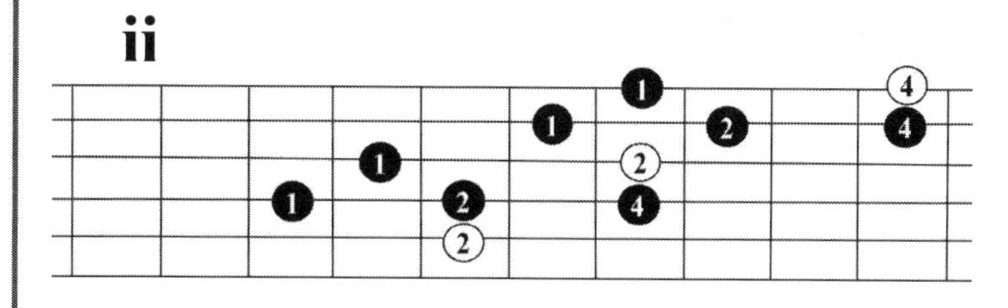

V

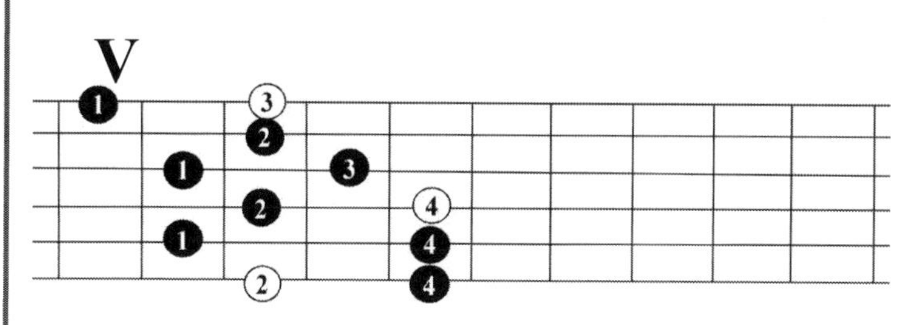

I

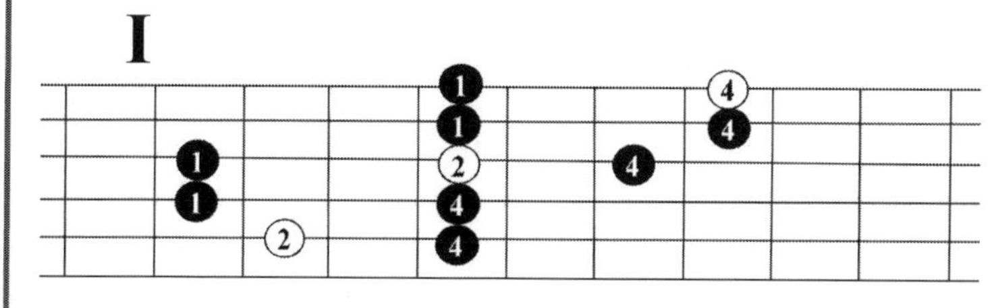

All Keys (v)

ii

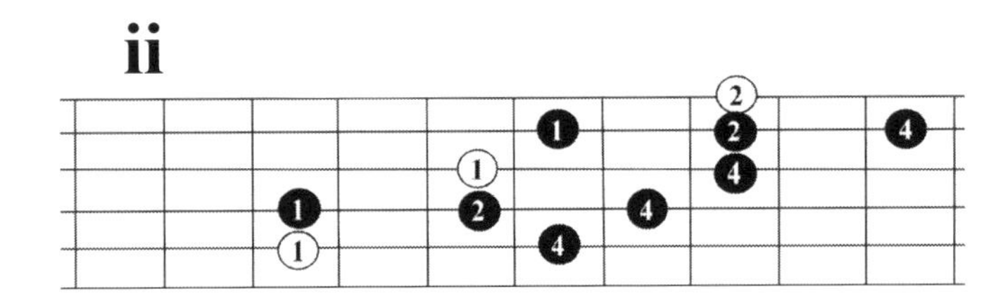

V

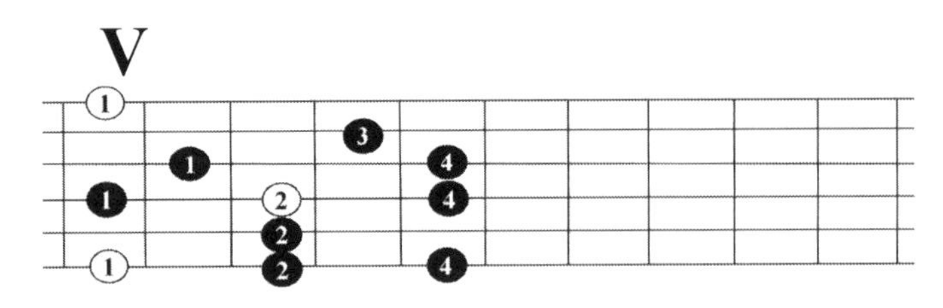

I

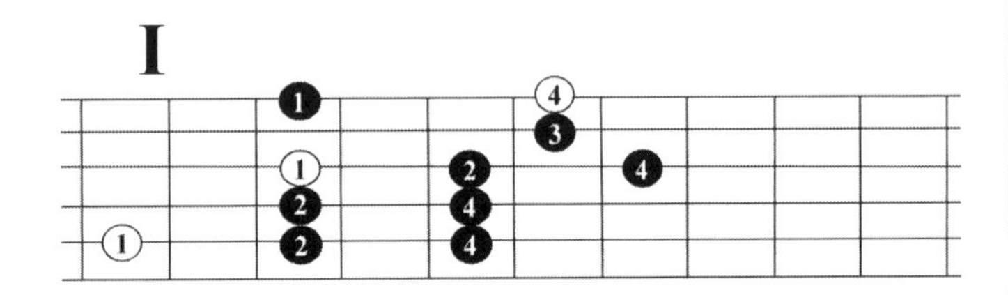

All Keys (vi)

ii

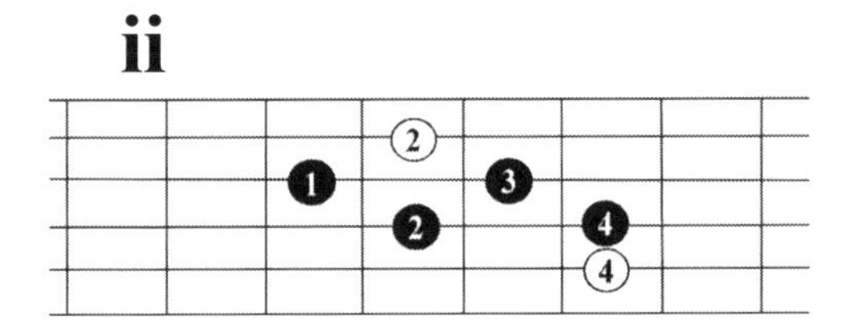

V

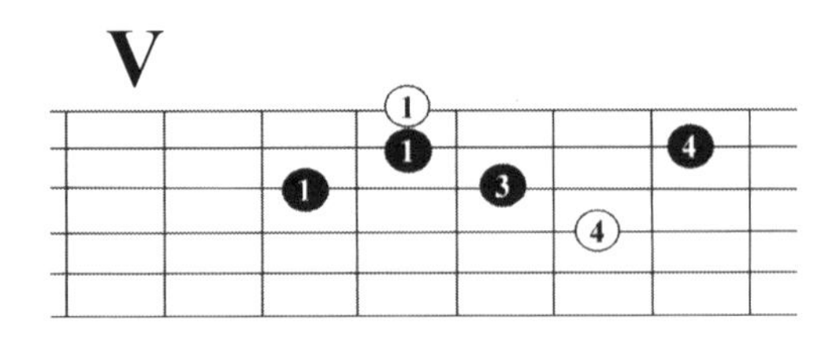

I

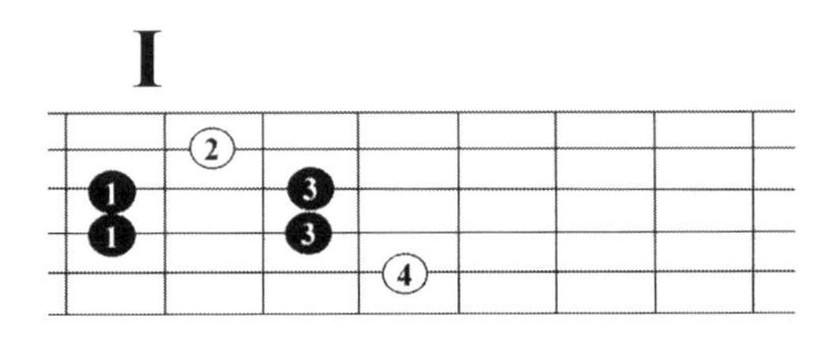

All Keys (vii)

ii

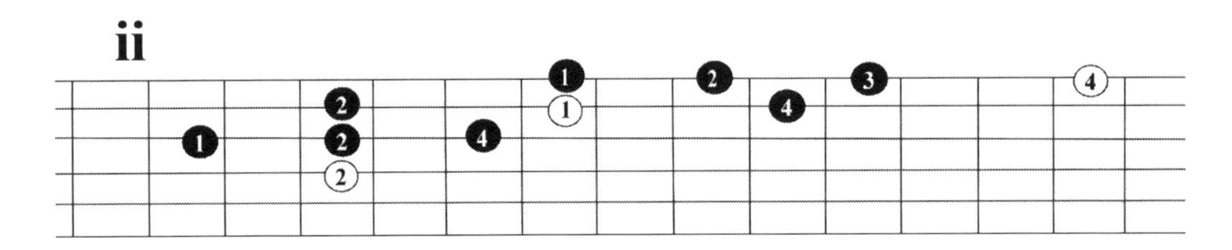

V

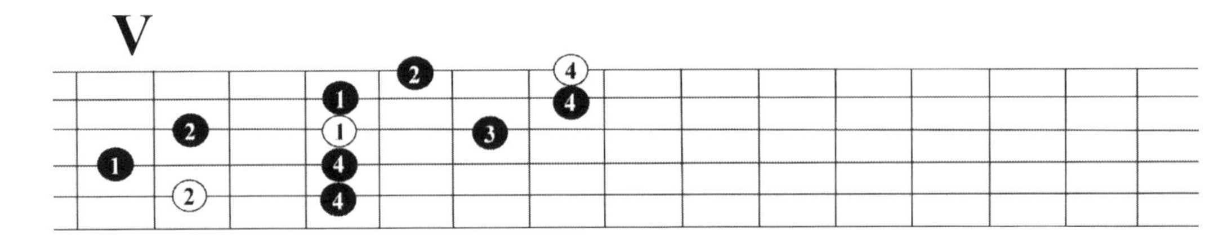

I

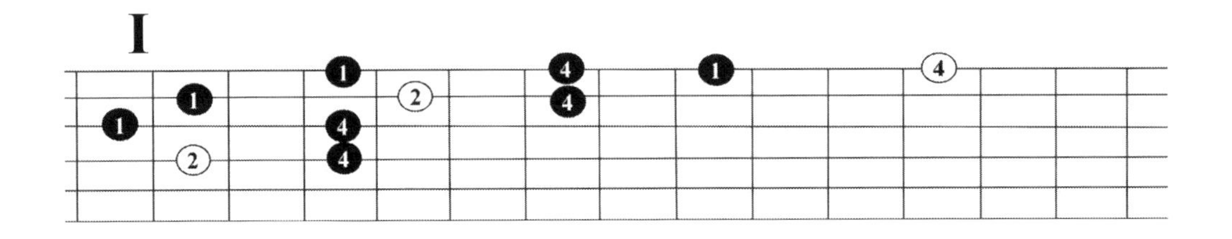

All Keys (viii)

ii

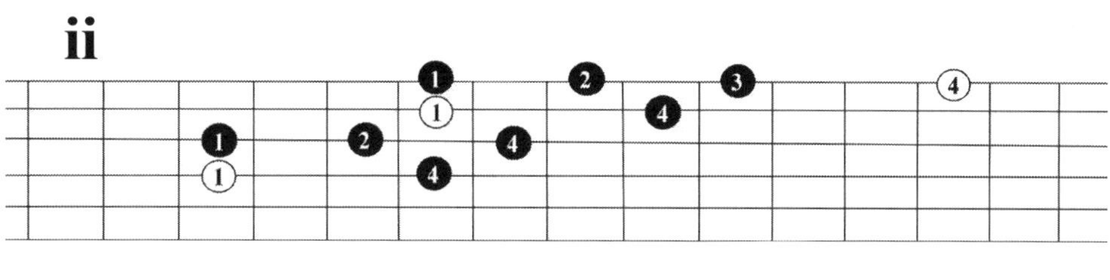

V

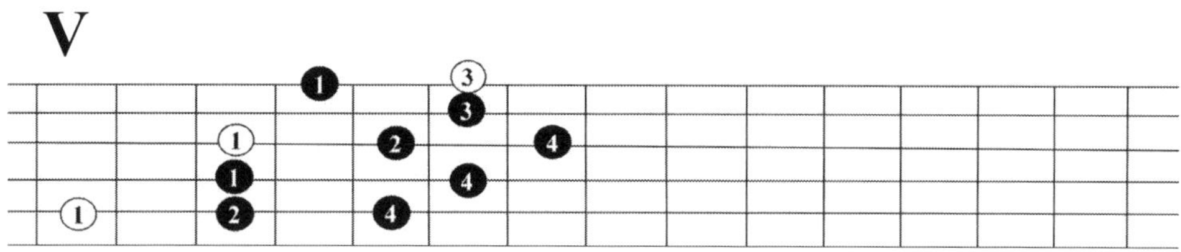

I

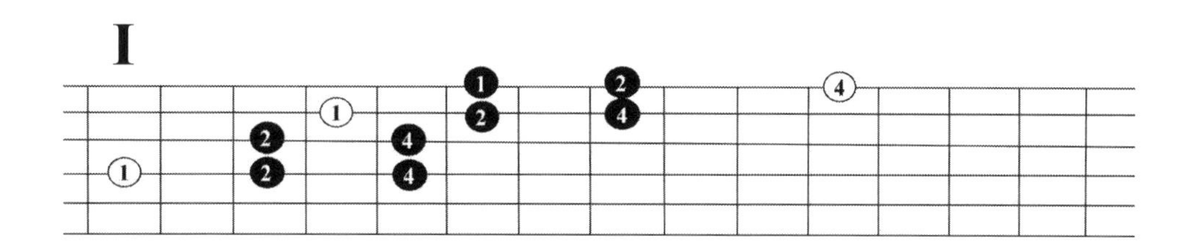

All Keys (ix)

ii

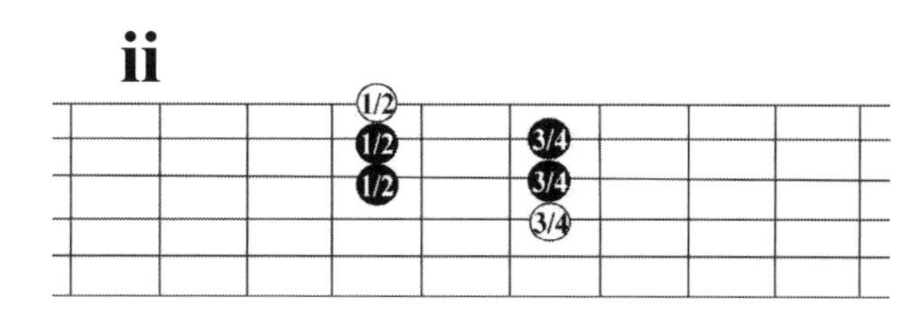

V

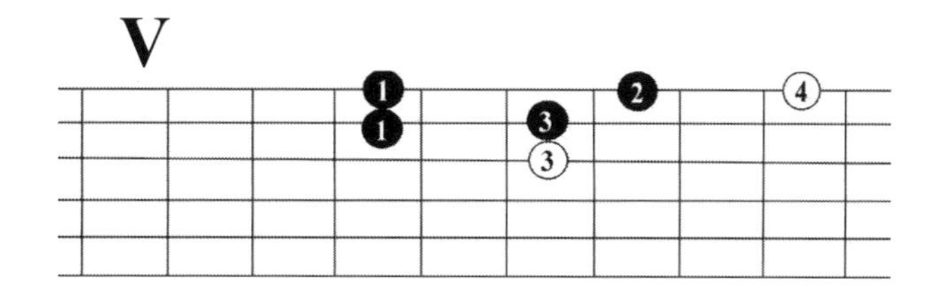

I

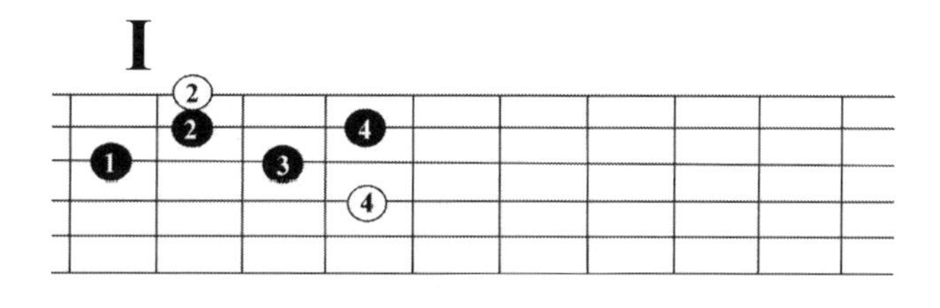

PART TWENTY-SEVEN

vi - ii - V - i

MAJOR KEYS PENTATONICS

THE vi (minor or m7) CHORD

The vi chord in a *major* key corresponds to the i chord in the relative *minor* key, and the pentatonic pattern used for these exercises contains a *root*, minor *third*, *fourth*, minor *sixth*, minor *seventh* and *octave*. e.g., for a chord of A in the key of C:

A *(minor third)* **C** *(tone)* **D** *(minor third)* **F** *(tone)* **G** *(tone)* **A**

Key of C

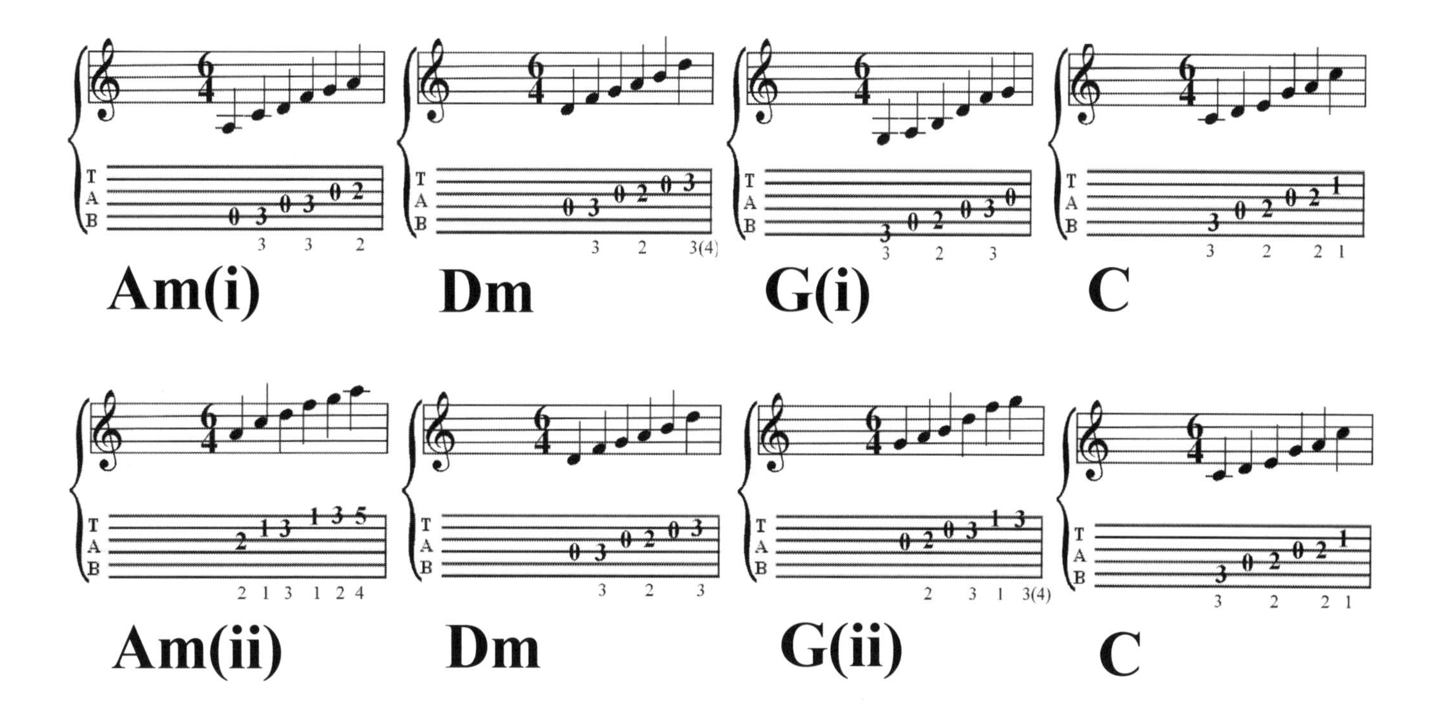

Key of G

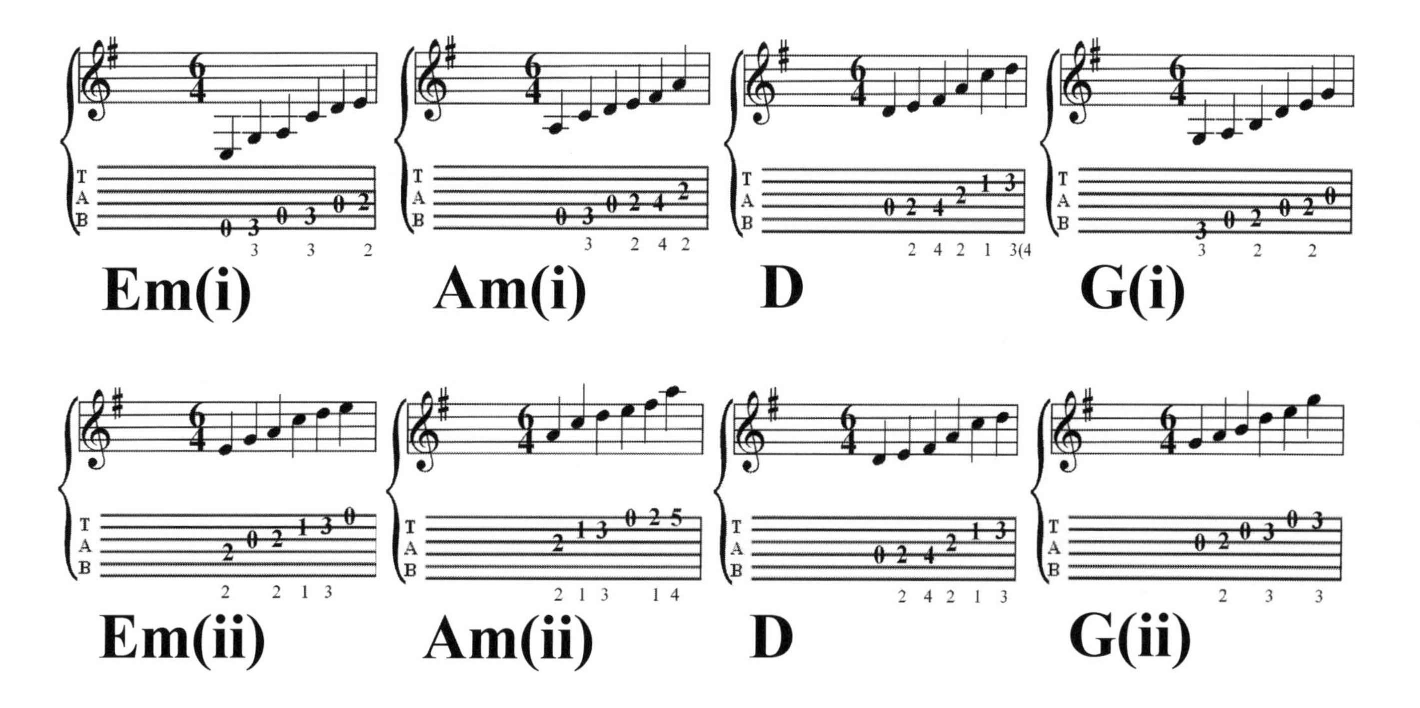

Key of D

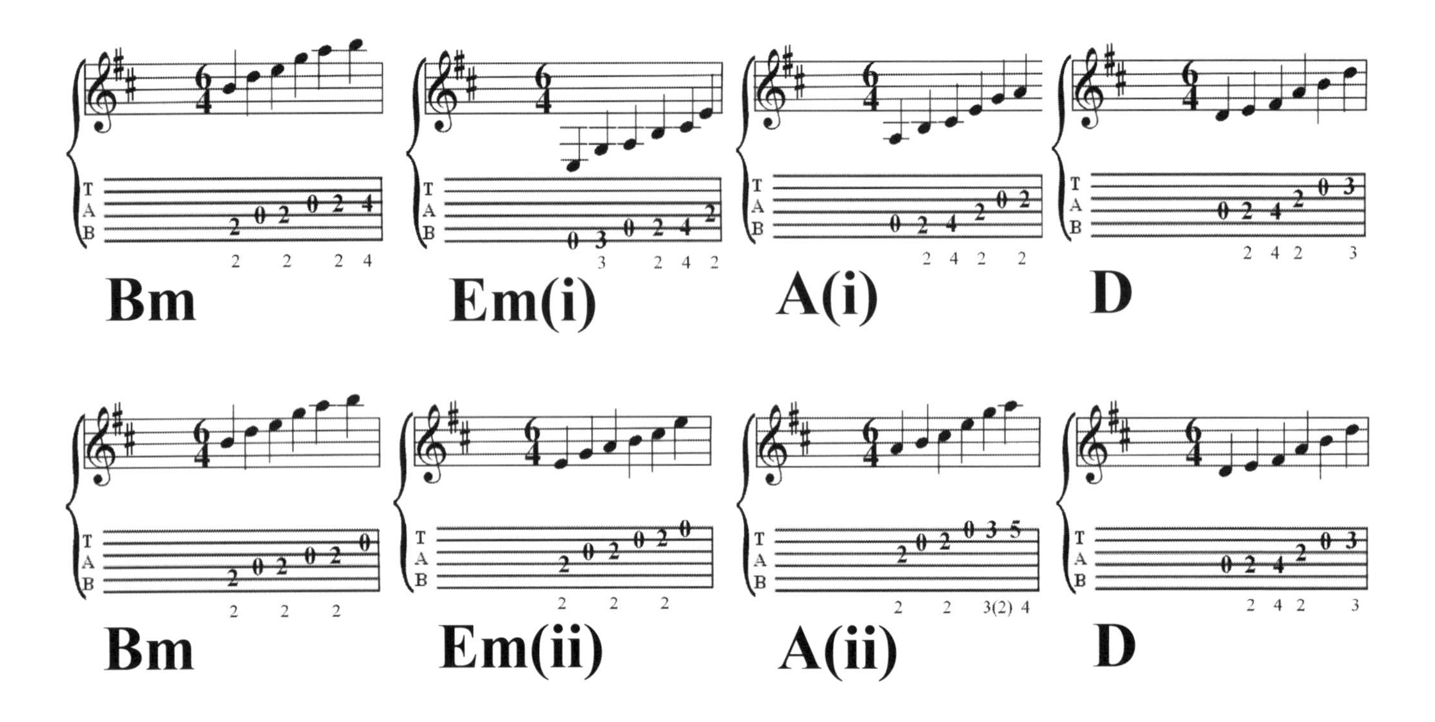

Key of A

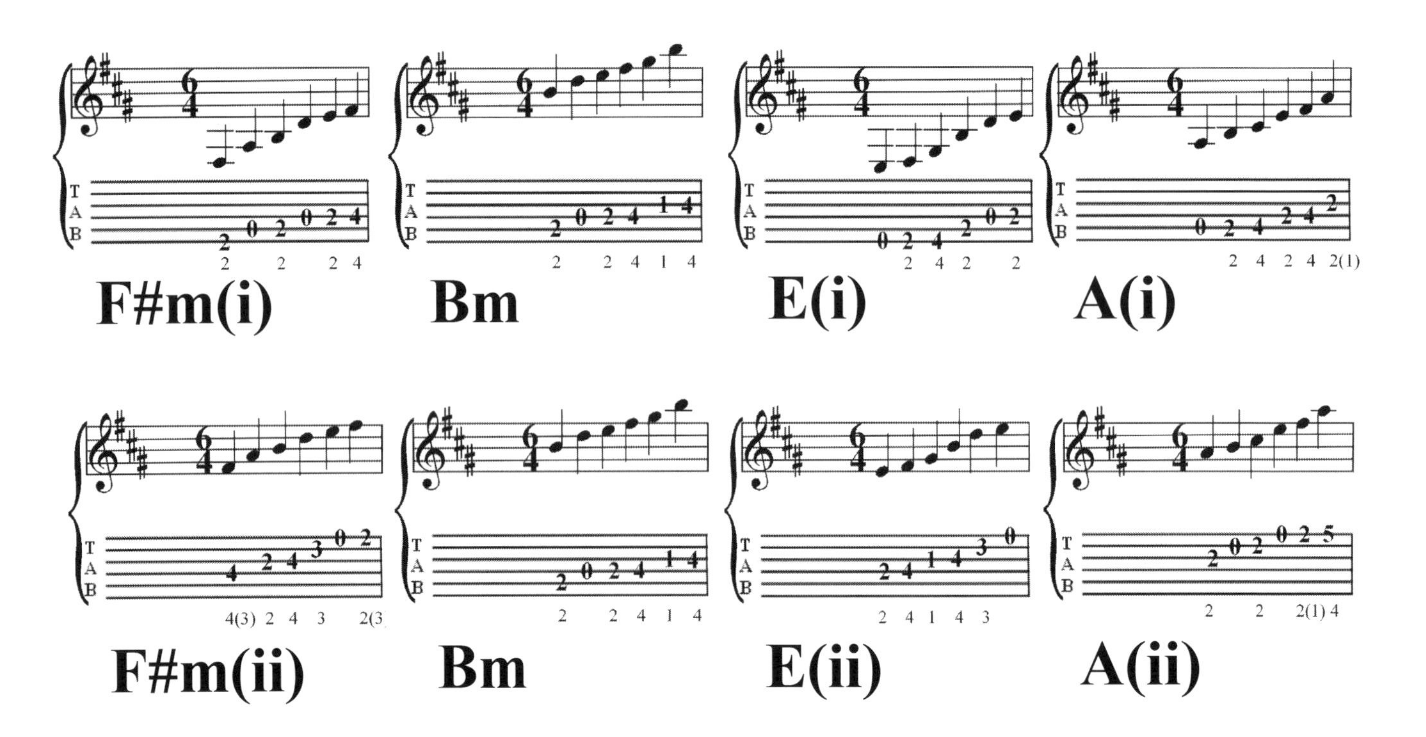

Key of E

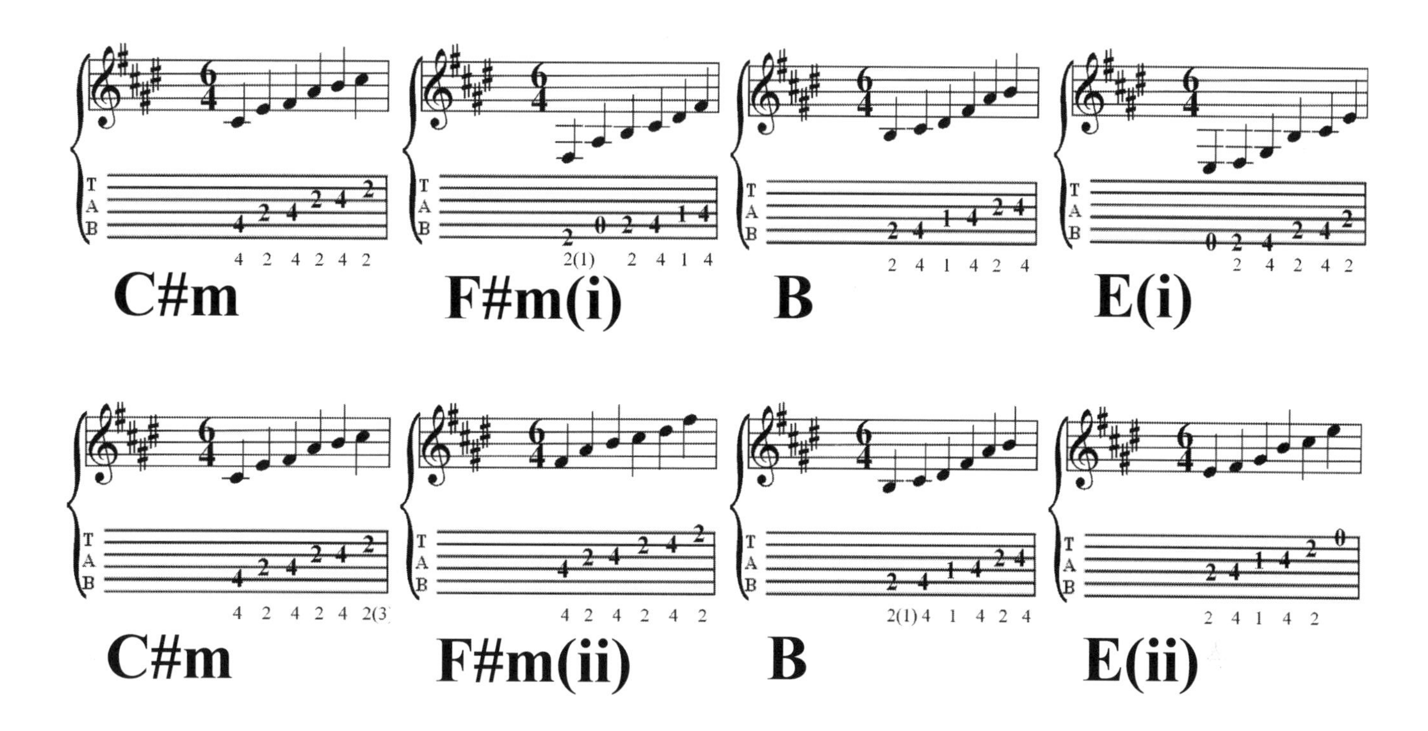

Key of B

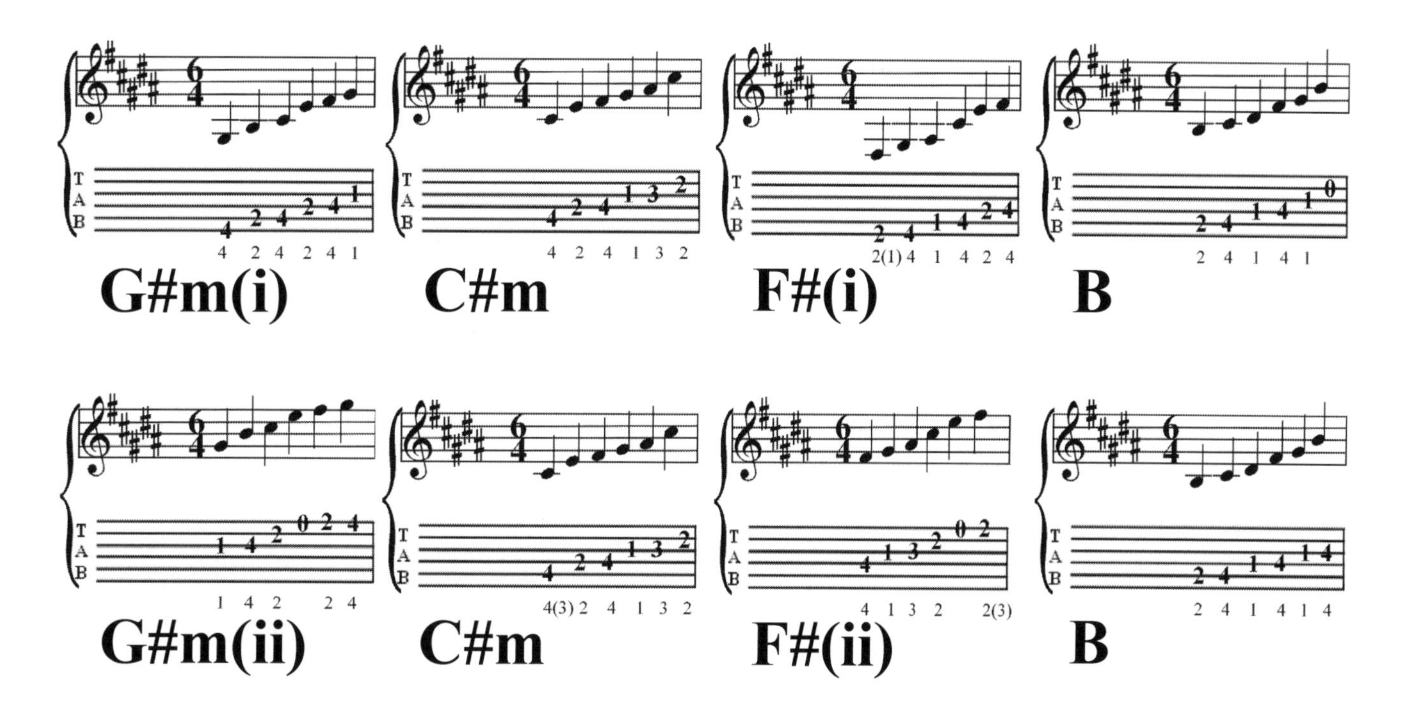

Key of F#

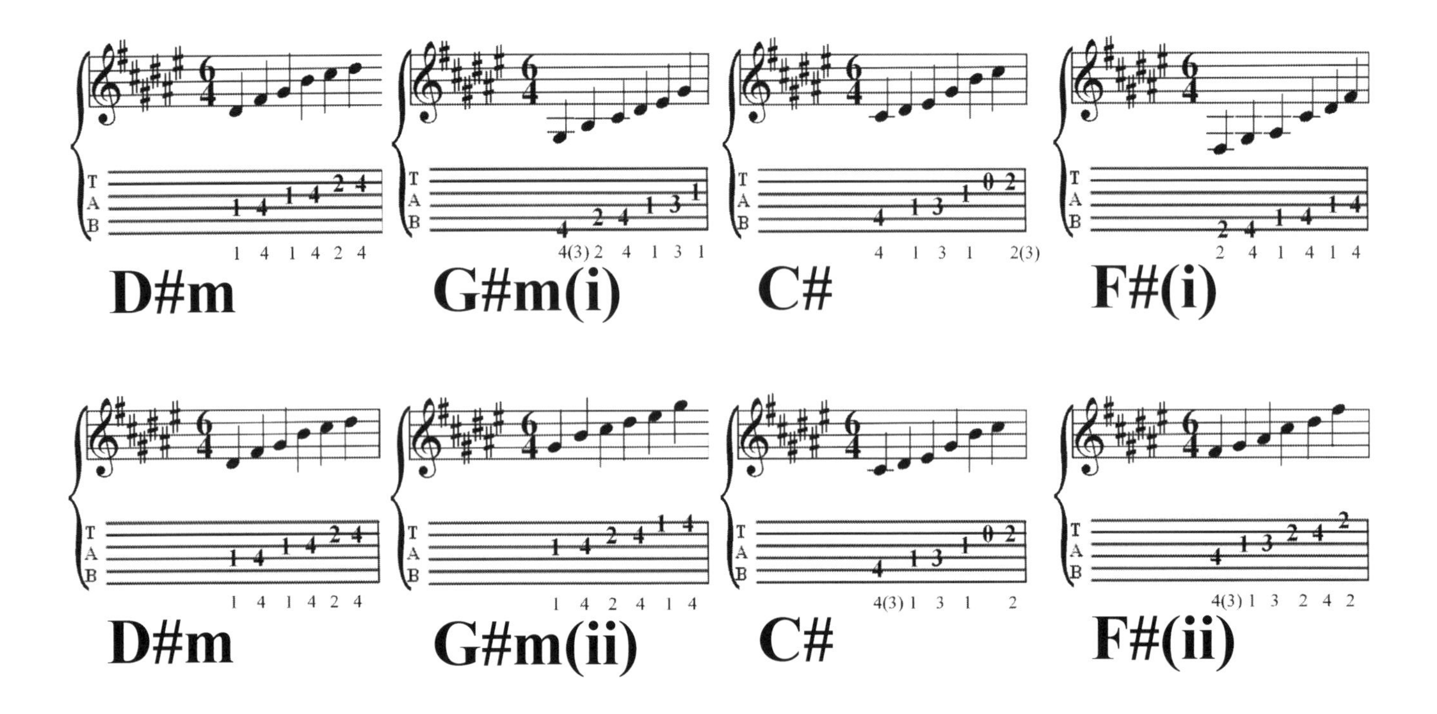

Key of C#

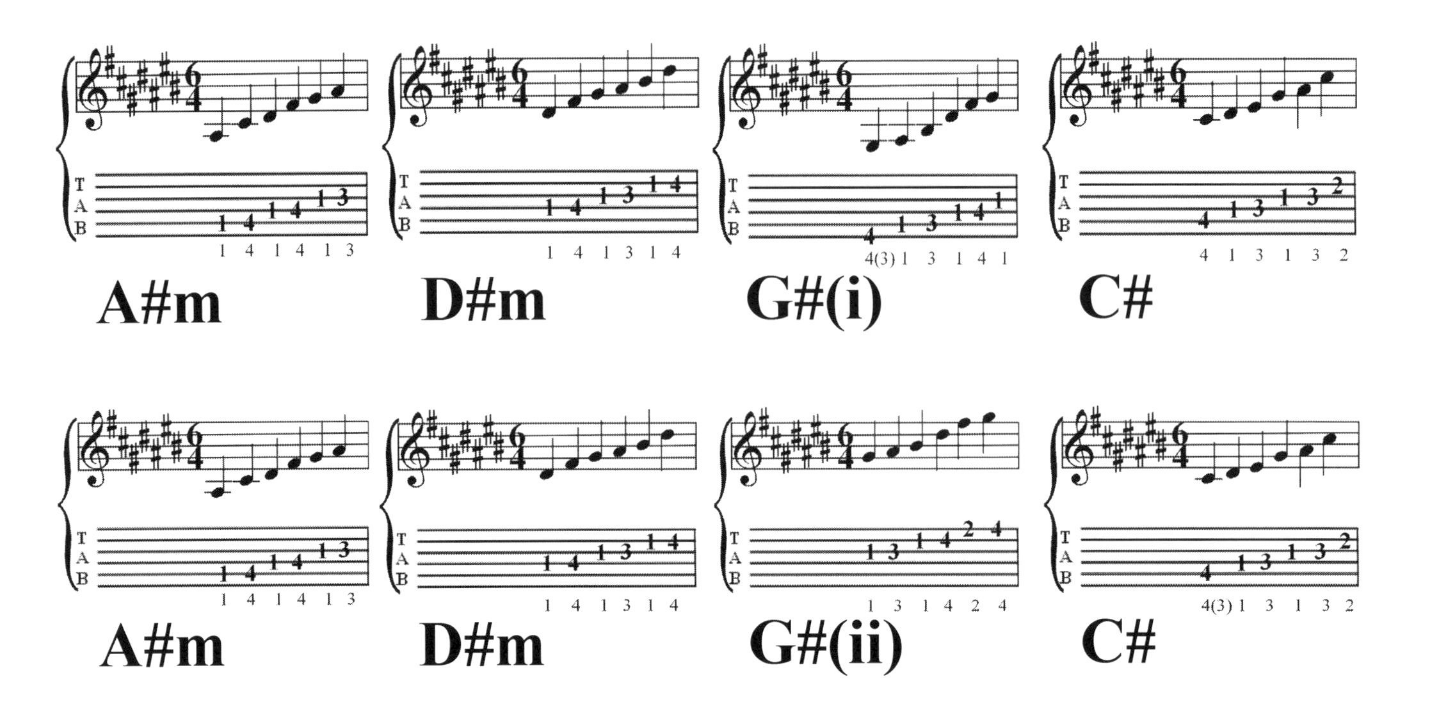

Key of A♭

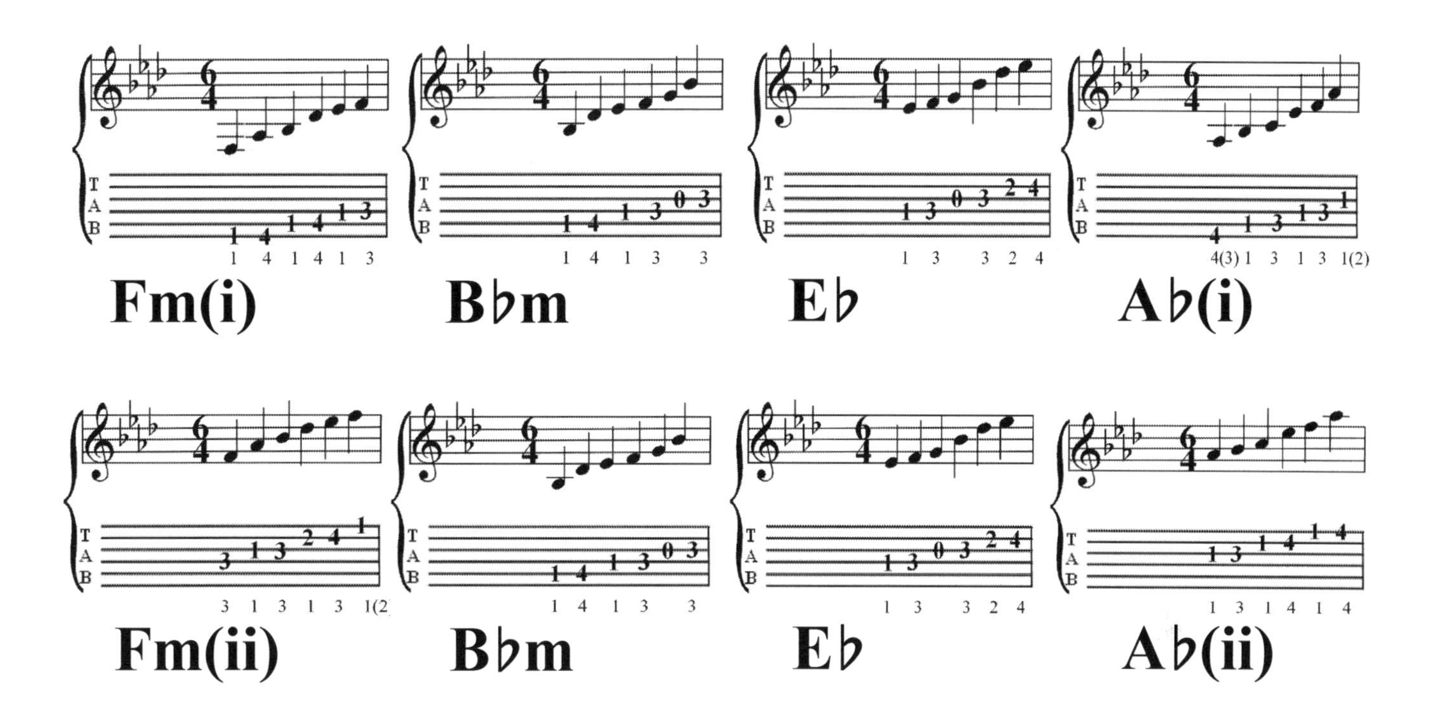

Key of E♭

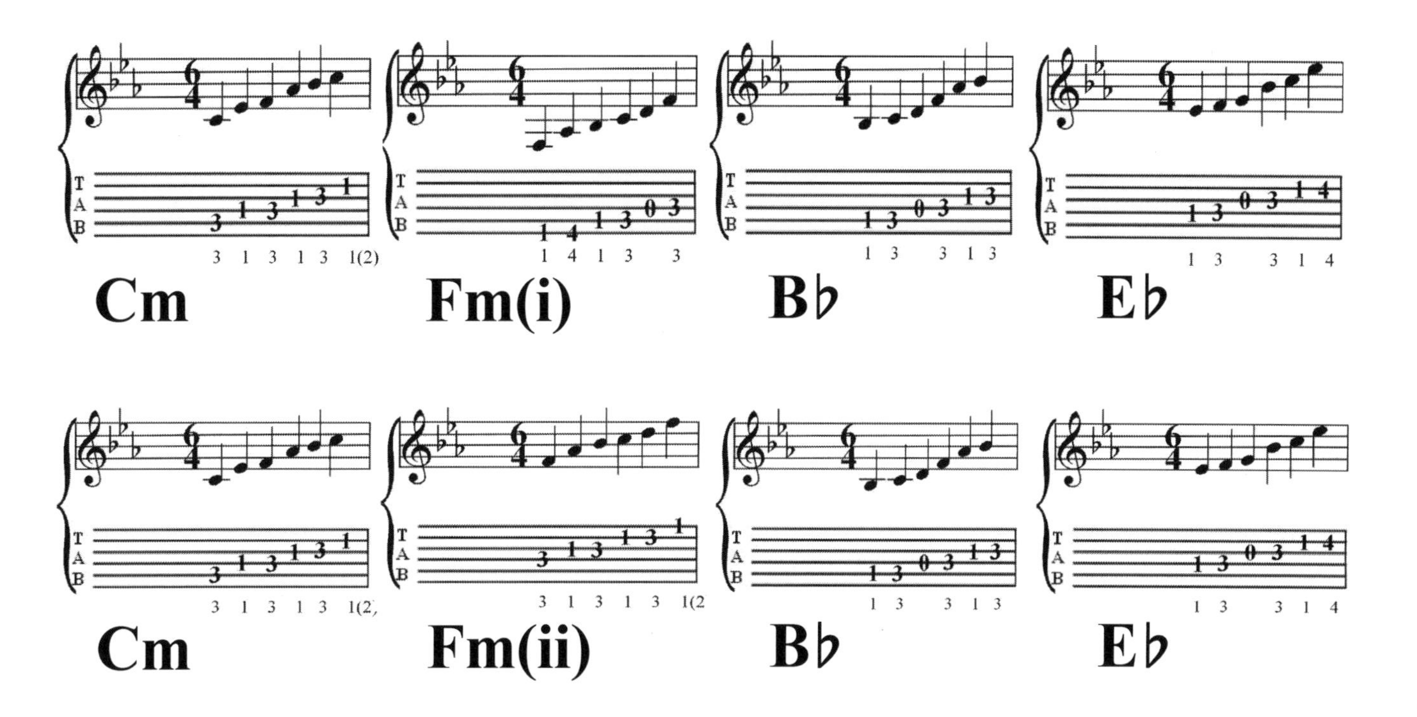

Key of B♭

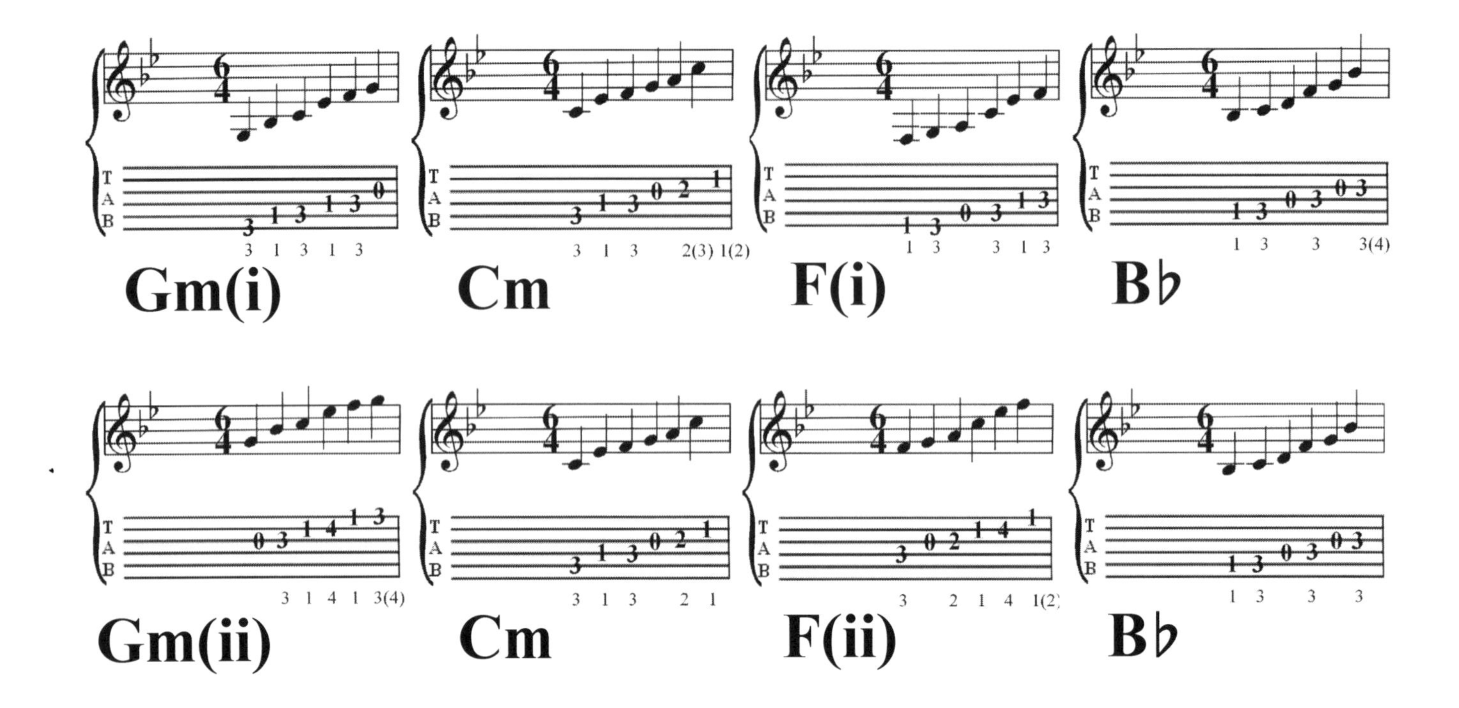

Key of F

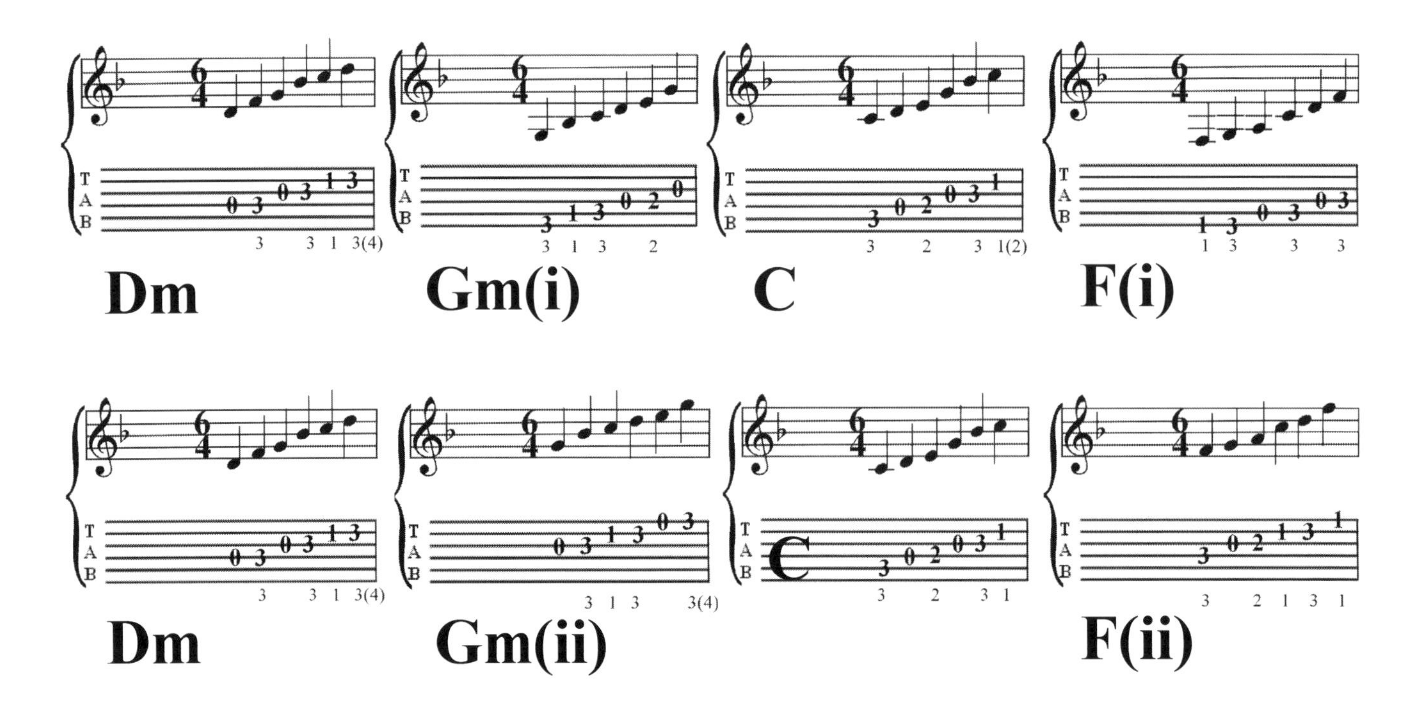

All Keys (i)

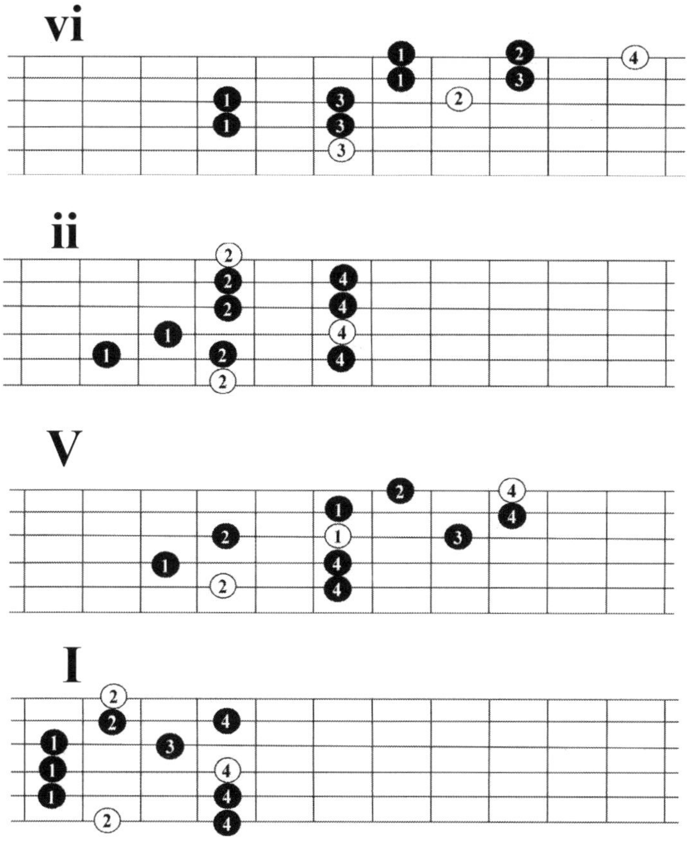

vi

ii

V

I

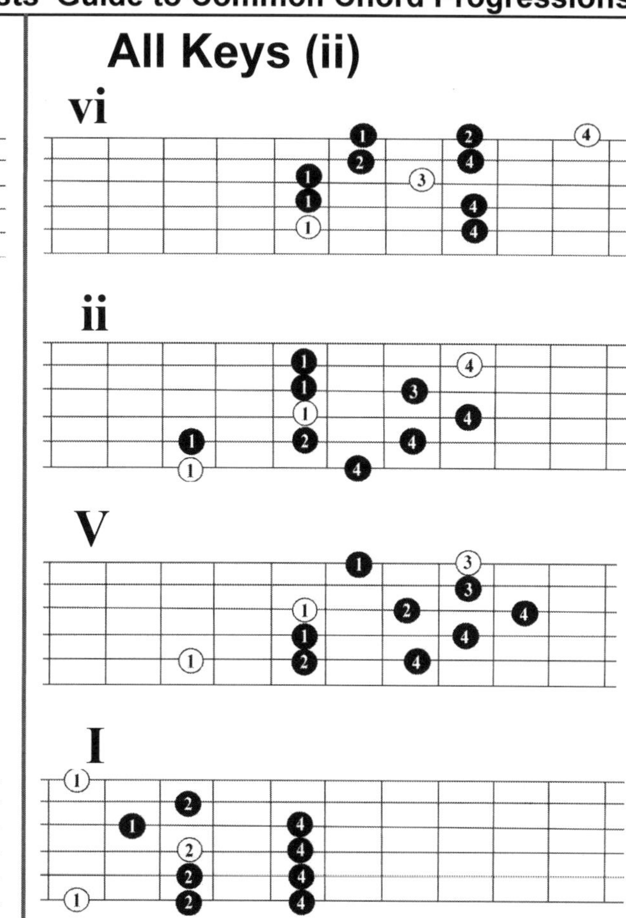

All Keys (iii)

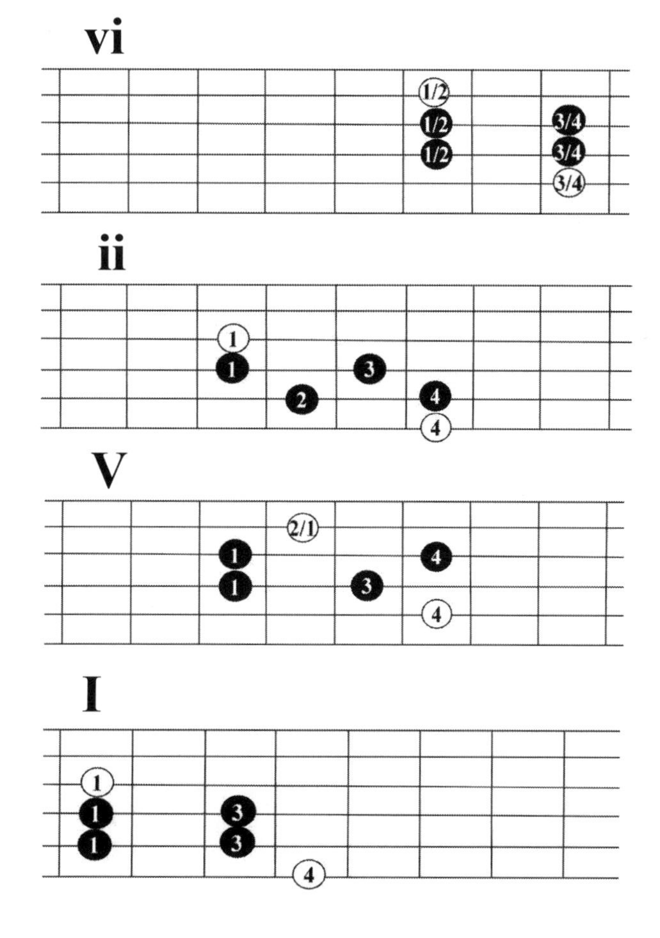

All Keys (iv)

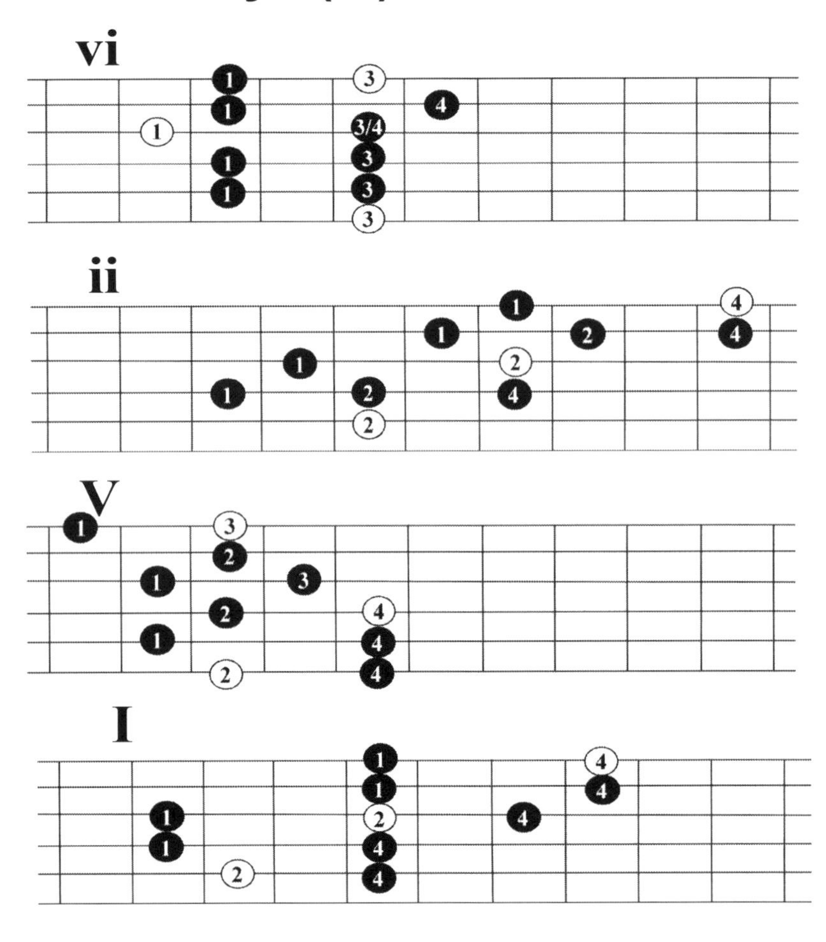

All Keys (v)

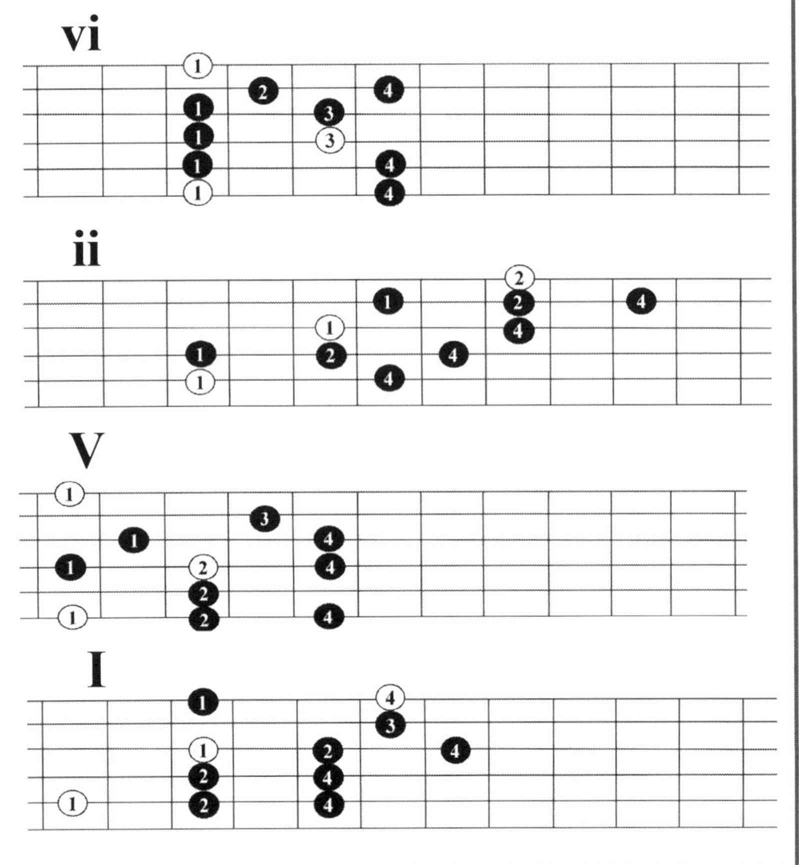

All Keys (vi)

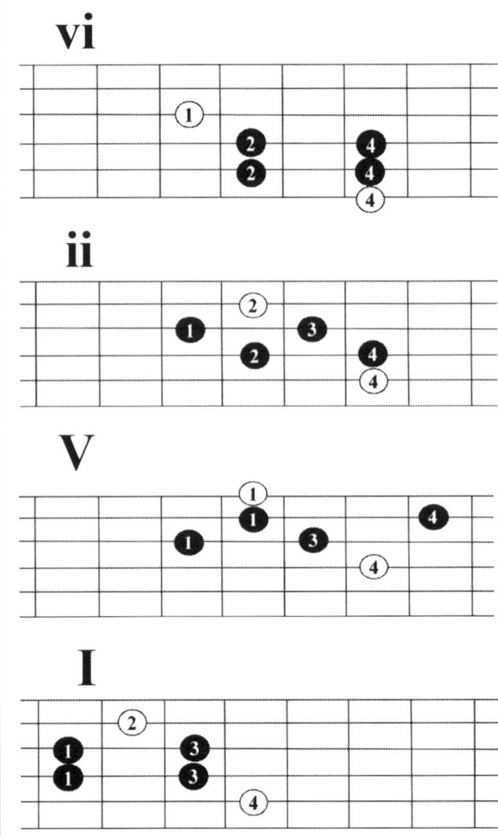

All Keys (vii)

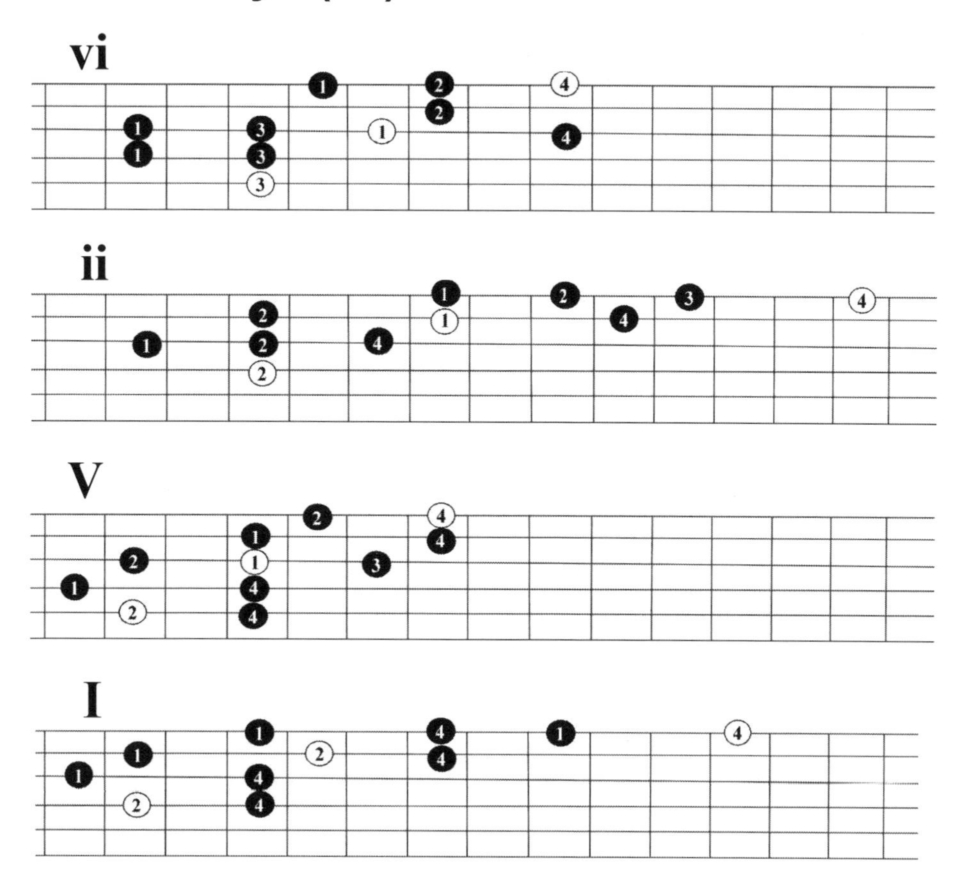

All Keys (viii)

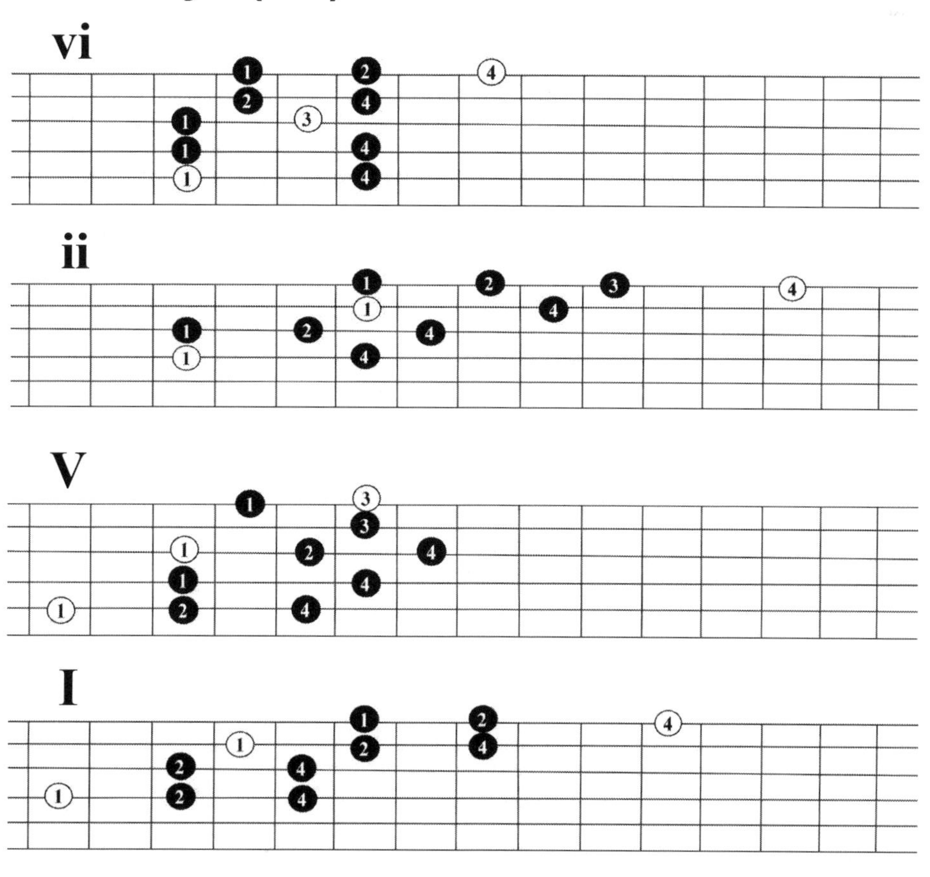

All Keys (ix)

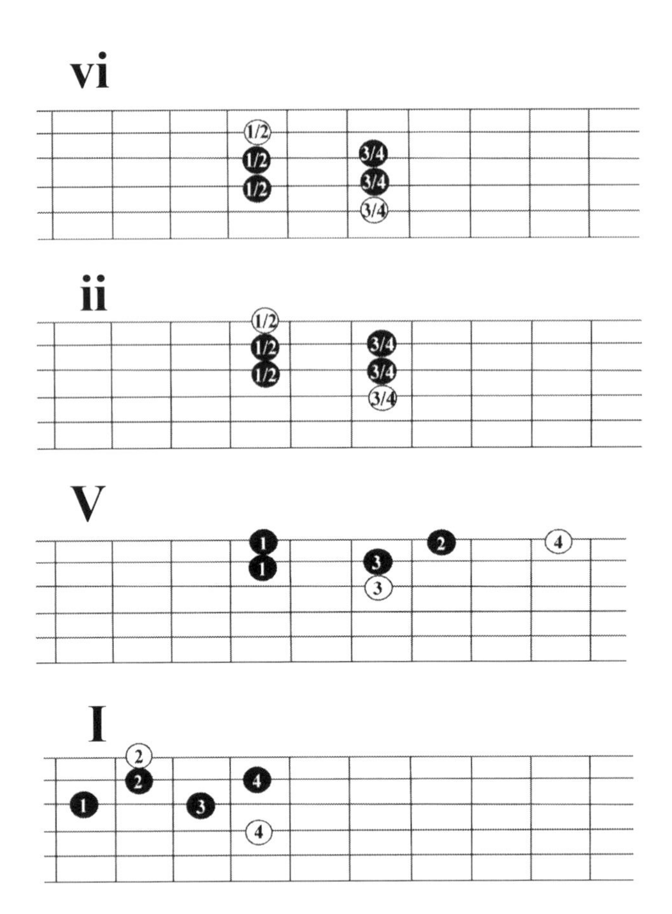

PART TWENTY-EIGHT

MINOR PENTATONIC SCALES - AN OVERVIEW

THE MINOR PENTATONIC SCALES

The construction of the *minor* pentatonic scales is treated in a separate section here, because there are some additional complications in their derivation, and also because, as we shall see, there is a useful variant of the minor pentatonic scale which will not be used in the chord progression exercises which follow.

THE i (minor or m7) CHORD

The *tonic* minor pentatonic scale is derived from the natural minor scale in the same way as the corresponding *major* pentatonic, i.e. by eliminating *semitone* intervals from the *diatonic* scale. We saw in the section on pentatonics in major keys that the choice of notes is constrained by the position of the semitone intervals in the scale. In the case of the natural minor scale, these appear between the *second* and *third*, and the *fifth* and *sixth degrees* of the scale. As with the major pentatonics, we shall retain the third as this is the note which invariably distinguishes major from minor (both chords and scales). However, in the case of the other semitone interval, we can choose to include **either** the fifth **or** the sixth. So in the key of A minor, for example, from the natural minor scale:

A *(tone)* **B** *(semitone)* **C** *(tone)* **D** *(tone)* **E** *(semitone)* **F** *(tone)* **G** *(tone)* **A**

We can create the following pentatonic scale (including the fifth):

A *(minor third)* **C** *(tone)* **D** *(tone)* **E** *(minor third)* **G** *(tone)* **A**

or the following (including the sixth):

A *(minor third)* **C** *(tone)* **D** *(minor third)* **F** *(tone)* **G** *(tone)* **A**

In the rest of this book, the exercises will use the second variant, firstly because it gives a clearer indication of tonality (remember the fifth is common to both major and minor chords and scales, whereas the minor sixth is distinctive in the minor scale), but also because, when played alongside the pentatonic scales formed on the other degrees of the scale, including the sixth gives us more distinctive variations of the pentatonic patterns for each chord, and hence a greater variety of fingering patterns to practise.

However, a closer look at the alternative form reveals:

A GENERIC MINOR PENTATONIC

If we examine the pentatonics derived from the modes of the natural minor scale for the minor/minor 7th chords formed by the harmonisation of this scale, it becomes apparent the the pentatonic pattern root/ minor third/fourth/fifth/minor seventh/octave is a generic form which is compatible with **all** the minor and minor 7th chords of the harmonised scale (including the v chord - equivalent to the iii chord in major keys, which does not appear in this book for the reasons discussed previously - and recapped in the next section).

This is obviously a very useful pattern to learn and practise, even though it is excluded from the chord progression exercises by the choices made above. Therefore, it is given its own section on the following pages, where you will find examples for each of the twelve minor/minor 7th chords, plus fingering charts *transposeable* to any position on the fretboard.

Minor pentatonic scales (generic)

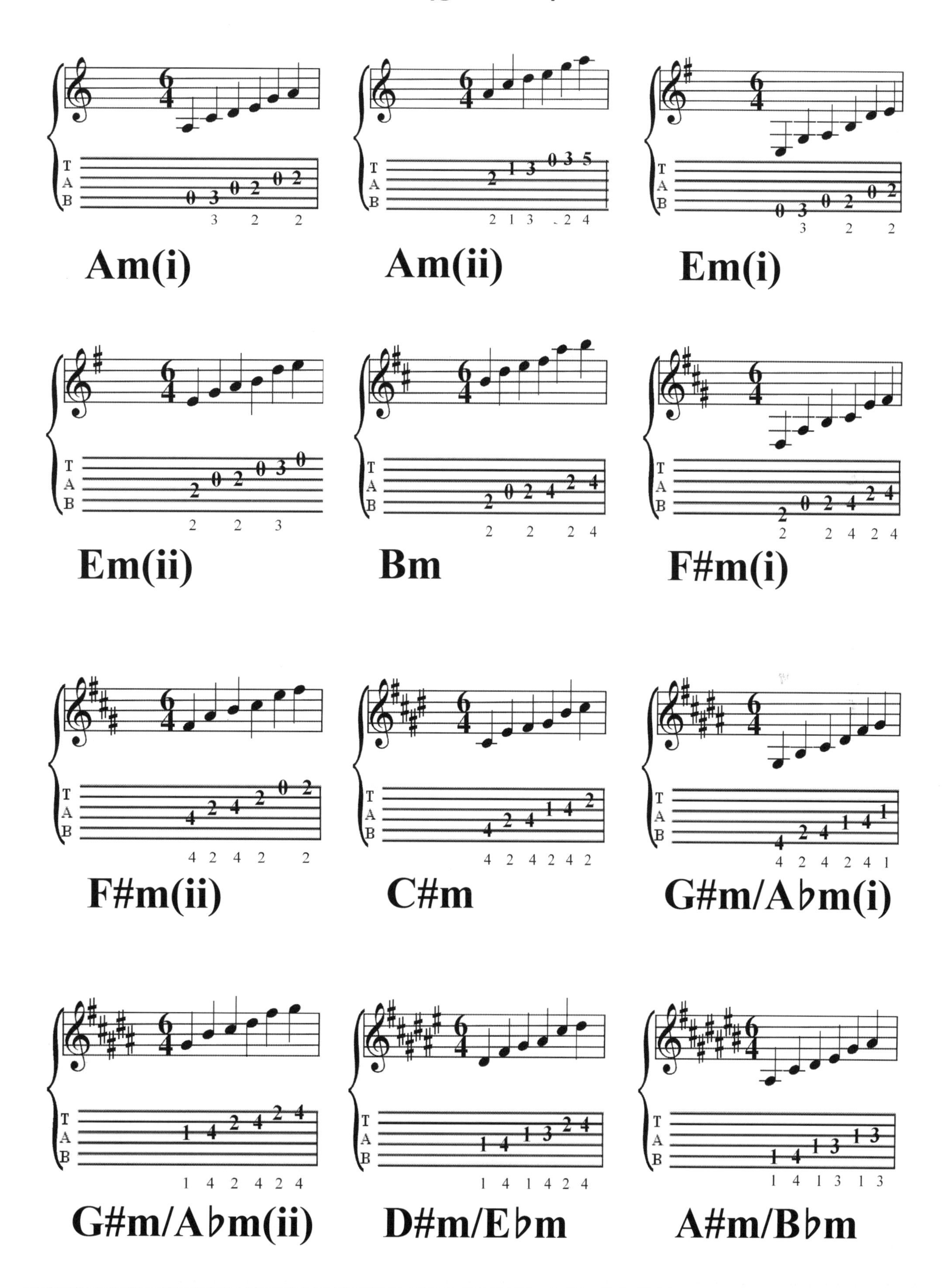

Minor pentatonic scales (generic)

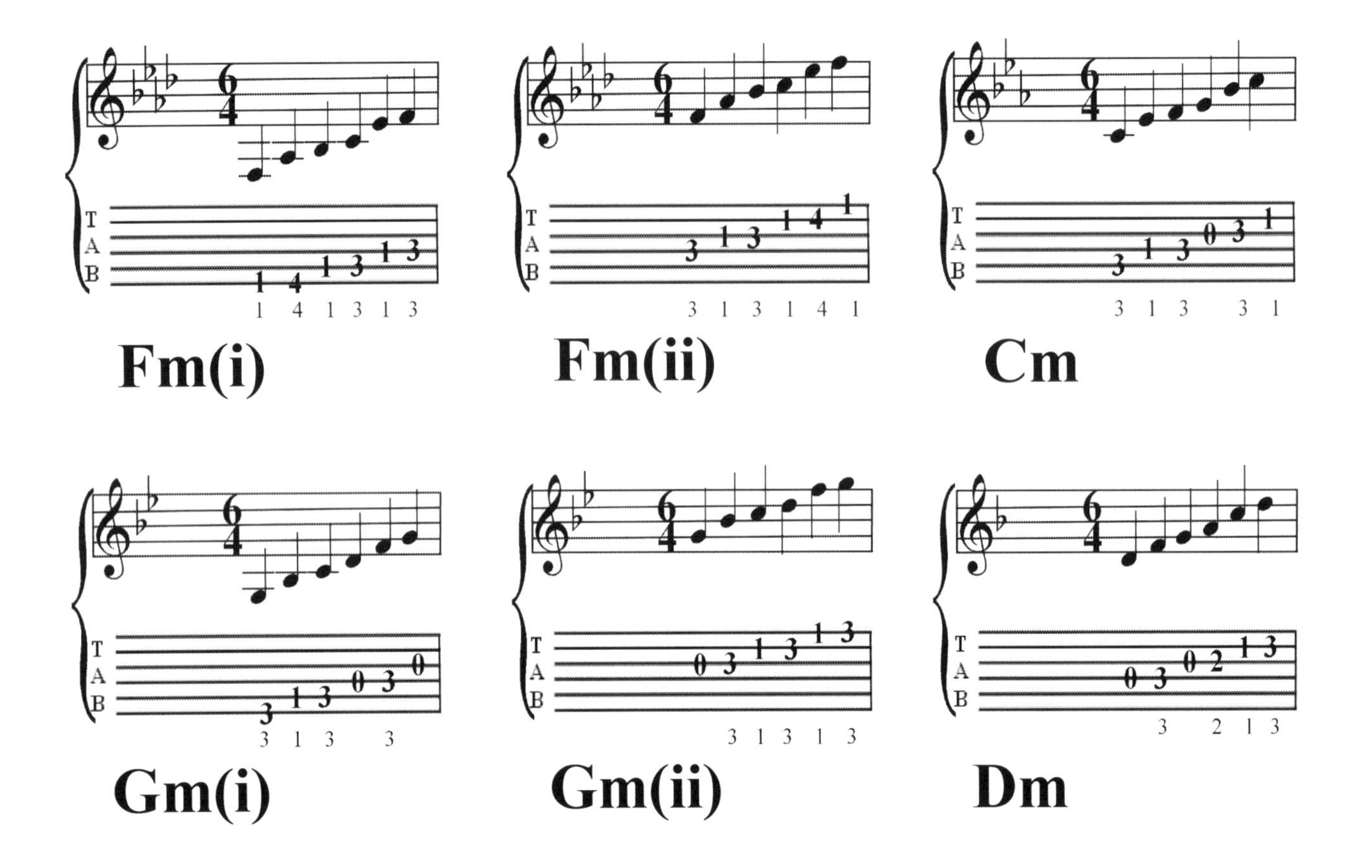

Minor pentatonic scales (generic)

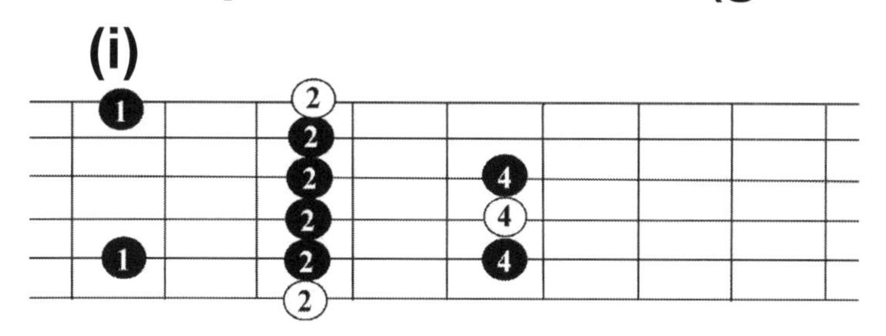

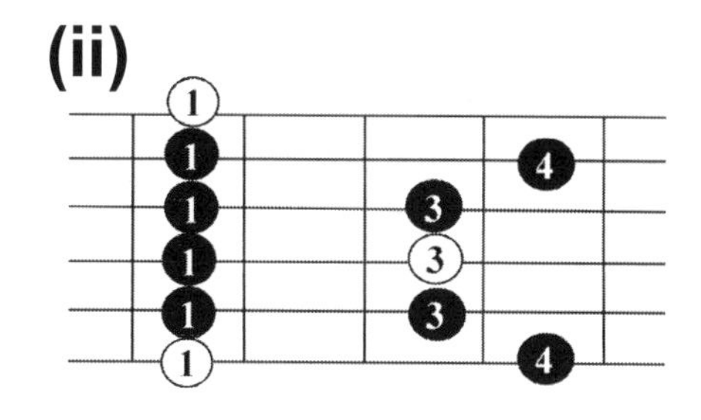

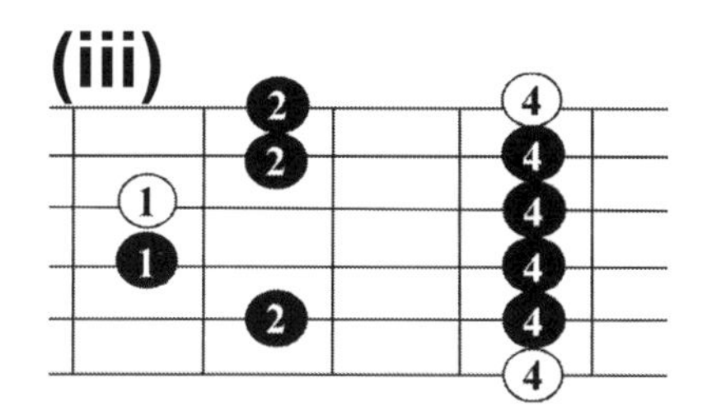

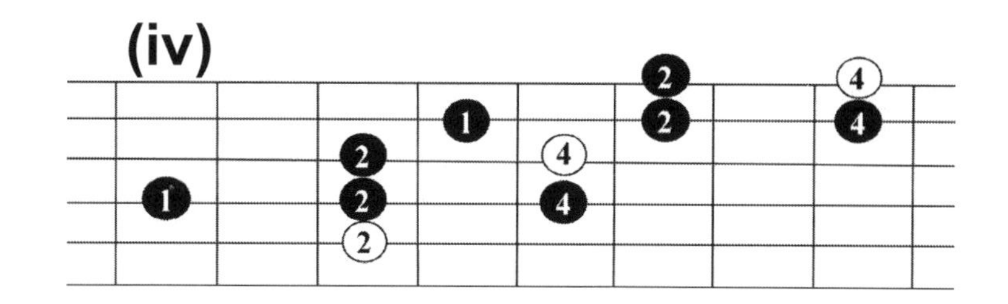

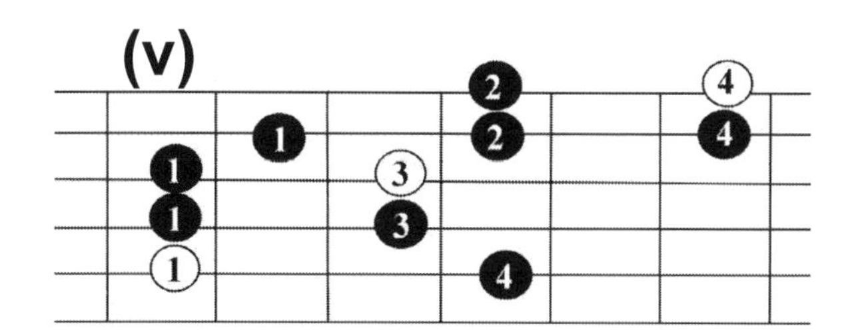

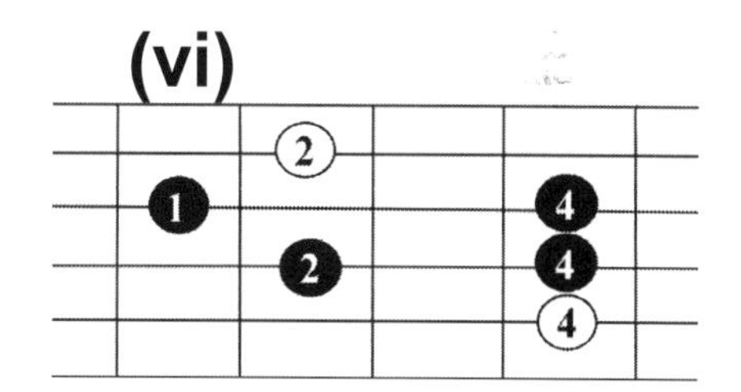

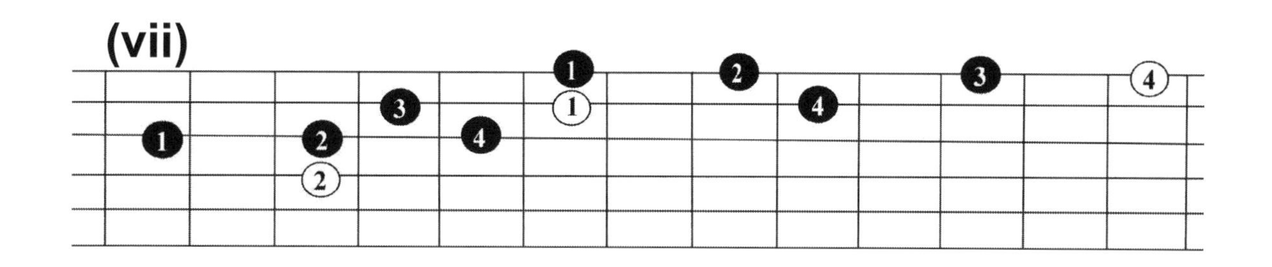

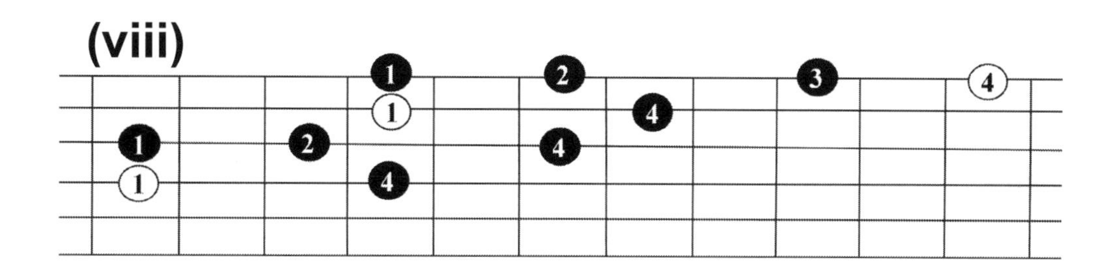

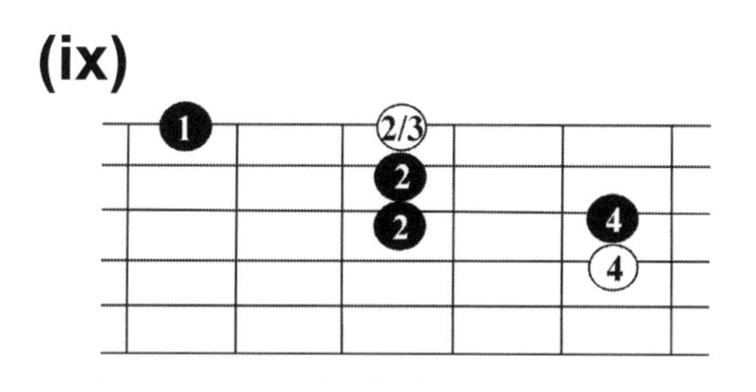

PART TWENTY-NINE

i - iv - V

MINOR KEYS
PENTATONICS

THE iv (minor or m7) CHORD

You have already met the pentatonic pattern for this chord, as it is the same as the ii chord in the relative *major* key.

The mode constructed on this *degree* of the scale is distinctive in containing a *minor third*, ***major** sixth*, and a minor *seventh*, so that the *semitone* intervals fall between the second and third, and sixth and seventh notes. The pentatonic scale, therefore, will contain the fifth and **either** the sixth **or** the seventh. Including the seventh creates our "generic" minor pentatonic: e.g, for a chord of D in the key of Am:

D *(minor third)* **F** *(tone)* **G** *(tone)* **A** *(minor third)* **C** *(tone)* **D**

In these exercises we will always use the pentatonic form containing the sixth, as being more distinctively characteristic of the tonality we are playing in (see previous discussion). Thus (e.g.):

D *(minor third)* **F** *(tone)* **G** *(tone)* **A** *(tone)* **B** *(minor third)* **D**

THE V (Major or 7) CHORD

We continue to follow the convention of substituting a major or dominant seventh (V7) chord for the v chord in minor keys. The pentatonic pattern for the V chord will, therefore be the same as that for major keys (i.e. root-2nd-3rd-5th-7th-octave). e.g., for a chord of E in the key of Am

E *(tone)* **F#** *(tone)* **G#** *(minor third)* **B** *(minor third)* **D** *(tone)* **E**

Comparing this pentatonic with the *tonic* natural minor scale, you will see that, in addition to the sharpened third, the second note of the pentatonic scale (corresponding to the sixth of the tonic minor scale) is also sharpened. This pentatonic scale can be derived from the **melodic minor scale** which is described in a later section of this book.

THE v (minor or m7) CHORD

Remember that the v minor seventh chord is also valid in minor keys. If this chord is used, then the appropriate pentatonic patterns are the same as those for the i (minor) chord, i.e. root-3rd-4th-6th-7th-octave, or the generic root-3rd-4th-5th-7th-octave. e.g., for a chord of Em in the key of Am

E *(minor third)* **G** *(tone)* **A** *(minor third)* **C** *(tone)* **D** *(tone)* **E**

or

E *(minor third)* **G** *(tone)* **A** *(tone)* **B** *(minor third)* **D** *(tone)* **E**

Key of Am

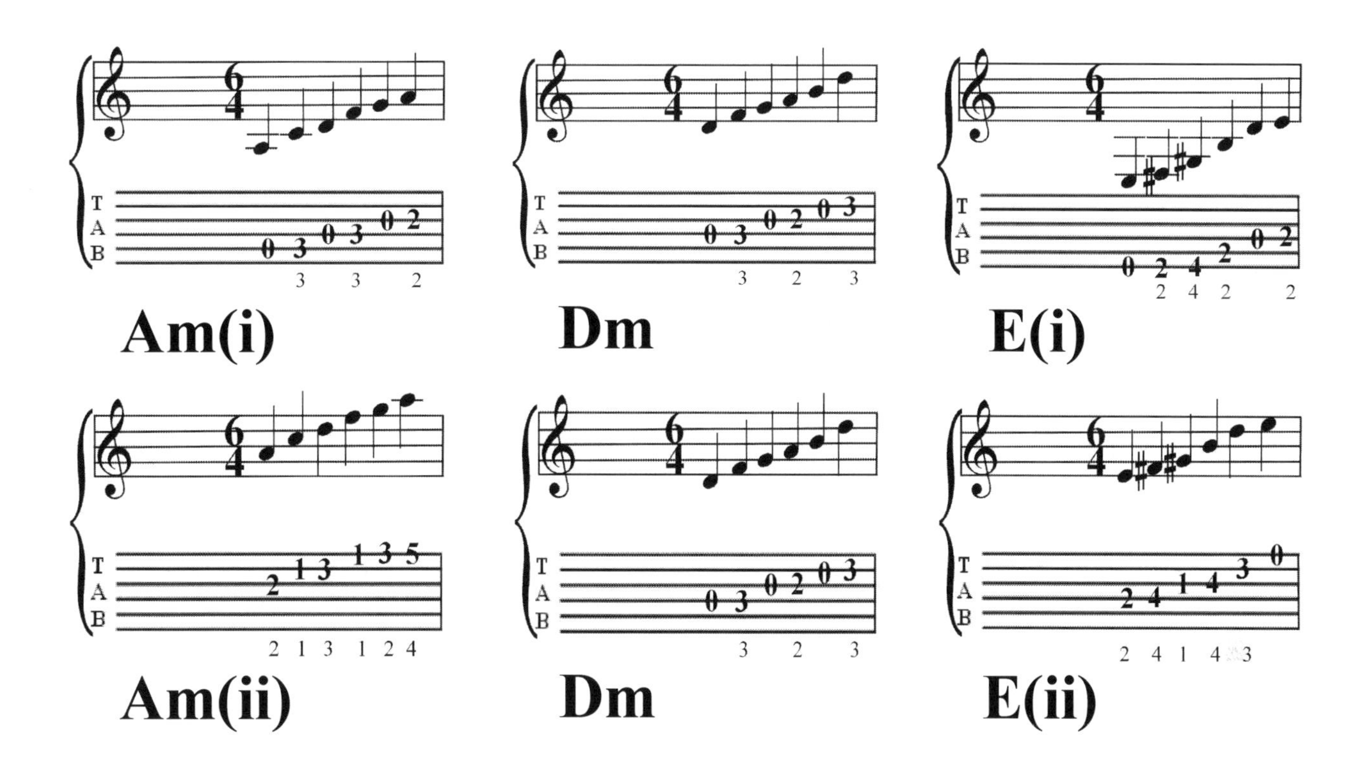

Key of Em

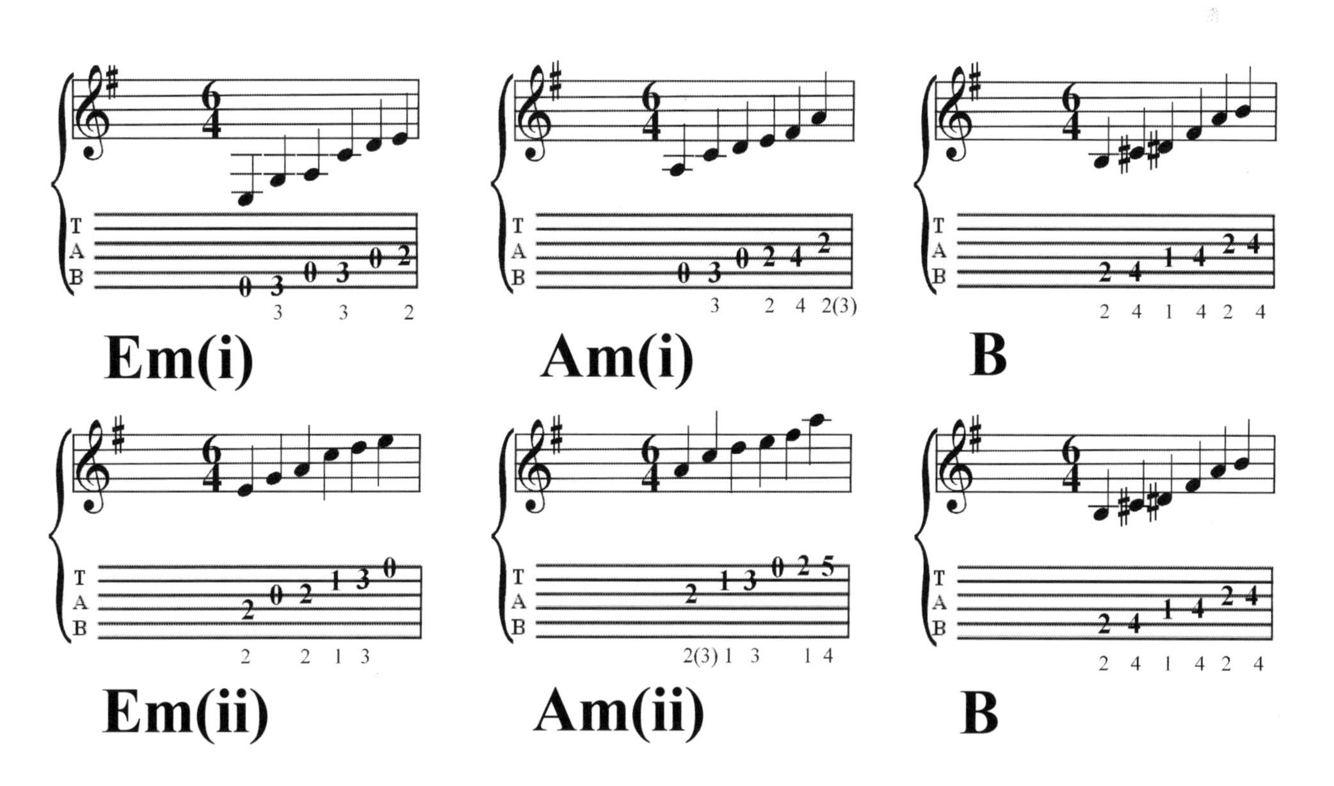

Key of Bm

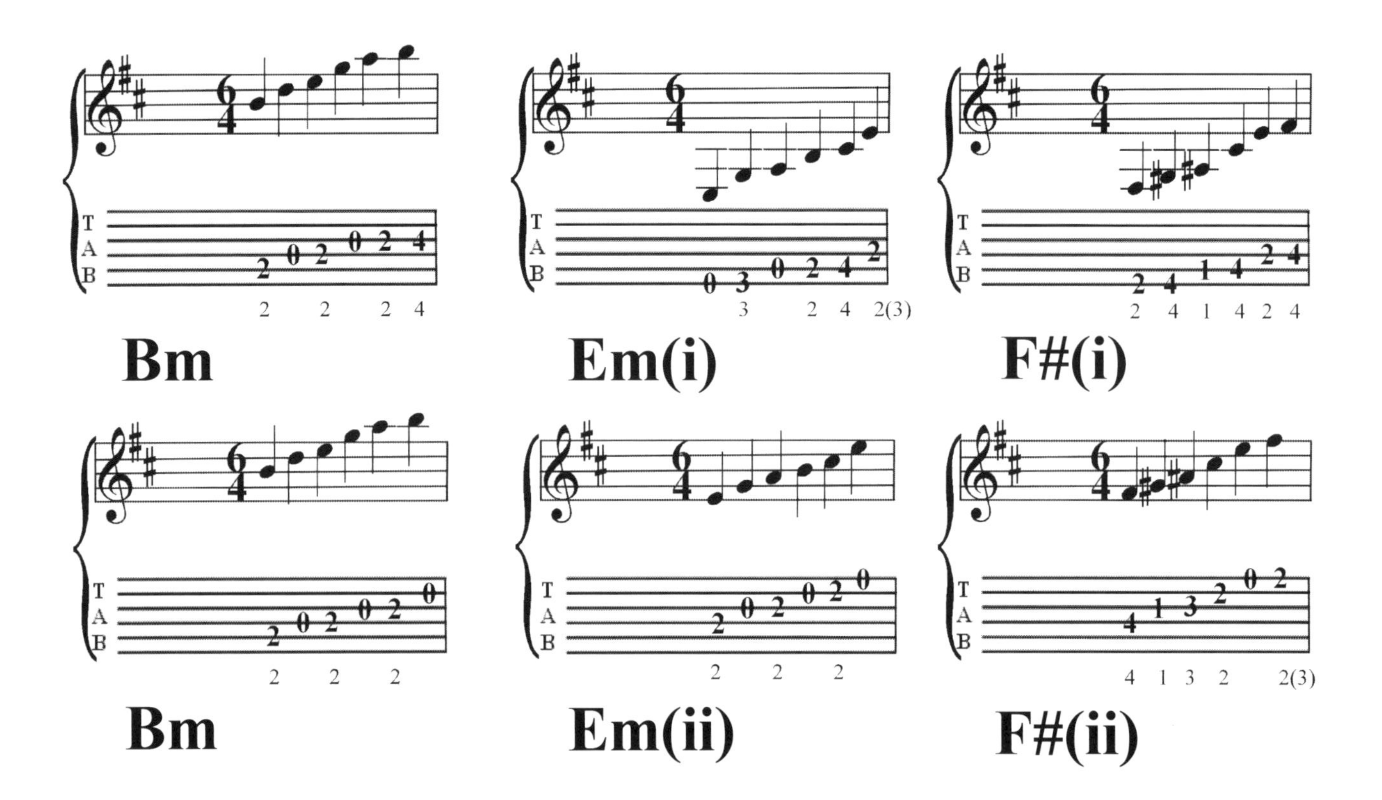

Key of F#m

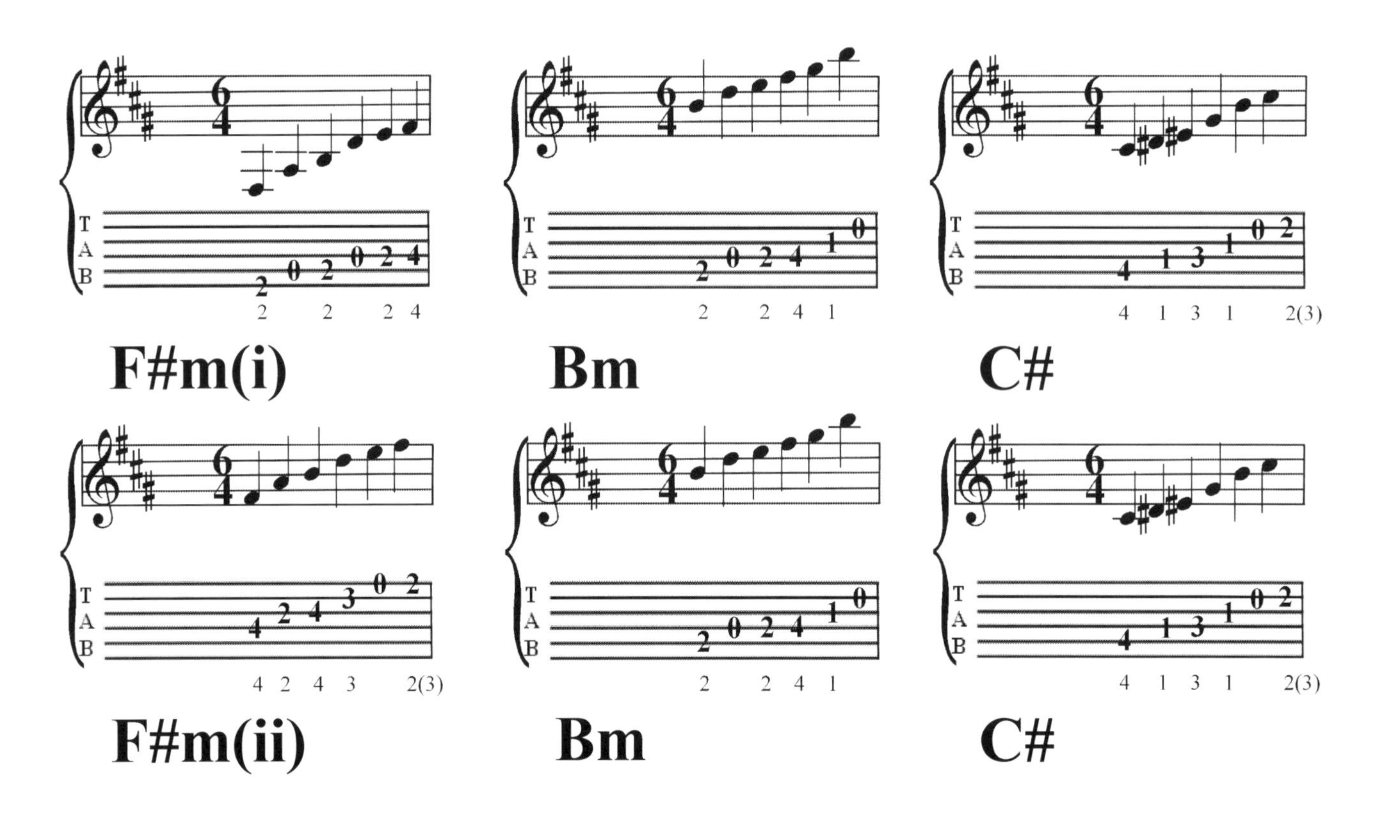

Key of C#m

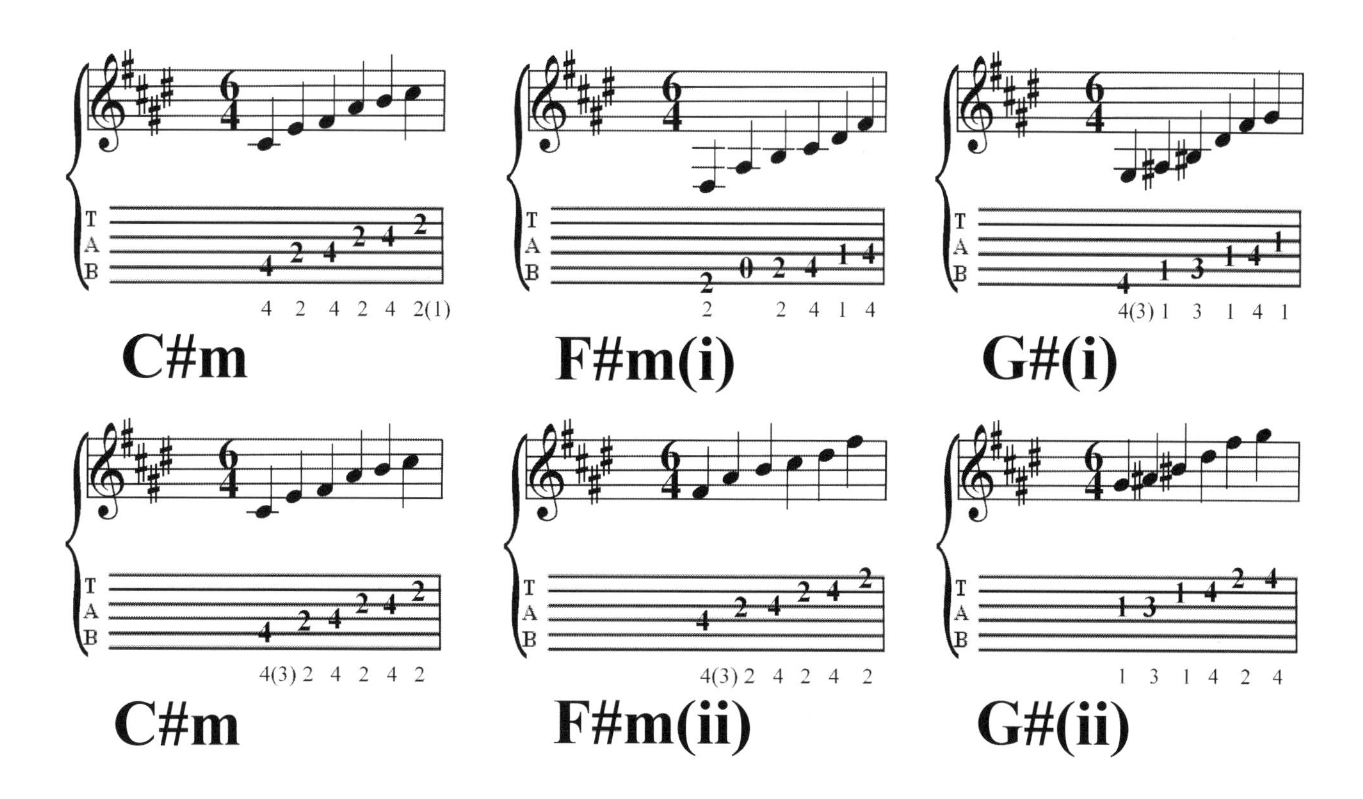

Key of A♭m

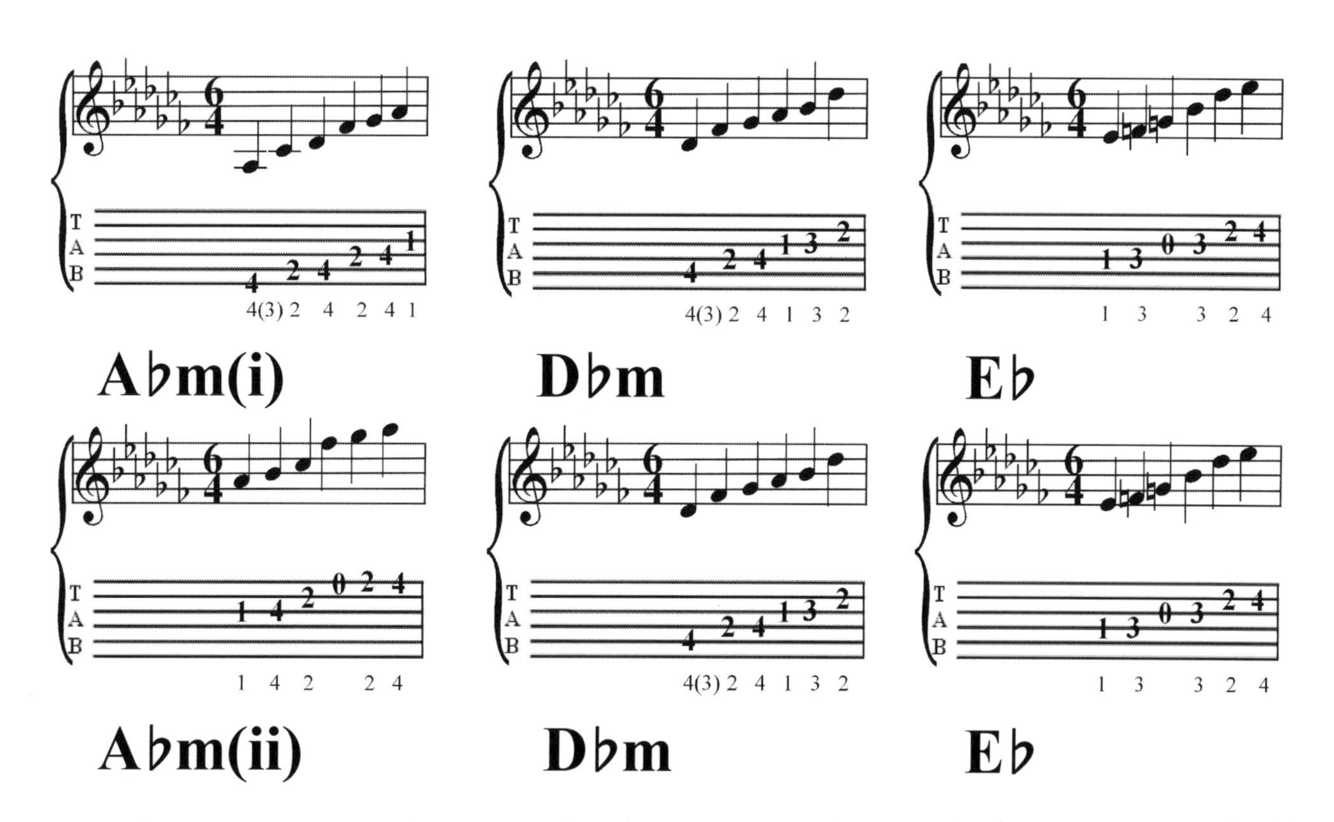

Key of E♭m

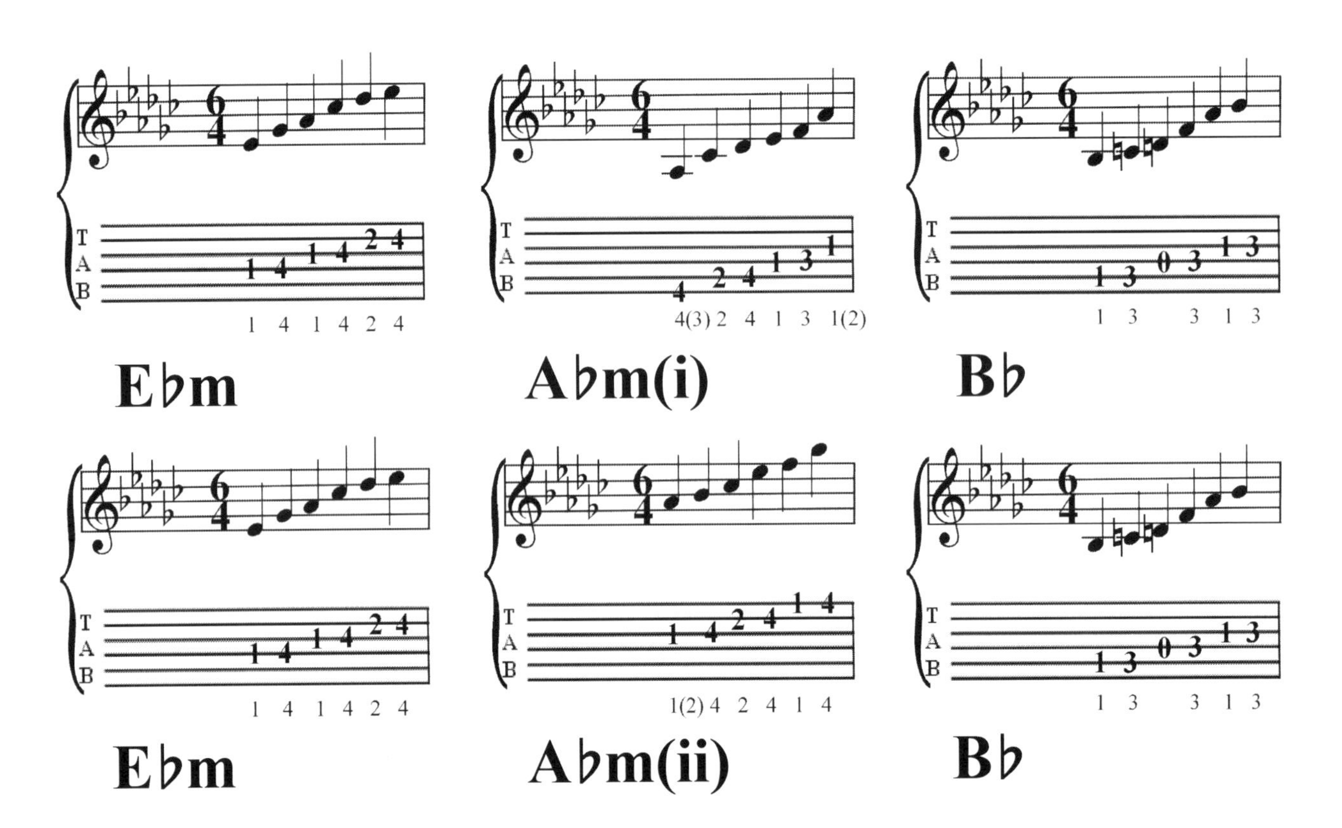

Key of B♭m

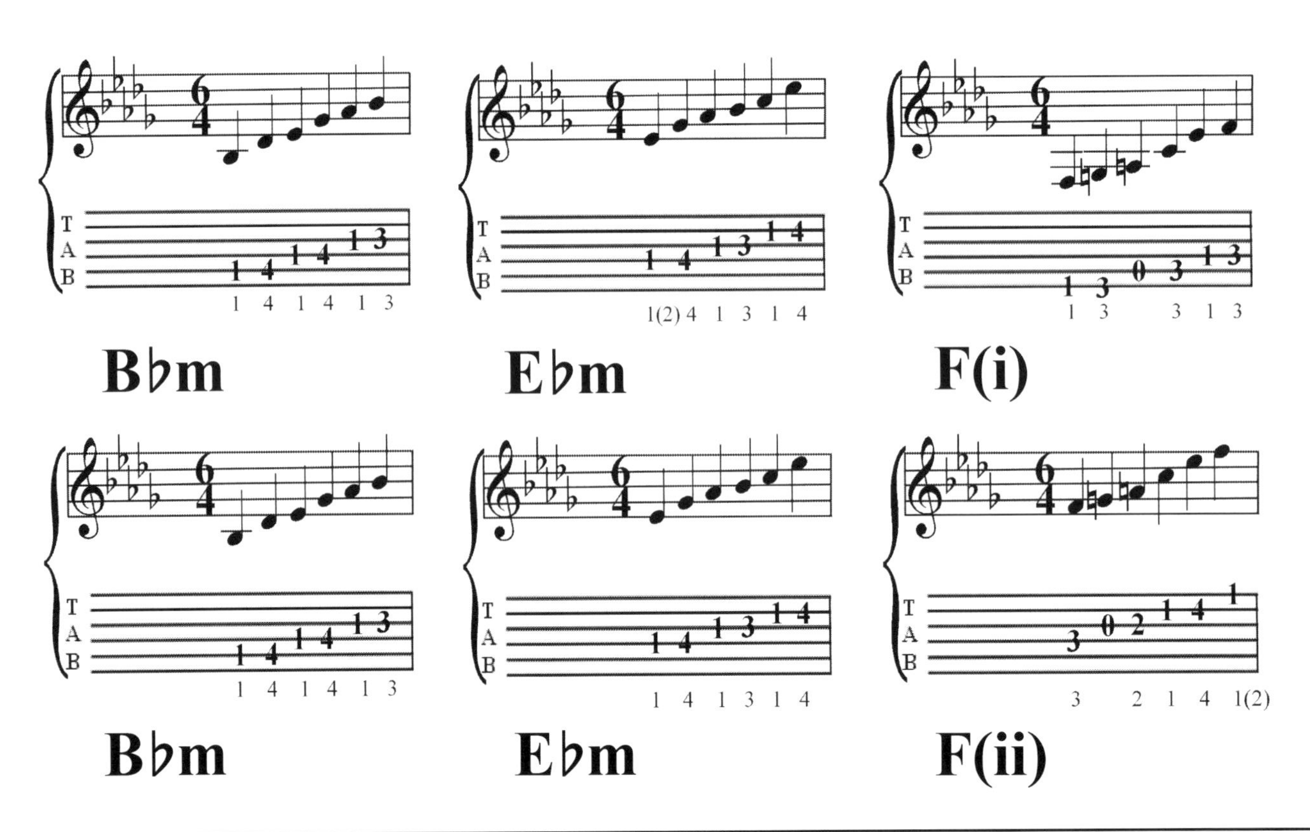

Key of Fm

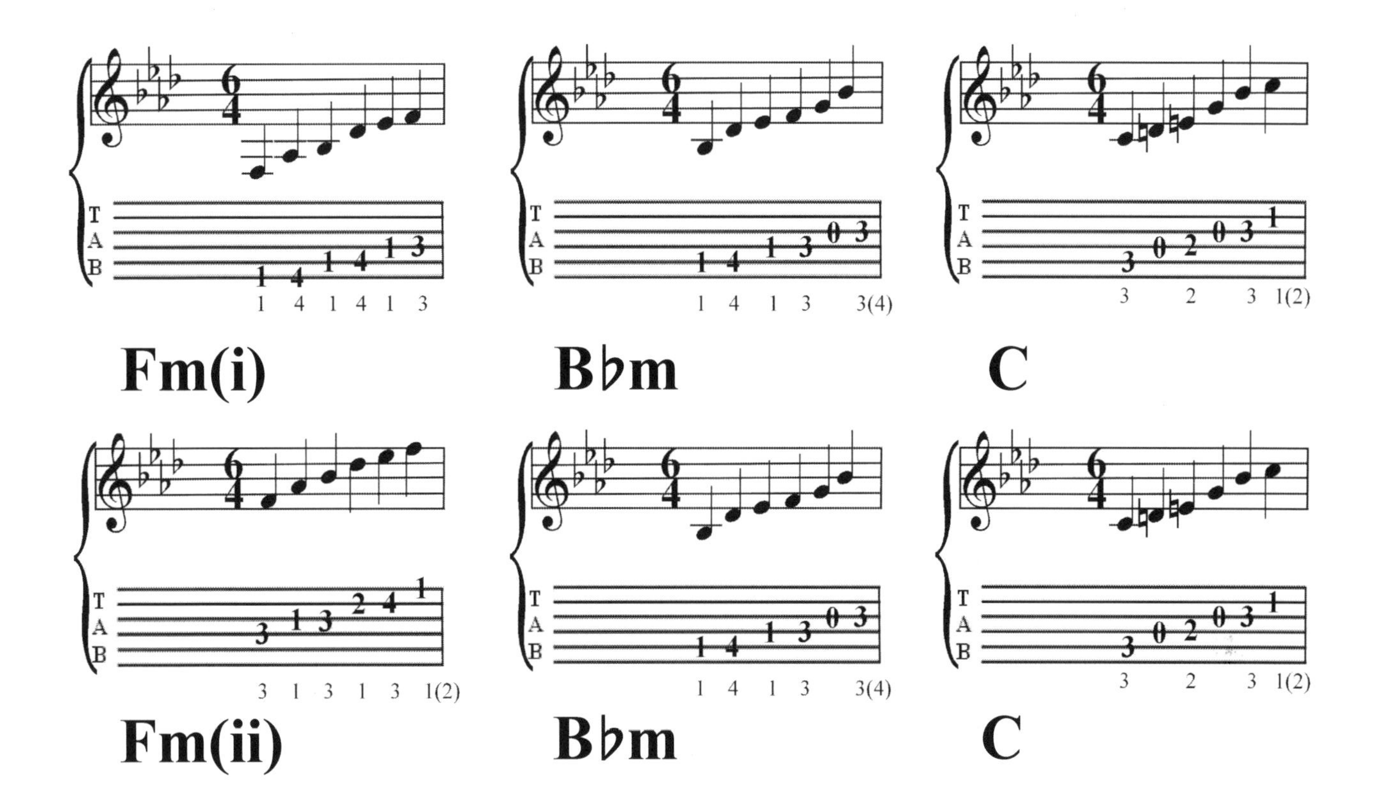

Key of Cm

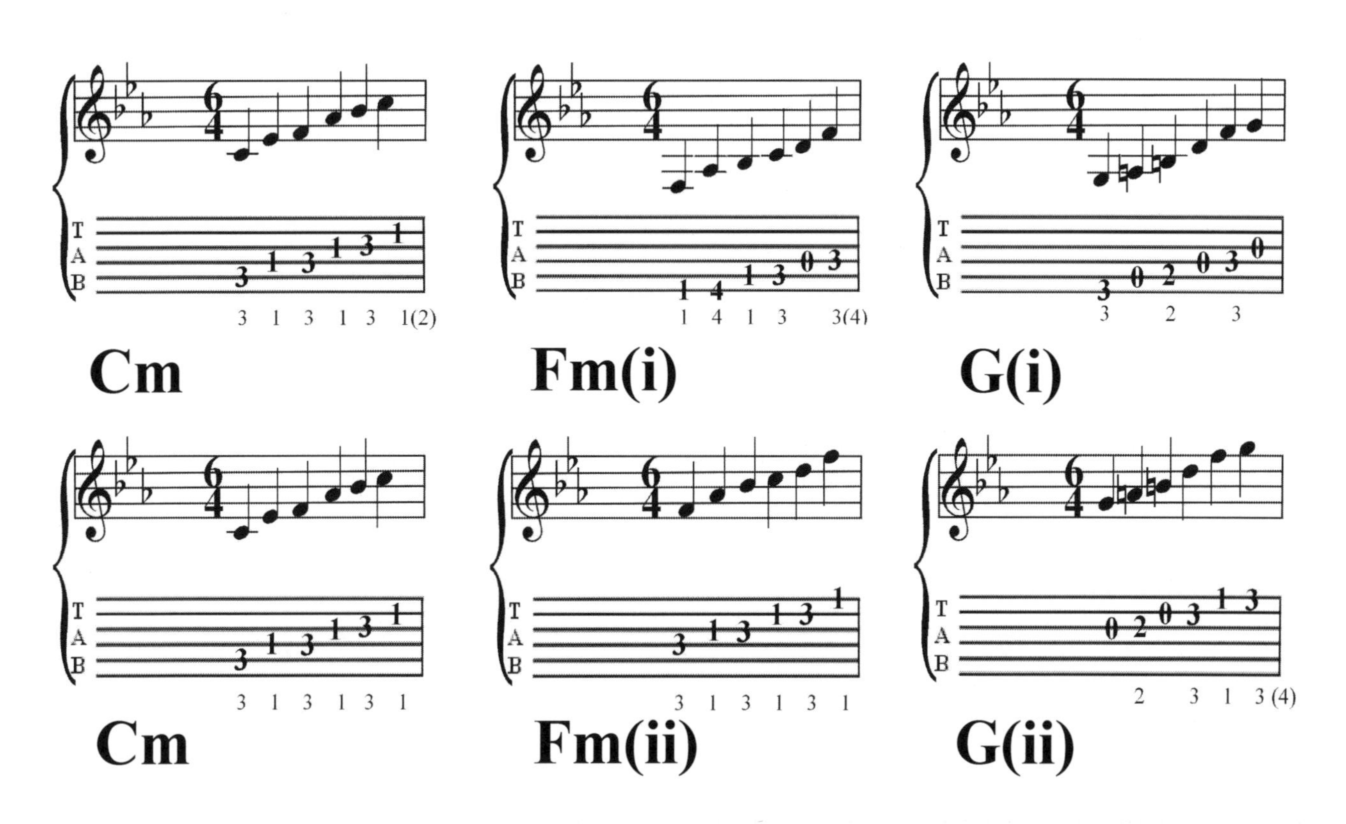

Key of Gm

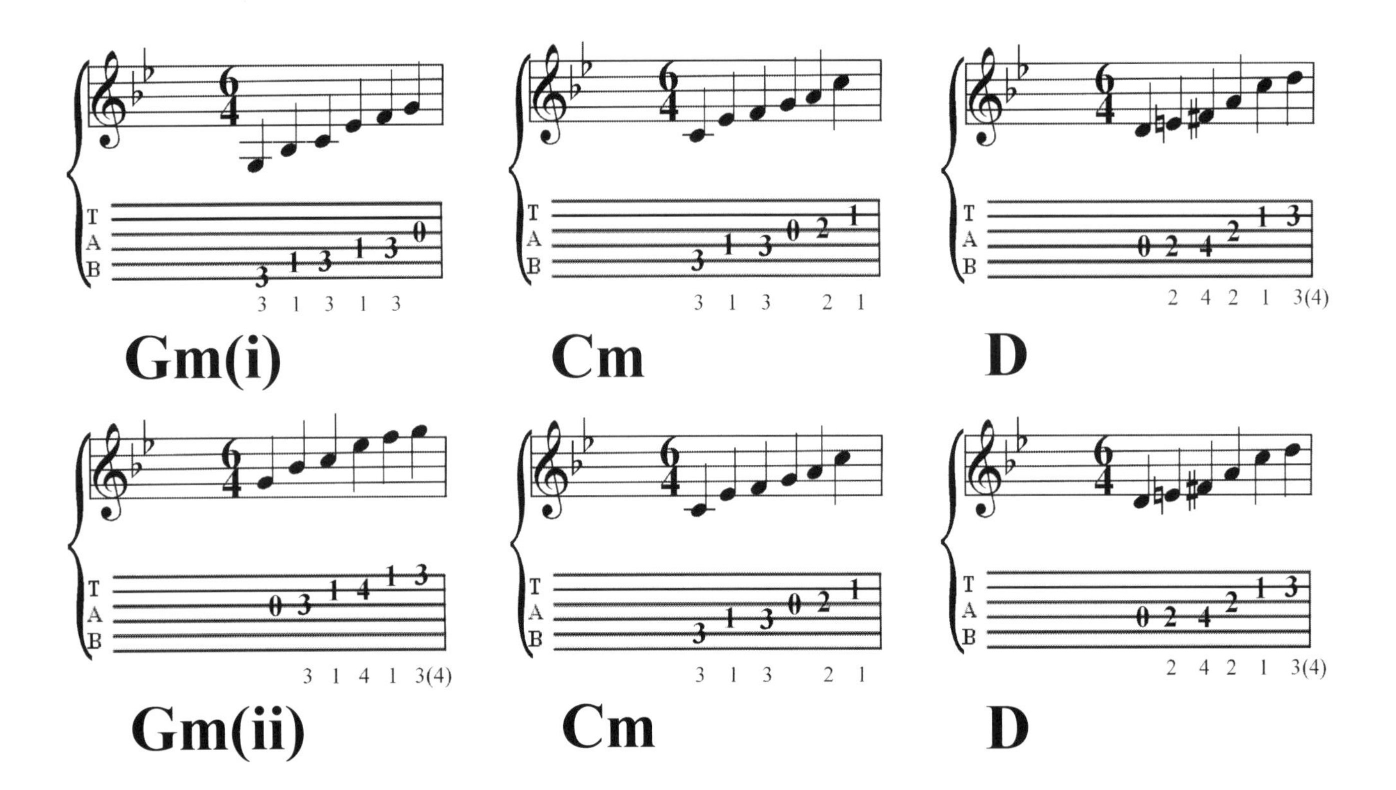

Key of Dm

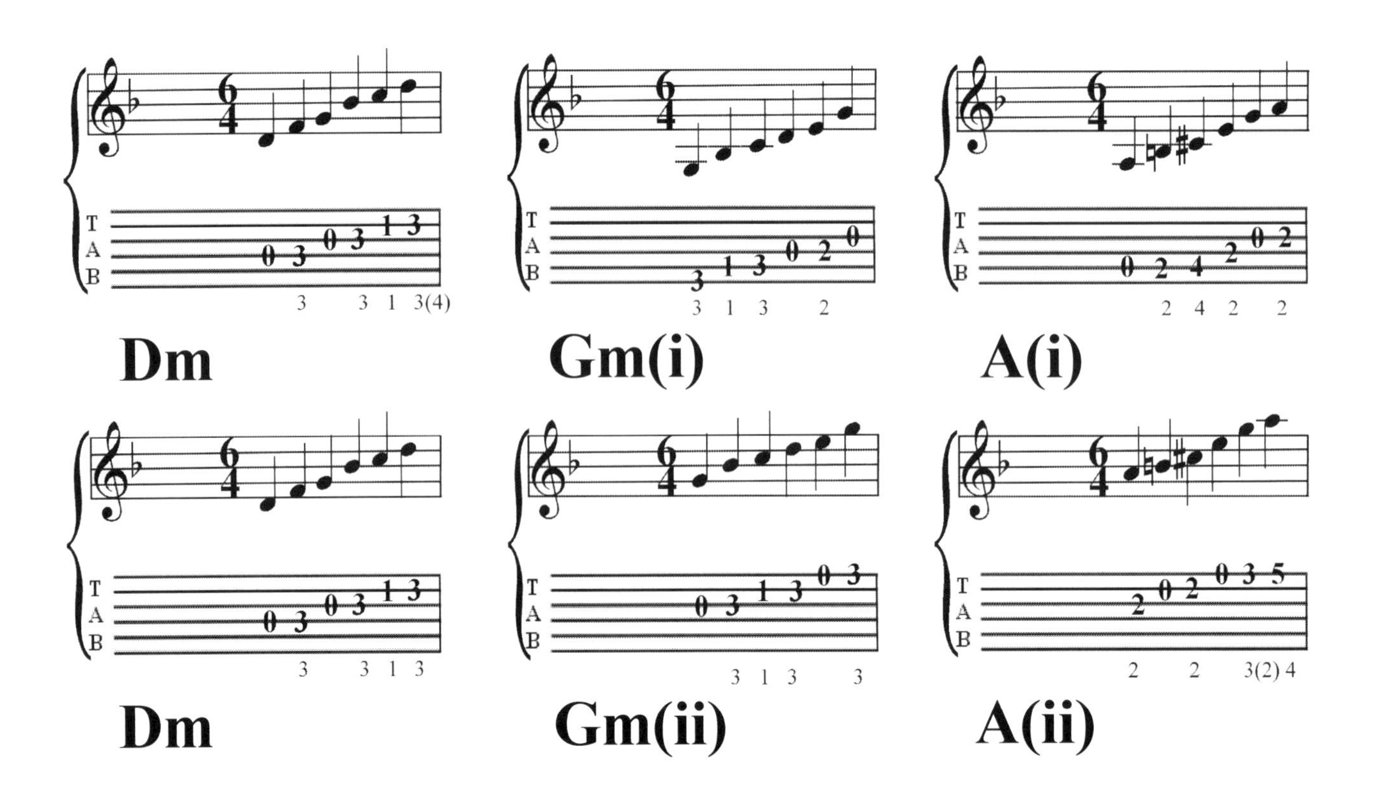

All Keys (i)

i

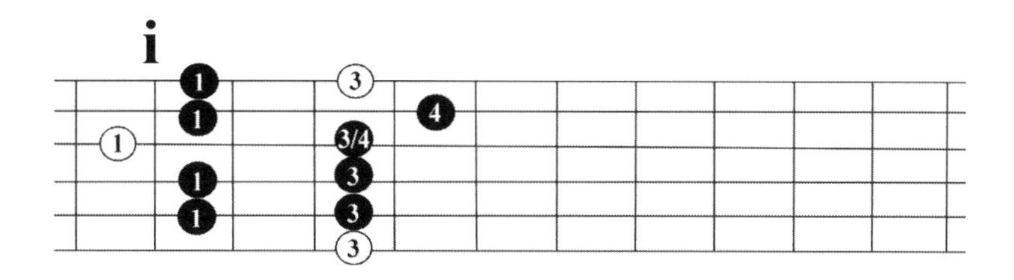

iv

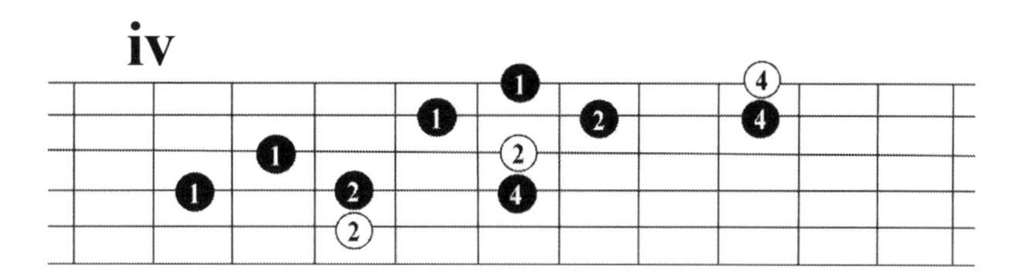

V

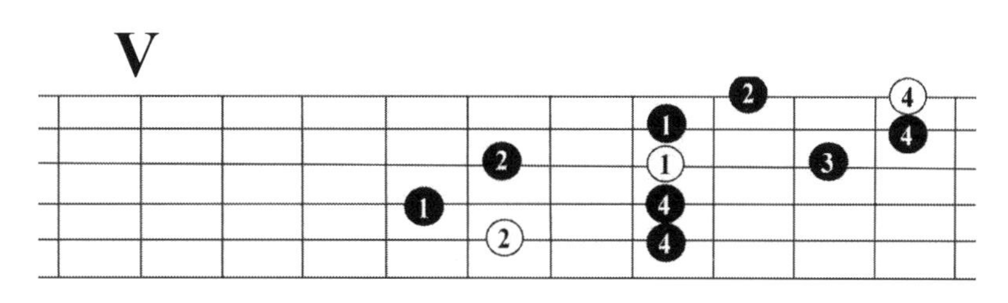

All Keys (ii)

i

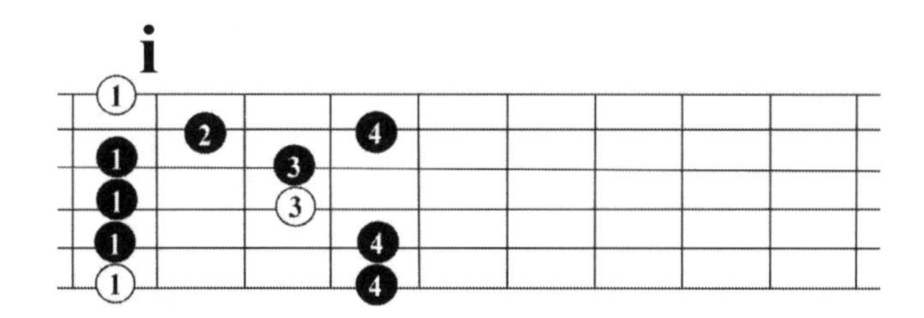

iv

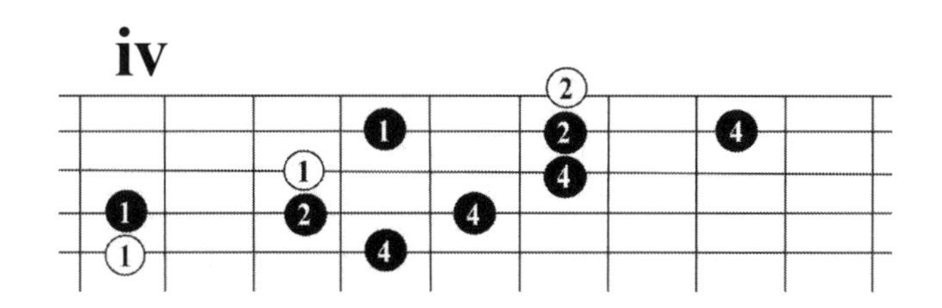

V

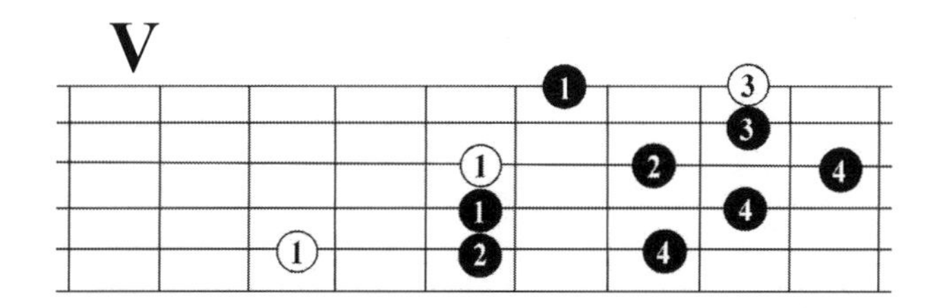

All Keys (iii)

i

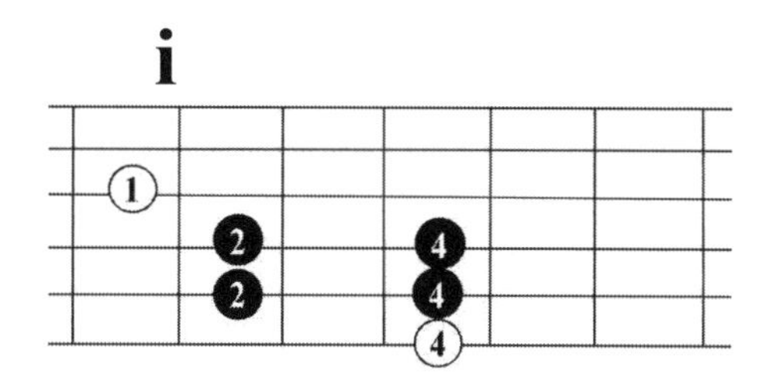

iv

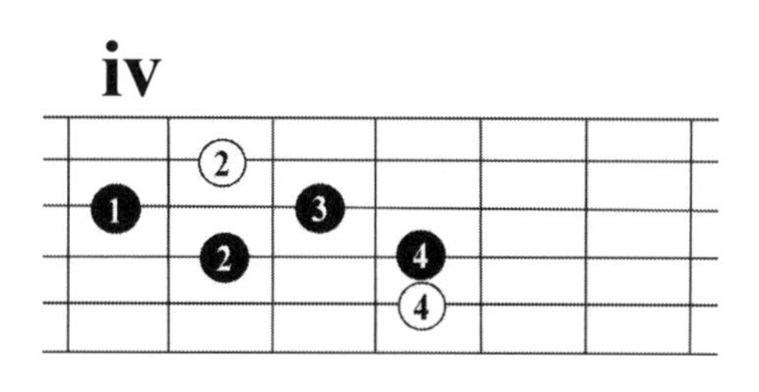

V

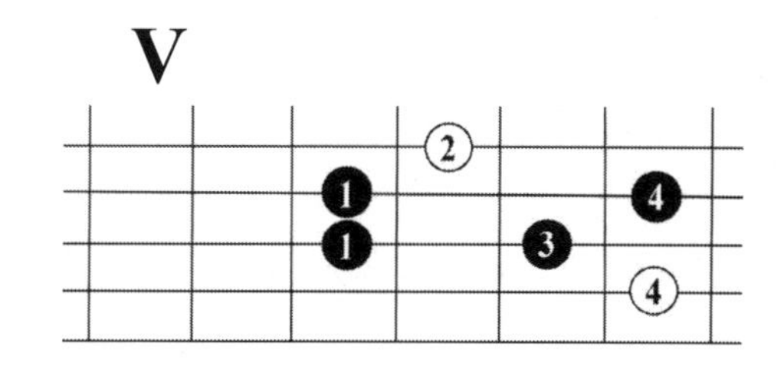

All Keys (iv)

i

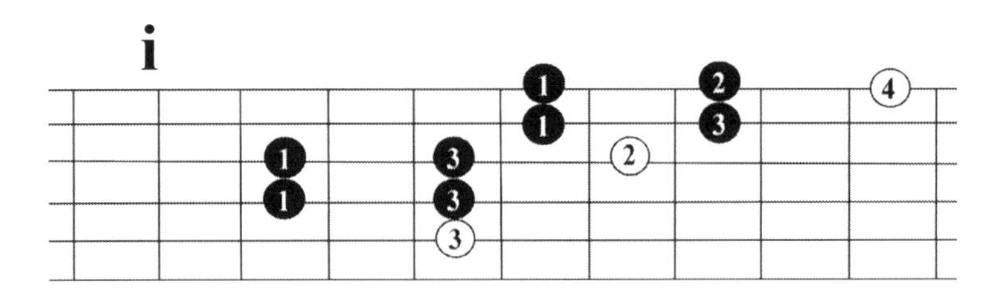

iv

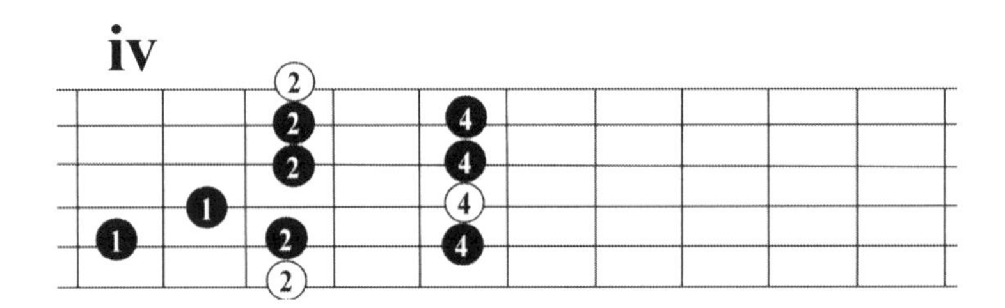

V

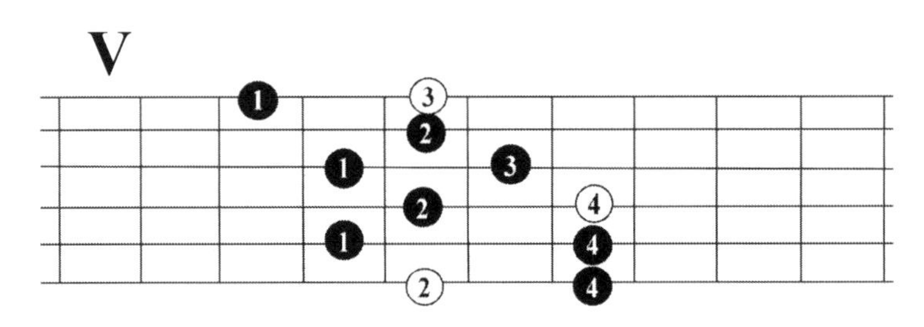

All Keys (v)

i

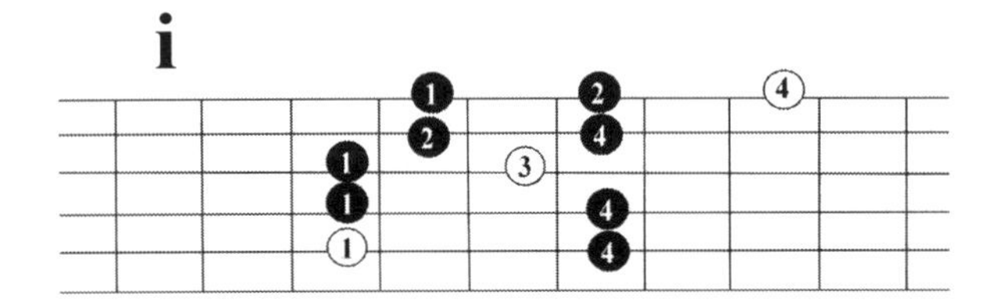

iv

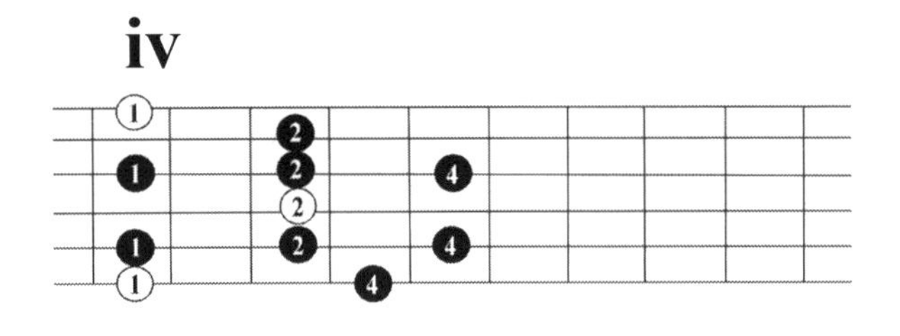

V

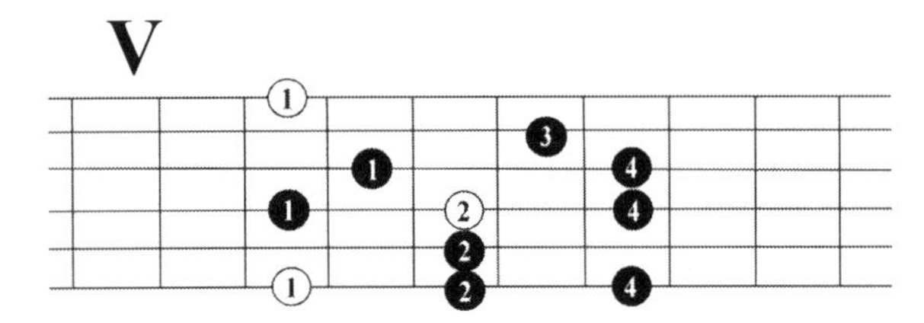

All Keys (vi)

i

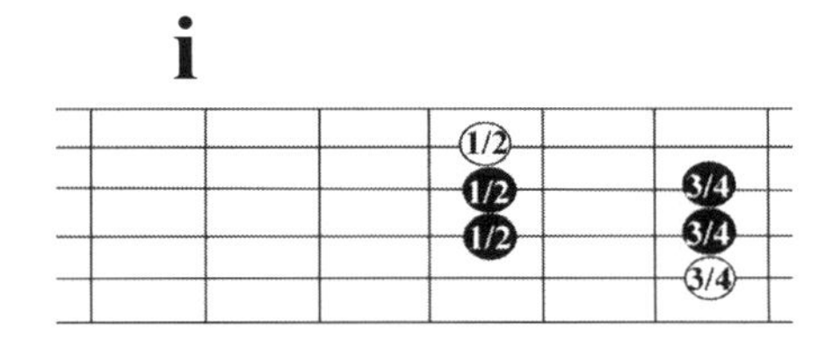

iv

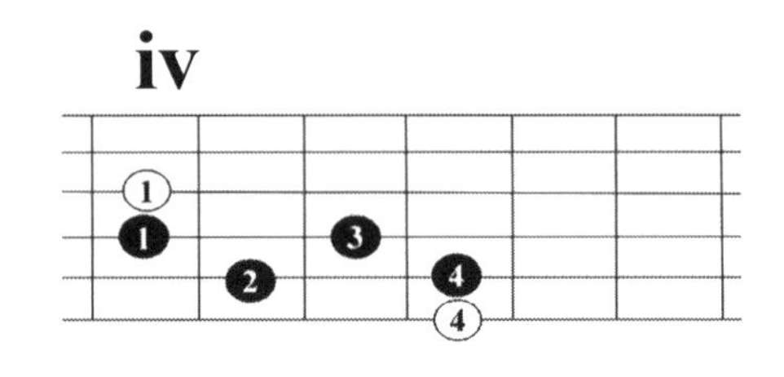

V

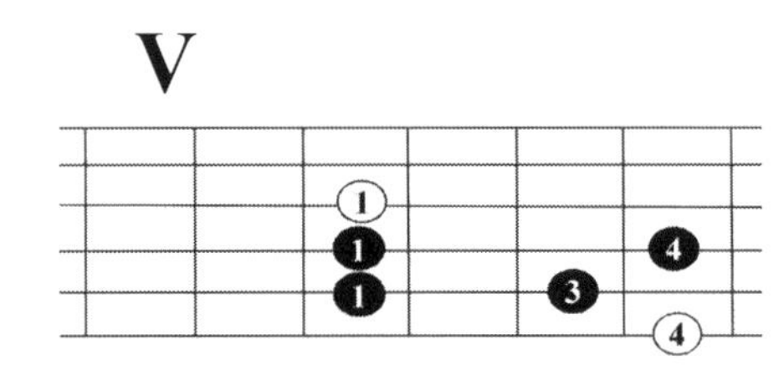

All Keys (vii)

i

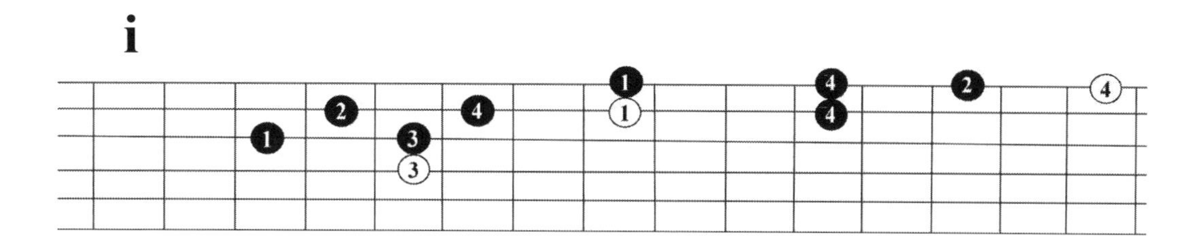

iv

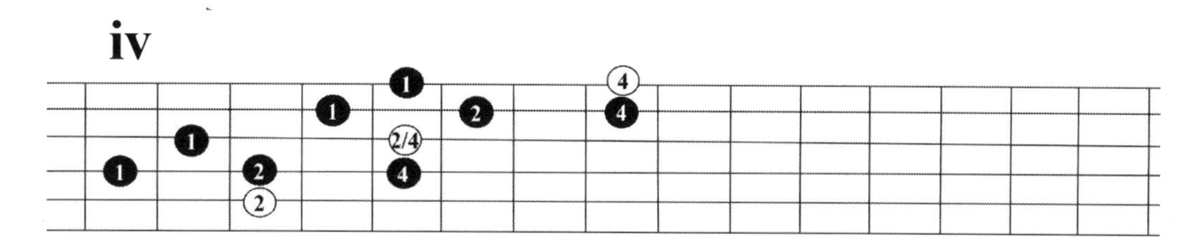

V

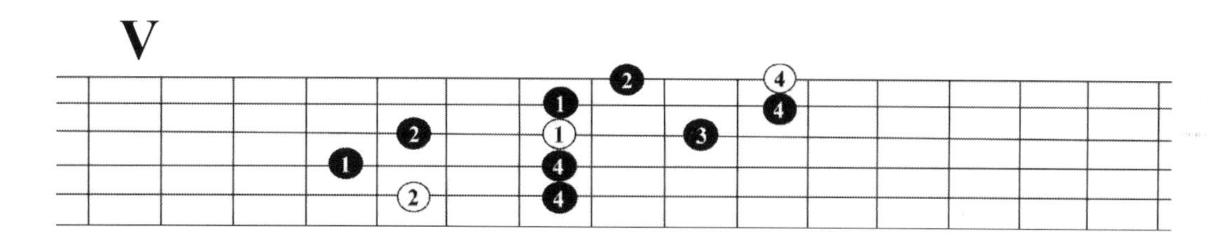

All Keys (viii)

i

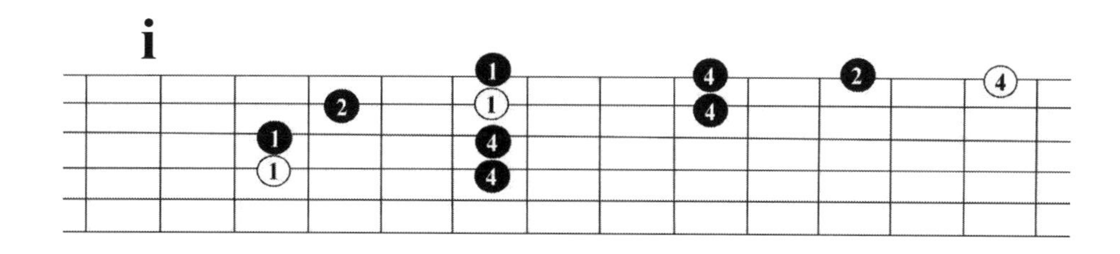

iv

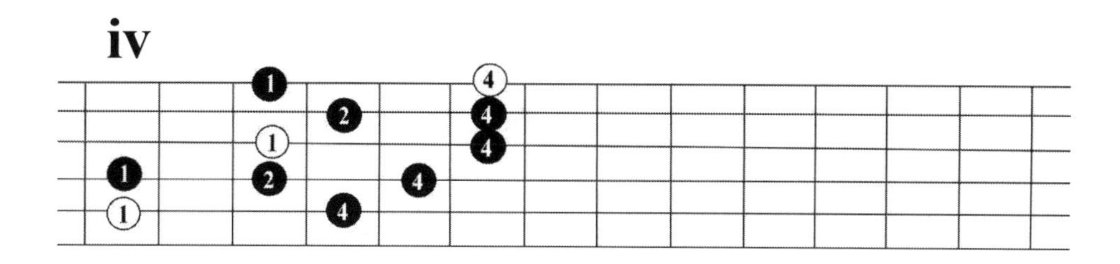

V

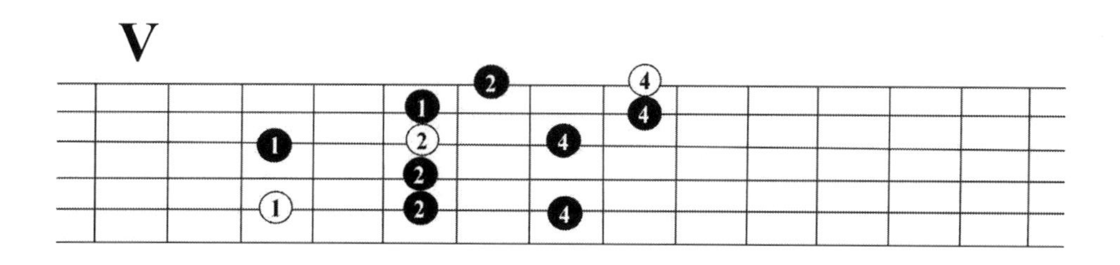

All Keys (ix)

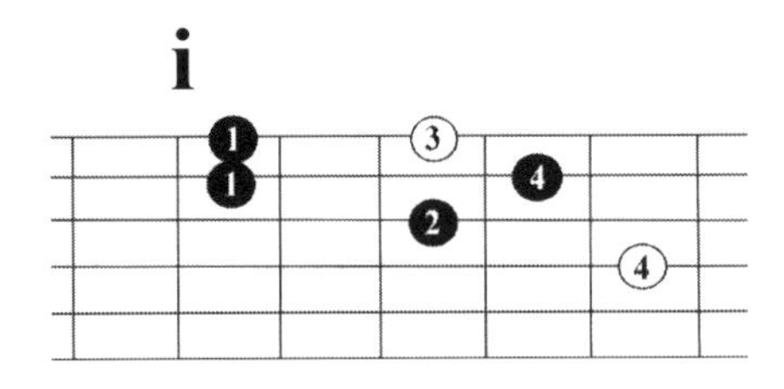

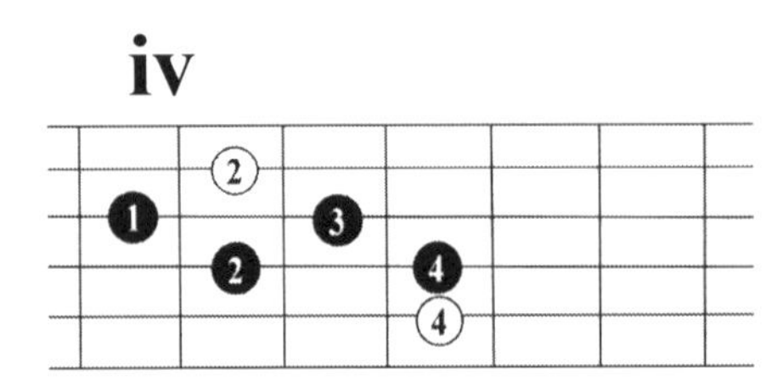

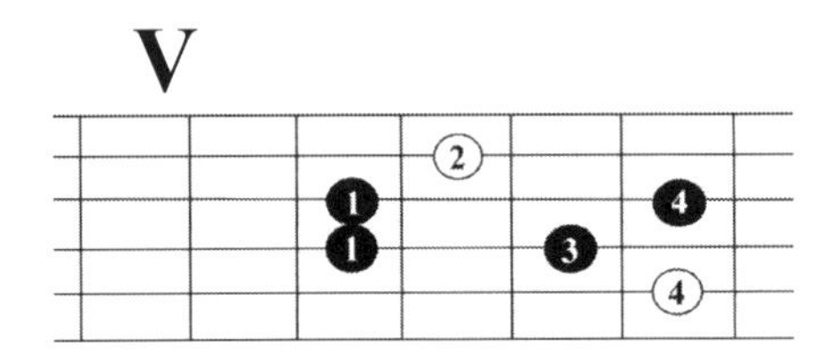

PART THIRTY

ii - V - i

MINOR KEYS PENTATONICS

THE ii (minor/flat 5 or m7♭5) CHORD

The second *degree* of the *minor* scale corresponds to the *seventh* of the relative *major* scale and the related mode contains *semitone* intervals between the *root* and *second*, and the *fourth* and *fifth*. Thus one possible pentatonic pattern is the root-3rd-4th-6th-7th-octave form which we have already used for the i (minor/m7) chord. e.g., for a chord of Bm♭5 in the key of Am:

B *(minor third)* **D** *(tone)* **E** *(minor third)* **G** *(tone)* **A** *(tone)* **B**

However, to bring out the unique character of the m♭5 chord (and add a new fingering pattern to your repertoire), we can replace the fourth with the flattened fifth, creating a pentatonic scale of the form root-3rd-5th-6th-7th-octave. e.g.:

B *(minor third)* **D** *(minor third)* **F** *(tone)* **G** *(tone)* **A** *(tone)* **B**

This is the form which is used in the following exercises.

Key of Am

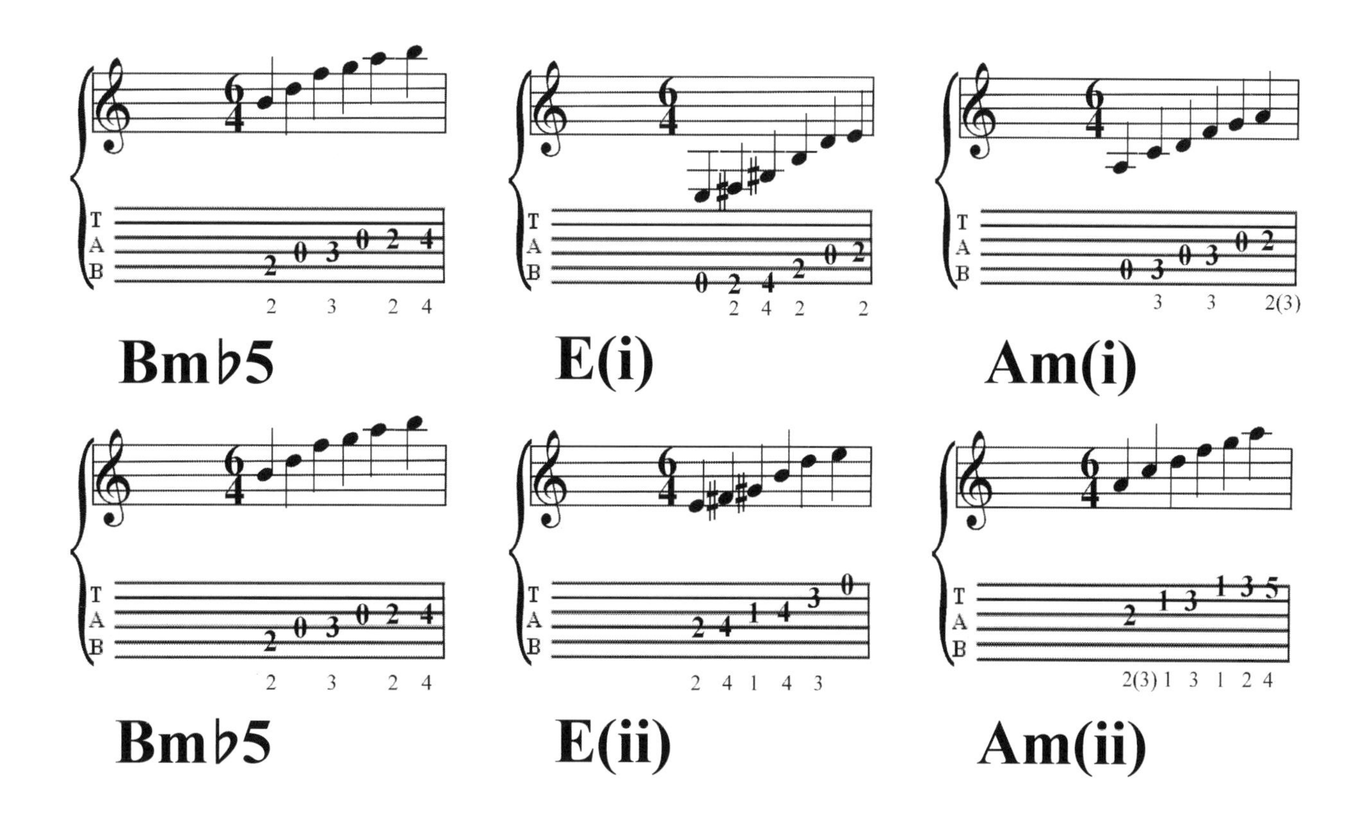

Key of Em

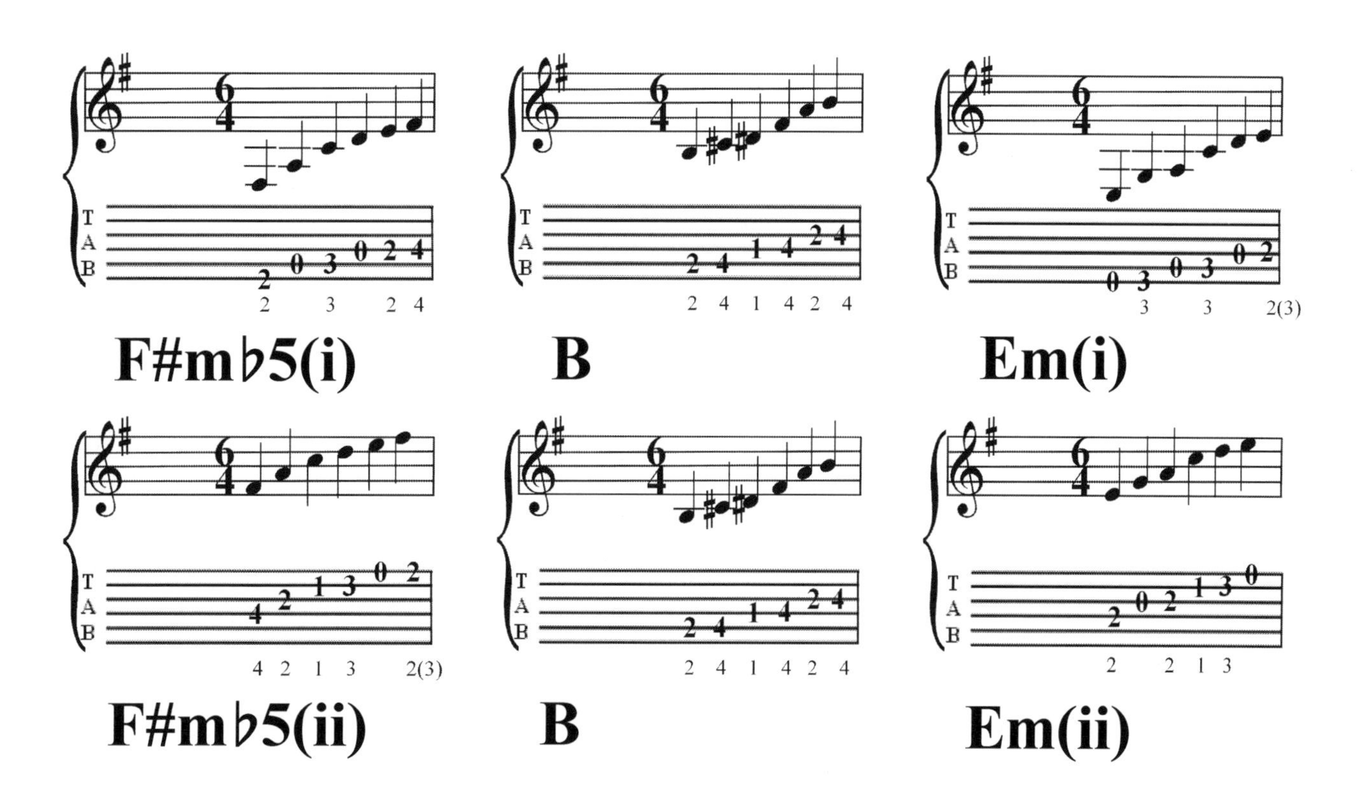

Key of Bm

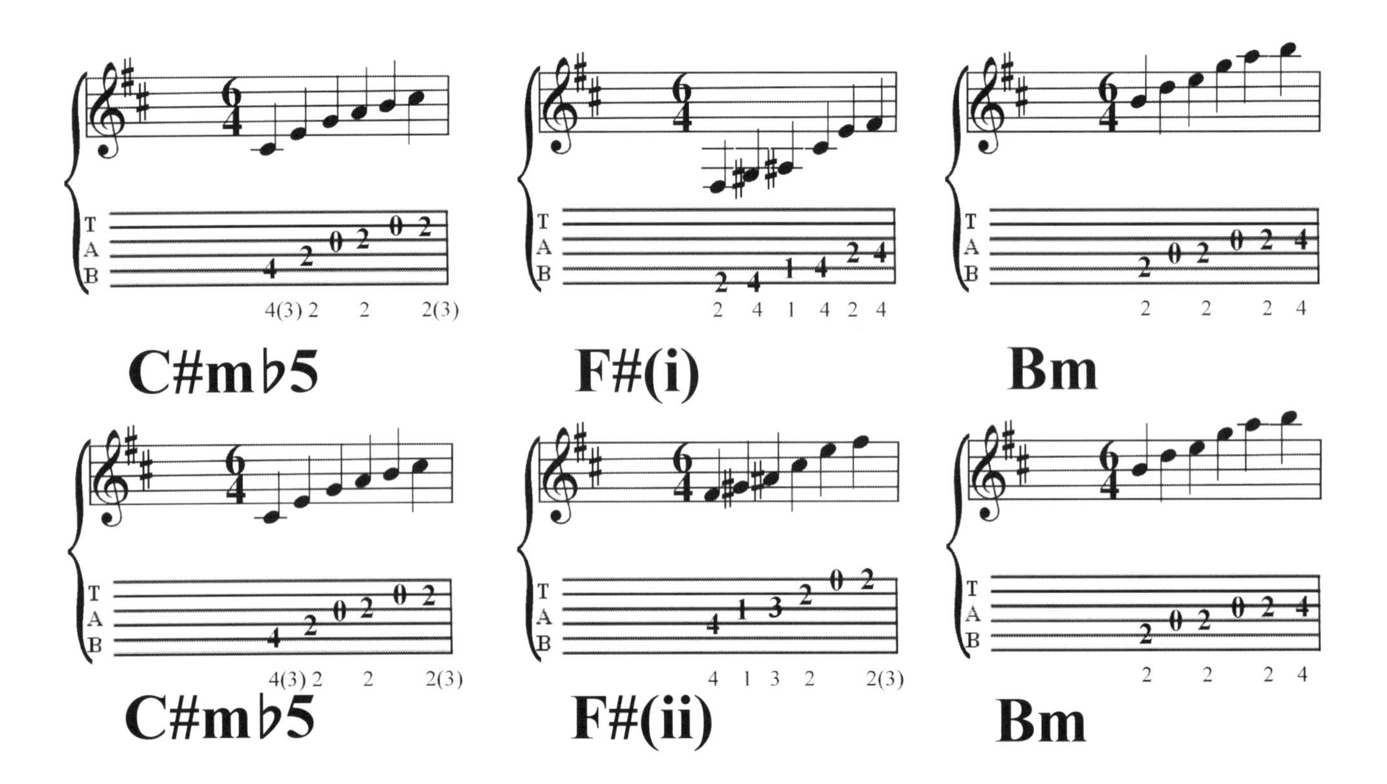

Key of F#m

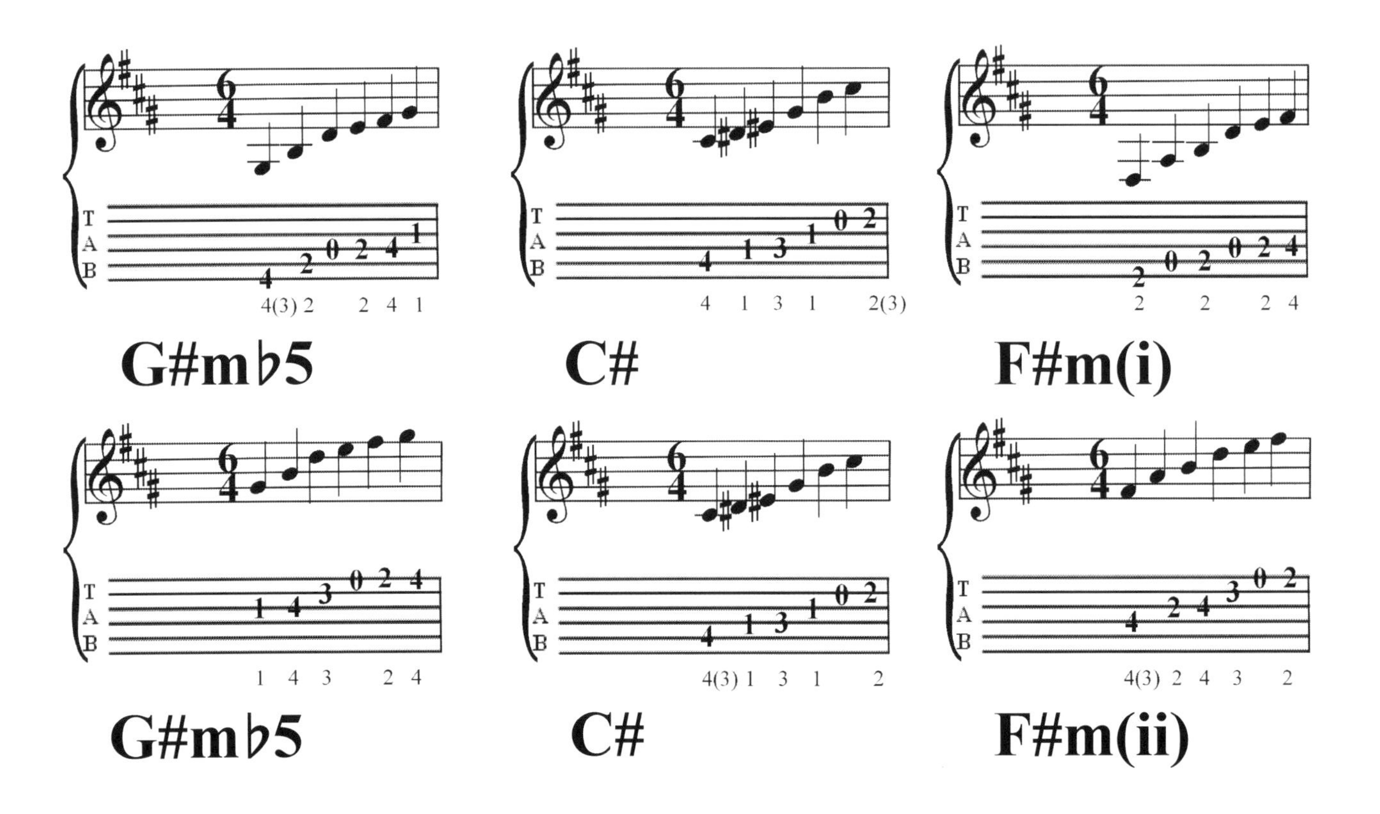

Key of C#m

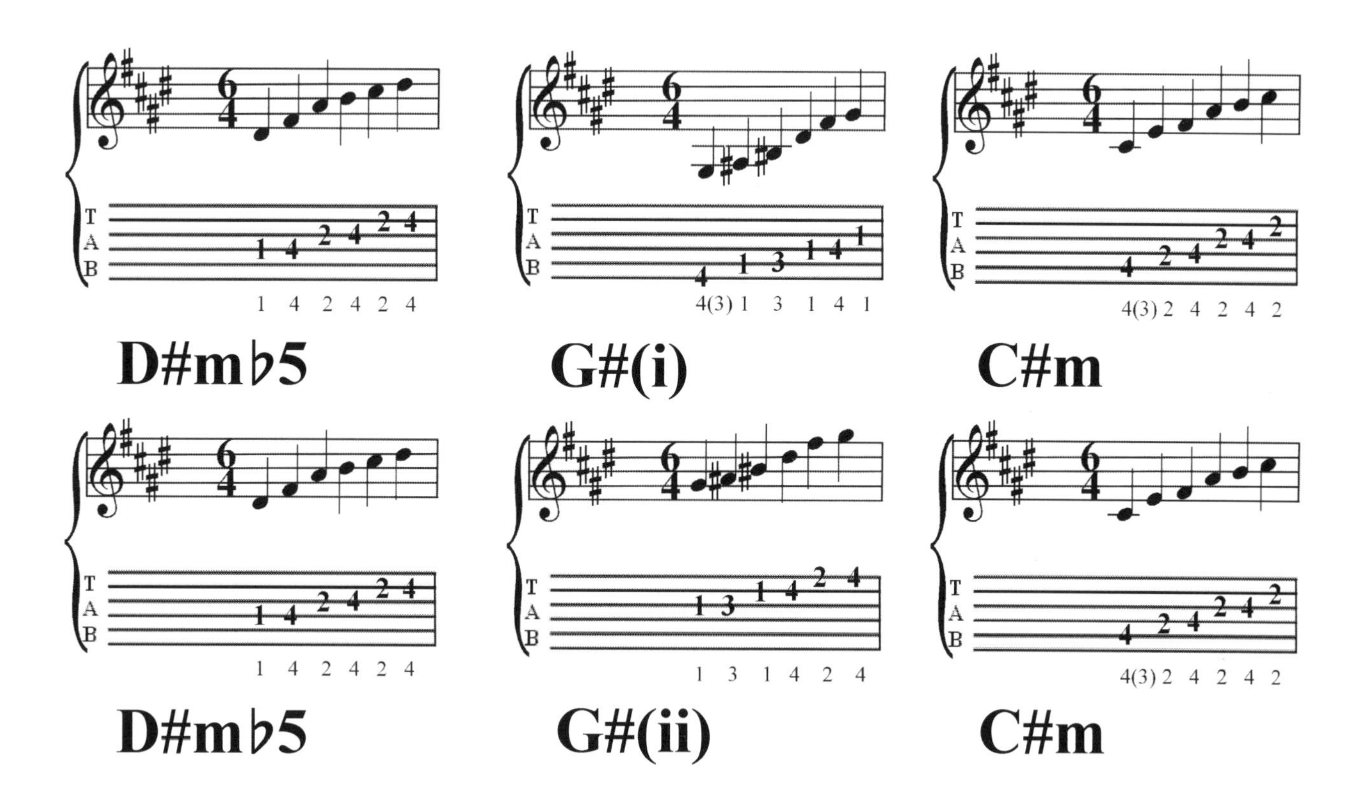

Key of A♭m

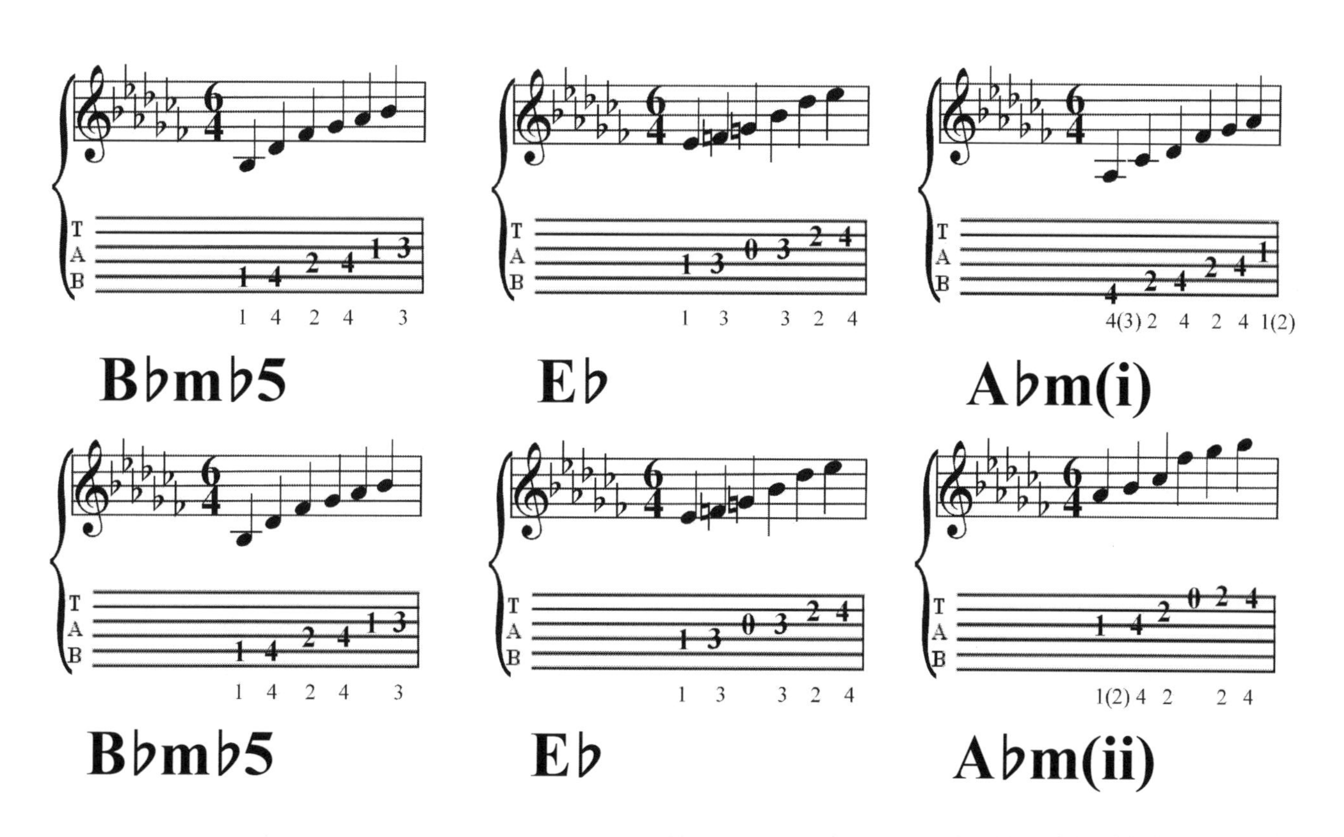

Key of E♭m

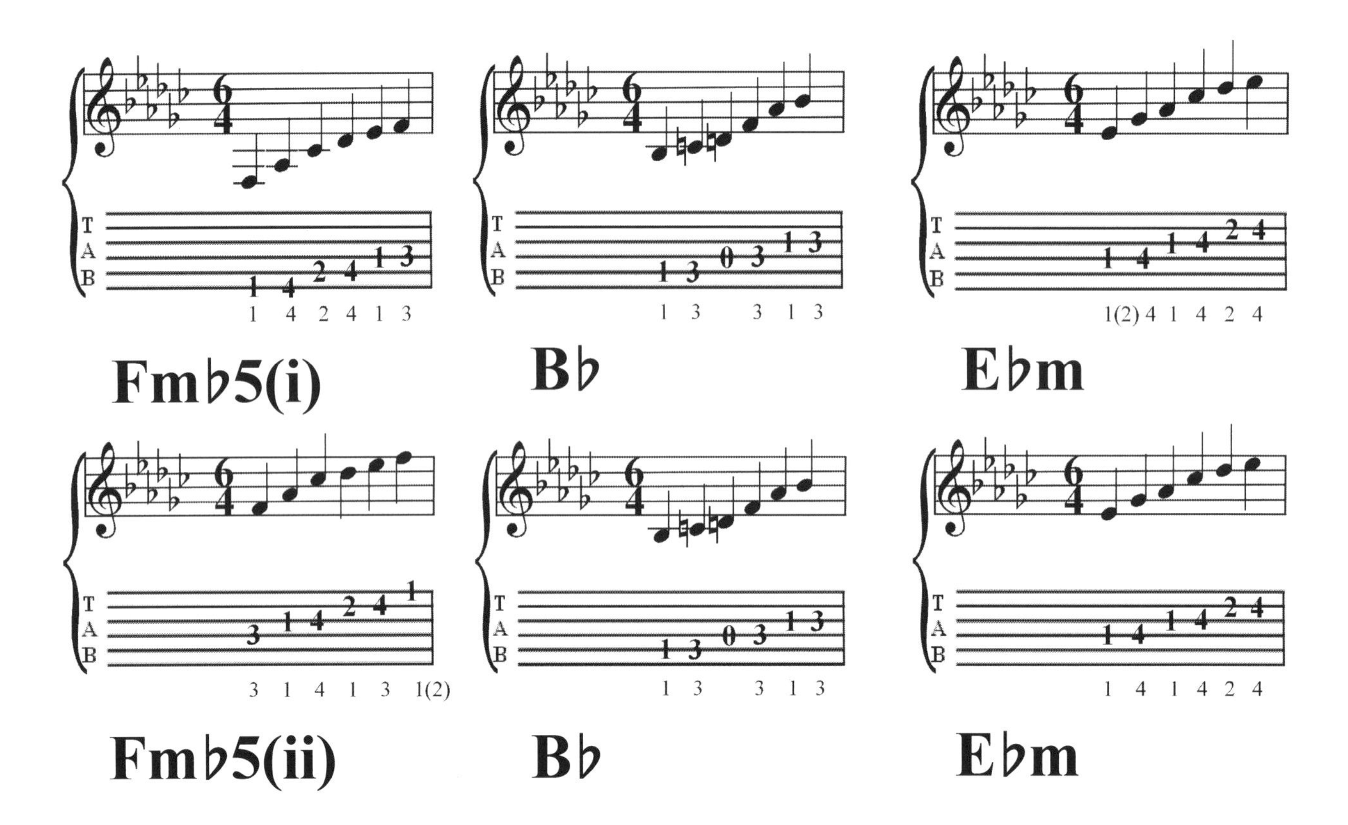

Key of B♭m

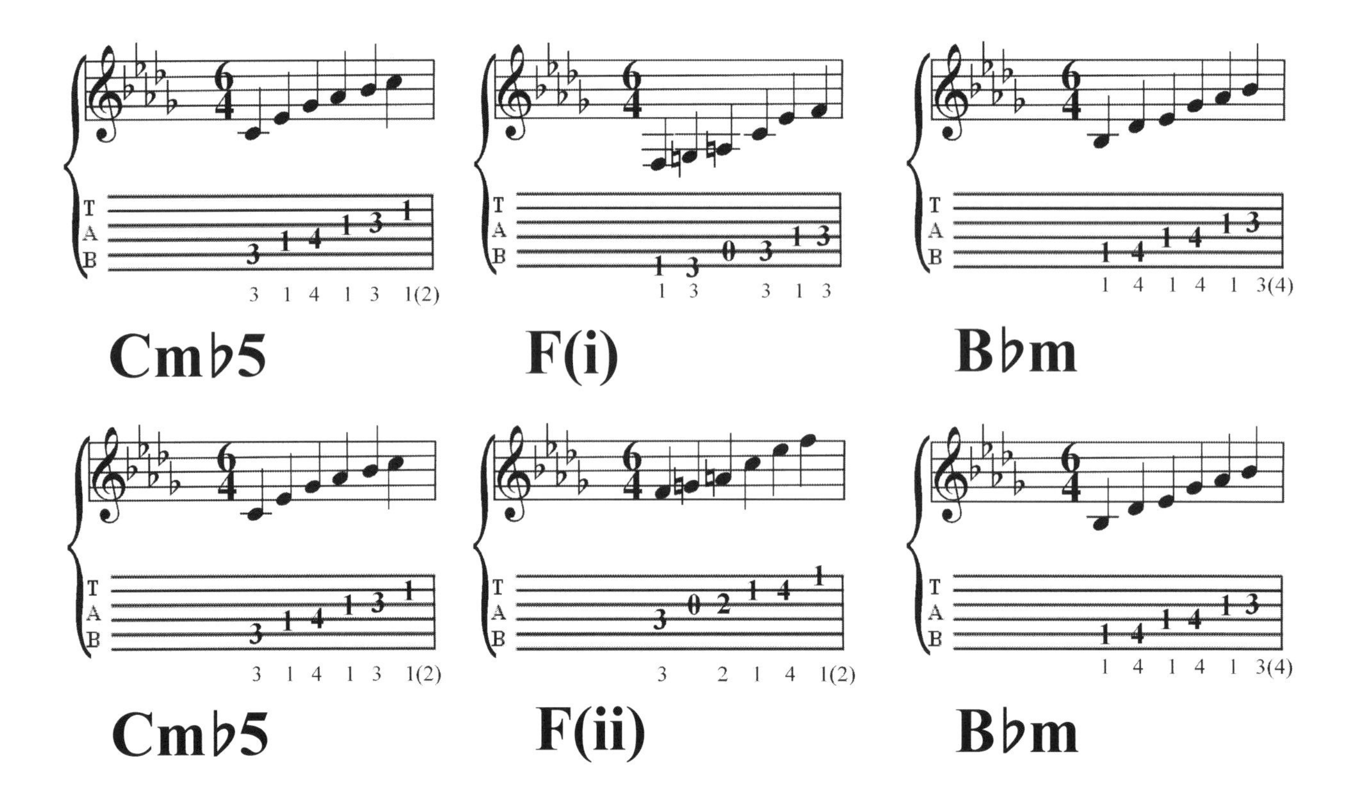

Key of Fm

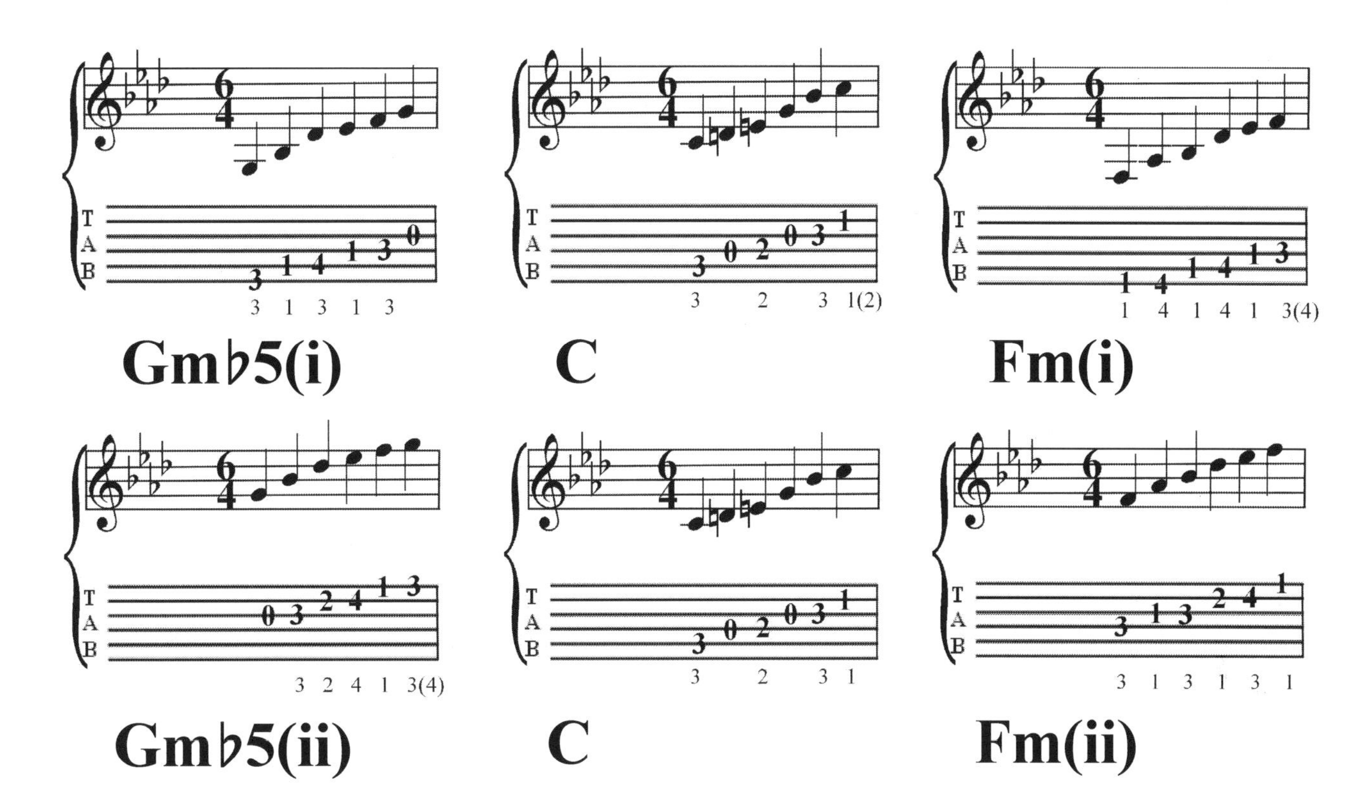

Key of Cm

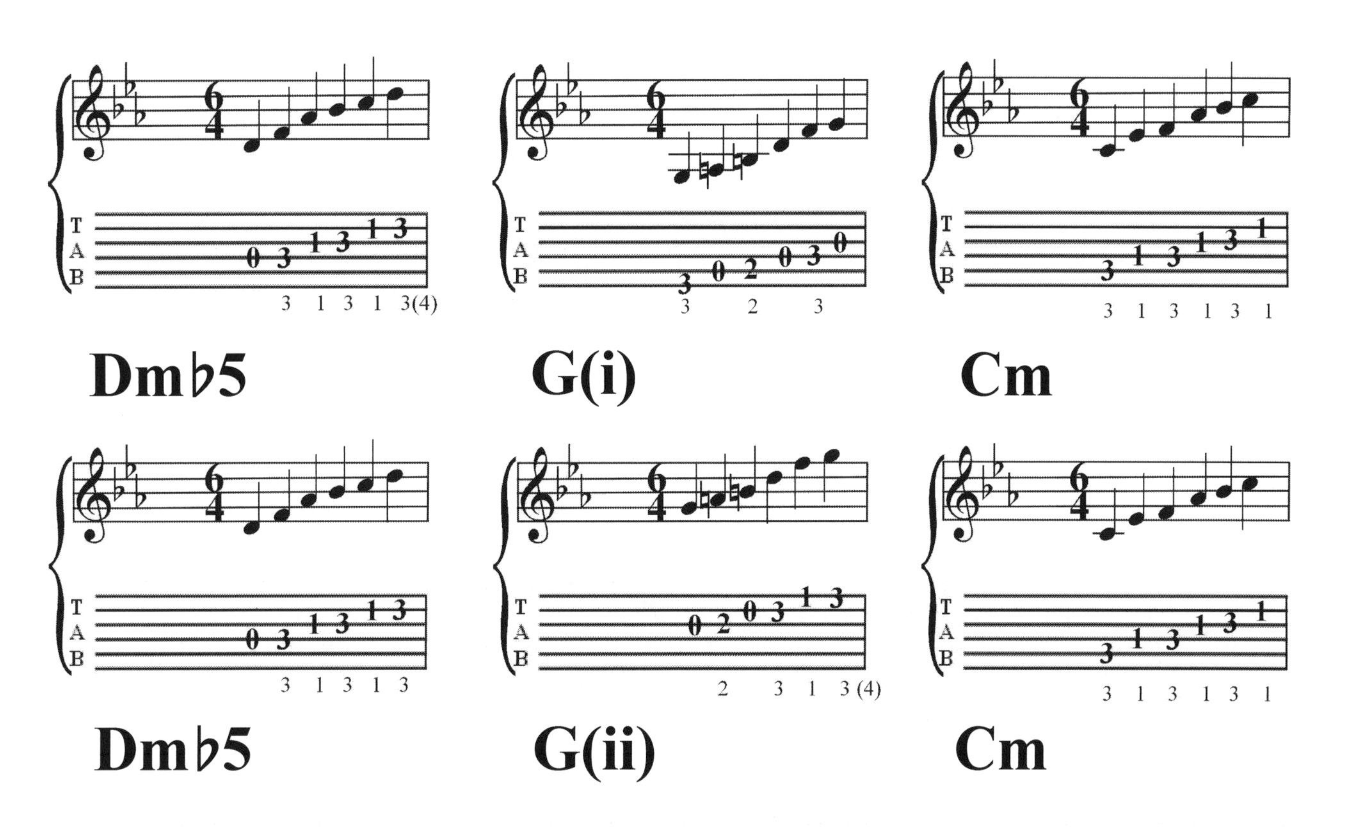

Key of Gm

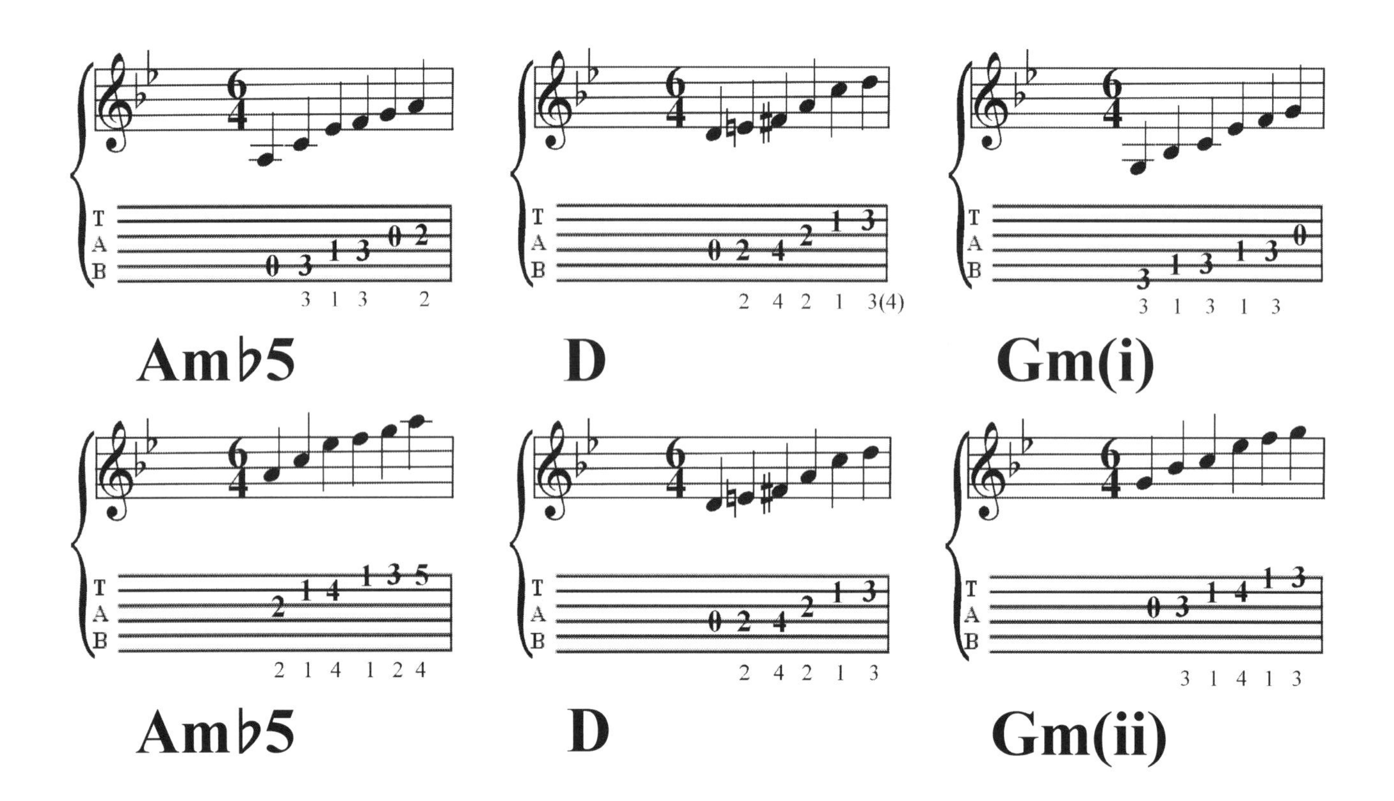

Key of Dm

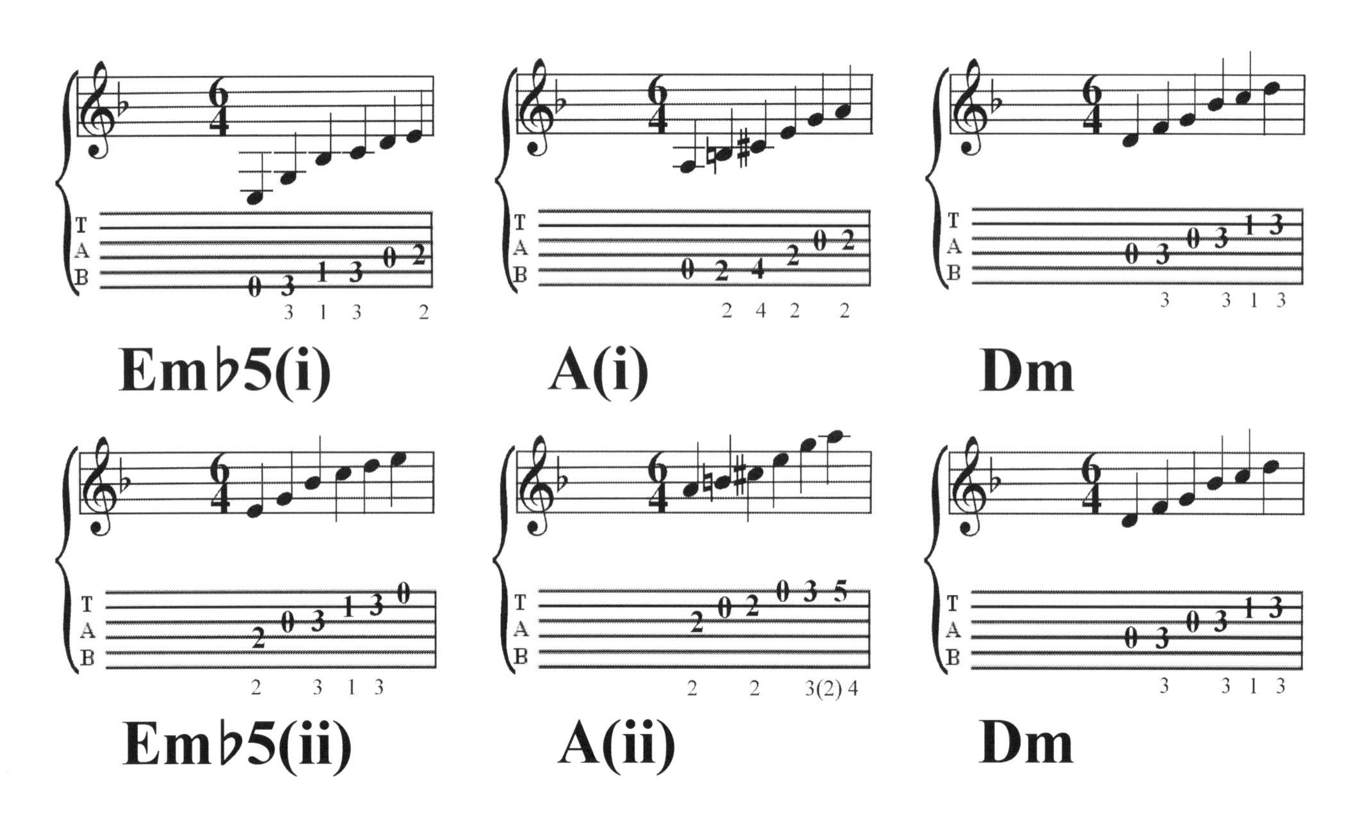

All Keys (i)

ii

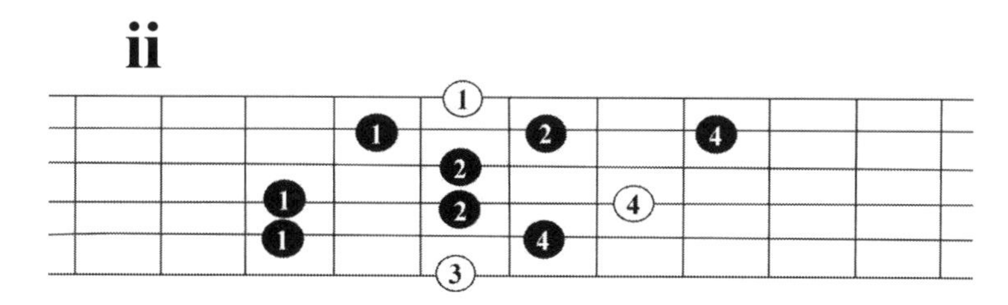

V

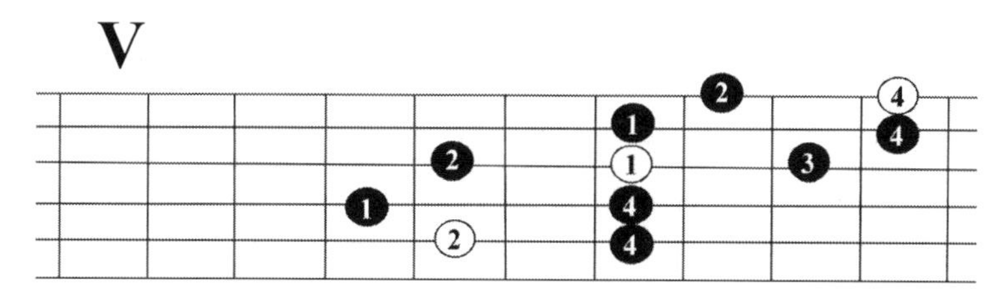

i

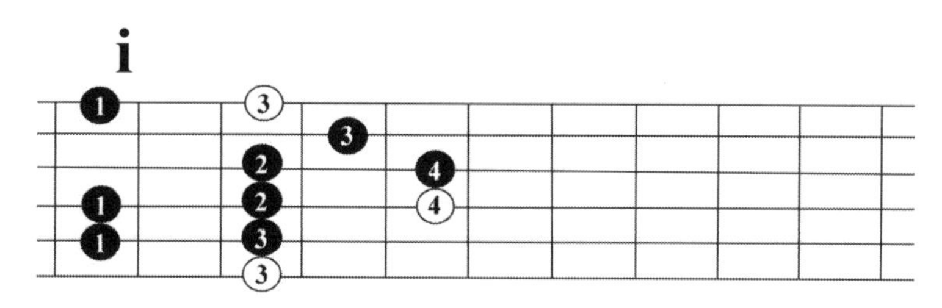

All Keys (ii)

ii

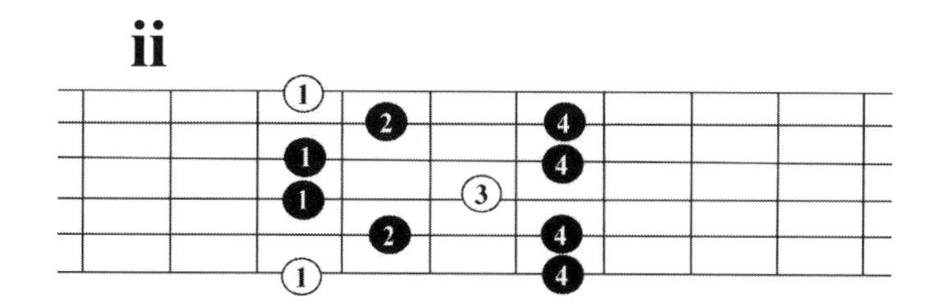

V

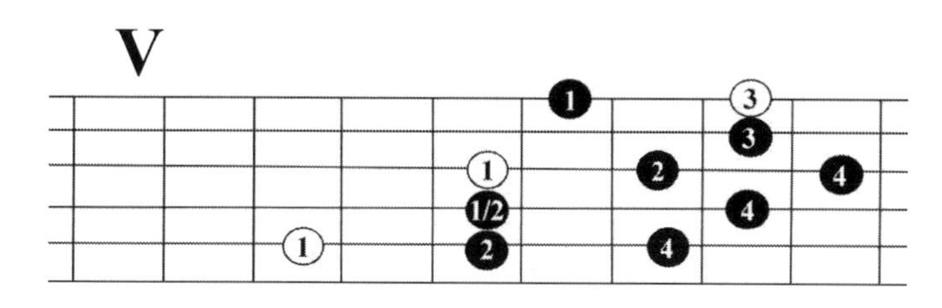

i

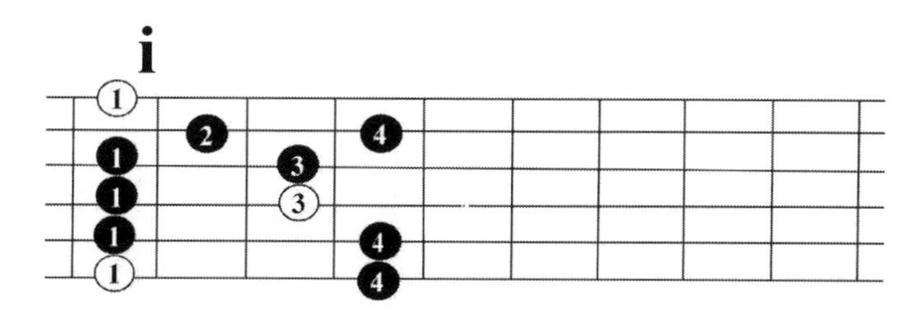

All Keys (iii)

ii

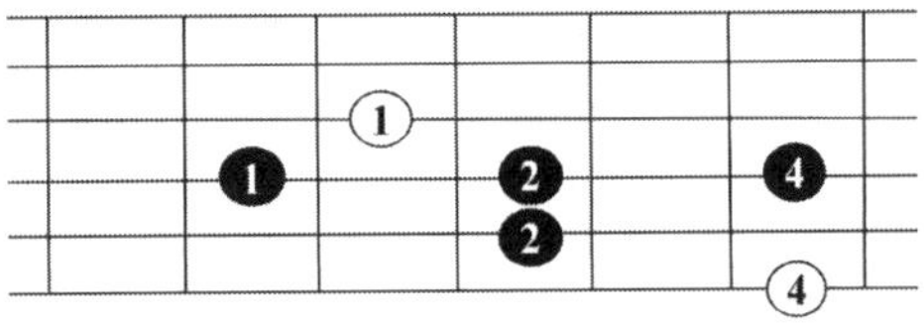

V

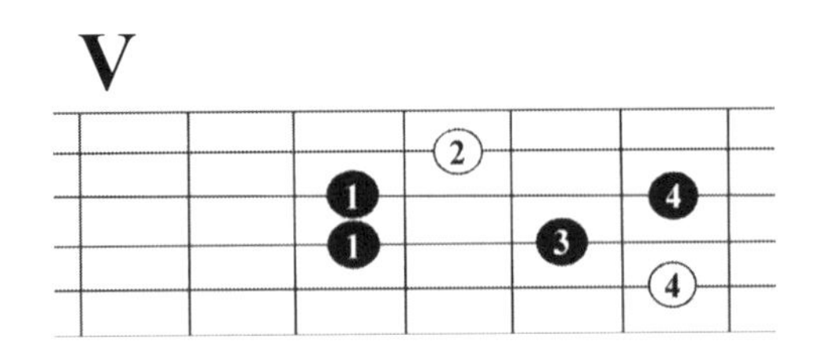

i

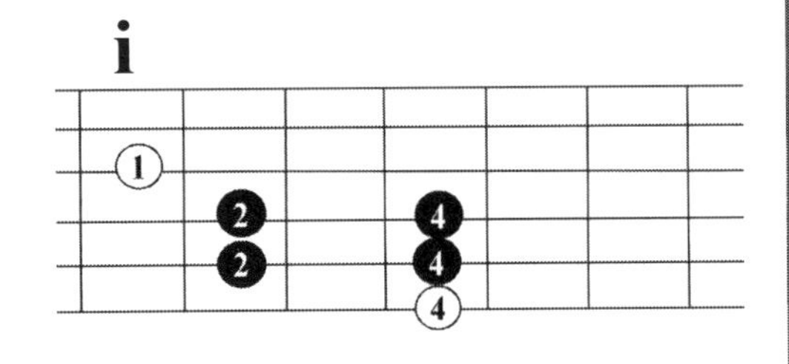

All Keys (iv)

ii

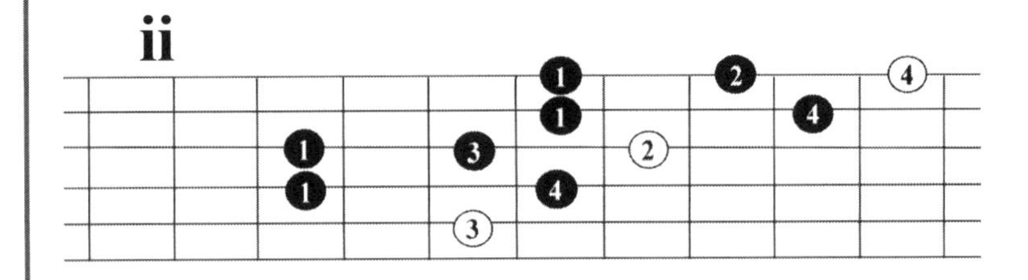

V

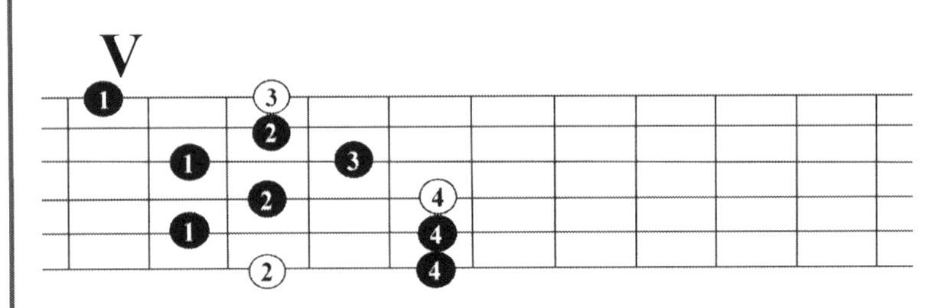

i

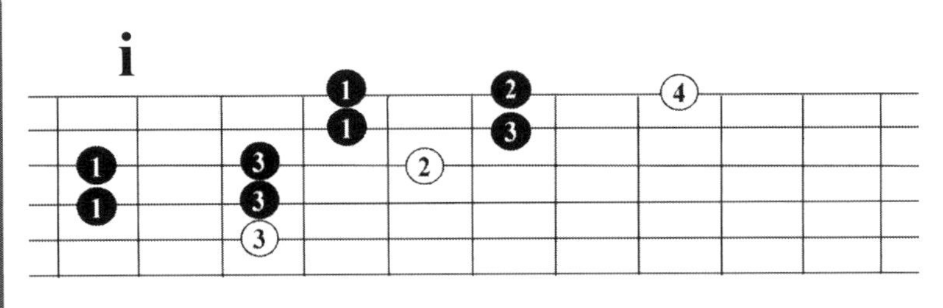

All Keys (v)

ii

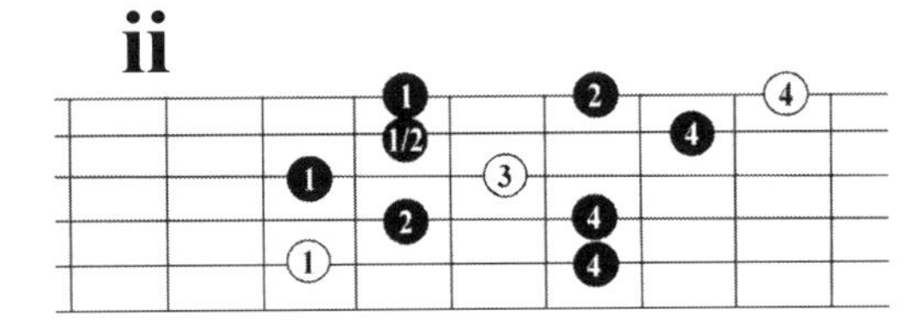

V

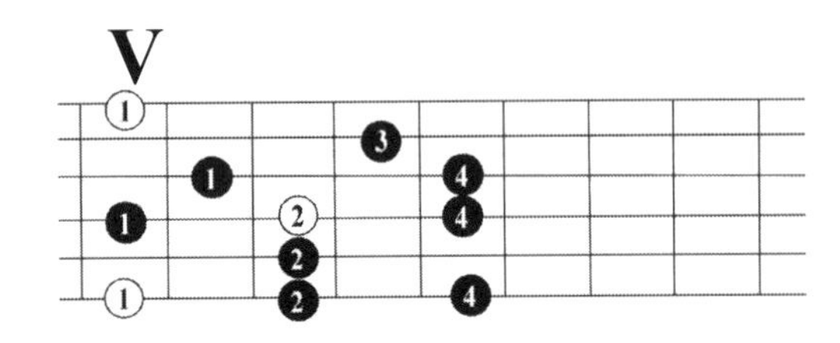

i

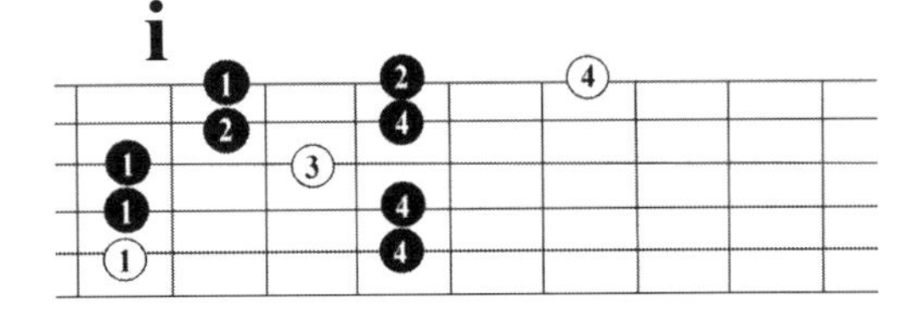

All Keys (vi)

ii

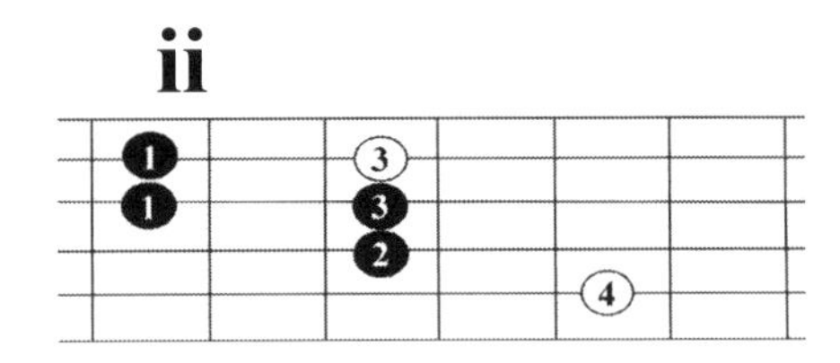

V

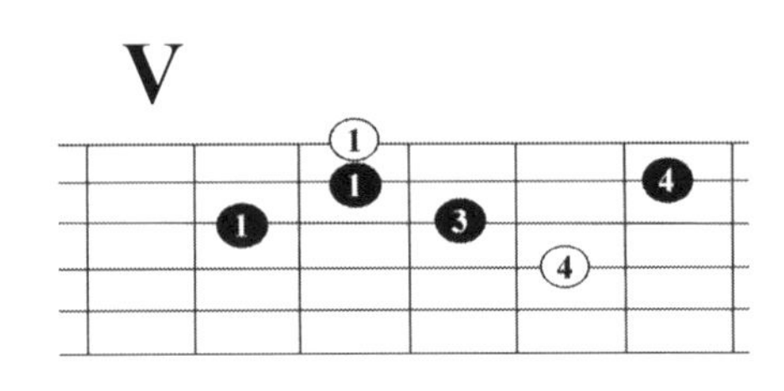

i

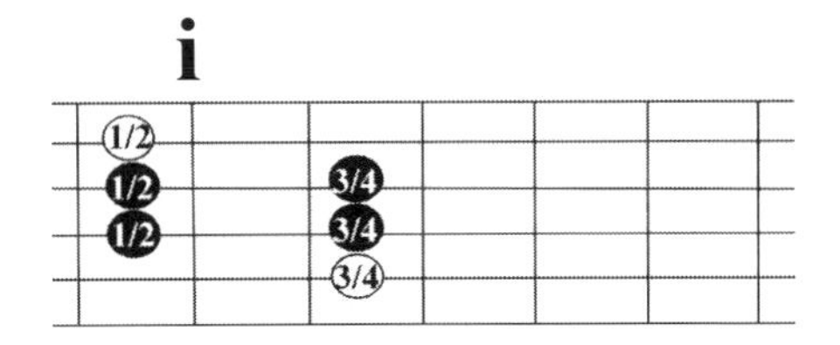

All Keys (vii)

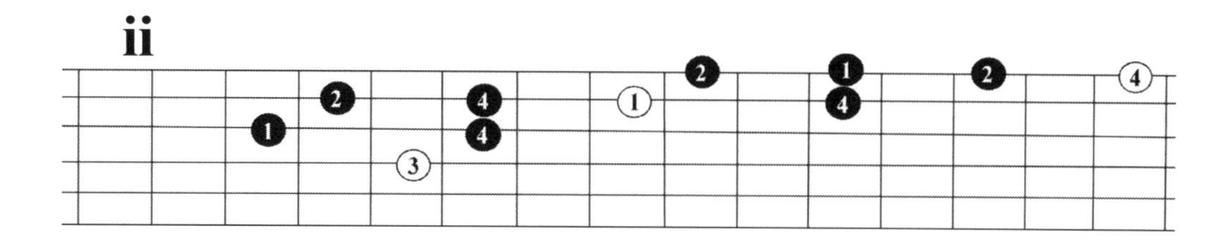

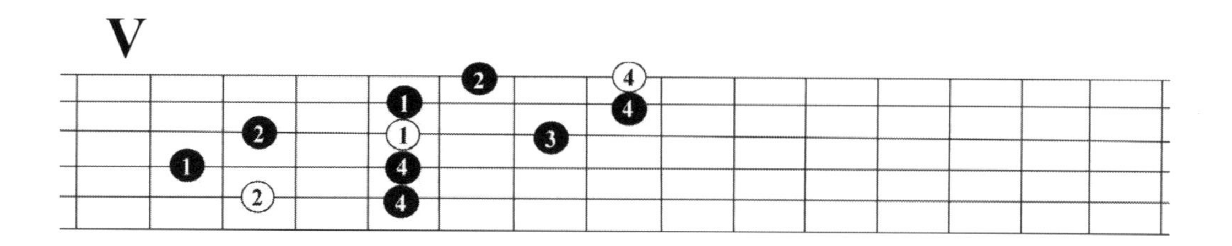

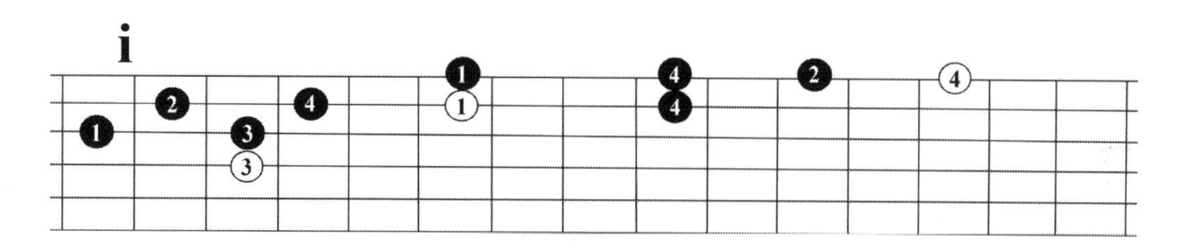

All Keys (viii)

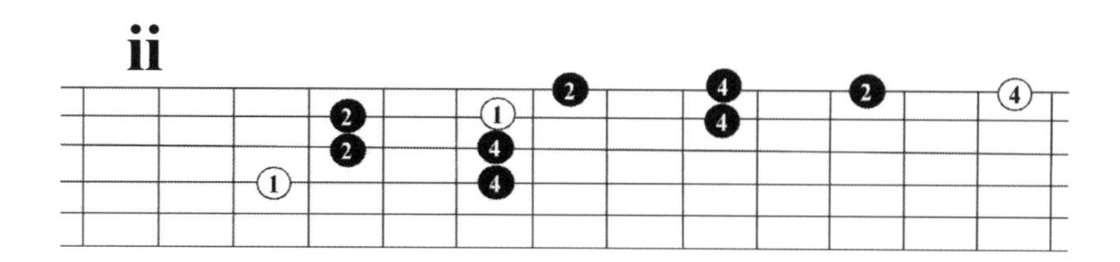

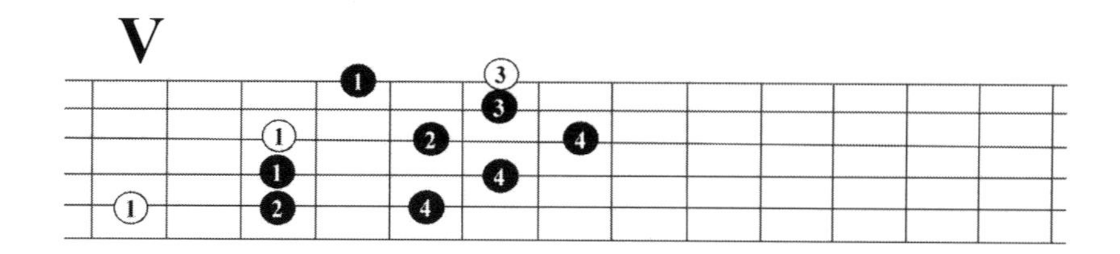

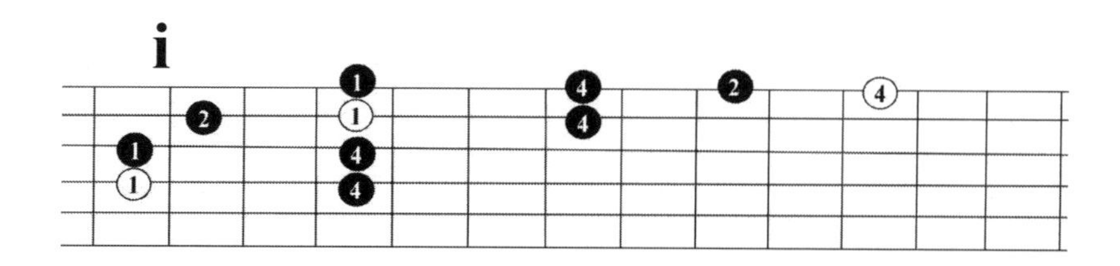

All Keys (ix)

ii

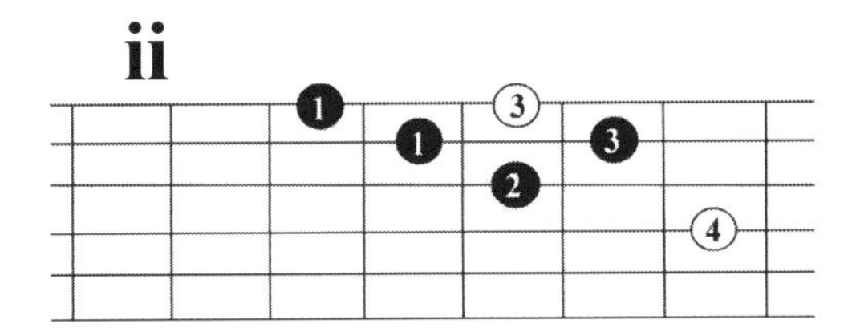

V

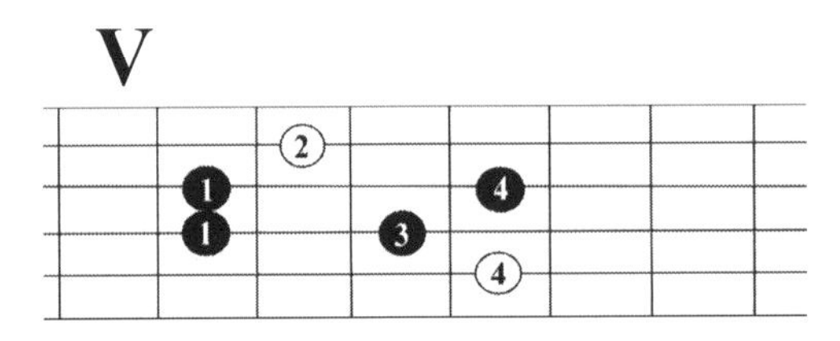

i

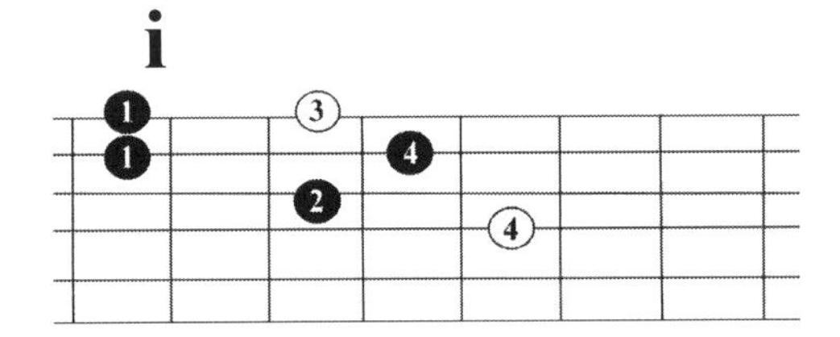

PART THIRTY-ONE

VI - ii - V - i

MINOR KEYS PENTATONICS

THE VI (Major or M7) CHORD

The sixth *degree* of the *minor* scale corresponds to the fourth of the relative *major* scale, and so uses the same pentatonic pattern, which includes the *root*, *second*, *third*, sharpened *fourth*, *sixth* and *octave*. e.g., for a chord of F in the key of Am:

F *(tone)* **G** *(tone)* **A** *(tone)* **B** *(minor third)* **D** *(minor third)* **F**

Key of Am

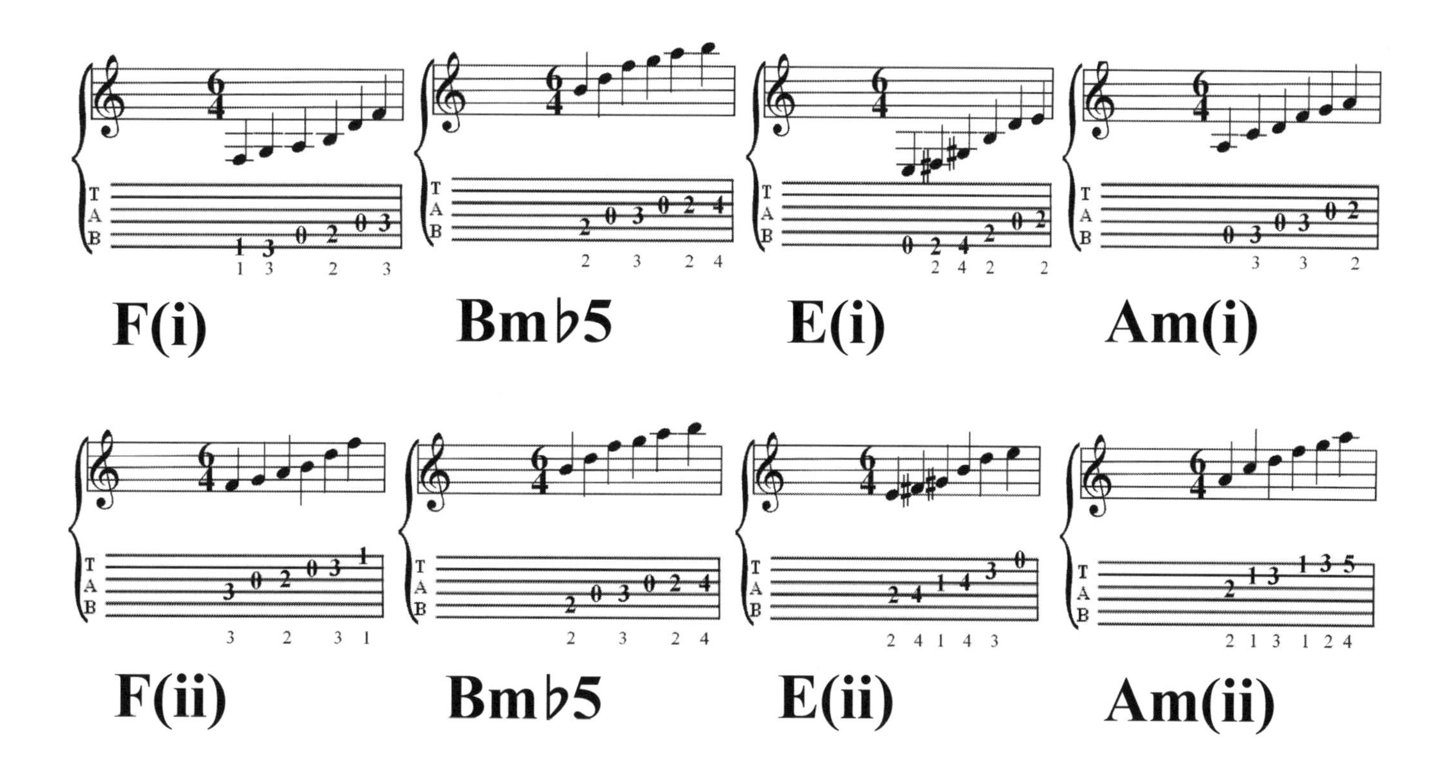

Key of Em

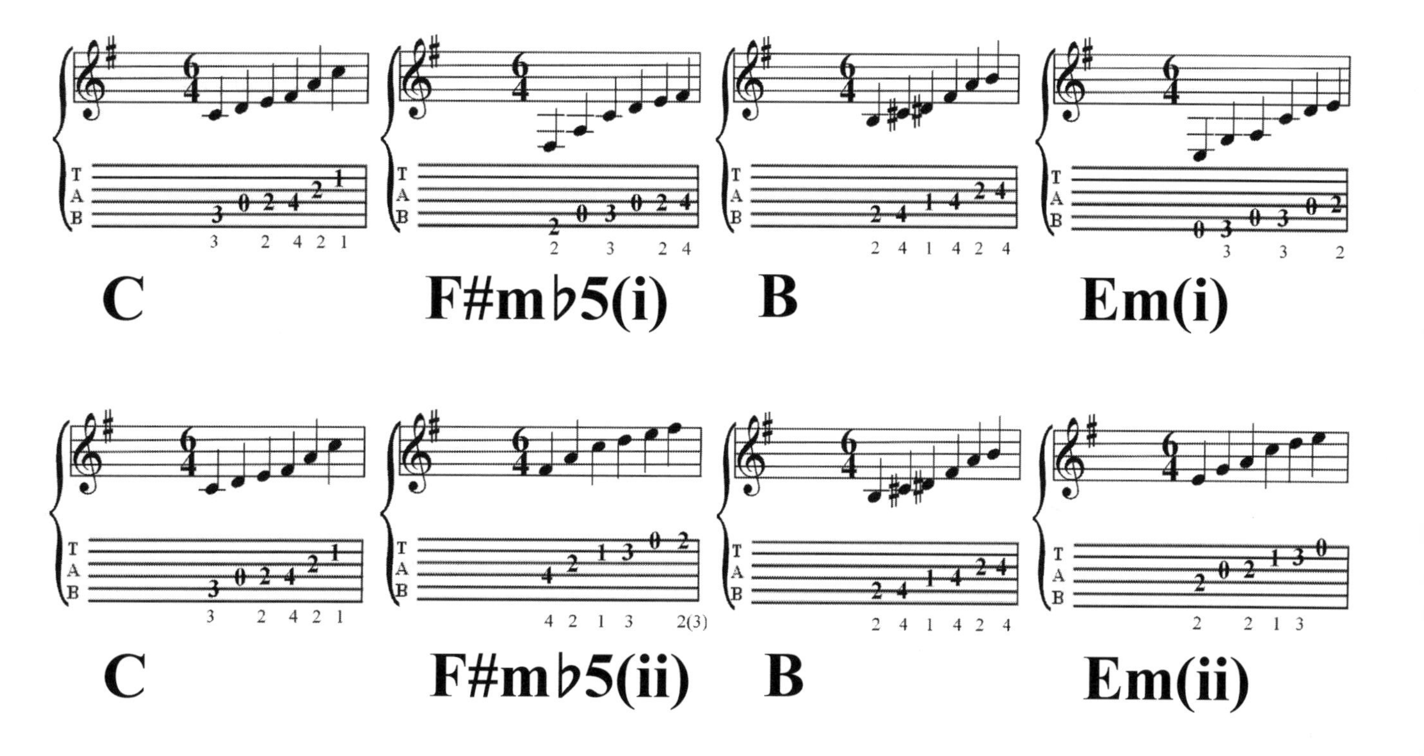

Key of Bm

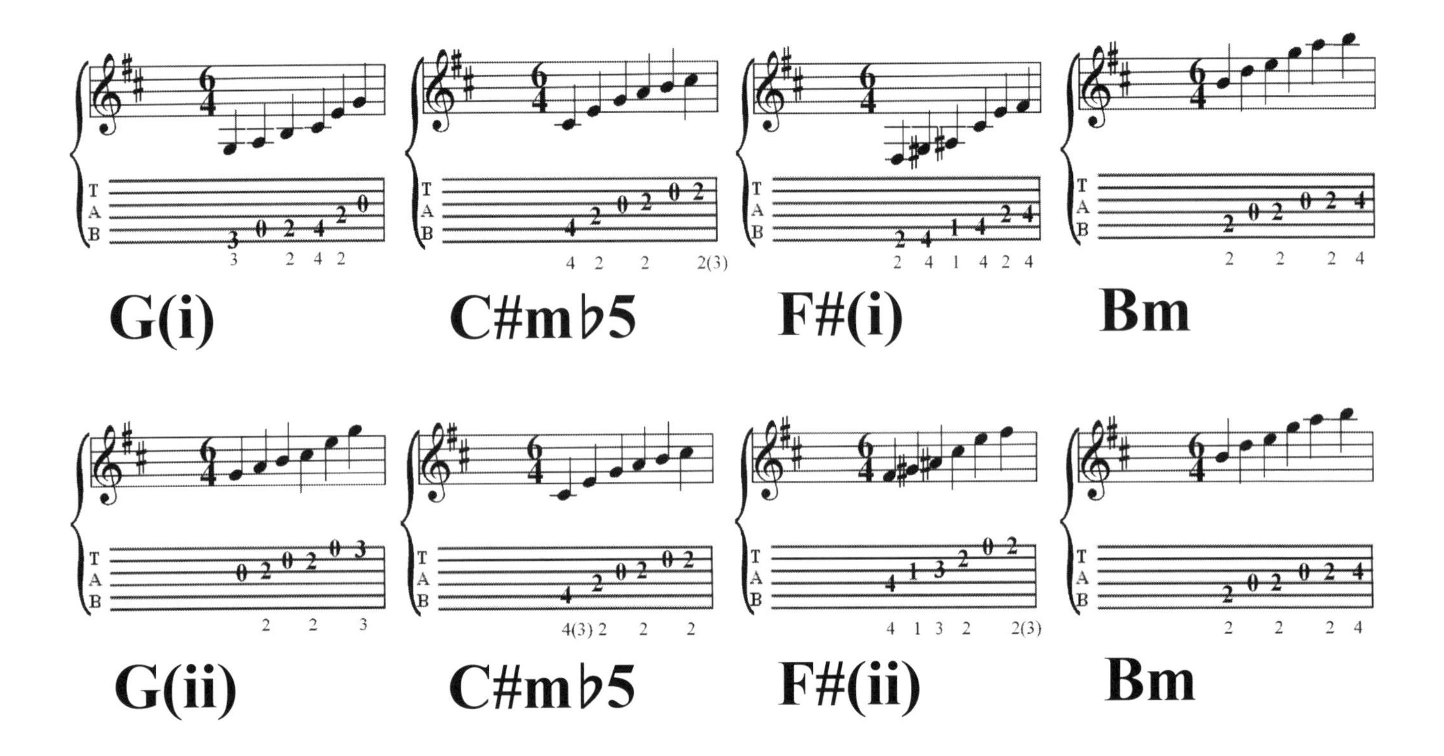

Key of F#m

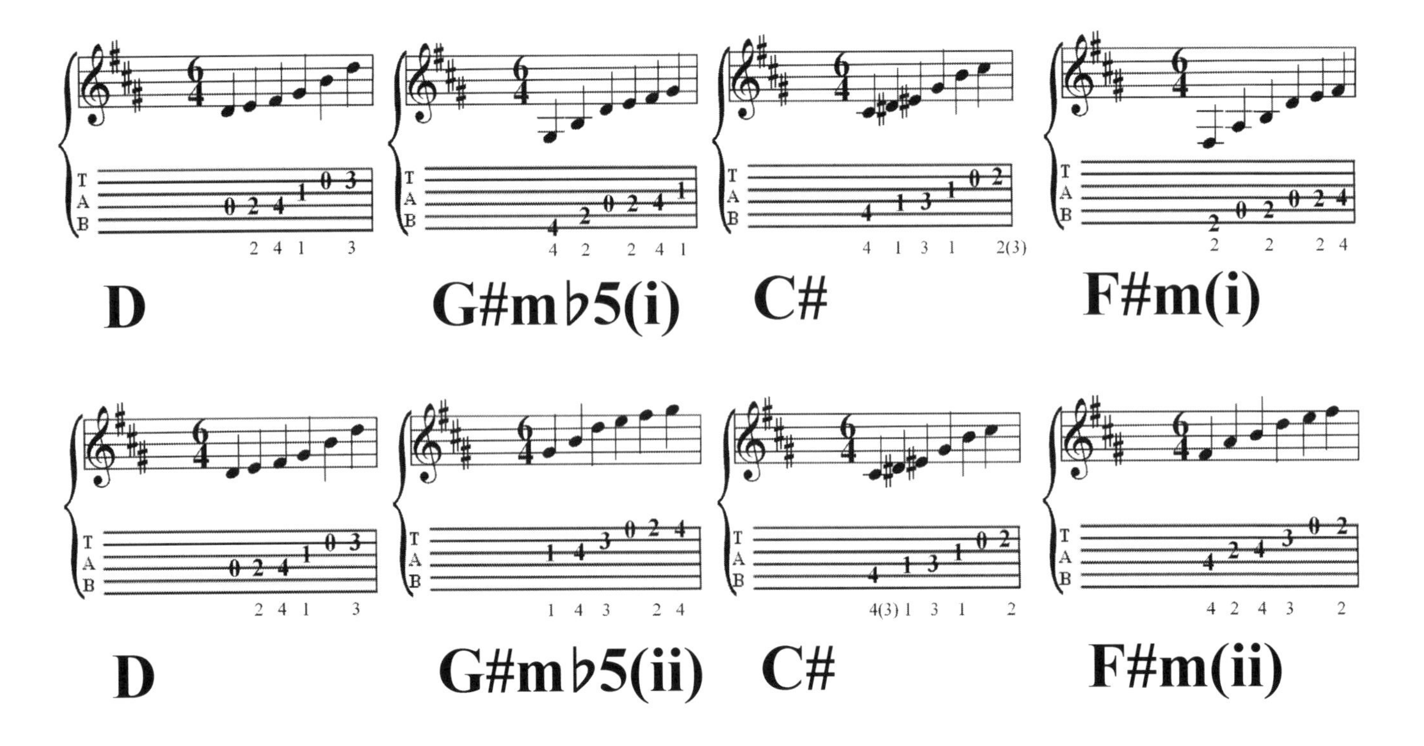

Key of C#m

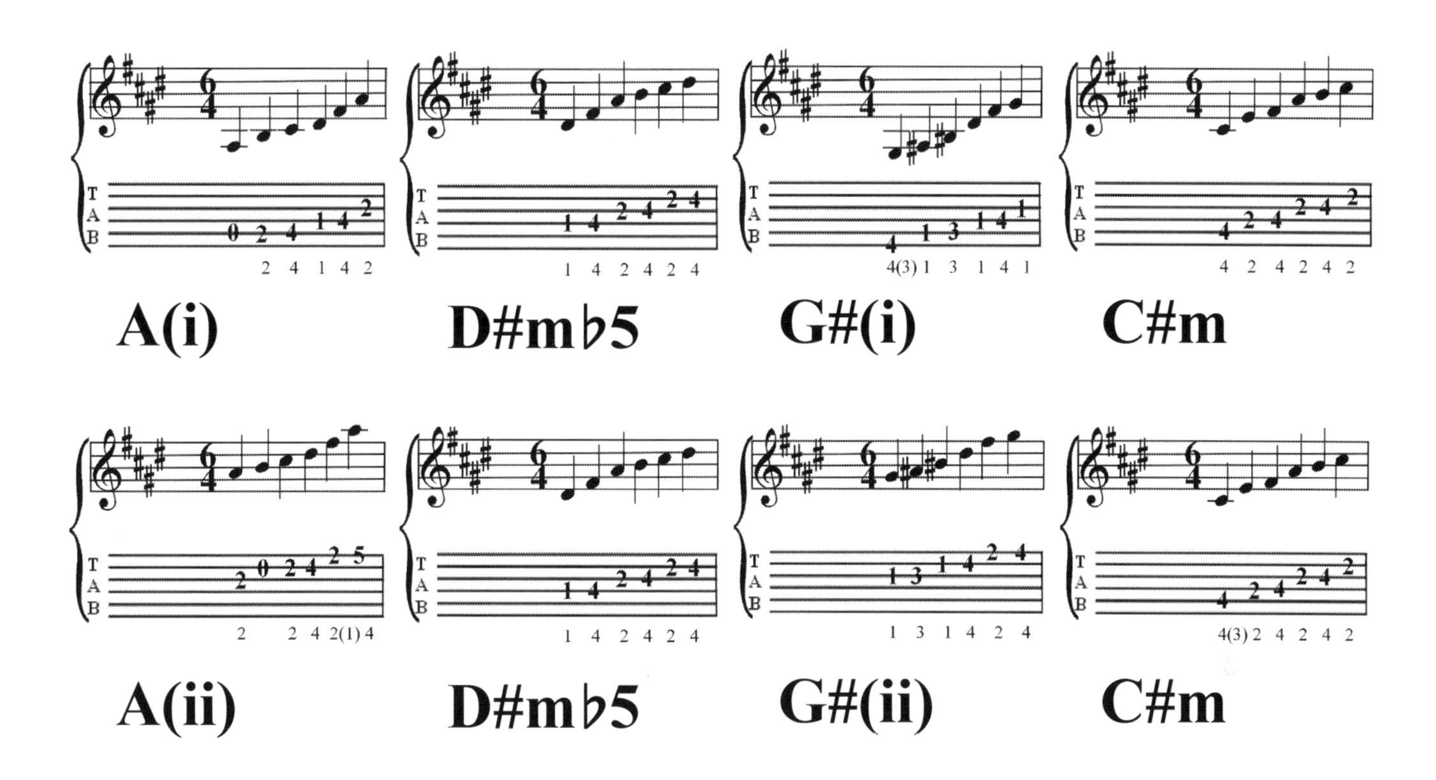

Key of A♭m

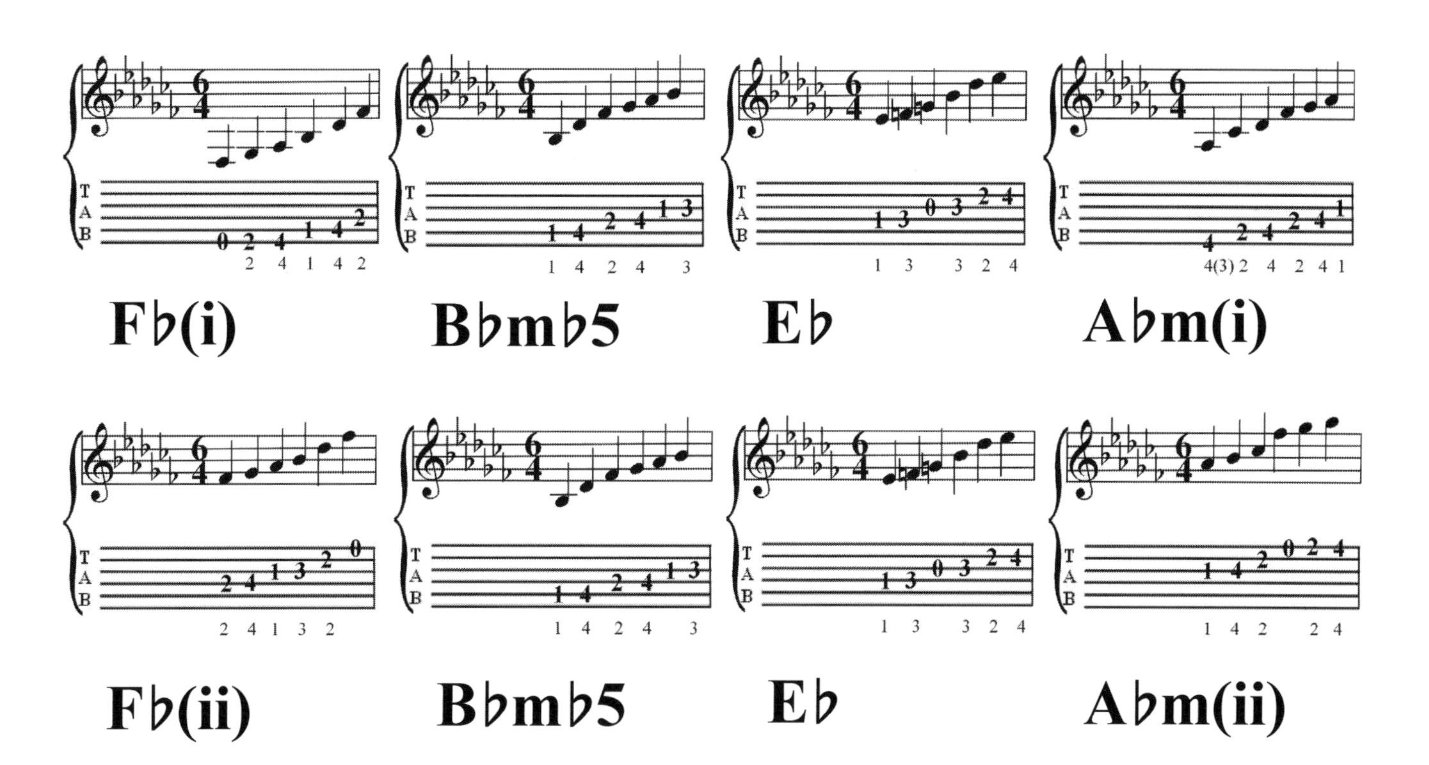

Key of E♭m

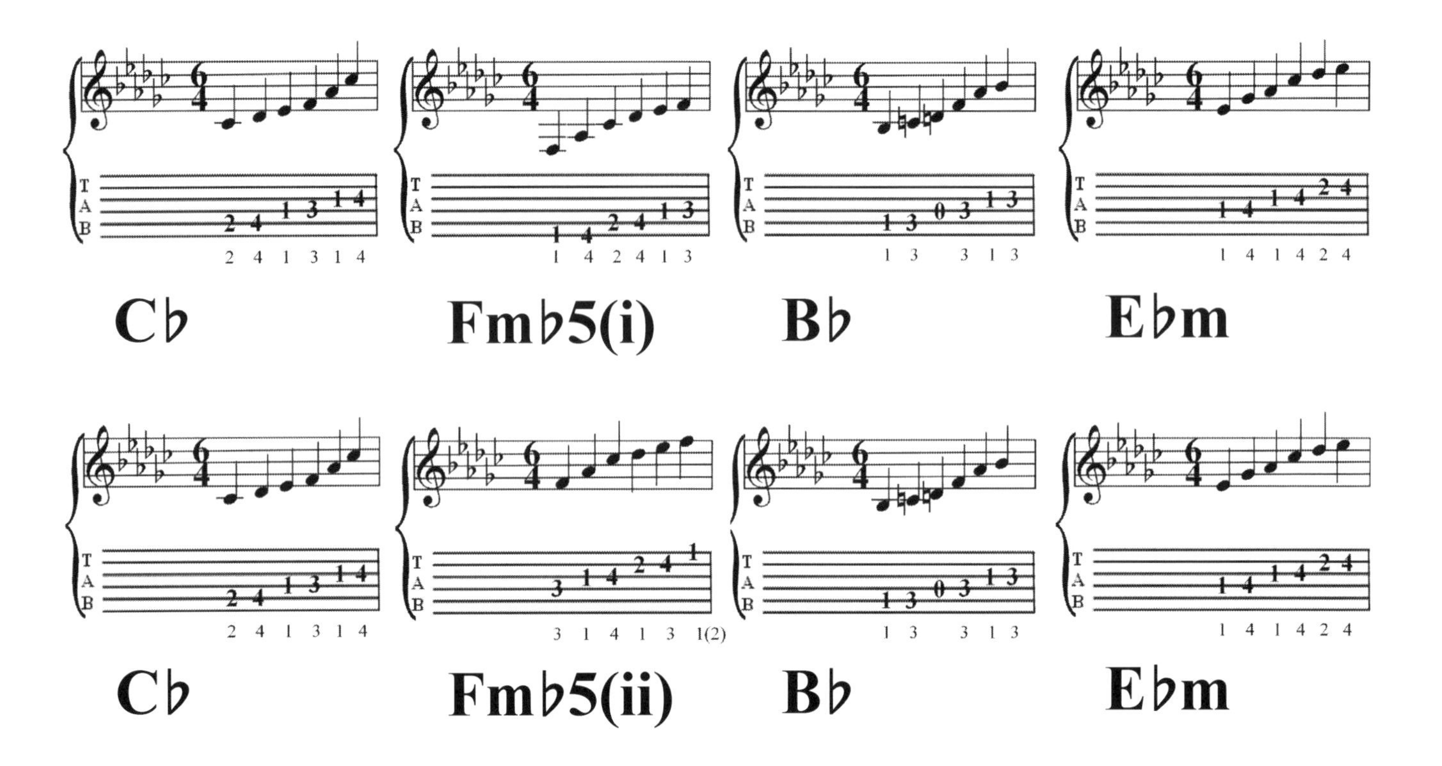

Key of B♭m

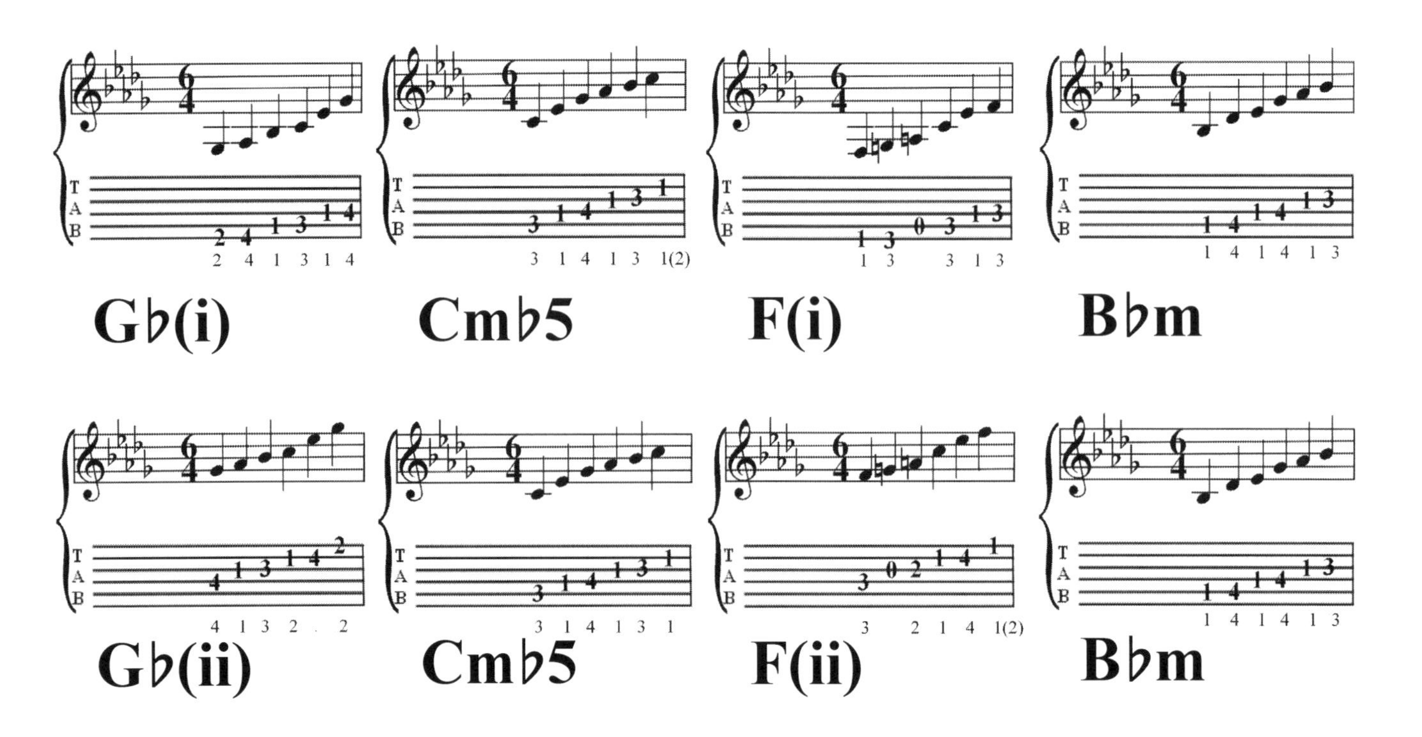

Key of Fm

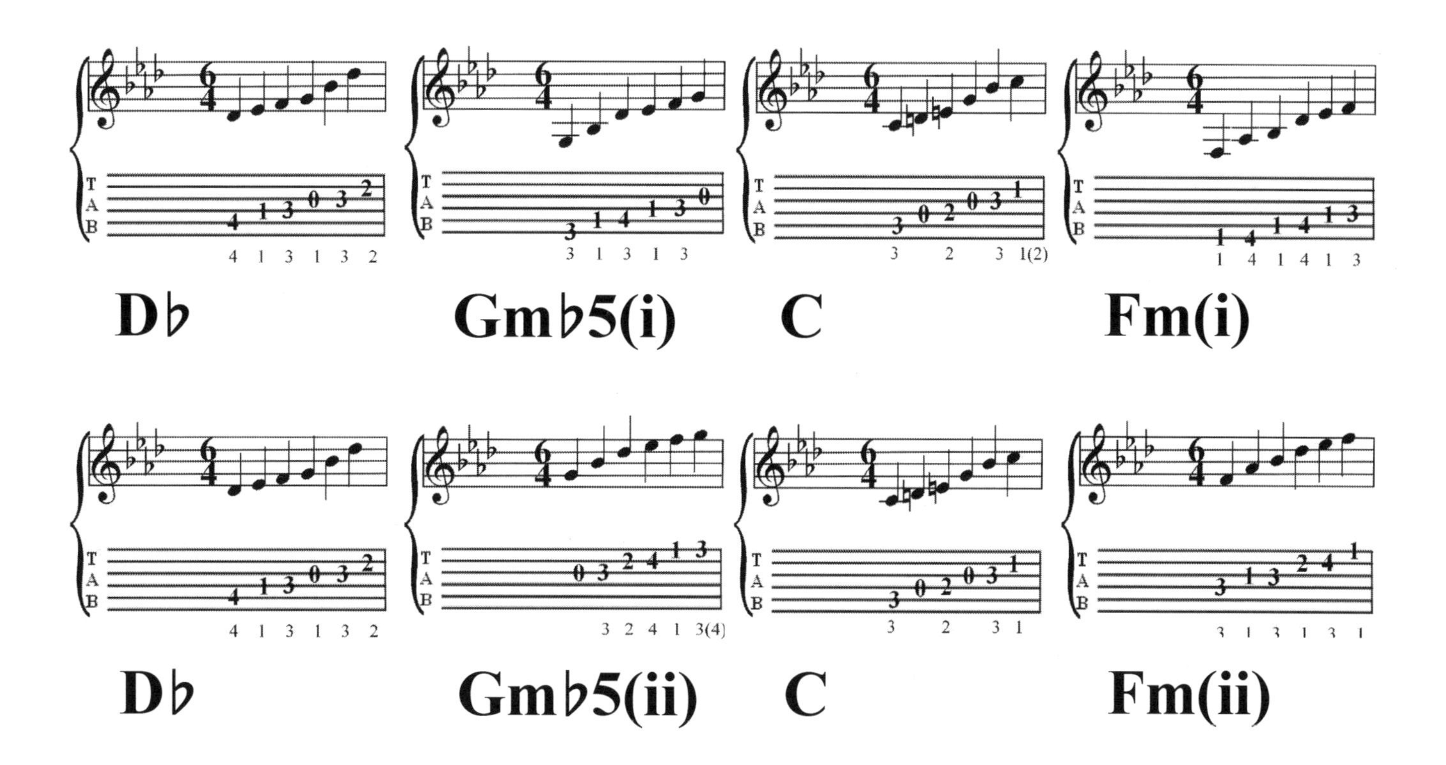

Key of Cm

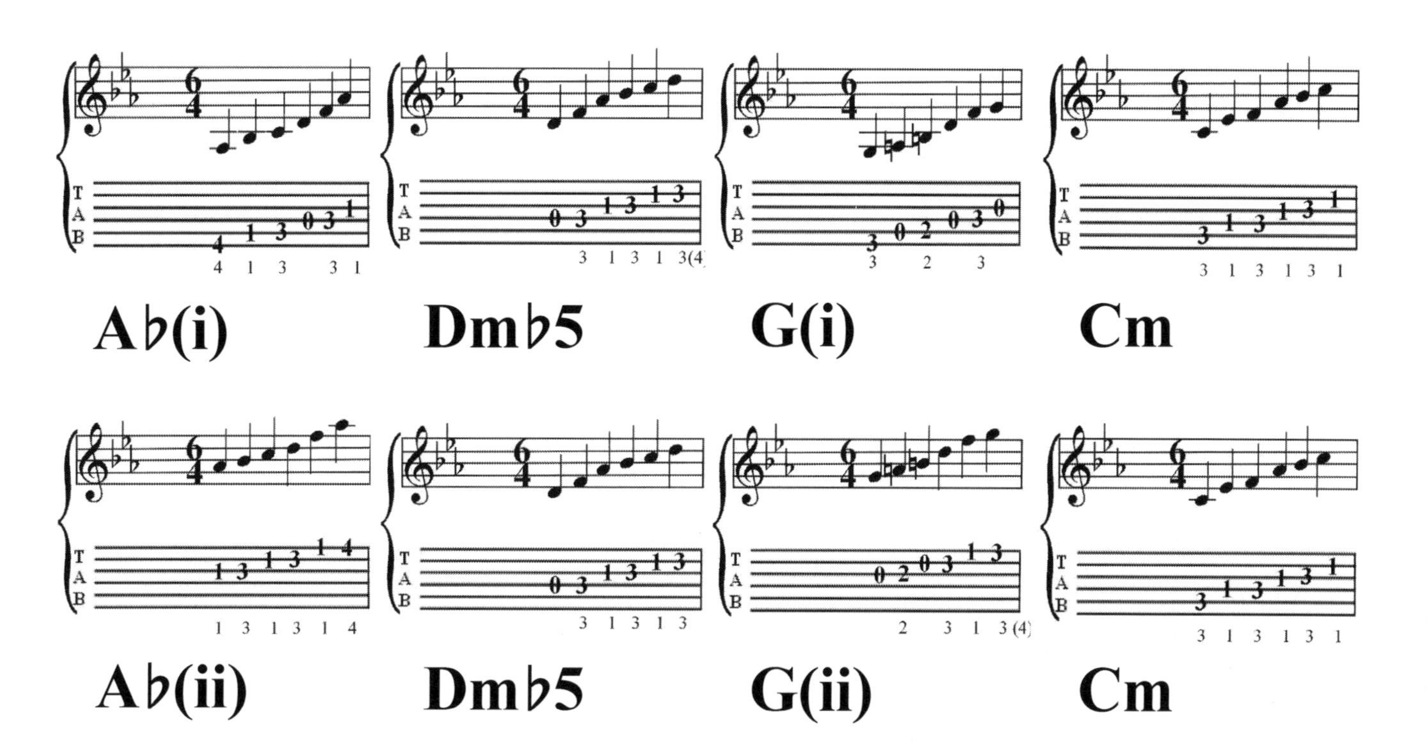

Key of Gm

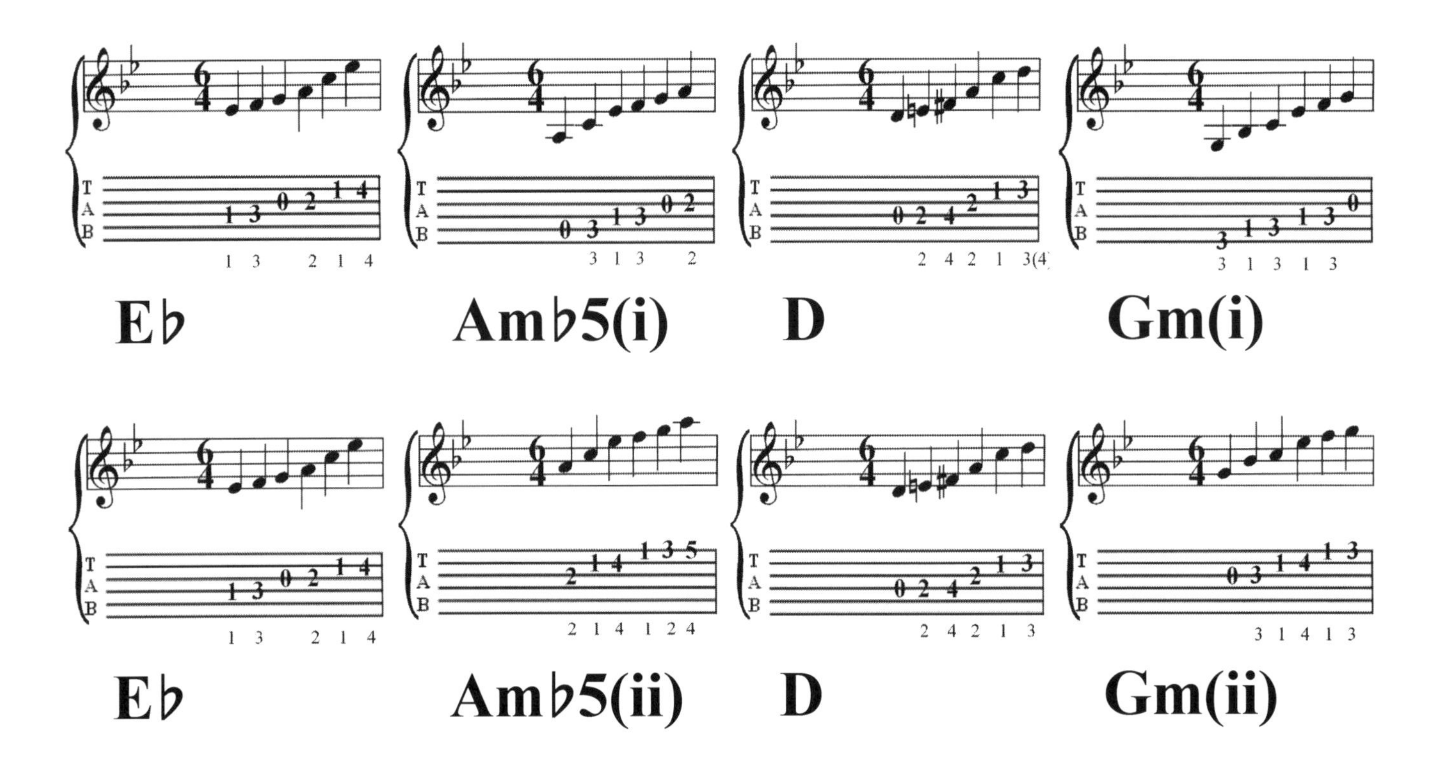

Key of Dm

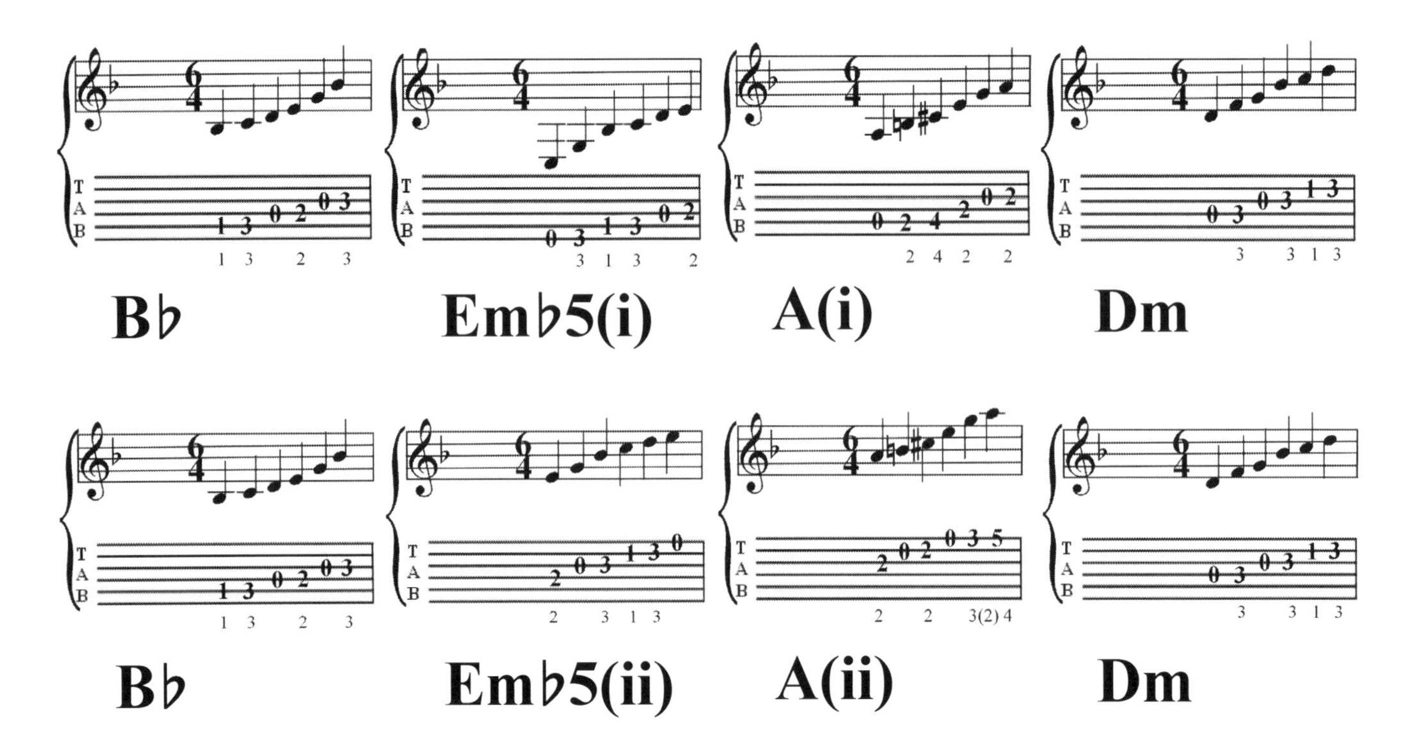

All Keys (i)

VI

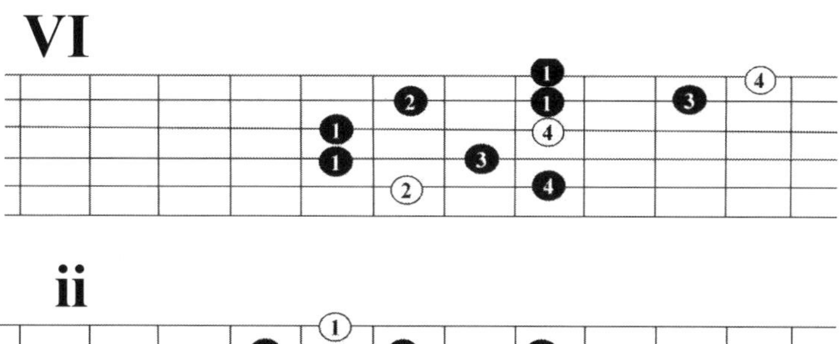

ii

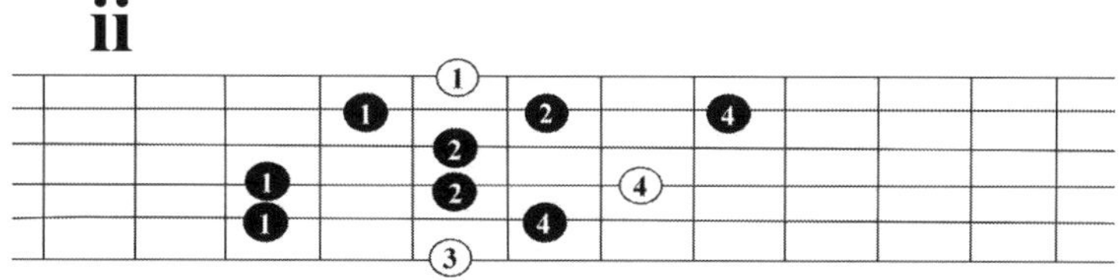

V

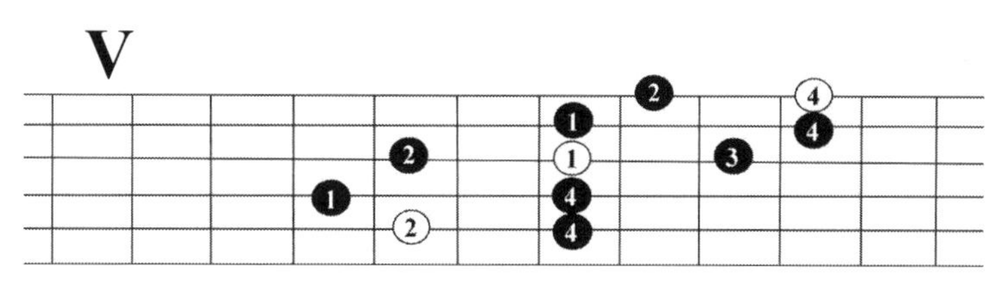

i

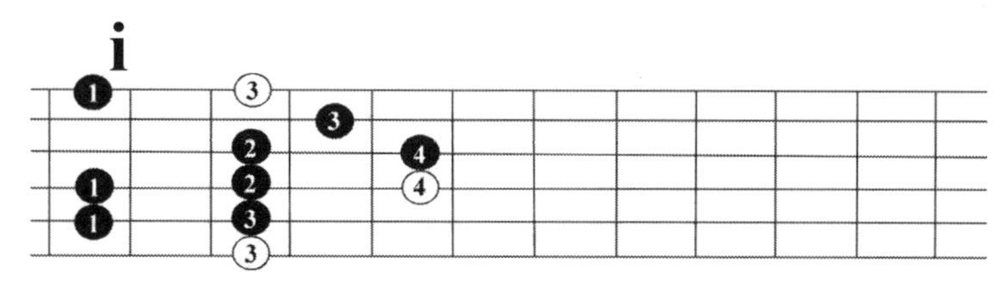

All Keys (ii)

VI

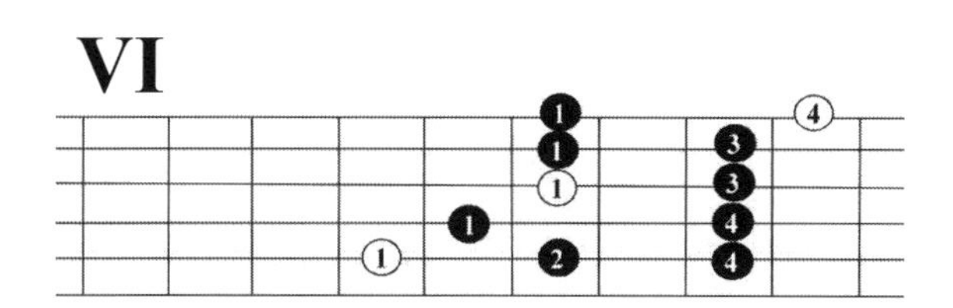

ii

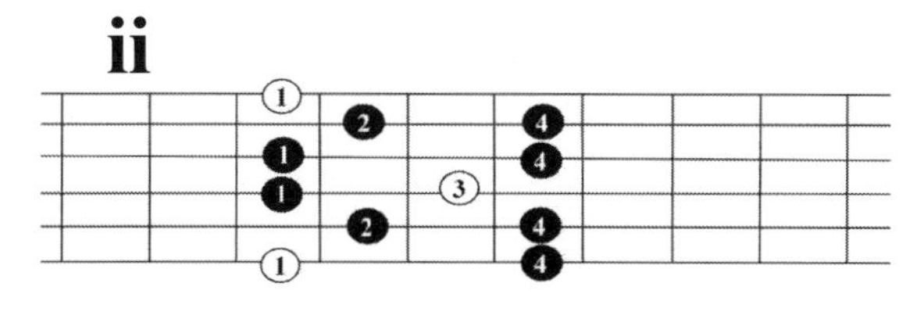

V

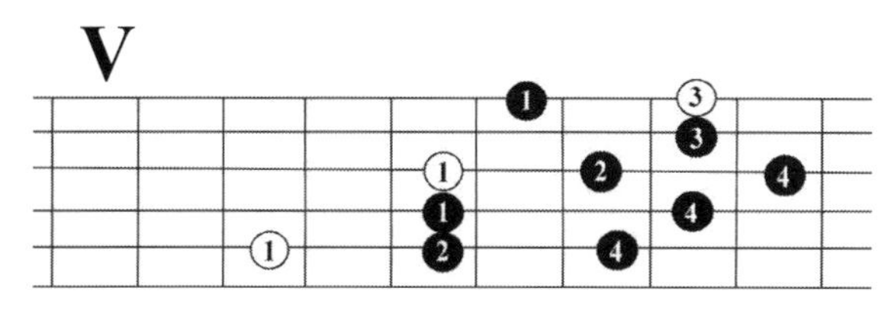

i

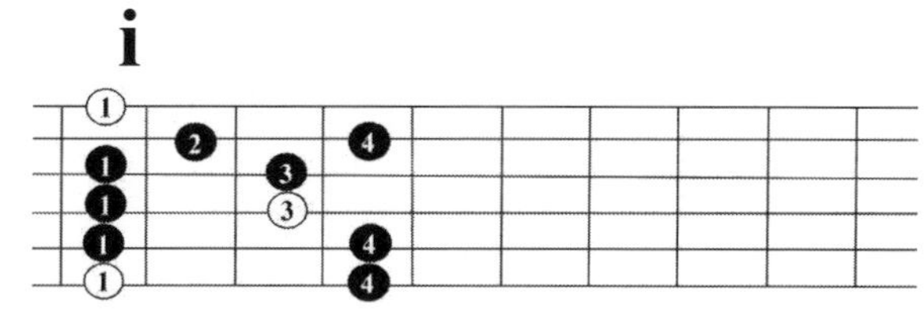

All Keys (iii)

VI

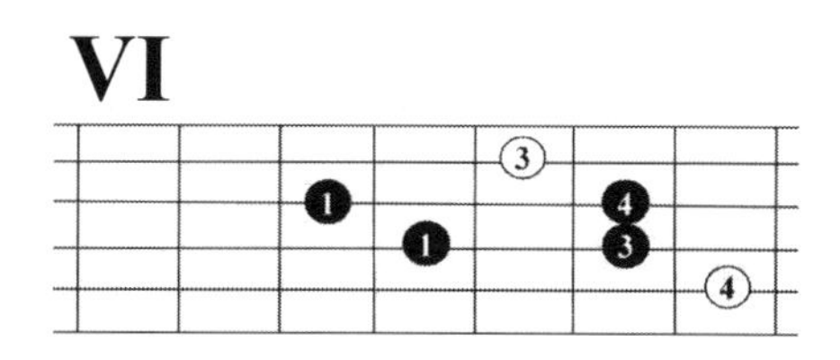

ii

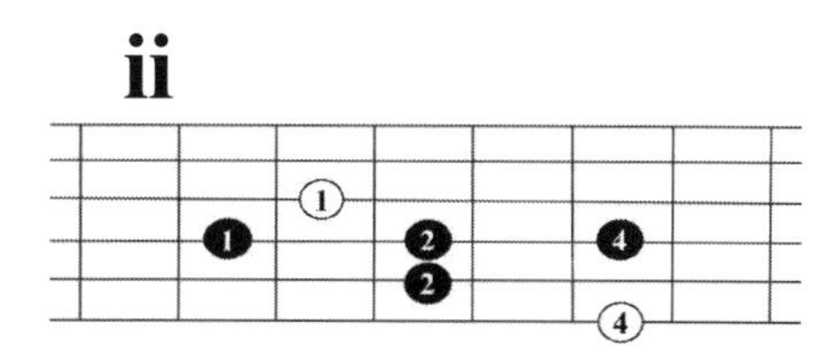

V

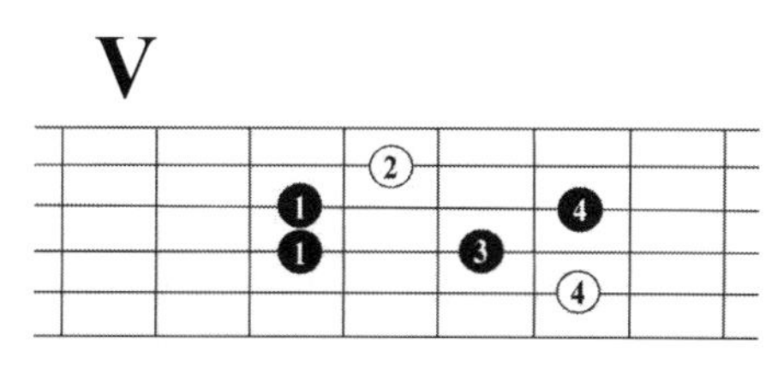

i

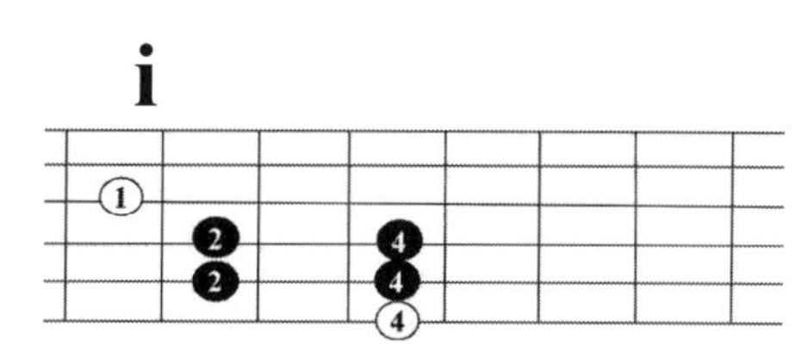

All Keys (iv)

VI

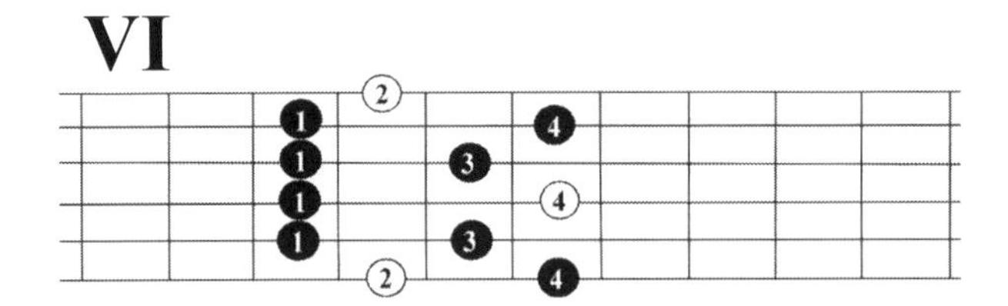

ii

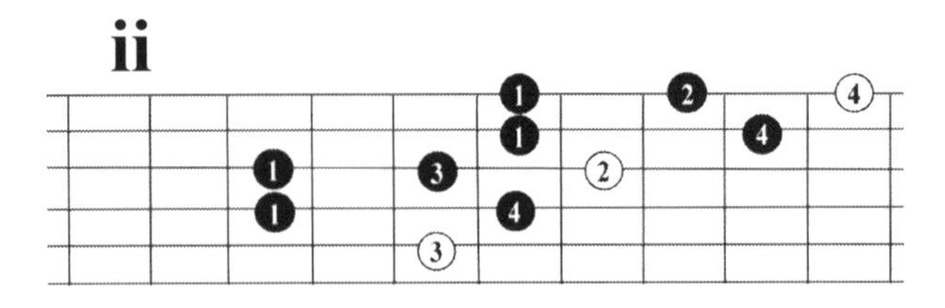

V

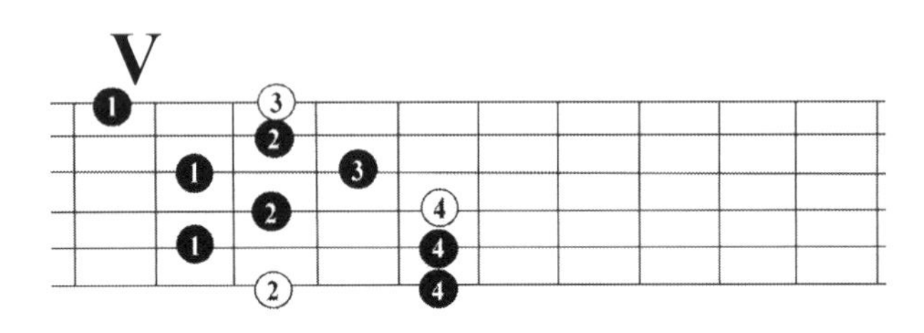

i

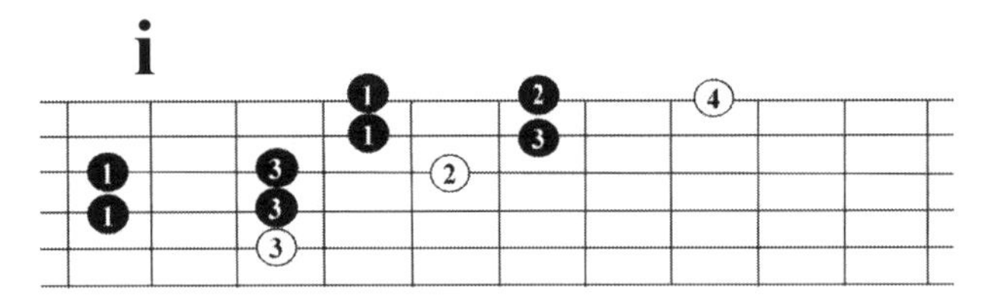

All Keys (v)

VI

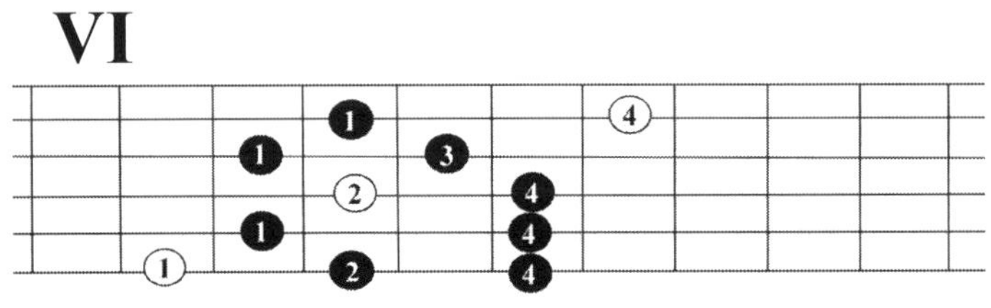

ii

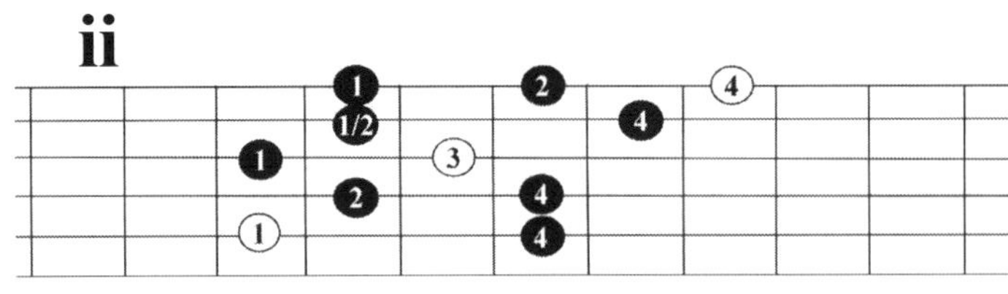

V

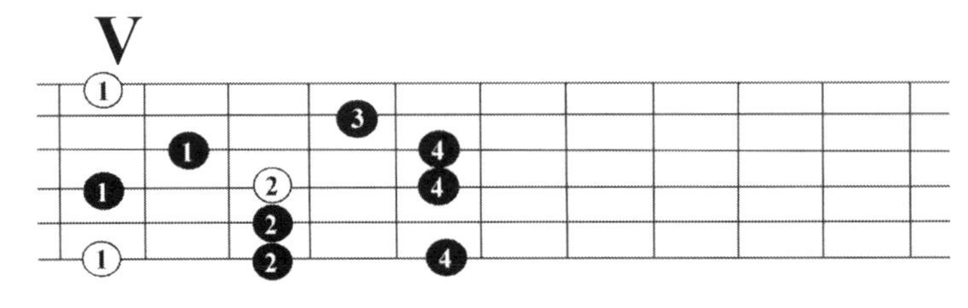

i

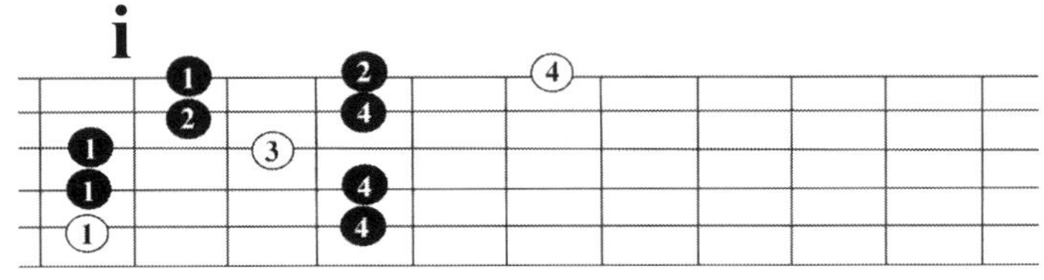

All Keys (vi)

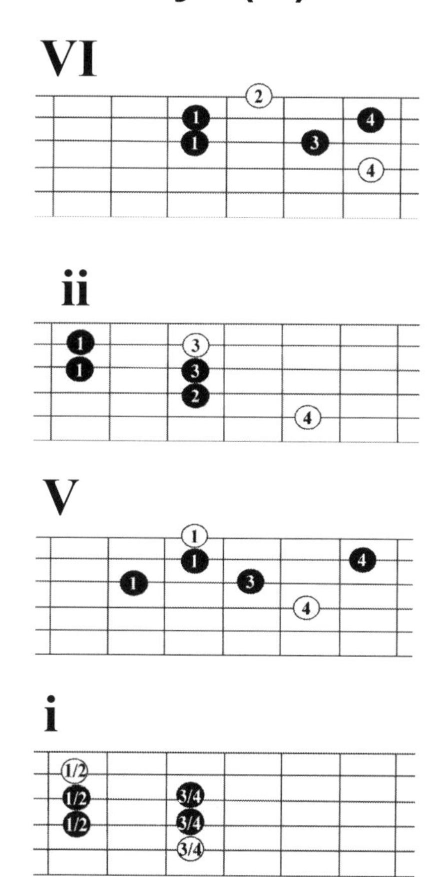

All Keys (vii)

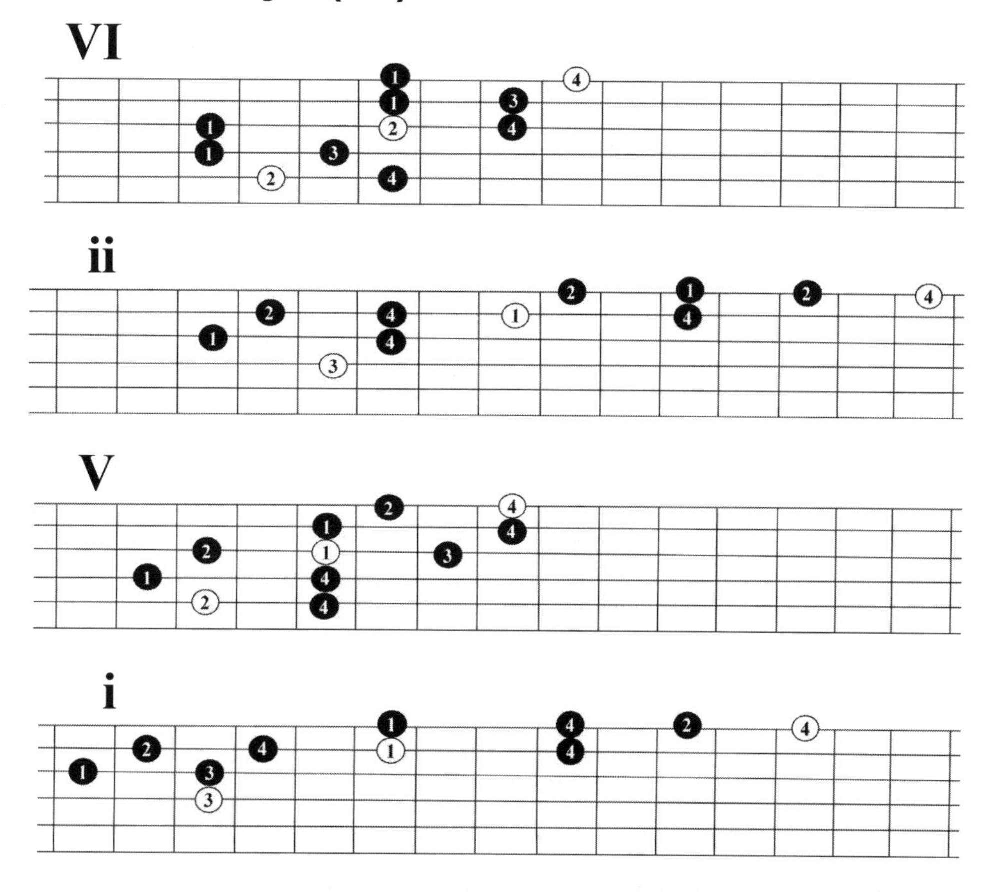

All Keys (viii)

VI

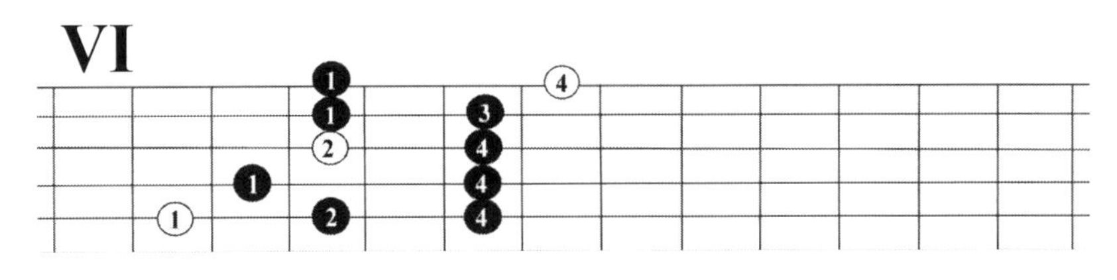

ii

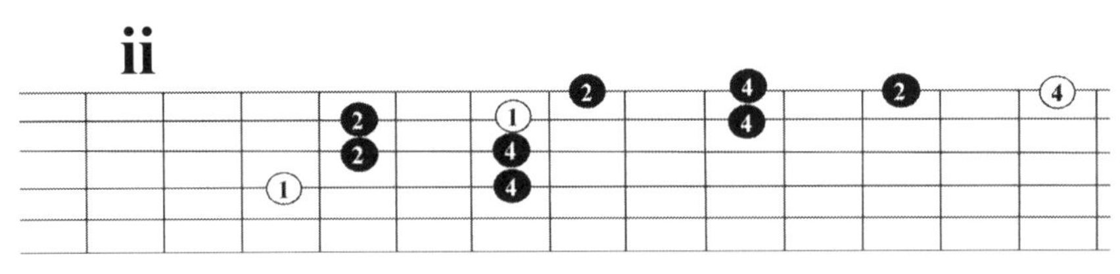

V

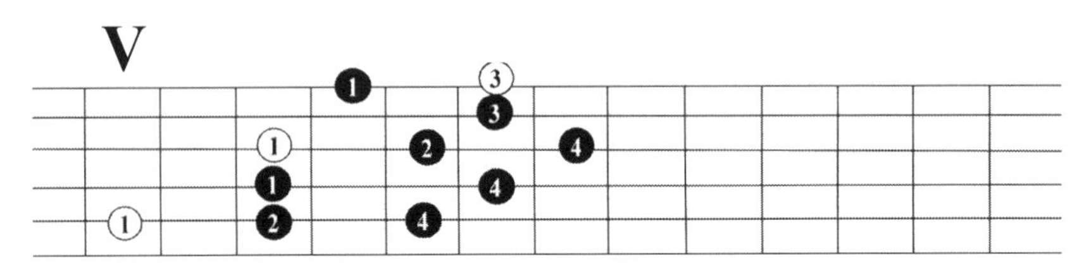

i

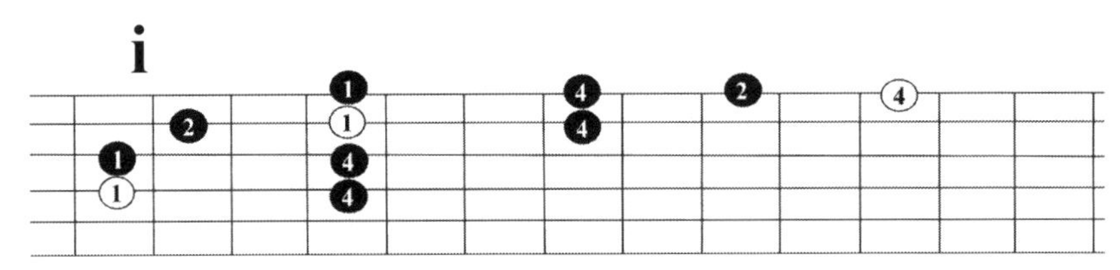

All Keys (ix)

VI

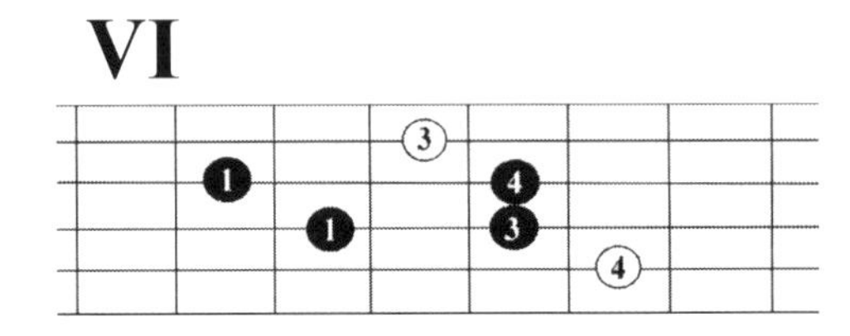

ii

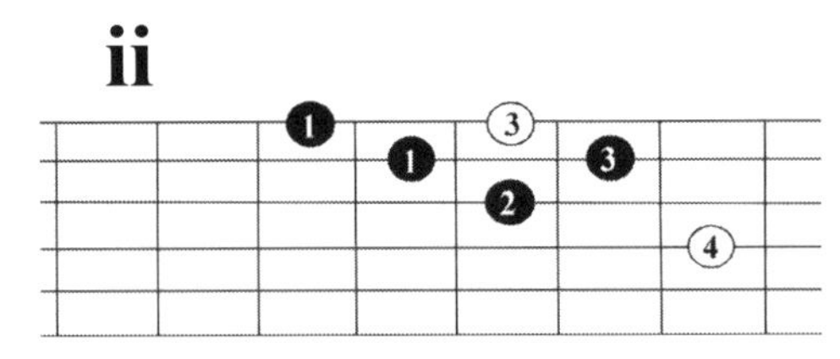

V

i

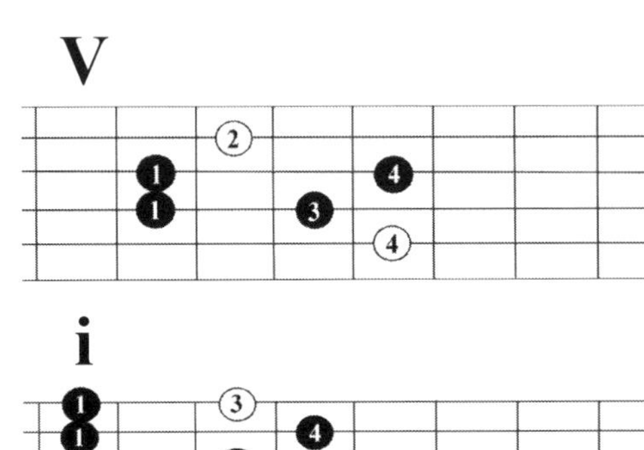

PART THIRTY-TWO

I - IV - V

MAJOR KEYS
MODES

MODES EXPLAINED

If you are not already familiar with the concept of "modes", the simplest way to understand them is as an extension of the system of relative *major* and relative *minor* keys. You should already be aware that for any major key there exists a relative minor key which has the same *key signature* (i.e. it contains exactly the same notes, but starts and ends on a different *tonic* note). For example, the scale of C major consists of the notes: C D E F G A B C; while the scale of A (natural) minor, the relative minor key, consists of the notes: A B C D E F G A.

In a similar fashion, it is possible to form a kind of scale, using the same notes, starting on each of the seven notes of any *diatonic* scale. It is these scales that are referred to as "modes". Each mode is given a name deriving from the culture of classical Greece (though the modes themselves do not). It is not essential to commit these names to memory, although it may be useful for future studies. At this stage the important thing is understand the principle on which they are constructed.

The examples below are given for the key of C major for convenience, as this key signature contains no sharps or flats. The same principles will apply to any major key, and the mode names will have the same correspondence to the *degrees* of the scale:

THE IONIAN MODE (built on the tonic note of the major scale)

This mode corresponds exactly to the familiar major scale and consists of the following *intervals*:
C *(tone)* **D** *(tone)* **E** *(semitone)* **F** *(tone)* **G** *(tone)* **A** *(tone)* **B** *(semitone)* **C**

THE DORIAN MODE (built on the second degree of the major scale)

This mode differs from the natural minor scale in containing a major *sixth*, and consists of the following intervals: **D** *(tone)* **E** *(semitone)* **F** *(tone)* **G** *(tone)* **A** *(tone)* **B** *(semitone)* **C** *(tone)* **D**

THE PHRYGIAN MODE (built on the third degree of the major scale)

This mode differs from the natural minor scale in containing a minor *second*, and consists of the following intervals: **E** *(semitone)* **F** *(tone)* **G** *(tone)* **A** *(tone)* **B** *(semitone)* **C** *(tone)* **D** *(tone)* **E**

THE LYDIAN MODE (built on the fourth degree of the major scale)

This mode differs from the major scale in containing an *augmented* (sharpened) *fourth*, and consists of the following intervals: **F** *(tone)* **G** *(tone)* **A** *(tone)* **B** *(semitone)* **C** *(tone)* **D** *(tone)* **E** *(semitone)* **F**

THE MIXOLYDIAN MODE (built on the fifth degree of the major scale)

This mode differs from the major scale in containing a minor *seventh*, and consists of the following intervals: **G** *(tone)* **A** *(tone)* **B** *(semitone)* **C** *(tone)* **D** *(tone)* **E** *(semitone)* **F** *(tone)* **G**

THE AEOLIAN MODE (built on the sixth degree of the major scale)

This mode corresponds exactly to the natural minor scale and contains the following intervals:
A *(tone)* **B** *(semitone)* **C** *(tone)* **D** *(tone)* **E** *(semitone)* **F** *(tone)* **G** *(tone)* **A**

THE LOCRIAN MODE (built on the seventh degree of the major scale)

This mode differs from the natural minor scale in containing a minor *second* and a *diminished* (flattened) *fifth*, and consists of the following intervals:
B *(semitone)* **C** *(tone)* **D** *(tone)* **E** *(semitone)* **F** *(tone)* **G** *(tone)* **A** *(tone)* **B**

HOW THE MODES ARE USED

The modes can be used as the basis of musical composition in the same way as the major and minor scales, and modal writing is the foundation of some modern jazz styles, as well as much of the early and traditional music of many cultures. However, in this book, we are concerned with the use of the modes as "chord scales".

WHY "CHORD SCALES"?

We can refer to the modes as "chord scales" because they provide a set of fingering patterns for each of the chords of the harmonised scale. Although, fundamentally, you are simply playing the scale of the underlying key signature, through diligent practice you will build a repertoire of fingerings which you can apply, almost without thinking, to each chord, based on the root note of the chord. For example, for the chord sequence I-IV-V in the key of C major, the appropriate modes would be:

C Ionian; F Lydian; G Mixolydian

Once these modal patterns are sufficiently "locked in", they will prove invaluable for fluent improvisation over the chord sequences.

PRACTISING THE MODES

The modes should be practised individually in ascending, descending and back-and-forth fingerings - then practised in sequence according to the chord progression exercises. The ascending and descending patterns can be mixed and matched across the chord sequences e.g. all one direction (ascending/descending); all back-and-forth; alternately ascending and descending; all ascending, then reversing the chord sequence in descending modes; etc.

If your practice schedule allows, try some more complex scale exercises, such as playing the modes in thirds (notes 1 - 3 - 2 - 4 - 3 - 5 - 4 - 6 - 5 - 7 - 6 - 8), or in groups of three (1-2-3; 2-3-4; 3-4-5; 4-5-6; 5-6-7; 6-7-8) or four (1-2-3-4; 2-3-4-5; 3-4-5-6; 4-5-6-7; 5-6-7-8) notes. Experiment with your own variations.

A NOTE ON THE EXERCISES

For the following exercises in the open position, no fingerings are given, since in almost all cases the fingering will correspond exactly to the fret numbers. The only exceptions are the higher (version ii) modes of A, in which cases the 3rd and 5th or 4th and 5th frets on the highest string are to be played with the 3rd and 4th fingers respectively.

As with the arpeggio and pentatonic exercises, varying the fingering when changing between modes can make the transitions smoother by avoiding jumps with the same finger.

Key of C

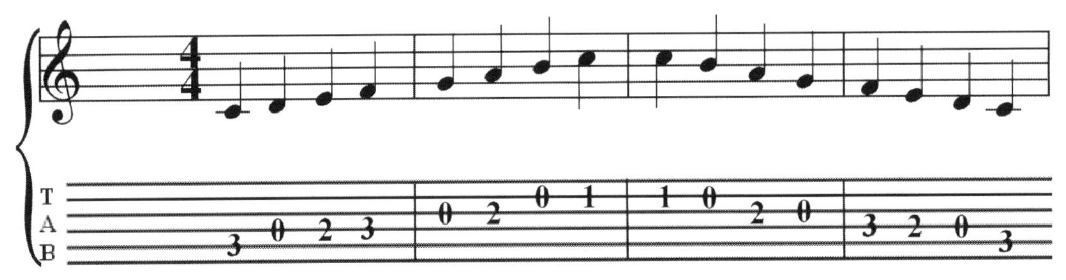

C Ionian - (Chord of C Major/CM7)

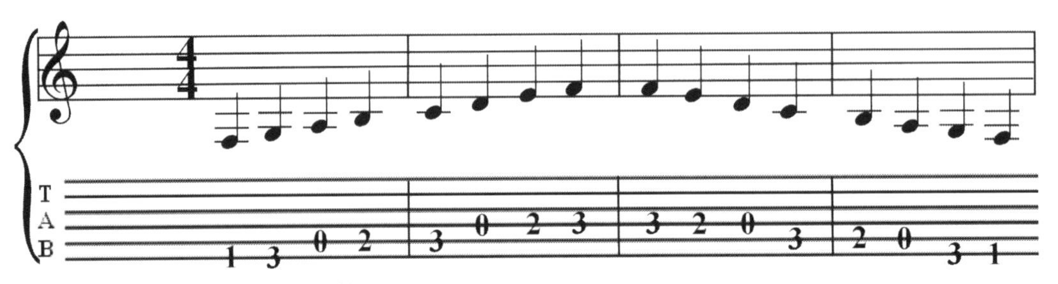

F Lydian (i) - (Chord of F Major/FM7)

F Lydian (ii) - (Chord of F Major/FM7)

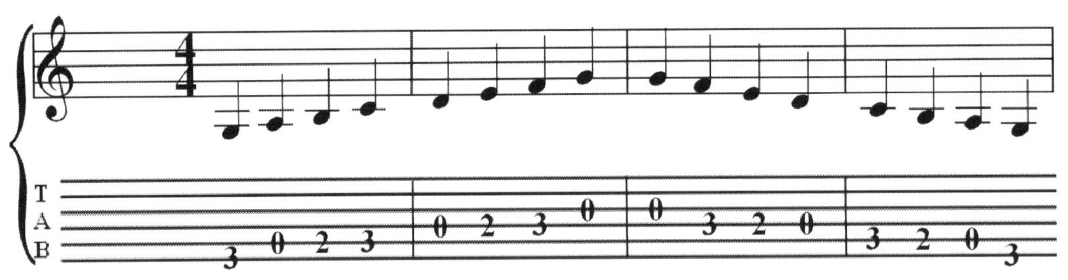

G Mixolydian (i) - (Chord of G Major/G7)

G Mixolydian (ii) - (Chord of G Major/G7)

Key of G

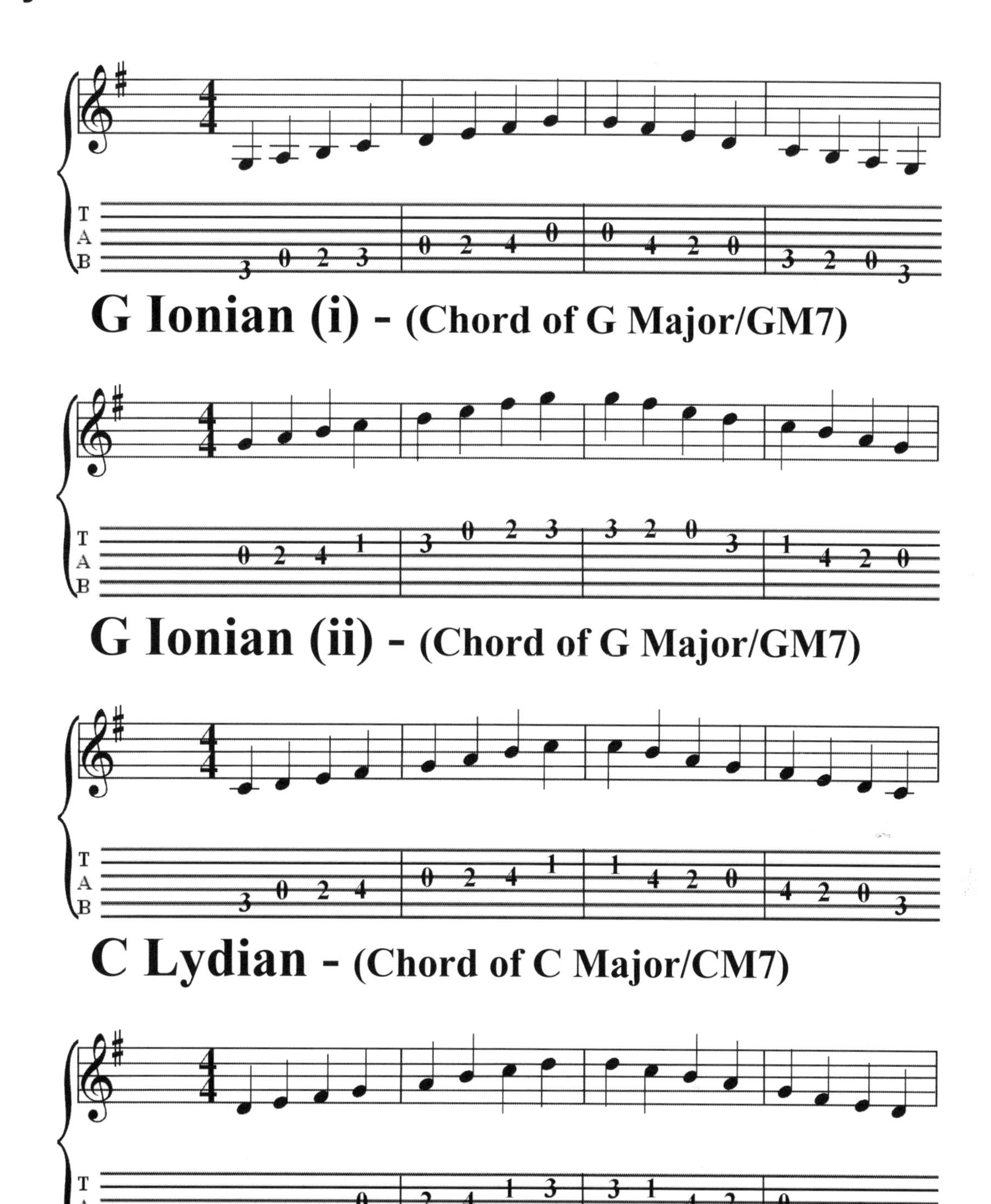

D Mixolydian - (Chord of D Major/D7)

Key of D

D Ionian - (Chord of D Major/DM7)

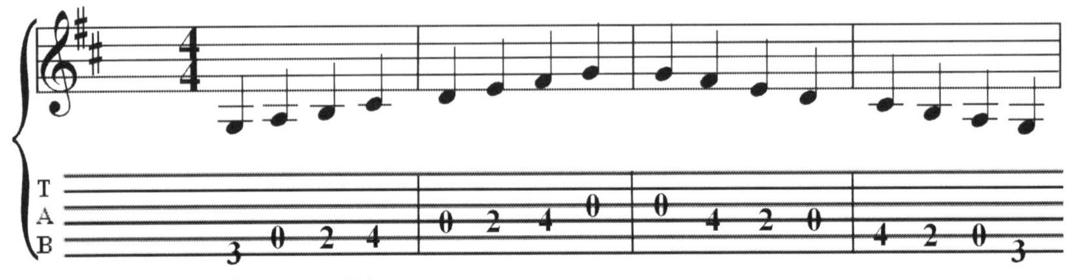

G Lydian (i) - (Chord of G Major/GM7)

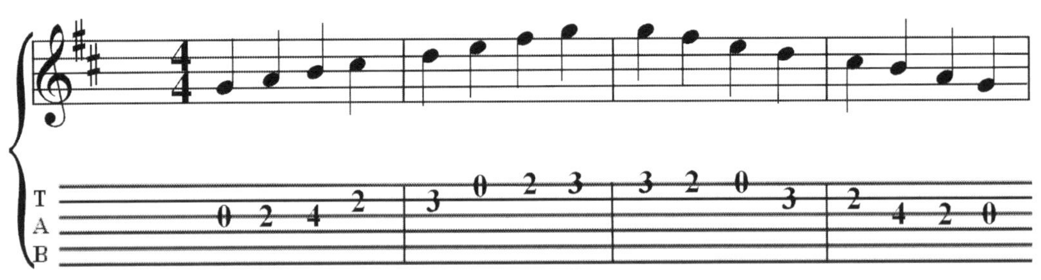

G Lydian (ii) - (Chord of G Major/GM7)

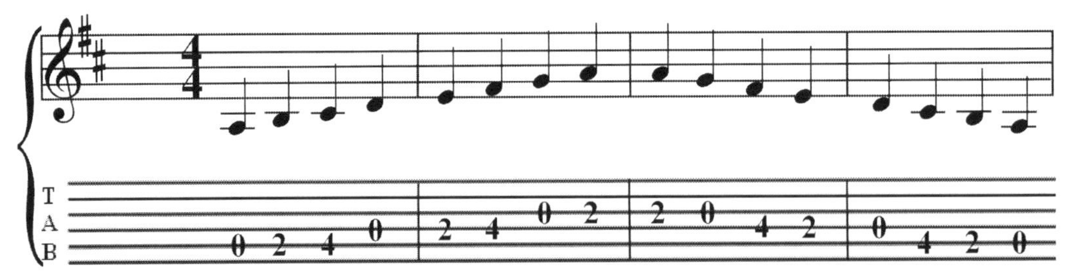

A Mixolydian (i) - (Chord of A Major/A7)

A Mixolydian (ii) - (Chord of A Major/A7)

Key of A

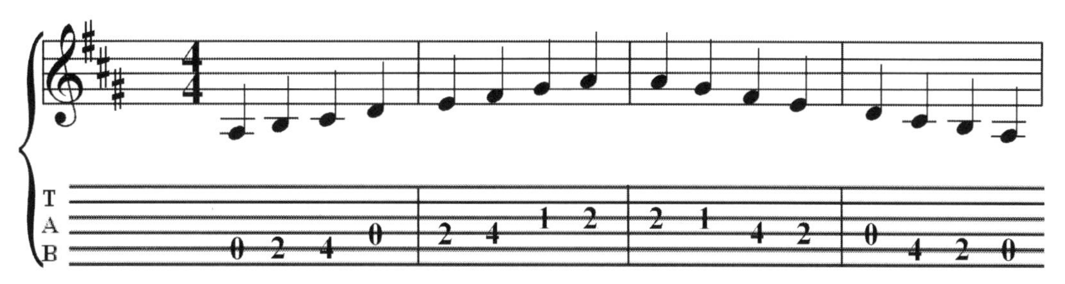

A Ionian (i) - (Chord of A Major/AM7)

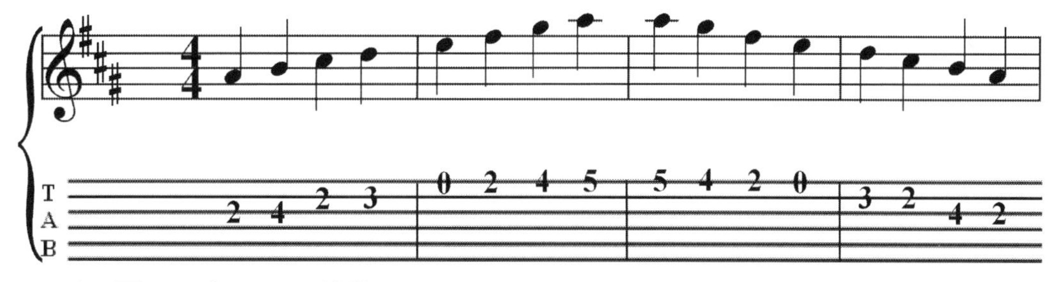

A Ionian (ii) - (Chord of A Major/AM7)

D Lydian - (Chord of D Major/DM7)

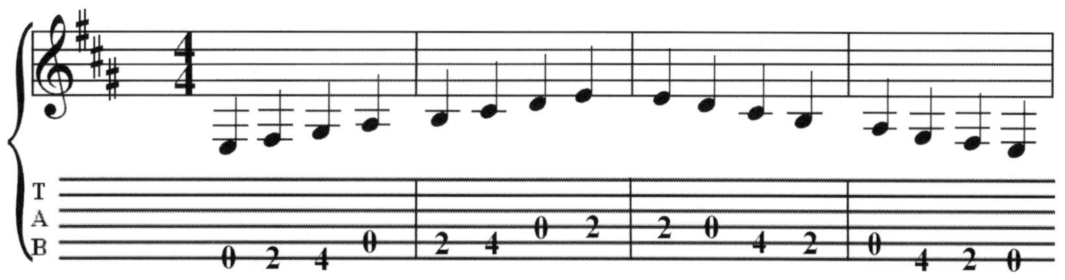

E Mixolydian (i) - (Chord of E Major/E7)

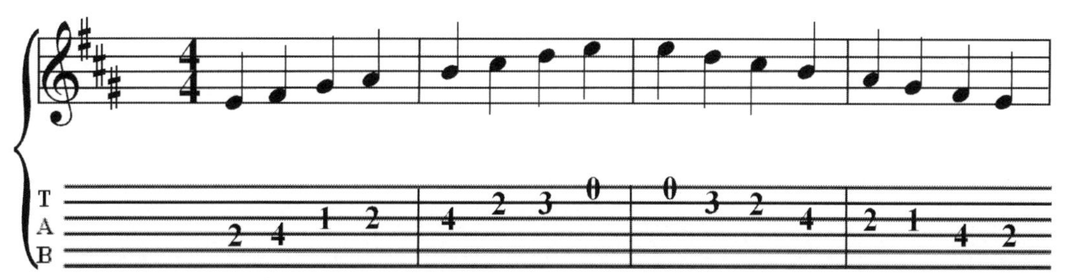

E Mixolydian (ii) - (Chord of E Major/E7)

Key of E

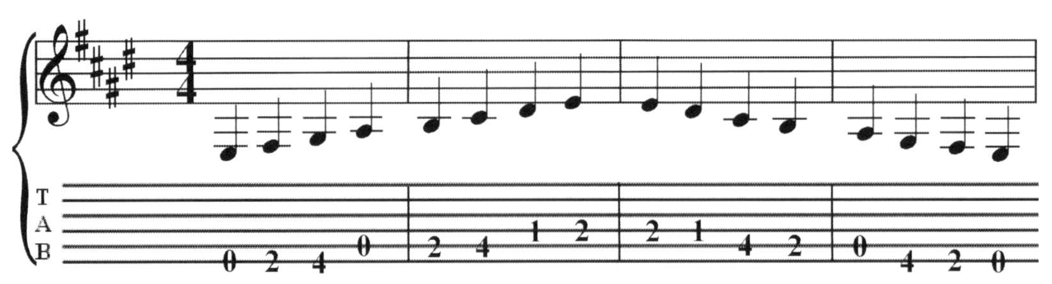

E Ionian (i) - (Chord of E Major/EM7)

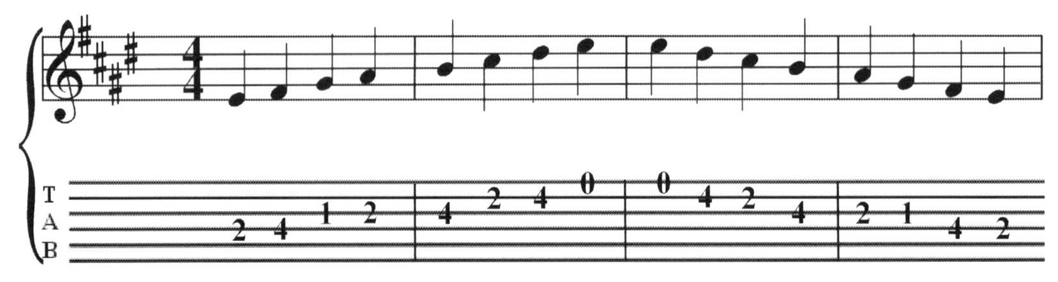

E Ionian (ii) - (Chord of E Major/EM7)

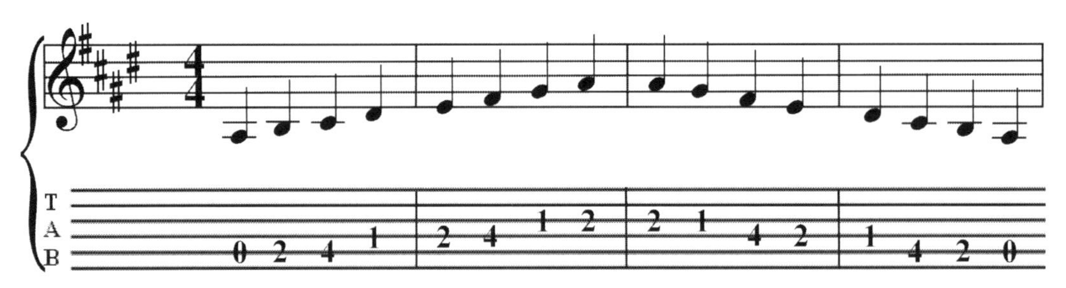

A Lydian (i) - (Chord of A Major/AM7)

A Lydian (ii) - (Chord of A Major/AM7)

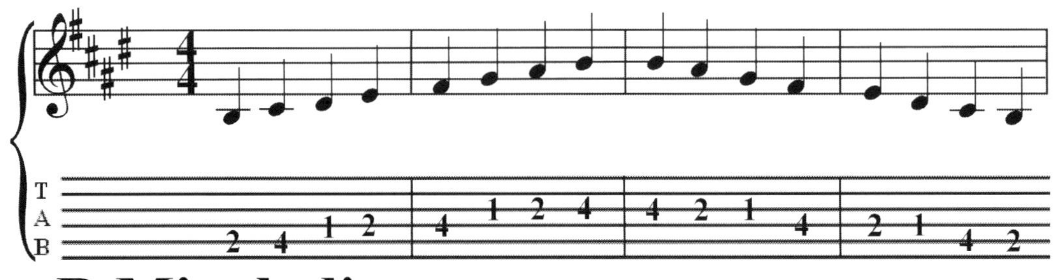

B Mixolydian - (Chord of B Major/B7)

Key of B

B Ionian - (Chord of B Major/BM7)

E Lydian (i) - (Chord of E Major/EM7)

E Lydian (ii) - (Chord of E Major/EM7)

F# Mixolydian (i) - (Chord of F# Major/F#7)

F# Mixolydian (ii) - (Chord of F# Major/F#7)

Key of F#

F# Ionian (i) - (Chord of F# Major/F#M7)

F# Ionian (ii) - (Chord of F# Major/F#M7)

B Lydian - (Chord of B Major/BM7)

C# Mixolydian - (Chord of C# Major/C#7)

Key of C#

C# Ionian - (Chord of C# Major/C#M7)

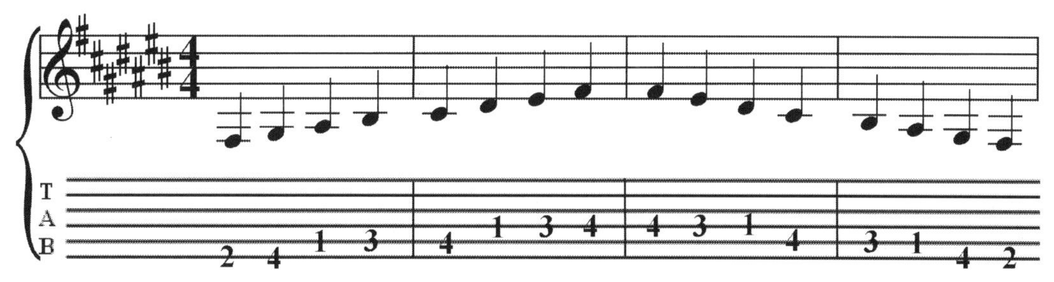

F# Lydian (i) - (Chord of F# Major/F#M7)

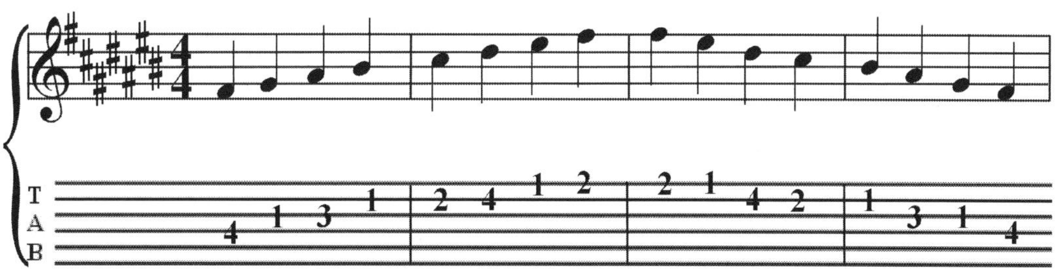

F# Lydian (ii) - (Chord of F# Major/F#M7)

G# Mixolydian (i) - (Chord of G# Major/G#7)

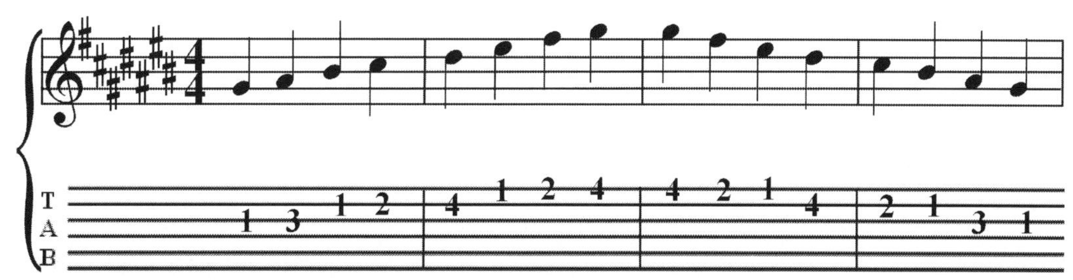

G# Mixolydian (ii) - (Chord of G# Major/G#7)

Key of A♭

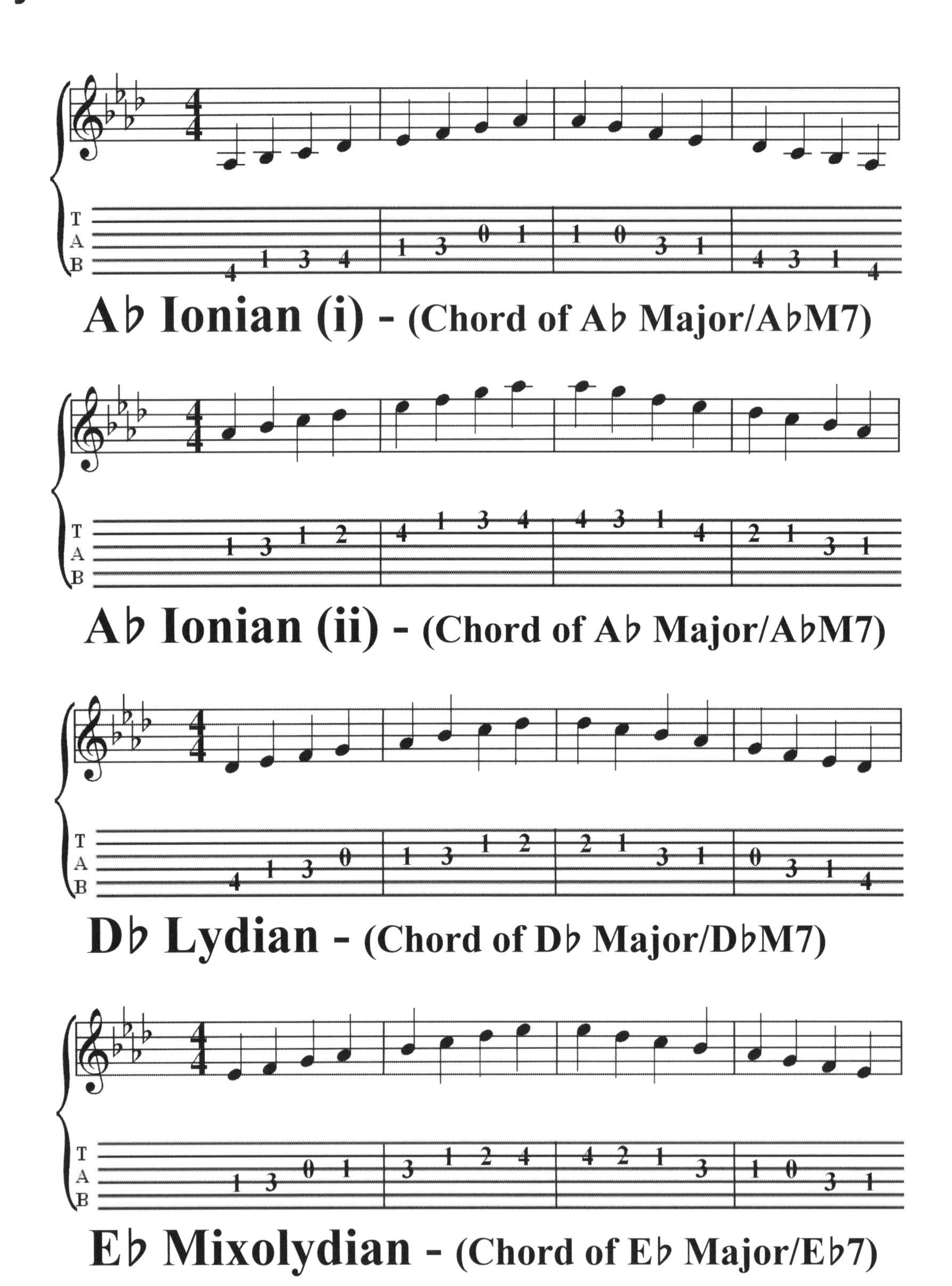
A♭ Ionian (i) - (Chord of A♭ Major/A♭M7)
A♭ Ionian (ii) - (Chord of A♭ Major/A♭M7)
D♭ Lydian - (Chord of D♭ Major/D♭M7)
E♭ Mixolydian - (Chord of E♭ Major/E♭7)

Key of E♭

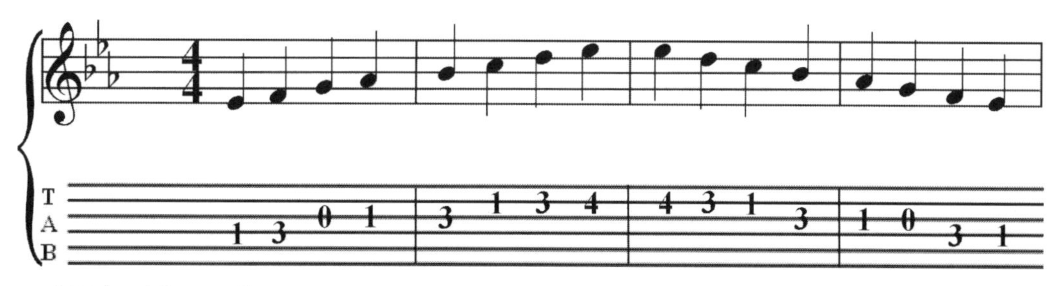

E♭ Ionian - (Chord of E♭ Major/E♭M7)

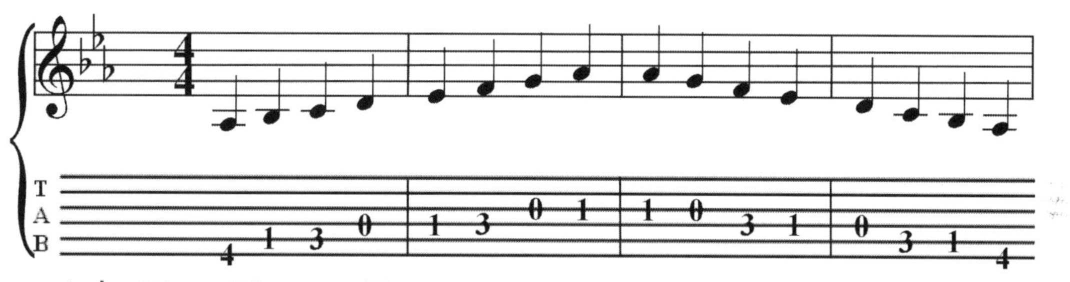

A♭ Lydian (i) - (Chord of A♭ Major/A♭M7)

A♭ Lydian (ii) - (Chord of A♭ Major/A♭M7)

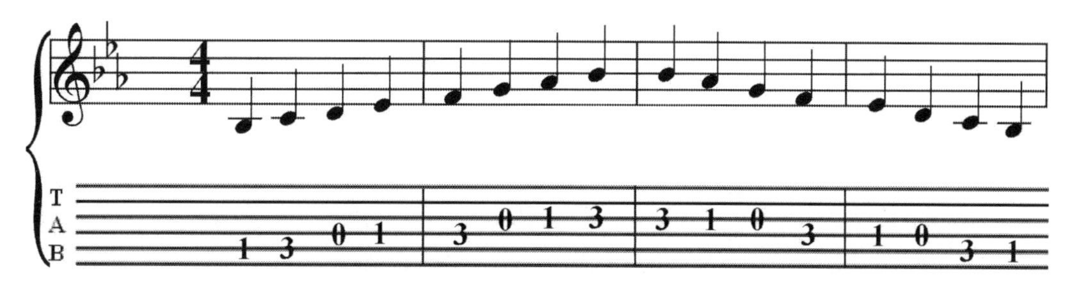

B♭ Mixolydian - (Chord of B♭ Major/B♭7)

Key of B♭

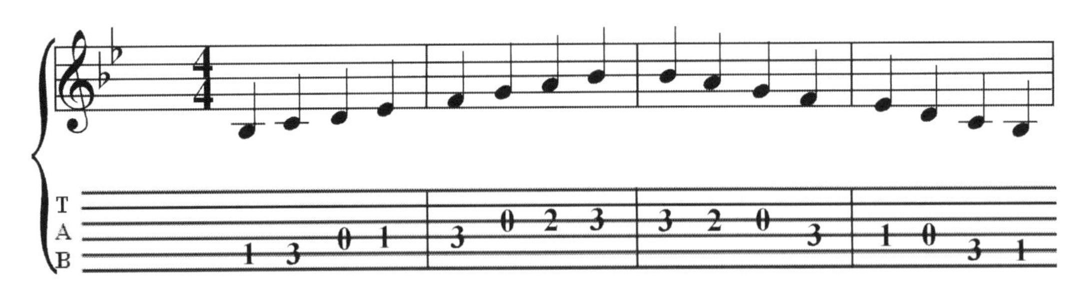

B♭ Ionian - (Chord of B Major/B♭M7)

E♭ Lydian - (Chord of E♭ Major/E♭M7)

F Mixolydian (i) - (Chord of F Major/F7)

F Mixolydian (ii) - (Chord of F Major/F7)

Key of F

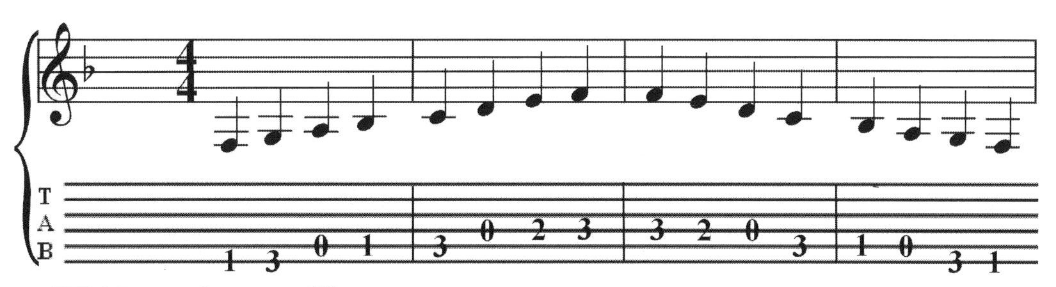

F Ionian (i) - (Chord of F Major/FM7)

F Ionian (ii) - (Chord of F Major/FM7)

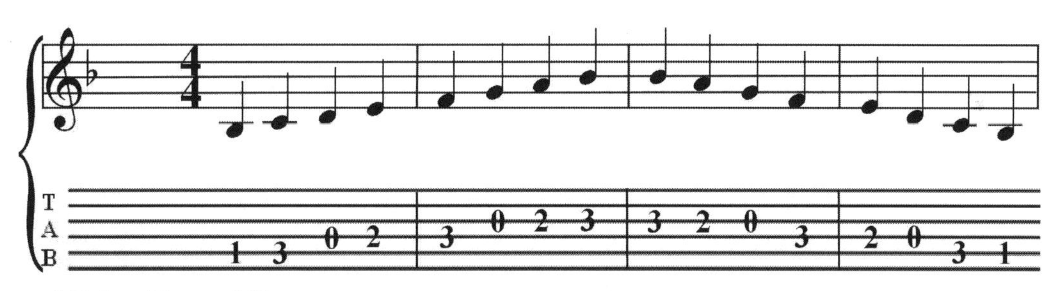

B♭ Lydian - (Chord of B♭ Major/B♭M7)

C Mixolydian - (Chord of C Major/C7)

All Keys (i)

I (Ionian / Major Scale)

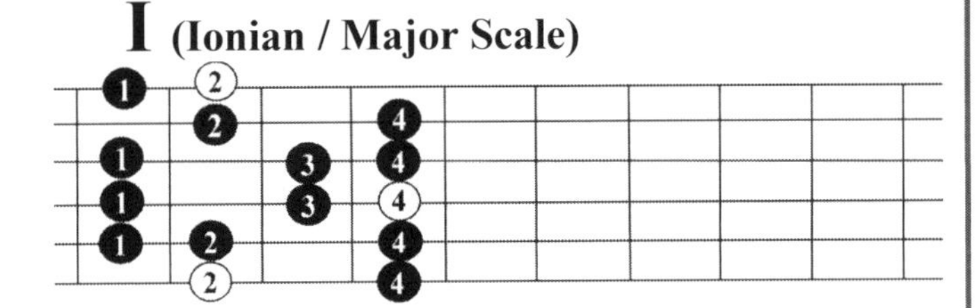

IV (Lydian)

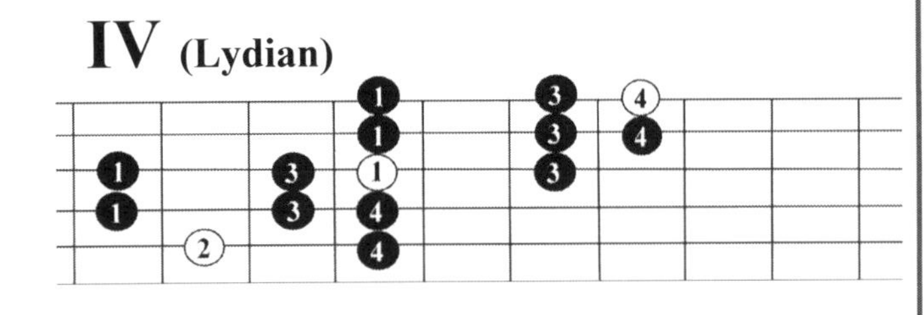

V (Mixolydian)

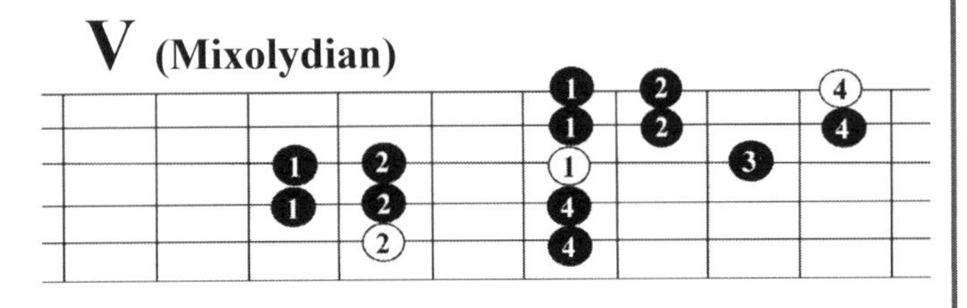

All Keys (ii)

I

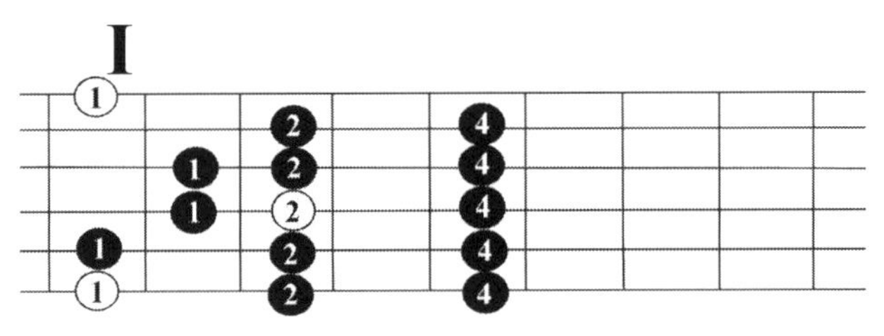

IV

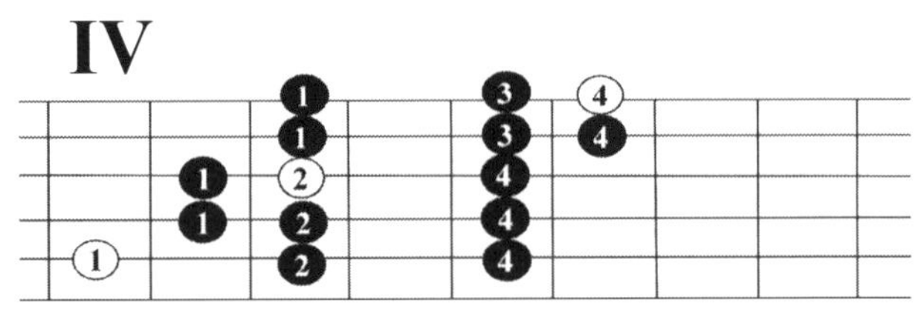

V

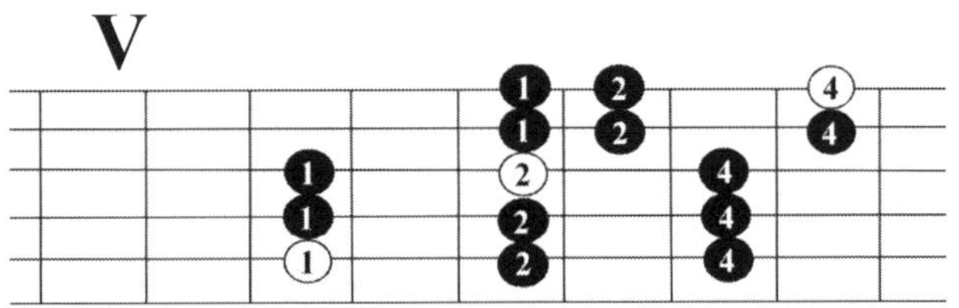

All Keys (iii)

I

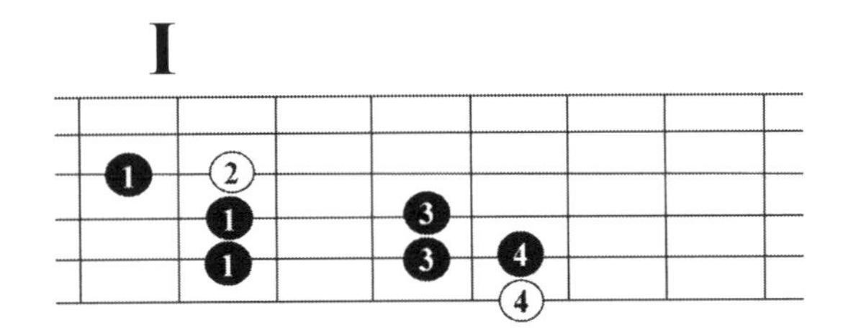

IV

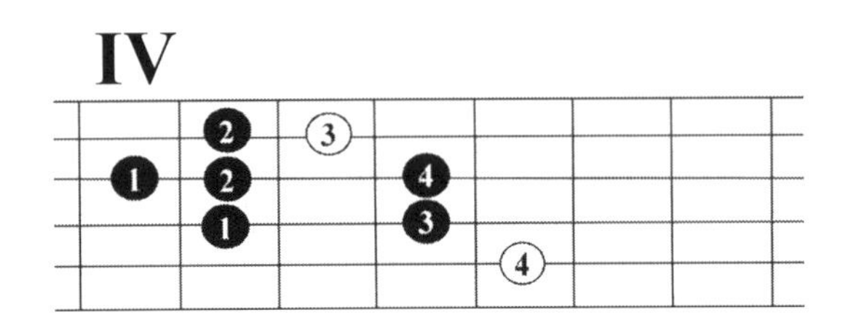

V

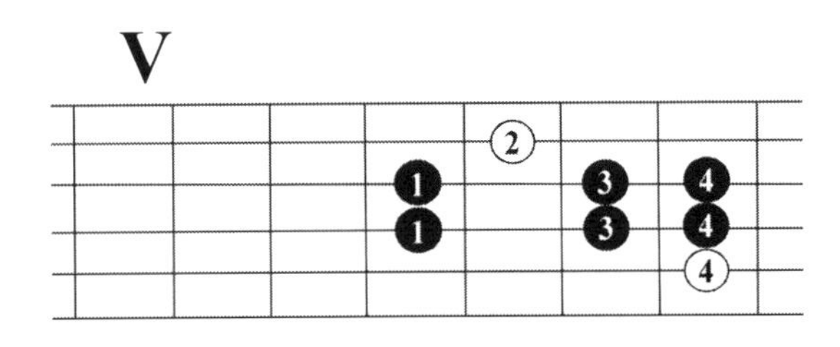

All Keys (iv)

I

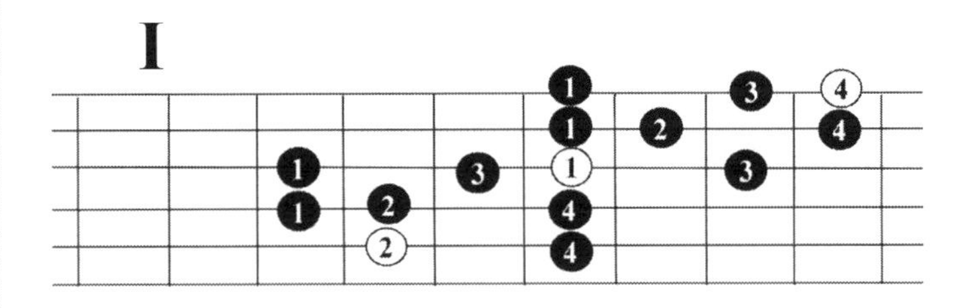

IV

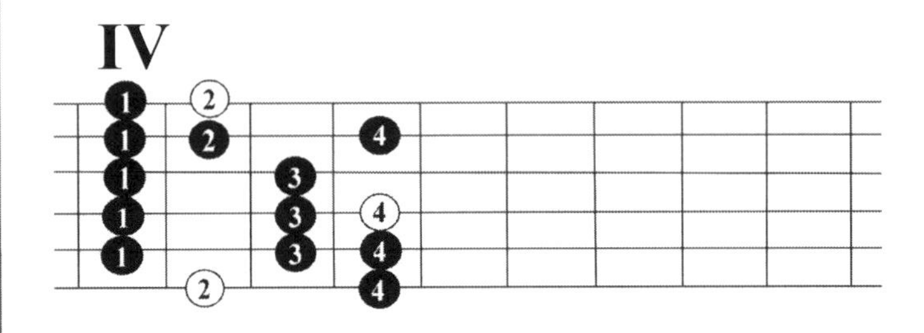

V

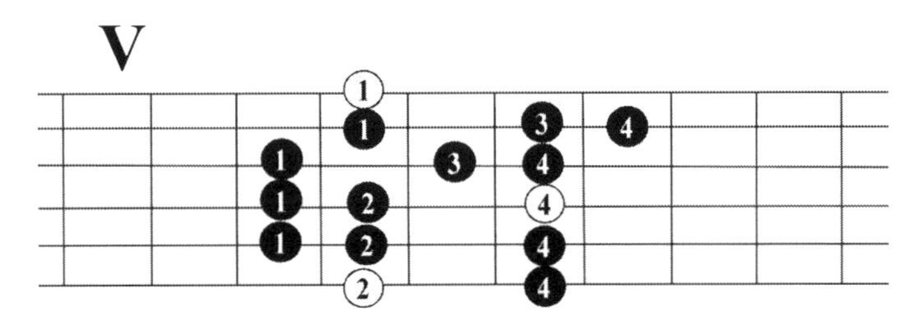

All Keys (v)

I

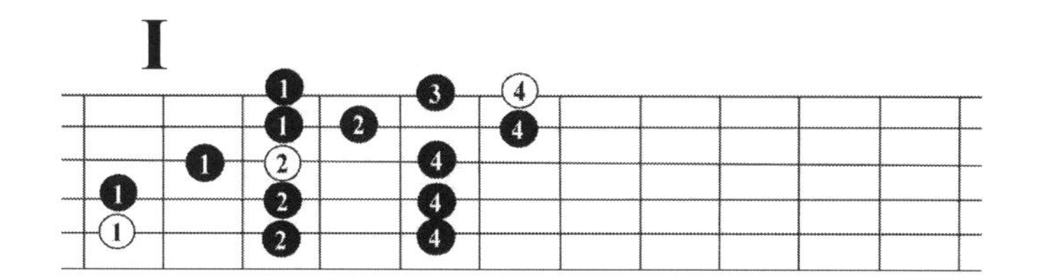

IV

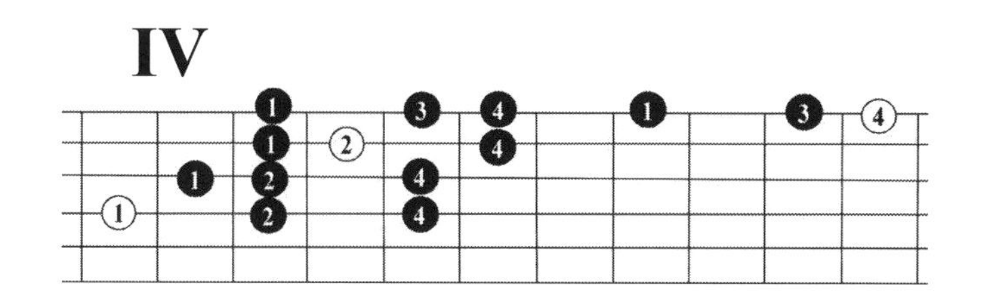

V

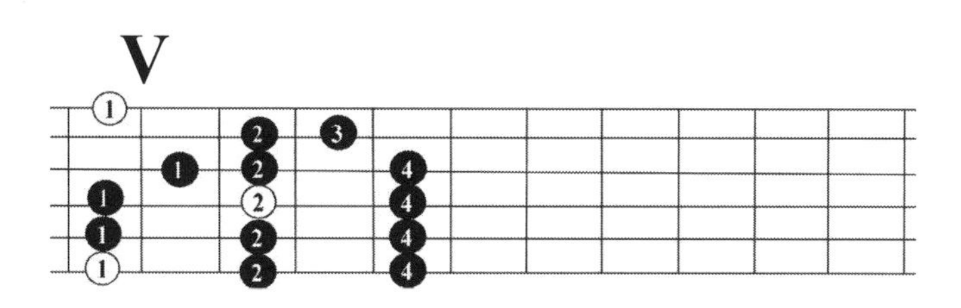

All Keys (vi)

I

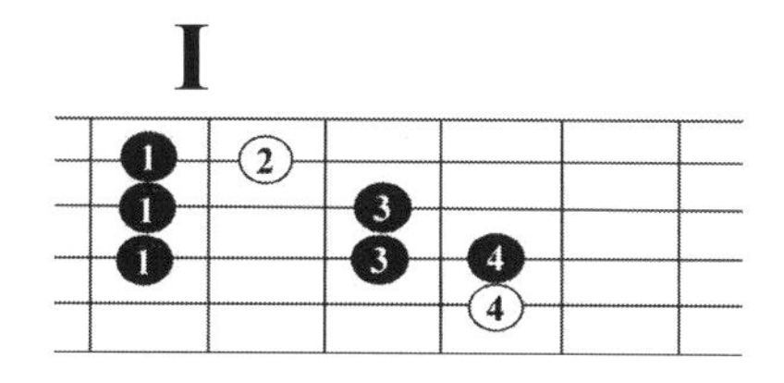

IV

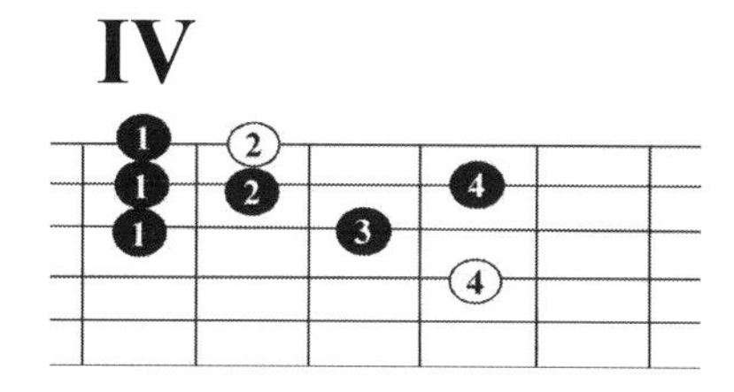

V

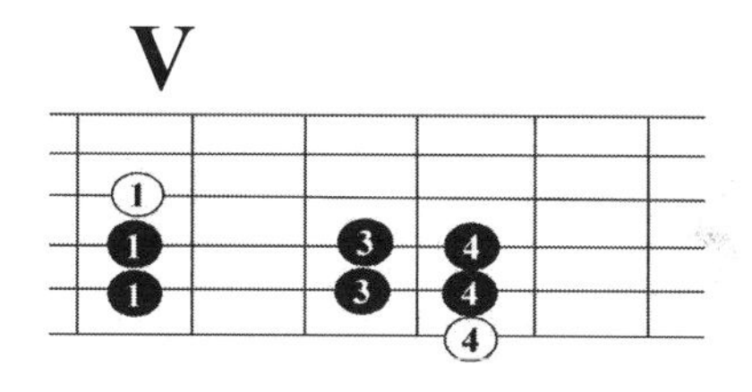

All Keys (vii)

I

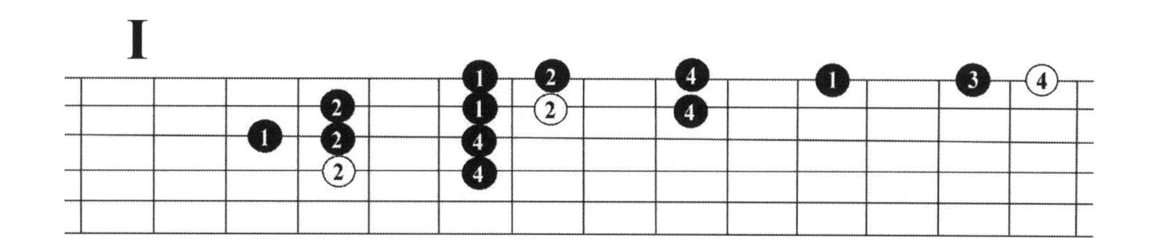

IV

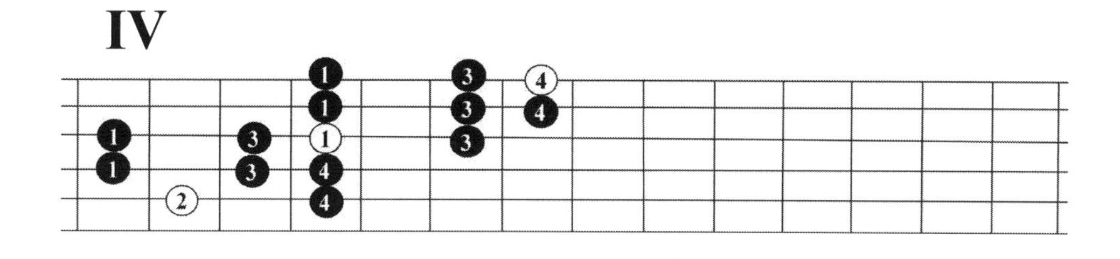

V

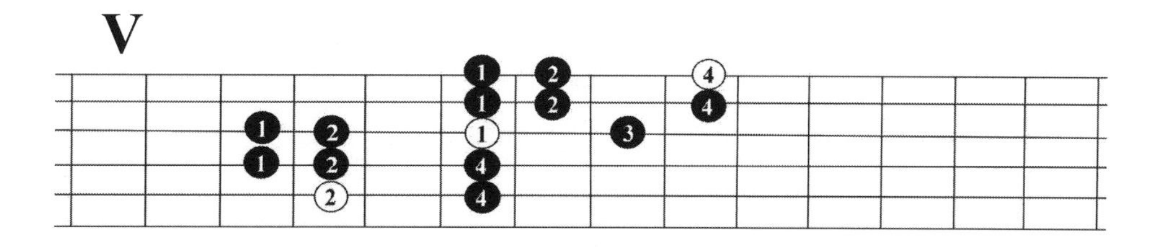

All Keys (viii)

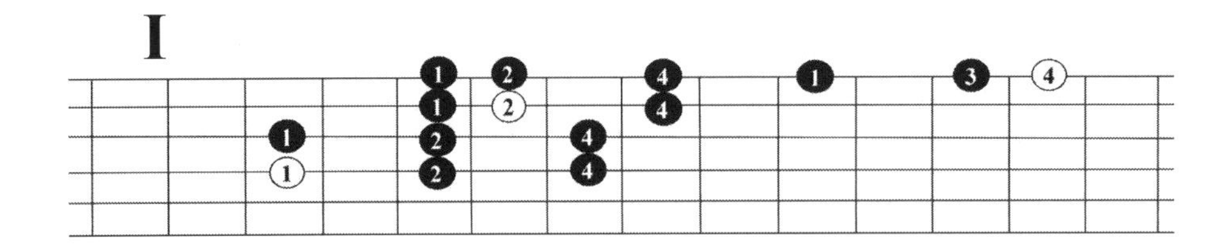

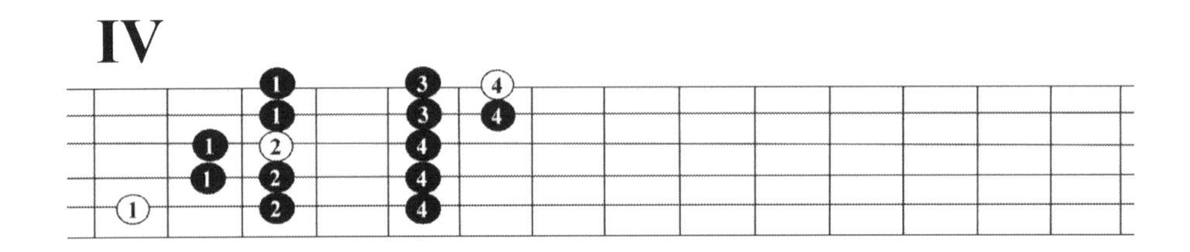

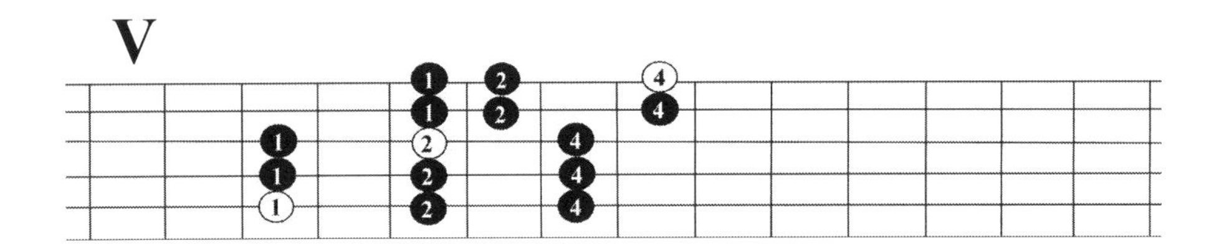

All Keys (ix)

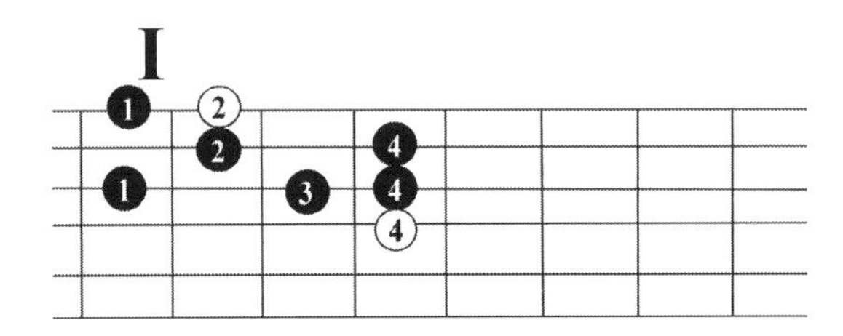

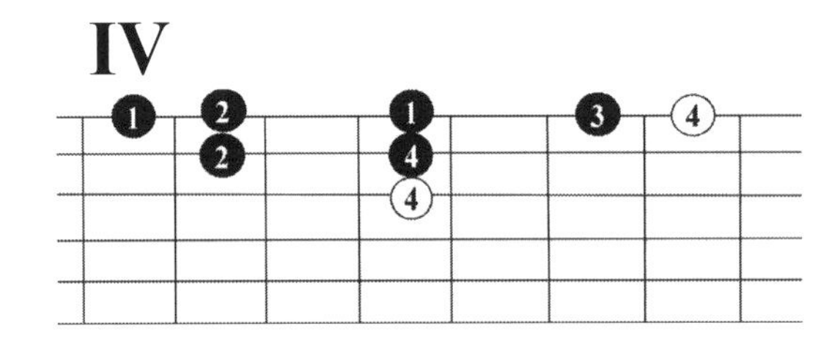

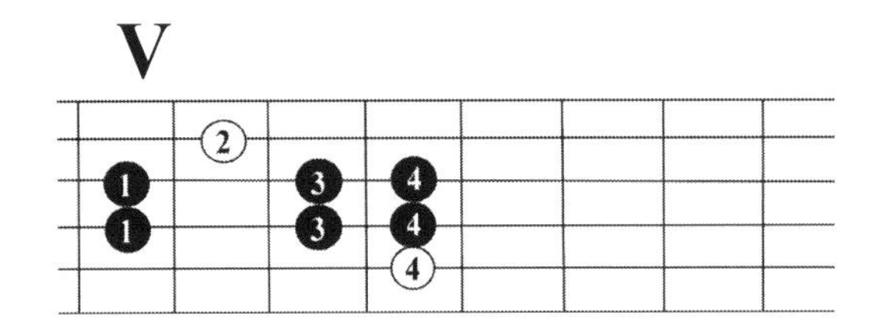

PART THIRTY-THREE

ii - V - I

MAJOR KEYS
MODES

Key of C

D Dorian - (Chord of D minor/Dm7)

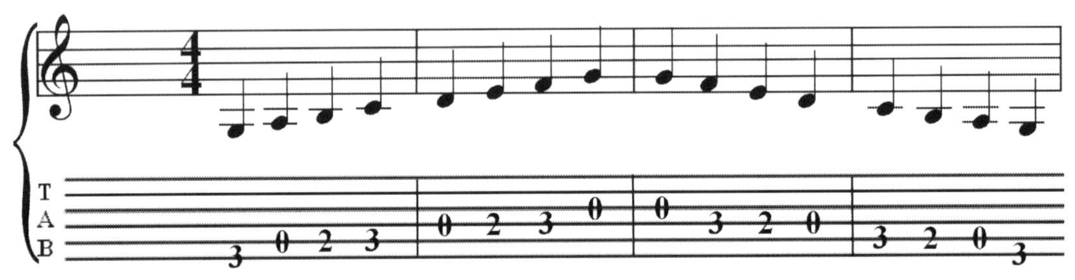

G Mixolydian (i) - (Chord of G Major/G7)

G Mixolydian (ii) - (Chord of G Major/G7)

C Ionian - (Chord of C Major/CM7)

Key of G

A Dorian (i) - (Chord of A minor/Am7)

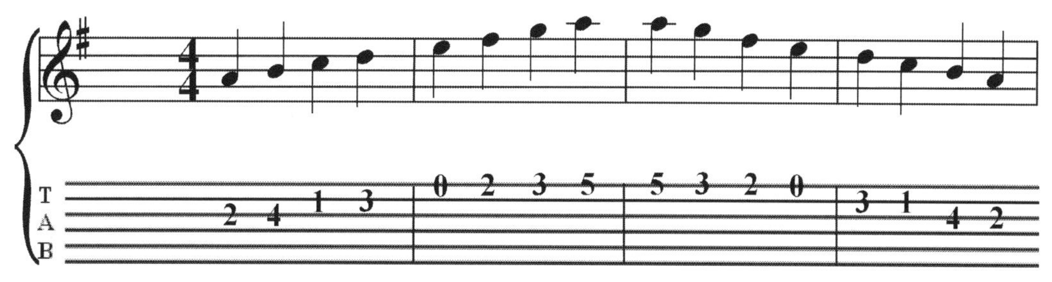

A Dorian (ii) - (Chord of A minor/Am7)

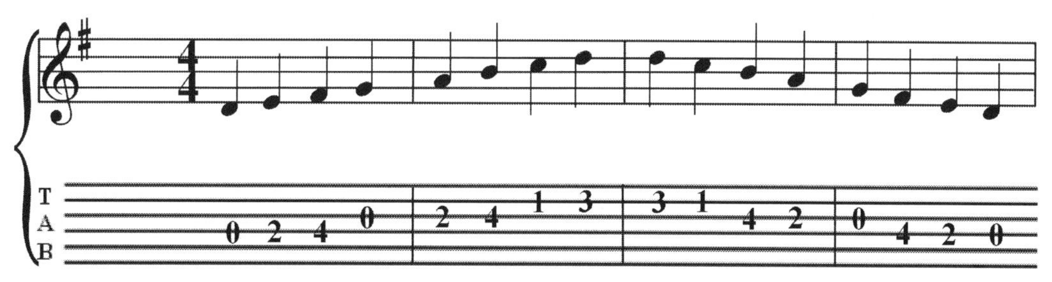

D Mixolydian - (Chord of D Major/D7)

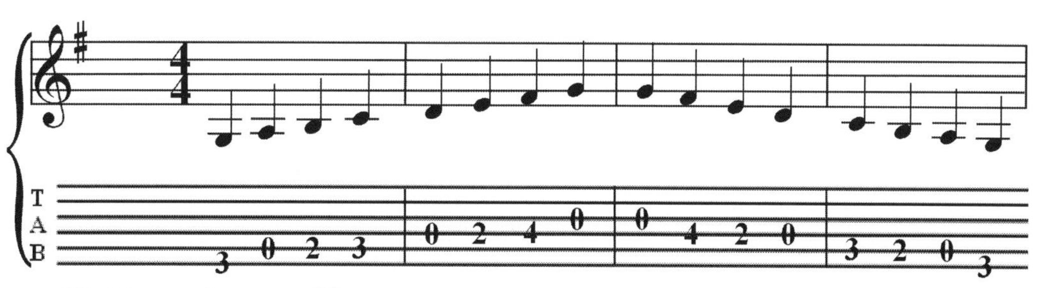

G Ionian (i) - (Chord of G Major/GM7)

G Ionian (ii) - (Chord of G Major/GM7)

Key of D

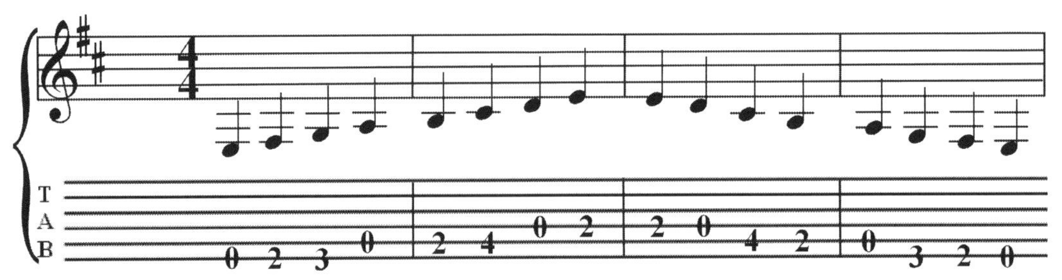

E Dorian (i) - (Chord of E minor/Em7)

E Dorian (ii) - (Chord of E minor/Em7)

A Mixolydian (i) - (Chord of A Major/A7)

A Mixolydian (ii) - (Chord of A Major/A7)

D Ionian - (Chord of D Major/DM7)

Key of A

B Dorian - (Chord of B minor/Bm7)

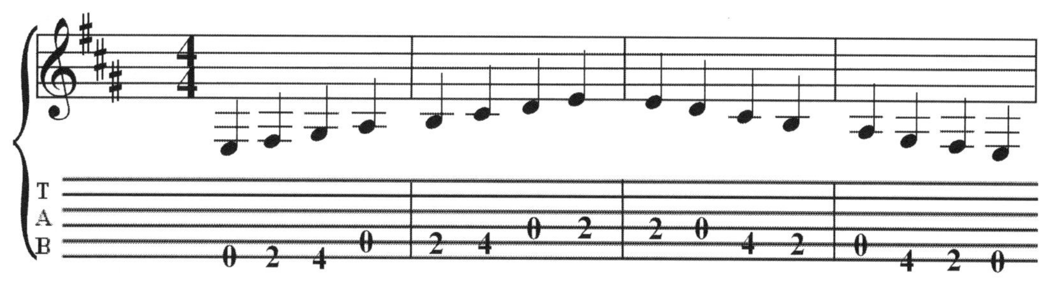

E Mixolydian (i) - (Chord of E Major/E7)

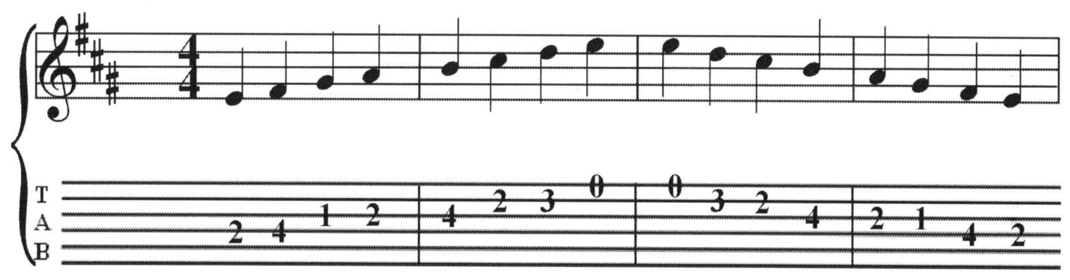

E Mixolydian (ii) - (Chord of E Major/E7)

A Ionian (i) - (Chord of A Major/AM7)

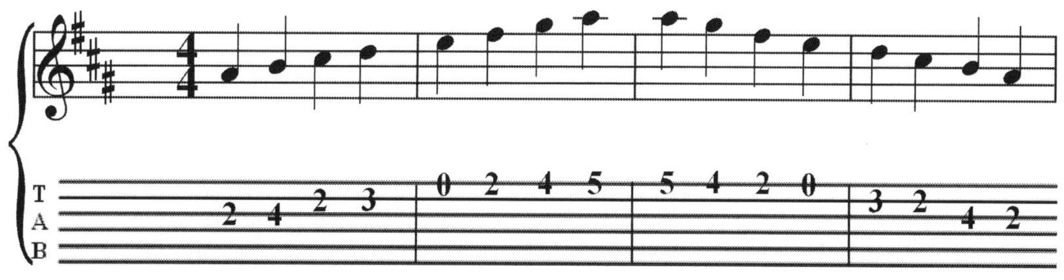

A Ionian (ii) - (Chord of A Major/AM7)

Key of E

F# Dorian (i) - (Chord of F# minor/F#m7)

F# Dorian (ii) - (Chord of F# minor/F#m7)

B Mixolydian - (Chord of B Major/B7)

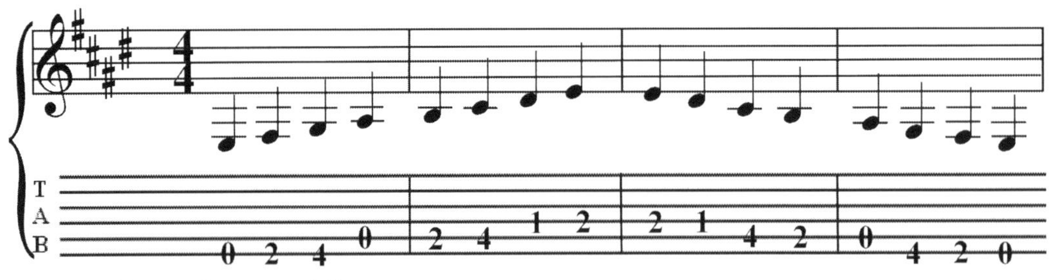

E Ionian (i) - (Chord of E Major/EM7)

E Ionian (ii) - (Chord of E Major/EM7)

Key of B

C# Dorian (ii) - (Chord of C# minor/C#m7)

F# Mixolydian (i) - (Chord of F# Major/F#7)

F# Mixolydian (ii) - (Chord of F# Major/F#7)

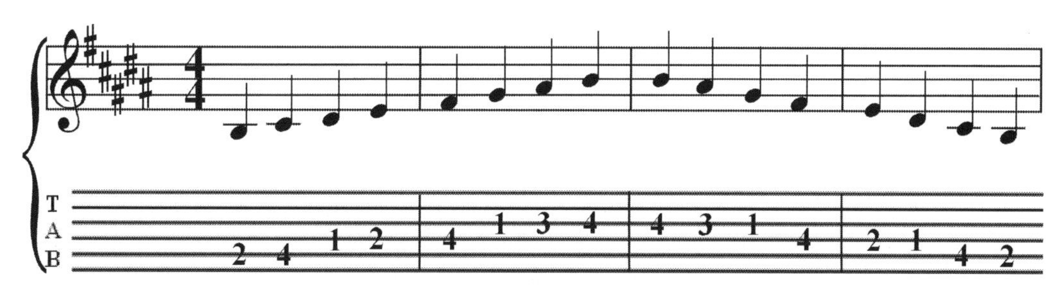

B Ionian - (Chord of B Major/BM7)

Key of F#

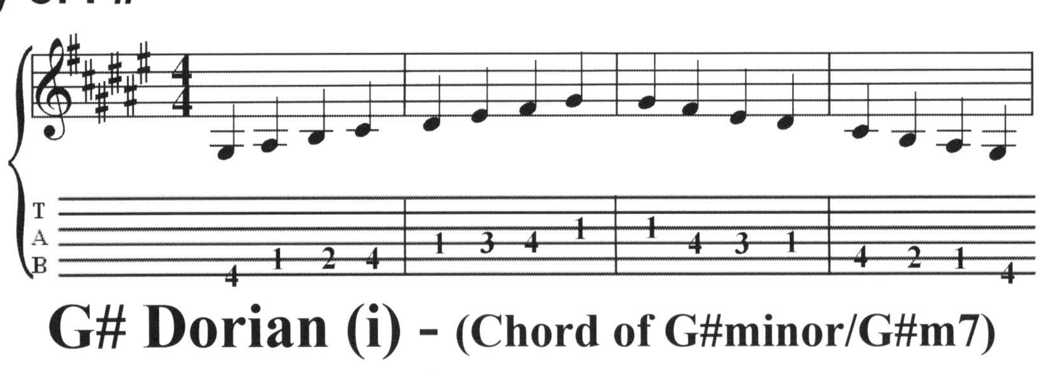

G# Dorian (i) - (Chord of G#minor/G#m7)

G# Dorian (ii) - (Chord of G#minor/G#m7)

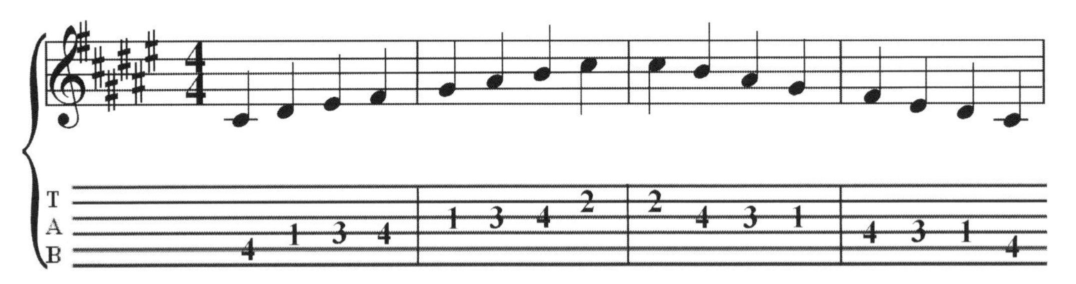

C# Mixolydian - (Chord of C# Major/C#7)

F# Ionian (i) - (Chord of F# Major/F#M7)

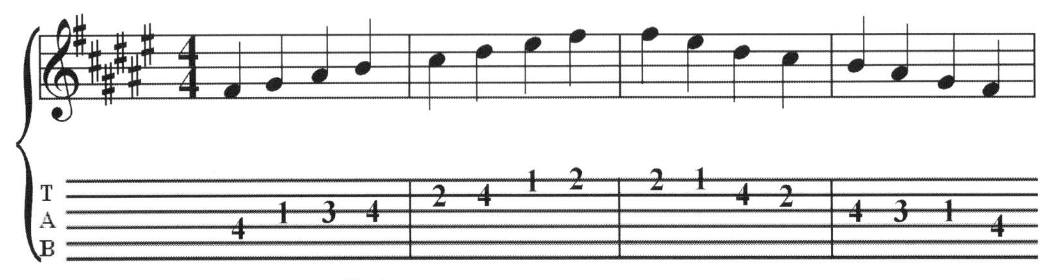

F# Ionian (ii) - (Chord of F# Major/F#M7)

Key of C#

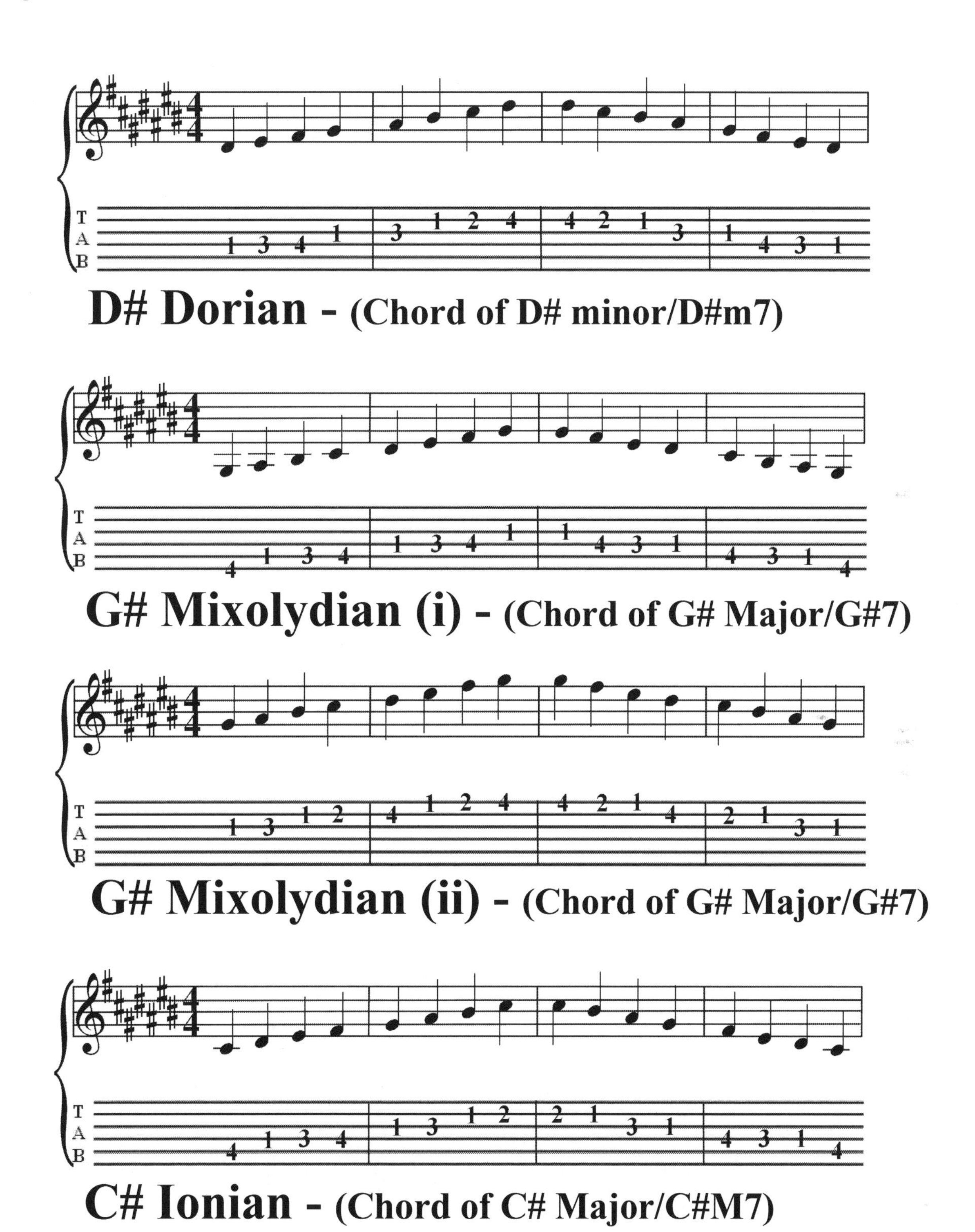

D# Dorian - (Chord of D# minor/D#m7)

G# Mixolydian (i) - (Chord of G# Major/G#7)

G# Mixolydian (ii) - (Chord of G# Major/G#7)

C# Ionian - (Chord of C# Major/C#M7)

Key of A♭

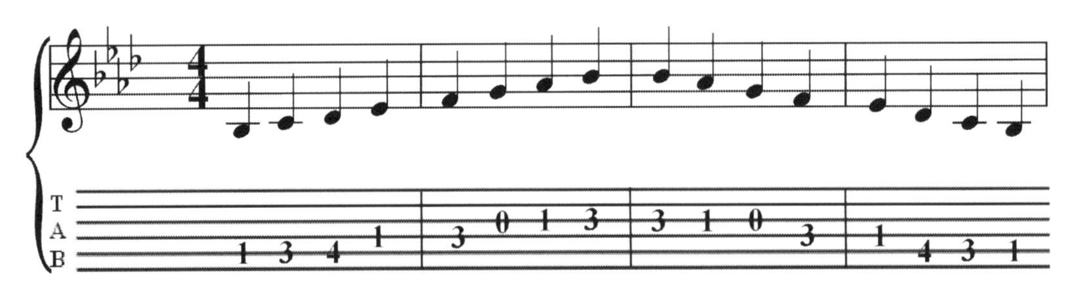

B♭ Dorian - (Chord of B♭ minor/B♭m7)

E♭ Mixolydian - (Chord of E♭ Major/E♭7)

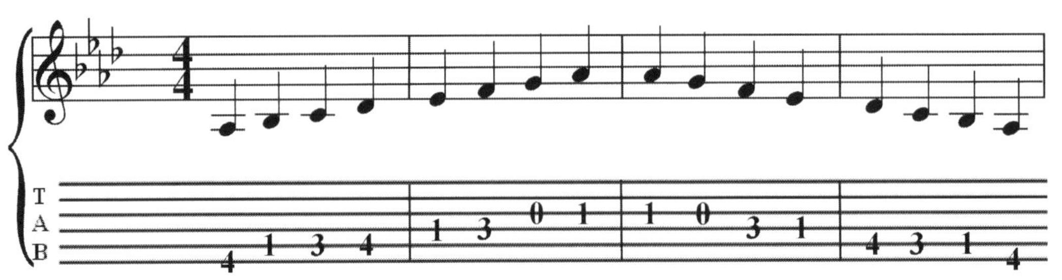

A♭ Ionian (i) - (Chord of A♭ Major/A♭M7)

A♭ Ionian (ii) - (Chord of A♭ Major/A♭M7)

Key of E♭

F Dorian (i) - (Chord of Fminor/Fm7)

F Dorian (ii) - (Chord of Fminor/Fm7)

B♭ Mixolydian - (Chord of B♭ Major/B♭7)

E♭ Ionian - (Chord of E♭ Major/E♭M7)

Key of B♭

C Dorian - (Chord of Cminor/Cm7)

F Mixolydian (i) - (Chord of F Major/F7)

F Mixolydian (ii) - (Chord of F Major/F7)

B♭ Ionian - (Chord of B♭ Major/B♭M7)

Key of F

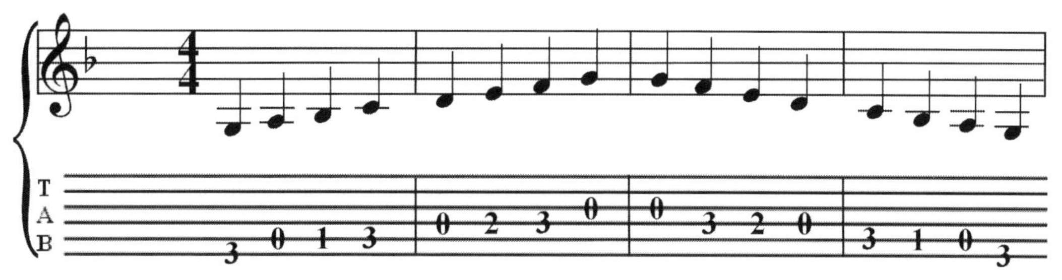

G Dorian (i) - (Chord of Gminor/Gm7)

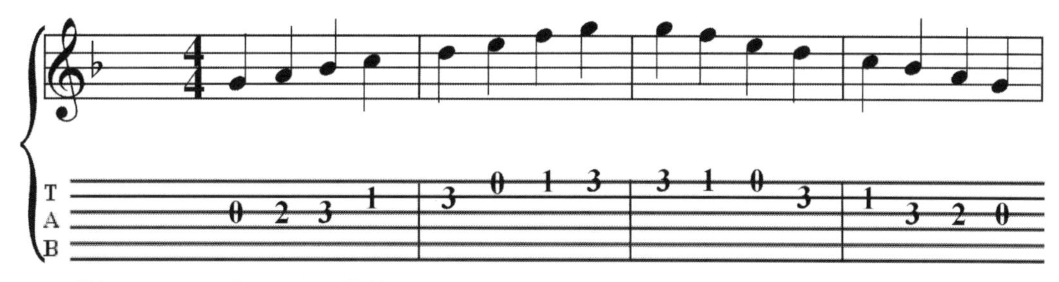

G Dorian (ii) - (Chord of Gminor/Gm7)

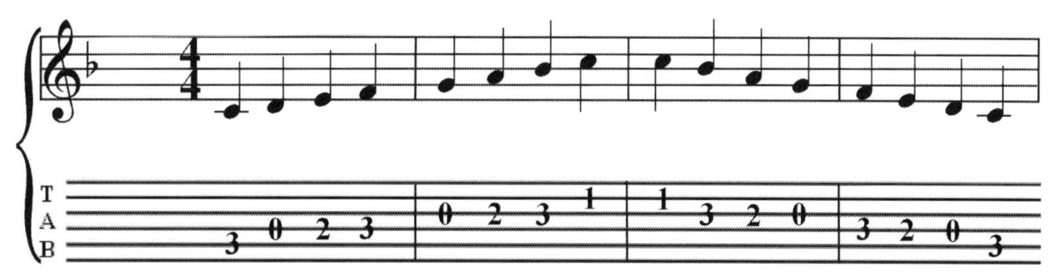

C Mixolydian - (Chord of C Major/C7)

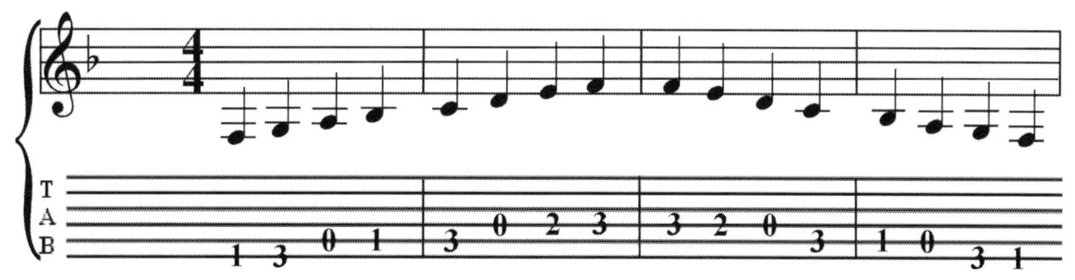

F Ionian (i) - (Chord of F Major/FM7)

F Ionian (ii) - (Chord of F Major/FM7)

All Keys (i)

ii (Dorian)

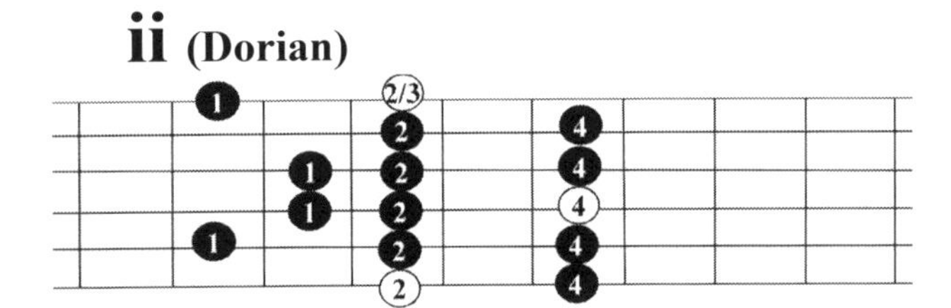

V (Mixolydian)

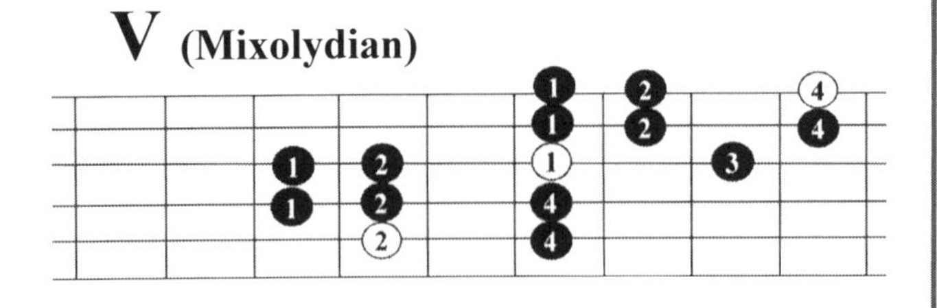

I (Ionian / Major Scale)

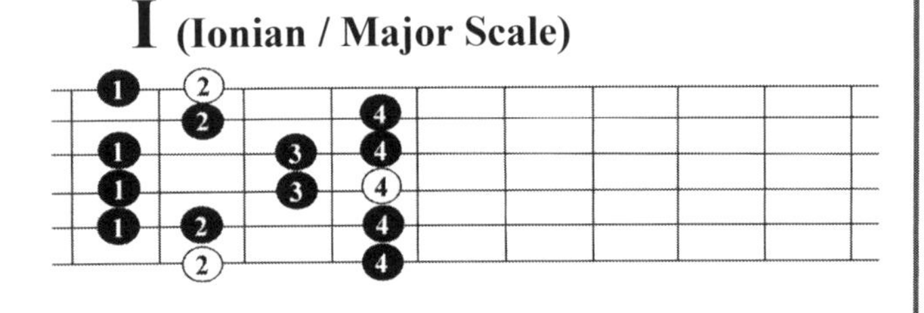

All Keys (ii)

ii

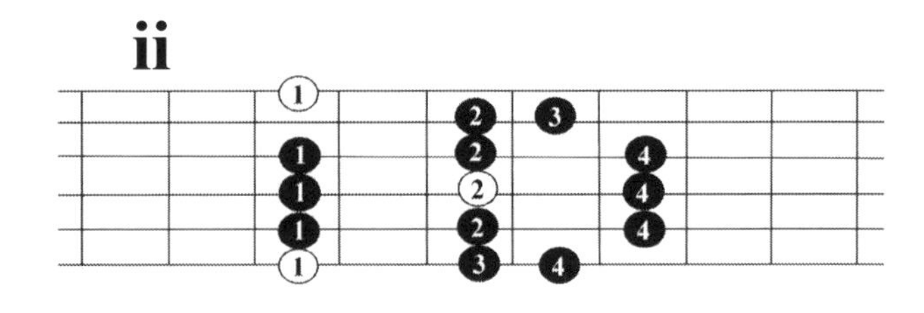

V

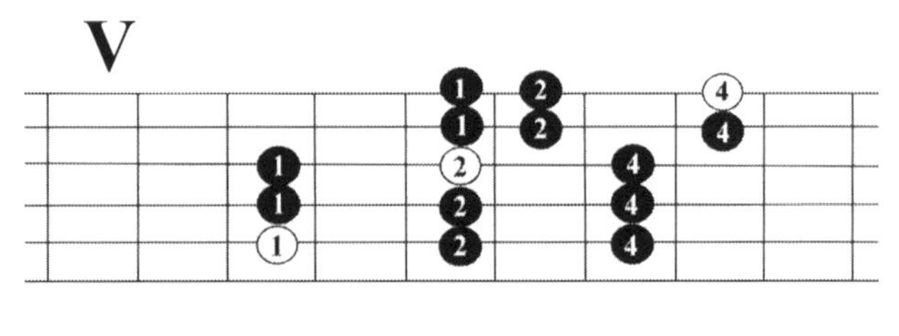

I

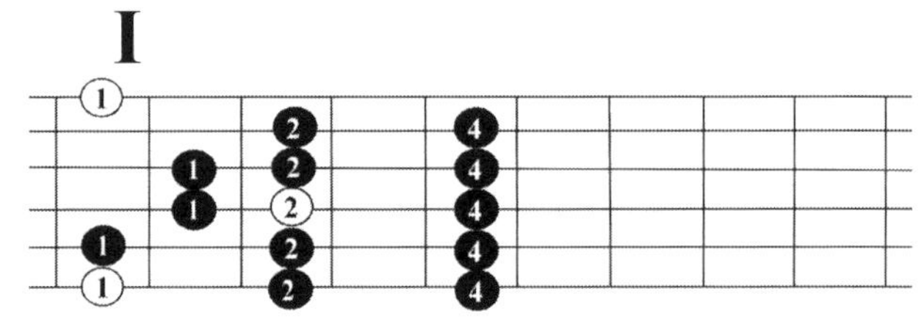

All Keys (iii)

ii

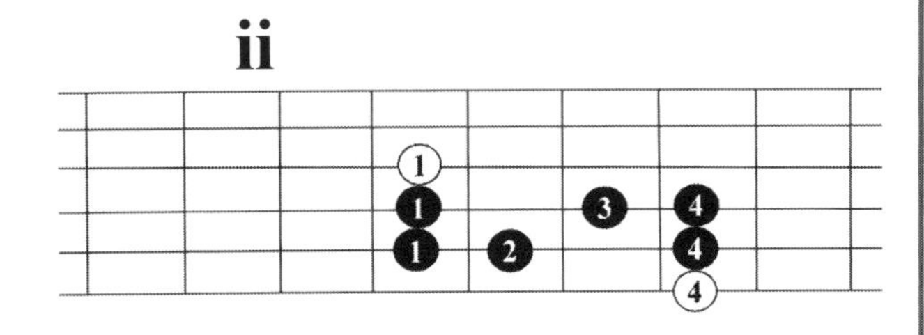

V

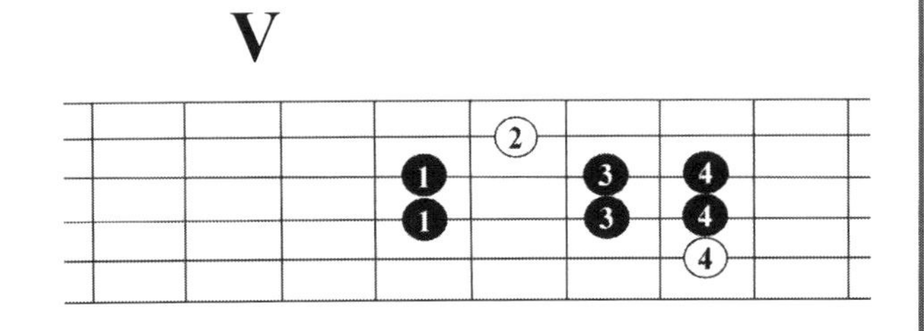

I

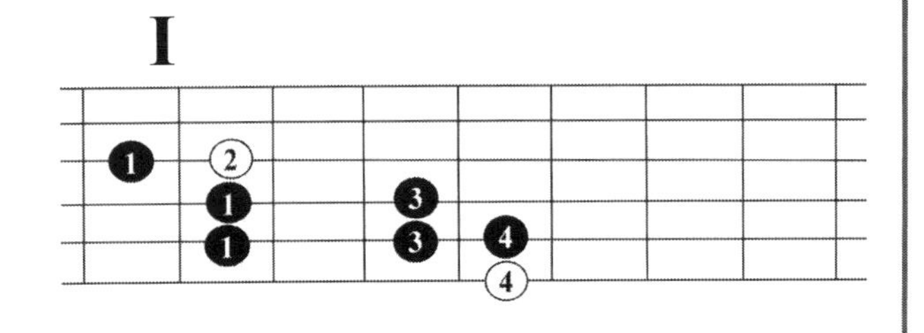

All Keys (iv)

ii

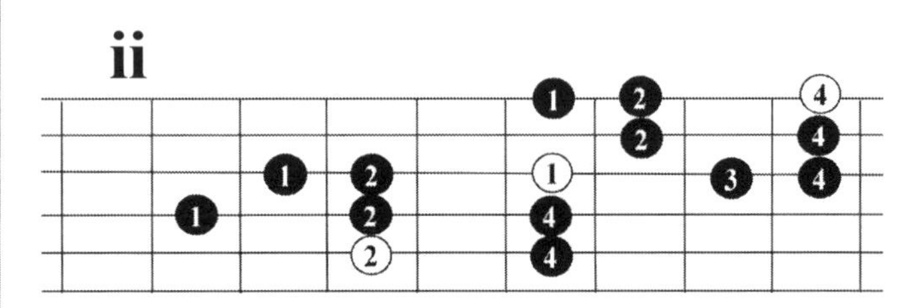

V

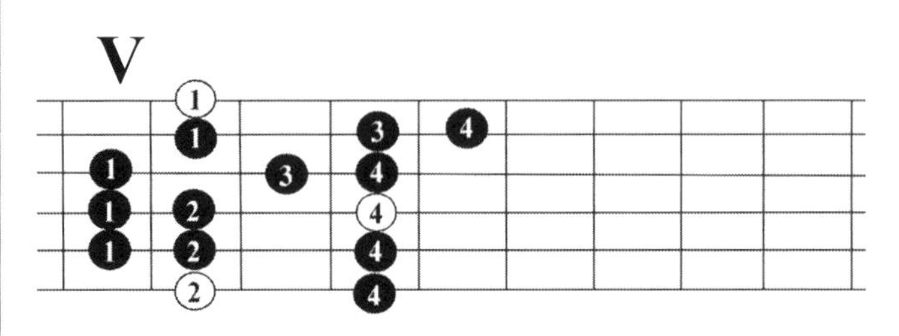

I

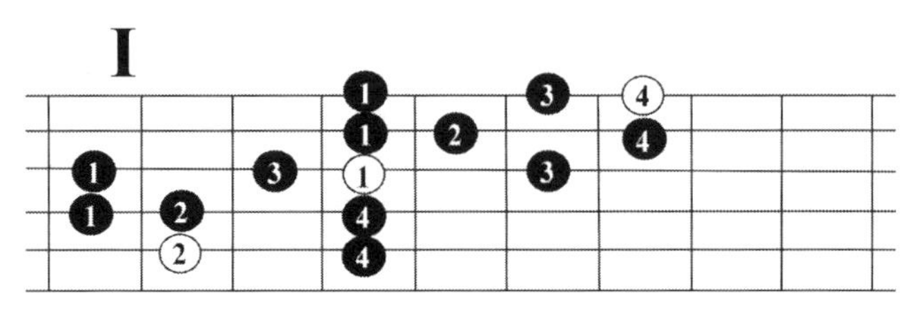

All Keys (v)

ii

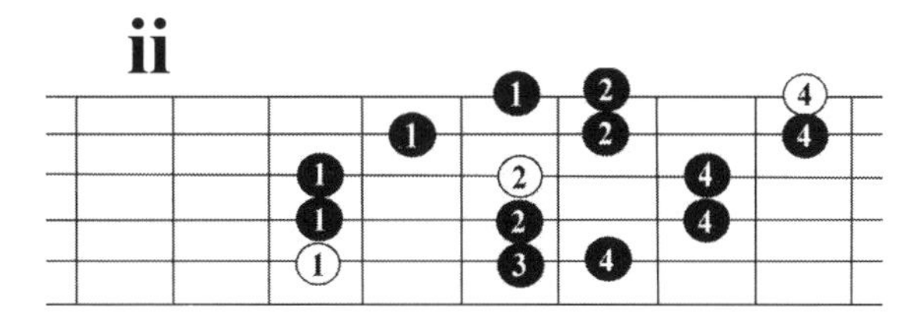

V

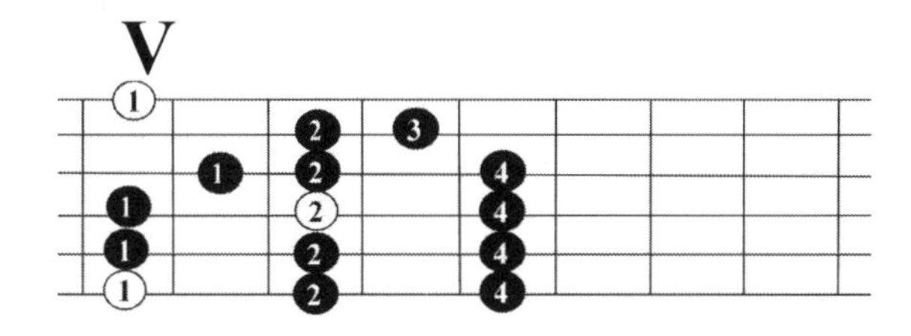

I

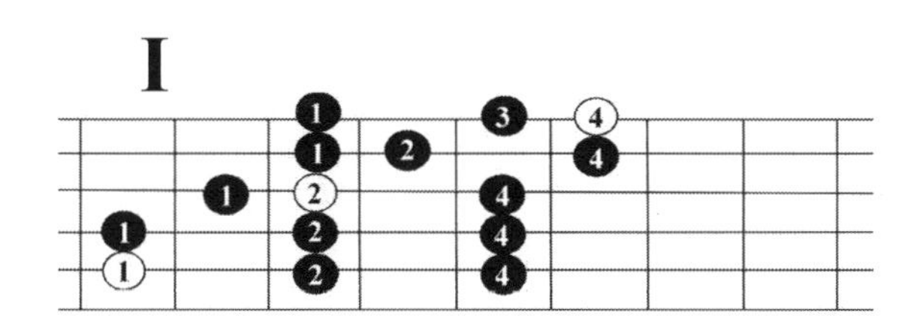

All Keys (vi)

ii

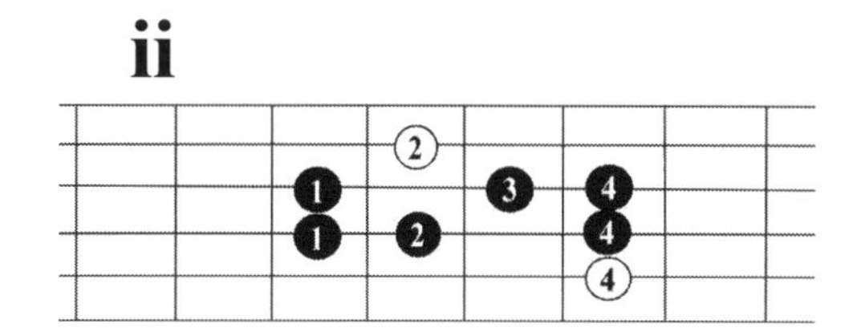

V

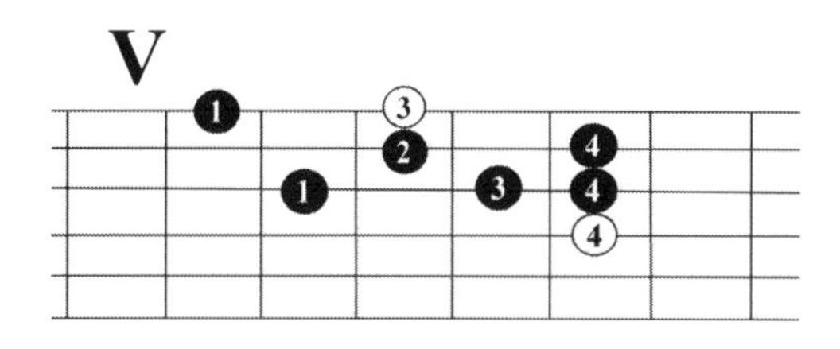

I

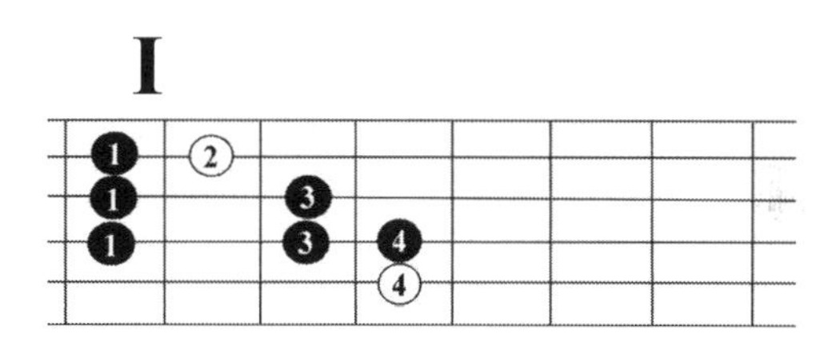

All Keys (vii)

ii

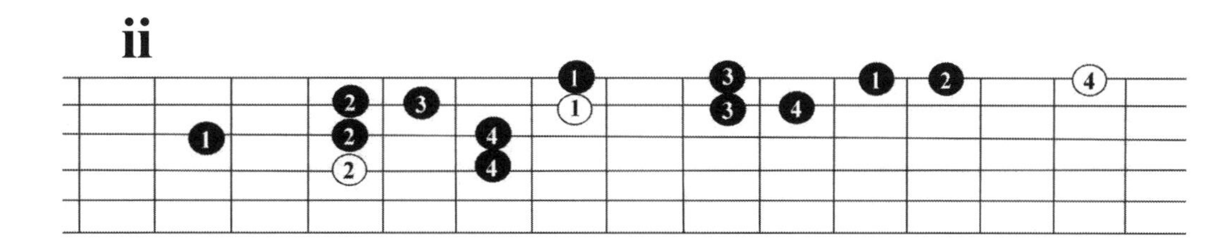

V

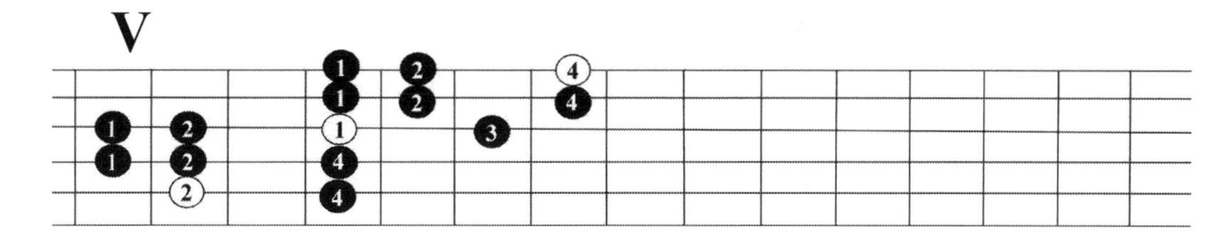

I

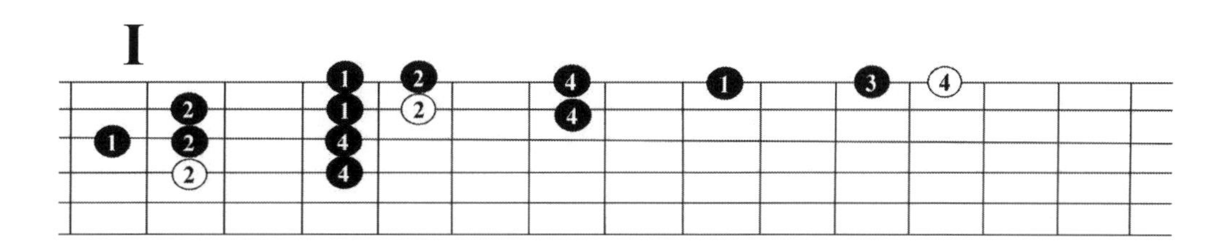

All Keys (viii)

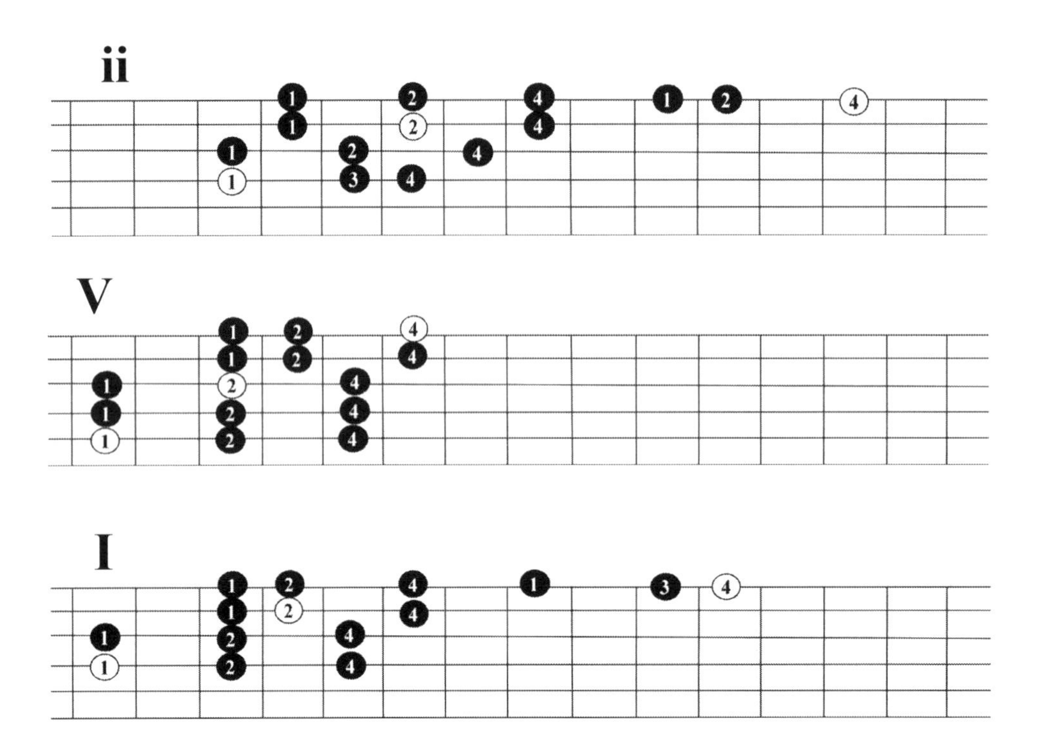

All Keys (ix)

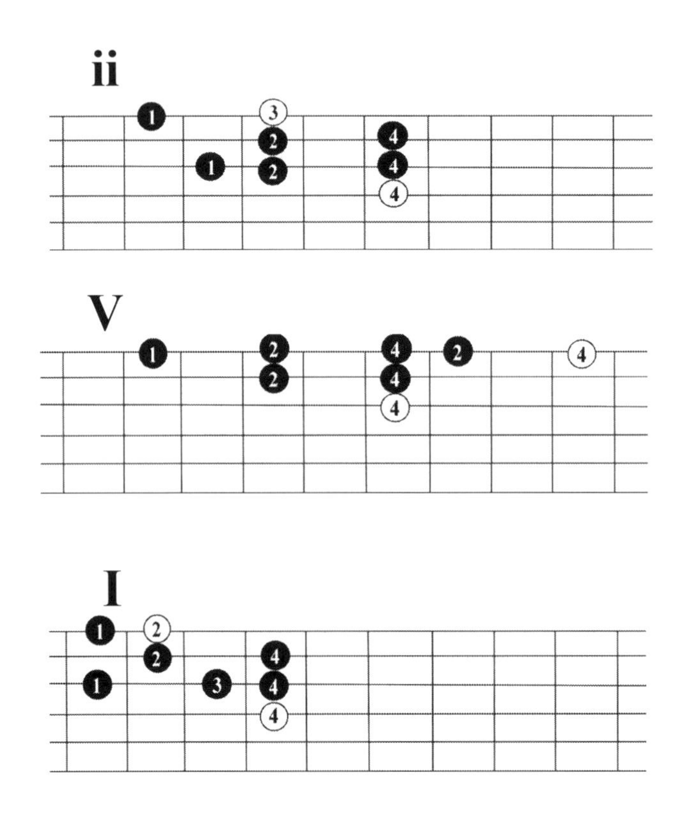

PART THIRTY-FOUR

vi - ii - V - I

MAJOR KEYS
MODES

Key of C

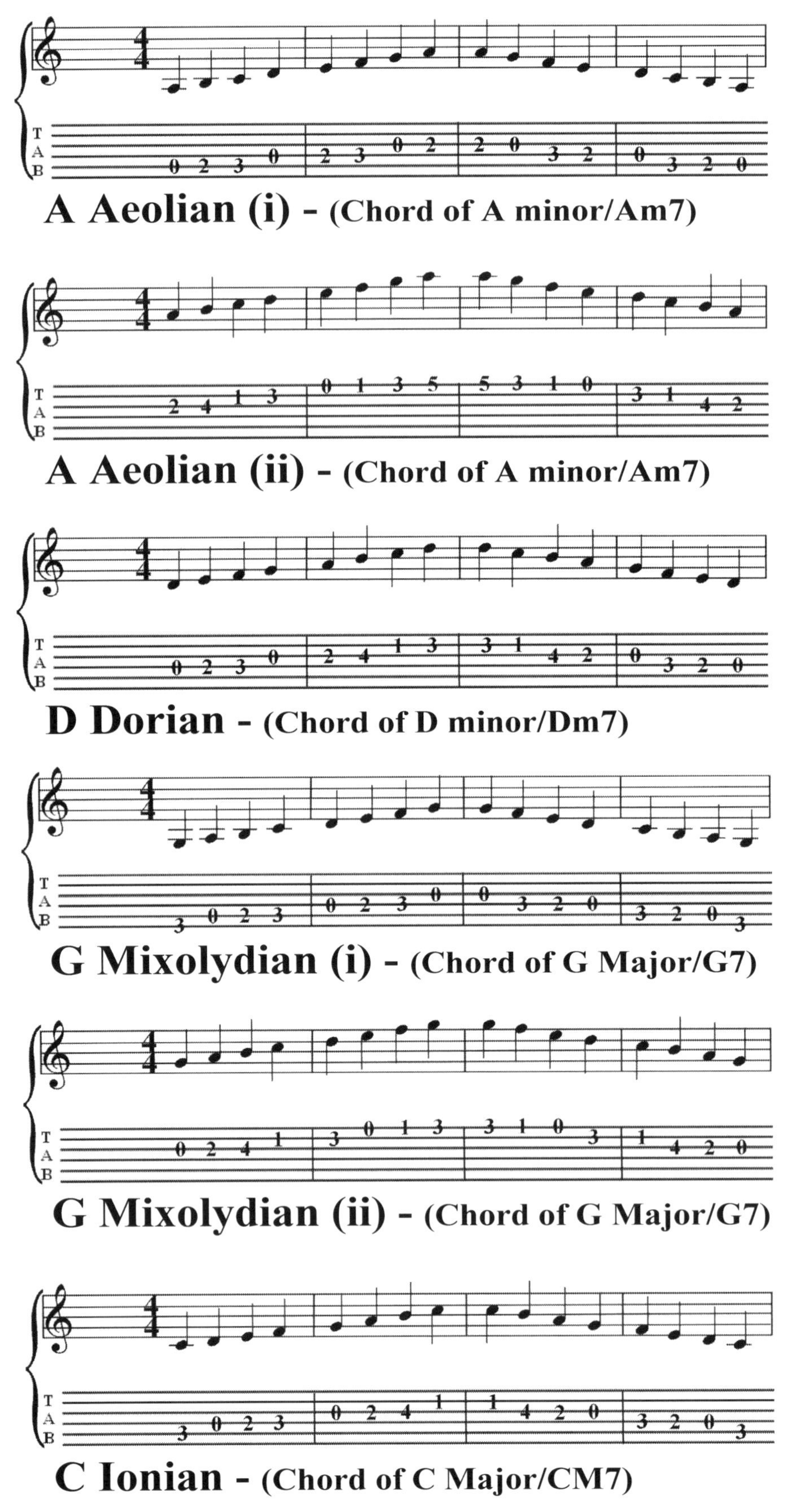

A Aeolian (i) - (Chord of A minor/Am7)

A Aeolian (ii) - (Chord of A minor/Am7)

D Dorian - (Chord of D minor/Dm7)

G Mixolydian (i) - (Chord of G Major/G7)

G Mixolydian (ii) - (Chord of G Major/G7)

C Ionian - (Chord of C Major/CM7)

Key of G

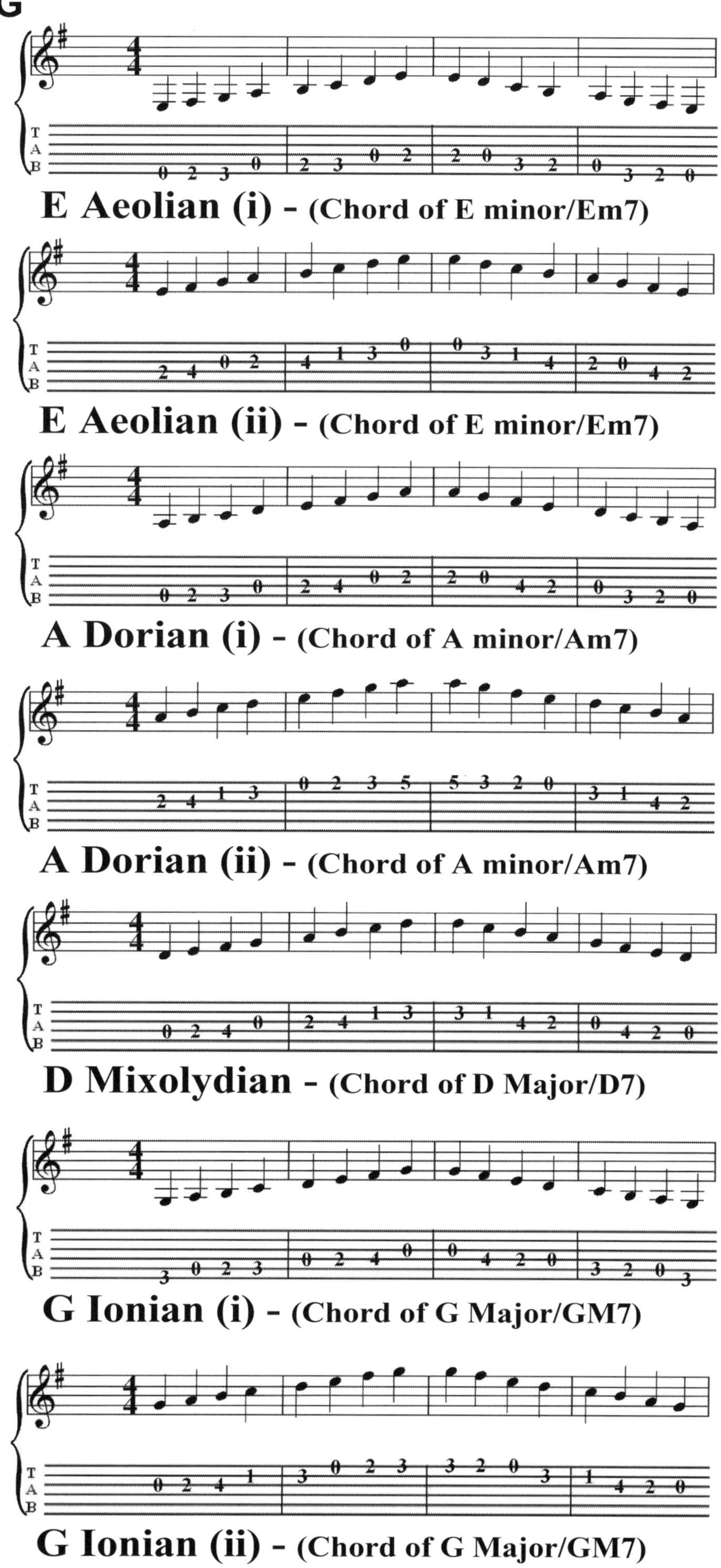
E Aeolian (i) - (Chord of E minor/Em7)
E Aeolian (ii) - (Chord of E minor/Em7)
A Dorian (i) - (Chord of A minor/Am7)
A Dorian (ii) - (Chord of A minor/Am7)
D Mixolydian - (Chord of D Major/D7)
G Ionian (i) - (Chord of G Major/GM7)
G Ionian (ii) - (Chord of G Major/GM7)

Key of D

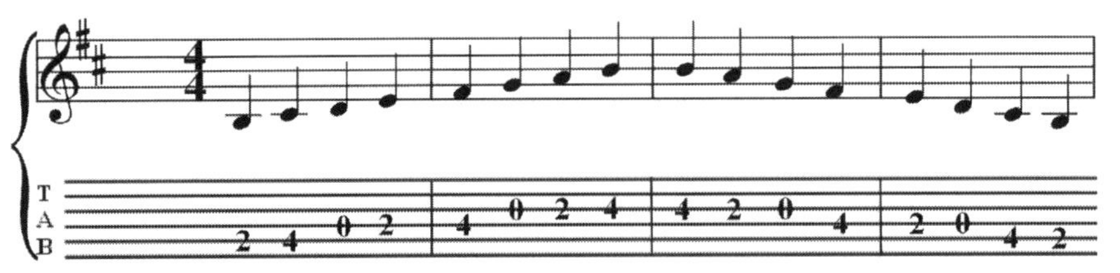

B Aeolian - (Chord of B minor/Bm7)

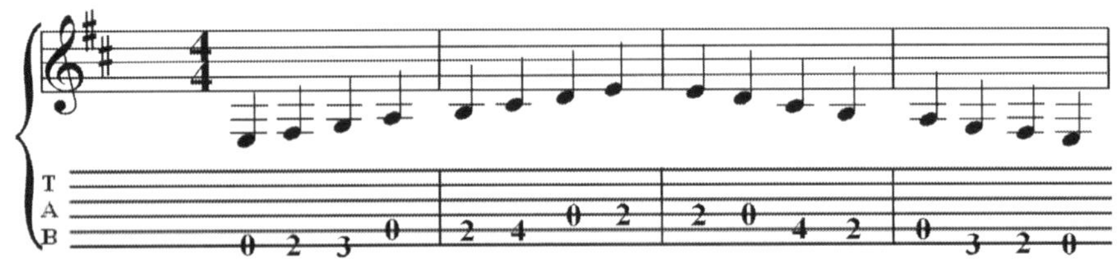

E Dorian (i) - (Chord of E minor/Em7)

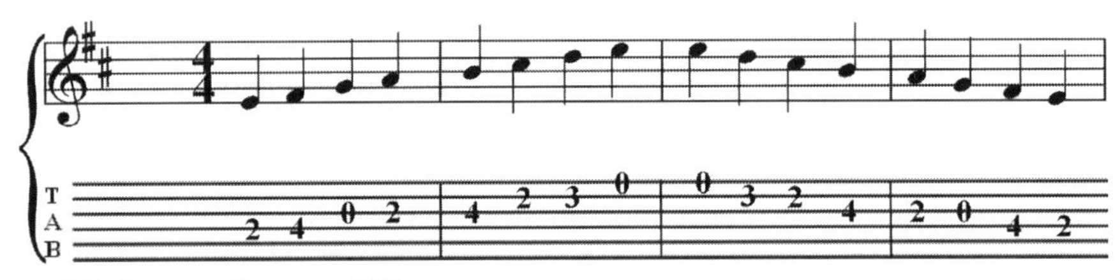

E Dorian (ii) - (Chord of E minor/Em7)

A Mixolydian (i) - (Chord of A Major/A7)

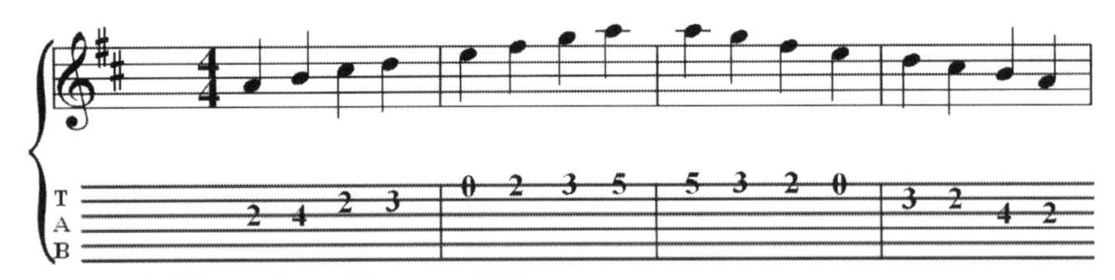

A Mixolydian (ii) - (Chord of A Major/A7)

D Ionian - (Chord of D Major/DM7)

Key of A

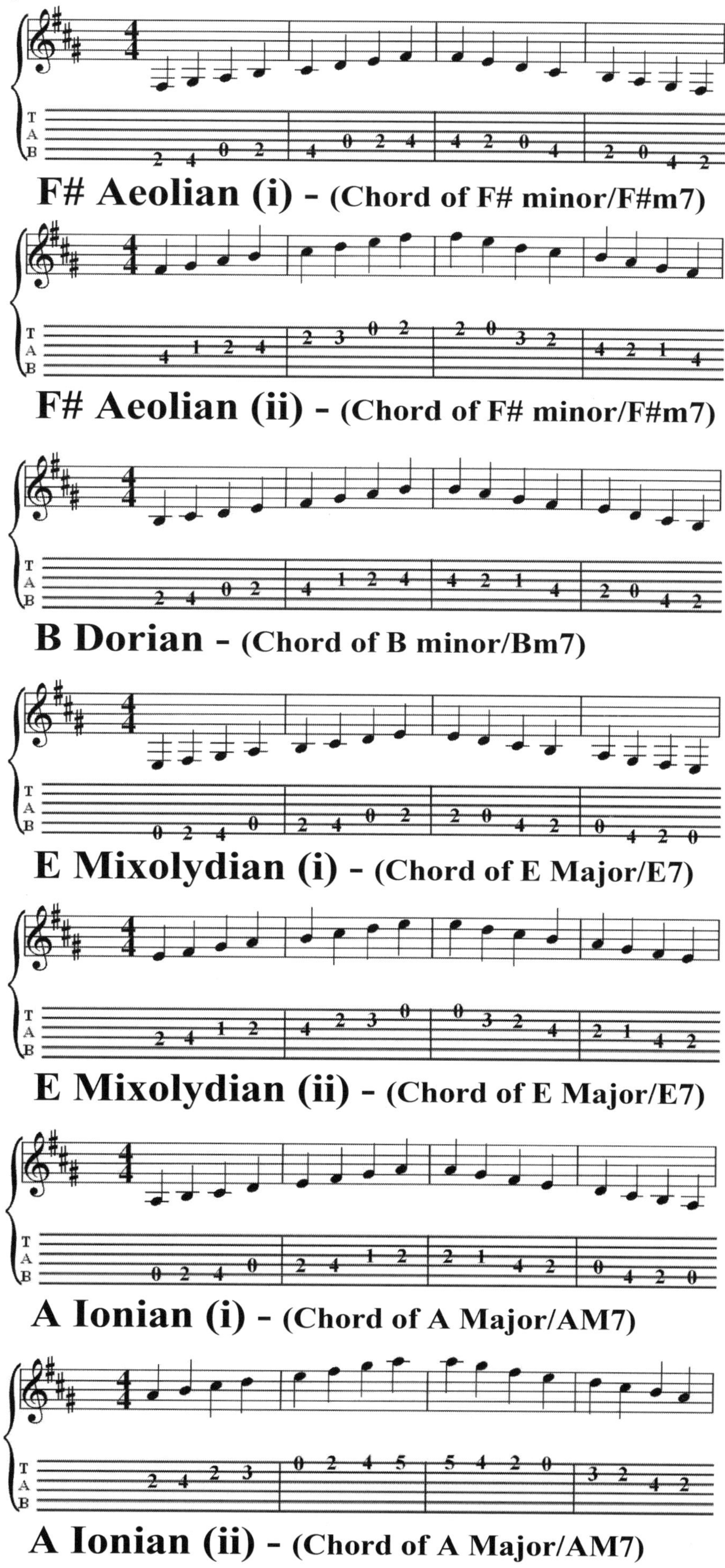
F# Aeolian (i) - (Chord of F# minor/F#m7)
F# Aeolian (ii) - (Chord of F# minor/F#m7)
B Dorian - (Chord of B minor/Bm7)
E Mixolydian (i) - (Chord of E Major/E7)
E Mixolydian (ii) - (Chord of E Major/E7)
A Ionian (i) - (Chord of A Major/AM7)
A Ionian (ii) - (Chord of A Major/AM7)

Key of E

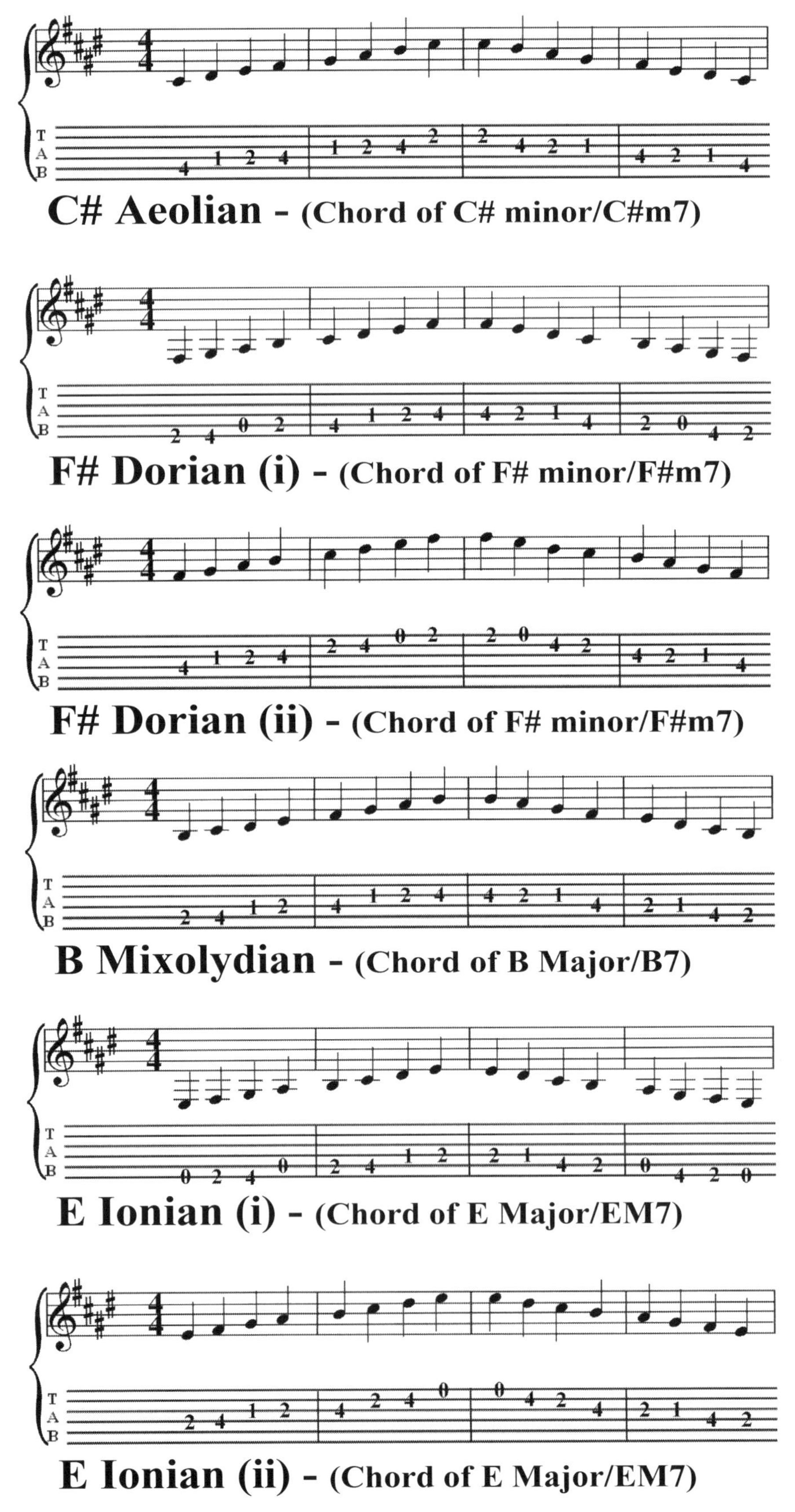

C# Aeolian - (Chord of C# minor/C#m7)

F# Dorian (i) - (Chord of F# minor/F#m7)

F# Dorian (ii) - (Chord of F# minor/F#m7)

B Mixolydian - (Chord of B Major/B7)

E Ionian (i) - (Chord of E Major/EM7)

E Ionian (ii) - (Chord of E Major/EM7)

Key of B

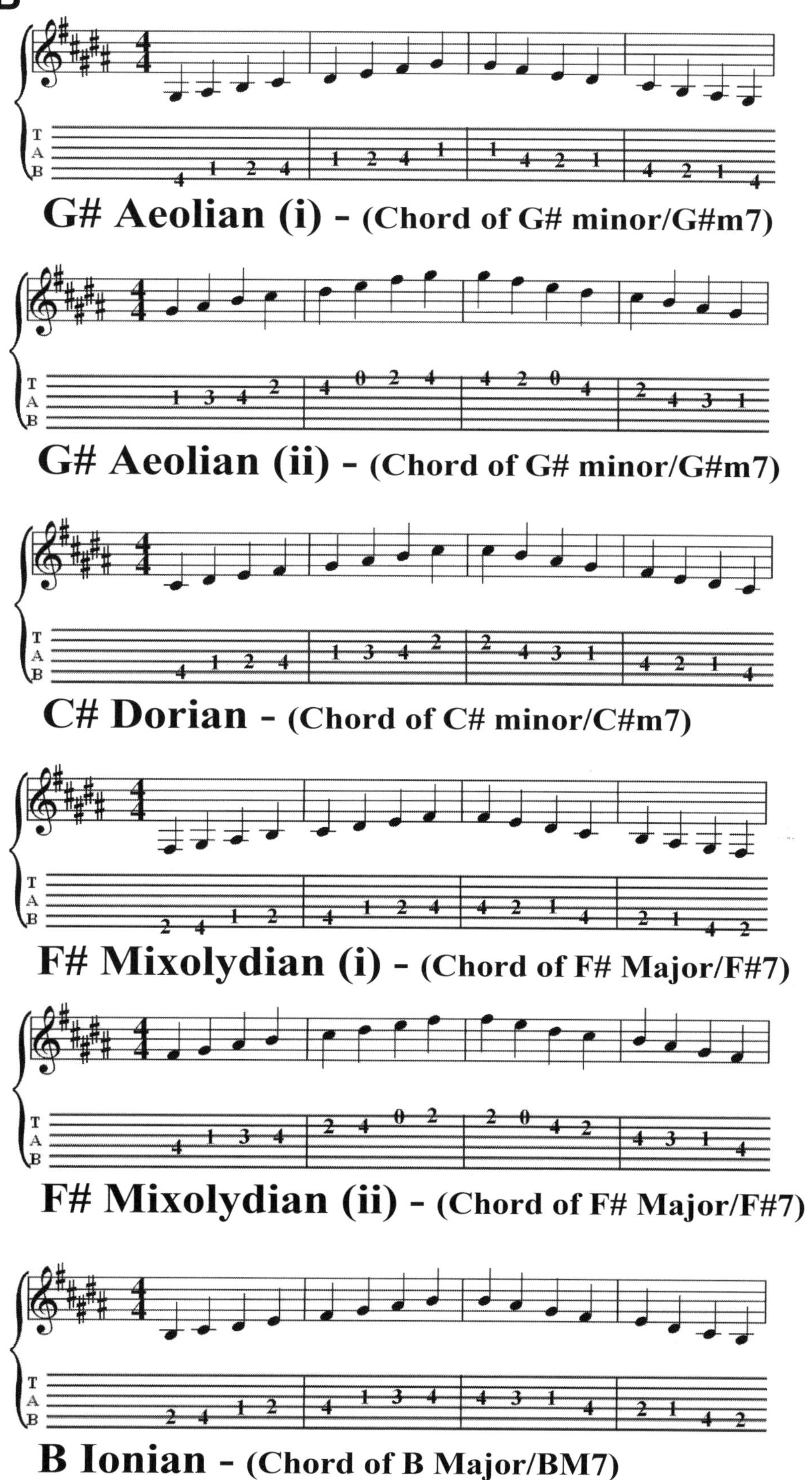

G# Aeolian (i) - (Chord of G# minor/G#m7)

G# Aeolian (ii) - (Chord of G# minor/G#m7)

C# Dorian - (Chord of C# minor/C#m7)

F# Mixolydian (i) - (Chord of F# Major/F#7)

F# Mixolydian (ii) - (Chord of F# Major/F#7)

B Ionian - (Chord of B Major/BM7)

Key of F#

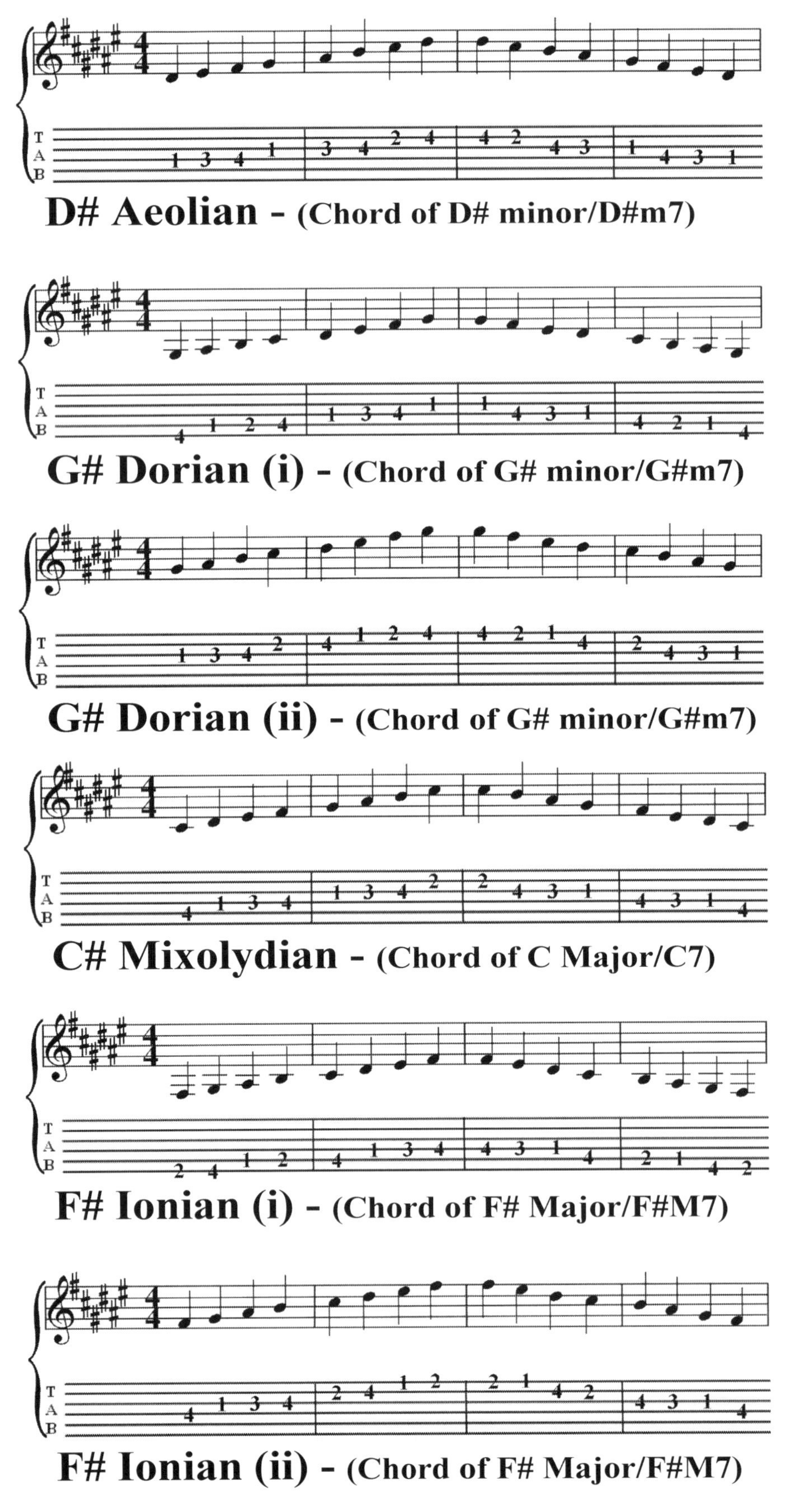

D# Aeolian - (Chord of D# minor/D#m7)

G# Dorian (i) - (Chord of G# minor/G#m7)

G# Dorian (ii) - (Chord of G# minor/G#m7)

C# Mixolydian - (Chord of C Major/C7)

F# Ionian (i) - (Chord of F# Major/F#M7)

F# Ionian (ii) - (Chord of F# Major/F#M7)

Key of C#

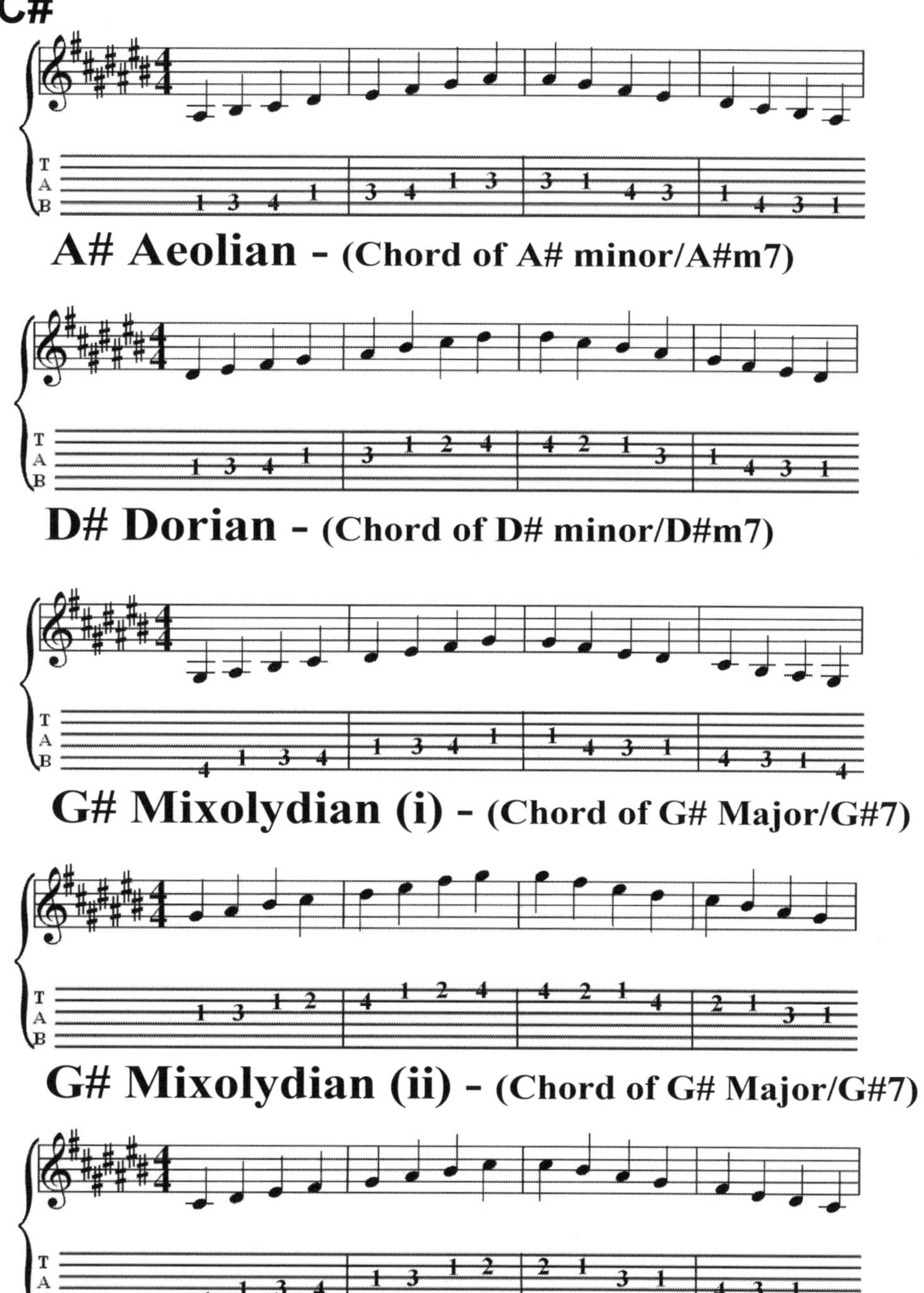
A# Aeolian - (Chord of A# minor/A#m7)
D# Dorian - (Chord of D# minor/D#m7)
G# Mixolydian (i) - (Chord of G# Major/G#7)
G# Mixolydian (ii) - (Chord of G# Major/G#7)
C# Ionian - (Chord of C# Major/C#M7)

Key of A♭

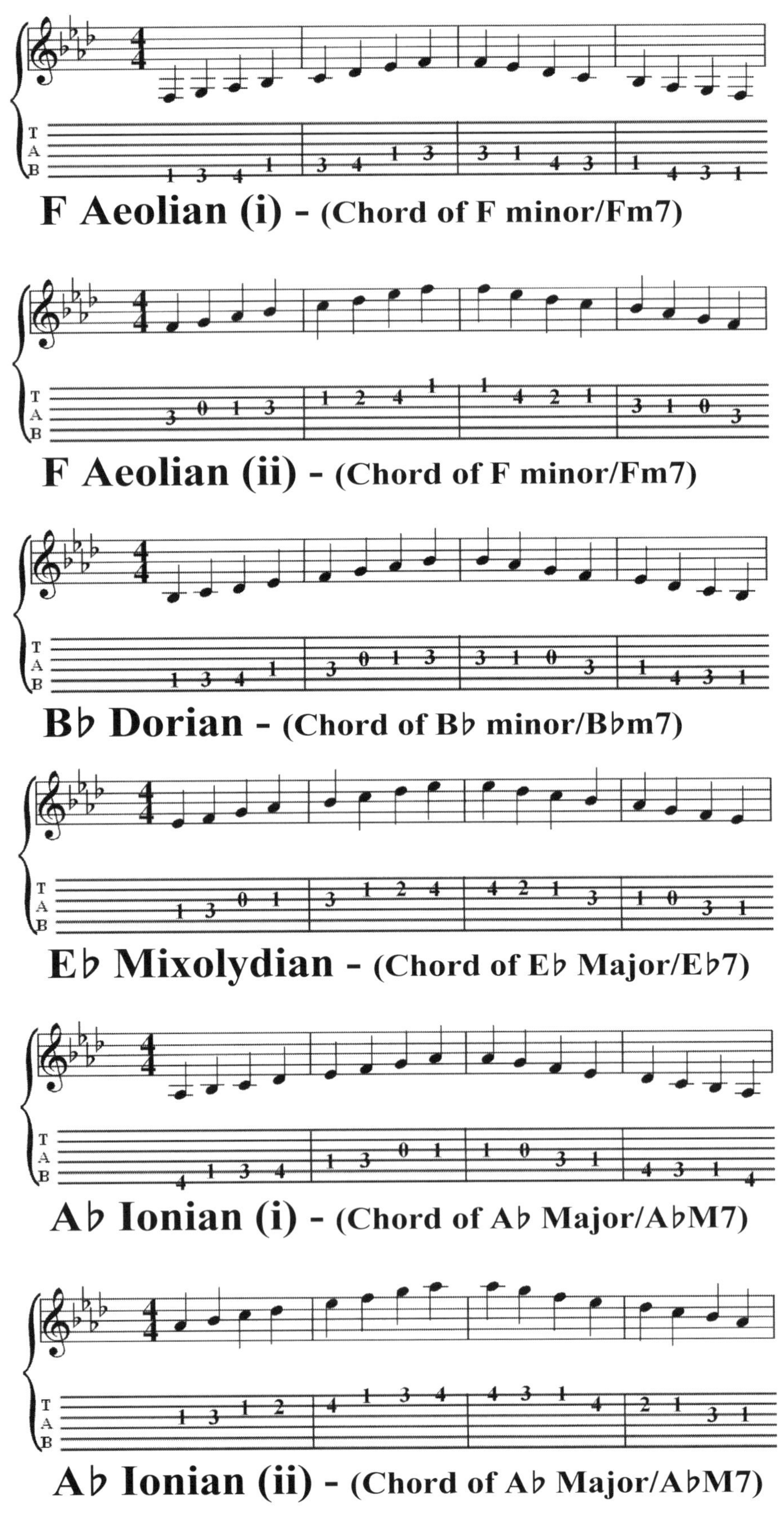
F Aeolian (i) - (Chord of F minor/Fm7)
F Aeolian (ii) - (Chord of F minor/Fm7)
B♭ Dorian - (Chord of B♭ minor/B♭m7)
E♭ Mixolydian - (Chord of E♭ Major/E♭7)
A♭ Ionian (i) - (Chord of A♭ Major/A♭M7)
A♭ Ionian (ii) - (Chord of A♭ Major/A♭M7)

Key of E♭

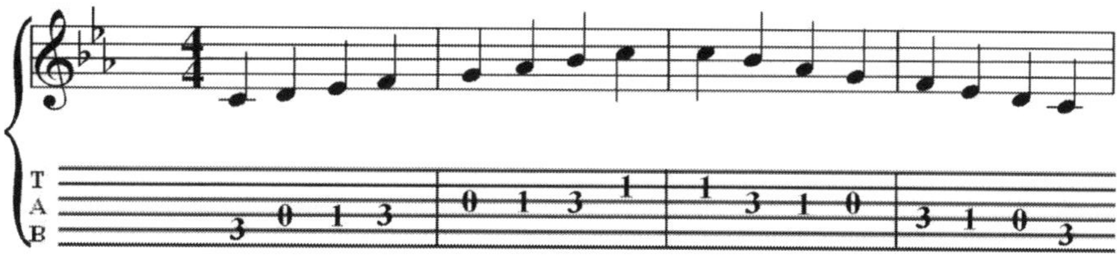

C Aeolian - (Chord of C minor/Cm7)

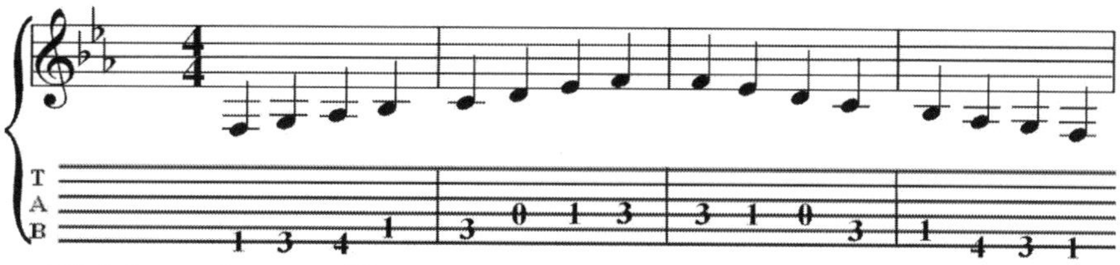

F Dorian (i) - (Chord of F minor/Fm7)

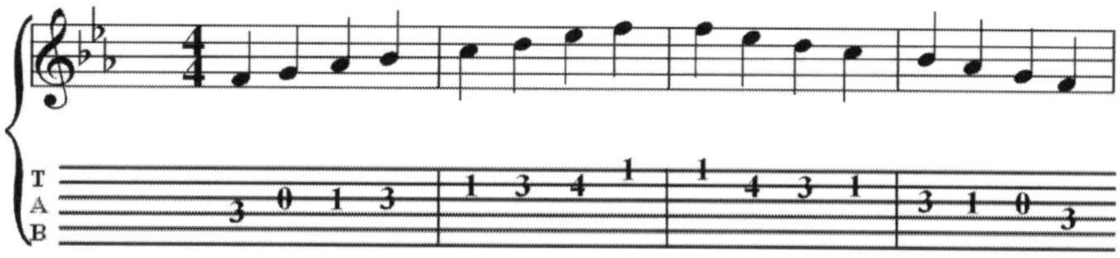

F Dorian (ii) - (Chord of F minor/Fm7)

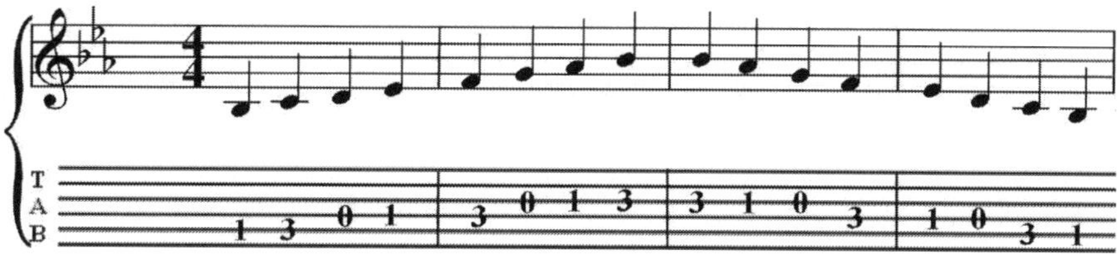

B♭ Mixolydian - (Chord of B♭ Major/B♭7)

E♭ Ionian - (Chord of E♭ Major/E♭♭M7)

Key of B♭

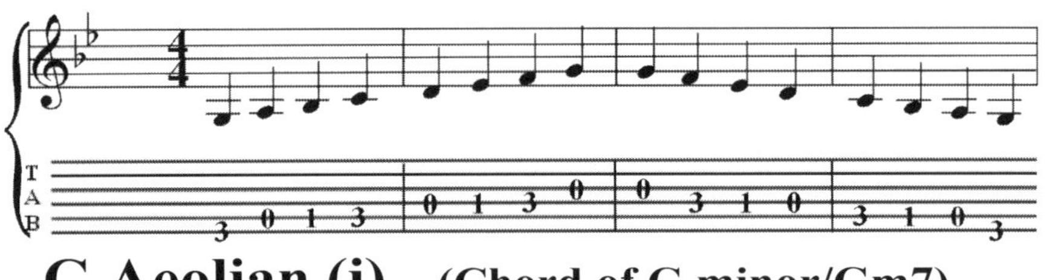

G Aeolian (i) - (Chord of G minor/Gm7)

G Aeolian (ii) - (Chord of G minor/Gm7)

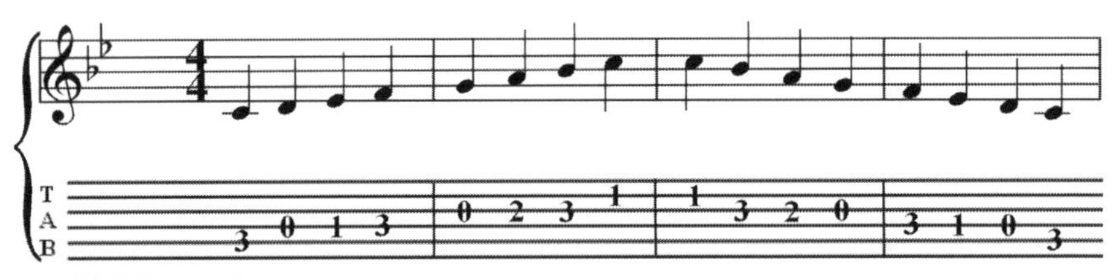

C Dorian - (Chord of C minor/Cm7)

F Mixolydian (i) - (Chord of F Major/F7)

F Mixolydian (ii) - (Chord of F Major/F7)

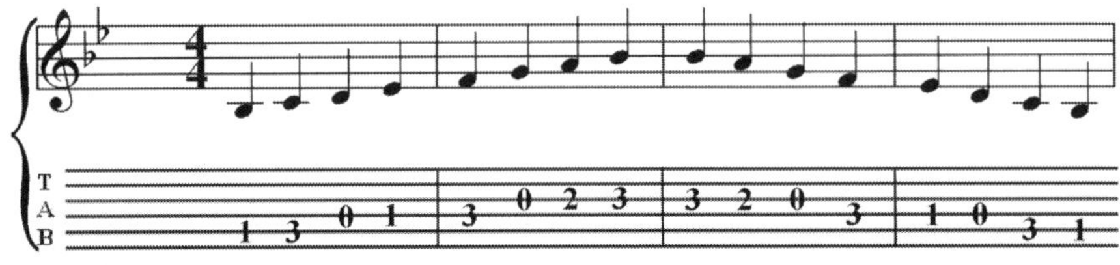

B♭ Ionian - (Chord of B♭ Major/B♭M7)

Key of F

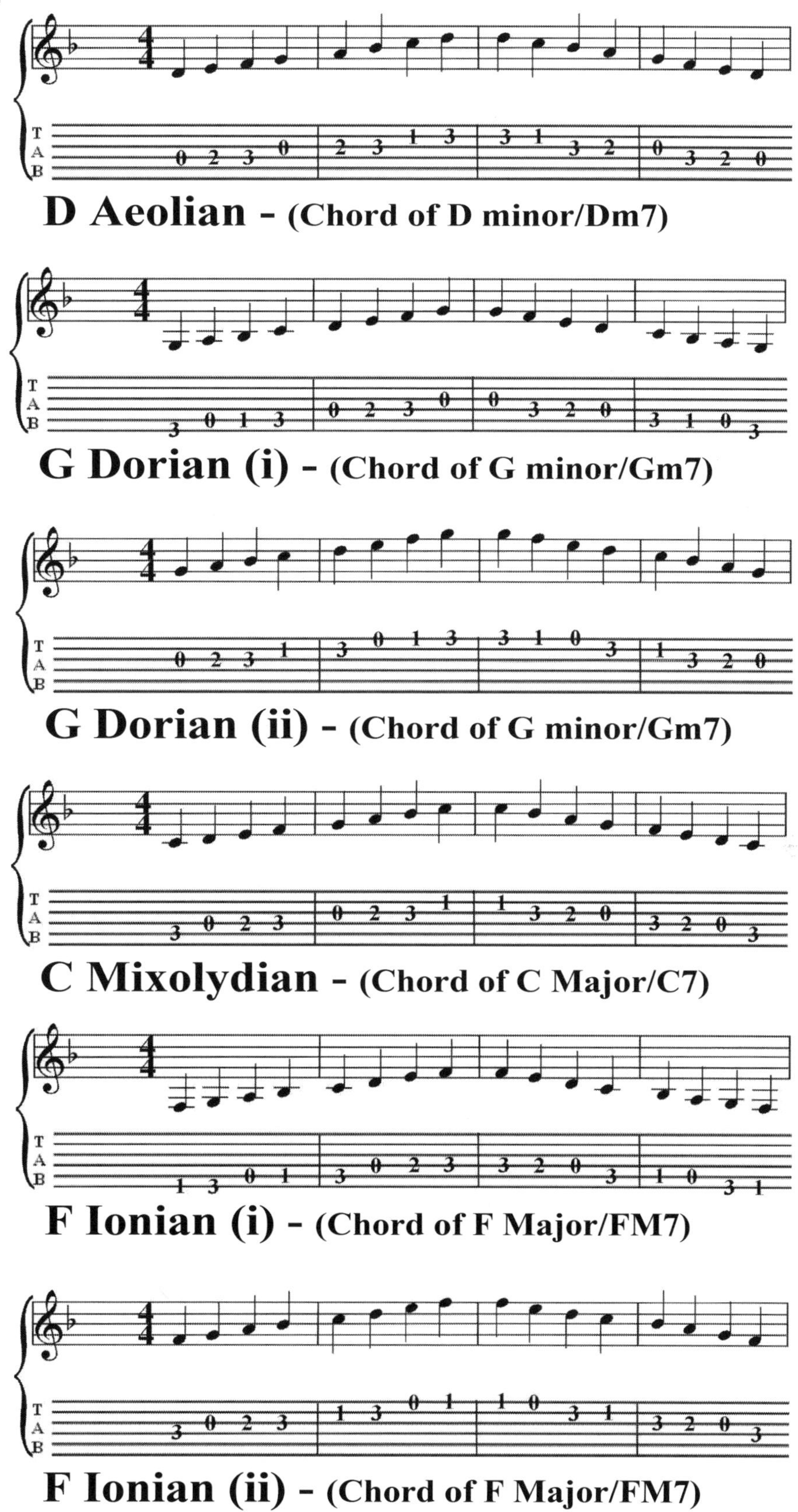

D Aeolian - (Chord of D minor/Dm7)

G Dorian (i) - (Chord of G minor/Gm7)

G Dorian (ii) - (Chord of G minor/Gm7)

C Mixolydian - (Chord of C Major/C7)

F Ionian (i) - (Chord of F Major/FM7)

F Ionian (ii) - (Chord of F Major/FM7)

All Keys (i)

vi (Aeolian / Natural Minor Scale)

ii (Dorian)

V (Mixolydian)

I (Ionian / Major Scale)

All Keys (ii)

vi

ii

V

I

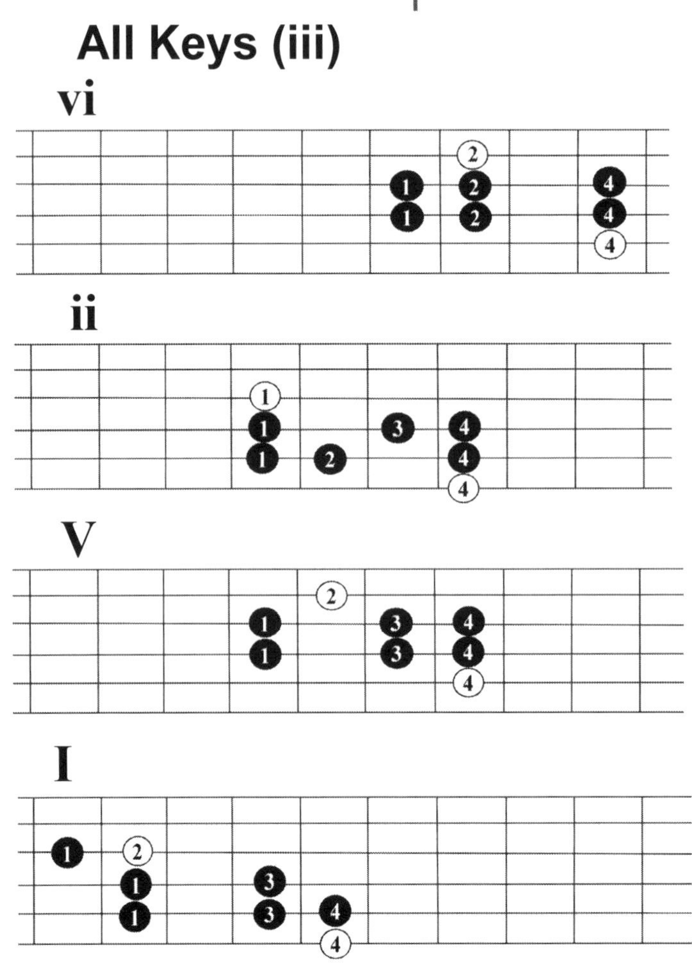

All Keys (iv)

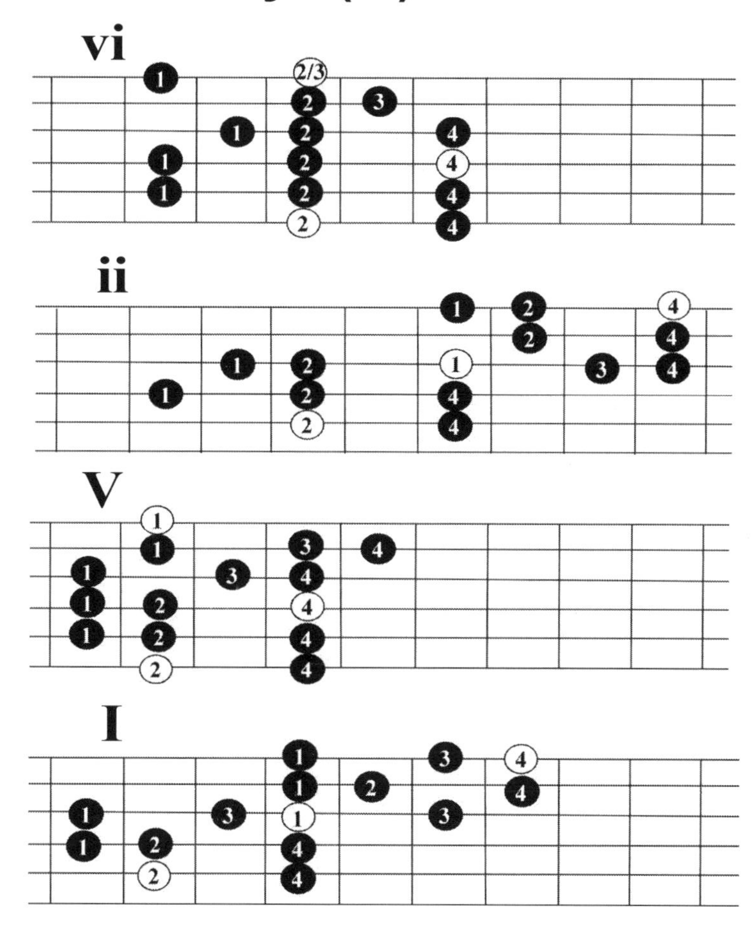

All Keys (v)

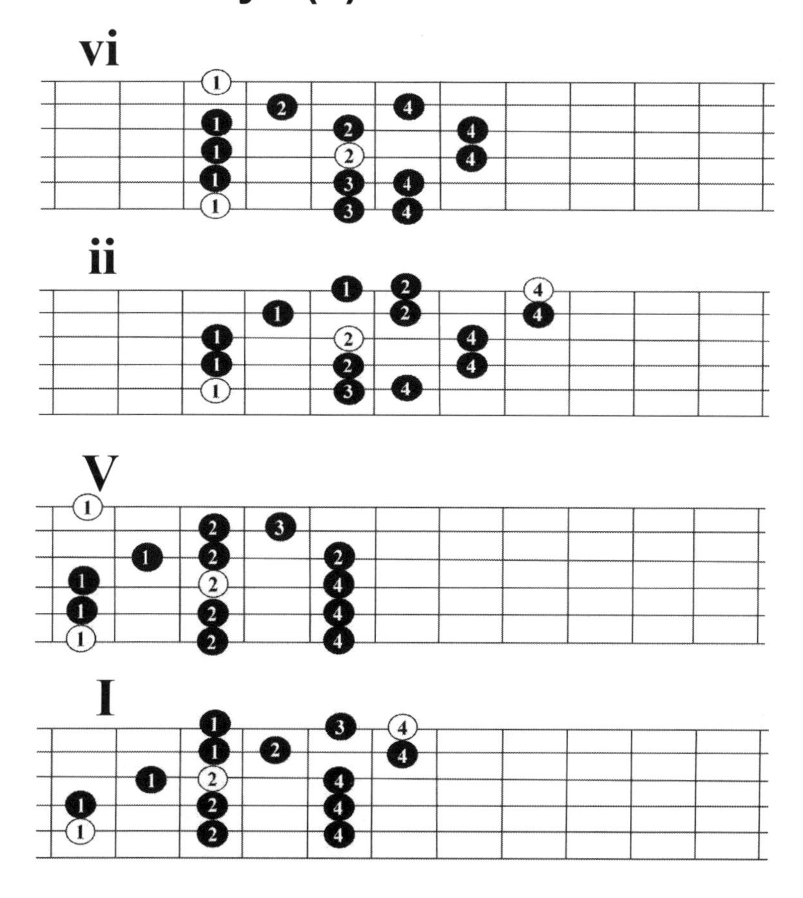

All Keys (vi)

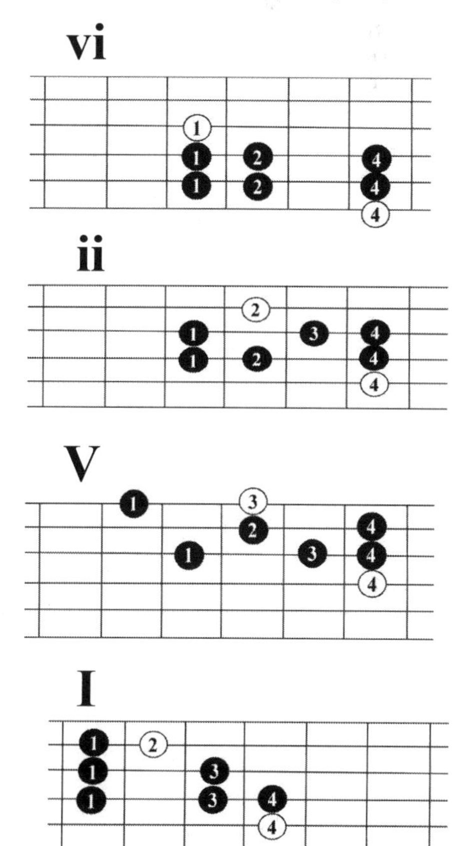

All Keys (vii)

vi

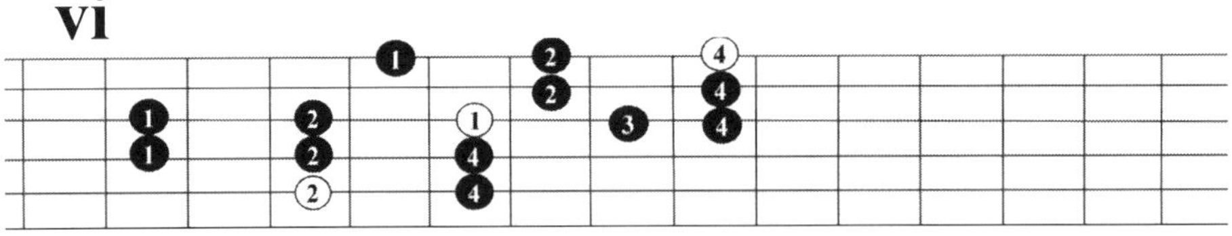

ii

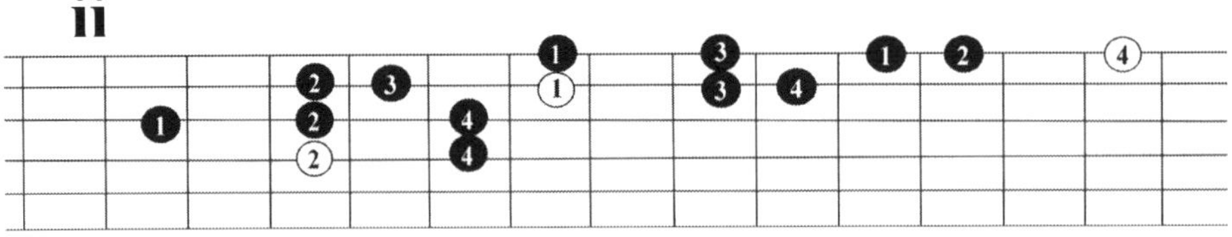

V

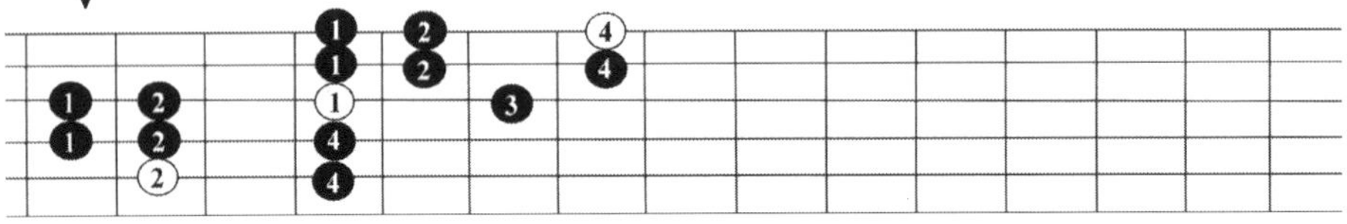

I

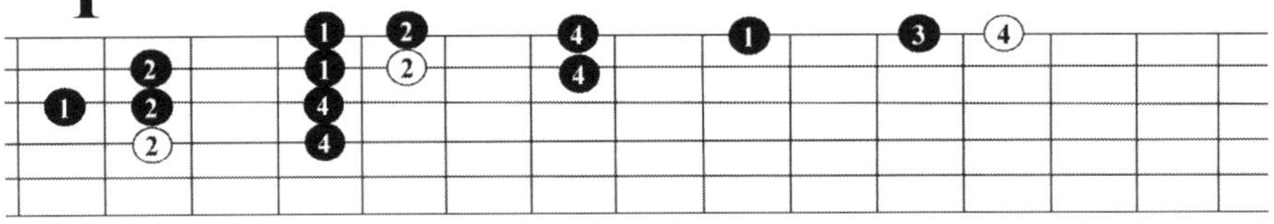

All Keys (viii)

vi

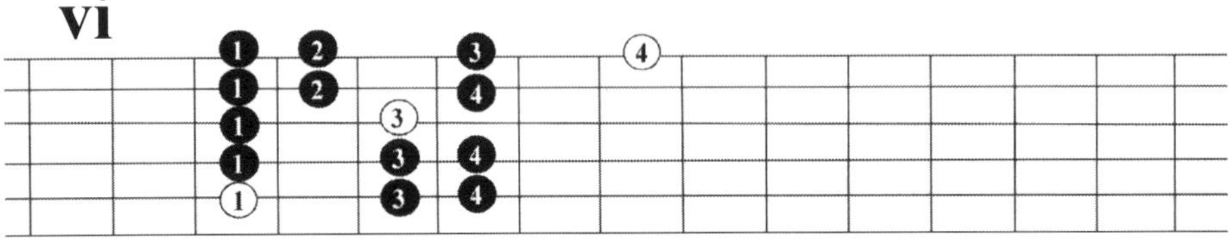

ii

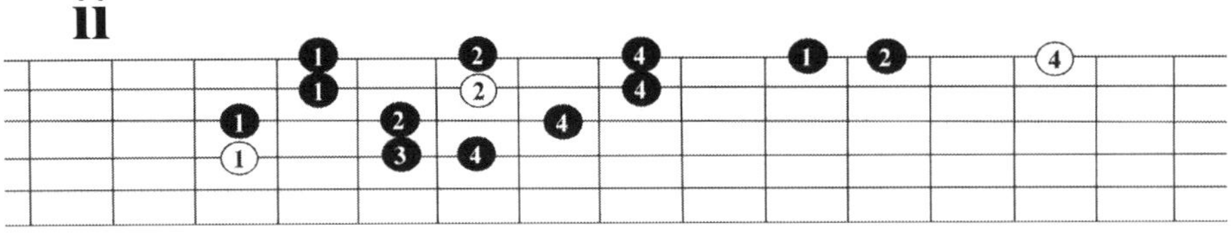

V

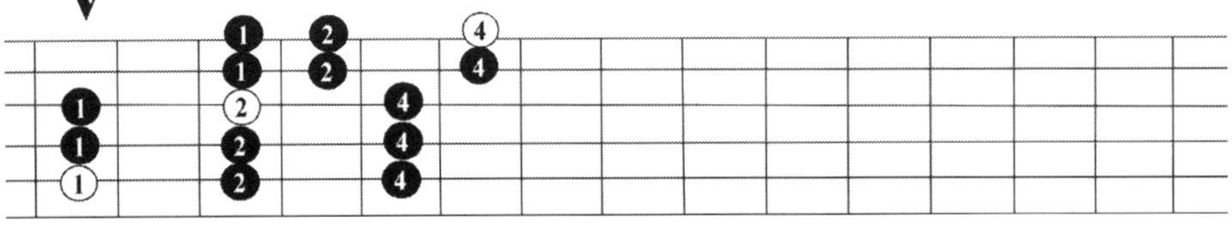

I

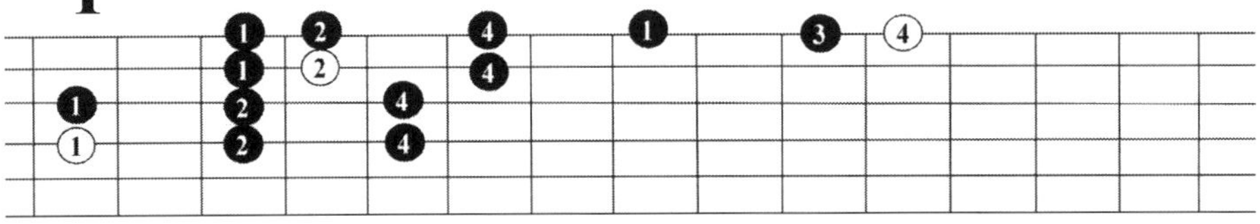

All Keys (ix)

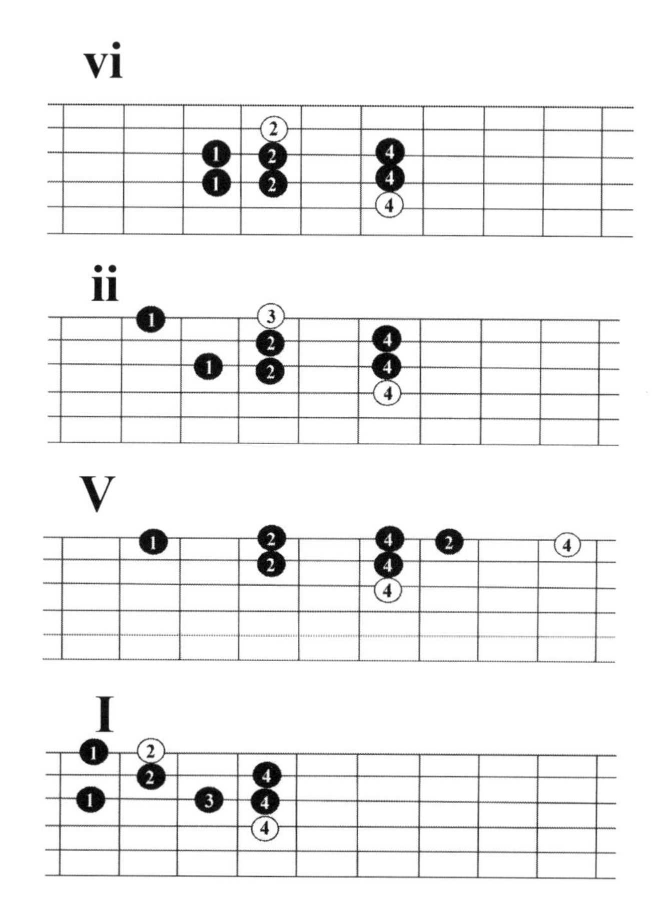

PART THIRTY-FIVE

THE PHRYGIAN MODE

MODES AND THE MINOR SCALE

The modes of a natural *minor* scale are the same as those of the relative *major* scale (since they share a *key signature*, all the notes are the same, but with a different starting point). Thus, in the key of A minor (the relative minor of C major), the sequence of modes will be:

i **A AEOLIAN (the natural minor scale)**

ii **B LOCRIAN**

III **C IONIAN (the C Major scale)**

iv **D DORIAN**

v **E PHRYGIAN**

VI **F LYDIAN**

VII **G MIXOLYDIAN**

THE PHRYGIAN MODE

You will see from the above that the appropriate mode for a v minor/minor seventh chord in a minor key is the Phrygian mode. Since this book follows the convention of using a V major/dominant seventh chord, we will not be using this mode in the chord progression exercises. Therefore, to avoid overlooking this mode altogether, it is treated to a separate subsection of its own in the following pages.

(The Phrygian mode is also the appropriate chord scale for a iii (minor or minor seventh) chord in a Major key.)

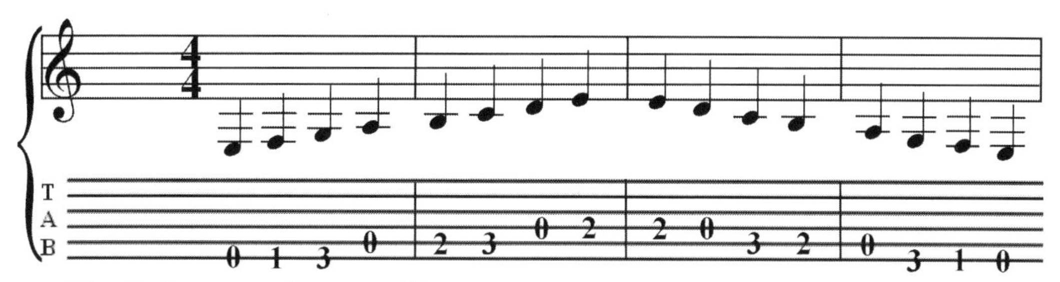

E Phrygian (i) - (Chord of E minor/Em7, key of Am)

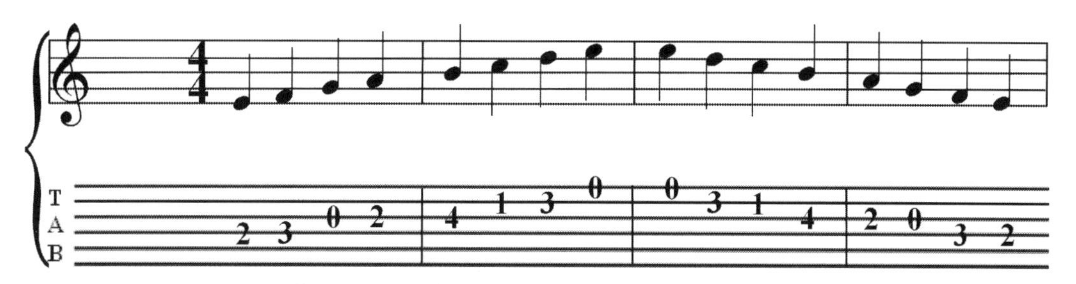

E Phrygian (ii) - (Chord of E minor/Em7, key of Am)

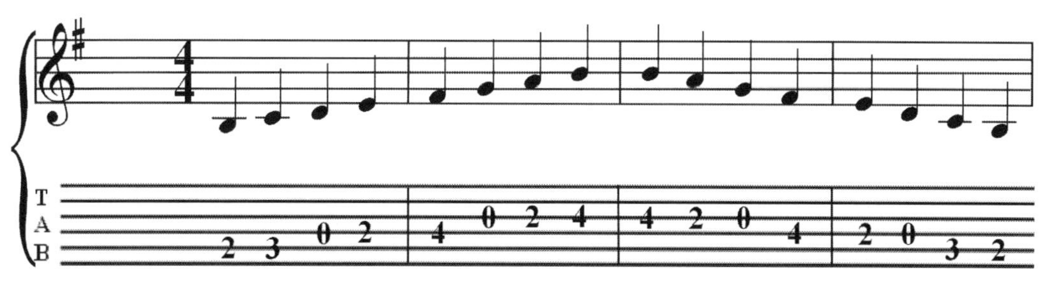

B Phrygian - (Chord of B minor/Bm7, key of Em)

F# Phrygian (i) - (Chord of F# minor/F#m7, key of Bm)

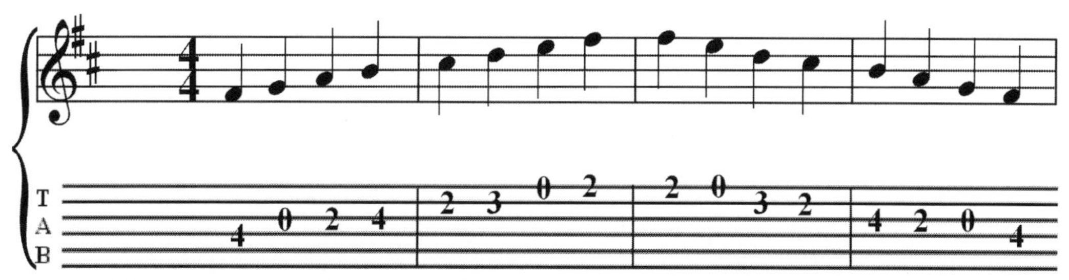

F# Phrygian (ii) - (Chord of F# minor/F#m7, key of Bm)

C# Phrygian - (Chord of C# minor/C#m7, key of F#m)

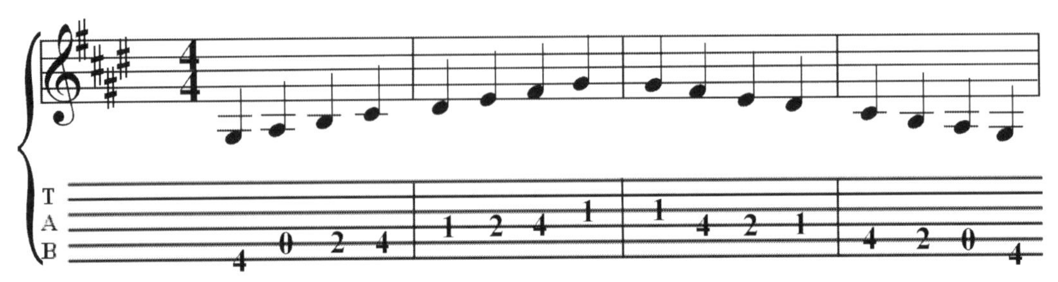

G# Phrygian (i) - (Chord of G# minor/G#m7, key of C#m)

G# Phrygian (ii) - (Chord of G# minor/G#m7, key of C#m)

E♭ Phrygian - (Chord of E♭ minor/E♭m7, key of A♭m)

B♭ Phrygian - (Chord of B♭ minor/B♭m7, key of E♭m)

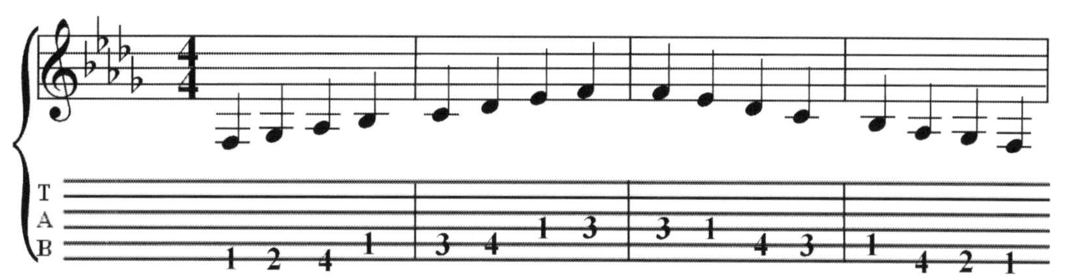

F Phrygian (i) - (Chord of F minor/Fm7, key of B♭m)

F Phrygian (ii) - (Chord of F minor/Fm7, key of B♭m)

C Phrygian - (Chord of C minor/Cm7, key of Fm)

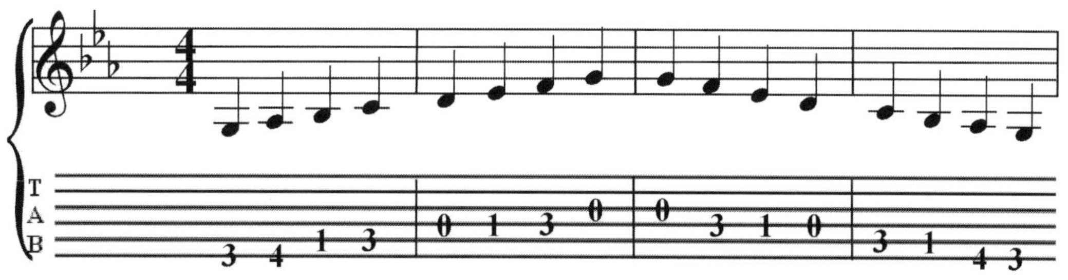

G Phrygian (i) - (Chord of G minor/Gm7, key of Cm)

G Phrygian (ii) - (Chord of G minor/Gm7, key of Cm)

D Phrygian - (Chord of D minor/Dm7, key of Gm)

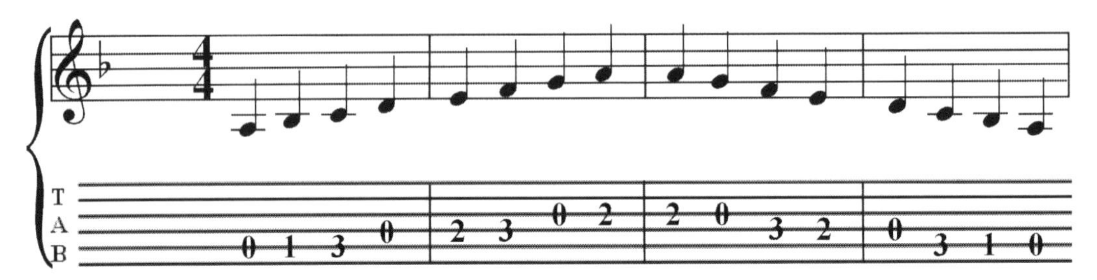

A Phrygian (i) - (Chord of A minor/Am7, key of Dm)

A Phrygian (ii) - (Chord of A minor/Am7, key of Dm)

PHRYGIAN MODE - ALL KEYS

(i)

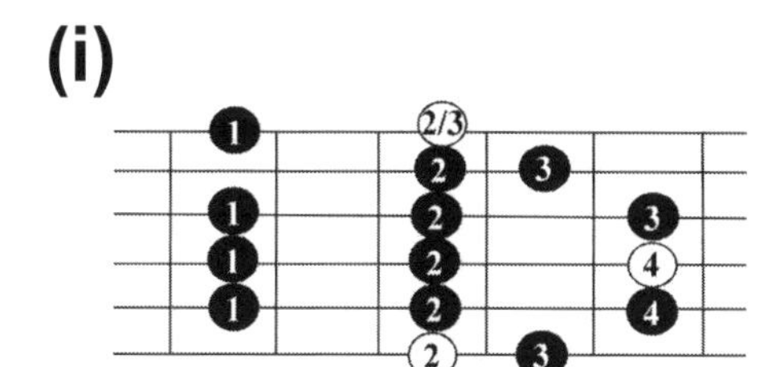

(ii)

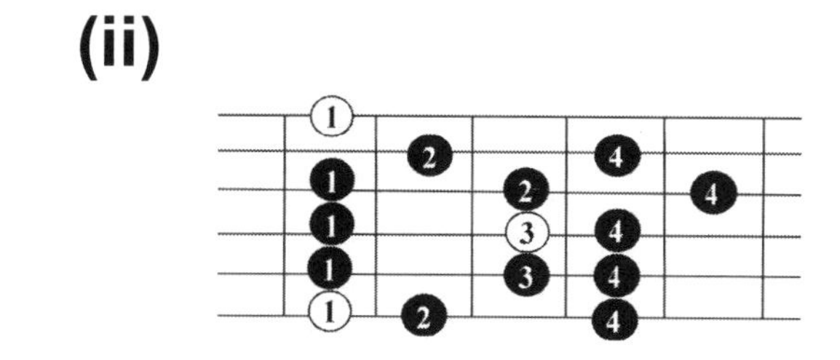

(iii)

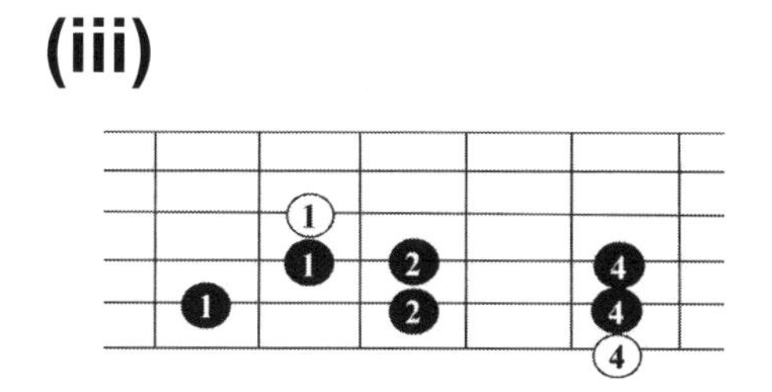

(iv)

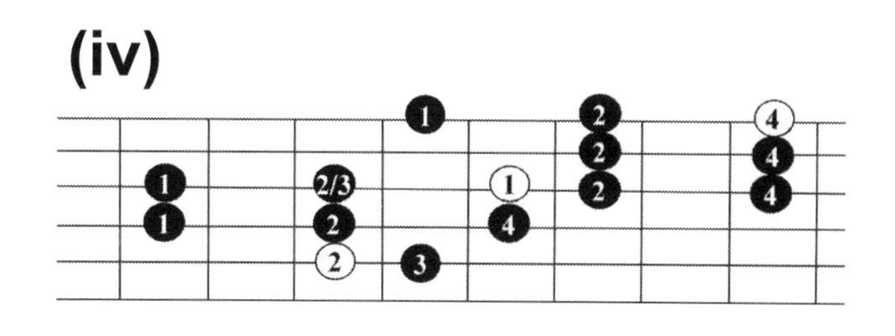

(v)

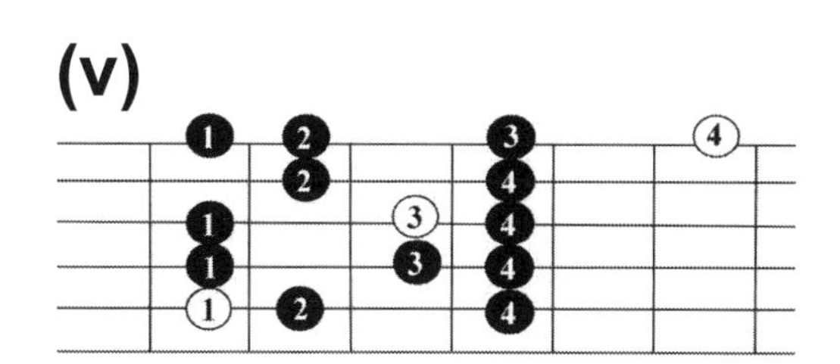

(vi)

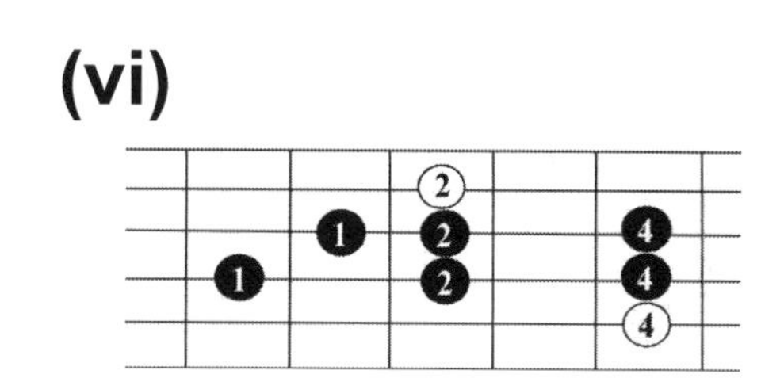

(vii)

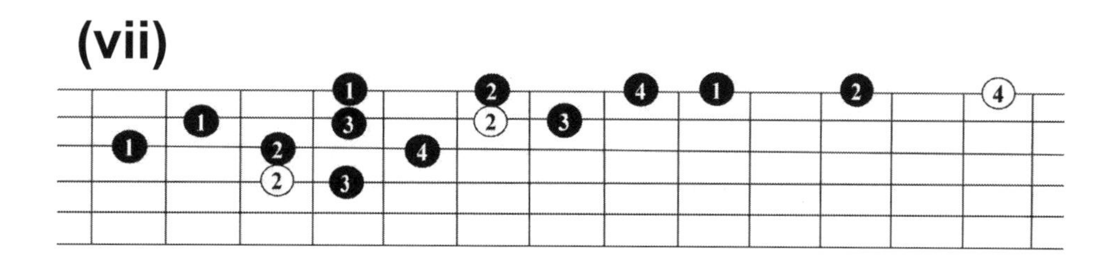

(viii)

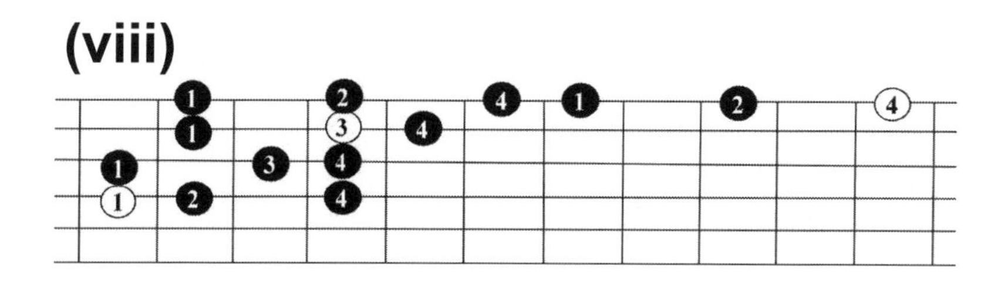

(xi)

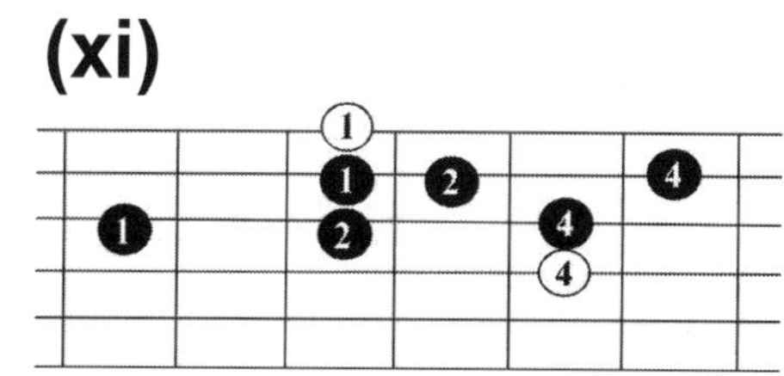

PART THIRTY-SIX

i - iv - V

MINOR KEYS
MODES

THE MIXOLYDIAN ♭6 MODE

To accompany the V *major*/dominant seventh chord in minor keys, a new mode is needed. This is the Mixolydian ♭6 mode, and as its name implies, differs from the normal Mixolydian mode in that the sixth note is flattened. This is the same note as the third of the corresponding *minor* scale. This mode is derived from the so-called "melodic minor scale" (see also the section on minor key pentatonics). A detailed discussion of the melodic minor scale, and its other modes, is beyond the scope of this book. However a brief summary is provided in the later section "Variant Minor Scales".

Key of Am

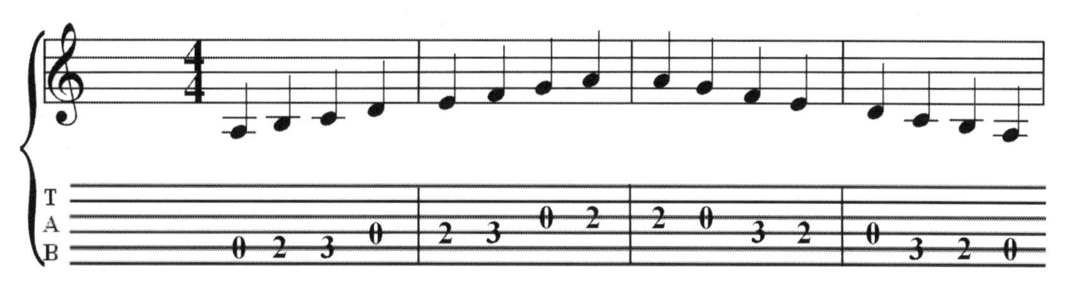

A Aeolian (i) - (Chord of A minor/Am7)

A Aeolian (ii) - (Chord of A minor/Am7)

D Dorian - (Chord of D minor/Dm7)

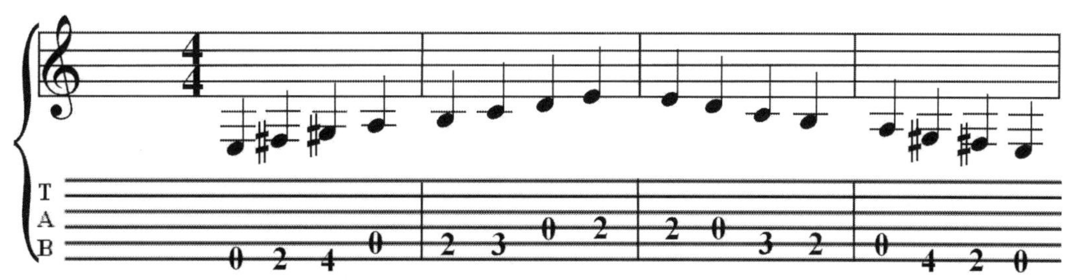

E Mixolydian ♭6 (i) - (Chord of E Major/E7)

E Mixolydian ♭6 (ii) - (Chord of E Major/E7)

Key of Em

E Aeolian (i) - (Chord of E minor/Em7)

E Aeolian (ii) - (Chord of E minor/Em7)

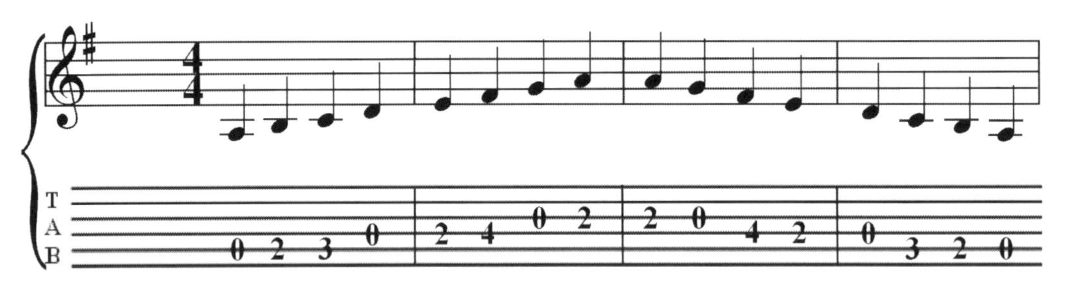

A Dorian (i) - (Chord of A minor/Am7)

A Dorian (ii) - (Chord of A minor/Am7)

B Mixolydian ♭6 - (Chord of B Major/B7)

Key of Bm

B Aeolian - (Chord of B minor/Bm7)

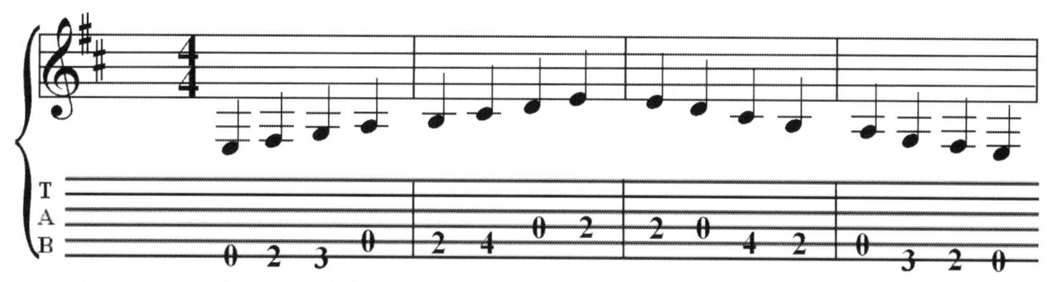

E Dorian (i) - (Chord of E minor/Em7)

E Dorian (ii) - (Chord of E minor/Em7)

F# Mixolydian ♭6 (i) - (Chord of F# Major/F#7)

F# Mixolydian ♭6 (i) - (Chord of F# Major/F#7)

Key of F#m

F# Aeolian (i) - (Chord of F# minor/F#m7)

F# Aeolian (ii) - (Chord of F# minor/F#m7)

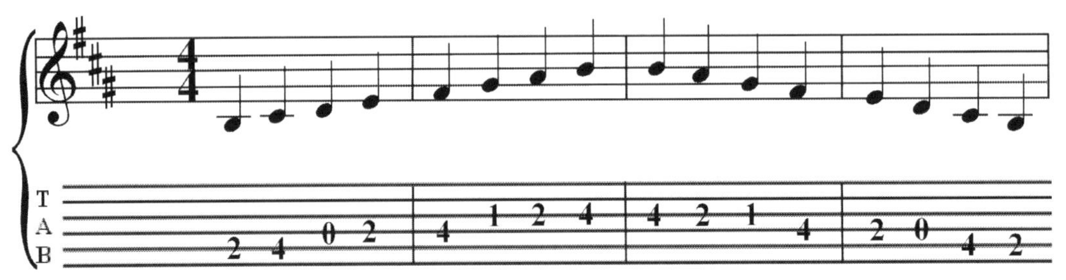

B Dorian - (Chord of B minor/Bm7)

C# Mixolydian ♭6 - (Chord of C# Major/C#7)

Key of C#m

C# Aeolian - (Chord of C# minor/C#m7)

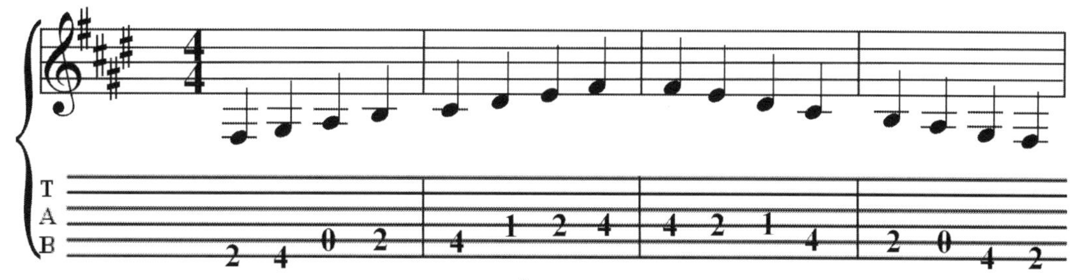

F# Dorian (i) - (Chord of F# minor/F#m7)

F# Dorian (ii) - (Chord of F# minor/F#m7)

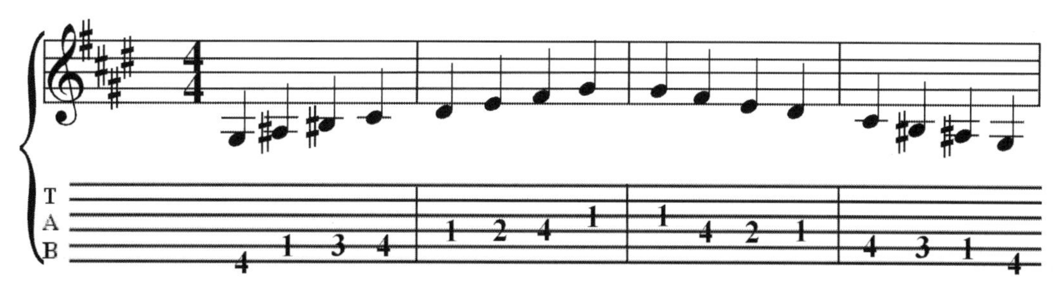

G# Mixolydian ♭6 (i) - (Chord of G# Major/G#7)

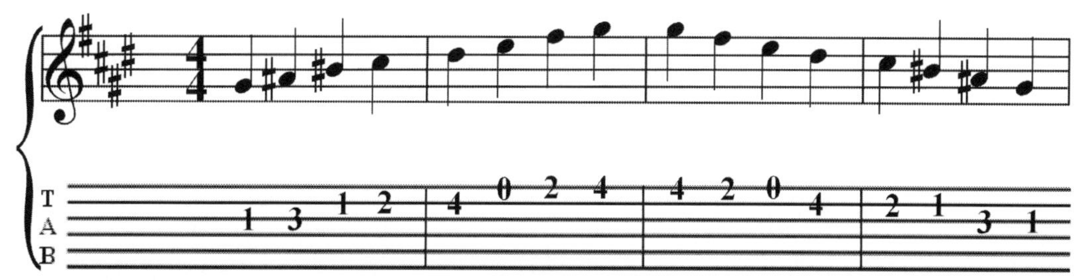

G# Mixolydian ♭6 (ii) - (Chord of G# Major/G#7)

Key of A♭m

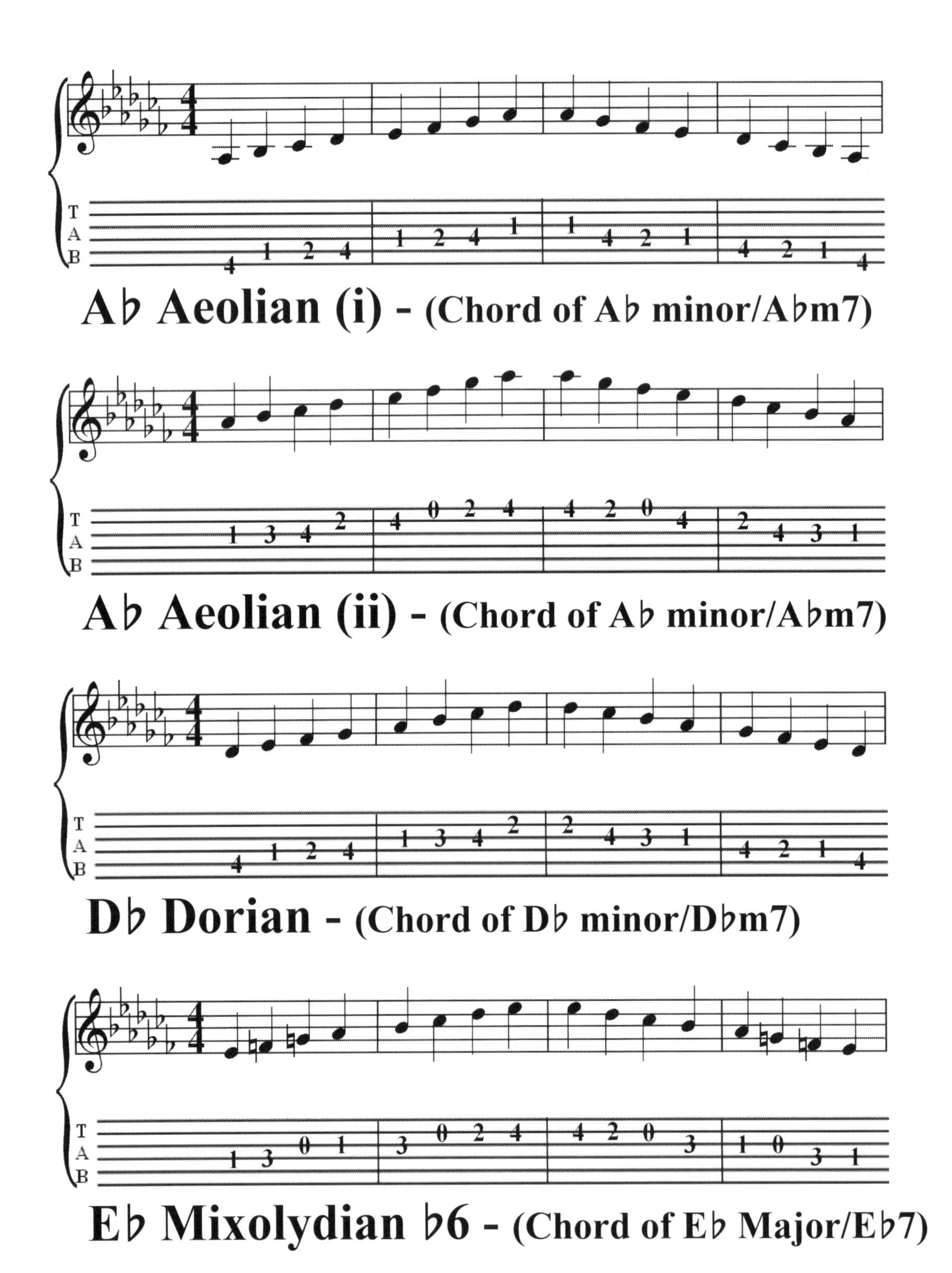

A♭ Aeolian (i) - (Chord of A♭ minor/A♭m7)

A♭ Aeolian (ii) - (Chord of A♭ minor/A♭m7)

D♭ Dorian - (Chord of D♭ minor/D♭m7)

E♭ Mixolydian ♭6 - (Chord of E♭ Major/E♭7)

Key of E♭m

E♭ Aeolian - (Chord of E♭ minor/E♭m7)

A♭ Dorian (i) - (Chord of A♭ minor/A♭m7)

A♭ Dorian (ii) - (Chord of A♭ minor/A♭m7)

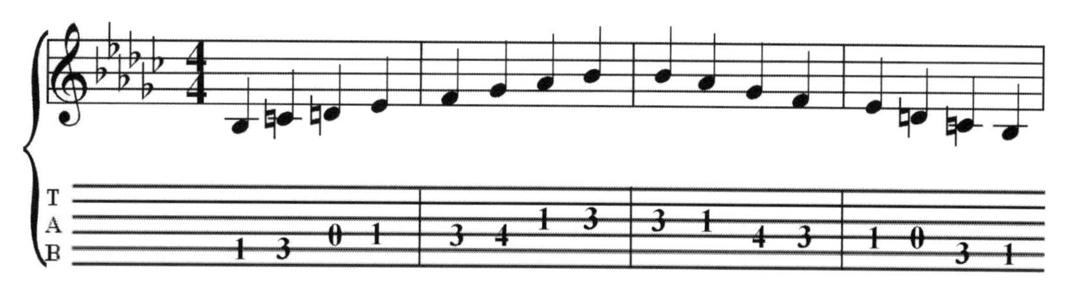

B♭ Mixolydian ♭6 - (Chord of B♭ Major/B♭7)

Key of B♭m

B♭ Aeolian - (Chord of B♭ minor/B♭m7)

E♭ Dorian - (Chord of E♭ minor/E♭m7)

F Mixolydian ♭6 (i) - (Chord of F Major/F7)

F Mixolydian ♭6 (ii) - (Chord of F Major/F7)

Key of Fm

F Aeolian (i) - (Chord of F minor/Fm7)

F Aeolian (ii) - (Chord of F minor/Fm7)

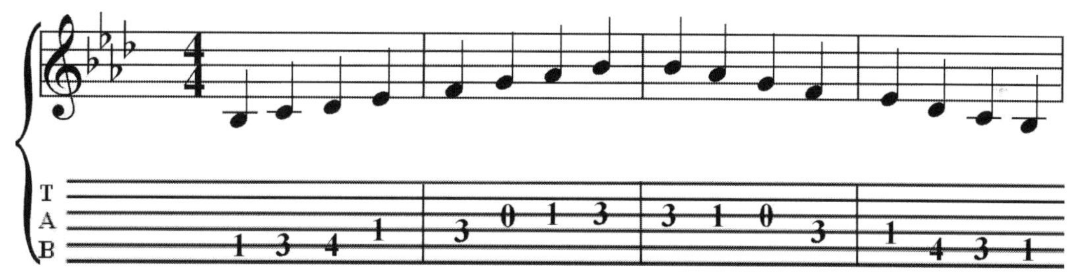

B♭ Dorian - (Chord of B♭ minor/B♭m7)

C Mixolydian ♭6 - (Chord of C Major/C7)

Key of Cm

C Aeolian - (Chord of C minor/Cm7)

F Dorian (i) - (Chord of F minor/Fm7)

F Dorian (ii) - (Chord of F minor/Fm7)

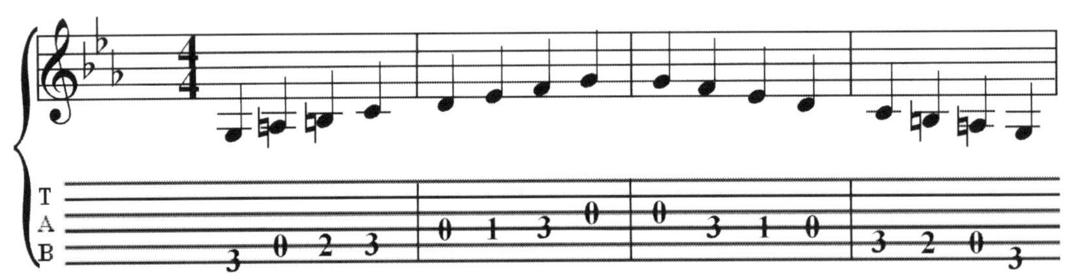

G Mixolydian ♭6 (i) - (Chord of G Major/G7)

G Mixolydian ♭6 (ii) - (Chord of G Major/G7)

Key of Gm

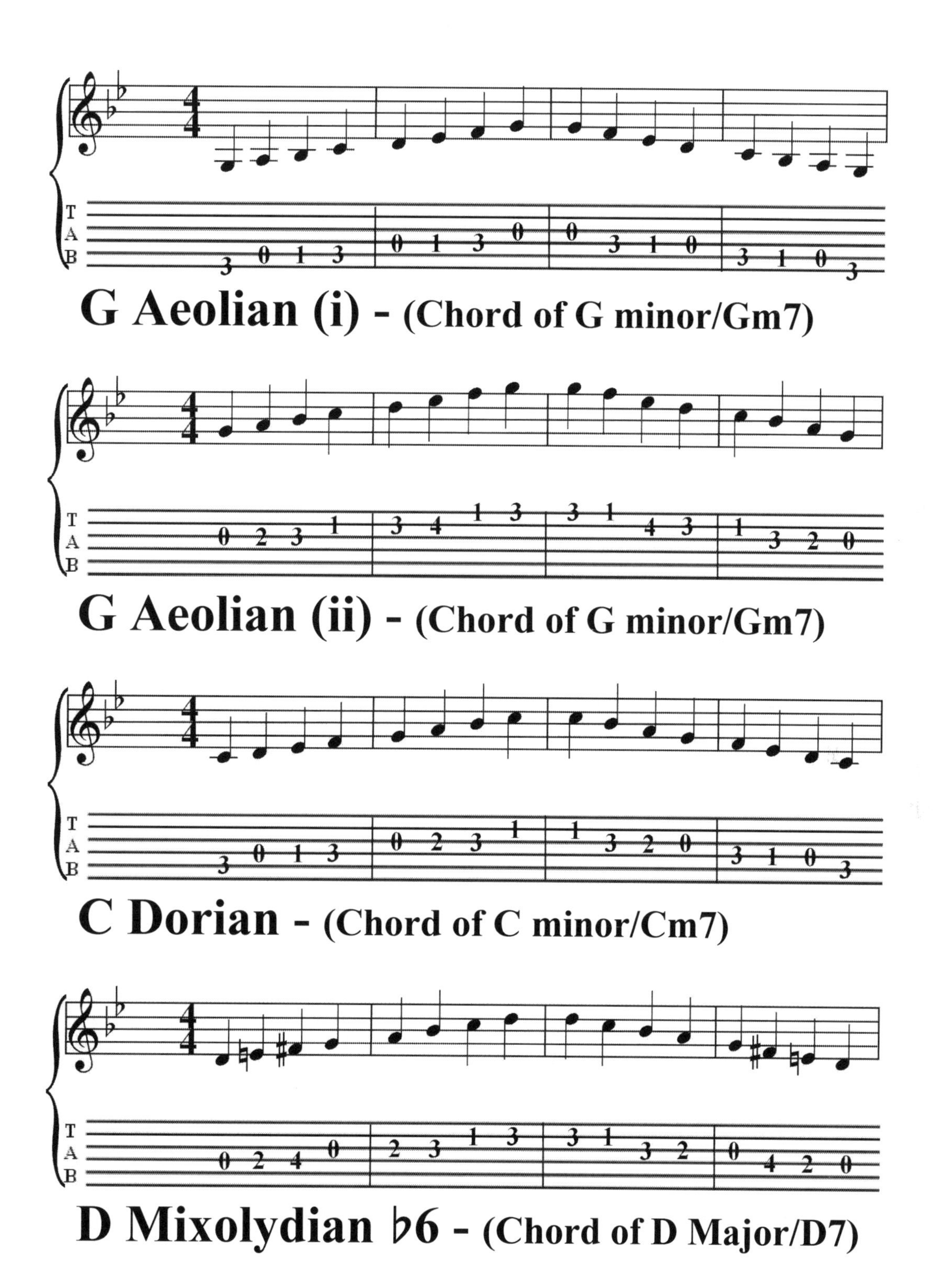
G Aeolian (i) - (Chord of G minor/Gm7)
G Aeolian (ii) - (Chord of G minor/Gm7)
C Dorian - (Chord of C minor/Cm7)
D Mixolydian ♭6 - (Chord of D Major/D7)

Key of Dm

D Aeolian - (Chord of D minor/Dm7)

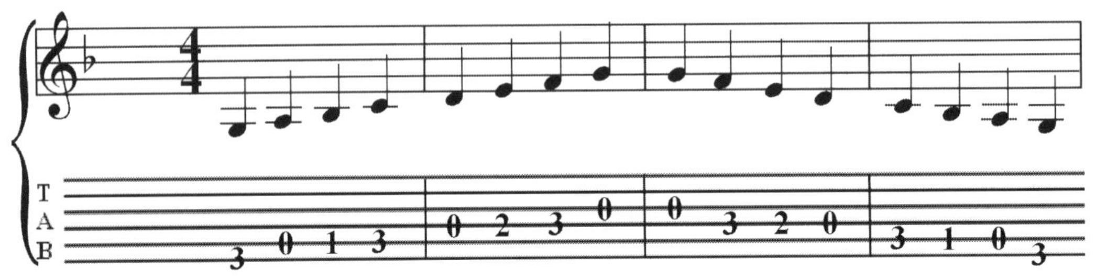

G Dorian (i) - (Chord of G minor/Gm7)

G Dorian (ii) - (Chord of G minor/Gm7)

A Mixolydian ♭6 (i) - (Chord of A Major/A7)

A Mixolydian ♭6 (ii) - (Chord of A Major/A7)

All Keys (i)

i (Aeolian / Natural Minor Scale)

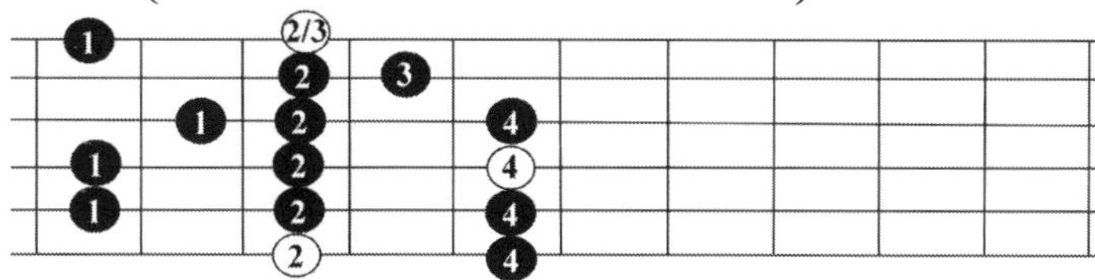

iv (Dorian)

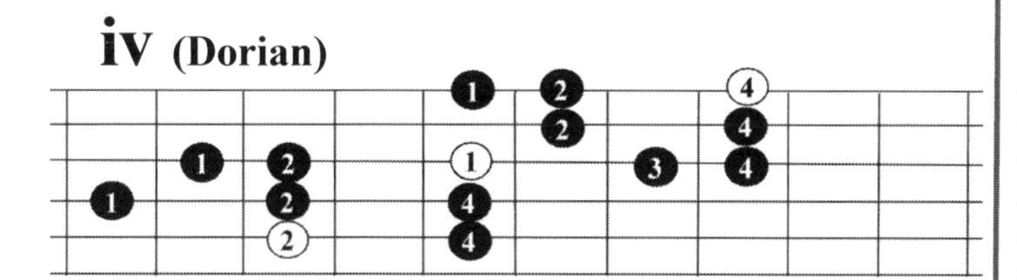

V (Mixolydian ♭6)

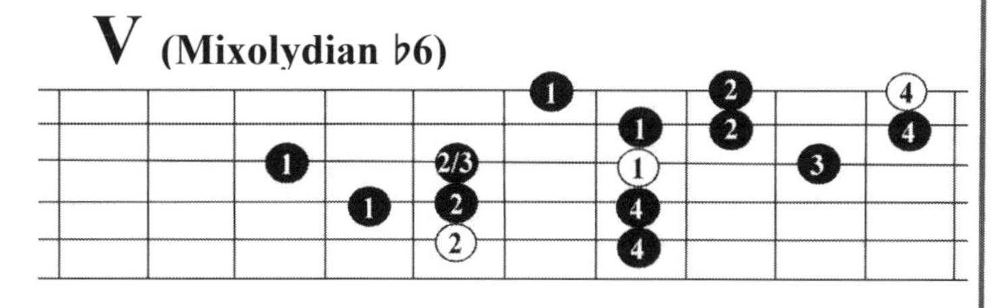

All Keys (ii)

i

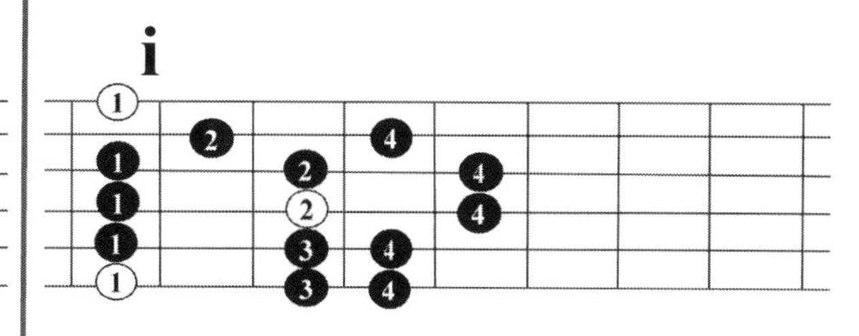

iv

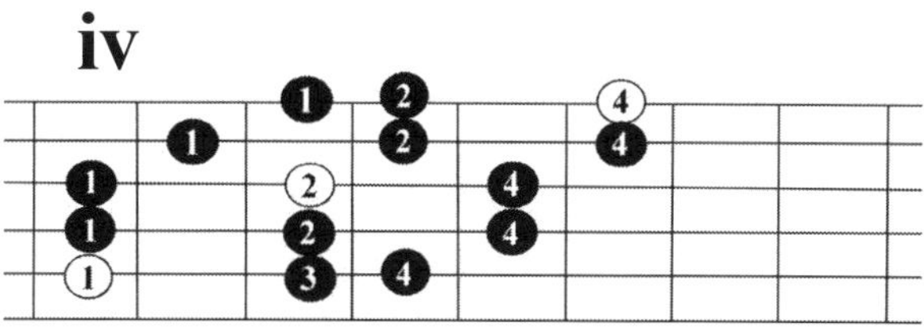

V

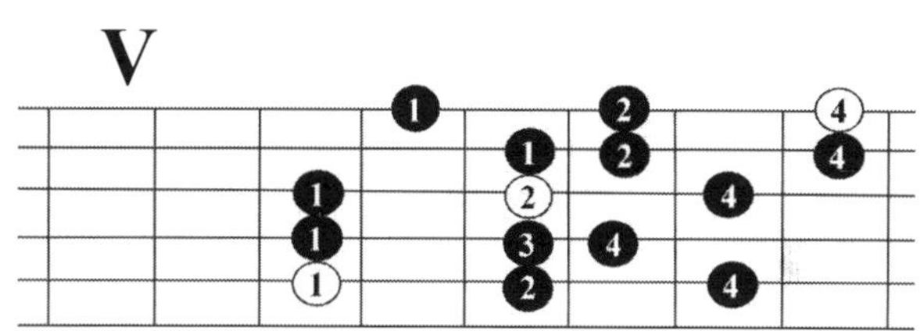

All Keys (iii)

i

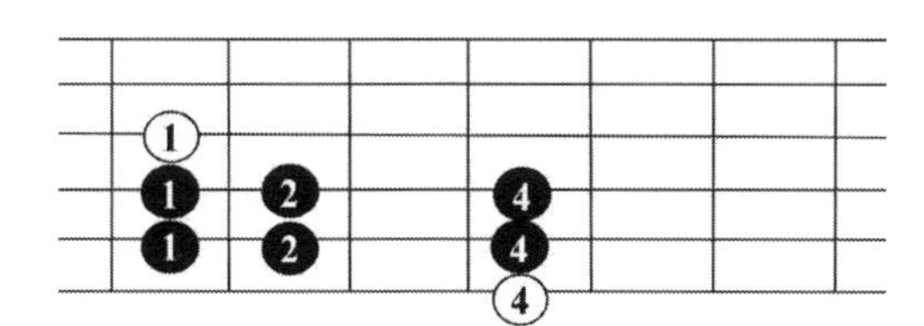

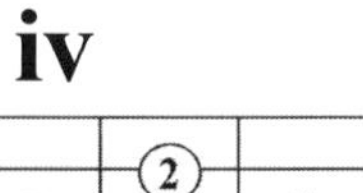

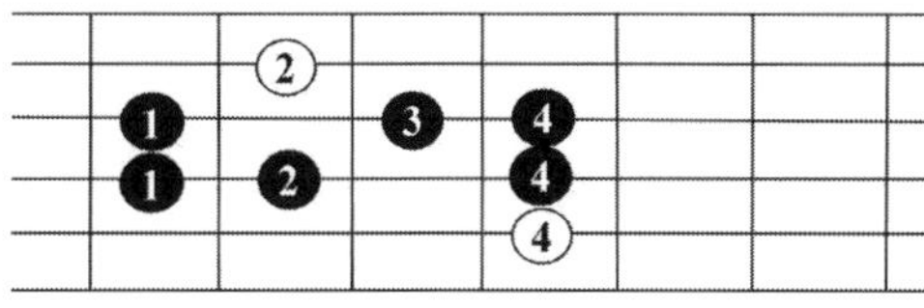

V

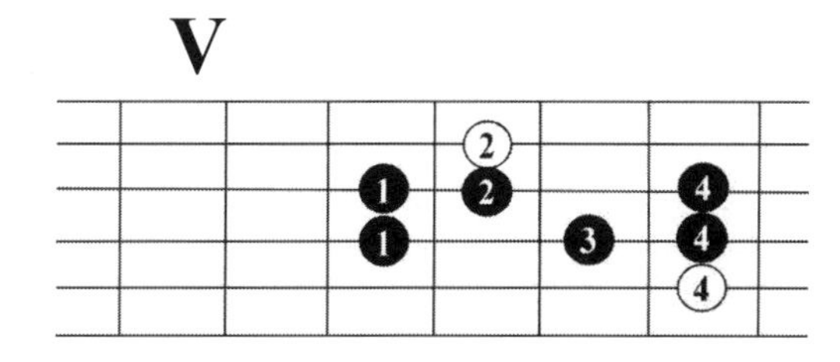

All Keys (iv)

i

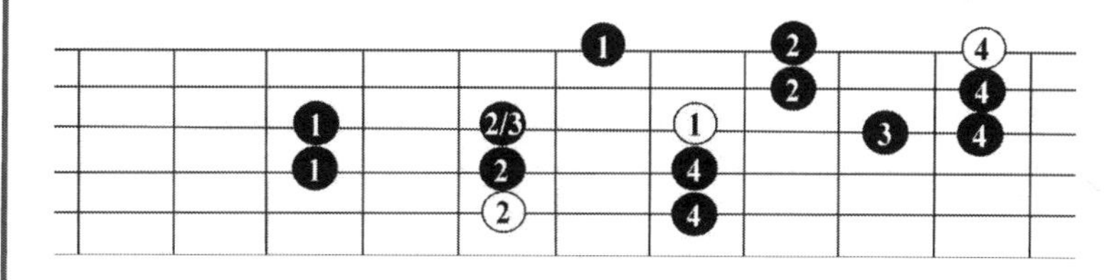

iv

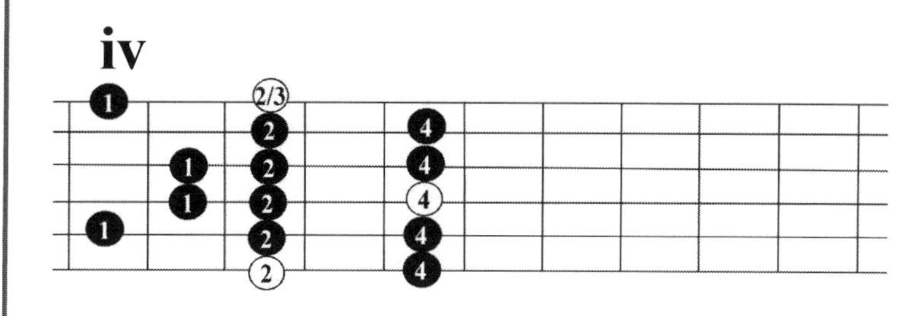

V

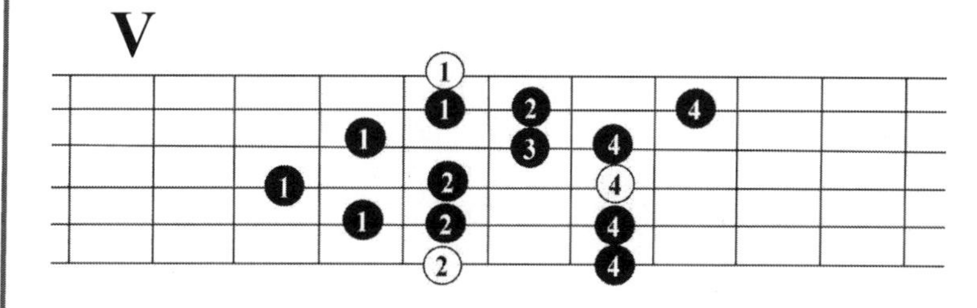

All Keys (v)

i

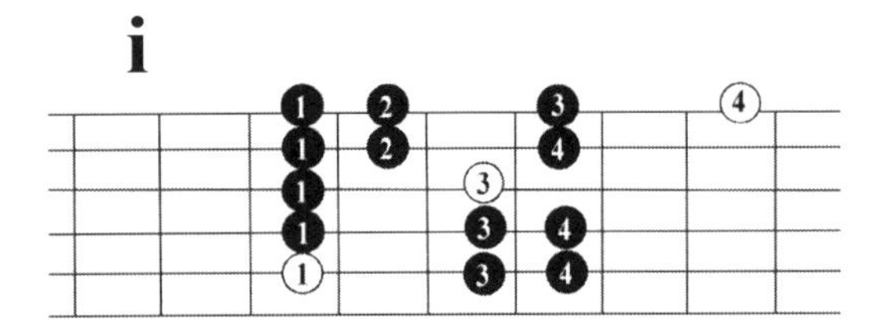

iv

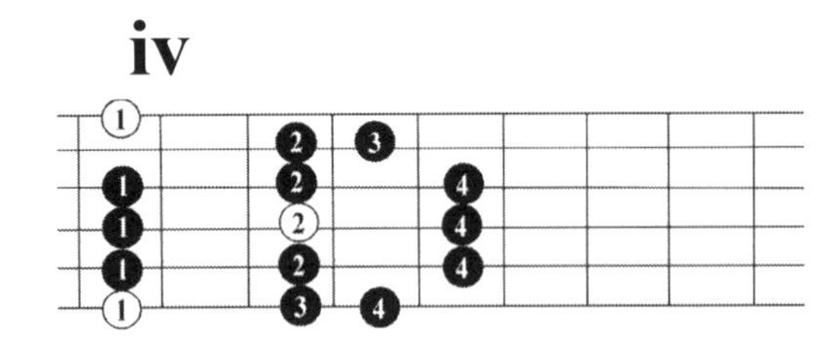

V

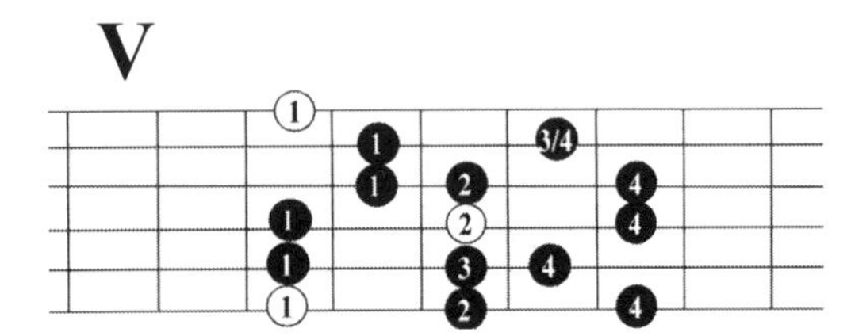

All Keys (vi)

i

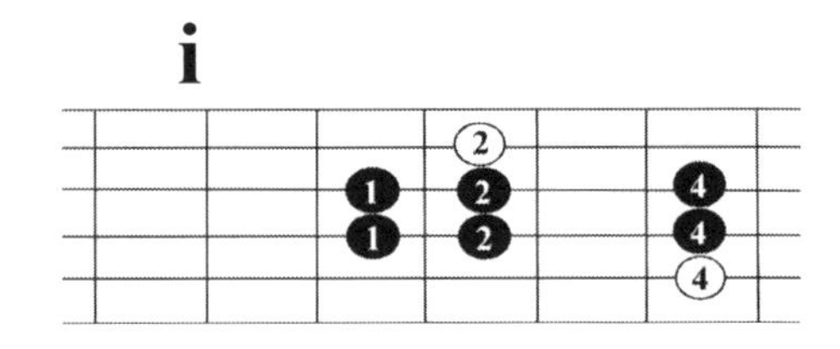

iv

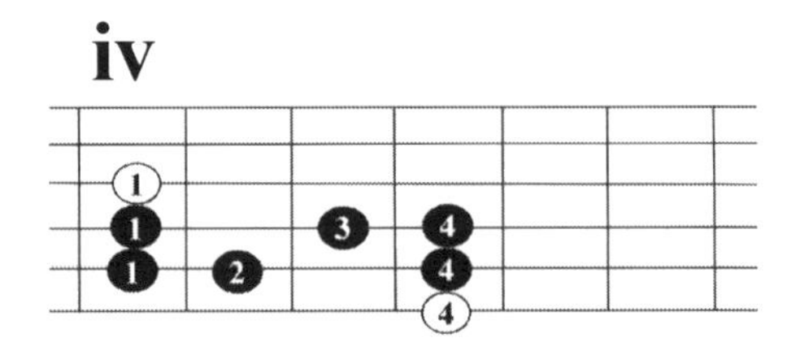

V

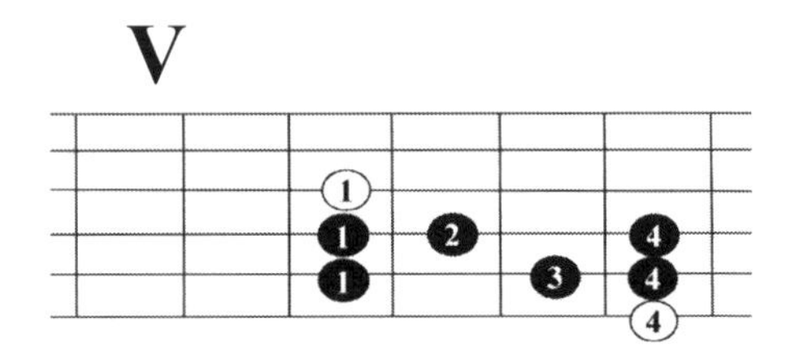

All Keys (vii)

i

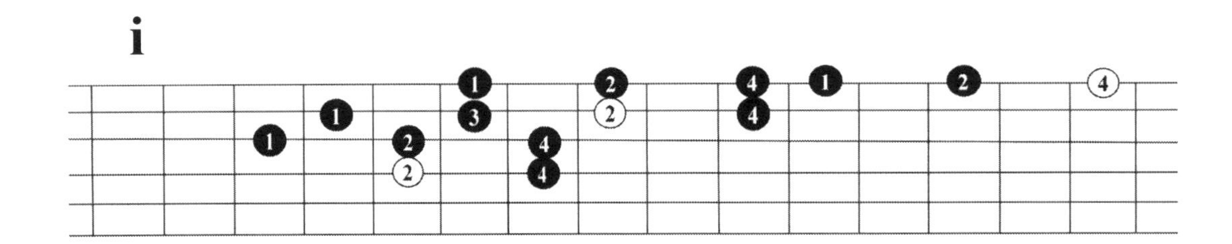

iv

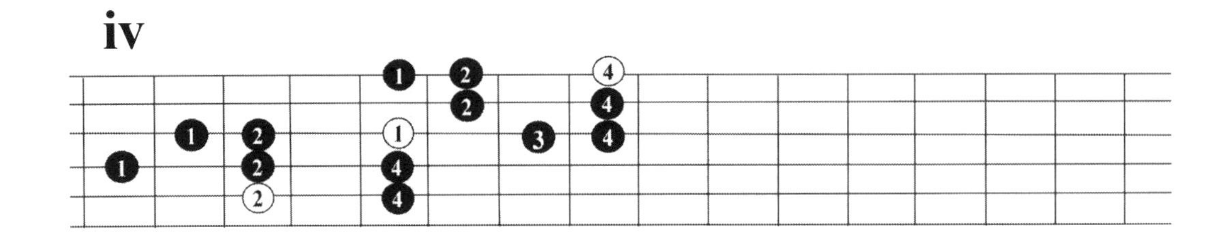

V

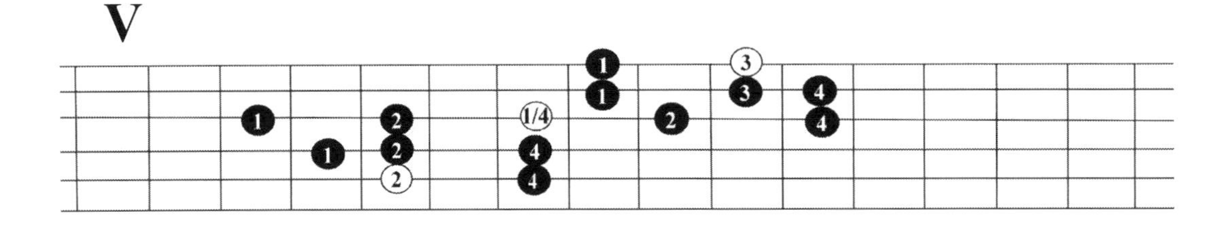

All Keys (viii)

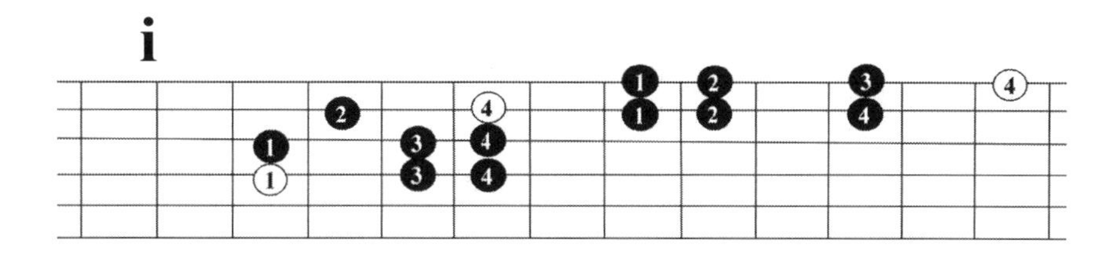

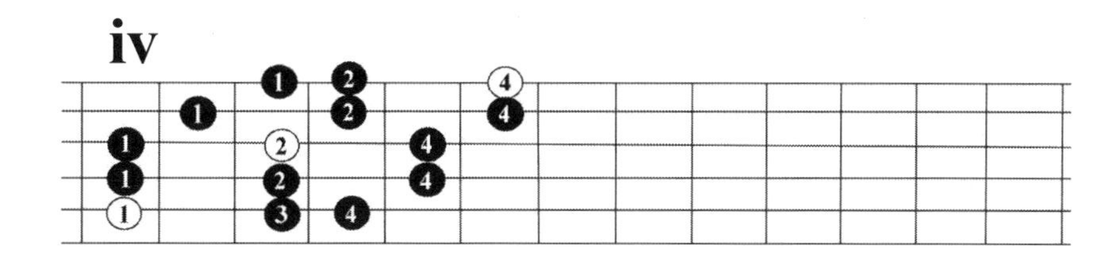

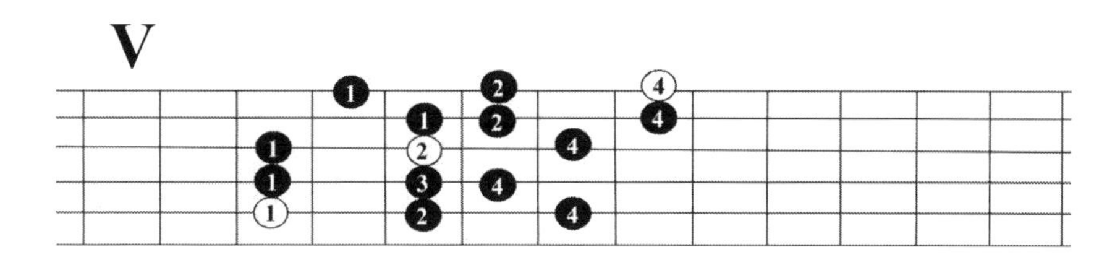

All Keys (ix)

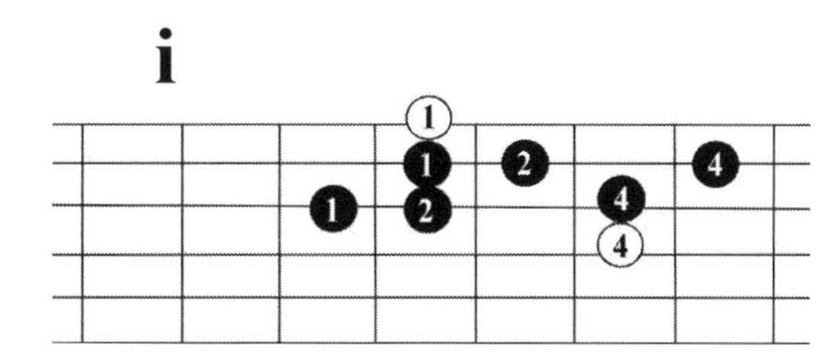

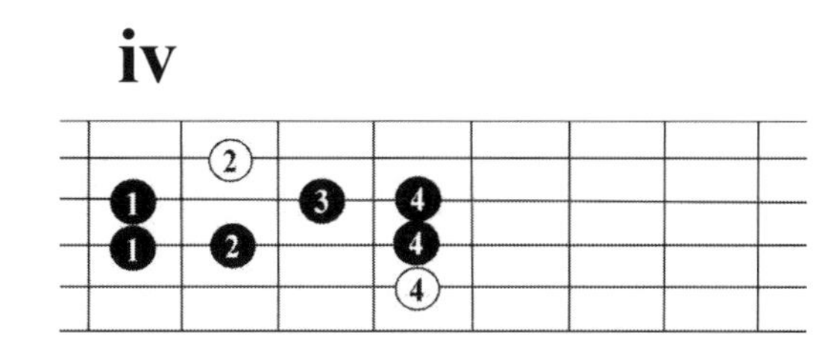

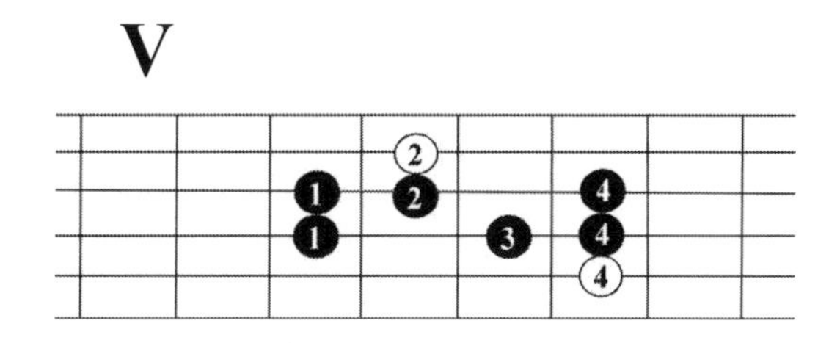

PART THIRTY-SEVEN

ii - V - i

MINOR KEYS
MODES

Key of Am

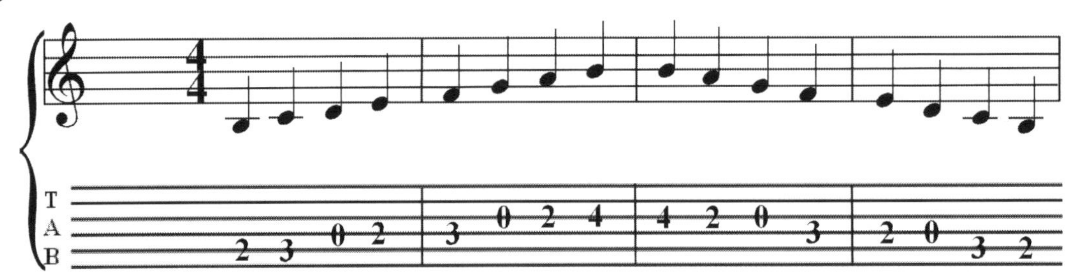

B Locrian - (Chord of B minor♭5/Bm7♭5)

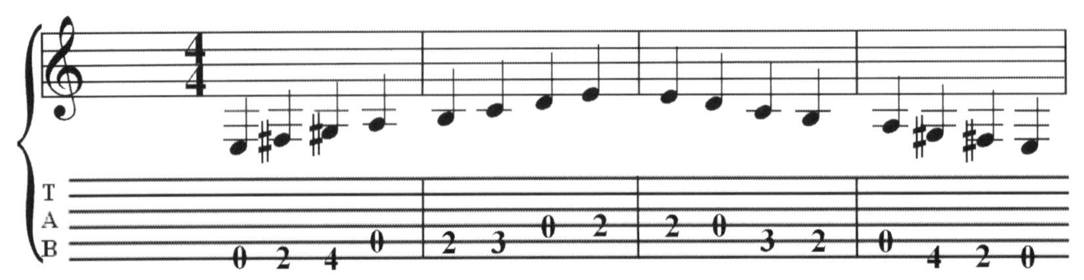

E Mixolydian ♭6 (i) - (Chord of E Major/E7)

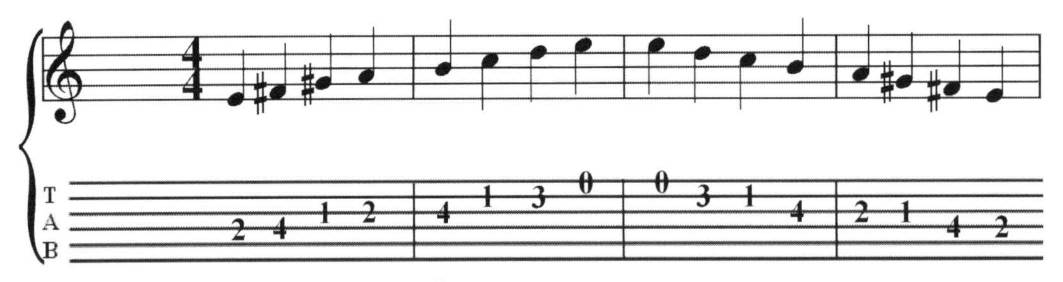

E Mixolydian ♭6 (ii) - (Chord of E Major/E7)

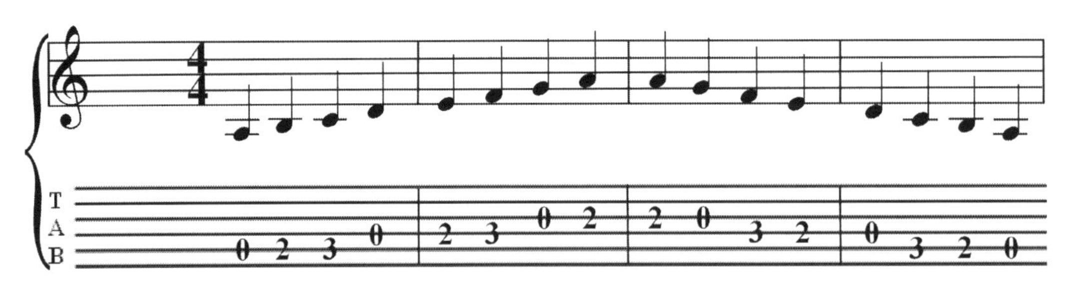

A Aeolian (i) - (Chord of A minor/Am7)

A Aeolian (ii) - (Chord of A minor/Am7)

Key of Em

F# Locrian (i) - (Chord of F# minor♭5/F#bm7♭5)

F# Locrian (ii) - (Chord of F# minor♭5/F#bm7♭5)

B Mixolydian ♭6 - (Chord of B Major/B7)

E Aeolian (i) - (Chord of E minor/Em7)

E Aeolian (ii) - (Chord of E minor/Em7)

Key of Bm

C# Locrian - (Chord of C# minor♭5/C#m7♭5)

F# Mixolydian ♭6 (i) - (Chord of F# Major/F#7)

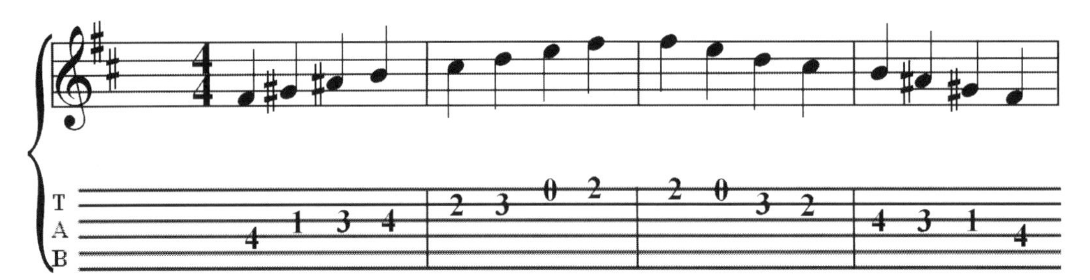

F# Mixolydian ♭6 (ii) - (Chord of F# Major/F#7)

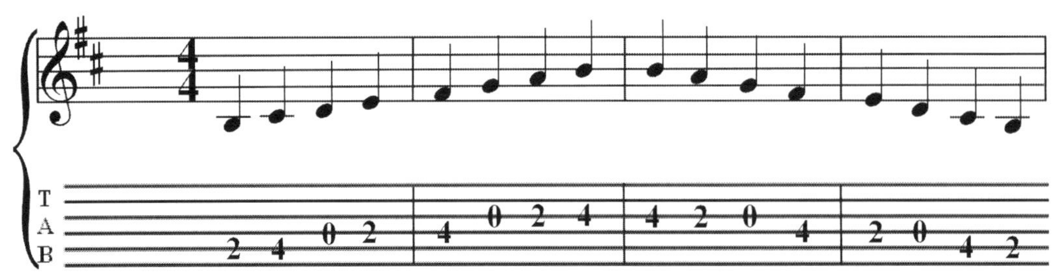

B Aeolian - (Chord of B minor/Bm7)

Key of F#m

G# Locrian (i) - (Chord of G# minor♭5/G#m7♭5)

G# Locrian (ii) - (Chord of G# minor♭5/G#m7♭5)

C# Mixolydian ♭6 - (Chord of C# Major/C#7)

F# Aeolian (i) - (Chord of F# minor/F#m7)

F# Aeolian (ii) - (Chord of F# minor/F#m7)

Key of C#m

D# Locrian - (Chord of D# minor♭5/D#m7♭5)

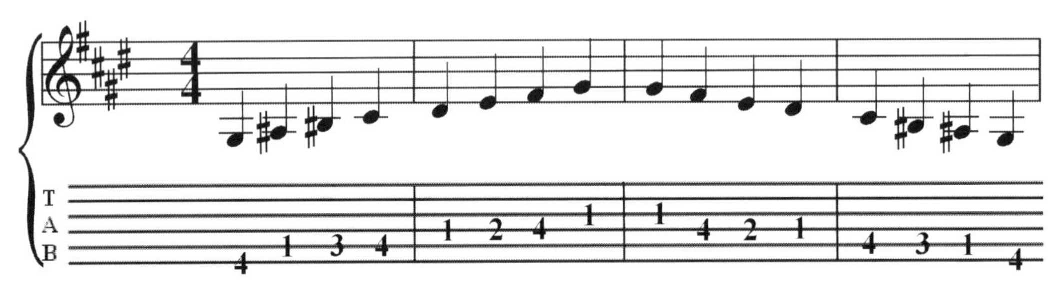

G# Mixolydian ♭6 (i) - (Chord of G# Major/G#7)

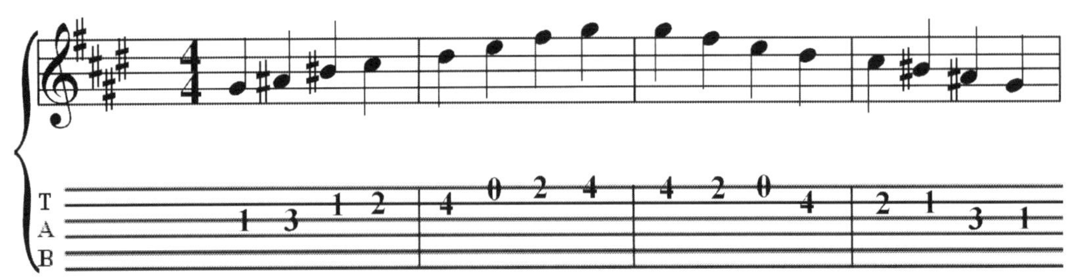

G# Mixolydian ♭6 (ii) - (Chord of G# Major/G#7)

C# Aeolian - (Chord of C# minor/C#m7)

Key of A♭m

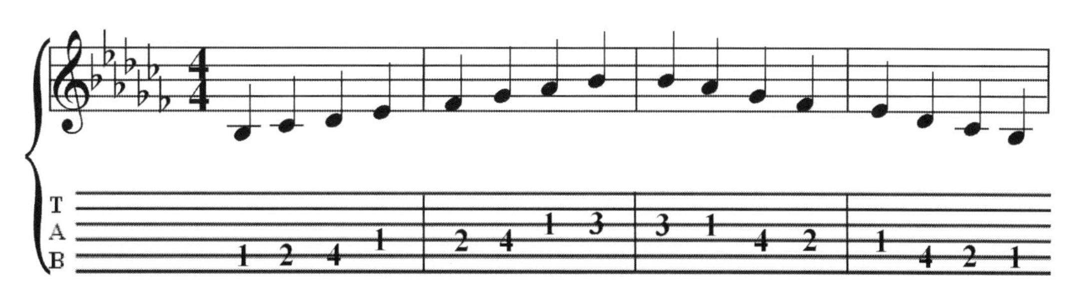

B♭ Locrian - (Chord of B♭ minor♭5/B♭m7♭5)

E♭ Mixolydian ♭6 - (Chord of E♭ Major/E♭7)

A♭ Aeolian (i) - (Chord of A♭ minor/A♭m7)

A♭ Aeolian (ii) - (Chord of A♭ minor/A♭m7)

Key of E♭m

F Locrian (i) - (Chord of F minor♭5/Fm7♭5)

F Locrian (ii) - (Chord of F minor♭5/Fm7♭5)

B♭ Mixolydian ♭6 - (Chord of B♭ Major/B7)

E♭ Aeolian - (Chord of E♭ minor/E♭m7)

Key of B♭m

C Locrian - (Chord of C minor♭5/Cm7♭5)

F Mixolydian ♭6 (i) - (Chord of F Major/F7)

F Mixolydian ♭6 (ii) - (Chord of F Major/F7)

B♭ Aeolian (i) - (Chord of B♭ minor/B♭m7)

Key of Fm

G Locrian (i) - (Chord of G minor♭5/Gm7♭5)

G Locrian (i) - (Chord of G minor♭5/Gm7♭5)

C Mixolydian ♭6 - (Chord of C Major/C7)

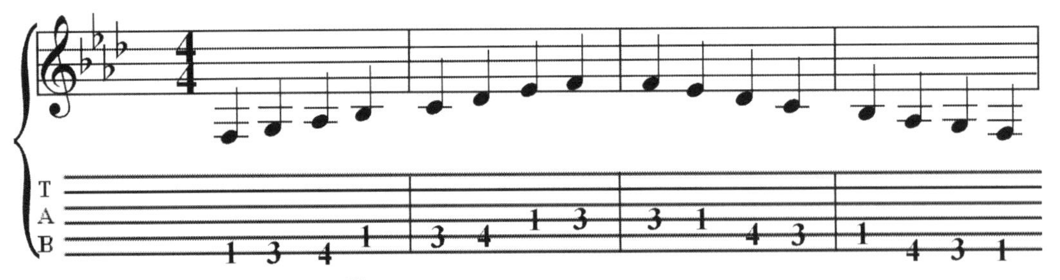

F Aeolian (i) - (Chord of F minor/Fm7)

F Aeolian (ii) - (Chord of F minor/Fm7)

Key of Cm

D Locrian - (Chord of D minor♭5/Dm7♭5)

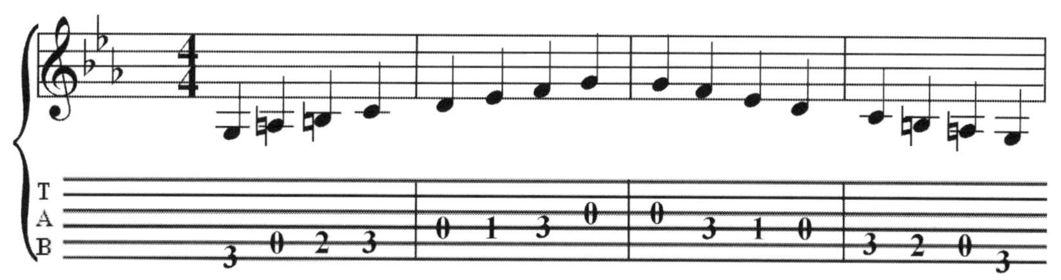

G Mixolydian ♭6 (i) - (Chord of G Major/G7)

G Mixolydian ♭6 (ii) - (Chord of G Major/G7)

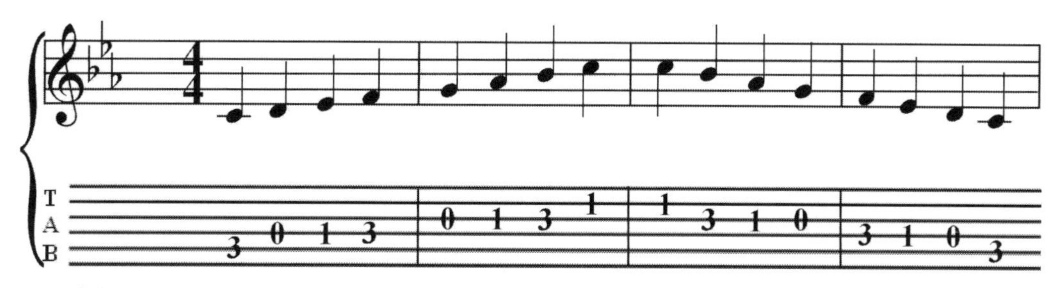

C Aeolian - (Chord of C minor/Cm7)

Key of Gm

A Locrian (i) - (Chord of A minor♭5/Am7♭5)

A Locrian (ii) - (Chord of A minor♭5/Am7♭5)

D Mixolydian ♭6 - (Chord of D Major/D7)

G Aeolian (i) - (Chord of F minor/Fm7)

G Aeolian (ii) - (Chord of F minor/Fm7)

Key of Dm

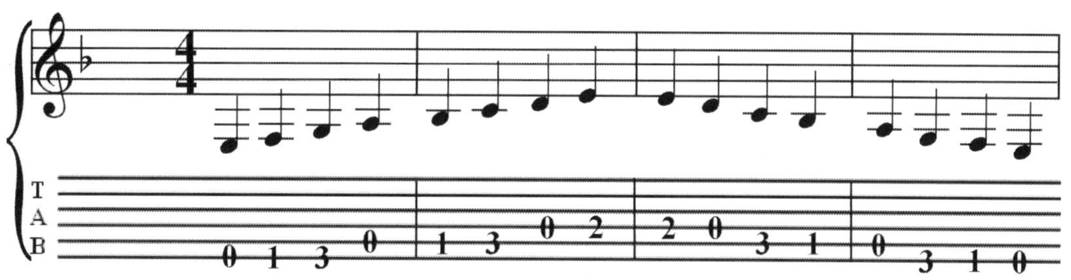

E Locrian (i) - (Chord of E minor♭5/Em7♭5)

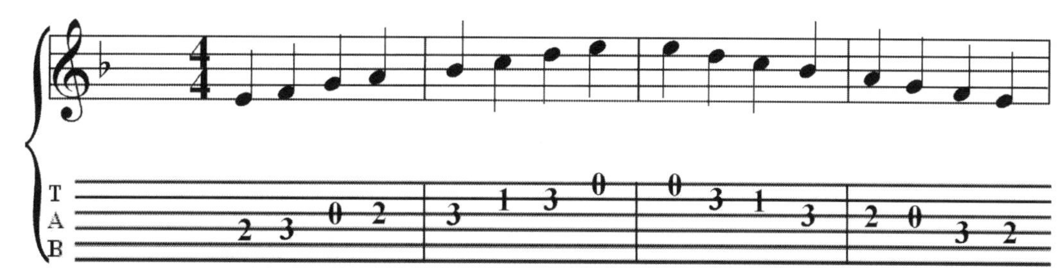

E Locrian (ii) - (Chord of E minor♭5/Em7♭5)

A Mixolydian ♭6 (i) - (Chord of A Major/A7)

A Mixolydian ♭6 (ii) - (Chord of A Major/A7)

D Aeolian - (Chord of D minor/Dm7)

All Keys (i)

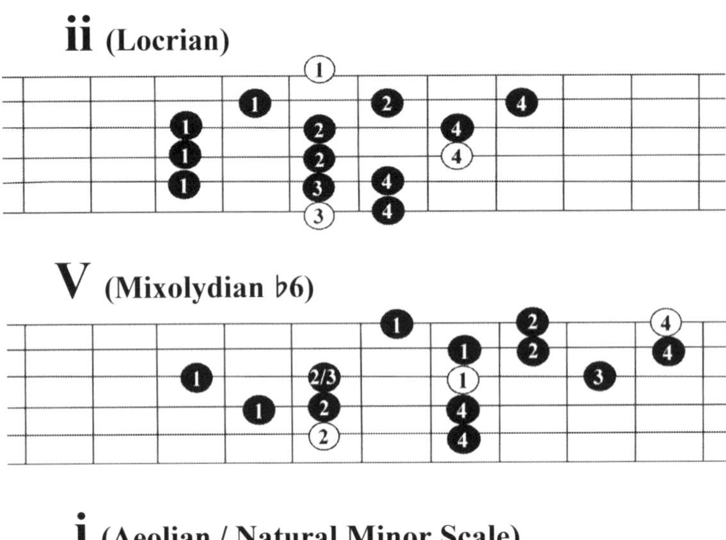

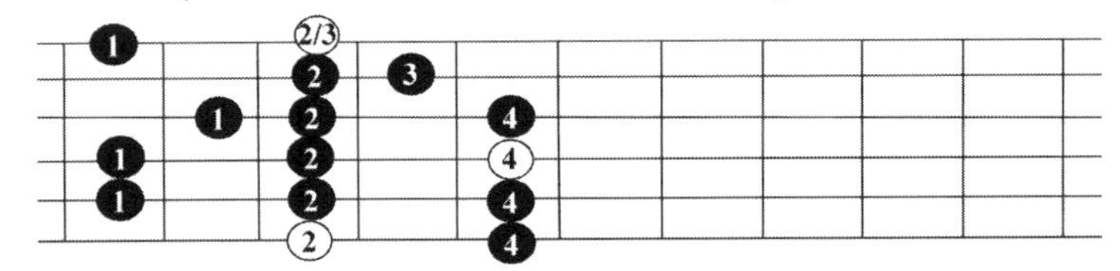

All Keys (ii)

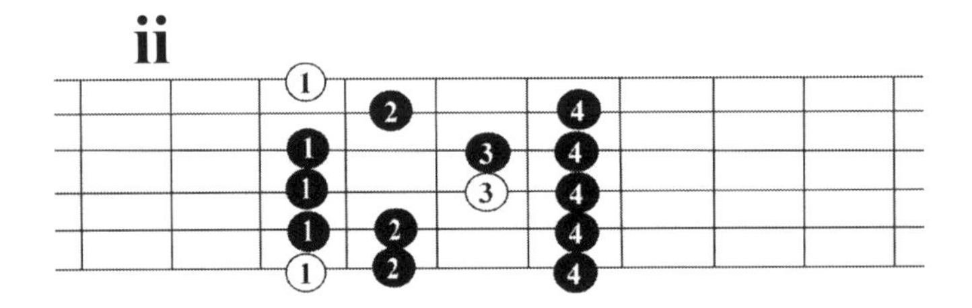

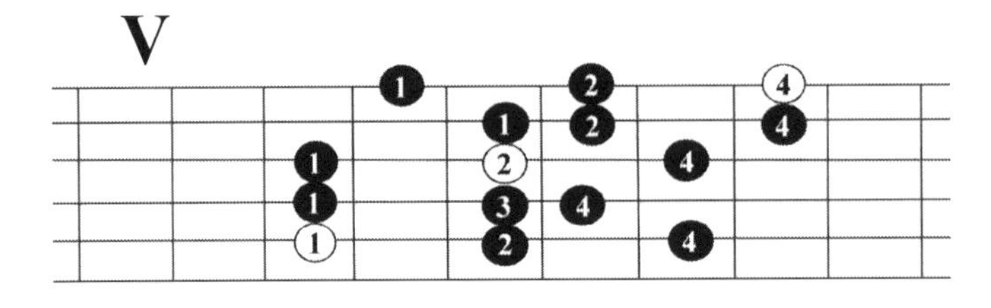

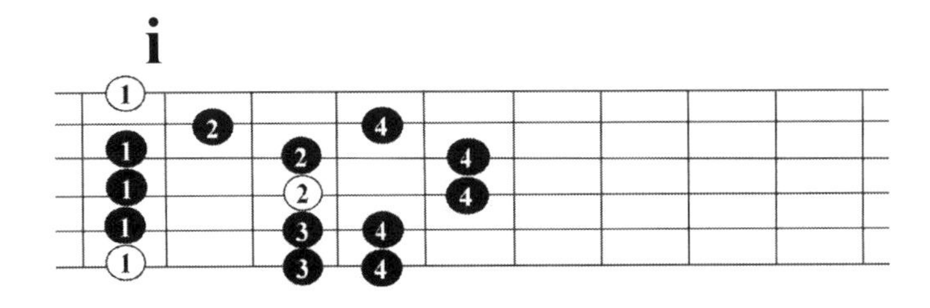

All Keys (iii)

ii

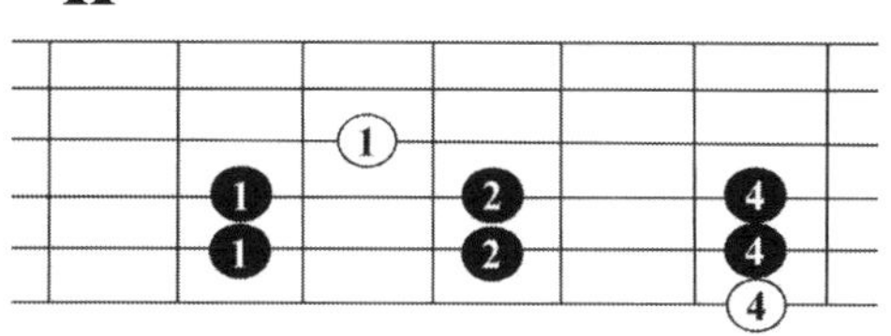

V

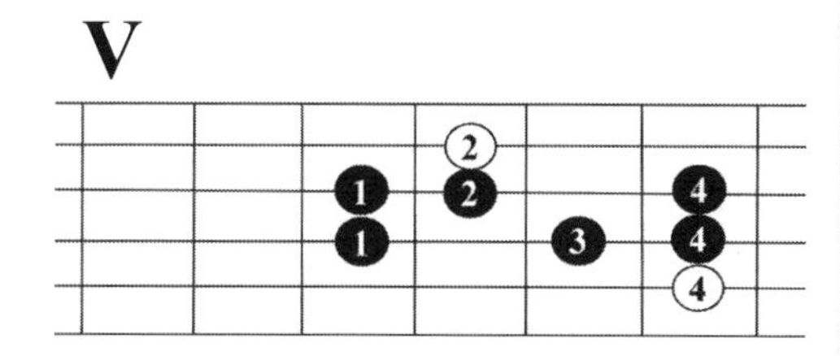

i

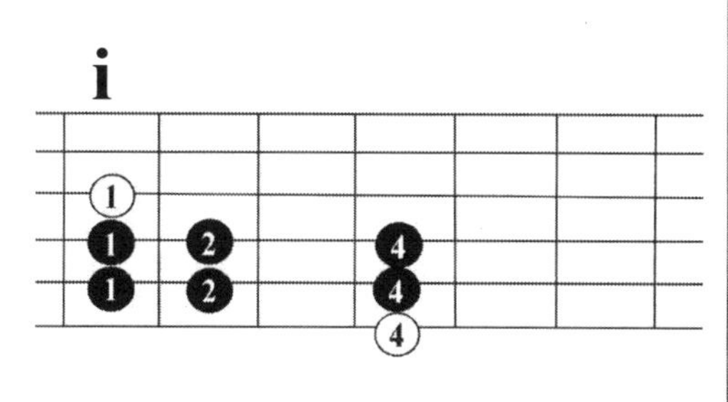

All Keys (iv)

ii

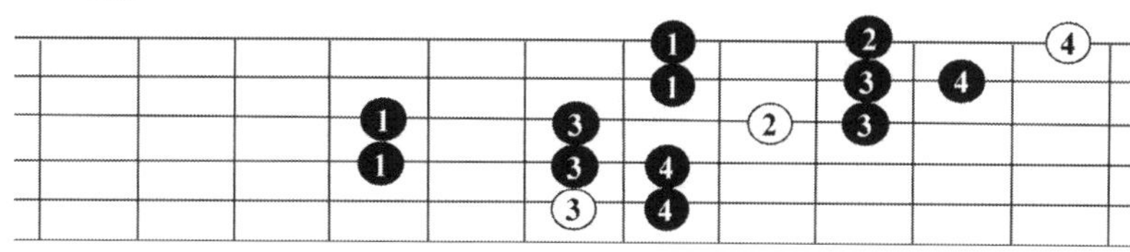

V

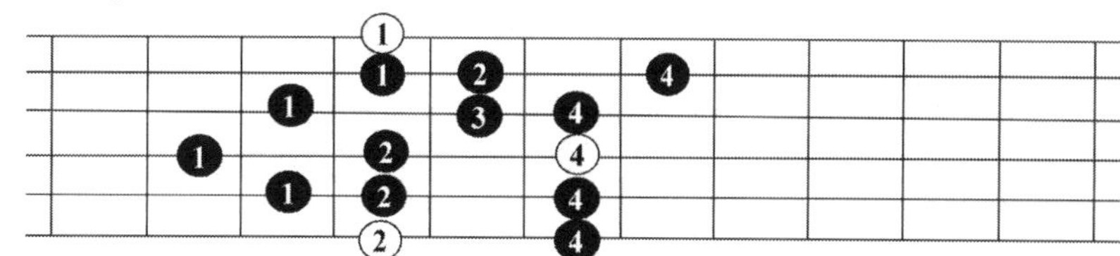

i

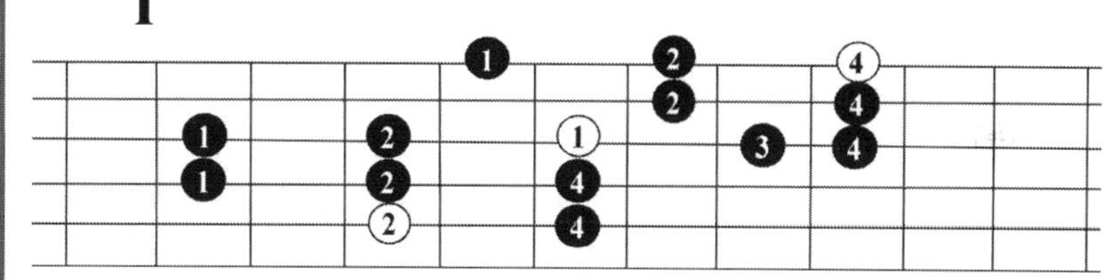

All Keys (v)

ii

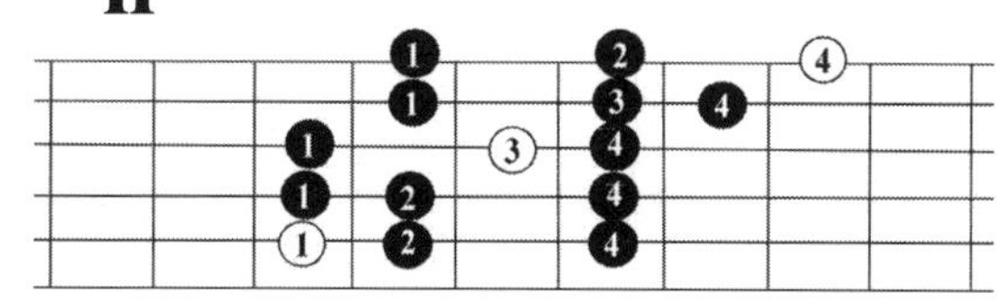

V

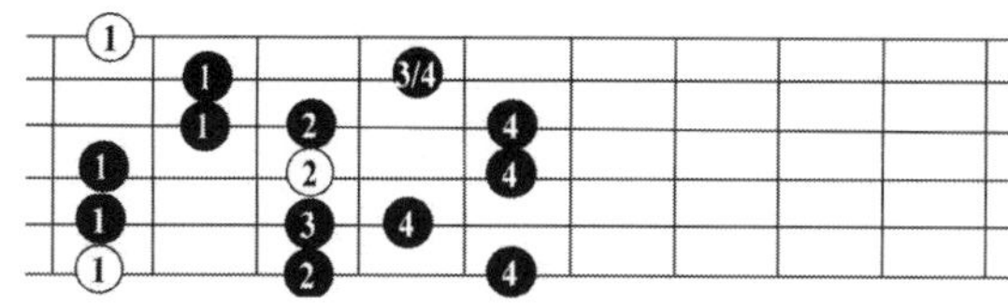

i

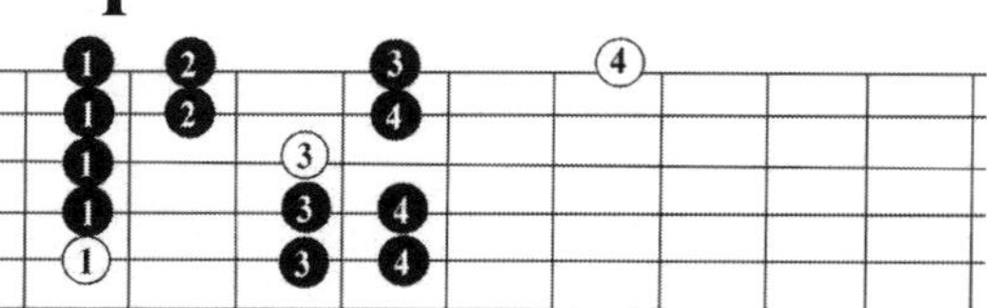

All Keys (vi)

ii

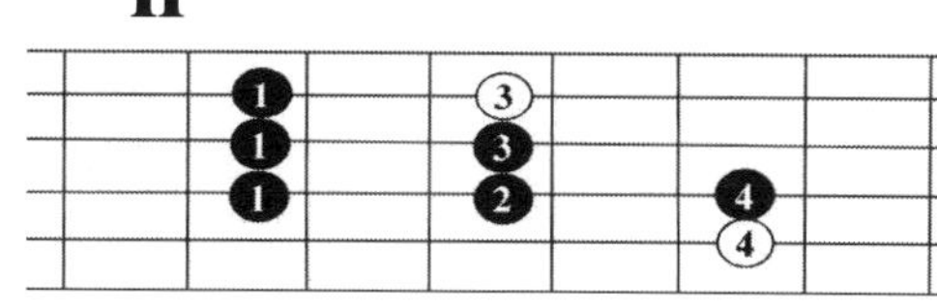

V

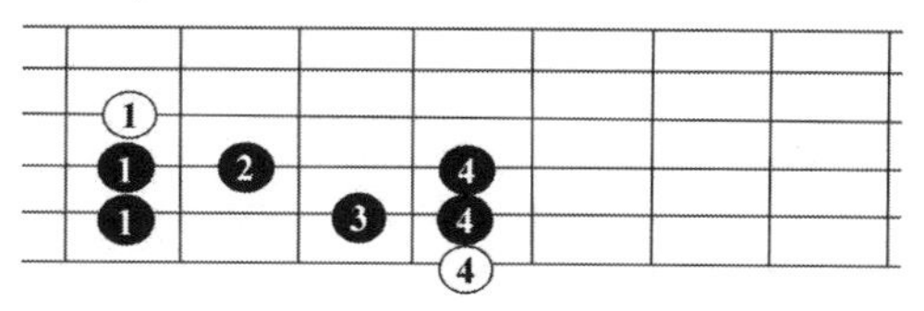

i

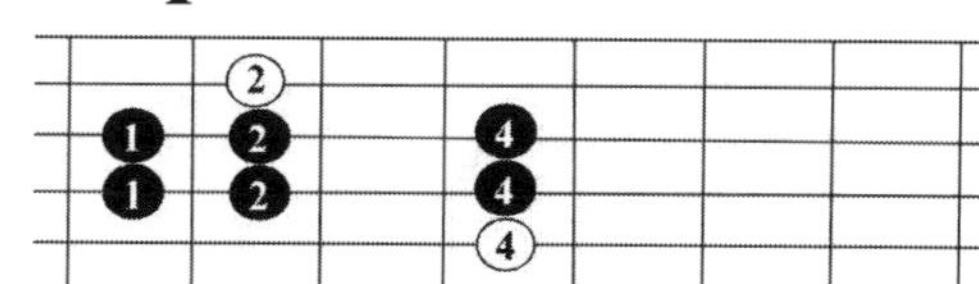

All Keys (vii)

ii

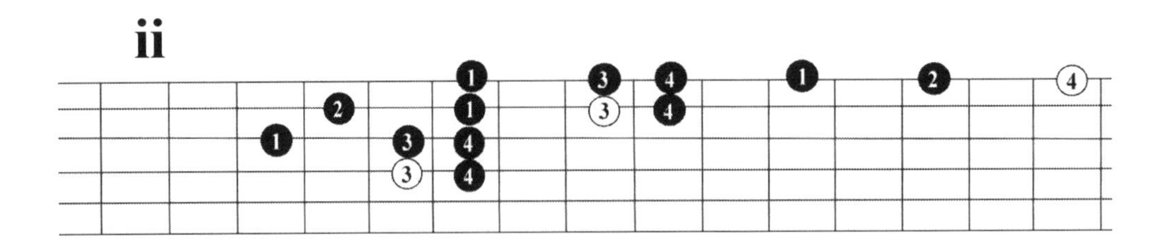

V

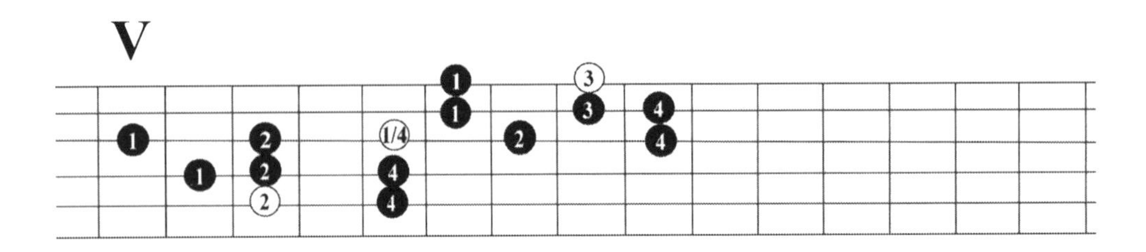

i

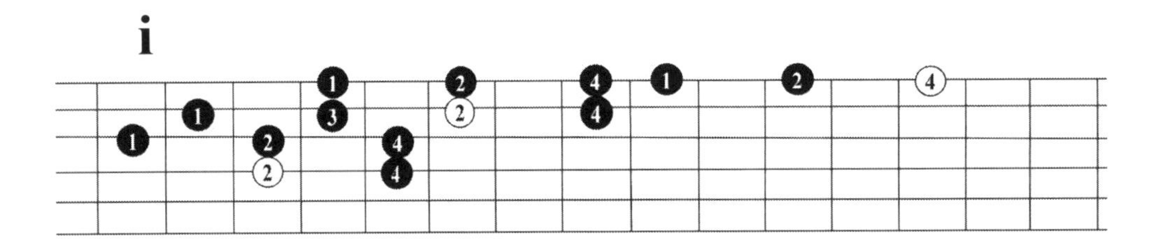

All Keys (viii)

ii

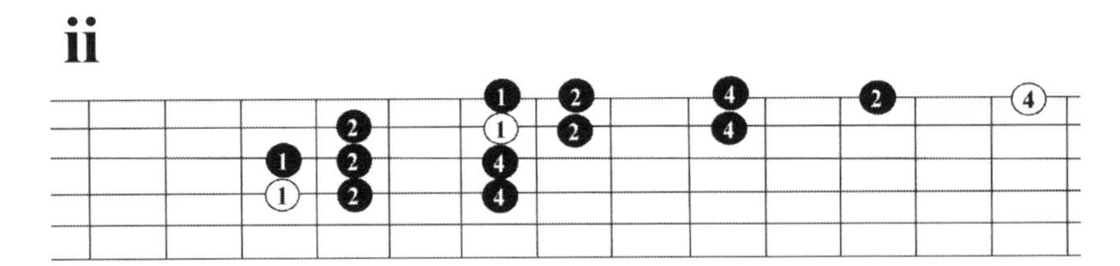

V

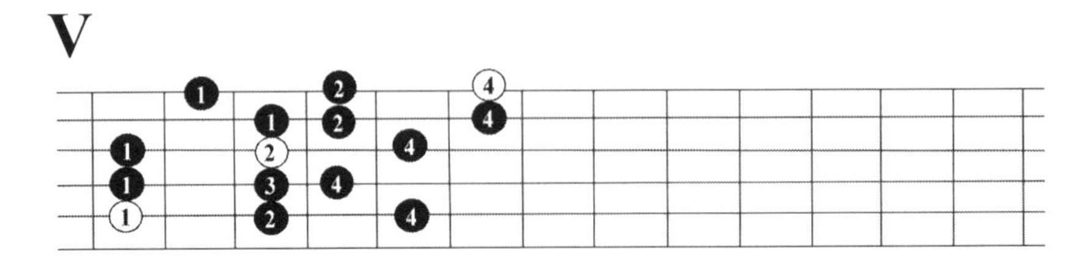

i

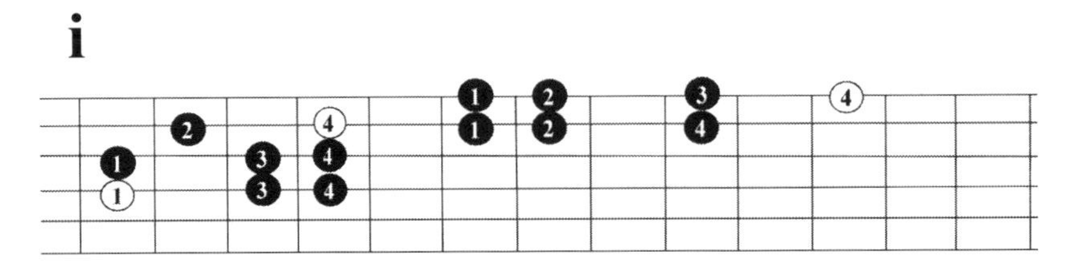

All Keys (ix)

ii

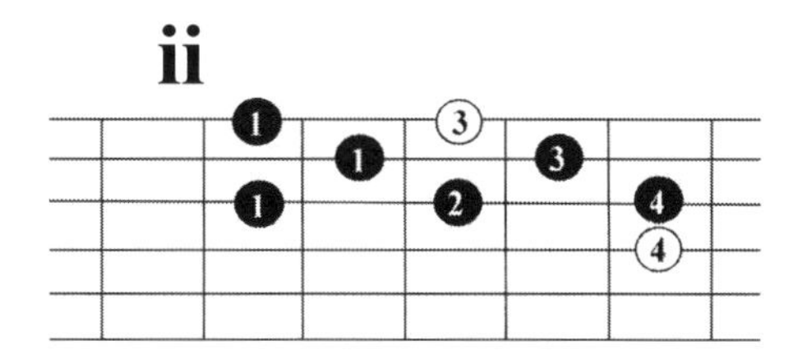

V

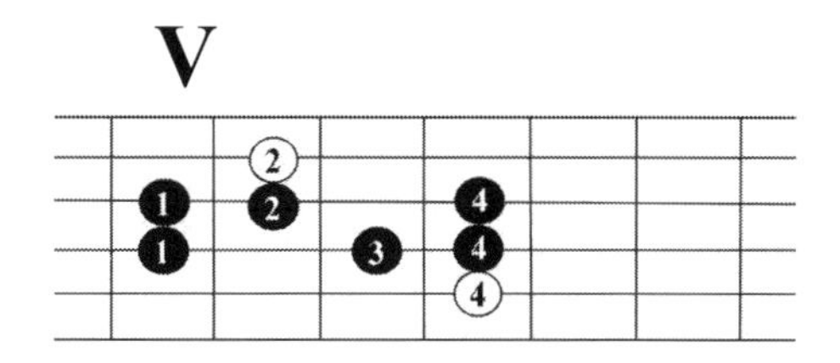

i

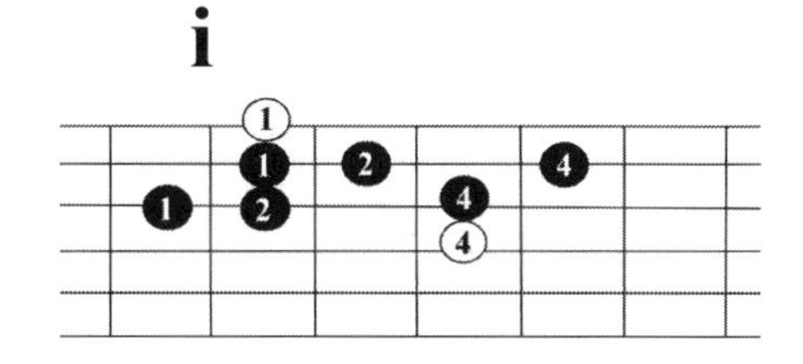

PART THIRTY-EIGHT

VI - ii - V - i

MINOR KEYS
MODES

Key of Am

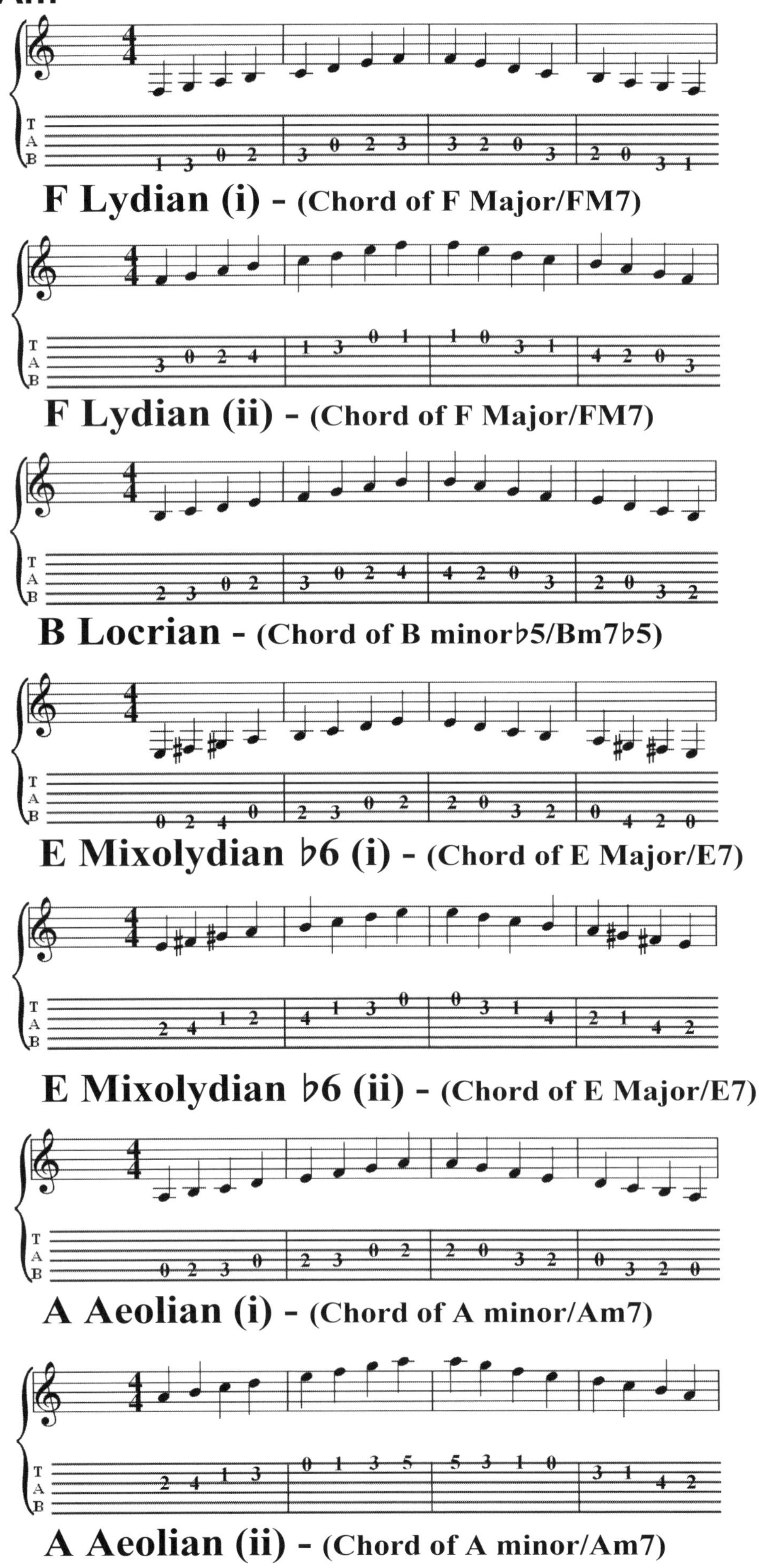

F Lydian (i) - (Chord of F Major/FM7)

F Lydian (ii) - (Chord of F Major/FM7)

B Locrian - (Chord of B minor♭5/Bm7♭5)

E Mixolydian ♭6 (i) - (Chord of E Major/E7)

E Mixolydian ♭6 (ii) - (Chord of E Major/E7)

A Aeolian (i) - (Chord of A minor/Am7)

A Aeolian (ii) - (Chord of A minor/Am7)

Key of Em

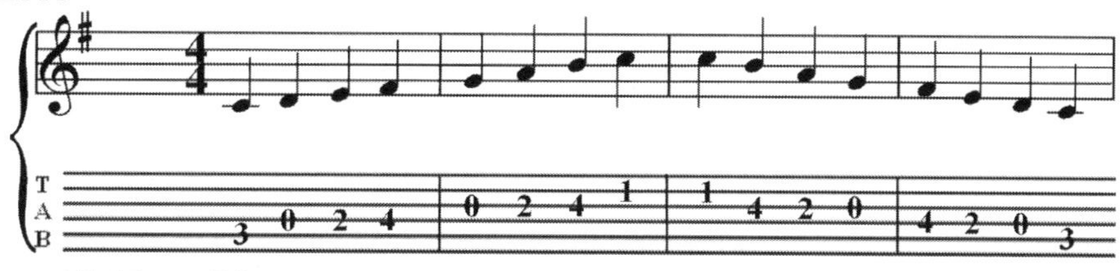

C Lydian - (Chord of C Major/CM7)

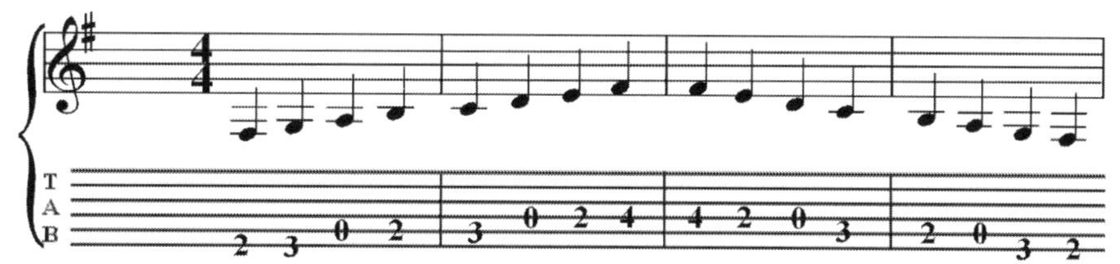

F# Locrian (i) - (Chord of F# minor♭5/F#m7♭5)

F# Locrian (ii) - (Chord of F# minor♭5/F#m7♭5)

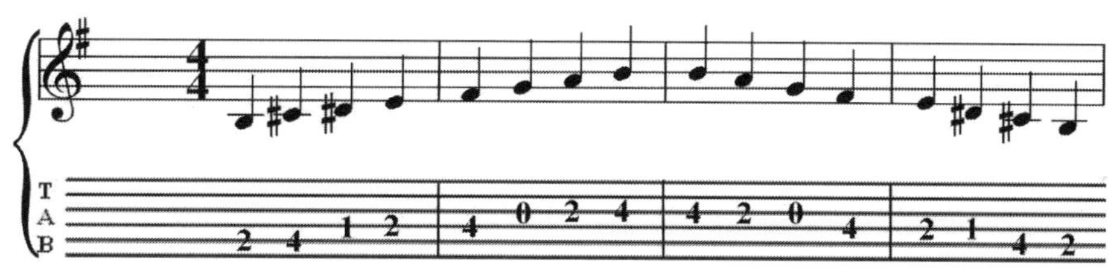

B Mixolydian ♭6 - (Chord of B Major/B7)

E Aeolian (i) - (Chord of E minor/Em7)

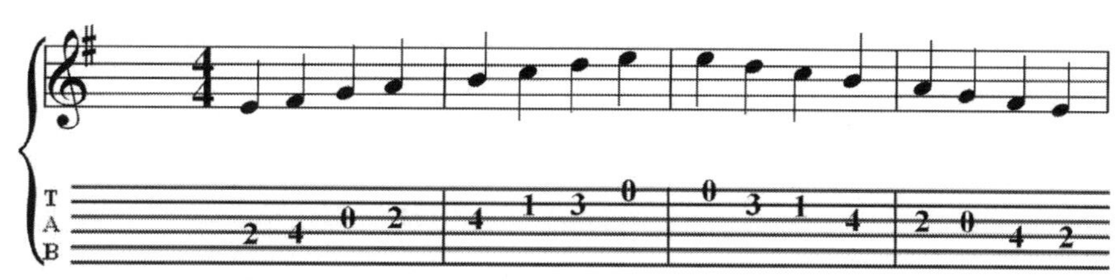

E Aeolian (ii) - (Chord of E minor/Em7)

Key of Bm

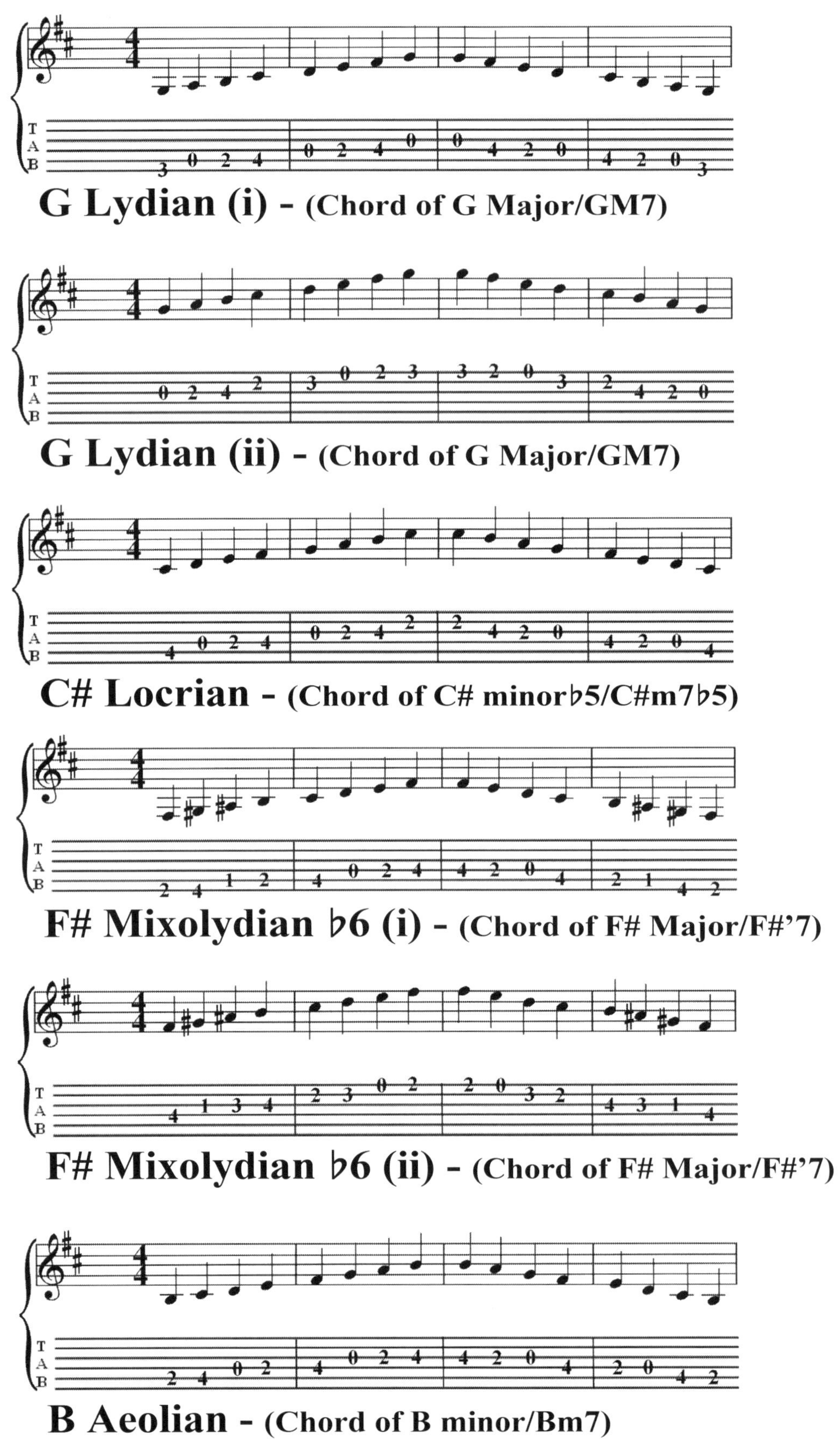
G Lydian (i) - (Chord of G Major/GM7)
G Lydian (ii) - (Chord of G Major/GM7)
C# Locrian - (Chord of C# minor♭5/C#m7♭5)
F# Mixolydian ♭6 (i) - (Chord of F# Major/F#'7)
F# Mixolydian ♭6 (ii) - (Chord of F# Major/F#'7)
B Aeolian - (Chord of B minor/Bm7)

Key of F#m

D Lydian - (Chord of D Major/DM7)

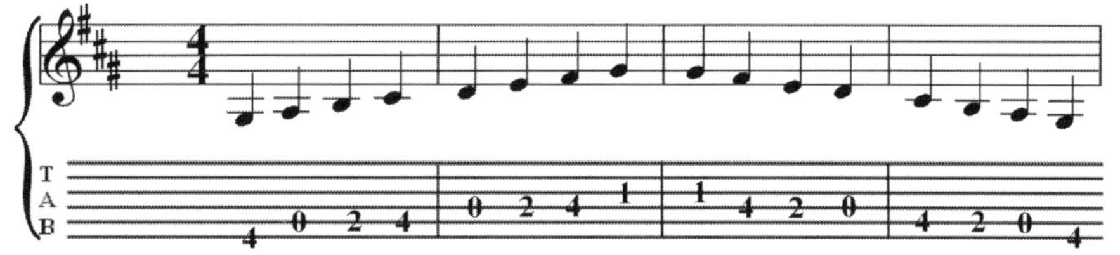

G# Locrian (i) - (Chord of G# minor♭5/G#m7♭5)

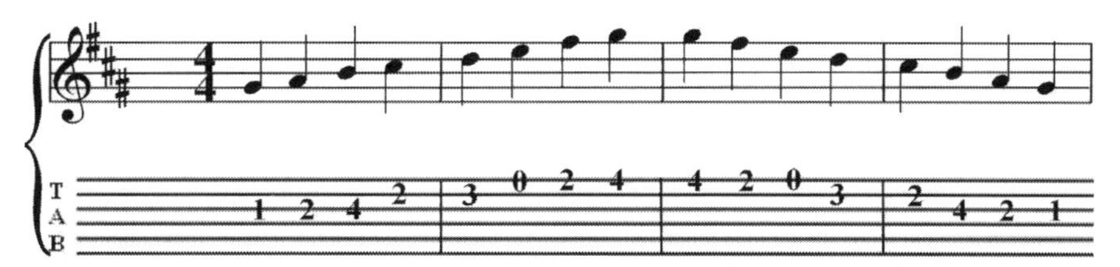

G# Locrian (ii) - (Chord of G# minor♭5/G#m7♭5)

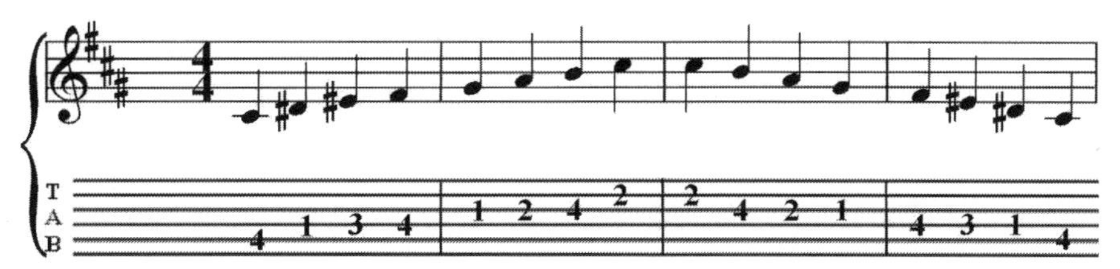

C# Mixolydian ♭6 - (Chord of C# Major/C#7)

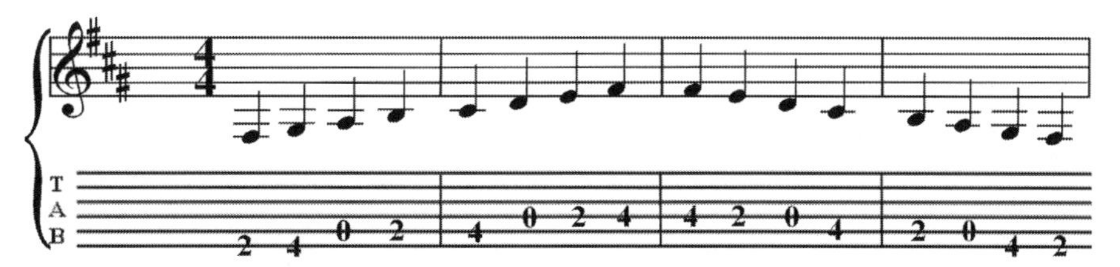

F# Aeolian (i) - (Chord of F# minor/F#m7)

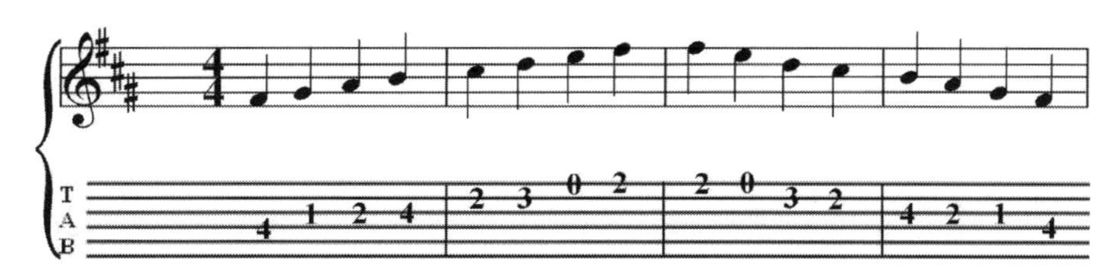

F# Aeolian (ii) - (Chord of F# minor/F#m7)

Key of C#m

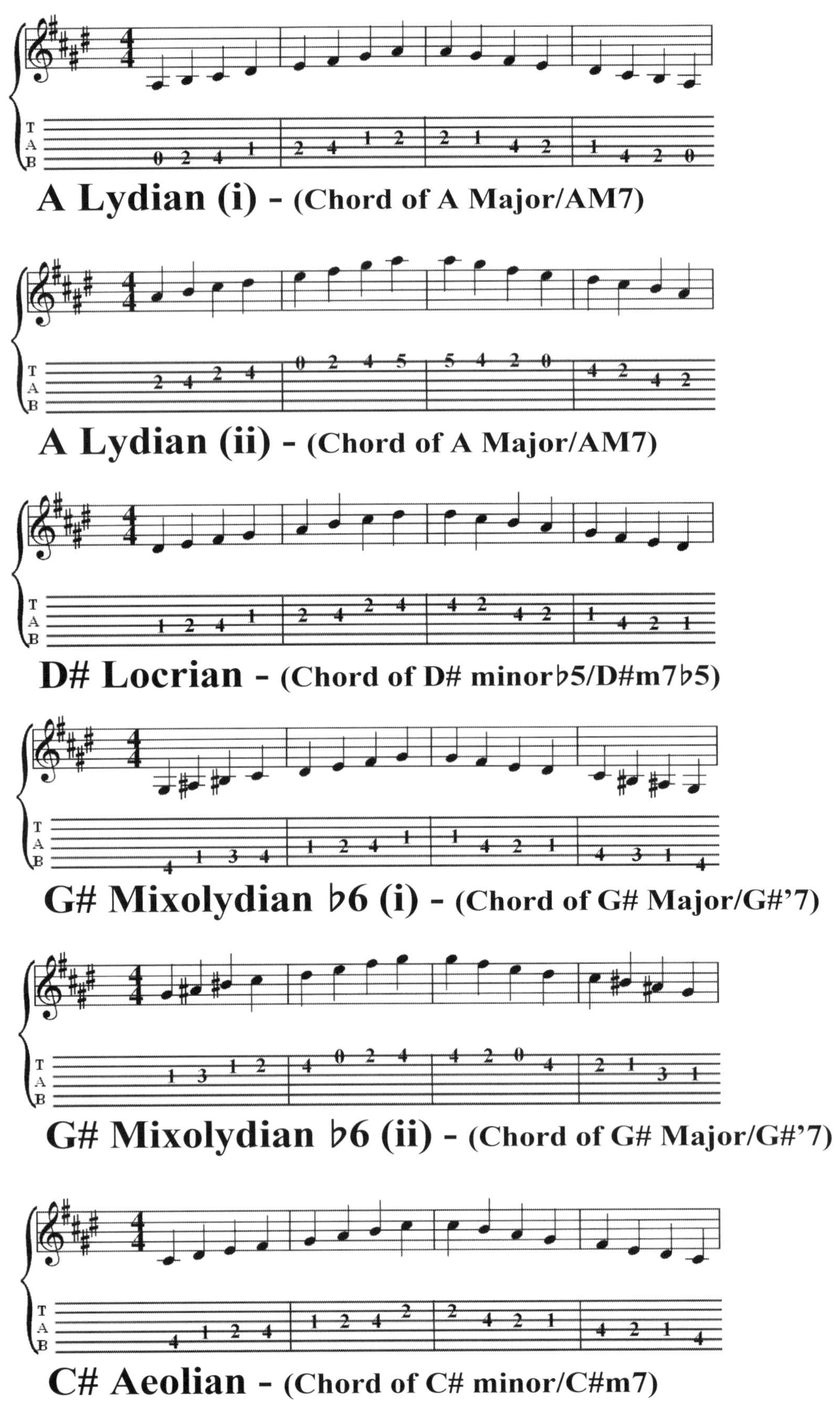

A Lydian (i) - (Chord of A Major/AM7)

A Lydian (ii) - (Chord of A Major/AM7)

D# Locrian - (Chord of D# minor♭5/D#m7♭5)

G# Mixolydian ♭6 (i) - (Chord of G# Major/G#'7)

G# Mixolydian ♭6 (ii) - (Chord of G# Major/G#'7)

C# Aeolian - (Chord of C# minor/C#m7)

Key of A♭m

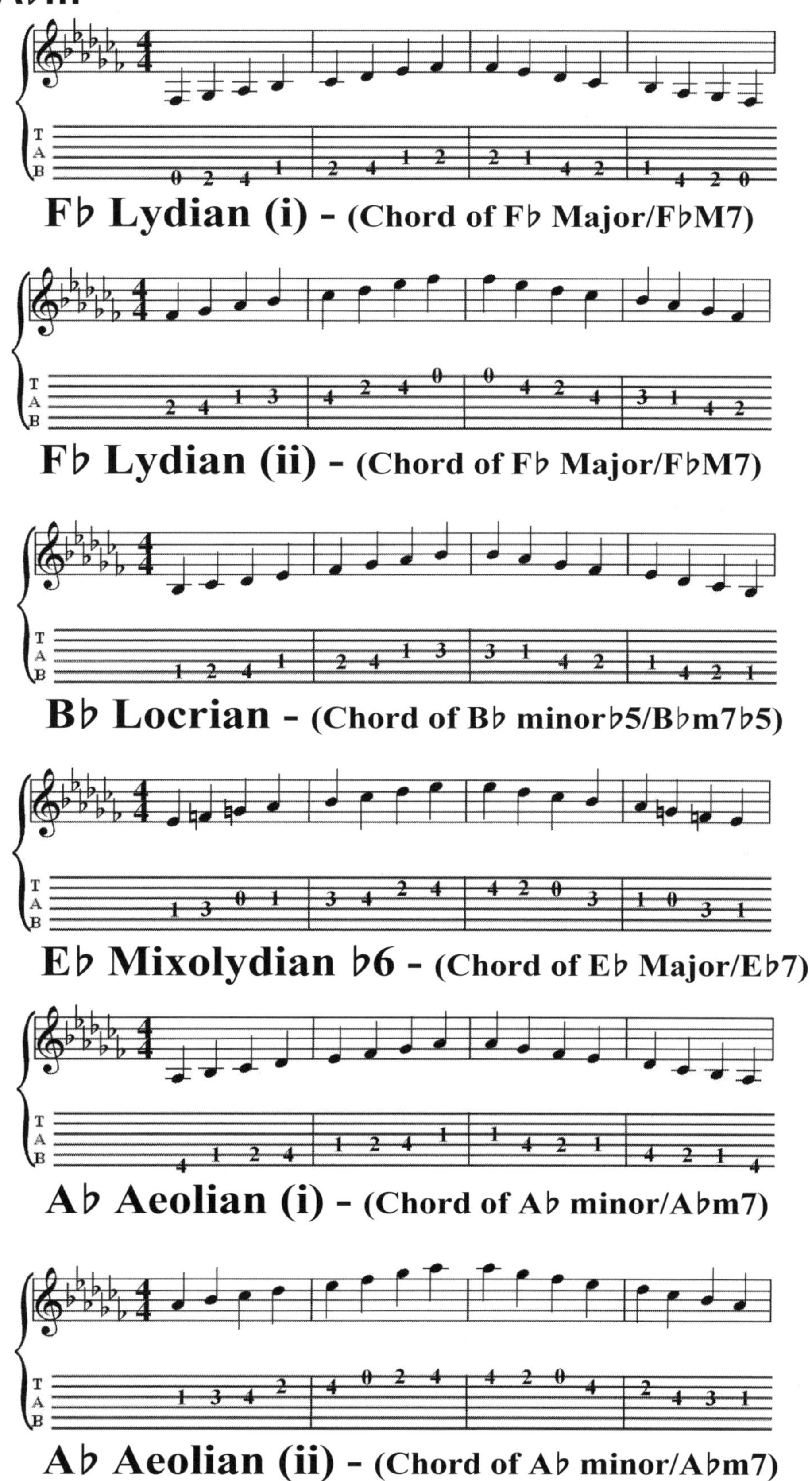

F♭ Lydian (i) - (Chord of F♭ Major/F♭M7)

F♭ Lydian (ii) - (Chord of F♭ Major/F♭M7)

B♭ Locrian - (Chord of B♭ minor♭5/B♭m7♭5)

E♭ Mixolydian ♭6 - (Chord of E♭ Major/E♭7)

A♭ Aeolian (i) - (Chord of A♭ minor/A♭m7)

A♭ Aeolian (ii) - (Chord of A♭ minor/A♭m7)

Key of E♭m

C♭ Lydian - (Chord of C♭ Major/C♭M7)

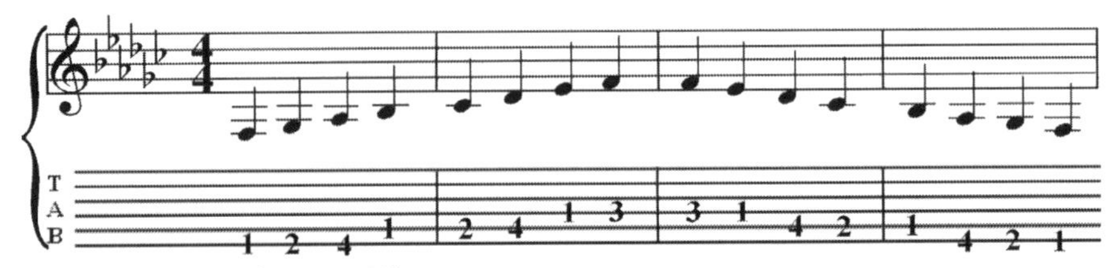

F Locrian (i) - (Chord of F minor♭5/Fm7♭5)

F Locrian (ii) - (Chord of F minor♭5/Fm7♭5)

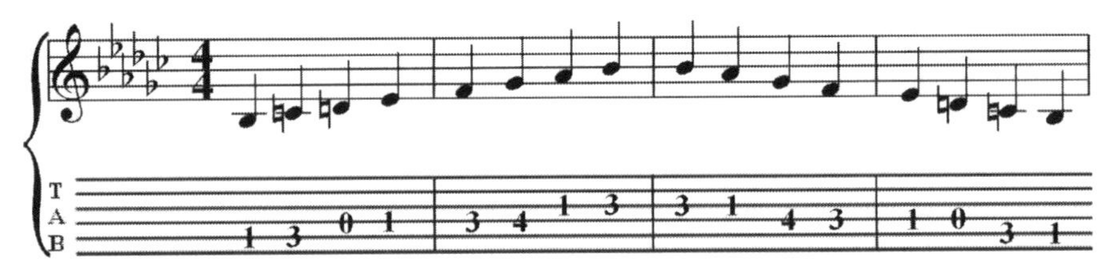

B♭ Mixolydian ♭6 - (Chord of B♭ Major/B♭7)

E♭ Aeolian - (Chord of E♭ minor/E♭m7)

Key of B♭m

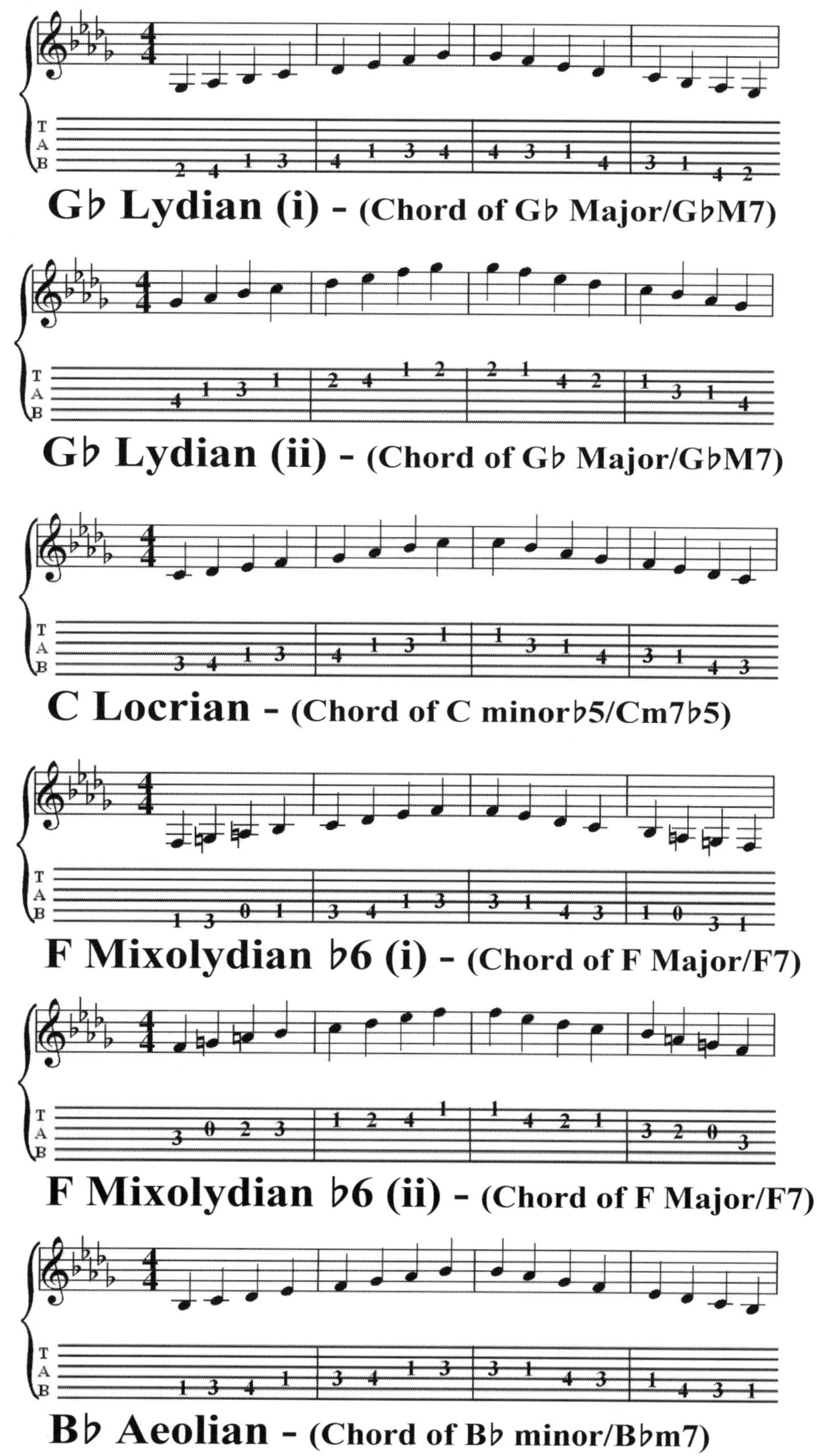

G♭ Lydian (i) - (Chord of G♭ Major/G♭M7)

G♭ Lydian (ii) - (Chord of G♭ Major/G♭M7)

C Locrian - (Chord of C minor♭5/Cm7♭5)

F Mixolydian ♭6 (i) - (Chord of F Major/F7)

F Mixolydian ♭6 (ii) - (Chord of F Major/F7)

B♭ Aeolian - (Chord of B♭ minor/B♭m7)

Key of Fm

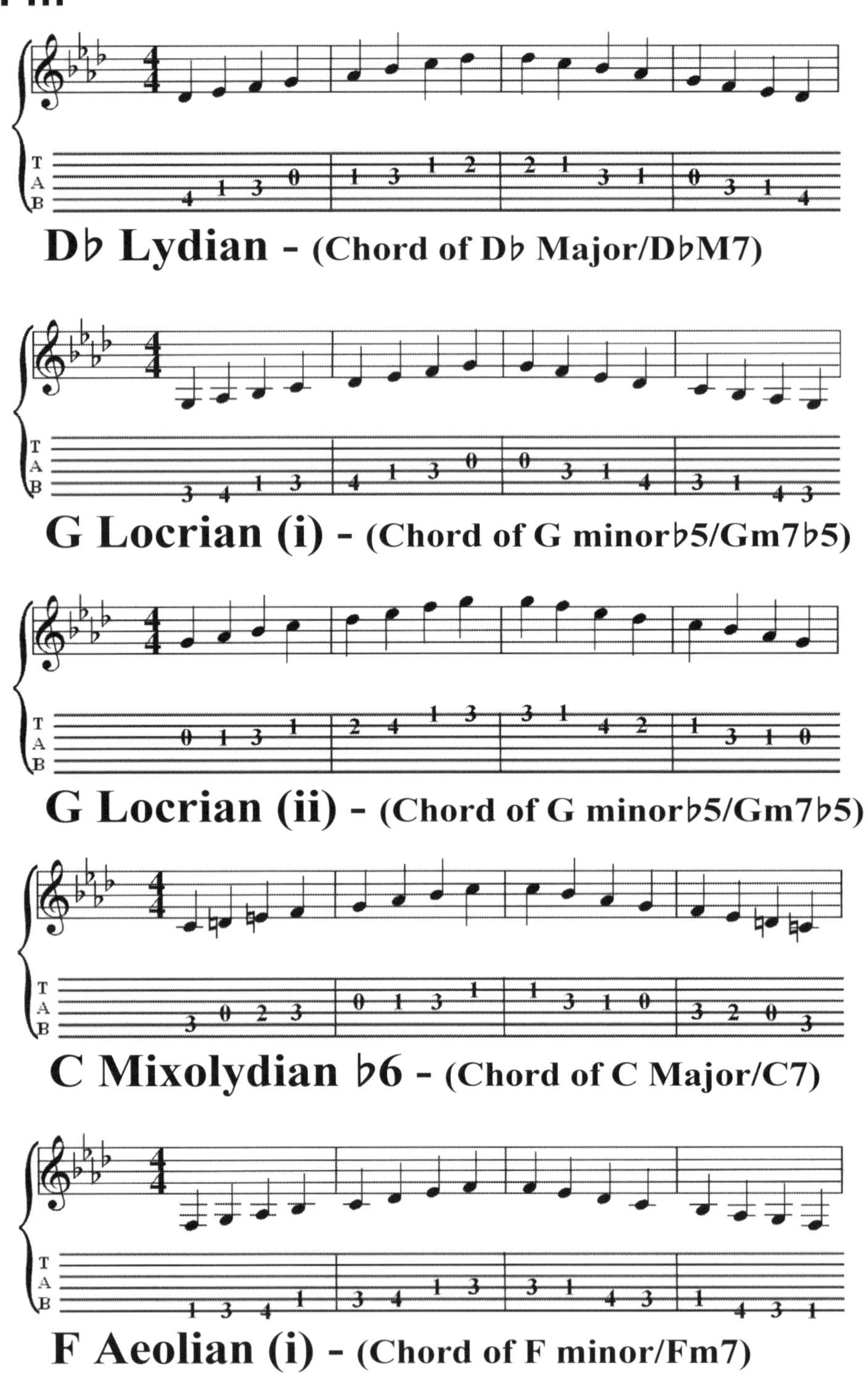

D♭ Lydian - (Chord of D♭ Major/D♭M7)

G Locrian (i) - (Chord of G minor♭5/Gm7♭5)

G Locrian (ii) - (Chord of G minor♭5/Gm7♭5)

C Mixolydian ♭6 - (Chord of C Major/C7)

F Aeolian (i) - (Chord of F minor/Fm7)

F Aeolian (ii) - (Chord of F minor/Fm7)

Key of Cm

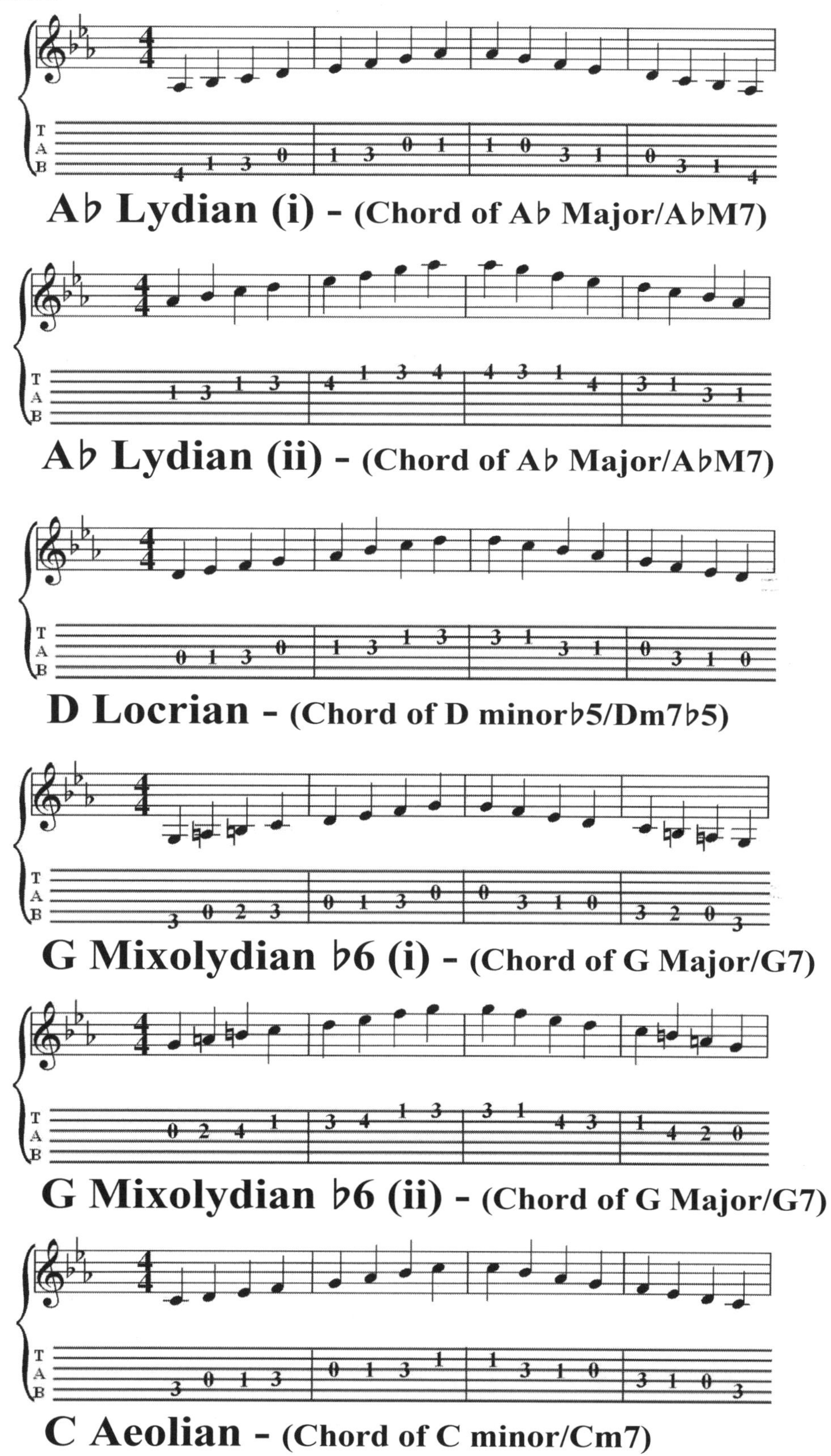

A♭ Lydian (i) - (Chord of A♭ Major/A♭M7)

A♭ Lydian (ii) - (Chord of A♭ Major/A♭M7)

D Locrian - (Chord of D minor♭5/Dm7♭5)

G Mixolydian ♭6 (i) - (Chord of G Major/G7)

G Mixolydian ♭6 (ii) - (Chord of G Major/G7)

C Aeolian - (Chord of C minor/Cm7)

Key of Gm

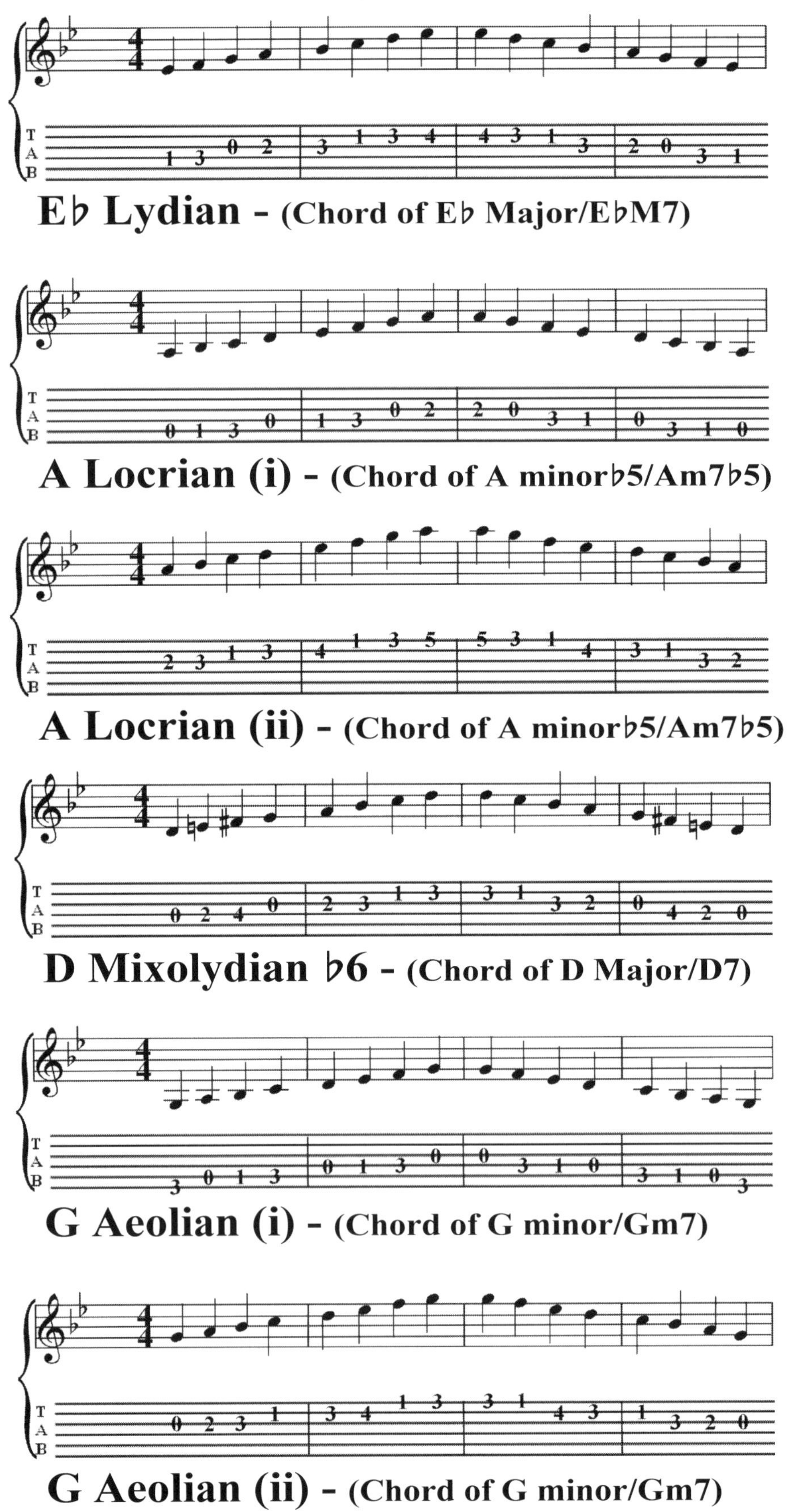
E♭ Lydian - (Chord of E♭ Major/E♭M7)
A Locrian (i) - (Chord of A minor♭5/Am7♭5)
A Locrian (ii) - (Chord of A minor♭5/Am7♭5)
D Mixolydian ♭6 - (Chord of D Major/D7)
G Aeolian (i) - (Chord of G minor/Gm7)
G Aeolian (ii) - (Chord of G minor/Gm7)

Key of Dm

B♭ Lydian - (Chord of B♭ Major/B♭M7)

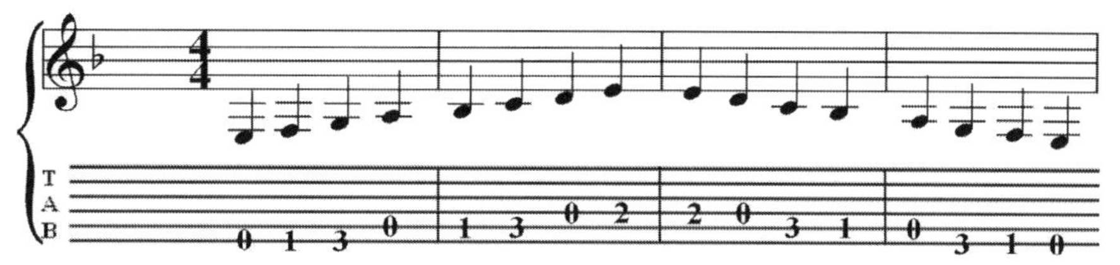

E Locrian (i) - (Chord of E minor♭5/Em7♭5)

E Locrian (ii) - (Chord of E minor♭5/Em7♭5)

A Mixolydian ♭6 (i) - (Chord of A Major/A7)

A Mixolydian ♭6 (ii) - (Chord of A Major/A7)

D Aeolian - (Chord of D minor/Dm7)

All Keys (i)

VI (Lydian)

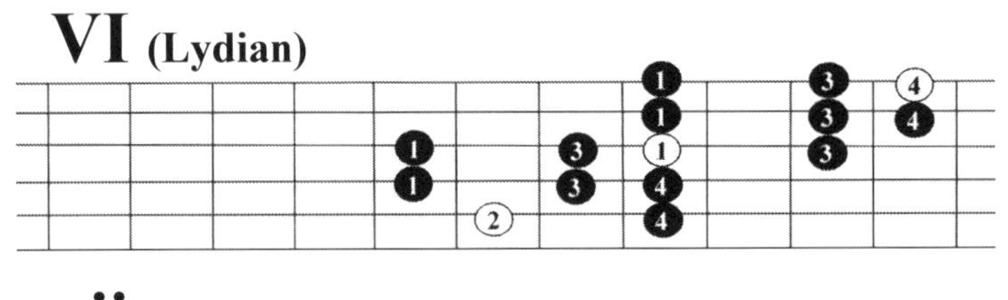

ii (Locrian)

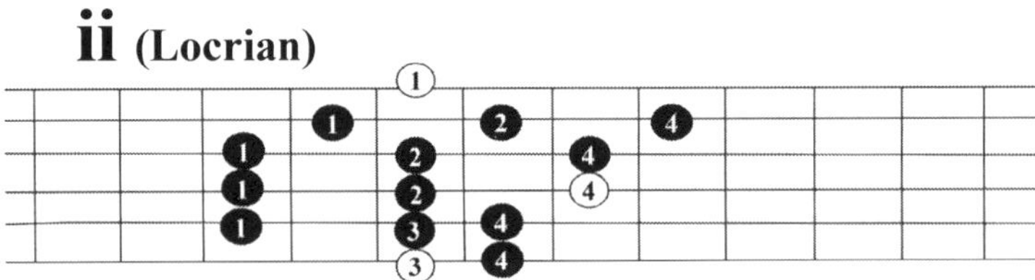

V (Mixolydian ♭6)

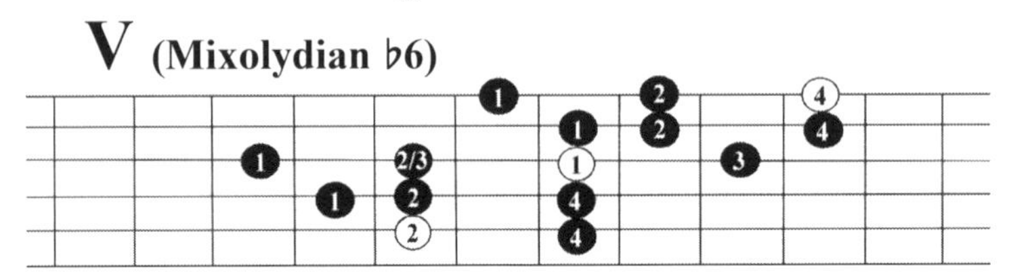

i (Aeolian / Natural Minor Scale)

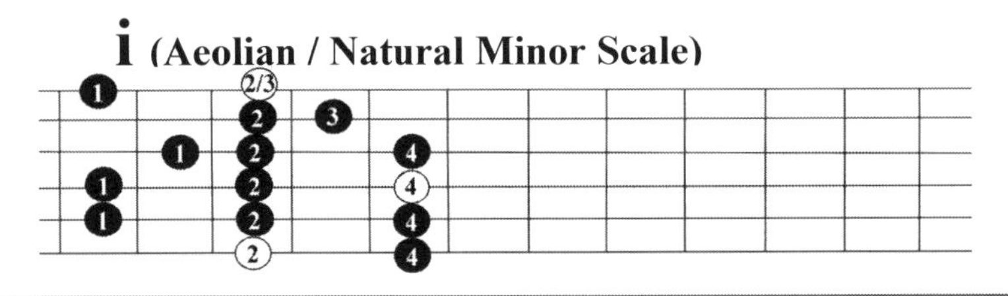

All Keys (ii)

VI

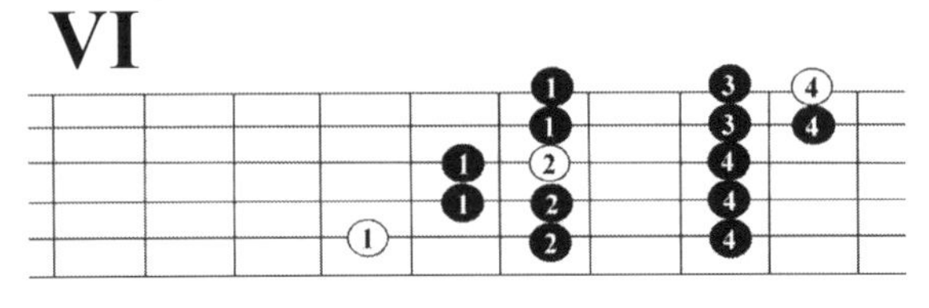

ii

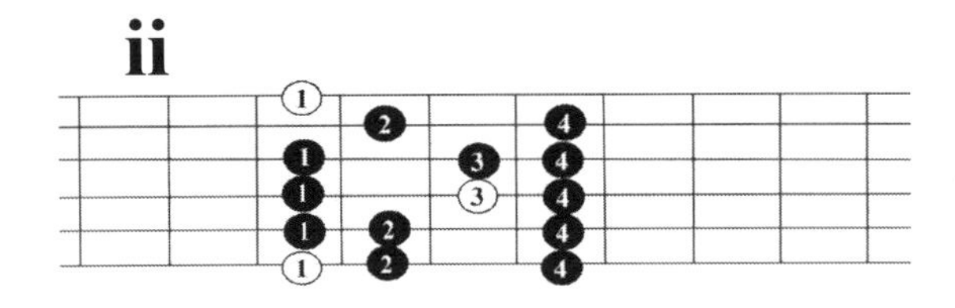

V

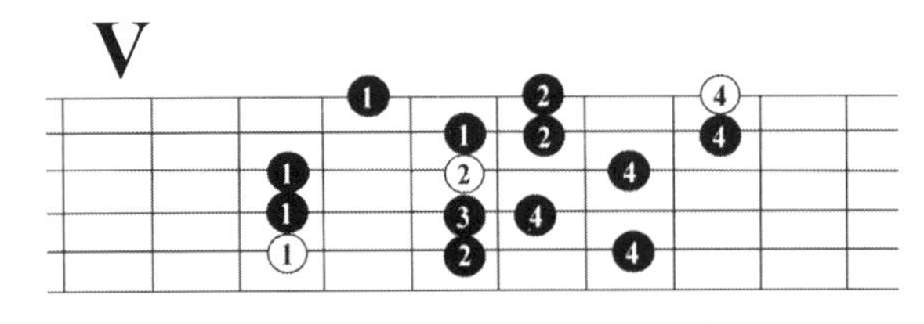

i

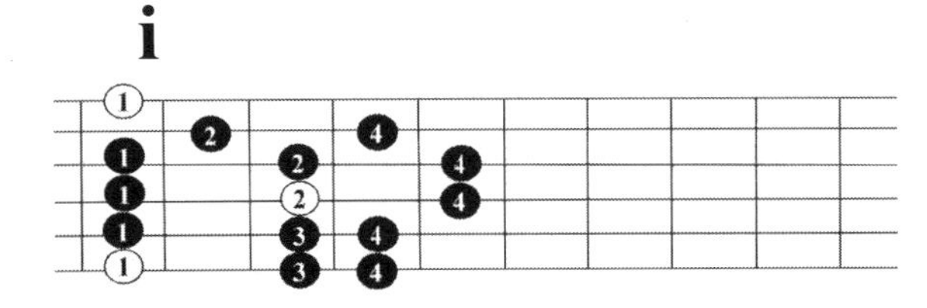

All Keys (iii)

VI

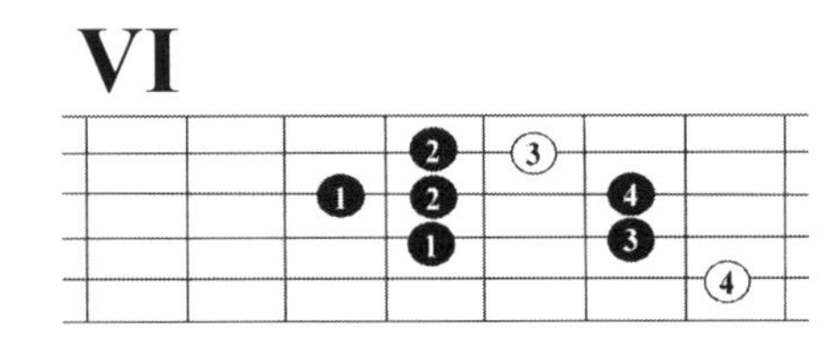

ii

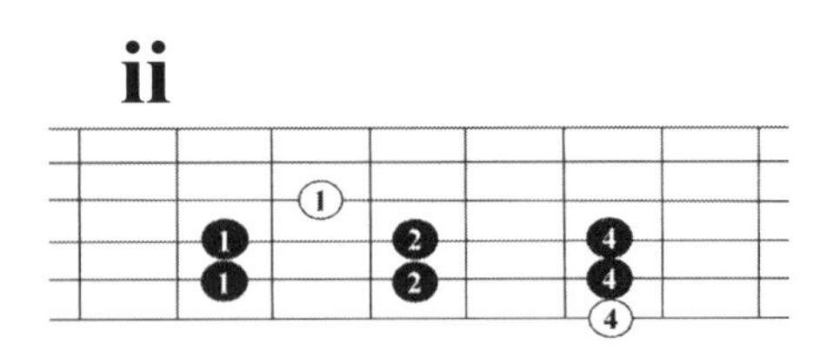

V

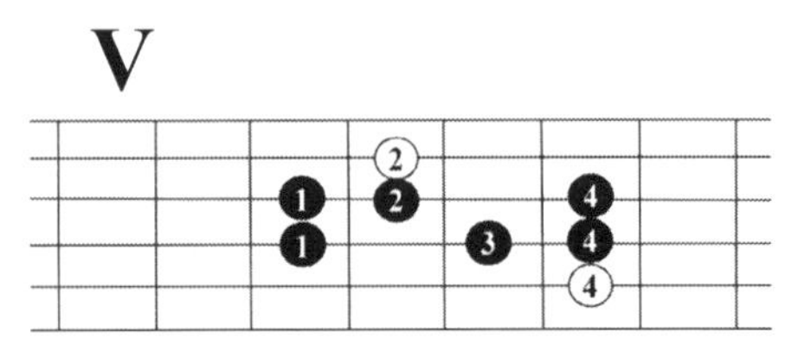

i

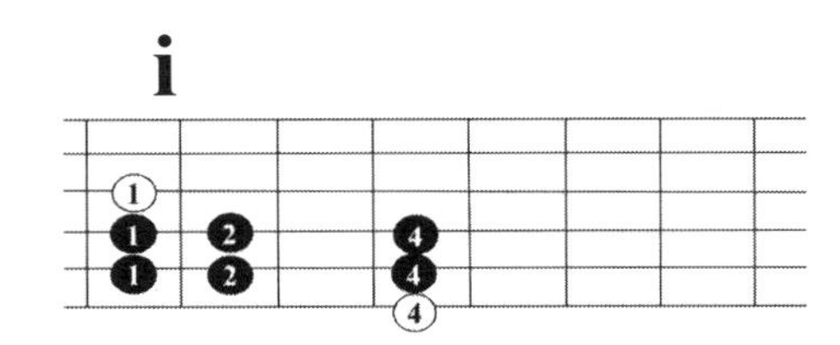

All Keys (iv)

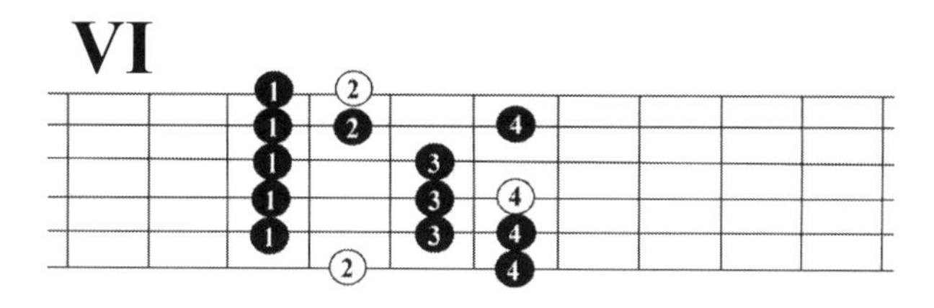

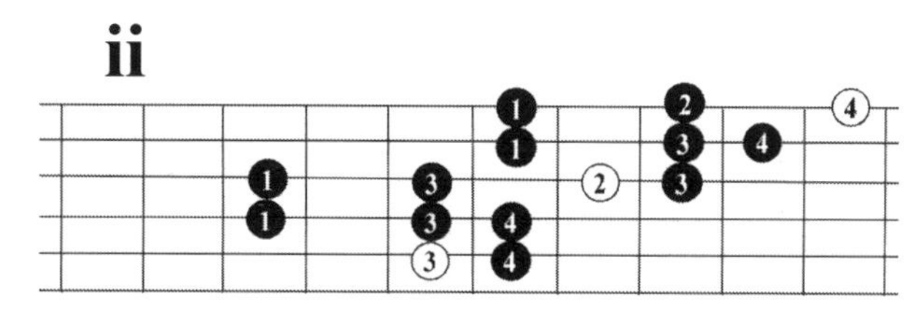

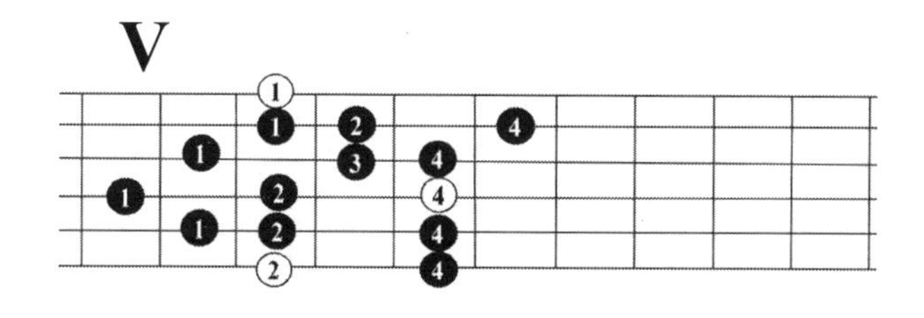

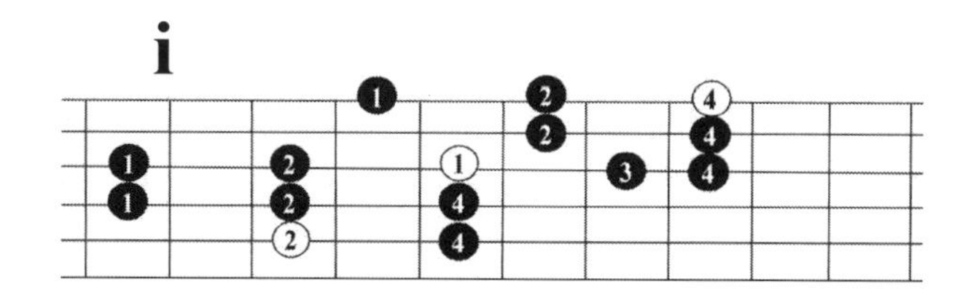

All Keys (v)

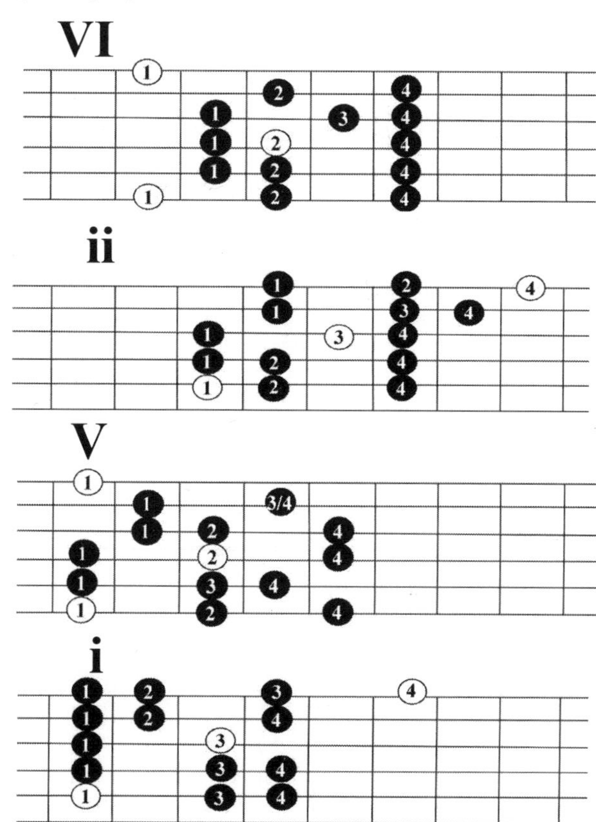

All Keys (vi)

VI

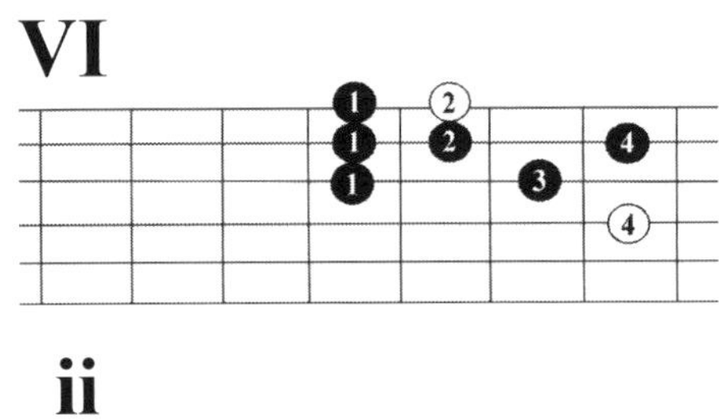

ii

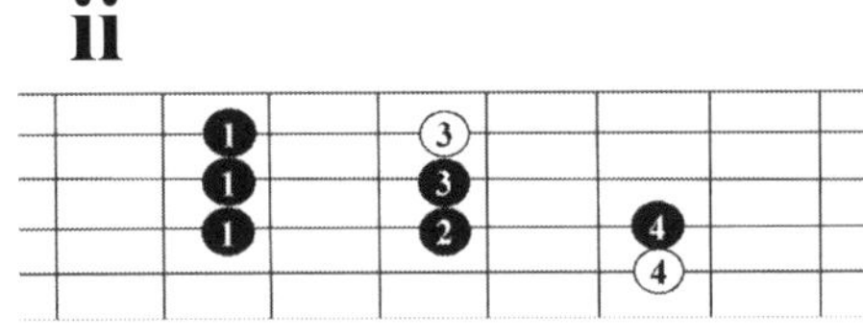

V

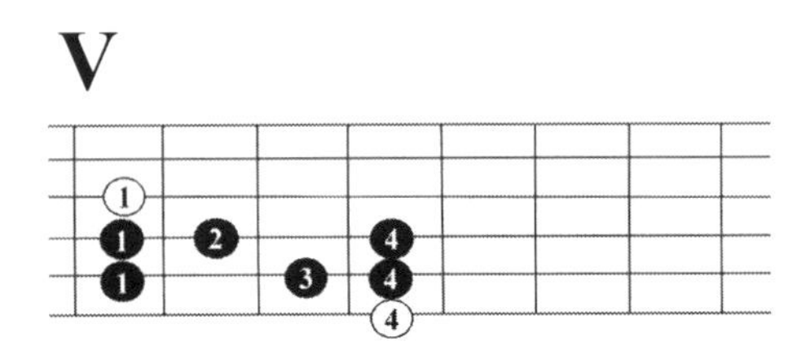

i

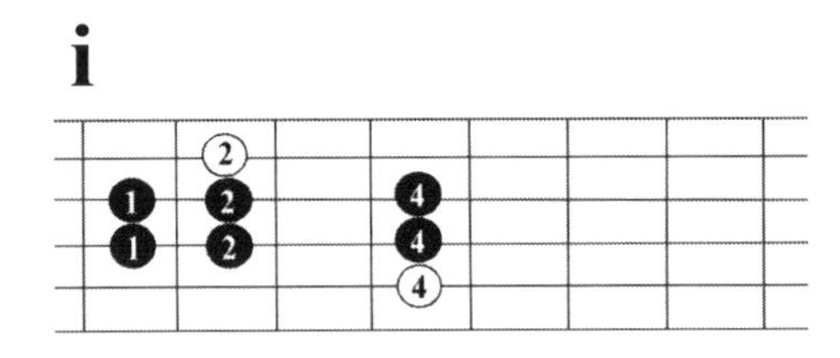

All Keys (vii)

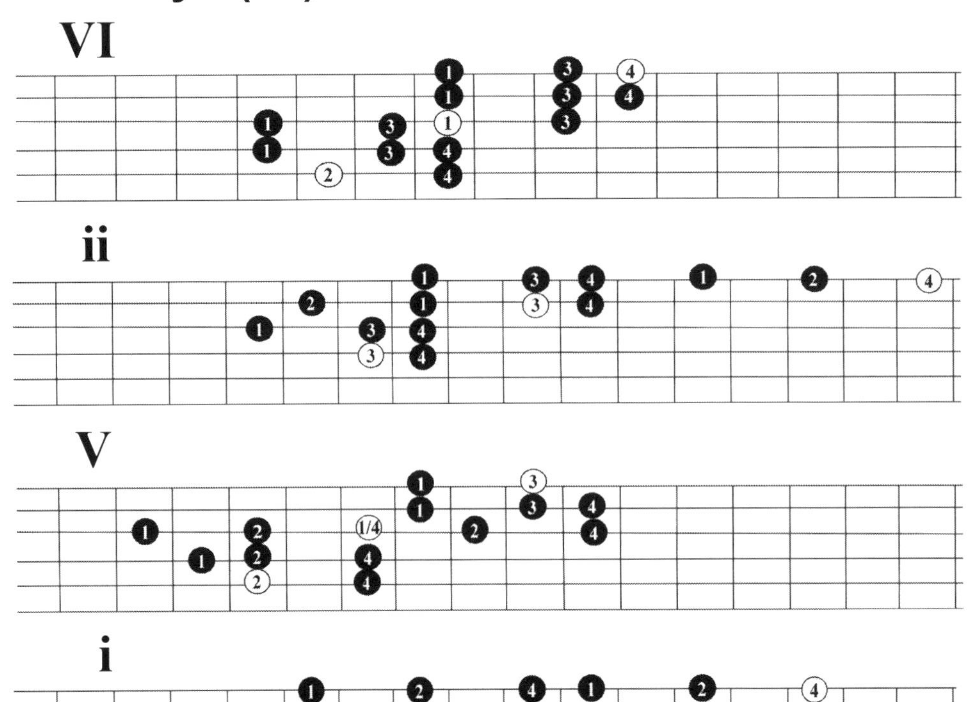

All Keys (viii)

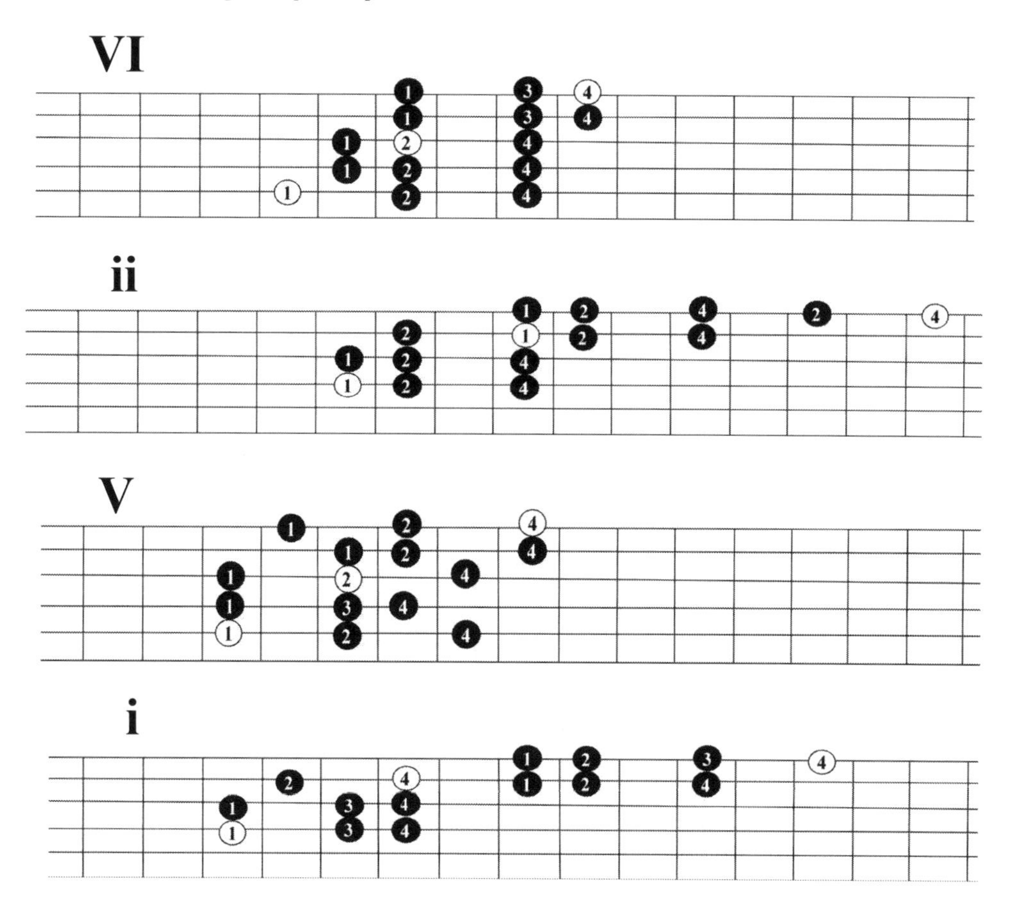

All Keys (ix)

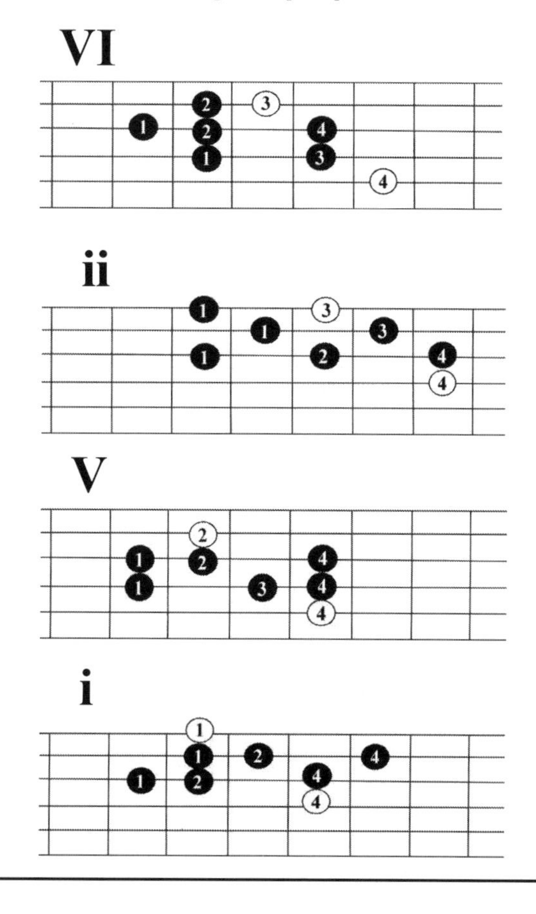

PART THIRTY-NINE

THE COMPLETE HARMONISED SCALE

HARMONISATION COMPLETED

In working through this book, you have now learned all the *triad* and *seventh* chords of the harmonised *major* and *minor* scales. The table below summarises the chord types and modes formed on each *degree* of the scale, and shows the correspondence between the degrees of any major scale and its relative minor.

MAJOR SCALE (DEGREE)	TRIAD	SEVENTH	MODE	MINOR SCALE (DEGREE)
I	Major	**M7**	Ionian	**III**
ii	minor	**m7**	Dorian	**iv**
iii	minor (Major)	**m7** **(7)**	Phrygian (Mixolydian ♭6)	**v** **(V)**
IV	Major	**M7**	Lydian	**VI**
V	Major	**7**	Mixolydian	**VII**
vi	minor	**m7**	Aeolian	**i**
vii	minor/♭5	**m7♭5**	Locrian	**ii**

PART FORTY

SUSPENSIONS AND SIXTHS

THE REMAINING SCALE INTERVALS

So far, all the chords we have studied have been formed by harmonising the scales and modes in *thirds* - i.e. stacking the first, third, fifth and seventh notes of each scale or mode. This has left the even-numbered *intervals* - the *second, fourth* and *sixth* - unused. You should be aware that if the system of harmonising in thirds is extended beyond the *octave*, these notes are added to form the more complex ninth, eleventh and thirteenth chords. In this section, however, we are looking at the cases where these notes are used **instead of** the odd-numbered intervals.

BACKGROUND

Historically, the odd-numbered intervals were regarded as "consonant" (i.e. harmonious) intervals, whereas the even-numbered intervals were considered to be "dissonant" and, if used, had to move to a consonant interval in the immediately following chord. In formal terms, the use of a dissonant interval is called a "suspension", and the chord containing it a "suspended chord", and the movement to a consonant interval is called the "resolution". The suspended chord "resolves" to a normal *major* or *minor* chord. In chord names, "suspended" is usually abbreviated to "sus" e.g. Csus4, or Asus2.

As music has evolved tastes have changed, and the sixth has been treated as a consonant interval since the late Classical period (so sixth chord names will always take the form C6, **not** Csus6), while fourths and seconds are used much more freely in contemporary and popular music. However, the traditional suspension/resolution formula is still frequently used, and the following examples should sound instantly familiar (see how many songs you can identify which use these patterns).

Asus4 - A Major

This is a popular suspension/resolution as the fingering is very easy on the guitar.

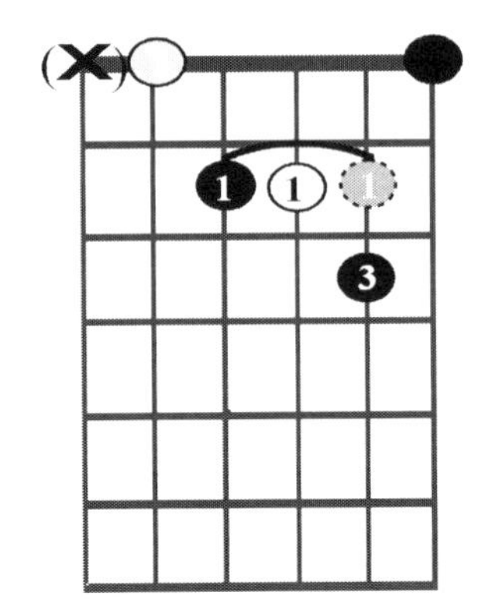

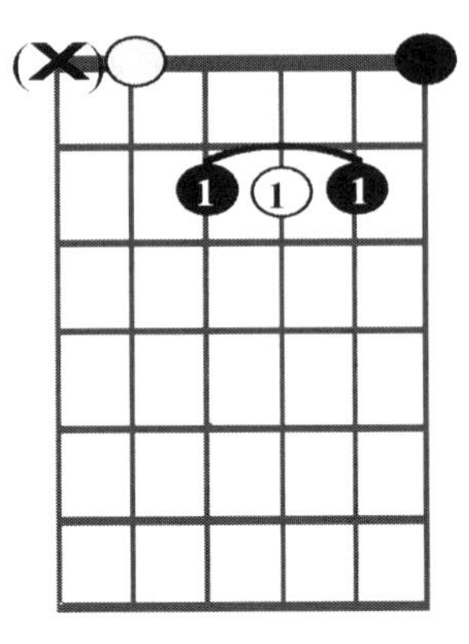

Once you are comfortable with barre chords, this pattern can be easily adapted as a barre chord and transposed to any key:

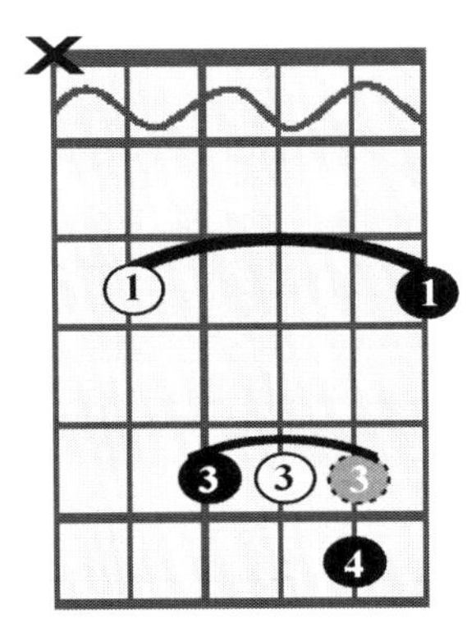

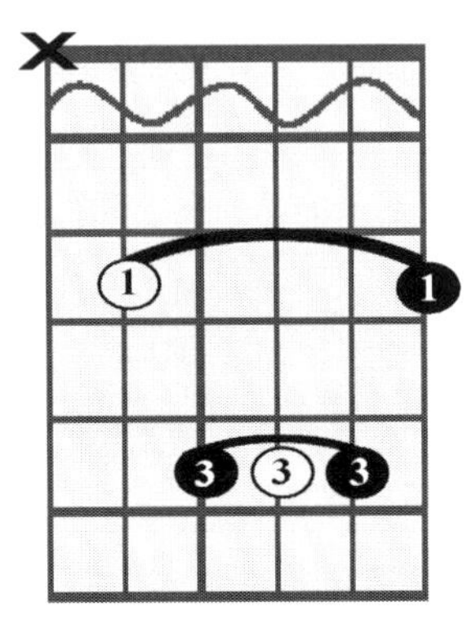

Dsus4 - D Major - Dsus2 - D Major

Ease of fingering also accounts for the popularity of this pattern, in which a Dsus4 chord resolves to D Major, followed immediately by Dsus2 before finally resolving back to the major:

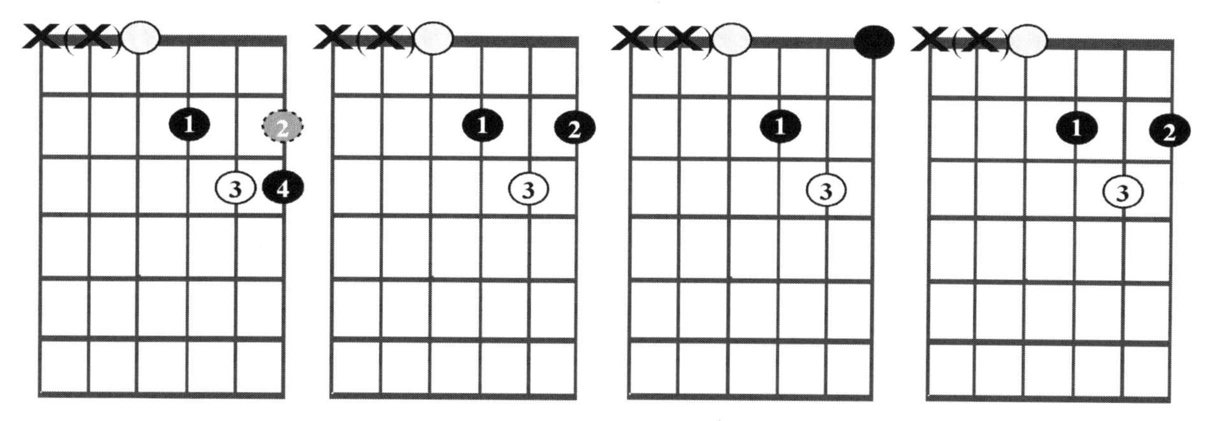

Major - 6sus4 - Major

In this final example, a major *triad* is followed by a chord including both a fourth and a sixth, which then resolve back to the third and fifth respectively. This pattern has the advantage of being playable on only three strings, and by keeping the first finger barre in place, is easily transposed up and down the fretboard (hint: try repeating the suspended chord before playing the final major triad on an off-beat).

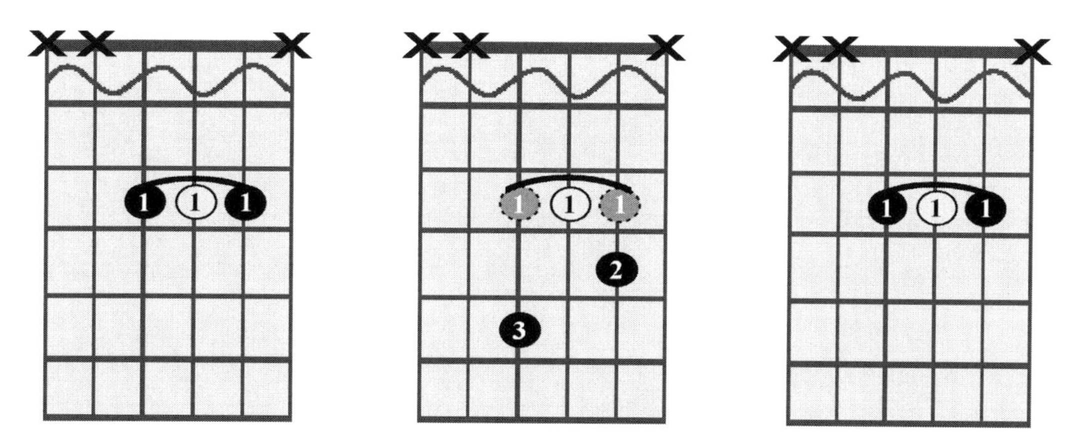

THE EXERCISES

In the following pages, examples are given of sus2, sus4 and sixth chords resolving to each of the *tonic* triads

(I Major and i minor). One fingering is given for each example - as always, experiment to find your own alternative fingerings. To give as wide a selection of alternatives as possible, I have included some fairly tricky voicings in some keys - remember you can always transpose from the easier examples.

A FINAL NOTE ON 6TH CHORDS

Since the sixth is considered to be a consonant interval, it is not uncommon for sixth chords to include the fifth as well. Where feasible optional fingerings with and without the fifth are indicated using brackets. In other cases, you should be aware that alternative fingerings may or may not include the fifth, at your discretion.

FURTHER STUDY

(i)

Using the modes as guides, investigate the implications of using seconds, fourths and sixths in chords where the chord *root* is not the tonic - find your own fingerings for the resulting chords. The second, fourth or sixth may be sharpened or flattened according the the underlying mode. The relevant alterations are:

Dorian mode (ii chord in major keys, iv chord in minor keys) - the sixth is sharpened (major 6th)

Phrygian mode (iii chord in major keys, v chord in minor keys) - the second is flattened (minor 2nd)

Lydian mode (IV chord in major keys, VI chord in minor keys) - the fourth is sharpened (augmented 4th)

Locrian mode (vii chord in major keys, ii chord in minor keys) - the second is flattened (minor 2nd)

Mixolydian ♭6 mode (V chord in minor keys) - the sixth is flattened (minor 6th)

(ii)

Try the effect of adding sevenths to the suspended and/or resolved chords. Once again, find your own fingerings for the chords - adding a major or minor seventh as appropriate to the degree of the scale represented by the root of the chord.

Csus2

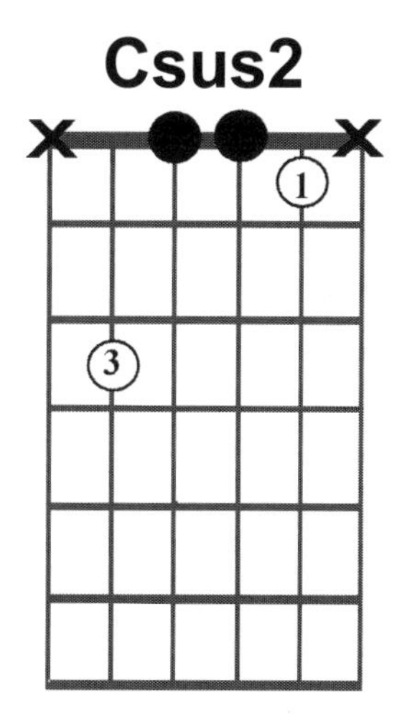

Csus4

C6

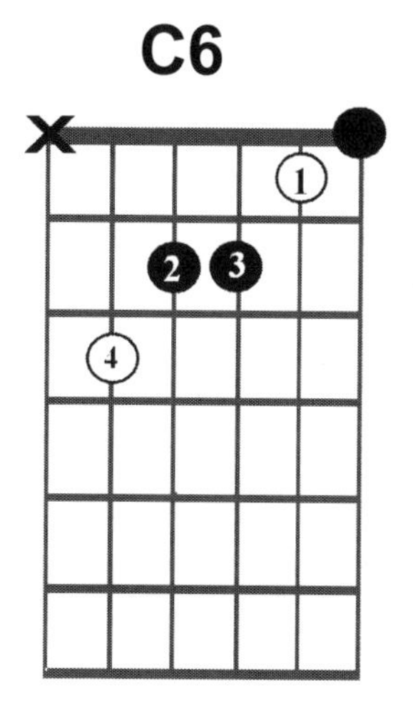

C Major

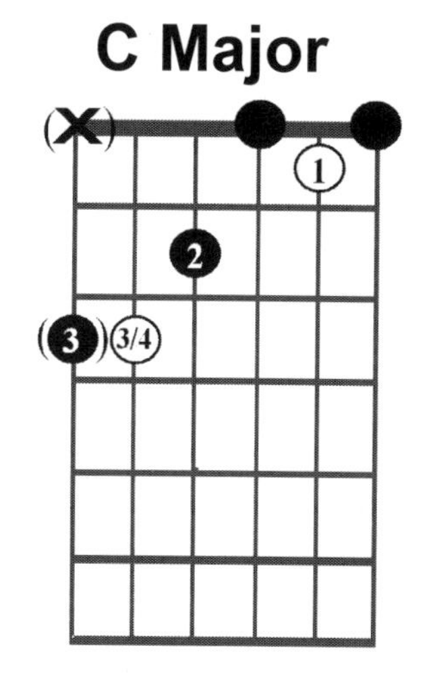

Gsus2

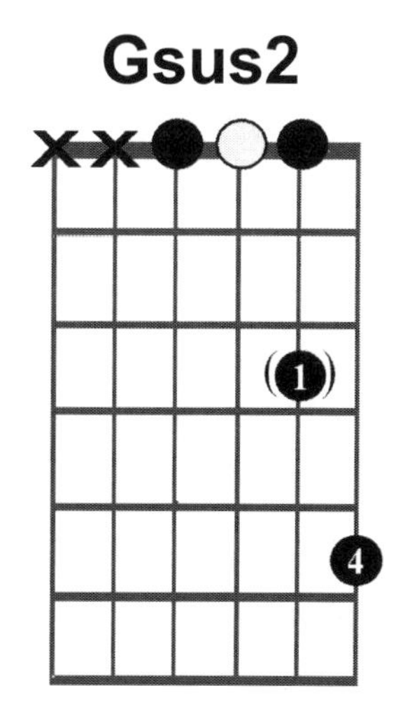

Gsus4

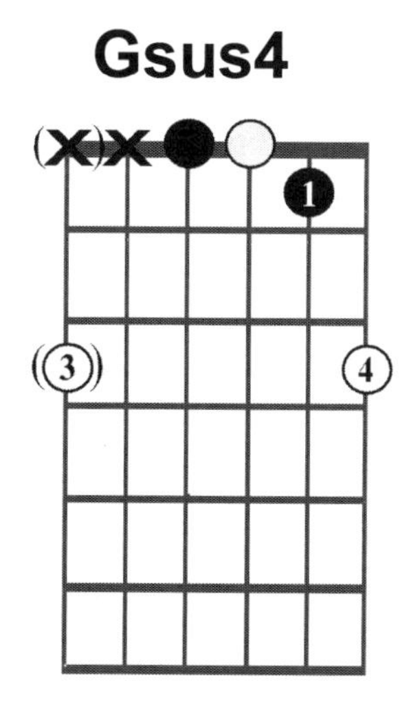

G6

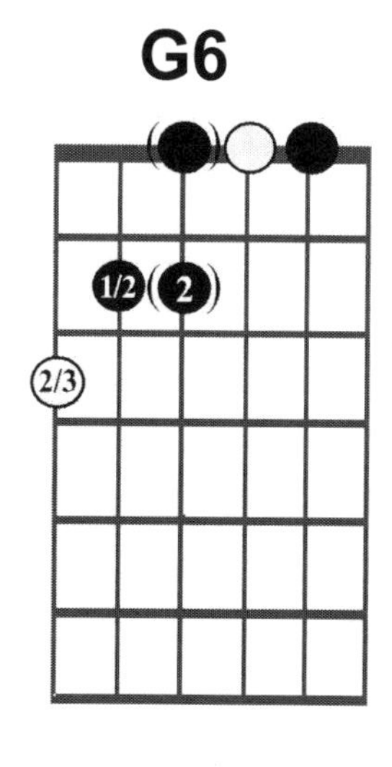

G Major

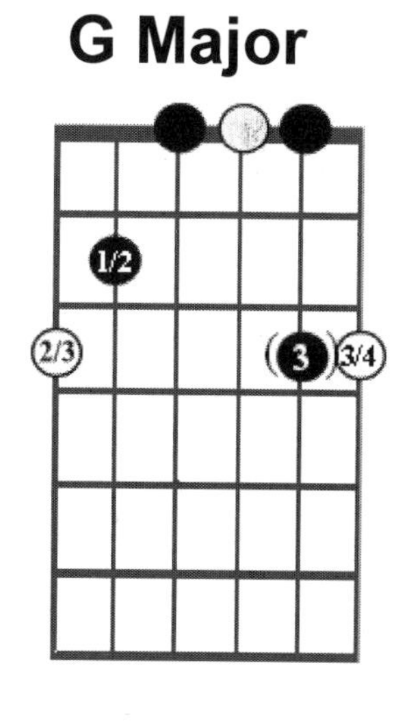

Dsus2

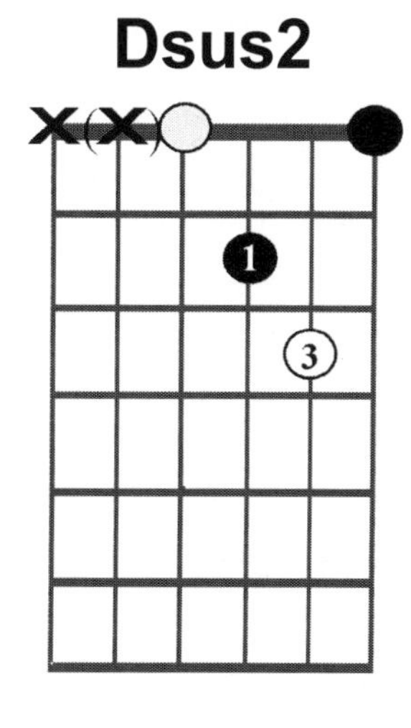

Dsus4

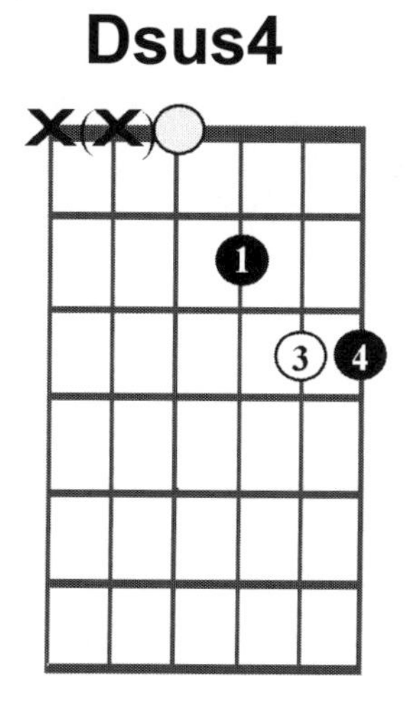

D6

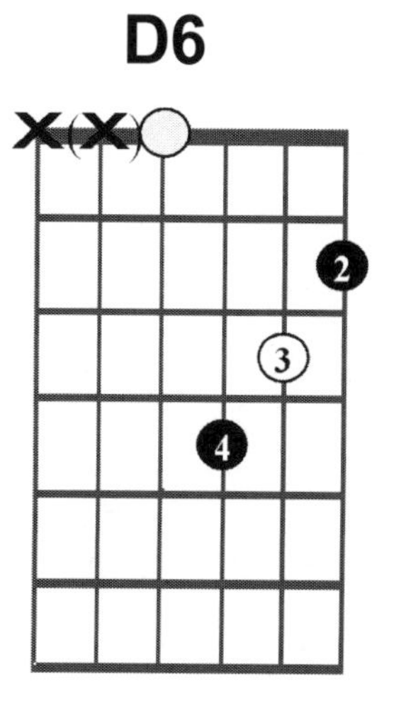

D Major

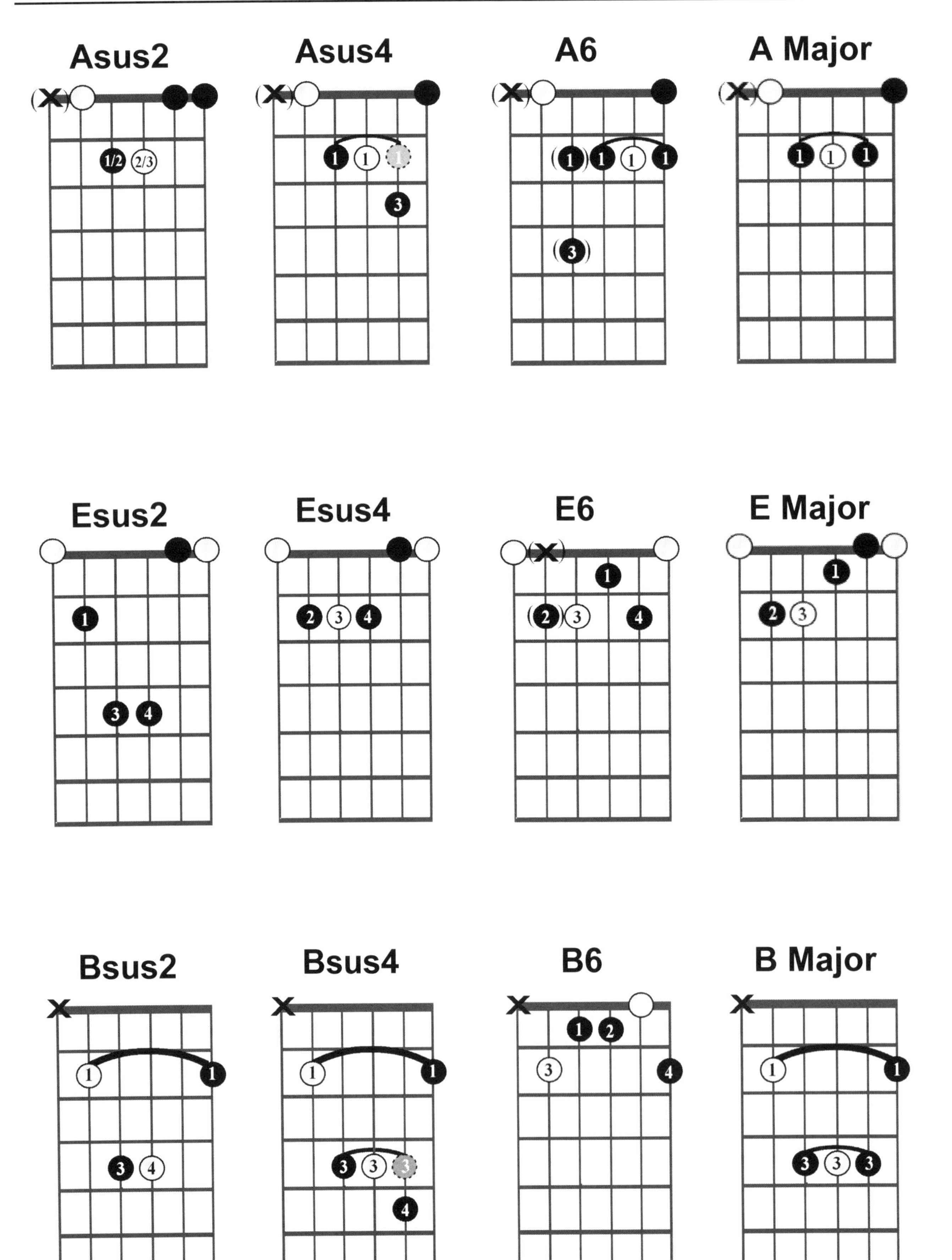

Asus2
1/2
2/3
Asus4
1
1
1
3
A6
1
1
1
1
3
A Major
1
1
1
Esus2
1
3
4
Esus4
2
3
4
E6
1
2
3
4
E Major
1
2
3
Bsus2
1
1
3
4
Bsus4
1
1
3
3
3
4
B6
1
2
3
4
B Major
1
1
3
3
3

F#sus2

F#sus4

F#6

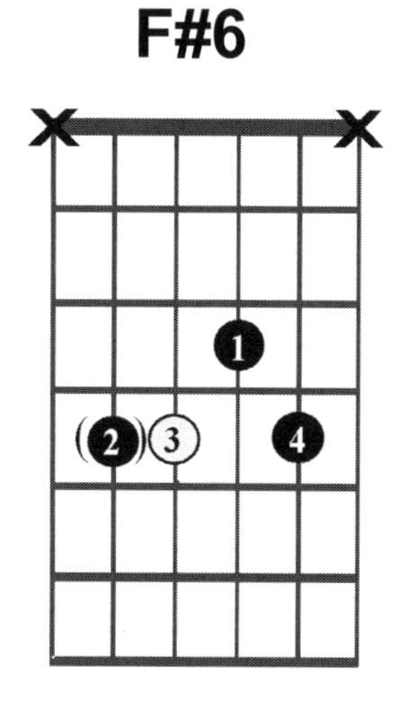

F# Major

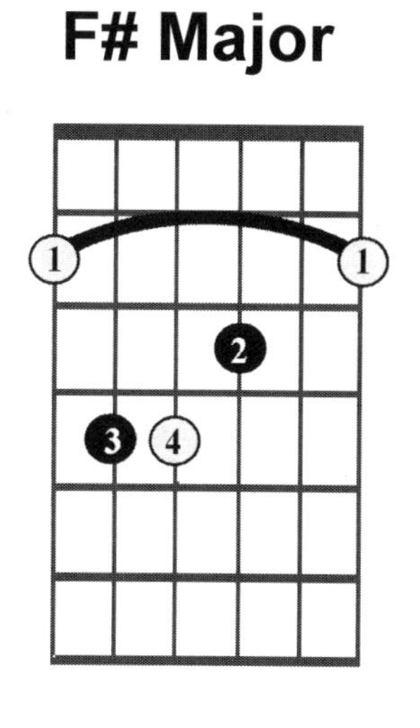

C#sus2

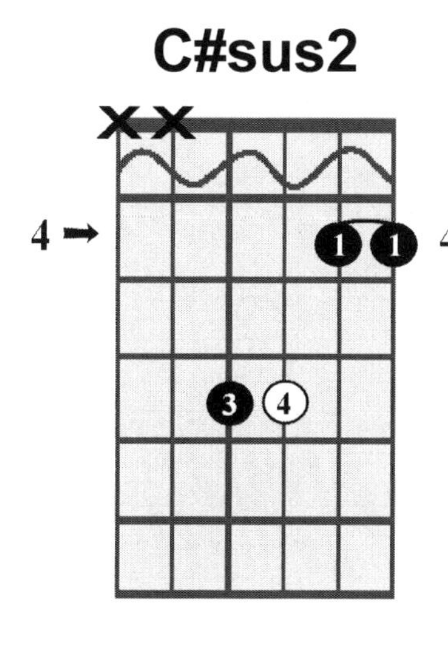

C#sus4

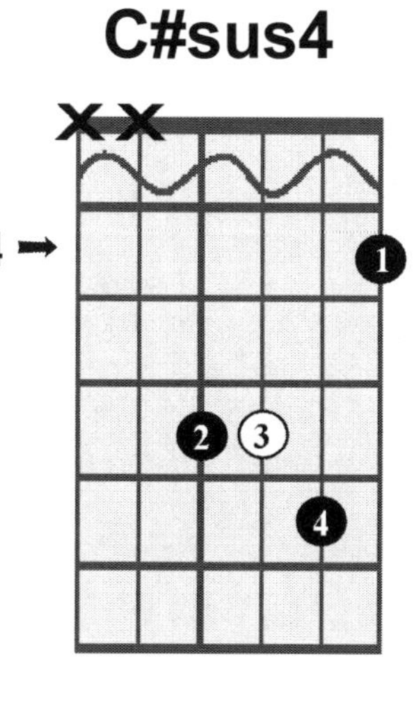

C#6

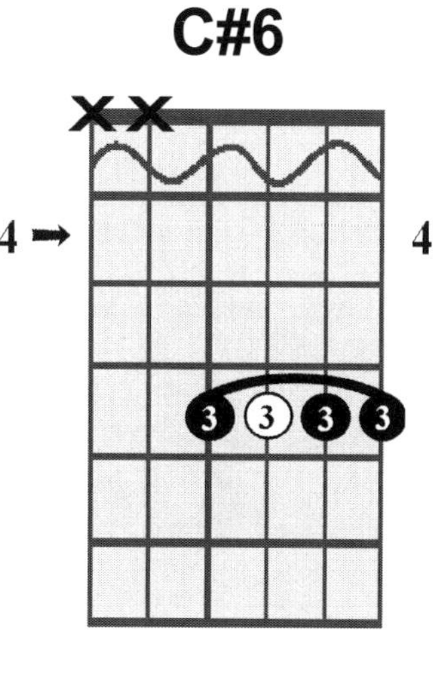

C# Major

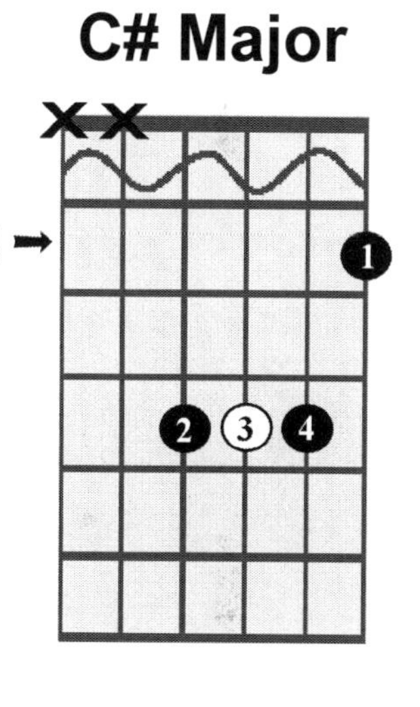

A♭sus2

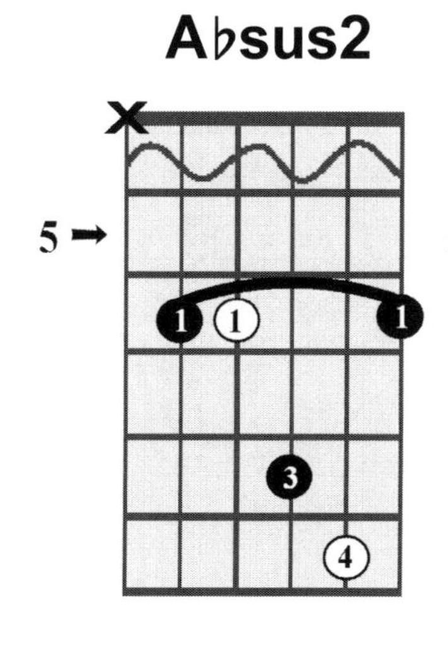

A♭sus4

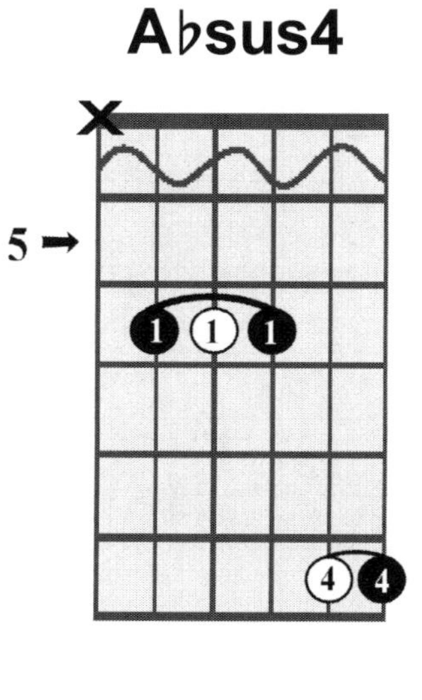

A♭6

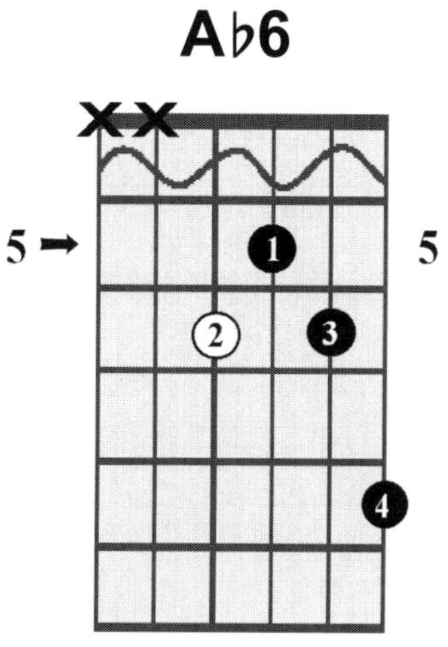

A♭ Major

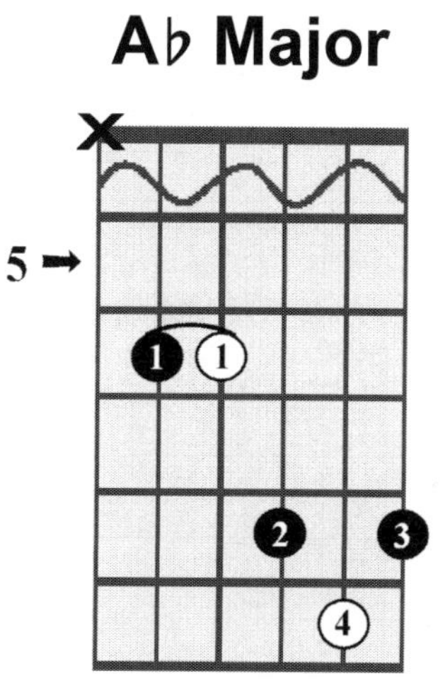

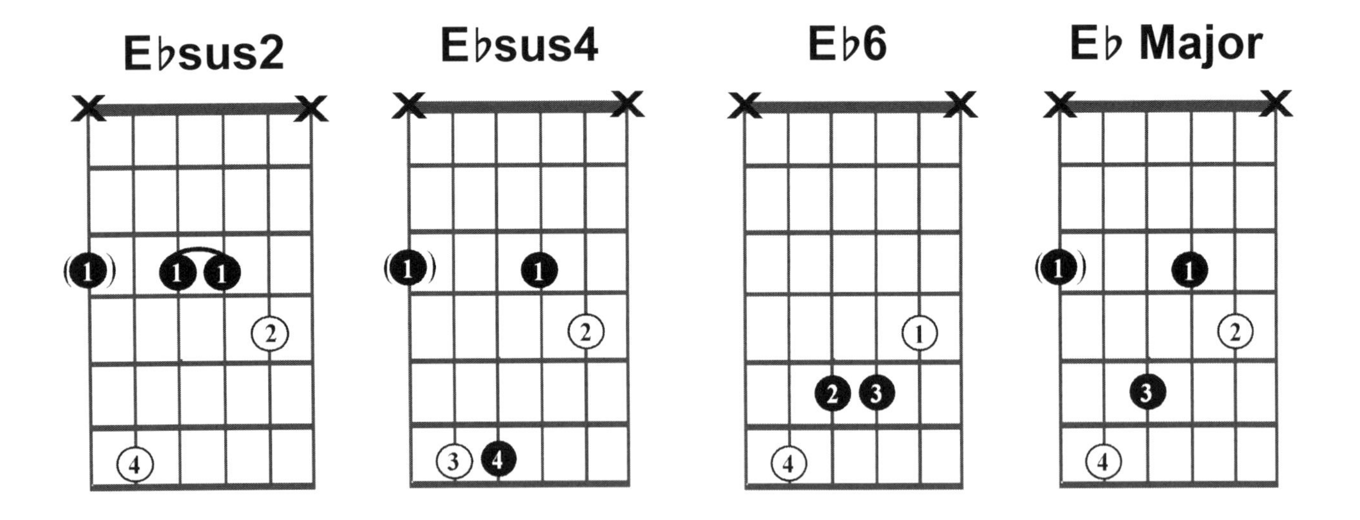
E♭sus2
E♭sus4
E♭6
E♭ Major

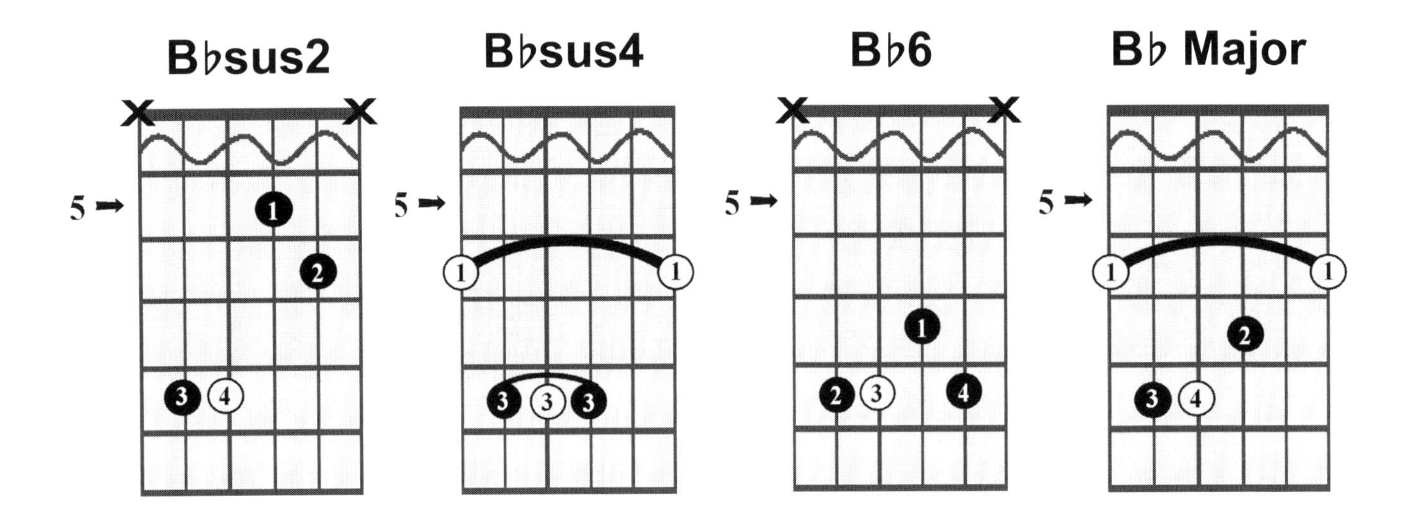
B♭sus2
B♭sus4
B♭6
B♭ Major
5
5
5
5

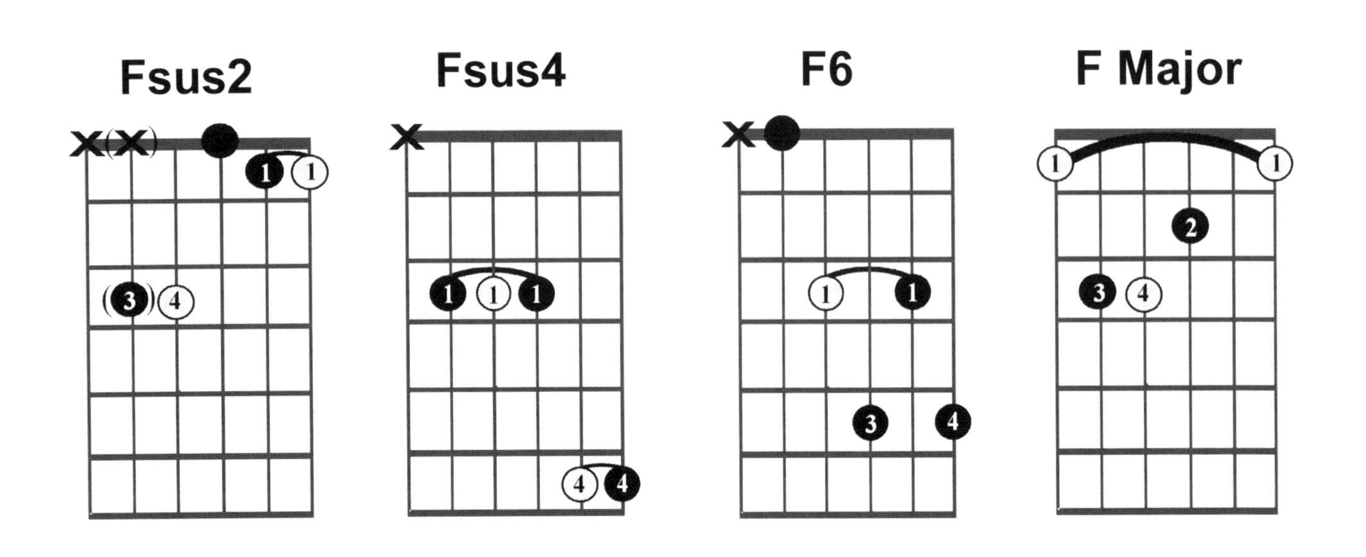
Fsus2
Fsus4
F6
F Major

THE MINOR SIXTH CHORD - AN IMPORTANT NOTE

By common convention, the designation minor sixth (m6) denotes a minor chord with a **major** sixth added. This is another chord derived from the melodic minor scale (see "Variant Minor Scales"), and is the chord used in the remaining exercises in this section.

The chord formed by adding a minor sixth to a minor chord is usually described as a minor (minor sixth) or m(min6). It is far less common, though you should be aware that it is a perfectly valid chord to use (try substituting m(min6) for m6 chords in the exercises).

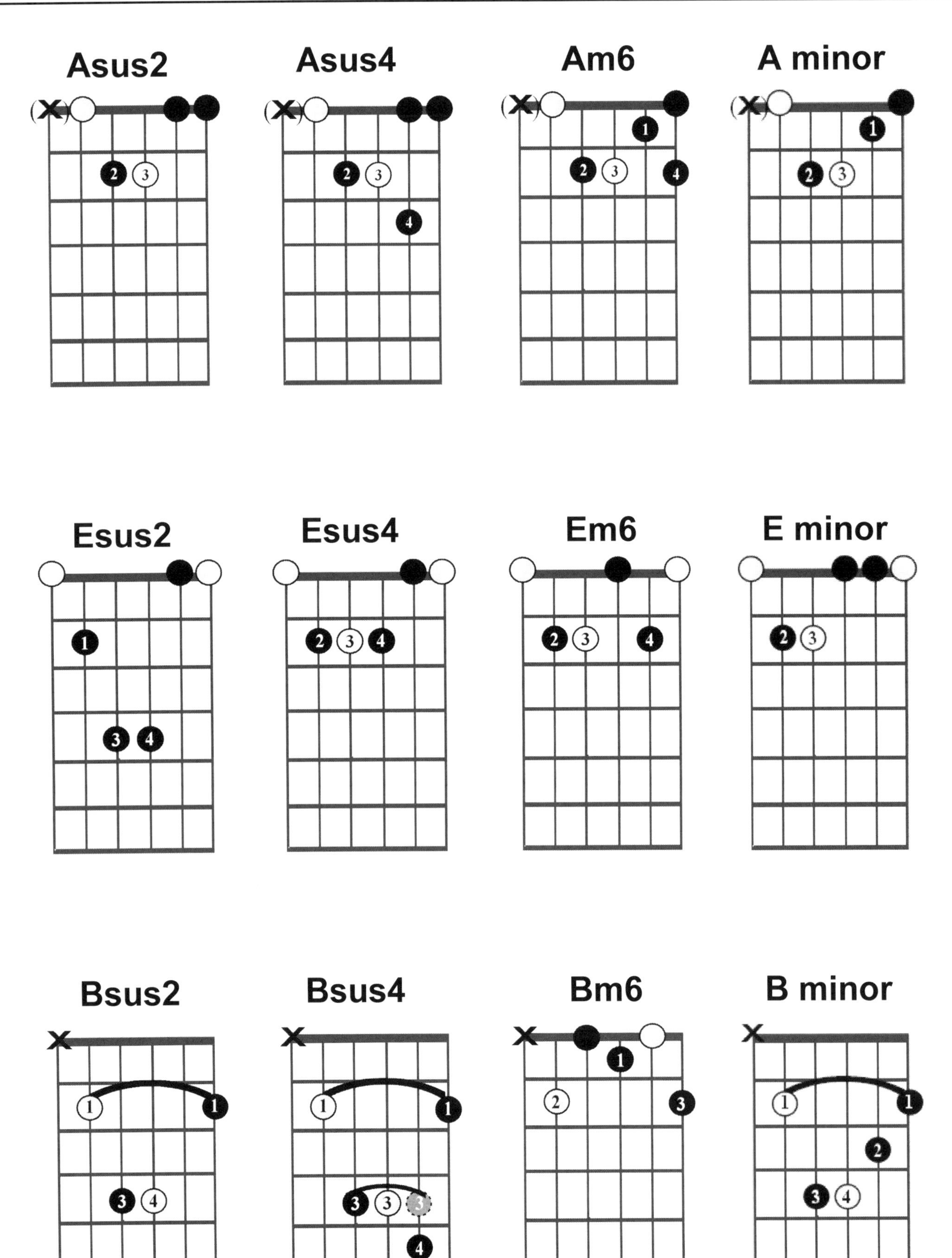
Asus2
Asus4
Am6
A minor
Esus2
Esus4
Em6
E minor
Bsus2
Bsus4
Bm6
B minor

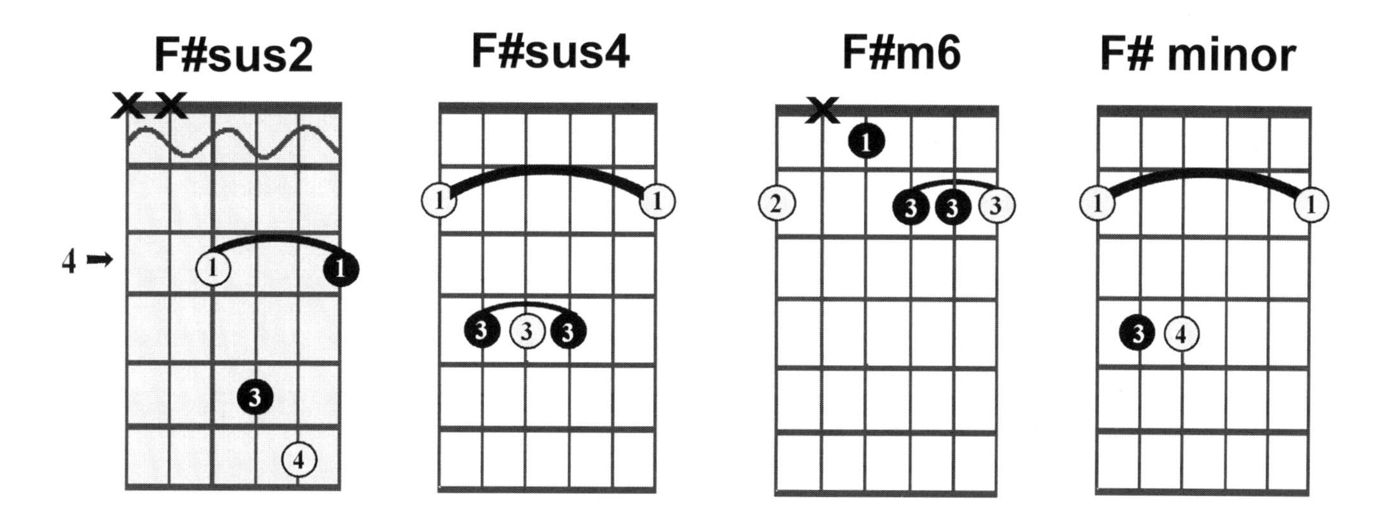
F#sus2
F#sus4
F#m6
F# minor
4

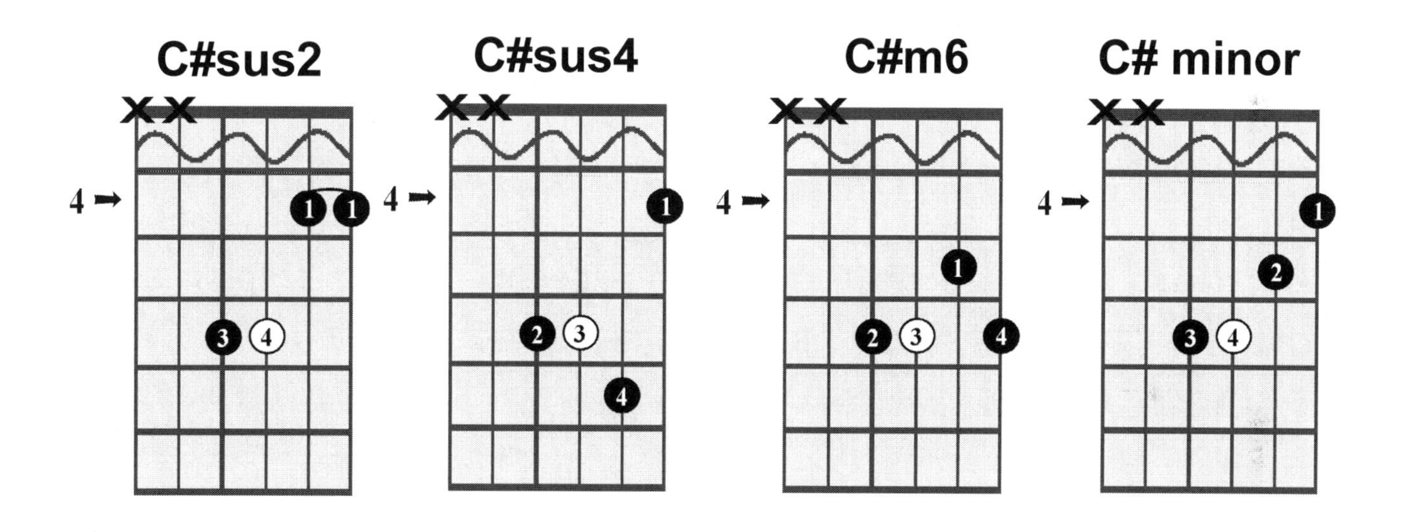
C#sus2
C#sus4
C#m6
C# minor
4
4
4
4

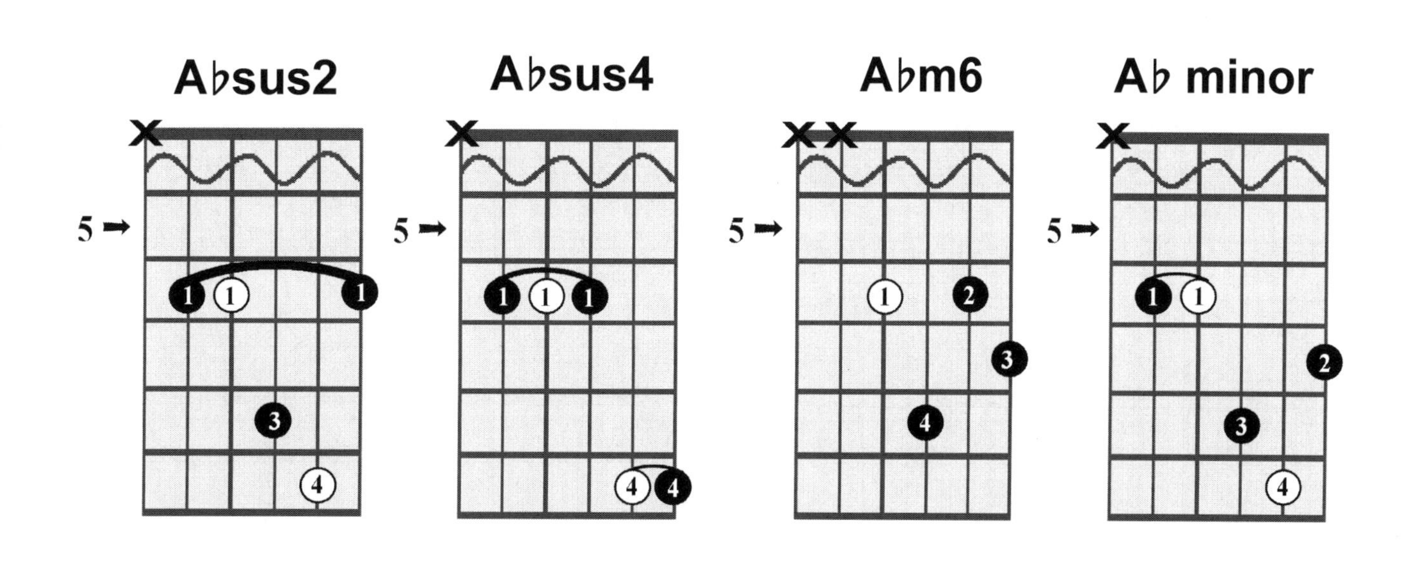
A♭sus2
A♭sus4
A♭m6
A♭ minor
5
5
5
5

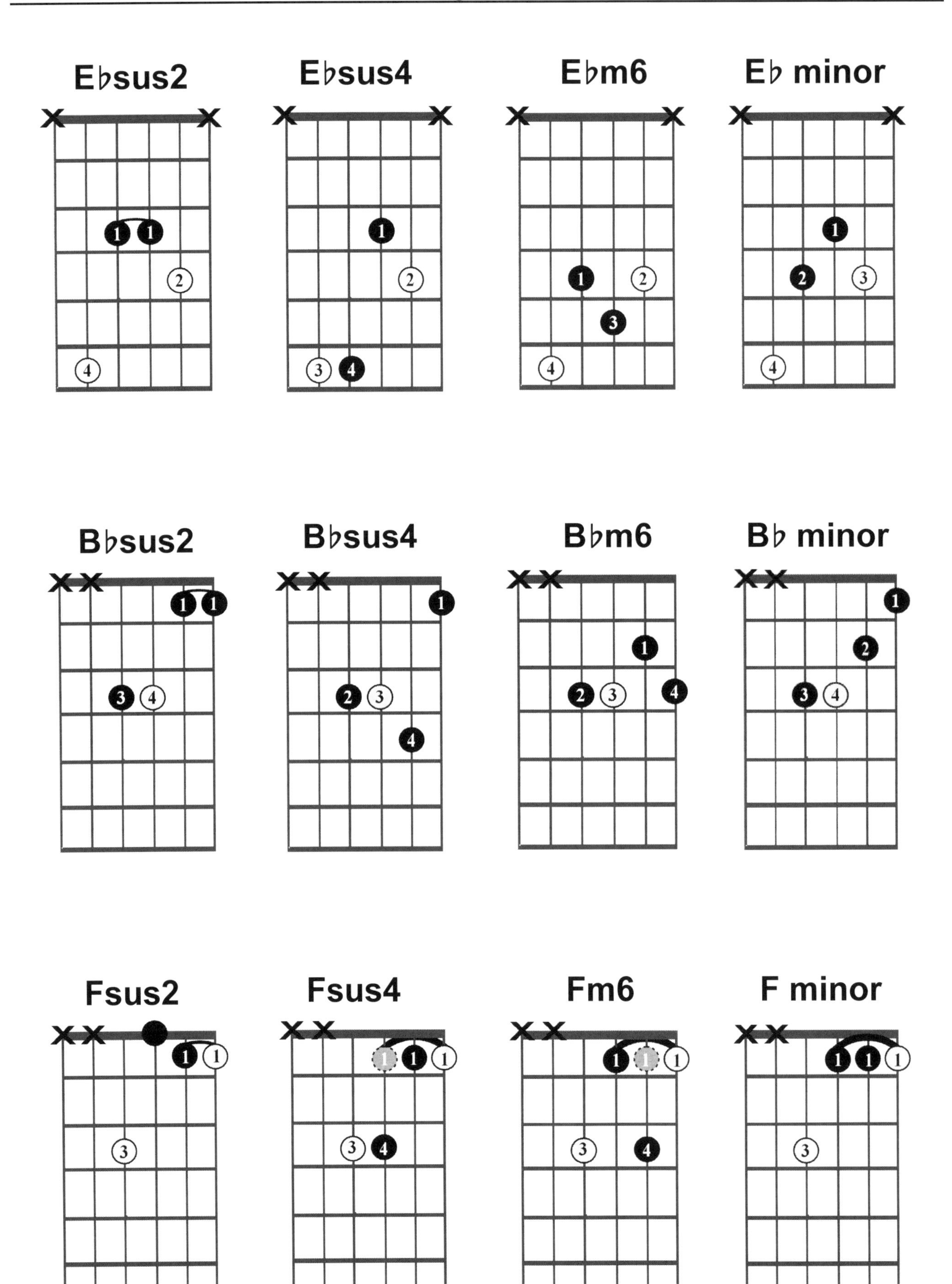
E♭sus2
E♭sus4
E♭m6
E♭ minor
B♭sus2
B♭sus4
B♭m6
B♭ minor
Fsus2
Fsus4
Fm6
F minor

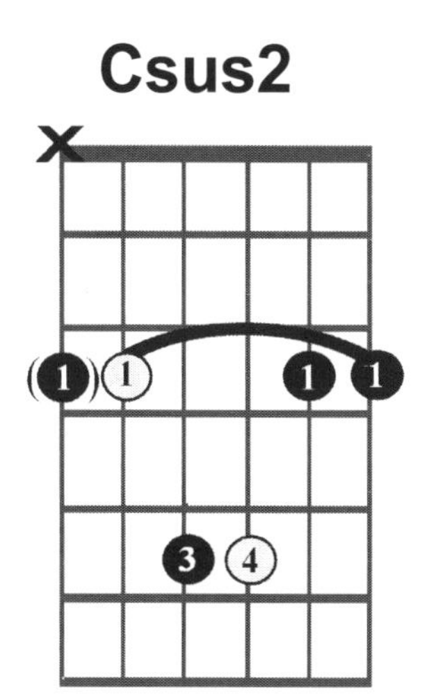

Csus4

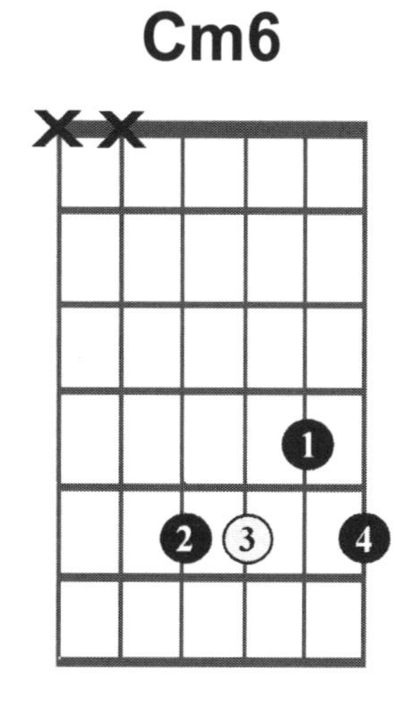

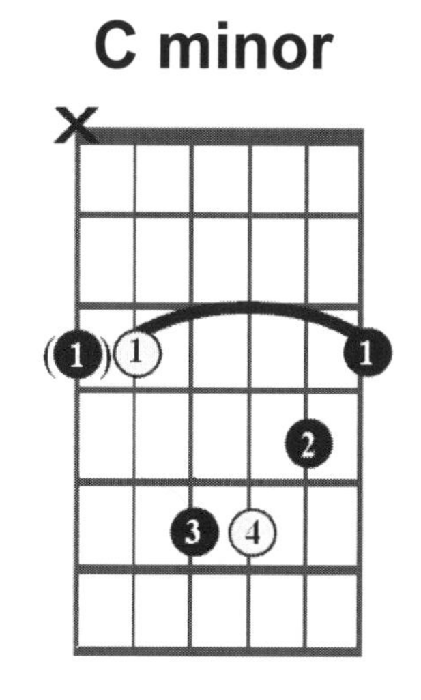

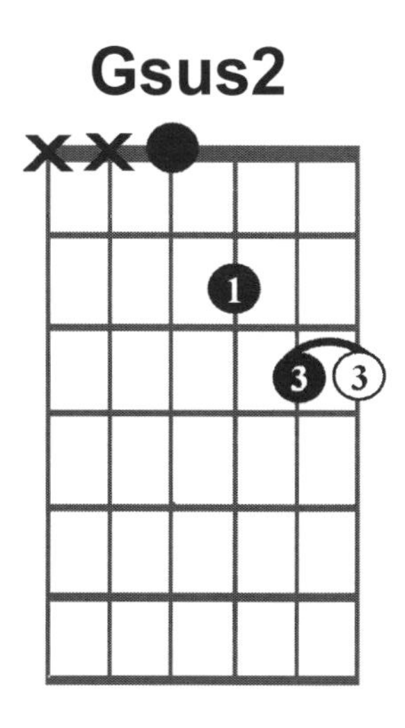

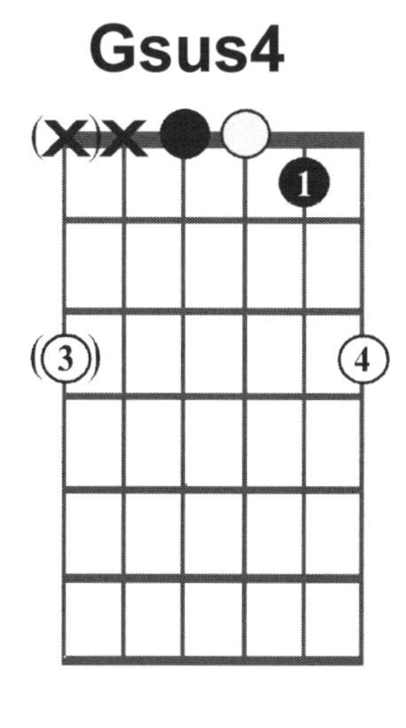

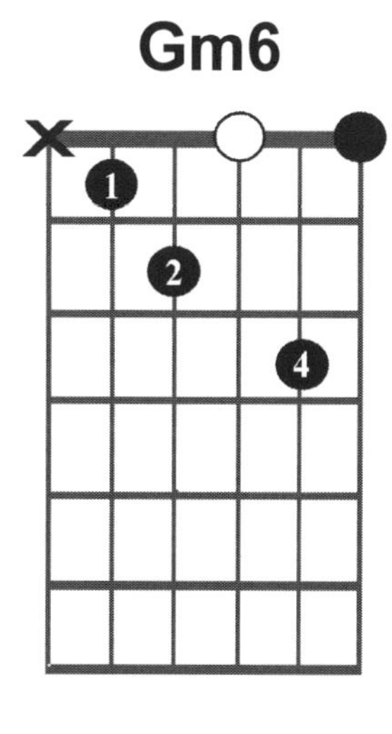

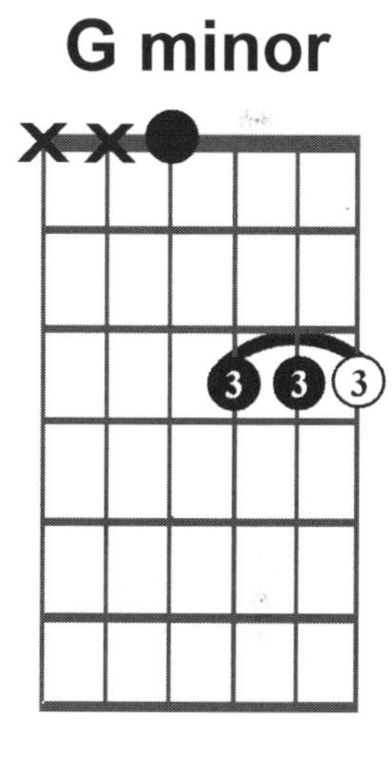

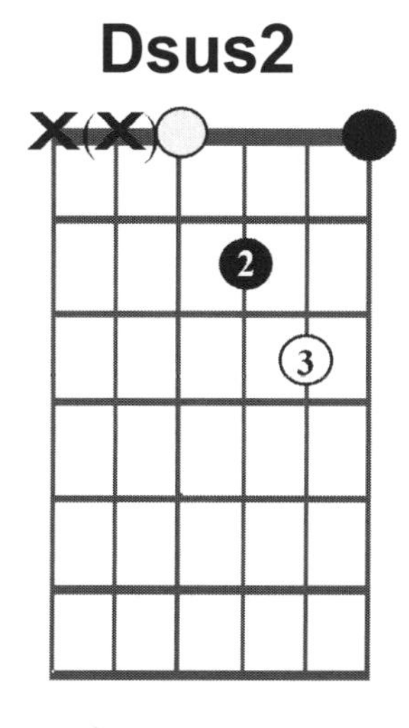

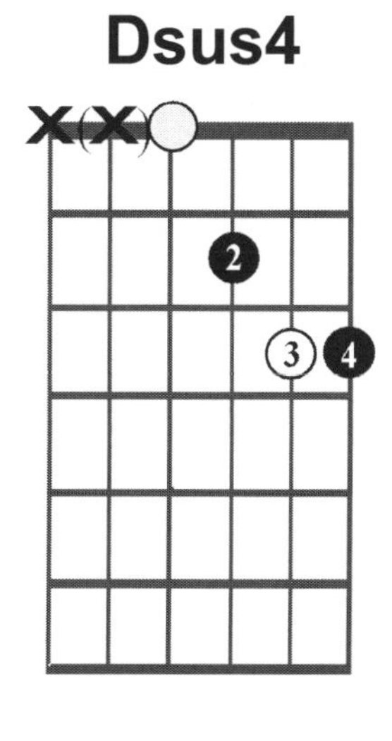

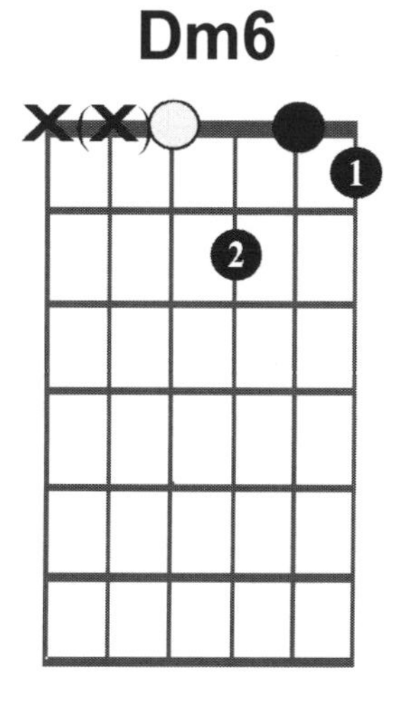

D minor

PART FORTY-ONE

VARIANT MINOR SCALES AND THE BLUES SCALE

THE HARMONIC MINOR SCALE

As we have seen, composers and songwriters have, historically, shown a preference for the *Major* or Dominant 7th V chord, over the *minor* or minor 7th v chord, in minor keys, and that the (major) *third* of this chord does not appear in the natural minor scale. In effect, the seventh note of the natural minor scale has been sharpened. If this substitution is made in the scale itself, a new scale results, called the "harmonic minor scale" - i.e. a minor scale with a major seventh. Thus in the key of Am, for example, the natural minor scale:

A *(tone)* **B** *(semitone)* **C** *(tone)* **D** *(tone)* **E** *(semitone)* **F** *(tone)* **G** *(tone)* **A**

becomes the harmonic minor scale

A *(tone)* **B** *(semitone)* **C** *(tone)* **D** *(tone)* **E** *(semitone)* **F** *(minor third)* **G#** *(semitone)* **A**

Since the sharpened seventh does not appear in the *key signature*, in music notation it must always be indicated by an "accidental"- i.e. a sharp sign, or natural sign if the key signature contains flats, in the score.

Examples in all keys are given in the following pages.

THE MELODIC MINOR SCALE

The harmonic minor scale has a problem, in that the normal *diatonic* pattern of mixed *tone* and *semitone intervals* has been broken, with a minor third (one-and-a-half tone interval) between the sixth and seventh notes. Constructing melodies from this scale (try some yourself) creates an unusual, vaguely oriental, sound which is at odds with the style of most western European music.

The solution was to devise a new scale: the "melodic minor scale" in which both the sixth and seventh notes are sharpened. Thus (e.g.) the A melodic minor scale:

A *(tone)* **B** *(semitone)* **C** *(tone)* **D** *(tone)* **E** *(tone)* **F#** *(tone)* **G#** *(semitone)* **A**

This melodic minor scale, however, has its own disadvantage in that it now differs in only one note (the third) from the major scale. To get round this problem the Classical melodic minor scale has different ascending and descending forms. When ascending the scale, the sixth and seventh are sharpened (major), but in the descending form they revert to minor intervals, making the descending form the same as the natural minor scale.

Jazz and popular musicians tend to disregard this difference, and a melodic minor scale with the sixth and seventh sharpened in both ascending and descending forms is sometimes referred to as the "jazz melodic minor scale".

Again, examples in all keys can be found in the following pages.

BLUES SCALES

Part of the character of the Blues as a style is an inherent ambiguity - it is in effect neither major nor minor in its tonality. "Blues scales" have been devised to exploit this ambiguity in constructing melodies and improvising solos. Examples are given at the end of this section

FURTHER STUDY

i) Harmonising the Melodic Minor Scale

Harmonising the ascending melodic minor scale, using the conventional system of stacking intervals of a third, naturally produces a slightly different set of chords to that formed from the natural minor scale - including the V/V7 chord we have been using in these exercises. The differences are summarised in the table below. By using your knowledge of chord construction (or consulting a good chord dictionary), find your own fingerings for these chords. If you wish to go further, investigate the forms of ninth, eleventh and thirteenth chords built from the melodic minor scale.

(Note: the notation "+5" signifies a chord with an *augmented* (sharpened) fifth).

The harmonised melodic minor scale increases the repertoire of chords available when writing music in minor keys. From the point of view of this book, the i, ii, IV, V and vi chords are of particular interest, and this topic will be revisited in the later section "Chord Substitution".

ii) Modes of the Melodic Minor Scale

The melodic minor scale also has its own modes. You have already met one, the "Mixolydian ♭6" mode which we used as the chord scale for the V chord in minor keys. The remaining modes are summarised in the table below and can be studied both as a separate topic in their own right, and as chord scales to accompany the chords of the harmonised melodic minor scale. Alternative names are sometimes used for these modes, and some common alternatives are given in smaller print in the table. I have chosen to use the names which indicate clearly which notes have been altered.

MELODIC MINOR SCALE (DEGREE)	TRIAD	SEVENTH	MODE
i	minor	**min/Maj7**	Melodic Minor Scale
ii	minor	**m7**	Dorian ♭2
III	Major+5	**M7+5**	Lydian #5
IV	Major	**7**	Lydian ♭7 (Lydian Dominant)
V	Major	**7**	Mixolydian ♭6
vi	minor/♭5	**m7♭5**	Aeolian ♭5
vii	minor/♭5	**m7♭5**	Locrian ♭4 (Altered/Superlocrian)

A Harmonic minor (i)

A Harmonic minor (ii)

E Harmonic minor (i)

E Harmonic minor (ii)

B Harmonic minor

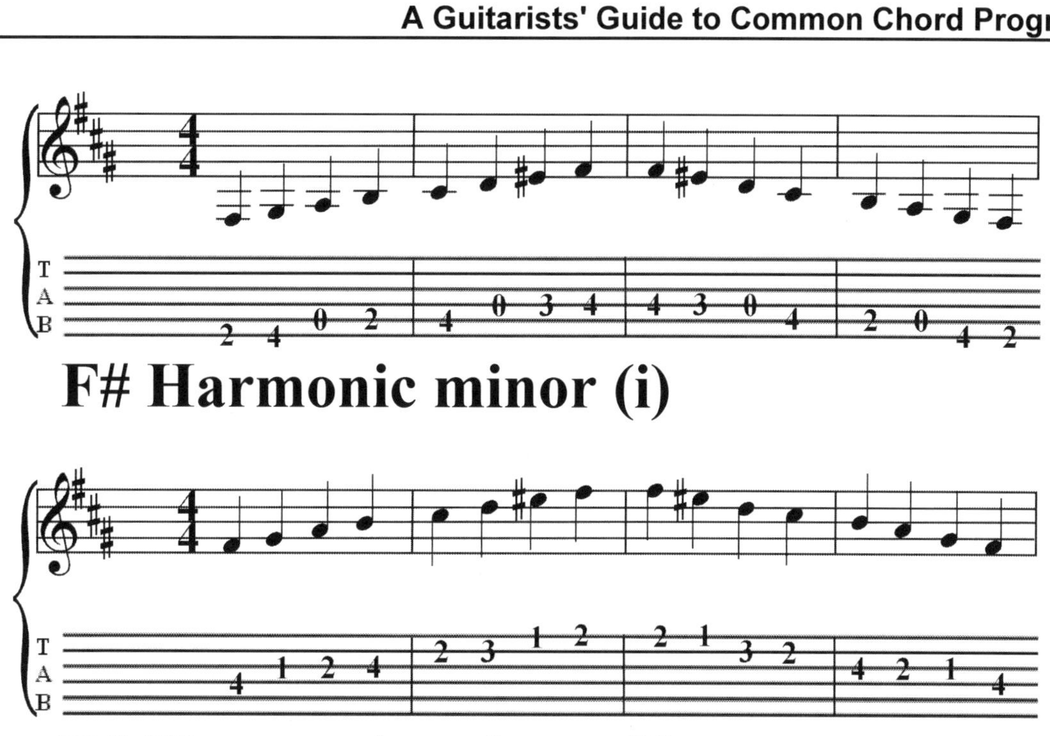

F# Harmonic minor (i)

F# Harmonic minor (ii)

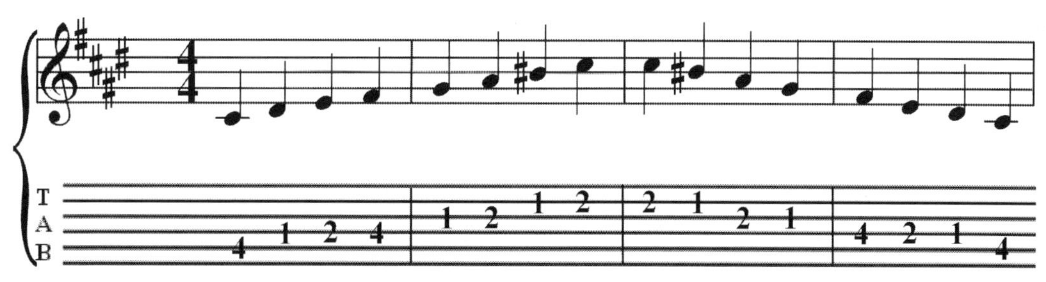

C# Harmonic minor

A♭ Harmonic minor (i)

A♭ Harmonic minor (ii)

E♭ Harmonic minor

B♭ Harmonic minor

F Harmonic minor (i)

F Harmonic minor (ii)

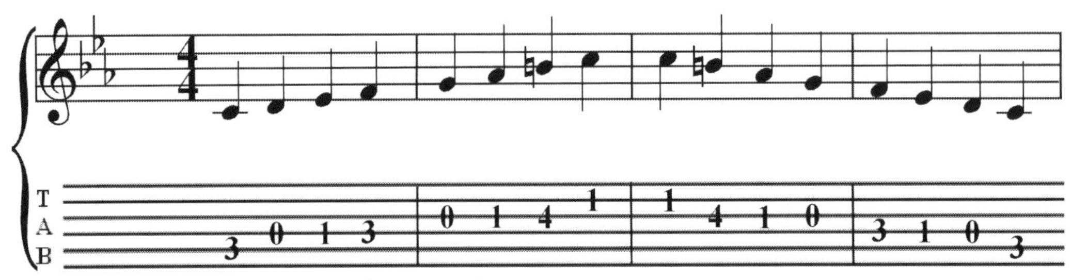

C Harmonic minor

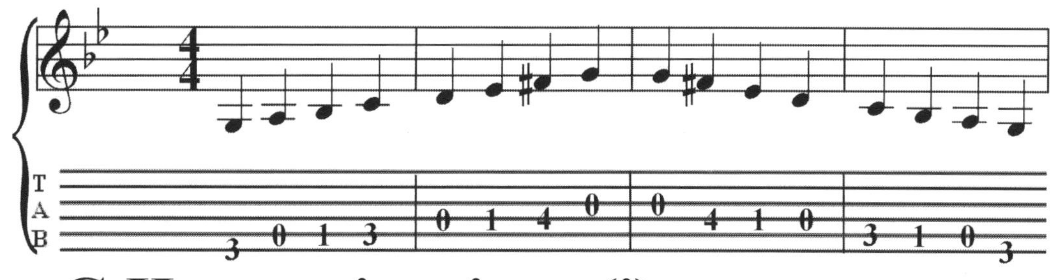

G Harmonic minor (i)

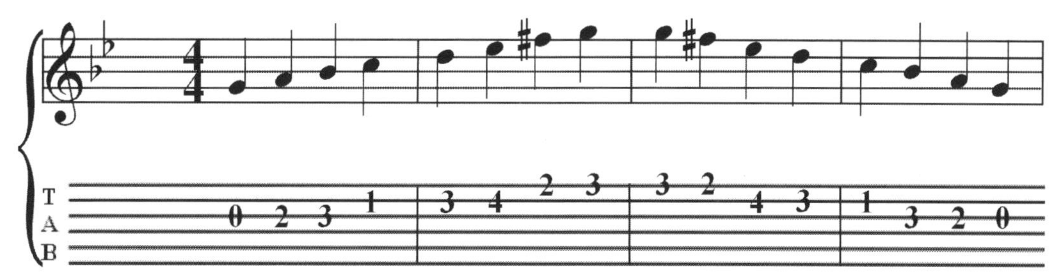

G Harmonic minor (ii)

D Harmonic minor

HARMONIC MINOR SCALE - ALL KEYS

(i)

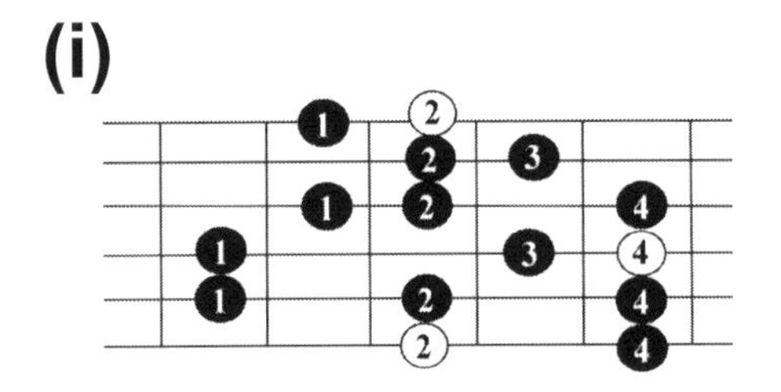

(ii)

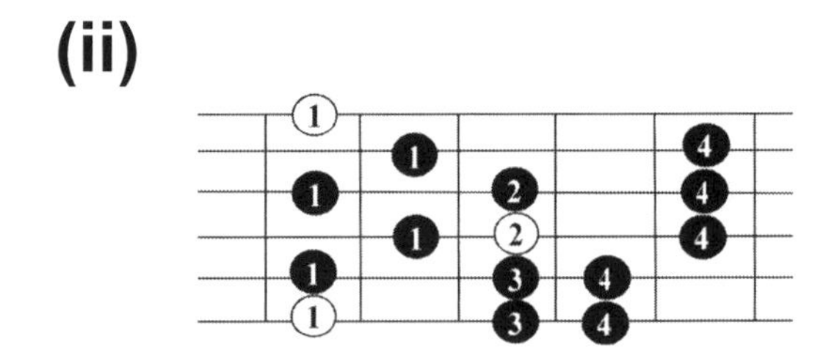

(iii)

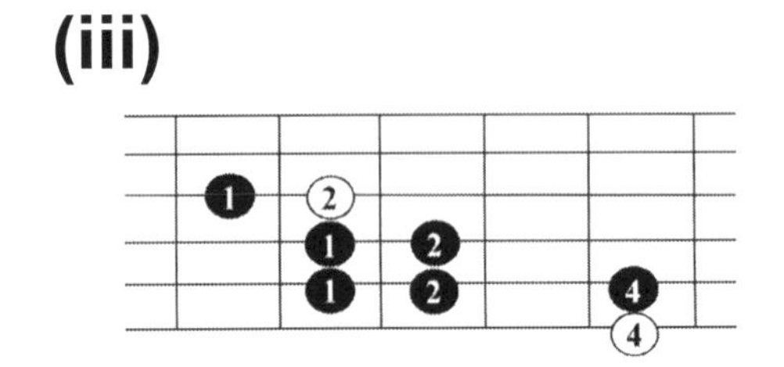

(iv)

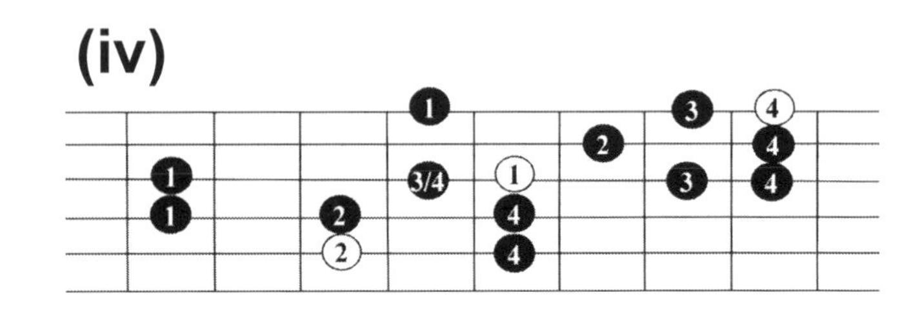

(v)

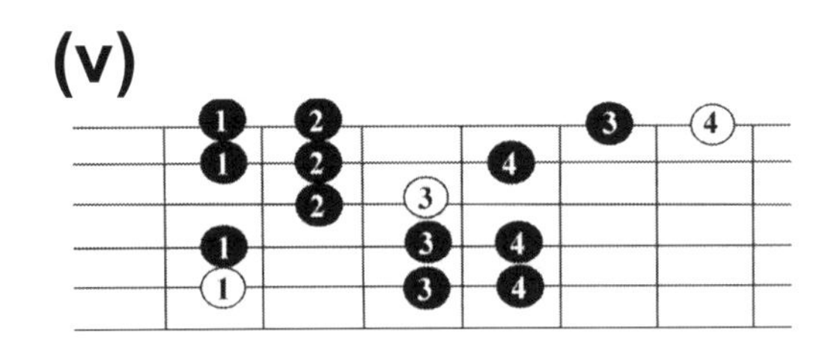

(vi)

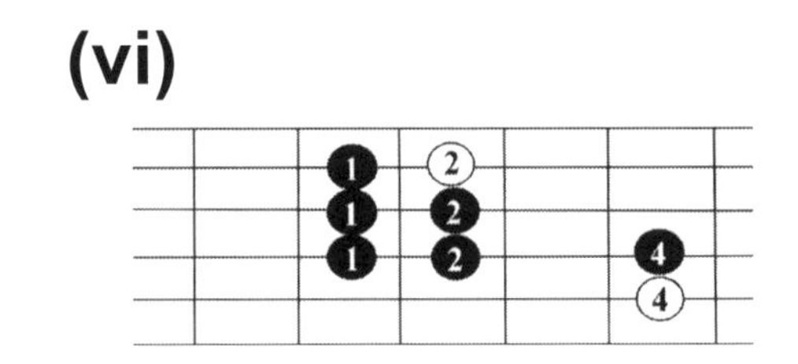

(vii)

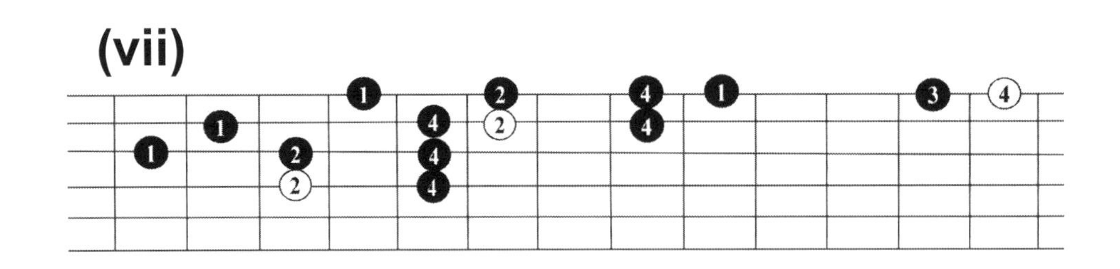

(viii)

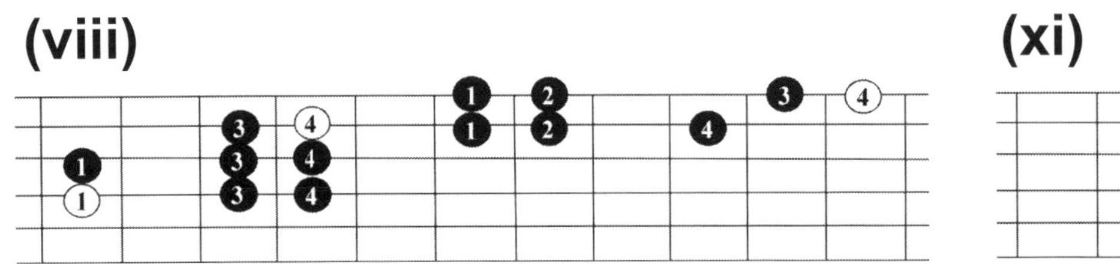

(xi)

A Melodic minor (i)

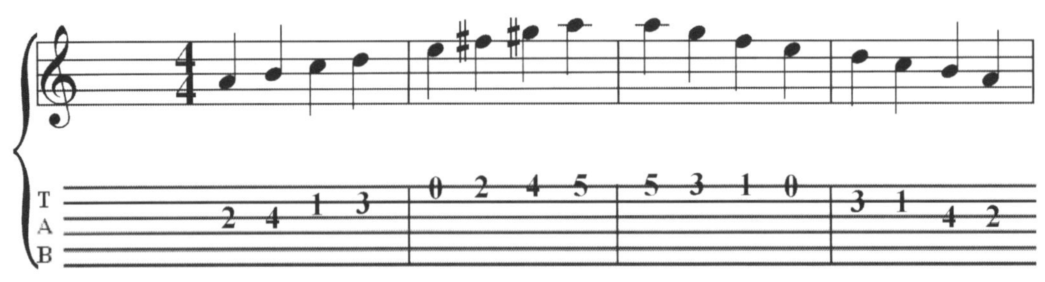

A Melodic minor (ii)

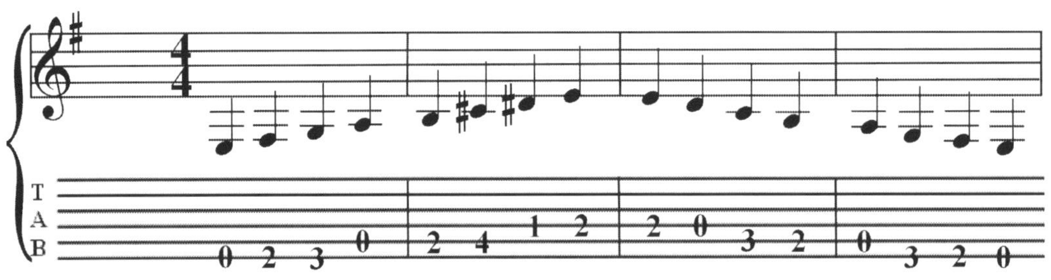

E Melodic minor (i)

E Melodic minor (ii)

B Melodic minor

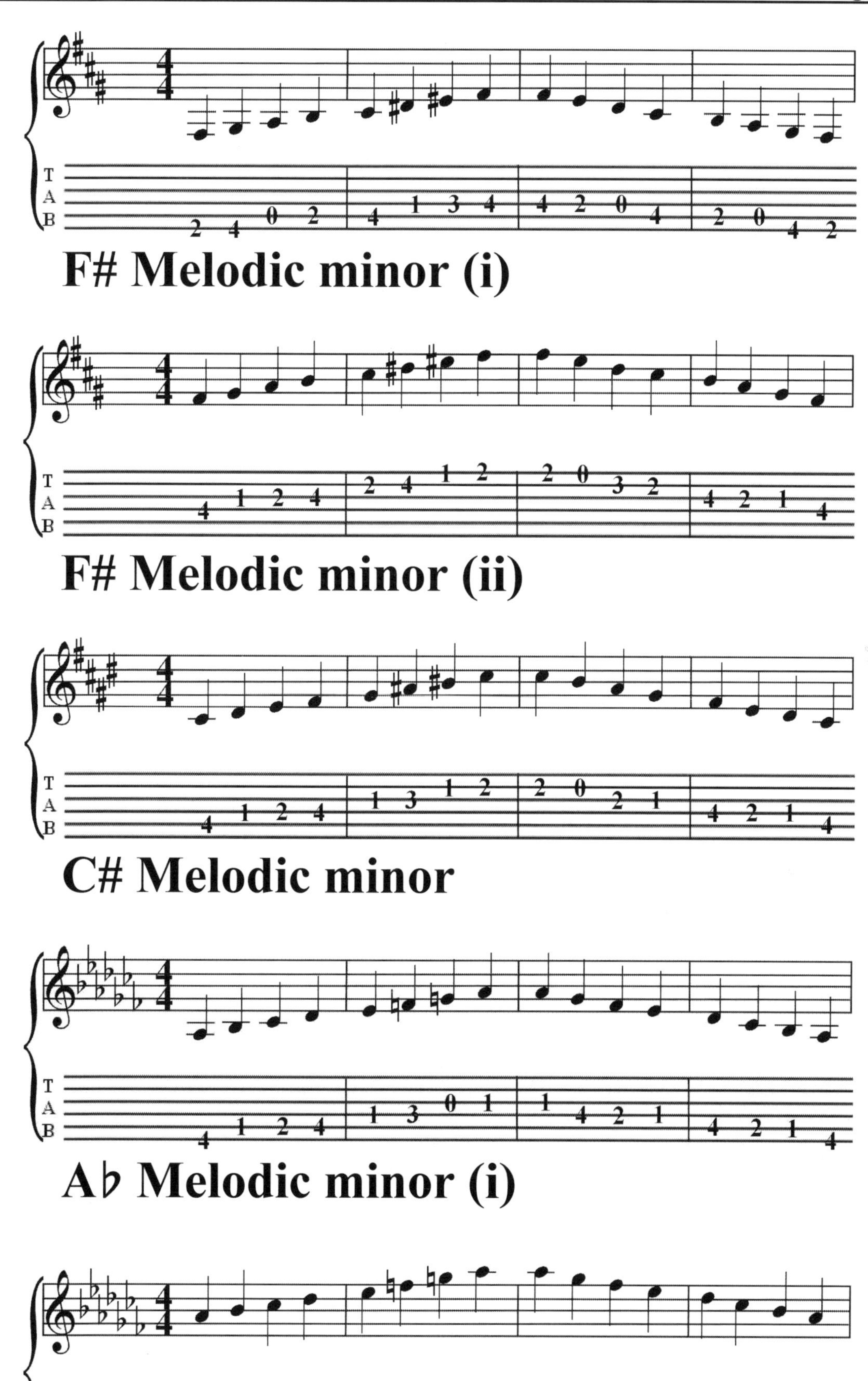
F# Melodic minor (i)
F# Melodic minor (ii)
C# Melodic minor
A♭ Melodic minor (i)
A♭ Melodic minor (ii)

E♭ Melodic minor

B♭ Melodic minor

F Melodic minor (i)

F Melodic minor (ii)

C Melodic minor

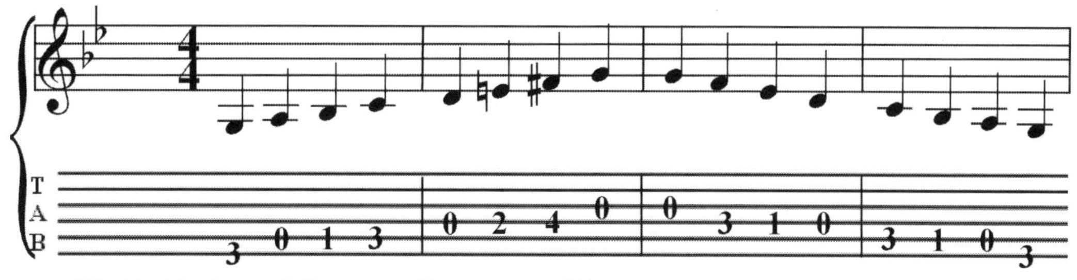

G Melodic minor (i)

G Melodic minor (ii)

D Melodic minor

MELODIC MINOR SCALE - ALL KEYS

Fingerings are given for the ascending form (or "jazz melodic minor"). Remember that the descending form of the Classical melodic minor scale is the same as the natural minor scale or Aeolian mode.

(i)

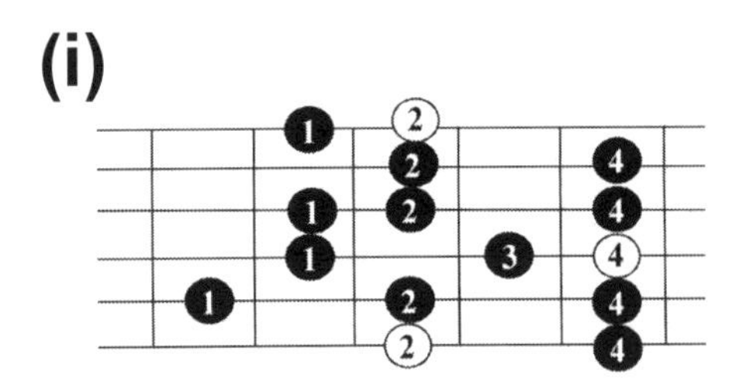

(ii)

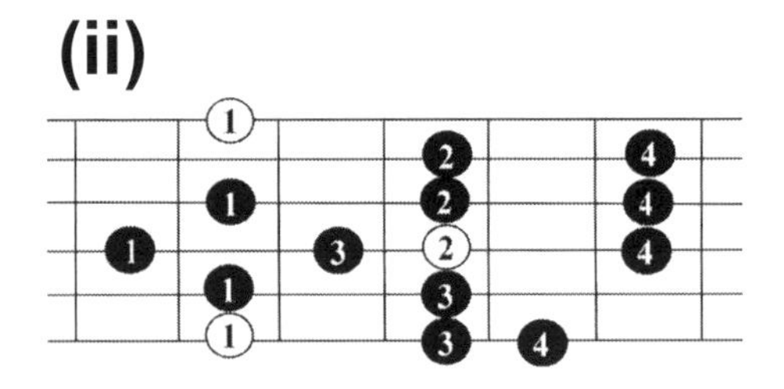

(iii)

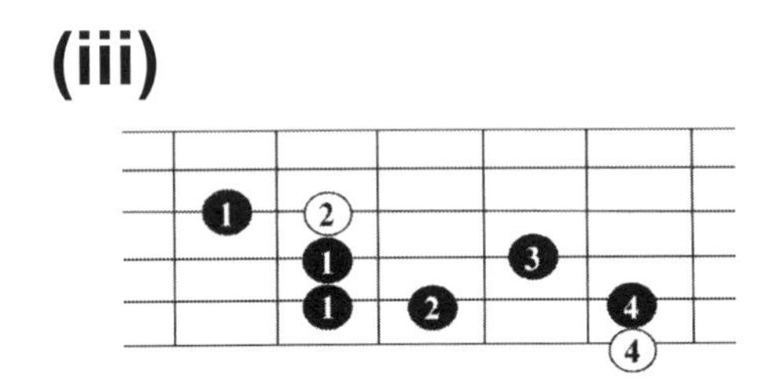

(iv)

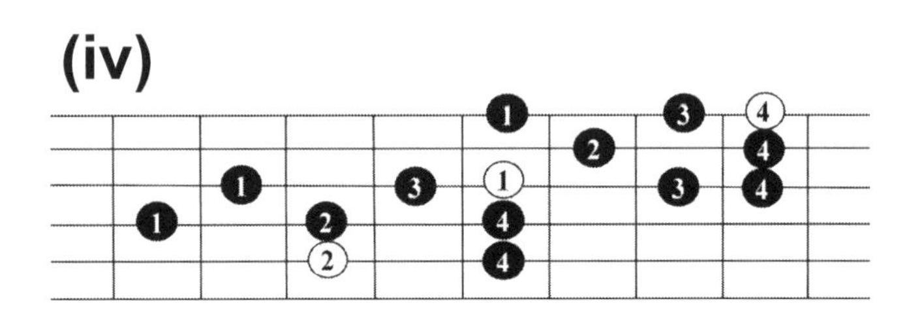

(v)

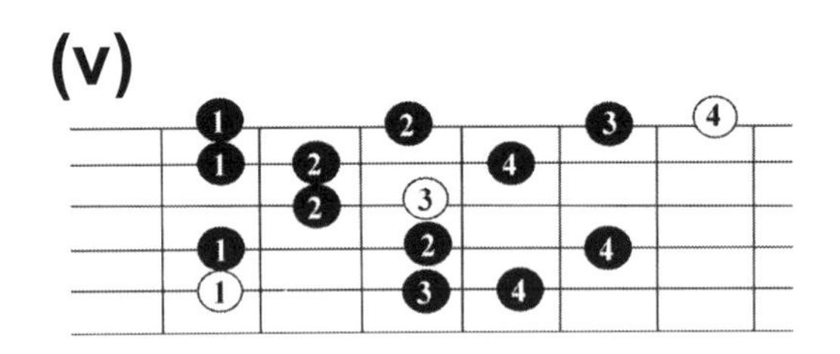

(vi)

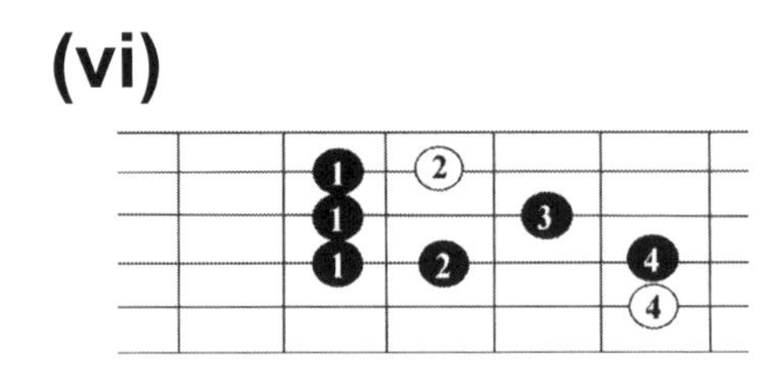

(vii)

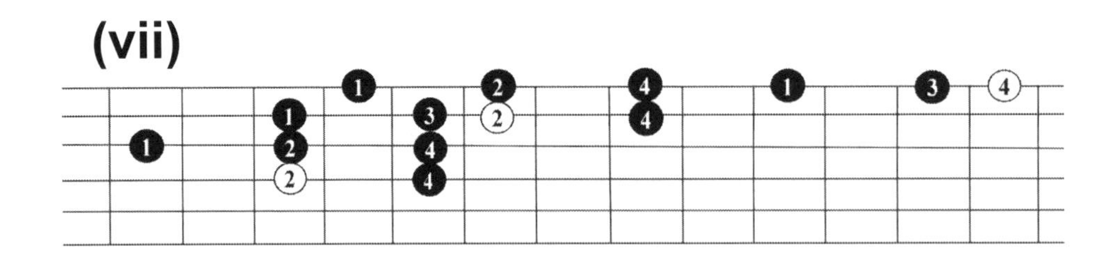

(viii)

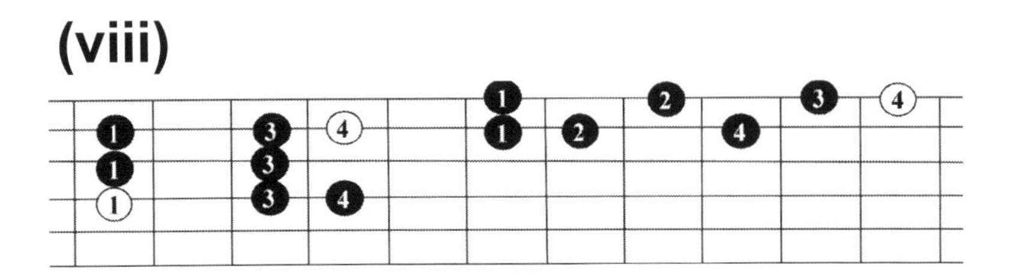

(xi)

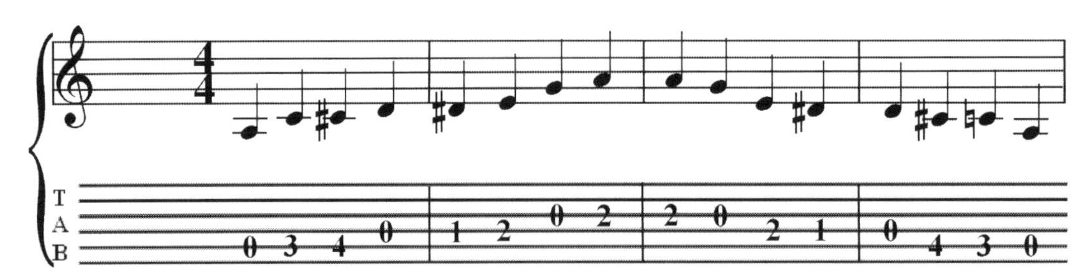

A Blues scale (i)

A Blues scale (ii)

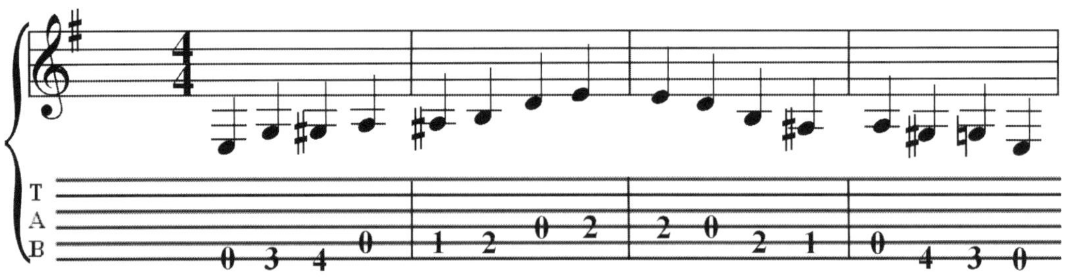

E Blues scale (i)

E Blues scale (ii)

B Blues scale

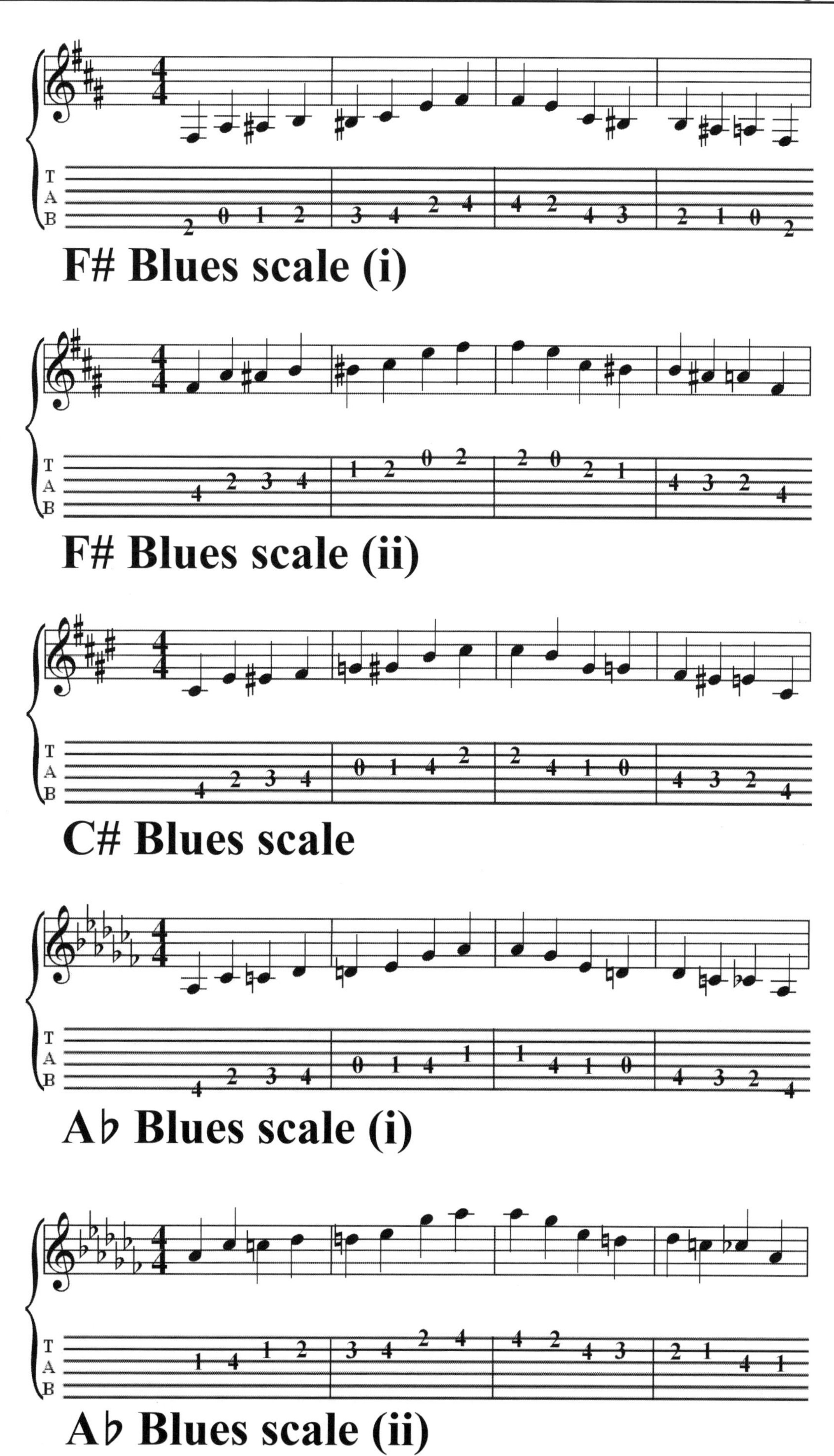

F# Blues scale (i)

F# Blues scale (ii)

C# Blues scale

A♭ Blues scale (i)

A♭ Blues scale (ii)

E♭ Blues scale

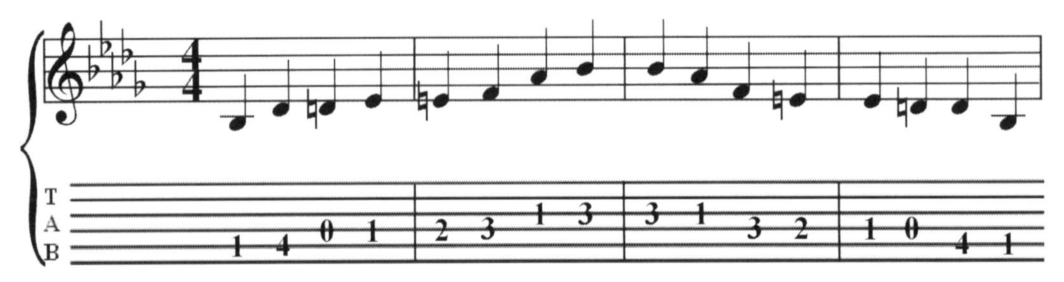

B♭ Blues scale

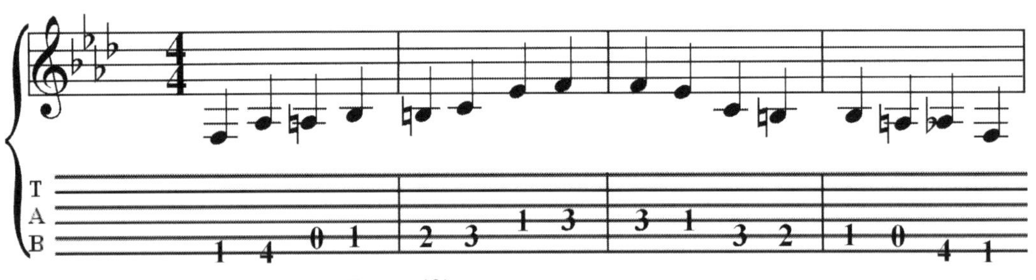

F Blues scale (i)

F Blues scale (ii)

C Blues scale

G Blues scale (i)

G Blues scale (ii)

D Blues scale

BLUES SCALE - ALL KEYS

(i)

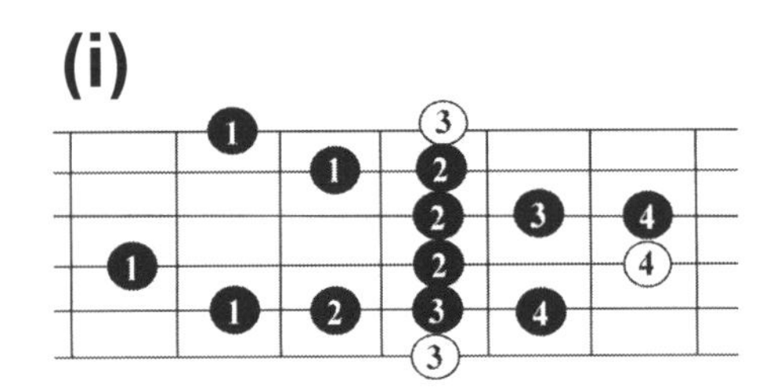

(ii)

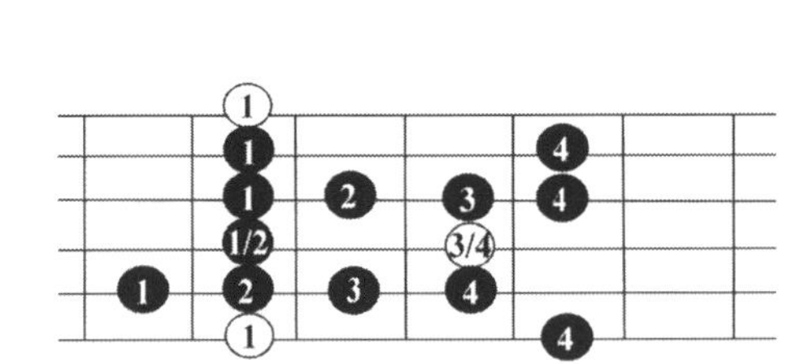

(iii)

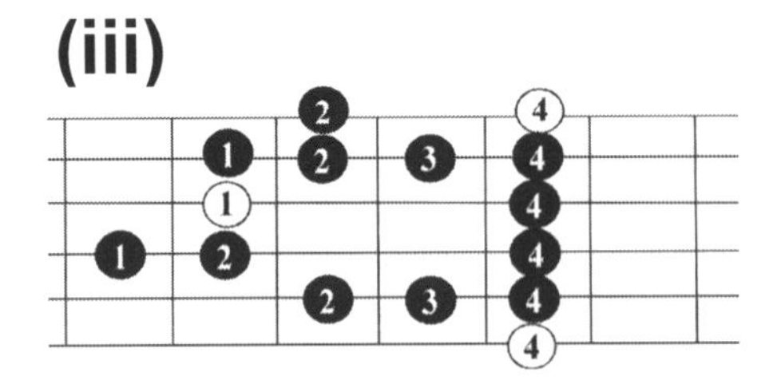

(iv)

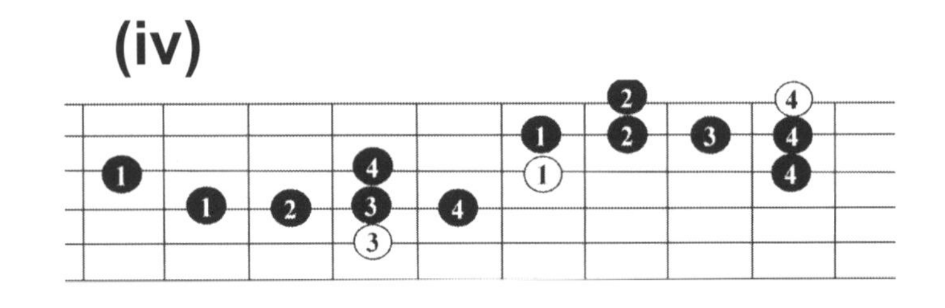

(v)

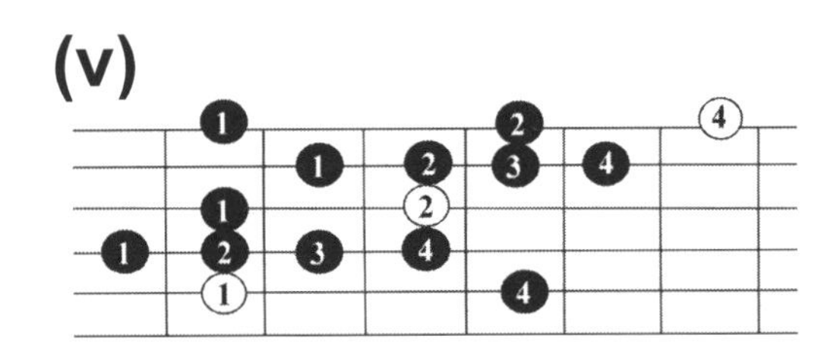

(vi)

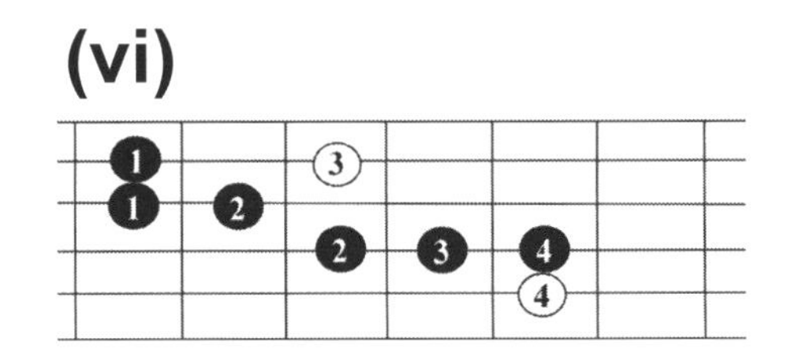

(vii)

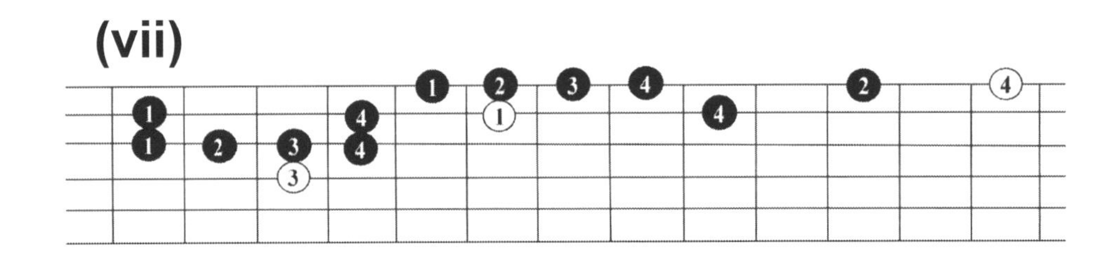

(viii)

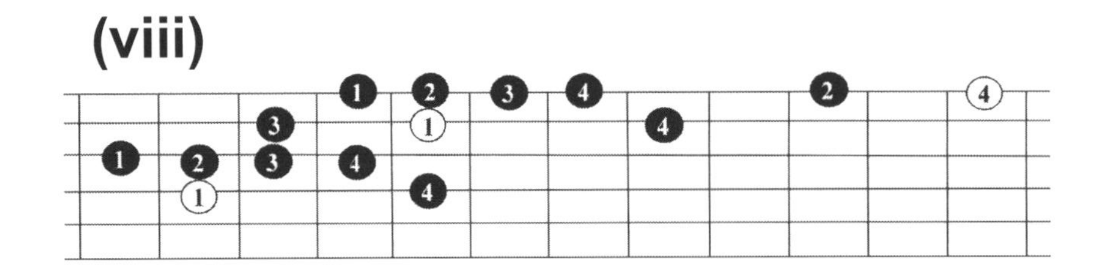

(ix)

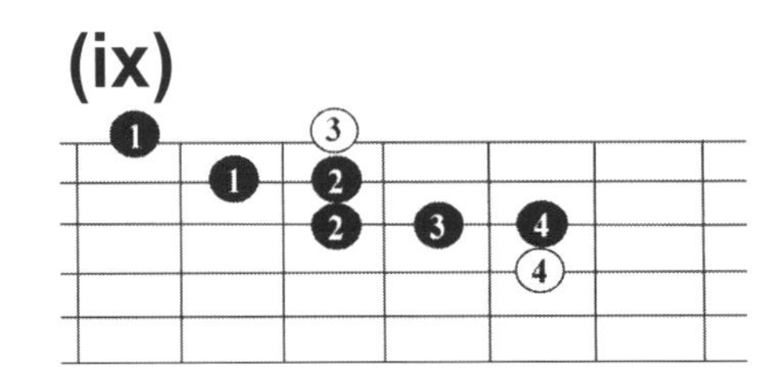

PART FORTY-TWO

DIMINISHED CHORDS AND THE DIMINISHED SCALE

DIMINISHED CHORDS

When chords are formed by harmonising the *major* or *minor* scale in *thirds*, the *intervals* making up the resulting chords are always a mixture of major and minor thirds, as determined by the intervals of the underlying scale - for example the major seventh chord contains:

Root *(major third)* **M3rd** *(minor third)* **5th** *(major third)* **M7th;**

whereas the minor seventh chord contains:

Root *(minor third)* **m3rd** *(major third)* **5th** *(minor third)* **m7th**

Diminished chords are a special case, in that all the intervals are **minor** thirds, giving them the structure:

Root *(minor third)* **m3rd** *(minor third)* **diminished 5th** *(minor third)* **diminished 7th**

The diminished 5th interval you have already met in minor/flat5 and minor seventh/flat 5 chords. The diminished 7th interval is equivalent to the major 6th (i.e. one semitone down from the minor seventh).

It follows that a diminished chord will always contain notes that do not appear in the *key signature.* Diminished chords can be used to add dramatic tension to a composition, and are also useful as transitional chords to introduce *chromatic* movement (i.e. movement by semitones) between chords and across key changes.

Diminished chords can also be substituted for dominant or dominant seventh (V/V7) chords. See section forty-four "Chord Substitution".

You will see that there are, in fact, only three distinct diminished chords, since the pattern of minor thirds repeats cyclically, so that (e.g.) C diminished (C, E♭, G♭, A) contains the same notes as E♭ (or D#) diminished (E♭, G♭, A, C), G♭ (or F#) diminished (G♭, A, C, E♭) and A diminished (A, C, E♭, G♭). When naming chords the lowest note is generally taken to be the root of chord, but in practice the *inversions* can often be used interchangeably, especially if another instrument such as bass or keyboard is playing the low root note.

When writing chord names, the word "diminished" is generally abbreviated to "dim", or represented by a minus sign (e.g. C-). An alternative notation uses a superscripted zero (e.g. C^0).

NOTE: To be strictly technically correct, we should refer to these chords as "diminished seventh" chords. In classical terminology, "diminished chord" refers only to the *triad*: Root - minor third - diminished fifth. However, in guitar chord charts the "dim" suffix almost invariably signifies a diminished seventh chord.

THE DIMINISHED SCALE

The structure of diminished chords is paralleled in the "diminished scale" - a scale in which all the thirds are minor. Thus the diminished scale consists of alternating tones and semitones. Like the diminished chords, there are really only three distinct diminished scales - in practice the scale takes its name from the starting note.

Diminished scales are appropriate to use as chord scales over diminished chords. Also, familiarity with the fingering patterns of the diminished scales will be useful in adding variety to your lead and melody playing by introducing chromatic elements (notes which are not in the key signature).

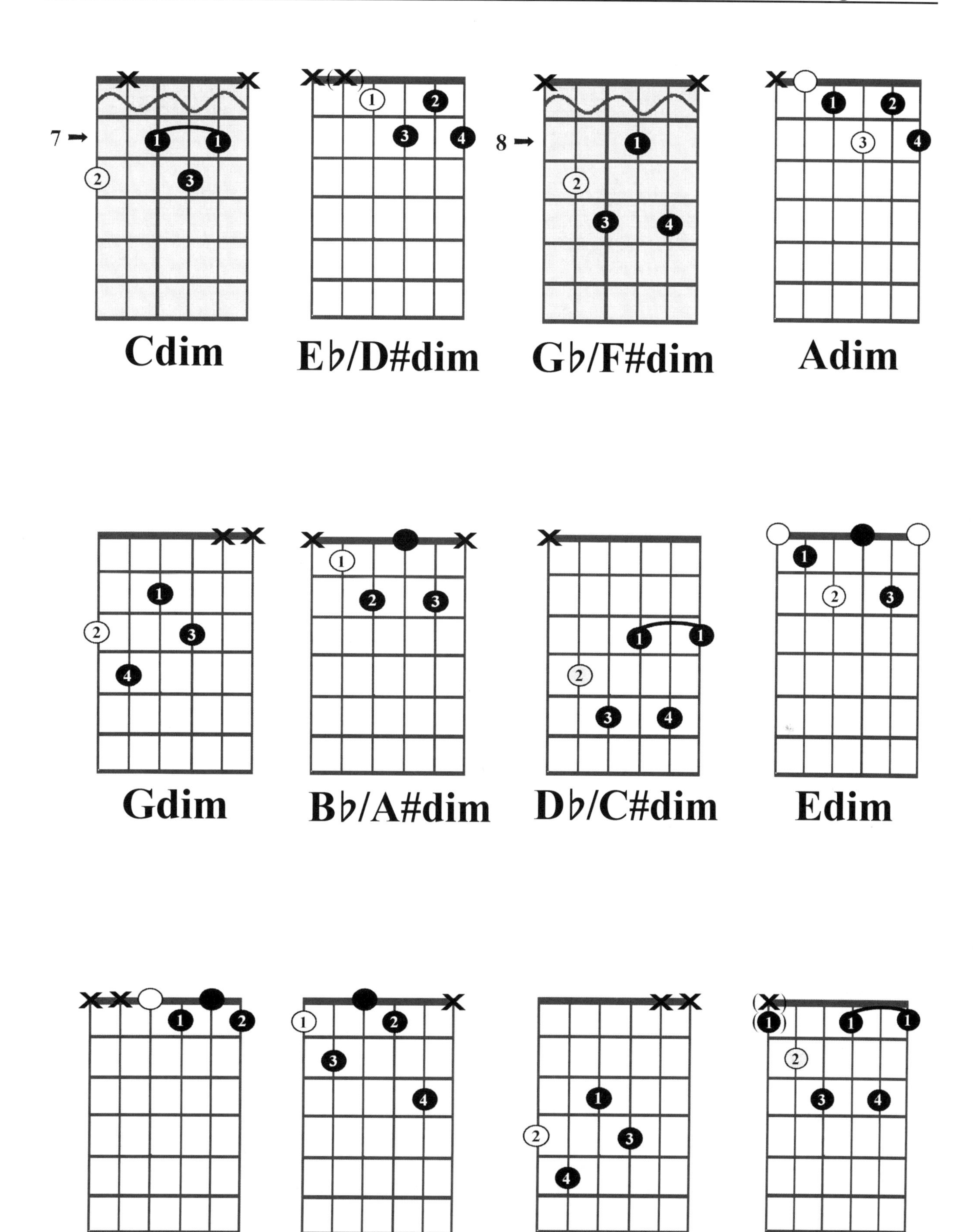

7
Cdim
Eb/D#dim
8
Gb/F#dim
Adim
Gdim
Bb/A#dim
Db/C#dim
Edim
Ddim
Fdim
Ab/G#dim
Bdim

E, G, A#/B♭, C#/D♭ Diminished Scale

F, G#/A♭, B, D Diminished Scale

F#/G♭, A, C, D#/E♭ Diminished Scale

Diminished Scale - any position - (i)

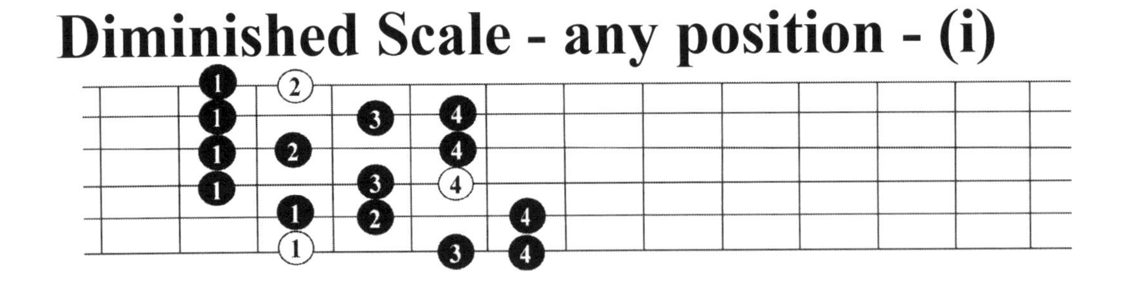

Diminished Scale - any position - (ii)

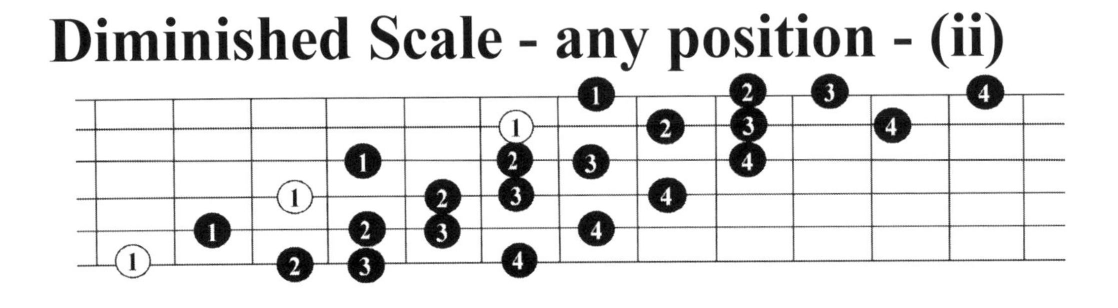

PART FORTY-THREE

AUGMENTED CHORDS AND THE WHOLE-TONE SCALE

AUGMENTED CHORDS

In contrast to the *diminished* chords, *augmented* chords contain only ***major*** *thirds*, giving them the structure:

Root *(major third)* **M3rd** *(major third)* **augmented 5th** *(major third)* **Octave**

Since this pattern is, again, cyclic, there are four distinct augmented chords. The bass note is normally taken to be the root, but the inversions can be freely used.

When writing chord names, the word "augmented" is generally abbreviated to "Aug", or represented by a plus sign (e.g. C+).

THE WHOLE-TONE SCALE

The scale which corresponds to the augmented chords is the "whole-tone" scale, in which, as the name implies, all the intervals are whole *tones*. This means that each whole-tone scale contains half the notes of the *chromatic* scale, so that there are two unique whole-tone scales.

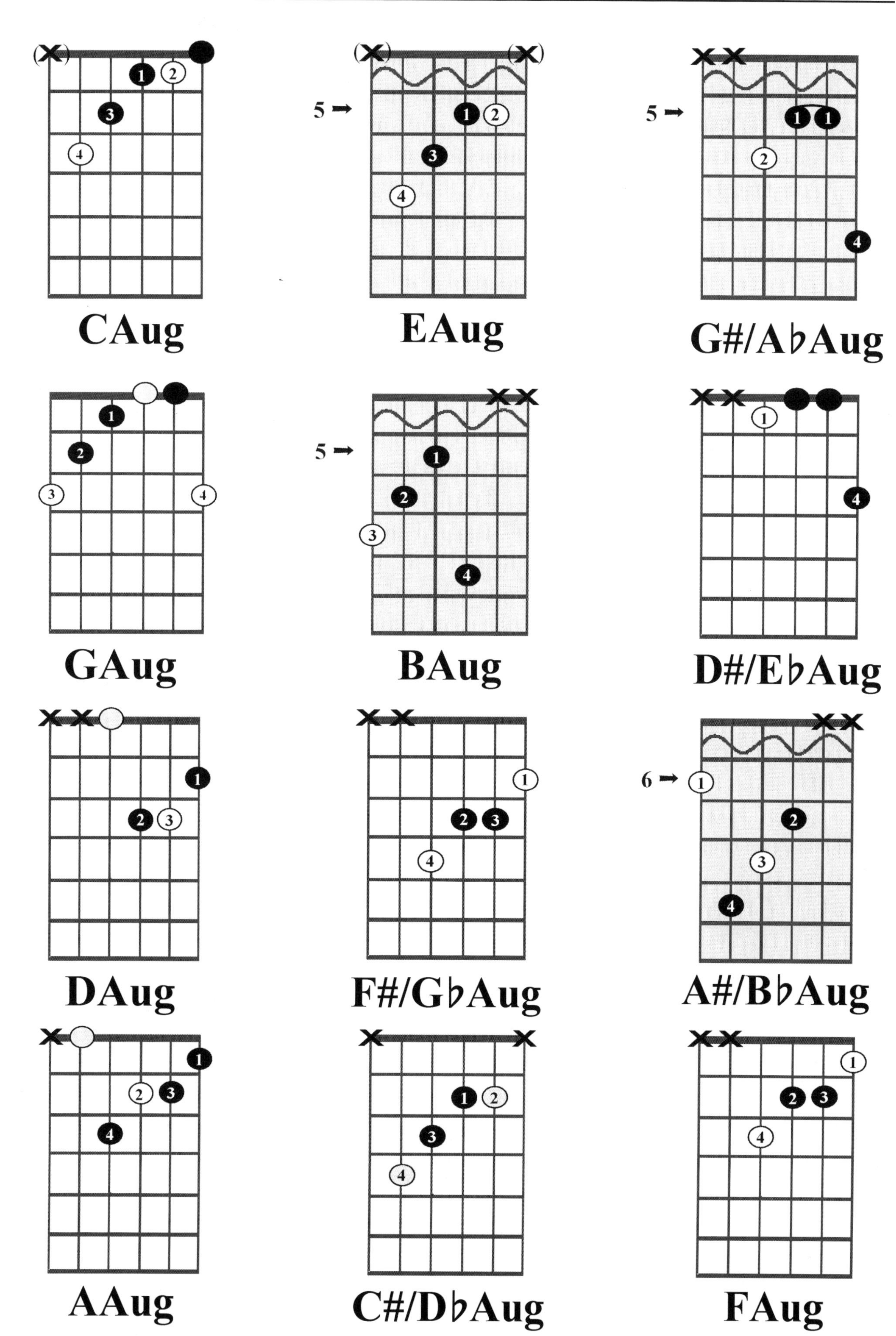
5 ➡
5 ➡
5 ➡
6 ➡
CAug
EAug
G#/A♭Aug
GAug
BAug
D#/E♭Aug
DAug
F#/G♭Aug
A#/B♭Aug
AAug
C#/D♭Aug
FAug

E, F#, G#/A♭, A#/B♭, C, D Whole-Tone Scale

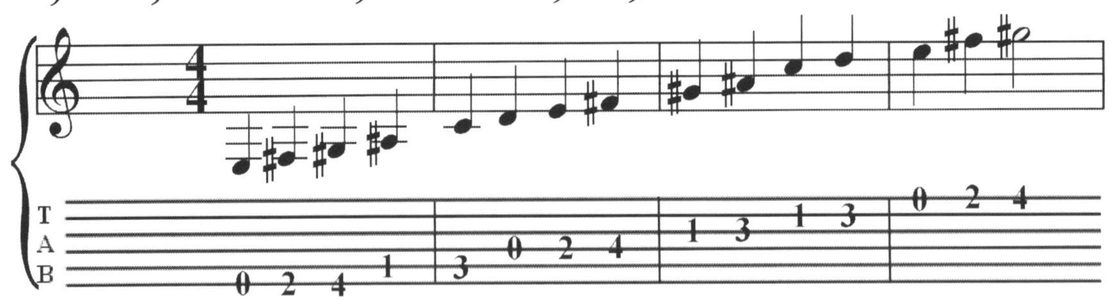

F, G, A, B, C#/D♭, D#/E♭ Whole-Tone Scale

Whole-Tone Scale - any position

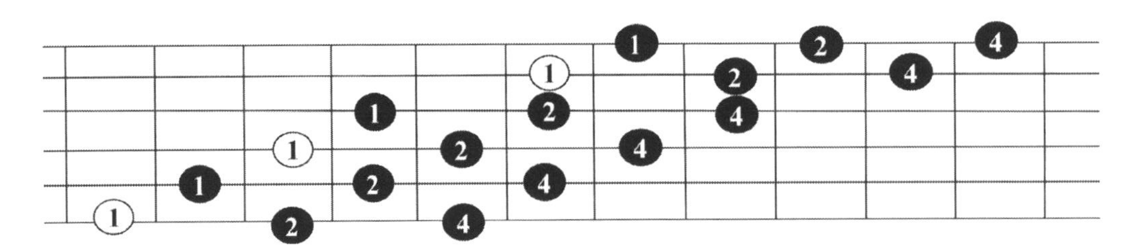

PART FORTY-FOUR

CHORD SUBSTITUTION

WHAT IS "CHORD SUBSTITUTION"

In this section we will be looking at alternative chords which can replace the conventional chords in our common chord progressions to add variety and interest to a composition. As this is intended as a broad overview, fingering charts will not generally be provided, although you will learn a new mode. If you need further guidance, there are several excellent chord dictionaries available, as well as numerous on-line resources which you can consult. (The Internet being what it is, you are advised to cross-check information across two or more sources to be sure of its accuracy).

i) DRONE (OR POWER) CHORDS

Drone chords, also known as power chords, are not, strictly speaking, chords at all, as they contain only two distinct notes: the *root* and *fifth*, doubled in octaves across four, five or six strings. Since the *third* is omitted, drone chords are neither *major* nor *minor*, and are useful in blues and blues-derived forms for underpinning the major/minor ambiguity which is characteristic of the blues. Power chords can also be used to create big, dramatic (if somewhat unsubtle) soundscapes, and so are also a staple of heavy rock styles. Drone/power chords can be substituted for any major or minor *triad.*

ii) FURTHER HARMONISATION

As I have mentioned in passing elsewhere in this book, the system of harmonisation in thirds can be extended beyond the *octave* to create ninth, eleventh and thirteenth chords. For example, the harmonisation of the tonic note C in the key of C major can generate all of the following chords:

C (Major)
C - E - G

C M7
C - E - G - B

CM9
C - E - G - B - D

CM11
C - E - G - B - D - F

CM13
C - E - G - B - D - F - A

Since the thirteenth chord contains all the notes of the C Major scale, no further harmonisation is possible.

In practice, seven-note chords are impossible on the guitar, while most six-note and many five-note chords are impractical. It will, therefore, be necessary to drop one or more of the lower chord tones in order to add the ninth, eleventh and thirteenth notes. Care should be taken to ensure that these chords can be differentiated from the sus2, sus4 and 6th chords, i.e. a ninth or eleventh chord should ideally always include the third, while a thirteenth chord should include the seventh. The safest note to omit is usually the fifth, and it is usual, on guitar, to omit the ninth from eleventh chords, and the ninth and eleventh from thirteenth chords.

CHROMATIC ALTERATIONS

As the possibilities of harmonising the major/natural minor scale have now been exhausted, the remaining examples of chord substitution will feature "*chromatic* alteration" - that is to say, replacing chord tones with notes which do not appear in the key signature.

iii) HARMONISING THE MELODIC MINOR SCALE

The chords of the harmonised melodic minor scale were listed in Part Forty-One "Variant Minor Scales and the Blues Scale". In minor keys, these can be substituted for the equivalent chords of the harmonised natural minor scale. In fact we have already used one such substitution, throughout this book, in using the major or dominant seventh form for the V (or V7) chord. Combining the chords of the harmonised natural and melodic minor scales, the following table lists all the possible alternatives for the chords of our three common progressions:

i	ii	iv	V	VI
minor or minor7 or min/Maj7	minor or minor7 or minor/flat5 or minor7/flat5	minor or minor7 or Major or (dominant) 7	minor or minor7 or Major or (dominant) 7	Major or Major7 or minor/flat5 or minor7/flat5

A more adventurous use of these chording possibilities would be to use substitute chords from the harmonised melodic minor scale in a chord progression in the relative **Major** key - or even the tonic Major key. (e.g. the relative Major key of A minor is C Major; the tonic Major key of A minor is A Major). I leave it to you to discover which of these substitutions yields useful results.

iv) SECONDARY DOMINANTS

To help to understand secondary dominants, take a moment to remind yourself why the dominant seventh (V7) chord was substituted for the minor seventh (vm7) chord in minor keys. By sharpening the third, the stepwise (semitone) movement from the third of the V chord to the root of the i chord, which is characteristic of the major key perfect *cadence* (V-I) is replicated in the minor key perfect cadence (V-i).

Another type of cadence is the so-called *imperfect cadence*, which ends on a V chord, rather than returning to the *tonic* (I). If the preceding chord is a ii (minor or minor seventh chord), sharpening the third will have a similar effect to the minor perfect cadence, creating a stepwise movement from the third of the II chord to the root of the V chord. Thus the sequence iim7 - V becomes II7 - V. The ii chord has been altered to take on the character of a dominant/dominant seventh chord - hence "secondary dominant".

This principle can be extended to any two-chord sequence where the first chord is a minor/minor seventh, and the chord root moves by an *interval* of a *fourth*. Thus: vim7 - iim7 can become VI7 - iim7, and (going beyond our set of common progressions) iiim7 - vim7 can become III7 - vim7

v) BLUES SEVENTHS

A common practice in blues, rhythm and blues, and rock-and-roll styles is to play the I - IV - V progression with each chord played as a dominant seventh form - i.e. I7 - IV7 - V7. This is often emphasised by a *riff* built from the dominant seventh arpeggio which follows the chord changes. The Mixolydian mode is an appropriate chord scale for the I7 and V7 chords, but the IV7 chord needs a new mode. This is the Lydian ♭7 (also called the "Lydian Dominant" mode), which contains a sharpened fourth and a flattened seventh.

The Lydian ♭7 mode is one of the modes of the melodic minor scale, and is also the appropriate mode for tritone substitutions (see below). A full set of examples is given at the end of this section.

v) TRITONE SUBSTITUTION (FLAT 5 SUBSTITUTION)

A tritone is an interval of three tones - i.e. a flattened (*diminished*) fifth or sharpened (*augmented*) fourth. Tritone substitution (also known as flat 5 substitution) replaces a V7 (dominant seventh) chord in a perfect cadence with a seventh chord having its root a tritone above (or below) the original.

In a perfect cadence (V7 - I) progression, the most significant notes in the V7 chord are the third and the seventh, and these are retained in the substituted chord, although their roles in the chord structure are reversed. Thus, in the key of C, the V7 chord G7 consists of the notes G, **B** (the third), D & **F** (the seventh). Moving this chord by a tritone creates a D♭7 chord containing D♭, **F** (now the third), A♭, and **B** (now the seventh).

Tritone substitutions are particularly associated with jazz styles.

The appropriate chord scale for a tritone substitute chord is the Lydian ♭7 (Lydian Dominant) mode, as described above - see the end of this section for examples.

vi) DIMINISHED SEVENTHS

Diminished seventh (dim) chords can also be substituted for a V7 (dominant seventh) chord. If you examine the structure of a dominant seventh chord, you will see that the third, fifth and seventh form a diminished triad. It follows that sharpening the root note will produce a diminished seventh chord which retains three out of four notes of the original dominant seventh chord, including the crucial third and seventh.

For example, in the key of C, the V7 chord G7 (G, B, D, F) can be replaced with the chord A♭dim (A♭, B, D, F - remember that the same notes form the Bdim, Ddim, and Fdim chords).

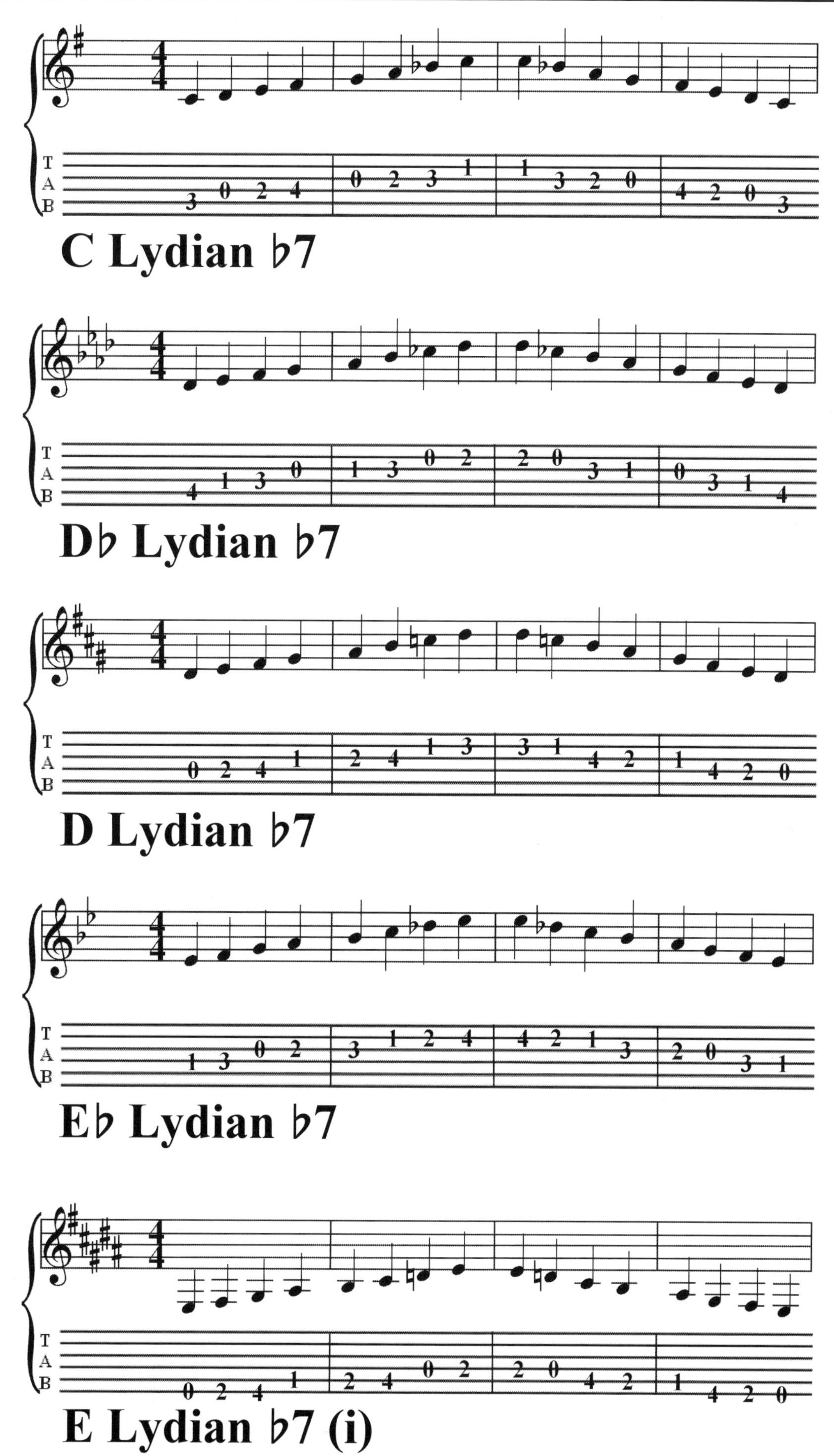
T
A
B
3 0 2 4
0 2 3 1
1 3 2 0
4 2 0 3
C Lydian ♭7
T
A
B
4 1 3 0
1 3 0 2
2 0 3 1
0 3 1 4
D♭ Lydian ♭7
T
A
B
0 2 4 1
2 4 1 3
3 1 4 2
1 4 2 0
D Lydian ♭7
T
A
B
1 3 0 2
3 1 2 4
4 2 1 3
2 0 3 1
E♭ Lydian ♭7
T
A
B
0 2 4 1
2 4 0 2
2 0 4 2
1 4 2 0
E Lydian ♭7 (i)

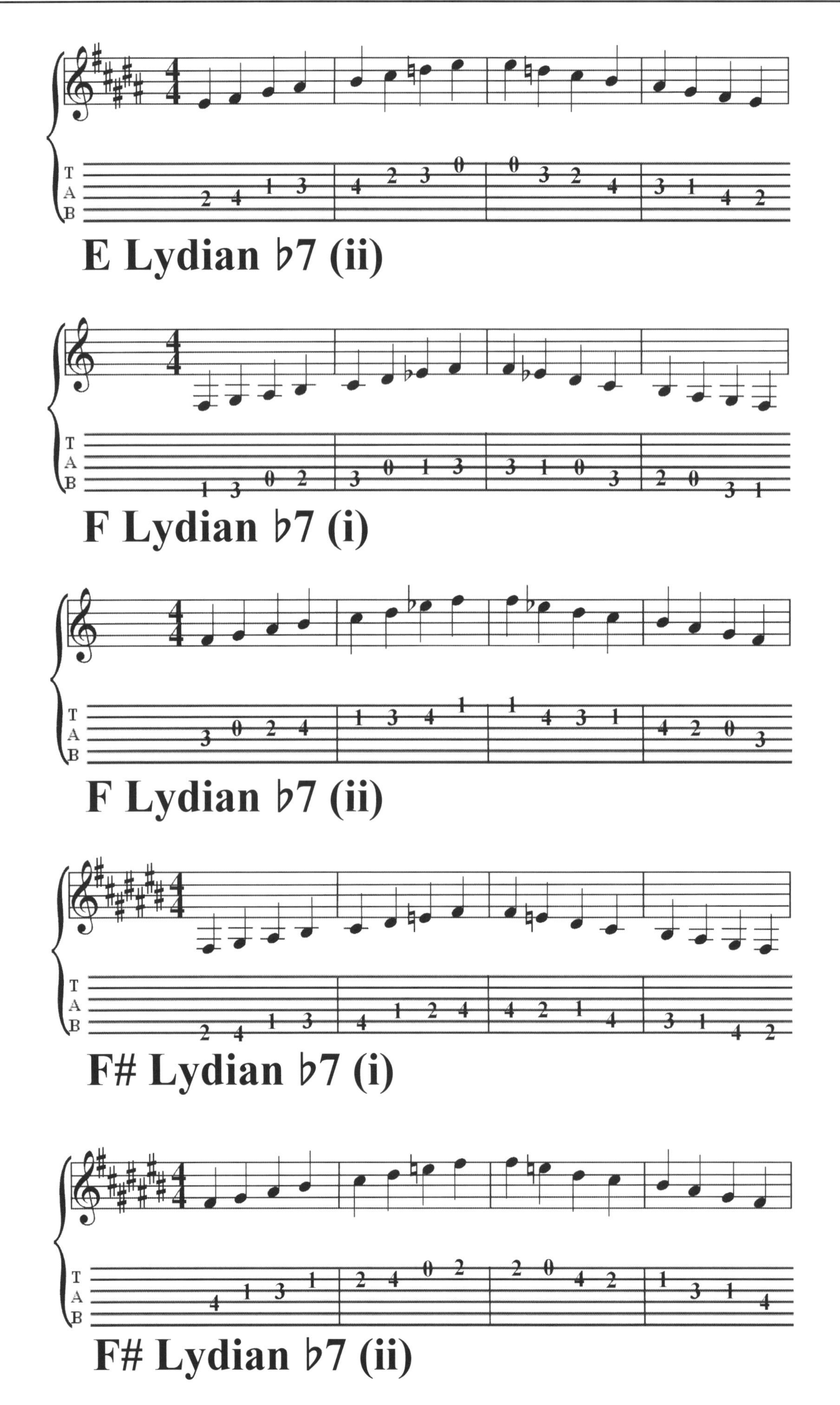
E Lydian ♭7 (ii)
F Lydian ♭7 (i)
F Lydian ♭7 (ii)
F# Lydian ♭7 (i)
F# Lydian ♭7 (ii)

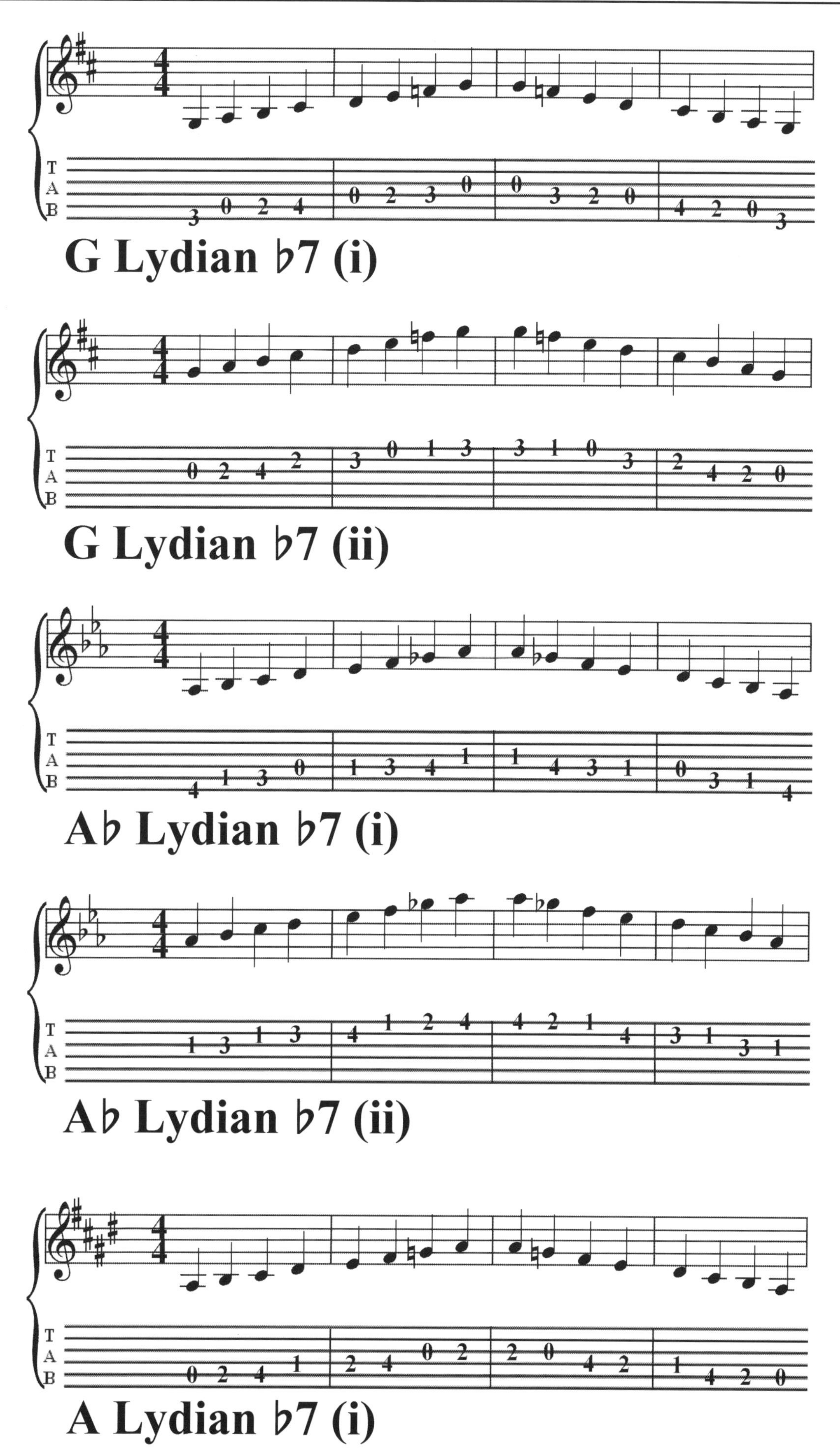
G Lydian ♭7 (i)
G Lydian ♭7 (ii)
A♭ Lydian ♭7 (i)
A♭ Lydian ♭7 (ii)
A Lydian ♭7 (i)

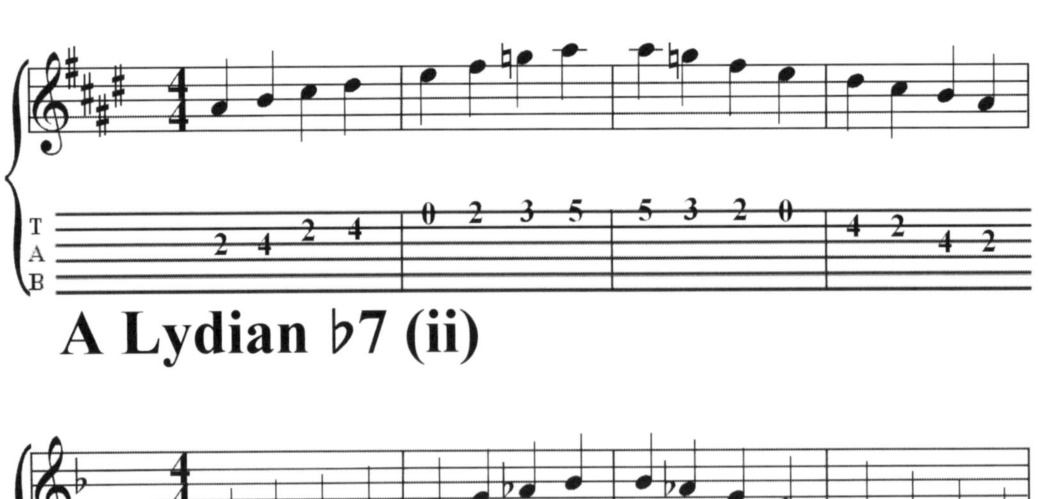

A Lydian ♭7 (ii)

T A B
1 3 0 2 | 3 0 1 3 | 3 1 0 3 | 2 0 3 1

B♭ Lydian ♭7

B Lydian ♭7

Lydian ♭7 MODE - ANY POSITION

(i)

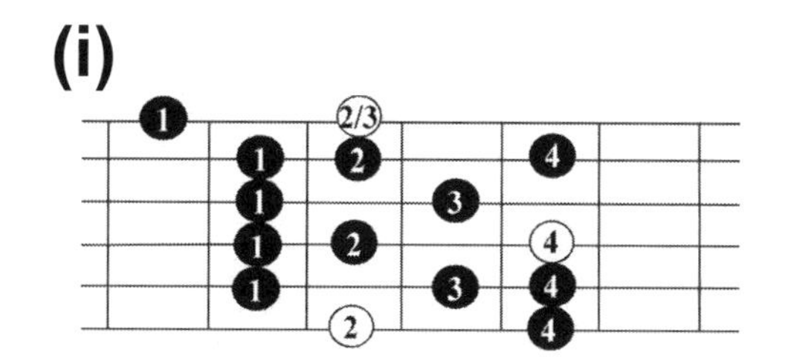

(ii)

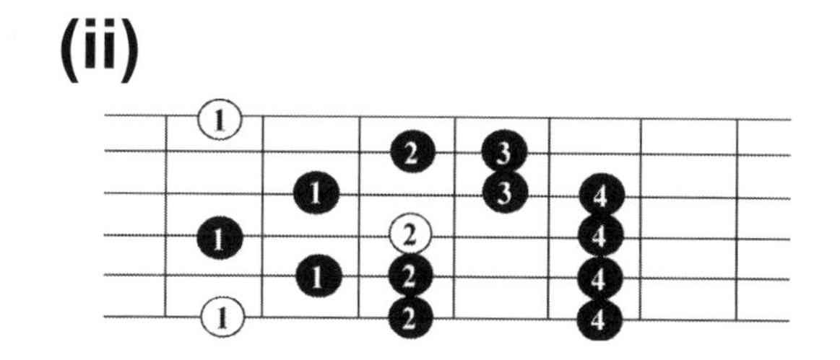

(iii)

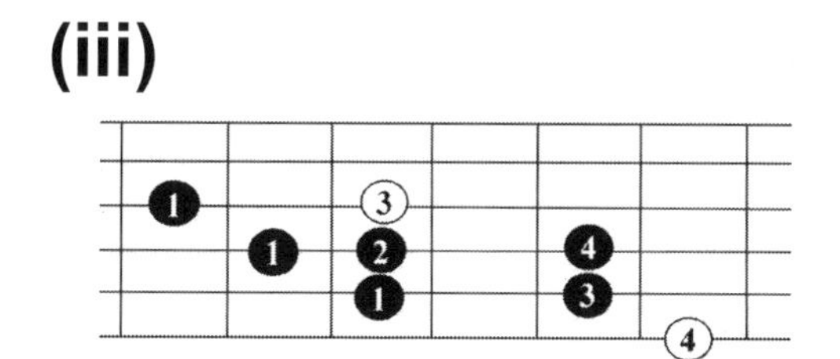

(iv)

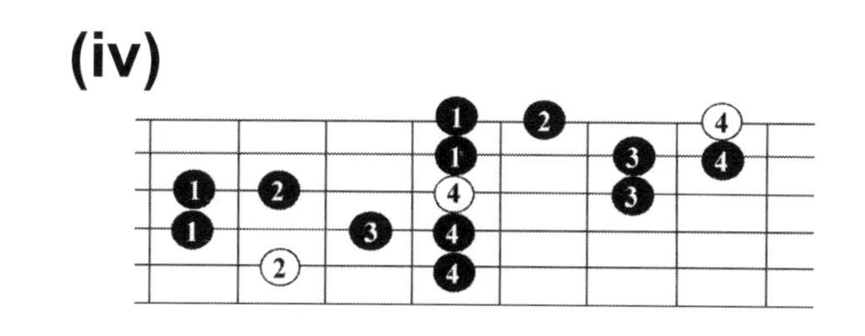

(v)

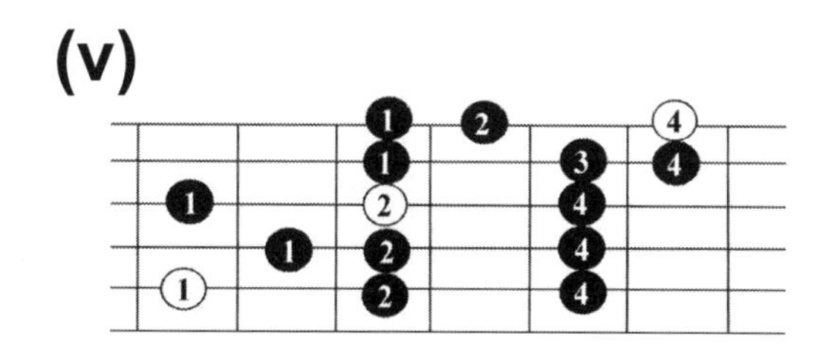

(vi)

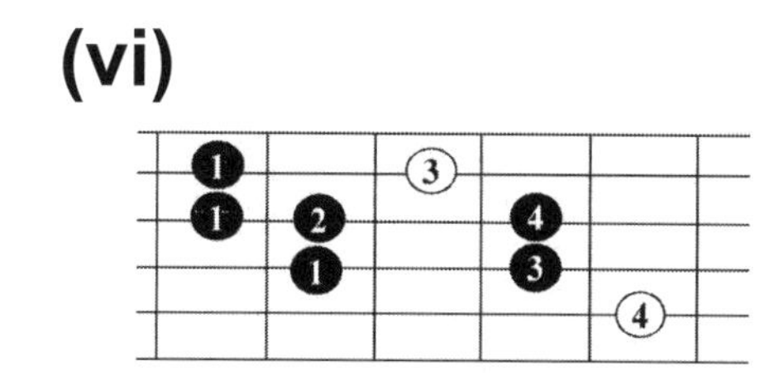

(vii)

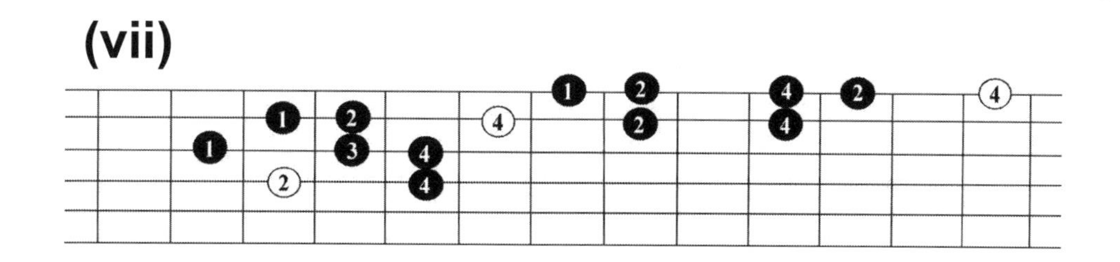

(viii)

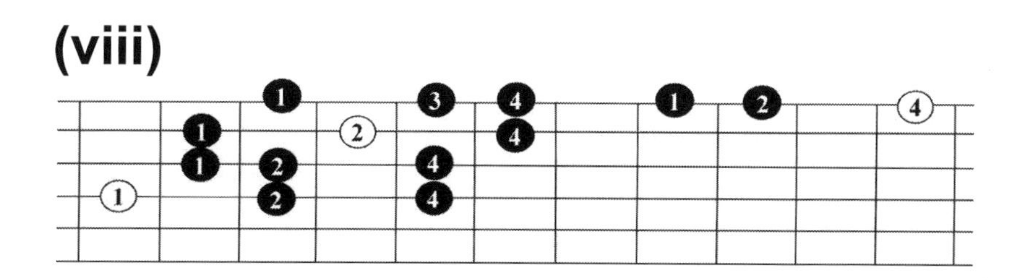

(xi)

PART FORTY-FIVE

GLOSSARY

augmented

A major or perfect interval becomes augmented when it is widened by sharpening (raising) the upper note by one semitone. An augmented chord is a chord containing a major third and augmented fifth, so that all the intervals within the chord are major thirds.

cadence

A melodic and chordal pattern which marks the end of a piece, or passage of music. For example, the “perfect cadence” describes a chord progression from the dominant (V) to the tonic (I); an “imperfect cadence” ends on the dominant, usually preceded by chord I, IV or ii; a “plagal cadence” moves from IV - I, and an “interrupted cadence” moves from the dominant to a chord other than the tonic, often the vi chord.

chromatic

Describes movement by semitone. Thus a “chromatic” scale contains all of the twelve notes comprising an octave divided into semitones (i.e. all the notes on your guitar). The term chromatic is also used to describe notes introduced into the harmony or melody of a piece which do not occur in the key signature (i.e. notes within the key have been sharpened or flattened by a semitone).

degree

The degrees of a scale are simply the scale notes, numbered relative to the tonic. Thus in the key of C (scale CDEFGABC), C is the first, D the second, E the third, etc. In classical terminology each degree of the scale also has a name:

1st = Tonic

2nd = Supertonic

3rd = Mediant

4th = Subdominant

5th = Dominant

6th = Submediant

7th = Leading Note

8th = Octave

In popular music, only the terms tonic, dominant and octave are in regular use.

diatonic

Refers to the conventional scales and modes of the European classical tradition. Each seven-note scale divides the octave into a pattern of tone and semitone intervals - the exception being the harmonic minor scale which contains one interval of a minor third.

diminished

A minor or perfect interval becomes diminished when it is narrowed by flattening (lowering) the upper note by one semitone. A diminished chord is a chord containing a minor third and diminished fifth - and more often than not, on the guitar, a diminished seventh (though this chord is more properly called a diminished-seventh chord) - so that all the intervals within the chord are minor thirds.

fifth

i) The note corresponding to the fifth degree of a scale;
ii) An interval corresponding to that between the tonic note of a scale and its fifth, equal to three and a half tones;
iii) A chord tone an interval of one fifth above the root note.

fourth

i) The note corresponding to the fourth degree of a scale;
ii) An interval corresponding to that between the tonic note of a scale and its fourth, equal to two and a half tones;
iii) A chord tone an interval of one fourth above the root note.

interval

The difference in pitch between two notes. Intervals are named by reference to the degrees of the scale. Thus, for example, a "major third" is any interval of the same magnitude as that between the first and third notes of a major scale (i.e. two tones).

inversion

Any chord voicing in which the root note of the chord is not the bass (lowest) note. If the third of the chord is the lowest note, then the chord is described as a "first-inversion" chord; if the fifth is the lowest note then it is a "second-inversion" chord.

key signature

The set of sharps and flats which define the notes available in a given key, and hence the scale of that key. In music notation, these are written at the start of the stave and do not need to be added to individual notes. Any sharp, flat or natural signs added to the score are called "accidentals" and represent chromatic (qv) elements.

Following the "cycle of fifths", one sharp is added to the key signature each time the tonic note moves by a fifth, until the maximum seven sharps is reached. The sharpened note is the seventh of the new key, thus:

Key	Key Signature
C Major/A minor	No sharps or flats
G Major/E minor	F#
D Major/B minor	F#, C#
A Major/F# minor	F#, C#, G#
E Major/C# minor	F#, C#, G#, D#
B Major/G# minor	F#, C#, G#, D#, A#
F# Major/D# minor	F#, C#, G#, D#, A#, E#
C# Major/A# minor	F#, C#, G#, D#, A#, E#, B#

Reversing this sequence results in a "cycle of fourths" - each time the tonic note moves by a fourth, one flat is added to the key signature. The flattened note is the fourth of the new key, thus:

Key	Key Signature
C Major/A minor	No sharps or flats
F Major/D minor	B♭
B♭ Major/G minor	B♭, E♭
E♭ Major/C minor	B♭, E♭, A♭
A♭ Major/F minor	B♭, E♭, A♭, D♭
D♭ Major/B♭ minor	B♭, E♭, A♭, D♭, G♭
G♭ Major/E♭ minor	B♭, E♭, A♭, D♭, G♭, C♭
C♭ Major/A♭ minor	B♭, E♭, A♭, D♭, G♭, C♭, F♭

Note that there is overlap between the two sequences and so C#/D♭, F#/G♭, & B/C♭ are alternative ways of representing the same keys.

See the diagram at the end of this book for a graphic representation of the cycle.

major

Scales/Keys: the major scale is one of the two principal scale types of the diatonic system (see also "minor"). The major scale contains only major and perfect (qv) intervals. Music written using mainly notes from a major scale is said to be in a major key, e.g. a piece written around the notes of the C major scale (CDEFGABC) is "in the key of C Major".

Intervals: the major intervals within the major scale are the second, third, sixth and seventh. Narrowing a major interval by one semitone results in the corresponding minor interval. Widening a major interval by one semitone results in an augmented interval.

Chords: The major or minor character of a chord is normally defined by its third - i.e. a chord containing a major third is usually called a Major chord. A noteable exception is the "dominant seventh", or just plain "seventh" chord, which contains a major third and a minor seventh.

minor

Scales/Keys: the minor scale is one of the two principal scale types of the diatonic system (see also "major"). The minor scale contains minor and perfect (qv) intervals, apart from the second, which is major. Music written using mainly notes from a minor scale is said to be in a minor key, e.g. a piece written around the notes of the A minor scale (ABCDEFGA) is "in the key of A minor". There are three main variants of the minor scale - the natural minor scale (containing the same notes as the relative major scale), and the harmonic and melodic minor scales, which contain altered notes. See part forty-one, "Variant Minor Scales and the Blues Scale".

Intervals: the minor intervals within the minor scale are the third, sixth and seventh. The second of the minor scale is something of an anomaly, as it is major (one tone). Minor seconds (one semitone) are found in some of the modes, but not in any of the natural, harmonic or melodic minor scales. Widening a minor interval by one semitone results in the corresponding major interval. Narrowing a minor interval by one semitone results in a diminished interval.

Chords: The major or minor character of a chord is normally defined by its third - i.e. a chord containing a minor third is usually called a minor chord.

modulation

The process of changing key within a piece of music by means of harmonic progressions. This might involve, for example, using chords whose notes are common to the two keys, or using transitional chords which introduce chromatic (qv) movement between the notes of the two keys.

octave

i) The note corresponding to the eighth degree of a scale, the same note name as the tonic (first). In physical terms an octave represents a doubling of the frequency of the note;
ii) An interval corresponding to that between the tonic note of a scale and its octave, equal to six tones;
iii) A chord tone an interval of one octave above the root note.

perfect

The perfect intervals within the major and minor scales are the fourth, fifth and octave. You will note that these intervals are common to both major and minor scales. The second is anomalous, as it too is common to both scales (it is equal to one tone), but by convention this interval is called a major second. Widening a perfect interval by one semitone results in an augmented interval. Narrowing a perfect interval by one semitone results in a diminished interval (though you are unlikely to encounter references to augmented or diminished octaves).

riff

A short melodic pattern played repeatedly to form the foundation of a piece of music. Typically a riff will follow the chord progression, transposing the pattern to a new position as the chord root changes. Characteristic of blues, rock and some jazz styles.

root

Of a chord, the note for which the chord is named. Often the bass (lowest) note, although chords can also be played as "inversions" (qv), with a note other than the root in the bass.

root-position

A chord played with the root in the bass is said to be in root-position.

second

i) The note corresponding to the second degree of a scale;
ii) An interval corresponding to that between the tonic note of a scale and its second, equal to one tone (major second) or one semitone (minor second);
iii) A chord tone an interval of one second above the root note.

semitone

Half a tone - the smallest interval of the diatonic system. Also the smallest interval playable on a guitar without bending strings, as it corresponds to one fret space on one string. Equivalent to a "minor second".

seventh

i) The note corresponding to the seventh degree of a scale;
ii) An interval corresponding to that between the tonic note of a scale and its seventh, equal to five and a half tones (major seventh) or five tones (minor seventh);
iii) A chord tone an interval of one seventh above the root note.

sixth

i) The note corresponding to the sixth degree of a scale;
ii) An interval corresponding to that between the tonic note of a scale and its sixth, equal to four and a half tones (major sixth) or four tones (minor sixth);
iii) A chord tone an interval of one sixth above the root note.

third

i) The note corresponding to the third degree of a scale;
ii) An interval corresponding to that between the tonic note of a scale and its third, equal to two tones (major third) or one and a half tones (minor third);
iii) A chord tone an interval of one third above the root note.

tone

Two semitones. On a guitar, this corresponds to two fret spaces on one string. Equivalent to a "major second".

tonic

The note for which a scale or key is named; the starting note of a scale. (Also the ending note of a scale, as the octave has the same note name as the tonic).

transpose

Transposition is the movement of a piece of music, chord or scale into a different key while keeping all the musical relationships (i.e. intervals) unchanged. Thus the absolute pitch is shifted, but the relative pitches of all the notes remain the same.

triad

A chord of three (different) notes. This is the minimum number of notes required to create a true chord.

THE CYCLE OF FIFTHS

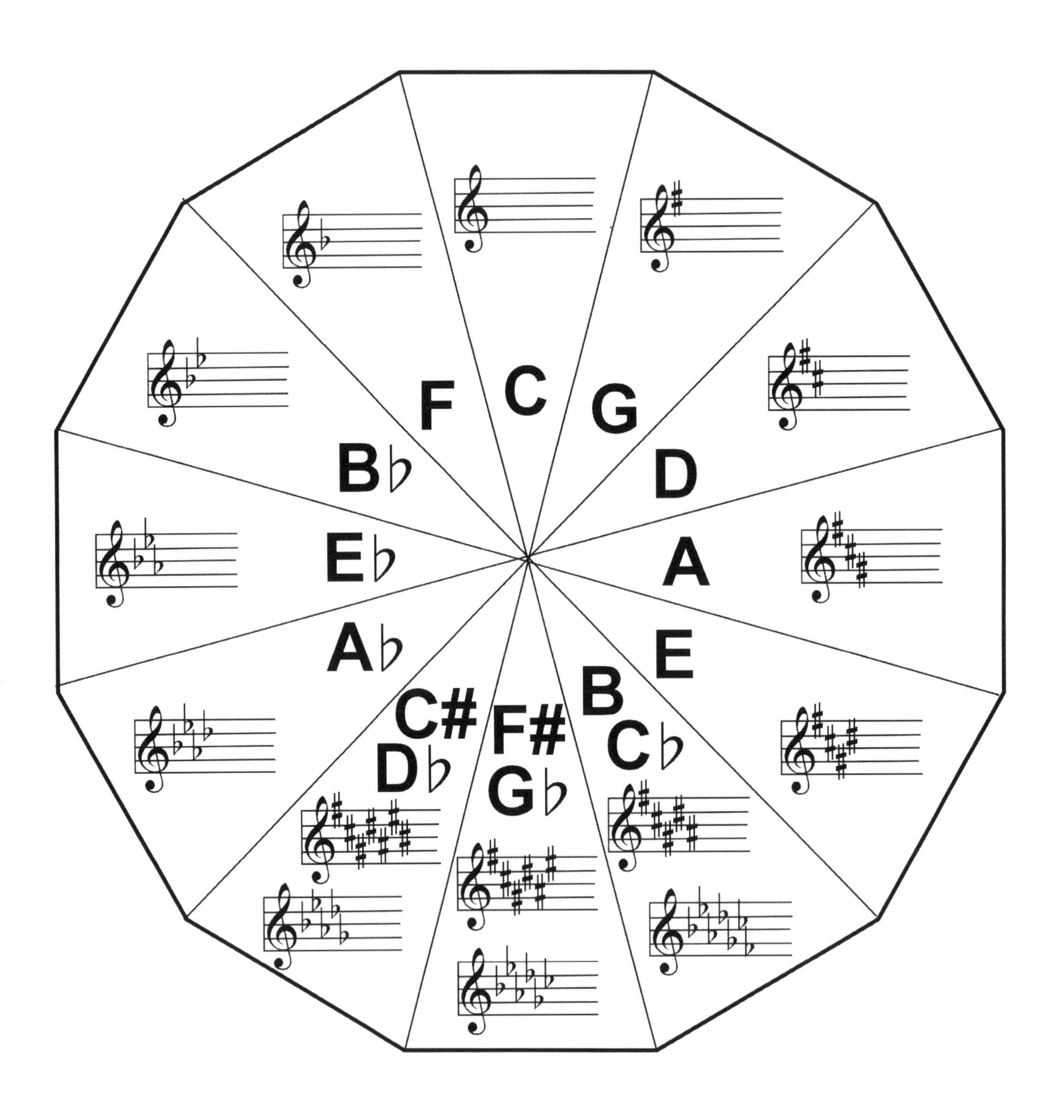

AFTERWORD

The chord progressions taught in this book have been the bedrock of European music for around four centuries. While they obviously still have some mileage in them, it can justifiably be argued that they have, by now, become somewhat stale and clichéd. Contemporary composers and songwriters, in all genres of music, are constantly searching for ways to keep music fresh and exciting, by getting away from these traditional forms. Some possibilities are:

- Alternative systems of harmonisation - for example based on intervals of a fourth, rather than a third.
- Using scales "borrowed" from non-European cultures, e.g. Asian, Middle-Eastern, African.
- "Atonal" music, which avoids the constraints of the key system by giving equal weight to all twelve notes of the chromatic scale.
- "Microtonal" music - using intervals of less than a semitone.

"When they sent a rocket to the stars, they brought it to the launch pad on wheels"

Even if your personal musical development is going to take you in these or other, uncharted, directions, I hope that you will still find some value in this book. Not only will the exercises herein help in developing the physical skills, dexterity, strength and stamina needed in guitar playing, but, perhaps more importantly, the grounding in basic harmony theory should give you a good working knowledge of what has gone before, so that your imagination and inspiration can take flight without needing to "reinvent the wheel".

Above all remember there are no right or wrong ways to compose and play music. Ultimately all that matters is that it feels good to you.

Acknowledgements

Thanks are due to Dave Bowmer and Martin Dix who reviewed early drafts of this book, corrected various errors and made some useful suggestions which are reflected in the final version. Also to Matt Allen who helped to prepare the finished product for publication.

Very special thanks to Veronica, who doesn't play guitar, but nevertheless supplied the necessary encouragement - and tolerance - for me to get this finished.